Psychology

Psychology

THIRD EDITION

Douglas A. Bernstein
University of Illinois at Urbana-Champaign

Alison Clarke-Stewart
University of California, Irvine

Edward J. Roy
University of Illinois at Urbana-Champaign

Thomas K. Srull
University of Illinois at Urbana-Champaign

Christopher D. Wickens
University of Illinois at Urbana-Champaign

HOUGHTON MIFFLIN COMPANY   BOSTON   TORONTO
Geneva, Illinois Palo Alto Princeton, New Jersey

To the researchers, past and present,

whose work embodies psychology today,

and to the students who will follow

in their footsteps to shape the psychology

of tomorrow.

Senior sponsoring editor: Michael DeRocco
Senior project editor: Carol Newman
Production/design coordinator: Sarah Ambrose
Senior manufacturing coordinator: Priscilla Bailey
Marketing manager: Becky Dudley

Cover photograph by Ralph Mercer Photography

Anatomical illustrations by Joel Ito

Illustrations by Steven Moore on pages 43, 53, 117, 143 (bottom), 149, 155, 170, 177 (bottom), 189, 194, 218, 251 (top), 260, 263, 273 (left), 317, 330, 338, 339 (bottom).

Photo research by Photosearch, Inc., New York City

Credits
Chapter opening photos: p. 2 Robert Llewellyn **p. 18** Mel Di Giacomo and Bob Masini/The Image Bank **p. 40** Bob Milne/First Light, Toronto **p. 92** Ted Horowitz/The Stock Market **p. 130** Kindra Clineff/The Picture Cube **p. 174** J. Paul Kennedy/The Stock Market **p. 212** Michael Melford/The Image Bank **p. 248** Kirk Weddle/Sipa Press **p. 286** Marc and Evelyn Bernheim/Woodfin Camp **p. 322** Gordon Gainer/The Stock Market **p. 364** Michael Newman/Photo Edit **p. 400** Frans Lanting/Minden Pictures **p. 450** Gerd Ludwig/Woodfin Camp **p. 482** Tom Owen Edmonds/The Image Bank **p. 520** Thomas Kitchin/First Light, Toronto **p. 566** Bob Daemmrich/The Image Works **p. 606** Dag Sunberg/The Image Bank **p. 638** Michael Smeltzer.

(Credits continue following references)

Printed in the U.S.A.

Library of Congress Catalog Card Number: 93-78678

ISBN: 0-395-64955-2

1 2 3 4 5 6 7 8 9-VH-97 96 95 94 93

Brief Contents

Contents

2

Research in Psychology   18

3

Human Development   40

4

Biological Aspects of Psychology   92

5

Sensation   130

9

Memory 286

10

Thought and Language 322

11

Mental Abilities 364

12

Motivation and Emotion 400

15

Psychological Disorders   520

16

Treatment of Psychological Disorders   566

17

Social Cognition   606

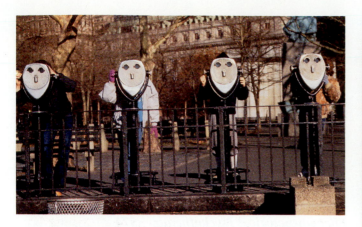

18

Social Behavior and Group Influences   638

Preface

In revising *Psychology* we have rededicated ourselves to the goals we pursued in the first two editions:

- To explore the full range of psychology, from cell to society, in an eclectic manner as free as possible from theoretical bias.
- To balance our need to explain the content of psychology with an emphasis on the *doing* of psychology, through a blend of conceptual discussion and description of research studies.
- To foster scientific attitudes and to help our readers learn to think critically by examining the ways that psychologists have solved, or failed to solve, fascinating puzzles of behavior and mental processes.
- To produce a text that, without oversimplifying psychology, is clear, accessible, and enjoyable for the student to read—even spiced now and again with humor.
- To demonstrate that, in spite of its breadth and diversity, psychology is a notably integrated discipline in which each subfield is linked to other subfields by common interests and overarching research questions. The productive cross-fertilization among social, clinical, and biological psychologists in researching health and illness is just one recent example of how different types of psychologists benefit from and build on one another's work.

Preparing the Third Edition provided us with new ways to do justice to our goals.

We sought to respond to the needs of instructors who wanted us to reduce or expand coverage of various topics. For example, many instructors asked us to expand our coverage of research methods. The result, a new Chapter 2, not only introduces students to the methodology of psychological research, it also grounds students in the rigors of critical thinking.

We sought to strike an ideal balance between classic and current research. The important historic findings of psychological research are here, but so is coverage of much recent work. Approximately one third of the research citations are new to the Third Edition, and we have added the latest information on such topics as:

- Quasi-experimental designs (Chapter 2)
- Identity and development of the self (Chapter 3)
- Plasticity in the brain (Chapter 4)
- Parallel and hierarchical processing of visual information (Chapter 5)

- Network processing of sensory information (Chapter 6)
- Attention and automatic processing (Chapter 6)
- Computational view of perception (Chapter 6)
- Mental processing without awareness (Chapter 7)
- Blindsight (Chapter 7)
- The neuropsychology of consciousness (Chapter 7)
- The role of neural networks in learning (Chapter 8)
- Explicit and implicit memory (Chapter 9)
- Transfer-appropriate and parallel distributed processing models of memory (Chapter 9)
- Semantic memory networks (Chapter 9)
- An ecological approach to mental abilities (Chapter 11)
- The role of the paraventricular nucleus in hunger and eating (Chapter 12)
- Sexual orientation (Chapter 12)
- Health-belief and stages-of-readiness models of health behavior (Chapter 13)
- The *Life Experience Survey* (Chapter 13)
- Preventing and coping with AIDS (Chapter 13)
- The MMPI-2 (Chapter 14)
- The DSM-IV classification of psychological disorders (Chapter 15)
- Seasonal affective disorder (Chapter 15)
- Social construction of the self (Chapter 17)
- Attraction and personality style (Chapter 17)
- Descriptive and injunctive norms (Chapter 18)
- Causes and management of interpersonal conflict (Chapter 18)

The Third Edition also contains abundant new material on human diversity. Throughout the text students will encounter recent research on multicultural phenomena both domestic and global. We introduce this multicultural emphasis in Chapter 1, and follow it through such topics as:

- Human diversity and research methods (Chapter 2)
- Culture and cognitive development (Chapter 3)
- Forming a personal and ethnic identity (Chapter 3)
- Culture, experience, and perception (Chapter 6)
- Cultural factors in learning and teaching (Chapter 8)
- Knowledge, language, and culture (Chapter 10)
- Cultural differences in logical reasoning (Chapter 10)
- Bilingualism (Chapter 10)
- Cultural bias in mental ability testing (Chapter 11)
- Ethnic differences in IQ (Chapter 11)

- Cultural aspects of emotional expression (Chapter 12)
- Cultural and gender differences in achievement motivation (Chapter 12)
- Cultural factors in personality development (Chapter 14)
- Sociocultural factors in psychological disorders (Chapter 15)
- Gender and cultural differences in depression and suicide (Chapter 15)
- Cultural factors in psychotherapy (Chapter 16)
- Human diversity and drug treatment (Chapter 16)
- Cultural factors in social norms (Chapter 18)
- Cultural factors in aggression (Chapter 18)

We also have increased our coverage of behavior genetics and evolutionary psychology. These topics are introduced in Chapters 1 and 2 and explored wherever appropriate—for example, when we discuss:

- Biopreparedness for learning (Chapter 8)
- Genetic components of intelligence (Chapter 11)
- Evolutionary explanations of mate selection (Chapter 12)
- Innate expressions of emotion (Chapter 12)
- The heritability of personality (Chapter 14)
- Genetic factors in psychological disorders (Chapter 15)
- Sociobiological explanations for helping and altruism (Chapter 18)

Chapter Organization

Three points are worth noting about the organization of the Third Edition.

First, we have refrained from grouping the eighteen chapters into sections. Indeed, we designed each chapter to be a freestanding unit so that you may assign chapters in any order you wish.

Many instructors who followed our chapter organization in the First and Second Editions found, as we have, that preceding physiology with human development had a salutary effect on their students. In the Third Edition we have retained this organizational feature. Wherever possible, we use Chapter 3 on development to show the reader how the principles and processes studied in each subfield come together across the human being's life span. Again, however, if you wish to assign the development chapter out of sequence you may do so comfortably.

Finally, in the Third Edition we have combined coverage of motivation and emotion in a single chapter (Chapter 12). Thus, even with the addition of Chapter 2 on research methods, the total number of chapters has not increased. We believe that we continue to cover mo-

tivation and emotion with appropriate breadth and rigor, but somewhat more concisely.

Special Features

Psychology contains a number of special features designed to promote efficient learning and students' mastery of the material. Features from the previous editions have been revised and enhanced in the Third.

Linkages

We have built into the book an integrating tool called Linkages, which highlights some of the relationships among the various subfields in psychology. In the Third Edition, this tool consists of four parts:

1. In the first few pages of each chapter, a linkage diagram (Linkages) illustrates how the chapter sheds light on other chapters and how material in other chapters helps illuminate the current one. Each contains six "linking questions" and carries a caption that helps students to use the diagram. The page numbers following each linking question direct the student to pages that carry further discussion of that question.
   Every linkage diagram contains at least one question new to the Third Edition.
2. To further reinforce the linkages concept as the student reads through each chapter, each linking question is repeated in the margin of the page where the discussion appears.
3. One such discussion appears in each chapter, in a linkages section that addresses at length a particularly timely or provocative question previously raised in that chapter's linkage diagram.
4. Each chapter contains at least one captioned photo that illustrates how the content of the chapter is related to that of another chapter.

By establishing ties among chapters, the Linkages material combines with the text narrative to highlight the network of relationships among psychology's subareas. However, the Linkages program does not require that you follow our text's chapter sequence.

Thinking Critically

A section in each chapter is called Thinking Critically. We try throughout the book to describe research on psychological phenomena in a way that reveals the logic of the scientific enterprise, that identifies possible flaws in design or interpretation, and that leaves room for more questions and further research. In other words, we try to display critical thinking processes. The Thinking Critically sections are designed to make these processes more explicit and accessible by providing a framework for analyzing evidence before drawing conclusions. The framework is built around five questions that the reader should find useful in analyzing not only studies in psychology but other forms of communication as well. These questions, first introduced when we discuss the importance of critical thinking in Chapter 2, are

1. What am I being asked to believe or accept?
2. What evidence is available to support the assertion?
3. Are there alternative ways of interpreting the evidence?
4. What additional evidence would help to evaluate the alternatives?
5. What conclusions are most reasonable?

Thinking Critically sections new to the Third Edition include:

■ Are there drugs that can make you smarter? (Chapter 4)
■ Can nonhumans use language? (Chapter 10)
■ Does evolution explain how people choose a marriage partner? (Chapter 12)
■ Does the hostile Type A behavior pattern increase the risk of heart disease? (Chapter 13)

In Review Charts

In Review charts summarize information in a convenient tabular format. We have placed two or three In Review charts strategically in each chapter to help students synthesize and assimilate large chunks of information—for example, on drug effects, key elements of personality theories, and stress responses and mediators. In Review charts new to the Third Edition include:

■ Neurons, neurotransmitters, and receptors (Chapter 4)
■ Organization of the brain (Chapter 4)
■ Principles of perceptual organization and constancy (Chapter 6)
■ Factors affecting retrieval from long-term memory (Chapter 9)

Future Directions

Each chapter concludes with Future Directions, a section intended to excite and inform students about new trends. Here we offer our views on the directions that theory, research, and applications are likely to take in future years. We also suggest courses that an interested student could take in psychology and other disciplines to learn more about the chapter's topic.

Chapter Summaries

These summaries are configured to reflect clearly the heading structure of each chapter. The chapters' key terms are integrated into the summaries rather than set off as a separate list. These terms are defined in the glossary.

Ancillary Package

Accompanying this book are, among other ancillaries, a *Test Bank*, an *Instructor's Resource Manual*, and a *Study Guide*. Because these items were prepared by the lead author and his colleagues from the University of Illinois psychology department, you will find an especially high level of coordination between the textbook and these supplements. All three are unified by a shared set of learning objectives. Equally important, all three have been significantly revised and enhanced for the Third Edition.

Test Bank (by Graeme McGufficke, Sandra S. Goss, and Douglas A. Bernstein)

The *Test Bank* contains more than 3,000 multiple-choice items (165 per chapter plus 45 on statistics), plus one to four essay questions for each chapter of the text. Half of these multiple-choice questions are new; in all others, the foils have been scrambled for the Third Edition.

All multiple-choice items are keyed to the learning objectives listed in the *Instructor's Resource Manual* and *Study Guide*. More than 1,000 questions have already been class-tested with approximately 2,000 students and are accompanied by graphs indicating the question's discriminative power, level of difficulty, the percentage of students who chose each response, and the relationship between students' performance on a given item and their overall performance on the test in which the item appeared.

Instructor's Resource Manual (by Sandra S. Goss, Joel I. Shenker, and Douglas A. Bernstein)

The *Instructor's Resource Manual* contains a complete set of lecture outlines and learning objectives. The manual contains 160 specific teaching aids—58 of them new to the Third Edition—including handouts, demonstrations, and classroom exercises. It also contains other material that will be useful to teachers of large introductory courses, such as a section on classroom management and administration of large multisection courses, and a discussion of careers in psychology that instructors may want to distribute to students.

Study Guide (by Bridget Schoppert, Marcia Graber, and Douglas A. Bernstein)

The *Study Guide* employs numerous techniques that help students to learn. Each chapter contains a detailed outline, a key-terms section that presents fresh examples and aids to remembering, learning objectives, and a "Concepts and Exercises" section that shows students how to apply their knowledge of psychology to everyday issues and concerns. In addition, each chapter concludes with a two-part self-quiz consisting of thirty multiple-choice questions. An answer key tells the student not only which response is correct but also why each of the other choices is wrong. The revised *Study Guide* also includes a write-in quiz for each chapter. New to the Third Edition guide is a package of critical-thinking exercises.

Other Ancillaries Available to Adopters

The *Test Bank, Instructor's Resource Manual,* and *Study Guide* are also available to adopters on disk for use on microcomputers. All are available in IBM and Macintosh formats.

The *Computer Test Bank* allows instructors to generate exams and to integrate their own test items with those on the disk.

The *Computer Lecture Outlines,* derived from the *Instructor's Resource Manual,* are available on disk in a generic ASCII-code version. This format allows instructors to use standard word-processing software to integrate their own lecture notes and ideas into the text lectures.

The *Computer Study Guide* is an interactive program that gives students feedback on incorrect as well as on correct answers.

These additional software items are available to qualified adopters:

- *Psychabilities* (by Sarah Ransdell, New College of the University of South Florida). These thirteen computer simulations, specially designed for use in either the classroom or the computer laboratory, illustrate intriguing phenomena and recreate important experiments. They include a multiple-choice self-quizzing program to test progress and encourage mastery.
- *Flash Card*, an interactive vocabulary-building program that helps students to master the technical language of psychology.

Also offered to adopters are:

- *The Psychology Show*, Houghton Mifflin's video supplement for introductory psychology, available in both videodisc and videotape formats. Containing nineteen motion segments plus nearly one hundred still images, *The Psychology Show* is designed to expand on text coverage and to stimulate class discussion through the length of your course. An accompanying instructor's guide offers information on each motion segment and still image, as well as advice on using a videodisc player. Available on adoption of a minimum number of new books.
- *Succeed in College!*, a skills-building booklet containing selected chapters from Walter Pauk's best-selling study skills text *How to Study in College*. This booklet, which offers time-tested advice on notetaking, test-taking, and other topics, can be shrinkwrapped free of charge with new copies of the student text.
- A range of videocassettes containing films on topics in psychology is available on adoption of a minimum number of new books.
- A transparency set containing 100 images from the text, most in full color; plus 50 images from outside the text.
- A film rental policy enabling qualified adopters to rent films or videos from a consortium of university film libraries.

Acknowledgments

Many people provided us with the help, criticism, and encouragement we needed to create the Third Edition.

Once again we must thank Katie Steele, who got the project off the ground in 1983 by encouraging us to stop talking about this book and start writing it.

We are indebted to Dennis Cannon (Indiana University/Purdue University—Fort Wayne) for his expert advice on revising Chapter 11, and to Ronald A. Kleinknecht (Western Washington University) for his similar advice on the revision of Chapters 13, 14, 15, and 16.

Joel I. Shenker of the University of Illinois also provided invaluable expertise on selected topics in Chapter 7.

Students, friends, and associates who evaluated parts of the Third Edition manuscript include Marie Banich, Martin Fishbein, Sandra Goss, Ann Harris, Meagan Harris, Lloyd Humphreys, Lisa Ochoa, Julian Rappaport, Mark Salzer, Harry Triandis, Ellen Wartella, and Gayle Wolfe.

We owe a special debt to the colleagues listed below, who provided prerevision evaluations of or reviewed the manuscript for the Third Edition as it was being developed. Their advice and suggestions for improvement were responsible for many of the good qualities you will find in the book. If you have any criticisms, they probably involve areas these people warned us about.

William Addison, Eastern Illinois University
Jeanne S. Albright, Loyola University of Chicago
Susan H. Bland, Niagara Community College
Linda Brannon, McNeese State University
John P. Broida, University of Southern Maine
Darrell L. Butler, Ball State University
Michael Crabtree, Washington and Jefferson College

Larry Christensen, Texas A&M University

Wendy Domjan, University of Texas

Wayne Dornan, Illinois Wesleyan University

Ernest Dzendolet, University of Massachusetts

G. Cynthia Fekken, Queens University, Ontario

Nelson Freedman, Queens University, Ontario

Howard Friedman, College of William and Mary

David C. Funder, University of California, Riverside

Alan G. Glaros, University of Missouri, Kansas City

Carol R. Glass, Catholic University

Constance Hammen, University of California, Los Angeles

Larry M. Leitner, Miami University, Ohio

Susan D. Lima, University of Wisconsin, Milwaukee

Douglas W. Matheson, University of the Pacific

Harold L. Miller, Jr., Brigham Young University

John B. Nezlek, College of William and Mary

Annemarie Nicols, Hunter College

David G. Payne, SUNY Binghamton

Constance J. Pilkington, College of William and Mary

James Prochaska, University of Rhode Island

Robert R. Prochnow, St. Cloud University

Charles K. Prokop, Trinity University

Sally A. Radmacher, Missouri Western State University

Richard Reardon, University of Oklahoma

Jill Rierdan, University of Massachusetts, Boston

Philippe Rochat, Emory University

Mark Sibicky, Marietta College

Marcia Smith, Washington University

Michael E. Smith, Texas A&M University

Paul Wellman, Texas A&M University

Burrton Woodruff, Butler University

The process of creating the Third Edition was greatly facilitated by the work of many dedicated people in the College Division at Houghton Mifflin Company. From the sales representatives and sales managers who told us of faculty members' suggestions for improvement to the marketing staff who developed innovative ways of telling our colleagues about the changes we have made, it seems that everyone in the division had a hand in shaping and improving the Third Edition. Four people deserve special thanks, however. Senior sponsoring editor, Mike DeRocco, gave us invaluable advice about structural, pedagogical, and content changes for the new edition and, as he has in past editions, continued to be the project's main shepherd. Kathy Field, our developmental editor, applied her editorial expertise and sparkling intellect to helping us create this manuscript, just as she had done in the two previous editions. She suggested changes based on reviewers' comments and our own goals, and she kept these suggestions and goals in mind as, chapter by chapter, she worked diligently to find ever better ways to organize the book and clarify its content. Carol Newman, project editor on the Second Edition, returned to star in the same role for the Third, bringing with her a set of organizational skills and a level of dedication to excellence that is, in our opinion, unmatched in college publishing. We also wish to thank Christine Arden for an outstanding job copyediting the manuscript. Without these people, and those who worked with them, this revision simply could not have happened.

Finally, we want to express our deepest appreciation to our families and friends. Once again, their love saw us through an exhilarating but demanding period of our lives. They endured our hours at the computer, missed meals, postponed vacations, and occasional irritability during the creation of the First Edition of this book, and they had to suffer all over again during the lengthy process of revising it again. Their faith in us is more important than they realize, and we will cherish it forever.

Psychology

Chapter 1

Introducing Psychology

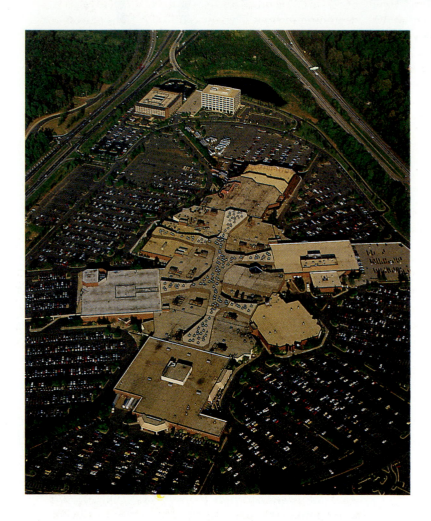

Have you ever wondered why the full moon looks so much larger near the horizon than it does high in the sky? Or what dreams mean? How about whether lie detectors really work or whether alcoholism is inherited? If so, you have entered the world of psychology, where scientists search for answers to these and many other fascinating questions.

Psychology is the science of behavior and mental processes. This means that psychologists conduct experiments and use other scientific methods to better understand the actions and thoughts of humans and animals, from the activity of a single nerve cell to the workings of memory to the social conflicts in a complex society. In this opening chapter we offer an overview of the field, including a description of the topics that psychologists examine and the approaches they use. We also describe how the varied interests of psychologists are linked with one another and with those of scientists in other fields. In later chapters we focus on how psychologists conduct research, on the results of that research, and on some of the many ways in which those results are being applied to improve the quality of life for many people.

The World of Psychology: An Overview

In 1879, in Leipzig, Germany, Wilhelm Wundt established the first formal psychology laboratory. Wundt, a physician and physiologist, used the methods of laboratory science, especially experiments, in an effort to identify the basic elements of human consciousness. Over the ensuing 115 years, psychologists expanded the range of their research to encompass hundreds of other phenomena—from colorblindness and racial prejudice to severe depression and job satisfaction. As a result of this diversity, psychology today has numerous areas of specialization, or *subfields*.

Subfields of Psychology

In March of 1991 television news programs aired a videotape showing four white police officers in Los Angeles kicking and severely beating Rodney King, an unarmed African-American motorist whom they were trying to arrest. A year later, when an all-white jury in the officers' state trial found the officers not guilty* of assault, live broadcasts showed parts of Los Angeles exploding in riots. These violent reflections of and reactions to prejudice against minorities in the United States provide but one example of the violence that is a distressing fact of public and private life in most countries around the world. In homes, children are abused and spouses are battered. In schools, there are fights and even shootings. Streets are the scene of murder and rape and conflicts between demonstrators and police. In some countries, rival militias clash, death squads torture and kill political opponents, and there is an endless procession of wars, large and small.

What causes violence? Why are some people so much more violent than others? What can be done to prevent violence? Some psychologists have addressed these important questions in their research (National Research Council, 1993). The particular aspects of violence they study illustrate the differences in the subject matter of psychology's subfields.

Experimental and cognitive psychologists, for example, study such basic components of behavior and mental processes as perception, learning, memory, motivation, and emotion, as well as judgment, decision making, and problem solving. Thus, their study of violence might focus on the effect of high temperatures on aggressiveness or how the information people recall about other people might affect the probability of physically attacking them. **Biological psychologists,** who are also called **physiological psychologists**, analyze how biology shapes behavior and mental processes. Their work has helped us understand, for example, how the brain controls physical movements, regulates eating, and receives information from the senses. With regard to violence, they have looked at whether differences in hormones account for the fact that men tend to be more violent than women; they also study how drugs or brain tumors can create episodes of aggression in normally peaceful people.

*Two of the officers were eventually found guilty in federal court of having violated Rodney King's civil rights.

Wilhelm Wundt (pictured here) and other early psychologists such as Edward Titchener and Hermann Ebbinghaus, used the term *experimental psychology* to distinguish their laboratory work from the endeavors of philosophers and others who thought and speculated about consciousness, memory, and other psychological matters but performed no experiments. Chapter 7, on consciousness, contains more on the early history of psychology.

While some psychologists seek laws that govern the behavior of people in general, **personality psychologists** focus on the characteristics that make each person unique. They have identified, for example, the personality dimension known as introversion-extraversion, and they study relationships between people's scores on personality tests and their tendency to display violent, shy, bold, or fearful behavior. **Social psychologists** study how people influence one another, especially in groups. They have found that the presence and actions of others affect a wide range of behaviors, from individual athletic performance and jury verdicts to group problem solving and mob violence. The research of **clinical and counseling psychologists** on violence is just one example of their interest in all forms of abnormal behavior; they also provide direct aid to troubled people.

Behavior and mental processes are always changing. **Developmental psychologists** describe these changes and try to understand their causes and effects throughout the life span. They ask, for example, whether differences in temperament at birth or variations in parenting patterns might be tied to, say, differences in dependency or aggressiveness in adulthood.

Research in yet other subfields—such as community, industrial-organizational, and quantitative psychology—has also shed light on various aspects of violence, as well as on many other behaviors and mental processes. Table 1.1 summarizes psychology's main subfields; we examine each of them much more closely in the chapters to come.

Approaches to Psychology

Suppose you were a psychologist trying to understand the origins of violence. Where would you look for answers? Do the origins lie in hormonal imbalances or brain disorders? Is its source an ancient instinct once necessary for survival, or do learned habits create violence? Each of these questions reflects a different approach to psychology, a different set of guiding assumptions, questions, and methods for understanding behavior and mental processes. Some psychologists adopt only one approach, but many are *eclectic,* combining features of two or more approaches because they believe that no one perspective can fully account for all aspects of every psychological phenomenon. Though they differ in their influence today, the approaches that have been most significant throughout the history of psychology are the biological, evolutionary, psychodynamic, behavioral, humanistic, and cognitive approaches. In this chapter we merely review the essential features of each approach; but throughout this book, we examine the value—and the limitations—of the various approaches for understanding many psychological phenomena.

The Biological Approach   The possibility that violent behavior might stem from a hormonal imbalance or brain disorder reflects the biological approach. Its roots can be traced back to Wilhelm Wundt. He studied biological processes only indirectly, by exploring, for example, how long it took people to react to a stimulus. Today, the **biological approach** focuses on biological processes more directly, examining how specific physiological processes shape behavior and mental processes.

As you might expect, the biological approach is prominent among biological psychologists, who study the psychological effects of hormones, genes, and electrical and chemical activity in the nervous system, especially the brain. However, psychologists in other subfields, such as cognitive or clinical psychology, may also take a biological approach. They try to understand how memories are stored in the brain; they look for patterns of physiological arousal associated with certain forms of thought; they analyze the degree to

Table 1.1
Subfields of Psychology

Here is a sample of general questions and issues that typically interest psychologists in various subfields. These subfields are not isolated, however. Each is linked to many others by psychologists' interests in different aspects of the same psychological phenomenon. For example, cognitive psychologists are not the only ones interested in memory; biological psychologists are concerned with the storage of memories in the brain, developmental psychologists might ask how memory changes with age, and social psychologists want to know how the presence of others influences what people remember. (You may find memory research especially valuable as you prepare for tests. Be sure to read about memory improvement and SQ3R study methods on pages 317–318 in Chapter 9, on memory.) Because behavior and mental processes do not fit neatly into specific subfields, the work of many, perhaps most, psychologists overlaps with and is linked to that of their colleagues in other areas of psychology and in other disciplines as well. We will be emphasizing these linkages throughout this book.

Subfield	Typical Questions
Experimental psychology	What rules govern what people perceive, how they learn, what they remember, and what they forget?
Cognitive psychology	What are the mental mechanisms through which people make judgments and decisions?
Biological psychology	How do the electrical and chemical activities in nerve cells influence behavior? Which parts of the brain control which kinds of behavior? What happens in the brain when people think or become emotional?
Personality psychology	How can personality differences be measured? To what extent is personality inherited? To what extent can it be altered?
Social psychology	How do people influence one another's attitudes, actions, emotions, and thoughts? What determines whether two people will be attracted to each other?
Industrial-organizational psychology	What factors influence job satisfaction? Are socioculturally diverse work groups more or less efficient than homogenous groups?
Clinical, counseling, and community psychology	In what ways can behavior and mental processes become disordered? What causes these disorders and how can they be treated? How can they be prevented?
Developmental psychology	How do attributes such as thinking, social skills, intelligence, language, and personality change throughout the life-span? What factors facilitate or distort their development?
Quantitative psychology	What mathematical tools can measure, describe, and predict intelligence, judgment, or decision making? How can research data best be analyzed?

which a tendency toward mental disorder is affected by the genes inherited from one's parents.

The enormous influence of the biological approach in modern psychology is evident in research described in nearly every chapter of this book. To help you appreciate that influence, we discuss some basic principles of genetics in the next chapter and devote Chapter 4 to other biological aspects of behavior.

The Evolutionary Approach Biological processes also figure prominently in the evolutionary approach. Charles Darwin's 1859 book, *The Origin of Species,* provided the foundation for this approach. Darwin argued that the forms of life we see today are the result of *evolution*—of changes in life forms over many generations—and, more specifically, that evolution occurs through natural selection. In *natural selection,* said Darwin, individuals whose appearance and patterns of action allow them to elude predators, withstand the elements, find food, and mate successfully are able to survive and produce offspring with similar characteristics. In other words, the inherited characteristics that allow individuals to remain alive by successfully adjusting, or *adapting,* to changing conditions are likely to survive in the species as well. Other, less adaptive attributes die out of the species along with the unfortunate creatures who carry them.

Darwin's work, as well as that of **ethologists**—scientists who study animal behavior in the natural environment—has provided thousands of examples from the animal world of how evolution, through natural selection, has sustained in a species those physical characteristics and behavior patterns that are adaptive for survival.

According to the evolutionary approach to psychology, patterns of behavior—like physical characteristics—that help individuals adapt and survive tend to be passed on from generation to generation. In animals such as insects, birds, and fish, species-specific behaviors often appear as relatively rigid rituals, called *fixed action patterns*, which are not altered much by learning and which tend to be triggered by specific cues called *sign stimuli*. For example: herring gull chicks peck for food in a characteristic way, but only when they see the red spot on their parents' beaks that serves as a target.

The effects of natural selection can be seen in inherited physical characteristics such as the camouflage coloration that helps animals escape predators, as well as in instinctive or, more properly, *species-specific* behaviors. Spiders build web patterns specific to their species. Allen's hummingbirds perform a trademark courtship flight that features repeated hundred-foot dives. Rats show characteristic "boxing" behaviors when fighting, cats arch their backs, and dogs bark. The fact that many animals perform species-specific behaviors successfully, often perfectly, the first time they try, even if isolation at birth prevents prior exposure to the behavior, suggests that these are unlearned, inherited patterns. Evolutionary biologists and psychologists have identified the adaptive value of these behaviors for the animal and, thus, for the species.

It was not until after Darwin's death that the discovery of genes filled in the story of how characteristics are transmitted from parents to offspring. In modern biology, knowledge about genetics is combined with the principle of natural selection to explain evolution and the structure of contemporary organisms. In psychology, the **evolutionary approach** holds that the *behavior* of animals and humans today is the result of evolution through natural selection. Psychologists who take an evolutionary approach therefore try to understand (1) the adaptive value of behavior, (2) the anatomical and biological mechanisms that make it possible, and (3) the environmental conditions that encourage or discourage it. Looking at violent behavior in humans from an evolutionary perspective, then, psychologists might think of it as an instinctive pattern stemming from the activity of certain brain centers and hormones, triggered by events such as frustration and kept under control by societal rules and traditions.

One application of the evolutionary approach is **sociobiology, which is the study of the relationship between a species' evolutionary heritage and its social behaviors, such as aggression, cooperation, child care, sexual behavior, and so on.** Building from research on animal behavior, some sociobiologists have suggested that the genetically encoded results of evolutionary history have programmed women to be cooperative, nurturing, and monogamous—and men to be competitive, violent, and sexually promiscuous.

These ideas have aroused a storm of controversy, including accusations that they vastly underplay the role of learning in social behavior. Indeed, the ability to learn through experience adds a vital layer of adaptive capacity as individuals strive to meet the demands of a changing environment. This ability is relatively limited in insects and other invertebrates, is more significant in mammals, and is absolutely crucial in humans. People inherit a species-specific capacity to walk upright and speak a complex, grammar-based language, for example, but they must still learn to do both.

Along with controversy, the evolutionary approach has generated a growing body of research (DeKay & Buss, 1992). Its increased influence in psychology will be apparent in later chapters.

The Psychodynamic Approach   The idea that people's aggressiveness might stem from an inherited instinct was taken in a different direction by a Viennese physician named Sigmund Freud, who began his work about fifteen years after the founding of Wundt's laboratory. Freud at first assumed that normal and abnormal behavior and mental processes have a physical cause somewhere in the nervous system. But Freud's work with people whose physical ailments had no apparent physical cause led him to create a new theory and form of treatment called *psychoanalysis*. His ideas are the foundation of the **psychodynamic approach, which holds that all behavior and mental processes reflect constant and mostly unconscious struggles within each person.** Usually, these struggles involve conflict between the impulse to satisfy instincts or wishes (for food, sex, or aggression, for example) and the restrictions

Sigmund Freud established the psychodynamic approach to human behavior and mental processes. In particular, he emphasized the role of instincts as a component of constant unconscious conflicts in the creation and alteration of human personality.

B. F. Skinner was the most notable contemporary champion of the behavioral approach to psychology. In spite of his reputation for being interested only in overt behaviors, Skinner recognized that mental events took place, and could be important, but argued that they could not be studied directly.

imposed by society. From this perspective, a display of violence (or hostility, or even anxiety) reflects the breakdown of civilizing defenses against the expression of primitive urges.

The psychodynamic approach is far less influential in psychology today than in the past, and most of its adherents prefer a revised version of Freud's original theories (Youngstrom, 1992). Still, Freud's ideas are critical to an understanding of contemporary views of personality, psychological disorders, and treatment, and we examine them in Chapters 14, 15, and 16.

The Behavioral Approach   In 1913, while Freud was pursuing his psychodynamic approach and gaining favor among American psychologists, a Harvard psychology professor named John B. Watson published a book called *Psychology as a Behaviorist Views It*. In it, Watson urged psychologists to ignore mental events (conscious as well as unconscious) and study instead only what they could observe directly. By focusing on observable, or *overt*, actions, said Watson, psychologists would not have to rely on people's potentially distorted reports about themselves. He also argued that environmental influences—the things that happen after birth—are paramount in shaping who people are and what they do.

Watson's views gave rise to the **behavioral approach** to psychology, which emphasizes the idea that behavior and mental processes are primarily the result of *learning*. From this perspective, biological, genetic, and evolutionary factors provide the raw material on which rewards, punishments, and other experiences act, molding each person. Thus, behaviorists examine a person's learning history, the pattern of rewards and punishments, to explain aggressive, dependent, or confident behavior. They assert that people can change problematic behaviors such as violence by unlearning old habits and developing new ones. For example, researchers using this approach have created programs to reduce antisocial behavior in children and to teach violent criminals the social skills they need to interact peacefully with other people (see, for example, Foxx, Faw & Weber, 1991; Hammond & Yung, 1991; Kazdin, Siegel & Bass, 1992).

Another Harvard psychologist, B. F. Skinner, spent decades perfecting methods for the *functional analysis of behavior,* mapping out the details of how rewards and punishments shape, maintain, and change behavior. His work helped explain, for example, how children's unruly behavior is sometimes inadvertently encouraged by the attention it attracts from parents and teachers, and how some people's virtual addiction to gambling can result from the occasional and unpredictable rewards it brings. Skinner's contributions helped behaviorism maintain in the 1950s and 1960s the dominant position in psychological research it had enjoyed in the United States since the 1920s. For some psychologists, however, behaviorism's near-exclusive focus on overt actions made it incomplete. They argued that we can never fully understand the nature of violence or altruism or any other behaviors, for that matter, without learning something about the thoughts that accompany them.

Since the 1970s, many behaviorists have come to endorse a *cognitive-behavioral* view, which adds the study of reportable mental processes to the traditional behaviorial emphasis on overt behavior (Hawkins et al., 1992; Thyer, 1992). Thus, the cognitive-behavioral approach explores how learning affects the development of thoughts and beliefs and how, in turn, these learned cognitive patterns affect overt behavior.

The Cognitive Approach   Recognition by many behaviorists of the importance of cognitive factors reflects a broader trend in the history of psychology. Nineteenth-century psychologists such as Wundt were interested in analyzing the basic elements of consciousness, much as chemists of the time were deter-

Cognitive scientists, including cognitive psychologists, try to understand intelligence and intelligent systems. They work on such projects as a "computational theory of the mind" in which computer programs model how humans perceive, remember, reason, and otherwise process information. In Chapter 10, on thought and language, we will discuss the progress that cognitive scientists have made in creating artificial intelligence in computers.

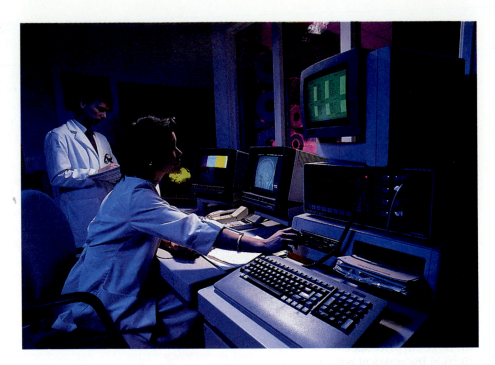

Carl Rogers, who died in 1987, was the most famous proponent of what came to be called the *humanistic approach* to psychology. Rogers believed that people's unique perceptions of the world and their innate tendency toward healthy growth were more important determinants of behavior than biological processes, unconscious conflicts, or learning. Behavior problems, from anxiety to violence, occur, said Rogers, when the environment—including other people—block this growth.

mining the basic elements of physical matter. Other psychologists, such as William James (1890), worked to understand how mental processes such as learning and memory function to help people get along in the world. Research on consciousness and cognitive activity all but ceased in the United States during the decades when the behavioral approach held sway. But dissatisfaction with the limitations of behaviorism and a renewed emphasis on mental processes have made the cognitive approach as influential today as behaviorism once was.

The cognitive approach not only emphasizes the importance of thoughts and other mental processes but also seeks to understand what they are and how they work. Specifically, the **cognitive approach** focuses on how people take in, mentally represent, and store information; how they perceive and process that information; and how integrated patterns of behavior occur. From this perspective, violent behavior is the outcome of a rapid sequence of mental events, components of which may occur outside of awareness. Thus, a person might (1) perceive that someone has cut into a theater line, for example, (2) use stored memories and concepts to decide that this act is inappropriate, (3) attribute the act to the culprit's obnoxiousness, (4) consider possible responses and their likely consequences, (5) decide that shoving the person is the best response, and (6) execute that response.

Psychologists taking the cognitive approach are interested in the role of information processing in areas ranging from decision making and interpersonal attraction to intelligence testing and group problem solving, to name but a few. Some of them work with researchers from computer science, the biological sciences, engineering, linguistics, philosophy, and other disciplines in a multidisciplinary field called *cognitive science,* which analyzes intelligent systems. Cognitive scientists attempt to discover the building blocks of cognition and to determine how these components produce complex behaviors such as remembering a fact, naming an object, or writing a word (Margolin, 1991).

The Humanistic Approach   Another slant on the role of mental events in psychology was offered in the early 1940s by Carl Rogers. Though trained in psychoanalysis, Rogers gradually rejected its assumptions that people are controlled by instincts, just as he rejected the notion that people are controlled

In Review: Approaches to Psychology

Approach	Characteristics
Biological	Emphasizes activity of the nervous system, especially the brain; the action of hormones and other chemicals; and genetics.
Evolutionary	Emphasizes the ways in which behavior and mental processes are adaptive for survival.
Psychodynamic	Emphasizes internal conflicts, mostly unconscious, which usually pit sexual or aggressive instincts against environmental obstacles to their expression.
Behavioral	Emphasizes learning, especially each person's experience with rewards and punishments.
Cognitive	Emphasizes mechanisms through which people receive, store, retrieve, and otherwise process information.
Humanistic	Emphasizes individual potential for growth and the role of unique perceptions in guiding behavior and mental processes.

Environmental psychologists study the effects of the physical environment on behavior and mental processes (Paulus & Nagar, 1989). Their research on how differing floor plans and other building features, such as the availability of natural light, affect occupants' behavior, mood, energy, and productivity helps architects create optimal designs for workplaces, nursing homes, schools, prisons, dormitories, and other structures. Psychology's many subfields offer a remarkably wide range of opportunities for careers in research and service relating to all stages of the lifespan and to all aspects of behavior.

mainly by biological forces or rewards and punishments. He advanced what has come to be called the **humanistic approach** (also known as the phenomenological approach). It holds that people control themselves and that each person is essentially good, with an innate tendency to grow toward his or her potential.

According to this approach, behavior is determined primarily by each person's capacity to *choose* how to think and act. These choices are dictated, say humanistic psychologists, by each individual's unique perception of the world. If you perceive the world as a friendly place, you are likely to feel happy and secure. If you view it as dangerous and hostile, you will probably be defensive and anxious. Seen from the humanistic perspective, then, aggressive behavior stems from the perception that aggression is justified in a given situation. However, unlike the cognitive approach, the humanistic approach does not lead to a search for laws that govern the perceptions, judgments, decisions, and actions of people in general. The humanistic approach celebrates immediate, individual experience. Many of its proponents assert that behavior and mental processes can be understood not through universal laws but, rather, through appreciating perceptions and feelings that can be fully experienced only by the person involved.

The humanistic approach was endorsed and elaborated by Abraham Maslow, Viktor Frankl, and others who became prominent theorists; but its influence in psychology today is limited, mainly because many psychologists find humanistic concepts and predictions too vague to be expressed and tested scientifically. (For a summary of the approaches we have discussed, see "In Review: Approaches to Psychology.")

Unity and Diversity in Psychology

Psychology's numerous subfields and approaches have led psychologists to varied activities and work settings, as Table 1.2 illustrates. They conduct re-

Work Setting	Percentage of Psychologists	Typical Activities
Colleges and Universities	28.6	Teaching, research, and writing, often in collaboration with colleagues from other disciplines
Mental health facilities (e.g. hospitals, clinics, counseling centers)	24.2	Testing and treatment of children and adults
Private Practice (alone or in a group of psychologists)	29.1	Testing and treatment of children and adults; consultation to business and other organizations
Business and industry	2.4	Testing potential employees; assessing employee satisfaction; identifying and resolving conflicts; improving leadership skills; offering stress management and other employee assistance programs; improving equipment design to maximize productivity and prevent accidents
Schools (including those for developmentally disabled and emotionally disturbed children)	4.5	Testing mental abilities and other characteristics; identifying problem children; consulting with parents; designing and implementing programs to improve academic performance
Other	10.5	Teaching prison inmates; research in private institutes; advising legislators on educational, research, or public policy; administering research funds; research on effectiveness of military personnel; etc.

Source: American Psychological Association, 1989.

Table 1.2
Typical Activities and Work Settings for Psychologists
The fact that psychologists can work in such a wide variety of settings and perform such a wide range of functions accounts for the popularity of psychology as an undergraduate major. The facts, concepts, theories, and methods studied in psychology courses have proven valuable to many students, whether they pursue graduate work in psychology or enter medicine, law, business, or other fields (Pauk & Fiore, 1989).

search; they apply the results of research to treat people with psychological disorders and to alleviate social problems; they teach and write about research findings and psychological knowledge. Beneath this diversity, however, lies a unity stemming from psychologists' common commitment to science and their tradition of linked interests (Kimble, 1989; Staats, 1991).

Research: The Foundation of Psychology

Psychology's historical roots in philosophy are reflected in the fundamental assumptions about behavior and mental processes that underlie its various approaches. But because psychology is a science, all of its subfields emphasize *empirical research*—in other words, research that goes beyond philosophical speculation and reasoning about behavior and mental processes to carefully gather and systematically analyze information about psychological phenomena. Thus, psychologists do more than form hypotheses about the causes of violence or depression or color vision, for example; they also test scientifically the validity of those hypotheses. For psychologists, it is not enough to merely suggest that, say, expressing your fears about an illness should reduce the symptoms of stress. They would want to objectively measure stress symptoms in people who had talked about their worries and compare them with the symptoms found in those who kept their worries to themselves. Even psychologists who do not conduct research themselves depend on psychological research discoveries to teach or write or provide up-to-date treatment.

The rules and methods of science that guide psychologists' research are discussed in the next chapter. Without them and the research foundation they

Linkages

The questions in this diagram illustrate some of the relationships between the topics discussed in this chapter and the topics of other chapters. Time and again throughout this book, you will see how psychologist's subfields and approaches are linked to one another. Diagrams like this one appear near the beginning of each chapter to illustrate some of these linkages. The page numbers indicating where the questions are discussed follow the questions. Of course, there are many more linkages than could be included in the diagrams. We hope that the diagrams will prompt you to look for these additional linkages. This kind of detective work can be enjoyable and useful. You may find it easier to remember material in one chapter by relating it to linked material in other chapters. You might also want to use the questions as a self-testing device when studying for quizzes and exams. Or you might want to read the discussions of some questions before reading the chapter to clarify how it relates to the rest of psychology. Most of all, by staying alert to linkages as you read this book, you will come away not only with threads of knowledge about each subfield but with an appreciation of the interwoven fabric of psychology as a whole. ■

HUMAN DEVELOPMENT
How is psychology's empirical tradition reflected in research on children's cognitive abilities? (p. 49)

BIOLOGICAL ASPECTS OF PSYCHOLOGY
What have biological psychologists discovered about brain structures and memory? (p. 109)

SOCIAL BEHAVIOR AND GROUP INFLUENCES
How do differing approaches to psychology explain aggression? (p. 654)

Introducing Psychology

MENTAL ABILITIES
What have psychologists done to make intelligence tests less culturally biased? (p. 374)

TREATMENT OF PSYCHOLOGICAL DISORDERS
How have clinical psychologists become more sensitive to culturally diverse clients? (p. 591)

HEALTH, STRESS, AND COPING
How have psychologists in biological and personality psychology helped to prevent heart disease? (p. 478)

provide, psychologists' statements would be no more credible than those of astrologers or the *National Enquirer*.

Linkages Within Psychology and Beyond

Psychology's subfields are not isolated areas of inquiry but overlapping frontiers of interest. Psychologists from many subfields may address a specific topic such as violence or language or an overarching issue such as how biological and cultural influences interact (Plomin & Neiderhiser, 1992). This overlap is exemplified by psychologists who work in more than one subfield and apply more than one approach (Cacioppo & Berntson, 1992). It is not surprising, for example, to meet a cognitive psychologist who combines biological and cognitive approaches in conducting research on the brain-wave patterns associated with thinking.

Even when psychologists do not themselves conduct research across subfields, they often draw on, and contribute to, the knowledge developed in other subfields. Their theories, methods, findings, and applications to daily life are inextricably linked. We illustrate a few of these linkages at the beginning of each chapter of this book in a "Linkages" diagram, similar to the one shown here. Each question in the diagram illustrates a linkage between the topics of two chapters; the page numbers indicate where the question is discussed. To help you keep these linkages in mind as you read the book, we have also placed each linking question in the margin next to the major discussion of that question (see, for example, p. 36). By examining the diagram in each chapter, you can see how the topic of that chapter is related to other subfields of psychology. In each chapter, one of these relationships is given special attention in a section entitled "Linkages."

Much as psychology's subfields are linked to one another, psychology is linked to many other academic disciplines. Sometimes these linkages occur because psychologists and researchers from other disciplines have common interests in a broad topic. Cognitive science, which we described earlier, is one example. Another is *neuroscience,* a multidisciplinary research enterprise that examines the structure and function of the nervous system, in animals and humans, at levels ranging from the individual cell to the behaving organism. This integrated field includes biological psychologists as well as specialists in neuroanatomy, neurophysiology, neurochemistry, genetics, and computer science. Some observers predict that biological psychologists, like the colleagues with whom they work, will soon be known simply as "neuroscientists."

Psychology is also linked with other disciplines because research and theory from one discipline is applicable to another. For example, psychologists are beginning to apply chaos theory—which was developed in physics and mathematics to understand natural systems such as weather—to detect underlying order in apparently random patterns of violence, drug abuse, or family conflict (Abraham, Abraham & Shaw, 1991; Chamberlain, 1990; Hawkins, 1990). Similarly, political scientists have applied research by social psychologists on cooperation, conflict, and negotiation to help them understand international tensions (see, for example, Tetlock, 1986; Worchel & Simpson, 1993).

This book is filled with examples of other ways in which psychological theories and research have been applied to fields as diverse as medicine, dentistry, law, business, engineering, architecture, aviation, public health, and sports. Cognitive psychologists' research on memory has influenced the ways in which attorneys question eyewitnesses and judges instruct juries; social psychologists' work on persuasion has shaped advertising campaigns for stemming the spread of AIDS; and research by industrial-organizational psychologists is helping budding businesses in Russia and other former Soviet states adjust to and survive in a market-driven economy.

Human Diversity and Psychology

The Soviet example is of more than passing interest because it provides an analogy for another important aspect of the diversity inherent in psychology. Until the Soviet Union dissolved in 1991, most westerners, and certainly most

Psychologists who specialize in *engineering, or human-factors, psychology* have helped to create computer-driven flight simulators like this one, which not only allow safer and more effective pilot training but also determine the arrangement of an airliner's vast array of instruments and warning lights so that the pilot can react to them quickly and correctly. Engineers and designers have applied experimental and cognitive psychologists' research on how people perceive the world and handle information as they strive to create computer keyboards, nuclear power plant control panels, and other vital equipment that is logically arranged and easy to use.

During Operation Desert Storm, many American soldiers were shocked by some of the cultural rules in Saudi Arabia, where alcohol is forbidden and women are not permitted to drive, much less vote. People differ greatly as a result of the culture in which they are raised. Particular ways of thinking and behaving that have been adaptive for the survival and satisfaction of certain groups tend to be passed down, often by example, from one generation to the next. Learned, culture-based behaviors, such as fishing for a living, can change more quickly than inherited characteristics, but their roots in tradition often cause them to change more slowly for the group as a whole than for any individual. This is why young people who reject their culture's traditional values tend to leave that culture rather than trying to endure or change it. Psychologists have become increasingly sensitive to the role of sociocultural variables such as gender, ethnicity, and culture in shaping human behavior and mental processes.

Americans, tended to perceive it as a single entity and the Soviet people as a relatively homogenous group. Yet it was actually a political and economic association of dozens of diverse states, each with distinct traditions, alliances, and animosities.

Similarly, many psychologists once implicitly assumed that all people are essentially the same, and that whatever principles emerged from research with local volunteer subjects would apply to people everywhere. Since about 90 percent of researchers in psychology work at universities in North America and Europe, they tended to study local college students, mostly white and middle class, and more often men than women (Crawford & Marecek, 1989; Graham, 1992). Most of the psychologists, too—including those traditionally identified as major figures in the history of psychology—tended to be white, middle class, and male (Walker, 1991).

From one perspective, studying a narrow sample of humankind need not threaten the generality of psychological research, because in many ways, people *are* very much alike. For example, all people tend to live in groups, develop religious beliefs, and create rules, music, and games. Similarly, the principles governing nerve-cell activity or reactions to heat or a sour taste are the same in men and women the world over, as is their recognition of a smile.

But are the forces that motivate people to achieve, or the development of their moral thought, or their patterns of interpersonal communication universal as well? Do the principles derived from research on European-American males in the Midwest apply to African-American women in inner-city ghettos or to people in Greece, Argentina, or Egypt? Not always. What people experience and what people learn through that experience are shaped by *sociocultural variables*, which are variations in social identity and background such as gender, ethnicity, social class, and culture. These variables create many significant differences in behavior and mental processes, especially from one culture to another (Berry et al., 1992; Lonner & Malpass, 1994).

A **culture** has been defined as the accumulation of values, rules of behavior, forms of expression, religious beliefs, occupational choices, and the like for a

Table 1.3
Some Characteristics of Behavior and Mental Processes Typical of Individualist vs. Collectivist Cultures

Cultural factors do not act as cookie-cutters that make everyone in a given culture the same, but certain broad tendencies in behavior and mental processes have been associated with particular kinds of cultures. For example, many people in individualist cultures, such as those typical of North America and Western Europe, tend to focus on and value personal rather than group goals and achievement. Competitiveness to distinguish oneself from others is common, as is a sense of isolation. Many people in collectivist cultures, such as Japan, tend to think of themselves mainly as part of family or work groups. Cooperative effort aimed at advancing the welfare of those groups is highly valued, and while loneliness is seldom a problem, fear of rejection by the group is common. Though we seldom think about it, many aspects of American culture—from self-reliant cowboy heroes and bonuses for "top" employees to the invitation to "help yourself" at a buffet table—reflect Americans' tendency toward an individualist orientation.

Variable	Individualist	Collectivist
Personal identity	Separate from others	Connected to others
Major goals	Self-defined; be unique; realize your personal potential; compete with others	Defined by others; belong; occupy your proper place; meet your obligations to others; be like others
Criteria for self-esteem	Ability to express unique aspects of the self; be self-assured	Ability to restrain the self and be part of a social unit; be self-effacing
Sources of success and failure	Success comes from personal effort, failure from external factors	Success due to help from others; failure due to personal faults
Major frame of reference	Personal attitudes, traits, and goals	Family, work group

group of people who share a common language and environment (Triandis, Kurowski & Gelfand, 1993). As such, culture is an organizing and stabilizing influence. It not only encourages or discourages particular behaviors and mental processes but also allows people to understand and anticipate the behavior of others in that culture. It is a kind of group adaptation, passed by tradition and example rather than genes from one generation to the next. Culture determines, for example, whether children's education will focus on skill at hunting or reading, how close people stand while having a conversation, and whether or not they form lines in public places (Munroe & Munroe, 1994).

Psychologists as well as anthropologists have isolated many ways in which cultures differ (Berry et al., 1992). Table 1.3 outlines one interesting way of analyzing these differences; it shows that many cultures can be described as either individualistic or collectivist. *Individualistic* cultures tend to accept people who place personal goals ahead of the goals of the collective (such as the family or work group), whereas *collectivist* cultures tend to reject such people and to encourage subordination of personal goals to the goals of collectives. Cultures also vary in the degree to which they impose tight or loose rules for social behavior, emphasize achievement or self-awareness, seek dominion over nature or integration with it, and emphasize the importance of time (see, for example, Markus & Kitayama, 1991; Triandis, 1990).

Culture is often associated with a particular country, but in fact most countries are *multicultural;* in other words, they host many *subcultures* within their borders. Often, these subcultures are formed by people with different ethnic origins. In the United States, the population includes African-Americans, Hispanic-Americans, Asian-Americans, and Native Americans as well as European-Americans with Italian, German, English, Polish, Irish, and other origins. The individuals in these groups who identify with their cultural heritage tend to share behaviors, values, and beliefs based on their culture of origin and, hence, form a subculture.

Like fish unaware of the water in which they are immersed, people often fail to notice how their culture or subculture has shaped their patterns of thinking and behavior until they come in contact with people whose culture or subculture has shaped different patterns. In southcentral Los Angeles, for example, Korean storekeepers' culturally correct but inadvertently insulting practice of placing change on the counter instead of in the customer's hand helped stir anger and resentment among customers from other cultural backgrounds. That anger led some lawbreakers to target Korean-owned businesses for destruction during the riots that followed the Rodney King verdict in 1992. Even some of the misunderstandings that occur between men and women in the same culture are traceable to subtle, culturally influenced differences in their communication patterns (Tannen, 1990). In the United States, for example, women's efforts to connect with others by talking may be perceived by many men as "pointless" unless the discussion is aimed at solving a specific problem; thus women often feel frustrated and misunderstood by men who tend to offer in lieu of conversation well-intentioned, but unwanted, advice.

Psychologists interested in *cross-cultural* research have studied cultural differences for decades (Triandis, 1964), but the influence of sociocultural variables is now of growing interest to psychologists in general (Albert, 1988; Bronstein & Quina, 1988; Lonner & Malpass, 1994). As psychology strives to be the science of *all* behavior and mental processes, its research will increasingly take gender and other sociocultural variables into account (Riger, 1992; Tavris, 1992; Triandis, Kurowski & Gelfand, 1993). The trend in this direction will be evident in much of the research described in the chapters to come.

Future Directions

Before you begin what we hope will be an exciting tour of psychology, we would like to point out a few things about how this book is organized and why. Because they are so fundamental to the development of psychological knowledge, we move next to a chapter on the methods that psychologists use to conduct their research and analyze their results. It is there, also, that we introduce the importance of *critical thinking* in dealing with psychology and the world in general. In Chapter 3, we cover developmental psychology, describing how a single cell develops into the complex and fascinating organism known as a human being. Examining developmental psychology early in the book provides both a preview of the many aspects of behavior and mental processes to be discussed in later chapters and a portrait of the human being as a unified whole—a creature who can act and react, feel and think, plan and imagine, learn and remember, and, above all, be consciously aware of the world and communicate with it. Through the rest of the book, we examine in more detail each of the major components of behavior and mental processes that ultimately come together in the whole human being.

This process of piecing together behavior and mental processes begins with cells and other biological structures. Thus, in Chapter 4 we examine biological aspects of psychology, showing how nerve cells communicate with one another to create behavior and mental activity. Next, in Chapter 5, on sensation, we consider how special groups of cells detect sound, light, and other forms of energy and how they convert this energy into the sensations of hearing, vision, taste, smell, and touch. How people organize, interpret, and attend to these sensations is the subject of Chapter 6, on perception. The analysis of how people experience the world is continued in Chapter 7, where we focus on consciousness and how it is affected by sleep, hypnosis, meditation, and drugs.

Having brought the complexities of consciousness into the picture, we next consider learning, memory, decision making, thinking, and the use of language, all of which are covered in Chapters 8 through 10. Of course, some people are better at these processes than others; in Chapter 11, we discuss individual differences in mental ability.

Psychology involves the study not only of what people do but also why they do it. This raises the topic of motivation, which is almost always accompanied by anger, joy, fear, hope, desperation, or any number of other emotions. Motivation and emotion are the subjects of Chapter 12.

At that point, we are ready to begin looking at how all the processes considered so far are integrated in functioning individuals and how those individuals relate to their environments. We begin this phase of study by considering in Chapter 13—on health, stress, and coping—how people's reactions to various forms of stress affect their health and how various lifestyles and ways of thinking promote or endanger health. We will see that some differences in people's stress responses and lifestyles are related to personality, the topic of Chapter 14. There we consider what personality is and how it relates to behavior and mental processes. In Chapter 15, on psychological disorders, we review some of the many ways in which human behavior and mental processes can go awry. In Chapter 16 we describe the major approaches and methods used in treating psychological problems. In Chapters 17 and 18 we examine social psychology—the ways in which one person's actions, thoughts, attitudes, emotions, and other processes influence and are influenced by other people.

By the end of your tour of psychology, we hope you might consider one of the many career opportunities offered in the field, or at least be curious enough to take more psychology courses.

Summary and Key Terms

Psychology is the science of behavior and mental processes. The topics included in this field range from the study of nerve cells to the interaction of people in families and other groups.

The World of Psychology: An Overview

What psychologists study depends largely on their chosen area of specialization; where they search for answers is guided by their theoretical approach.

Subfields of Psychology

Because the subject matter of psychology is so diverse, most psychologists work in particular subfields within the discipline. For example, *experimental and cognitive psychologists* focus on basic psychological processes such as learning, memory, and perception in both animals and humans; they also study judgment, decision making, and problem solving. *Biological psychologists,* also called *physiological psychologists,* study topics such as how nerve cells communicate with one another and the role played by the nervous system in regulating behavior. *Personality psychologists* focus on the unique characteristics that determine individuals' behavior. *Social psychologists* examine questions regarding how people influence one another, especially in groups. *Clinical and counseling psychologists* provide direct service to troubled people and conduct research on abnormal behavior. *Developmental psy-*

chologists specialize in trying to understand the development of behavior and mental processes over a lifetime.

Approaches to Psychology

Psychologists also differ in their theoretical approaches. Those adopting a *biological approach* examine how physiological processes shape behavior and mental processes. The *evolutionary approach* emphasizes the inherited, adaptive aspects of behavior and mental processes. The application of this approach to social behavior is known as *sociobiology.* The *psychodynamic approach* sees behavior and mental processes as a struggle to resolve conflicts between impulses and the demands made by society to control those impulses. Psychologists who take the *behavioral approach* see behavior as determined primarily by learning based on past experiences with rewards and punishments. The *cognitive approach* advocates the idea that behavior cannot be understood until the basic mental processes that underlie it are understood. The *humanistic approach* views behavior as controlled by the decisions that people make about their lives based on their perceptions of the world.

Unity and Diversity in Psychology

In spite of the diversity of its subfields and theoretical approaches, psychology is unified by a commitment to scientific methods and by shared interests.

Research: The Foundation of Psychology

Because psychology is a science, all of its subfields emphasize empirical research.

Linkages Within Psychology and Beyond

Psychologists often work in more than one subfield and usually share knowledge with colleagues in many subfields. Psychologists also draw on and contribute to knowledge in other disciplines such as biology, chemistry, physics, anthropology, and political science.

Human Diversity and Psychology

Psychologists are increasingly taking into account the influence of *culture* and other sociocultural variables such as gender and ethnicity in shaping human behavior and mental processes.

Chapter 2

Research in Psychology

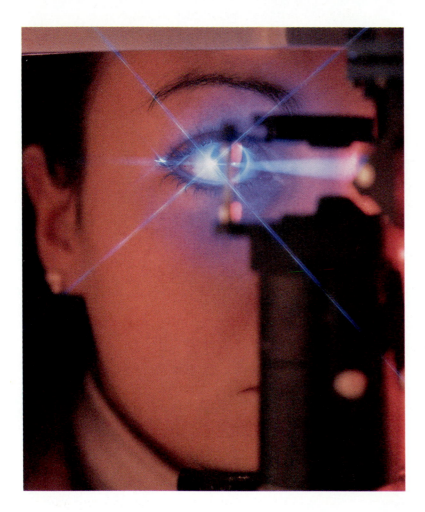

Outline

Francine Shapiro, a clinical psychologist practicing in northern California, had an odd experience one day in 1987. She was walking in a park, thinking about some distressing events, when she noticed that her emotional reaction to them was fading away. Upon reflection, she realized that she had been involuntarily moving her eyes back and forth. Did the eye movements have anything to do with the change? When she made the eye movements deliberately, the emotion-reducing effect was even stronger. Curious, she examined the effect in others, first among friends and colleagues, then with clients who had suffered childhood sexual abuse, rape, or other traumas. She asked these people to think about their unpleasant experiences while following her finger with their eyes as she moved it back and forth in front of their faces. Like her, they said that their reactions to the memories faded. And her clients reported that emotional flashbacks, nightmares, fears, and other trauma-related problems dropped dramatically, often after only one session (Shapiro, 1989a).

Dr. Shapiro eventually called her new treatment *eye movement desensitization and reprocessing,* or *EMD/R* (Shapiro, 1991). Today, Dr. Shapiro and other therapists are using EMD/R to treat a wide range of anxiety-related problems. But could anxiety be reduced by anything as simple as eye movements?

Psychologists do not yet know what to make of EMD/R. As is the case when examining any phenomenon, it is vital to know first what questions to ask and then how to go about searching for the answers. Knowing what to ask depends on an ability to think critically about the world; making progress toward answers depends on translating critical thinking into scientific research methods. As the Linkages diagram illustrates, psychologists use these methods to study a wide range of behavior and mental processes. In this chapter, we summarize some of the basic questions that flow from thinking critically about psychology, and we describe the methods of science.

Thinking Critically About Psychology (or Anything Else)

Often, people simply accept what they are told. Indeed, advertisers, politicians, TV evangelists, pop-psychologists, and activists of all kinds who seek your money, votes, or allegiance hope that you will believe their promises or claims without careful thought. Especially if they have made misleading statements, they hope you will not think critically.

Critical thinking is the process of assessing claims and making judgments on the basis of well-supported evidence (Wade, 1988). Consider our description of Shapiro's EMD/R treatment. Does it reduce anxiety-related problems, as Shapiro's report suggests? One strategy for applying critical thinking to this or any other topic is to ask the following five questions:

1. *What am I being asked to believe or accept?* In this case, the assertion to be examined is that EMD/R causes the reduction or elimination of certain anxiety-related problems.
2. *What evidence is available to support the assertion?* Shapiro began her research on EMD/R by gathering information about whether the reduction of her own emotional distress was related to the eye movements or simply a coincidence. When she found the same effect in others, coincidence became a less plausible explanation.
3. *Are there alternative ways of interpreting the evidence?* The dramatic effects experienced by Shapiro's friends and clients might be due not to EMD/R but to factors such as their motivation to change or their desire to please her. Even the most remarkable evidence cannot be accepted as confirming an assertion until all equally plausible alternative assertions have been ruled out, which leads to the next step in critical thinking.
4. *What additional evidence would help to evaluate the alternatives?* It would be ideal to identify three groups of people who are identical in every way except for the anxiety treatment they received. If a group receiving EMD/R improved to a much greater extent than those given an equally motivating but inherently useless treatment, or no treatment at all, it would become less likely that EMD/R effects could be explained on the basis of clients' motivation or the mere passage of time. The ways in which psychologists and other scientists collect evidence to test alternative explanations constitute the methods of scientific research, which we describe in detail later.
5. *What conclusions are most reasonable?* Because the evidence actually available so far does not rule out

Linkages

The questions in this diagram illustrate some of the relationships between the topic of this chapter, research methods, and the topics of other chapters. The linkages are many. Indeed, virtually all the research and conclusions discussed in this book flow from the methods and techniques described in this chapter. Remember that some of the questions in the diagram are examined in this chapter and some are answered in other chapters; the page numbers indicate where the questions are discussed. ■

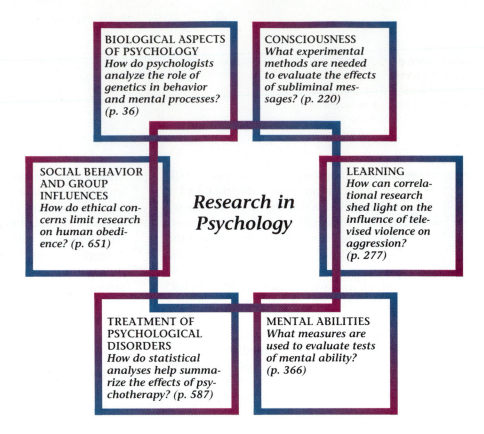

BIOLOGICAL ASPECTS OF PSYCHOLOGY
How do psychologists analyze the role of genetics in behavior and mental processes? (p. 36)

CONSCIOUSNESS
What experimental methods are needed to evaluate the effects of subliminal messages? (p. 220)

SOCIAL BEHAVIOR AND GROUP INFLUENCES
How do ethical concerns limit research on human obedience? (p. 651)

Research in Psychology

LEARNING
How can correlational research shed light on the influence of televised violence on aggression? (p. 277)

TREATMENT OF PSYCHOLOGICAL DISORDERS
How do statistical analyses help summarize the effects of psychotherapy? (p. 587)

MENTAL ABILITIES
What measures are used to evaluate tests of mental ability? (p. 366)

alternative explanations for the effects of EMD/R, the only reasonable conclusions to be drawn at this point are that EMD/R seems to have an impact and that further research is needed in order to understand it.

Does that sound wishy-washy? Critical thinking sometimes does create the appearance of indecisiveness because conclusions must be tempered by the evidence available. But critical thinking opens the way to understanding. To help you hone your critical thinking skills, we include in each chapter of this book a section called "Thinking Critically" in which we examine an issue by considering the same five questions we used here to examine EMD/R.

Critical Thinking and Scientific Research

Imagine that you are Dr. Francine Shapiro: you begin, as scientific work often does, with curiosity about a phenomenon. Curiosity frequently provokes stimulating questions, but they may be too general to be investigated scientifically. In Dr. Shapiro's place, you might at first wonder, can eye movements help with anxiety? However, critical thinking requires that you make your question more specific, in order to clarify the assertion to be evaluated.

Psychologists and other scientists typically phrase their questions about a phenomenon in terms of a **hypothesis**—a specific, testable proposition about a phenomenon. Researchers state hypotheses in order to establish in clear, precise terms what they think may be true, and how they will know if it is not. In this case, the hypothesis might be: *EMD/R treatment causes significant improvement in anxiety.* To make it easier to understand and evaluate hypotheses, scientists employ **operational definitions,** which are statements describing the exact operations or methods used in their research. Thus, in the hypothesis just stated, "EMD/R treatment" might be operationally defined as creating a certain number of back-and-forth eye movements per second for a particular period of time, while "significant improvement in anxiety" might be defined

Acceptance of unsubstantiated information merely because it is cleverly or confidently stated, comes from prominent people, or is endorsed by many others can be dangerous—not just for those who get stuck with useless products but also for citizens at large. Whether the claim is for the value of astrology, the effectiveness of a new therapy method, or the wisdom of a government policy, critical thinkers carefully evaluate evidence before accepting a claim or assertion as fact. Abandoning uncritical acceptance of stated "facts" and even long-held beliefs for the more laborious but vital task of critically evaluating evidence can open the way to a fuller understanding of a broad range of issues, including research in psychology and other fields.

as a certain amount of reduction in clients' self-reported discomfort. The kind of treatment a subject is given and the results of that treatment are examples of research **variables**, specific factors or characteristics that can take on different values in research.

In evaluating a hypothesis, scientists look not only for evidence that supports it but also for evidence that refutes it. They not only gather evidence but also assess its quality. Usually, the quality of evidence is evaluated in terms of two characteristics: reliability and validity. In essence, *reliability* is the degree to which the evidence is repeatable; the *validity* of evidence is the degree to which it actually supports an assertion. For example, the initial claims for EMD/R stemmed from Dr. Shapiro's use of the treatment with her colleagues and clients. If she had not been able to repeat, or *replicate,* the initial effects, or if only a few clients showed improvement, you might question the reliability of the evidence. If the clients' reports of improvement were not checked for accuracy, you might doubt the validity of the evidence.

The Role of Theories

After examining the evidence from research on particular phenomena, scientists often begin to favor certain explanations. Sometimes, they organize these explanations into a **theory,** which is an integrated set of propositions that can be used to account for, predict, and even control certain phenomena. For example, evidence that people under stress often smoke more, overeat, or increase alcohol consumption has led to the theory that apparently self-abusive behaviors may actually be forms of stress management. Broader and more famous theories include Charles Darwin's theory of evolution and Sigmund Freud's theory of psychoanalysis, discussed in Chapter 1. Throughout this book you will encounter numerous other theories designed to explain phenomena such as color vision, memory, aggression, and sleep.

Theories are tentative explanations that must themselves be subjected to scientific evaluation based on critical thinking. In other words, theories are built on research results, but they also generate hypotheses for further research. Without research results, there would be nothing to explain; without explanatory theories, the results might never be organized in a usable way. The continuing interaction of theory and research lies at the heart of the process that has created the knowledge generated in psychology over the past century. Predictions flowing from a theory proposed by one psychologist will be tested by many other psychologists. If research does not support a theory, it is revised or, sometimes, abandoned.

As coming chapters illustrate, the constant formulation, evaluation, reformulation, and abandonment of theories has generated many competing explanations of behavior and mental processes. The resulting absence of absolute conclusions can be frustrating. While promoters of pop-psychology are happy

Curiosity about important everyday phenomena, such as what factors determine whether two people will be attracted to each other, is often the basis for psychological research. In many cases, the results not only contribute to knowledge about the phenomenon originally studied but also provoke additional questions that help clarify principles governing other aspects of human behavior, such as how people perceive one another.

to haunt the talk shows, confidently espousing sweeping theories about pyramid power or flying-saucer abductions, scientists must be more careful. Conclusions about many of the phenomena described in this book are tentative and almost always accompanied by a call for additional research. In fact, it is the rare piece of research that does not raise more questions than it answers.

Still, current knowledge and tentative conclusions can be put to good use. EMD/R and many other forms of treatment, for example, are being applied and studied every day. Indeed, psychologists in all subfields are using today's knowledge as the foundation for the research that will increase tomorrow's understanding. In the rest of this chapter, we describe their research methods and some of the pitfalls threatening progress toward their goals.

Research Methods in Psychology

Like other scientists, psychologists strive to achieve four main goals in their research: to *describe* a phenomenon, to *make predictions* about it, and to introduce enough *control* in their research to allow them to *explain* the phenomenon with some degree of confidence. Certain methods are especially useful for gathering the evidence needed to attain each of these goals. Specifically, psychologists tend to describe and predict behavior and mental processes through *naturalistic observation, case studies,* and *surveys;* they use *experiments* to introduce the control necessary to rule out alternative explanations for the evidence they collect and thus help establish *cause-effect relationships,* in which one variable can be shown to have actually caused a change in another. Thus, Francine Shapiro initially *described* the EMD/R effect on the basis of observations of her own reactions; then she tested the *prediction* that similar results might occur in other cases. Later we discuss an experiment Dr. Shapiro conducted in an effort to introduce enough *control* into the treatment situation to begin evaluating alternative *explanations* for the effect, and thus to explore whether EMD/R itself is actually the cause of clients' improvement. Let's look at how these goals and methods are blended in psychologists' work.

In the "classic" scientific research sequence, explanations result when initial observations of a phenomenon suggest a hypothesis about it, thus leading to predictions, further observations, more precise predictions, and then experiments to eliminate alternative explanations and establish cause-effect relations between variables. However, psychologists follow no fixed sequence in working toward their goals of description, prediction, control, and explanation. Sometimes explanatory theories spark the curiosity that begins new research and guides researchers in their choice of topics to explore. Or, as in Francine Shapiro's case, the first step might come from observation.

Naturalistic Observation

Sometimes, the best way to gather descriptive data is through naturalistic observation, the process of watching without interfering as a phenomenon occurs in the natural environment. This method is especially valuable in cases where other methods are likely to be disruptive or misleading. For example, if you studied animals only by observing them in the laboratory, you might conclude that learning alone determines most of what they do, because you would not see how they normally use cues in their natural environment. In fact, as noted in Chapter 1, many animals display inherited patterns of behavior that are predictable, stereotyped, and triggered automatically by environmental events.

Naturalistic observation of people can also be revealing. For example, when John Gottman and other psychologists observed married couples discussing their conflicts, they discovered that distressed pairs tend to assume the worst about each other and to exchange increasingly negative messages that eventually halt communication (Bradbury & Fincham, 1992; Gottman & Levenson, 1986). Some marital treatment programs now focus on preventing such emotional escalation (Baucom & Epstein, 1990).

Naturalistic observation can provide large amounts of rich information, but it is not problem-free (Nietzel, Bernstein & Milich, 1994). For one thing, when people know they are being observed (and ethics usually require that they do know), they tend to act differently than they otherwise would. Researchers typically combat this problem by observing long enough for subjects to get used to the situation and begin behaving more naturally. Observations can also be distorted if observers expect to see certain behaviors. Thus, if observers in a study evaluating a treatment for social anxiety know which subjects at a social gathering had received treatment and which had not, they might tend to rate treated subjects as more socially skilled. To get the most out of naturalistic observation, psychologists must counteract problems such as these.

Case Studies

Observations are often an important part of a case study, which is an intensive examination of a phenomenon in a particular individual, group, or situation. Often, case studies combine observations, tests, interviews, and analysis of written records. Case studies are especially useful when a phenomenon is new, complex, or relatively rare. The EMD/R method, for example, first attracted psychologists' attention through case-study reports (Shapiro, 1989a).

Case studies have a long tradition in clinical work. Freud's development of psychoanalysis, for example, was based on case studies of people whose paralysis or other physical symptoms disappeared when they were hypnotized or asleep. Case studies have also played a special role in neuropsychology, the study of the relationships among brain activity, thinking, and behavior. Consider the case of Dr. P., a patient described by Oliver Sacks (1985). A distinguished musician with superior intelligence, Dr. P. began to display odd symptoms, such as the inability to recognize familiar people or to distinguish between people and inanimate objects. During a visit to a neurologist, Dr. P. mistook his foot for his shoe. When he rose to leave, he tried to lift off his wife's head and put it, like a hat, on his own. He could not name even the most common objects when he looked at them, although he could describe them. When handed a glove, for example, he said, "A continuous surface, infolded on itself. It appears to have . . . five outpouchings, if this is the word. . . . A container of some sort." Only later, when he put it on his hand, did he exclaim, "My God, it's a glove!" (Sacks, 1985, p. 13).

Linkages: Konrad Lorenz, one of the founders of ethology, used naturalistic observation to describe many examples of inborn but environmentally triggered behaviors, discussed under the evolutionary approach in Chapter 1. One of the most delightful of these is shown here. Baby geese follow their mother because her movement and honking provide signals that are naturally attractive. After Lorenz squatted and made mother-goose noises in front of newborn geese whose real mother was not present, the goslings began following him wherever he went, much to the amusement of his neighbors.

Guaranteed anonymity may help improve the validity of survey data. For example, a confidential telephone survey by the Crime Victims Research and Treatment Center found that the frequency of rape in the United States in 1990 may have been five times higher than that found in a Justice Department survey of rapes reported to the police that year (Associated Press, 1992).

Using case studies like this one, pioneers in neuropsychology noted the deficits suffered by people with particular kinds of brain damage or disease. Eventually, neuropsychologists were able to tie specific disorders to certain types of injuries, tumors, poisons, and other causes. (The cause of Dr. P.'s symptoms was apparently a large brain tumor.) Case studies do have their limitations, however. They may contain only the evidence that a particular researcher considered important, and, of course, they are unlikely to be representative of people in general. Still, case studies can provide valuable raw material for further research. They can also be vital sources of information about particular people, and they serve as the testing ground for new treatments, training programs, and other applications of research.

Surveys

Case studies provide close-up views of individuals; surveys give broad portraits of large groups. A **survey** involves asking people questions, in interviews or on questionnaires, in order to obtain descriptions of their behavior, attitudes, beliefs, opinions, and intentions.

To conduct a useful survey, researchers must phrase their questions clearly and select their subjects carefully. Consider a survey conducted several years ago by Ann Landers. She asked her female readers whether they would prefer to have sexual relations with their partners or just to be held and cuddled. The results showed a preference for cuddling. Does this mean that sex is going out of style? Very unlikely. Several other explanations are possible. Perhaps the preference for cuddling emerged because the question was phrased in a way that left no room for people to indicate that they liked both cuddling and sex. Or perhaps the women who answered the question were not representative of women in general.

Other problems that may lurk within the survey method are more difficult to avoid. People may be reluctant to admit undesirable or embarrassing things about themselves or may say what they feel they *should* say about an issue. For example, people may be reluctant to admit negative attitudes toward minorities or may understate the strength of those attitudes (Ottati et al., 1989). In spite of these problems, surveys provide an excellent way of gathering large amounts of data from a large number of people at relatively low cost.

Testing Hypotheses Through Correlational Research

Data from naturalistic observations, case studies, and surveys help psychologists to describe behavior and mental processes and to formulate predictions and other hypotheses. To test a prediction or hypothesis, they often gather additional data and then analyze the data in order to measure the correlation between variables.

Correlation means just what it says—"co-relation"; it is a measure both of the degree to which one variable is related to another and of the direction of the relationship. In a *positive correlation,* two variables increase together or decrease together. In a *negative correlation,* the variables move in opposite directions: when one increases, the other decreases. For example, James Schaefer noticed that the tempo of jukebox music seemed to be related to the rate at which bar customers drink alcohol. This relationship was replicated in observations of 4,500 people in 65 bars (Schaefer et al., 1988). Schaefer found that the musical tempo and drinking rate were negatively correlated: as musical tempo decreased, the drinking rate increased.

The accuracy of predictions about one variable from knowledge of another depends on the strength of the correlation. If the correlation is very weak, then knowing something about one variable tells you very little about the

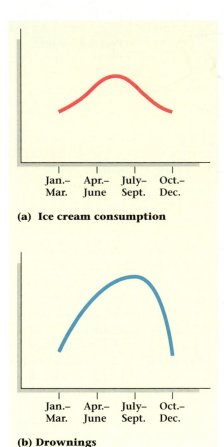

(a) Ice cream consumption

(b) Drownings

Figure 2.1
Correlation and Causation
This graph shows that, in the United States, ice cream consumption and drownings tend to rise and fall together during the year. However, this *correlation* does not mean that eating ice cream *causes* people to drown. Indeed, correlation between two variables says nothing about whether one variable actually exerts an impact on the other. In this case, the correlation probably reflects a third variable—time of year—which affects both ice cream sales and the likelihood that people are swimming and boating.

other. Later in this chapter and in the Appendix we discuss how the strength of correlations are measured.

The variables of interest in psychology are seldom perfectly correlated or utterly uncorrelated. Suppose you want to test the hypothesis that people enjoy social dates more when the dating couple holds similar beliefs. You operationally define "amount of enjoyment" as ratings on a ten-point scale and "shared beliefs" as the number of similar scores on attitude tests about important issues; you find a strong, but not perfect, positive correlation between the similarity scores and the enjoyment ratings. (Researchers have in fact found this correlation; see Chapter 17.) The correlation suggests that knowing how similar a couple's beliefs are would allow you to predict their enjoyment better than you could by random guessing, but that the predictions would not be perfectly accurate.

Correlational methods greatly enhance psychologists' ability to describe and predict phenomena; they help in the evaluation of existing hypotheses; and they often lead to new hypotheses. But correlational research does not indicate *why* two variables are related. For example, the fact that the amount of alcohol consumed and the intensity of a hangover are strongly correlated by itself says nothing about the biochemical processes underlying the relationship. Indeed, as Figure 2.1 illustrates, the fact that two variables are correlated cannot even tell you whether one variable actually influences the other or, if it does, which one is doing the influencing.

Consider some explanations for the relationship between watching violent television programs and acting violently. Researchers have found that there is a positive correlation between these variables. But does seeing violence on TV cause viewers to be violent, or does being violent to begin with cause a preference for violent shows? Or perhaps neither causes the other; violent behavior *and* TV choices could both be due to a third factor, such as stress. In the chapter on learning we discuss how researchers have evaluated these possibilities.

In order to choose among alternative hypotheses and establish cause-effect relationships, psychologists must go beyond *correlating* the variables they measure and actually manipulate those variables. In doing so, they try to create situations in which they can control the influence of unwanted factors. If they do this properly, they create conditions that more clearly indicate whether a cause-effect relationship exists between variables, which influences which, and perhaps even why. Usually, this kind of research takes the form of an experiment.

Experimental Research

Experiments are situations in which the researcher manipulates one variable and then observes the effect of that manipulation on another variable, while holding all other variables constant. The variable manipulated by the experimenter is called the **independent variable.** The variable to be observed is called the **dependent variable** because it is affected by, or *depends on,* the independent variable.

Francine Shapiro performed an experiment to try to better understand the apparent effects of EMD/R. As illustrated in Figure 2.2, she first identified twenty-two people suffering ill-effects from traumas such as rape or military combat, then divided them into two groups. The first group received a single session of EMD/R treatment for about fifty minutes; the second focused on their unpleasant memories for eight minutes, but without moving their eyes back and forth (Shapiro, 1989b). The experimenter controlled whether EMD/R treatment was administered to each subject, so the presence or absence

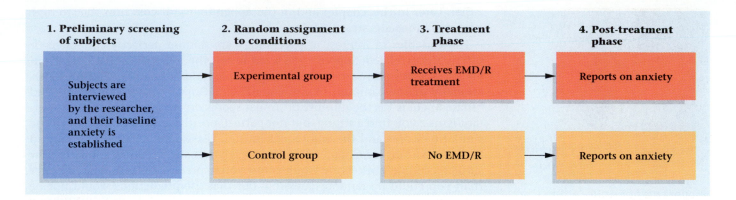

Figure 2.2
Design of a Simple
Two-Group Experiment
Ideally, the only difference between
the experimental and control group
in experiments like this one is
whether the subjects receive the
treatment the experimenter wishes
to evaluate. Under such ideal circumstances, any difference in the results should be attributable to the
treatment.

of treatment was the independent variable. The subjects' anxiety level while
thinking about their traumatic memories was the dependent variable.

The group that receives the experimental treatment is called, naturally
enough, the **experimental group.** The people who receive no treatment or
some other comparison treatment are called the **control group.** Control
groups provide baselines against which to compare the performance of others.
In Shapiro's experiment, having a control group allowed the experimenter to
measure how much change in anxiety can be expected from exposure to bad
memories without EMD/R treatment. If everything about the two groups is
exactly the same except for exposure to treatment, then any difference in anxiety between the groups at the end of the experiment should be caused by the
treatment, not merely correlated with it. In turn, hypotheses about alternative
causes become less plausible.

The results of Dr. Shapiro's (1989b) experiment showed that subjects receiving EMD/R treatment experienced a complete and nearly immediate reduction
in anxiety over their traumatic memories, while the controls showed no
change. At this point, you might be ready to believe that the treatment caused
the difference. Before coming to that conclusion, however, look again at the
design of the experiment. The treatment group's session lasted about fifty minutes, but the control group focused on their memories for only eight minutes.
Would the people in the control group have improved if they had spent fifty
minutes focusing on their memories? We don't know, because the design of
the experiment did not compare methods of equal duration.

Designers and consumers of research must be on guard for such flaws in
experimental control. Before drawing any conclusions from research, you
must consider other factors—especially confounding variables—that might account for the results. **Confounding variables** confuse, or confound, interpretation of the results of an experiment. Any factor that might have affected the
dependent variable, along with or instead of the independent variable, may be
a confounding variable. When confounding variables are present, you cannot
know whether the independent variable or the confounding variable produced
the results. Here we examine three sources of confounding variables: random
variables, subjects' expectations, and experimenter bias.

Random Variables In an ideal research world, the experimental and the
control conditions would be identical except for the amounts of the independent variable, such as the presence or absence of treatment. In reality, however,
there are always other differences, especially in **random variables.** These are
uncontrolled, sometimes uncontrollable, factors such as differences in the
subjects—in their backgrounds, personalities, physical health, or vulnerability
to stress, for example—as well as differences in conditions such as the time of
day and noise level.

Proponents of mental techniques known as Transcendental Meditation (TM) claim that when enough people practice TM at once, it causes an "influence of harmony" throughout the world called the "Maharishi Effect." It has been asserted that this effect—named for TM's founder, Maharishi Mahesh Yogi—is "the only scientific explanation for why U.S.-Soviet relations improved so rapidly in recent years" (Gelderloos et al., 1988; Orme-Johnson, 1992). This is an interesting hypothesis, but is it accurate? Perhaps, but the collapse of the Soviet economy, increasing social unrest in the Soviet Republics, and conflicts within the Soviet government are some of the many plausible alternative hypotheses capable of explaining the reduction of East-West tensions. The causal role of TM can be made more plausible only through experimental methods capable of ruling out these alternative hypotheses.

Random variables are so numerous that no experimenter can create groups that are equivalent on all of them. A common solution to this problem is to flip a coin or use some other random process to assign each subject to experimental or control groups. Such procedures tend to distribute the impact of uncontrolled variables randomly—and probably about evenly—across groups, thus minimizing the chance that they will distort the results of the experiment.

Placebo Effects In Shapiro's experiment, after eight minutes of focusing on negative memories, control subjects were asked to begin moving their eyes; then they, too, started to improve. Was this because of the eye movements themselves, or could it be that the instructions made the subjects feel more confident that they were getting real treatment? This question illustrates a second source of confounding: differences in what subjects think about the experimental situation. If subjects expect that a treatment will help them, they may try harder to improve than those in a control group who receive no treatment, or a less impressive one. In medical and psychological treatments, improvement created by a subject's knowledge and expectations is called the *placebo effect*. A **placebo** (pronounced "pla-see-bow") is a treatment that contains no active ingredient but nevertheless produces an effect because a person *believes* it will have that effect. Patients may improve after they are given a drug, not because the drug contains an effective treatment for their illness but because they believe that the drug will help them.

How can researchers determine the extent to which a result is caused by the independent variable or by a placebo effect? Often they include a special control group that receives *only* a placebo. Then they compare results for the experimental group, the placebo group, and those receiving no treatment. In one smoking-cessation study (Bernstein, 1970), for example, subjects in a placebo group took sugar pills described by the experimenter as "fast-acting tranquilizers" that would help them learn to endure the stress of giving up cigarettes. These subjects did as well at quitting as those in the experimental group, who received extensive treatment. This result suggests that the success of the experimental group may have been due largely to the subjects' expectations, not to the treatment methods. Complete evaluation of the EMD/R treatment must await further research, including placebo-controlled experiments. A number of psychologists are now conducting such research (Boudewyns et al., 1993).

Experimenter Bias Another potential confounding variable comes from **experimenter bias,** the unintentional effect that experimenters may exert on results. Robert Rosenthal (1966) demonstrated the power of experimenter bias. His subjects were laboratory assistants who were asked to run rats in a maze. Rosenthal told some of the assistants that their rats were bred to be particularly "maze-bright"; he told the others that their rats were "maze-dull." In fact, both groups of rats were randomly drawn from the same population and had equal maze-learning capabilities. But the maze-bright animals learned the maze significantly faster than the maze-dull rats. How was this possible? Rosenthal concluded that the result had nothing to do with the rats and everything to do with the experimenters. He suggested that the assistants' expectations about their rats' supposedly superior (or inferior) capabilities caused them to subtly alter their training and handling techniques, which in turn speeded or slowed the animals' learning. Similarly, when administering different kinds of anxiety treatments to different groups, an experimenter's beliefs about which will be the best treatment may lead him or her to do a slightly better job with that treatment and, thus, unintentionally improve its effects.

To prevent experimenter bias from confounding results, experimenters often use a **double-blind design,** an arrangement in which both the subjects and those giving the treatments are unaware of, or "blind" to, who is receiving a placebo and what results are expected. Only the director of the study—a person with no direct contact with the subjects—knows the hypotheses, who is in the experimental group, and who is in the placebo group.

In short, experiments are vital tools for examining cause-and-effect relationships between variables, but like the other methods we have described, they are vulnerable to error. Scientists try to maximize the value of experimental methods by designing experiments to eliminate as many confounding variables as possible, repeating their studies to ensure consistent results, then tempering their interpretation of the results to take into account the limitations or problems that remain.

Quasi-Experiments   Sometimes an experiment is flawed not because the experimenter failed to create the conditions needed to eliminate alternative hypotheses but because it would have been impossible or unethical to do so. Consider the problem of testing the hypothesis that a pregnant woman's use of drugs causes abnormalities in her developing baby. From an experimental design standpoint, it would be ideal to take a large group of newly pregnant women, randomly assign them to either use or not use, say, cocaine, then observe the condition of the babies they deliver. Such an experiment would be unthinkable, however; so in evaluating such hypotheses, psychologists conduct **quasi-experiments**, which are studies whose designs approximate the control of a true experiment (*quasi-* means "resembling") but may not include manipulation of the independent variable, assignment of subjects to groups, or other elements of true experimental control (Campbell & Stanley, 1966). Even when subjects cannot, for example, be randomly assigned to different conditions, the experimenter can still measure differences in dependent variables between subjects who have or have not been exposed to particular conditions. Thus, a researcher can measure differences in the mental, physical, and behavioral characteristics of children whose mothers did or did not use drugs during pregnancy.

The conclusions that can be drawn from quasi-experiments are usually not as firm as those from true experiments, but, especially when their results are replicated many times with large numbers of subjects, they can inspire considerable confidence. They also allow scientific research to be conducted on topics and in settings that would otherwise be impossible.

Human Diversity and Research Methods

One of the ways in which the results of experiments, naturalistic observations, case studies, and surveys might be limited relates to the representativeness of the subjects. (For a review of these methods, see "In Review: Methods of Psychological Research.") Just as visitors from another galaxy would err wildly if they tried to describe the typical earthling after meeting only Arsenio Hall, Geraldo Rivera, and Roseanne Arnold, psychologists can wander astray if they do not have access to a sample of subjects that provides a fair representation of the population about which they want to draw conclusions.

The process of selecting subjects for research is called **sampling.** Sampling should not be taken lightly. If the subjects come from a particular subgroup (say, male European-American construction workers), the research results might apply, or *generalize,* only to people like them. This is especially likely if the researcher is studying a behavior or mental process that is affected by age, gender, ethnicity, cultural background, socioeconomic status, sexual orientation, disability, or similar characteristics of subjects. When these *subject variables* are likely to be significant, the sample of subjects studied must be representative of people in general if the researcher wants results that reveal something about people in general (Lips, 1988).

In Review: Methods of Psychological Research

Method	Features	Strengths	Pitfalls
Naturalistic observations	Observation of human or animal behavior in the environment where it typically occurs	Provides descriptive and correlational data about behavior presumably uncontaminated by outside influences	Observer bias and subject self-consciousness can distort results
Case studies	Intensive examination of the behavior and mental processes associated with a specific person or situation	Provides detailed descriptive and correlational analyses of new, complex, or rare phenomena	May not provide representative picture of phenomena
Surveys	Standard sets of questions asked of a large number of subjects	Gathers large amounts of descriptive or correlational data relatively quickly and inexpensively	Sampling errors, poorly phrased questions, and response biases can distort results
Experiments	Manipulation of an independent variable and measurement of its effects on a dependent variable	Can establish a cause-effect relationship between dependent and independent variables	Sampling biases may restrict generality of results; confounding variables may prevent valid conclusions
Quasi-experiments	Measurement of dependent variables when independent variables were not entirely under the experimenter's control	Can provide strong evidence suggesting cause-effect relationships	Lack of full control may weaken conclusions
All of the above	Choosing among alternative hypotheses; sometimes generating theories	Can expand our understanding of behavior and mental processes	Errors, limitations, and biases in research evidence can lead to incorrect or incomplete explanations

When every member of the population has an equal chance of being chosen for study, the individuals selected constitute a **random sample.** If not everyone in a population has an equal chance of being selected, the sample is said to be a **biased sample.** In reality, no researcher is likely to draw a truly random sample, unless it is from a very restricted population, which might be of very limited interest. *Representative samples,* which contain people who represent significant subject variables in the overall population, are the practical alternative.

Sometimes representative samples are not necessary, or even desirable. In studying how children develop language, for example, the most valuable case study may be one that examines not the average youngster but the unfortunate child raised in solitary confinement by a parent who provided no language instruction (Rymer, 1992). Further, if you *want* to learn about male European-American construction workers, or pregnant teenagers, or Hispanic-American women executives, all your subjects should be randomly selected from those groups, not from the general population.

For convenience, researchers often begin their work by studying a particular population, such as local college students or, as in Dr. Shapiro's case, friends and colleagues; then they attempt to replicate their results with broader, more representative samples. If outcomes are consistent across a diverse group of subjects, researchers can more confidently draw future samples from whatever willing group is at hand without worrying too much about subject diversity. However, it is vital to show, rather than merely to assume, that subject variables do not limit the breadth of conclusions that can be drawn from research data.

Psychologists must also guard against allowing preconceptions about gender, ethnicity, and other variables to influence the questions they ask, the research designs they create, and the way they analyze, interpret, and report their data (Denmark et al., 1988; McHugh, Koeske & Frieze, 1986). When designing a study on gender and job commitment, for example, the researcher must be sure to look at men and women in jobs of equal status. Comparing male executives with female secretaries might create a false impression of greater male commitment, because people in lower-status jobs (whether male *or* female) tend to change jobs more often. Furthermore, it is important to report whatever results appear. It is just as valuable to know that men and women, or Mexican-Americans and European-Americans, did *not* differ on a test of leadership ability as to know that they did. Perhaps Stephanie Riger (1992) put it best when she said that one of psychologists' greatest challenges is to "disengage themselves sufficiently from commonly shared beliefs so that those beliefs do not predetermine research findings" (p. 732).

Statistical Analysis of Research Results

Whether psychologists conduct naturalistic observations, case studies, surveys, or experiments, their investigations usually generate a large amount of **data:** numbers that represent research findings and provide the basis for conclusions. *Statistical analyses* are the methods most often used to summarize and analyze data. These methods include *descriptive statistics,* which are the numbers that psychologists use to describe and present a set of data, and *inferential statistics,* which are mathematical procedures used to draw conclusions from data and to make inferences about what they mean. Here, we describe a few statistical terms that you will encounter in the coming chapters; you can find more information about statistics in the Appendix.

Descriptive Statistics

The three most important descriptive statistics are *correlation coefficients,* which describe relationships between variables; *measures of central tendency,* which describe the typical value of a set of data; and *measures of variability,* which describe the spread, or dispersion, in a set of data.

The Correlation Coefficient   The strength and direction of correlations between variables can be summarized by calculating a statistic called the **correlation coefficient** (procedures for doing so appear in the Appendix). The correlation coefficient is given the symbol *r.* It can vary from 0.00 to $+1.00$ or -1.00. Thus, the coefficient includes (1) an absolute value, such as 0, .20, or .50, and (2) either a plus sign or a minus sign.

The absolute value of *r* indicates the strength of the relationship. An *r* of 0.00 between people's hat size and the age of their cars, for example, indicates that there is no relationship between the variables. A correlation of $+1.00$ or -1.00 indicates a *perfect correlation,* which means that if you know the value of one variable, you can predict the value of the other variable with certainty (see Figure 2.3). An *r* of $+.50$ or $-.50$ suggests a relationship of intermediate strength.

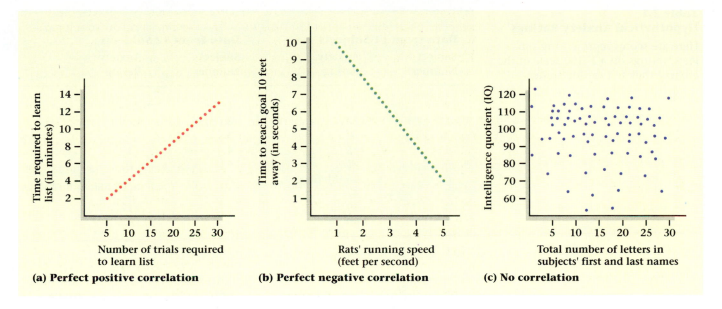

(a) Perfect positive correlation

(b) Perfect negative correlation

(c) No correlation

Figure 2.3
Three Correlations

The strength and direction of the correlation between variables can be pictured in a graph called a *scatter-plot*. Here are three examples. In part (a), we have plotted the number of thirty-second trials that subjects took to learn a list of meaningless words against the number of minutes the subjects participated in the experiment. Since time in the lab and the number of trials are positively and perfectly correlated, the scatterplot appears as a straight line; you can predict the value of either variable once the value of the other is known. Part (b) shows the scatterplot representing the perfect negative correlation between rats' running speeds and the time it took them to reach a goal ten feet away. The higher the animals' speeds, the lower their running times; again one variable can be predicted perfectly from the other. Part (c) illustrates the scatterplot of the zero correlation (no relationship) between IQ and the length of people's names. Higher and higher correlations are represented by ever-tighter patterns of dots that begin to approximate straight lines.

The sign of a correlation coefficient indicates its direction. A plus sign means that the relationship between variables is *positive*—that is, as one variable changes, the other variable changes in the same direction. For example, the correlation between the cost of a particular gasoline purchase and the number of gallons pumped is positive; as gallons increase or decrease, so does the cost. A minus sign in the correlation coefficient indicates that the relationship is *negative,* which means that as one variable increases or decreases, the other changes in the opposite direction. The tavern observations described earlier gave an example of a negative correlation: recall that as musical tempo decreased, drinking speed increased.

Measures of Central Tendency The left side of Table 2.1 contains ratings of the amount of anxiety each of 11 subjects felt about spiders. What is the typical value, the central tendency, that best represents the group's anxiety level? There are three measures designed to capture this typical value: the mode, the median, and the mean.

The **mode** is the value or score that occurs most frequently in the data set. You can find it by ordering the scores from lowest to highest. In the left side of Table 2.1, the mode is 50, because the score of 50 occurs more often than any other. Notice, however, that in this data set, the mode is actually an extreme score. Sometimes, the mode acts like a microphone for a small but vocal minority, which, though speaking most frequently, does not represent the views of the majority.

Unlike the mode, the median takes all of the scores into account. The **median** is the halfway point in a set of data: half the scores fall above the median, half fall below it. For the scores in the left side of Table 2.1, the halfway point—the median—is 45.

The third measure of central tendency is the **mean**, which is the *arithmetic average.* When people talk about the "average" in everyday conversation, they are usually referring to the mean. To find the mean, add the values of all the scores and divide by the number of scores. For the scores in the left side of Table 2.1, the mean is $436/11 = 39.6$.

Like the median (and unlike the mode), the mean reflects all the data to some degree, not just the most frequent data. Notice, however, that the mean reflects the actual value of all the scores, whereas the median gives each score

Table 2.1
Hypothetical Anxiety Ratings
Here are scores representing subjects' ratings on a 1–100 scale of the anxiety they felt toward spiders.

Data from 11 Subjects		Data from 12 Subjects	
Subject Number	Anxiety Rating	Subject Number	Anxiety Rating
1	20	1	20
2	22	2	22
3	28	3	28
4	35	4	35
5	40	5	40
6	45 (Median)	6	45 Median = 46*
7	47	7	47
8	49	8	49
9	50	9	50
10	50	10	50
11	50	11	50
		12	100
Mode = 50		Mode = 50	
Median = 45		Median = 46	
Mean = 436/11 = 39.6		Mean = 536/12 = 44.7	

*When there is an even number of scores, the exact middle of the list lies between two numbers. The median is the value halfway between those numbers.

equal weight, whatever its size. This difference can have a big effect on how well the mean and median reflect the values of a particular set of data. Suppose, for example, that a twelfth subject was added to the sample and gave an anxiety rating of 100. When you re-analyze the rating data (see the right side of Table 2.1), the median will hardly change, because the new subject counts as just one more score added to the list. However, when you compute the new mean, the actual *amount* of the new subject's rating is added to everyone else's ratings; as a result, the mean jumps 5 points. Sometimes, as in this example, the median is a better measure of central tendency than the mean because the median is less sensitive to extreme scores. But because the mean is more representative than the median of the value of all the data, it is often the preferred measure of central tendency.

Measures of Variability   The variability (also known as spread or dispersion) in a set of data can be quantified by the range and the standard deviation. The **range** is simply the difference between the highest and the lowest value in the data set. In contrast, the **standard deviation**, or **SD**, measures the average difference between each score and the mean of the data set. The higher the standard deviation, the more variability there is in the data. In the Appendix we show how to calculate the standard deviation.

Inferential Statistics

One of the most difficult tasks psychologists face is to understand the meaning of the results summarized in descriptive statistics. Is a correlation between college grade-point average and eating certain foods large enough to support the hypothesis that diet is important for mental functioning? Is the anxiety reduction following EMD/R sufficiently greater than that following other treatments to recommend one over the other? The answers to questions like these are based largely on the results of analyses through inferential statistics.

Suppose you are a substitute teacher who comes to a new school hoping for an easy day's work. You are offered either of two classes. In each, the students' mean IQ is 100. At first glance, there would appear to be no major difference between the classes, but it turns out that the standard deviation (SD) of IQs in one class is 16; the SD in the other is 32. Since a higher standard deviation means more variability, the class with the SD of 32 is likely to be more difficult to teach because its students vary more in ability. The standard deviation is a particularly important descriptive statistic in any data set.

Inferential statistics employ certain conventional rules to evaluate the likelihood that a difference between groups or a correlation reflects an important relationship rather than the operation of chance factors. Suppose, for example, that subjects who received EMD/R showed a mean decrease of 10 points on a test of anxiety while scores of the control group decreased a mean of 7 points. How likely is it that the difference between 10 and 7 was due to chance alone? Analysis through inferential statistics can provide an answer. When a correlation coefficient or the difference between the means of two groups is larger than would be expected by chance alone, it is said to be **statistically significant.** In the Appendix we discuss how the size of mean differences or correlations, the number of subjects studied, and the amount of variability in the data affect statistical significance.

Traditionally, scientists do not consider correlations or other research results to be worthy of much attention if they are not statistically significant (Powell, Nabers & Knight, 1992). Thus, in thinking critically about research, part of the process of evaluating the evidence requires asking about the statistical significance of a researcher's results.

Ethical Guidelines for Psychologists

The obligation to analyze and report research fairly and accurately is one of the ethical requirements that guide psychologists. Preservation of the welfare and dignity of their subjects, animal and human, is another. Though researchers *could* measure severe anxiety by putting a loaded gun to people's heads, or study marital conflicts by telling one partner that the other has been unfaithful, such methods are potentially harmful and, therefore, unethical.

In each of these examples, the ethical course of action is obvious: the psychologist must find another way to conduct the research. In practice, however, ethical choices are often more complicated, and psychologists must decide how to balance conflicting values. Many experiments reflect a compromise between the need to protect subjects from harm and the need to know about the unknown. In finding ways to help people cope with anxiety, for example, researchers may ask them to try new coping skills while enduring an anxiety-provoking, but not traumatic, situation.

When research does create risks or discomfort for subjects, researchers must determine that the potential benefits of the work in terms of new knowledge and human welfare outweigh any potential harm. They must also minimize the discomfort and risk, and they must act to prevent subjects from suffering any long-term negative consequences from participation. When people are the research subjects, researchers must inform them about every aspect of the study that might influence their decision to participate and also ensure that the subjects' involvement is voluntary. If a researcher deceives people about an experiment because full disclosure beforehand would bias their behavior, the researcher must reveal and justify the deception afterward.

The obligation to protect subjects' welfare also extends to animals, which are used as subjects in about 8 percent of psychological research (Shapiro, 1991). Psychologists study animals partly because their behavior is interesting in and of itself and partly because studies of animals can yield information that would be impossible or unethical to collect from humans.

Contrary to the allegations of some animal-rights activists, animals used in psychological research are not routinely subjected to extreme pain, starvation, or other inhumane conditions (Coile & Miller, 1984; Novak, 1991). Even in the small proportion of studies that require the use of electric shock, the dis-

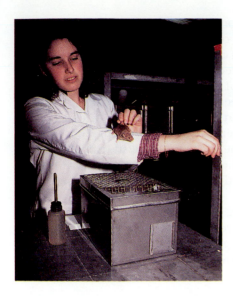

Psychologists are highly motivated to protect the welfare of animal subjects. Like most of us, they take no pleasure in animals' suffering. Furthermore, inflicting undue stress on animal subjects is likely to create reactions that can act as confounding variables. For example, in an experiment on how the amount of food offered as a reward affects learning in rats, the researcher might reduce the animals' food intake in order to make them hungry enough to want the experimental rewards. But starving the subjects would introduce discomfort that may make it impossible to separate the effects of the reward from the effects of starvation.

comfort created is mild, brief, and not harmful. The recently revised Animal Welfare Act, the National Institutes of Health *Guide for the Care and Use of Laboratory Animals,* the American Psychological Association's *Principles on Animal Use,* and other laws and regulations set high standards for the care and treatment of animal subjects. In those relatively rare studies that require animals to undergo short-lived pain or other forms of moderate stress, legal and ethical standards require the psychologist to persuade funding agencies—as well as local committees charged with monitoring animal research—that the discomfort is justified by the expected benefits to human welfare.

The responsibility for conducting research in the most humane fashion possible forms just one aspect of the *Ethical Principles of Psychologists and Code of Conduct* developed by the APA (American Psychological Association, 1992). The main purpose of these standards is to protect and promote the welfare of society and those with whom psychologists work. For example, as teachers, psychologists should strive to give students a complete, accurate, and up-to-date view of each topic rather than a narrow, biased point of view. Psychologists should perform only those services and use only those techniques for which they are adequately trained; a biological psychologist untrained in clinical methods should not try to offer psychotherapy. Except in the most unusual circumstances (to be discussed in Chapter 16), psychologists should not reveal information obtained from clients or students, and they should avoid situations in which a conflict of interest might impair their judgment or harm someone else. They should not, for example, have sexual relations with their clients, their students, or their employees.

Despite these guidelines, doubt and controversy arise in some cases about whether a proposed experiment or a particular practice, such as deceiving subjects, is ethical (Baumrind, 1985; Christensen, 1988; Tabachnick, Keith-Spiegel & Pope, 1991). Indeed, ethical principles for psychologists will continue to evolve as psychologists face new and more complex ethical issues (Kimmel, 1991; Pope & Vetter, 1992).

Linkages: Psychological Research and Genetics

One of the greatest challenges in psychology is to understand the ways in which what people bring into the world—their biological *nature*—and the environmental events and conditions that affect them after they arrive—often called *nurture*—intertwine to shape behavior and mental processes. Psychologists interested in everything from perception to personality, from mental disorder to mental ability, face the problem of how to design research that can illuminate, if not separate, these two primary influences. Designing or interpreting this research requires knowledge about **genetics**, the biology of inheritance. Because questions about nature and nurture, and the genetic principles that underlie them, surface in relation to many topics in this book, we should consider in more detail this important linkage between psychological research and biological science.

Principles of Genetics and Heredity

What does it mean to say that someone has genetically inherited some physical feature or behavioral trait? The story begins with **chromosomes**, which are long, thin structures within each cell that are made up of thousands of genes. **Genes** are composed of **deoxyribonucleic acid (DNA)**—strands of sugar, phosphate, and nitrogen-containing molecules twisted around each other in a double spiral (see Figure 2.4). It is the particular order in which the nitrogen-containing molecules are arranged in the DNA that determines, through the

Figure 2.4
The Structure of DNA
Genes are actually segments of DNA, which is formed from two strands of molecules intertwined in a double spiral. The sides of the spiral are made up of sugar and phosphate; they are connected by "rungs" composed of two of four nitrogen-containing molecules: adenine, thymine, guanine, and cytosine. Differing sequences of the molecules on the "rungs" act as coded instructions to create different proteins, which, in turn, direct the creation of differing new cells (Watson, 1976).

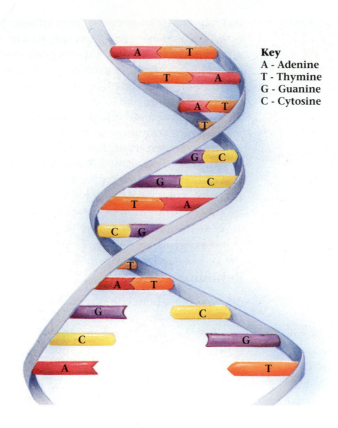

Key
A - Adenine
T - Thymine
G - Guanine
C - Cytosine

In most human cells, there are 23 pairs of chromosomes that carry the genetic code. Diversity in this genetic makeup produces the infinite variability that provides the raw material for the process of evolution through natural selection described in Chapter 1. Abnormalities in genetic makeup can lead to a wide range of problems, however. Consider, for example, the 23rd chromosome pair, called the *sex chromosomes*. Males' cells contain a large sex chromosome, designated X, and a smaller one, called Y. Females' cells contain two X chromosomes. Females born with only one X chromosome and males born with an extra X chromosome do not show normal sexual development. Similarly, children born with a trio instead of a pair of chromosome 21 develop the distinctive physical appearance and slowed intellectual growth known as Down syndrome.

production of *ribonucleic acid (RNA),* which protein each gene will produce. Protein molecules, in turn, form the physical structure of each cell and also direct the activity of the cell. Thus, through DNA, the genes contain a coded message that provides a blueprint for constructing every aspect of a physical human being, including eye color, height, blood type, inherited disorders, and the like—and all in less space than the period that ends this sentence.

Most human cells contain forty-six chromosomes, arranged in twenty-three matching pairs. New cells are produced by the division of existing cells. Most of the body's cells divide through a process in which the cell's chromosomes duplicate themselves, so that each new cell contains copies of the twenty-three pairs of chromosomes in the original. However, when males' sperm cells and females' egg cells (called *ova*) are formed, a special kind of cell division, called *meiosis*, occurs.

In meiosis, instead of being copied, the chromosome pairs are randomly split and rearranged, leaving each new sperm and egg cell with just *one* member of each chromosome pair, or twenty-three *single* chromosomes. No two of these special new cells are quite the same, and none contains an exact copy of the person who produced it. So when, at conception, a male's sperm cell penetrates, or *fertilizes,* the female's ovum, a truly new cell is formed. This fertilized cell, called a *zygote,* carries twenty-three pairs of chromosomes—half of each pair from the mother and half from the father—which represent a unique heritage, a complete genetic code for a new person that combines randomly selected aspects from both parents. As described in the next chapter, the zygote divides first into copies of itself and then into the billions of specialized cells that form a new human being.

Not all genes get to express themselves. *Dominant* genes are expressed whenever they are present; *recessive* genes are expressed outwardly only when they are paired with a similar gene from the other parent. Consider eye color, for example. Genes for brown eyes are dominant, so you will have brown eyes if you have a brown-eye gene from either parent. Blue-eye genes are recessive, so getting a blue-eye gene from one parent will not give you blue eyes unless it is paired with a second blue-eye gene from the other parent. Other eye colors, such as hazel, are the result of more complicated gene combinations. In fact, few human characteristics are controlled by just one gene or pair of genes; in other words, most characteristics are **polygenic.** Even a person's height is affected by more than one pair of genes.

The genes contained in the forty-six chromosomes inherited from parents make up the **genotype.** Because they develop from the same fertilized egg cell, identical twins are called *monozygotic* and have exactly the same genes. So why don't all identical twins look exactly alike? Because, in twins and nontwins alike, how people actually look and act—their **phenotype**—is influenced both by the combination of genes they carry and by environmental factors—in other words, by both nature and nurture.

Behavior Genetics

Linkages: How do psychologists analyze the role of genetics in human behavior and mental processes? (a link to Biological Aspects of Psychology)

Because most behavioral tendencies are polygenic and heavily influenced by the environment, researchers do not expect to find specific genes that control, say, aggression or shyness. Instead, researchers in **behavior genetics**—the study of the effect of genes on behavior—explore the relative roles of genetic and environmental factors in creating differences in behavioral tendencies in groups of subjects.

Early research in behavior genetics relied on selective breeding of animals. For example, Robert Tryon (1940) mated rats who were fast maze learners with other fast learners and mated slower learners with other slow learners. After repeating this procedure for several generations, he found that the offspring of the fast learners were significantly better at maze learning than those of the slow learners.

Selective-breeding studies must be interpreted with caution, however, because it is not specific behaviors that are inherited. Instead, what is inherited are differing sets of physical structures, sensory and motor capacities, and the like, which, in turn, make certain behaviors more or less likely to occur. These behavioral tendencies are often narrow, and they can be altered by the environment. For example, "maze-dull" rats were just as good as "maze-bright" rats on many tasks other than maze learning (Searle, 1949). And, when raised in an environment containing tunnels and other stimulating features, "dull" animals did as well at maze learning as "bright" ones; both groups did equally poorly in the maze after being raised in a boring environment (Cooper & Zubek, 1958).

Research on behavior genetics in humans must be interpreted with even more caution because environmental influences have an enormous impact on human behavior and because legal, moral, and ethical considerations prohibit manipulations such as selective breeding. Instead, research in human behavior genetics depends on quasi-experiments, where control is imperfect. Some of the most important quasi-experimental designs are family studies, adoption studies, and twin studies.

In *family studies,* researchers examine whether similarities in behavior and mental processes are greater in people who are closely related as compared to more distant relatives or unrelated individuals. If increasing similarity is associated with closer family ties, the similarities might be inherited. For example, data from family studies suggest a genetic basis for schizophrenia because this severe mental disorder appears much more often in the closest relatives of schizophrenics than in other people (see Figure 2.5). Family studies alone cannot establish the role of genetic factors in mental disorders or other characteristics, however, because close relatives tend to share environments as well

Figure 2.5
Family Studies of Schizophrenia
Data from family studies show that the risk of developing schizophrenia, a severe mental disorder described in Chapter 15, is highest for the siblings and children of schizophrenics and decreases progressively with genetic distance; the risk is lowest for people with no genetic relationship to a schizophrenic. Does this mean that schizophrenia is inherited? The data are certainly consistent with that interpretation, but the question cannot be answered through family studies alone. Other factors, including environmental stressors that close relatives share, could also play an important role in the development of the disorder.

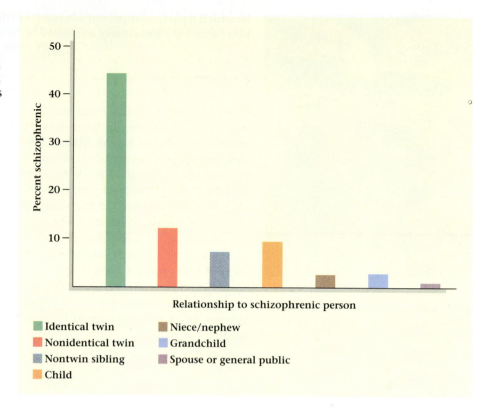

as genes. Thus, similarities in close relatives might stem from environmental factors instead of, or in addition to, genetic ones.

Twin studies explore the heredity-environment mix by comparing the similarities seen in identical twins with those of nonidentical pairs. Twins usually share the same environment and may also be treated very much the same by parents and others, so if identical twins—whose genes are exactly the same— are more alike on some characteristic than nonidentical twins (whose genes are no more similar than those of other siblings), that characteristic may have a significant genetic component. We will see in later chapters that this pattern of results holds for a number of characteristics, including some measures of intelligence and some mental disorders.

Adoption studies take advantage of the naturally occurring quasi-experiments that take place when babies are adopted very early in life. The logic underlying these studies is that if adopted children's characteristics are more like those of their biological parents than those of their adoptive parents, genetically inherited ingredients in the nature-nurture mix play a clear role in that characteristic. As described in Chapter 14, for example, the personalities of young adults who were adopted at birth tend to be more like those of their biological parents than those of their adoptive parents. Adoption studies can be especially valuable when they focus on identical twins who were separated at or near birth. If identical twins show similar characteristics after years of living in very different environments, the role of heredity in that characteristic is highlighted. Adoption studies of intelligence, for example, tend to support the role of genetics in variations in mental ability, but they show that environmental influences are important as well (see Chapters 3 and 11 for more on this issue).

When reading about the role of genetics in human development and in differences in personality and mental abilities, remember that research on human behavior genetics can help illuminate the relative roles of heredity and environment that underlie *group differences,* but it cannot determine the degree

Twin studies and adoption studies employ quasi-experimental designs that help illuminate the interaction of genetic and environmental influences on human behavior and mental processes. Cases in which identical twins who had been separated at birth but have similar interests, personality traits, and mental abilities suggest that these characteristics have a significant genetic component.

to which a particular person's behavior is due to heredity or environment. The two factors are too closely entwined to be separated that way.

Future Directions

Through new technology and new ideas, psychologists are creating ever better ways of manipulating independent variables and measuring dependent variables. For example, Joseph Malpeli created a tiny device for use with animals that temporarily deactivates cells in particular parts of the lateral geniculate nucleus (LGN), an area of the brain vital to vision. The ability to "turn off" various parts of the LGN and to observe the effects on vision has greatly enhanced understanding of the visual system (Mignard & Malpeli, 1991). Another example is provided by Thomas Borkovec. While evaluating treatments for insomnia, Borkovec found a way to control for placebo effects without giving anyone a phony treatment. He told some treated subjects that the effects of their therapy would not occur until after four sessions (Borkovec & Bauer, 1982; Steinmark & Borkovec, 1974). Because all treated subjects, including those who were led to expect delayed effects, improved before the fourth session, placebo effects could be largely ruled out as an explanation of the results.

As psychologists follow new research directions, they will continue to develop new research designs, methods, and analytical techniques. Each chapter of this book describes research that uses advanced methods for collecting and analyzing data. For example, in Chapter 14 we discuss correlational procedures known as *factor analysis* that help psychologists identify the basic components of human personality. And in Chapter 16 we describe *meta-analysis,* a method for evaluating the results of many research studies on many forms of therapy for many kinds of problems. If you would like to learn more about the basic principles of psychological research and about the innovations that are constantly appearing in the research literature, consider taking a course in research methods.

Summary and Key Terms

Thinking Critically About Psychology (or Anything Else)
Critical thinking is the process of assessing claims and making judgments on the basis of well-supported evidence.

Critical Thinking and Scientific Research
Often, questions about psychological phenomena are phrased in terms of *hypotheses* about *operationally defined variables,* which must be evaluated for reliability and validity.

The Role of Theories
Explanations of phenomena sometimes take the form of *theories,* which are integrated sets of propositions that can be used to account for, predict, and even control certain phenomena. Theories must also be subjected to rigorous evaluation.

Research Methods in Psychology

Research in psychology, as in other sciences, focuses on four main goals: description, prediction, control, and explanation.

Naturalistic Observation
Naturalistic observation entails watching without interfering as behavior occurs in the natural environment. This method can be revealing, but care must be taken to ensure that observers are unbiased and do not alter the behavior of interest.

Case Studies
Case studies are intensive examinations of a particular individual, group, or situation. Case studies are useful for studying new or rare phenomena and can also help evaluate new treatments or training programs.

Surveys
Surveys ask questions, through interviews or questionnaires, about behavior, attitudes, beliefs, opinions, and intentions. They provide an excellent way of gathering large amounts of data from a large number of people at relatively low cost, but their results can be distorted if questions are poorly phrased or if respondents do not answer honestly.

Testing Hypotheses Through Correlational Research
Many relationships between variables involve *correlations.* Though they can be very valuable, correlational data alone cannot establish that two correlated variables are causally related, which variable might affect which, or why.

Experimental Research
In *experiments,* researchers manipulate an *independent variable* and observe the effect of that manipulation on a *dependent variable.* Subjects receiving experimental treatment are called the *experimental group;* those in comparison conditions are called *control groups.* Experiments can reveal cause-and-

effect relationships between variables, but only if researchers use *placebo* conditions, *double-blind designs,* and other strategies to avoid being misled by *random variables, experimenter bias,* and other *confounding variables.* When ethics or other obstacles prevent full experimental control, researchers sometimes employ *quasi-experiments.*

Human Diversity and Research Methods

Psychologists' research can be limited if their subject *sampling* procedures do not give them a fair cross-section of the population they want to study and about which they want to draw conclusions. Anything less than a *random sample* is said to be a *biased sample* of subjects; but in most cases, a representative sample is adequate.

Statistical Analysis of Research Results

Psychologists use descriptive and inferential statistical analyses to summarize and analyze *data,* the numbers that represent research findings and provide the basis for conclusions.

Descriptive Statistics

Descriptive statistics include *correlation coefficients,* measures of central tendency (such as the *mode, median,* and *mean*), and measures of variability, such as the *range* and *standard deviation.*

Inferential Statistics

Psychologists employ inferential statistics to guide conclusions about data, especially to determine if correlations or differences between means are *statistically significant*—that is, larger than would be expected by chance alone.

Ethical Guidelines for Psychologists

Ethical guidelines promote the protection of human and animal subjects in psychological research, and set the highest standards for behavior in all other aspects of psychologists' professional lives.

Linkages: Psychological Research and Genetics

Research on the ways in which nature and nurture interact to shape behavior and mental processes requires knowledge about *genetics,* the biology of inheritance.

Principles of Genetics and Heredity

The genetic code that transmits characteristics from one generation to the next is contained in the *DNA* that comprises the *genes* that make up *chromosomes.* Most human characteristics are controlled by more than one gene or gene pair; they are *polygenic.* The genes in one's forty-six chromosomes make up the *genotype;* the *phenotype*—how people actually look and act—is influenced by genes and the environment.

Behavior Genetics

Behavior genetics, the study of the effect of genes on behavior, uses family studies, twin studies, and adoption studies to explore the interaction of heredity and environment in shaping human behavior and mental processes.

Chapter 3

Human Development

For several years in the late 1700s, people living in and around the Caune Woods of Aveyron, France, reported sighting a wild boy running naked with the animals. Supposedly, he had been lost or abandoned by his parents at a very early age and had grown up with animals. Eventually, when this Wild Boy of Aveyron was about eleven, hunters captured him, and he was sent to Paris.

The scientists in Paris expected to observe what philosopher Jean-Jacques Rousseau had called the "noble savage." After all, here was a human being who had grown up uncontaminated by the evils and arbitrary rules of society. But what the scientists found was a dirty, frightened creature who crawled and trotted like a wild animal, who would eat the filthiest of garbage, and who preferred raw to cooked meat. He spent most of his time silently rocking back and forth. He would snarl at and attack anyone who tried to touch him. Though the scientists worked with the boy for more than ten years, they produced only minor changes in his behavior. He never learned to speak. He was never able to live unguarded among other people.

If a child like the Wild Boy were found today, could modern psychologists "cure" him? Probably not. In recent times there have been children who were rescued after having been confined for years in closets and other environments that cut them off from other people (Rymer, 1992). Invariably, these children find it extremely difficult to interact with others. Often they are unable to learn language.

These cases highlight the importance of early contacts with other people for normal human development. They underscore the need to know as much as possible about early development and what can help or hinder it. And they bear on what is arguably the most salient issue in developmental psychology—the *nature-nurture issue* introduced in Chapter 2. That is, to what extent is a person's development a product of what he or she arrives with—his or her inherited, biological *nature*—and to what extent is it a product of what the world provides—the *nurture* of the environment?

Developmental psychology is the psychological subfield that documents the course and causes of physical, social, emotional, moral, and intellectual development over a person's life span. *Development* refers to age-related changes that are systematic, sequential, and long lasting. It does not include changes that are brief or reversible, such as those resulting from illness, accidents, or drugs. It does not include fluctuations in mood or behavior that are related to the time of day or the season of the year. Developmental psychologists study when certain kinds of behavior first appear, how they change with age, and whether they change in a sudden spurt or gradually. They look at how development in one domain, say, cognitive abilities, is related to development in another domain, such as social relations. They want to know whether everyone develops abilities at the same rate and, if not, whether slow starters ever catch up. They are interested in the *processes* of development. How do transitions from lower to higher levels of skill occur? How much of development is determined by children's inheritance of abilities? How much can the environment alter the rate of development or the level an individual reaches? How much does culture alter the environment?

In this chapter, you will read about how a person develops from a fertilized egg into a mature adult and how adults, too, change as they get older. You will preview the milestones of growth in sensation, emotion, thinking, social behavior, and other domains that are examined in later chapters (see the Linkages diagram). Throughout, you will consider evidence relating to the issue of nature and nurture.

Exploring Human Development

Arguments about the nature-nurture issue can be traced back to philosophers' statements centuries ago. In essays published in the 1690s, British philosopher John Locke argued for the dominance of nurture, suggesting that what happens during childhood has a profound and permanent effect on the individual. He proposed that the newborn infant is like a blank slate, or *tabula rasa,* on which experience writes its story. Adults write on that slate, he said, as they teach children about the world and how to behave in it. Some seventy years later, French philosopher Jean-Jacques Rousseau made the opposite argument; he claimed that children are capable of discovering how the world operates and how they should behave without instruction from adults. Accordingly, he advocated

Linkages

The questions in this diagram illustrate some of the relationships between the topic of this chapter, human development, and the topics of other chapters. The study of developmental psychology is interesting in its own right, but it also illuminates other areas of psychology, as this diagram suggests. Differences between men and women and among members of various cultures are one example. Studies by developmental psychologists shed light on what these differences are, when they emerge, and how variable they are. Linking their work with research by specialists in other subfields gives a more detailed picture of the mechanisms behind these differences—showing how some differences might be inherited and how some might be learned. Remember that some of the questions in the diagram are examined in this chapter and some are answered in other chapters. The page numbers indicate where the questions are discussed; each Linkages question is repeated in the margin where it appears in the text. ■

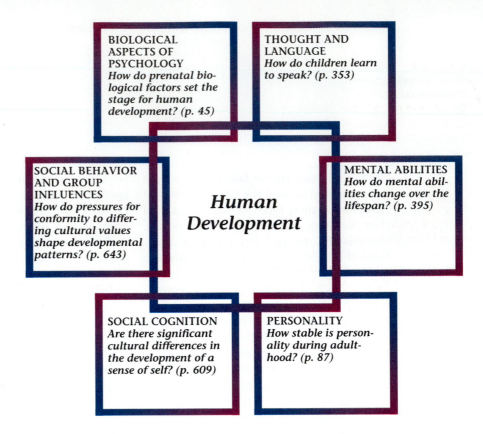

BIOLOGICAL ASPECTS OF PSYCHOLOGY
How do prenatal biological factors set the stage for human development? (p. 45)

THOUGHT AND LANGUAGE
How do children learn to speak? (p. 353)

SOCIAL BEHAVIOR AND GROUP INFLUENCES
How do pressures for conformity to differing cultural values shape developmental patterns? (p. 643)

Human Development

MENTAL ABILITIES
How do mental abilities change over the lifespan? (p. 395)

SOCIAL COGNITION
Are there significant cultural differences in the development of a sense of self? (p. 609)

PERSONALITY
How stable is personality during adulthood? (p. 87)

the idea that children should be allowed to grow as nature dictates, with little guidance or pressure from parents.

The first American psychologist to follow up on Rousseau's view was Arnold Gesell. Early in this century Gesell made many observations of children of all ages. He demonstrated that motor skills, such as standing and walking, picking up a cube, and throwing a ball, develop in a fixed sequence of stages in all children, as Figure 3.1 illustrates. The order of the stages and the age at which they develop, he showed, are determined by nature and relatively unaffected by nurture. Only under extreme conditions—such as famine, war, or poverty—are children thrown off this biologically programmed timetable. This type of natural growth or change, which unfolds in a fixed sequence relatively independent of the environment, is called **maturation**. It clearly reflects the influence of nature on development.

The environment, not nature, was the key to development in the view of a second American psychologist, John B. Watson. As we mentioned in Chapter 1, Watson was the founder of the behavioral approach to psychology. Early in this century he began conducting experiments with children. From his experiments Watson inferred that children *learn* everything, from skills to fears. "Give me a dozen healthy infants," he wrote,

well formed, and my own specified world to bring them up in and I'll guarantee to take any one at random and train him to become any type of specialist I might select—doctor, lawyer, artist, merchant chief, and, yes, even beggar-man and thief, regardless of his talents, penchants, tendencies, abilities, vocations, and race of his ancestors. (Watson, 1930, p. 104)

Watson's view stimulated much debate and much research, which we examine in other chapters of this book.

Later psychologists did not take such strong "either-or" positions about nature and nurture. According to Sigmund Freud's (1930) theory, development

Figure 3.1
Motor Development: An Example of Maturation
The left end of each bar indicates the age at which 25 percent of the infants tested were able to perform the behavior; 50 percent of the babies were performing the behavior at the age indicated by the vertical line in the bars; the right end indicates the age at which 90 percent could do so (Frankenberg & Dodds, 1967). Although different infants, especially in different cultures, achieve milestones of motor development at slightly different ages, all infants—regardless of their ethnicity, social class, or temperament—achieve them in the same order. Thus, motor development during infancy is maturational.

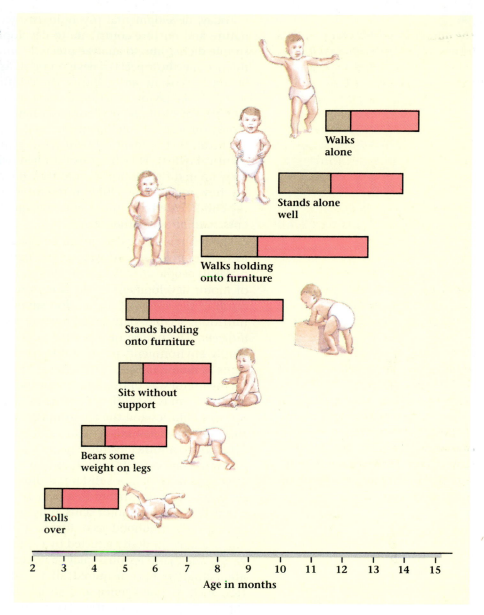

Walks alone

Stands alone well

Walks holding onto furniture

Stands holding onto furniture

Sits without support

Bears some weight on legs

Rolls over

Age in months

was neither the simple result of benign growth toward maturity, as Gesell suggested, nor the product of environmental experiences alone, as Watson claimed. Instead, said Freud, development is the product of *both* internal urges and external conditions, particularly children's sexual and aggressive urges and how parents handle them. Thus, Freud's theory incorporated both nature and nurture.

The combined contributions of nature and nurture were explored most thoroughly, however, by a Swiss psychologist, Jean Piaget. His views influenced the field of developmental psychology more than any other person's before or since (Beilin, 1992). Piaget suggested that the influences of nature and nurture are inseparable and interactive. As children manipulate and explore the objects around them, they are guided by mental images of the objects and of their own actions. At the same time, their experiences with the objects modify these images.

Today, developmental psychologists accept as given the notion that both nature and nurture contribute to development. They have gone beyond this simple dichotomy to analyze precisely how inheritance and environment influence specific aspects of development. As described in Chapter 2, one way of trying to separate and identify these influences is through correlational research in behavior genetics, especially through family, twin, and adoption studies. For example, psychologists have compared the correlations between scores on tests of intelligence or personality of people who are genetically identical (that is, identical twins) and genetically different (for example, nonidentical twins). They have also studied twins who were separated at birth and grew up in different homes, and they have studied adopted children, examining how much these children resemble their adoptive parents, who provide the children's environment, and how much they resemble their biological parents, who provided their genes.

These studies have demonstrated that nature and nurture contribute jointly to development in two ways. First, nature and nurture operate together to make all people *alike* as human beings. For example, we all achieve milestones of motor development in the same order and at roughly the same rate as a result of the *nature* of maturation supported by the *nurture* of basic care and nutrition. Second, nature and nurture also both operate to make each person *different.* The nature of inherited genes and the nurture of widely different family environments produce differences among individuals in such dimensions as motor abilities, intelligence, speech patterns, and personality.

One useful way of thinking about the relative contributions of heredity and environment is to think of genetics as roughly defining a fairly broad potential *range* of abilities and the environment as pushing a child up or down within this range. Just *how much* nature and nurture contribute varies from one characteristic to another. Nature shapes some characteristics, such as physical size and appearance, so strongly that only extreme environmental conditions can affect them. It takes a substantial difference in diet, for instance, to make a difference of a few inches in a person's ultimate height. Nature affects other characteristics, like motor skills, only slightly less strongly; these skills develop during early childhood according to a maturational timetable (see Figure 3.1) and are only modestly affected by experience. Nurture—in the form of soccer games and piano lessons—plays a larger role in children's motor abilities only after children have acquired all the basic motor skills. Other characteristics, such as intelligence and social skills, may be more easily affected by the environment from the very beginning than either physical and motor development.

For *all* human characteristics, the influences of nature and nurture are always inextricably intertwined. This is because, first, heredity and environment are usually *confounded.* For example, parents with higher intelligence may provide their children both with genes for more intelligent behavior *and* with more stimulating environments; parents with special athletic skills may pass on genes that facilitate athletic skill *and* play more sports with their children. In addition, heredity and environments *interact;* that is, the environment encourages or discourages the expression of an individual's inherited characteristics while, at the same time, those inherited characteristics to some extent determine that individual's environment. For example, a stimulating environment—toys, books, lessons—encourages children's mental development and increases the chances of developing their full inherited intellectual potential. At the same time, more intelligent children seek out more stimulating environments, ask more questions, and evoke more attention from adults; their innate abilities influence and help them take advantage of their environments. The interplay between nature and nurture is a busy two-way street.

An environment full of new and interesting stimuli provides the ideal circumstances for the fullest development of a child's inherited intellectual potential.

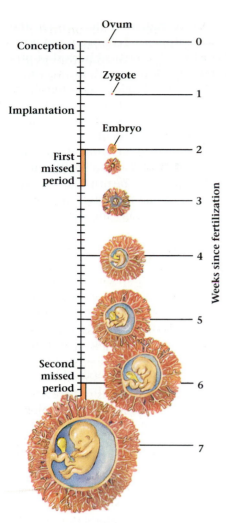

Ovum

Conception

Zygote

Implantation

Embryo

First
missed
period

Weeks since fertilization

Second
missed
period

0

1

2

3

4

5

6

7

Figure 3.2
Prenatal Development:
The First Weeks
These drawings show the ovum, zygote, and embryo only slightly
smaller than their actual sizes during
the first seven weeks of life.

*Linkages: How do prenatal
biological factors set the stage for
human development? (a link to
Biological Aspects of Psychology)*

Beginnings

Nowhere are the complementary contributions of heredity and environment
clearer than during the eventful nine months before birth, when a single fertilized egg becomes a functioning newborn infant.

Prenatal Development

The process of the newborn's development begins when a sperm from the
father-to-be fertilizes the ovum of the mother-to-be and forms a brand-new
cell, called a *zygote*. As described in Chapter 2, this new cell carries a genetic
heritage from both mother and father.

Stages of Development   During the first week after fertilization, the zygote
divides into cells, any one of which has the potential to become a complete
human being. During the second week, these cells separate into sections that
will become the **embryo** (the part that will be the infant), the *placenta* (which
will transmit nutrients from the mother and carry away wastes from the infant), the *amnion* (the "bag of waters" surrounding the embryo), and the *yolk
sac* (which will produce blood). From this time on, each new cell formed has
a specialized function.

At the end of the second week after fertilization, the *embryonic stage* of prenatal development begins. During this stage the basic plan for the body
emerges, and all the organs are created, as the cells continue to divide and take
on increasingly specialized functions. The placenta begins to "breathe," digest,
and excrete for the embryo. By the end of the second month, the inch-long
embryo has a heart, nervous system, stomach, esophagus, and ovaries or testes
(see Figure 3.2). It looks decidedly human, with eyes, ears, and nose, jaw,
mouth, and lips. The tiny arms have elbows, hands, and stubby fingers; the
legs have knees, ankles, and toes.

The embryo becomes a **fetus** in the third prenatal stage, when the cartilage
in the bones starts to harden. In the *fetal stage,* which extends until birth, the
various organs grow and function more efficiently. By the end of the third
month after conception, the fetus can kick, make a fist, turn its head, open its
mouth, swallow, and frown. In the sixth month, the eyelids, which have been
sealed, open. The fetus now has a well-developed grasp and abundant taste
buds and can breathe regularly for as long as twenty-four hours at a time.

By the end of the seventh month, the organ systems, though immature, are
all functional. In the eighth and ninth months, the fetus becomes sensitive to
a variety of outside sounds and responds to light and touch. It can lift its head,
and it may even be able to learn. In one study, for example, Anthony DeCasper
demonstrated that infants whose mothers repeatedly read them a Dr. Seuss
story before they were born preferred the sound of this story to the sound of
other conversation after they were born (Spence & DeCasper, 1982).

Prenatal Risks   During prenatal development the placenta is selective. It
allows beneficial materials such as nutrients in and screens out many potentially harmful substances, including most bacteria. But this screening is imperfect. Gases, viruses, nicotine, alcohol, and other drugs can pass through.
Severe damage can occur if the baby's mother takes certain drugs or is exposed
to certain toxic substances or has certain illnesses during the embryonic period. A baby whose mother has rubella (German measles) during the third or
fourth week after conception, for example, has a 50 percent chance of being
blind, deaf, or mentally retarded or of having a heart malformation. If the
mother has rubella later in the pregnancy, after the eyes, ears, brain, and heart
have formed, the likelihood that the baby will have one of these defects drops
substantially.

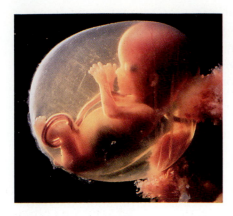

A fetus at twelve weeks. At this point in prenatal development, the fetus can kick its legs, curl its toes, make a fist, turn its head, squint, open its mouth, swallow, and take a few "breaths" of amniotic fluid.

Harmful external substances such as drugs or radiation that invade the womb and result in birth defects are called **teratogens.** Teratogens are especially damaging in the embryonic stage because it is a **critical period** in prenatal development, a time during which certain kinds of growth must occur if development is to proceed normally. Specific physical developments must take place during the embryonic stage, or they never will. If the heart, eyes, ears, hands, and feet do not appear in the embryonic period, they cannot form later on, and if they form incorrectly, the defects will be permanent.

During the fetal stage of prenatal development, the environment provided by the mother affects the baby's size, behavior, intelligence, and health, rather than the formation of organs and limbs. The mother's health and age, her nutrition before and during pregnancy, the emotional and physical stresses she undergoes, and the nicotine, alcohol, and other drugs she consumes all make a difference to the infant.

Of special concern today are the effects of alcohol and cocaine on prenatal development. Babies born to women who are alcoholics have a 44 percent chance of suffering from **fetal alcohol syndrome,** a pattern of defects that includes physical malformations of the face and mental retardation. Fetal alcohol syndrome is linked to heavy drinking, but even moderate drinking—a glass or two of wine a day—can harm infants' intellectual functioning (Streissguth et al., 1989). Mothers addicted to drugs like cocaine also put their infants at risk. They pass on their addiction to the fetus, and their babies are born premature, underweight, tense, and fussy (Jeremy & Hans, 1985). Many are brain damaged and have serious problems learning and concentrating (Revkin, 1989). Organs such as kidneys or genitals may be malformed because the mother's use of cocaine leads to a loss of blood to the developing organ. A little drug for the mother is a lot for the fetus, who does not have the enzymes necessary to break it down. Today, more than 10 percent of the babies born in some city hospitals have cocaine-addicted mothers (Revkin, 1989).

The likelihood that potentially harmful conditions and substances will affect a particular infant depends on nature and nurture—on the infant's genetic inheritance, the stage of prenatal development during which the infant is exposed to the teratogen, and the intensity of the harmful condition. Malformation or deficiency is most likely when the effects of nature and nurture

"Cocaine babies," sometimes called "crack babies," are born with numerous physical defects as a result of their mothers' drug use during pregnancy. To make matters worse, these mothers are likely to respond negatively to their infants because, for example, these babies often turn their heads away when the mother tries to play. This unfortunate reaction can impair the mother-child relationship and lead to a vicious cycle of child abuse in already fragile families.

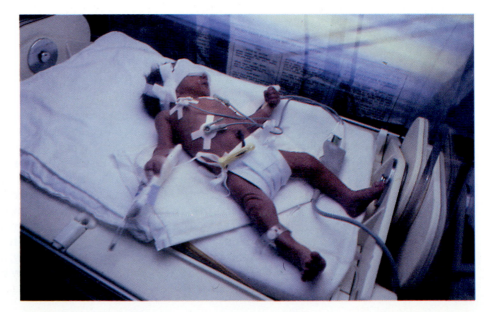

summate, as when a genetically susceptible infant receives a strong dose of a damaging substance during a critical period of prenatal development.

Despite these vulnerabilities, mental or physical problems resulting from all harmful factors affect fewer than 10 percent of the babies born in the United States. Mechanisms built into the human organism maintain normal development under all but the most adverse conditions. The vast majority of fetuses arrive at the end of their nine-month gestation averaging a healthy seven pounds and ready to continue a normal course of development in the world.

The Newborn

As soon as they arrive on the scene, newborn infants actively use their senses to explore the world around them. At first they can attend to sights and sounds for only short periods, but gradually their attention lengthens and their exploration becomes more focused and systematic.

Determining just what newborns see and hear provides quite a challenge because they are extremely difficult to study. If they are held upright, their heads fall forward or backward; if they are lying down, they are likely to fall asleep. If the lights are too bright, they shut their eyes; if the lights are too dim, back to sleep they go. About 70 percent of the time, newborns are asleep. When they are not sleeping, they are drowsy, crying, awake and active, or awake and inactive. It is only when they are in this last state, which occurs infrequently in segments only a few minutes long, that infants observe their surroundings and seem most capable of learning. This is the time when researchers must assess infants' abilities.

To conduct these assessments, psychologists have shown infants objects or pictures and watched where they look and for how long. They film infants' eye movements and record changes in infants' heart rates, sucking rates, brain waves, movements, and skin conductance (a measure of perspiration associated with emotion) when objects are shown or sounds are made. From studies using all these techniques, researchers have gleaned a fair picture of what infants can sense at birth and soon after.

Vision and Other Senses At birth, the infant's vision is limited by immaturities in both the eye and the brain. Their eyes do not yet have a *fovea*—the area on which images are focused. Their eye movements are slow and jerky. Pathways in the nervous system connecting the eyes to the brain are still inefficient, as is the processing of visual information within the brain. A very rough estimate is that the newborn has 20:600 eyesight; that is, an object 20 feet away looks as clear as it would if it were viewed from 600 feet away by an adult with normal vision.

But infants are by no means blind. Although they cannot see small objects on the other side of the room, infants can see large objects close up—the distance at which most interaction with parents takes place. They particularly seem to enjoy looking at faces. In the early weeks, their eyes will follow a moving face-like drawing (Johnson et al., 1991), and by one month of age they will stare at a human face longer than at other figures (Olson & Sherman, 1983). Infants, it seems, look longest at what they can see best: patterns with the largest visible elements, the most movement, the clearest contours, and the greatest amount of contrast (Banks & Salapatek, 1983).

Newborns do more than take in visual sensations. They actively search for things to look at. They scan the visual field, moving their eyes back and forth, looking for lines and corners. At first they focus only on the edges of objects, but by two months of age, they scan whole objects systematically (Banks & Salapatek, 1983). Then, when they see an object, they get all the information they can from it before going on to something new (Hunter & Ames, 1988).

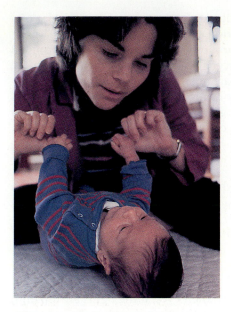

Figure 3.3
Reflexes in the Newborn
When a finger is pressed into the newborn's palm, the *grasping reflex* causes the infant to hold on tightly enough to suspend its entire weight. The *Moro reflex* is a response to the sudden sensation of falling: the arms and legs are flung to the sides, hands open and fingers spread, then the arms are brought in toward the body in a hugging motion, hands now fisted, back arched, and legs fully extended. Other reflexes include the *stepping reflex* and the *swimming reflex.*

Can they tell if something is near or far, steep or shallow? We consider these questions in Chapter 6, where we examine the principles that guide these perceptions.

What can the newborn hear? At birth, hearing is somewhat impaired by amniotic fluid left in the ear, but this fluid is soon gone. At two or three days of age, newborns can hear soft voices and can notice the difference between tones about one note apart on the musical scale (Aslin, Pisoni & Jusczyk, 1983). They can also locate sounds that are to their left or their right.

Interestingly, newborns are more sensitive to sounds that are in the range of speech than to other sounds. When they hear speech, babies open their eyes wider and look around for the sound. Judging from where infants look or how fast they suck in order to hear recordings of different voices, researchers have concluded that infants also prefer certain *kinds* of speech. They like rising tones, spoken by women or children (Sullivan & Horowitz, 1983). They also like speech that is high-pitched, exaggerated, and expressive. In short, they like to hear the *baby talk* used by nearly all adults in all cultures when they talk to babies (Fernald, 1981, 1990; Glenn & Cunningham, 1983).

Newborns also like certain smells and tastes better than others. Within a few days after birth, breast-fed babies prefer the odor of their own mother's milk to that of another mother's (Russell, 1976). Newborns can also taste the difference between water, sugar water, and milk, and they react differently depending on the concentration of sweet and bitter solutions (Ganchrow, Steiner & Daher, 1983). They suck longer and slower, pause for shorter periods, and smile and lick their upper lips when given a sweet solution.

Reflexes   In the first few weeks and months of life, babies' actions are dominated by involuntary, unlearned reactions called **reflexes.** These are swift, automatic movements in response to external stimuli. Figure 3.3 shows an example of the *grasping reflex;* more than twenty other reflexes have been observed in newborn infants. For example, in the *rooting reflex* the infant turns its mouth toward a finger or nipple that touches its cheek. In the *sucking reflex* the newborn sucks on anything that touches its lips. The infant is not consciously controlling these behaviors; they are automatic. As brain development allows the infant to control muscles voluntarily, reflexes fade. Most reflexes disappear within three or four months. The absence of reflexes in the newborn, or their failure to disappear within a few months, signals problems in brain development.

Infancy and Childhood: Cognitive Development

From conception through childhood, children's bodies and brains increase in size, complexity, and efficiency. These changes are related to advances in behavior and in *cognitive development*—the development of thinking, knowing, and remembering. Do changes in the brain cause the advances in thinking, or vice versa? It is likely that each affects the other in a constantly evolving fashion (Cacioppo & Berntson, 1992). In the Linkages section of the next chapter we describe how scientists are mapping out the intermingling effects of nature and nurture on the brain, but the puzzle is far from solved. Still, psychologists have documented the radical developments in cognition that occur from infancy through childhood, changes that transform the infant struggling to figure out how to reach the bottle just beyond reach into the competent creature who can read a book, write a poem, and compose a logical argument for going to computer camp.

Linkages: How is psychology's empirical tradition reflected in research on children's cognitive abilities? (a link to Introducing Psychology)

One explanation of cognitive development, *learning theory,* grew out of Watson's behavioral approach and its emphasis on nurture's role in development. Some learning theorists argue that children's thought develops as a result of the consequences of their behaviors (Bijou & Baer, 1961). These theorists suggest that if children are rewarded for speaking in long sentences, for learning the alphabet, or for saying that tulips are flowers, they are likely to repeat those behaviors and will thus learn cognitive skills. Indeed, within hours of birth, infants can learn associations between events. For example, they start puckering up when the researcher touches their forehead if that kind of touching has regularly preceded feeding (Rovee-Collier, 1987). As discussed in other chapters, learning theory has value for understanding many aspects of behavior. However, because it focuses on environmental factors rather than on both nature and nurture, learning theory provides an incomplete explanation of cognitive development. The theory of cognitive development formulated by Jean Piaget appears more complete.

The Development of Knowledge: Piaget's Theory

We mentioned earlier that Piaget was the first psychologist to fully integrate the contributions of both nature and nurture into his explanation of development. From the 1920s until his death in 1980, Piaget charted the fascinating journey of cognitive development, from the simple reflexes of the newborn to the complex understanding of the adult.

Piaget proposed that this journey proceeds in a series of distinct stages, which are outlined in Table 3.1. Note that a stage is more than just a step in a sequence. A *stage* involves a *qualitative* change from whatever preceded it, as when a butterfly passes through the distinct stages of larva, pupa, and caterpillar. Each stage builds on the preceding stages, and the order of stages cannot change. According to Piaget, the thinking of infants is qualitatively different from the thinking of children, and the thinking of children is qualitatively different from that of adolescents—because they are at different stages of development. Thus, children are not miniature adults and they are not dumber than adults; they just think in completely different ways.

Building Blocks of Development   With age and experience, said Piaget, all children's thinking goes through the same stages—in the same order, without skipping, building on previous stages and moving to a higher stage when new information won't fit the mental images of the old stage. Piaget called these mental images "schemas." **Schemas** are the basic units of knowledge, the building blocks of intellectual development. They are generalizations formed as people experience the world. Schemas organize past experiences and provide a framework for understanding future experiences. They may involve patterns of action, simple thoughts about objects, or complex ideas.

At first, infants form simple schemas, such as a sucking schema, by which they consolidate their experiences of sucking into images of what objects can be sucked on—bottles, fingers, pacifiers. Later, children form more complex schemas, such as a schema for tying a knot or making a bed. Still later, adolescents form schemas about what it is to be in love. According to Piaget, as children are driven by their desire to make sense of the world they form many and varied schemas, which appear in distinct stages marked by increasingly sophisticated modes of thought.

Two complementary processes guide this development: assimilation and accommodation. In **assimilation,** people take in information about new objects by trying out existing schemas and finding schemas that the new objects will fit. They *assimilate* the new object into their existing schemas. A baby boy is

Table 3.1
Piaget's Periods of Cognitive Development

According to Piaget, a predictable set of features characterizes each period of children's cognitive development. Note that the ages associated with the stages are approximate; Piaget realized that some children move through the stages slightly faster or slower than others.

Period	Activities and Achievements
Sensorimotor Birth–2 years	Infants discover aspects of the world through their sensory impressions, motor activities, and coordination of the two.
	They learn to differentiate themselves from the external world. They learn that objects exist even when they are not visible and that they are independent of the infant's own actions. They gain some appreciation of cause and effect.
Preoperational 2–4 years	Children cannot yet manipulate and transform information in logical ways, but they now can think in images and symbols.
4–7 years	They become able to represent something with something else, acquire language, and play games of pretend. Intelligence at this stage is said to be intuitive, because children cannot make general, logical statements.
Concrete operational 7–11 years	Children can understand logical principles that apply to concrete external objects.
	They can appreciate that certain properties of an object remain the same, despite changes in appearance, and sort objects into categories. They can appreciate the perspective of another viewer. They can think about two concepts, such as longer and wider, at the same time.
Formal operational Over 11 years	Only adolescents and adults can think logically about abstractions, can speculate, and can consider what might or what ought to be.
	They can work in probabilities and possibilities. They can imagine other worlds, especially ideal ones. They can reason about purely verbal or logical statements. They can relate any element or statement to any other, manipulate variables in a scientific experiment, and deal with proportions and analogies. They reflect on their own activity of thinking.

given a new toy. He examines it, sucks on it, waves it, and throws it—and discovers that this toy, like his familiar rattle, is suckable, wavable, and throwable. A toddler encounters a large dog. How she assimilates this new experience depends on her existing schema of dogs. If she has had positive experiences with a family pet she will have a schema different from that of a child whose only experience with dogs has been watching *101 Dalmatians.* Thus past experiences affect what and how children think about new ones. Sometimes, like Cinderella's sisters squeezing their oversized feet into the glass slipper, people distort information about a new object to make it fit their existing schemas. When squeezing won't work, though, people are forced to change, or *accommodate,* their schemas to the new objects.

In **accommodation,** the person tries out familiar schemas on a new object, finds that the schemas cannot be made to fit the object, and changes the schema so that it will fit (see Figure 3.4). The baby boy is given a cup. He

**Figure 3.4
Accommodation**
Because the bars of the playpen are in the way, this child discovers that her schema for grasping and pulling objects toward her will not work. Thus she adjusts, or accommodates, her schema in order to achieve her goal.

examines it, sucks on it, waves it, and throws it. He discovers that to suck on it, he can put only the edge in his mouth; to wave it, he must hold onto the handle; and throwing it will not work at all, because Mother removes the cup from his playpen. Similarly, the toddler refines her "doggie" schema when she meets a nasty pit bull and discovers that her original schema does not extend to all dogs.

Sensorimotor Development   Piaget (1952) called the first stage of cognitive development the **sensorimotor period** because, he claimed, the infant's mental activity is confined to sensory functions, like seeing and hearing, and to motor skills, like grasping and sucking. The infant's early schemas involve simple sensory and motor functions such as these. As motor skills develop and voluntary actions replace reflexes, babies elaborate these simple schemas into complex ones of waving or shaking and, later, of inserting or building.

At first, infants repeat these actions for the sheer pleasure of it. Later, they begin to use their schemas to achieve a goal—to get a toy that is out of reach, to put two objects together. By the end of the sensorimotor period, they begin to experiment, repeating and modifying actions to see the effects. The toddler picks up a spoon full of grape jelly. She holds it flat, she tips it one way, she tips it the other way, she slowly turns it upside down. She stirs the jelly on the tray. She smears it on her hands, in her hair, and on everything else within reach. All the while, she is refining her schema for grape jelly.

According to Piaget, in the sensorimotor stage of development, infants can form schemas only of objects and actions that are present, things they can see or hear or touch. They cannot think about absent objects because they cannot act on them; thinking, for infants, is doing. They do not lie in the crib with Mother's face or a favorite toy in their mind's eye. What is distinctive about the sensorimotor stage is that infants are not yet able to form schemas that are *mental representations* of objects and actions.

The sensorimotor period ends when infants can form mental representations so that they can think about objects and actions even while the objects are not visible or the actions are not occurring. This is a remarkable milestone.

It frees the child from the here-and-now of the sensory environment and allows for the development of thought. One sign that children have reached this milestone occurs when they are able to find a hidden object. This behavior was of particular interest to Piaget because, for him, it reflected infants' knowledge that they do not have to look at, touch, or suck an object to know that it exists; it exists even when out of sight. Piaget called this knowledge **object permanence.** He tested the development of this concept by hiding small objects under little covers and then letting infants try to find them.

Before they acquire a knowledge of object permanence, infants do not search under the covers, just as young infants do not search if you hide a toy behind your back or hide their bottle under a blanket, hungry as they may be. According to Piaget, out of sight is literally out of mind for infants in this stage. The first evidence that object permanence is developing, he said, appears when infants are four to eight months old. At this age, for the first time, they can recognize a familiar object even if part of it is hidden—they know it's the bottle even if they can see only the nipple peeking out from under the blanket. This shows that infants have some primitive mental representation of objects. If an object is completely hidden, however, they will not search for it.

Several months later, infants will search briefly for a hidden object, but their search is haphazard and ineffective. Even when infants watch an object being moved from one hiding place to another, they may search for it in the first place it was hidden. Not until they are eighteen to twenty-four months old, said Piaget, do infants appear able to picture and follow events in their minds. They look for the object in places other than where they saw it last, sometimes in completely new places. They have a mental representation of the object that is completely separate from their immediate perception of it. According to Piaget, their concept of objects as permanent is now fully developed.

Preoperational Development For Piaget, the ability to form mental representations marks the end of the sensorimotor period and the beginning of the second major stage of cognitive development. In this **preoperational period,** children begin to think for the first time. They understand, create, and use *symbols* to represent things that are not present; they can draw, pretend, and talk. (How children learn to talk is described in Chapter 10, on thought and language.)

The ability to symbolize opens up vast new domains for two- to four-year-olds. Two-year-olds might use a finger for a horse, or pretend to be Mommy or Daddy. They watch a television show and, next day, playfully imitate what they saw. At the age of three or four, children can symbolize intricate roles and events, as they play house, doctor, Ninja Turtles, or Batman. They can appreciate the symbolic function of a model. In one study, for example, three-year-olds shown a scale-model room in which a miniature dog was hidden behind a miniature sofa could then find an actual stuffed dog in a real room (DeLoache, 1987).

According to Piaget, in the second half of the preoperational stage, from ages four to seven, children's thinking is dominated not by logical thought but by intuition, by guesses. They know many things about people, toys, animals, vehicles, and food, but only what they have seen and touched for themselves. Their reasoning about things with which they have no hands-on experience is often wrong or even bizarre by adult standards. As Piaget discovered in his conversations with children, they may assume that dreams are real and take place outside of themselves as "pictures on the window," "a circus in the room," or "something from the sky." They may believe that some inanimate objects are alive and have intentions, feelings, and consciousness. The clouds go slowly because they have no paws or legs. Flowers grow because they want to. Empty cars feel lonely.

Children's thinking at this stage is so dominated by what they can see and touch for themselves that they do not realize that something is the same if its appearance is changed. In one study, for example, preoperational children thought that a cat wearing a dog mask was actually a dog, because that's what it looked like (DeVries, 1969). In short, they do not yet have what Piaget called **conservation**, the ability to recognize that important properties of a substance—including its volume, weight, and species—remain constant despite changes in its shape.

Figure 3.5 illustrates two tests of conservation. In yet another test, Piaget showed children water from two equal-sized glasses being poured into a tall, thin glass and a short, wide one and then asked them if one glass contained more water than the other. Children at this stage of development guessed that one glass (usually the taller one) contained more. They were dominated by the evidence of their eyes. If the glass looked bigger, then it contained more. Children at this stage did not understand the logic of *reversibility* (you just poured the water from one container to another, so you can pour it back and it will still be the same amount) or *complementarity* (one glass is taller but also narrower; the other is shorter but also wider). They focused on only one dimension at a time—the most salient one—and made their best intuitive guess. Indeed, Piaget named this stage "*pre*operational" because children at this stage do not yet understand logical mental *operations* such as reversibility and complementarity.

Concrete Operational Thought   Sometime around the age of six or seven, children do develop the ability to conserve number and amount. When they do so, they enter what Piaget called the stage of **concrete operations**. Now they can count, measure, add, and subtract; their thinking is no longer dominated by the visual appearance of things. They can use simple logic and perform simple mental manipulations and mental operations on things. They can sort objects into classes (such as tools, fruit, and vehicles) or series (such as largest to smallest) by systematic searching and ordering. They realize that if A is larger than B and B is larger than C, then A is larger than C.

Figure 3.5
Conservation
Here are two of the procedures that have been used to test children's ability to conserve length and substance amount. Conservation of area, liquid quantity, and volume may be tested in a similar way.

Type of conservation	First display	Second display	Child is asked
Length	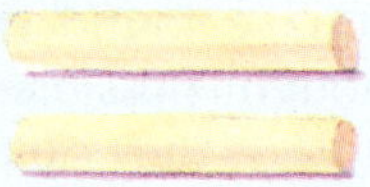 The child sees two sticks of equal length and agrees that they are of equal length.	 The experimenter moves one stick over.	Is one stick longer? Preconserving child will say that one of the sticks is longer. Conserving child will say that they are both the same length.
Substance amount	 The child sees two identical clay balls and acknowledges that the two have equal amounts of clay.	 The experimenter rolls out one of the balls.	Do the two pieces have the same amount of clay? Preconserving child will say that the long piece has more clay. Conserving child will say that the two pieces have the same amount of clay.

Still, concrete operational children can perform their logical operations only on real, concrete objects—sticks and glasses, tools and fruit—not on abstract concepts like justice and freedom. They can reason only about what *is*, not about what is *possible*. The ability to think logically about abstract ideas comes in the next stage of cognitive development. This *formal operational period* occurs during adolescence, which we discuss later in this chapter.

Modifying Piaget's Theory

Piaget's observations and demonstrations of children's cognitive development are vivid and fascinating. Many psychologists have tested his findings and theory with experiments of their own. On the basis of these experiments it appears that, just as children accommodate their schemas to take account of new information, Piaget's theory needs some modification.

What needs to be modified most is Piaget's notion of developmental stages. Piaget did *not* hold that stages were tightly tied to chronological age or that children wake up one day totally changed from the day before. Still, other psychologists have found the changes to be even less consistent and global than Piaget suggested. They have discovered that children can sometimes perform the behaviors Piaget talked about at earlier ages than he demonstrated— if the test conditions are changed slightly. If, in tests of object permanence, for example, the experimenter simply turns the light out and does not use a cover to hide the object, infants as young as five months old may reach for the object in the dark (Bower & Wishart, 1972; Rochat et al., 1989). And if infants are allowed to search under a cover immediately after the object is hidden, those as young as seven months are likely to find the object, although they lose track if you make them wait for several seconds before letting them search (Diamond, 1985). Researchers now recognize that finding a hidden object requires two things: mentally representing the hidden object, and figuring out where it might be. Piaget's tests did not allow for the possibility that an infant might know that an object exists but not have adequate strategies for finding it.

Recent research has tested the depth of infants' knowledge about objects. In one set of experiments, Renee Baillargeon (1987, 1992; Baillargeon et al., 1990) has demonstrated that infants as young as four or five months of age act surprised when experimenters perform visual "tricks" that make it look, for example, as if one solid object has passed right through another. She suggests that this surprise reflects a violation of the infant's expectations about the properties of objects. The general consensus now seems to be that infants develop some mental representations earlier than Piaget's demonstrations suggested, even though they lack the ability to solve the particular problems he set for them.

With older children, too, researchers have found evidence of advanced thinking at younger ages than Piaget thought possible. Preoperational children can do conservation tasks, for example, if they can count the number of objects or if they have been trained to focus on relevant dimensions, such as number, height, and width. They also can solve some kinds of conservation problems before others—for example, number before substance and weight before volume (Gelman & Baillargeon, 1983). Taken together, these studies suggest that knowledge appears unevenly, not all at once and across the board, but at different ages in different domains, and at earlier ages if the children are given specific domain-related experience.

So Piaget was right in pointing out that there are significant shifts with age in children's thinking and that thinking becomes more systematic, consistent, and integrated as children get older. His descriptions of assimilation and accommodation as mechanisms by which development occurs remain one of the strong, if untestable, contributions of his theory. But developmental psychologists have concluded that cognitive abilities appear more gradually than Piaget originally suggested and that knowledge develops in "pockets" rather than in global levels of understanding (Sternberg, 1989).

It appears, then, that children's reasoning in any particular situation depends not only on their general level of development but also on how easy the task is, how familiar they are with the objects involved, how well they understand the language the adult uses, and what experiences they have had in similar situations. Eventually, of course, most children do achieve levels of cognitive development at which they are capable of understanding problems and solving tasks under *all* circumstances, not just when the objects are familiar and the wording of the question is simple. Thus, both Piaget's developmental framework and the overall processes of development he first described remain uniquely useful for understanding cognitive development.

Information Processing During Childhood

An alternative to Piaget's approach to cognitive development is to describe children's cognitive activities in terms of **information processing**, examining how they take in information, use it, and remember or forget it. Like Piaget, developmental psychologists taking this approach attempt to describe the processes that go on inside the child's head. But unlike Piaget, they focus on gradual quantitative changes in children's mental capacities, rather than on qualitative advances or stages. They use the analogy that people are like computers, at least in the way they process information.

As children get older, their information-processing skills gradually get better. Older children, for example, can take in information and shift their attention from one task to another more rapidly than younger ones (Manis, Keating & Morrison, 1980). They also become more selective in terms of what they take in as they learn to focus on the relevant parts of incoming information and ignore the rest (Hagen & Hale, 1973). Their attention spans increase in length. In short, for the first five or six years, children's ability to receive information improves. There are also marked improvements in children's memory storage capacity. For example, preschoolers can keep only two or three pieces of information in mind at the same time; older children can remember more (Morrison, Holmes & Haith, 1974). Their memory capacities get larger every year, though only up to a point. Unlike computers, people's brains can't just keep adding "memory boards" indefinitely; even most adults can hold only about seven pieces of information in mind at any one time (see Chapter 9).

We don't yet know what causes the increase in children's memory storage capacities. It may relate to nature—specifically, to maturation of the brain (Case, Kurland & Goldberg, 1982)—or to effects of nurture, such as increased familiarity with the items to be memorized. Children's memory abilities improve dramatically when they are asked to remember familiar rather than unfamiliar items. In one experiment, Mayan children in Mexico lagged behind their American age-mates on typical memory tests, but their performance was greatly enhanced when researchers gave them a task that was more familiar, such as recalling miniature objects in a model of a Mayan village (Rogoff & Waddell, 1982).

Linkages: Why do children's memories improve during the school years? (a link to Memory)

Better memorization strategies may also help account for the improvement in children's memories—another explanation based on nurture. To a great extent, children learn these strategies in school; research in different cultures around the world has shown that children who attend school have better immediate memories than those who do not (Wagner, 1978). Schoolchildren learn how to memorize and how to study. They learn to repeat information over and over to help fix it in memory, to place information into categories,

Memory abilities depend, to some extent, on the familiarity of the items to be remembered. In one experiment, children who were chess experts had much better memories for the placement of chess pieces than did adults who did not have expertise in chess—even though adults usually perform better than children on memory tests (Chi, 1978).

and, as discussed in Chapter 9, to use memory aids like "*i* before *e* except after *c*" to help them remember. They also learn what situations call for deliberate memorization and what factors, such as the length of a list, affect memory.

After about age seven, schoolchildren are also better at remembering more complex and abstract information, such as the gist of what several people have said during a conversation. Their memories are more accurate, extensive, and well organized. The knowledge they have accumulated allows them to draw more inferences and to integrate new information into a more complete network of facts, a more complete mental filing system. It is this slow and steady improvement on a number of different fronts that is emphasized and analyzed by psychologists who take an information-processing view of cognitive development. (See "In Review: Milestones of Cognitive Development in Infancy and Childhood.")

Culture and Cognitive Development

Just as Piaget's focus in explaining development was on the physical world of objects, Russian psychologist Lev Vygotsky (1934/1962) focused on the social world of people. He viewed the human mind as a product of cultural history. The child's mind, said Vygotsky, grows through interaction with other minds. Indeed, cases like the Wild Boy of Aveyron show that, without society, children's minds do not develop much beyond those of animals. Vygotsky proposed that through their interaction with parents, teachers, and other representatives of their culture, children acquire the ideas of that culture.

Researchers in the West have pursued Vygotsky's ideas by studying the effects of the social world on children's development. For example, Katherine Nelson (1986) has studied how participation in social routines affects children's developing knowledge of the world. In North American culture, such routines include going shopping, eating at McDonald's, going to birthday parties, attending religious services, and so on. In another culture they might include helping to make pottery, going hunting, and weaving baskets. Quite early, children develop mental representations, or **scripts**, of these activities. By the time they are three, children can describe routine activities quite ac-

In Review: Milestones of Cognitive Development in Infancy and Childhood

Age*	Achievement	Description
3–4 months	Maturation of senses	Immaturities that limit the newborn's vision and hearing are overcome.
	Voluntary movement	Reflexes disappear and infants begin to gain voluntary control over their movements.
12–18 months	Mental representation	Infants can form images of objects and actions in their minds.
	Object permanence	Infants understand that objects exist even when out of sight.
18–24 months	Symbolic thought	Young children use symbols to represent things that are not present in their pretend play, drawing, and talk.
4 years	Intuitive thought	Children reason about events, real and imagined, by guessing rather than by logical analysis.
6–7 years	Concrete operations	Children can apply simple logical operations to real objects. For example, children recognize that important properties of a substance, such as number or amount, remain constant despite changes in shape or position.
	Conservation	
7–8 years	Information processing	Children can remember about seven pieces of information; they begin to learn strategies for memorization.

*These ages are approximate; they indicate the order in which children first reach these milestones of cognitive development rather than the exact ages.

curately. Scripts, in turn, affect children's knowledge and understanding of Piaget's cognitive tasks. Thus, middle-class children can understand conservation problems earlier than inner-city children if the problems are presented, as Piaget's were, like miniature science experiments. But the performance of inner-city children is improved when the task is presented via a script that is more familiar to them, such as one involving what a "slick trickster" would do to fool someone (White & Glick, described by Nelson, 1986).

Children's cognitive abilities are influenced by the very language of their culture. Korean children, for instance, show exceptional ability at adding and subtracting large numbers (Fuson & Kwon, 1992). Korean third-graders can do in their heads three-digit problems (for example, 702 minus 125) that their American peers labor over or fail. The difference seems traceable in part to the fact that the Korean language explicitly names numbers between ten and nineteen as "ten and some ones." In English, the number words between ten and nineteen are not so clear. The meaning of the word *eleven,* for instance, is not as clear as *ten and one one.* In addition to the hints thus contained in their language, Koreans use the metric system of measurement and the abacus—both of which are structured around the number ten. Moreover, Korean math textbooks emphasize the tens structure by presenting the ones digits in red, the tens in blue, and the hundreds in green. On top of this, for children in Asian cultures, educational achievement, especially in mathematics, is both strongly encouraged by parents at home and emphatically supported by teachers at school (Stevenson, Azuma & Hakuta, 1986; Stigler, 1992). Children's cognitive development is thus affected in ways large and small by the culture in which they are enmeshed, including the family environments in which they live.

Individual Variations in Cognitive Development

Even within a single culture, some children are mentally precocious while others lag behind their peers. Why? As already suggested, heredity is an important factor (Plomin, 1989). Genes do not fix the child's cognitive development, but they do set some general limits on it. Within those limits, experience plays its role. To explore just how significant that role is, psychologists have studied the cognitive development of children in many different rearing environments.

Children raised in barren environments—deprived of the everyday sights, sounds, and feelings provided by conversation and loving interaction with family members, by pictures and books, even by television and radio—develop more slowly than children in more normal family environments (Rymer, 1992). Such severe deprivation can noticeably impair intellectual development by the time children are two or three years old. Children's development may also be impaired by less extreme deprivation and despair. In one study, children were observed and repeatedly tested from the time they were born until they were adolescents (Seifer & Sameroff, 1989). Cognitive development was below normal among those children who faced an abundance of negative experiences—for example, having a mother who was mentally ill, anxious, uneducated, unmarried, and poor, and who did not interact much with the child.

In average homes, too, children's cognitive development is related to their surroundings and experiences. For example, Asian-American students get better grades on average than their European- or African- or Hispanic-American classmates (Steinberg, Dornbusch & Brown, 1992). They do better on tests, and teachers have a higher opinion of them (Farkas, Grobe & Shuan, 1990). The most likely explanation for their superior performance seems to be that they have better work habits and that these are based on cultural traditions continued by their families. Asian parents provide help with homework, extra workbooks, and special after-school lessons (Fuson & Kwon, 1992). Some Japanese-American mothers even buy two sets of textbooks, one of which they study themselves so that they can better help their children (White, 1987).

Parents can often make the difference between a child's getting A's and getting C's. To help children achieve those A's, parents can expose them, from the early years, to a variety of interesting materials and experiences—though not so many that the child is overwhelmed (Clarke-Stewart, 1988a; Gottfried, 1984). One set of crayons, some blocks, an electric train, a doll, a tea set, a puzzle or two, and some books will do more for the child's cognitive development than *all* the dolls *or* puzzles *or* trains at the toy store. Children's cognitive development is promoted also when parents read and talk to them, encourage and help them to explore, and actively teach them (Gottfried, 1984)—in short, when they provide both support and challenge for their children's talents (Wong & Csikszentmihali, 1992).

To improve the cognitive skills of children whose parents are not able to provide these kinds of stimulation, developmental psychologists have provided some children with extra lessons, materials, and educational contact with sensitive adults. In the United States, the most comprehensive effort to provide this kind of help has been through Head Start, a preschool program for poor children. Numerous smaller, more intensive programs have also been carried out. In a variety of such programs, children's cognitive abilities are enhanced (Ramey & Ramey, 1992).

In Chapter 11, on mental abilities, we examine more closely how heredity, the environment, and efforts like Head Start affect cognitive development. Though important for cognitive development, experiences in the early years of childhood are not absolutely critical in the same way that the embryonic period of prenatal development is critical for organ formation. The effects of positive *or* negative early experience on cognitive development are, to some extent, reversible, so later gains—or losses—are possible (Clarke & Clarke, 1976a; Kagan, 1984).

Infancy and Childhood: Social and Emotional Development

Life for the child is more than learning about physical objects and social scripts, doing math problems and getting good grades. There are people to be explored, feelings to be experienced, and relationships to be formed. From the first months of life, infants are attracted by the faces, voices, and actions of people. Most babies are immensely attractive creatures themselves, with their tiny bodies, large eyes, chubby cheeks, rosebud mouths, and soft gurgles. These qualities exert a powerful pull on people around them, especially parents.

During the first hour or so after birth, babies are usually awake. During this time, researchers have observed, if they are with their mother, infants gaze at her face while she gazes back and gives gentle touches (Klaus & Kennell, 1976).

Mutual eye contact, exaggerated facial expressions, and shared baby talk are an important part of the early social interactions that promote an enduring bond of attachment between parent and child.

This is the first opportunity we have to see the mother's *bond* to her infant— an emotional tie that begins even before the baby is born and continues to grow over the first few months. Over these months, a strong relationship between both parents and the infant develops, as the infant responds to the parents' behavior and the parents respond to the infant.

Infants respond even to subtle behaviors like facial expressions. They gaze at a beaming face (Malatesta & Izard, 1984), smile at a toothy grin (Oster, 1981), and look angry when the mother does (Lelwica & Haviland, 1983). In one study (Cohn & Tronick, 1983) researchers tested the ability of three-month-olds to respond to emotional cues from their mothers. Some mothers acted normally, whereas others were asked to act depressed. Babies of the "depressed" mothers spent more time protesting, reacting warily, looking away, or giving only fleeting smiles. If mothers actually are depressed, their infants also turn away or protest (Cohn et al., 1990).

Infants also communicate their feelings to their parents, not only by crying and screaming but also more subtly. They signal when they want to interact by looking and smiling; they indicate that they do not want to interact by turning away and sucking their thumbs (Tronick, 1989). Infants enjoy being in control and will repeat things they can control (Watson, 1972). If parents do not respond to their infants' emotional signals, the babies will not learn that their behavior has consequences, and their development will be hindered (Lewis & Goldberg, 1969). In families where infants are generally healthy and parents are attentive and responsive, where infants are part of a mutual communication system in which parents aid their attempts to achieve a goal, emotional development has a strong foundation and the children will thrive.

Individual Temperament

Sometimes, characteristics of infants or parents, or both, give rise to problems. From the moment they are born, infants differ from one another in the emotions they express. Some infants are happy, active, and vigorous; they splash, thrash, and wriggle. Others lie still most of the time. Some infants approach a new object with enthusiasm; others turn away or fuss. Some infants whimper; others kick, scream, and wail. Characteristics like these make up the infant's temperament. **Temperament** refers to the infant's individual style and frequency of expressing needs and emotions; it is constitutional, biological, and genetically based. In other words, it reflects a contribution by nature to the beginning of an individual's personality.

In some of the earliest research on infant temperament, Alexander Thomas and Stella Chess (1977) found three main temperament patterns. *Easy babies,* the most common kind, get hungry and sleepy at predictable times, react to new situations cheerfully, and seldom fuss. *Difficult babies* are irregular and irritable. Those in the third group, *slow-to-warm-up babies,* react warily to new situations but eventually come to enjoy them.

Traces of early temperamental characteristics weave their way throughout childhood (McNeil & Persson-Blennow, 1988). Easy infants usually stay easy, and difficult infants remain difficult (Guerin & Gottfried, 1986; Riese, 1986). Timid toddlers tend to become shy preschoolers and are restrained and inhibited as eight-year-olds (Kagan et al., 1988). However, not every cautious infant ends up painfully shy, not every difficult baby becomes an elderly curmudgeon, nor does each easy baby develop into Miss Congeniality. In temperament, as in cognitive development, nature interacts with nurture. Many events take place between infancy and adulthood to shift the individual's development in one direction or another.

One possibly influential factor suggested by Thomas and Chess is the match between the infant's temperament and the parents' expectations, desires, and personal styles. When parents believe they are responsible for the infant's behavior, an easy child might reassure them. If parents are looking for signs of assertiveness, a difficult child might prove welcome. If parent and infant are in tune, chances increase that temperamental qualities will be stable. Consider, for example, the temperament patterns of Chinese-American and European-American children. At birth, Chinese-American infants are calmer, less changeable, less perturbable, and more easily consoled when upset than European-American infants, suggesting that there may be an inherited predisposition toward self-control among the Chinese. This tendency is then powerfully reinforced by the Chinese culture. Compared with European-American parents, Chinese parents are less likely to reward and stimulate babbling and smiling, and more likely to maintain close control of their young children (Kagan, Kearsley & Zelazo, 1978; Kriger & Kroes, 1972; Smith & Freedman, 1983). The children, in turn, are more dependent on their mothers and less likely to play by themselves; they are less vocal, noisy, and active than European-American children.

These temperamental differences between children in different ethnic groups illustrate the combined contributions of nature and nurture. Many other illustrations are available in the cross-cultural literature. Mayan infants, for example, are relatively inactive from birth. The Zinacantecos, a Mayan group in southern Mexico, reinforce this innate predisposition toward restrained motor activity by swaddling their infants and by nursing at the slightest sign of movement (Greenfield & Childs, 1991). This combination of genetic predisposition and cultural reinforcement is culturally *adaptive:* quiet infants do not kick off their covers at night, which is important in the cold highlands where they live; quiet infants are able to spend long periods on their mother's back as she works at the loom; infants who do not begin to walk until they can understand some language do not wander into the open fire at the center of the house. This adaptive interplay of innate and cultural factors in the development of temperament operates in all cultures.

The Infant Grows Attached

Over the first year of life, while parents are responding to the infant and the infant is responding to the parents, the infant begins to form an **attachment**— a deep, affectionate, close, and enduring relationship—to these important figures. John Bowlby (1951, 1973), a British psychoanalyst, drew attention to the importance of attachment after he observed the dire effects of separation from parents on orphans who had lost their parents in World War II. These children's depression and other emotional scars led Bowlby to develop a theory about the importance of developing a strong attachment to one's primary caregivers, a tie that normally keeps infants close to their caregivers and, therefore, safe. Soon after Bowlby first described his theory, researchers in the United States began to investigate how such attachments are formed and what happens when they are not formed, or when they are broken by loss or separation. Perhaps the most dramatic of these studies was conducted with monkeys by Harry Harlow.

Motherless Monkeys Harlow (1959) separated newborn monkeys from their mothers and reared them in cages containing two artificial mothers. One "mother" was made of wire with a rubber nipple from which the infant could get milk (see Figure 3.6); it provided food but no physical comfort. The other artificial mother had no nipple but was made of soft, comfortable terrycloth. If attachments form entirely because caregivers provide food, the infants would be expected to prefer the wire mother. In fact, they spent most of their time with the terrycloth mother. And when they were frightened by a me-

Figure 3.6
Wire and Terrycloth "Mothers"
Here are the two types of artificial
mothers used in Harlow's research.
Although baby monkeys received
milk from the wire mother, they
spent most of their time with the
terrycloth version and would cling
to it when frightened.

Source: Harlow Primate Laboratory, University of Wisconsin.

Figure 3.7
Monkeys Raised in Isolation
Monkeys reared without any social
contact develop a variety of disorders. As shown at left, many of them
spend most of their time huddled in
the corner of the cage. At right, one
of these animals began to bite himself when a stranger approached.

chanical robot, the infants immediately ran to their terrycloth mother and
clung to it. Harlow concluded that the monkeys were motivated by the need
for contact comfort. The terrycloth mother provided feelings of softness and
cuddling, which were things the infants needed when their safety was in
jeopardy.

Harlow also investigated what happens when attachments do not form. He
isolated some monkeys from all social stimuli from birth. After a year of this
isolation, the monkeys showed dramatic disturbances (see Figure 3.7). When
visited by normally active, playful monkeys, they withdrew to a corner, hud-

Source: Harlow Primate Laboratory, University of Wisconsin.

dling or rocking back and forth for hours. If one of the normal monkeys approached, those that had been isolated often bit themselves until left alone. These monkeys' problems continued into adulthood. The males seldom got further than touching a potential sexual partner; the females quickly ran from any male who made a sexual advance. When some of the females were made pregnant through artificial insemination, their maternal behaviors were woefully inadequate. In most cases, these mothers totally ignored their infants. When the infants began to send distress signals, the mothers physically abused and sometimes even killed them.

In short, it seems that when early attachment in monkeys is prevented by social isolation, the animals are deficient, both socially and emotionally. The degree to which this research might apply to humans is not entirely clear. Still, Harlow's work does demonstrate the effects of extreme deprivation, and one might expect that human babies would also suffer if their caregivers were unavailable or unresponsive.

Forming an Attachment Researchers would never raise human babies like Harlow's monkeys, without social contact; but they *have* investigated the development of attachment in human babies as it occurs naturally under different conditions. After observing infants in Uganda and Baltimore, for example, Mary Ainsworth concluded that with normal care the attachment relationship develops in several phases (Ainsworth, 1973).

At first, infants respond to anyone who comes around: all faces are beautiful, all arms can give comfort. This phase lasts only a few weeks or months; it ends when the infant can discriminate among people and pick out parents from the crowd. In the second phase, infants respond differently to familiar and unfamiliar people, smiling or vocalizing to those whom they recognize, crying when those people leave, and finding comfort in their soothing. The third. phase begins sometime around six or seven months, when the baby shows evidence of forming a true attachment to the single person with whom the baby has shared many experiences.

As you will recall from our discussion of cognitive development, this is the time when infants are beginning to realize that objects are permanent. They also realize that people are permanent; but when the person to whom they are attached disappears, the child doesn't have a blanket to search under and therefore gets upset (Corter, Zucker & Galligan, 1980). The baby seeks contact with this person—crawling after her, calling her, embracing her, clambering up into her lap, or protesting when she leaves. This phase of development continues through the second and third years.

In most cultures in which the attachment process has been studied, the person to whom the baby forms an attachment first is usually the mother. Infants also develop attachments to their fathers, but often this occurs a little later than the attachment to the mother (Kotelchuck, 1976; Lamb, 1976). Not only is father-infant interaction less frequent than mother-infant interaction, but most studies show that it has a somewhat different nature. Mothers tend to feed, bathe, dress, cuddle, and talk to their infants, whereas fathers are more likely to play with, jiggle, and toss them, especially sons (Clarke-Stewart, 1980; Lamb, 1977). Fathers are usually just as sensitive and responsive to their infant's expressions while things are going well; but when the baby gets bored or distressed, fathers may not do as well as mothers (Frodi et al., 1978; Power & Parke, 1983). After the attachment to the father has formed, though, the father often becomes the toddler's preferred play partner (Clarke-Stewart, 1980; Lynn & Cross, 1974).

Variations in Attachment The amount of closeness and contact the infant seeks with mother or father depends to some extent on characteristics of the infant. Those who are ill or tired or slow to warm up may require more closeness. Closeness also depends to some extent on the parent. An infant whose parent has been absent, aloof, or unresponsive is likely to need more closeness than one whose parent has been accessible and responsive. Again, we see the contributions of both nature—the infant's temperament—and nurture—the parent's availability.

All infants develop an attachment to their primary caregiver, but not all attachments are created equal. Researchers have studied the differences in infants' attachments in a special situation that simulates the natural comings and goings of parents and infants—the so-called *Strange Situation* (Ainsworth et al., 1978). Mother and infant come to an unfamiliar playroom in a laboratory, where the infant interacts with the mother and an unfamiliar woman in brief episodes, which include the infant playing with the mother and stranger in the room, the mother and stranger leaving, the baby staying alone in the room, and the mother returning to the room.

Researchers have found that most infants in the United States display a *secure attachment* to the mother in the Strange Situation. Their urge to be close is balanced by their urge to explore the environment. In the unfamiliar room, the infant uses the mother as a home base, leaving her side to explore and play but returning to her periodically for comfort or contact. Securely attached children can tolerate the brief separations from their mother, but they are always happy to see her return and they are always receptive to her overtures of contact. These mother-child pairs, researchers have found, tend to have harmonious interactions from the earliest months (Isabella, Belsky & von Eye, 1989). The mothers themselves tend to be sensitive and responsive (Clarke-Stewart, 1988a).

Some infants, however, form an *anxious insecure attachment.* Their relationship may be (1) *avoidant*—they avoid or ignore the mother when she approaches or when she returns after the brief separation; (2) *ambivalent*—they are upset when their mother leaves, but when she returns they act angry and reject her efforts at contact, and when picked up they squirm to get down; or (3) *disorganized*—their behavior is inconsistent, disturbed, and disturbing; they may begin to cry again after the mother has returned and comforted them, or they may reach out for the mother while looking away from her. Mothers who are rejecting, abusive, or neglectful are likely to have children with insecure attachments (Schneider-Rosen et al., 1985).

In Japan, good mothers are expected to be completely devoted to the child, giving unconditional love and affection, and rarely separating from the infant (Miyake, Chen & Campos, 1985; White, 1987). In Japan, as in many other cultures, infants sleep with their parents. All these factors lead to extremely close mother-child attachments.

The security of a child's attachment to parents has a number of far-reaching implications. Compared with insecurely attached children, those who are securely attached tend to be more socially and emotionally competent; more cooperative, enthusiastic, and persistent; better at solving problems; more compliant and controlled; and more popular and playful (Clarke-Stewart, 1988a; Elicker & Sroufe, 1992/3). However, attachment is just one of a number of factors—including stressful events and family characteristics—that affect the course of a child's development. A secure attachment does not guarantee confidence and competence, nor does an insecure attachment predestine pathology.

Indeed, patterns of child care and attachment vary widely in different parts of the world. In northern Germany, for example, the proportion of infants who display avoidant behavior in the Strange Situation is much higher than in the United States (Grossmann et al., 1985). In Japan, it is impossible for many mothers to leave their infants in the Strange Situation because the infants are so distressed by separation (Miyake, Chen & Campos, 1985). Yet another pattern is seen among the Efe, a pygmy people. Efe infants spend almost all their time in social contact with other people, but only about half of it is with their mothers (Tronick, Morelli & Ivey, 1992). As a consequence, their attachments are not as focused on a single maternal figure as are those of infants in other cultures.

Thinking Critically

Does Day Care Harm the Emotional Development of Infants?

With the mothers of half the infants in the United States working outside the home, concern has been expressed about how daily separations from their mothers affect infants. Some have argued that putting infants in day care, with a babysitter or in a day-care center, damages the quality of the mother-infant relationship and increases the babies' risk for psychological problems later on (Belsky, 1988, 1992). The steps for critical thinking presented in Chapter 2 offer a strategy for evaluating this issue.

What am I being asked to believe or accept?

The claim to be evaluated here is that the daily separations created by day care damage the formation of an attachment between the mother and infant and harm the infant's emotional development.

What evidence is available to support the assertion?

There is clear evidence that separation from the mother is painful for young children. Furthermore, if separation lasts a week or more, young children who have formed an attachment to their mother tend to protest, then become apathetic and mournful, and finally seem to lose interest in the missing mother (Robertson & Robertson, 1971). But day care does not involve such lasting separations, and research has shown that infants who are in day care *do* form attachments to their mothers. In fact, they prefer their mothers to their babysitters or daytime caregivers (Clarke-Stewart & Fein, 1983).

Are these attachments as secure as the attachments formed by infants who are raised at home? Researchers have examined this question by comparing how infants react to brief separations from their mother in the Strange Situation. Infants who are relatively unperturbed and ignore or avoid their mothers after the separations are rated as insecurely attached. Combined data from about twenty studies reveal that infants in full-time day care are somewhat more likely to be classified as insecurely attached. About 36 percent of them are classified as insecure in this assessment of attachment; only 29 percent of the infants who were not in full-time day care were counted as insecure (Clarke-Stewart, 1989a). These results appear to support the suggestion that day care harms infants' attachments to their mothers.

Are there alternative ways of interpreting the evidence?

Perhaps factors other than day care are at work, and the difference between infants in day care and those at home with their mothers is only apparent, not real. What could these other factors be?

One factor is the method that was used to assess attachment. Recall that infants in these studies were judged insecure if they were relatively unperturbed by a brief separation from their mothers in an unfamiliar room with an unfamiliar woman. Maybe infants who experienced routine separations from their mothers when they were left in day care felt more comfortable in this situation and therefore sought out less closeness with their mothers. Maybe they were expressing their independence, not their insecurity. A second factor is the possible differences between the infants' mothers. Perhaps mothers who value independence in themselves and in their children are more likely to be working and to place their children in day care, whereas mothers who value closeness with their children are more likely to stay home. This *self-selection* could have led more infants of working mothers to be classified as insecure.

What additional evidence would help to evaluate the alternatives?

Finding a heightened rate of insecure attachment among the infants of working mothers does not, by itself, demonstrate that day care is harmful. To judge the effects of day care, other measures of emotional adjustment are necessary. If infants in day care showed consistent signs of impaired emotional relations in other situations (at home, say) and with other caregivers (for example, with the father), this evidence would support the argument that day care harms children's emotional development. Investigation of the behavior and attitudes of parents who use day care for their infants and those who do not would also be useful. If both groups of parents were comparable in every measurable way except for their use of day care, this too would support the argument. Finally, useful information might come from experimental research in which infants were randomly assigned to be in day care or to stay at home with Mother. But this kind of study has practical and ethical problems, and it is unlikely ever to be done.

What conclusions are most reasonable?

Psychologists cannot yet say whether day care, *per se,* is harmless or harmful. The most reasonable conclusion at present is that there is an increased likelihood that infants in day care will ignore or avoid their mothers after a brief separation. Until we have figured out why, we should study the development of infants in day care with great care. Some day-care situations may be more harmful than others, and some infants may be more vulnerable than others to negative effects. For example, it seems likely that infants would be harmed if they were in unstable or low-quality day care, if they spent more than eight hours a day in the day-care setting, if they were temperamentally difficult, and if their parents were insensitive.

Relationships with Parents and Peers

Erik Erikson (1968) saw the first year of life as the time when infants develop a feeling of basic trust (or mistrust) about the world. According to his theory, an infant's first year represents the first of eight stages of lifelong psychosocial development, which are outlined in Table 3.2. Each stage focuses on an issue or crisis that is especially important at that time of life. Erikson believed that the ways in which people resolve these issues shape their personalities and social relationships. Positive resolution of an issue provides the foundation for characteristics such as trust, autonomy, initiative, and industry. But if the crisis is not resolved positively, according to Erikson, the person will be psychologically troubled and cope less effectively with later crises. Thus, in Erikson's theory, forming basic feelings of trust during infancy is the bedrock for all future emotional development.

After children have formed strong emotional attachments to their parents, their next psychological task is to begin to develop a more autonomous relationship with them. In Erikson's theory, this task is reflected in stage 2 (see Table 3.2): after developing a trusting relationship, children begin to exercise their wills, to develop some independence from their all-powerful parents, and to initiate activities on their own. According to Erikson, children who are not allowed to exercise their wills or initiate their own activities will feel uncertain about doing things for themselves and guilty about seeking independence.

Researchers have observed that from two to four years, children in the United States do become more self-reliant and autonomous from their parents (Mahler, Pine & Bergman, 1975). They spend more time apart from the parents, pursuing their own activities, are less distressed by separation, assert their desires, and say "no." At the same time, parents start saying "no" to the children. Freud characterized childhood as an ongoing conflict between the child's wishes and the parents' rules. It is up to parents to channel the child's impulses into socially accepted outlets.

Table 3.2
Erikson's Stages of Psychosocial Development

In each of Erikson's stages of development, a different psychological issue presents a new crisis for the person to resolve. The person focuses his or her attention on the issue and by the end of the period has worked through the crisis and resolved it either positively, in the direction of healthy development, or negatively, hindering further psychological development.

Age	Central Psychological Issue or Crisis
First year	**Trust versus mistrust** Infants learn to trust that their needs will be met by the world, especially by the mother—or they learn to mistrust the world.
Second year	**Autonomy versus shame and doubt** Children learn to exercise will, to make choices, and to control themselves—or they become uncertain and doubt that they can do things by themselves.
Third to fifth year	**Initiative versus guilt** Children learn to initiate activities and enjoy their accomplishments, acquiring direction and purpose. Or, if they are not allowed initiative, they feel guilty for their attempts at independence.
Sixth year through puberty	**Industry versus inferiority** Children develop a sense of industry and curiosity and are eager to learn—or they feel inferior and lose interest in the tasks before them.
Adolescence	**Identity versus role confusion** Adolescents come to see themselves as unique and integrated persons with an ideology—or they become confused about what they want out of life.
Early adulthood	**Intimacy versus isolation** Young people become able to commit themselves to another person—or they develop a sense of isolation and feel they have no one in the world but themselves.
Middle age	**Generativity versus stagnation** Adults are willing to have and care for children and to devote themselves to their work and the common good—or they become self-centered and inactive.
Old age	**Integrity versus despair** Older people enter a period of reflection, becoming assured that their lives have been meaningful and ready to face death with acceptance and dignity. Or they are in despair for their unaccomplished goals, failures, and ill-spent lives.

Socialization Styles   The process by which parents and others in authority channel children's impulses and teach them the skills and rules needed to function in their society is called **socialization.** Cultural values and environmental conditions clearly shape this process. In the Mexican and Mayan cultures, for example, children are supposed to respect their elders, not learn how to question, negotiate, and argue as middle-class European-American children are expected to do; good children are children who obey their elders (Greenfield & Childs, 1991).

Studying a sample of parents in Berkeley, California, Diana Baumrind found three distinct patterns that describe the socialization styles of the majority of U.S. parents (Baumrind, 1971). **Authoritarian parents** were strict, punitive, and unsympathetic. They valued obedience from their children and tried to shape their children's behavior to meet a set standard and to curb the children's wills. They did not encourage independence. They were detached and seldom praised their youngsters. In contrast, **permissive parents** gave their children complete freedom, and their discipline was lax. The third group, **authoritative parents**, fell between these two extremes. They reasoned with their children, encouraging give and take. They allowed children increasing responsibility as they got older and better at making decisions. They were firm but understanding. They set limits but also encouraged independence. Their demands were reasonable, rational, and consistent.

Baumrind found that these three socialization styles were consistently related to children's social and emotional development. Authoritarian parents had children who were unfriendly, distrustful, and withdrawn. The children of permissive parents were immature, dependent, and unhappy; they were likely to have tantrums or to ask for help when they encountered even slight difficulties. Children raised by authoritative parents were friendly, cooperative, self-reliant, and socially responsible. A follow-up study of the same children at age nine showed that the advantages of authoritative discipline were still present (Baumrind, 1986).

Other researchers have found authoritative socialization styles associated with other positive outcomes, including better school achievement and better psychological adjustment to parental divorce (Dornbusch et al., 1987; Hetherington & Clingempeel, 1992; Steinberg, Dornbusch & Brown, 1992). Socialization styles may also help mold children's moral behavior. Children who are given orders, threats, and punishments are more likely than others to cheat and less likely to experience guilt or to accept blame after doing something wrong (Hoffman, 1970). Still, you cannot predict whether children, or adults, will help or hurt someone just by knowing how they were raised. In Chapter 18 we look at other factors that help determine whether people will obey the law or break it, help someone or turn their backs.

Indeed, studies of socialization are limited in several ways. First, they are based on correlations—and, as discussed in Chapter 2, correlations do not tell you about causation. Finding consistent correlations between parents' and children's behavior does not establish that parents are creating the differences in their children. In fact, to some extent socialization styles are shaped by children, and especially by their temperaments. Mothers of difficult or aggressive children do more controlling, warning, prohibiting, and removing of objects than mothers of children with easy dispositions (Bates, 1980; Lytton, 1987). Difficult children persist in their troublesome actions longer and ignore, protest, or fuss at their mothers' attempts to control them. In some extreme cases, qualities in the child can trigger physical abuse, especially when parents are overburdened or psychologically disturbed. Children who are underweight, handicapped, difficult, or aggressive, who cry often, mature slowly, and need special care, are more likely to be victims of abuse (Kochanek, 1986). Just like cognitive development, then, the socialization of children depends on the forces of both nature and nurture.

Second, the correlations between socialization styles and children's behavior, though statistically significant, are not terribly strong. Thus, expected outcomes do not always appear. For example, Baumrind (1971) found a small group of families in which, like the permissive families, discipline was never observed, yet the children were thriving. These harmonious families seemed

Linkages: Research in developmental psychology on the relationship between parents' socialization styles and behavior patterns has helped shape parent-training programs such as the one described in Chapter 14, on personality. These programs are designed to help the parents of unruly children, for example, to adopt more systematic and authoritative methods that can minimize the frequency of scenes like this.

to have achieved an optimal balance without authoritative discipline; the children had developed their own internalized values early so that direct parental control was rarely necessary.

A third limitation is that most socialization research has been done in the United States, generally with middle-class parents. Therefore, the findings do not necessarily represent universal principles. As psychologists broaden their research to include families of diverse subcultures and different cultural groups, they are finding that authoritative discipline may not be the ideal socialization style for all groups. For example, the correlation Baumrind found between authoritarian discipline and poor social development did not hold up for the African-American families she observed. In a larger-scale study, youngsters from authoritative homes had better psychosocial outcomes than children from nonauthoritative homes in all ethnic groups, but in terms of school performance, European-American and Hispanic-American children were more likely to benefit from authoritative parenting than were African-American or Asian-American youngsters (Steinberg et al., 1992). Socialization obviously occurs in a cultural context. Both the effectiveness of the parents' socialization efforts and their socialization styles themselves are affected by the living and working conditions in which parents find themselves (Greenberg, O'Neil & Goldberg, 1991).

Relationships with Peers

The saga of social development over the years of childhood is the story of an enlarging social world, which broadens to include brothers and sisters, playmates and classmates. From a remarkably early age—as young as one—children are interested in the behavior of other children, usually their siblings, and by the time they are a year and a half, they know how to hurt or comfort other children (Dunn, 1992).

Though social interests and expressions appear early on, social skills, like cognitive skills, must be learned. At two years old, the most children can do is to exchange—or fight over—toys. In these interactions, their interest really is the toys, not the peer (Mueller & Lucas, 1975). By the time children are three, toys have become a means to an end, helping to elicit responses from peers;

Though relationships with peers may not always be cordial, they are often among the closest and most positive in a child's life. In North American cultures, children's friendships are almost always with children of the same sex. The reasons, presumably, are that children of the same sex share the same play interests and that children are attracted to others who are like themselves and want to avoid those who are different. Friends are more interactive than nonfriends; they smile and laugh together more, pay closer attention to equality in their conversations, and talk about mutual rather than their own idiosyncratic ends.

by age four, children begin to converse about the toys they are playing with (Mueller & Lucas, 1975). It is not until the end of the preschool period, however, that children are able to share toys and tasks cooperatively (Parten, 1932, 1971). In the school years, peer interaction becomes more complex and structured. School children play games with rules. They play on teams. They tutor each other. They cooperate—and compete—in achieving goals.

The school years are also the time when friends become important and friendships become long-lasting. Children begin to understand that feelings, not things, keep friends together (Selman, 1981). Friendships appear to be the best contexts for learning social skills such as cooperation and intimacy. Children who have supportive friends become more popular with other kids as well (Berndt & Hawkins, 1987). Children who do not have friends usually have problems in later life (Parker & Asher, 1987).

Social Skills and Understanding

The changes in peer interactions and relationships over the years can be traced in part to children's increasing social competence and understanding. At first, children need an adult partner such as their mother or father to have a significant social interaction. Very young children do not have the social skills to engage in sustained, responsive interactions with other children. They develop these skills gradually over the preschool years as their interest in peers and their ability to communicate with them increase. It appears that parents can aid the process—for example, by initiating lots of pretend play (Vandell, Ramanan & Lederberg, 1991).

As children get older, they play, smile, and laugh more (Blurton-Jones, 1972). They become better able to follow the rules in games and to act together in groups. They grow increasingly sensitive to the rights of minorities (Selman et al., 1983). They learn more elaborate and appropriate ways of helping and comforting each other (Zahn-Waxler, Iannotti & Chapman, 1982). They increase the frequency with which they help, share, and provide comfort (Zahn-Waxler et al., 1992). They learn the rules that govern social interactions and society at large. For example, they learn to be polite. By six years of age, children begin to say "Can I swing?" or "Please may I swing?" instead of "Let me swing" or "Get off that swing!" (Bates, 1976; Garvey, 1975). They also learn to control their emotional expressions to conform to social norms (Ekman, 1980); they smile when greeting Grandmother and try not to cry when hurt or angry. Through the school years, children become aware of subtle distinctions among types of rules and become more flexible in complying with arbitrary ones.

Linkages: How does a child's social perception differ from an adult's (a link to Social Cognition)

Children's increased social competence is due in part to their growing ability to detect and interpret emotional signals and social situations. At three or four, children can name typical facial expressions of happiness, sadness, anger, and fear (Camras, 1977). Girls are able to do this at younger ages than boys; their understanding of people's feelings is related to talking about feelings with their parents and having cooperative interactions with their siblings (Dunn et al., 1991). As they get older, children learn to recognize a wider range of emotions and to predict how a person will feel in emotion-provoking situations. For one thing, they learn that people do not always express what they feel (Gnepp, 1983; Selman, 1980). They also come to realize that individuals have abiding personal dispositions, or personalities. By the end of elementary school, they begin to describe people in terms of psychological attributes, such as "really conceited; he thinks he's great," or "real sensitive, a lot more than most people" (Barenboim, 1981; Rholes & Ruble, 1984). Children's understanding of people and their feelings parallels the development of their understanding of the nonsocial world (Marini & Case, 1989); they learn rules governing objects and rules applying to feelings at the same time.

Part of understanding people is knowing about social roles. Toddlers pretend to perform imaginary acts such as bathing the baby or hosing the fire, but they are not aware that these acts are part of social roles. Later, they begin to understand that parents buy things, make phone calls, and clean house; that doctors wear white coats, ask to look at your tongue, and give injections. At age four, children understand how two or three roles fit together, and they can play family. By age six, children understand whole networks of roles, such as teachers, students, principal, and janitor, allowing them to play school (Watson, 1981).

Gender Roles

Linkages: How do boys learn to be men and girls learn to be women? (a link to Learning)

Many of the roles children learn about are linked to being male or female. In all societies, some roles, like firefighter, have traditionally been male, whereas others, like nurse, have traditionally been female. These traditions are not nearly as strong in North American culture as they once were, but all cultures, North American included, do establish expectations about **gender roles**, which are general patterns of work, appearance, and behavior associated with being a man or a woman. Research by Deborah Best suggests that children learn gender-role expectations earliest in Muslim countries (where the roles are perhaps most extreme), but children in all twenty-five countries she studied eventually developed them (Best, 1992; Williams & Best, 1990). Gender roles persist because they are deeply rooted in both nature and nurture.

Gender roles, first, are rooted in biological differences between males and females. Even before children have learned gender roles, there are some physical and behavioral differences between the sexes, which then increase with age (Feingold, 1988; Hyde, 1992; Jacklin, 1989; Maccoby & Jacklin, 1974; Shepherd-Look, 1982). Girls are, on the average, physically more mature than boys and less susceptible to illness. They suffer less from speech, learning, and behavior disorders, mental retardation, emotional problems, and sleep disorders. As a group, girls speak and write earlier, and are better at grammar and spelling. Boys are more skilled at manipulating objects, constructing three-dimensional forms, and mentally manipulating figures and pictures. They are more physically active and aggressive and more inclined to hit obstacles or people; they play in larger groups and spaces, enjoying noisier, more strenuous physical games like soccer and football. Girls are more nurturant and emotionally empathic; their play tends to be more orderly (DiPietro, 1981).

The biological foundation of these male-female differences is supported by studies of differences in anatomy, hormones, and brain organization, as well as by cross-cultural research showing consistency in gender patterns even in the face of different socialization. In virtually every culture, for example, males are more violent than females. In one survey, there was not a single culture in which the number of women who killed women was even one-tenth as great as the number of men who killed men; on average, men's homicides outnumbered women's by more than 30 to 1 (Daly & Wilson, 1988). Research in neuroscience has found some differences in the brain structure of males and females (Hines & Green, 1991), and gender differences have also been linked to hormonal factors, as discussed in the next chapter (Berenbaum & Hines, 1992; Resnick et al., 1986).

As always, however, it is difficult if not impossible to untangle biologically based gender differences from the socially created ones—to separate nature and nurture—because, from the moment they are born, boys and girls are treated differently. In Western cultures, for example, parents perceive their newborn girls as softer, smaller, more beautiful, and their sons as firm, strong, and well coordinated (Rubin, Provenzano & Luria, 1974)—even though the infants are not observably different (Plomin & DeFries, 1985). Adults play more gently and talk more to infants they believe to be girls than infants they

Socialization by parents and others typically encourages interests and activities traditionally associated with a child's own gender.

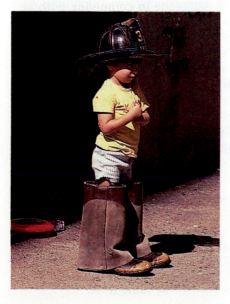

In Review: Social and Emotional Development During Infancy and Childhood

Age	Relationships with Parents	Relationships with Other Children	Social Understanding
Birth–2 years	Infants form an attachment to the primary caregiver.	Play focuses on toys, not on other children.	Infants respond to emotional expressions of others.
2–4 years	Children become more autonomous and no longer need their parents' constant attention.	Toys are a way of eliciting responses from other children.	Young children can recognize emotions of others.
4–10 years	Parents actively socialize their children.	Children begin to cooperate, compete, play games, and form friendships with peers.	Children learn social rules, like politeness, and roles, like being a male or female; they learn to control their emotions.

believe to be boys (Culp, Cook & Housley, 1983). They shower their daughters with dolls and doll clothes, lace and roses, their sons with trucks and teddy bears, balls and ballistics (Rheingold & Cook, 1975). They tend to encourage boys to achieve, compete, and explore; to control their feelings, act independent, and assume personal responsibility. They more often encourage girls to be expressive, nurturant, reflective, dependent, domestic, obedient, and unselfish (Archer & Lloyd, 1985; Block, 1983; Hoffman, 1977; Shepherd-Look, 1982; Huston, Carpenter & Atwater, 1986). Thus parents consciously or inadvertently pass on their ideas about "appropriate" behaviors for boys and girls. Parents are not the only source of these lessons. Teachers and other authorities (including influential figures on television) reinforce the parents' efforts.

Children also pick up notions of what is gender-appropriate behavior from their peers. Peer pressure exaggerates whatever differences may exist to begin with. Even in nursery school, children are less likely to play with a toy associated with the other gender if another child is watching (Serbin et al., 1979). Children are more likely to play with other children of the same sex, and in gender-typical ways, on the playground than they are in private, at home, or in the classroom (Luria, 1992; Maccoby & Jacklin, 1987; Thorne, 1986). An analysis of 143 studies of sex differences in aggression showed that boys were significantly and consistently more aggressive than girls (especially in the preschool years), but especially so when they were being watched (Hyde, 1986).

In short, social training by both adults and peers tends to bolster and amplify any biological predispositions that distinguish boys and girls, thus creating gender roles that are the joint—and inextricably linked—products of nature and nurture. This and other elements of early development are summarized in "In Review: Social and Emotional Development During Infancy and Childhood." In Chapter 8, on learning, we examine the mechanisms by which children learn gender roles, among other things.

Adolescence

The years of middle childhood usually pass smoothly, as children busy themselves with schoolwork, hobbies, friends, and clubs. But adolescence changes

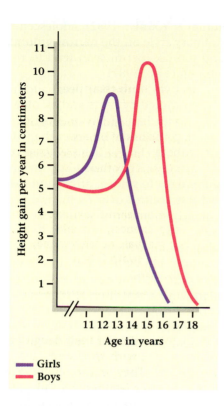

Source: Adapted from Tanner, Whitehouse & Takaishi, 1960.

Figure 3.8
Adolescent Growth
At about ten and a half years, girls begin their growth spurt and are temporarily taller than their male peers. When boys, at about age twelve, begin their growth spurt, they usually grow faster and for a longer period of time than girls. Adolescents may grow as much as 5 inches a year.

things drastically. All adolescents undergo significant changes in size, shape, and physical capacities. In Western cultures many adolescents also experience substantial changes in their social life, reasoning abilities, and views of themselves.

The Big Shakeup

The first and most visible sign that adolescence has begun is a sudden spurt in physical growth. Beginning at about age ten and a half for girls and at about twelve for boys, weight and height increase dramatically (see Figure 3.8). Suddenly, adolescents find themselves in new bodies. At the end of the growth spurt, menstruation begins in females and live sperm are produced in males. **Puberty**—the condition of being able for the first time to reproduce—is also characterized by changes such as fuller breasts and rounder curves in females, broad shoulders and narrow hips in males.

There are psychological changes as well. Young adolescents begin to realize that they are no longer children; yet they are far from adult. In Western cultures, *early adolescence*—the period from age twelve to sixteen or so—is fraught with ups and downs. Moods often swing wildly from one extreme to the other: from elation at a girlfriend's kiss to dejection at a failed exam (Csikszentmihalyi & Larson, 1984). Sexual interest stirs, and there are opportunities to smoke, drink alcohol, and take other drugs. All of this can be very disorienting. For adolescents, this is their first big shakeup; it changes how they act, how they feel, and how they think.

Early adolescence challenges the child's *self-esteem,* the sense of being worthy, capable, and deserving of respect—especially if other stresses occur at the same time. Youths who experience more or greater stressors—from inadequate study space at home to parental divorce or unemployment—have more difficulty adapting to adolescence (DuBois et al., 1992). The effects of such stressors can be offset, however, if teachers or parents offer the young adolescent social and emotional support (DuBois & Hirsch, 1990; DuBois et al., 1992).

Another factor affecting self-esteem is physical maturity. In Western cultures, boys who go through puberty early are accepted by their peers and teachers as mature; they tend to have higher status, to become leaders, and to be happy, poised, and relaxed. Those who reach puberty late feel rejected, dependent, and dominated by others (Duke et al., 1982; Peterson, 1987). For girls, maturing early is likely to lead to embarrassment, to sexual activity, and to increased distance between the girls and their parents (Brooks-Gunn, 1988; Peterson, 1987). These differences between early and late maturers may persist into adulthood (Jones, 1957).

Although adolescence was once considered to be a period of inevitable storm and stress, contemporary research suggests that in Western cultures more than half of today's teens find early adolescence relatively trouble free; only about 15 percent of the adolescents studied experience serious turmoil (Peterson, 1987). For girls, the turmoil typically results in depression; for boys, rebellion.

The changes and pressures of adolescence are often reflected in family conflicts. Teenagers are no longer content to accept all their parents' rules and values. This can lead to bickering over everything from taking out the garbage to who left the gallon of milk on top of the refrigerator. Serious conflicts often lead to serious problems, including running away, pregnancy, stealing, even suicide (Montemayor, 1983). Conflict with families and a desire for the company of people with common interests lead many teenagers to "hang out" with other teenagers. Adolescents influence one another to look and act alike in many ways, from musical tastes and dancing to smoking and skipping school (Condry & Siman, 1974; Krosnick & Judd, 1982). By ninth grade, adolescents say that their relationships with their peers are closer than those with their parents (Bowerman & Kinch, 1956; Hunter & Youniss, 1982). Adolescents whose parents retain an authoritative disciplinary style on the narrow ground between being too strict (authoritarian) and too lax (permissive) tend to remain well-adjusted (Baumrind, 1991; Dornbusch et al., 1987).

Sexuality is one area in which adolescents feel closer to their peers and in conflict with their parents. Sexual activity is promoted by peers and by older brothers and sisters (Rodgers & Rowe, 1988). About half of North America's youth has had sexual intercourse by age sixteen, compared with fewer than 10 percent fifty years ago (Brooks-Gunn & Furstenberg, 1989). Teens who have sex differ from those who do not in a number of ways. They hold less conventional attitudes and values, and they are more likely to smoke, drink, and use drugs. Their parents are less educated, exert less control over them, and are less likely to talk openly with them. A substantial number of sexually active girls were sexually abused as children (Musick, 1987).

Too often, sexual activity leads to declining school achievement and interest, sexually transmitted diseases, and, of course, unplanned and unwanted pregnancies. Teenagers have the highest rates of sexually transmitted diseases (such as gonorrhea, chlamydia, and pelvic inflammatory disease) of any age group (Brooks-Gunn & Furstenberg, 1989). One-fifth of all AIDS cases start in adolescence. Nearly one-quarter of all teenage girls in the United States get pregnant before they reach age eighteen (Furstenberg, Brooks-Gunn & Chase-Lansdale, 1989).

In fact, the United States has the highest rate of teenage pregnancy in the industrialized world. This is not because U.S. adolescents are more sexually active than other teenagers but because they do not use effective contraception. In cultures where attitudes toward sex are more liberal, sex education more thorough, and contraceptives more readily available, rates of teenage pregnancy are lower (Furstenberg, Brooks-Gunn & Chase-Lansdale, 1989).

About 40 percent of U.S. adolescents who become pregnant have an abortion, 12 percent get married, and 4 percent give up their baby for adoption. The largest number of pregnant teens become single mothers, who face serious medical, social, and economic risks. When the girl raises a child alone, she ends up with less education, poorer economic opportunities, and, usually, more children than she wants or can afford to support (Furstenberg, Brooks-Gunn & Chase-Lansdale, 1989).

Identity and Development of the Self

In many Third World cultures today and in the United States during earlier times, the end of early adolescence, around the age of sixteen, marks the beginning of adulthood: of work, parenting, and grown-up responsibilities. In modern North America, the transition from childhood to adulthood often lasts into the early twenties. Adolescents spend a substantial amount of time being students, trainees, and apprentices. This lengthened adolescence has created special problems—among them, finding or forming an identity. The journey through early adolescence behind them, adolescents' major psychological task is to answer the critical question: Who am I?

Forming a Personal and Ethnic Identity   Most adolescents have not previously thought about who they are. As young children, their self-concepts were based on fleeting, sometimes inaccurate, perceptions. When preschool children are asked to describe themselves, they often mention a favorite or habitual activity: "I watch TV," "I walk to school," or "I do the dishes" (Keller, Ford & Meacham, 1978). At eight or nine, children identify themselves by giving facts such as their sex, age, name, physical appearance, likes, and dislikes. They may still describe themselves in terms of what they do, but they now

Teenage mothers tend to be less positive and stimulating with their children than older mothers (Garcia Coll, Oh & Hoffman, 1987); they more often abuse them. The children of teenage mothers, in turn, are likely to develop behavior problems and to do poorly in school (Furstenberg, Brooks-Gunn & Chase-Lansdale, 1989).

include how well they do it compared with other children (Secord & Peevers, 1974). By age eleven, children begin to describe themselves in terms of social relationships and personality characteristics. A sense of a unique self develops gradually over the years of middle childhood, then erupts during adolescence in the form of dramatically increased self-consciousness and self-awareness. Adolescents begin to think of themselves in terms of general, stable psychological characteristics (Damon & Hart, 1982).

Interestingly, girls develop ideas about themselves and others faster than boys. According to the responses of more than 9,000 subjects on a personality questionnaire, girls outgrew seeing themselves and others egocentrically and entered a stage of social conformity sooner than boys did; then, as boys entered the conformity stage, girls moved to a higher level of self-awareness (Cohn, 1991). Girls' faster development may have biological or social causes: girls' physical development is faster than boys', and girls tend to have more interpersonal awareness because their social interactions are more likely to occur in pairs rather than in large groups.

A person's self-concept includes a social as well as a personal identity—an identification with one or more groups. Often the group is based on ethnicity or nationality. In the melting pot of the United States, some members of ethnic minorities may identify with their ethnic group—Chinese, Mexican, or Italian, for example—even more than with being an American. Children are aware of ethnic cues such as skin color before they reach the age of three—minority-group children earlier than other children—and prefer to play with children from their own group (Hartup, 1983; Milner, 1983). In high school, students hang out in ethnically homogeneous groups and do not know classmates from other ethnic groups well, seeing them more as members of other groups than as individuals (Steinberg, Dornbusch & Brown, 1992). These social processes solidify ethnic identity. A positive ethnic identity contributes to self-esteem; seeing their own group as superior makes people feel good about themselves (Turner, 1987). *Bicultural people,* who affirm both their ethnic and their national identities, also typically have a positive self-concept (Phinney, 1990). However, as described in Chapters 17 and 18, the same processes that solidify ethnic identity can also sow the seeds of ethnic prejudice.

Erikson's Identity Crisis Identity formation is the central task of adolescence in Erikson's theory of psychosocial development. According to Erikson, events of late adolescence—graduating from high school, going to college, and forging new relationships—challenge the adolescent's self-concept, precipitating an **identity crisis** (see Table 3.2). In this crisis, the adolescent must develop an integrated image of himself or herself as a unique person. This is done by pulling together self-knowledge acquired during childhood. If infancy and childhood brought trust, autonomy, and initiative, according to Erikson, the adolescent will resolve the identity crisis positively, feeling self-confident and competent. If, however, infancy and childhood resulted in feelings of mistrust, shame, guilt, and inferiority, the adolescent will be confused about his or her identity and goals.

There is some limited empirical support for Erikson's ideas about the identity crisis in Western cultures. In late adolescence, young people do consider alternative identities (Waterman, 1982). They "try out" being rebellious, studious, or detached, as they attempt to resolve questions about sexuality, self-worth, industriousness, and independence. By the time they are twenty-one, about half of the adolescents studied have resolved the identity crisis in a way that is consistent with their self-image and the historical era in which they are living. They are ready to enter adulthood with self-confidence. Basically the same people who entered adolescence, they have more mature attitudes and behavior, more consistent goals and values, and a clearer idea of who they are (Adams & Jones, 1983; Dusek & Flaherty, 1981; Savin-Williams & Demo, 1984). For those who fail to resolve identity issues—either because they avoided the identity crisis by accepting whatever identity their parents set for them or because they postponed dealing with the crisis and remain uncommitted and lacking in direction—there are often problems ahead.

Abstract Thought and Moral Reasoning

One reason that adolescents can develop a conscious identity is that at this age it is possible for the first time to think and reason about abstract concepts. For many young people in Western cultures, adolescence begins a stage of cognitive development that Piaget called the **formal operational period**, a stage marked by the ability to engage in hypothetical thinking, including the imagining of logical consequences. For example, adolescents who have reached the level of formal operations can consider various strategies for finding a part-time job and recognize that some methods are more likely to lead to success than others. They can form general concepts and understand the impact of the past on the present and the present on the future. They can question social institutions, think about the world as it might be and ought to be, and consider the ramifications of love, morality, work, politics, philosophy, and religion. They can think logically and systematically about symbols and propositions, regardless of whether the propositions are true. For example, they might evaluate the idea "Suppose there were no money in the world" logically to determine the possible consequences. They can reflect on and analyze their own mental processes, recognizing that, for example, they tend to be too optimistic or trusting. They can focus on form and symbolism in art and literature, going beyond the content of a painting or a book to see what the artist or author was trying to say about the world.

Piaget explored adolescents' formal operational abilities by asking them to perform science experiments that involved formulating and systematically investigating hypotheses. Research indicates that only about half the people in Western cultures ever reach the formal operational level necessary to succeed in Piaget's experiments; those who have not had high school science and math are less likely to succeed (Keating, 1980; Neimark, 1982). In other cultures, too, people who have not gone to school are less likely to exhibit formal operations. Here, for example, is an exchange between a researcher and an illiterate Kpelle farmer in a Liberian village (Scribner, 1977):

Researcher: All Kpelle men are rice farmers. Mr. Smith is not a rice farmer. Is he a Kpelle man?

Kpelle farmer: I don't know the man. I have not laid eyes on the man myself.

Kpelle villagers who had had formal schooling answered the question logically: "No, Mr. Smith is not a Kpelle man."

Even people who have been to school do not use a single mode of thinking in all situations. Just because they use formal operations in a chemistry lab, they may not do so all the time. People are more likely to use formal operations for problems based on their own occupations; this is one reason that people whose logic is impeccable at work may still become the victim of a home-repair or investment con artist (Carraher, Schliemann & Carraher, 1988).

Kohlberg's Stages of Moral Reasoning   One domain in which adolescents can apply their advanced cognitive skills is morality. To examine how people think about morality, psychologists have presented subjects with hypothetical moral dilemmas and then asked them how they would resolve the dilemmas and why. Perhaps the most famous of these is the "Heinz dilemma":

In Europe, a woman was near death from a special kind of cancer. There was one drug that the doctors thought might save her. It was a form of radium that a druggist in the same town had recently discovered. The drug was expensive to make, but the druggist was charging ten times what the drug cost him to make. He paid $200 for the radium and charged $2000 for a small dose of the drug. The sick woman's husband, Heinz, went to everyone he knew to borrow the money, but could only get together about $1000, which was half of what it cost. He told the druggist that his wife was dying and asked him to sell it cheaper or let him pay later. But the druggist said, "No, I discovered the drug and I'm going to make money from it." So Heinz got desperate and considered breaking into the man's store to steal the drug for his wife. Should Heinz steal the radium? (Kohlberg & Gilligan, 1971, pp. 1072–1073)

Using moral dilemmas like this one, Lawrence Kohlberg found that the reasons given for moral choices change systematically and consistently with age. Young children make moral judgments that are different from those of older children, adolescents, or adults. Kohlberg proposed that moral reasoning develops in six stages, which are summarized in Table 3.3. Like Piaget's stages, these stages are not tightly linked to the person's chronological age; there is a range of ages for reaching each stage, and not everyone reaches the highest level. But people do progress through the stages in the same order; they do not jump from Stage 1 to Stage 3 or from Stage 3 to Stage 2.

Table 3.3
Kohlberg's Stages of Moral Development

Kohlberg's stages of moral reasoning describe differences in how people think about moral issues. Here are some examples of answers that people at different stages of development might give to the "Heinz dilemma" described in the text.

Stage	What Is Right?	Should Heinz Steal the Drug?
1	Obeying and avoiding punishment from a superior authority	Heinz should not steal the drug because he will be jailed.
2	Making a fair exchange, a good deal	Heinz should steal the drug because his wife will repay him later.
3	Pleasing others and getting their approval	Heinz should steal the drug because he loves his wife and because she and the rest of the family will approve.
4	Doing your duty, following rules and social order	Heinz should steal the drug for his wife because he has a duty to care for her, or he should not steal the drug because stealing is illegal.
5	Respecting rules and laws, but recognizing that they may have limits	Heinz should steal the drug because life is more important than property.
6	Following universal ethical principles, such as justice, reciprocity, equality, and respect for human life and rights	Heinz should steal the drug because of the principle of preserving and respecting life.

Which of Kohlberg's stages of moral reasoning is represented here?

"Quit complaining and eat it! ... Number one, chicken soup is good for the flu – and number two, it's nobody we know."

Stage 1 and Stage 2 moral judgments, which are most typical for children under the age of nine, tend to be selfish in nature. Kohlberg called this level of moral reasoning **preconventional** because reasoning at this level is not based on the conventions or rules that guide social interactions in society. People at this level of moral development are concerned with avoiding punishment or following rules when it is to their own advantage. At the next higher, **conventional** level of moral reasoning, Stages 3 and 4, people are concerned about other people; they think that morality consists of following rules and conventions such as duty to the family, to marriage vows, to the country. The moral reasoning of children from nine to nineteen is most often at this level. Stages 5 and 6 represent the highest level of moral reasoning, which Kohlberg called **postconventional** because it occurs after conventional reasoning. Moral judgments at this level are based on personal standards or on universal principles of justice, equality, and respect for human life, not on the dictates of authority figures or society. People who have reached this level view rules and laws as arbitrary but respect them because they protect human welfare. They believe that individual rights can sometimes supersede these laws if the laws become destructive. People do not usually reach this level until after the end of adolescence. Stage 6 is seen only rarely in extraordinary individuals.

To test the validity of his stages of moral development, Kohlberg and his associates studied the moral reasoning of males as they developed from age ten to thirty-six (Colby et al., 1983; see Figure 3.9). The subjects proceeded through the stages in the order Kohlberg proposed. None of them skipped a stage; only rarely did any seem to move back a stage, although they moved through the stages at different rates and reached different levels. Other tests of Kohlberg's stages (for example, Walker, 1989) generally support the sequence he proposed.

Limitations of Kohlberg's Stages   Kohlberg's research on stages focused on males in the United States, but attempts have been made to replicate his findings in other cultures. In forty-five studies in twenty-seven cultures from Alaska to Zambia, researchers found that their subjects tend to make upward progress through Kohlberg's stages, without reversals (Snarey, 1987). Further, though Stages 5 and 6 did not always appear, Stages 1 through 4 did and thus appear universal. The reason may be that these lower levels of reasoning are more closely linked to cognitive development than is the highest level. Some moral judgments in other cultures, however, simply did not fit into Kohlberg's

**Figure 3.9
The Development of
Moral Reasoning**
The results of a longitudinal study by
Colby et al. (1983) showed that, as
adolescents, most of the male sub-
jects reasoned at a Stage 3 level.
Some of those tested never rose
above Stage 2; only about 20 percent
of the subjects tested as adults
reached Stage 5; none reached
Stage 6.

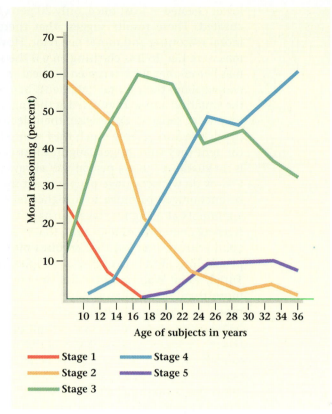

Source: Adapted from Colby et al., 1983.

stages. Some subjects in collectivist cultures like Papua-New Guinea, Taiwan, and Israeli kibbutzim, for example, explained their answers to moral dilemmas by pointing to the importance of the community. This kind of reasoning did not appear in Kohlberg's U.S. males, suggesting that culture plays a significant role in determining the factors that shape moral judgments.

Similarly, Carol Gilligan (1982; Gilligan & Wiggins, 1987) has suggested that for North American females the moral ideal is not the abstract, impersonal concept of justice that Kohlberg documented in males but, rather, the need to protect enduring relationships and fulfill human needs. Gilligan questioned Kohlberg's assumption that the highest level of morality is based on justice. When she asked people about moral conflicts, the majority of men focused on justice, but only half of the women did so. The other half focused on caring. This difference between men and women has not been found in all studies (see, for example, Miller & Bersoff, 1992) but has appeared in some (for example, Rogers, 1987).

Taken together, the results of research in different countries and with both genders suggest that moral ideals are *not* absolute and universal. Moral development is apparently an adaptation to the moral world in which one finds oneself. It is not a milestone like puberty or an achievement like graduation. Formal operational reasoning may be necessary for people to reach the highest level of moral reasoning, but this alone is not sufficient. To some extent, at the highest levels, moral reasoning is a product of culture and history.

Moral Reasoning and Moral Action   How is a person's level of moral reasoning related to the way he or she behaves? In one study, junior high school students were given the opportunity to cheat on tests and games (Krebs & Kohlberg, 1973). The majority of those whose reasoning was at Stage 4 or lower cheated at least once; only 20 percent of those who had reached Stage 5 cheated. These results suggest that there is indeed a relationship between moral reasoning and moral behavior. However, higher scores on moral dilemmas were tied to less cheating *only* if the subjects were asked about the dilemmas before they were tempted to cheat (Krebs, 1967). Apparently, interviewing people about their moral judgments before a test made them suspicious about the situation and so they acted at the highest level of moral reasoning of which they were capable. Otherwise, their decision to cheat or not was determined by such factors as how much they wanted to pass the test and how likely they thought they were to get caught. Clearly, having high moral reasoning *ability* is no guarantee that a person will always *act* morally.

How do we encourage people to act morally? Children and adolescents can be encouraged to move to a higher level of reasoning by exposing them to arguments at a higher stage, perhaps as they argue issues with one another. Hearing about moral reasoning that is one stage higher than their own or encountering a situation that requires more advanced reasoning seems to push people into moral reasoning at a higher level (Enright, Lapsley & Levy, 1983; Turiel, 1966; Walker, 1982). But the development of moral behavior involves more than abstract knowledge. Vivid emotional experiences in solving real moral problems—like being asked by a friend to help with a plan to cheat, being asked to sell drugs, or getting pregnant—have a major impact as well (Haan, Aerts & Cooper, 1985). Children and adolescents need to see consistent models of moral reasoning and behavior in the *actions* of their parents and peers. They also need parents who promote moral behavior through authoritative socialization. Finally, as discussed in Chapter 18, the situation itself may have a large effect on whether a person acts morally. For example, moral reasoning, as well as moral behavior, tends to be lower among people who are out drinking with friends (Denton & Krebs, 1990). Not only do we sometimes fail to act at the highest level of which we are capable, we sometimes fail even to reason at this level.

Adulthood

Development does not end with adolescence. Adults, too, go through transitions and experience physical and cognitive changes. For our purposes, adulthood can be divided into three periods: *early adulthood* (ages twenty to forty), *middle adulthood* (ages forty to sixty-five), and *late adulthood* (from age sixty-five on).

The Aging Body

In early adulthood, physical growth continues. Shoulder width, height, and chest size increase. People continue to develop their athletic abilities. By their mid-thirties nearly everyone shows some hearing impairment, but, for most people, these years are the prime of life.

Signs of aging typically appear in middle adulthood. The first place most people notice the change is in the mirror. They see sagging skin under the chin, crows' feet, dryness, and flabbiness. Shoulder width, height, and chest size decrease. Muscle, too, decreases, and fat increases, especially around the midriff. The body of the average sixty-year-old woman is 42 percent fat, compared to about 26 percent fat when she was twenty (Henig, 1988).

For many, the impact of these images in the mirror is softened because the senses begin to lose acuity in middle adulthood (Fozard et al., 1977). People become less sensitive to light, less accurate at perceiving differences in distance, and slower and less acute at seeing details. Increased farsightedness is

Linkages: Do the senses improve during adulthood? (a link to Sensation)

an inevitable change that begins around age forty. You know you're getting older when you find yourself reading in the position your parents once did, holding the book farther and farther from your face.

Inside the body, bone mass is dwindling. The risk of heart disease increases. In the reproductive system, fertility declines quickly during a woman's forties, as menstrual periods get shorter and less regular. Eventually, menstruation stops altogether, and a woman has reached **menopause.** Although some women suffer through menopause with hot flashes and night sweats, bursts of temper and bouts of depression, only one-quarter of the women in one survey suffered any of these symptoms (Corby & Solnick, 1980). Moreover, hormone replacement therapy is now commonly used to reduce or eliminate the symptoms of menopause (Sheehy, 1992). In men, the middle years see sexual responsiveness slowing and the number of sperm produced in the testes dropping to about half. The orgasms of both men and women become weaker, and the frequency of intercourse may decline.

Despite these signs of an aging body, most people are well into late adulthood before their bodily functions are noticeably impaired. In late adulthood men shrink about an inch, and women about two inches, as their posture changes and cartilage disks between the spinal vertebra become thinner. Hardening of the arteries and a build-up of fat deposits on the artery walls may lead to heart disease. The digestive system slows down and becomes less efficient. Both digestive disorders and heart disease sometimes result from problems of diet—too little fluid, too little fiber—and inactivity. In addition, the brain shrinks during late adulthood. Reflexes (such as the knee-jerk reflex) that remained after infancy grow weak or disappear. The flow of blood to the brain slows.

The Experienced Mind

Despite the aging of the brain, cognition undergoes little change for the worse until late adulthood. Alert older people can think just as quickly as alert younger people. In fact, older people may function as well as or better than younger adults in everyday situations that tap their memories and learning skills. The experienced teacher may deal with an unruly child more skillfully than the novice, and the senior lawyer may understand the implications of a new law more quickly and thoroughly than the recent graduate. Their years of accumulating and organizing information can make older adults practiced, skillful, learned, and wise.

Early and Middle Adulthood   Cognitive changes in early and middle adulthood are generally improvements. During this period, adults' performance improves on tests of vocabulary, comprehension, and general knowledge, especially if they use these abilities in their daily lives or engage in enriching activities such as travel or reading (Botwinick, 1977; Eichorn et al., 1981). Young and middle-aged adults learn new information and new skills; they remember old information and hone old skills.

The nature of thought may also change during adulthood. Adult thought is often more complex and adaptive than adolescent thought (Labouvie-Vief, 1982). For some, a stage of *problem-finding* occurs in adulthood, following the problem-solving level of Piaget's formal operational period (Arlin, 1980). In this stage, the rules of logic that are intellectual toys for adolescents come to be applied to the real world. Further, adults can understand, as adolescents cannot, the contradictions inherent in thinking. They see both the possibilities and the problems in every course of action (Riegel, 1975)—in deciding whether to start a new business or back a political candidate, whether to move to a new place, change jobs, and so on. Middle-aged adults are more expert than adolescents or young adults at making rational decisions and at relating logic and abstractions to actions, emotions, social issues, and personal relationships (Tversky & Kahneman, 1981). As they appreciate these relationships, their thought becomes more global, more concerned with broad moral and practical concerns (Labouvie-Vief, 1982).

Late Adulthood   It is not until late in adulthood—after sixty-five or so—that some intellectual abilities decline in some people. Psychologists who specialize in the study of cognitive abilities have analyzed why this decline occurs; we examine their findings in Chapter 11, on mental abilities. They have found that for some cognitive tasks, old age is usually not a hindrance.

Which mental abilities tend to suffer during late adulthood? Generally it is the abilities that require rapid and flexible manipulation of ideas and symbols. Most older adults can repeat information they have just heard, but they may have difficulty if they must think about the information as well as remember it. For example, it is difficult for many older people to repeat a series of numbers backward, to do a mathematical calculation in their heads, or to recall an address they were given several days ago (Fozard, 1980; Whitla, 1991). If they are asked to do something they know how to do well—like naming familiar objects—older adults do just as well as younger ones (Poon & Fozard, 1978). There is no decline in abilities that depend on recalling information and facts about the world, but older adults are slower and less effective when asked to perform an unfamiliar task or to solve a complex problem they have not seen before (Craik & Rabinowitz, 1984).

When facing complex problems, older people apparently suffer from having too much information to sift through (Arenberg, 1982). They have trouble going over the possible choices and planning and executing their next choice. As people age, they grow less efficient at organizing the elements of a problem and at holding and manipulating more than one idea at a time (Hebb, 1978). They have difficulty doing tasks that require them to divide their attention between two activities at the same time and are slower at shifting their attention back and forth between two activities (Korteling, 1991; McDowd, Vercruyssen & Birrin, 1991). If older adults have enough time, though, and can separate the two activities, they can perform just as well as younger adults (Hawkins, Kramer & Capaldi, 1993).

For some unfortunate people, the decline in intellectual abilities is dramatically hastened and intensified by brain disorders such as Alzheimer's disease, a disorder in which older adults gradually lose their memory and other cognitive abilities and, eventually, their capacity to function independently. But in most cases, the loss of intellectual abilities is slow and need not produce severe problems. Continued mental exercise can help people think and remember effectively and creatively. With mental abilities the principle is "use it or lose it" or, to paraphrase one psychologist's wry comment, "Those who live by their wits, die with their wits" (Krech, 1978).

Just as it can help maintain an aging body, physical exercise can also reduce the ravages of age on mental abilities. In one study, ten weeks of aquatic exercises and swimming were found to improve older people's performance on tasks that required them to divide or shift their attention (Hawkins, Kramer & Capaldi, 1993). Other research suggests the positive effects of a lifetime of aerobic-exercise fitness on a variety of mental tasks, including reaction time and reasoning (Offenbach, Chodzko-Zajko & Ringel, 1990; Clarkson-Smith & Hartley, 1989; Dustman et al., 1990).

In short, if older adults have kept in touch with their inspiring passions and kept their skills up to date and their bodies fit and active, they can continue to be creative thinkers. If they spend their old age achieving a new understanding of the self and the world, they grow in wisdom. Only when old age is fraught with unresolved conflicts and physical passivity does inspiration die and creativity wither.

The Social Clock

Changes in social relationships and positions also occur in adulthood. Do these changes occur in systematic stages? Research by Daniel Levinson and his colleagues (1978) suggested that men go through progressive, predictable, age-linked stages, each offering challenges that must be met before moving on to the next stage. His proposed timetable allowed no more than four years' leeway for each transition. Other researchers, however, have found that development in adulthood does not fall neatly into stages; instead, people follow any of several developmental paths (Schlossberg, 1987). What seems to matter most is the individual's experiences—such as being dumped by a husband, fired from a job, going back to school, getting remarried.

Even the differences between early, middle, and late adulthood are blurring in contemporary society (Neugarten & Neugarten, 1987). In Western cultures, many milestones were traditionally expected to occur within particular age ranges, according to the beat of a **social clock** (Neugarten, 1968). The markers on the social clock included completing school, leaving home, getting married, having a child, and becoming a grandparent. There were never absolute ages on the social clock; it ticked at different rates in different classes and subcultures and for men and women. For example, these events tended to occur earlier in traditional than in unconventional or "sophisticated" groups (Olsen, 1969). But whatever age was considered normal, being "on time" in achieving these milestones was less stressful than being either early or late (Neugarten & Neugarten, 1987). Getting married early, for example, could create problems with peers if they were not also getting married. Getting married late was a sign of failure.

In Western cultures today, the ticking of the social clock is quieter than in the past (Neugarten & Neugarten, 1987). More men and women marry, divorce, remarry, and divorce again up through their seventies. More stay single. More women have their first child before they are fifteen, and more do so after thirty-five. More men and women exit and re-enter school, enter and re-enter the work force, and begin second and third careers through their seventies. All across adulthood, age has become a poor predictor of the timing of life events.

Nevertheless, in all cultures the influence of traditional timetables has not disappeared. Today, as in the past, most people have expectations about major life events and turning points and when they should occur. If their lives are noticeably out of sync—as when a parent dies during one's childhood rather than in one's middle age or when the birth of a child comes unusually early in life—people (or those around them) often feel discomfort. Accordingly, it still makes sense to discuss adults' social and psychological development in terms of broad age periods.

Early Adulthood   Men and women in Western cultures usually enter the adult world in their twenties. They decide on an occupation, or at least take a job, and often become preoccupied with their careers. They also become concerned with love. Having resolved their identity crisis, they develop a capacity for and concern with intimacy, as Erikson's theory describes (Vaillant, 1977; Whitbourne et al., 1992). This intimacy may include sexual intimacy, friendship, or mutual intellectual stimulation. It may lead to marriage or some other form of committed relationship. All this comes at a time when, having sepa-

Middle adulthood tends to be a time during which people become deeply committed to building personal monuments, by raising children, through occupational achievements, or even by seeking political office. Some people manage to do all these things, and more. In 1992, Carol Mosley Braun became the first African-American woman ever elected to the U.S. Senate.

rated from their parents, young adults may be experiencing isolation and loneliness. They may view the future with anticipation, fear, and insecurity (Levinson et al., 1978).

Just how willing and able people are to make intimate commitments may depend on their earlier attachment relationships (Bartholomew & Horowitz, 1991). Researchers have discovered that young adults' views of intimate relationships parallel the patterns of infant attachment that we described earlier. If their view reflects a secure attachment, they tend to feel valued and worthy of support and affection, develop closeness easily, and have relationships characterized by joy, trust, and commitment. If their view is ambivalent, they may feel misunderstood, underappreciated, and worried about being abandoned; their relationships are often negative, obsessive, jealous. A third group of people express an avoidant attitude toward relationships: they are aloof, cannot commit or trust and, although they desire intimacy, they fear it. Researchers have videotaped the behavior of young adults with a dating partner in slightly anxiety-provoking situations that in some ways resemble the Strange Situation used with infants (Simpson, Rholes & Nelligan, 1992). Their results showed that as anxiety increases, people with secure views increase their requests for or offers of support to their partner; those with avoidant views decrease support-seeking behaviors. In Chapter 16, we discuss some methods aimed at correcting the effects of attachment difficulties.

In their thirties, adults tend to settle down and decide what is important in life (Levinson et al., 1978). According to Erikson, this is the time when people become concerned with producing something that will outlast them, usually through parenthood or job achievements. Erikson called this concern the crisis of **generativity** because people are focused on producing or generating something. If people do not resolve this crisis, he suggested, they stagnate.

For many North American adults, however, the greatest tension occurs between two types of generativity—parenthood versus achievement. Especially for women, the demands of children and career often pull in opposite directions. Devotion to a job may lead to guilt about depriving children of attention; too much emphasis on home life may impair productivity at work. This stressful balancing act can lead to anxiety, frustration, and conflicts at home and on the job. Most women, though, find satisfaction in work: they are more satisfied if they do work; they like the respect, the independence, the stimulation (Crosby, 1991).

Middle Adulthood   Sometime around age forty, between early and middle adulthood, people experience a **midlife transition.** They reappraise and may modify their lives and relationships. Some feel invigorated and liberated; others may feel upset and have a midlife crisis (Levinson et al., 1978; Vaillant, 1977).

No one knows how many people experience a crisis during the midlife transition. The contrast between youth and middle age may be especially upsetting for men who matured early in adolescence and were sociable and athletic rather than intellectual (Block, 1971). Women who chose a career over a family now hear the biological clock ticking out their last childbearing years. Women who have had children, however, become more independent and confident, oriented toward achievement and events outside the family (Helson & Moane, 1987). For both men and women, the emerging sexuality of teenage children, the emptiness of the nest as children leave home, or the declining health or death of an elderly parent may precipitate a crisis. People in the midlife transition may feel caught between the generations, pressured by the expenses of college on one side and nursing homes on the other. After the midlife transition, the middle years of adulthood are often a time of satisfaction and happiness.

Sometimes, though, they are a time of divorce. Currently, the divorce rate in the United States is about 50 percent (Bureau of the Census, 1992). Neither age nor income seems to determine whether a couple will be satisfied with their marriage (Spanier & Lewis, 1980). What matters to women is intimacy and emotional security; what matters to men is loyalty and commitment to the future of the marriage (Reedy, Birren & Schaie, 1981). For both men and women, a successful marriage is related to liking each other and thinking of each other as best friends (Lauer & Lauer, 1985), having the same view of each other's responsibilities (Bahr, Chappell & Leigh, 1983; Bowen & Orthner, 1983), and being able to understand each other's thoughts and feelings and to argue in constructive ways (Gottman & Krokoff, 1989; Gottman & Levenson, 1992). (For more on the characteristics of satisfying marriages, see Chapter 17.)

Divorce may free people from a bad relationship, but it is also likely to make them feel anxious, guilty, incompetent, depressed, and lonely; it may even lead to health problems (Brody, 1983; Cargan & Melko, 1982). Furthermore, 70 percent of divorces in the United States involve couples with children (Furstenberg & Cherlin, 1991). When parents divorce, the effects on children may be even more dramatic than those on the adults. The good news is that the negative effects are not inevitable and do not have to be permanent. By two or three years after the divorce, in most families, routines are back to normal, physical symptoms have disappeared, the intense psychological stress is over, and adults and children have improved self-esteem and are functioning competently (Furstenberg & Cherlin, 1991). Still there may be long-lasting effects, especially during adolescence; some behavior problems may be delayed until the child whose parents had divorced earlier reaches early adolescence (Amato & Keith, 1991; Baumrind, 1989; Hetherington & Clingempeel, 1992). In one study, those who were early adolescents when their parents divorced were still not, as young adults ten years later, able to form committed relationships (Wallerstein & Blakeslee, 1989). However, other research suggests that it is worse for the child to experience continued conflict between their parents, married or not (Garber, 1992).

Most people who divorce remarry within three years (Glick, 1980). These marriages seem to be about as satisfying, happy, and worrisome as first marriages (Furstenberg, 1982). They are just as likely to end in divorce, and remarriage does not improve the chances of psychological recovery for the children (Hetherington & Clingempeel, 1992).

Late Adulthood   From sixty-five to seventy-five, most people think of themselves as middle-aged, not old (Neugarten, 1977). They are active and influential politically and socially; they often are physically vigorous. Men and women who have been employed usually retire from their jobs in this period. They adjust most easily to retirement if they view it as a choice (Neugarten, Havighurst & Tobin, 1968). Ratings of life satisfaction and self-esteem are on average as high in old age as during any other period of adulthood (Costa et al., 1987). Even after seventy-five, many seniors continue active lives, and they resist the suggestion that they shouldn't drive (Wood, 1992). In fact, they perform as well on driving tests as younger drivers, and their accident rate is lower (far lower than that of teenagers), largely because they drive many fewer miles.

During late adulthood, people generally become more inward looking, cautious, and conforming (Neugarten, 1977; Reedy, 1983). Many also become more *androgynous,* showing some of the characteristics of the other gender in addition to their own. Women become more assertive and men more nurturant, especially if they are grandparents (Fiske, 1980; Hyde & Phillis, 1979).

In Review: Milestones of Adolescence and Adulthood

Age	Physical Changes	Cognitive Changes	Social Events and Psychological Changes
Early adolescence (11–15 years)	Puberty brings reproductive capacity and marked bodily changes.	Formal operations and principled moral reasoning become possible for the first time (this occurs only for some people).	A social and emotional shakeup results from growing sexual awareness, mood swings, physical changes, conflicts with parents.
Late adolescence (16–20 years)	Physical growth continues.	Formal operations and principled moral reasoning become more likely.	An identity crisis accompanies graduation from high school.
Early adulthood (20–39 years)	Physical growth continues; hearing impairment begins.	Increases continue in knowledge, problem-finding ability, and moral reasoning.	People choose a job and often a mate; they may become parents.
Middle adulthood (40–65 years)	Size and muscle mass decrease, fat increases, eyesight declines, reproductive capacity in women ends.	Thought becomes more complex, adaptive, and global.	Midlife transition may lead to change; for most, the middle years are satisfying.
Late adulthood (over 65 years)	Size decreases; organs become less efficient.	Reasoning, mathematical ability, comprehension, novel problem solving, and memory may decline.	Retirement requires adjustments; people look inward; awareness of death precipitates life review.

Death and Dying

The many changes associated with adolescence and adulthood are summarized in "In Review: Milestones of Adolescence and Adulthood." With the onset of old age, people become aware that death is approaching. They watch as their friends disappear. They feel their health deteriorating, their strength waning, and their intellectual capabilities declining. A few years or a few months before death, people experience a sharp decline in mental functioning known as **terminal drop** (Berkowitz, 1965).

The awareness of impending death brings about the last psychological crisis, according to Erikson's theory, in which people evaluate their lives and accomplishments and affirm them as meaningful (leading to a feeling of integrity) or meaningless (leading to a feeling of despair). They tend to become more philosophical and reflective. They attempt to put their lives into perspective. They reminisce, resolve past conflicts, and integrate past events. They may also become more interested in the religious and spiritual side of life (Butler, 1963). This "life review" may trigger anxiety, regret, guilt, and despair, or it may allow people to face their own death and the deaths of friends and relatives with a feeling of peace and acceptance (Butler, 1975; Erikson, 1968; Lieberman & Tobin, 1983).

The elderly can be helped to feel better physically and psychologically if they continue to be socially active and useful. For example, old people who are given parties, plants, or pets are happier and more alert and do not die as soon as those who receive less attention (Kastenbaum, 1965; Rodin & Langer, 1977). Withdrawing care, control, and social contact from people who are sick is likely to make them sicker.

Even the actual confrontation with death does not have to bring despair and depression. People generally want to be told if they are dying (Hinton, 1967). When death finally is imminent, old people strive for a death with dignity, love, affection, physical contact, and no pain (Schulz, 1978). As they think about death, they are comforted by their religious faith, their achievements, and the love of their friends and family (Kastenbaum, Kastenbaum & Morris, 1989). Interestingly, very few take comfort from the thought that their children and grandchildren will survive and carry on their name and tradition.

Linkages: Human Development and Personality

How stable is personality during adulthood?

Marriage, childbirth, divorce, promotion, firing, illness, the death of loved ones—these events and others mark the lives of adults. We have described how people tend to change during their lives. But in what respects are the people sitting in class with you going to be the *same* ten years from now? Will the young man who is sociable at parties also seek out people in his old age? Will the woman who was apprehensive before marrying at age forty feel nervous before she retires at seventy? Twenty years from now, are *you* likely to be much the same person you are today?

These questions interest both developmental and personality psychologists. One way to answer them is to examine a person's distinguishing characteristics, or *traits,* over the years. Personality psychologists have developed tools for doing this, including personality tests such as the Personality Research Form (PRF) and the California Psychological Inventory (CPI). These tests consist of questions or statements like "I am often very tense on the job," to which the test taker answers *true, false,* or *cannot say.* Analysis of the answers allows the tester to compile an inventory of how one person compares with other people—whether, for example, compared with others an individual tends to be hostile or trusting, confident or anxious, and so on.

In some ways each of us changes greatly during our lives, but in other ways we stay essentially the same.

To examine the stability of personality traits, developmental psychologists have tested individuals repeatedly over many years. The results indicate that three basic personality traits—shyness, sociability, aggressiveness—change very little during adulthood (Costa & McCrae, 1988; McCrae & Costa, 1982; Costa, 1992). However, these data might reflect stable self-portraits, not stable traits. Perhaps people's *views* of their personalities stay the same even when their personalities change. To test this hypothesis, researchers asked spouses to rate the personality of subjects. If people really change and only their ideas about themselves stay stable, then their self-ratings and their spouses' ratings of them should become more and more dissimilar over time. This divergence does not occur, however (McCrae & Costa, 1983).

Thus, there is good evidence that shyness, sociability, and aggressiveness remain quite stable during the adult years, just as they did across childhood and as they do from childhood into adulthood (Caspi, Elder & Bem, 1988; Dubow, Huesmann & Eron, 1987; West & Graziano, 1989). The woman who, at thirty, was more outgoing than other thirty-year-olds is likely to be more outgoing at seventy-five than others her age, although she may not be as sociable as she was at thirty. The boy who was painfully shy may delay, or even avoid, marriage and parenthood. The altruistic adolescent probably becomes a compassionate adult.

Other aspects of personality, however, seem to be less stable than these basic traits. A confident seventy-five-year-old woman may have been insecure twenty years ago. She may be anxious with teenagers but relaxed with everyone else. Whether you see a particular personality as stable may depend both on what aspects of personality you look at and whether you consider stability through the years or stability in different situations.

Furthermore, different people show varying degrees of stability (Bem & Allen, 1974). This variation depends in part on events. An unexpected crisis—a spouse leaving, a child dying—may change an adult's outlook on life. When personalities do change, it is often in response to such events (Moss & Susman, 1980). More often, however, personality is not permanently altered by major stressors, especially when people live in stable environments.

Indeed, among the majority of people who remain healthy and socially involved, most aspects of personality do not change markedly from early to later adulthood (Thomae, 1980; West & Graziano, 1989; Costa, 1992). Why? One possibility is that certain basic traits, such as sociability or emotionality, might be inherited and less likely to be altered by life experiences. Other theories suggest that recurring psychological defense mechanisms, well-entrenched behavior patterns, and consistent ways of perceiving create relatively unchanging personalities. We examine these explanations in Chapter 14, on personality.

In the details behind these generalizations lie some of the most interesting questions and findings about personality and its development. Why, for example, would a man who was apparently happy and involved with his work at thirty sink into a deep depression and consider life to be meaningless at age fifty? If you are generous and cheerful and confident with acquaintances but anxious and angry at home, is there a "real you"? If you want to become less anxious when you meet strangers, can you? In Chapters 14 through 16 we examine theories and research that provide a closer look at adult personality, at what it is and why and how it may change, for better or worse.

Future Directions

We have traced the journey of human development from conception to death. Researchers over the past eighty years have charted this developmental journey and some of its variations. Psychologists now know what newborns can see and hear, when babies start to walk and talk, how well preschoolers run and read, what changes puberty brings, and which mental faculties are the first to fail. They are learning more and more about the processes of development, about how people learn new habits, incorporate new information, and form new relationships, and about how these processes depend on inheritance (nature) and experience (nurture). They have replaced the notion of global developmental stages with a looser notion of developmental levels in particular areas of development.

Still, there is much to learn. The future of developmental psychology will involve further elaboration and more sophisticated analysis of both the biological underpinnings of development and the social contexts that influence it. Thus, the nature-nurture issue will continue to anchor, motivate, and extend research in this field (Beilin, 1992).

We can expect to see much more research exploring the significance of cultural differences in the ways children are reared and in the extent to which these differences affect the children's knowledge, behavior, and attitudes. We can look forward to more studies documenting and assessing new worlds of childhood: the world of day care, the world of living with a single, employed, and highly educated mother, and, unfortunately, the world of homelessness. We can also expect to see more research probing the limits—and limitations—of early education. When should it start? At age five? At two? Prenatally? And what should it consist of? "Discovery learning" or fact-filled flash cards? Parents and psychologists often differ on what they see as the pros and cons of early education (Bjorkland & Green, 1992). These new studies will extend our understanding of nature and nurture, of cognitive development, and of variations in social relationships.

You will be able to follow the progress of research in this fascinating field by taking courses in infancy, child development, adolescence, life-span development, language acquisition, cognitive development, and social development.

Summary and Key Terms

Developmental psychology is the study of the course and causes of systematic, sequential age-related changes in mental abilities, social relationships, emotions, and moral understanding over the life span.

Exploring Human Development
A central question in developmental psychology is the relative influences of nature and nurture, a theme that had its origins in the philosophies of John Locke and Jean-Jacques Rousseau. In the early part of the twentieth century, Arnold Gesell stressed nature in his theory of development, proposing that development is *maturation*—the natural unfolding of abilities with age. John Watson took the opposite view, claiming that development is learning—shaped by the external environment. Sigmund Freud began to bring nature and nurture together by suggesting that development depends on both internal forces (children's sexual and aggressive urges) and external conditions (how parents handle the children's urges). Jean Piaget fully integrated the influences of nature and nurture in his theory of cognitive development. According to Piaget, knowledge develops as children actively explore the environment guided by internal mental images. To-

day we accept as given the notion that both nature and nurture affect development and ask not whether but how much and how each contributes. The intertwined influences of heredity and environment on human development have been revealed by behavior genetics researchers who have conducted correlational studies of the similarities of identical twins vs. less closely related siblings, and of children who have been adopted into different environments.

Beginnings
Prenatal Development
Development begins with the union of an ovum and a sperm. In the first two weeks after fertilization, the new cell develops into an *embryo*. The embryonic stage is a *critical period* for development, a time when certain organs must develop properly, or they never will. Development of organs at this stage is markedly and irrevocably affected by harmful *teratogens* like drugs and alcohol. The embryo develops into a *fetus* in the fetal stage of prenatal development, when adverse conditions may harm the infant's size, behavior, intelligence, or health. Babies born to women who drink heavily have a strong chance of suffering from *fetal alcohol syndrome*.

The Newborn

Newborn infants have limited but effective senses of vision, hearing, and smell. Motor behavior in the first few months of life is dominated by *reflexes*: swift, automatic responses to external stimuli.

Infancy and Childhood: Cognitive Development

Cognitive development refers to the development of thinking, knowing, and remembering.

The Development of Knowledge: Piaget's Theory

According to Piaget, with experience, *schemas* are modified through the complementary processes of *assimilation* (fitting new objects or events into existing schemas) and *accommodation* (changing schemas when new objects will not fit the existing schemas). Cognitive development occurs in a fixed sequence of stages. During the first stage, the *sensorimotor period,* infants progress from using only simple senses and reflexes to forming mental representations of objects and actions. This allows the child to think about objects that are not immediately present. The ability to recognize that objects continue to exist even when they are hidden from view Piaget called *object permanence*. Once children have developed this knowledge, they move to the second stage of cognitive development, the *preoperational period.* During this period, children can use symbols, but they do not have the ability to think logically and rationally. Their understanding of the world is intuitive. When children develop the ability to think logically about concrete objects, they enter the period of *concrete operations*. They can solve simple problems and have a knowledge of *conservation*, recognizing that, for example, the amount of a substance does not change even when its shape changes.

Modifying Piaget's Theory

Recent research has led to a modification of Piaget's proposal that cognitive development progresses in sharply marked stages of global understanding. Developmental psychologists now believe that levels of understanding are reached more gradually, in specific areas rather than across the board, and that children's reasoning in any situation is affected by how easy the task is and how familiar the child is with the objects and language.

Information Processing During Childhood

Psychologists who explain cognitive development in terms of *information processing* have documented age-related improvements in children's attention, their abilities to explore and focus on features of the environment, and their memories.

Culture and Cognitive Development

The specific content of cognitive development, including the development of *scripts,* depends on the cultural context in which children live.

Individual Variations in Cognitive Development

How fast children develop cognitive abilities depends to a certain extent on how stimulating and supportive their environments are.

Infancy and Childhood: Social and Emotional Development

Infants and their caregivers, from the early months, respond to each other's emotional expressions.

Individual Temperament

Most infants can be classified as having easy, difficult, or slow-to-warm-up *temperaments*. Whether they retain these traits may depend to some extent on the meshing of the traits with the parents' expectations and demands.

The Infant Grows Attached

Over the first six or seven months of life, infants form deep and abiding emotional *attachments* to their parents. These attachments may be secure or anxious-insecure, depending to a large extent on whether the parents are responsive and loving, or rejecting.

Relationships with Parents and Peers

From age two on, children seek and are given more autonomy from their parents. Parents begin to teach their children the skills and rules needed in their culture using styles of *socialization* that are *authoritarian, permissive,* or *authoritative*. Authoritative parents tend to have more competent and cooperative children. Patterns of socialization depend upon the culture and conditions in which parents find themselves. Over the childhood years, interactions with peers increase in cooperation and competition. Children come to base their friendships on feelings, not things.

Social Skills and Understanding

Changes in children's relationships grow in part from their growing social competence. They learn to interpret and understand social situations and emotional signals. They learn social rules and roles, including those related to gender.

Gender Roles

Gender roles are based on both biological differences between the sexes and, to a larger extent, on implicit and explicit socialization by parents, teachers, peers, and the media.

Adolescence

Adolescents undergo significant changes in size, shape, and physical capacities and, typically, in their social lives, reasoning abilities, and views of themselves.

The Big Shakeup

Puberty brings about physical changes that lead to psychological changes. Early adolescence is a period of wide mood swings and shaky self-esteem. Adolescence is also a period of conflict with parents and closeness and conformity to friends. Pregnancy is an acute problem in this period.

Identity and Development of the Self

Later adolescence focuses on finding an answer to the question: Who am I? Events like graduating from high school and going to college challenge the adolescent's self-concept, precipitating an *identity crisis*. To resolve this crisis the adolescent must develop an integrated image of himself or herself as a unique person, which often includes ethnic identity.

Abstract Thought and Moral Reasoning

For many people, adolescence begins a stage of cognitive development that Piaget called the *formal operational period*. Formal abstract reasoning now becomes more sophisticated, moral reasoning may begin its progress through *preconventional, conventional,* and *postconventional* stages; principled moral judgment—shaped by gender and culture—becomes possible for the first time. Such advanced understanding may be reflected in moral action—if there are no other more compelling circumstances.

Adulthood

Physical, cognitive, and social changes occur throughout adulthood.

The Aging Body

Middle adulthood sees changes that include decreased acuity of the senses, increased risk of heart disease, and the end of fertility in women, signaled by *menopause.* Nevertheless, most people do not have major health problems until they pass the age of seventy-five.

The Experienced Mind

In early and middle adulthood, cognitive changes are generally positive, including advanced reasoning and problem-finding ability. In late adulthood, some intellectual abilities decline. This is particularly true for tasks that are unfamiliar, complex, or difficult, and for people who have not kept mentally active. Other abilities, such as recalling facts, tend not to decline.

The Social Clock

Although the ticking of the *social clock* is quieter now than it was in past generations, there are still social and psychological changes associated with different periods of adulthood. In their twenties, young adults make occupational choices and form intimate commitments. In their thirties, they settle down and decide what is important. They become concerned with producing something that will outlast them in a crisis of *generativity.* Sometime around age forty, adults experience a *midlife transition,* which may or may not be a crisis. The forties and fifties are often a time of satisfaction and sometimes a time for divorce. In their sixties, people contend with the issue of retirement. They generally become more inward looking, cautious, and conforming.

Death and Dying

In their seventies and eighties, people confront their own mortality. They may become more philosophical and reflective as they review their lives. A few years or months before death, they experience a sharp decline in mental functioning known as *terminal drop.* Still, they strive for a death with dignity, love, and no pain.

Linkages: Human Development and Personality

Shyness, sociability, and aggressiveness are personality traits that are stable across the life span for most people. Other personality characteristics, like anxiety or insecurity, are more affected by life events.

Chapter 4

Biological Aspects of Psychology

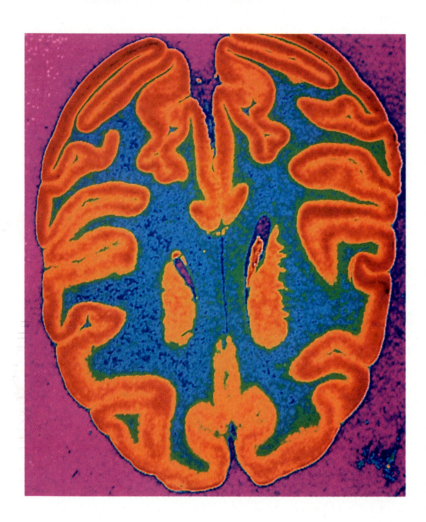

Outline

Imagine something you enjoy doing. Maybe it's eating chocolate, or listening to your favorite music, or having sex. Maybe it's eating chocolate while listening to music and having sex. All of these activities depend on your cells and organs and how they influence your behaviors and mental processes (see the Linkages diagram). Why? Because, first, many of the things that motivate behavior, such as eating, reflect basic biological needs. Second, certain stimuli—such as chocolate or electric shock—activate specific brain regions that result in pleasure or pain. Third, it is your nervous system that allows you to do what is necessary to hear the music, or eat the chocolate, or find the one you love. The nervous system is a complex combination of cells that allows an organism to gain information about what is going on inside and outside the body and to respond appropriately. It allows you to learn about and react to the world.

In learning about the world and reacting to it, the nervous system displays the components of an information-processing system: it has input, processing, and output activities (see Figure 4.1). *Input* occurs in the form of the sensory signals you receive from the world. *Processing* occurs as you integrate the information with past experiences and decide what to do about it. And *output* occurs as your brain activates your muscles to act on the information. All three of these activities work in the service of your motivational state and your goals. For example, when you see chocolate, you may remember that it is edible and delicious, and if you are hungry, you may reach out and take a bite to satisfy that hunger. Many of these goals are biological in origin.

Indeed, the biological aspects of our being are crucial from conception onward. A genetic contribution has been found in everything from reaction times to religiosity (Bouchard et al., 1990). Even the environmental factors (nurture) that constantly interact with your genetic background (nature) to shape lifelong development do so through biological processes. Whether these environmental influences come in the form of music lessons, parental praise, math classes, or the traditions of your country or ethnic group, they have their effects by changing your brain, an organ that is extremely responsive to the environment. It is a fundamental tenet of scientific psychology that every thought, every feeling, every action, is represented somehow in the nervous system and that none of these events could occur without it. **Biological psychology** is the study of the cells and organs and physical and chemical changes involved in behavior and mental processes.

Does the proposition that "All mental activity requires the brain" mean we can understand behavior and mental processes by studying biological processes alone? Does it mean that behavioral problems that have a biological component can be cured only by biological therapies such as drugs? No. Attempts to reduce all of psychology to the study of brain chemicals oversimplify the interactions between our biological selves and our experiences. For example, brain scans show unusual activity in specific brain regions in people suffering from obsessive-compulsive disorder (which involves a disabling need to repeat certain behaviors over and over). These scans are sometimes used to argue that the disorder has a biological cause best treated with drugs. Drug treatments can correct the disordered behavior and make the brain scans look normal, but so can treatments that help clients learn new, more adaptive behaviors (Baxter et al., 1992). In such cases, new experiences alone change both behavior and biology, without using drugs to directly alter brain activity. At the same time, it would be shortsighted to ignore the biological level of analysis. Some severe behavioral abnormalities, such as schizophrenia, appear to have a major biological component; nonbiological therapies for schizophrenia tend to be much less effective compared to drug therapies.

In short, behavior and mental life are best understood by synthesizing information from many levels of analysis, and in this chapter we focus on the biological level.

Levels of Analysis: From Molecules to Memories

Modern revolutions are occurring in the study of nervous systems from their most basic to their most complex levels of organization. Researchers are learning how molecules and cells work, as well as how vast networks of brain cells accomplish such complex tasks as recognizing visual patterns and learning a language. We begin our exploration of the nervous

Linkages

This diagram illustrates some of the relationships between the topic of this chapter—biological aspects of psychology—and other chapter topics. Because all thoughts, feelings, and actions take place through the body, understanding its biological structures and functions is important to understanding psychology. In this chapter we introduce some basic facts about biological structures and processes that underlie behavior and mental activity. In later chapters we build on this information to examine more specifically how biological factors influence a wide variety of psychological phenomena. ■

HUMAN DEVELOPMENT
How does the brain change throughout life, and how do these changes affect people? (p. 120)

CONSCIOUSNESS
How do drugs act in the nervous system to alter consciousness? (p. 233)

TREATMENT OF PSYCHOLOGICAL DISORDERS
What biological mechanisms underlie drug treatment of psychological disorders? (p. 600)

Biological Aspects of Psychology

MEMORY
What chemicals and brain structures are involved when people form and store memories? (p. 313)

PSYCHOLOGICAL DISORDERS
Is depression caused by a chemical imbalance in the brain? (p. 548)

THOUGHT AND LANGUAGE
What parts of the brain make language possible? (p. 114)

system at the "bottom," with a description of the individual cells and molecules that compose it. Then we consider how these cells are organized to form the structures of the human nervous system.

Cells of the Nervous System

One of the most striking findings in current research on the cells of the nervous system is how similar they are to other cells in the body, and how similar all cells are in all living organisms, from bacteria to plants to humans. For example, bacteria, plant cells, and brain cells all synthesize similar proteins when they are subjected to reduced oxygen or elevated temperatures. Whether one sees such similarities across life forms as the product of shared evolutionary processes or as the work of an efficient Creator, the implications are the same: much can be learned about humans by studying animals, and much can be learned about brain cells by studying cells in simple organisms. For example, studies of viruses by cancer researchers led to the discovery of proteins that may be involved in the formation of memories in the brain (Morgan & Curran, 1991; Alcantara et al., 1993).

Another common thread to life is the ability of cells to respond to the environment and adapt to environmental changes. A change in the internal workings of a cell in response to stimuli from outside it is known as *signal transduction.* Much of the signal transduction in the body occurs as cells respond to chemicals released by other cells. Even as various cells specialize after conception to become skin, bones, hair, and other tissues, they "stay in touch" to some extent through their ability to respond to chemical signals from other cells. For example, bone cells add or lose calcium in response to hormones secreted in another part of the body.

Some cells are specialized for even more complex signaling, and for the ability to respond to stimuli from outside of the body. These include cells of the nervous system, as well as cells of the endocrine and immune systems.

Figure 4.1
Three Functions of the
Nervous System
The nervous system's three main
functions involve receiving information (input), integrating that information with past experiences and
motivational states (processing), and
guiding actions (output). Here, the
auditory information received—
the sound generated by the alarm
clock—is integrated with past knowledge that the sound means it is time
to get up. The action generated by
the brain includes neural signals
causing the arm to reach out.

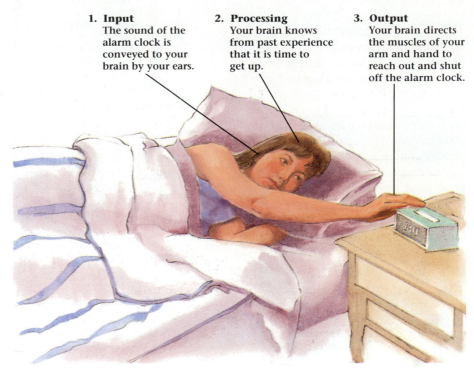

1. Input
The sound of the
alarm clock is
conveyed to your
brain by your ears.

2. Processing
Your brain knows
from past experience
that it is time to
get up.

3. Output
Your brain directs
the muscles of your
arm and hand to
reach out and shut
off the alarm clock.

Through the communication abilities of the cells of these three systems, the
body becomes an integrated whole capable of detecting and responding to
what is in the world. The nervous system and immune system also have the
ability to form memories and to compare current experiences with past experiences. Later in this chapter we examine the endocrine and immune systems;
for now, we focus on the nervous system.

Two major types of cells in the nervous system allow it to carry out its signaling tasks: neurons and glial cells. **Neurons** are cells that are specialized to
rapidly respond to signals and quickly send signals of their own. *Glial* means
"glue," and until recently scientists thought glial cells were in the nervous
system only to hold neurons together. However, research now suggests that
glial cells also help neurons communicate (Cornell-Bell et al., 1990).

Neurons and glial cells share many characteristics with every other kind of
cell in the body. First, as Figure 4.2 illustrates, they have an *outer membrane*
that, like a fine screen, lets some substances pass in and out while blocking
others. Second, each neuron and glial cell has a *cell body*, which contains a
nucleus. The nucleus carries the genetic information that, as mentioned in
Chapter 2, determines how a cell will function. Third, neurons contain *mitochondria,* which are structures that turn oxygen and glucose into energy. This
process is especially vital to brain cells. Although the brain accounts for only
2 percent of the body's weight, it consumes more than 20 percent of the body's
oxygen (Sokoloff, 1981). All of this energy is required because neurons transmit signals among themselves to an even greater extent than do cells in the
rest of the body.

Three special features enable neurons to communicate signals efficiently.
The first is their structure. Although neurons come in many shapes and sizes,
all have long, thin fibers that extend outward from the cell body (see Figure
4.2). When these fibers get close to other neurons, communication between
the cells can occur. The intertwining of all these fibers with fibers from other
neurons allows each neuron to be in close proximity to thousands or even
hundreds of thousands of other neurons (Guroff, 1980).

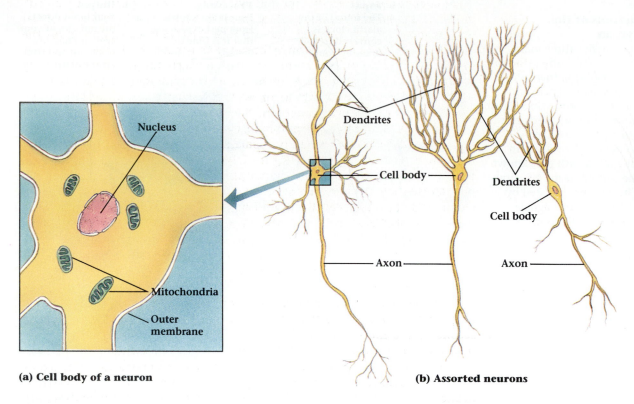

(a) Cell body of a neuron

(b) Assorted neurons

Figure 4.2
The Neuron
Part (a) shows the cell body of a neuron, enlarged from one of the whole neurons shown in part (b). The cell body of a neuron has typical cell elements, including an outer membrane and mitochondria. Part (b) shows some of the shapes neurons can take. The fibers extending outward from each cell body, the axons and dendrites, are among the features that make neurons unique.

The fibers extending from a neuron's cell body fall into two categories: axons and dendrites. **Axons** are the fibers that carry signals away from the cell body, out to where communication occurs with other neurons. Each neuron generally has only one axon leaving the cell body, but that one axon may have many branches. Axons can be very short or several feet long, like the axon that sends signals from the spinal cord all the way down to the big toe. **Dendrites** are the fibers that receive signals from the axons of other neurons and carry those signals to the cell body. A neuron can have many dendrites. Dendrites, too, usually have many branches. Remember that *axons* carry signals *away* from the cell body, whereas *dendrites* *detect* those signals.

The neuron's ability to communicate also depends on two other features: the "excitable" surface membrane of some of its fibers, and the minute gap, called a **synapse**, between neurons. In the following sections we examine how these features allow a signal to be sent rapidly from one end of the neuron to the other and from one neuron to another.

Action Potentials

To understand the signals in the nervous system, you first need to know something about cell membranes and the chemical molecules within and outside the cell. The cell membrane is *selectively permeable;* that is, it lets some molecules pass through, yet excludes others. Many molecules carry a positive or negative electrochemical charge and are referred to as **ions.** Normally, the membrane maintains an uneven distribution of positively and negatively charged ions inside and outside the cell. The result is that the inside of the cell is slightly negative compared with the outside, and the membrane is said to be *polarized*. Because molecules with a positive charge are attracted to those with a negative charge, a force called an *electrochemical potential* drives positively charged molecules toward the inside of the cell; but many are kept outside by the membrane.

For communication in the nervous system the most important "excluded" molecule is sodium (the same sodium found in table salt), which is symbolized Na+ when positively charged. Sodium ions are highly concentrated on the outside of the cell and are strongly attracted to negatively charged molecules inside the cell. However, sodium can pass through the membrane only by going through special *channels,* or holes, in the membrane. These channels, which are distributed along the axon, act as *gates* that can be opened or closed.

Normally the sodium channels are closed, but changes in the environment of the cell can *depolarize* the membrane, making the area inside the membrane less negative. If the membrane is depolarized to a point called the *threshold,* then the gate swings open (see Figure 4.3). As sodium ions rush into the cell, the adjacent area of the axon becomes more depolarized, thereby causing the neighboring gate to open. This sequence continues, and the change in electro-chemical potential spreads like a wild rumor all the way down the axon.

This abrupt change in the potential of an axon is called an **action potential**, and its "contagious" nature is referred to as its *self-propagating* property. When an action potential shoots down an axon, the neuron is said to have *fired.* This is an *all-or-none* type of communication: the cell either fires at full strength or does not fire at all.

The speed of the action potential as it moves down an axon is constant for a particular cell, but in different cells the speed ranges from 0.2 meters per second to 120 meters per second (about 260 miles per hour). The speed depends on the diameter of the axon—larger ones are faster—and on whether myelin is present. **Myelin** is a fatty substance that wraps around some axons and speeds action potentials. Larger, myelinated cells usually occur in the parts of the nervous system that carry the most urgently needed information. For example, the sensory neurons that receive information from the environment about onrushing trains, hot irons, and other dangers are fast-acting, myelinated cells.

Although each neuron fires or does not fire in an "all-or-none" fashion, its *rate* of firing varies. It can fire over and over because the sodium gates open only briefly and then close. Between firings there is a very brief rest, called a **refractory period**. During this time, gates for positively charged potassium (K+) open briefly; because of their high concentration on the inside of the axon, these ions flow out of the axon, and the membrane becomes re-polarized. At that point the neuron can fire again. Because the refractory period is quite short, a neuron can send action potentials down its axon at rates of up to one thousand per second. The *pattern* of repeated action potentials amounts to a coded message. We describe some of the codes used by the nervous system in Chapter 5, on sensation.

Figure 4.3
The Beginning of an Action Potential
This very diagrammatic view of a polarized nerve cell axon shows the normally closed sodium gates in the cell membrane. Much of the negative charge inside the axon is produced by proteins, P⁻. If stimulation of the cell causes depolarization near a particular gate, that gate may swing open, allowing sodium (Na⁺) to rush into the axon, stimulating the next gate to open, and so on down the axon. This spread of depolarization and the consequent progressive entry of sodium into the cell is called an action potential; when it occurs, the cell is said to have fired. The action potential fired by one cell may subsequently stimulate other cells to fire. The cell is repolarized when the Na⁺ gates are closed and gates are opened for potassium, K⁺, to flow out.

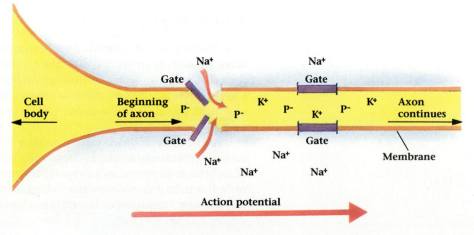

Figure 4.4
A Synapse
This photograph taken through an electron microscope shows part of a neural synapse magnified 50,000 times. Clearly visible are the mitochondria; the neurotransmitter-containing vesicles in the ending of the presynaptic cell's axon; the synapse itself, which is the narrow gap between the cells; and the dendrite of the postsynaptic cell.

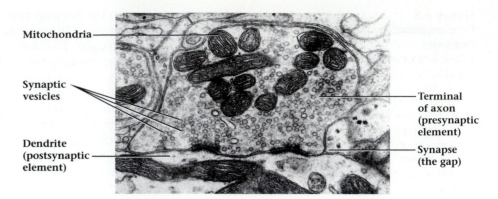

Mitochondria

Synaptic vesicles

Dendrite (postsynaptic element)

Terminal of axon (presynaptic element)

Synapse (the gap)

Synapses and Communication Between Neurons

How does the action potential in one neuron have an effect on the next neuron? For communication to occur *between* cells, the signal must be transferred across the synapse between neurons. Most often, the axon of one cell delivers its signals across a synapse to the dendrites of a second cell; those dendrites in turn transmit the signal to their cell body, which may relay the signal down its axon and thus on to a third cell, and so on. But other communication patterns also occur. Axons can signal to other axons or even directly to the cell body of another neuron; dendrites of one cell can send signals to the dendrites of other cells (Glowinski, 1981). These varied communication patterns allow the brain to conduct extremely complex information-processing tasks.

Neurotransmitters   Unlike the communication down the axon, which uses electrochemical signals, communication at the synapse between neurons relies solely on chemicals. The transfer of information across a synapse is accomplished by chemicals called **neurotransmitters**. These chemicals are stored in numerous little "bags," called *vesicles,* at the tips of axons (see Figure 4.4). When an action potential reaches a synapse at the end of an axon, a neurotransmitter is released.

More than fifty different neurotransmitters have been identified, and more are discovered every year. The most recently discovered neurotransmitters are—surprisingly—the gases nitric oxide and carbon monoxide (Snyder, 1992; Verma et al., 1993). When a neurotransmitter is released into a synapse, it spreads across the synapse to reach the next, or *postsynaptic,* cell (see Figure 4.5).

At the postsynaptic membrane, neurotransmitters bind to proteins called **receptors.** Like a puzzle piece fitting into its proper place, a neurotransmitter fits snugly into its own receptors but not into receptors for other neurotransmitters (see Figure 4.6). The receptors "recognize" only one type of neurotransmitter, and they are vital in conveying signals between cells.

As a result of a neurotransmitter binding to a receptor, channels in the postsynaptic cell open (much like the sodium channels involved in action potentials), allowing ions to flow in or out. The flow of ions into and out of the postsynaptic cell produces a change in its membrane potential; thus, the chemical signal at the synapse creates an electrochemical signal within the postsynaptic cell.

Some of the chemical substances that act on receptors at synapses have been called **neuromodulators,** because they act slowly and often modify or "modulate" the response to more rapidly acting neurotransmitters. However, we use only the term *neurotransmitter,* because the distinction between "neurotransmitter" and "neuromodulator" is not always clear. Depending on the type of

Figure 4.5
Communication Between Neurons

When a neuron fires, a self-propagating action potential shoots to the end of its axon, triggering the release of a neurotransmitter into the synapse. This stimulates neighboring cells. One type of stimulation is *excitatory,* causing depolarization of the neighboring cells. This depolarization, in turn, will cause those neurons to fire an action potential if threshold is reached.

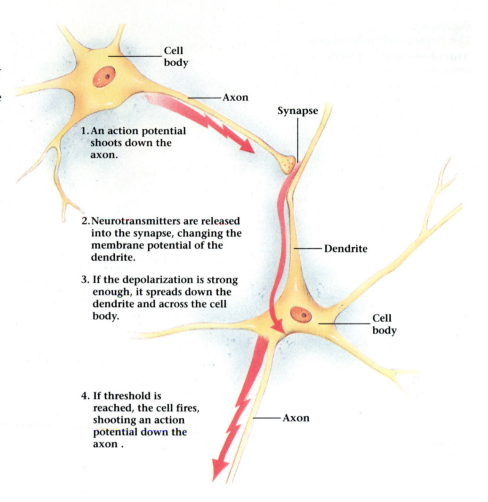

Cell body

Axon

Synapse

1. An action potential shoots down the axon.

2. Neurotransmitters are released into the synapse, changing the membrane potential of the dendrite.

3. If the depolarization is strong enough, it spreads down the dendrite and across the cell body.

Dendrite

Cell body

4. If threshold is reached, the cell fires, shooting an action potential down the axon .

Axon

receptor it acts on at a given synapse, the same neurotransmitter can function as either a neuromodulator or a neurotransmitter.

Excitatory and Inhibitory Signals   Today, scientists can record the extremely small electrochemical changes that occur as ions flow through one ion channel, as Figure 4.7 illustrates (Sakmann, 1992). The change in the membrane potential of the dendrite or cell body of the postsynaptic cell is called the **postsynaptic potential.** It can make the cell either more likely or less likely to fire. If positively charged ions (like sodium or calcium) flow *into* the neuron, it becomes slightly *less* polarized, or *depolarized.* Because depolarization of the membrane can lead the neuron to fire an action potential, a depolarizing postsynaptic potential is called an **excitatory postsynaptic potential,** or EPSP. However, if positively charged ions (like potassium) flow *out* of the neuron, or if negatively charged ions flow *in,* the neuron becomes slightly more polarized, or *hyperpolarized.* Hyperpolarization diminishes the likelihood that the neuron will fire an action potential. Thus, a hyperpolarizing postsynaptic potential is called an **inhibitory postsynaptic potential,** or **IPSP.**

The postsynaptic potential spreads along the membrane of the postsynaptic cell. But unlike the action potential in an axon, which remains at a constant strength, the postsynaptic potential fades as it goes along. Usually, it is not strong enough to pass all the way along the dendrite and through the cell body to the axon, so a single EPSP is not enough to cause a neuron to fire. However, each neuron is constantly receiving EPSPs and IPSPs. The combined effect of rapidly repeated potentials or potentials from many locations can create a sig-

Figure 4.6
The Relationship Between Neurotransmitters and Receptors
Neurotransmitters influence postsynaptic cells by stimulating special receptors on the surface of those cells' membranes. Each type of receptor receives only one type of neurotransmitter, the two fitting together like puzzle pieces or like a key in a lock. Stimulation of these receptors by their neurotransmitter causes them, in turn, to either help or hinder the generation of a wave of depolarization in their cell's dendrites.

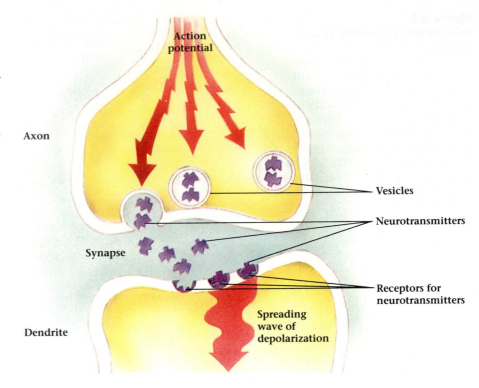

Figure 4.7
Electrical Recording of a Single Sodium Channel
Scientists are now able to record the electrical changes that occur when a single sodium channel opens and closes. Using a tiny glass tube only 1/25,000th the diameter of a human hair, they suck up a small "patch" of cell membrane that contains a channel. When the channel opens, sodium ions flow through and cause the section of membrane to be less polarized. Amazingly, when neurotransmitter-sensitive ion channels are inserted into non-neural cells, those cells begin to behave like neurons when neurotransmitters are applied.

nal strong enough to reach the junction of the axon and cell body, a specialized region where new action potentials are generated.

Whether or not the postsynaptic cell fires and how rapidly it fires depend on whether, from moment to moment, excitatory ("fire") or inhibitory ("don't fire") signals from many other neurons predominate at this junction (see Figure 4.8). Thus, each neuron constantly integrates or processes information from many other neurons, mediated by multiple neurotransmitters.

Specific neurotransmitters will be mentioned throughout this book, because their effects touch on virtually every aspect of psychology. For example, the sensation of pain is discussed in the next chapter. Several neurotransmitters called **endorphins** are used in many of the pathways that convey pain messages throughout the brain and spinal cord. Receptors for endorphins are the sites at which *opiate* drugs such as heroin and morphine produce their pain-relieving and euphoric effects. In Chapter 7, on consciousness, we describe other drugs that affect thinking and behavior by altering the activity of neu-

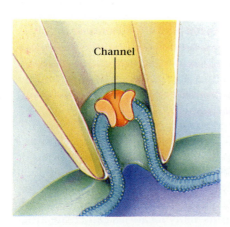

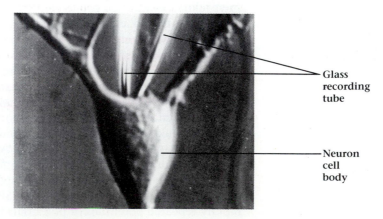

Source: Neher / Sakmann, 1992.

Figure 4.8
Integration of Neural Signals
Most of the signals that a neuron receives arrive at its dendrites or at its cell body. These signals, which typically come from many neighboring cells, can be conflicting. Some are excitatory, stimulating the cell to fire; others are inhibitory signals that tell the cell not to fire. Whether the cell actually fires or not at any given moment depends on whether excitatory or inhibitory messages predominate at the junction of the cell body and the axon.

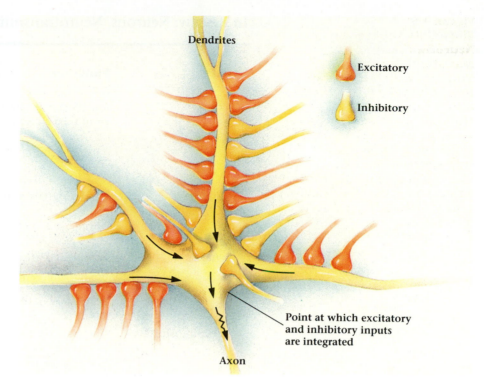

Dendrites

Excitatory

Inhibitory

Point at which excitatory and inhibitory inputs are integrated

Axon

rotransmitters. In Chapter 15, on psychological disorders, we discuss the role that malfunctioning neurotransmitter systems play in schizophrenia and depression. And in Chapter 16, on treatment, we discuss how therapeutic drugs act on neurotransmitter systems. Thinking itself requires communication among neurons, and neurotransmitters and their receptors are key links in this vital process.

Organization and Functions of the Nervous System

Impressive as individual neurons are (see "In Review: Neurons, Neurotransmitters, and Receptors"), understanding their functions requires looking at the organization of groups of neurons. Neurons in the brain and spinal cord are organized into groups called *networks*. Many neurons in a network are reciprocally connected, sending axons to the dendrites of every other neuron in the network. Signals from one network also go to other networks, and small networks are organized into bigger collections.

These collections of neurons perform the input, processing, and output tasks that make it possible for you to gain information about what is going on inside and outside the body and to respond adaptively. The parts of the nervous system that provide input about the environment are known as the senses, or sensory systems. These systems—including hearing, vision, taste, smell, and touch—are described in the next chapter. Integration and processing of information occur mainly in the brain. Output flows through motor systems, which are the parts of the nervous system that influence muscles and other organs to respond to the environment.

The nervous system has two major divisions, which work together: the peripheral nervous system and the central nervous system (see Figure 4.9). The peripheral nervous system, which includes all of the nervous system that is not housed in bone, carries out sensory and motor functions. The central nervous system (CNS) is by definition the part encased in bone. It includes the brain, which is inside the skull, and the spinal cord, which is inside the spinal column (backbone). The CNS is the "central executive" of the body; in

In Review: Neurons, Neurotransmitters, and Receptors

Part	Function	Type of Signal Carried
Axon	Carries signals away from the cell body	The action potential, an all-or-none electrochemical signal, that shoots down the axon to vesicles at the tip of the axon, releasing neurotransmitters
Dendrite	Carries signals to the cell body	The postsynaptic potential, an electrochemical signal that fades as it moves toward the cell body
Synapse	Provides an area for the transfer of signals, usually between axon and dendrite	Chemicals that cross the synapse and reach receptors on another cell
Neurotransmitter	Chemical released by one cell that binds to the receptors on another cell	A chemical message telling the next cell either to fire or not to fire its own action potential
Receptor	Proteins on cell membrane that receive chemical signals	Changes in the flow of ions through the cell membrane

other words, information is usually sent to the CNS to be processed and acted on.

The Peripheral Nervous System: Keeping in Touch with the World

As shown in Figure 4.9, the peripheral nervous system has two components, each of which performs both sensory and motor functions.

The Somatic Nervous System

The first is the somatic nervous system, which transmits information from the senses to the CNS and carries signals from the CNS to the muscles that move the skeleton. The somatic nervous system is involved, for example, in sending signals from the skin to the brain that become sensations of warmth when you lie in the sun at the beach. The somatic nervous system is also involved in every move you make. Neurons extend from the spinal cord to the muscles, where the release of the neurotransmitter *acetylcholine* onto them causes the muscles to contract. In fact, much of what we know about neurotransmitters was discovered by laboratory studies of this "neuromuscular junction," especially in the frog's hind leg. At the neuromuscular junction, the action of acetylcholine allows a quick response that can mean the difference between life and death, for a frog or anyone else.

**Figure 4.9
Organization of the
Nervous System**
The bone-encased central nervous system (CNS) is made up of the brain and spinal cord and acts as the body's central information processor, decision maker, and director of actions. The peripheral nervous system includes all nerves not housed in bone and functions mainly to carry messages. The somatic subsystem of the peripheral nervous system transmits sensory information to the CNS from the outside world and conveys instructions from the CNS to the muscles. The autonomic subsystem conveys messages from the CNS that alter the activity of organs and glands, and sends information about that activity back to the brain.

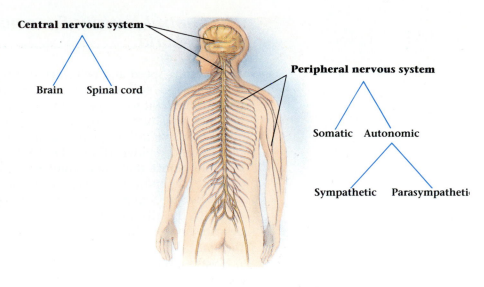

The Autonomic Nervous System

The second component of the peripheral nervous system is the autonomic nervous system (ANS); it carries messages back and forth between the CNS and the heart, lungs, and other organs and glands (Cechetto & Saper, 1990). These messages increase or decrease the activity of the organs and glands to meet varying demands placed on the body. As you lie on the beach, it is your autonomic nervous system that makes your heart beat a little faster when an attractive person walks by and smiles.

The name *autonomic* means "autonomous" and suggests independent operation. The name is appropriate because, although the ANS is influenced by the brain, it controls activities that are normally outside of conscious control, such as digestion and perspiration. The ANS has two divisions to exercise this control: the sympathetic and parasympathetic branches. Generally, the *sympathetic system* mobilizes the body for action; the responses that result are sometimes collectively referred to as the "fight or flight" response. The *parasympathetic system* regulates the body's functions to conserve energy. Thus, these two branches often create opposite effects. For example, the sympathetic nervous system can make the heart beat faster, whereas the parasympathetic nervous system can slow it down. The neurotransmitters in the sympathetic nervous system are *norepinephrine* and *epinephrine* (also known as *adrenaline*); the neurotransmitter in the parasympathetic nervous system is *acetylcholine*, the same substance used at the neuromuscular junction.

The functions of the autonomic nervous system may not get star billing, but you would miss them if they were gone. Just as a race-car driver is nothing without a good pit crew, the somatic nervous system depends on the autonomic nervous system in order to get its job done. For example, when you want to move your muscles, you create a demand for energy; the autonomic nervous system fills the bill by increasing sugar fuels in the bloodstream. If you decide to stand up, you need increased blood pressure so that your blood does not flow out of your brain and settle in your feet. Again, the autonomic nervous system makes the adjustment. Disorders of the autonomic nervous system can make people sweat uncontrollably or faint whenever they stand up; they can also lead to other problems, such as an inability to have sex. We examine the autonomic nervous system in more detail in Chapter 12, on motivation and emotion.

The Central Nervous System: Making Sense of the World

The amazing speed and efficiency of the neural networks that make up the central nervous system—the brain and spinal cord—have prompted many people to compare it to the central processor in a computer. In fact, to better understand how human and other brains work and how they relate to sensory and motor systems, *computational neuroscientists* have created neural network models on computers (Churchland & Sejnowski, 1992). Figure 4.10 shows an example. Notice that input simultaneously activates several paths in the network, so that information is processed at various places at the same time. Accordingly, the activity of these models is described as *parallel distributed processing.* In the chapters on sensation, perception, learning, and memory, we describe how parallel distributed processing often characterizes the activity of the brain.

However, the flesh-and-blood central nervous system is not neatly laid out like computer circuits or the carefully planned streets of a new suburb. In fact, the central nervous system looks more like Boston or Montreal, with distinct neighborhoods, winding back streets, and multi-laned expressways. Its "neighborhoods" are collections of neuronal cell bodies called **nuclei.** The "highways" of the central nervous system are made up of axons that travel together in bundles called **fiber tracts** or **pathways.** Like a freeway ramp, the axon from a given cell may merge with and leave fiber tracts, and it may send branches into other tracts. The pathways travel from one nucleus to other nuclei, and scientists have learned much of how the brain works by determining the anatomical connections among nuclei. We will describe some of these nuclei and anatomical connections, beginning with a practical example of nervous system function.

At 6 A.M., your alarm goes off. The day begins innocently enough with what appears to be a simple case of information processing. Input in the form of sounds from the alarm clock is received by your ears, which convert the sounds into neural signals that reach your brain. Your brain compares these signals with previous experiences stored in memory and correctly associates the sound with "alarm clock" and "coffee." However, your output is somewhat impaired because your brain's activity has not yet reached the waking state. It directs your muscles poorly: stumbling into the kitchen, you touch the glowing heating element as you reach for the coffee pot. Now things get more lively. Heat energy activates sensory neurons in your fingers, which generate action potentials that flash along fiber tracts going into the spinal cord.

Figure 4.10
A Neural Network Model
A simple, computer-based neural network model includes three fundamental components: an input layer, a processing layer, and an output layer. More complex models may have additional processing layers. Each element in each layer is connected to every other element in the other layers. In a typical model, the connections can be either excitatory or inhibitory, and the strengths of connections between the elements can be modified depending on the results of the output; in other words, the network has the capacity to learn. Research on neural network models is part of *cognitive science,* whose linkages with psychology were mentioned in Chapter 1.

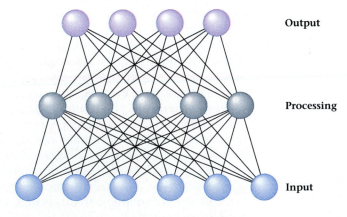

Output

Processing

Input

Source: Hinton, 1989.

The Spinal Cord

The **spinal cord** receives signals from peripheral senses, including pain and touch from the fingertips, and relays the signals to the brain through fibers within the cord. Neurons in the spinal cord also carry signals downward, from the brain to the muscles. In addition, cells of the spinal cord can direct some simple behaviors without instructions from the brain. These behaviors are called **reflexes** because the response to an incoming signal is directly "reflected" back out.

For example, when you touched that heating element, impulses from sensory neurons in your fingers reflexively activated motor neurons, which caused muscles in your arm to contract and quickly withdraw your hand. Because spinal reflexes like this one include few time-consuming synaptic links, they are very fast. And because spinal reflexes occur without instructions from the brain, they are considered involuntary; but they also send action potentials along fiber tracts going to the brain. Thus, you officially "know" you have been burned a fraction of a second after your reflex got you out of trouble.

The story does not end there, however. When a simple reflex set off by touching something hot causes one set of arm muscles to contract, an opposing set of muscles relaxes. If this did not happen, the arm would go rigid. Furthermore, muscles have receptors that send impulses to the spinal cord to let it know how extended they are, so that a reflex pathway can adjust the muscle contraction to allow smooth movement. Thus, the spinal cord is an example of a *feedback system,* a series of processes in which information about the consequences of an action goes back to the source of the action, so that adjustments can be made.

In the spinal cord, sensory neurons are often called *afferent* neurons and motor neurons are termed *efferent* neurons, because *afferent* means "coming toward" and *efferent,* "going away." To remember these terms, notice that *afferent* and *approach* both begin with *a; efferent* and *exit* both begin with *e.*

The Brain

The brain has three major subdivisions: the hindbrain, the midbrain, and the forebrain, the last of which has an outer surface known as the cerebral cortex. Table 4.1 and Figures 4.11 and 4.12 describe and illustrate some of the techniques scientists use to learn about these structures and how they function.

Figure 4.11
PET Scans of Brain Activity While Viewing Words and Nonwords

These patterns of brain activity were revealed by PET scans as a subject looked at four types of stimuli: a "word" made up of geometrical patterns that resemble letters but are not; a word made of letter patterns that cannot be pronounced; a pseudo-word that follows the rules of spelling; and a meaningful word. Note that some areas of the brain are activated by all four tasks, that some areas are activated only by the pseudo-word and the real word, and that the real word creates the most intense activity in these regions (Petersen et al., 1990). Similar studies using auditory (sound) stimuli show that different parts of the brain are activated depending on whether sounds convey words or not, and on whether the listener is trying to decide about the sound of words (for example, was it *pig* or *big*?) or about which of two sounds had a higher pitch (Zatorre et al., 1992).

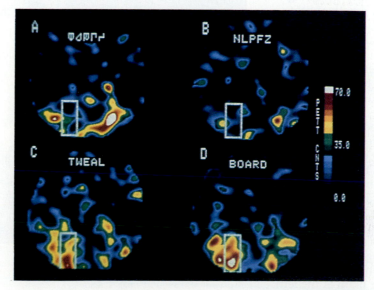

Technique	What It Shows	Advantages (+) and Disadvantages (−)
EEG (electroencephalogram) Multiple electrodes are pasted to outside of head.	A single line that charts the summated electrical fields resulting from the activity of billions of neurons.	+ High temporal resolution (thousandths of seconds) to monitor stages of cognitive processing. − No indication of anatomical source of activity.
PET (positron emission tomography) and SPECT (Single Photon Emission Computed Tomography) Positrons and photons are emissions from radioactive substances.	An image of the concentration and localization of any molecule that can be injected in a radioactive form: for example, drugs, neurotransmitters, or tracers for blood flow or oxygen consumption (which reflect local changes in neuronal activity).	+ Allows functional and biochemical studies. + Concentration is color-coded, making activity easy to visualize. − Requires exposure to low levels of radioactivity. − Spatial resolution is not as good as with MRI. − Rapid changes (faster than 30 seconds) cannot be followed.
MRI (magnetic resonance imaging) Exposes the brain to magnetic field and measures radiofrequency waves.	An image of structure: fibers appear white and nuclei appear gray. Newer "high-speed MRI" also reveals changes in blood flow (which reflect changes in neuronal activity).	+ No radioactivity. + High spatial resolution of anatomical details (< 1 mm). + High-speed MRI has higher temporal resolution than PET (< 1/10 of a second).

Table 4.1
Noninvasive Techniques for Studying Human Brain Function and Structure

Neuroscientists have developed a number of techniques for studying the structure and functions of the brain.

Figure 4.12
Combining PET Scans and Magnetic Resonance Imaging
PET scans provide excellent data about the brain's activity but imprecise information about structures. Much clearer pictures of structures come from magnetic resonance imaging (MRI), which detects the magnetic fields that surround the atoms in brain tissue. Recently, researchers have superimposed images from both techniques to construct a three-dimensional view of the living brain. This figure shows the brain of a young epileptic girl. The picture of the outer surface of the brain is from the MRI; the pink area is from PET and shows the source of epileptic activity. The images at the right are the MRI and PET images at one plane, or "slice," through the brain (indicated by the line on the brain at the left).

The Hindbrain Incoming signals first reach the **hindbrain,** which is actually a continuation of the spinal cord. As you can see in Figure 4.13, the hindbrain lies inside the skull. Blood pressure, heart rate, breathing, and many other vital autonomic functions are controlled by nuclei in the hindbrain, particularly in an area called the **medulla.**

Threading throughout the hindbrain and into the midbrain is a collection of cells that are not arranged in any well-defined nucleus. Because the collec-

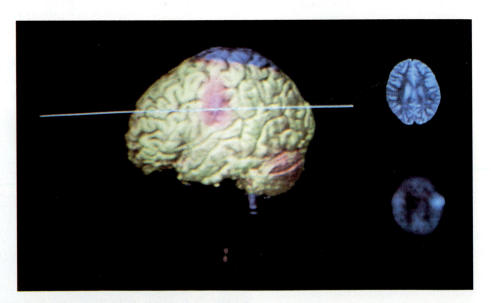

Source: D. N. Levin, H. Xiaoping, K. K. Tan, S. Galhotra, C. A. Pelizzari, G. T. Y. Chen, R. N. Beck, C-T. Chen, M. D. Cooper, J. F. Mullan, J. Hekmatpanah (1989). The brain: Integrated three-dimensional display of MRI and PET images. *Radiology, 172,* 783–789. By permission of the author.

Figure 4.13
Major Structures of the Brain
This view from the side of a section cut down the middle of the brain reveals the forebrain, midbrain, hindbrain, and spinal cord. Many of these subdivisions do not have clear-cut borders, since they are all interconnected by fiber tracts. Indeed, though beautifully adapted to its functions, the brain was not the work of a city planner. Its anatomy reflects its evolution over millions of years. Newer structures (such as the cerebral cortex, which is the outer surface of the forebrain) that handle higher mental functions were built on older ones (like the medulla) that coordinate heart rate, breathing, and other more basic functions. To the left of the drawing is the same view of a living brain, as created by magnetic resonance imaging.

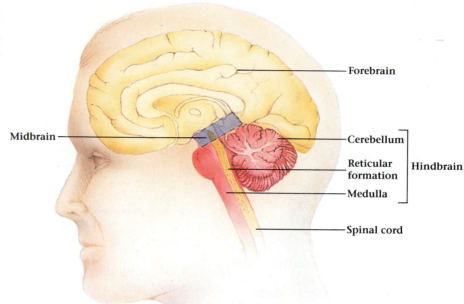

tion looks like a net, it is called the **reticular formation** (*reticular* means "net-like"). This network is very important in altering the activity of the rest of the brain. It is involved, for example, in arousal and attention; if the fibers from the reticular system are disconnected from the rest of the brain, a person goes into a permanent coma. Some of the fibers carrying pain signals from the spinal cord make connections in the reticular formation, which immediately arouses the rest of the brain from sleep. Within seconds, the hindbrain causes your heart rate and blood pressure to increase.

Activity of the reticular formation also leads to activity in a small nucleus called the **locus coeruleus**, which means "blue spot" (Aston-Jones et al., 1991a). There are relatively few cells in the locus coeruleus—only about 30,000 of the 100 billion or so in the human brain (Foote, Bloom & Aston-Jones, 1983)—but each sends out an axon that branches extensively, making contact with as many as 100,000 other cells (Moore & Bloom, 1979; Swanson, 1976). All of the neurons of the locus coeruleus use *norepinephrine* as their neurotransmitter (see Figure 4.14). Norepinephrine is also called *noradrenaline,* and neurons that use noradrenaline are referred to as *adrenergic.* Approximately half of the norepinephrine in the brain is contained in cells of the locus coeruleus. Norepinephrine systems are involved in the appearance of wakefulness and sleep, in learning, and in the regulation of mood. Studies of rats and monkeys suggest that the locus coeruleus is involved in the state of vigilance (Aston-Jones, Chiang & Alexinsky, 1991b). In humans, abnormalities in norepinephrine systems have been linked to depression but, as we discuss in the chapter on psychological disorders, the exact nature of the link is not clear.

The **cerebellum** is also part of the hindbrain. Its primary function is to control finely coordinated movements, such as threading a needle. The cerebellum also allows the eyes to track a moving target accurately (Krauzlis & Lisberger, 1991), and it may be the storehouse for well-rehearsed movements, such as those associated with ballet, piano playing, and athletics (McCormick & Thompson, 1984).

Reflexes and feedback systems are important to the functioning of the hindbrain, as they are in the spinal cord. For example, if blood pressure drops, heart action increases reflexively to compensate for that drop. If you stand up very quickly, your blood pressure can drop so suddenly that it produces lighthead-

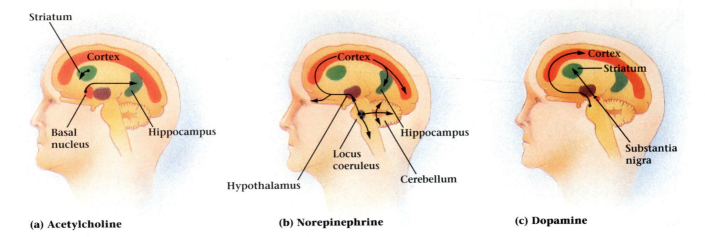

(a) **Acetylcholine**   (b) **Norepinephrine**   (c) **Dopamine**

Figure 4.14
Examples of Neurotransmitter Pathways
Neurons that release a certain neurotransmitter may be concentrated in one particular region (indicated by dots) and send fibers into other regions, to which they communicate across synapses (arrows).

Linkages: Neurons that use dopamine, called dopaminergic systems, send axons from the midbrain to the forebrain, including the cerebral cortex. Some of these neurons are important in the experience of reward, or pleasure, which is vital in shaping and motivating behavior (Wise & Rompre, 1989). Animals will work intensively to receive a direct infusion of dopamine into the forebrain. These dopaminergic systems play a role in the rewarding properties of many drugs, including cocaine (Wise, 1988; Gawin, 1991). Malfunctioning of other dopaminergic neurons that go to the cortex may be partly responsible for *schizophrenia,* a psychological disorder (described in Chapter 15) in which perception, emotional expression, and thought are severely distorted (Weinberger, 1988).

edness until the hindbrain reflex "catches up." If the hindbrain does not activate ANS mechanisms to increase blood pressure, you will faint.

The Midbrain   Continuing upward from the hindbrain, we reach the **midbrain.** In humans it is a small structure, but it serves some very important functions. Certain types of automatic behaviors that integrate simple movements with sensory input are controlled there. For example, when you move your head, midbrain circuits allow you to move your eyes smoothly in the opposite direction, so that you can keep your eyes focused sharply on an object despite the movement of your head. And when a loud noise causes you to turn your head reflexively and look in the direction of the sound, your midbrain circuits are at work.

One vital midbrain nucleus is the **substantia nigra,** meaning "black substance." This small area and its connections to the **striatum** (named for its "striped" appearance) in the forebrain are necessary for the smooth initiation of movement. Without it, you would find it difficult, if not impossible, to get up out of a chair, lift your hand to swat a fly, move your mouth to form words, or, yes, reach for that coffee pot.

Figure 4.14 shows that dopamine is the neurotransmitter used in the substantia nigra and striatum. Indeed, malfunctioning of the dopamine system in these regions contributes to movement disorders. In *Parkinson's disease,* for example, dopamine cells in the substantia nigra completely degenerate; the victim experiences severe shakiness and has difficulty beginning any movement. Parkinson's is most common in elderly people. Scientists are looking for possible environmental causes of the disease (Tanner, 1989). Dopamine pathways also extend to other areas of the forebrain, which we discuss next.

The Forebrain   In humans the **forebrain** has grown so out of proportion to the rest of the brain that it folds back over and completely covers the other parts. It is responsible for the most complex aspects of behavior and mental life. As Figure 4.15 shows, the forebrain includes parts known as the *diencephalon* and the *cerebrum;* the latter is covered by the *cerebral cortex.*

The diencephalon includes two structures deep within the brain—the hypothalamus and the thalamus—that are involved in emotion, basic drives, and sensation. The **thalamus** relays pain signals from the spinal cord as well as signals from the eyes and other sense organs to upper levels in the brain, and it plays an important role in processing and making sense out of this information. Under the thalamus lies the **hypothalamus** (*hypo-* means "under"), which plays an important role in regulating hunger, thirst, and sex drives. It has many connections to and from the autonomic nervous system and the endocrine system (described later in this chapter), as well as to other parts of

Figure 4.15
Some Structures of the Forebrain

The forebrain is divided into the cerebrum and the diencephalon. The structures of the cerebrum are covered by the outer "bark" of the cerebral cortex. This diagram shows some of the structures that lie deep within the cerebrum, as well as structures of the diencephalon.

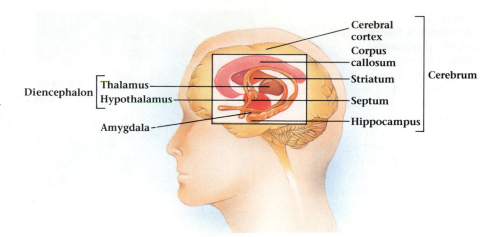

Linkages: What have biological psychologists discovered about brain structures and memory? (a link to Introducing Psychology)

the brain. Destruction of one section of the hypothalamus results in an overwhelming urge to eat. Damage to another area of the male's hypothalamus causes the sex organs to degenerate and the sex drive to decrease drastically. There is also a fascinating part of the hypothalamus that contains the brain's own clock: the **suprachiasmatic nuclei.** The suprachiasmatic nuclei keep an approximately twenty-four-hour clock that determines your biological rhythms. Studies of the suprachiasmatic nuclei in animals suggest that many people are "morning people" or "night people," with different periods of greatest alertness, for biological reasons. This characteristic is stable throughout a lifetime (Cofer et al., 1992). We discuss the functions of the hypothalamus in more detail in Chapter 12, on motivation and emotion.

The largest part of the forebrain is the **cerebrum.** Two structures within it, the **amygdala** and **hippocampus,** are important in memory and emotion. For example, the amygdala is important in associating features of stimuli from two sensory modalities, such as linking the shape and feel of objects in memory (Murray & Mishkin, 1985). Damage to the hippocampus results in the inability to form new memories of events. In one case, a patient known as R.B. suffered a stroke (an interruption of blood flow to the brain) that damaged only his hippocampus. Although tests indicated that his intelligence was above average and he could recall old memories, he was almost totally unable to build new memories (Squire, 1986). Animal studies have also shown that damage to the hippocampus within a day of a mildly painful experience erases memories of the experience, but that removal of the hippocampus several days after the experience has no effect on the memory. Thus, memories are not permanently stored in the hippocampus but, rather, are transferred elsewhere.

In fact, how memories are stored, as well as how they are formed, seems to depend partly on the type of memory involved. For example, the hippocampus is critical in associating an unpleasant experience with a particular *place,* but it is not involved in associating the unpleasant experience with particular *sounds* (Kim & Fanselow, 1992). As we discuss in Chapter 9, your varied memories depend on the activities of many parts of the brain.

The hippocampus and amygdala are both part of the **limbic system,** which is a set of interconnected structures that play important roles in regulating emotion and memory. Among the other structures in the limbic system are the hypothalamus and the septum. As Figure 4.14 shows, axons of neurons that use acetylcholine make up major pathways in the limbic system. Severe degeneration of these cholinergic systems in the hippocampus and other limbic structures occurs in victims of Alzheimer's disease (see Figure 4.16). Alzheimer's disease is a major cause of dementia, the deterioration of cognitive capabilities often associated with aging. About 10 percent of people over the

Figure 4.16
Alzheimer's Disease and the Hippocampus
These magnetic resonance images of living brains show that, compared to the normal person (top), a patient with Alzheimer's disease shows degeneration in the hippocampus (marked *H*). On average, the hippocampus of Alzheimer's patients has been found to be 40 percent smaller than in normal people. Damage to the hippocampus may be responsible for the severe memory impairments in Alzheimer's disease.

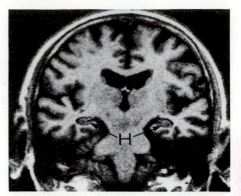
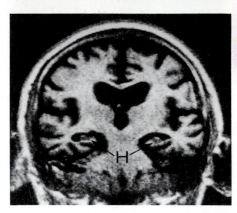
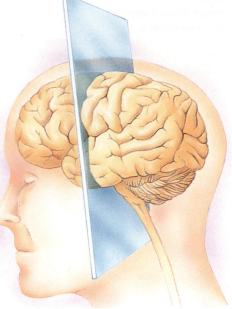

Source: Seab et al., 1988.

age of sixty-five, and 47 percent of people over eighty-five, suffer from this disorder (Evans et al., 1989). The financial cost of Alzheimer's disease is more than $80 billion a year in the United States alone (Selkoe, 1991); the cost in human suffering is incalculable.

Substantial efforts are under way to develop drugs that will slow the relentless progression of Alzheimer's or improve its victims' deteriorating memory capacities. Progress has been frustratingly slow. But a few drugs have been shown to have modestly beneficial effects in animals, and there have even been occasional reports of clinical improvement following drug treatment of Alzheimer's patients. Drugs that are intended to improve cognitive functioning are called *nootropic* drugs (from *noos,* which is Greek for "mind").

Thinking Critically

Are There Drugs That Can Make You Smarter?

If nootropics can improve memory in elderly people with dementia, why not in younger people who are just a little forgetful? In some cities around the world, nootropics, referred to as "smart drugs," are sold at "smart bars" in combination with vitamins and other ingredients. Are "smart drugs" really effective, or are they modern-day snake oil, giving no more than the illusion of a sharpened mind?

What am I being asked to believe or accept?
The belief that certain drugs can enhance memory was widened by a popular 1991 book by John Morgenthaler and Ward Dean, *Smart Drugs and Nutrients.* In an interview that year, thirty-one-year-old Morgenthaler said he had been taking "smart drugs" for ten years, about eight pills twice a day. "It's not a

scientific study; I may have gotten smarter just from growing up, educating myself and stimulating my brain. But I do stop taking the drugs every now and then, and I know that I have better concentration, attention and memory when I'm on them" (Greenwald, 1991). Can nootropics improve your memory and other aspects of your intellect?

What evidence is available to support the assertion?

There is certainly an element of truth to the idea that some of these drugs can improve cognitive performance under some circumstances. Animals given the drugs under controlled conditions show statistically significant improvements in performance on tasks requiring attention and memory. The chemicals used in these drugs include piracetam, vinpocetine, codergocrine (Hydergine), and vasopressin. Actually, piracetam was shown to improve the acquisition of new information in rats more than twenty years ago (Wolthius, 1971). Pramiracetam and other new variants of piracetam have been shown to be more effective than piracetam in facilitating the formation of new memories and the retrieval of old ones (Nicholson, 1990).

Consistent with their behavioral effects, these drugs have measurable biochemical effects on the brain. Some drugs have general effects on brain metabolism and also increase blood sugar levels (Wenk, 1989); others affect acetylcholine activity (Pepeu et al., 1989).

Do "smart drugs" work with people? One study of elderly people with general cerebral impairment found significant improvement after twelve weeks of treatment with piracetam. There have also been reports that the drugs have positive effects on memory and cognition in normal persons as well. For example, tenilsetam, a piracetam-like drug, was associated with improved performance on several tests of cognitive performance in eighteen-year-old college students (Wesnes, Simpson & Kidd, 1987). And vinpocetine has been shown to improve memory in normal volunteers (Subhan & Hindmarch, 1985) as well as in elderly people with memory impairments due to poor blood circulation to the brain (Balestreri, Fontana & Astengo, 1987).

Are there alternative ways of interpreting the evidence?

Glowing testimonials from individuals who feel they are helped by a drug may reflect their *belief* in the drug, not the drug itself. For example, in 1894, when the scientist Charles Edouard Brown-Sequard was feeling old and tired, he gave himself injections of an extract made of ground-up dog testicles. He reported a return of youthful energy and sharpened cognitive abilities, but it was all a placebo effect. As described in Chapter 2, on research methods, only carefully controlled double-blind studies can separate the effect of patients' expectancies from the specific effects of drug or other treatments.

Some double-blind studies have found positive effects of nootropic drugs on memory and cognitive performance, but a closer look at these reports shows that the effects, though perhaps statistically significant, do not result in major changes. The amount of improvement in memory is often very small and occurs on only some of the tests used. Overall, the evidence coming from properly designed studies shows nootropic drugs to be a major disappointment (Bartus et al., 1982; Schindler, 1989). Further, the beneficial effects for Alzheimer's patients may be temporary (Claus et al., 1991).

What additional evidence would help to evaluate the alternatives?

Researchers are evaluating several new and promising categories of drugs. It will take many studies over many years to determine which drugs are truly effective for memory enhancement, and under what circumstances. It will also take time to learn whether the drugs affect memory or related processes such as motivation or attention. In addition, research will have to be done on side-effects. For example, tacrine, one of the more effective drugs for Alzheimer's, was found to cause serious liver damage in about one-third of those who took it (Molloy et al., 1991). And vasopressin, which has occasionally been found to improve memory in humans, may create nausea and increased blood pressure (Goodman-Gilman et al., 1990).

What conclusions are most reasonable?

In spite of their unimpressive showing overall, nootropic drugs are still occasionally used with Alzheimer's patients, mainly for lack of better alternatives (Cooper, 1991). Currently available drugs for improving memory are limited in effectiveness, but proponents argue that even if the drugs only delay the institutionalization of Alzheimer's patients for several months, the savings to society are substantial. As for the drinks you can buy in "smart bars," be sure they taste good, because their effect on your mental powers is likely to be minimal. Indeed, the memory strategies described in Chapter 9 are likely to be far more effective in helping you remember our description of the parts of the brain, to which we now return. ▪

The Cerebral Cortex

Figure 4.17
The Cerebral Cortex (viewed from the left side)
The ridges (gyri) and valleys (sulci) are landmarks that divide the cortex into four lobes: the frontal, the parietal, the occipital, and the temporal. These terms describe anatomical regions, but the cortex is also divided in terms of function. These functional areas include the motor cortex (which controls movement), sensory cortex (which receives information from the senses), and association cortex (which integrates information). Also illustrated are Wernicke's area, which is involved in the interpretation of speech, and Broca's area, a region vital to the production of speech. (These two areas are found only on the left side of the cortex.)

So far, we have described some key structures within the forebrain, but not those on its surface. The outermost part of the cerebrum appears rather round and has right and left halves that are similar in appearance. These halves are called the **cerebral hemispheres.** The outer surface of the cerebral hemispheres, the **cerebral cortex,** has a surface area of one to two square feet—an area that is larger than it looks because of the folds that allow the cortex to fit compactly inside the skull. The cerebral cortex is much larger in humans than in other animals (with a few exceptions, such as dolphins). It is associated with the analysis of information from all the senses, control of voluntary movements, higher-order thought, and other complex aspects of human behavior and mental processes.

The folds of the cerebral cortex give the surface of the human brain its wrinkled appearance, its ridges and valleys. The ridges are called *gyri* and the valleys, *sulci* or *fissures.* As you can see in Figure 4.17, several deep sulci divide the cortex into four areas: the *frontal, parietal, occipital,* and *temporal lobes.* Thus, the gyri and sulci provide landmarks for describing the cortex, although the

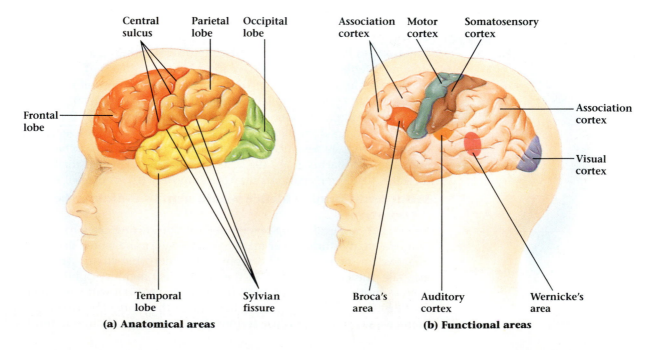

Central sulcus   Parietal lobe   Occipital lobe   Association cortex   Motor cortex   Somatosensory cortex

Frontal lobe   Association cortex

                                                                                          Visual cortex

Temporal lobe   Sylvian fissure   Broca's area   Auditory cortex   Wernicke's area

(a) Anatomical areas   **(b) Functional areas**

Figure 4.18
Motor and Somatosensory Cortex

The areas of cortex that move parts of the body (motor cortex) and receive sensory input from body parts (somatosensory cortex) occupy neighboring regions on each side of the central sulcus. These regions appear in both hemispheres; here we show only those on the left side, looking from the back of the brain toward the front. The cross-sections also show how areas controlling movement of neighboring parts of the body, like the foot and leg, occupy neighboring parts of the motor cortex. Areas receiving input from neighboring body parts, such as the lips and tongue, are near one another in the sensory cortex.

functions of the cortex do not follow these boundaries. Divided according to functions, the cortex includes areas called the sensory cortex, association cortex, and motor cortex.

Sensory and Motor Cortex Different regions of the **sensory cortex** receive information about different senses. As Figure 4.17 shows, the sensory cortex lies in the parietal, occipital, and temporal lobes. Cells in the occipital lobe receive visual information; information from the ears reaches cells in the temporal lobe. Cells in the parietal lobe take in information from the skin about touch, pain, and temperature; these areas are called the *somatosensory cortex*. Information about skin sensations from neighboring parts of the body comes to neighboring parts of the somatosensory cortex, as Figure 4.18 illustrates. It is as if the outline of a tiny person, dangling upside down, determined the location of the information. This pattern is called the *homunculus,* which means "little man."

Neurons in specific areas of the **motor cortex,** which is in the frontal lobe, initiate voluntary movements in specific parts of the body. Some control movement of the hand; others stimulate movement of the foot, the knee, the head, and so on. The motor cortex is arranged in a way that mirrors the somatosensory cortex. For example, as you can see in Figure 4.18, the parts of

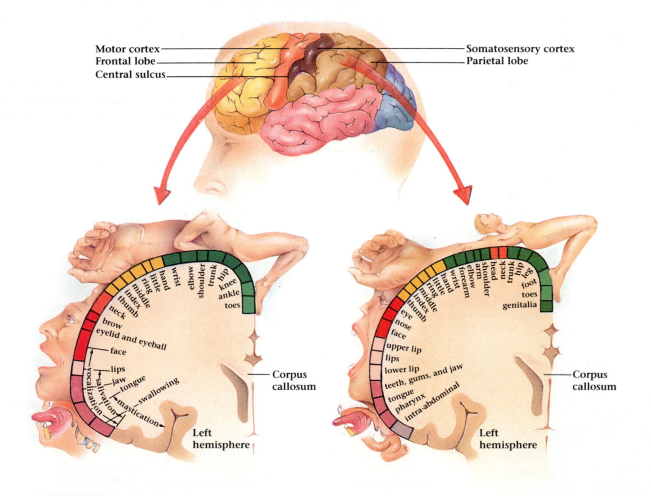

(a) Motor areas (end view)   **(b) Sensory areas (end view)**

Source: Penfield & Rasmussen, 1978.
Note: Can you find the error in this classic drawing? (The figure shows the right side of the body, but the left hand and left side of the face.)

"Whoa! *That* was a good one! Try it, Hobbs — just poke his brain right where my finger is."

> Linkages: What parts of the brain
> make language possible? (a link to
> Thought and Language)

Smooth movements require the co-ordination of neural activity in both the brain and the spinal cord. Without this coordination, walking would be a jerky affair, similar to the movements created in paralyzed people by computer-controlled electrical stimulation of the legs.

the motor cortex that control the hands are near parts of the sensory cortex that receive sensory information from the hands.

Controlling the movement of body parts may seem simple: you have a map of body parts in the cortex, and you activate cells in the hand region if you want to move your hand. But the actual process is much more complex. Recall again your sleepy reach for the coffee pot. The cortex must first translate the coffee pot's location in space into coordinates relative to your body; for example, your hand must be moved to the right or left of your body. Next, the cortex must determine which muscles must be contracted to produce those movements. Populations of neurons work together to produce just the right combinations of direction and force in the particular muscle groups necessary to create the desired effects. Many interconnected areas of the cortex are involved in making these determinations. Artificial neural networks are demonstrating how these exquisitely complex problem-solving processes might occur (Kalaska & Crammond, 1992).

Association Cortex   Parts of the cerebral cortex that are not directly involved with either receiving specific sensory information or initiating movement are called the **association cortex.** These are the areas that perform such complex cognitive tasks as associating words with images. The term *association* is appropriate because these areas either receive information from more than one sense or combine sensory and motor information. Association cortex occurs in all of the lobes and forms a large part of the cerebral cortex in human beings. This is one reason why damage to association areas can create severe deficits in all kinds of mental abilities.

One of the most devastating deficits, called *aphasia,* involves difficulty in producing or understanding speech. Language information comes from the auditory cortex (for spoken language) or from the visual cortex (for written language); areas of the motor cortex produce speech (Geschwind, 1979). But the complex function known as language also involves activity in the association cortex. In the 1860s Paul Broca described the difficulties that result from damage to the association cortex in the frontal lobe near motor areas that control facial muscles. This part of the cortex on the left side of the brain is called *Broca's area* (see Figure 4.17). When Broca's area is damaged, the mental organization of speech suffers. Victims have great difficulty speaking, and what they say is often grammatically incorrect. Each word comes slowly. One patient who was asked about a dental appointment said haltingly, "Yes . . . Monday . . . Dad and Dick . . . Wednesday 9 o'clock . . . 10 o'clock . . . doctors . . . and . . . teeth" (Geschwind, 1979). The ideas—dentists and teeth— are right, but the fluency is gone. A fascinating aspect of the disorder is that when a person with Broca's aphasia sings, the words come fluently and correctly. The words to music presumably are handled by a different part of the brain.

Other language problems result from damage to a portion of the association cortex described in the 1870s by Carl Wernicke. Like Broca's area, *Wernicke's area* is also on the left side; it is in the temporal lobe, near the area of sensory cortex that receives information from the ears, as Figure 4.17 shows. Wernicke's area also receives input from the visual cortex. It is involved in the interpretation of both speech and written words. Damage to Wernicke's area produces complicated symptoms. It can leave fluency intact but disrupt the ability to understand the meaning of words or to speak comprehensibly. One patient who was asked to describe a picture of two boys stealing cookies behind a woman's back said, "Mother is away here working her work to get her better, but when she's looking the two boys looking in the other part. She's working another time" (Geschwind, 1979).

It appears that differing areas of cortex are activated depending on whether language is spoken or written and whether particular grammatical and conceptual categories are involved (see Figure 4.11). For example, two women (H.W. and S.J.D.) each had a stroke in 1985, causing damage to different language-related parts of the association cortex. Neither woman has difficulty speaking or writing nouns, but both have difficulty with verbs (Caramazza & Hillis, 1991). H.W. can write verbs but cannot speak them. S.J.D can speak verbs but has difficulty writing them. Furthermore, H.W. had difficulty pronouncing *watch* when it was used as a verb in the sentence "I watch TV" but spoke the same word easily when it appeared as a noun in "My watch is slow." Another person with damage in a different language area lost the ability to name certain nouns, specifically fruits and vegetables! He could name an abacus or a sphinx, but when presented with an apple or an artichoke he was dumbfounded (Hart, Berndt & Caramazza, 1985). Cases like these indicate that the meaning of language plays a role in determining what structures of the brain process it, thus providing further clues to the complexity of the biological basis of language abilities.

The Divided Brain in a Unified Self

A striking idea emerged from observations of people with damage to the language areas of the brain. Researchers noticed that damage to limited areas of the left hemisphere impaired the ability to use or comprehend language, while damage to corresponding parts of the right hemisphere usually did not. Perhaps, then, the right and left halves of the brain serve different functions.

This concept was not entirely new. It had long been understood, for example, that most sensory and motor pathways cross over as they enter or leave the brain. As a result, the *left hemisphere* receives information from and controls movements of the *right* side of the body, while the *right hemisphere* receives input from and controls the *left* side of the body. However, *both* sides of the brain perform these functions. In contrast, the fact that language centers, such as Broca's area and Wernicke's area, are almost exclusively on the left side of the brain suggested that each hemisphere might be specialized to perform some functions almost independently of the other hemisphere.

In the late 1800s there was much interest in this idea that the hemispheres might be specialized, but techniques were not available to test it. Renewed interest in this issue grew out of studies during the 1960s by Roger Sperry, Michael Gazzaniga, and their colleagues.

Split-Brain Studies   Sperry studied *split-brain* patients—people who had undergone a radical surgical procedure in an attempt to control severe epilepsy. Before surgery their seizures began in one hemisphere and then spread to engulf the whole brain. As a last resort, the two hemispheres in these people were isolated from each other by severing the **corpus callosum, a massive bundle of more than a million fibers that connects the two hemispheres** (see Figure 4.19).

After the surgery, researchers used a special apparatus to present visual images to only *one* side of these patients' split brains (see Figure 4.20). They found that severing the tie between the hemispheres had dramatically affected the way these people thought about and dealt with the world. For example, when the image of a spoon was presented to the left, language-oriented side of patient N.G.'s split brain, she could say what the spoon was; but when the spoon was presented to the right side of her brain, she could not describe the spoon in words. She still knew what the object was, however. Using her left hand (controlled by the right hemisphere), N.G. could pick out the spoon from a group of other objects by its shape. But when asked what she had just grasped,

Figure 4.19
The Brain's Left and Right
Hemispheres
The brain's two hemispheres are
joined by a core bundle of nerve fibers known as the corpus callosum;
in this figure the corpus callosum
has been cut and the two hemispheres are separated. The two cerebral hemispheres look nearly the
same but perform somewhat different tasks. For one thing, the left
hemisphere receives sensory input
from and controls movement on the
right side of the body. The right
hemisphere senses and controls the
left side of the body.

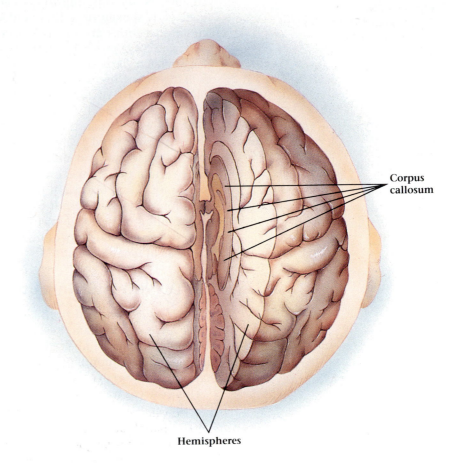

Corpus
callosum

Hemispheres

she replied, "A pencil." The right hemisphere recognized the object, but the
patient could not describe it because the left (language) half of her brain did
not see or feel it (Sperry, 1968).

Though the right hemisphere has no control over spoken language in split-
brain patients, it does have important capabilities, including some related to
nonspoken language. For example, a split-brain patient's right hemisphere can
guide the left hand in spelling out words with Scrabble tiles (Gazzaniga &
LeDoux, 1978). Thanks to this ability, researchers discovered that the right
hemisphere of split-brain patients has self-awareness and normal learning abilities. In addition, it is superior to the left on tasks dealing with spatial relations, especially drawing three-dimensional shapes, and at recognizing human
faces.

*Linkages: Are spatial and verbal
abilities controlled by different
parts of the brain? (a link to
Mental Abilities)*

Lateralization of Normal Brains   Sperry concluded from his studies that
each hemisphere in the split-brain patient has its own "private sensations, perceptions, thoughts, and ideas all of which are cut off from the corresponding
experiences in the opposite hemisphere. . . . In many respects each disconnected hemisphere appears to have a separate mind of its own" (Sperry, 1974).
But when the hemispheres are *not* disconnected, are their functions different?
Are certain functions, such as mathematical reasoning or language skills, lateralized? A **lateralized** task is one that is performed more efficiently by one
hemisphere than by the other.

To find out, researchers presented images to just one hemisphere of people
with normal brains and then measured how fast they could analyze information. If information is presented to one side of the brain and that side is spe-

Figure 4.20
Apparatus for Studying Split-Brain Patients
When the subject stares at the dot on the screen, images briefly presented on one side of the dot go to only one side of the brain. For example, a picture of a spoon presented on the left side of the screen goes to the right side of the brain. Thus the right side of the brain could find the spoon and direct the left hand to touch it; but because the language areas on the left side of the brain did not see it, the subject would not be able to identify the spoon verbally.

cialized to analyze that type of information, a person's responses will be faster than if the information must first be transferred to the other hemisphere for analysis. These studies have confirmed that the left hemisphere has better logical and language abilities than the right, whereas the right hemisphere has better spatial, artistic, and musical abilities (Springer & Deutsch, 1989). PET scans of normal people receiving varying kinds of auditory stimulation also demonstrate these asymmetries of function (see Figure 4.21). The language abilities of the left hemisphere are not specifically related to auditory information, since deaf people also use the left hemisphere more than the right for sign language (Corina, Vaid & Bellugi, 1992).

The precise nature and degree of lateralization vary quite a bit among individuals. For example, in about a third of left-handed people, either the right hemisphere or both hemispheres control language functions (Springer & Deutsch, 1989). In contrast, only about 5 percent of right-handed people have language controlled by the right hemisphere. Evidence about sex differences in brain laterality comes from studies on the cognitive abilities of normal men and women, the effects of brain damage on cognitive function, and anatomical differences between the sexes. Among normal individuals there are sex differences in the ability to perform tasks that are known to be lateralized in the brain. For example, women are better than men at perceptual fluency tasks, such as rapidly identifying matching items, and at arithmetic calculations. Men are better at imagining the rotations of an object in space and in target-directed motor skills, such as guiding projectiles or intercepting them. As demonstrated in any video-game arcade, however, males tend to practice this type of skill more than females; the performance difference might be reduced if practice effects were equated (Law, Pellegrino & Hunt, 1993). Damage to just one side of the brain is more debilitating to men than to women. In particular, men show larger deficits in language ability than women when the left side is damaged (McGlone, 1980), but recent evidence suggests that this sex difference might not be due entirely to differences in lateralization. Women are more dependent on the front part of the left hemisphere, and men are more dependent on the back part (Kimura, 1992), so the consequences also depend

Figure 4.21
Lateralization of the Cerebral Hemispheres: Evidence from PET Scans

These PET scans show overhead views of a section of a person's brain that was receiving different kinds of stimulation. At the upper left, the subject was resting, with eyes open and ears plugged. Note that the greatest brain activity, as indicated by the red color, is in the visual cortex, which is receiving input from the eyes. As shown at the lower left, when the subject listened to spoken language, the left (more language-oriented) side of the brain, especially the auditory cortex in the temporal lobe, became more active, but the right temporal lobe did not; the visual and frontal areas were also active. However, when the subject was listening to music (lower right), there is intense activity in the right temporal lobe but little in the left. When the subject heard both words and music, the temporal cortex on both sides of the brain became activated. Here is visual evidence of the involvement of each side of the brain in processing different kinds of information (Phelps & Mazziotta, 1985, p. 804).

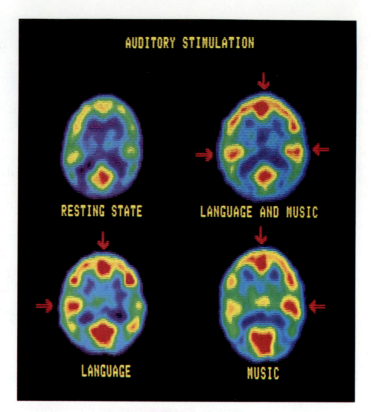

Source: Mazziota & Phelps, 1982.

on *where* the left hemisphere damage occurs. Though humans and animals show definite sex differences in brain anatomy (Allen et al., 1989), no particular anatomical feature has been identified as underlying sex differences in lateralization. One highly publicized report claimed that the corpus callosum is larger in women than men (de Lacoste-Utamsing & Holloway, 1982), but nineteen subsequent investigations failed to replicate this finding (Witelson, 1992). Nevertheless, the original report of a sex difference in the corpus callosum continues to be cited in spite of overwhelming evidence against it, suggesting that scientists are sometimes not entirely unbiased.

Although the two hemispheres are somewhat specialized, the differences between them should not be exaggerated. Normally the corpus callosum integrates the functions of the two hemispheres so that people are not aware of their "two brains." The hemispheres work so closely together, and each makes up so well for whatever lack of ability the other may have, that people are normally unaware that their brains are made up of two partially independent, somewhat specialized halves. There is no evidence that programs designed to train one hemisphere or to synchronize the two hemispheres can enhance performance (Druckman & Swets, 1988).

Plasticity in the Brain

The brain has a remarkable property called **synaptic plasticity**, which is the ability to strengthen neural connections at synapses as well as to establish new synapses. This property provides the basis for the capacity to form memories and learn from experiences, as described in Chapters 8 and 9. However, the brain's plasticity is severely limited when it comes to repairing damage. There are heroic recoveries from brain damage following a stroke, but more often the victim is permanently enfeebled in some way. Brain damage caused by Parkinson's disease and Alzheimer's disease shows unremitting progression as specific populations of neurons degenerate; no one has yet figured out a way to reverse the process.

Why is it difficult for the brain to heal damaged neurons? There are several reasons. First, the brain of an adult animal generally cannot make new neurons. During prenatal development, neurons divide and multiply as other cells do, but as the brain matures the neurons stop dividing and cannot produce more cells in response to injury. Glial cells continue to divide; neurons do not. A second problem arises from the fact that, even if new neurons could be grown, their axons and dendrites would have to reestablish all their former communication links. In the peripheral nervous system, the glial cells form "tunnels" that guide the regrowth of the axons. But in the central nervous system, reestablishing communication links is almost impossible, because glial cells "clean up" after brain damage, consuming injured neurons and forming a barrier to new connections. Nevertheless, the brain does try to heal itself. Undamaged tissue tries to take over for lost tissue, partly by changing its function and partly by sprouting new axons and dendrites to make new connections. Unfortunately, these changes rarely result in total restoration of lost functions.

Several new methods are being employed to help people recover from brain damage. One approach is to replace lost tissue with tissue from another brain. Scientists have transplanted tissue from a still-developing fetal brain into the brain of an adult animal of the same species. If the receiving animal does not reject it, the graft sends axons out into the brain and makes some functional connections. This treatment has reversed animals' learning difficulties, movement disorders, and other results of brain damage. The technique has also been used to treat a very small number of Parkinson's disease patients, with very encouraging results (Lindvall et al., 1992). These patients maintained some improvement a year after the transplant, and PET scans showed an increase in the amount of dopamine synthesized in the striatum. Because the transplanted tissue must come from aborted fetuses, however, there has been considerable ethical and political controversy about this promising procedure.

An alternative treatment for Parkinson's disease uses cells of the person's own adrenal gland, instead of fetal tissue. Cells of the adrenal gland may act like neurons when placed in the brain, and people can live with just one adrenal gland. Unfortunately, fewer than 20 percent of fifty-eight patients who received grafted adrenal cells still exhibited improved conditions after two years; further, a significant number died from surgical complications (Goetz et al., 1991).

Another approach seeks ways to guide newly sprouted axons in the central nervous system. Researchers have "engineered" cells from rats to produce nerve growth factor, a substance that helps stimulate and guide the growth of axons. When the engineered cells were implanted into the brains of rats with brain damage or disease, the cells secreted nerve growth factor. In many cases, brain damage was reversed, with surviving neurons sprouting axons that grew toward the graft (Rosenberg et al., 1988). Based on these animal studies, nerve growth factor has been infused directly into the brain of a person with Alzheimer's disease (Olson et al., 1992). The results were very encouraging, and trials with other patients are in progress. In addition, studies of nerve growth factor led to the discovery of other growth factors (such as brain-derived neurotrophic factor and neurotrophin-3) that may provide new avenues for treatment.

Yet another prospect for reversing brain damage was originally suggested by studies of bird brains (Nottebohm, 1985). Each year, the male canary learns new songs, then forgets many of them at the end of the breeding season. Also, each year, a part of his brain related to the learning of songs grows by neuronal cell division. Later, the neurons die, and the cycle repeats during the next season. If scientists could discover what is different about this part of the bird brain, perhaps the same processes could be generated in the human brain, allowing it to heal itself by producing new neurons.

Some progress has already been made in discovering factors that might allow the birth of new neurons in adult mammals. For example, cells were taken from the striatum of mice and maintained in a dish with nutrients and oxygen. When the cells were treated with a growth factor known as *epidermal growth factor (EGF)*, some of them divided and produced immature forms of neurons and glial cells. Some cells then developed into new neurons (Reynolds & Weiss, 1992), thus showing that, if conditions are right, the mammalian brain does have the potential to form new neurons. This effect has not yet been produced in the intact brain, but scientists are trying to accomplish that goal. We are clearly approaching the time when brain degeneration can be more effectively treated.

Linkages: Human Development and the Changing Brain

How does the brain change throughout life, and how do these changes affect people?

Fortunately, most of the changes that take place in the brain throughout life are not the kind that produce Parkinson's disease and Alzheimer's disease. What are these changes, and what are their effects? How are they related to the developments in sensory and motor capabilities, mental abilities, and other characteristics that we described in Chapter 3?

PET scans are one technique that researchers have used to begin to answer these questions. They have uncovered some interesting correlations between changes in neural activity and the behavior of human newborns and young infants. Among newborns, activity is relatively high in the thalamus but low in the striatum. This pattern may be related to the way newborns move: they make nonpurposeful, sweeping movements of the arms and legs, much like patients with Huntington's disease, who have a hyperactive thalamus and a degenerated striatum (Chugani & Phelps, 1986). During the second and third months of life, activity increases in many regions of the cortex, a change that is correlated with the loss of subcortically controlled reflexes such as the grasping reflex. When infants are around eight or nine months old, activity in the frontal cortex increases, a development that correlates well with the apparent beginnings of cognitive activity in infants (Chugani & Phelps, 1986).

These changes reflect brain plasticity, not the appearance of new cells: essentially all the neurons the brain will ever have are present at birth. After birth, the number of dendrites and synapses increases. In one area of the cortex the number of synapses increases tenfold from birth to twelve months of age (Huttenlocher, 1979). In fact, by the time children are six or seven years old, their brains have more dendrites and use twice as much metabolic fuel as those of adults (Chugani & Phelps, 1986; Huttenlocher, 1979). In early adolescence, the number of dendrites and neural connections actually drops, so that the adult level is reached by about the age of fourteen.

Figure 4.22 shows how the brain overproduces neural connections, establishes the usefulness of certain connections, and then "prunes" the extra connections (Cowan, 1979). One possible explanation for this overproduction is

Figure 4.22
Changes in Neurons of the Cerebral Cortex During Development
Neurons generate an overabundance of dendrites during childhood. During adolescence, extra dendrites are "pruned" until they reach a level characteristic of the adult.

(a) At birth

(b) Six years old

(c) Fourteen years old

Source: Conel, 1939/1967.

that when there are many neural connections, development can take many paths. Overproduction of synapses, especially in the frontal cortex, may be essential for infants to develop certain intellectual abilities (Goldman-Rakic, 1987). Surgically produced lesions of an adult monkey cortex cause the monkey to revert to infant-level performance on some tasks. Some scientists believe that the pruning of connections may reflect a process whereby those connections that are used survive, while others die.

Even as dendrites are pruned, the brain retains its plasticity and "rewires" itself to form new connections throughout life. Genes apparently determine the basic pattern of growth and the major lines of connections, the "highways" of the brain and its general architecture. (For a summary of this architecture, see "In Review: Organization of the Brain.") But the details of the connections seem to depend on factors such as how complex and interesting the environment is. For example, researchers have compared the brains of rats raised in individual cages with only a boring view of the side of the cage to the brains of rats raised with interesting toys and stimulating playmates. The cerebral cortex of those from the enriched environment had more and longer dendrites as well as more synapses than the cortex of animals from barren, individual housing (Turner & Greenough, 1985; Volkmar & Greenough, 1972). Furthermore, the number of cortical synapses increased when old animals who had always lived in boring individual cages were moved to an enriched environment (Green, Greenough & Schlumpf, 1983). Environmentally influenced neuronal changes may help explain why, as described in Chapter 2, the maze-learning ability of genetically "maze-dull" rats raised in stimulating cages can equal that of genetically "maze-bright" animals.

Researchers have not yet determined whether an enriched environment stimulates the development of new connections or slows down normal pruning; also not yet known is whether animals will lose synaptic complexity if they are moved from an enriched to a barren environment. To the extent that these ideas and research findings apply to humans, however, they hold ob-

In Review: Organization of the Brain

Major Division	Some Important Structures	Some Major Functions
Hindbrain	Medulla	Regulation of breathing, heart rate, and blood pressure
	Reticular formation (also extends into midbrain)	Regulation of arousal and attention
	Cerebellum	Control of finely coordinated movements
Midbrain	Various nuclei	Relay of sensory signals to forebrain; creation of automatic responses to certain stimuli
	Substantia nigra	Smooth initiation of movement
Forebrain	Hypothalamus	Regulation of hunger, thirst, and sex drives
	Thalamus	Interpretation and relaying of sensory information
	Hippocampus	Formation of new memories
	Cerebral cortex	Analysis of sensory information; control over voluntary movements, abstract thinking, and other complex cognitive activity
	Corpus callosum	Transfer of information between the two cerebral hemispheres

vious implications for how people raise children and treat the elderly. These findings may someday help explain why, as discussed in Chapter 3, children raised in stimulating environments tend to show faster and more extensive cognitive development than those from barren backgrounds.

In any event, this line of research highlights the interaction of environmental and genetic factors. Some overproduced synapses may reflect genetically directed preparation for certain types of experiences. Generation of these synapses is an "experience-expectant" process, and it accounts for sensitive periods during development when certain things can be most easily learned. But overproduction of synapses also occurs in response to totally new experiences; this process is "experience dependent" (Greenough, Black & Wallace, 1987). Within constraints set by genetics, interactions with the world appear to mold the brain itself.

The Endocrine System: Coordinating the Internal World

Neurons are not the only cells that can communicate with one another in ways that affect behavior and mental processes. Another class of cells with this ability occurs in the **endocrine system,** which regulates functions ranging from stress responses to physical growth. The cells of endocrine organs, or **glands,** communicate by secreting chemicals, much as neurons do. In the case of endocrine organs, the chemicals are called **hormones.** Figure 4.23 shows the location and functions of some of the major endocrine glands.

Hormones from the endocrine organs are similar to neurotransmitters. In fact, many such chemicals, including norepinephrine and endorphin, act both as hormones and as neurotransmitters. However, whereas neurons secrete neurotransmitters into synapses, endocrine organs put their chemicals into the blood stream, which carries them throughout the body. In this way, endocrine glands can stimulate cells with which they have no direct connection. But not all cells receive the hormonal message. Hormones, like neurotransmitters, can influence only those cells with receptors that can receive them (McEwen, 1991). Organs whose cells have receptors for a hormone are called *target organs.*

Each hormone acts on many target organs, producing coordinated effects throughout the body. For example, when the sex hormone *estrogen* is secreted by a woman's ovaries, it activates her reproductive system. It causes the uterus to grow in preparation for nurturing an embryo; it enlarges the breasts to prepare them for nursing; it stimulates the brain to enhance interest in sexual activity; and it stimulates the pituitary gland to release another hormone that causes a mature egg to be released by the ovary for fertilization.

Figure 4.23
Some Major Glands of the Endocrine System
Each of the glands shown releases its hormones into the bloodstream. Even the hypothalamus, a part of the brain, regulates the adjacent pituitary gland by secreting hormones.

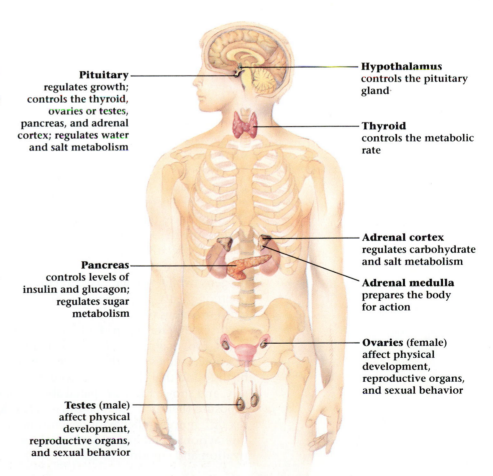

Pituitary
regulates growth; controls the thyroid, ovaries or testes, pancreas, and adrenal cortex; regulates water and salt metabolism

Hypothalamus
controls the pituitary gland

Thyroid
controls the metabolic rate

Adrenal cortex
regulates carbohydrate and salt metabolism

Pancreas
controls levels of insulin and glucagon; regulates sugar metabolism

Adrenal medulla
prepares the body for action

Ovaries (female)
affect physical development, reproductive organs, and sexual behavior

Testes (male)
affect physical development, reproductive organs, and sexual behavior

The brain has ultimate control over the secretion of hormones. Through the hypothalamus, it controls the pituitary gland, which in turn controls endocrine organs in the body. The brain is also one of the target organs for most endocrine systems. Thus, the typical endocrine system involves four elements: the brain, the pituitary gland, the endocrine organ, and the target organs, which include the brain. Each element in the system uses hormones to signal the next element, and the secretion of each hormone is stimulated or suppressed by other hormones.

For example, in stress-hormone systems, the brain controls the pituitary gland by signaling the hypothalamus to release hormones that stimulate receptors of the pituitary gland, which secretes another hormone, which stimulates another endocrine gland to secrete *its* hormones. Specifically, when the brain interprets a situation as threatening, the pituitary releases the hormone *ACTH*, which causes the adrenal glands to release the hormone *cortisol* into the blood stream. These hormones in turn act on cells throughout the body. The combined effects of the adrenal hormones and the activation of the sympathetic system result in a set of responses called the **fight-or-flight syndrome**, which, as mentioned earlier, prepares the animal or person for action in response to danger. The heart beats faster, the liver releases glucose into the bloodstream, fuels are mobilized from fat stores, and the organism is generally placed in a state of high arousal.

However, the hormones also provide feedback to the brain as well as to the pituitary gland. Just as a thermostat and furnace regulate heat, this feedback system regulates hormone secretion so as to keep it within a certain range. If a hormone rises above a certain level, feedback about this situation signals the brain and pituitary to stop stimulating its secretion. Thus, after the immediate threat is over, feedback about cortisol's action in the brain and in the pituitary terminates the secretion of ACTH and, in turn, cortisol. Because the feedback suppresses further action, this arrangement is called a **negative feedback system.**

As an additional example of the effect of hormones, consider another class of sex hormones, the *androgens.* Pituitary hormones cause the male sex organs to secrete androgens, stimulate the maturation of sperm, increase a male's motivation for sexual activity, and increase his aggressiveness (Davidson, Camargo & Smith, 1979; Archer, 1991). The relationship between androgens and aggressiveness in humans is complicated and controversial; we discuss it further in Chapter 18.

Can differences between hormones in men and women account for some of the differences between the sexes that we mentioned in the chapter on human development? During development and in adulthood, sex differences in hormones are relative rather than absolute: both men and women have both androgens and estrogens, but men have relatively higher concentrations of androgens while women have relatively higher concentrations of estrogens. There is plenty of evidence from animal studies that the presence of higher concentrations of androgens in males during development creates both structural sex differences in the brain and sex differences in adult behaviors. Humans, too, may be similarly affected by hormones early in development. For example, studies of girls who were exposed to high levels of androgen before birth found that they later played more with "boys'" toys, were more aggressive, and showed greater spatial ability than their sisters who had not had such exposure (Reinisch, Ziemba-Davis & Sanders, 1991). However, the creation of sex differences in behavior depends not on hormones alone, but on complex interactions of biological and social forces, as described in the chapter on motivation and emotion.

The Immune System: Linking the Brain and the Body's Defense System

With many similarities to the nervous system and endocrine systems, the **immune system** serves as both a sensory system and a surveillance system. It monitors the internal state of the body and detects unwanted cells and toxic substances that may invade the body. It recognizes and remembers foreign substances, and engulfs and destroys foreign cells, and cancer cells. People such as AIDS patients, whose immune system is underresponsive, face certain death from invading bacteria or malignant tumors. However, if the system becomes overzealous, the results can be just as devastating: many diseases, including arthritis and cancer, are now recognized as **autoimmune disorders,** in which cells of the immune system attack normal cells of the body, including cells of the brain.

The immune system is perhaps as complex as the nervous system, and it contains as many cells as the brain (Guyton, 1991). Some of these cells are in identifiable organs like the thymus and spleen, and some circulate in the bloodstream and enter tissues throughout the body (see Figure 4.24). In Chapter 13, on health, stress, and coping, we describe a few of the immune system's many cell types and how they work.

Traditionally, the nervous system and the immune system were thought of as completely separate (Ader, Felten & Cohen, 1990). This view stemmed in part from the fact that various types of immune cells seem to act on their own. However, four lines of evidence suggest important interactions between the nervous system and immune systems (Dunn, 1989).

First, stress can alter the outcome of disease in animals, and, as we discuss in Chapter 13, there is growing evidence that psychological stressors also affect disease processes in humans. Second, immune responses can be "taught" using some of the principles of learning outlined in Chapter 8. In one study with humans, for example, exposure to the taste of sherbet was repeatedly associated with an injection of epinephrine, which increases immune system activity. Eventually, an increase in immune system activity could be prompted by the taste of sherbet alone (Buske-Kirschbaum et al., 1992). Animal studies show that learning can also play a part in the appearance of allergic responses (MacQueen et al., 1989). Similarly, for some allergic people, the mere sight of pollen-laden flowers associated with their allergy may eventually be enough to prompt a round of sneezing. Learned *suppression* of immune function has also been demonstrated; conditioning has been shown to prolong the life of mice that are vulnerable to autoimmune disorders (Ader & Cohen, 1982). Third, animal studies have shown that electrical stimulation or lesions of specific parts of the hypothalamus, the cortex, or the brain stem that control the autonomic nervous system can enhance or impair immune functions (Felten et al., 1991).

Finally, activation of the immune system produces changes in the electrical activity of the brain, neurotransmitter activity, hormonal secretion, and behavior. For example, many of the symptoms associated with routine "sickness"—sleepiness, nausea, and fever—are actually a result of chemicals released by immune cells, collectively called **cytokines,** which act directly on the brain through specific receptors (Kent et al., 1992). Immune cells also produce some of the same substances that are used by the brain as neurotransmitters and by the endocrine system as hormones (Blalock, 1989). These include endorphins, which are the body's natural painkillers, and ACTH, the hormone that stimulates the adrenal gland to produce glucocorticoids during stress.

Figure 4.24
Relations Among the Nervous System, Endocrine System, and Immune System
All three systems interact and influence one another. The nervous system affects the endocrine system by controlling secretion of hormones via the pituitary gland. It also affects the immune system via the autonomic nervous system's action on the thymus gland. The thymus and bone marrow are sites of generation and development of immune cells. Hormones of the pituitary gland and adrenal gland modulate immune cells. Immune cells secrete cytokines and antibodies to fight foreign invaders; cytokines are blood-borne messengers that regulate development of immune cells and also influence the central nervous system.

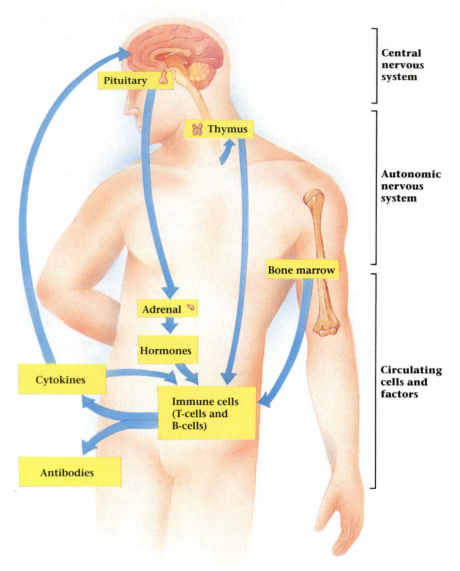

These converging lines of evidence point to important relationships that illustrate the intertwining of biological and psychological functions, the interaction of body and mind. They highlight the ways in which the immune system, nervous system, and endocrine system—all systems of communication between and among cells—are integrated to form the biological basis for a smoothly functioning self that is filled with interacting thoughts, emotions, and memories and is capable of responding to life's challenges and opportunities with purposeful and adaptive behavior.

Future Directions

Today, information about the brain is increasing at an explosive rate. Medical researchers, biochemists, computer scientists, physiologists, and psychologists are all applying specialized techniques to the study of the nervous system and approaching questions about the brain and behavior from complementary angles.

Technical breakthroughs have allowed a tremendous amount of information to be gathered in an amazingly short time, and each year impressive new research capabilities will continue to appear. For example, ever-improving PET scans, "fast" MRI, and other advanced imaging techniques will allow increasingly rapid and detailed monitoring of brain activity (Belliveau et al., 1992). At the same time, techniques from molecular biology will allow the dissection and manipulation of genes that shape behavior (Grant et al., 1992).

Some of the most exciting work in coming years is likely to focus on biological factors in diseases. Scientists may soon be able to answer questions such as What specific biological processes occur in Alzheimer's disease and schizophrenia? and What genetic differences can be used to predict who is susceptible to alcoholism or other disorders? Better ways of treating or even preventing many disorders will be found.

There will also be greater understanding of the biological aspects of cognitive functioning. A molecular basis for learning and memory will be found, though it appears unlikely that a single mechanism will account for all types of memory. The ways in which complex neural networks allow the brain to solve complicated problems will be unraveled, and the principles derived will allow computers to be programmed to do a better job of understanding language. As computer-based models of mental activity more closely approximate the way real brains work, these models will be useful in understanding abnormalities in cognitive functions. For example, neural network models for language abilities have been shown to respond to changes in the computer program in much the same way that human language is affected by brain damage; the models even have potential for developing rehabilitation strategies (Margolin, 1991).

The larger question of how the functioning of the nervous system translates into what people experience as the mind will be more difficult to answer. How do all the details fit together? More information than any individual can master is being generated about such questions. It will take some great minds, probably working with great computers, to synthesize this information into a vision of how the brain generates experience and behavior.

If you are interested in taking part in this collective adventure, either as a participant scientist or as an informed spectator, you can prepare yourself by learning more about both physical and psychological sciences. Relevant courses offered by most psychology departments include physiological psychology, sensation and perception, learning and memory, motivation and emotion, and abnormal psychology. Many departments now offer courses in drugs and behavior. Courses in chemistry, physiology, anatomy, and computer science are also relevant. Studying the relationships between body and mind is an interdisciplinary adventure, so having a broad background will help you greatly.

Summary and Key Terms

The *nervous system* is a system of cells that allows an organism to gain information about what is going on inside and outside the body and to respond appropriately. *Biological psychology* focuses on the biological aspects of our being, including the nervous system, which provide the physical basis for behavior and mental processes.

Levels of Analysis: From Molecules to Memories

Much of our understanding of biological aspects of psychology has stemmed from research on animal and human nervous systems at levels ranging from single cells to complex organizations of cells.

Cells of the Nervous System

The fundamental units of the nervous system are cells called *neurons*. They are especially good at signal transduction, which, in the nervous system, means the ability to receive signals from, and transmit signals to, other neurons. Neurons have cell bodies and two types of fibers, called *axons* and *dendrites*. Axons carry signals away from the cell body; dendrites carry signals to the cell body. Neurons can transmit signals because of the structure of these fibers, the excitable surface of some of the fibers, and the *synapses,* or gaps, between cells.

Action Potentials

The selectively permeable membrane of neurons normally keeps the distribution of electrochemically charged molecules, or *ions,* uneven between the inside of cells and the outside, creating an electrochemical force called a potential. The membrane surface of the axon can transmit a disturbance in this potential, called an *action potential,* from one end of the axon to the other. The speed of the action potential is fastest in neurons sheathed in *myelin.* Between firings there is a very brief rest, called a *refractory period.*

Synapses and Communication Between Neurons

When an action potential reaches the end of an axon, the axon releases a chemical called a *neurotransmitter* (some neurotransmitters are also referred to as *neuromodulators*). It crosses the synapse and interacts with the postsynaptic cell at special sites called *receptors,* creating either an *excitatory* or an *inhibitory postsynaptic potential* that makes the postsynaptic cell more likely or less likely to fire an action potential. Thus, whereas communication within a neuron is electrochemical, communication between neurons is chemical. Because the fibers of neurons have many branches, each neuron can interact with thousands of other neurons. Each neuron constantly integrates signals received at its many synapses; the result of this integration determines how often the neuron fires an action potential.

Organization and Functions of the Nervous System

Neurons are organized in networks of reciprocally connected cells, forming *sensory systems,* which receive information from the environment, and *motor systems,* which influence the actions of muscles and other organs. The two major divisions of the nervous system are the *central nervous system* (CNS), which includes the brain and spinal cord, and the *peripheral nervous system.*

The Peripheral Nervous System: Keeping in Touch with the World

The peripheral nervous system has two components.

The Somatic Nervous System

The first is the *somatic nervous system,* which transmits information from the senses to the CNS and carries signals from the CNS to the muscles that move the skeleton.

The Autonomic Nervous System

The second is the *autonomic nervous system* (ANS); it carries messages back and forth between the CNS and the heart, lungs, and other organs and glands.

The Central Nervous System: Making Sense of the World

Although artificial neural network models are being run on computers to understand it, the CNS is laid out, not in neat circuits, but in intertwined groups of neuron cell bodies, called *nuclei,* whose collections of axons travel together in *fiber tracts* or *pathways.*

The Spinal Cord

The *spinal cord* receives information from the peripheral senses and sends it to the brain; it also relays messages from the brain to the periphery. In addition, cells of the spinal cord can direct simple behaviors, called *reflexes,* without instructions from the brain.

The Brain

The brain's major subdivisions are the *hindbrain, midbrain,* and *forebrain.* The hindbrain includes the *medulla, cerebellum,* and the *locus coeruleus.* The midbrain includes the *substantia nigra.* The *reticular formation* is found in both the hindbrain and midbrain. The forebrain is the largest and most highly developed part of the brain; it includes the diencephalon and cerebrum. The diencephalon includes the *hypothalamus* and *thalamus.* A part of the hypothalamus called the *suprachiasmatic nuclei* maintains a clock that determines biological rhythms. Structures within the *cerebrum* include the *striatum, hippocampus,* and *amygdala.* Several of these structures form the *limbic system,* which plays an important role in regulating emotion and memory.

The Cerebral Cortex

The outer surface of the *cerebral hemispheres* is called the *cerebral cortex;* it is responsible for many of the higher functions of the brain, including speech and reasoning. The functional areas of the cortex consist of the *sensory cortex, motor cortex,* and *association cortex.*

The Divided Brain in a Unified Self

The right and left hemispheres of the cerebral cortex are specialized to some degree in their functions. In most people, the left hemisphere is more active in language and logical tasks; the right hemisphere, in spatial, musical, and artistic tasks. A task that is performed more efficiently by one hemisphere than the other is said to be *lateralized.* The hemispheres are connected through the *corpus callosum,* allowing them to operate in a coordinated fashion.

Plasticity in the Brain

The brain's *synaptic plasticity,* the ability to strengthen neural connections at its synapses as well as to establish new synapses, forms the basis for learning and memory. Scientists are studying ways to increase plasticity following brain damage.

Linkages: Human Development and the Changing Brain

A child's growing and changing intellectual abilities are based on changing synaptic connections in the brain, not on an increase in the number of brain cells. The brain produces many more synaptic connections than it needs, pruning extra connections as experience strengthens useful connections. The ability to form new synapses nevertheless continues even into old age.

The Endocrine System: Coordinating the Internal World

Like nervous-system cells, those of the *endocrine system* communicate by releasing a chemical that is a signal to other cells. However, the chemicals released by endocrine organs, or *glands,* are called *hormones* and are carried by the bloodstream to remote target organs. *Negative feedback systems* are involved in the control of most endocrine functions. The brain is the main controller: through the hypothalamus, it controls the pituitary gland, which in turn controls endocrine organs in the body. The brain is also a target organ for most endocrine systems. The target organs often produce a coordinated response to hormonal stimulation. One of these is the *fight-or-flight syndrome,* which is set off by adrenal hormones that prepare for action in times of stress. Hormones also modulate the development of the brain, creating sex differences in brain and behavior.

The Immune System: Linking the Brain and the Body's Defense System

The *immune system* serves as a sensory system that monitors the internal state of the body and as a protective system for detecting, then destroying, unwanted cells and toxic substances that may invade the body. *Autoimmune disorders* result when cells of the immune system attack normal cells of the body. There are important relationships among the immune system, nervous system, and endocrine systems. For example, many of the symptoms of illness are actually a result of immune-system chemicals called *cytokines,* which act directly on the brain through specific receptors.

Chapter 5

Sensation

Outline

In your everyday life you probably assume that there is an objective reality that is the same for everyone. The seat that you sit on, the ground that you walk on, are solid objects. You can see and feel them with your senses. But sensory psychologists tell us that reality is not so simple, that the senses do not reflect an objective reality. The senses of each individual, they point out, actively shape information about the outside world to create a *personal* reality. The sensory experiences of various species—and individual humans—vary, so that you do not see the same world a fly sees, and people from California may not hear music quite the same way that British people do.

In order to explain how sensory systems create reality, we must consider some basic information about the senses. A **sense** is a system that translates information from outside the nervous system into neural activity. For example, vision is the system through which the eyes convert light into neural activity. This neural activity tells the brain something about the source of the light (for example, that it is bright) or about objects from which light is reflected (for example, that a round, red object appears to be out there). These messages from the senses are called **sensations.** Since they provide the link between the self and the world outside the brain, sensations help shape many kinds of behavior and mental processes (see the Linkages diagram).

Traditionally, psychologists have distinguished between sensation—the initial message from the senses—and *perception,* the process through which messages from the senses are given meaning. Thus, you do not actually "sense" a cat lying on the sofa; you sense shapes and colors—visual sensations. Because of your knowledge of the world, you interpret, or perceive, these sensations as a cat (or a pillow if you are especially tired). However, it is difficult to draw a clear line between sensation and perception. Research shows that the process of interpreting sensations begins in the sense organs themselves. For example, the frog's eye immediately interprets any small black object as "fly!"—thus enabling the frog to attack the fly with its tongue without waiting for its brain to process the sensory information (Lettvin et al., 1959).

In this chapter we cover the first steps of the sensation-perception process, examining the ways in which the senses pick up information and convert it into forms the brain can use. In the next chapter we discuss the later phases of the sensation-perception process. Together, these chapters illustrate how human beings create, with the sense organs and the brain, their own worlds and their own realities.

Sensory Systems

The senses gather information about the world by detecting various forms of *energy,* such as sound, light, heat, and physical pressure. For example, the eyes detect light energy, the ears detect the energy of sound, and the skin detects the energy of heat and pressure. Humans depend primarily on vision, hearing, and the skin senses to gain information about the world; they depend less than other animals on smell and taste. To your brain, "the world" also includes the rest of your body, and there are sensory systems that provide information about the status of your body parts.

All of these senses must detect stimuli, encode them into neural activity, and transfer this coded information to the brain. Figure 5.1 illustrates these basic steps in sensation. At each step, sensory information is "processed" in some way: the information that arrives at one point in the system is not the same as the information that goes to the next step.

In some sensory systems, the first step in sensation involves **accessory structures,** which modify the stimulus. The lens of the eye is an accessory structure that changes incoming light by focusing it; the outer part of the ear is an accessory structure that collects sound.

The second step in sensation is **transduction,** which is the process of converting incoming energy into neural activity. Just as a radio receives energy and transduces it into sounds, the ears receive sound energy and transduce it into neural activity that people recognize as voices, music, and other auditory experiences. Transduction takes place at structures called **receptors,** cells that are specialized to detect certain forms of energy. Sensory receptors are somewhat like the neurons that we described in Chapter 4, in that they respond to incoming energy by changing their membrane potential and can release neurotransmitters to send a signal to neighboring cells. Sensory receptors respond best to *changes* in energy. A constant

Linkages

The questions in this diagram illustrate some of the relationships between the topic of this chapter, sensation, and other chapter topics. The senses—vision, hearing, smell, taste, and touch—put people in touch with their environment and, hence, with the arena for all aspects of human behavior and mental processes. Understanding sensory systems is therefore vital to understanding how people think, feel, and act. In describing these systems, we will encounter many of the biological processes presented in Chapter 4. The page numbers in the diagram indicate where the linkages are discussed; we repeat each Linkage question in the margin next to the discussion. Keep in mind that the diagram shows only a sampling of the linkages between sensation and other aspects of psychology. ■

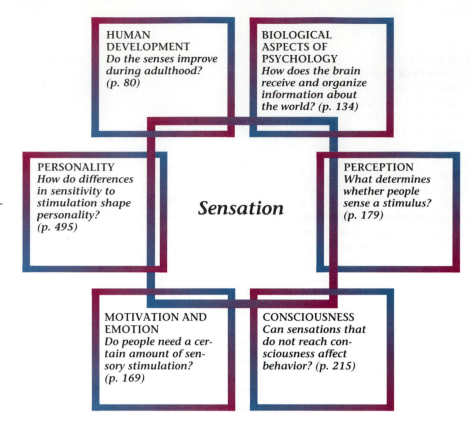

HUMAN DEVELOPMENT
Do the senses improve during adulthood? (p. 80)

BIOLOGICAL ASPECTS OF PSYCHOLOGY
How does the brain receive and organize information about the world? (p. 134)

PERSONALITY
How do differences in sensitivity to stimulation shape personality? (p. 495)

Sensation

PERCEPTION
What determines whether people sense a stimulus? (p. 179)

MOTIVATION AND EMOTION
Do people need a certain amount of sensory stimulation? (p. 169)

CONSCIOUSNESS
Can sensations that do not reach consciousness affect behavior? (p. 215)

---

level of stimulation usually produces **adaptation**, a process through which responsiveness to an unchanging stimulus decreases over time.

Next, sensory nerves carry the output from receptors to the brain. For all the senses but smell, the information is taken first to the thalamus, which relays it to the cerebral cortex. It is in the cortex that the most complex processing occurs.

The Problem of Coding

Linkages: How do sensory processes contribute to people's perception of the world? (a link to Perception)

When receptors transduce energy, they must somehow code the physical properties of the stimulus into firing patterns that, when organized by the brain, allow you to make sense of the stimulus—to tell, for example, whether you are looking at a dog or a cat. Each psychological dimension of a sensation, such as the brightness or color of light, must have a corresponding physical dimension that is coded by sensory receptors.

As a way of thinking about the problem of coding, suppose that, for your birthday, you are given a Pet Brain, a new product inspired by the people who brought us Pet Rocks, The Clapper, and Jurassic Park. Your Pet Brain is definitely alive (the guarantee says so), but it does not seem to respond when you talk to it. You show it an ice cream sundae; no response. You show it pictures of other highly attractive brains; no response. You are about to deposit your Pet Brain in the garbage disposal when you suddenly realize that you and your Pet Brain are not talking the same language. You should be buzzing the brain's sensory nerves to send it messages and recording from its motor nerves to discern its responses.

After having this brilliant insight and setting up a little electric stimulator, you are faced with an even more awesome problem. How do you describe a

Figure 5.1
Elements of a Sensory System
Sensory systems have many features in common. Objects in the world generate energy that is focused by accessory structures and detected by sensory receptors, which convert the energy into neural signals. As the signals are transferred through parts of the brain, information is extracted and analyzed. In the cerebral cortex, the information is further analyzed and compared with sensory experiences stored in memory.

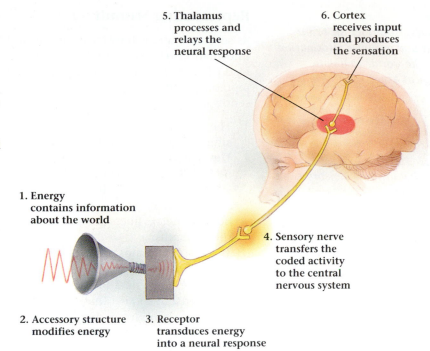

5. Thalamus processes and relays the neural response

6. Cortex receives input and produces the sensation

1. Energy contains information about the world

4. Sensory nerve transfers the coded activity to the central nervous system

2. Accessory structure modifies energy

3. Receptor transduces energy into a neural response

hot-fudge sundae in terms of action potentials? This is the problem of coding. **Coding** is the translation of the physical properties of a stimulus into a pattern of neural activity that specifically identifies those physical properties.

Now you realize that if you want the brain to see the sundae, you should probably stimulate its optic nerve (the nerve from the eye to the brain) rather than its auditory nerve (the nerve from the ear to the brain). This idea is based on the doctrine of **specific nerve energies:** stimulation of a particular sensory nerve provides codes for that one sense, no matter how the stimulation takes place. For example, if you apply gentle pressure to your eyeball, you will produce activity in the optic nerve and sense little spots of light. Similarly, electrical stimulation of the optic nerve is sensed as light.

Having chosen the optic nerve to convey visual information, you must next code the specific attributes of the sundae stimulus: the soft white curves of the vanilla ice cream, the dark richness of the chocolate, the bright redness of the cherry on top. These dimensions must be coded in the language of neural activity. As described in the previous chapter, this language is made up of membrane potentials in dendrites and cell bodies and of action potentials in axons.

Some attributes of a stimulus are coded fairly simply. For example, a bright light will cause some neurons in the visual system to fire faster than will a dim light. This is a **temporal code,** because it involves changes in the *timing* of firing. Temporal codes can be more complex as well; for example, a burst of firing followed by a slower firing rate means something different than a steady rate. The other basic type of code is **spatial,** in which the *location* of firing neurons relative to their neighbors provides information about the stimulus. For example, neurons that carry sensations from the fingers travel close to those carrying information from the arms, but far from those carrying information from the feet. Information can be recoded at several relay points as it makes its way through the brain. Sensory psychologists are still working on deciphering the codes that the brain uses; your Pet Brain may have to wait a while to appreciate the beauty of that sundae.

Linkages: How does the brain receive and organize information about the world? (a link to Biological Aspects of Psychology)

Representing Stimuli

As sensory systems transfer information to the brain, they also organize that information. This organized information is called a *representation*. If you have read Chapter 4, you are already familiar with some characteristics of sensory representations. In humans, representations of vision, hearing, and the skin senses in the cerebral cortex share the following features:

1. The information from each of these senses reaches the cortex via the thalamus. (Figures 4.13 and 4.15 show where these areas of the brain are.)
2. The representation of the sensory world in the cortex is *contralateral* to the part of the world being sensed. For example, the left side of the primary visual cortex "sees" the right side of the world, and the right side of the somatosensory cortex "feels" the left side of the body. This happens because nerve fibers from each side of the body cross on their way to the thalamus.
3. The cortex contains maps, or **topographical representations,** of each sense. This means that any two points that are next to each other in the stimulus are represented next to each other in the brain. There are multiple maps of each sense. The area that receives the input directly from the thalamus is called the **primary cortex** for that sense.
4. The density of nerve fibers at any particular part of a sense organ determines the extent of its representation in the cortex. For example, the finger tips, which have a higher density of receptors for touch than the skin on the back does, have a larger area of cortex representing them than does the skin on the back.
5. Each region of primary sensory cortex is divided into columns of cells that have similar properties. For example, some columns of cells in the visual cortex respond most to diagonal lines.
6. For each of the senses, regions of cortex other than the primary areas do additional processing of sensory information. Called **association cortex,** some of these areas contain representations of more than one sense.

In short, sensory systems convert some form of energy into neural activity. Often the energy is first modified by accessory structures; then a sensory receptor converts the energy to neural activity. The pattern of neural activity encodes physical properties of the energy. The codes are modified as the information is transferred to the brain and processed further. In the rest of this chapter we describe these processes in specific sensory systems.

Hearing

When Neil Armstrong stepped onto the moon in 1969, he proclaimed, "That's one small step for a man, one giant leap for mankind." Many people heard him because the words were transmitted back to earth by radio. But if Armstrong had taken off his space helmet, thrown it high over his head, and shouted, "Whoo-ee! I can moonwalk!" not even an astronaut three feet away could have heard him. Why? Because he would have been speaking into airless, empty space. **Sound** is a repetitive fluctuation in the pressure of a medium like air, and it cannot exist in a place like the moon, which has almost no atmosphere.

Sound

The fluctuations in pressure that constitute sound are produced by the vibrations of an object. Each time the object moves outward, it increases the pressure in the medium around it. As the object moves back, the pressure drops. In speech, for example, the vibrating object is the vocal cord, and the medium is air. When you speak, your vocal cords vibrate, producing fluctuations in air pressure that spread as waves. A *wave* is a repetitive variation in pressure that spreads out in three dimensions. The wave can move great distances, but the air itself barely moves. Imagine a jam-packed line of people waiting for a movie. If someone at the rear of the line violently shoves the next person, a wave of people jostling against people may spread all the way to the front of the line, but the person who shoved first is still no closer to getting into the theater.

The Physical Characteristics of Sound   Sound is represented graphically by waveforms like those in Figure 5.2. A waveform represents in two dimensions the wave that moves through the air in three dimensions.

Three characteristics of the waveform are important in understanding sounds. First, the difference in air pressure from the baseline to the peak of the wave is the **amplitude** of the sound, or its intensity. Second, the distance from one peak to the next is the **wavelength.** Third, **frequency** is the number of complete waves, or cycles, that pass by a given point in space every second. Frequency is described in a unit called *hertz,* abbreviated Hz (for Heinrich Hertz, a nineteenth-century physicist). One cycle per second is 1 hertz. Because the speed of sound is constant in a given medium, wavelength and frequency are related: the longer the wavelength, the lower the frequency. Likewise, high-frequency sound is short-wavelength sound.

Most sounds are mixtures of many frequencies and amplitudes. In contrast, a *pure tone* is made up of only one frequency and can be represented by what is known as a *sine wave.* The waveforms in Figure 5.2 are sine waves; each has just one frequency. A complex sound can be analyzed into its component, simple sine waves by a mathematical process called *Fourier analysis.* This technique can be used to eliminate noises that are regular, like engine noises: after the waveforms are analyzed, a sound synthesizer produces the *opposite* waveforms. The opposing waves cancel each other out, and the amazing result is silence.

Psychological Dimensions of Sound   The amplitude and frequency of sound waves determine the sounds that you hear. These *physical* characteristics

Figure 5.2
Sound Waves and Waveforms
The molecules of air around a sound source are unevenly distributed. Regions of greater compression of air molecules alternate with regions of lesser compression because of the to-and-fro vibrations of the object generating the sound. These variations in compression can be represented as a *waveform.* The point where the air is compressed the most is the peak of the graph. The lowest point, or trough, is where the air pressure is lowest.

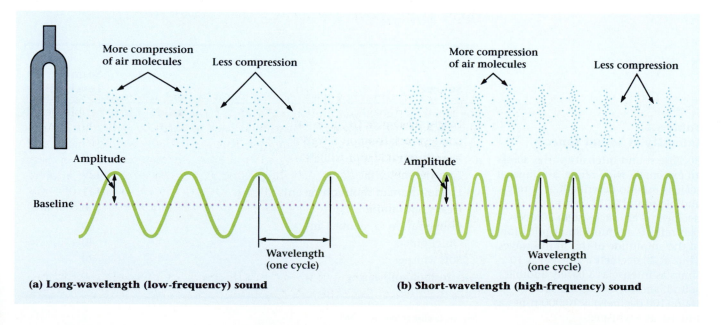

(a) Long-wavelength (low-frequency) sound

(b) Short-wavelength (high-frequency) sound

A musical synthesizer can produce the sounds of different instruments—say, a piano and a trumpet—by combining sine waves in various ways. The auditory system takes the opposite approach: it can analyze the mixture that makes up a sound into its component sine waves.

of the waves produce the *psychological* dimensions of sound known as loudness, pitch, and timbre.

Loudness is determined by the amplitude of the sound wave; waves with greater amplitude produce sensations of louder sounds. Loudness is described in units called *decibels,* abbreviated Db. By definition, 0 decibels is the minimal detectable sound for normal hearing. Table 5.1 gives examples of the loudness of some common sounds.

Pitch—how high or low a tone sounds—depends on the frequency of sound waves. High-frequency waves are sensed as sounds of high pitch. The highest note on a piano has a frequency of about 4,000 hertz; the lowest note has a frequency of about 50 hertz. Humans can hear sounds from about 20 hertz to about 20,000 hertz. Almost everyone experiences pitch as a relative dimension—that is, they can tell whether one note is higher or lower than another—but almost no one can identify specific frequencies, for example, that a 262 Hz tone is middle C. Even with training, adults are unable to learn this "perfect pitch" skill, but if taught before the age of six, children can learn that specific frequencies are particular notes (Takeuchi & Hulse, 1993).

Timbre is the quality of sound; it is determined by complex wave patterns that are added onto the lowest, or *fundamental,* frequency of a sound. The extra waves allow you to tell, for example, the difference between a note played on a flute and a note played on a clarinet. Figure 5.3(a) shows that a musical note played on an instrument has one fundamental frequency as well as other added waves; the other waves give the tone its timbre. Because the added waves are multiples of the fundamental frequency of the note, the sound is musical. In contrast, a *noise* is a sum of unrelated waveforms, as Figure 5.3(b) illustrates.

The Ear

Sharks can "hear" underwater sounds through simple nerve endings in their skin. Their "hearing" is good enough to get by in the sea, but hardly adequate to appreciate Mozart or U2. By contrast, humans have very sophisticated ears that detect sounds with great sensitivity and precision. The ear converts sound into neural activity through a fascinating series of accessory structures and transduction mechanisms.

Table 5.1
Intensity of Sound Sources

Because sound intensity varies across an extremely wide range, an unusual scale is used to describe it. A barely audible sound is, by definition, 0 decibels; every increase of 20 decibels reflects a tenfold multiplication of the amplitude of the sound waves. Thus at 20 decibels a whisper is 10 times as intense as a barely audible sound, and the noise of a subway train (100 decibels) is 10,000 times as intense as a whisper.

Source	Sound Level (dB)
Spacecraft launch (from 45 m)	180
Loudest rock band on record	160
Pain threshold (approximate)	140
Large jet motor (at 22 m)	120
Loudest human shout on record	111
Heavy auto traffic	100
Conversation (at about 1 m)	60
Quiet office	40
Soft whisper	20
Threshold of hearing	0

Source: Levine & Shefner, 1981.

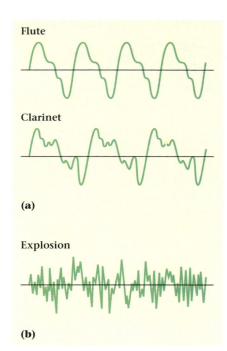

Source: Miller, 1926.

Figure 5.3
Timbre
Because most sounds are not pure tones, they have complex waveforms. Even when a single note is played, musical instruments produce complex waveforms. Part (a) shows the waveforms produced by a flute and a clarinet playing one note. Because the components of the complex waves have a systematic relationship to the fundamental frequency, the sound is musical. Part (b) shows the waveform produced by an explosion. Explosions are normally considered noise rather than music, because their waveforms are very irregular.

Auditory Accessory Structures Sound waves are collected in the outer ear, beginning with the **pinna,** the crumpled, oddly shaped part of the ear on the side of the head. The pinna funnels sound down through the ear canal (see Figure 5.4). At the end of the ear canal, the sound waves reach the middle ear, where they strike a tightly stretched membrane known as the eardrum, or **tympanic membrane.** The sound waves set up vibrations in the tympanic membrane.

Next the vibrations of the tympanic membrane are passed on by a chain of three tiny bones named for their shapes: the *malleus,* or *hammer;* the *incus,* or *anvil;* and the *stapes,* or *stirrup* (see Figure 5.4). The bones focus the vibrations of the tympanic membrane onto a smaller membrane, the *oval window,* thereby amplifying the changes in pressure produced by the original sound waves.

Auditory Transduction When sound vibrations pass through the oval window, they enter the inner ear, or **cochlea,** the structure in which transduction occurs. The cochlea is wrapped into a coiled spiral. (*Cochlea* is derived from the Greek word for "snail.") If you unwrapped it, you would see that a fluid-filled duct runs down its length. The **basilar membrane** forms the floor of this long duct (see Figure 5.5). Whenever a sound wave passes through the fluid in the duct, it moves the basilar membrane, and this movement deforms *hair cells* of the *organ of Corti,* a group of cells that rests on the membrane. These hair cells make connections with fibers from the **auditory nerve,** a bundle of axons that go into the brain. Mechanical deformation of the hair cells stimulates the auditory nerve, changing the electrical activity of some of its neurons and thus sending a coded signal to the brain about the amplitude and frequency of sound waves, which you sense as loudness and pitch.

Deafness Problems with the tiny bones of the middle ear are one cause of deafness. Sometimes the bones of the middle ear fuse together, preventing accurate reproduction of vibrations. This is called *conduction deafness.* It may be treated by breaking the bones apart or replacing the natural bones with plastic ones; a hearing aid that amplifies the input can also be helpful.

Figure 5.4
Structures of the Ear
The outer ear (pinna and ear canal) channel sound waves into the middle ear, where the vibrations of the tympanic membrane are amplified by the delicate bones that stimulate the cochlea. In the cochlea the vibrations are transduced into changes in neural activity, which are sent along the auditory nerve to the brain.

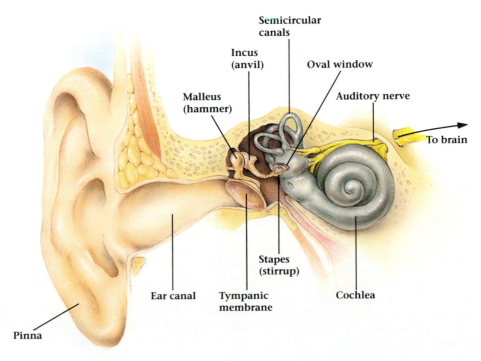

Figure 5.5
The Cochlea
The vibrations of the stirrup set up vibrations in the fluid inside the cochlea. The coils of the cochlea are unfolded in this illustration to show the path of the fluid waves along the basilar membrane. Movements of the basilar membrane stimulate the hair cells of the organ of Corti, which transduce the vibrations into changes in neural firing patterns.

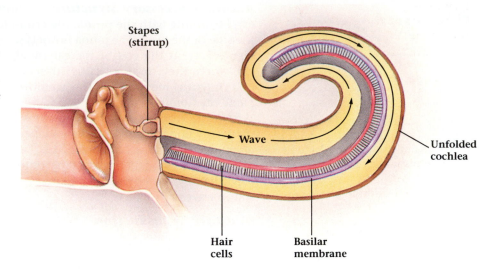

If the auditory nerve or the hair cells are damaged, *nerve deafness* results. Hair cells are destroyed by loud noises (including intense rock music); they can be regenerated in chickens (who seldom listen to loud rock music), but most researchers believe that mammals are not capable of hair cell regeneration (Corwin, 1992). Still, recent results showing regeneration of inner ear hair cells that, as described later, contribute to the sense of balance, have fueled optimism about finding a way to stimulate regeneration of human auditory hair cells (Warchol et al., 1993). Nerve deafness cannot be improved by conventional hearing aids, but an artificial cochlea has been developed that stimulates the auditory nerve (Mulder et al., 1992). The sensations derived from these devices are still crude, but the possibilities are exciting.

Coding Intensity and Frequency

People can hear an incredibly wide range of sound intensities. The faintest sound that can be heard moves the hair cells less than the diameter of a single hydrogen atom (Hudspeth, 1983). Sounds more than a trillion times more intense can also be heard. Between these extremes, the auditory system codes intensity in a straightforward way: the more intense the sound, the more rapid the firing of a given neuron.

Recall that the pitch of a sound depends on its frequency. How do people tell the difference between frequencies? Differences in frequency appear to be coded in two ways, which are described by the place theory and the frequency-matching theory.

Place Theory   Georg von Bekesy did some pioneering experiments in the 1930s and 40s to figure out how frequency is coded (von Bekesy, 1960). He opened the skulls of human cadavers, exposed the cochlea, and made a hole in the cochlear wall to observe the basilar membrane. He then presented his "volunteers" with sounds of different frequencies by mechanically vibrating a rubber membrane that was installed in place of the oval window. With sensitive optical instruments, von Bekesy observed ripples of waves moving down the basilar membrane. He noticed something very important. The outline of the waves, called the *envelope,* grows and reaches a peak; then it quickly tapers off to smaller and smaller fluctuations, much like an ocean wave that crests and then dissolves.

Figure 5.6 illustrates this wave. The critical feature of this wave is that the place on the basilar membrane where the envelope peaks depends on the fre-

Figure 5.6
Movements of the Basilar Membrane
As vibrations of the cochlear fluid spread along the basilar membrane, the membrane is deflected and then recovers. The point at which the bending of the basilar membrane reaches a maximum is different for each sound frequency. This graph shows the deflections that occur in response to sounds of three frequencies. The arrows indicate the location of greatest deflection in each case; according to place theory, these are the locations at which the hair cells receive the greatest stimulation.

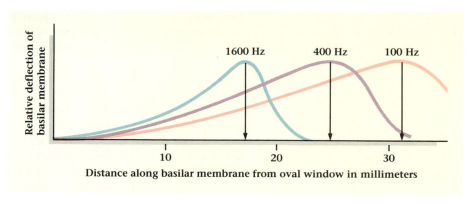

Source: From G.L. Rasmussen and W.F. Windle, *Neural Mechanisms of the Auditory and Vestibular Systems*, 1960. Courtesy Charles C. Thomas, Publisher, Springfield, Illinois.

quency of the sound. High-frequency sounds produce a wave that peaks soon after it starts down the basilar membrane. Lower-frequency sounds produce a wave that peaks farther along the basilar membrane, farther from the stirrup.

How does the location of the peak affect the coding of frequency? According to **place theory**, also called *traveling wave theory,* the greatest response by hair cells occurs at the peak of the wave. Because the location of the peak varies with the frequency of the sound, it follows that hair cells at a particular place on the basilar membrane respond most to a particular frequency of sound, called a *characteristic frequency.* Thus, place theory describes a spatial code for frequency. One important result of this arrangement is that exposure to a very loud noise of a particular frequency for a long time destroys hair cells at one spot on the basilar membrane, as well as the ability to hear sounds of that frequency (see Figure 5.7).

Frequency-Matching Theory   Though place theory accounts for a great deal of data on hearing, it cannot explain the coding of very low frequencies, such as that of a deep bass note, because there are no auditory nerve fibers that have very low characteristic frequencies. Since humans can hear frequencies as low as 20 hertz, however, they must be coded somehow. How?

Frequency matching seems to be the answer. **Frequency matching** refers to the fact that the firing *rate* of a neuron in the auditory nerve matches the

Figure 5.7
Effects of Loud Sounds
High-intensity sounds can actually rip off the hair cells of the organ of Corti on the basilar membrane. Generally, any sound that is loud enough to produce a ringing sensation in the ears causes some damage. Small amounts of damage can accumulate over many years to produce a significant hearing loss. These scanning electron micrographs illustrate the effect of intense sound on the inner ear. Part (a): Cochlea of a normal guinea pig, showing three rows of outer hair cells and one row of inner hair cells. Part (b): Cochlea of a guinea pig after twenty-four-hour exposure to a sound level approached by loud rock music (2000 hertz at 120 decibels).

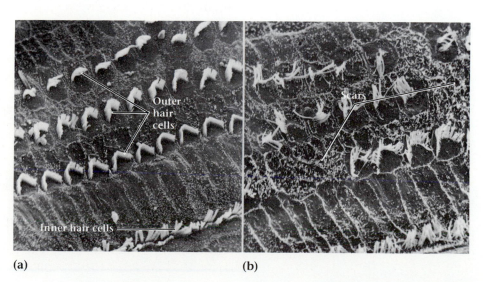

(a)   (b)

frequency of a sound wave. Frequency matching provides a temporal code for frequency. For example, one neuron might fire at every peak of a wave. Thus, a sound of 20 hertz could be coded by a neuron that fires twenty times per second.

In this simple form, however, frequency matching would apply to few sounds, because no neuron can fire faster than 1,000 times per second. A slightly more complicated process can account for the coding of moderate frequencies above 1,000 hertz. These frequencies can be matched, not by a single neuron, but by the summed activity of a group of neurons firing in concert. Some neurons in the group might fire, for example, at every other wave peak, others at every fifth peak, and so on, producing a *volley* of firing at a combined frequency higher than any could manage alone. Indeed, the frequency-matching theory is sometimes called the **volley theory** of frequency coding.

In summary, the nervous system apparently uses more than one way to code the range of audible frequencies. The lowest sound frequencies are coded by matching the frequency with the firing rate of auditory nerve fibers (frequency matching). Low to moderate frequencies are coded by both frequency matching and the place on the basilar membrane where the wave peaks. High frequencies are coded exclusively by the place where the wave peaks.

Mixtures of frequencies can produce sounds of ambiguous pitch. In fact, the same sequence of notes can sound like an ascending scale to one person and a descending scale to another. Recent work has shown that cultural factors are partly responsible for which way the pitch is sensed; American and British people, for example, hear the ambiguous scales progressing in opposite directions (Deutsch, 1992).

In Review: Hearing

Aspect of Sensory System	Elements	Key Characteristics
Energy	Sound—pressure fluctuations of air produced by vibrations	Amplitude, frequency, and complexity of the sound waves determine the loudness, pitch, and timbre of sounds.
Accessory structures	Ear—pinna, tympanic membrane, malleus, incus, stapes, oval window, basilar membrane	Changes in pressure produced by the original wave are amplified.
Transduction mechanism	Hair cells of the organ of Corti	Frequencies are coded by the location of the hair cells receiving the greatest stimulation (place theory) and by the firing rate of neurons (frequency matching).
Pathways and representations	Auditory nerve to thalamus to primary auditory cortex	Neighboring cells in auditory cortex have similar preferred frequencies, thus providing a map of sound frequencies.

Auditory Pathways and Representations

Before sounds can be heard, the information coded in the activity of auditory nerve fibers must be conveyed to the brain and processed further. (For a review of how changes in air pressure become signals in the brain that are perceived as sounds, see "In Review: Hearing.") The auditory nerve, the bundle of axons that conveys this information, makes one or two synapses and crosses the midline before reaching the thalamus. From there, the information is relayed to the **primary auditory cortex,** an area in the temporal lobe of the brain.

Cells in the auditory cortex have preferred frequencies, just as neurons in the auditory nerve do. Neighboring cells in the cortex have similar preferred frequencies; thus, the auditory cortex provides a map of sound frequencies. However, although each neuron in the auditory nerve has a "favorite" or characteristic frequency, each responds to some extent to a range of frequencies. Therefore, the cortex must examine the pattern of activity of a number of neurons in order to determine the frequency of a sound.

Vision

Soaring eagles have the incredible ability to see a mouse move in the grass from a mile away. Cats have special "reflectors" at the back of their eyes that help them to see even in very dim light. Nature has provided each species with a visual system uniquely adapted to its way of life. The human visual system is also adapted to do many things well: it combines great sensitivity and great sharpness, enabling people to see objects near and far, during the day and night. Our night vision is not as acute as that of some animals, but our color vision is excellent. This is not a bad tradeoff, since being able to experience a sunset's splendor seems worth an occasional stumble in the dark. In this section, we consider the human visual sense and how it responds to light.

Light

Light is a form of energy known as *electromagnetic radiation.* Most electromagnetic radiation—including x-rays, radio waves, television signals, and radar—passes through space undetected by the human eye. As Figure 5.8 shows, **visible light** is electromagnetic radiation that has a wavelength from just under 400 nanometers to about 750 nanometers. (A *nanometer* is one-billionth of a meter.) Unlike sound, light does not need a medium to pass through; light waves are like particles that pass through space, but they vibrate with a certain wavelength. Thus light has some properties of waves and some properties of particles, and it is correct to refer to light as either *light waves* or *light rays.*

Sensations of light depend on two physical dimensions of light waves: intensity and wavelength. **Light intensity** refers to how much energy the light contains; it determines the brightness of light. What color you sense depends mainly on **light wavelength.** At a given intensity, different wavelengths produce sensations of different colors. For instance, 440-nanometer light appears violet-blue, and 600-nanometer light appears orangish-red.

Focusing Light

Light energy is transduced into neural activity in the eye. First, the accessory structures of the eye focus light rays into a sharp image. The light rays enter the eye by passing through the curved, transparent protective layer called the **cornea** (see Figure 5.9). Then the light passes through the **pupil,** the opening just behind the cornea. The **iris,** which gives the eye its color, adjusts the amount of light allowed into the eye by constricting to reduce the size of the

Figure 5.8
The Spectrum of Electromagnetic Energy
The eye is sensitive to a very limited range of wavelengths. Electronic instruments have detectors for other ranges of wavelengths and, in effect, "see" their own kind of light, just as the eye sees visible light.

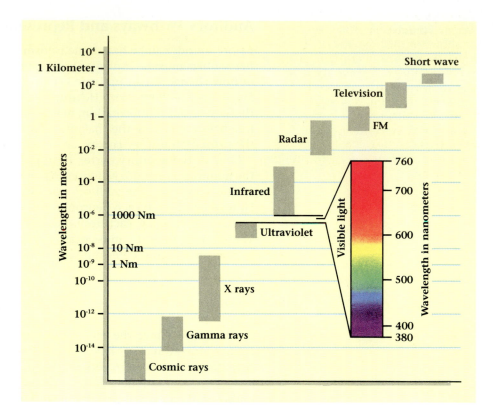

pupil or relaxing to enlarge it. Directly behind the pupil is the **lens.** The cornea and the lens of the eye are both curved so that, like the lens of a camera, they bend light rays. The light rays are focused into an image on the surface at the back of the eye; this surface is called the **retina**. This arrangement of lens and retina is not the only way to create an image; ten distinct types of eyes are found in nature (Land & Fernald, 1992), from simple eyes with a pinhole opening instead of a lens to the compound eyes of flies, which have hundreds of separate eyes.

Figure 5.10 illustrates how the lens of the human eye bends light rays from a point source so that they meet at a point on the retina. If the rays meet either in front of the retina or behind it, the image will be out of focus. The muscles that hold the lens adjust its shape so that either near or far objects can be focused on the retina. If you peer at something very close, for example, your muscles must tighten the lens, making it more curved, to obtain a focused image. This ability to change the shape of the lens to bend light rays is called **accommodation**. Over time, the lens loses some of its flexibility, and accommodation becomes more difficult. This is why most older people need glasses for reading or close work.

Converting Light into Images

Visual transduction, the conversion of light energy into neural activity, takes place in the retina, which contains neurons that actually constitute an extension of the brain. The word *retina* is Latin for "net"; the retina is an intricate network of cells. Before transduction can occur, light rays must actually pass *through* several layers in this network to reach photoreceptor cells. First we will describe how the photoreceptors work; then we will explain how other cells in the retina operate.

Photoreceptors The **photoreceptors** are specialized cells in the retina that convert light energy into neural activity. They contain **photopigments**, which

Figure 5.9
Major Structures of the Eye
As shown in this top view of the eye, light rays are bent by the combined actions of the cornea and the lens and focused on the retina at the back of the eye. Transduction of light energy into neural activity takes place in the retina. Nerve fibers known collectively as the optic nerve pass out the back of the eye and continue to the brain.

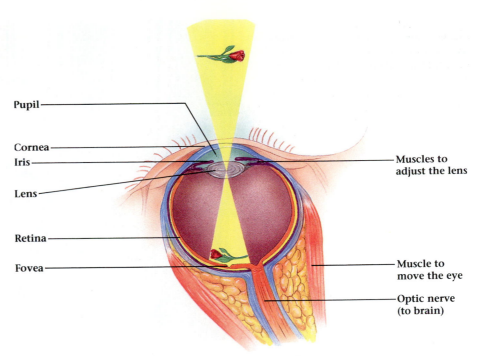

Pupil

Cornea
Iris

Lens

Retina

Fovea

Muscles to
adjust the lens

Muscle to
move the eye

Optic nerve
(to brain)

are chemicals that respond to light. When light strikes a photopigment, the photopigment breaks apart, changing the membrane potential of the photoreceptor cell. This change in membrane potential provides a signal that can be transferred to the brain.

After a photopigment has broken down in response to light, new photopigment molecules are put together. This takes a little time, however. So when you first come from bright sunshine into, say, a dark theater, you cannot see because your photoreceptors do not yet have enough photopigment. In the dark, your photoreceptors synthesize more photopigments, and your ability to see gradually increases. This increasing ability to see in the dark as time passes is called **dark adaptation.** Overall, your sensitivity to light increases some ten thousand fold after half an hour or so in a darkened room. A fully dark-adapted photoreceptor is incredibly sensitive to light; it can even respond to a single photon, the smallest division of light energy. Vision is not accurate at this low level of light, however, because photoreceptors are occasionally activated by

Figure 5.10
The Lens and the Retinal Image
Objects in the world can be thought of as consisting of many point sources of light. Light rays from the top of an object are focused at the bottom of the image on the retinal surface. Similarly, rays from the right side of the object end up on the left side of the retinal image. The brain rearranges this upside down and reversed image so that people see the object as it is. For the image to be in focus, rays from each point of the object must converge at a point on the retinal surface.

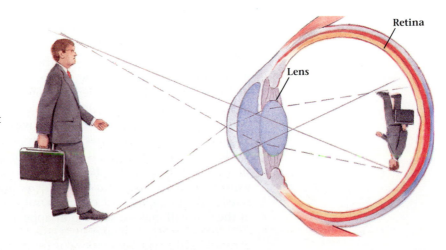

Retina

Lens

Cone cells in the retina allow people to see color, but they do not operate well in low-light conditions. This is why it is so difficult to see colors in dim light.

the warmth of the body (Schnapf & Baylor, 1987). This thermal activation of photoreceptors is sensed as light, so you sense some light even in complete darkness.

The retina has two basic types of photoreceptors: **rods** and **cones.** As their names imply, these cells differ in shape. They also differ in composition, response to light, and location in the eye. For one thing, the photopigment in rods includes a substance called *rhodopsin,* whereas the photopigment in cones includes one of three varieties of *iodopsin.* The multiple forms of iodopsin provide the basis for color vision, which we explain later. Because rods have only one pigment, they are unable to discriminate colors. However, the rods are more sensitive to light than cones. Thus, rods allow you to see even when there is very little light, as on a moonlit night. But if you have trouble trying to match a pair of socks in a darkened bedroom, you now know the reason: because the light is dim, you are seeing with your rods, which cannot discriminate colors. At higher light intensities, the cones, with their ability to detect colors, become most active.

The rods and cones also differ in their distribution in the eye. Cones are concentrated in the center of the retina, a region called the **fovea.** This concentration makes the ability to see details, or **acuity,** greatest in the fovea. Indeed, the fovea is precisely where the eye focuses the light coming from objects you look at. Variations in the density of cones in the fovea probably account for individual differences in visual acuity (Curcio et al., 1987). Interestingly, animals who live where the topography is very flat (cheetahs on the plains and sea birds near the ocean, for example) have, not a circular fovea, but a horizontal streak of dense photoreceptors corresponding to the unbroken horizon (Land & Fernald, 1992).

There are no rods in the human fovea. With increasing distance from the fovea, the number of cones gradually decreases and the proportion of rods gradually increases. Thus, if you are trying to detect a small amount of light, such as that from a faint star, it is better to look slightly away from where you expect to see it. This focuses the weak light on the very light-sensitive rods outside the fovea. Because cones do not work well in low light, looking directly at the star will make it seem to disappear.

Visual experience can modify the retina. For example, large amounts of reading may lead to nearsightedness (Young et al., 1969). Why? In studies with chickens, the birds were outfitted with special goggles that presented part of their retinas with an unpatterned image; that part of the eyeball became elongated, or myopic (Wallman et al., 1987). The researchers suggested that when humans read, the areas around the fovea are constantly presented with a relatively unpatterned image, causing the eyeball to elongate. (We urge you to continue reading this chapter, but perhaps rest your eyes now and then.)

Interactions in the Retina   If the eye simply transferred to the brain the stimuli that are focused on the retina, the images would appear like a somewhat blurred TV image. Instead, the eye actually sharpens visual images. How? The key lies in the interactions among the cells of the retina, which are illustrated in Figure 5.11. The most direct connections from the photoreceptor cells to the brain go first to **bipolar cells** and then to *ganglion cells;* the axons of ganglion cells form the optic nerve, which extends out of the eye and into the brain. However, interactions with other cells modify this direct path. Two types of interactions are especially important.

First, most bipolar cells receive input from many photoreceptors, as illustrated in Figure 5.12(a); this arrangement is called convergence. **Convergence** increases the sensitivity of each bipolar cell, because light striking any of the photoreceptors to which the cell is connected will stimulate it. However, convergence reduces acuity, because information about exactly *which* photoreceptor was stimulated is lost. Thus, it is not surprising that there is little convergence among the cones of the fovea, an area that is good at detecting fine details but is not very sensitive to light.

Figure 5.11
Cells in the Retina
Light rays actually pass through several layers of cells before striking the photoreceptive rods and cones. Signals generated by the rods and cones then go back toward the surface of the retina, passing through the bipolar cells and on to the ganglion cells. Axons from the ganglion cells form the optic nerve, which sends signals to the brain. Interconnections among the interneurons, the bipolar cells, and the ganglion cells allow the eye to begin analyzing visual information even before that information leaves the retina. In effect, the cells of the retina are outposts of the brain.

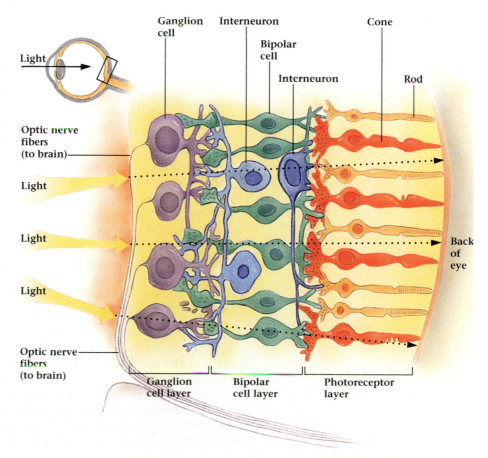

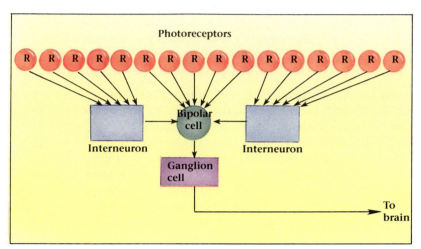

(a) Convergence

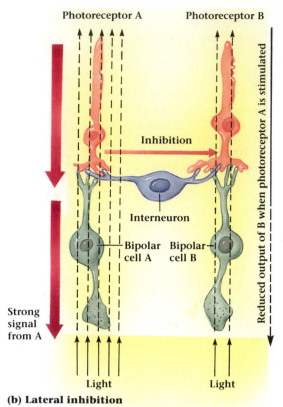

(b) Lateral inhibition

Figure 5.12
Convergence and Lateral Inhibition Among Retinal Cells
Input from many photoreceptors converges onto bipolar cells in the retina. Many receptors feed directly into a given bipolar cell, as part (a) shows, and many receptors have indirect input to bipolar cells by influencing interneurons. As part (b) illustrates, this influence is often inhibitory. The bipolar cell of photoreceptor A makes a lateral connection to an interneuron that synapses on the bipolar cell of photoreceptor B. When A is stimulated, it excites the interneuron, which inhibits the bipolar cell of B. Thus, light shining on photoreceptor A actually inhibits the signal that photoreceptor B sends to the brain. Light striking photoreceptor A both sends a signal to the brain that there is light at point A and makes it appear as if there is less light at point B than there really is.

Second, photoreceptor cells make connections to other types of cells in the retina, **interneurons**, which make lateral (sideways) connections between bipolar cells. Through these lateral connections, the response to light by one cell can excite or, more commonly, inhibit the response of a neighboring cell. Figure 5.12(b) illustrates **lateral inhibition**.

Lateral interactions have the important result of enhancing the sensation of contrast. Why? Most of the time, the amounts of light reaching two photoreceptors will differ. As Figure 5.12(b) illustrates, through its lateral connections the photoreceptor receiving more light inhibits the output to the brain from the photoreceptor receiving less light, making it seem as if there is less light at that cell than there really is. Therefore, the brain actually receives a *comparison* of the light hitting two neighboring points, and whatever difference exists between the light reaching the two photoreceptors is exaggerated. This exaggeration is important, because specific features of objects can create differences in amounts of incoming light. For example, the visual image of the edge of an object contains a transition from a lighter region to a darker region. Lateral inhibition in the retina enhances this difference, creating contrast that sharpens the edge and makes it more noticeable.

Ganglion Cells and Their Receptive Fields Photoreceptors, bipolar cells, and interneurons communicate by releasing neurotransmitters. But, as discussed in Chapter 4, neurotransmitters cause only small, graded changes in the membrane potential of the next cell, which cannot travel the distance from eye to brain. **Ganglion cells** are the cells in the retina that generate action potentials capable of traveling that distance. Ganglion cells are stimulated by bipolar cells and modulated by interneurons, and their axons extend out of the retina to the brain.

Figure 5.13
Center-Surround Receptive Fields of Ganglion Cells
Light falling on photoreceptors in the center of the receptive field of a center-on ganglion cell increases its firing activity, whereas light falling on photoreceptors in the area surrounding the center (the surround) decreases that activity. As part (a) shows, the arrangement is just the opposite in a center-off ganglion cell, where light falling on photoreceptors in the center of the receptive field decreases the activity of the cell. Part (b) shows that these center-surround receptive fields allow ganglion cells to act as edge detectors. An edge is a region of light next to a region of relative darkness. If an edge is outside the receptive field of a center-on ganglion cell, there will be a uniform amount of light on both the excitatory center and the inhibitory surround, thus creating a moderate amount of activity. If, as shown in the middle drawing, the dark side of an edge covers a large portion of the inhibitory surround but leaves light on the excitatory center, the output of the cell will be high, signaling an edge in its receptive field. When, as shown at right, the dark area covers both the center and the surround of the ganglion cell, its activity will be lower, because neither segment of the cell's receptive field is receiving much stimulation.

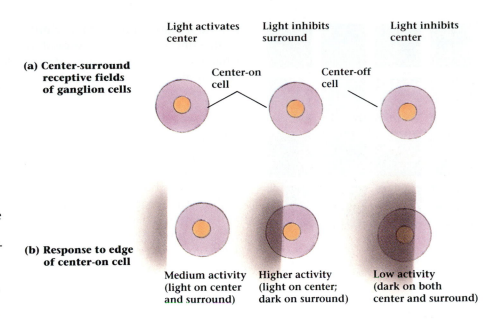

(a) **Center-surround receptive fields of ganglion cells**

Light activates center — Center-on cell

Light inhibits surround — Center-off cell

Light inhibits center

(b) **Response to edge of center-on cell**

Medium activity (light on center and surround)

Higher activity (light on center; dark on surround)

Low activity (dark on both center and surround)

What message do ganglion cells send on to the brain? The answer depends on the **receptive field** of each cell, which is that part of the retina *and* the corresponding part of the visual world to which a cell responds. Most ganglion cells have a *center-surround receptive field*. That is, most ganglion cells compare the amount of light stimulating the photoreceptors in the center of their receptive fields with the amount of light stimulating the photoreceptors in the area surrounding the center. This comparison results from the lateral interactions in the retina that enhance contrast. As Figure 5.13 illustrates, some center-surround ganglion cells (*center-on cells*) are activated by light in the center of their receptive field; light in the regions surrounding the center inhibits their activity. Other center-surround ganglion cells (*center-off cells*) work in just the opposite way. They are inhibited by light in the center and activated by light in the surrounding area.

The result of the center-surround receptive fields, as Figure 5.13(b) illustrates, is to optimize the detection of variations, such as edges and small spots of light or dark. In fact, as Figure 5.14 demonstrates, people see a sharper contrast between darker and lighter areas than actually exists. By enhancing the sensation of edges and other important features, the retina gives your brain an "improved" version of the visual world.

Seeing Color

Like beauty, color is in the eye of the beholder. Many animals see only shades of gray even when they look at a rainbow, but for humans color is a highly salient feature of vision. An advertising agent might tell you about the impact of color on buying preferences, a poet might tell you about the emotional power of color, but we will tell you about how you see colors—a process that is itself a thing of elegance and beauty.

Wavelengths and Color Sensations We noted earlier that, at a given intensity, each wavelength of light is sensed as a certain color (look again at Figure 5.8). However, the eye is seldom if ever presented with pure light of a single wavelength. Sunlight, for example, is a mixture of all wavelengths of light. When sunlight passes through a droplet of water, the different wavelengths of light are bent to different degrees, separating into a colorful rainbow. The spectrum of color found in the rainbow illustrates an important con-

Figure 5.14
Visual Effects of Lateral Inhibition
One effect of lateral inhibition among retinal cells is the appearance of dark spots at the intersections of the black boxes in this figure, called the Hermann grid. When you look directly at an intersection, the dark spot disappears, because ganglion cells in the fovea have smaller receptive fields than those elsewhere in the retina. The receptive fields of two ganglion cells projected onto the pattern show how, at the intersection, the ganglion cell on the left has more whiteness shining on the inhibitory surround. Thus, the output of the cell is reduced compared to that of the one on the right, and the spot on the left appears darker.

Figure 5.15
The Color Circle
Ordering the colors according to their psychological similarities results in a circle that reveals some interesting things about color vision. Among other things, the color circle allows one to predict the result of additive mixing of two colored lights. The resulting color will be on a line between the two starting colors, the exact location on the line depending on the relative proportions of the two colors. For example, mixing equal amounts of pure green and pure red light will produce yellow, the color that lies at the midpoint of the line connecting red and green.

cept: the sensation produced by a mixture of different wavelengths of light is not the same as the sensations produced by separate wavelengths.

Characteristics of the mixture of wavelengths striking the eyes determine the color sensation. There are three separate aspects of this sensation: hue, saturation, and brightness. These are *psychological* dimensions that correspond roughly to the physical properties of light. **Hue** is the essential "color," determined by the dominant wavelength in the mixture of the light. Black, white, and gray are not considered hues because no wavelength predominates in them. **Saturation** is related to the purity of a color. A color is more saturated and more pure if just one wavelength is relatively more intense—contains more energy—than other wavelengths. If many wavelengths are added to a pure hue, the color is said to be *desaturated*. For example, pastels are colors that have been desaturated by the addition of whiteness. **Brightness** refers to the overall intensity of all of the wavelengths making up light.

The color circle shown in Figure 5.15 arranges hues according to their perceived similarities. If lights of two different wavelengths but equal intensity are mixed, the color you sense is at the midpoint of a line drawn between the two original colors on the color circle. This process is known as *additive color mixing,* because the effects of the wavelengths from each light are added together. If you keep adding different colored lights, you eventually get white (the combination of all wavelengths). You are probably familiar with a very different form of color mixing called *subtractive color mixing,* which occurs when paints are combined. Like other physical objects, paints reflect certain

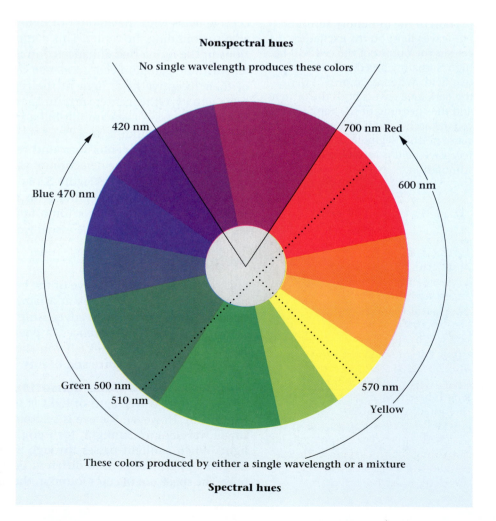

wavelengths and absorb all others. For example, grass is green because it absorbs all wavelengths *except* wavelengths that are preceived as green. White objects are white because they reflect all wavelengths. Light reflected from paints or other colored objects is seldom a pure wavelength, so predicting the color resulting from mixing paint is not as straightforward as combining pure wavelengths of light. But if you keep combining different colored paints, all of the wavelengths will eventually be subtracted, resulting in black. (The discussion to follow refers to additive color mixing, the mixing of light.)

By mixing lights of just a few wavelengths, we can produce different color sensations. How many wavelengths are needed to create any possible color? Figure 5.16 illustrates an experiment that addresses this question, using a white piece of paper, which reflects all wavelengths and therefore appears to be the color of the light shined upon it. The answer to the question of how many lights are needed to create all colors helped lead scientists to an important theory of how people sense color.

The Trichromatic Theory of Color Vision   Early in the nineteenth century, Thomas Young and, later, Hermann von Helmholtz established that any color could be matched by mixing pure lights of just three wavelengths. For example, by mixing blue light (about 440 nanometers), green light (about 510 nanometers), and red light (about 600 nanometers) in different ratios, *any* other color can be produced. Young and Helmholtz interpreted this evidence to mean that there must be three types of visual elements, each of which is most sensitive to different wavelengths, and that information from these three elements combines to produce the sensation of color. This theory of color vision is called the *Young-Helmholtz theory,* or the **trichromatic theory.**

Support for the trichromatic theory has come from recordings of the responses of individual photoreceptors to particular wavelengths of light and from electrical recordings from human cones (Schnapf, Kraft & Baylor, 1987). This research reveals that there are three types of cones. Although each type responds to a broad range of wavelengths, each is most sensitive to particular wavelengths. *Short-wavelength cones* respond most to light of about 440 nanometers (a shade of blue). *Medium-wavelength cones* are most sensitive to light of about 530 nanometers (a shade of green). Finally, *long-wavelength cones* respond best to light of about 560 nanometers (a shade of red).

Figure 5.16
Matching a Color by Mixing Lights of Pure Wavelengths
Experiments like this generated the information that led Young to propose the trichromatic theory of color vision. The subject is presented with a target color on the left side of the display; the subject's task is to adjust the intensity of different pure-wavelength lights until the resultant mixture looks exactly like the target. A large number of colors can be matched with just two mixing lights, but Young found that *any* color can be matched by mixing *three* pure-wavelength lights.

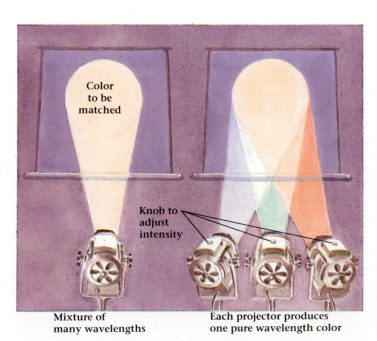

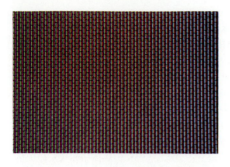

The discovery of three types of cones and the ways in which their activity can combine was put to use in color television. Color television screens have microscopic dots, or elements, that are either red, green, or blue. The television broadcast excites these elements to varying degrees, mixing their colors to produce many other colors. You see these color mixtures rather than patterns of red, green, and blue because the dots are too small and close together to be seen individually.

Note that no single cone, by itself, can signal the color of a light. It is the *ratio* of the activities of the three types of cones that indicates what color will be sensed. Color vision is therefore coded by the pattern of activity of the different cones. For example, a light is sensed as yellow if it has a pure wavelength of 570 nanometers; this light stimulates both medium- and long-wavelength cones, as illustrated by arrow A in Figure 5.17. But yellow is also sensed whenever any mixture of other lights stimulates the same pattern of activity in these two types of cones.

The Opponent-Process Theory of Color Vision

Brilliant as it is, the trichromatic theory in its simplest form cannot explain some aspects of color vision. For example, it cannot account for color afterimages. If you stare at Figure 5.18 for thirty seconds and then look at the blank white space below it, you will see an afterimage. What was yellow in the original image will be blue in the afterimage, what was green before will appear red, and what was black will now appear white.

This type of observation led Ewald Hering to offer an alternative to the trichromatic theory of color vision, called the **opponent-process theory.** It holds that the visual elements sensitive to color are grouped into three pairs and that the members of each pair oppose, or inhibit, each other. The three pairs are a *red-green* element, a *blue-yellow* element, and a *black-white* element. Each element signals one color or the other—red or green, for example—but never both. This explains color afterimages. When one part of an opponent pair is no longer stimulated, the other is activated. Thus, if the original image you looked at were green, the afterimage would be red (see Figure 5.18).

The opponent-process theory also explains the phenomenon of complementary colors. Two colors are **complementary** if gray results when lights of the two colors are mixed together. Actually the neutral color of gray can appear as anything from white to gray to black depending on the intensity of the light. On the color circle (see Figure 5.15), complementary colors are roughly opposite. Red and green are complementary, as are yellow and blue. Notice that

Figure 5.17
Relative Responses of Three Cone Types to Different Wavelengths of Light
Each type of cone responds to a range of wavelengths but responds more to some wavelengths than to others. Because each cone type responds to a range of wavelengths, it is possible to generate the same pattern of output—and hence the same sensation of color—by more than one combination of wavelengths. For example, a pure light of 570 nanometers (A in the figure) stimulates long-wavelength cones at 1.0 relative units and medium-wavelength cones at 0.7 relative units. This ratio of cone activity (1/0.7 = 1.4) yields the sensation of yellow. Any combination of wavelengths at the proper intensity that generates the same ratio of activity in these cone types will produce the sensation of yellow.

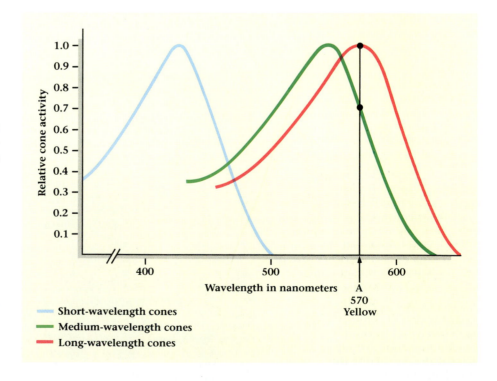

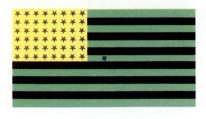

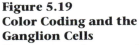

complementary colors are *opponent* colors in Hering's theory. According to opponent-process theory, complementary colors stimulate the same visual element (for example, red-green) in opposite directions, canceling each other out. Thus, the theory helps explain why mixing lights of complementary colors produces gray.

A Synthesis   The trichromatic and opponent-process theories seem quite different, but both are correct to some extent, and together, they can explain most of what is now known about color vision. Electrical recordings made from different types of cells in the retina paved the way for a synthesis of the two theories.

At the level of the photoreceptors, the trichromatic theory is right: as we said, there are three types of cones. However, we also noted that output from many photoreceptors feeds into each ganglion cell, and the output from the ganglion cell goes to the brain. Recall that the receptive fields of most ganglion cells are arranged in center-surround patterns. The center and the surround are color coded, as illustrated in Figure 5.19. The center responds best to one color, and the surround responds best to a different color. This color coding arises because varying proportions of the three cone types feed into the center and the surround of the ganglion cell.

When either the center or the surround of the ganglion cell is stimulated, the other area is inhibited. In other words, the colors to which the center and the surround of a given ganglion cell are most responsive are opponent colors. Recordings from many ganglion cells show that three very common pairs of opponent colors are those predicted by Hering's opponent-process theory: red-green, blue-yellow, and black-white. Stimulating both the center and the surround cancels the effects of either light, producing gray. Black-white cells receive input from all types of cones, so it does not matter what color stimulates them.

In summary, color vision is possible because the three types of cones have different sensitivities to different wavelengths, as the trichromatic theory suggests. The sensation of different colors results from stimulating the three cone types in different ratios. Because there are three types of cones, any color can be produced by mixing three different wavelengths of light. But the story does

Figure 5.18
Afterimages Produced by the Opponent-Process Nature of Color Vision
Stare at the dot in the figure for at least 30 seconds, then fixate on the dot in the white space below it.

Figure 5.19
Color Coding and the Ganglion Cells
The center and surround of the receptive fields of ganglion cells form the anatomical basis for opponent colors. Some ganglion cells, like G_2, have a center whose photoreceptors respond best to red wavelengths and a surround whose photoreceptors respond best to green wavelengths. Other ganglion cells pair blue and yellow. Some ganglion cells have receptive fields that are not particular about color; they receive input from all types of photoreceptors. The receptive fields of some ganglion cells overlap.

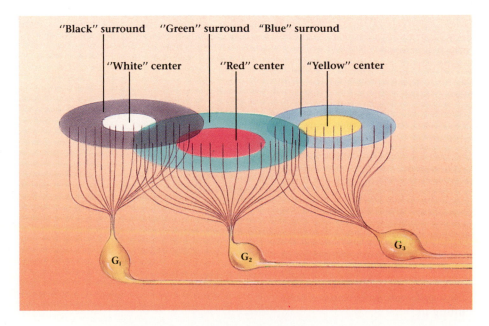

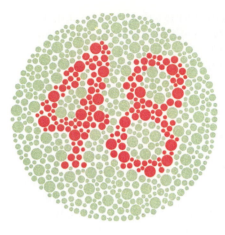

Figure 5.20
A Test for Red-Green Colorblindness
Because people with red-green color-blindness cannot discriminate red from green, they do not see the red 48 embedded in the green dots. However, they are still able to discriminate red from blue.

not end there. The output from cones is fed into ganglion cells, and the center and surround of the ganglion cells respond to different colors and inhibit each other. This activity provides the basis for afterimages. Therefore, the trichromatic theory embodies the properties of the photoreceptors, while the opponent-process theory embodies the properties of the ganglion cells. Both theories are needed to account for the complexity of visual sensations of color.

Colorblindness   What kind of color vision would people have if they had cones containing only two of the three color-sensitive pigments mentioned earlier? Many people do have this condition, and they are described as *color-blind* (see Figure 5.20). They are not actually blind to all color; they simply discriminate fewer colors than other people. Scientists have found the genes that direct different cones to produce pigments sensitive to blue, green, or red; colorblind people do not have the genes that code one or more of the pigments (Nathans, Thomas & Hogness, 1986).

Visual Pathways

In addition to all the processing by the retina that we have described, even more elaborate processing takes place within the brain. Information is brought there by axons from ganglion cells. These axons, which are several inches long, leave the eye as a bundle of fibers called the **optic nerve.** The axons from all of the ganglion cells converge and exit the eyeball at one point (see Figures 5.9 and 5.11). This exit point has no photoreceptors and is therefore insensitive to light, creating a **blind spot,** as Figure 5.21 demonstrates. The fact that you do not notice this "hole" in your visual world provides clues about how the brain perceives visual information, as we discuss in Chapter 6.

After leaving the retina, about half the fibers of the optic nerve cross over to the opposite side of the brain at a structure called the **optic chiasm.** (*Chiasm* means "cross.") Fibers from the inside half of each eye, nearest to the nose, cross over; fibers from the outside half of each eye do not, as Figure 5.22 shows. This arrangement makes sense when you realize that the same half of each eye is looking at the same part of the visual field. Thus, the crossing at the optic chiasm brings all the visual information about the right half of the visual world to the left hemisphere of the brain and information from the left half of the visual world to the right hemisphere of the brain.

Figure 5.21
The Blind Spot
The blind spot occurs in the region of the retina where the axons from the ganglion cells leave the eye as the optic nerve; the area is devoid of photoreceptors. To "see" your blind spot, cover your left eye and stare at the cross. Move the page closer and farther away, and at some point (less than one foot from your face), the dot to the right should disappear from view. When this happens, the vertical lines around the dot will probably look as if they are continuous, since the brain tends to fill in visual information at the blind spot. We are not normally aware of the blind spot, mainly because of this "filling in."

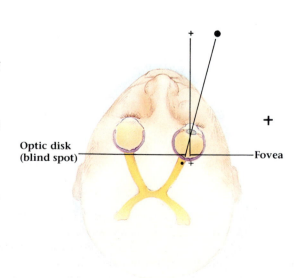

Optic disk (blind spot)   Fovea

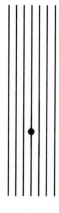

Figure 5.22
Pathways from the Ganglion Cells into the Brain
Light rays from the right side of the visual field (everything on the right side of what you are looking at) end up on the left half of the retina. In order to unite information from both eyes about the right visual field in the same part of the brain, one of the pathways must cross over to the other side of the brain. From the right eye, the axons from the nasal side of the retina (the side nearer the nose, which receives input from the right visual field) cross over the midline and travel with those fibers from the left eye that also receive input from the right side of the visual world. A similar arrangement unites left visual-field information from both eyes in the right side of the brain. Fibers from the nasal side of the retina of the left eye cross the midline, while fibers from the part of it toward the ear do not cross. The axons have a synapse in the thalamus, in the lateral geniculate nucleus. From there, neurons send axons to the visual cortex in the occipital lobe.

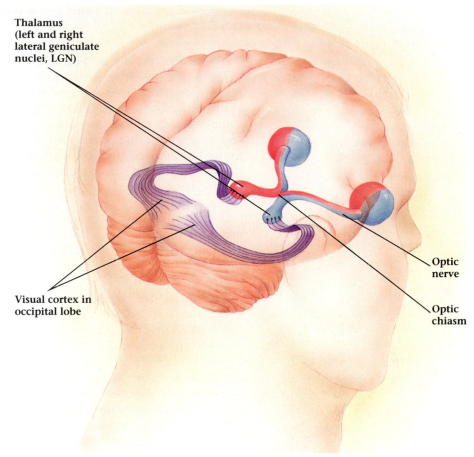

Thalamus (left and right lateral geniculate nuclei, LGN)

Visual cortex in occipital lobe

Optic nerve

Optic chiasm

The optic chiasm is part of the bottom surface of the brain; beyond the chiasm, the fibers ascend into the brain itself. The axons from most of the ganglion cells in the retina form synapses in the thalamus, in a specific region called the **lateral geniculate nucleus (LGN).** Neurons in the LGN then relay the visual input to the **primary visual cortex,** which lies in the occipital lobe at the back of the brain. From the primary visual cortex, many more areas of cortex process visual information. In monkeys, 32 separate visual areas interconnected by more than 300 pathways have been identified so far (Van Essen, Anderson & Felleman, 1992).

The retina has a topographical map of the visual world, which means that neighboring points on the retina receive information from neighboring points in the visual world. This topographical map is maintained in the brain, in the primary visual cortex, and in each of the many other visual areas of the cortex. That is, neighboring points in the retina are represented in neighboring cells in the brain: this is a spatial coding system. The map is a distorted one, however. A larger area of cortex is devoted to the areas of the retina that have many photoreceptors. For example, the fovea, which is densely packed with photoreceptors, is represented in an especially large segment of cortex.

Visual Representations

The normally effortless experience of sight provides no clues to the complexities involved as visual sensations are transmitted from the retina through various cortical regions. We can appreciate some of these complexities by considering the receptive fields of neurons at each point along the way. These receptive fields are characterized by *parallel processing of visual properties, hierarchical processing of visual information,* and *spatial frequency processing of visual information.*

Parallel Processing of Visual Properties   Like ganglion cells, neurons of the LGN have center-surround receptive fields. However, the LGN is organized in multiple layers of neurons, and each layer contains a complete map of the retina. Neurons of different layers respond to particular aspects of visual stimuli. In fact, four separate aspects of the visual scene are handled by *parallel processing systems* that extend into the cortex (Livingstone & Hubel, 1988). The form of objects and their color are handled by one system, while their movement and cues to distance are handled by another system (Livingstone & Hubel, 1988).

You might expect that somewhere in the cortex the puzzle of these separate sensations would finally be assembled in order to provide the basis for a unified conscious experience. However, current evidence suggests that there is no one region where the separate streams of processing converge (Engel et al., 1992). Instead, horizontal connections among the regions of cortex that process separate aspects of visual sensation appear to integrate their activity, making possible a distributed but unified experience (Gilbert, 1992).

PET scans provide evidence of these separate processing channels in humans (see Figure 5.23). For example, one area of visual cortex is activated when a person views a colorful abstract painting; a different area is activated by viewing black-and-white moving images (Zeki, 1992). Brain damage may also reveal the separate channels. Damage in one area can produce a person who is no longer able to see colors, or even remember them, although the person can still see and recognize objects. Damage in another area produces a person who can see only stationary objects; as soon as the object moves, it disappears. People with brain damage in still other regions can see only moving objects, not stationary ones (Zeki, 1992). Even in visual imagination, the same separate processing channels apparently operate. Thus, some patients with brain damage can recall parts of a visual image, but not their correct spatial relationship. For example, they may be able to "see" a mental image of a cow's horn and ears, but cannnot assemble them mentally to form a cow's head (Kosslyn, 1988).

Another way of thinking about parallel channels of visual processing is that different parts of the visual system determine the "what is it?" (form and color) and "where is it?" (movement and distance) of a visual image (Mishkin & Ungerleider, 1982). In evolutionary terms, the more primitive "where is it?" systems are critical for being able to *act* on visual information, by avoiding a predator or grasping an object, for example (Goodale & Milner, 1992).

Hierarchical Processing of Visual Information   Multiple inputs from the LGN converge on single cells of the cortex, as Figure 5.24 illustrates. Cells of the cortex that receive input from the LGN have more complex receptive fields than the center-surround fields of LGN cells. For example, a specific cell in the cortex might respond only to vertical edges, but it responds to vertical edges anywhere in its receptive field. Another class of cells responds only to moving objects; a third class responds only to objects with corners. Because cortical cells respond to specific characteristics of objects in the visual field, they have been described as **feature detectors** (Hubel & Wiesel, 1979).

Feature detectors illustrate how cortical processing is partly *hierarchial* in nature. Complex feature detectors may be built up out of more and more complex connections of simpler feature detectors (Hubel & Wiesel, 1979). For example, several center-surround cells might feed into one cortical cell to make a line detector, and several line detectors might feed into another cortical cell

Figure 5.23
Separate Processing of Color and Movement
Different aspects of a visual image are processed in parallel by different parts of the visual system. A brightly colored image causes one part of the brain on the medial surface to be activated, and the activity can be gauged by PET scans. Black-and-white moving images trigger activity in a completely different area on the lateral surface. Both types of images activate the primary visual cortex, but within that region the neurons stimulated by each type of image are segregated.

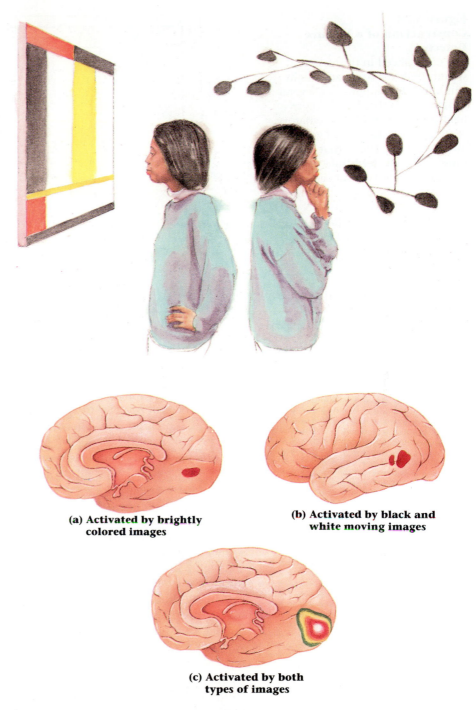

(a) Activated by brightly colored images

(b) Activated by black and white moving images

(c) Activated by both types of images

Source: From "The Visual Image in Mind and Brain," by Semir Zeki. Copyright © 1992 by Scientific American, Inc. All rights reserved.

to make a cell that responds to a particular spatial orientation, such as the vertical. With further connections, a more complex detector, such as a "box detector," might be built from the simpler line and corner detectors.

Cells with similar receptive-field properties are organized into columns in the cortex. The columns are arranged perpendicular to the surface of the cortex. For example, if you locate a cell that responds to diagonal lines in a particular spot in the visual field, most of the cells in a column above and below that cell will also respond to diagonal lines. Other properties are represented

Figure 5.24
Construction of a Feature Detector
The cortical cell in this case responds best to a bar-shaped light stimulus. The output from several ganglion cells that have receptive fields in a row and have excitatory centers goes to the lateral geniculate nucleus (LGN). The output from those LGN cells feeds into one cell in the cortex. This cortical cell responds best when all of the LGN cells are excited, and the LGN cells are excited when light falls on the center of the receptive fields of the ganglion cells—in other words, when a bar-shaped light is oriented so that it stimulates the centers of the receptive fields. Rotating the bar to a different orientation would no longer stimulate this particular cortical cell.

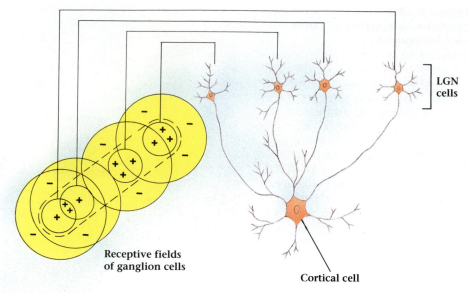

Receptive fields
of ganglion cells

LGN
cells

Cortical cell

Source: Hubel & Wiesel, 1962, 1965; redrawn by Kuffler & Nicholls, 1976.

by whole columns of cells, so, for example, there are columns in which all of the cells are most sensitive to a particular color.

Spatial Frequency Analysis   According to the *spatial frequency filter model* of visual representation, the brain analyzes patterns not only by putting together information about lines, edges, and other features, but by analyzing gradual changes in brightness over broader areas. Spatial frequency analysis is a radically different way of describing what the cortex does with visual information.

This model points out that *any* pattern, no matter how complex, can be decomposed into regions of light and dark, which can be represented by sine waves, as Figure 5.25(a) illustrates. The pattern of bars in the figure is called a *sine-wave grating.* Narrow areas of light and dark are represented by a high-frequency sine wave, and broader areas of light and dark are represented by a lower-frequency sine wave.

If many different sine-wave gratings like those in Figure 5.25(a) are combined in different orientations, a complex pattern results. The spatial frequency filter model suggests that the brain does the opposite, analyzing the complex visual world into alternating regions of light and dark and, in effect, representing those patterns as a collection of sine waves of many different frequencies. Large areas of uniform light or dark correspond to low-frequency components; areas of detailed pattern correspond to high-frequency components. The theory says that the brain, in effect, undertakes a complex Fourier analysis (see page 135) and decomposes a complicated waveform into simple sine waves. Even if a pattern of light and dark did not start out as sine waves, it can be *represented* in the brain as a collection of many sine waves.

What evidence is there that the visual cortex might do this complicated processing? If a series of gratings like those in Figure 5.25(a) is shined on the retina, each neuron in the visual cortex responds best to a grating with a particular frequency; in effect, each has a preferred sine wave (Kelly & Burbeck, 1984). Further, removing one part of the cortex does not eliminate the ability to see a certain type of object. This suggests that a large part of the visual cortex might participate, possibly through Fourier analysis, in sensing each object.

Figure 5.25
Spatial Frequency
The gratings in part (a) illustrate two different "pure" spatial frequencies, analogous to two pure tones. The one on the left is of low spatial frequency and high amplitude; the one on the right is of higher spatial frequency and low amplitude. By adding together appropriate sine waves representing pure spatial frequencies, it is possible to represent images that do not initially appear anything like sine waves. Part (b) illustrates how the visual system can extract information based on a spatial frequency analysis of a visual pattern. The image on the right was generated by a computer, which took an average of the light-dark level within each block of the figure on the left. The blocks are a low spatial frequency analysis of the figure, but the edges of the blocks are a high spatial frequency component that interferes with "seeing" the figure. To see just the low spatial frequency components, take off your glasses (if you wear them), and blur your vision by squinting. The right-hand figure will now look like Abraham Lincoln.

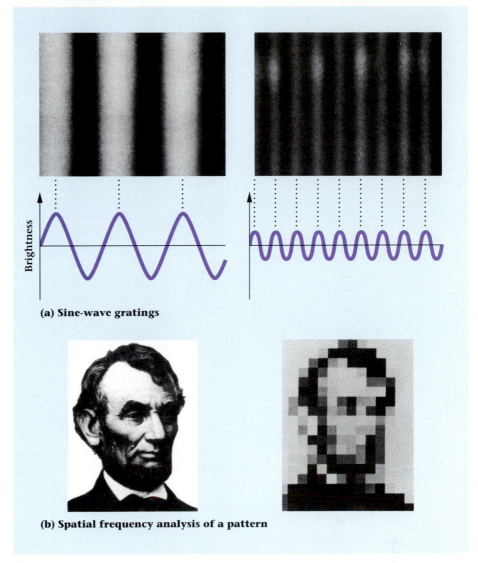

(a) Sine-wave gratings

(b) Spatial frequency analysis of a pattern

Source: (part a) From *Fundamentals of Sensation and Perception* by M. W. Levine and J. M. Schefner, Addison-Wesley, 1981; (part b) Leon B. Harmon and Bela Julesz, *Science*, 180: 1194–1197 (1973).

Our description of spatial frequency analysis demonstrates that there is still a great deal to learn about the way the brain makes use of visual information. The mysteries are by no means solved, and evidence suggests that two very different processes, hierarchical feature detection and spatial frequency analysis, contribute to how the brain sees things. ("In Review: Seeing" summarizes how the nervous system gathers the information that allows people to see.)

The Chemical Senses: Smell and Taste

There are animals without vision, and there are animals without hearing, but there are no animals without some form of chemical sense, some sense that arises from the interaction of chemicals and receptors. **Olfaction** (smell) detects chemicals that are airborne, or *volatile*. Gustation (taste) detects chemicals in solution that come into contact with receptors inside the mouth.

In Review: Seeing

Aspect of Sensory System	Elements	Key Characteristics
Energy	Light—electromagnetic radiation from almost 400 nm to about 750 nm	The intensity, wavelength, and complexity of light waves determine the brightness, hue, and saturation of visual sensations.
Accessory structures	Eye—cornea, pupil, iris, lens	Light rays are bent to focus on the retina.
Transduction mechanism	Photoreceptors (rods and cones) in the retina	Rods are more sensitive to light than cones, but cones discriminate among colors. Sensations of color depend first on the cones, which respond differently to different light wavelengths, and then on processing by ganglion cells. Interactions among cells of the retina exaggerate differences in the light stimuli reaching the photoreceptors, enhancing the sensation of contrast.
Pathways and representations	Optic nerve to optic chiasm to LGN of thalamus to primary visual cortex	Neighboring points in the visual world are represented at neighboring points in the LGN and primary visual cortex. Neurons there respond to particular aspects of the visual stimulus—such as color, movement, distance, or form.

Olfaction

People sense odors in the upper part of the nose (see Figure 5.26). Odor molecules can pass either through the nose or through an opening in the palate at the back of the mouth into the moisture of the lining of the nose. There, the molecules bind to receptors and cause depolarization of the membrane, leading to an action potential in the olfactory nerve (Firestein & Werblin, 1989).

Substances that have similar chemical structures tend to have similar odors, but the precise means by which olfactory receptors in the nose discriminate various smells and code them in ways the brain can interpret is still unknown. We do know that the cells of the nasal cavity have thousands of different re-

Figure 5.26
The Olfactory System: The Nose and the Rose
Airborne chemicals from the rose reach the olfactory area through the nostrils and through the back of the mouth. Fibers pass directly from the olfactory area to the olfactory bulb in the brain, and from there signals pass to areas such as the hypothalamus and amygdala, which are involved in emotion.

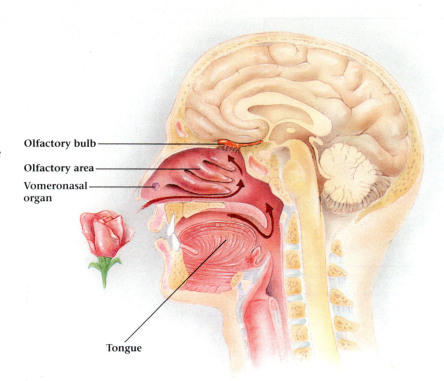

Olfactory bulb

Olfactory area

Vomeronasal organ

Tongue

ceptors that detect the more than 10,000 different odors that humans can discriminate (Buck & Axel, 1991). This arrangement contrasts sharply with the visual system, where only three different receptors allow discrimination of hundreds of colors.

Olfaction is the only sense that does not send its messages through the thalamus. Instead, axons from the nose extend directly to a synapse in a structure called the **olfactory bulb.** Connections from the olfactory bulb spread diffusely through the brain, but they are especially plentiful in the amygdala, a part of the brain involved in emotional experience.

These unusual anatomical features of the olfactory system may account for the unique relationship between olfaction and memory. For example, associations between a certain experience and a particular odor are not weakened much by time or subsequent experiences (Lawless & Engen, 1977). Thus, catching a whiff of the cologne once worn by a lost loved one can reactivate intense feelings of love or sadness associated with that person. Odors can also bring back very accurate memories of significant experiences linked with them; sights, sounds, and other sensory experiences are less capable of doing this (Engen, Gilmore & Mair, 1991). Yet despite the enduring nature of olfactory memories, people have a curious difficulty in associating a name with a particular odor. They may recognize an odor as familiar but be unable to name it, a phenomenon called the "tip-of-the-nose" state (Engen, 1987).

For many animals, olfaction plays an important role in social behavior. Chemicals called **pheromones** that are released by one animal and detected by another can shape the second animal's behavior or physiology. For example, male snakes detect a chemical exuded on the skin of female snakes that causes them to "court" the female (Mason et al., 1989). Literally hundreds of male snakes wrap themselves around a single female, forming a "mating ball." In mammals, pheromones can be nonvolatile chemicals that animals lick and

"Hold it right there, young lady! Before you go out, you take off some of that makeup and wash off that gallon of pheromones!"

pass into a portion of the olfactory system called the **vomeronasal organ.** In female mice, for example, the vomeronasal organ detects chemicals in the male's urine; by this means a male can cause a female to ovulate and become sexually receptive, and an unfamiliar male can cause a pregnant female to abort her pregnancy (Bruce, 1969). In humans the vomeronasal organ was once thought to be nonfunctional, but recent studies show that it responds to suspected human pheromones with neural firing (Monti-Bloch & Grosser, 1991), suggesting that there may be undiscovered human pheromones.

Although there is not yet any solid evidence that humans give off or can detect pheromones that act as sexual attractants, learned associations between certain odors and emotional experiences may enhance a person's readiness for sex. People also use olfactory information in other social situations. For example, after just a few hours of contact, mothers can usually identify their newborn babies by the infants' smell (Porter, Cernich & McLaughlin, 1983). If infants are breast fed, they can discriminate their mothers' odor from the odor of other breast-feeding women, and appear to be comforted by it (Porter, 1991).

Gustation

The chemical sense system in the mouth is **gustation,** or taste. The receptors for taste are in the taste buds, which are grouped together in structures called **papillae.** Normally, there are about ten thousand taste buds in a person's mouth, mostly on the tongue but also on the back of the throat.

In contrast to the olfactory system, which can discriminate thousands of different odors, the human taste system detects only a very few elementary sensations: sweet, sour, bitter, and salty. Each taste bud responds best to one or two of these categories, but it also responds weakly to others. The sensation of a particular substance results from the coded *pattern* of responses by many taste buds. A possible fifth taste, called *umami,* enhances other tastes and is produced by monosodium glutamate (MSG), but its status as a separate taste sensation is controversial (Bartoshuk, 1990; Kinnamon & Cummings, 1992).

Scientists are still trying to determine the properties that allow chemicals to stimulate specific types of taste receptors. They do know that sweetness is signaled when a chemical fits into receptor sites at up to eight points (Tinti & Nofre, 1991). Although the sweet properties of saccharin and aspartame (NutraSweet) were discovered by accident (Mazur, 1991), knowledge of the chemistry of sweetness is allowing scientists to design new chemicals that fit the sweetness receptors and taste thousands of times sweeter than sugar (Tinti & Nofre, 1991). Many of these substances are now being tested for safety and may soon allow people to enjoy low-calorie hot-fudge sundaes. The issue of whether such low-calorie treats will satisfy hunger is discussed in Chapter 12, on motivation and emotion.

Salty is another important dimension of taste. Most people like a certain degree of saltiness in their food, but excessive salt intake can contribute to high blood pressure and heart disease. At least in animals, taste responses to salt are determined during early development, before and after birth. If the mother is put on a low-salt diet, the offspring are less likely to prefer salt (Hill & Przekop, 1988). In humans, experiences with salty foods over the first four years of life may alter the sensory systems that detect salt and contribute to enduring preferences for salty foods (Hill & Mistretta, 1990).

Smell, Taste, and Flavor

If you have a stuffy nose, everything tastes like cardboard. Why? Because smell and taste act as two components of a single system, known as *flavor* (Rozin,

1982). Most of the properties that make food taste good are actually odors detected by the olfactory system, not activities of the taste system. The olfactory and gustatory pathways converge in some areas of the brain (Van Buskirk & Erickson, 1977), but no one knows yet how smell and taste come to seem like one sensation.

Both taste and odors prompt strong emotional responses. For tastes, the repugnance of bitter flavors is inborn, but the associations of emotions with odors are all learned (Bartoshuk, 1991). Many animals easily learn taste aversions to particular foods when the taste is associated with nausea, but humans learn aversions to odors more readily than to tastes (Bartoshuk & Wolfe, 1990).

Variations in one's nutritional state affect taste and flavor, as well as motivation to consume particular foods. Food deprivation or salt deficiency makes sweet or salty things taste better. Intake of protein and fat are influenced more indirectly. Molecules of protein and fat have no inherent taste or smell; the tastes and smells of foods that contain these nutrients actually come from trace amounts of other volatile substances. So adjustments in intake of these nutrients are based on associations between olfactory cues from the volatile substances and the nutritional consequences of eating the foods (Bartoshuk, 1991). These findings have implications for dieting, also discussed in Chapter 12.

Flavor includes other characteristics of food as well: its tactile properties (how it feels in your mouth) and especially its temperature. Warm foods are experienced as sweeter, but temperature does not alter saltiness (Frankmann & Green, 1987). Also, warming releases aromas that rise from the mouth into the nose and create more flavor sensations. This is why many people find hot pizza delicious and cold pizza disgusting. The texture and the heat of food are detected by nerve endings in the mouth that are sensitive to temperature, touch, and pain—sensations that we examine in the next section.

Somatic Senses and the Vestibular System

Some senses are not located in a specific organ, such as the eye or the ear. These are the **somatic senses**, also called **somatosensory systems**, which are spread throughout the body. The somatic senses include the skin senses of touch, temperature, and pain as well as kinesthesia, the sense that tells the brain where the parts of the body are. The vestibular system will also be considered in this section, even though it is not strictly a somatosensory system, because its function—telling the brain about the position and movements of the head—is closely related to kinesthesia.

Touch and Temperature

Touch is vitally important. Blind people survive and prosper, as do deaf people and people who cannot taste or smell. But a person without touch would have difficulty surviving. Without a sense of touch, you could not even swallow food.

Stimulus and Receptors for Touch   The energy detected by the sense of touch is a mechanical deformation of tissue, usually of the skin. The skin covers nearly two square yards of surface and weighs more than twenty pounds. The hairs distributed virtually everywhere on the skin do not sense anything directly, but when hairs are bent, they deform the skin beneath them. The receptors that transduce this deformation into neural activity are in, or somewhere near, the skin.

Many nerve endings in the skin are candidates for the role of touch receptor. Some neurons come from the spinal cord, enter the skin, and simply end; these

The sense of touch provides information about the world that is vital to survival. Its importance is revealed in many other aspects of behavior as well. For example, this sculptor can create without his sight, but not without touch.

are called *free nerve endings.* Many other neurons end in a variety of elaborate, specialized structures. However, there is generally little relationship between the type of nerve ending and the type of sensory information carried by the neuron. Many types of nerve endings respond to mechanical stimuli, but the exact process through which they transduce mechanical energy is still unknown.

People do more than just passively respond to whatever happens to come in contact with their bodies; jellyfish can do that much. For humans, touch is also an active sense that is used to get specific information. Much as you can look as well as just see, you can also touch as well as feel. When people are involved in active sensing, they usually use the part of the sensory apparatus that has the greatest sensitivity. For vision, this is the fovea; for touch, the finger tips. (The area of primary somatosensory cortex devoted to the finger tips is correspondingly large, as you can see in Figure 4.18.) Finger-tip touch is the main way people explore the textures of surfaces. It can be extremely sensitive, as evidenced by the fact that blind people can read Braille as rapidly as 200 words per minute (Foulke, 1991).

Adaptation of Touch Receptors   Constant input from all the touch neurons would provide an abundance of unnecessary information. Once you get dressed, for example, you do not need to be constantly reminded that you are wearing clothes and in fact do not continue to feel your clothes against your skin. *Changes* in touch (for example, if your jeans suddenly drop to your knees) constitute the most important sensory information.

The touch sense emphasizes changes and filters out excess information partly through adaptation, which, as mentioned earlier, results in reduced responding to constant stimulation. Typically, a touch neuron responds with a burst of firing when a stimulus is applied, then quickly returns to baseline firing rates, even though the stimulus may still be in contact with the skin. If the touch pressure increases, the neuron again responds with an increase in firing rate, but then it again slows down. A few neurons adapt more slowly, continuing to fire at an elevated rate as long as pressure is applied to the skin. By attending to this input, you can sense a constant stimulus.

Coding and Representation of Touch Information   The sense of touch codes information about three aspects of an object in contact with the skin: How heavy is it? Is it vibrating? Where is it? The *intensity* of the stimulus—how heavy it is—is coded by both the firing rate of individual neurons and the number of neurons stimulated. A heavy object produces a higher rate of firing and stimulates more neurons than a light object. *Vibrations* are simply rapid fluctuations in pressure, and information about them is also coded by changes in the firing rate. *Location* is coded much as it is for vision: by the spatial organization of the information.

Touch information is organized such that signals from neighboring points on the skin stay next to each other, even as they ascend from the skin through the spinal cord to the thalamus and on to the somatosensory cortex. Accordingly, just as there is a topographical map of the visual field in the brain, the area of cortex that receives touch information resembles a map of the surface of the body. (To confirm this, look again at Figure 4.18.) As with the other senses, these representations are contralateral; input from the left side of the body goes to the right side of the brain, and vice versa.

Temperature   When you lie on a beach in the summer and dig your toes in the sand, you experience a pleasant stimulation, part of which comes from the sensation of the warmth of the sand. Touch and temperature seem to be separate senses, and to some extent they are, but the difference between the two senses is not always clear.

Some of the skin's sensory neurons clearly respond to a change in temperature, but not to simple contact by a thermally neutral stimulus. There are "warm fibers" that increase their firing rates when the temperature changes in the range of about 95° to 115° F (35° to 47° C). Temperatures above this range are painful and stimulate different fibers. Other fibers are "cold fibers"; they respond to a broad range of cool temperatures. However, many of the fibers that respond to temperature also respond to touch, so sensations of touch and temperature sometimes interact. For example, warm and cold objects feel much heavier than thermally neutral objects—up to 250 percent heavier (Stevens & Hooper, 1982).

Though different patterns of activity in a single nerve fiber in the skin can code different stimuli, no one knows how the different stimuli create different patterns of firing. Thus, scientists have so far been unable to resolve whether each of the skin senses has a separate existence or whether they are just aspects of the touch sense.

Pain

The skin senses can convey a great deal of pleasure, but a change in the intensity of the same kind of stimulation can create a distinctly different sensation: pain. Pain provides you with information about the impact of the world on your body; it can tell you, "You have just crushed your left thumb with a hammer." Pain also has a distinctly negative emotional component. Pain researchers have focused on the information-carrying aspects of pain, its emotional components, and the various ways that the brain can adjust the amount of pain that reaches consciousness.

Pain as an Information Sense The information-carrying aspect of pain is very similar to that of touch and temperature. The receptors for pain are free

If pain were based only on the nature of incoming stimuli, this Hindu fakir (religious mendicant) would be hurting. However, the experience of pain is a complex phenomenon that is affected by psychological and biological variables that can make it more or, as in this case, less intense.

nerve endings. Painful stimuli cause the release of chemicals that fit into specialized receptors in pain neurons, causing them to fire.

Two types of nerve fibers carry pain signals from the skin to the spinal cord. *A-delta fibers* carry sharp, pricking pain sensations; they are myelinated to carry the sharp pain message quickly. *C fibers* carry chronic, dull aches and burning sensations. Some of these same C fibers also respond to nonpainful touch, but with a different pattern of firing.

Both A-delta and C fibers carry pain impulses into the spinal cord, where they form synapses with neurons that carry the pain signals to the thalamus and other parts of the brain (see Figure 5.27). Different pain neurons respond to different degrees of painful stimuli, but each neuron will respond to many types of stimuli, such as heat, intense mechanical pressure, or chemical irritation. Numerous types of neurotransmitters are used by different pain neurons, a phenomenon that has allowed the development of a variety of new drugs for pain management (Foley & Macaluso, 1992).

The role of the cerebral cortex in experiencing pain is still being defined. Earlier studies of humans undergoing brain surgery for epilepsy concluded that pain has little, if any, cortical representation (Penfield & Rasmussen, 1968). More recently, PET scans of healthy volunteers compared cortical activity during the experience of "warm" versus "painful but tolerable heat" (Talbot et al., 1991). The scans show activation of the somatosensory cortex under both conditions, and additional activity during pain in the cingulate cortex, a region thought to be important in emotions.

Figure 5.27
Pain Pathways
Pain messages are carried from the periphery to the brain by way of the spinal cord. *A-delta* fibers carry information about sharp pain. *C fibers* are unmyelinated fibers that carry several types of pain sensations, including chronic, dull aches. Pain fibers make synapses in the reticular formation, causing arousal. They also project to the thalamus and from there to the cortex. Incoming pain messages can be "gated," or blocked, in several ways, including by signals that descend from the brain to the spinal cord.

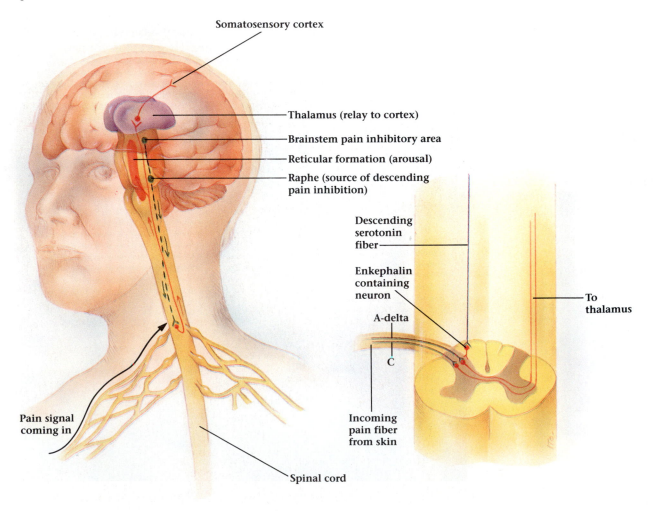

Somatosensory cortex

Thalamus (relay to cortex)

Brainstem pain inhibitory area

Reticular formation (arousal)

Raphe (source of descending pain inhibition)

Descending serotonin fiber

Enkephalin containing neuron

A-delta

C

To thalamus

Incoming pain fiber from skin

Pain signal coming in

Spinal cord

Emotional Aspects of Pain   All senses can have emotional components, most of which are learned responses. For example, the smell of baking cookies may make you feel good because it has been associated with happy childhood times. The emotional response to pain is more direct. Specific pathways carry an emotional component of the painful stimulus to areas of the hindbrain and reticular formation (see Figure 5.27), activating emotional responses.

Nevertheless, the overall emotional response to pain depends greatly on cognitive factors. For example, experimenters compared responses to a painful stimulus in people who were informed about the nature of the stimulus and when to expect it, and in people who were not informed. Knowing about pain seemed to make it less objectionable, even though the sensation was reported to be just as noticeable (Mayer & Price, 1982). Other factors that affect the emotional responses to pain sensations include whether people use pain-reducing strategies (such as distracting thoughts or mental images of pleasant stimuli) and whether they expect these strategies to succeed (Marino, Gwynn & Spanos, 1989).

Modulation of Pain: The Gate Control Theory   Pain is extremely useful, because in the long run it protects you from harm. However, there are times when enough is enough. Fortunately, the nervous system has several mechanisms for controlling the experience of pain.

One explanation of how the nervous system controls the amount of pain that reaches the brain is the **gate control theory** (Melzack & Wall, 1965). It holds that there is a functional "gate" in the spinal cord that either lets pain impulses travel upward to the brain or blocks their progress. The details of the original formulation of this theory turned out to be incorrect, but recent work

Linkages: As described in Chapter 7, hypnosis can create circumstances in which a person is temporarily insensitive to pain. This patient's only anesthesia during the surgical removal of her appendix consisted of tape-recorded hypnotic suggestions that she would feel no pain.

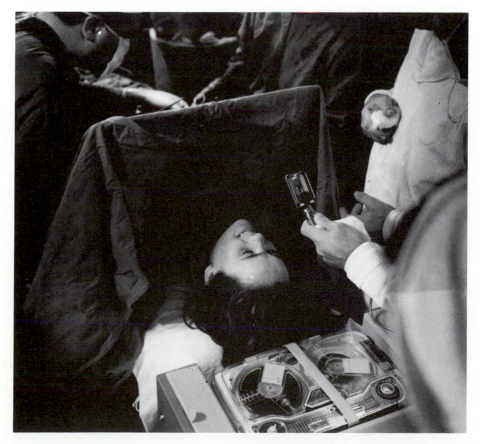

Bruno

SEE, MANDY, IT DOESN'T EVEN HURT

ARF!

Little Endorphin Annie

supports the idea that natural mechanisms can block pain sensations (Hoffert, 1992; Yeh et al., 1992).

For example, input from other skin senses can come into the spinal cord at the same time the pain gets there and "take over" the pathways that the pain impulses would have used. This appears to be why rubbing the skin around a wound reduces the pain that is felt, why electrical stimulation of the skin around a painful spot relieves the pain, and why scratching relieves itching. (Itching is actually low-level activity in pain fibers.)

The brain can also close the gate to pain impulses by sending signals down the spinal cord. The control of sensation by messages descending from the brain is a common aspect of sensory systems (Willis, 1988). In the case of pain, these messages from the brain block incoming pain signals where they synapse in the spinal cord. The result is **analgesia,** the absence of the sensation of pain in the presence of a normally painful stimulus. For example, if part of a rat's brain stem is electrically stimulated, pain signals generated in the skin never reach the brain (Reynolds, 1969). Permanently implanting stimulating electrodes in the same region of the human brain has reduced severe pain in some patients, but unfortunately it also produces a profound sense of impending doom (Hoffert, 1992).

Natural Analgesics   At least two substances play a role in the brain's ability to block pain signals: (1) the neurotransmitter *serotonin,* which is released by neurons descending from the brain, and (2) natural opiates called *endorphins.* Endorphins are natural painkillers that act as neurotransmitters at many levels of the pain pathway, including the spinal cord, where they block the synapses of the fibers that carry pain signals. Endorphins may also relieve pain when the adrenal and pituitary glands secrete them into the bloodstream as hormones.

Most of the time, the endorphin system is not active as an analgesic. This makes sense; chronic analgesia would defeat the purpose of pain, which is to prompt you to escape or avoid damaging stimuli. Constant activity of the endorphin system would not solve the problem of pain anyway, since tolerance and addiction can develop to endorphins as with the opiate drugs discussed in Chapter 7. That is, chronically high levels of endorphins would lose their effectiveness.

Several conditions are known to cause the body to ease its own pain. For example, during the late stages of pregnancy an endorphin system reduces the mother's labor pains (Facchinetti et al., 1982). An endorphin system may also be activated by eating hot chili peppers; people who like hot foods no longer can tolerate them when they receive *naloxone,* a drug that blocks the action of endorphins (Etscorn, 1992, cited in Stern & Stern, 1992). Further, an endorphin system is activated when people *believe* they are receiving a painkiller even when they are not; this may be the basis for the placebo effect, discussed in Chapter 2. Physical or psychological stress can activate natural analgesic systems as well. Different types of stress apparently bring different analgesic systems into action (Watkins & Mayer, 1982). For example, ridiculous as it may seem, shocking a rat's front feet activates a different system than shocking its hind feet. Stress-induced release of endorphins may account for instances in which severely injured soldiers and athletes continue to perform in the heat of battle or competition with no apparent pain.

There are also mechanisms for reactivating pain sensitivity once a crisis is past. Recent work shows that animals can learn that certain situations signal "safety," and that these safety signals prompt the release of a neurotransmitter that counteracts endorphins' analgesic effects (Wiertelak, Maier & Watkins, 1992).

Thinking Critically

Does Acupuncture Relieve Pain?

Acupuncture is an ancient and widely used treatment in Oriental medicine that is alleged to relieve pain. The method is based on the idea that body energy flows along lines called *channels* (Vincent & Richardson, 1986). There are fourteen main channels, and a person's health supposedly depends on the balance of energy flowing in them. Stimulating the channels by inserting very fine needles into the skin and twirling them is said to restore a balanced flow of energy. Modern practitioners of acupuncture also use electrical stimulation through needles at the same points. The needles produce an aching and tingling sensation called *Teh-ch'i* at the site of stimulation, but they relieve pain at distant, seemingly unrelated parts of the body.

What am I being asked to believe or accept?

Acupuncturists assert that twirling a needle in the skin can relieve pain caused by everything from tooth extraction to cancer.

What evidence is available to support the assertion?

There is no scientific evidence to verify the theory underlying acupuncture regarding the existence of channels of energy. However, there is evidence regarding the more specific assertions that acupuncture relieves pain and that it does so through direct physical mechanisms.

In studying acupuncture, it is very difficult to control for the placebo effect, especially in double-blind fashion. (How could a therapist not know whether the treatment being given is acupuncture or not? And from the patient's perspective, what placebo treatment could look and feel like having a needle inserted and twirled in the skin?) Nevertheless, researchers have tried to separate the psychological and physical effects of acupuncture by, for example, using mock electrical nerve stimulation.

Overall, well-controlled studies are surprisingly rare, and the results are contradictory (Ter Riet, Kleijnen & Knipschild, 1990). In studies showing positive results, 50 to 80 percent of patients are helped by acupuncture (Richardson & Vincent, 1986). In one such controlled study of headache pain, 33 percent of the patients in a placebo group improved following mock electrical nerve stimulation (which is about the usual proportion of people responding to a placebo), but 53 percent reported reduced pain following real acupuncture (Dowson, Lewith & Machin, 1985).

There is evidence that acupuncture activates the endorphin system. It is associated with the release of endorphins into the fluid surrounding the brain, and drugs that slow the breakdown of opiates also prolong the analgesia produced by acupuncture (He, 1987). Furthermore, the pain-reducing effects of acupuncture during electrical stimulation of a tooth can be reversed by naloxone, the substance mentioned earlier as blocking the painkilling effects of endorphins (and other opiate drugs). This finding suggests that acupuncture somehow activates the body's natural painkilling system. However, not all studies have found that naloxone reverses acupuncture analgesia (see, for example, Chapman et al., 1983). In the cases where acupuncture activates endorphins, is this activation brought about through the placebo effect? Probably not entirely, because acupuncture produces naloxone-reversible analgesia in monkeys, who are much less likely than humans to have developed positive expectancies by reading about acupuncture (Ha et al., 1981).

Are there alternative ways of interpreting the evidence?

Yes. Evidence about acupuncture might be interpreted as simply confirming that the body's painkilling system can be stimulated by external means. Acupuncture may merely provide one activating method; there may be other, even more efficient methods for doing so. We already know, for example, that successful placebo treatments for human pain appear to operate by activating the endorphin system. Perhaps acupuncture is an especially effective placebo.

What additional evidence would be helpful to evaluate the alternatives?

Researchers need to focus not just on the effects of acupuncture but on the general relationship between internal painkilling systems and external methods for stimulating them. Regarding acupuncture itself, scientists do not yet know what factors govern whether it will activate the endorphin system. Other important unknowns include the types of pain for which acupuncture is most effective, the types of patients who respond best, and the precise procedures that are most effective.

What conclusions are most reasonable?

There seems little doubt that, in some circumstances, acupuncture relieves pain. It is even effective for some types of pain that resist other forms of treatment (Terenius, 1988). Acupuncture is not a panacea, however. For example, acupuncture does not appear to be useful for relieving the pain following major surgery (He, 1987).

If scientists can determine how natural analgesic systems are brought into play by acupuncture and other means, the total amount of medication necessary to relieve pain could be reduced. There is certainly a need for better methods of pain control. The pain of arthritis, migraine headaches, back disorders, cancer, and other physical ailments imposes a heavy burden, causing disability for millions and costing more than $70 billion a year in medical and other costs (Bonica, 1992).

Proprioception

Most sensory systems receive information from the external world, such as the light reflected off green grass or the feeling of cool water. But as far as the brain is concerned, the rest of the body is "out there" too, and you know about the position of your body and what each part of your body is doing only because sensory systems provide this information to the brain. These sensory systems are called **proprioceptive** ("received from one's own").

Kinesthesia   The sense that tells you where the parts of your body are with respect to each other is **kinesthesia.** You probably do not think much about kinesthetic information, but you definitely use it. For example, even with your eyes closed, you can usually do a decent job of touching two index fingers together in front of you. To do this, you must know where each finger is with respect to your body. You also depend on kinesthetic information to guide all your movements. Otherwise, it would be impossible to develop or improve any motor skill, from basic walking to complex athletic movements. These movement patterns become simple and fluid because, with practice, the brain uses kinesthetic information automatically.

Kinesthesia also plays an important role in a person's sense of self. Consider the case of Christina. Christina has a rare neurological disease that, for unknown reasons, causes degeneration of the spinal neurons that provide kinesthetic information (Sacks, 1985). When the disorder began, Christina had difficulty holding onto objects. Then she had trouble moving; she would rise from bed and flop onto the ground like a rag doll. Soon she began to feel she

The smooth coordination of all physical movement, from scratching your nose to complex dance steps, depends on kinesthesia, the sense that provides information about where each part of the body is in relation to all the others.

was losing her body; she was becoming disembodied, like a ghost. One time she became annoyed when she thought her roommate was tapping her fingers on a table top, but then saw that she was doing it herself. Her hands were on their own, and her body was doing things she did not know about. The disease progressed until she lost her sense of self and became a stranger in her own body.

Normally, kinesthetic information comes primarily from the joints but also from muscles. Receptors in muscle fibers send information to the brain about the stretching of muscles (McCloskey, 1978). When the position of the bones changes, receptors in the joints transduce this mechanical energy into neural activity, providing information about both the rate of change and the angle of the bones. This coded information goes to the spinal cord and is sent from there to the thalamus along with sensory information from the skin. Eventually it goes to the cerebellum and to the somatosensory cortex (see Figures 4.13 and 4.17), both of which are involved in the smooth coordination of movements.

Vestibular Sense   Whereas kinesthesia tells the brain about where body parts are in relation to one another, the **vestibular sense** tells the brain about the position of the head (and hence the body) in space and about its general movements. It is often thought of as the sense of balance. People usually become aware of the vestibular sense only when they overstimulate it and become dizzy.

Two vestibular sacs and three semicircular canals that are part of the inner ear are the organs for the vestibular sense. (You can see the semicircular canals in Figure 5.4; the vestibular sacs connect these canals and the cochlea.) The **vestibular sacs** are filled with fluid and contain small crystals called **otoliths** ("ear stones") that rest on hair endings. The **semicircular canals** are fluid-filled, arc-shaped tubes; tiny hairs extend into the fluid in the canals. When your head moves, the otoliths shift in the vestibular sacs and the fluid moves in the semicircular canals, stimulating hair endings. This activates neurons that travel with the auditory nerve, signaling to the brain the amount and direction of head movement.

The vestibular system has neural connections to the cerebellum, to the part of the autonomic nervous system (ANS) that affects the digestive system, and to the muscles of the eyes. The connections to the cerebellum help coordinate bodily movements. The connections to the ANS help create the nausea that sometimes follows overstimulation of the vestibular system, by amusement park rides, for example. The connections to the eye muscles create *vestibular-ocular reflexes.* For example, when your head moves in one direction, your eyes reflexively move in the opposite direction. This reflex allows your eyes to fixate on a point in space even when your head is moving around, so you can track a flying baseball while you are running. You can dramatize this reflex by having a friend spin you around on a stool for a while; when you stop, try to fix your gaze on one point in the room. You will be unable to do so, because the excitation of the vestibular system will cause your eyes to move repeatedly in the direction opposite to that in which you were spinning.

Do people need a certain amount of sensory stimulation?

Linkages: Sensation and Motivation/Emotion

So far, we have described particular types of sensation—sights and sounds, smells and tastes, and so on—but the overall *amount* of sensory stimulation available has strong motivational and emotional properties. Solitary confinement in prison, for example, is extremely unpleasant. In the laboratory, psy-

Figure 5.28
A Sensory Deprivation Chamber
Subjects in early sensory deprivation experiments were asked to lie for days at a time on a soft cot while wearing translucent, vision-blurring goggles as well as gloves and padded arm tubes that minimized touch sensations. Their heads were surrounded by U-shaped pillows and an air conditioner provided constant, dull background noise.

chologists have found that *sensory deprivation,* a prolonged reduction in exposure to sensory stimuli, has wide-ranging effects.

In one of the first experiments on sensory deprivation, student volunteers were told that they would be paid about one hundred dollars for every day they remained in a small room that was soundproofed and dimly lighted (Bexton, Heron & Scott, 1954). Food, water, and toilet facilities were available on request, but the subjects spent most of their time on a cot, seeing, hearing, and doing almost nothing (see Figure 5.28). How did the students react? The first day was usually easy; they slept most of the time. But it did not take long for the volunteers to become extremely bored and restless; many experienced irritability and dramatic mood shifts. In spite of the large monetary incentive, few students remained in sensory deprivation for more than two or three days.

An extended period of sensory deprivation temporarily impairs the ability to react quickly to visual or auditory signals, to solve mental problems efficiently, and to perform other complex tasks (Suedfeld, 1980; Zubek, 1969). Some people react to sensory deprivation by creating their own sensations in the form of imagined sights and sounds (Heron, 1957; Suedfeld, 1980). Indeed, while they are deprived of normal levels of sensory stimulation, subjects are motivated to obtain any kind of stimulation they can get. Deprived subjects will gladly listen to a monotonous recording of old stock market price reports (Bexton, 1953).

These findings regarding the effects of sensory deprivation suggest that everyone is motivated to obtain at least some sensory stimulation most of the time. Why? Sensory stimulation produces not only specific information about stimuli but also an increase in *arousal,* the general activation of physiological systems. According to one prominent theory of motivation, discussed in Chapter 12, people are motivated to behave in ways that keep the level of arousal within an optimal range. When arousal is too high, people seek to reduce it; when arousal is too low, they seek to increase it.

Thus, too much sensory input, as well as too little, may create discomfort and interfere with the ability to perform physical or mental tasks. In fact, a form of sensory deprivation known as restricted environmental stimulation (REST) is used to reduce overarousal and some of the problems it may cause. REST consists of floating for a few hours in a large, dark, soundproofed tank of body-temperature water (Suedfeld, 1980). REST has been used to treat high blood pressure, low back pain, smoking, and drug abuse (Fine & Turner, 1982; Shea et al., 1991; Suedfeld & Baker-Brown, 1986; Borrie, 1991).

How much stimulation is enough and how much is too much? People differ in their optimal level of arousal. Furthermore, there are individual differences in sensitivity to sensory stimulation; the same sensory input therefore produces different levels of arousal in different people. Whether people are motivated to increase stimulation through social contacts or skydiving, or to reduce stimulation by seeking solitude or quiet activities, depends on their optimal level of arousal and their sensitivity to sensory stimulation. Thus, the constant regulation of arousal and the stimulation underlying it helps account for the endless decisions that people make about how to spend their time.

Future Directions

In this chapter we have described how sensory systems allow people to make contact with the outside world as well as with what is going on within their own bodies. The study of these systems has been somewhat unusual. On one hand, it is tied up with very abstract issues, with questions at the core of philosophy, such as: What is reality? How can we know what it is? On the other hand, the study of sensory systems has led to some of the most concrete, down-to-earth research in psychology. This work focuses on learning more about just how sensory systems detect energy, transduce it, and send it to the brain in a usable form.

Psychologists have accumulated a vast body of knowledge in these areas, but much remains unknown or poorly understood, and the research goes on. For some senses, such as olfaction, we still need to learn more about transduction. For other senses, the major questions concern how the brain processes the information it receives. When it comes to the transition from sensation to perception, to how the pathways and connections give rise to perception and subjective reality, we still know very little. Nevertheless, our detailed knowledge of the visual system in particular, has opened the way for new theorizing about the basis of consciousness (Dennet, 1991; Churchland & Sejnowski, 1992).

This task has practical applications: researchers would like to build computers that can see and recognize objects. But building a computer that can extract the relevant features of an image and recognize objects from any angle has turned out to be difficult. Some recently understood principles about the brain, such as the independent processing of several dimensions of visual sensation (for example, edge detection, movement, and color), are being applied in computer modeling of vision (Becker & Hinton, 1992). These principles have also been applied in the development of artificial sensory organs that can be integrated into the nervous system.

There are many as-yet-unsolved mysteries of sensation and many practical applications of the information to come. For more detailed information on sensory systems and how they work, consider taking courses on sensation and perception, biological psychology, vision, speech and hearing, or computer science.

Summary and Key Terms

A *sense* is a system that translates information from outside the nervous system into neural activity. Messages from the senses are called *sensations*.

Sensory Systems

Accessory structures first collect and modify sensory stimuli. *Transduction* is the process of converting incoming energy into neural activity; it is accomplished by sensory *receptors*, neural cells specialized to detect energy of some type. *Adaptation* takes place when receptors receive unchanging stimulation. Neural activity is transferred through the thalamus (except in the case of olfaction) and on to the cortex.

The Problem of Coding

Coding is the translation of physical properties of a stimulus into a pattern of neural activity that specifically identifies those physical properties. It is the language the brain uses to describe sensations. Coding is characterized by *specific nerve energies*: stimulation of a particular sensory nerve provides codes for that one sense no matter how the stimulation takes place. There are two basic types of sensory codes: *temporal* and *spatial*.

Representing Stimuli

The *topographical representations* of sensory information in the central nervous system maintain the topographical relationships of the stimuli. Information from the left side of the sensory world is represented in the right side of the cerebral cortex, and vice versa. The region of cerebral cortex in which a sense is first represented is called the *primary cortex* for that sense. Neurons in primary cortex are organized in columns that have similar response properties. The density of sensory receptors in an area determines how much of the cortex is devoted to representing that part of the sensory world. There are multiple topographical representations of the sensory world, as well as areas of cortex, called *association cortex,* that integrate information from more than one sense.

Hearing

Sound is a repetitive fluctuation in the pressure of a medium like air; it travels in waves.

Sound

The *frequency* (which is related to *wavelength*) and *amplitude* of sound waves produce the psychological dimensions of *pitch* and *loudness,* respectively. *Timbre,* the quality of sound, depends on complex wave patterns added to the basic frequency of the sound.

The Ear
The energy from sound waves is collected and transmitted to the *cochlea* through a series of accessory structures, including the *pinna, tympanic membrane,* malleus (hammer), incus (anvil), stapes (stirrup), and oval window. Transduction occurs when sound energy stimulates hair cells on the organ of Corti on the *basilar membrane* of the cochlea, which in turn stimulate the *auditory nerve.*

Coding Intensity and Frequency
The intensity of a sound stimulus is coded by the firing rate of auditory neurons. *Place theory* describes the coding of high frequencies: they are coded by the place on the basilar membrane where the wave envelope peaks. Each neuron in the auditory nerve is most sensitive to a specific frequency (its characteristic frequency). Very low frequencies are coded by *frequency matching,* which refers to the fact that the firing rate of a neuron matches the frequency of a sound wave; according to *volley theory,* some frequencies may be matched by the firing rate of a group of neurons. Low to moderate frequencies are coded through a combination of these methods.

Auditory Pathways and Representations
Auditory information is relayed through the thalamus to the *primary auditory cortex* and to other areas of auditory cortex. Sounds of similar frequency activate neighboring cells in the cortex.

Vision

Light
Visible light is electromagnetic radiation with a wavelength from about 400 to about 750 nanometers. *Light intensity,* or the amount of energy in light, determines its brightness. Differing light *wavelengths* are sensed as different colors.

Focusing Light
Accessory structures of the eye include the *cornea, pupil, iris,* and *lens.* Through *accommodation* and other means, these structures focus light rays on the *retina,* the netlike structure of cells at the back of the eye.

Converting Light into Images
Photoreceptors in the retina—*rods* and *cones*—have *photopigments* and can transduce light into neural activity. Rods and cones differ in their shape, their sensitivity to light, their ability to discriminate colors, and their distribution across the retina. The *fovea,* the area of highest *acuity,* has only cones, which are color sensitive. Rods are more sensitive to light but do not discriminate colors; they are distributed in areas around the fovea. Both types of photoreceptors contribute to *dark adaptation.* From the photoreceptors, energy transduced from light is transferred to *bipolar cells* and then to *ganglion cells,* with *interneurons* making lateral connections between the bipolar and ganglion cells. As a result of *convergence* and *lateral inhibition,* most ganglion cells in effect compare the amount of light falling on the center of their *receptive fields* with that falling on the surrounding area.

The result is that the retina enhances the contrast between dark and light areas.

Seeing Color
The color of an object depends on which of the wavelengths striking it are absorbed and which are reflected. The sensation of color has three psychological dimensions: *hue, saturation,* and *brightness.* According to the *trichromatic* (or Young-Helmholtz) *theory,* color vision results from the fact that the eye includes three types of cones, each of which is most sensitive to short, medium, or long wavelengths; information from the three types combines to produce the sensation of color. According to the *opponent-process* (or Hering) *theory,* there are red-green, blue-yellow, and black-white visual elements; the members of each pair inhibit each other so that only one member of a pair may produce a signal at a time. This theory explains color afterimages as well as the fact that lights of *complementary* colors cancel each other out and produce gray when mixed together.

Visual Pathways
The ganglion cells send action potentials out of the eye, at a point that creates a *blind spot.* Axons of ganglion cells travel as the *optic nerve* through the *optic chiasm* and terminate in the *lateral geniculate nucleus (LGN)* of the thalamus. Neurons in the LGN send visual information on to the *primary visual cortex,* where cells detect and respond to features such as lines, edges, and orientations.

Visual Representations
Visual form, color, movement, and depth are processed by parallel systems. *Feature detectors* are hierarchically built out of simpler units. The visual system also analyzes input into spatial frequencies of light and dark.

The Chemical Senses: Smell and Taste

Olfaction
Olfaction detects volatile chemicals that come into contact with olfactory receptors in the nose. Olfactory signals are sent to the *olfactory bulb* in the brain without passing through the thalamus. *Pheromones* are odors from one animal that change the physiology or behavior of another animal, sometimes acting through the *vomeronasal organ.*

Gustation
Gustation detects chemicals that come into contact with taste receptors in *papillae* on the tongue. Elementary taste sensations are limited to sweet, sour, bitter, and salty. The pattern of responses by many taste buds determines a taste sensation.

Smell, Taste, and Flavor
The senses of smell and taste interact to produce flavor.

Somatic Senses and the Vestibular System

The *somatic senses,* or *somatosensory systems,* include skin senses and proprioceptive senses. The skin senses include touch, temperature, and pain.

Touch and Temperature
Nerve endings in the skin generate touch sensations when they are mechanically stimulated. Some nerve endings are

sensitive to temperature, and some respond to both temperature and touch. Signals from neighboring points on the skin stay next to each other even in the cortex.

Pain

Pain provides information about damaging stimuli. Sharp pain and dull, chronic pain are carried by different fibers—A-delta and C fibers, respectively. The emotional response to pain depends on how the painful stimulus is interpreted. According to the *gate control theory,* pain signals can be blocked by messages sent from the brain down the spinal cord, producing *analgesia.* Endorphins act at several levels of the pain systems to reduce sensations of pain.

Proprioception

Proprioceptive senses provide information about the body. *Kinesthesia* provides information about the positions of body parts with respect to one another, and the *vestibular sense* provides information about the position of the head in space through the *otoliths* in *vestibular sacs* and the *semicircular canals.*

Linkages: Sensation and Motivation/Emotion

People are motivated to maintain an optimal level of sensory stimulation; the optimal level differs among individuals.

Chapter 6

Perception

Outline

At one traffic circle in Scotland, fourteen fatal accidents occurred in a twelve-month period, at least in part because drivers failed to slow down as they approached the circle. When warning signs failed to solve the problem, Gordon Denton, a British psychologist, proposed an ingenious solution. White lines were painted across the road leading to the circle, in a pattern that looked something like this:

/   /   /   /   /   / ///

Crossing these ever-closer spaced lines at a constant speed gave drivers the impression that their car was accelerating, and their automatic response was to slow down (Denton, 1980). During the fourteen months after implementation of Denton's idea, there were only two fatalities at the traffic circle. To reach this solution, Denton depended partly on his knowledge of *sensation,* the process (described in Chapter 5) through which energy from outside the nervous system is translated into neural signals that are sent to the brain. He relied even more on his knowledge of the principles of human *perception.*

Perception is the process through which sensations are interpreted, using knowledge and understanding of the world, so that they become meaningful experiences. Thus, perception is not a passive process of simply absorbing and decoding incoming sensations. If it were, people's understanding of the environment would be poor indeed. The visual scene would be a constantly changing, confusing mosaic of lights and color. The auditory world would be a din of buzzing, clicking, humming, and shrieking noises; "a blooming, buzzing confusion," in William James's words. Instead, human brains take sensations and create a coherent world. People fill in missing information and draw on past experiences to give meaning to what they see, hear, or touch. For example, the raw sensations coming from the stimuli in Figure 6.1 convey only the information that there is a series of lines and angles, with no parallel lines and no right-angle intersections. But your perceptual system automatically interprets this image as a rectangle (or window frame) lying on its side.

Perception is so quick and familiar that it is difficult to appreciate the processes that allow you to turn the signals from sensory receptors into your personal experience of reality. By shaping experience, perceptions influence thoughts, feelings, and actions (see the Linkages diagram). In this chapter, we explore the wondrous processes of perception, examining how people detect incoming energy, organize sensations into distinct and stable patterns, and recognize those patterns. We also explore the role of attention in guiding the perceptual system to analyze some parts of the experienced world more closely than others. First, however, we take a closer look at the nature of perception itself.

Three Views of Perception

Most of the time, your perceptions are a faithful reflection of the objects, spaces, sounds, and other stimuli that your senses detect. They allow you to deftly swat a fly on a cluttered counter, guide a vehicle on a crowded freeway, rack up high scores on a video game, or land a helicopter on the rolling deck of a ship. Scientists discovered just how impressive human perceptual abilities are when they tried to program computers to perform simple perceptual tasks, like recognizing a cup among objects on a crowded desk. Every system has limitations, however, and your perceptual interpretations of the world are sometimes mistaken, or illusory. For example, in the case of the dangerous traffic circle described earlier, Gordon Denton took advantage of one type of illusion to give drivers the false impression that they were accelerating.

Ironically, illusions come about in part because the perceptual system is so active, constantly filling in gaps and providing interpretations that go beyond information provided by the senses. As was the case for drivers who slowed down at Denton's traffic circle, much of this perceptual work is done automatically, without conscious awareness. Other aspects of perception are quite conscious and effortful, as when a young child struggles to recognize each letter on a printed page, and then mentally pieces them together and perceives them as words and sentences. The magnitude of the automatic and conscious perceptual work humans do every day is awesome.

Linkages

The questions in this diagram illustrate some of the relationships between the topic of this chapter, perception, and the topics of other chapters. The ways people behave, feel, and think are governed to a large extent by the way they perceive, or interpret, the stimulation that comes to them through the senses. Thus, the capacities and limitations of perception have far-reaching effects on how people react to and interact with objects, situations, and other people. Some of the questions in the diagram are examined in this chapter and some are answered in other chapters; the page numbers indicate where the questions are discussed. ■

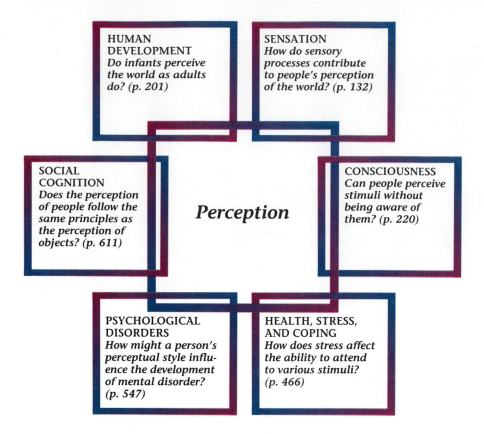

HUMAN DEVELOPMENT
Do infants perceive the world as adults do? (p. 201)

SENSATION
How do sensory processes contribute to people's perception of the world? (p. 132)

SOCIAL COGNITION
Does the perception of people follow the same principles as the perception of objects? (p. 611)

Perception

CONSCIOUSNESS
Can people perceive stimuli without being aware of them? (p. 220)

PSYCHOLOGICAL DISORDERS
How might a person's perceptual style influence the development of mental disorder? (p. 547)

HEALTH, STRESS, AND COPING
How does stress affect the ability to attend to various stimuli? (p. 466)

**Figure 6.1
What Do You See?**

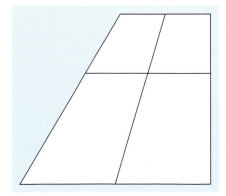

Psychologists agree on the complexity of human perceptual work and on many of the principles that govern perception, but there is some disagreement about where and when this work takes place. Three views are prominent today.

According to the **ecological view** of perception, most of what is perceived is already present in the rich array of stimulation that the environment provides. Psychologist James J. Gibson, founder of the ecological view, noted, for example, how accurately the skilled pilot can bring an aircraft to a gentle touchdown precisely at the end of the runway. Gibson showed that the pilot's perceptual system is tuned to the information arising from the landscape below in a way that precisely establishes the plane's location and movement through the air (Gibson, 1979). According to the ecological view, the primary goal of perception is to support actions, such as walking, by "tuning in" to the part of the stimulus array that is most important for performing the tasks at hand (Warren & Werthheimer, 1990). Most psychologists who take the ecological perspective like to use the kinds of stimuli that people encounter in everyday life. They focus on what the perceptual system does correctly, often automatically, rather than on the ways in which it fails (Banks & Krajicek, 1990).

A very different view of perception is held by **constructionists,** who argue that the perceptual system must often construct an image of reality from fragments of sensory information, much as a paleontologist constructs an entire dinosaur from a few bits of bone (Rock, 1983). This constructive process, they say, explains how you can perceive the images in Figure 6.2 as a triangle and a face even though the sensory information is incomplete. We can predict what people will perceive in this display, say constructionists, because perceptual processes do not build reality randomly. The construction is heavily influenced by past experience and knowledge, which build up *expectations* of what you will see or hear. These expectations make perception easier, particularly when sensory evidence is weak or ambiguous. For example, it is your knowledge of the typical size of a male human that tells you that the two figures in

**Figure 6.2
The Constructionist View of Perception**
These stimuli demonstrate the constructionist view of perception: when you look at them, you perceive more than the raw sensory information provides.

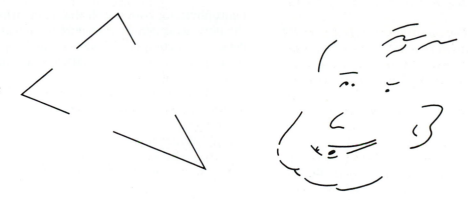

Figure 6.3 are about the same height and, therefore, must be at different distances. As this example shows, constructionists argue that most aspects of perception involve *inferences* about reality based on the available sensory information. Accordingly, many constructionist psychologists are less concerned about how perception supports action than about how perception supports people's *understanding* of the world.

Recently, a third approach to perception has emerged. This **computational view** focuses on how perception occurs; it tries to explain how *computations* by the nervous system might turn raw sensory stimulation into an experience of reality (Green, 1991). Unlike the ecological view, this new approach assumes that the nervous system creates reality by altering incoming stimuli. And unlike the constructionist view, the computational approach places a relatively greater emphasis on how the perceptual system will *compute* the expectancy of a given perceptual category, given the number of times that category has been experienced in the past. This third approach relies partly on research in

**Figure 6.3
The Knowledge-Based Nature of Perception**
Why don't you see the person on the left as twice as tall as the person on the right? Primarily because perception is knowledge based, and you know it is unlikely that two people would be so different in height.

neurophysiology—research that is identifying structures and mechanisms in the nervous system that analyze basic features of the perceptual scene. It also depends on computer models capable of making the computations that, according to the computational view, are like those carried out by the human brain (Grossberg, 1988).

In short, in order to explain perception the ecological view emphasizes the information provided by the environment itself, the constructionist perspective emphasizes how people make inferences about that environment, and the computational approach focuses on how the nervous system manipulates signals. You will see evidence for each of these views in the rest of this chapter as we examine the effects of perception.

Psychophysics

Human perceptual processes range from the very simple, such as listening for a faint sound in a quiet house, to the very complex, such as evaluating and appreciating an architect's design. The most basic perceptual processes assess whether a stimulus is present and, if present, how strong or intense it is.

Absolute Thresholds: Is Something Out There?

The minimum detectable amount of light, sound, pressure, or other physical energy is called the *absolute threshold.* This threshold can be amazingly low. Normal human vision, for example, can detect the light of a single candle flame burning on a dark night thirty miles away. Table 6.1 lists thresholds for human vision, hearing, taste, smell, and touch.

The information in Table 6.1 was compiled by psychologists whose specialty is **psychophysics**, an area that focuses on the relationship between the *physical* energy of stimuli and the *psychological* experience those stimuli produce. Psychophysical research examines not only what stimuli people can detect but also what changes in intensity or other qualities of those stimuli they can perceive. These questions get at the foundation of how people make contact with and become conscious of the world, and they were the focus of research by the pioneers of psychology.

Suppose you are a subject in a typical psychophysical experiment on the absolute threshold for vision. You are brought into a laboratory, and the lights are turned out. After your eyes have adapted to the darkness, brief flashes of

Table 6.1
Value of the Absolute Threshold
Examples of stimuli at the absolute threshold for the five primary senses.

Human Sense	Absolute Threshold
Vision	A candle flame seen at 30 miles on a clear night
Hearing	The tick of a watch under quiet conditions at 20 feet
Taste	1 teaspoon of sugar in 2 gallons of water
Smell	1 drop of perfume diffused into the entire volume of air in a 6-room apartment
Touch	The wing of a fly falling on your cheek from a distance of 1 centimeter

Source: Galanter, 1962.

light are presented one at a time at varying intensities. Each time, you are asked if you saw the stimulus.

Your responses would probably form a curve like the one shown in Figure 6.4. As you can see, the "absolute" threshold is actually not absolute. Sometimes a stimulus of a particular intensity will be perceived; at other times, it will not. Because of this variability, psychophysicists have redefined the **absolute threshold** as the minimum amount of energy that can be detected 50 percent of the time. Why should there be variability in an "absolute" threshold? Psychologists have long been aware of two reasons: internal noise and response criterion.

Internal noise is the spontaneous, random firing of neurons. It occurs because the nervous system is never inactive. This firing is a little like "snow" on a television screen or static between radio stations. If the level of internal noise happens to be high at a particular moment, it may be mistaken for an external light or sound. If the level of internal noise is extremely low, the energy added by a faint light or sound may not create enough total neural activity to make that stimulus noticeable.

The second source of variation in absolute threshold, the **response criterion**, is a person's willingness or reluctance to respond to a stimulus. The response criterion reflects a person's *motivation*—wants and needs—as well as expectancies. For example, if people are penalized when they incorrectly report seeing a faint light, they may report detected signals only when they are very confident about them. Similarly, people who expect a stimulus to occur are more likely to detect it than people who do not.

Going Beyond the Threshold: Signal-Detection Theory

Obviously, the characteristics of a stimulus do not by themselves determine whether you detect that stimulus; the effects of neural noise and response criterion can never be entirely eliminated. Accordingly, researchers have gone beyond trying to determine thresholds. They have turned to **signal-detection theory** (Green & Swets, 1965), which is a mathematical model of what determines people's decisions that a near-threshold stimulus has or has not oc-

Linkages: What determines whether people sense a stimulus? (a link to Sensation)

Figure 6.4
The Absolute Threshold
The curve shows the relationship between the percentage of times that a signal is detected and the physical intensity of that stimulus. If the absolute threshold were indeed absolute, a signal of a particular intensity would always be detected, and any signal below that intensity would never be detected. In that case, the red line would represent the relationship, with no reports when the stimulus is below the threshold and 100 percent of the reports above it. Instead, the absolute threshold is defined as the intensity at which the signal is detected with 50 percent accuracy.

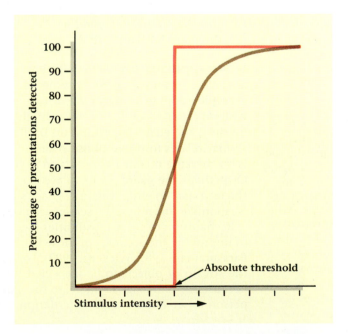

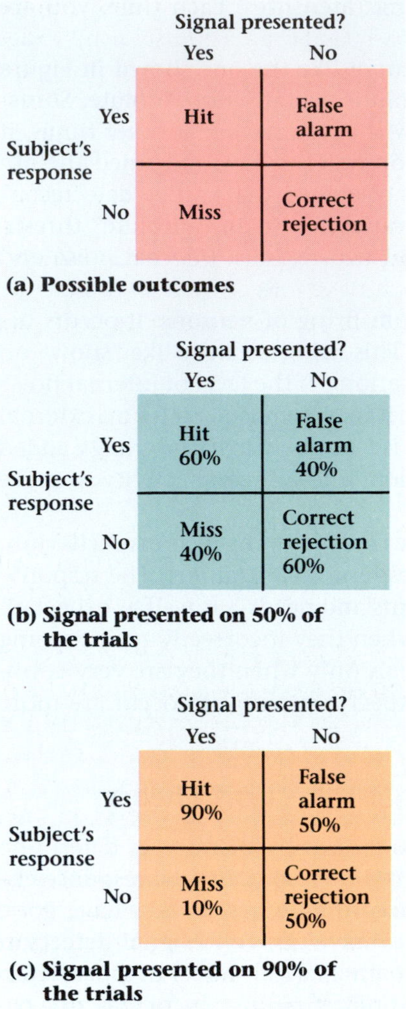

Signal presented?

	Yes	No
Subject's response **Yes**	Hit	False alarm
No	Miss	Correct rejection

(a) Possible outcomes

Signal presented?

	Yes	No
Subject's response **Yes**	Hit 60%	False alarm 40%
No	Miss 40%	Correct rejection 60%

(b) Signal presented on 50% of the trials

Signal presented?

	Yes	No
Subject's response **Yes**	Hit 90%	False alarm 50%
No	Miss 10%	Correct rejection 50%

(c) Signal presented on 90% of the trials

Figure 6.5
Signal Detection
On any trial in a typical signal-detection task, the subject might score a *hit* (a correct detection), a *miss* (a failure to report a stimulus), a *correct rejection,* or a *false alarm* (reporting a signal when none occurred). Part (a) outlines these possible outcomes. One way in which experimenters examine sensitivity is to manipulate the response criterion by altering the percentage of trials on which a signal is presented. Parts (b) and (c) compare the likely outcomes when a signal is presented on 50 percent of the trials and on 90 percent of the trials.

curred. This theory permits psychologists to identify the effects of the response criterion and to compare people's ability to detect stimuli of any kind. How good are you at finding typing errors in your term paper? How likely is a referee to see a player's foul? Will an airport security guard spot the weapon in a hijacker's x-rayed luggage? Signal-detection theory provides a way to understand and predict responses in these and many other situations.

Signal-detection theory begins by doing away with the notion of an absolute threshold. It assumes instead that detection of a faint signal depends on two factors: sensitivity and response criterion. **Sensitivity** refers to the ability to discriminate a stimulus from its background; it is influenced by neural noise, the intensity of the stimulus, and the capacity of the person's sensory system. The *response criterion* determines the amount of energy necessary for a person to justify reporting that a signal has occurred. It is the internal rule, also known as *bias,* that a person uses in deciding whether to report a signal; as already noted, it reflects the person's motivation and expectations.

Analyzing Signal Detection   To separate and measure the effects of sensitivity and the response criterion, researchers use two key procedures. First, as shown in Figure 6.5(a), they present signals on some trials but not on others. The no-signal trials are called *catch trials,* because they are designed to catch the subject's tendency to respond when nothing is there (perhaps as a result of sensory noise or a low response criterion). Second, researchers *manipulate* the response criterion, the bias to report a signal. For example, they might alter the person's motivation by offering money, or they might alter the person's expectations by changing the percentage of trials on which the stimulus occurs. Then they look at what happens to the person's responses.

As an example, suppose a signal is presented on 50 percent of the trials, and you respond as in Figure 6.5(b). You might then be told that signals will occur, say, 90 percent of the time. This change *increases* your expectancy of a stimulus, which would *lower* your response criterion, which would increase the number of times you report detecting a signal—even when you are unsure about its occurrence. Thus, the percentage of correct detections, or *hits,* goes up, but the percentage of *false alarms* increases, too (see Figure 6.5c).

Researchers estimate a subject's sensitivity to signals by examining the pattern of hits and false alarms that occurs as the experimenter manipulates the response criterion. When performance on the trials is plotted, the resulting curve is called a *receiver operating characteristic (ROC) curve.* As shown in Figure 6.6, the more bowed the ROC curve, the greater the subject's sensitivity.

Some Applications   Signal-detection theory has given psychologists an important tool for analyzing why people sometimes fail to detect signals. For example, suppose an airport security guard overlooks the image of a concealed weapon on an x-ray. The problem might be inadequate sensitivity. After hours on duty, the guard might nod off briefly just as a signal occurs. Another possibility relates to the response criterion. Perhaps the guard's expectancy level is low because no one has ever tried to conceal a weapon at the guard's airport. Or perhaps the guard wants to avoid a false alarm that might cause panic in the terminal. In either case, the guard's response criterion is high; thus mildly weaponlike images on the screen are not likely to provoke a search.

Recognition of these possibilities has led psychologists to recommend ways of improving the accuracy of those working at signal-detection tasks (Warm & Parasuraman, 1987; Wickens, 1992). For example, inserting "false signals" into the stream of objects to be inspected improves detection of the true signals because the extra signals increase the expectation of a signal and so lead the person to set a lower response criterion.

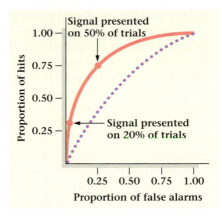

Figure 6.6
Receiver Operating Characteristic (ROC) Curves
These two curves compare the signal-detection performance of two subjects as the expectancy for a stimulus was changed. Each curve shows the proportion of hits and false alarms given by a subject as the experimenter changed the percentage of trials on which a signal was presented. For example, when a signal was presented only 20 percent of the time, there were few hits but also almost no false alarms. The bowed shape of the solid curve indicates that this subject is quite sensitive to the signal; as it became more frequent, hits were more common than false alarms. The "flatter" dotted curve indicates performance by an observer with lower sensitivity in discriminating signals from nonsignals; false alarms appeared about as often as hits. This may occur either because the observer is trying to detect signals that are fainter or because the observer's eyes or ears are less keen.

Signal-detection theory has also produced ideas for dealing with the response bias that witnesses bring to police line-ups. Some witnesses want to see someone, anyone, convicted of a crime; their response criterion may be so low that they are likely to identify someone in any line-up as the criminal. These people have what is called a *risky bias.* Psychologists recommend that officers remind witnesses that the criminal might *not* be in the line-up (Wells, 1993). This reminder tends to lower the witness's expectation of seeing the criminal, thus raising the response criterion. Also, the suspect and others in the line-up should look equally dissimilar from one another. If the suspect looks markedly different from the others in the line-up, a witness with a risky bias—likely to find a culprit in any group—might select the suspect merely by guessing (Ellison & Buckhout, 1981).

Judging Differences Between Stimuli: Weber's, Fechner's, and Stevens's Laws

Often people must not only detect a stimulus but also determine whether two stimuli are the same or different. For example, when tuning up, musicians must decide if notes played by two instruments have the same pitch. When repainting part of a wall, you may need to decide if the new paint matches the old.

It turns out that people's ability to judge differences in the amount of a stimulus depends on how much of that stimulus there is to begin with. More specifically, the ability to detect differences declines as the magnitude of the stimulus increases. For example, if you are comparing the weight of two envelopes, you will be able to detect a difference of as little as a fraction of an ounce. But if you are comparing two boxes weighing around fifty pounds, you may not notice a difference unless it is a pound or more.

One of the oldest laws in psychology gives a precise description of the relationship between the intensity of a stimulus and the ability to detect a change in its magnitude. Named after the nineteenth-century German physiologist Ernst Weber (pronounced "vayber"), **Weber's law** states that the smallest detectable difference in stimulus energy is a constant fraction of the intensity of the stimulus. The smallest detectable difference in the stimulus is called the **difference threshold** or **just-noticeable difference (JND)**. The constant fraction, which is different for different types of sensory input, is given the symbol K.

In algebraic terms, Weber's law is $JND = KI$, where K is the constant fraction and I is the amount, or intensity, of the stimulus. For example, the value of K for weight is .02. If an object weighs 25 pounds (I), the JND is only half a pound (.02 × 25 pounds). In other words, for 25 pounds of luggage, groceries, or other liftable object, an increase or decrease of half a pound is necessary before you can detect a change.

Table 6.2 lists the value of K for a variety of human sense modalities. The smaller the value of K, the more sensitive a sense is to stimulus differences. For example, K for vision is .017, which indicates a high degree of sensitivity; only a small change in the intensity of light is needed for a difference in its brightness to be noticeable. Differences in K demonstrate the *adaptive* nature of perception. For example, humans, who depend more heavily on vision than on taste for survival, have a greater sensitivity (smaller K) for vision than for taste.

Weber's law does not hold when stimuli are very intense or very weak, but it does apply to complex as well as simple stimuli. Thus you would surely notice a fifty-cent increase in a one-dollar bus fare; this 50 percent increase is well above the JND for noticing changes in cost. But the same fifty-cent in-

Table 6.2
Weber Constants (*K*) for Different Sensory Inputs
The value of Weber's constant fraction differs from one sense to another. Senses that are most important for survival tend to be the most sensitive.

Pitch	.003
Brightness	.017
Weight	.020
Loudness	.100
Pressure on skin	.140
Saltiness of taste	.200

crease in monthly rent would be less than a JND and thus unlikely to cause notice, let alone concern.

How much must the rent increase before it would seem twice as high? How many pounds could you add to a package before it would seem twice as heavy? Weber's law does not address questions like these, but it helped Gustav Fechner look for an answer. In 1860 Fechner proposed that Weber's law could be used to understand the perception of stimulus magnitude. He applied the concept of a JND in an attempt to describe the relationship between the intensity of a stimulus and the perception of its magnitude.

According to *Fechner's law,* as physical magnitude increases, larger and larger increases in physical energy are necessary to obtain equal changes in *perceived* magnitude. In other words, constant increases in physical energy will produce progressively smaller increases in perceived magnitude. For example, the perceived difference in brightness between a 75-watt bulb and a 100-watt bulb will be greater than the perceived difference between a 100-watt bulb and a 125-watt bulb.

Fechner's law describes fairly well how people judge the loudness of sounds, the brightness of lights, and the intensity of many other sensations; but it does not apply to some stimuli. For example, contrary to Fechner's law, each successive increase in the perceived intensity of electric shock takes *less and less* of an increase in physical energy. S. S. Stevens later offered a formula (known as *Stevens's power law*) in order to correct the failings of Fechner's law. The details of these laws are not significant for our purposes. What is important is the theme they echo: the perception of magnitude is not absolute but relative. Your experience of one stimulus depends on its relationship to others.

Thinking Critically

Can People Perceive What Cannot Normally Be Sensed?

Weber's law is based on the assumption that people experience the world through the sensory systems. Throughout history, however, various people have claimed *extrasensory perception,* the ability to perceive stimuli from the past, present, or future through a mechanism beyond vision, hearing, touch, taste, and smell. Key forms of extrasensory perception (ESP) have been called clairvoyance, telepathy, and psychokinesis. *Clairvoyance* involves perceiving signals from objects obscured from view or out of earshot—for example, being able to "see" the face of a card that is face-down in another room. Reading another person's thoughts is an example of *telepathy,* which is communication between individuals using extrasensory signals. *Psychokinesis,* although not actually perception, refers to the use of mental processes to move or control objects—for example, bending a spoon merely by looking at it or influencing the roll of dice (Swets & Bjork, 1990). Claims for ESP are widely believed (Gallup & Newport, 1991; Lett, 1992). Research on them is called *parapsychology,* meaning an area that alters or "goes beyond" psychology.

What am I being asked to believe or accept?
Proponents of ESP ask you to believe that information can be transmitted from the outside world to the brain (and back again, in the case of psychokinesis) while bypassing traditional sensory receptors.

What evidence is available to support the assertion?
Many apparent parapsychological phenomena are weak and difficult to replicate. Under close scrutiny by outside observers in the researcher's own labo-

When a stereo is playing very softly, even a very small increase in volume is noticeable. But if the music is blaring, it takes a much larger increase in volume before the music *sounds* louder. Weber's law describes this relationship between the initial amount of a stimulus and the amount of energy that must be added to produce a noticeable change.

ratory, reported ESP phenomena often fail to occur (Swets & Druckman, 1990). However, several experiments have apparently demonstrated clairvoyance, psychokinesis, or telepathy in the laboratory (see, for example, Rao & Palmer, 1987). In a typical experiment on clairvoyance, for example, a subject is blindfolded and asked to report the colors of a stack of cards by feeling them with his or her finger tips (Youtz, 1968). Some subjects do far better at color naming than would be expected by the laws of chance alone. In other experiments, a subject is placed in an isolated room and asked either to use clairvoyance to "read" the output of a machine that is generating random numbers in another room or, using psychokinesis, to influence the machine's output. Some investigators have reported that some people perform at slightly greater than chance levels of accuracy on clairvoyance tasks, or that in a psychokinesis task they can make machine-generated numbers less random (see, for example, Honorton & Harper, 1974; Jahn, 1982; Schmidt, 1969).

In one series of experiments, subjects were asked to predict which of four randomly illuminated lights would appear next (Schmidt, 1969). After several thousand trials, a few subjects correctly predicted the illumination up to 26.3 percent of the time, which is significantly more often than the 25 percent that would be expected on the basis of chance alone (Rao & Palmer, 1987).

Are there alternative ways of interpreting the evidence?

Consider first the experiments on color naming by clairvoyance. It turns out that different colors give off different amounts of radiant energy. Is it possible that certain subjects' sense of touch is particularly sensitive to differences in heat? Some evidence for this possibility comes from experiments in which color-guessing performance drops to chance levels after heat-blocking filters are placed over the cards. In addition, the reading speed of blind readers of Braille is affected by the color of the paper on which the Braille is printed (Duplessis, 1979). Thus, the claims made about color guessing, at least, can be accounted for by extra*sensitive* rather than extrasensory perception.

Many psychologists have also challenged the use of nonrandom machine output as a criterion for establishing psychokinesis because randomness is not an all-or-none concept. If you flip a coin seven times and it comes up heads each time, is the pattern really nonrandom? Does it mean you have psychokinetic ability? A sequence of seven heads in a row is unlikely (it will occur only once in 128 tries), but it certainly can happen. Indeed, a seven-heads sequence is just as likely as any of the 127 other possible seven-flip sequences. In other words, it is far more difficult than one might think to determine that something really is "nonrandom" (Hansel, 1980). Thus, a very plausible interpretion of apparently nonrandom events in ESP experiments is that they are random after all.

Finally, some apparently remarkable results of ESP experiments can be attributed to fraud. A few researchers have tampered with their equipment and measurements, thus destroying their credibility and raising suspicions about all parapsychological research.

What evidence would help to evaluate the alternatives?

As a science, psychology depends for evidence on clear, reliable, and replicated observations. Skeptical scientists place the burden of proof for the existence of ESP on parapsychologists, who must be able to show robust, replicable ESP effects that do not depend on interpretations of nonrandomness and that occur under tightly controlled conditions. Until and unless such new evidence is available, most scientists will interpret existing evidence as suggesting the operation of non-ESP factors. Indeed, since 1964 James Randi, an expert magician and ESP skeptic, has carried a $10,000 check that he will give to anyone who can perform a genuine act of ESP under scientific conditions. After hundreds of challenges, he still has his money (Randi, 1987). Claims for ESP would also be more plausible if scientific evidence could be found for a form of energy—and a system to send it to and from the brain—that could provide the psychophysical basis for ESP (Alcock, 1987).

What conclusions are most reasonable?

Given relatively weak and unreplicated laboratory effects, numerous negative findings in the presence of neutral observers, and absence of additional supporting evidence, a strong scientific case for the existence of ESP cannot be made.

Does this mean that parapsychological phenomena have been disproven? No. In the first place, scientists in the past have been surprised by the existence of phenomena, such as subatomic particles, that they once believed nonexistent or impossible. Furthermore, reputable and honest researchers continue to report phenomena that are not easily explained by known sensory or perceptual mechanisms (Honorton et al., 1990). A distinguished panel of scientists assembled by the National Research Council in the United States reviewed much of the literature in this area and visited the most respected laboratories (Swets & Bjork, 1990). The panel concluded that the data offered were not convincing enough to warrant efforts to use ESP to improve performance in, say, air traffic control; but the panel did recognize the possible value of additional research on ESP. Until such research identifies plausible and scientifically respectable mechanisms through which ESP signals could be transmitted, the majority of the scientific community is likely to remain skeptical.

Organizing the Perceptual World

Suppose for a moment that you are driving down a busy road while searching for Barney's Diner, an unfamiliar restaurant where you are to meet a friend. The roadside is crammed with signs of all shapes and colors, some flashing, some rotating, and some standing still. If you are ever to recognize the one sign that says "Barney's Diner," you must impose some sort of organization on this overwhelming array of visual information.

How do you do this? How do you know where one sign ends and another begins? And how do you know that an apparently tiny sign is not too small to read but is just far away? In this section, we describe some of the organizational processes that allow people to understand which parts of the visual array are objects and which are not, how far away these objects are, how bright or colorful they are, which ones are moving and which are still.

Principles of Perceptual Organization

Before you can recognize the "Barney's Diner" sign, your perceptual system must separate that sign from its background of lights, colors, letters, and other competing stimuli. Two basic principles—*figure-ground perception* and *grouping*—guide this initial organization.

Figure and Ground   When you look at a complex scene or listen to a noisy environment, your perceptual apparatus automatically picks out certain objects or sounds to be figures (that is, the features to be emphasized) and relegates others to be **ground**—the meaningless, contourless background. For example, as you drive toward an intersection, a stop sign becomes a figure, standing out clearly against the background of trees, houses, and cars. A **figure** is the part of the visual field that has meaning, stands in front of the rest, and

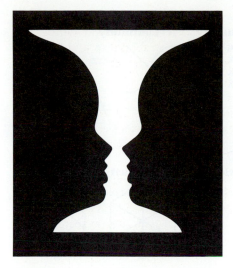

Figure 6.7
Figure-Ground Perception
What do you see? At first, you may perceive two people facing each other. If so, the space between their two faces is the ground—the background behind the faces that form the figure. But look again. You may also perceive the figure as a vase or candle holder. Now the spaces on each side, which had been meaningful figures, take on the meaningless properties of ground.

The fact that you perceive a cat behind the railing and a tree outside the window—even though neither object can be seen in its entirety—illustrates the perceptual tendency known as closure. Without it, the world would appear to be a confusing array of fragmented images.

always seems to include the contours or borders that separate it from the relatively meaningless background (Rubin, 1915).

The relationship between figure and ground is usually, but not always, clearcut. Consider Figure 6.7. What do you see? You can repeatedly reverse figure and ground to see faces, then a vase, then faces again. Figure 6.7 illustrates that perception is not only an active process but a *categorical* one. People usually assign sensory stimulation to one perceptual category or another, rarely to both or to something in between. You cannot, for instance, easily perceive Figure 6.7 as both a vase and two faces at the same time. The figure is *ambiguous* because the identical sensory information can give rise to two very different perceptual interpretations.

Grouping   Why is it that certain parts of the world become figure and others become background, even when nothing in particular stands out in the physical pattern of light that falls on the retina? The answer is that certain inherent properties of stimuli lead people to group them together, more or less automatically.

Early in this century, German psychologists described the principles behind this grouping of stimuli. They argued that people perceive sights and sounds as organized wholes. These wholes, they said, are different from and more than just the sum of the individual sensations, much as water is something more than just an assortment of hydrogen and oxygen atoms. Because the German word meaning (roughly) "whole figure" is *Gestalt,* these researchers became known as **Gestalt psychologists.** They proposed a number of principles or properties that lead the perceptual system to "glue" raw sensations together in particular ways, organizing stimuli into a world of shapes and patterns. For example:

1. **Proximity.** The closer objects are to one another, the more likely they are to be perceived as belonging together, as Figure 6.8(a) illustrates.
2. **Similarity.** Similar elements are perceived to be part of a group, as in Figure 6.8(b). People wearing the same school colors at a stadium will be perceived as belonging together even if they are not seated close together. Similarity also affects the perception of sound. For example, a flute and a tuba that are both playing a rising scale will be perceived together even though the pitches of their notes are quite distinct.
3. **Continuity.** Sensations that appear to create a continuous form are perceived as belonging together, as in Figure 6.8(c).
4. **Closure.** People tend to fill in missing contours to form a complete object, as in Figure 6.8(d).
5. **Texture.** When basic features of stimuli have the same texture (such as the orientation or "grain size" of certain elements), people tend to group those stimuli together (Bergen & Adelson, 1988; Olson & Attneave, 1970). Thus you group the vertical lines of a grove of standing trees together and see those trees separately from their fallen neighbors in the undergrowth. Figure 6.8(e) provides another example. Feature-detecting cells in the visual cortex, described in the chapter on sensation, appear to be responsible for this aspect of perceptual grouping.
6. **Simplicity.** People tend to group features of a stimulus in a way that provides the simplest interpretation of the world (Hatfield & Epstein, 1985; Biederman, 1987). Consider, for example, what it takes to describe each pattern in Figure 6.8(f). To describe the figure on the left in two dimensions, you need only say that it is a hexagon with six radii. To describe it as a three-dimensional figure, you would have to say that it is a cube with sides of equal length, which is being viewed from a certain unusual angle. The simpler, more economical, two-dimensional perception will prevail. For the

Figure 6.8
Gestalt Principles of Perceptual Grouping
You probably perceive (a) as being made up of two groups of two circles plus two single circles, rather than as three groups of two circles or some other arrangement. In (b), you see two columns of X's and two columns of O's, not four rows of XOXO. You see the large symbol in (c) as being made out of two continuous lines—one straight and one curved—rather than being composed of the other discontinuous forms shown in the figure. You immediately perceive the disconnected line segments of (d) as a triangle and a circle. In (e), the different orientation of the lines and different size of the circles in one quadrant of each of the two rectangles makes that quadrant stand out from the others. In (f), both figures are the same three-dimensional cube viewed from different angles, but the one on the left is normally perceived as a two-dimensional hexagon with lines running through it; the other, as a three-dimensional cube. (In each case, perception is based on the simpler explanation.)

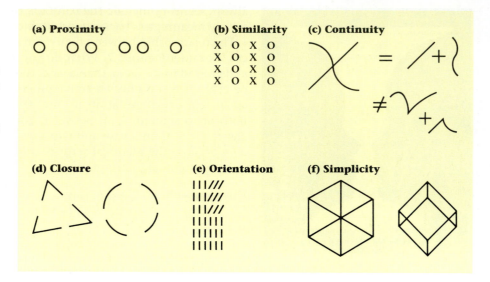

second figure, however, the two-dimensional interpretation is not nearly as simple to describe, because the shape is no longer a simple hexagon. You would have to describe it as "two over-lapping squares with lines connecting their corresponding corners." The three-dimensional interpretation (a cube) is now simpler and more naturally perceived.

7. **Common fate.** Sets of objects that are moving in the same direction at the same speed are perceived together. Thus, a flock of birds, although separated in space, will be perceived as a group. Choreographers and marching band directors often use the principle of common fate, arranging for groups of dancers or musicians to move identically, causing the audience to perceive waves of motion.

These principles are generally consistent with both the ecological and computational views of perception. The properties of the stimulus environment can account quite well for most of these principles of perceptual organization, as ecological psychologists have argued. At the same time, research on neurophysiology is demonstrating how neural pathways detect edges, lines, and texture in a way that can allow these organizational processes to be carried out early in perception, in an essentially automatic way.

Gestalt principles of perceptual organization describe how people organize the world into identifiable shapes and patterns. But these patterns keep changing from moment to moment. You interpret the patterns as being stable because of perceptual constancy, to which we turn next.

Perceptual Constancy

Suppose that one sunny day you are watching a friend walking toward you along a tree-lined sidewalk. The visual sensations produced by this movement are actually rather bizarre. For one thing, the size of the image on your retinas keeps getting larger as your friend gets closer. To demonstrate this effect to yourself, look at a distant person and hold your hand out at arm's length in front of your eyes. The image of your hand will completely block your view of the person, because the retinal image of the person is so small. Try the same thing when the person is three feet away. Your retinal image of the person will now be so large that your hand can no longer cover all of it. But you perceive the person as being closer now, not bigger. Similarly, as your friend walks along, passing from bright sunshine through the shadows of trees, the sensa-

THE FAR SIDE   By GARY LARSON

The deadly couch cobra — coiled and alert in its
natural habitat.

The natural camouflage of certain animals, as well as the kind printed on military uniforms for jungle fighting, works by taking advantage of Gestalt principles of perceptual organization, often by blurring cues for figure and ground and making objects much less noticeable.

If you were to trace the outline of this floating object, you would see that its image is oval-shaped. However, the perceptual principle of shape constancy causes you to perceive it as the perfectly circular life ring that it is.

tions reaching your eyes suggest that your friend becomes darker, then lighter, then darker again. But you perceive an individual whose coloring remains the same.

This example illustrates **perceptual constancy**, the perception of objects as constant in size, shape, color, and other properties despite changes in their retinal image. Without this aspect of perception, the world would be an Alice-in-Wonderland kind of place in which objects continuously changed their properties.

Size Constancy   Why does the perceived size of objects stay more or less constant, no matter what changes occur in the size of the retinal image? One view, which emphasizes the computational aspects of perception, suggests that as objects move closer or farther away, the brain perceives the change in distance and automatically adjusts the perception. (Later we describe how changes in distance are perceived.) Thus, the *perceived size* of an object is equal to the size of the retinal image multiplied by the perceived distance (Holway & Boring, 1941). As an object moves closer, its retinal image increases, but the perceived distance decreases at the same rate, so the perceived size remains constant. If, instead, a balloon is inflated in front of your eyes, perceived distance remains constant, and the perceived size (correctly) increases as the retinal image increases.

This computational perspective is reasonably good at explaining most instances of size constancy, but it cannot fully account for the fact that people are better at judging the true size (and distance) of familiar objects than unfamiliar ones. This phenomenon suggests that there is an additional mechanism for size constancy, one that is consistent with the constructionists' emphasis on the knowledge-based aspects of perception. Indeed, it is your knowledge and experience that tell you that objects (aside from balloons) do not suddenly change size.

The perceptual system usually produces size constancy correctly and automatically, but it can sometimes fail. For example, people may perceive objects with smaller retinal images to be farther away than those with larger images even when the distance is actually the same. This error may explain why, in countries where cars vary greatly in size, small cars have higher accident rates than large ones (Eberts & MacMillan, 1985). A small car produces a smaller retinal image at a given distance than a larger one, possibly causing the driver of a following vehicle to overestimate the distance to the small car and therefore fail to brake in time to avoid a collision. Such misjudgments illustrate the *inferential* nature of perception emphasized by constructionists: people make logical inferences or hypotheses about the world based on the available cues. Unfortunately, if the cues are misleading, or the inferences are wrong, perceptual errors may occur.

Shape Constancy   The principles behind shape constancy are closely related to those of size constancy. To see shape constancy at work, remember what page you are on, close this book, and tilt it toward and away from you several times. The book will continue to look rectangular, even though the shape of its retinal image changed dramatically as you moved it. The brain automatically integrates information about retinal images and distance as movement occurs. In this case, the distance information involved the difference in distance between the near and the far edges of the book.

As with size constancy, much of the ability to judge shape constancy depends on automatic computational mechanisms in the nervous system, but expectations about the shape of objects also play a role. For example, in Western cultures, most corners are at right angles, and most curved surfaces are circular or spherical. Knowledge of these facts helps make "rectangle" the most likely interpretation of the retinal image shown in Figure 6.1.

Brightness Constancy No matter how the amount of light striking an object changes, the object's perceived brightness remains relatively constant. You could demonstrate this brightness constancy by placing a lump of coal in sunlight and a piece of white paper in nearby shade. The coal would still look very dark and the paper very bright, even though a light meter would reveal much more light energy reflected to the eyes from the sun-bathed coal than from the shaded paper.

Of course, one reason the coal would continue to look dark, no matter the illumination, is that you know that coal is black, illustrating once again the knowledge-based nature of perception. Another reason is that the coal is still the darkest object *relative* to its background in the sunlight, and the paper is the brightest object *relative* to its background in the shade. The brightness of an object is perceived in relation to its background (see Figure 6.9).

Depth Perception

Thanks to the constancies of perception, people perceive coherent, stable objects. Imagine trying to deal with a world in which objects changed their form as often as their images changed on your retinas. But Figure 6.10 shows a case in which perceptual constancy fails. Why does the nearer baseball player seem larger? Why does size constancy fail here?

The answer lies in perceived distance, one of the most important factors underlying size and shape constancy. Perception of distance, or **depth perception**, allows people to experience the world in three-dimensional depth. How can this occur, when all visual information comes through a set of two-dimensional retinas? There are two reasons: cues provided by the environment, sometimes described as *stimulus cues,* and properties of the visual system itself.

Stimulus Cues To some extent, people perceive depth through the same cues that artists use to create the impression of depth and distance on a two-dimensional canvas. These cues are actually characteristics of visual stimuli and therefore illustrate the ecological view of perception. Figure 6.11 demonstrates several of these cues.

- Look first at the two men at the far left of Figure 6.11. They illustrate the principle of **relative size:** if two objects are assumed to be the same size, the object producing a larger image on the retina is perceived as closer than the one producing a smaller image.
- Another cue comes from **height in the visual field:** on the ground, more distant objects are usually higher in the visual field than those nearby. The woman near the man at the front of Figure 6.11 therefore appears to be farther away.

Figure 6.9
Brightness Constancy
You probably perceive the inner ring on the left to be brighter than the inner ring on the right. But if you carefully examine the inner circles alone, by covering their surroundings, you will see that the two are of equal intensity. The brighter surround in the right-hand drawing leads you to perceive its inner circle as relatively darker.

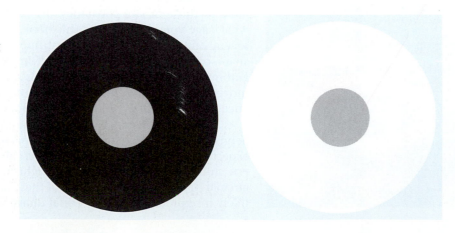

■ The woman walking by the car in the middle of Figure 6.11 illustrates another depth cue called **interposition**, or *occlusion*. Closer objects block the view of things farther away. Because of misleading cues from both height in the visual field and interposition, size constancy was violated in Figure 6.10. The more distant ballplayer is lower, not higher in the visual field; also the runner's leg appears to be in front of, not behind the pitcher's leg, thereby providing a misleading interposition cue. Together, these misleading cues make the runner appear smaller than normal rather than farther away.

■ The figure at the far right of Figure 6.11 is seen as still farther away, in part because she is standing near a point in the road where its edges, like all parallel lines that recede into the distance, appear to converge toward a single point. This apparent convergence provides a cue called **linear perspective**. The closer together two converging lines are, the greater the perceived distance.

■ Notice that the road in the picture disappears into a hazy background. Since greater distances usually produce less clarity, **reduced clarity** is interpreted as a cue for greater distance. The effect of clarity on perceived distance explains why a mountain viewed on a hazy day appears to loom larger than the same mountain on a clear day. The haze acts as a cue for greater distance, but the size of the mountain's retinal image is unchanged. The same retinal image accompanied by a greater perceived distance produces a larger perceived size.

■ **Light and shadow** also contribute to the perception of three dimensions (Ramachandran, 1988). The buildings in the background of Figure 6.11 are seen as three-dimensional cubes, not flat billboards, because of the shadows on their right faces. Figure 6.12 gives another example of shadows' effect on depth perception.

Two additional stimulus cues for depth come from **gradients**, which are continuous changes across the visual field. A **textural gradient** is a graduated change in the texture, or "grain," of the visual field, as you can see from the sidewalk and the centerline of the road in Figure 6.11. Texture appears less detailed as distance increases; so as the texture of a surface changes across the retinal image, people perceive a change in distance.

Figure 6.10
A Violation of Size Constancy
The two baseball players in the picture appear to be of very different sizes, even though you know that their heights are probably much the same. The discussion of stimulus cues to depth explains why.

Figure 6.11
Stimulus Cues for Depth Perception
See if you can identify how cues of relative size, interposition, linear perspective, height in the visual field, textural gradient, and shadows combine to create a sense of three-dimensionality.

Figure 6.12
Light, Shadow, and Depth Perception
Here you perceive the three-dimensionality of a series of protruding rivets. But hold the book upside down and look again. The rivets now look like dents and the dents look like bumps. This reversal occurs, in part, because people normally assume that illumination comes from above and interpret the pattern of light and shadows from the perspective of this assumption (Berbaum, Bevert & Chung, 1983; Reichel & Todd, 1990). When the picture is turned upside down, light coming from the top would produce the observed pattern of shadows only if the circles were dents, not rivets.

The second gradient cue is the **movement gradient,** which is the difference in the apparent movement of objects. As you move your head back and forth, things closer to you appear to move farther and faster than things farther away. The next time you are riding in a car through an open area, look out the side window at an object of intermediate distance (for example, a house). The objects closest to you will appear to fly rapidly across your visual field; in contrast, distant objects will look as if they are motionless or moving along with you. This difference in relative movement, sometimes called *motion parallax,* provides cues to the difference in distance. Faster relative movement across the visual field indicates less distance.

Yet another cue to the three-dimensional properties of an object comes from a phenomenon called *structure from motion* (Braunstein, 1990). Hold a twisted wire behind a paper illuminated from behind and look at the two-dimensional shadow cast by the wire. Now slowly twist the wire and watch the three-dimensional properties of the image come to life. You "see" the three-dimensional figure rotating in depth.

Cues Based on Properties of the Visual System   Several cues to depth result from the way human eyes are built and positioned. One of these cues is related to facts discussed in Chapter 5, on sensation. To bring an image into focus on the retina, the lens of the eye changes shape, or *accommodates.* To accomplish this feat, muscles surrounding the lens either must tighten, to make the lens more curved for focusing on close objects, or must relax, to flatten the lens for focusing on more distant objects. Information about the activity of the muscles is relayed to the brain, and this accommodation cue helps create the perception of distance.

The location of each eye at a different spot on the head produces two other depth cues. One is **convergence:** because each eye is located at a slightly different place, the eyes must converge, or rotate inward, in order to project the image on each retina. The brain receives and processes information from the eye muscles about this activity. The closer the object, the more the eyes must converge, and the greater the proprioceptive information going to the brain.

Parallel lines seem to converge as they extend into the distance. This illusion provides linear perspective cues for distance; objects near where the lines "meet" are perceived as farther away than those located where the lines appear farther apart.

Second, because of their differing locations, each eye receives a slightly different view of the world, as Figure 6.13 illustrates. The difference between the two retinal images of an object is called **binocular disparity.** For any particular object, this disparity decreases with increasing distance. The brain combines

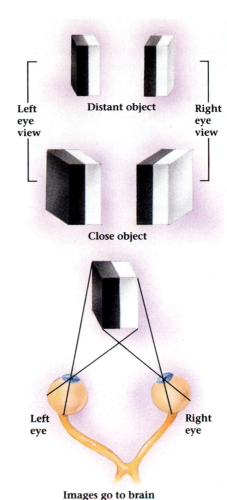

Left eye view   Distant object   Right eye view

Close object

Left eye   Right eye

Images go to brain where they are compared

Figure 6.13
Binocular Disparity
Each eye has a slightly different view of the cube. The difference between views is greater when the cube is close than when it is far away. For a quick demonstration, hold a pencil vertically about six inches in front of you. Close one eye and take note of where the pencil is relative to the objects in the background. Now open that eye and close the other one. Notice how the pencil seems to shift slightly and how it obscures slightly different parts of the background. These are the two views your eyes have of that pencil. If you now hold the pencil at arm's length or look at some other narrow vertical object some distance away, there is less difference in the angles at which the two eyes see the object, and the amount of disparity (or shift) decreases.

the two images, processes information about the amount of disparity, and generates the impression of a single object having depth as well as height and width. Thus, Viewmaster slide viewers and 3-D movies can create the appearance of depth by displaying to each eye a separate photograph of an object or scene, each taken from a slightly different angle.

What binocular disparity does for depth perception, the placement of the ears does for sound localization: it provides a cue for locating the source of sounds. If a sound is continuous, the peak of sound waves coming toward the right side of the head will reach the right ear before reaching the left ear. Similarly, a sound coming toward the right side of the head will be a little bit louder to the right ear than to the left ear, because the head blocks some of the sound from the left ear. Thus, the brain can use both the timing and intensity of sounds as cues to locate their source.

In short, there are a host of cues—some present in the environment and in retinal images, others arising from the structure of the visual system—that combine to give us a powerful and accurate sense of depth and distance. In turn, precise judgments of depth and distance, when coupled with experience, create perceptual constancy.

Perception of Motion

Sometimes the critical property of an object is not its size or shape or distance but its motion—how fast it is going and where it is heading. People often get a lot of additional information about the world from seeing it in motion. For example, a still photograph of twelve points of light attached to the hands, elbows, shoulders, ankles, knees, and hips of a person in a dark room cannot be recognized as a human figure. However, if these same points of light are seen in a movie of the person walking, they are instantly recognized as a human; even the sex of the figure can be identified (Johansson, Hofsten & Jansson, 1980).

Usually the perception of motion occurs as visual patterns from objects move across the surface of the retina. People somehow translate this two-dimensional retinal image into a three-dimensional experience. As in the case of depth perception, people make this translation automatically.

One example is the response to **looming**, which is a rapid expansion in the size of an image so that it fills the available space on the retina. When an image looms, there is an automatic tendency to perceive it as an approaching stimulus, not an expanding object viewed at a constant distance. Furthermore, if the expansion is as fast to the right as to the left, and as fast above as below, this information signals that the object is directly approaching the eyes. In other words: duck! (Regan, Kaufman & Lincoln, 1986).

If movement of the retinal image were the only factor contributing to motion perception, however, swinging your head around or even rotating your eyeballs should create the perception that everything in the visual field is moving. This is not the case because the brain also receives and processes information about the motion of the eye and head. If the brain determines that such bodily movement accounts for all of the movement of light on the retina, then the outside world is perceived as stable, not moving. To demonstrate this, close one eye and wiggle your open eyeball by gently pushing your lower eyelid. Now the brain no longer receives the usual signals that the eye is being moved by its own muscles, and the *world* is perceived as the unstable, moving element.

When you *are* moving, the movement gradient discussed in the section on depth perception can provide another cue to this fact. Imagine you are in a car riding forward toward the horizon. As you look forward, objects appear to diverge from the point where the road disappears into the horizon and to move faster as they move away from this vanishing point. You automatically perceive this pattern as the forward movement of your own body toward and past unmoving objects. Further, the magnitude and pattern of texture moving across the retina provide a cue to your speed and to whether you are accelerating, decelerating, or holding a steady rate. (The safety measure at the traffic circle described in the chapter opening relied on this phenomenon.) The fact that the accurate perception of self-motion depends greatly on "tuning in" to information already in the environment illustrates the value of the ecological view of perception (Warren & Wertheimer, 1990).

Normally, as you move through an environment, the flow of visual information across the retina is also combined with information from the vestibular and tactile senses. For example, if you accelerate in a car, you feel pressure from the back of the seat and you feel your head tilt backwards. When visual flow is perceived without appropriate sensations from other parts of the body, motion sickness may be the result. This explains why people sometimes feel sick while operating motion simulators and even while playing some video games; the moving images suggest that they are in motion when there is no real motion (Andersen, 1986).

Perceptual Illusions

Car owners are often unaware of the complex operations that allow their engines to run properly, until the car breaks down. Similarly, it is difficult to appreciate the complexities underlying the normally smooth and automatic functioning of the perceptual system until it fails. One category of perceptual failures, called *optical illusions,* is particularly helpful in revealing the wonders, and vulnerabilities, of your perceptual system. Some of these are shown in Figure 6.14. (For a discussion of illusions, see Block & Yuker, 1989.)

Figure 6.14
Five Perceptual Illusions
In the Zollner illusion (a), you can focus attention directly on a pair of parallel lines to establish that they are in fact parallel, but if you draw back to consider the entire figure, you get the clear impression that they are not parallel. The horizontal lines in the Wundt illusion (b) are actually parallel, and the twisted cord (c) is actually made up of concentric circles. The Ebbinghaus illusion (d) is a direct analogy to the misjudgment of brightness shown in Figure 6.9. The circle in the center of the pattern on the left probably looks smaller to you than the one on the right because of the sizes of the surrounding circles. In the Ponzo illusion (e), the two horizontal lines are in fact the same length.

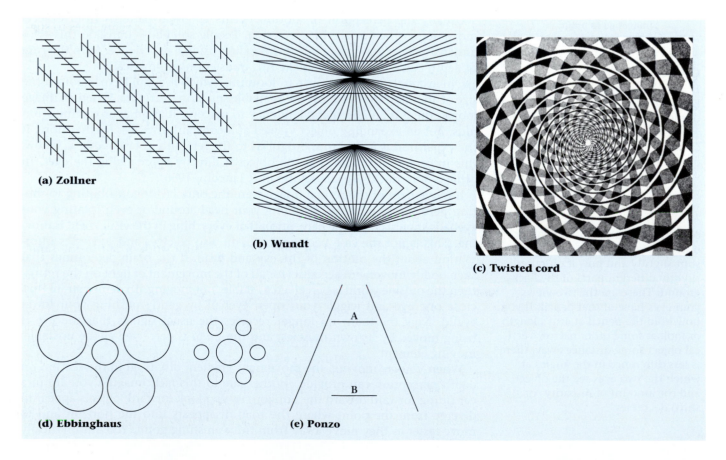

(a) Zollner

(b) Wundt

(c) Twisted cord

(d) Ebbinghaus

(e) Ponzo

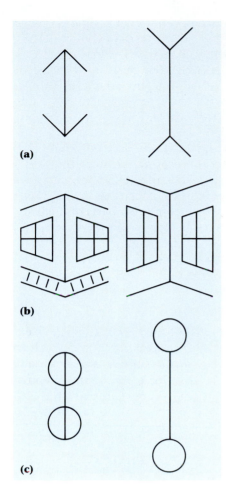

Figure 6.15
Variations on the Müller-Lyer Illusion
Part (a) shows the Müller-Lyer illusion. In (b) the illusion is placed in a three-dimensional context, in which the vertical line is used to form the outside corner of a house and the inside corner of a room. The inside corner looks taller. Part (c) shows a demonstration of the illusion that does not involve perception of three dimensions.

For psychologists, some of the most fascinating illusions are those related to depth, distance, and size constancy. Consider, for example, the *Ponzo illusion* shown in Figure 6.14(e). Why is line A perceived to be longer than line B, even though both are actually the same length? The principles behind size constancy provide one explanation. The converging lines provide a strong cue (linear perspective) that tells the perceptual system that A must be farther away than B, but both lines form images of the same length on the retina. Recall the size constancy principle: that when two objects have retinal images of the same size, the one that seems farther away is perceived as larger. Consistent with past perceptual experience and size constancy principles, then, most people perceive A to be longer than B (Rock, 1983). This explanation supports the constructionist view of perception. It also highlights the degree to which depth cues based on linear perspective automatically capture perception and signal a slanting, three-dimensional surface even when it is not there.

Similarly, Richard Gregory (1968, 1973) has argued that the *Müller-Lyer illusion* shown in Figure 6.15(a) represents a misapplication of the depth cue of linear perspective. The convergence of the arrowheads on each side of the shaft on the left makes the shaft appear to be the closest part of the scene—like the outside corner of the house in Figure 6.15(b)—whereas the divergence of the arrowheads on the right makes that shaft seem to be toward the back. By the logic applied to the Ponzo illusion, the more "distant" shaft appears to be larger.

The idea that depth cues underlie the Müller-Lyer and Ponzo illusions is supported by the fact that increasing the amount of three-dimensional information in the drawing increases the magnitude of the illusion (Leibowitz et al., 1969). For example, when the arrows in Figure 6.15(a) are created with luminous paint and viewed in a darkened room, the illusion is greatly magnified (Gregory, 1973).

Attractive as the depth perception theory of the Müller-Lyer illusion may seem, it cannot account for some phenomena (Nijhawan, 1991). A striking example is shown in Figure 6.15(c). The figure has no converging lines to suggest distance, and the figure does not give a feeling of three-dimensionality, yet it still creates a misjudgment like that in the Müller-Lyer illusion. Why? One proposed explanation is that the perceived length of an object is based on its "frame." When the frame is perceived as larger, as it is in the right side of Figure 6.15(c), so is the line segment within it (Rock, 1978).

Perhaps the best conclusion at this point is that illusions such as the Müller-Lyer illusion are multiply determined. (Figure 6.16 shows another common and equally fascinating illusion.) After all, since perception is based on many principles, it seems reasonable that illusions could reflect the violation of more than one of them.

Culture, Experience, and Perception

So far, we have talked as if all aspects of perception work or fail in the same way for everyone. Differing experiences, however, do affect how people perceive the world. To the extent that people in different cultures are exposed to substantially different visual environments, some of their perceptual experiences may be different as well. For example, researchers have compared responses to pictures containing depth cues by people from cultures that do and do not use pictures and paintings to represent reality (Derogowski, 1989). This research suggests that people in cultures that provide minimal experience with pictorial representations, like the Me'n or the Nupa in Africa, have a more difficult time judging distances shown in pictures (see Figure 6.17). These individuals also tend to have a harder time sorting *pictures* of three-dimensional objects into categories, even though they can easily sort the objects themselves (Derogowski, 1989).

Figure 6.16
The Moon Illusion
Why does the moon appear so large on the horizon? Kaufman and Rock (1962) suggest that this illusion occurs because the horizon moon seen across a space filled with distance cues appears farther away than when seen overhead. Since the retinal images of the horizon moon and the overhead moon are nearly the same size, greater perceived distance causes the horizon moon to look larger. This explanation is probably incomplete because sometimes the horizon moon seems larger even when the observer cannot see the intervening terrain (Suzuki, 1991). The illusion may be thus related to how the eye accommodates when viewing horizon and zenith moons (Roscoe, 1989). A complete explanation of this illusion continues to elude psychologists.

Figure 6.17
The Hudson Test
Cross-cultural differences in picture perception often appear on the Hudson test. Subjects are shown pictures like these and asked to judge which animal is closer to the hunter. Those familiar with pictures select the animal to the right, near the same depth as the hunter. Those less familiar with pictorial depth cues tend to select that on the left, which, though physically closer on the page, is more distant when depth cues are considered.

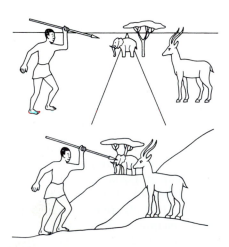

Source: Hudson, 1960.

Other studies have shown that the intensity of optical illusions varies from culture to culture and is related to cultural differences in perceptual experiences. Consider again the Ponzo illusion. Figure 6.18 shows materials that were used to test the intensity of this illusion. For Americans, the more depth cues, the greater the illusion, perhaps because their perceptual systems automatically grab onto the cue of converging lines and interpret it as a depth cue. But adding depth cues had no effect on the intensity of the illusion for people on Guam, where the flat textured fields and railroad tracks shown in Figure 6.18 were, at that time, absent (Leibowitz et al., 1969). The structure and principles of human perceptual systems do tend to create generally similar views of the world for each person. (For a summary of these principles, see "In Review: Principles of Perceptual Organization and Constancy.") But because culture shapes experience, it may help create different versions of reality.

Some psychologists have argued that reported cross-cultural differences in perception are related to factors other than perceptual experience. For example, differences in experience with the test materials, or in the amount of attention subjects' devoted to the tests might account for reported differences (Biederman, 1987). It is often difficult to find groups of people who differ in cultural background but are similar enough on other variables, such as educational background, to allow any observed differences to be attributed to cultural factors (in this case, differences in perceptual experience). Still, the perceptual differences that have been attributed to cultural experience are consistent with what we know about the role of experience in perception. Unfortunately, as more and more cultures become "westernized," the visual stimulation they present to their children will become less distinctive; eventually, research on the impact of differential experience on perception may become impossible.

Figure 6.18
Testing for the Ponzo Illusion
These images were used in Leibowitz's (1969) experiment on the Ponzo
illusion. They vary in the number of
cues that convey depth. Section (a)
shows only differing height in the
visual field, (b) adds textural gradient
cues for distance, (c) adds linear perspective cues alone, and (d) adds
both linear perspective and textural
gradient cues.

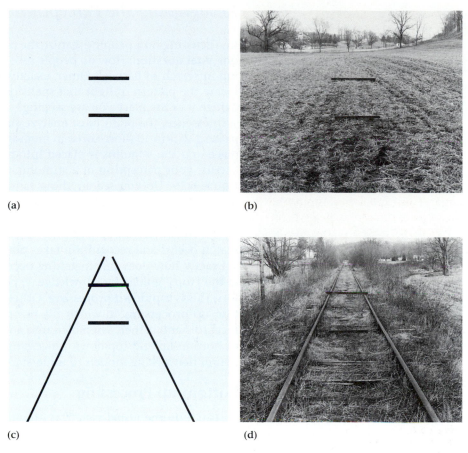

(a)   (b)

(c)   (d)

Source: Leibowitz et al., 1969.

In Review: Principles of Perceptual Organization and Constancy

Principle	Description	Example
Figure-ground	Certain objects or sounds automatically be-come identified as figures while others become meaningless background.	You see a person standing against a build-ing, not a building with a person-shaped hole in it.
Grouping	Properties of stimuli lead us to automatically group them together. These include proximity, similarity, continuity, closure, texture, simplic-ity, and common fate.	People who are sitting together, or are dressed similarly, are perceived as a group.
Perceptual constancy	Objects are perceived as constant in size, shape, color, and other properties, despite changes in their retinal images.	A train coming toward you is perceived as getting closer, not larger; a gas station sign is perceived as rotating, not changing shape.
Depth perception	The world is perceived as three-dimensional, with help from stimulus cues—such as relative size, height in the visual field, interposition, linear perspective, reduced clarity, light and shadow, and gradients—and from visual system cues, such as accommodation, convergence, and binocular disparity.	A person who looks tiny and appears high in the visual field will be perceived as being of normal size, but at a great distance.

Recognizing the Perceptual World

In discussing how people organize the perceptual world, we have so far ignored one vital question: How do people recognize what objects are? If you are driving in search of Barney's Diner, exactly what happens when your eyes finally locate the pattern of light that spells out "Barney's Diner"? How do you recognize it as the place you are seeking?

In essence, the brain must analyze the incoming pattern and compare that pattern to information stored in memory. If it finds a match, recognition takes place and the stimulus is placed into a *perceptual category*. Once recognition occurs, your perception of a stimulus may never be the same again. Look at Figure 6.19. Do you see anything familiar? If not, turn to Figure 6.21, then look at Figure 6.19 a second time. You should now see it in an entirely new light. The difference between your "before" and "after" experience of Figure 6.19 is the difference between the sensory world before and after a perceptual match occurs and recognition takes place.

Exactly how does this matching occur? Some aspects of recognition begin at the "top," guided by knowledge, expectations, and other psychological factors; this is **top-down processing**. Other aspects of recognition depend on **bottom-up processing**, in which the information comes "up" from the sensory receptors and is then assembled into a whole. Let's consider the contributions of bottom-up and top-down processing to recognition, as well as the use of neural networking models to understand both.

Bottom-up Processing

Research on the visual system is providing a detailed picture of how bottom-up processing works. As described in Chapter 5, on sensation, research suggests that all along the path from the eye to the optic nerve to the brain, certain cells respond to selected features of a stimulus, so that the stimulus is actually *analyzed* into *basic features* before these features are recombined to create the perceptual experience.

Figure 6.19
Perceptual Categorization
For the identity of this figure, turn the page.

What features are subjected to separate analysis? Again, as discussed in Chapter 5, on sensation, there is strong evidence that certain cells specialize in responding to stimuli having specific orientations in space (Hubel & Weisel, 1979). For example, one cell in the cortex might fire only in response to a diagonal line, so it acts as a *feature detector* for diagonal lines. Figure 6.20 illustrates how the analysis by such feature detectors, early in the information-processing sequence, may contribute to recognition of letters or judgments of shape. Color and motion are other sensory features that appear to be analyzed separately—in different parts of the brain—prior to full perceptual recognition (Baylis & Driver, 1992; Livingston & Hubel, 1987; Treisman, 1988).

In addition, the brain apparently analyzes *spatial frequencies*—that is, patterns of light and darkness in the visual scene. Analyzing the difference between low and high spatial frequencies may allow you to perceive texture gradients that help in making depth judgments and to recognize the general shape of blurry images or an object's fine details.

How do psychologists know that these kinds of feature analysis are actually involved in pattern recognition? As noted in the chapter on sensation, recordings of brain activity indicate that the sensory features we have listed here cause particular sets of neurons to fire. Further, people with damage in certain regions of the brain show selective impairment in the ability to perceive certain sets of sensory features, such as an object's color or movement (Banks & Krajicek, 1991).

Irving Biederman (1987) has suggested that, just as the features of lines and angles might be used for recognizing letters, a slightly more complex set of features provides the basis for recognizing natural objects. He has proposed that people recognize three-dimensional objects by detecting and then combining simple forms, which he calls *geons;* Figure 6.22 shows some of these geons. Evidence for Biederman's theory comes from experiments in which people must identify drawings when some of the details have been eliminated. Recognition becomes particularly difficult when the geons are no longer intact, as Figure 6.23 demonstrates.

Top-down Processing

Bottom-up feature analysis can explain why you recognize the letters in a sign for Barney's Diner. But why is it that you will recognize the sign more easily if

Figure 6.20
Feature Analysis in the Perception of Letters and Distance
Feature detectors that operate at lower levels of the visual system detect component features of incoming stimuli, like the corners and particular angles shown on the left side of the figure. Later in the perceptual sequence, bottom-up processing might recombine these features to aid in pattern recognition, as in the examples on the right side of the figure.

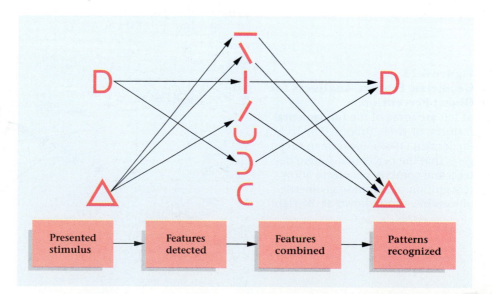

Figure 6.21
Another Version of Figure 6.19
Now that you can identify the figure clearly, look back to the previous figure, which should now be much easier to recognize.

it appears precisely at the corner where your map says you should expect it rather than a block earlier? And why can you recognize it even if a few letters are missing from the sign? Top-down processing seems to be at work in these cases. In top-down processing, people use their knowledge in making inferences or "educated guesses" to recognize objects, words, or melodies, especially when sensory information is vague or ambiguous (DeWitt & Samuel, 1990; Rock, 1983). For example, your knowledge that there is a dog in Figure 6.19 makes it much easier for you to perceive one.

Many aspects of perception can best be explained by higher-level cognitive influences, especially by expectancy and motivation. Consider Figure 6.24, for example. Some people immediately see an attractive young woman wearing a feathered hat and turning her head away. Others see an old woman with a large nose and a protruding chin (Boring, 1930). Which one you recognize first can be influenced by what you expect to see. Robert Leeper (1935) showed people either Figure 6.24(b), in which the young woman is strongly empha-

Figure 6.22
Geometric Feature Analyzers for Object Perception
At left are some of the fundamental features, or *geons,* proposed by Irving Biederman (1987). Biederman suggests that the perceptual system detects and combines geons to allow recognition of common geometric objects like those shown at the right.

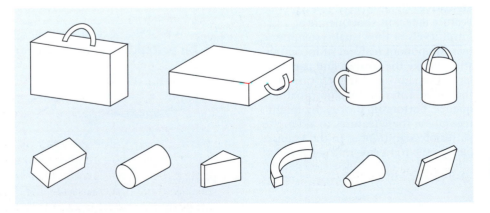

Source: Biederman, 1985.

Figure 6.23
Recognition of Objects With and Without Their Geons Destroyed
Which column of pictures is hardest to recognize? Those in columns 2 and 3 have had the same amount of ink removed, but the ink has been removed from column 3 figures so as to destroy the integrity of many of the geons used in object recognition. Because geons in the column 2 figures are intact, and it is easy to see where each one starts and stops, the objects are far easier to recognize.

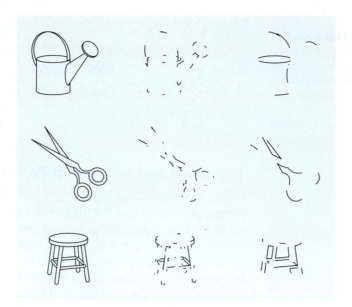

Source: Biederman, 1987.

Figure 6.24
An Ambiguous Figure
Which face do you see in part (a)? Unambiguous portraits of the young and old women are shown in parts (b) and (c).

(a)

(b)   (c)

Source: Rumelhart & McClelland, 1986.

sized, or Figure 6.24(c), which makes the old woman stand out. Then he showed Figure 6.24(a), the ambiguous drawing, to everyone. Most of those who had first seen the "young woman" version continued to see her in the ambiguous figure, whereas the old woman was more often identified by those who had first seen the version emphasizing her.

Thus, past experience can create expectancy. Expectancy, in turn, can bias perception toward one recognition or another by creating a *perceptual set,* a readiness or predisposition to perceive a stimulus in a certain way. Expectancy may also be shaped by the immediate *context* in which a stimulus occurs. For example, people would be more likely to perceive the ambiguous drawing in Figure 6.24(a) as a young woman if it appeared in a set of unambiguous drawings of young women. Context and expectancy have biasing effects for sounds as well as sights. The raw sound "eye screem" takes on very different meanings when heard in the context of "I scream whenever I am angry" rather than "I love ice cream."

Like the perception of objects and words, the perception of people can be influenced by expectancies. You may initially categorize someone as a certain type of person because he or she belongs to a certain ethnic group or social organization; then you may interpret that person's behavior in the light of your initial perception. In the chapter on social cognition we explore some of the consequences of this process.

Top-down processing also provides good explanations for the effects of motivation on perception. Suppose you are very hungry as you drive the streets of an unfamiliar city. You don't care if you find Barney's Diner or not; you'll eat anywhere. In this state of mind, you are likely to experience many false alarms, slamming on the brakes and salivating at the sight of "McDonald's Furniture," "Burger's Body Shop," "Chicken Little Antiques," or any other sign that even hints at food.

Many motives can alter perceptions. If you have ever watched an athletic contest, you probably remember a time when an obviously demented referee incorrectly called a foul on the team you wanted to win. You knew the call was wrong because you clearly saw the other team's player at fault. But suppose you had been cheering for the other team. The chances are good that you would have seen the referee's call as the right one.

Figure 6.25
Interaction of Top-down and Bottom-up Processing
Top-down processing assists in reading the obscured text on the top line. However, in the bottom line, the words are not coherently related, so top-down processing cannot operate.

it is very easy to read this redundant sentence
BUT NOT
better resist reading that grammar a/saw writing)

Top-down and Bottom-up Processing Together

Often, bottom-up and top-down processing work together to aid in recognizing the perceptual world. This interaction is beautifully illustrated by the process of reading. When the quality of the raw stimulus on the page is poor, as in Figure 6.25, top-down processes compensate to make continued reading possible. They allow you to fill in where words are not well perceived and processed, thus giving a general idea of the meaning of the text.

You can fill in the gaps left by stimuli because the world is *redundant,* giving multiple clues about what is going on. If you lose or miss one stimulus in a pattern, others can fill in the gaps so that you can still recognize the total pattern. There is so much redundancy in written language, for example, that many of the words and letters you see are not needed. Fo- ex-mp-e y-u c-n r-ad -hi- se-te-ce -it- ev-ry -hi-d l-tt-r m-ss-ng. Similarly, vision in three dimensions normally provides multiple redundant cues to depth, making recognition of distance easy and clear. It is only when many of these cues are eliminated that ambiguous stimuli, subject to multiple interpretations, create the sort of depth illusions discussed earlier.

For the spoken word, too, top-down processing can compensate for ambiguous stimuli. This fact was nicely illustrated in an experiment in which strings of five words in meaningless order, such as "wet brought who socks some," were read to subjects. There was so much noise in the background that an average of only 75 percent of the words could be recognized (Miller, Heise & Lichten, 1951). Under these conditions, bottom-up processing was difficult, because the quality of the raw stimuli was poor. But when the same words, presented under the same noisy conditions, were reordered to make a meaningful sentence (for example, "who brought some wet socks"), a second group of subjects was able to recognize almost every word. In fact, in order to reduce their performance to that of the first group, the noise level had to be doubled! Why? When the words were in meaningless order, only bottom-up processing was available, and recognizing one word was no help in identifying the next. The meaningful sentence, however, provided a more familiar context, allowing for some top-down processing in which hearing one word helped the listener make a reasonable guess (based on knowledge and experience) about the others.

Network Processing

An experiment on pattern recognition suggests another way of explaining how recognition occurs. Subjects were asked to detect whether a particular feature, like the dot and angle shown in Figure 6.26, occurred within a pattern that was briefly flashed on a computer screen (Weisstein & Harris, 1974; Purcell & Stewart, 1991). Sometimes this feature was flashed on the screen alone, sometimes in a random set of features, and sometimes it was embedded among features that resembled a three-dimensional object. Detection of the feature was faster when it was part of a whole object, a result called the *object superiority effect.* Similarly, researchers have found a *word superiority effect:* when

Linkages: Research on the effects of top-down processing supports the idea that "beauty is in the eye of the beholder." Perhaps you have come to perceive someone as physically more attractive or less attractive as you got to know him or her better. Assuming no cosmetic surgery, this change in perception occurs largely because the new information interacts with and alters, in top-down fashion, the raw sensations arising from the person's "real" appearance. Here, then, is another example of how reality is actually somewhat different for each person. Appreciating these "personal realities" can help us understand how people perceive and react to one another (see Chapter 17).

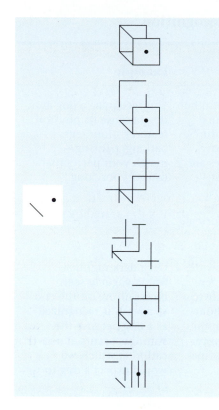

Source: Weisstein & Harris, 1974.

Figure 6.26
The Object Superiority Effect
Subjects were asked to say whether the feature at left appears in the patterns at right when those patterns were briefly flashed on a computer screen. The feature was more likely to be detected when it appeared in patterns, like those at the top right, which most resemble three-dimensional objects. This "object superiority effect" tends to support the importance of network processing in perception.

strings of letters were briefly flashed on a screen, people's ability to detect target letters was better if the string formed a word (Reicher, 1970; Prinzmetal, 1992).

These and related findings appear to be best explained in terms of *network processing,* which involves interaction among the various feature analyzers we have discussed (Green, 1991; Rumelhart & McClelland, 1986; Rumelhart & Todd, 1992). Like bottom-up processing, network processing is relatively automatic and does not require inferences, expectancies, or other cognitive processes. But like top-down processing, network processing does reflect the effects of learning, experience, and context. The communication among feature analyzers is richer and more informative to the extent that the combinations of features creates a context that has been experienced before.

More specifically, some researchers explain recognition by **parallel distributed processing (PDP) models** (Rumelhart & McClelland, 1986). These are neural network models, which we introduced in Chapter 4. Recall that in a neural network model each element is connected to every other element, and each connection has a specific weight or strength. According to PDP models, the units in a network operate in parallel—simultaneously. Connections between units either excite or inhibit other units. If the connection is excitatory, activating one unit spreads the activation to connected units. Using a connection may strengthen it.

How does this apply to recognition? According to PDP models, recognition occurs as a result of the simultaneous operation of connected units. Units are activated when matched by features in a stimulus. To the extent that features such as letters in a word or the angles in a box have occurred together in the past, their connective links will be stronger, and detection of any of them will be made more likely by the presence of all the others. This appears to be what happens in the word and object superiority effects, as Figure 6.27 explains.

PDP models, sometimes called *connectionist* models, clearly represent the computational view of perception. Indeed, many of the advances in theories of pattern recognition have been achieved by programming computers to carry out the kinds of computations that neural networks are assumed to perform in the human perceptual system (Grossberg, 1988). These computers have "learned" to read and recognize speech and even faces, in a manner that is strikingly similar to how humans learn and perform the same perceptual tasks. Research on such *artificial intelligence* is discussed in more detail in Chapter 10, on thought and language.

In summary, we have described three kinds of perceptual processing for pattern recognition (see "In Review: Mechanisms of Pattern Recognition"). Bottom-up processing analyzes and combines raw stimulus features. Top-down processing uses higher-level knowledge—including past experience, expectations, and context—to guide recognition. Network processing combines aspects of the other two; each feature in a stimulus array is more likely to be perceived as belonging to a particular pattern if it is activated by another feature with which it has been paired in the past.

Do infants perceive the world as adults do?

Linkages: Perception and Human Development

We have seen the important role that knowledge and experience of the world play in recognition. But what evidence is there that knowledge or experience is in fact necessary for basic aspects of perception, such as perceptual constancy or pattern recognition? If perception is knowledge based, does that mean that heredity is not important or that infants perceive the world much differently from adults? Philosophers have long debated whether babies are

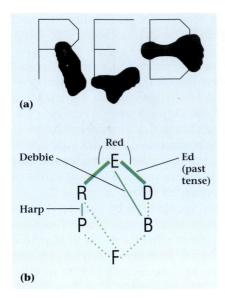

(a)

(b)

Source: Rumelhart & McClelland, 1985.

Figure 6.27
Recognizing a Word
Each letter of the word shown in (a) is ambiguous. The first could be *R* or *P,* the second *E* or *F,* and the third *D* or *B.* Yet, together, the letters are quickly recognized as the word *RED.* According to PDP models, recognition occurs because, *together,* the letters excite one another's appropriate and correct interpretation. This mutual excitation process is illustrated in (b) by a set of letter "nodes" (corresponding to activity sites in the brain), surrounded by some of the words they might activate. These nodes will be activated in the perceptual centers of the brain if evidence for their presence appears in the stimulus array. They will also be activated if nodes with which they are linked become active. The stronger the link between nodes, the more activation will occur. Strong links are formed if units have been activated together in the past. Thus, links combining R-E and E-D will be quite strong; others, like F-B, will be weak. Thus, all six letters shown in (b) will initially be excited when the stimulus in (a) is presented, but mutual excitement along the strongest links will guarantee that the word *RED* is perceived (Rumelhart & Mc-Clelland, 1985).

In Review: Mechanisms of Pattern Recognition

Mechanism	Description	Example
Bottom-up processing	Raw sensations from the eye or the ear are analyzed into basic features, such as color or movement; these features are then recombined at higher brain centers, where they are compared to stored information about objects or sounds.	You recognize a dog as a dog because its physical features—four legs, barking, panting—match your perceptual category for "dog."
Top-down processing	Knowledge of the world and experience in perceiving allow people to make inferences about the identity of stimuli, even when the quality of raw sensory information is low.	On a dark night, a small, vaguely seen blob pulling on the end of a leash is recognized as a dog because the stimulus occurs at a location at which we would expect a dog to be.
Network, or PDP, processing	Recognition depends on communication among feature analysis systems operating simultaneously, and enlightened by past experience.	A dog standing behind a picket fence will be recognized even though each disjointed "slice" of the stimulus may not look like a dog.

born with perceptual abilities or whether they acquire them by seeing, hearing, smelling, touching, and tasting things. Developmental psychologists have provided some answers, thereby also shaping understanding of the nature of perception.

Determining what infants perceive is not easy. Psychologists have studied infants' perception by observing their eye movements, especially two inborn patterns called *inhibition* and *disinhibition.* If an infant repeatedly sees stimuli that are perceived to be the same, the infant will stop looking at them. This is inhibition. If a stimulus appears that is perceived to be different, looking resumes. This is disinhibition.

Using the inhibition/disinhibition technique, Russell Adams and his associates (1986) found that newborns could perceive the difference between black-and-white versus colored displays and concluded that they had color vision within one to five days after birth. Other researchers used the same methods to show that newborns can perceive differences in the angles of lines (Slater et al., 1991). These and other studies suggest that people are born with the basic components of feature detection at birth. Do they also have an innate ability to combine these into the perception of whole objects? Apparently not. At one month of age, infants concentrate their gaze on one part of an object, like the corner of a triangle (Goldstein, 1989). At two months, however, the eyes systematically scan the perimeter of the object, suggesting that the infant is perceiving the pattern, or shape of the object, not just its basic features.

Figure 6.28
Infants' Perception of Human Faces
These are examples of stimuli used to study infants' perception of faces (Johnson et al., 1991). Newborns show significantly greater interest in the facelike pattern at the far left than in any of the other patterns. It thus appears that some aspects of face perception are innate.

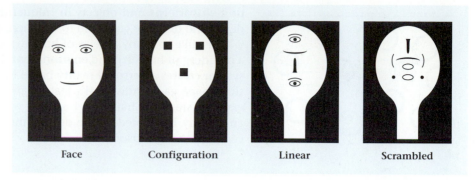

| Face | Configuration | Linear | Scrambled |

Source: Johnson et al., 1991.

Figure 6.29
The Visual Cliff
The pattern beneath this glass-topped table makes one side seem to be a high cliff. The crawling infant readily crosses the shallow side of the test apparatus but hesitates to crawl over what appears to be a cliff. When infants too young to crawl are placed on the "deep" side, they show reduced heart rate and crying, and increased attentiveness to what is below them (Campos, Langer & Krowitz, 1970).

While the ability to recognize complex patterns seems to come only with experience, there is some evidence that infants may be innately tuned to perceive at least one important complex pattern: the human face. In one study of newborns, some less than an hour old, patterns like those in Figure 6.28 were moved slowly past the infants' faces (Johnson et al., 1991). The infants moved their heads and eyes to follow these patterns, but they tracked the facelike pattern shown on the left side of Figure 6.28 significantly farther than any of the nonfaces. The difference in tracking indicates that the infants could discriminate between faces and nonfaces, and are more interested in the former. Why should this be? The investigators suggest that an interest in human faces is adaptive, in evolutionary terms, because it helps newborns focus on their only source of food and care.

Other research on perceptual development suggests that the infant's ability to accurately perceive depth and distance probably develops more slowly than object recognition. For example, the infant's ability to use binocular disparity and relative motion cues to judge depth appears to develop some time after about three months of age (Yonas, Artiberry & Granrud, 1987). Infants do not use texture gradient and linear perspective as cues to depth until they are around five to seven months old (Artiberry, Yonas & Bensen, 1989).

One of the most popular techniques for studying infants' depth perception uses the *visual cliff,* a glass-topped table that has a pattern placed beneath it in a way that makes one side of the table seem to be a high cliff. A ten-month-old infant placed in the middle of the apparatus will calmly crawl across the shallow side to reach a parent, but will hesitate and cry rather than crawl over what appears to be a cliff (Gibson & Walk, 1960). As Figure 6.29 describes, infants too young to crawl act as if they can perceive depth but are not frightened by it (Campos, Langer & Krowitz, 1970). Here is a fascinating, and evolutionarily sensible, interaction of nature and nurture. It appears that depth perception is present at or near birth, but that fear and avoidance of the danger sometimes associated with depth do not develop until an infant is old enough to crawl into trouble.

In summary, there is little doubt that many of the basic building blocks of perception are present within the first few days of life, and so, possibly, are certain more complex abilities, such as face recognition. The basics include such organ-based cues to depth as accommodation, convergence, and binocular disparity, as well as the stimulus cue of relative motion. These components make it possible for infants to perceive many aspects of their surroundings in ways that approximate adult perception. Maturation of the visual system adds to these basics as time goes by. For example, over the first few months after birth, the eye's fovea gradually develops the number of cone cells necessary for high visual acuity and perception of fine details (Goldstein, 1989). However, visual experience is also necessary if the infant is to recognize

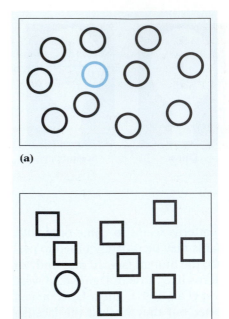

(a)

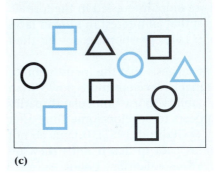

(b)

(c)

Figure 6.30
Parallel Visual Search
Look at each part of the figure and search for the blue shape in section (a), search for the circle in (b), and search for the blue circle in (c). In (a) and (b), your search is parallel. That is, you searched all locations at once for the blue target or the circle target, and the target probably "popped out" at you. In (c), however, your search for the blue circle was serial. That is, you probably had to examine each stimulus in turn until the target was found. The more nontarget elements there are, the longer a serial search will take.

unified patterns and objects in frequently encountered stimuli, to interpret depth and distance cues, and to use them in moving safely through the world.

Thus, like so many aspects of human psychology, perception is the result of a blending of heredity and environment. From infancy onward, the perceptual system creates a personal reality based in part on the learning and experience that shape each individual's feature-analysis networks and knowledge-based expectancies. In Chapters 14 and 15 we discuss how such perceptual differences may be related to the development of individual personalities and to certain behavior disorders.

Attention

Believe it or not, you still haven't found Barney's Diner. As you continue driving, you turn on the radio and catch a news story about a trainload of New York City garbage being sent from town to town in search of a landfill. After listening intently to the story, you realize that you have not been paying attention to your own search for Barney's. Did you miss it? The fact that you are not sure demonstrates that although some perceptual processes—like analyzing objects into features—occur "automatically" or *preattentively* (Kinchla, 1992), it is often necessary to pay attention to something in order to perceive it.

Attention is the process of directing and focusing certain psychological resources, usually by voluntary control, to enhance perception, performance, and mental experience. Some psychological disorders such as attention deficit hyperactivity disorder (ADHD) appear to be related to malfunctions in attentional systems (see Chapter 15). As a resource, attention has three characteristics. First, it *improves mental processing;* you often need to concentrate your attention on a task to do your best at it. Second, attention is associated with a sense of *effort.* Prolonged concentration of attention can leave you drained, and when you are fatigued, focusing attention on anything becomes more difficult. Third, attentional resources are *limited.* When your attention is focused on reading this book, for example, you have less attention left over to listen to a conversation in the next room.

Attention and Automatic Processing

A flashing red light on the control panel will automatically attract the attention of a nuclear power plant operator, just as your bright red wallet will attract your attention as you search for it in the grass. Psychologists describe this ability to search rapidly and automatically for targets as *parallel processing;* it is as if you can examine all nearby locations at once (in parallel) and rapidly detect the target if it appears at any location. Figure 6.30 provides another example. If you look for the blue target in Figure 6.30(a) or the circle in Figure 6.30(b), each one "pops out" at you from its background. The automatic, parallel processing that allows detection of the features of blueness or circularity suggests that such features are analyzed before the point at which attention is required.

Now search for the blue circle in Figure 6.30(c). It does not "pop out" to the same extent as the other targets. Why? The search for this "two-feature" target demands *serial processing,* in which attention must be focused on each item in turn, to determine if it is or is not the target (Treisman, 1988; Treisman & Gelade, 1980). The "pop-out" test offers a good way to determine which kinds of information are processed in parallel, leaving spare attention for use elsewhere, and which require serial processing and thus more focused attention.

Where's Waldo? This game provides an example of the need for serial processing of information in order to find a target.

Advertisers know that certain stimulus features—such as movement, contrast, color, and intensity—capture attention, and they use this knowledge to call attention to their products. Magicians also capitalize on selective attention by creating compelling visual events that pull the audience's attention away from the actions that lie behind their tricks.

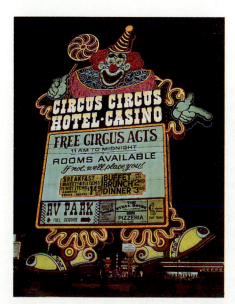

Allocating Attention

Because attentional resources are limited, people cannot attend to everything at once. Attention is *selective;* it is like a spotlight that illuminates different parts of the external environment or various mental processes. For example, you can attend to the words of a lecturer, or to your thoughts or daydreams, but not to both at once.

Sometimes the spotlight of attention is guided by features of sensory information that are processed preattentively. If your name is mentioned across a noisy, crowded room, it may capture your attention and, in the process, disrupt your ability to attend to the conversation you were having (Moray, 1960). With the limits of human attentional resources in mind, engineering psychologists try to determine the kinds of stimuli most likely to automatically attract attention to warnings of danger in complex systems (Bettman, Payne & Staelin, 1986; Wogalter et al., 1991). For example, the most effective auditory warning signal in an aircraft might be a personalized one that calls out the pilot's name.

Attention can also be guided by factors other than external stimuli. For example, you can choose to attend to a book rather than to the TV, or *vice versa.* Also, in developing certain skills, people learn to direct their attention to critical sources of information that they once ignored. The skilled baseball player attends to subtle characteristics of the pitcher's delivery, the skilled driver looks farther down the road than the novice, and the skilled pilot will selectively attend to the flight instruments in a more efficient manner than will a trainee (Abernethy, 1988; Mourant & Rockwell, 1972; Wickens, 1992).

Divided Attention   Although attentional resources are limited, the spotlight of attention is sometimes wide enough to allow people to perceive, or do, more than one very specific thing at a time. In many familiar situations, people divide attention efficiently enough to perform more than one activity at a time (Damos, 1992). In fact, as Figure 6.31 illustrates, it is sometimes difficult to keep attention focused rather than divided. People can walk while talking, or drive while listening to music. People can even divide attention between two visual stimuli, as when a driver recognizes Barney's Diner while perceiving the flow of information necessary to keep the car in its lane. Even reading involves divided attention; perceptual processes recognize words while memory processes hold them in awareness long enough for the reader to combine them into sentences and understand the author's meaning (Just & Carpenter, 1992). But try reading a book while having a conversation. It is virtually impossible.

Why is it sometimes so easy and sometimes so difficult to do two things at once? We have already seen that if one task is *automatic,* like signing your name or searching for a bright target on a dark background, it can easily be performed along with another task (Schneider, 1985). Automatic processing tends to occur on tasks that either have been extensively practiced or, like feature analysis, take place out of awareness at lower levels of perceptual processing (Treisman, Viera & Hayes, 1992). When one of two simultaneous tasks requires little or no attention, there is usually no problem doing both tasks at once.

Even when two tasks require attention, it may still be possible to perform them simultaneously, as long as each taps into different kinds of attentional resources (Wickens, 1992). For example, some attentional resources are devoted to perceiving incoming stimuli, while others handle making responses. This specialization of attention allows a skilled pianist to read musical notes and press keys simultaneously even the first time through a piece. Apparently,

BLUE   GREEN

GREEN   ORANGE

PURPLE ORANGE

GREEN   BLUE

RED   RED

GRAY   GRAY

RED   BLUE

BLUE   PURPLE

Figure 6.31
The Stroop Task
Stimuli that are processed automatically can't easily be "turned off." As you look at this list of words, try, as rapidly as possible, to call out the color of the *ink* in which each word is presented. This *Stroop task* (Stroop, 1935) is not easy because the brain automatically processes the *meaning* of these familiar words, which then competes with the response you are supposed to give. To do well, you must focus attention on color alone and not allow your attention to be divided between color and meaning. A child who is just learning to read will have far less trouble with this task, because the child does not yet process the meaning of words as automatically as experienced readers do. For experienced readers, the difficulty of the Stroop task lies in the fact that it requires you to focus on just one stimulus characteristic and ignore others, whereas your general tendency is to divide attention between the two.

the human brain has more than one type of attentional resources and more than one spotlight of attention (Navon & Gopher, 1979; Wickens, 1989).

This notion of different types of attention also helps explain why a driver can listen to the radio while steering safely and why voice control can be an effective way of performing a second task in an aircraft while the pilot's hands are busy manipulating the control stick (Wickens, 1992). The relative ease with which people can speak while using their hands is one reason why so many car phones now feature voice dialing; saying the desired number is far less likely to cause an accident than dialing it manually.

Divided Attention and Stress   Suppose your job is to operate the controls of a modern, automated power plant. You face a vast array of dials, meters, graphs, charts, and warning lights. Should a serious problem occur, many of these stimuli will compete for your attention. To perceive all of them correctly, your beam of attention must be divided as widely as possible. But the stress of emergency situations tends to narrow attention, not broaden it (Easterbrook, 1959; Hockey, 1986).

Nowhere have the limits of the ability to divide attention under stress been more clearly and tragically demonstrated than just prior to the crash of an Eastern Airlines L1011 into the Florida Everglades in 1972 (Wiener, 1977). The plane was approaching Miami's airport at night when the crew became aware of a warning light indicating that the landing gear was malfunctioning. They set the autopilot for level flight and then directed their attention to diagnosing the cause of the warning light. Somehow the autopilot setting was moved so that it produced a gradual descent. As the plane came closer to the ground, air traffic controllers, as well as signals in the cockpit, warned the crew of their situation. But their attention was so intently focused on the landing gear problem that they did not attend to these signals until it was too late to avoid disaster.

A decrease in the ability to divide attention is only one of many consequences of stress discussed in Chapter 13. Exactly why this ability is impaired under stress is not fully understood, but awareness of the problem has led engineering psychologists to recommend steps to counteract it. They have suggested that instrument displays be better integrated physically so that, as attention narrows, critical pieces of information are less likely to be ignored (Vicente & Rasmussen, 1990).

Attention and the Brain

If directing attention to a task causes extra mental "work" to be done, there should be evidence of that work in brain activity. Such evidence has been provided by positron emission tomography (PET) scans, which reveal increased blood flow to regions of the brain associated with the mental processing necessary for the task. In one study, for example, subjects were asked either to focus attention on reporting only the color of a stimulus, or to divide attention between reporting its color, speed of motion, and shape (Corbetta et al., 1991). When attention was focused on color alone, increased blood flow appeared only in the part of the brain where that stimulus feature was analyzed; when attention was divided, the added supply of blood was shared between two locations. Similarly, particular patterns of blood flow have been observed in different areas of the brain involved in different reading processes such as attending to the shape, sound, or meaning of words (Peterson et al., 1990).

Other research using PET scans, surgery on animal subjects, and case studies of humans with brain damage has shown that switching the spotlight of visual attention involves at least three different parts of the brain (see, for example,

LaBerge, 1991; Posner & Peterson, 1990). An area in the posterior parietal lobe of the cerebral cortex appears responsible for disengaging attention from its present focus. A region in the midbrain's superior colliculus is involved in shifting the focus of attention. Interestingly, this region is also involved in eye movements. A third area deep in the thalamus, called the pulvinar, focuses attention on a new location (Posner & Peterson, 1990). Finally, there is evidence that the right cerebral hemisphere, more than the left, is responsible for sustaining or concentrating attention on a particular task (Pardo, Fox & Raichle, 1991). Because attention appears to be a linked set of resources that improve information processing at several levels and locations in the brain, it is not surprising that no single brain region has been identified as an "attention center" (Posner & Peterson, 1990).

Applications of Research on Perception

Throughout this chapter we have mentioned ways in which the perceptual system shapes people's ability to handle a variety of tasks, from recognizing restaurant signs to detecting weapons at an airport security checkpoint. In this section we examine the application of perception research to two areas in which perception is particularly important: aviation and reading.

Aviation Psychology

Much of the impetus for research on perception in aviation has come from accidents caused in part by failures of perception (Wiener & Nagel, 1988; O'Hare & Roscoe, 1991). To land an aircraft safely, for example, pilots must make very accurate perceptual judgments of how far they are from the ground, and how fast and from what angle they are approaching a runway. Normally, the bottom-up perceptual cues providing this information are rich and redundant, and the pilots' perception is accurate (Gibson, 1979). Further, the ground surface they are approaching matches their expectations based on experience, thus adding top-down processing to produce a correct perception of reality. But suppose there are few depth cues because the landing is occurring at night, and suppose the lay of the land is different from the pilot's normal experience. With both bottom-up and top-down processing impaired, the pilot's interpretation of reality may be disastrously incorrect.

The pilot of a modern commercial jetliner is faced with a potentially overwhelming array of visual and auditory signals that must be correctly perceived and interpreted to ensure a safe landing.

If, for example, the runway is much smaller than a pilot expects, it might be perceived as farther away than it actually is—especially at night—and thus may be approached too fast (O'Hare & Roscoe, 1991). (This illusion is similar to the one mentioned earlier in which drivers overestimate their distance from small cars.) Or if a pilot expects the runway terrain to be flat but it actually slopes upward, the pilot might falsely perceive that the aircraft is too high. Misguided attempts to "correct" a plane's altitude under these circumstances have caused pilots to fly in too low, producing a series of major nighttime crashes in the 1960s (Kraft, 1978). Psychologists helped to prevent similar tragedies by recommending that airline training programs remind pilots about the dangers of visual illusions and the importance of relying on their flight instruments during landings, especially at night.

Unfortunately, the instruments in a typical aircraft cockpit present information that bears little resemblance to the perceptual world. A pilot depending on these instruments must do a lot of time-consuming and effortful serial processing in order to perceive and piece together the information necessary to understand the aircraft's position and movement. To address this problem, engineering psychologists have helped to develop displays that present a realistic three-dimensional image of the flight environment—similar in some ways to a video game display. This image more accurately captures the many cues for depth perception that the pilot needs (Lintern, 1991; Haskell & Wickens, 1993).

Research on auditory perception has also contributed to aviation safety, both in the creation of warning signals that are most likely to catch the pilot's attention and in efforts to minimize errors in cockpit communications. Air traffic control communications use a special vocabulary and standardized phrases in order to avoid ambiguity. But as a result, the communications are also usually short, with little of the built-in redundancy that, in normal conversation, allows people to understand a sentence even if some words are missing. If a pilot anxious to depart on time perceives an expected message as "take off" when the actual message is "hold for takeoff," the results can be catastrophic. Just such an error was responsible for the death of hundreds of people in the 1979 runway collision of two 747s in the Canary Islands (Hawkins, 1987). Problems like these are being addressed, "bottom-up," through "noise canceling" microphones and visual message displays (Kerns, 1991), as well as through the use of slightly longer messages that aid top-down processing by providing more contextual cues.

Reading

Few would disagree that reading is one of the most important abilities in the human repertoire. Visual perception plays a vital role in making this skill possible.

Normally when you read, your eyes scan across the page, stopping to fixate at various points, then making short jumps from one position to the next. Two factors place physical limits on the speed with which you can read coherent text: (1) how rapidly you can shift from one fixation to the next (that is, the minimum time you can spend on one fixation before moving on) and (2) how much print you can take in at a single fixation.

The minimum time people can spend on one fixation and then move to the next is around 250 milliseconds, meaning that humans can make no more than about four fixations per second. The amount people can perceive during one fixation is roughly ten characters to the left and right of the fixation point for each eye. Thus, if we assume that twenty characters is roughly equivalent to three words, the maximum possible reading speed would be around seven hundred words per minute. Actually, fixations are usually longer than 250 milliseconds when words are less familiar, and people rarely move their eyes a full twenty characters. Thus, a normal reader typically reads only about three hundred words per minute.

To read faster than seven hundred words per minute, you must *skim,* skipping some letters and words altogether. This technique works because of top-down processing and the redundancy of language. Still, skimming disrupts comprehension, especially if the material is difficult and its information content is high (that is, not very redundant). This is not to suggest that skimming and speed reading are bad habits. In fact, one of the most important reading skills is **adaptive reading**, which means speeding up and slowing down according to the content of the material and the level of comprehension required (Anderson, 1979).

When you read, your brain not only analyzes the visual pattern of the letters, in parallel, but also determines the sound of the word (Adams, 1990). In fact, the ability to quickly identify the meaning of each word seems to depend on close communication between the auditory and visual systems. This communication appears to be accomplished through parallel distributed processing (PDP), as described earlier (Seidenberg & McClelland, 1989). It is the development of this rapid parallel processing, rather than any substantial differences in visual scanning, that governs the acquisition of skilled, rapid reading (Adams, 1990).

Understanding that both visual and auditory systems are involved in reading skill has helped researchers learn more about various reading disabilities. For example, **dyslexia** is a condition in which a person with normal intelligence and full comprehension of spoken words has difficulty understanding written words. A dyslexic child could follow your spoken instruction to "Go over to the table and take the apples out of the bag" but might be mystified by the same request made in writing. Obviously, this disruption in the process of translating letters on the page into meaningful interpretations can create major obstacles to learning. There is now strong evidence that dyslexia is not the result of a single breakdown in the perceptual process, so the term actually refers to a number of different reading deficiencies (Tyler & Elliott, 1988; Pennington, 1991).

One possible cause of dyslexia is difficulty in translating the visual form of a written word into the corresponding auditory, or *phonetic,* representation (the sound), a process that normal readers do automatically and fluently (Miles & Miles, 1990). If this breakdown in visual-auditory perception is indeed responsible for some forms of dyslexia, it may explain why reading disorders appear to be less frequent in cultures that use a purely pictorial (not a phonetic) representation of words, such as the Kanji symbols in Japanese (Miles & Miles, 1990).

Other researchers have suggested that some forms of dyslexia can be explained by problems in the brain while learning to read. Normally, a child shifts from the right-hemisphere-dominated task of learning the shapes of letters to the left-hemisphere-dominated task of associating letters with speech sounds (Bakker, 1990). According to this view, some children remain "stuck" for too long on the shape-learning task and never fully develop the phonetic analysis skills necessary for normal reading abilities. Other children may shift too soon, without fully learning the visual characteristics of the letters. Despite intense study, psychologists are not yet sure what causes dyslexia, but perceptual processes are undoubtedly involved.

Future Directions

We have outlined how perception translates raw sensations into information that is meaningful and useful to the perceiver. The process is elaborate, involving both bottom-up and top-down processing. Many of the principles of perception are well documented; yet questions and debates remain.

The most active trend in perceptual research, and one that is likely to engage researchers for years to come, is modeling on computers the computational processes thought to be involved in perception. To shed light on human perception, these computational models must work in a way that is faithful to the ways in which the brain actually carries out perceptual analysis—relying, for example, on neural networks and parallel distributed processing (McClelland, 1992). This computer modeling will be part of a larger effort to determine which aspects of perception can be explained purely by characteristics of the incoming stimulus array, which can be explained by neural computations, and which must be accounted for by complex cognitive and motivational variables.

The issue of attention will also continue to intrigue psychologists (Dulany, 1992; Kinchla, 1992; Vellmans, 1991). They will study its complex relation to the structure of the brain, and they will try to clarify exactly which aspects of perception require attention and which do not. Researchers will also seek to identify those forms of automatic perceptual processing which are fundamen-

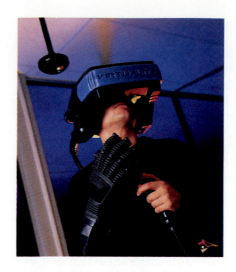

In virtual reality systems, the user wears the computer-generated display as a mask, which senses head movements. Using this movement information, the computer creates an image of wherever the user looks in the virtual world. The user also wears "data gloves," which can both sense hand position (and so display a "virtual hand" to the eyes) and provide sensations to the finger tips, creating the perception of touch when the virtual hand makes contact with a virtual object.

tal to the hardware of the nervous system and those which *become* automatic through experience and practice (Treisman, Viera & Hayes, 1992).

The coming years will also see a new approach to the age-old question of "what is reality?" If reality lies in perceptions of sensory input, it may be possible to manufacture sensory cues that can give people the experience of many different realities, much as an electronic synthesizer creates the sound of many different musical instruments. Capitalizing on recent advances in computer technology, scientists are working on the creation of *virtual reality,* a set of sensations so compelling that observers feel that they are really "in" the computer-generated world, not just perceiving its image (Ellis, 1991; Rheingold, 1991; Reveaux, 1993). Part of the effect is created by computer graphics, which produce the most startlingly faithful images possible. The sense of reality is enhanced by other sensory inputs, such as three-dimensional sound that surrounds the listener (Baughman & Wenzel, 1992). Research conducted so far suggests that these coordinated sensory inputs create a strong feeling of reality, not just an impressive show.

Though it is already being exploited for entertainment, virtual reality technology also has valuable applications in architectural planning, space exploration, medicine, and other fields. Designers and clients may someday "walk through" a virtual model of a planned building. Scientists might explore a "virtual" Martian surface created by data from space probes (McGreevy, 1991). And before actually performing certain operations, surgeons may first explore relevant anatomical details, and even practice the procedure, using a virtual human body whose characteristics have been digitized on a computer.

If you want to learn more about these and other aspects of perception, consider taking the basic course in the area, which is usually called "Sensation and Perception." Many psychology departments also offer advanced courses in perception. If the idea of programming computers to perceive intrigues you, look for courses in artificial intelligence; they are commonly offered by computer science departments. And for more on the nature of reality, take some philosophy courses.

Summary and Key Terms

Perception is the active process through which people use knowledge and understanding of the world to interpret sensations as meaningful experiences.

Three Views of Perception

The *ecological* view of perception holds that the environment itself provides the cues that people use to form perceptions. The *constructionist* view suggests that the perceptual system constructs the experience of reality, making inferences and applying knowledge in order to interpret sensations. The *computational* view emphasizes the computations performed by the nervous system.

Psychophysics

Absolute Thresholds: Is Something Out There?
Psychophysics is the study of the relationship between stimulus energy and the psychological experience of that energy. It has traditionally been concerned with matters such as determining *absolute thresholds* for the detection of stimuli. *Internal noise* and one's *response criterion* cause variation in the absolute threshold.

Going Beyond the Threshold: Signal-Detection Theory
Signal-detection theory describes how detection is affected by *sensitivity* and the response criterion. Sensitivity and response criterion can be graphed in the receiver operating characteristic curve. Signal-detection theory has been applied to problems in areas such as airport security and eyewitness testimony.

Judging Differences Between Stimuli: Weber's, Fechner's, and Stevens's Laws
Weber's law states that the minimum detectable amount of change in a stimulus, the *difference threshold* or *just-noticeable difference (JND),* increases in proportion to the initial amount of the stimulus. The less the initial stimulation, the smaller the change must be in order to be detected. Fechner's law and Stevens's power law describe the relation between the magnitude of a stimulus and its perceived intensity.

Organizing the Perceptual World

Principles of Perceptual Organization
When people perceive objects or sounds, they automatically discriminate *figure* from *ground.* In addition, the perceptual

system automatically groups stimuli into patterns on the basis of the *Gestalt* principles of *proximity, similarity, continuity, closure, texture, simplicity,* and *common fate.*

Perceptual Constancy
Because of *perceptual constancy,* the brightness, size, and shape of objects can be seen as constant even though the sensations received from those objects may change. Size and shape constancy depend on the relationship between the retinal image of the object and the knowledge-based perception of its distance. Brightness constancy depends on the perceived relationship between the brightness of an object and its background.

Depth Perception
The perception of distance, or *depth perception,* depends partly on stimulus cues and partly on the physical structure of the visual system. Some of the stimulus cues are *relative size, height in the visual field, interposition, linear perspective, reduced clarity, light and shadow, textural gradients,* and *movement gradients.* Cues based on the structure of the visual system include *convergence* of the eyes (the fact that the eyes must move to focus on the same object), *binocular disparity* (the fact that the eyes are set slightly apart), and *accommodation* (the change in the shape of the lenses as objects are brought into focus).

Perception of Motion
The perception of motion results, in part, from the movement of stimuli across the retina. Expanding or *looming* stimulation is perceived as an approaching object. Movement of the retinal image is interpreted along with information about movement of the head, eyes, and other parts of the body, so that one's own movement can be discriminated from the movement of external objects.

Perceptual Illusions
Perceptual illusions are distortions of reality that result when principles of perception are applied inappropriately. Many illusions are caused by misreading depth cues and by evaluating stimuli in the context of their surroundings.

Culture, Experience, and Perception
To the extent that the visual environments of people in different cultures differ, their perceptual experiences—as evidenced by their responses to perceptual illusions—may differ as well.

Recognizing the Perceptual World
Both *bottom-up processing* and *top-down processing* may contribute to recognition of the world. The ability to recognize objects is based on finding a match between the pattern of sensations organized by the perceptual system and a pattern that is stored in memory.

Bottom-up Processing
Bottom-up processing seems to be accomplished by the analysis of stimulus features, or combinations of features, such as form, color, motion, depth, and spatial frequencies.

Top-down Processing
Top-down processing is influenced by expectancy and motivation. Expectancy produces a perceptual set to make a particular categorization.

Top-down and Bottom-up Processing Together
Top-down and bottom-up processing commonly work together to create recognition. Top-down processing can fill in gaps in physical stimuli, in part because the environment provides redundant stimuli.

Network Processing
Recent research on pattern recognition has focused attention on network, or *parallel distributed processing (PDP),* models of perception. These emphasize the simultaneous activation and interaction of feature-analysis systems and the role of experience.

Linkages: Perception and Human Development
The ability to perceive color, basic shape features, and possibly the face are present at or near birth. Other abilities, like recognition of form, are acquired later. Depth is perceived early, but its meaning is learned later. Perceptual abilities are modified by both experience and maturation.

Attention
Attention is the process of focusing psychological resources to enhance perception, performance, and mental experience.

Attention and Automatic Processing
Some information can be processed more or less automatically, leaving spare attention for use elsewhere and allowing for parallel processing; other situations demand focused attention.

Allocating Attention
Attention is selective; it is like a spotlight that illuminates different parts of the external environment or various mental processes. What people attend to depends partly on the stimuli in the environment and partly on their choices. People can sometimes attend to two tasks at once, especially if a task has been extensively practiced or if different attentional resources are involved. However, there are limits to how well people can divide attention. These limits are particularly great under stressful conditions, when the focus of attention tends to narrow.

Attention and the Brain
Psychologists are identifying various brain regions responsible for different aspects of attention. No single brain region has been identified as an "attention center."

Applications of Research on Perception
Research on human perception has numerous practical applications.

Aviation
Accurate size and distance judgments, top-down processing, and attention are all important to safety in aviation.

Reading
The number of letters or words perceived during a fixation and the minimum time spent on each fixation put physical limitations on reading speed. Skimming usually results in some loss of comprehension; *adaptive reading* maximizes both overall speed and comprehension. Reading problems such as *dyslexia* may result from several different, but not fully understood, causes.

Chapter 7

Consciousness

Outline

A woman with the initials P.S. suffered brain damage resulting in a syndrome called *hemi-neglect,* which caused her to ignore one entire side of her world. When copying a stick-figure or drawing a picture from memory, for example, she included only the details of objects' right sides, yet she thought her drawings were complete. When reading, she skipped or changed the left-most letters in words (thus she read *simile* as *mile* and *facade* as *arcade*). But neurological testing showed that P.S. could still see both sides of objects. If there was nothing wrong with her eyes, or with the nerves connecting them to her brain, what was her problem?

Neuropsychologists John Marshall and Peter Halligan argue that although hemi-neglect patients like P.S. can still see both sides of objects, they have problems becoming *conscious* of the left-sided visual information they receive. To test this idea, they asked P.S. to look at two drawings of a house that were identical except that one showed flames coming from the house's left side. P.S. insisted that both houses looked the same, but when asked "Which house would you rather live in?," she consistently pointed to the house without the flames. Apparently, her brain had received, understood, and guided responses to left-sided visual information, but P.S. was unaware of it (Marshall & Halligan, 1988).

Cases like P.S. illustrate that in some circumstances people can detect and respond to stimuli without being aware of having done so. If mental processing can proceed without awareness, what is gained when we *are* conscious of the world around us? Exactly what does it mean to say that one is conscious or aware? Just what is consciousness, and what does it do for us?

Consciousness can be defined as the process of being aware of the outside world as well as of one's own mental processes, thoughts, feelings, and perceptions. It is at the heart of psychology (see the Linkages diagram). Consciousness is a property of many mental processes rather than a unique mental process. Thus, memories can be conscious, but consciousness is not memory; perceptions can be conscious, but consciousness is not perception. In this chapter we describe the nature of consciousness and consider how it affects mental activity. We also explore the changes in consciousness that occur as people sleep, dream, undergo hypnosis, meditate, or use certain drugs.

Analyzing Consciousness

As noted in Chapter 1, the formal psychological study of consciousness began in 1879 with Wilhelm Wundt, founder of European psychology. Wundt's approach, called *structuralism,* sought to describe the *structure* of consciousness—its basic building blocks—by carefully observing conscious experience. Structuralists used the technique of *introspection.* In this method, trained subjects were given a stimulus (such as a bright red object) and tried to describe the sensations (for example, brightness, redness) that made up their conscious experience of that stimulus. Introspection can be misleading, however, as exemplified by the perceptual illusions described in Chapter 6, and by the experience of movement created by films, which actually consist of a series of still photographs.

In the late 1800s, American psychologist William James offered an alternative to structuralism by studying how consciousness *functions* to help people adapt to their environments (James, 1890, 1892). His approach, called *functionalism,* focused on the ongoing "stream" of consciousness—the ever-changing pattern of images, sensations, memories, and other mental events. He wanted to know how the whole process works. Why, for example, do most people remember recent events better than things that happened in the remote past?

In the early 1900s, John B. Watson argued that psychologists should ignore consciousness and focus instead on observable stimuli and behavior. Watson's approach, known as *behaviorism,* admitted the existence of consciousness, but considered it useless as a target of research since it cannot be observed directly. This view dominated psychological research for several decades, during which time the study of consciousness became unpopular, especially in the United States.

Mainstream psychology has now come full circle, once again accepting consciousness as a legitimate topic for research. As always, psychologists are committed to examining consciousness scientifically, using the empirical methods and principles we described in Chapter 2 (Libet, 1992).

213

Linkages

The questions in this diagram illustrate some of the relationships between the topic of this chapter, consciousness, and other chapter topics. Research in biological psychology, for example, provides a wealth of information about what your brain is doing while you sleep and how chemicals in the brain change if you drink alcohol or coffee. These activities alter your consciousness, your awareness of the world, and your own mental processes. That awareness has often been compared to a flowing stream, because it changes constantly. Many of the changes reflect variations in attention, discussed in the chapter on perception. These and other linkages between consciousness and other aspects of psychology are discussed in the text. The diagram shows a sampling of these links; the numbers in parentheses indicate where the questions are discussed. ■

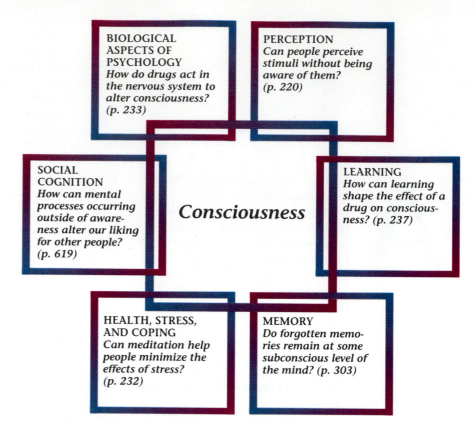

BIOLOGICAL ASPECTS OF PSYCHOLOGY
How do drugs act in the nervous system to alter consciousness? (p. 233)

PERCEPTION
Can people perceive stimuli without being aware of them? (p. 220)

SOCIAL COGNITION
How can mental processes occurring outside of awareness alter our liking for other people? (p. 619)

Consciousness

LEARNING
How can learning shape the effect of a drug on consciousness? (p. 237)

HEALTH, STRESS, AND COPING
Can meditation help people minimize the effects of stress? (p. 232)

MEMORY
Do forgotten memories remain at some subconscious level of the mind? (p. 303)

Three questions dominate the psychological study of consciousness today. First, like the philosophers who preceded them, psychologists grapple with the *mind-body problem,* the question of the relationship between the conscious mind and the physical brain (Efron, 1992; Rossetti, 1992). According to one approach, known as *dualism,* the mind is entirely separate from the physical brain. This idea was advanced in the seventeenth century by French philosopher René Descartes. Descartes claimed that a person's soul, though separate from the brain, could "view" and interact with brain events through the pineal gland, a brain structure about the size of a grape. In contrast, *materialism* argues that mind *is* brain. Materialists suggest that the complex interconnections among the brain's nerve cells somehow produce consciousness, much as the components of a television set interact to produce a picture. Materialists support their claim by arguing that because brain damage sometimes removes awareness of certain mental activities (as in the case of P.S.), the damaged tissue must have provided a physical basis for consciousness. In response, dualists note that brain injuries impair only isolated pockets of awareness while consciousness of other mental activities remains intact.

A second question is whether nonhuman intelligence can support consciousness. Some psychologists believe that animals may possess consciousness (Radner & Radner, 1989), and others speculate that computers might develop the capacity to "think" about the information they process (Churchland & Churchland, 1990). If, as some believe, "humans are machines of a special biological kind" that can think, then "it might be possible to produce a thinking machine out of different materials altogether—say, out of silicon chips or vacuum tubes" (Searle, 1990, p. 26).

A third question focuses on the nature of consciousness. Is it one thing, or many? The *Cartesian theater* view sees consciousness as a unitary thing, a kind of stage where all the diverse experiences that make up awareness converge to "play" before the "audience" of your mind. Those adopting this view point to the fact that the subjective intensity of lights, sounds, weights, and other stimuli follows similar psychophysical laws (as described in the chapter on perception), as if each sensory system passes its inputs to a single "monitor" that coordinates the experience of magnitude (Teghtsoonian, 1992). Those adopting the *multiple drafts* view argue that the mind simultaneously processes many parallel streams of information, each of which can independently contribute to conscious experience (Dennett, 1991; Dennett & Kinsbourne, 1992). The multiple drafts view is supported by research on parallel processing models of sensation, perception, memory, and thought described in Chapters 5, 6, 9, and 10. These models emphasize the brain's separate and somewhat independent systems for processing different aspects of information at the same time (Goodale & Milner, 1992; Sejnowski, 1991). For example, in the visual system, the form and color of objects are processed separately, and there is no evidence that the separate streams of processing ever converge in a single place within the brain.

The Role of Consciousness

Consciousness improves and expands many mental abilities. It is your conscious awareness that the face in front of you belongs to your lover that allows you bestow a kiss without having to wait to hear the person speak. Further, awareness of mental operations can act as a "bridge" to take those operations into new realms (Reber, 1992; Rozin, 1976). Thus, by being aware of where and how you learned to play tennis, you will have a good idea of where to refer others who wish to do the same.

One way to understand the importance and the limits of consciousness is to consider the mental processing that can occur outside of consciousness. Evidence about the extent to which people can perform mental operations without awareness comes from both normal subjects and those with certain kinds of brain damage.

Mental Processing Without Awareness

Linkages: Can sensations that do not reach consciousness affect behavior? (a link to Sensation)

Many important mental operations proceed without our being aware of them. A fascinating experiment demonstrated this point with patients who were under anesthesia for surgical procedures. While the still-unconscious patients were in a postoperative recovery room, an audiotape player presented a list of fifteen word pairs, over and over. After the patients regained consciousness, they could not say what words had been played while they were in the recovery room—or even whether an audiotape had been presented. Yet when given one word from each of the fifteen word pairs and asked to say the first word that came to mind, the patients were able to produce the other member of the audiotaped word pair. Thus, the patients *had* heard the audiotape, and could use their memory of it, but they were unaware of the mental processes involved as they did so (Cork, Kihlstrom, & Hameroff, 1992; Kihlstrom, et al., 1990).

Even when you are awake and alert, mental processing can occur without your awareness. One example is provided by the *mere-exposure effect,* the tendency to like previously encountered stimuli more than new ones. In one experiment, subjects viewed slides of complex and unfamiliar characters used in Japanese writing. Then they saw another set of characters and were asked to rate their liking for each character and to say which ones they had seen earlier and which were new. The subjects liked the previously viewed characters more than the new ones, even when they could not say which characters they had seen before and which were new. In other words, the subjects' ratings revealed

Evidence for the operation of subconscious mental processing includes research showing that surgery patients may be able to hear and later comply with instructions or suggestions given while they are under anesthesia and of which they have no memory (Bennett, Giannini & Davis, 1985). In another study, people showed physiological arousal to emotionally charged words even when they were not paying attention to them (Von Wright, Anderson & Stenman, 1975).

a better memory of their prior experience than their conscious reports did (Moreland & Zajonc, 1977).

Similar results have been found in experiments on *priming* (Schacter, Chiu & Ochsner, 1993). In a typical priming demonstration (see Figure 7.1), people respond faster or more accurately to a previously seen stimulus, even if they are unaware that it had been encountered before (Schacter et al., 1991; Cooper et al., 1992). Thus data from mere-exposure and priming experiments suggest that an encounter with a specific stimulus can—without your conscious awareness—affect how you respond to that stimulus in the future.

It also appears that some kinds of learning can occur without awareness. This phenomenon was demonstrated by a study in which subjects watched a computer screen as an *X* flashed in one of four locations. The subjects' task was to indicate where the *X* appeared by pushing one of four buttons as quickly as possible. Though the *X*'s location seemed to vary randomly, the placement sequence actually followed a set of complex rules, such as "If the *X* moves horizontally twice in a row, then it will move vertically next." The subjects' responses became progressively faster and more accurate until the rules were secretly abandoned and the *X*s began appearing in *truly* random locations. In other words, the subjects had learned a complex rule-bound strategy that improved their performance. However, even when offered $100 to state the rules that had guided the location sequence, they could not do so, nor were they sure that any such rules existed (Lewicki, 1992).

Figure 7.1
A Priming Experiment
Subjects viewed figures like these, one at a time, and were asked to decide which of them could actually exist in three-dimensional space and which could not (the upper ones can, the lower ones cannot). Subjects were better at classifying pictures that they had seen before, even when they could not remember having seen them (Cooper et al., 1992; Schacter et al., 1991).

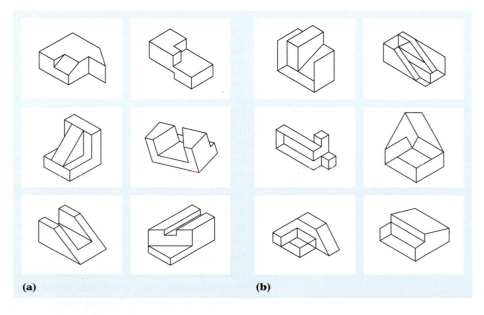

(a)   (b)

Source: Schacter et al., 1991.

The Neuropsychology of Consciousness

The degree to which mental activity occurs without conscious awareness is often exaggerated by brain damage. Victims such as P.S., for example, are left unaware of even the fact that certain mental processes exist (see, for example, Heller, 1989; Milner & Rugg, 1992).

Such an impairment in consciousness is also seen in cases of *prosopagnosia,* a condition usually due to damage in the brain's temporal lobes (Damasio et al., 1982). People with prosopagnosia lose the ability to consciously recognize faces—even their own face in the mirror—yet they can still see and recognize many other objects, and they can still recognize people by their voices (Young & De Haan, 1992). Amazingly, however, when looking at a familiar—but not consciously recognized—face, prosopagnosics show eye movement patterns, changes in the brain's electrical activity, and autonomic nervous system responses that do not occur when viewing an unfamiliar face (Trannel & Damasio, 1985; Renault et al., 1989). Thus, some vestige of face recognition is preserved, but it is unavailable to conscious experience.

Brain damage can also create a more general impairment in visual perception. For example, patients with *visual form agnosia* do not perceive the correct size, shape, or orientation of objects. One such patient could not judge the orientation of lines, causing her to judge a vertical line to be horizontal. Nor could she judge the width of blocks, either verbally or by estimating sizes with her thumb and index finger. Yet despite having no conscious awareness of objects' orientation or size, she could reach for and grasp them; her movements were adjusted to the objects' orientation, and she correctly varied the distance between her thumb and index finger to accommodate each object's size (Goodale et al., 1991). Thus, visual perception of features occurred, and the patient used it to guide her behavior, all without awareness.

Visual processing without awareness may even occur in certain cases of blindness. For example, when destruction of the visual cortex causes clinical blindness, victims report no longer seeing anything at all. But if the damage is limited to the primary visual cortex, nerve fibers from the eyes will still be connected to other brain areas capable of processing visual information (see Chapter 5, on sensation). Some of these surviving pathways appear to permit visual processing, but without creating visual awareness—a condition known as *blindsight* (Weiskrantz, 1986). Thus, even though such patients say they see nothing, if forced to guess, they can still detect and locate objects, identify the direction and orientation of moving targets, accurately reach for objects, and name the color of flashing lights (Cowey & Stoerig, 1992; Stoerig & Cowey, 1992).

Brain damage can also impair conscious access to mental abilities outside the visual realm. Consider *anterograde amnesia,* an inability to form new memories that is usually due to damage to the hippocampus (Cohen & Eichenbaum, 1993). Anterograde amnesics seem unable to remember *any* new information, even about the passage of time. One man who developed this condition in 1957 still needed to be reminded more than thirty years later that it was no longer 1957 (Smith, 1988). Yet as Figure 7.2 shows, anterograde amnesics can learn new skills, even though they can't consciously recall the practice sessions (Milner, 1962). A 1911 case report provides another dramatic, though rather cruel, example: a doctor hid a pin in his hand while shaking the hand of a patient with anterograde amnesia. The patient quickly lost the conscious memory of the episode, but thereafter refused to shake hands with anyone, stating without further explanation that "sometimes pins are hidden in people's hands" (Cleparede, 1911, cited in Schacter & Tulving, 1982). So these amnesics *can* form some memories, but they remain unaware of them.

Even when brain damage leaves some unconscious functions intact, however, it is often quite debilitating. Anterograde amnesics, for example, live in a

Figure 7.2
Memory Formation in Anterograde Amnesia
A patient known as H.M., who had anterograde amnesia, was asked to learn to trace the outline of an object using only a mirror (which reverses left and right) for visual feedback. H.M.'s performance on this task improved over time, indicating that he learned and remembered how to do the task. Yet H.M. had no conscious memory of the practice that allowed his skill to develop (Milner, 1965). In Chapter 9 we examine different types of memory and how they are formed and retrieved.

(a) Mirror-tracing task

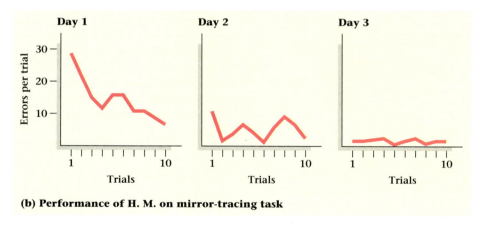

(b) Performance of H. M. on mirror-tracing task

Source: Data from Milner, 1965.

perpetual "here and now," not knowing what occurred minutes ago, and always remaining only moments away from forgetting the present. As one victim put it: "Every day is alone in itself, whatever enjoyment I've had, and whatever sorrow I've had. . . . Right now, I'm wondering, have I done or said anything amiss? You see, at this moment everything looks clear to me, but what happened just before? That's what worries me" (Milner, 1970).

Much like the stream to which it has been compared, consciousness is an ever-changing, multilayered phenomenon. Consciousness varies in both quantity and quality. Variations in its quantity—that is, in *how much* awareness one has for mental events—create different *levels of consciousness.* Variations in quality—in the *nature* of the mental processing available to awareness—are called *states of consciousness.* Let's look first at the levels of consciousness.

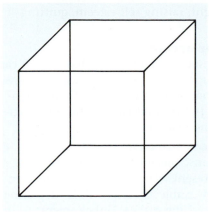

Figure 7.3
The Necker Cube
Each of the two squares in the Necker cube can be perceived as either the front or rear surface of the cube. Take a few seconds and try to make the cube switch back and forth between the two perspectives. Now try to hold one perspective in view and prevent the cube from switching to the other perspective. How long could you hold it in one perspective? If the whole cube is maintained in consciousness, it usually cannot be held for longer than about 3 seconds before it "flips" to the other.

Levels of Consciousness

At any moment, the mental events that you are currently aware of are said to exist at the **conscious level.** For example, look at the *Necker cube* shown in Figure 7.3. You can hold the cube in one configuration for only a few seconds before the second configuration "pops" out at you. The configuration that you experience at any moment is at your conscious level of awareness for that moment.

In contrast, some events cannot be experienced consciously. For example, you are not directly aware of the fact that your brain is constantly regulating your blood pressure. This kind of mental processing occurs at the **nonconscious level**—it is totally removed from conscious awareness. As described in the chapter on health, stress, and coping, some people learn to alter a nonconscious process through *biofeedback training,* a special method in which a measuring device tracks and provides information about biological processes such as blood pressure; but the process itself remains outside of conscious awareness.

Some mental events are not conscious but either can become so or can influence conscious experience, thought, and action; these mental events make up the *cognitive unconscious* (Kihlstrom, 1987), which is further divided into preconscious and subconscious (or unconscious) levels. Mental events that are outside of awareness but can easily be brought into awareness exist at the **preconscious level.** For example, think about last night's dinner. As you do so, you become aware of what and where you ate, whom you were with, and the like. But before you read this paragraph, you were probably not thinking about that information; it was still at the preconscious level, ready to be brought to the conscious level when needed. Similarly, in a trivia game you may draw on your large storehouse of preconscious memories to come up with obscure facts.

Other mental activities alter thoughts, feelings, and behavior but are more difficult than preconscious material to bring into awareness. Most psychologists use the term **subconscious** to describe the level of consciousness at which important but normally inaccessible mental processes—such as mere-exposure effects and priming—take place. Sigmund Freud, the founder of psychoanalysis, referred to this activity as the **unconscious** level of mental processing, and suggested that some thoughts are actively kept away from the conscious level. In the unconscious, he said, reside sexual and aggressive impulses, as well as once-conscious but unacceptable thoughts, feelings, and memories. Material at this level, he claimed, determines most human behavior and is the source of mental disorders. (We examine Freud's ideas in Chapter 14, on personality.)

Thinking Critically

Can You Be Influenced by Subliminal Perceptions?

To what extent can your thoughts, emotions, and actions be affected by stimuli perceived at a *subliminal* level, below your conscious awareness? In the 1950s advertisers allegedly used subliminal messages to promote sales. A New Jersey theater claimed to have flashed messages such as "buy popcorn" and "drink Coke" on a movie screen, too fast to be noticed, while customers viewed the movie *Picnic*. The theater claimed a rise of 15 percent in Coke sales and 58 percent in popcorn sales during this time. Can such "mind control" really work? Over 50 percent of people in the United States seem to think so (Synodinos, 1988; Zanot, Pincus, & Lamp, 1983), fueling multi-million dollar industries that provide "self-help" tapes supposedly containing subliminal encouragement for losing weight, raising self-esteem, quitting smoking, and the like.

What am I being asked to believe or accept?

The claim underlying the alleged value of subliminal tapes is that stimuli can be detected, perceived, and overtly acted upon without conscious awareness. The strong version of this claim implies that others might secretly try to influence people's emotions, buying habits, political decisions, and other attitudes and actions, all without their awareness or consent.

What evidence is available to support the assertion?

Linkages: Can people perceive stimuli without being aware of them? (a link to Perception)

Evidence that subliminal messages alter conscious judgments comes from studies using *tachistoscopes,* devices that present visual stimuli too briefly to be perceived consciously. In one such study, subjects viewed slides depicting people performing ordinary acts such as washing dishes. Unbeknownst to the subjects, each slide was preceded by a subliminal (9 millisecond) exposure to a photo showing "positive" stimuli (such as a child playing) or "negative" stimuli (such as a monster). Later, the subjects rated the people on the visible slides as more likable, polite, friendly, successful, and reputable when their images had been preceded by a positive rather than a negative subliminal photo (Krosnick, Jussim & Lynn, 1992). Thus, the subliminal photos not only affected subjects' liking of the people they saw but also shaped beliefs about their personalities.

An early study showed that subliminal messages can also affect emotional responses (Bach & Klein, 1957). Subjects saw slides of faces paired with a subliminally flashed word (*happy* or *sad*). Later, subjects described the faces that had been associated with the word *sad* as sadder than those that had been paired with *happy.* More recently, subjects were shown written messages at subliminal (4 millisecond) speed while researchers recorded their *galvanic skin resistance* (GSR), a measure of autonomic arousal. Though the slides were flashed too quickly to be consciously perceived, subjects showed increased arousal after messages like "no one loves me," but not after equally long nonemotional messages like "no one lifts it." This result suggests that the meaning of subliminal messages can be understood (Masling & Bornstein, 1991).

The quality of evidence for the subliminal effects mentioned so far contrasts sharply with that available for the effects of subliminal self-help tapes. Reports supporting the use of subliminal tapes in promoting self-esteem, weight loss, and other self-improvement goals comes not from experimental research but from anecdotal reports by satisfied customers and advertisers (see, for example, McGarvey, 1989).

Are there alternative ways of interpreting the evidence?

Linkages: What experimental methods are needed to evaluate the effects of subliminal messages? (a link to Research in Psychology)

Many commercial claims for subliminal persuasion—including the New Jersey theater story mentioned earlier—have turned out to be publicity stunts using fabricated data (Pratkanis, 1992). Other claims may be based on what statisticians call a *Type 1 error,* which occurs when researchers collect so many data sets that the desired result finally appears by chance. Clearly, it is misleading to publicize the one positive result without mentioning all the negative results.

What about user testimonials supporting the effectiveness of subliminal self-help tapes? They could be based on positive expectations, not subliminal effects. This possibility is made more plausible by the results of a double-blind placebo-controlled study in which subjects listened to self-help tapes designed to improve memory or self-esteem. Some heard the standard commercially marketed version, while others got "placebo" tapes—identical to the commercial versions, but with the subliminal messages deleted. Special coding procedures ensured that, until the experiment was over, neither the subjects nor the research staff knew which subjects got which kind of tape. The results showed that the commercial self-help tapes were no better than the placebo versions in producing changes in memory or self-esteem (Greenwald & Spangenberg, 1991). Thus, customers' reports about the value of subliminal self-help tapes may reflect placebo effects based on optimistic expectations that were engendered, in part, by reports that they themselves had heard (see Chapter 2).

What additional evidence would help to evaluate the alternatives?

The effects of subliminal persuasion methods must be assessed via controlled experiments of the kind described in Chapter 2, on research methods. Those advocating the development and use of such methods will have to provide supporting evidence based on the kind of double-blind, placebo-controlled studies just described.

What conclusions are most reasonable?

The evidence available thus far suggests that subliminal perception does occur, but has no potential for "mind control." Subliminal effects are usually modest and short-lived, and affect only such general measures as overall arousal. Most psychologists agree that subliminal messages have no special power to create needs, goals, skills, or actions (Pratkanis, 1992). Indeed, advertisements, political speeches, and other messages that people can perceive consciously are likely to have far stronger effects. ■

States of Consciousness

Mental activity is always changing. The features of consciousness at any moment—what reaches your awareness, the decisions you are making, and the like—make up your **state of consciousness** at that moment. Possible states range from deep sleep to alert wakefulness, with many gradations in between. Imagine for a moment that you know everything that is going on in an airplane en route from New York to Los Angeles. In the cockpit, the pilot calmly scans the instruments while talking to an air-traffic controller on the ground. In seat 37B, a sales representative has just polished off her second Scotch as she works on plans for the next day's sales meeting. Nearby, a young mother gazes out the window, daydreaming, while her small son sleeps in her lap, dreaming dreams of his own.

Each of these people is experiencing a different state of consciousness. Some states are active and some passive (Hilgard, 1980). The daydreaming mother is simply letting her mind wander, passively observing the images, memories, and other mental events that come unbidden to mind. In contrast, the sales representative is actively manipulating her mental activity, considering various courses of action and speculating about their likely outcomes.

Most people spend most of their time in a *waking* state of consciousness. The mental processes in this state vary with shifts in attention and changes in arousal. Thus, while reading, you may temporarily ignore sounds in the world around you. Similarly, if you are upset or bored, you may miss important environmental cues, making it dangerous to drive a car.

When changes in mental processes are great enough for you or others to notice significant differences in how you function, you have entered an **altered state of consciousness** (Ludwig, 1969; Zinberg, 1974). In an altered state, mental processing shows distinct changes unique to that particular state. Cognitive processes as well as perceptions of yourself or the world may change, and normal inhibitions or self-control may weaken (Martindale, 1981).

The phrase *altered states of consciousness* acknowledges waking consciousness as the most common state, a baseline against which the "altered" states are compared. However, this is not to say that waking consciousness is universally considered more normal or proper or valued than other possible states. In fact, value judgments about different states of consciousness vary considerably from culture to culture (Ward, 1989; 1994). Some cultures regard any shifts away from the standard waking state as deviant; other cultures sometimes encourage the production of nonordinary states of consciousness (Davidson, 1980, p. 36).

For instance, culture shapes opinions about *hallucinations,* which are perceptual experiences (such as hearing voices) that occur in the absence of sensory stimuli. In the United States, hallucinations are viewed quite negatively. As a result, mental patients who hallucinate may experience added anxiety and self-blame over their symptoms, may try to hide their hallucinatory experiences, and may receive poorer prognoses and more drastic treatments (Wallace, 1959). But in the Moche culture in coastal Peru, for example, hallucinations have a culturally sanctioned place. When someone is beset by illness or misfortune, a healer conducts an elaborate ritual to determine the causes and treatments for the affliction. During the ceremony, the healer drinks a brew that includes mescaline, a drug that causes hallucinations. These hallucinations are deeply respected by all present, and are thought to give the healer spiritual insight into the patient's problems (de Rios, 1989). In this cultural context, purposeful hallucinations are revered, not demeaned.

Thus, states of consciousness differ not only in terms of their basic characteristics but also in their value to members of particular cultures. In the sections to follow, we describe some of the most interesting altered states of consciousness, beginning with the most common one, sleep.

Sleeping and Dreaming

The electroencephalogram (EEG) allows scientists to record brain activity through electrodes attached to the skull. The advent of this technology opened the door to the scientific study of sleep. This subject's brain waves will be monitored throughout the night in a sleep laboratory.

According to ancient myths, sleepers lose control of their minds, flirting with death as their souls wander freely. Early researchers thought sleep was a time of mental inactivity. Modern research shows that it is actually a very active, complex state.

Stages of Sleep

In 1919 Hans Berger developed the *electroencephalogram,* or *EEG,* which provides a record of the electrical activity in the brain. EEG recordings, often called *brain waves,* show variations in height (amplitude) and speed (frequency) as behavior or mental processes change. The brain waves of an awake, alert person have high frequency and low amplitude; they appear as small, closely spaced, irregular EEG spikes. A relaxed person with closed eyes shows *alpha waves*—rhythmic brain waves at speeds of 8 to 12 cycles per second (cps).

During the night, brain waves undergo distinctive and systematic changes in amplitude and frequency (Loomis, Harvey & Hobart, 1937). In the 1950s, these EEG changes, along with changes in muscle activity and eye movement, were used to describe six stages of sleep: stage 0, which is a prelude to sleep, four stages of quiet sleep, and rapid eye movement (REM) sleep (Dement & Kleitman, 1957). This remains the primary sleep classification system today (see, for example, Keenan, 1992).

Stage 0 and Quiet Sleep   In stage 0, you are relaxed, with eyes closed, but awake. Here, EEG activity is mixed but includes some alpha waves. During this stage, the body may remain tense and the eyes move normally. The next stages, stages 1 through 4, are called **quiet sleep** or **slow-wave sleep;** all are accompanied by slower brain waves, deep breathing, a calm heartbeat, and low blood pressure. Because they contrast with REM sleep, these stages are sometimes referred to as non-REM, or NREM, sleep.

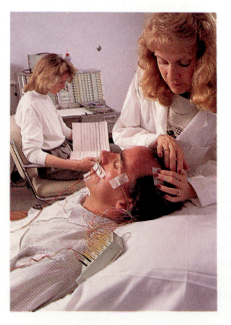

Figure 7.4
EEGs During Sleep
Notice the regular patterns of alpha waves in stage 0 (relaxed wakefulness), the sleep spindles and K-complexes in stage 2, and the slower delta waves in stages 3 and 4 (Webb, 1968, p. 15).

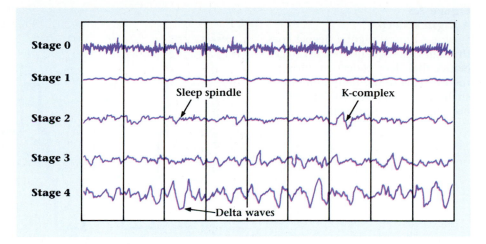

Source: Webb, 1968.

As you enter stage 1 sleep, your eyes begin to roll lazily. Rhythmic alpha waves give way to irregular waves, similar to those seen in an awake and mentally active person (see Figure 7.4). A few minutes later, stage 2 sleep begins. The EEG shows sharply pointed waves called *sleep spindles,* as well as occasional *K-complexes,* waves with high peaks and deep valleys. Stage 3 sleep shows fewer spindles and K-complexes, but it adds *delta waves,* which are much slower (0.5 to 0.3 cps) and larger in amplitude. When delta waves begin to occur more than 50 percent of the time, you enter stage 4 sleep, from which it is quite difficult to be roused. If you are roused from this stage of deep sleep, you will be groggy and confused. The journey from stage 1 to stage 4 has taken you about thirty minutes.

REM Sleep   After thirty to forty minutes in stage 4, you quickly pass back to stage 2 sleep and then begin a special stage in which your eyes move rapidly under closed lids (Aserinsky & Kleitman, 1953). This stage is called **REM (rapid eye movement) sleep,** or **active sleep.** As in stage 1, the EEG resembles that of a person who is awake and mentally active, but now physiological arousal—heart rate, breathing, blood pressure—is also similar to that of the waking state. Paradoxically, while brain waves and other measures resemble those of an awake person, muscle tone decreases to the point of virtual paralysis. Sudden, twitchy spasms appear, especially in the face and hands.

In early attempts to determine what goes on during this *paradoxical sleep,* researchers wakened sleeping subjects when the EEG revealed they were in REM. In about 80 percent of these REM interruptions, subjects said they had been dreaming. In contrast, dream reports followed only 7 percent of non-REM awakenings (Dement & Kleitman, 1957).

A Night's Sleep   Most people pass through the cycle of sleep stages four to six times each night. Each cycle lasts about 90 minutes, but with a somewhat different itinerary (see Figure 7.5). Early in the night most of the time is spent in stages 3 and 4, with only a few minutes in REM. As sleep continues, though, it is dominated by stage 2 and REM, from which sleepers finally awaken.

Sleep patterns change with age. An average infant sleeps about sixteen hours a day; an average seventy-year-old, only about six hours (Roffwarg, Muzio & Dement, 1966). Most of the decreased sleeping time comes out of REM sleep, as Figure 7.6 shows. REM accounts for half of total sleep at birth, but less than 25 percent in later life. Individual sleeping patterns may vary widely from these averages, however; some people feel well rested after four or five hours

Figure 7.5
A Night's Sleep
During a typical night a sleeper goes
through this sequence of EEG stages.
Notice that sleep is deepest during
the first part of the night and more
shallow later on, when REM sleep
becomes more prominent.

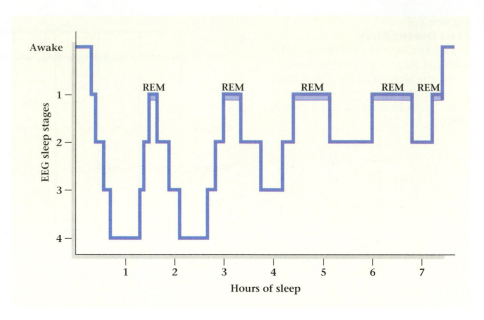

Source: Cartwright, 1978.

sleep while others of similar age feel satisfied only after nine or ten hours
(Clausen, Sersen & Lidsky, 1974). Moreover, there is wide variation from cul-
ture to culture in the tendency to take daytime naps (Cartwright, 1978;
Webb, 1968).

Sleep Disorders

The most common sleeping problem is **insomnia**, in which one feels tired
during the day due to trouble falling asleep or staying asleep. Besides being
tiring, insomnia is tied to mental distress. A review of 177 studies covering
7,151 patients found that psychiatric patients sleep less than nonpsychiatric
patients (Benca et al., 1992). In one study, insomniacs were three times as
likely to show a mental disorder as those with no sleep complaints (Ford &
Kamerow, 1989). In animals, long-term sleep deprivation causes physiological
changes resembling those seen in human depression (Patchev, Felszeghy &
Korranyi, 1991). Note, however, that it is still not clear from human data
whether insomnia contributes directly to mental disorders or whether factors
that eventually lead to disorders also disrupt sleep.

Sleeping pills temporarily relieve insomnia, but they interact dangerously
with alcohol and are addictive. More helpful approaches include biofeedback,
relaxation training, and stress management, which are described in the chapter
on health, stress, and coping. Insomniacs may also benefit by going to bed
only when sleepy and staying out of bed when they cannot sleep (Lacks et al.,
1983). In this way they come to associate being in bed with sleeping rather
than with wakefulness.

Narcolepsy is a disturbing daytime sleep disorder. Its victims abruptly
switch from active, often emotional waking states into several minutes of REM
sleep. Because of the drastic decrease in muscle tone during REM, the narco-
leptic collapses and remains briefly immobile even after awakening. The exact
cause of narcolepsy is unknown, but it appears to have a genetic basis (Parkes
& Lock, 1989). Stimulants and napping have both been effective treatments
for narcolepsy.

In **sleep apnea**, sleepers briefly stop breathing hundreds of times during the
night, waking up each time long enough to resume breathing. In the morning,
victims do not feel rested, but also do not recall their nighttime awakenings.

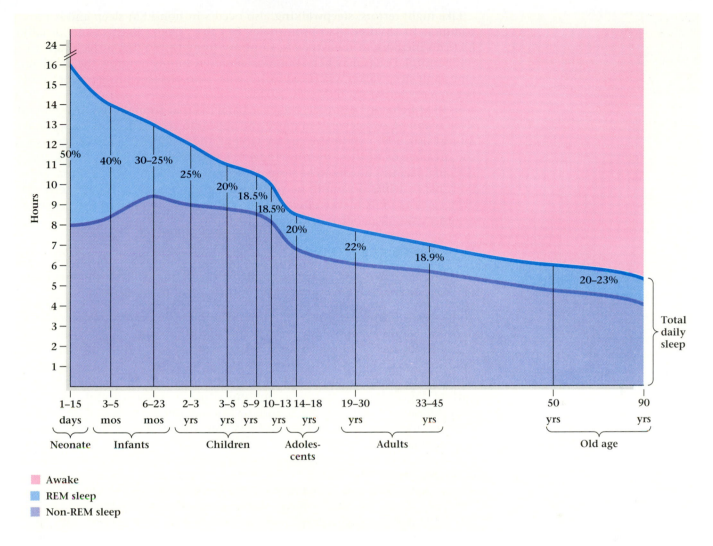

Note: Percentages indicate portion of total sleep time spent in REM.
Source: Roffwarg, Muzio & Dement, 1966 (revised 1969).

Figure 7.6
Sleep and Dreaming Over the Lifespan

From infancy to old age, certain changes typically occur in total daily sleep, non-REM sleep, REM sleep, and the percentage of REM sleep. Notice first that people tend to sleep less as they get older. Notice as well the sharp reduction in the percentage of REM sleep, from about eight hours per day in infancy to less than an hour per day by age seventy. Non-REM sleep time also decreases somewhat but, compared to the drop in REM, remains relatively stable. After age twenty, however, non-REM sleep contains less and less of the deepest, or stage 4, sleep.

Apnea can be caused by compression of the windpipe or problems in the brainstem's control of breathing (Guilleminault, Stroohs & Quera-Salva, 1992). Effective treatments include brainstem-stimulating drugs or a nasal mask that provides a steady stream of air (Mann et al., 1992; Hoijer et al., 1992).

In **sudden infant death syndrome (SIDS)**, a sleeping baby stops breathing but does not awaken and suffocates. An estimated 28 to 52 percent of apparent SIDS cases may actually be accidental suffocation caused when infants sleep face down on soft cushions (Kemp & Thach, 1991; Guntheroth & Spiers, 1992). The cause of true SIDS cases is still unknown. The problem may lie in the brain systems normally responsible for arousing a sleeper who stops breathing (Harper et al., 1988). The finding that certain sleeping patterns may predict SIDS could make it possible to identify and save at-risk infants (Schechtman et al., 1992).

Nightmares are frightening dreams in REM sleep, while **night terrors** are horrific non-REM dream images occurring during stage 4 sleep. The sleeper often awakens from a night terror with a bloodcurdling scream and remains intensely afraid for up to thirty minutes. In the morning, the person may not remember the episode. Night terrors are especially common in boys, but adults can suffer milder versions. Night terrors are sometimes treated with hypnosis or drugs (Kohen, Mahowald & Rosen, 1992).

Like night terrors, **sleepwalking** also occurs in non-REM sleep and is most common in children (Jacobson, Kales & Kales, 1969). Sleepwalkers usually have no memory of their travels. Contrary to myth, waking a sleepwalker is not harmful. Drugs may help, but most children simply outgrow the problem. One adult sleepwalker was cured by his wife, who blew a whistle whenever he began a nocturnal stroll (Meyer, 1975).

In **REM behavior disorder,** the near paralysis that should accompany REM sleep is absent, so sleepers can move and appear to act out dreams (Lappiere & Montplaisir, 1992). If the dreams are violent, the disorder can be dangerous to the dreamer or to those nearby. Indeed, 44 percent of sufferers attack their sleeping partners during REM sleep. One man grabbed his wife's throat with both hands while dreaming he was breaking a deer's neck. Fortunately, the drug *clonazepam* is highly effective, controlling 90 percent of REM behavior disorder cases (Schenck & Mahowald, 1990).

Why Do People Sleep?

In trying to understand sleep, psychologists have studied both the functions that sleep serves and how brain mechanisms shape its characteristics.

Sleep as a Circadian Rhythm　　The sleep-wake cycle is one example of the rhythmic nature of life. Many physiological processes also exhibit cycles that repeat about every 24 hours in a **circadian rhythm** (from the Latin *circa dies,* meaning "about a day"). Longer and shorter rhythms also occur, but less commonly. These rhythms are linked, or *entrained,* to signals such as the light and dark of day and night, but some rhythms continue even without such time cues. Volunteers who live for months without external cues maintain daily rhythms, including sleep and wakefulness. But when the sleep-wake rhythm is not externally entrained, most people maintain an approximately 25-hour day.

The effects of disrupting the sleep-wake cycle are seen in **jet lag,** a syndrome of fatigue, irritability, inattention, and sleeping problems caused by air travel across several time zones. The traveler's body feels ready to sleep at the wrong time for the new location. Similar problems affect workers who must change from day shifts to night shifts, and back (Gold et al., 1992). Generally, it is easier to make yourself stay awake later rather than go to sleep earlier. Thus, sleep-wake rhythms readjust more readily when sleep is shifted to a later rather than an earlier time. As a result, west-to-east travel is more difficult than east-to-west, as Figure 7.7 illustrates.

Figure 7.7
Westward/Eastward Travel and Jet Lag
Changing time zones causes more intense symptoms of "jet lag" after eastward travel (when time is lost) than after westward travel (when time is gained). The data shown here come from a study of people flying between London and Detroit, which involves a five-hour time change. Researchers studied the time it took travelers to fall asleep once in bed, both on the night before traveling (B1) and on the five nights after traveling (1–5). Travelers who flew eastward, from Detroit to London, needed more time to fall asleep than travelers who flew westward, from London to Detroit (Nicholson et al., 1986).

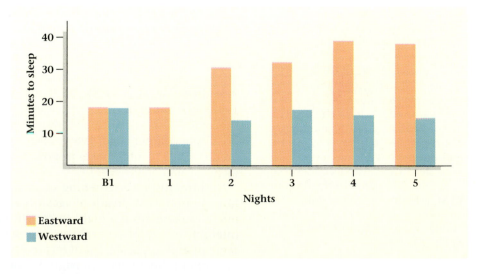

Source: Adapted from Nicholson et al., 1986.

Since circadian-like rhythms continue without external cues, there must be an internal "biological clock" to keep track of time. This clock appears to be the *suprachiasmatic nucleus (SCN)* of the hypothalamus (see Figure 7.8). Signals from the SCN reach areas of the hindbrain that activate sleep or wakefulness (McCarley, 1987). SCN neurons show a 24- to 25-hour rhythm in firing even when they are removed from the brain and put in a dish (Gillette, 1986). And when animals with lesions in the SCN receive transplanted SCN tissue, the restored circadian rhythms parallel those of the donor animal (Hurd & Ralph, 1992; Ralph et al., 1990).

Pathways from the eyes to the SCN may help the SCN entrain its rhythmicity to the light-dark cycle. This may be why exposure to properly timed bright light can be helpful in "resetting" the biological clock in cases of jet lag (Culebras, 1992).

The Functions of Sleep   Examining the effects of sleep deprivation may help explain why people sleep at all. People who go without sleep for as long as a week usually do not display serious effects, but sleeplessness does lead to fatigue, irritability, and inattention (Linde & Bergstrom, 1992). More than 60 percent of fatal auto accidents on U.S. roads occur during the "fatigue hazard" hours of midnight to 6 A.M. (Coleman, 1992).

Some researchers believe that sleep, especially non-REM sleep, helps to restore the body for future activity (Adam & Oswald, 1977). They point out that non-REM sleeping time remains fairly stable with age and that both short and long sleepers get their non-REM sleep first and in about the same amounts (Hartman, Baekeland & Zwilling, 1972). Animal studies also support a restorative role for sleep (see, for example, Rechtschaffen et al., 1983).

After total sleep deprivation, people do not make up lost sleep hour for hour. Instead, they get about twice a normal night's sleep, then awake feeling rested. But if people are deprived only of REM sleep, they later compensate more directly. In a classic study, subjects were awakened on several nights whenever their EEG showed REM sleep. When allowed to sleep without interruption the next night, the subjects tended to "rebound" by spending about twice the normal amount of time in REM (Dement, 1960). People's apparently strong need for REM sleep suggests that REM has special functions.

First, REM may help maintain the activity of neurons that use norepinephrine (Siegel & Rogawski, 1988). Norepinephrine is a neurotransmitter released by nerve cells of the locus coeruleus (see Figure 7.8). These cells are very active

Figure 7.8
Sleep, Dreaming, and the Brain
This diagram shows the location of some of the brain structures thought to be involved in sleep and dreaming as well as in other altered states discussed later in the chapter.

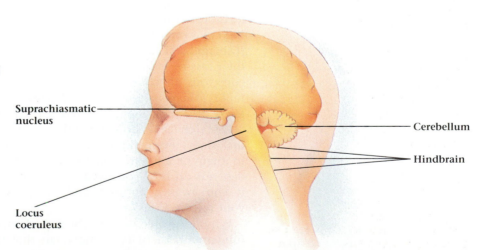

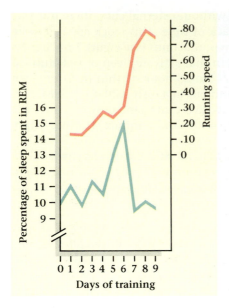

Source: Drucker-Colin & McGaugh, 1977.

Figure 7.9
REM Sleep and Learning
The upper curve shows the average running speed of rats as they learned their way around a maze over several days. The lower curve shows the average percentage of REM sleep during the nights between practice sessions. Notice that the rats spent more time in REM on nights during the learning phase than after learning was complete.

during waking, affecting alertness and mood. But the brain's neurons become less sensitive to norepinephrine if it is released continuously for too long. Because the locus coeruleus is almost completely inactive during REM sleep, researchers have suggested that REM helps restore sensitivity to norepinephrine (Steriade & McCarley, 1990). In this way, REM sleep may help maintain waking alertness.

Second, REM may be a time for developing, checking, and expanding the brain's nerve connections (Roffwarg, Muzio & Dement, 1966). This notion would explain why children and infants, whose brains are still developing, spend so much time in REM (see Figure 7.6). In contrast, guinea pigs and other animals born with well-developed brains spend very little sleep time in REM early in their lives (Cartwright, 1978).

A third, possibly related function of REM sleep may be to help solidify and assimilate the day's learning experiences and mental efforts. In one study, people who were REM-deprived showed poorer retention of a skill learned the day before than people who were either deprived of non-REM sleep or allowed to sleep normally (Karni et al., 1992). As Figure 7.9 shows, animals that spend daytime hours engaged in various learning tasks display more frequent and longer REM episodes than those that spend the day in their cages (Ambrosini et al., 1992; Langella et al., 1992).

Since REM and dreaming so often occur together, could their underlying purposes be related? We cannot really know, since dreaming is such a subjective experience. Also, dreams sometimes do occur in non-REM sleep as well.

Dreams and Dreaming

The mind is active during all stages of sleep, not just during dreams. But **dreams** differ from other mental activity in sleep because they are usually storylike, generally lasting from several seconds to several minutes. Dreams may be organized or chaotic, realistic or bizarre, boring or fascinating. Dreams can provide creative insights to waking problems. For example, after trying for days to write a story about good and evil in the same person, author Robert Louis Stevenson had a dream about a man who drank a substance that turned him into a monster (Hill, 1968). The dream inspired *The Strange Case of Dr. Jekyll and Mr. Hyde.*

Daytime activities clearly influence the content of dreams. In one study, subjects wore red-tinted goggles for a few minutes just before going to sleep. Although subjects did not know the purpose of the experiment, the next morning they reported more red images in their dreams than people who had not worn the goggles (Roffwarg, Hermann & Bowe-Anders, 1978). It may even be possible to intentionally direct the content of dreams. Reports of **lucid dreaming**, in which the sleeper is aware of dreaming *while a dream is happening* (Laberge et al., 1981), provide further evidence that sleep does not involve a total loss of self-awareness or mental functioning and may thus be open to conscious direction. In one study, for example, subjects were more likely to report dreams about a desired personality trait after receiving instructions to try dreaming about that trait (Cartwright, 1974).

Research leaves little doubt that everyone dreams during every night of normal sleep. Even blind people dream, although the perceptual experiences in their dreams are usually not visual. Whether you remember a dream depends on how you sleep and wake up (Cartwright, 1978). Recall is better if you awaken abruptly and lie quietly while writing or tape-recording your recollections.

Why do people dream? Theories abound. Some suggest that dreaming is a fundamental activity of mammals that helps them process and consolidate information of great personal significance or survival value. In fact, research

This 1931 painting by Thomas Hart Benton illustrates the fact that the content of dreams often relates to the events and concerns of the dreamer's life. Why dreams occur and what they might mean are subjects of continuing research and debate.

suggests that nonhuman animals do dream. After neurons that cause paralysis during REM sleep were disabled, sleeping cats walked around and attacked or seemed alarmed by unseen objects, presumably the images from dreams (Winson, 1990).

Some believe that dreams provide clues about a dreamer's hidden mental processes. Freud (1900) called dreams the "royal road to a knowledge of the unconscious." He theorized that during sleep, normally unconscious impulses and wishes appear disguised in dreams. If this is true, then unconscious psychological problems might reveal themselves in dreams. We discuss this idea further in the chapter on treatment of psychological disorders.

Others see dreams as inherently meaningless by-products of REM sleep. One theory holds that changes in brain activity during REM sleep allow certain brain circuits to transport essentially random messages from a hindbrain "dream-state generator" to the cerebral cortex (Quattrochi et al., 1989). According to this view, dreams result when the cortex tries to use memories and feelings to make sense of these messages, much as people do when trying to find meaningful shapes in cloud formations.

Whatever their physiological explanation, dreams may still be important psychologically. One study investigated the dreams of 29 divorcing or recently divorced women, 19 of whom were depressed (Cartwright et al., 1984). The depressed women dreamed repeatedly of the past, whereas the nondepressed women more often had problem-solving dreams and dreams spanning the distant and recent past, the present, and the future. Thus, even if dream content is physiologically determined, the mental style or current concerns of the dreamer can affect the ways in which dreams are organized and recalled.

Hypnosis

The word *hypnosis* comes from the Greek word *hypnos,* which means "sleep," but hypnotized people are not truly asleep. People who have been hypnotized report that their bodies felt "asleep," but their minds remained active and alert. **Hypnosis** is an altered state of consciousness brought on by special tech-

Mesmerism was a forerunner of hypnosis named for its chief proponent, Franz Anton Mesmer, an Austrian physician. Mesmerism was used in the late eighteenth century to treat all sorts of physical disorders. Patients would place their afflicted body parts against magnetized metal rods extending from a tub of water. Then, upon being touched by Mesmer, the patients would fall into a curative "crisis" or trance, sometimes accompanied by convulsions. We now know that hypnosis can be induced by staring at an object or in other ways that are much simpler than Mesmer's elaborate rituals.

niques and characterized by responsiveness to suggestions for changes in experience and behavior (Orne, 1977, 1980). Most hypnotized people do not feel forced to follow the hypnotist's instructions; they simply see no reason to refuse (Gill & Brenman, 1959; Hilgard, 1965).

Experiencing Hypnosis

Usually, hypnosis begins with suggestions that the subject feels relaxed and sleepy. The hypnotist then gradually focuses the subject's attention on a restricted, often monotonous set of stimuli while suggesting that the subject ignore everything else and imagine certain feelings.

Not everyone can be hypnotized. Special tests measure **hypnotic susceptibility,** the degree to which people respond to hypnotic suggestions (Weitzenhoffer & Hilgard, 1962; Shor & Orne, 1963). These tests show that about 10 percent of adults are difficult or impossible to hypnotize (Hilgard, 1982). Hypnotically susceptible people appear to differ from others in having more active imaginations (Wilson & Barber, 1978), a tendency to fantasize (Lynn & Rhue, 1986), an ability to focus attention for long periods (Graham & Evans, 1977), and an ability to process information quickly and effortlessly (Dixon, Brunet & Laurence, 1990). You can become more susceptible by adopting more positive attitudes toward hypnosis, watching what susceptible subjects do, and practicing (Gfeller, Lynn & Pribble, 1987; Gorassini et al., 1991; Spanos, Lush & Gwynn, 1989; Wickless & Kirsch, 1990). Your *willingness* to be hypnotized is the most important factor. Contrary to myth, you cannot be hypnotized against your will.

The results of hypnosis can be fascinating. People told that their eyes cannot open may struggle fruitlessly to open them. They may appear deaf or blind or less sensitive to pain. They may forget their own names. Some appear to remember things they were unable to recall before. Others display **age regression,** in which they seem to recall and even re-enact childhood themes (see Figure 7.10). Hypnotic effects can last for hours or days through **posthypnotic suggestions**—instructions about behavior to take place after hypnosis has ended (say, smiling whenever someone says "Oregon"). Some subjects show **posthypnotic amnesia,** which is a failure to recall what happened while they were hypnotized, even after being told what happened.

Ernest Hilgard (1965, 1992) has described the main changes people display during hypnosis. First, hypnotized people show *reduced planfulness.* They tend not to initiate actions, waiting instead for the hypnotist's instructions. One subject said, "I was trying to decide if my legs were crossed, but I couldn't tell, and didn't quite have the initiative to move to find out" (Hilgard, 1965, p. 6). Second, subjects tend to ignore everything but the hypnotist's voice and whatever it points out; their *attention is redistributed.* Third, hypnosis enhances the ability to *fantasize,* leaving subjects able to more vividly imagine a scene or relive a memory. Fourth, hypnotized people show an increased ability at *role-taking;* they can more easily act like a person of a different age or a member of the opposite sex, for example. Fifth, hypnotic subjects show *reduced reality testing,* tending not to question if statements are true and showing a willingness to accept apparent distortions of reality. Thus, a hypnotized person might shiver in a warm room after a hypnotist says it is snowing. Although these experiences seem vivid and real, hypnotized subjects can otherwise still distinguish reality from nonreality (Lynn, Weekes & Milano, 1989).

Explaining Hypnosis

Hypnotized people often look and act differently from those who are not hypnotized (Hilgard, 1965). Do these differences actually reflect an altered state of

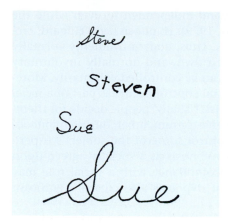

Source: Hilgard, 1965.

Figure 7.10
Hypnotic Age Regression
Here are the signatures of a man and a woman before hypnotically induced age regression (top) and while age-regressed (bottom). Notice that the lower signatures look less mature; one is even printed rather than written. In spite of such changes in behavior, the things people "recall" during age regression are not especially accurate and are subject to the usual distortions associated with attempts to retrieve old memories (Nash et al., 1986).

consciousness? Several well-supported theories offer different answers (Lynn & Rhue, 1991).

According to **role theory**, hypnosis does not create a special state of consciousness; hypnotized subjects merely comply with social demands and act in accordance with a special social role (Kirsch et al., 1992; Sarbin, 1950). From this perspective, hypnosis merely provides a socially acceptable reason to follow another person's suggestions, much as a doctor's white coat provides a good reason for patients to remove their clothing on command.

Support for role theory comes from several sources. First, unhypnotized people sometimes behave in bizarre ways associated with hypnosis. On television game shows, for example, apparently normal people scream, jump around, kiss strangers, and otherwise make fools of themselves, all without benefit of hypnosis. In the laboratory, motivated but unhypnotized volunteers can duplicate virtually every aspect of hypnotic behavior, from arm rigidity to age regression (Baker, 1990; Barber, 1969; Orne, 1970; Orne & Evans, 1965). And in some studies (one of which is illustrated in Figure 7.11), people whom hypnosis had made blind, deaf, or insensitive to touch could actually see, hear, and feel, in spite of the fact that they otherwise behaved (and believed) that they could not (Pattie, 1935; Bryant & McConkey, 1989). Even expert psychologists who believe that hypnosis is a special altered state cannot tell the difference between true and fabricated accounts of hypnotic experiences (Kirsch et al., 1992).

Advocates of **state theory** argue that hypnosis *does* create an altered state of consciousness. They point to subtle differences in the way hypnotized and nonhypnotized people carry out suggestions (see, for example, Spanos, James & de Groot, 1990). In one study, for example, hypnotized people and those who had been asked to simulate hypnosis were told that they would run their hands through their hair whenever they heard the word *experiment* (Orne, Sheehan & Evans, 1968). Simulators did so only when the hypnotist said the cue word; hypnotized subjects complied no matter who said it. State theorists see such differences between hypnotized and nonhypnotized people as evidence that hypnotized people are not just role-taking, that their mental processes change significantly, and in ways not seen in unhypnotized people (Orne, 1980).

Hilgard (1977, 1979, 1992) proposed **dissociation theory** to blend role and state theories. He suggested that hypnosis is not one specific state but a general condition in which a person reorganizes control over behavior. The normal, centralized control over how to act or think can be temporarily broken up by a process called *dissociation*. Dissociation occurs when two or more thoughts

Figure 7.11
Can Hypnosis Produce Blindness?
The top row in this figure looks like gibberish, but it can be read as the numbers and letters in the lower row if viewed through special glasses with one eye closed. Frank Pattie (1935) found that hypnotized subjects who had been given suggestions for blindness in one eye were unable to read the numbers and letters while wearing the special glasses with both eyes open, a result indicating that both eyes were in fact working normally.

Source: Pattie, 1935.

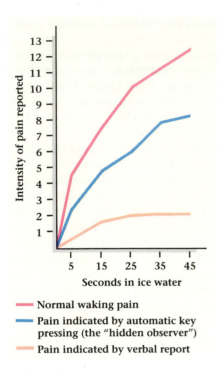

Source: Hilgard, 1977.

Figure 7.12
Reports of Pain in Hypnosis
This graph compares the average reports of pain when a person's hand is immersed in ice water. The red line shows the reports by nonhypnotized subjects. The orange line shows the reports by hypnotized subjects who were told they would experience no pain. The green line shows key-presses made by hypnotized subjects who were told they would experience no pain but were asked to press a key if "any part of them" felt pain. The nonverbal reports by this "hidden observer" suggest that under hypnosis the experience of pain was dissociated from conscious awareness.

Can meditation help people minimize the effects of stress?

or perceptions take place simultaneously and independently, even while the person may be aware of only one (Hilgard, 1979). Hypnosis, says Hilgard, creates a dissociation, a split in consciousness. Thus, body movements normally under voluntary control can occur on their own, and normally involuntary processes (such as overt reactions to pain) can be controlled voluntarily. Moreover, Hilgard argues, the relaxation of central control occurs as part of a *social agreement* to share control with the hypnotist. Usually, people decide for themselves how to act or what to attend to, perceive, or remember; during hypnosis, however, the hypnotist is "allowed" to control some of the subject's experiences and actions. In short, Hilgard sees hypnosis as a socially agreed-upon display of dissociated mental functions. Compliance with a social role may account for part of the story, he says, but hypnosis also creates significant changes in mental processes.

Evidence for dissociation comes from a study in which hypnotized subjects immersed one hand in ice-cold water after being told that they would feel no pain (Hilgard, Morgan & MacDonald, 1975). With the other, nonimmersed hand, subjects were told to press a key to indicate if "any part of them" felt pain. Subjects' oral reports indicated almost no pain, but their key-pressing told a different story (see Figure 7.12). Hilgard concluded that a "hidden observer" was reporting on pain that was reaching the person but had been separated, or dissociated, from conscious awareness (Hilgard, 1977).

Appealing as dissociation theory may be, further research will be necessary to establish its validity and to explore the roles of social and cognitive factors in hypnotic phenomena. In sum, there is much left to learn about the nature of hypnosis.

Some Uses of Hypnosis

Whatever hypnosis is, it has proven useful, especially in the control of pain. Hypnosis seems to be the only anesthetic some people need to prevent the pain of dental work, childbirth, burns, abdominal surgery, and spinal taps (Finer, 1980; Patterson et al., 1992; Van Sickel, 1992). For other people, hypnosis relieves the chronic pain of arthritis, nerve damage, migraine headaches, and cancer (Hilgard, 1980; Long, 1986). Hypnotic suggestion can reduce nausea and vomiting due to chemotherapy (Redd, 1984), and it can help reduce surgical bleeding (Gerschman, Reade & Burrows, 1980). Hypnosis has also had moderate success in helping clients to stop using cigarettes, alcohol, or other drugs by virtue of posthypnotic suggestions that link such substances with nausea or disgust.

Other applications of hypnosis are controversial, especially the use of hypnosis to enhance memory. Certainly, when hypnotized people show age regression, they are not actually becoming younger. They are probably reconstructing early memories, as well as imagining and acting out past actions (Foenander & Burrows, 1980). Similarly, it is questionable whether hypnotizing witnesses helps them to recall a crime. Instead, their confidence in hypnosis may cause them to unintentionally distort information or reconstruct memory for the events in question (Loftus & Loftus, 1980; McCann & Sheehan, 1988; Murrey, Cross & Whipple, 1992; Orne, 1979; Weekes et al., 1992).

Linkages: Meditation, Health, and Stress

Separation of mind and body, a sense of timelessness, a feeling of oneness with the universe, increased self-knowledge, and ecstasy have all been sought through *meditation,* a set of techniques designed to create an altered state of consciousness characterized by inner peace and tranquillity (Shapiro & Walsh, 1984). Many believe that meditation increases awareness and understanding of themselves and their surroundings, decreases stress and anxiety, improves physical and mental health, and even aids performance in everything from work to tennis.

There is no one "right" way to create a meditative state. Most common are *focusing* methods (Ornstein, 1977). These methods aim to narrow attention to just one thing—a word, a sound, or an object—long enough for the meditator to stop thinking about *anything* and to experience nothing but pure awareness. They call for the meditator to (1) find a quiet environment, (2) assume a comfortable position, (3) organize attention through some mental device, and (4) take a passive attitude (Benson, 1975).

What a meditator focuses on is far less important than doing so with a passive attitude. To organize attention, meditators may, for example, inwardly name every sound or thought that reaches consciousness, focus on the sound of their own breathing, or slowly repeat a *mantra,* which is a soothing word or phrase such as *om* (meaning "I am"). If attention begins to wander, there is a natural tendency to try to refocus it, but such active efforts block the way to the meditative state (Shapiro, 1980). Instead, new meditators are encouraged to observe any distractions but to make no effort to get rid of them, instead letting them fall away on their own. In effect, you achieve a passive attitude by not trying to achieve it!

During a typical meditation session, breathing, heart rate, muscle tension, blood pressure, and oxygen consumption decrease (Shapiro & Giber, 1978; Wallace & Benson, 1972). Most forms of meditation also produce a considerable amount of alpha-wave activity, the brain-wave pattern commonly found in a relaxed, eyes-closed, waking state (see Figure 7.4). Meditators often report significant reductions in stress-related problems such as general anxiety, high blood pressure, and insomnia (Carrington, 1986; Eppley, Abrams & Shear, 1989; Smith, 1975). More generally, meditators' scores on personality tests indicate increases in general mental health, self-esteem, and social openness (Alexander, Rainforth & Gelderloos, 1991; Shapiro & Giber, 1978). Exactly how meditation produces its effects is unclear. Many of its effects can also be achieved by biofeedback, hypnosis, and just relaxing (Holmes, 1984). (For a comparison of meditation and the other altered states we have discussed, see "In Review: Some Altered States of Consciousness").

Psychoactive Drugs

Each day, most people in the world use drugs that alter brain activity and consciousness. For example, in North America 80 to 90 percent of people use caffeine, the stimulant contained in coffee, tea, and some soft drinks (Gilbert, 1984). A drug is a chemical that is not normally needed for physiological activity and that can affect the body upon entering it. (Some people reserve the word *drug* for therapeutic, medicinal substances, while referring to nonmedicinal drugs as *substances.*) Some drugs affect the brain, changing consciousness and other psychological processes; these drugs are called **psychoactive drugs.** The study of psychoactive drugs is called **psychopharmacology.**

Psychopharmacology

Most psychoactive drugs affect the brain by altering the interaction between neurotransmitters and receptors. As described in the chapter on biological aspects of psychology, *neurotransmitters* are chemicals that are released by a neu-

Linkages: Can meditation help people deal with psychological problems? (a link to the Treatment of Psychological Disorders)

Linkages: How do drugs act in the nervous system to alter consciousness? (a link to Biological Aspects of Psychology)

In Review: Some Altered States of Consciousness

State	Characteristics	Postulated Benefits
Quiet sleep		Restores body and brain
Stage 1	Irregular EEG, rolling eyes	
Stage 2	Sleep spindles, K-complexes in EEG	
Stage 3	Addition of delta waves to EEG	
Stage 4	More than 50% delta waves in EEG	
REM sleep	EEG, heart rate, and other physiological patterns characteristic of the waking state combined with rapid eye movements and reduced muscle tone	Allows dreams to occur; allows norepinephrine sensitivity to restore itself; allows new connections between neurons to be consolidated or unused connections to be pruned
Hypnosis	Increased susceptibility to suggestions for changes in experience or behavior	Pain control, for example
Meditative state	Passive mental processes with alpha activity in brain waves	Reduces stress and anxiety

ron, cross a synapse, bind to the next neuron's receptors, and can affect its firing pattern. That effect may be *excitatory,* making the neuron more likely to fire, or *inhibitory.* The neurotransmitter, GABA, for example, is inhibitory, suppressing the firing of other neurons. Drugs that enhance the binding of GABA to its receptors reduce anxiety at low doses and induce a sleep-like state of sedation at higher doses.

Specific neurotransmitters tend to affect certain behaviors because, to some extent, different brain systems tend to use different neurotransmitters. A set of neurons that tends to use the same neurotransmitter is called a **neurotransmitter system.** For example, the neurons that we described in Chapter 4 in relation to Alzheimer's disease use acetylcholine and are thus known as a cholinergic system. Some of the most important neurotransmitter systems are summarized in Table 7.1.

The structure of the blood vessels supplying the brain creates a **blood-brain barrier** that allows only certain substances to leave the blood and interact with brain tissue. Psychoactive drugs penetrate this barrier. Once exposed to brain tissue, a psychoactive drug's effects depend on several factors: With which neurotransmitter systems does the drug interact? How does the drug affect neurotransmitters or their receptors? What psychological functions are performed by the brain systems that use these neurotransmitters?

Drugs can affect neurotransmitters or their receptors through several mechanisms. Recall that neurotransmitters fit into their own receptors, as Figure

Table 7.1
Major Neurotransmitter Systems
Here is a summary of the characteristics of seven major neurotransmitter systems. Usually, the suffix *-ergic* is added to the neurotransmitter name to make it an adjective. (For example, a dopamine-using system is a *dopaminergic* system, and an acetylcholine-using system is a *cholinergic* system.)

Neurotransmitter	Normal Function	Impact of Drugs
Acetylcholine	Memory	Blocking impairs memory; enhancing may improve memory (in Alzheimer's disease)
Norepinephrine	Mood, sleep	Cocaine and antidepressants block inactivation
Serotonin	Mood, appetite, sensory systems	Antidepressants and appetite suppressants block inactivation; hallucinogens activate receptors
Dopamine	Reward, movement	Drugs of abuse enhance; antipsychotics block receptors
GABA	Reduction of general excitability	Sedatives and anxiolytics enhance binding to receptors
Glutamate	Memory	May be related to drug tolerance
Endorphin	Modulation of pain	Mimicked by opiates (heroin, morphine)

7.13 shows. Some drugs are similar enough to a particular neurotransmitter to fool its receptors. These drugs, called **agonists**, bind to the receptor and mimic the effects of the normal neurotransmitter. Other drugs, called **antagonists**, are similar enough to a neurotransmitter to occupy its receptors but cannot mimic its effects; they bind to a receptor and prevent the normal neurotransmitter from binding. Certain snake venoms, for example, paralyze prey by blocking acetylcholine receptors that normally produce movement of muscles. Other drugs work by increasing or decreasing the release of a specific neurotransmitter. Finally, some drugs work by speeding or slowing the removal of a neurotransmitter from synapses.

Predicting a drug's behavioral effects is complicated by the fact that a drug sometimes interacts with more than one neurotransmitter system. Also, the nervous system usually compensates for any disturbance. For example, repeated exposure to a drug that blocks receptors for a certain neurotransmitter leads to a compensatory increase in the number of receptors available to respond to the neurotransmitter.

The Varying Effects of Drugs

Drugs don't "know" what we want them to do; they just affect biological systems in accordance with their chemical properties. Unfortunately, their medically desirable *main effects,* such as pain relief, are often accompanied by undesirable *side effects,* which may include the potential for abuse. **Drug abuse** is the self-administration of drugs in ways that deviate from a culture's medical or social norms (Gilman et al., 1985). Thus the definition of excessive or inappropriate drug use can vary across cultures and over time within a culture (Weiss & Moore, 1990). For example, in the United States cocaine was once a respectable, commercially available drug; today, it is illegal.

Figure 7.13
Agonists and Antagonists
Part (a) depicts a molecule of neuro-transmitter interacting with a recep-tor on a neuron's dendrites. Note that it fits into the receptor and stimulates it. If, as shown in part (b), a drug molecule is similar enough to the neurotransmitter that normally stimulates the receptor, the drug can act as an *agonist,* affecting the recep-tor in the same way the neurotrans-mitter would. An *antagonist* is a drug molecule that is similar enough to occupy a receptor site but not similar enough to stimulate it. The drug blocks the natural neurotransmitter from reaching and acting upon the receptor, as part (c) shows. Other drugs indirectly affect receptor stim-ulation by increasing or decreasing the release of natural neurotransmit-ters into the synapse or by altering the speed at which a neurotransmit-ter is removed from the synapse. Thus, these drugs alter the amount of neurotransmitter available in the synapse to stimulate receptors. As de-scribed in Chapter 16, the drugs used to treat various mental disorders act by altering neurotransmitters and/or receptors.

Linkages: How do the effects of psychoactive drugs lead to addiction and other problems? (a link to Psychological Disorders)

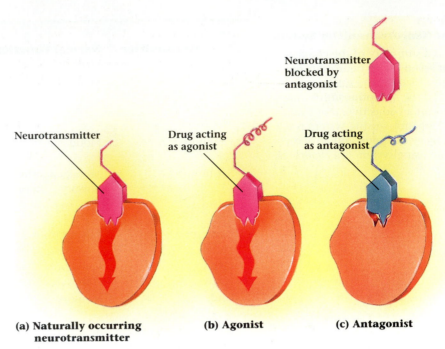

(a) Naturally occurring neurotransmitter   **(b) Agonist**   **(c) Antagonist**

Drug abuse sometimes leads to psychological or physical dependence. **Psy-chological dependence** is a condition in which a person continues drug use despite adverse effects, needs the drug for a sense of well-being, and becomes preoccupied with obtaining the drug if it becomes unavailable. Psychological dependence can occur with or without **physical dependence**, or **addiction,** which is a physiological state in which drug use is needed to prevent a **with-drawal syndrome.** Withdrawal symptoms vary from drug to drug but often include an intense craving for the drug and effects generally opposite to those produced by the drug. Physical dependence can develop gradually and without awareness. As addiction progresses, drug tolerance may appear. **Tolerance** is a condition in which increasingly larger drug doses are needed to produce a given effect (Gilman et al., 1985). With the development of tolerance, many addicts need the drug just to prevent the negative effects of not taking it (see the Linkages section in Chapter 8). However, most researchers now believe that a craving for the positive effects of drugs is what keeps addicts coming back to drug use (Wise, 1988).

The potential for "normal" people to develop drug dependence should not be underestimated. All potentially addictive drugs stimulate a dopaminergic system known as the brain's "pleasure center." Neuronal activity in this area produces intensely pleasurable feelings; the same system helps generate the pleasant feelings of a good meal, a "runner's high," or sex (Kalivas & Nemeroff, 1988). Thus, addictive drugs have the capacity to create rewarding effects in most people. Even rats that have become addicted to cocaine will choose it over food, and may starve (Bozarth & Wise, 1985).

Expectations and Drug Effects   Still, drug effects are determined by more than biochemistry; *learned expectations* also play a role. In one study (Lang et al., 1975), subjects drank tonic water with or without alcohol (the alcohol could not be tasted). Those drinking alcohol got enough to make them legally drunk as defined by most of the United States. Half of those drinking each beverage were told what they were drinking. The other half were misin-formed; they were told they were drinking alcohol, when in fact they were not, or that they were drinking only tonic water when in fact their drink contained alcohol. Then a research assistant, posing as an obnoxious subject, angered the subjects. Subjects later could hurt him by giving electric shocks (the shocks were only simulated but the assistant pretended to be shocked). Figure 7.14 shows the results of this experiment. Alcohol's effect on aggressiveness (that is, on the strength of the shocks the subjects gave) depended not on whether the subjects were *actually* drunk or sober but on their *expectations*. Other studies have produced similar findings and show that learned expectancies can affect the consequences of taking other drugs, including heroin, cocaine, and marijuana (Goldman et al., 1991; Schafer & Brown, 1991; Stacy, Widaman & Marlatt, 1990).

Expectations about drug effects develop in part as people watch other people react to drugs. Because what they see can vary from person to person and from culture to culture, the effects of some drugs vary considerably across people and cultures (MacAndrew & Edgerton, 1969). For example, the loss of inhibition, increased aggressiveness, and sexual promiscuity commonly associated with the use of alcohol in the United States is probably attributable in large part to custom. This custom is not universal. Members of the Camba culture in Bolivia drink, in extended binges, a potent brew that is 89 percent alcohol (178 proof). During their revels, these people repeatedly pass out, wake up, and then start drinking again—all the while maintaining tranquil social relations.

The learned nature of responses to alcohol is also demonstrated by cases in which there are *changes* in the model for appropriate "drunken comportment." When Europeans brought alcohol to Tahiti in the 1700s, the Tahitians' initial response to drinking it was to become relaxed and slightly befuddled, much as they did when drinking *kava*, their traditional nonalcoholic, tranquilizing drink. But after several years of watching European sailors' drunken violence, Tahitian drinkers became quite violent themselves. Fortunately, subsequent learning experiences have once again made their response to alcohol more pacific (MacAndrew & Edgerton, 1969).

These case examples and experiments show that the effects of psychoactive drugs are complex and variable. In Chapter 16 we discuss psychoactive drugs that are used in the treatment of psychological problems. In the sections that follow we consider several major categories of psychoactive drugs that are used primarily for the alterations they produce in consciousness, including depressants, stimulants, narcotics, and psychedelics.

Depressants

Depressant drugs reduce activity of the central nervous system. Examples are alcohol, sedatives, and anxiolytics, all three of which increase activity of the neurotransmitter GABA. Since GABA reduces postsynaptic neuron activity, enhancing GABA function reduces the excitability of many neural circuits.

Alcohol In the United States alone, more than 100 million people drink alcohol, and this drug is popular in many other countries as well (see, for example, Engs, Slawinska & Hanson, 1991). Alcohol's effects involve the neurotransmitters dopamine, norepinephrine, serotonin, endorphins, and GABA (Koob & Bloom, 1988). The GABA effect is notable; indeed, drugs that interact with GABA receptors can block some of alcohol's effects, as shown in Figure 7.15 (Suzdak et al., 1986). Alcohol enhances the effect of endorphins (the body's natural painkillers, described in Chapter 5). This action may underlie the "high" that most people feel when drinking alcohol and may explain why *naltrexone*, an endorphin antagonist, is significantly better than placebos at reducing both alcohol craving and relapse rates in recovering alcoholics (O'Malley et al., 1992; Volpicelli et al., 1992).

Figure 7.14
Expectancy and Alcohol's Effects on Aggressiveness
In this experiment, aggression was measured by the intensity of shocks that subjects delivered to another person over several trials. Shocks given by people who thought they had been drinking (brown and blue lines) were significantly more intense, whether the subjects actually had alcohol or not, than those given by subjects who were sober or at least thought they were (red and green lines). Thus, aggression was influenced more by the subjects' expectancies than by alcohol itself.

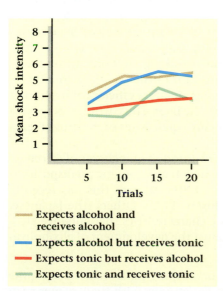

— Expects alcohol and receives alcohol

— Expects alcohol but receives tonic

— Expects tonic but receives alcohol

— Expects tonic and receives tonic

Source: Lang et al., 1975.

Figure 7.15
GABA Receptors and Alcohol
Both rats in this photograph received the same amount of alcohol, enough to incapacitate them with drunkenness. But the rat on the right also received a drug that reverses the intoxicating effect of alcohol; within two minutes it was acting completely sober. The drug, Ro15-4513, binds to part of the brain's GABA receptor complex, blocking the ability of alcohol to stimulate GABA receptors. The company that developed Ro15-4513 decided to discontinue work on the drug because of ethical and legal concerns. Before lamenting this decision, note that the drug does not reverse the effects of alcohol on the hindbrain's breathing centers. So if you were drinking to become intoxicated and Ro was frustrating your attempts, you could more easily ingest a lethal overdose.

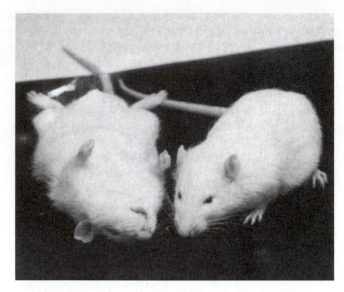

Source: Kolata, 1986.

Alcohol depresses activity in specific brain regions. Lowered activity in the cerebral cortex causes cognitive changes and a release of inhibitions. Some drinkers begin talking too loudly, acting silly, or telling others what they think of them. Emotional reactions range from euphoria to deep sadness. Normally shy and mild-mannered people may become impulsive or violent (Steele, 1986). Alcohol also depresses activity in the locus coeruleus, a brain region that helps activate the cortex (Koob & Bloom, 1988). Alcohol impairs the cerebellum as well, causing poor motor coordination (Rogers et al., 1986). Alcohol's ability to depress hindbrain mechanisms that control breathing and heartbeat can make overdoses fatal.

As suggested earlier, some effects of alcohol—such as happiness, sadness, adventurousness, lust, anger—depend on a combination of biochemical factors and learned expectations (Keane, Lisman & Kreutzer, 1980; Marlatt & Rohsenow, 1980; McMillen, 1991). But many effects—particularly disruptions in motor coordination, speech, and thought—are the result of biochemical factors alone (Vuchinich & Sobell, 1978). These biological effects depend on the amount of alcohol the blood carries to the brain. Since the liver breaks down about one ounce of alcohol in an hour, alcohol has little effect if consumed that slowly. Effects increase with faster drinking, or if one drinks on an empty stomach, thus speeding drug absorption into the blood. Even after allowing for differences in body size, male bodies are more efficient at beginning to break down alcohol even before it reaches the liver. Thus, women may have higher blood alcohol levels than men following equal doses of the drug (Frezza et al., 1990).

Genetics also seems to play a role in determining the biochemical effects of alcohol. There is evidence that some people may have a genetic predisposition toward alcohol dependence (Pickens et al., 1991), though this has recently been questioned (Gelernter, Goldman & Risch, 1993). Others (the Japanese, for example) may have inherited metabolic characteristics that enhance alcohol's adverse effects, which might work against the development of alcoholism (Harda et al., 1980).

Sedatives   Sometimes called "downers" or sleeping pills, *sedatives* are quite addictive. The most common sedatives are *barbiturates* with trade names such as Seconal or Nembutal, but methaqualone (Quaalude) has similar effects.

Linkages: Though practice may make it seem easy, driving a car is a complex information-processing task that, as described in the chapter on thought and language, requires the driver to be constantly alert to a wide range of incoming stimuli, to make fast and accurate decisions about how to respond, and to execute those responses in a skillful, coordinated fashion. Alcohol can impair all these processes (as well as the ability to judge the degree of impairment), thus making drinking and driving a deadly combination that kills tens of thousands of people each year in the United States alone.

Small doses cause relaxation, mild euphoria, disrupted muscle coordination, poor mental concentration, and lowered attention. Higher doses cause very deep sleep, but continued sedative use actually distorts sleep patterns (see Figure 7.16). Thus, the long-term use of sedatives as sleeping pills is unwise. Overdoses can be fatal. Withdrawal symptoms are among the most severe for any drug and can include intense agitation, violent outbursts, convulsions, hallucinations, and even sudden death.

Anxiolytics   Once called *tranquilizers* or *anti-anxiety* drugs, *anxiolytics* are used to help patients with anxiety, but they also have sedative properties. For example, the anxiolytic meprobamate (Miltown) can be taken in small daily doses for anxiety, but it has barbiturate-like effects (overdoses can cause sleep or death). The *benzodiazepines* (for example, Librium, Valium) relieve anxiety but cause less sleepiness. It is very difficult to commit suicide by taking an overdose of benzodiazepines. Like alcohol, benzodiazepines affect the GABA receptor system, but they do not bind directly to GABA receptors (Squires & Braestrup, 1977). Instead, benzodiazepines enhance the binding of GABA to its receptors, resulting in increased inhibition whenever GABA is released.

Many people become psychologically and physically dependent on anxiolytics and suffer symptoms similar to barbiturate withdrawal when they discontinue use (Gilman et al., 1985). Many long-term users experience confusion, anger, and memory loss. These effects are exaggerated if anxiolytics are used with alcohol, an often fatal combination.

Stimulants

Amphetamines, cocaine, MDMA, caffeine, and nicotine are all examples of **stimulants**, which are drugs that increase behavioral and mental activity.

Amphetamines   Also called "uppers" or "speed," the *amphetamines* (for example, Benzedrine, Dexedrine, Methadrine) increase the release, and decrease the removal, of norepinephrine and dopamine at synapses. The result is increased activity at these neurotransmitters' receptors. The dopamine activity probably causes the drugs' rewarding properties, since taking dopamine antagonists reduces amphetamine use (Wise, 1978, 1988).

Figure 7.16
The Effects of Sedatives on Sleep
Long-term use of sedatives disrupts the normal pattern of sleep, as is illustrated when people abruptly stop taking them. Sudden withdrawal results in a dramatic "rebound" of previously suppressed REM sleep, as well as a reported increase in the intensity and frequency of dreams. Stage 3 and stage 4 sleep increase to normal levels more gradually (Kales & Kales, 1973).

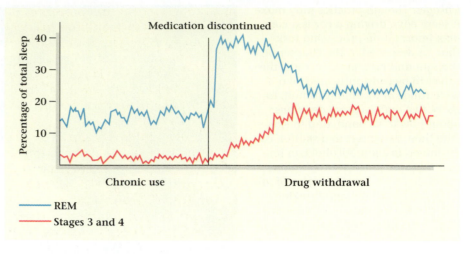

Source: Adapted from Kales & Kales, 1973.

Amphetamines stimulate both the brain and the sympathetic branch of the autonomic nervous system, raising heart rate and blood pressure, constricting blood vessels, shrinking mucous membranes (thus relieving stuffy noses), and reducing appetite. Amphetamines seem to increase alertness and speed up reaction times, but they also increase decision-making errors (Naylor, Halliday & Callaway, 1992).

Amphetamine abuse is usually due to a desire to lose weight, stay awake, or experience a "high." Continued use leads to severe restlessness, sleeplessness, heart problems, mental confusion, suspiciousness, nonstop talking, and, in some cases, symptoms virtually indistinguishable from those of paranoid schizophrenia.

Cocaine produces euphoria and increased physiological activation, but its users run a high risk of ruining their lives by becoming dependent on the drug.

Cocaine Like amphetamines, *cocaine* increases norepinephrine and dopamine activity, although cocaine acts mainly by blocking the removal of neurotransmitters. Thus, amphetamine and cocaine produce psychological effects that may be indistinguishable. Cocaine's powerful effect on dopamine and its special affinity for certain brain regions may underlie its remarkably addictive nature (Museo, Zocchi & Pert, 1992; Wise, 1988).

Cocaine's effects are more rapid than amphetamines', which may also explain its addictiveness. In animal studies, drugs with rapid onset and short duration are more highly addictive than others (Kato, Wakasa & Yanagita, 1987). This fact may help explain why *crack*—a purified, very potent, smokable form of cocaine—is especially addictive. Crack's fast onset and short duration cause a rapid "rush," followed quickly by a depressed mood that can be relieved by more crack.

Cocaine stimulates self-confidence, well-being, and optimism. Continued use can lead to nausea, overactivity, sleeplessness, paranoid thinking, a sudden depressive "crash," hallucinations, and permanent brain damage (Pascual-Leone et al., 1990). Overdoses, especially of crack, can be fatal (Kozel, Grider & Adams, 1982). Even small doses can cause a fatal heart attack or stroke. Cocaine is both physically and psychologically addictive (Jones, 1984).

Because of cocaine's strong effect on the dopaminergic "pleasure centers," ending a cocaine addiction is especially difficult. A possible treatment may involve *buprenorphine,* an opiate antagonist that suppresses cocaine self-administration in addicted monkeys (Mello et al., 1989). Other drug treatments for addicts have had mixed but promising success (Meyer, 1992).

MDMA "Ecstasy," or *MDMA* (an abbreviation for 3,4–Methylenedioxymethamphetamine), has properties of both the stimulants and the psyche-delics. Its effects include visual hallucinations, a feeling of enhanced closeness with others, increased heart rate, dry mouth, hyperactivity, and jaw muscle spasms causing "lockjaw." On the day after using MDMA, people often complain of muscle aches, fatigue, depression, and poor concentration (Downing, 1986; Peroutka et al., 1988). With continued use, positive effects diminish while negative effects persist. MDMA does not appear to be physically addictive (Peroutka, 1989).

MDMA increases the activity of neurons that use dopamine or serotonin (McKenna & Peroutka, 1990). Its impact on dopamine parallels that of cocaine and amphetamine and causes many of the same effects (Gold, Hubner & Koob, 1989; White & Paros, 1992). At serotonin synapses, MDMA is a receptor agonist and also causes neurotransmitter release; this probably accounts for the drug's hallucinatory effects (Nichols & Oberlender, 1990).

The negative effects of MDMA are many. Of greatest concern, MDMA permanently damages the brain, killing serotonergic neurons in the cortex and other forebrain areas (McKenna & Peroutka, 1990; Slikker et al., 1989). Brain damage seems to increase with dosage and frequency of use (Battaglia, Yeh & De Souza, 1988). MDMA users may also develop *panic disorder,* a problem discussed in Chapter 15 that includes symptoms of intense anxiety and a sense of impending death (Pallanti & Mazzi, 1992).

Caffeine   The potent stimulant *caffeine* is probably the world's most popular psychoactive drug (Gilbert, 1984). It occurs in coffee, tea, chocolate, and many soft drinks. Caffeine decreases drowsiness, makes thought more rapid (Goodman-Gilman et al., 1990), increases the capacity for physical work, and raises urine production. At high doses it induces anxiety and tremors. Tolerance develops to caffeine's effects, and it can induce physical dependence (Evans & Griffiths, 1992; Griffiths & Woodson, 1988). Withdrawal symptoms—including headaches, fatigue, anxiety, shakiness, and craving—begin to appear twelve to twenty-four hours after abstinence, peak at about forty-eight hours, and last about a week (Silverman et al., 1992).

Nicotine   A powerful stimulant of the autonomic nervous system, the acetylcholine agonist *nicotine* is the main psychoactive ingredient in tobacco. Nicotine's psychoactive effects are rather subtle, yet the drug has vast worldwide appeal. There is controversy over nicotine's potential for creating dependence. In 1988 the U.S. Surgeon General declared that nicotine, like heroin or cocaine, is physically addictive (USDHHS, 1988). This claim is supported by the presence of a withdrawal syndrome, which includes nicotine craving, restlessness, irritability, lowered heart rate, and weight gain (Hughes et al., 1991). Reactions do vary, however, and others see nicotine as creating psychological rather than physical dependence for many people. Whatever blend of physical and psychological dependence is involved, there is no doubt that the smoking habit is very hard for most smokers to break (see, for example, Robinson & Pritchard, 1992). Nor is there any doubt that smoking increases smokers' risks for cancer, heart disease, respiratory disorders, and a number of other life-threatening illnesses (USDHHS, 1990), as discussed in Chapter 13, on health, stress, and coping.

Narcotics

The **narcotics** (opium, morphine, heroin, codeine) are unique in inducing sleep and relieving pain (Julien, 1988); they are also called *opiates. Opium,* which comes from the poppy plant, relieves pain and causes feelings of well-being and dreamy relaxation. One of its most active ingredients is *morphine,* which was first isolated in the early 1800s and is used worldwide for pain relief.

Percodan and Demoral are some common morphinelike drugs. *Heroin* is derived from morphine but is three times more powerful, causing an intensely pleasurable reaction.

Narcotics have complex effects on consciousness. Drowsy, cloudy feelings occur because the opiates depress activity in areas of the cerebral cortex. But they also create excitation in other parts, causing some users to experience euphoria (Bozarth & Wise, 1984). Narcotics exert many of their effects through their role as agonists for endorphins. When opiates activate endorphin receptors, they are "tricking" the brain into an exaggerated activation of its pain-killing and mood-altering systems (Julien, 1988).

Narcotics are quite addictive, perhaps as a result of their ability to stimulate receptors in the brain for the neurotransmitter glutamate. Activation of a particular type of glutamate receptor appears to induce physical changes in a neuron's structure; as discussed in Chapter 9, such changes may be the basis for certain kinds of memories. It may be that opiates' activation of glutamate alters neurons so that they come to require the drug for proper functioning. Supporting this idea are data showing that glutamate antagonists appear to block the development of morphine dependence but leave the drug's pain-killing effects intact (Marek et al., 1989; Trujillo & Akil, 1991). Beyond the hazards of addiction itself, heroin addicts risk death through overdoses, contaminated drugs, or AIDS contracted by sharing drug-injection needles.

Psychedelics

A loss of contact with reality is one effect of **psychedelics.** They also produce changes in other aspects of emotion, perception, and thought that may include distortions in body image (one may feel gigantic or very tiny), loss of identity (confusion about who one actually is), dreamlike fantasies, and hallucinations. Since these effects resemble many severe forms of mental disorder, psychedelics are sometimes called *hallucinogens* or *psychotomimetics* (mimicking psychosis).

One of the most powerful psychedelics is *lysergic acid diethylamide,* or *LSD.* It was first synthesized from a rye grain fungus by Swiss chemist Albert Hofmann. In 1938, after Hofmann accidentally ingested a minuscule amount of the substance, he discovered the drug's strange effects in the world's first LSD "trip" (Julien, 1988). LSD's hallucinations can be quite bizarre. Time may seem distorted, sounds may cause visual sensations, and users may feel as if they have left their bodies. These experiences probably result from LSD's action as a serotonin agonist (Jacobs, 1987), since serotonin antagonists greatly reduce the hallucinatory effects of LSD (Nielson et al., 1985).

The precise effects of LSD are rather unpredictable. Unpleasant hallucinations and delusions can occur in a person's first LSD experience or the 200th. Although LSD is not addictive, tolerance to its effects does develop. Some users suffer lasting side effects, including severe short-term memory loss, paranoia, violent outbursts, nightmares, and panic attacks (Seligmann, 1992). Distortions in visual sensations can remain even two years after the end of heavy use (Abraham & Wolf, 1988). Sometimes flashbacks occur, in which a person suddenly returns to an LSD-like state of consciousness weeks or even years after using the drug.

Another psychedelic is *phencyclidine,* or *PCP,* which is often called angel dust. PCP attaches to specific binding sites in the brain that are not related to any known neurotransmitter (Vincent et al., 1979). PCP's effects include agitated excitement, disorientation, and hallucinations. It is very dangerous. Relatively small doses create insensitivity to pain, psychological separation from the world and from one's own body, rigidity, a blank stare, and an inability to speak. The drug also kills neurons in the cerebral cortex (Olney, Labruyere &

Price, 1989). Higher doses bring stupor and mental confusion for hours or days. PCP users have been known to jump off buildings because they do not recognize danger or feel pain. The drug can also cause the user to injure or kill others.

A mixture of crushed leaves, flowers, and stems from the hemp plant (*Cannabis sativa*) makes up *marijuana.* The active ingredient is *tetrahydrocannabinol,* or *THC.* When inhaled from a marijuana cigarette, THC reaches peak concentrations in the blood in ten to thirty minutes. It is absorbed by many organs, including the brain, through which it continues to affect consciousness for a few hours. THC tends to collect in fatty deposits (for example, in the brain or reproductive organs), where it can be detected for weeks. Scientists have recently discovered specific receptors for THC, and isolated a naturally occuring substance in the brain that binds to THC receptors; this substance, called anandamide (from a Sanskrit word meaning bliss), may be a new neurotransmitter (Devanne et al., 1988; Devane et al., 1992; Fride & Mechoulam, 1993).

Low doses of marijuana cause relaxation and reduce anxiety. Initial restlessness and hilarity may be followed by a dreamy, carefree state of relaxation; expansion of space and time; more vivid sensations; food cravings, especially for sweets; and subtle changes in thought formation and expression (National Commission on Marijuana and Drug Abuse, 1972). Marijuana may also disrupt the ability to remember what happened a few seconds ago, making it difficult to carry out mental or physical tasks (Jaffe, 1975). These effects intensify with the dose. Following very large doses, a person may occasionally experience vivid LSD-like phenomena.

Numerous government groups have summarized research on marijuana (Commission of Inquiry into the Non-medical Use of Drugs, 1970, 1972, 1973; National Academy of Sciences, 1982; National Commission on Marijuana and Drug Abuse, 1972; Report of the British Advisory Committee on Drug Dependence, 1968). They find that compared with other psychoactive drugs, marijuana is the least potent (see "In Review: Major Classes of Psychoactive Drugs"). There are no known major health hazards associated with *moderate* marijuana use, but there may be significant hazards associated with smoking large amounts of marijuana for long periods. These include the closing of breathing passages, risking bronchitis and asthma; suppression of the immune system; and stress on the heart. In rats, THC also kills cells in the brain's hippocampus, an area vital for the formation of new memories (Eldridge, Murphy & Landfield, 1991). Because marijuana interferes with muscle coordination, people should not drive after using it. Some motor impairment continues well after the subjective effects of the drug have worn off. In one study, pilots had impaired ability to land a simulated aircraft even twenty-four hours after smoking one marijuana cigarette (Yesavage et al., 1985). Like all psychoactive drugs, marijuana easily reaches a developing fetus and thus should not be used by pregnant women. Marijuana actually has some positive therapeutic uses: it is sometimes a helpful treatment for asthma, glaucoma, epilepsy, and the nausea caused by cancer chemotherapy.

Future Directions

The most influential psychological theories today view human behavior as guided by both conscious and subconscious mental events and processes that mediate the effects of the external consequences of behavior. As a result, the study of consciousness provides a kind of conceptual meeting place for ideas and findings from many areas of psychology. In fact, as noted in Chapter 1, investigators and researchers from disciplines as diverse as biology, psychol-

In Review: Major Classes of Psychoactive Drugs

Drug	Trade/Street Name	Main Effects	Potential for Physical/ Psychological Dependence
Depressants			
Alcohol	"booze"		High/High
Sedatives (barbiturates)	Seconal, Tuinal ("downers"), Nembutal	Relaxation, anxiety reduction, sleep	High/High
Anxiolytics (meprobamate, benzodiazepines)	Miltown, Equanil, Librium, Valium		Moderate to high/High
Stimulants			
Amphetamines	Benzedrine, Dexedrine, Methadrine ("speed," "uppers," "ice")	Alertness, euphoria	Moderate/High
Cocaine	"coke"		Moderate to high/High
Caffeine			Moderate/Moderate
Nicotine		Alertness	High (?)
MDMA	Ecstasy	Alertness Hallucinations	Low
Narcotics			
Opium		Euphoria	High/High
Morphine	Percodan, Demoral	Euphoria, pain control	High/High
Heroin	"junk," "smack"	Euphoria, pain control	High/High
Psychedelics			
LSD	"acid"	Mind expansion, hallucinations	Low/Low
Phencyclidine	"PCP," "angel dust"	Exhilaration	Unknown/High
Marijuana (cannabis)	"pot," "dope," "reefer"	Euphoria, relaxation	Low/Moderate

ogy, linguistics, electrical engineering, and computer science—all interested in the broad field called *cognitive science*—work together in special programs to better understand human consciousness. There is a long way to go. Psychologists still do not know where or how self-referent properties occur in the human brain. And intense research is under way to understand how drugs affect consciousness.

Current research may open the way for significant improvements in the understanding and treatment of various disorders. For example, if investigators find the natural substance that normally fits into the binding site of the benzodiazepines, they may learn more about the chemistry of anxiety. New drugs will likely be developed that will reduce the craving for addictive drugs without themselves producing addiction. Earlier we noted that naltrexone may serve this role in recovering alcoholics. And buprenorphine seems to be effective for treating not only cocaine abuse but also narcotic dependence (Johnson, Jaffe & Fudala, 1992). The fact that drugs like buprenorphine appear to block the craving for more than one type of abused drug supports the notion that there may be common (and perhaps treatable) mechanisms underlying all drugs of abuse. Research on circadian rhythms is also promising new therapies for those mental disorders, such as bipolar disorder, that may be caused by disruptions of these rhythms. And if sleep disorders are found to reliably predict psychological disorders, perhaps this link may allow early intervention, assuming that better sleep therapies can be developed.

Future research will also help answer questions about the possibility of undiscovered potential in human consciousness. For example, we already know that peaceful mental images can block the perception of pain (Elton, Burrows & Stanley, 1980; Turk, 1978). In one experiment, cancer patients who used self-hypnosis to reduce their pain and group psychotherapy to reduce their anxiety about death lived an average of eighteen months longer than patients receiving only conventional therapy (Spiegel et al., 1989). The author of this study has emphasized that *all* of the patients received conventional radiation and drug therapy, and that this work in no way implies that one can "wish away your cancer." But the work does suggest that it will be valuable to learn how psychological processes can affect the course of the disease.

For more detailed information about the study of consciousness, consider taking courses in neuropsychology, cognitive psychology, psychopharmacology, and sleep. Also look for courses that offer lectures and direct experience with meditation and hypnosis.

Summary and Key Terms

Consciousness can be defined as the mental process of being aware of the outside world as well as of one's own thoughts, feelings, and perceptions.

Analyzing Consciousness

Early psychologists—structuralists—tried through introspection to understand the structure of consciousness, the mental building blocks that create mental life. Functionalists emphasized studying how mental processes operate and function in a person's environment. Recently, the study of consciousness has made a comeback. Current research on consciousness embraces several themes. First, researchers ask questions about the mind-body problem. Dualists see the mind as separate and distinct from the brain; materialists argue that the brain itself is the complete basis for the mind. Second, psychologists are exploring whether animals or computers can be conscious. Third, researchers study whether consciousness occurs as a single "point" in the stream of mental processing or as several parallel mental operations that operate simultaneously and independently.

The Role of Consciousness

Consciousness extends mental capacity and acts as a kind of "bridge" to unite various aspects of mental life. But it is not always required for mental operations.

Mental Processing Without Awareness

In the mere-exposure effect, people tend to judge stimuli more favorably if the stimuli have been previously encountered, even when people are unaware of having seen the stimuli before. Similarly, in the priming phenomenon, responses to stimuli are speeded and improved as stimuli are repeated, even when people have no conscious memory of which stimuli are old and which are new. It also appears that certain cognitive decision-making strategies can be learned and executed without conscious awareness.

The Neuropsychology of Consciousness

Brain injuries often reveal ways in which mental processing can occur without conscious awareness. In prosopagnosia, people do not consciously recognize faces yet continue to discriminate unconsciously between familiar and unfamiliar faces. In visual agnosia, brain-damaged patients do not consciously understand some visual sensations, though they can interpret and use them without awareness. In blindsight, a patient experiencing blindness can still "guess" details of visual stimuli. In anterograde amnesia, patients do not consciously form new memories but continue to acquire new skills without later awareness of how or where their new abilities were learned.

Levels of Consciousness

Variations in how much awareness you have for a mental function are described by different levels of consciousness. The *preconscious* includes mental activities that are outside of awareness but can be easily brought to the *conscious level*. *Subconscious* or *unconscious* mental activity contains thoughts, memories, and processes that are more difficult to bring to awareness. Mental processes that cannot be brought into awareness are called *nonconscious*.

States of Consciousness

Like the varying flow of a stream, a person's *state of consciousness* is constantly changing. When the changes are particularly noticeable, they are called *altered states of consciousness*. Examples include sleep, hypnosis, meditation, and some drug-induced states. Different cultures vary considerably in the value placed on different states of consciousness.

Sleeping and Dreaming
Sleep is a very active and complex state.

Stages of Sleep
Different stages of sleep are defined on the basis of changes in brain activity (as seen in an electroencephalograph, or EEG) and physiological arousal. Sleep normally begins with stage 1 sleep and progresses gradually to stage 4 sleep. Sleep stages 1 through 4 constitute *quiet sleep, slow-wave sleep,* or non-REM sleep. After passing back to stage 2, people enter REM (*rapid eye movement*) *sleep,* or *active sleep.* This is when most dreaming occurs. The sleeper cycles up and down through these stages several times each night, gradually spending more time in stage 2 and REM sleep later in the night.

Sleep Disorders
Sleep disorders can disrupt the natural rhythm of sleep. Among the most common is *insomnia,* in which one feels tired because of trouble falling or staying asleep. *Narcolepsy* produces sudden daytime sleeping episodes. In *sleep apnea,* people briefly but repeatedly stop breathing during sleep. *Sudden infant death syndrome (SIDS)* may be due to brainstem abnormalities. *Nightmares* and *night terrors* are different kinds of frightening dreams. *Sleepwalking* happens most frequently during childhood. *REM behavior disorder* is potentially dangerous because the decrease in muscle tone that normally prevents people from acting out REM dreams is absent.

Why Do People Sleep?
The cycle of waking and sleeping is a natural *circadian rhythm,* possibly controlled by the suprachiasmatic nucleus of the brain. *Jet lag*—a temporary appearance of sleeping problems, irritability, and inattention caused by traveling to new time zones—can be one result of disrupting the normal sleep-wake cycle. The purpose of sleep is much debated. Non-REM sleep may aid bodily rest and repair. REM sleep may help maintain activity in brain areas that provide daytime alertness, or it may allow the brain to "check circuits," eliminate useless information, and solidify learning from the previous day.

Dreams and Dreaming
Dreams are storylike sequences of images, sensations, and perceptions that occur during sleep. Evidence for *lucid dreaming* suggests that people may be able to control their own dreams. Some claim that dreams may be no more than the meaningless by-products of brain activity. But the way in which one recalls and organizes dreams may still reflect one's mental style and current concerns.

Hypnosis
Hypnosis is a well-known but still poorly understood phenomenon.

Experiencing Hypnosis
Tests of *hypnotic susceptibility* suggest that some people cannot be hypnotized. Hypnotized people tend to focus attention on the hypnotist and then passively follow his or her instructions. They become very good at fantasizing and role

taking. They may exhibit apparent *age regression,* experience *posthypnotic amnesia,* and obey *posthypnotic suggestions.*

Explaining Hypnosis
Role theory suggests that hypnosis creates a special social role that gives people permission to act in unusual ways. *State theory* sees hypnosis as a special state of consciousness. Hilgard's *dissociation theory* combines aspects of role and state theories. It says that hypnotic subjects enter into an implicit social contract with the hypnotist in which they agree to allow normally well-integrated mental processes to become dissociated and to share control over their mental processes.

Some Uses of Hypnosis
Hypnosis is useful in many ways, including the control of pain, and reduction of the discomfort associated with cancer chemotherapy.

Linkages: Meditation, Health, and Stress
Meditation is a set of techniques designed to create an altered state of consciousness characterized by inner peace but with increased awareness. During meditation, muscle tension and blood pressure decrease, and alpha waves appear on the EEG. The consistent practice of meditation reportedly reduces stress-related health problems such as anxiety and high blood pressure.

Psychoactive Drugs
Psychoactive drugs affect the brain, changing consciousness and other psychological processes. *Psychopharmacology* is the field that studies drug effects and their mechanisms.

Psychopharmacology
A *neurotransmitter system* is a set of neurons that use the same neurotransmitter. Psychoactive drugs exert their effects primarily by affecting some specific neurotransmitter system and, hence, certain brain activities. To reach brain tissue, drugs must cross the *blood-brain-barrier.* Drugs that mimic the receptor effects of a neurotransmitter are called *agonists,* and drugs that block the receptor effects of a neurotransmitter are called *antagonists.* Some drugs alter the release or inactivation of specific neurotransmitters, thus affecting the amount of neurotransmitter available for receptor effects.

The Varying Effects of Drugs
Adverse effects often accompany psychoactive drugs, especially when drug use becomes *drug abuse. Psychological dependence, physical dependence (addiction), tolerance,* and a *withdrawal syndrome* may result. Drugs that produce dependence share the property of directly stimulating certain dopamine-containing areas of the brain, the so-called pleasure centers. The consequences of using a psychoactive drug depend both on how the drug affects neurotransmitters and on the user's learned expectations and responses.

Depressants
Alcohol, sedatives, and anxiolytics are all *depressants.* They reduce activity in the central nervous system, often by enhancing the action of inhibitory neurotransmitters. They have considerable potential for producing both psychological and physical dependence.

Stimulants
Stimulants such as amphetamines and cocaine increase be-

havioral and mental activity mainly by increasing the action of the neurotransmitters dopamine and norepinephrine. These drugs can also produce both psychological and physical dependency. MDMA exhibits properties of both the stimulants and psychedelics and is one of several psychoactive drugs that can permanently damage brain tissue. Caffeine, one of the world's most popular stimulants, may also create dependency. Nicotine is a potent stimulant.

Narcotics

Narcotics such as opium, morphine, and heroin are highly addictive drugs that induce sleep and relieve pain.

Psychedelics

LSD, PCP, and marijuana are examples of *psychedelics,* or hallucinogens. Psychedelics alter consciousness by producing a temporary loss of contact with reality and changes in emotion, perception, and thought. PCP is particularly dangerous.

Chapter 8

Learning

Outline

For most preschoolers, the first few days of kindergarten are a bewildering, often frightening excursion in which the comforting familiarity of home or day care is replaced by an environment filled with new names and faces, rules and events. Before long, however, most youngsters *adapt* to this new environment.

The adaptation occurs in many ways. Some are simple, as when once-startling sounds from a balky heating system are eventually ignored. Others are more complex. Ringing bells, roll call, and other strange new events become part of children's pattern of expectancies about the world. Youngsters come to expect that certain events, such as the arrival of the juice cart, signal the likely occurrence of other events that are going to be pleasant or unpleasant. They also develop expectancies about which aspects of their school behavior are likely to be rewarded and which are likely to be punished. Talking at will, for example, may not be as acceptable in class as at home, but enthusiastic finger painting—perhaps forbidden at home—may bring praise at school. Finally, schoolchildren acquire facts about the world and develop skills ranging from reading to kickball.

Adaptation is not confined to school. As described in Chapter 3, the entire process of development, from birth to death, involves adapting to increasingly complex, ever-changing environments, using continuously updated knowledge gained through experience. Though perhaps most highly developed in humans, the ability to adapt to changing environments appears to varying degrees in members of all species. According to the evolutionary approach to psychology discussed in Chapter 1, it is individual variability in the capacity to adapt, and thus to survive and reproduce, that shapes the evolution of animal and human appearance and behavior.

Many forms of animal and human adaptation follow the principles of **learning**, which is the modification through experience of pre-existing behavior and understanding. The pre-existing behavior and understanding may have been present at birth, acquired through maturation, or learned earlier. People learn primarily by identifying relationships between events and noting the regularity in the world around them. When two things repeatedly occur together, people can predict the occurrence of one from knowledge of the other. They learn that a clear blue sky means dry weather, that too little sleep makes them irritable, that they can reach someone on the telephone by dialing a certain number, that screaming orders motivates some people and angers others. (The Linkages diagram shows just a few of the many ways in which learning plays a role in other areas of psychology.)

Which relationships do people identify, and how do they do it? What determines whether and how people learn? These and other basic questions about learning are among the most frequently and intensively studied topics in psychology. For several decades, much of the research on learning was guided by the behaviorist approach (discussed in Chapter 1), which stresses the importance of reward and punishment in altering the frequency of different forms of observable behavior. That approach was inspired by the hope that all behavior could be explained by a few basic principles of learning and by the idea that all learning amounted to the automatic formation of associations between stimuli and responses. Research on learning, and on the role that various cognitive processes play in it, eventually showed that these ideas about unthinking, automatic associations were oversimplified. Still, an understanding of how associations are formed is basic to an understanding of learning. Thus, we first consider two models of how basic associations develop and how cognitive factors can influence them; these models are called classical and instrumental conditioning.

Classical Conditioning: Learning Signals and Associations

At the opening bars of the national anthem, a young ballplayer's heart may begin pounding; those sounds signal that the game is about to begin. A flashing light on a control panel may make an airplane pilot's adrenaline flow, because it means that something has gone seriously wrong. These people were not born with such reactions; they learned them from associations between events in the world. The experimental study of this kind of learning was begun, almost by accident, by Ivan Petrovich Pavlov.

Linkages

The questions in this diagram illustrate some of the relationships between the topic of this chapter, learning, and other chapter topics. In psychology, learning means far more than acquiring academic information or skills. When, as described in Chapter 3, boys and girls begin to act in ways that their culture considers right for men and women, that, too, is learning; so is the change that occurs when a person develops a fear of dogs (see Chapter 15), or overcomes it through the learning-based treatments described in Chapter 16. Like other Linkages diagrams, this one shows just a sampling of the links with other topics. There are many others. For example, our examination in Chapter 9 of the physiology of memory also sheds light on the biological basis of learning. Page numbers in the diagram indicate where its questions are discussed, and each linkage question is repeated in the margin near where the discussion appears. ■

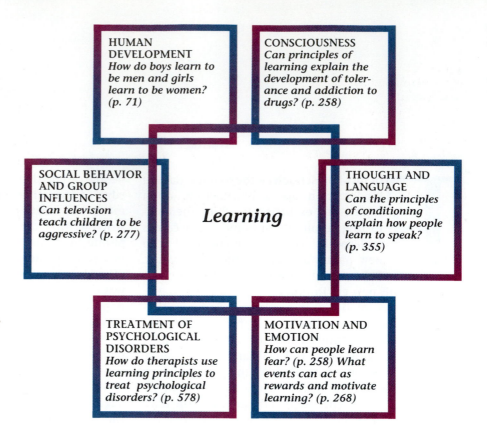

HUMAN DEVELOPMENT
How do boys learn to be men and girls learn to be women? (p. 71)

CONSCIOUSNESS
Can principles of learning explain the development of tolerance and addiction to drugs? (p. 258)

SOCIAL BEHAVIOR AND GROUP INFLUENCES
Can television teach children to be aggressive? (p. 277)

Learning

THOUGHT AND LANGUAGE
Can the principles of conditioning explain how people learn to speak? (p. 355)

TREATMENT OF PSYCHOLOGICAL DISORDERS
How do therapists use learning principles to treat psychological disorders? (p. 578)

MOTIVATION AND EMOTION
How can people learn fear? (p. 258) *What events can act as rewards and motivate learning?* (p. 268)

Pavlov's Discovery

Pavlov is one of the best-known figures in psychology, but he was not a psychologist. A Russian physiologist, Pavlov won a Nobel Prize in 1904 for his work on the physiology of dogs' digestive systems. During his research, Pavlov noticed a strange phenomenon: his dogs sometimes salivated when no food was present—for example, when they saw the assistant who normally brought their food.

Pavlov devised a simple experiment to determine how salivation could occur in the absence of an obvious physical cause. First he performed an operation to divert a dog's saliva into a container, so that the amount secreted could be measured precisely. He then confined the dog in the apparatus shown in Figure 8.1. The experiment had three phases.

In the first phase of the experiment, Pavlov and his associates (Anrep, 1920) confirmed that when meat powder was placed on the dog's tongue, the dog salivated, but that it did not salivate in response to a neutral stimulus—a white lab coat or a musical tone, for example. Thus, the researchers established the existence of the two basic components for Pavlov's experiment: a natural reflex (the dog's salivation when food was placed on its tongue) and a neutral stimulus (the sound of the tone). A *reflex* is the swift, automatic response to a stimulus, such as shivering in the cold or jumping when you are jabbed with a needle. A *neutral stimulus* is one that initially does not elicit the reflex being studied, although it may elicit other responses. For example, when the tone is first sounded, the dog pricks up its ears, turns toward the sound, and sniffs around; but it does not salivate.

It was the second and third phases of the experiment that showed how one type of learning can occur. In the second phase, the tone was sounded and then meat powder was quickly placed in the dog's mouth. The dog salivated. This *pairing*—the tone followed immediately by meat powder—was repeated several times. In the third phase of the experiment the tone was sounded

Figure 8.1
Apparatus Used in Pavlov's Experiments

Dogs were surgically prepared and then placed in a harness. Saliva flowed into a tube inserted in the dog's cheek. The amount of saliva secreted was then recorded by a pen attached to a slowly moving drum of paper.

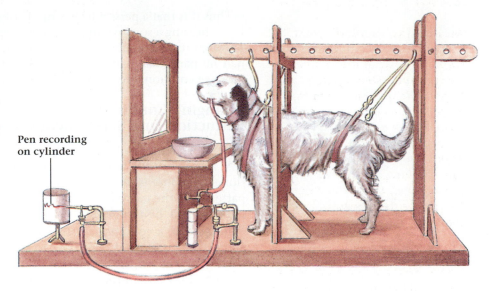

Pen recording on cylinder

alone, and the dog again salivated, even though no meat powder was presented. In other words, the tone by itself now elicited salivation, as if the tone predicted the presentation of the meat powder.

Pavlov's experiment was the first demonstration of what today is called **classical conditioning**—a procedure in which a neutral stimulus is paired with a stimulus that already triggers a reflexive response until the previously neutral stimulus alone provokes a similar response. Figure 8.2 shows the basic elements of classical conditioning. The stimulus that elicits a response without conditioning, like the meat powder in Pavlov's experiment, is called the **unconditioned stimulus (UCS)**. The automatic, unlearned reaction to this stimulus is called the **unconditioned response (UCR)**. The new stimulus after being paired with the unconditioned stimulus is called the **conditioned stimulus (CS)**, and the response it comes to elicit is a **conditioned response (CR)**.

Figure 8.2
Classical Conditioning

Before classical conditioning has occurred, meat powder on a dog's tongue produces salivation, but the sound of a musical tone—a neutral stimulus—does not. During the process of conditioning, the tone is paired on numerous trials with the meat powder. After classical conditioning has taken place, the sound of the tone alone acts as a conditioned stimulus, producing salivation.

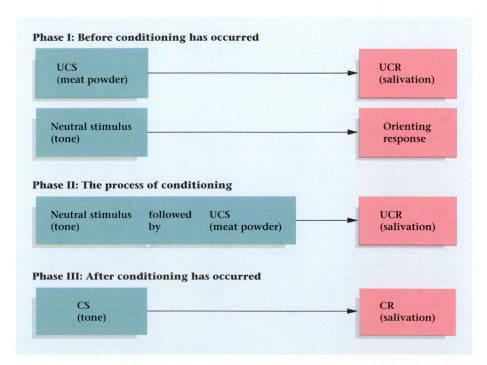

Phase I: Before conditioning has occurred

| UCS (meat powder) | → | UCR (salivation) |
| Neutral stimulus (tone) | → | Orienting response |

Phase II: The process of conditioning

| Neutral stimulus (tone) followed by UCS (meat powder) | → | UCR (salivation) |

Phase III: After conditioning has occurred

| CS (tone) | → | CR (salivation) |

Thus it is that a person feels a ripple of emotion—a conditioned response—when hearing a song or smelling the cologne associated with a long-lost lover. Through its association with that person, the song or fragrance, which once had no particular significance, has become a conditioned stimulus that can provoke emotional reactions experienced in the past.

Changing Conditioned Responses Over Time: Learning, Extinction, and Spontaneous Recovery

When researchers in Pavlov's lab continued to pair the conditioned stimulus (CS: tone) with the unconditioned stimulus (UCS: meat powder), the conditioned response (CR: salivation) to the tone gradually increased, following a pattern like the curve at the left in Figure 8.3. The conditioned response had been learned, or *acquired.*

In general, a conditioned stimulus continues to elicit the conditioned response only if the UCS continues to appear, at least periodically. For example, dogs in one experiment were conditioned to salivate at the sound of a buzzer (Pavlov, 1927). Then the buzzer was repeatedly sounded, but no meat powder was presented. As the CS was presented repeatedly without the UCS, the strength of the conditioned response decreased. As the center section of Figure 8.3 shows, salivation was almost completely eliminated by the sixth trial. This gradual disappearance of a conditioned response by eliminating the association between conditioned and unconditioned stimuli is called **extinction**.

Extinction does not simply erase learning, however. If the CS and the UCS are again paired after the conditioned response has been extinguished, the conditioned response returns to its original strength very quickly, often after only one or two trials. This quick relearning of a conditioned response after extinction is called **reconditioning**. Because reconditioning takes much less time than the original conditioning, some change in the organism must have persisted even after extinction.

Additional evidence for this conclusion comes from the phenomenon illustrated on the right side of Figure 8.3. Suppose that after extinction the CS does not appear for a while and then again recurs without the UCS. What will happen? As Figure 8.3 shows, the conditioned response temporarily reappears. This reappearance of the conditioned response after extinction (and without further CS-UCS pairings) is called **spontaneous recovery**. In general, the longer the time between extinction and the reappearance of the CS, the

Figure 8.3
Changes Over Time in the Strength of a CR
As the CS and UCS are repeatedly paired during the initial conditioning, the strength of the CR increases. During extinction, the strength drops as more trials occur in which the CS is presented without the UCS; eventually the CR disappears completely. However, after a brief period, the CR reappears when the CS is again presented. In general, the longer the time before the new presentation of the CS, the stronger the CR.

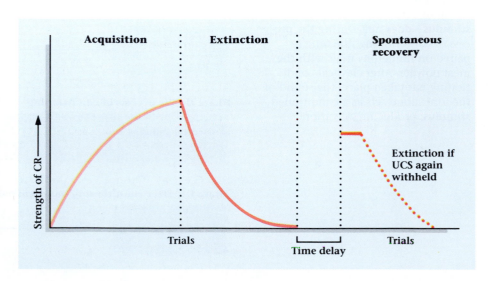

stronger the recovered conditioned response. However, unless the UCS is again paired with the CS, extinction rapidly occurs again.

The Signaling of Significant Events

What is learned in classical conditioning? Pavlov's research suggests that classical conditioning allows the substitution of one stimulus (the CS) for another (the UCS) in producing a reflexive response, a substitution that prepares the animal or person for the arrival of the UCS. It is certainly useful and adaptive for the dog to prepare for the arrival of food; having saliva flowing in advance makes it easier to swallow the meat. For years much of the study of classical conditioning focused on its importance in the control of such automatic, involuntary behavior. Recently, however, psychologists have recognized the far wider implications of classical conditioning (Rescorla, 1988; Turkkan, 1989). According to this view, the appearance of conditioned responses provides evidence that organisms learn that one event reliably predicts, or *signals,* the appearance of another. In other words, in this view classical conditioning creates, not robotlike reflexes, but a means through which animals and people develop *mental models* of the relation between events in their environment, models that help them to adapt and survive.

What determines whether and how a conditioned response is learned? Important factors include the timing, predictability, and strength of signals, the amount of attention they receive, how broad or narrow their effects are, and how easily the signals can be associated with other stimuli.

Timing   A signal cannot prepare you for something that has already happened, so it is not surprising that classical conditioning works best when the conditioned stimulus *precedes* the unconditioned stimulus, an arrangement known as *forward conditioning. Backward conditioning,* in which the CS signal (the tone) *follows* the UCS (the meat powder), takes place very slowly, if at all. Even *simultaneous conditioning,* in which the CS and UCS arrive at the same time, works much less well than forward conditioning. We will explain why shortly.

Research on forward conditioning shows that it works best when there is a delay of about one-half to one second between the CS and the UCS (Ross & Ross, 1971). Notice that this "optimum interval" makes adaptive sense. Normally, the presence of food, predators, or other significant stimuli is most reliably signaled by smells or growls or similar events that come just before their appearance (Einhorn & Hogarth, 1982). Thus, it is logical that the brain should be "wired" to form associations most easily between things that occur in a tight time sequence.

Predictability   Is it enough that the CS precedes the UCS—that two events are *contiguous* in time—in order for classical conditioning to occur? Think about it. Suppose you have a dog that growls all the time. Most of the growls mean little but, occasionally, the growl precedes a bite. If the growl, a CS, does not *reliably* signal the danger of a bite (a UCS), you will probably not develop a conditioned response to the growl, or will do so very slowly. Now suppose you get another dog who growls *only* before biting. Even if both dogs provide the same number of pairings of the CS (growl) and UCS (bite), it is only in the second dog that the CS *reliably* predicts the UCS (Rescorla, 1968). Accordingly, you are likely to quickly develop a classically conditioned fear response to the second dog's growls, because classical conditioning proceeds most rapidly when the CS *always* signals the UCS, and *only* the UCS.

Signal Strength   A conditioned response will be learned more rapidly if the UCS is strong than if it is weak. Thus a predictive signal will be more rapidly associated with a strong shock (a UCS) than with a weak one. Like timing and predictability, the effect of signal strength on classical conditioning makes adaptive sense: it is more important to be prepared for major events than for those that have little impact.

The speed with which a conditioned response is learned also depends on the strength or "salience" of the conditioned stimulus (CS). Because louder tones, brighter lights, or other more salient events are most likely to be noticed, they are most rapidly associated with a UCS, as long as they remain reliable predictive signals.

Attention   The fact that stronger stimuli are more likely to be associated with a UCS highlights the role of attention in classical conditioning. In the natural environment, more than one potential conditioned stimulus often precedes a UCS. For example, a person might have been tasting a sandwich, reading a book, and enjoying the smell of newly mown grass just before being attacked by a mugger in the park. Which of these stimuli is most likely to become a conditioned stimulus for fear? It depends in part on where the person's attention was focused. In line with the perceptual principles governing attention described in Chapter 6, not all of these potential CSs were being fully perceived just before the beating; thus, the one most closely attended to at that moment may dominate the others in forming a conditioned response.

Two additional phenomena demonstrate the importance of attention in classical conditioning: the inefficiency of simultaneous conditioning and the appearance of blocking. We noted earlier that presenting the CS and the UCS at the same time—simultaneous conditioning—does not lead to very effective learning. This is partly because the CS does not *predict* the appearance of the UCS and partly because, when a CS and a UCS are presented simultaneously, attention will probably be directed to the most salient one, usually the reflex-producing UCS (such as food or pain). With few attentional resources left to perceive the CS, an association between it and the UCS is slow to develop.

To understand the phenomenon of *blocking*, suppose that a CS always occurs just before a UCS and that a conditioned response to the CS has been established; then another stimulus is paired with the UCS, so that both CSs are presented at the same time. Will the new stimulus also come to elicit a conditioned response? To find out, Leon Kamin (1969) used the procedure illustrated in Figure 8.4. To take a human example, consider a child who develops a conditioned fear response (CR) by repeatedly associating the smell of the doctor's office (CS) with the pain of injections (UCS). After this conditioned fear response has been formed, the child visits the doctor again, and this time the office has new wallpaper. Will the wallpaper become a CS as the smell did? No, its conditioning power has been blocked. In general, once a CS is linked to a UCS, pairing a second stimulus with the UCS will not create a conditioned response to the new stimulus. Once people (and animals) have one useful predictor of a UCS, they fail to attend to others that may be just as good.

Figure 8.4
Blocking
In Kamin's study of blocking, one group of rats learned a fear response to both light and noise; they later showed a conditioned fear response to either the light or the noise. A second group of rats first learned a conditioned fear response to noise; then the light was added as an additional potential CS. Even though the light was repeatedly paired with shock, these rats later showed no fear response to the light. The training with one CS apparently *blocked* the rats from learning another CS that was subsequently added.

	Phase 1	Phase 2	Test phase	Result
Group 1	(no treatment)	CS = light and noise UCS = shock	light ⟶ CR? noise ⟶ CR?	Yes Yes
Group 2	CS = noise UCS = shock	CS = light and noise UCS = shock	noise ⟶ CR? light ⟶ CR?	Yes No

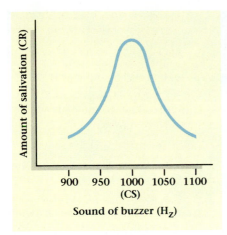

Figure 8.5
Stimulus Generalization
The strength of a conditioned response is greatest when a new stimulus closely resembles the CS. Here, the CS is the sound of a buzzer at 1,000 hertz, and the CR is salivation. As the new stimulus becomes less similar to the CS, or farther away from 1,000 hertz, the strength of the CR—in this case, amount of salivation—is reduced.

Signal Breadth: Stimulus Generalization and Discrimination   After a conditioned response is acquired, stimuli that are similar but not identical to the conditioned stimulus also elicit it. This phenomenon is called **stimulus generalization.** Usually the greater the similarity between a new stimulus and the conditioned stimulus, the stronger the conditioned response will be. Figure 8.5 shows an example.

Stimulus generalization has obvious adaptive advantages. It is important for survival, for example, that a person who becomes sick after drinking sour-smelling milk later avoids dairy products that give off an odor resembling the smell associated with the illness. Generalization, however, would be problematic if it had no limits. Most people would be frightened to see a real lion in their home, but imagine the inconvenience if you became fearful every time you saw a cat or a picture of a lion.

Stimulus generalization does not run amok because it is balanced by a complementary process called **stimulus discrimination.** Through stimulus discrimination, organisms learn to differentiate among similar stimuli. An infant's crying commonly becomes a conditioned stimulus for its mother, whose conditioned response might include waking out of a deep sleep at the baby's slightest fussing. Yet the same mother might sleep soundly while someone else's baby cries.

Second-Order Conditioning   When a child suffers the pain of an injection (a UCS) at a doctor's office, salient stimuli—like the doctor's white coat—that precede and predict the UCS can become conditioned stimuli for fear. Interestingly, once the white coat evokes a conditioned fear response, it may take on some properties of a UCS. Thus, at future visits, the once-neutral sound of a nurse calling the child's name can become a conditioned stimulus for fear because it signals the appearance of the white coat, which in turn signals pain. When a conditioned stimulus acts like a UCS, creating conditioned stimuli out of events associated with it, the phenomenon is called **second-order conditioning.** Conditioned fear, and the second-order conditioning that can be based on it, illustrates one of the most important adaptive characteristics of classical conditioning: the ability to prepare the organism for damaging or life-threatening events (a UCS) when these are predictably signaled by a CS.

Conditioning New Associations: Are All Signals Created Equal?

After Pavlov's initial demonstration of classical conditioning, many psychologists believed that forming new associations through classical conditioning was a bit like working with tinker-toys. Just as tinker-toy rods of any length or color can be attached with equal ease, it was believed that any conditioned stimulus had an equal potential for becoming associated with any unconditioned stimulus, as long as the two occurred in the right time sequence. But this *equipotential* view was later challenged by experiments showing that certain signals or events are especially suited to form associations with other events (Donjan & Wilson, 1972; Logue, 1985; Rescorla & Gillian, 1980). This apparent natural affinity for certain events to become linked suggests that organisms are "biologically prepared" or "genetically tuned" to develop certain conditioned associations.

The most dramatic example of the *biopreparedness* of organisms is conditioned taste aversion. Consider the results of a study in which rats were either shocked or made nauseous in the combined presence of a bright light, a loud buzzer, and saccharin-flavored water. Only certain conditioned associations were formed. Specifically, the animals that had been shocked developed a conditioned fear response to the light and the buzzer, but not to the flavored

After learning to associate the taste of mutton with severe nausea created by lithium chloride, wolves and coyotes were placed in a pen with live sheep (mutton on the hoof, the CS). At first they started to attack, but after biting and smelling the sheep several times, they withdrew (the CR). Later, the doors of the pen were opened, and a dramatic role reversal occurred: the predators were literally chased away by the sheep! Now ranchers often lace a carcass with enough lithium chloride to make wolves and coyotes ill, thus "teaching" them not to kill sheep.

water. Those who had been made nauseous developed a conditioned avoidance of the flavored water, but showed no particular response to the light or buzzer (Garcia & Koelling, 1966). Notice that these results are adaptive: nausea is more likely to be produced by something that is eaten or drunk than by an external stimulus like noise. Accordingly, nausea is more likely to become a conditioned response to an internal stimulus, such as a saccharin flavor, than to an external stimulus, such as a sound. In contrast, the sudden pain of a shock is more likely to have been caused by an external stimulus, and so it makes evolutionary sense that the organism should be "tuned" to associate shock with a sight or a sound.

The power of taste-aversion learning has been put to work to help ranchers in the western United States who are plagued by wolves and coyotes that kill and eat their sheep. To alleviate this problem without killing the predators, some ranchers have set out lithium-laced mutton for marauding wolves and coyotes to eat. The dizziness and severe nausea (UCR) created by the lithium becomes associated with the mutton taste (a CS), thus making sheep an undesirable meal for these predators and protecting the ranchers' livelihood (Garcia, Rusiniak & Brett, 1977; Gustavson et al., 1974).

People, too, develop classically conditioned taste aversions, as Ilene Bernstein (1978) demonstrated. She gave one group of cancer patients a unique flavor of ice cream, Mapletoff, one hour before they received chemotherapy, which produces nausea as a side effect. A second group was given the same ice cream on a day they did not receive chemotherapy. A third group was not given any ice cream. Approximately five months later, all three groups were asked to taste several flavors of ice cream and select their favorite. Two groups chose the Mapletoff: those who had not previously tasted it and those who had eaten it when they did not receive chemotherapy. In contrast, those who had eaten Mapletoff before receiving chemotherapy found the flavor very distasteful.

Notice that conditioned taste aversion violates the usual timing rules of classical conditioning. In taste aversion, strong conditioning develops despite the long delay between the CS (the taste) and the UCS (the nauseous sensation). Poisons do not usually produce their effects until minutes or hours after being ingested, but people who experience food poisoning may never again eat the type of food that made them so ill—even though that illness was delayed far longer than the optimal CS-UCS interval of one-half to one second. In evolutionary terms, organisms that are biologically prepared to link taste signals with illness, even if it occurs after considerable delays, are more likely to survive than those not so prepared.

Evidence from several sources suggests other ways in which animals and people are innately prepared to learn associations between certain stimuli and certain responses. People, for example, are much more likely to develop a conditioned fear of harmless dogs, snakes, and rats than of equally harmless doorknobs or stereos (Kleinknecht, 1986). Experiments with animals suggest that they are prone to learn the type of associations that are most common in or most relevant to their environment (Staddon & Ettinger, 1989). For example, unlike coyotes and rats, birds of prey, so strongly dependent upon their visual sense in foraging for food, may develop taste aversions on the basis of visual stimuli.

Some Applications of Classical Conditioning

"In Review: Basic Processes of Classical Conditioning" summarizes the principles of classical conditioning. In addition to broadening our understanding of drug effects and addictive processes, these principles have proven useful in fighting diseases and overcoming fears.

Learned Immune Responses   Research suggests that decreases in the body's *immune response*—the biological mechanisms described in Chapter 4 that protect the body from infection—can be classically conditioned (Ader & Cohen, 1985; Cohen & Ader, 1988). This research raises the possibility that

In Review: Basic Processes of Classical Conditioning

Process	Description	Example
Acquisition	A neutral stimulus and a UCS are paired. The neutral stimulus becomes a CS, eliciting a CR.	A child learns to fear (CR) the doctor's office (CS) by associating it with the reflexive emotional reaction (UCR) to a painful injection (UCS).
Stimulus generalization	A CR is elicited not only by the CS but also by stimuli similar to the CS.	A child fears all doctors' offices and places that smell like them.
Stimulus discrimination	Generalization is limited so that some stimuli similar to the CS do not elicit the CR.	A child learns that his mother's doctor's office is not associated with the UCS.
Extinction	The CS is presented alone, without the UCS. Eventually the CS no longer elicits the CR.	A child visits the doctor's office several times for a checkup, but does not receive a shot. Fear may eventually cease.

increases in the immune response might also be conditioned. For example, one group of researchers paired the taste of sweet sherbet with an injection of adrenaline, whose unconditioned effect is to increase the activity of the immune system's natural killer cells. Eventually the sherbet flavor alone elicited this immune response (Buske-Kirschbaum et al., 1992).

Someday doctors may treat disease by using stimuli associated with a drug's effects to enhance a person's immune response, so that less actual medication is needed and side effects are minimized. For example, there are drugs that control allergic reactions, but the drugs themselves usually create severe drowsiness. By pairing these drugs with a unique stimulus such as a strange odor, researchers have tried to teach people a conditioned response that will, by itself, alleviate the allergic reaction. The results of this research suggest that a response that reduces allergy symptoms can be conditioned (Russell et al., 1984; Sampson & Jolie, 1984). Another possibility is to associate placebos (inactive medications) with active drugs and then administer the placebos alone in the hope that they might trigger beneficial effects as a conditioned response (Turkkan, 1989).

Phobias   *Phobias* are strong fears of objects or situations that either are not objectively dangerous—public speaking, for example—or are less dangerous than the phobic person's reaction suggests. Classical conditioning often plays a role in the development of such fears; a child who is frightened by a large dog may learn a dog phobia that is so intense and generalized that it creates avoidance of *all* dogs. A truly dangerous situation can also produce classical conditioning of very long-lasting fears. Decades after their war experiences, some military veterans still respond to simulated battle sounds with large changes in heart rate, blood pressure, galvanic skin responses, and other signs of emotional arousal (Edwards & Acker, 1972).

Classical conditioning has also been employed to treat phobias. Joseph Wolpe (1958) pioneered the development of these procedures. Using techniques first developed with laboratory animals, Wolpe showed that irrational fears could be relieved through *systematic desensitization,* a procedure that associates a new response, such as relaxation, with a feared stimulus. For example, to treat a thunderstorm phobia, a therapist might first teach the client to relax deeply and then associate that relaxation with gradually more intense sights and sounds of thunderstorms presented on videotape (Öst, 1978). Desensitization is discussed in more detail in Chapter 16, on treatment of psychological disorders.

Linkages: Learning and Consciousness

People are constantly bombarded by stimuli in a changing world. If you tried to pay attention to every sight and sound, your information-processing system would be overloaded, and you couldn't concentrate on anything. People appear to be genetically tuned to attend to and orient toward certain kinds of events, such as loud sounds or pain. *Novel* stimuli are also very likely to attract attention. At the same time, people adapt, or become *habituated,* to events that are repeated often; in other words, their responsiveness to an unchanging stimulus decreases over time. For example, you will eventually cease to notice the loud ticking of a clock; in fact, you may become aware of the clock again only when it stops, because now something has changed.

Habituation is sometimes considered to be the simplest form of learning, and it has been observed even in the sea slug (Kandel, 1976). Habituation provides yet another example of how learning helps organisms adapt to their environments (Schwartz & Reisberg, 1991). And according to a theory proposed by Richard Solomon, it has a very direct connection to classical conditioning,

Linkages: How can people learn fear? (a link to Motivation and Emotion)

Can principles of learning explain the development of tolerance and addiction to drugs?

as well as to the impact created by some of the drugs described in Chapter 7, on consciousness.

According to Solomon's (1980) *opponent-process theory,* habituation to repeated stimuli is the result of two processes in the organism that are triggered by those stimuli. One is a relatively automatic, involuntary response, called the *A-Process,* which is essentially an unconditioned response. The second, or *B-Process,* is a conditioned response that follows and counteracts the A-Process. For example, an injection of adrenaline produces an increase in heart rate, the A-Process; the B-Process will then decrease the heart rate. In other words, the B-Process is a conditioned response to the same stimulus that produced the unconditioned A-Process. The B-Process occurs progressively more quickly and with greater intensity as the UCS (for example, the injection) is repeated (see Figure 8.6). Thus, the net effect of the opposing A and B processes becomes smaller and smaller with repeated exposure to a stimulus; habituation results.

Consider now what happens when someone first uses a drug such as heroin or crack cocaine. The unconditioned, pleasant reaction (the A-Process) is eventually countered or neutralized as the unpleasant B-Process becomes quicker and stronger. Thus progressively larger doses of the drug are required to obtain the same drug "high." According to Solomon, these opponent processes form the basis for the development of drug tolerance and addiction described in Chapter 7.

Solomon's analysis may also explain some accidental drug overdoses. Because the B-Process is a conditioned response, stimuli that are regularly present when the drug is taken may become conditioned stimuli, triggering the B-Process by themselves. Suppose that a person takes a normal dose in a very different environment. The strength of the A-Process (the unconditioned drug effect) will still be the same, but without the environmental cues that normally help create the B-process, that counteracting process may be diminished. The net effect may be a stronger-than-usual drug reaction, possibly leading to the trauma of an overdose (Siegel et al., 1982; Turkkan, 1989).

Instrumental and Operant Conditioning: Learning the Consequences of Behavior

Much of what people learn cannot be described as classical conditioning. In classical conditioning, neutral and unconditioned stimuli are predictably

Figure 8.6
Solomon's Opponent-Process Theory
Solomon's theory explains habituation to repeated stimuli as follows. The unconditioned response to an unconditioned stimulus (the A-Process) is followed by a small, but opposite, B-Process, which acts to reduce the size of the unconditioned response. Over time, the B-Process occurs more quickly and with greater intensity, eventually resulting in a minimal net response.

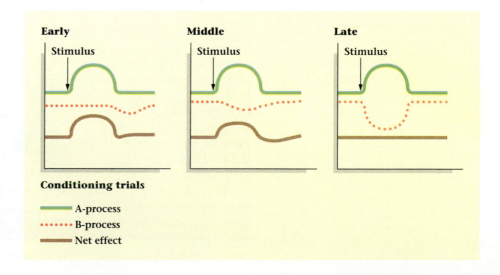

paired, and the result is an automatic association between the two, as evidenced by the conditioned response elicited when the conditioned stimulus appears. Notice that both stimuli occur before or along with the conditioned response. But people also learn associations between responses and the stimuli that *follow* them—in other words, between behavior and its consequences. A child learns to say "please" in order to get a piece of candy; a headache sufferer learns to take a pill in order to escape pain; a dog learns to "shake hands" in order to get a treat. All of these responses are *instrumental* in obtaining something rewarding for the person or animal. **Instrumental conditioning** is a process through which responses are learned that help produce some rewarding or desired effect.

From the Puzzle Box to the Skinner Box

At just about the time that Pavlov was conducting his experiments in Russia, American psychologist Edward L. Thorndike was discovering the principles of instrumental learning. To study whether animals can think and reason, Thorndike devised an elaborate cage called a *puzzle box* (see Figure 8.7). An animal, usually a hungry cat, was placed in the puzzle box and had to learn some response—say, stepping on a small lever—in order to unlock the door and get out. When the cat succeeded, it was rewarded with food and then placed back inside the box. After several trials, the cat walked calmly to the lever, pushed it down with its paw, strolled through the opened door, and ate.

It is clear that cats in this situation learned something, because over the course of the trials they took less time to get out of the cage. But did they understand the task? During the first few trials the cats took a long time to discover the secret of opening the door. Thorndike thought that at some point a cat would suddenly understand, or gain *insight* about, the task and perform the response very quickly. In fact, however, he found no such quick change (Thorndike, 1898). Instead, the amount of time a cat took to open the door declined very gradually over the trials. In some cases, a cat actually took longer on one trial than it did on the previous trial. In other words, there was no evidence that the cats suddenly understood the task.

Figure 8.7
Thorndike's Puzzle Box
A sample "puzzle box," as used in Thorndike's research. Because a rope is connected to both the door latch and the pedal, a cat can open the door by pressing down on the pedal.

What, then, were Thorndike's cats learning? On the first few trials, the cats performed a great many responses, almost at random. They might run back and forth, scratch at the bars, meow, rub their faces, and so on. Eventually, they stepped on the lever, and the door opened. Any response that did not produce a rewarding effect (opening the door) became weaker over time, and any response that did have a rewarding effect became stronger over time, so that eventually the cat required less time to open the door. Learning, said Thorndike, is governed by the **law of effect.** According to this law, if a response made in the presence of a particular stimulus is followed by a reward, that response is more likely to be made the next time the stimulus is encountered. Responses that are not rewarded are less likely to be performed again.

Decades after Thorndike published his work, another American psychologist, B. F. Skinner, extended and formalized many of Thorndike's ideas. Skinner emphasized that during instrumental conditioning an organism learns a response by *operating on* the environment, so he called the process of learning these responses **operant conditioning.** His primary aim was to analyze how behavior is changed by its consequences.

To study operant conditioning, Skinner devised some new tools. One was a chamber known as the *Skinner box.* The experimenter can control it completely. It contains a device that the animal can operate in order to get a reward. For example, rats are usually placed in a box like the one shown in Figure 8.8, which has a lever; when the lever is pressed, a food pellet drops through a thin tube. Skinner also developed the *cumulative recorder,* a device that monitors a particular response, producing a graph like the one in Figure 8.9. The graph provides a precise picture of the rate of the response over time.

Instrumental and operant conditioning differ from each other in one important respect. In instrumental conditioning, the experimenter defines each opportunity for the subject to produce a response, and conditioning is usually measured by how long it takes for the response to appear. In operant conditioning, the subject is free to make responses at any time, so conditioning is

Figure 8.8
Skinner Boxes
Shown here are two common forms of the Skinner box. In (a), a rat presses a bar to obtain food pellets from a tube. In (b), a pigeon pecks a plastic key; this action briefly opens a door that gives the pigeon access to a tray of food.

(a)   (b)

Figure 8.9
A Cumulative Record
Graphs like this one, produced by a cumulative recorder, allow researchers to see how much time elapsed between one response and the next. For example, responses 1 and 2 were separated by a considerable amount of time; but little time passed between responses 3, 4, 5, and 6. The record shows exactly how the pattern of responses changed over time.

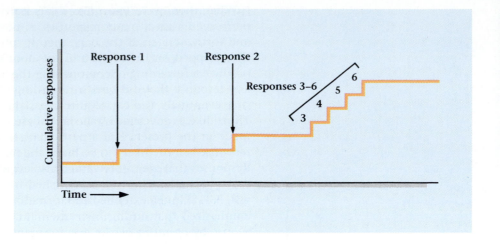

measured by the *rate* of responding. In most other ways, however, these forms of learning are essentially the same. Thus, in the following sections, the term *operant conditioning* refers to both.

Basic Components of Operant Conditioning

The tools Skinner devised allowed him and other researchers to arrange relationships between an arbitrary response and its consequences and then to analyze how those consequences affected behavior. They found that the basic phenomena of classical conditioning—stimulus generalization, stimulus discrimination, extinction, and spontaneous recovery—also occur in operant conditioning. In operant conditioning, however, the basic components are operants, reinforcers, and discriminative stimuli.

Operants and Reinforcers   Skinner introduced the term *operant* or *operant response* to distinguish the responses in operant conditioning from those in classical conditioning. Recall that in classical conditioning the conditioned response does not affect whether or when the stimulus occurs. Dogs salivated when a buzzer sounded, but the salivation had no effect on the buzzer or on whether food was presented. In contrast, an **operant** is a response that has some effect on the world; it is a response that *operates on* the environment. For example, when a child says, "Momma, I'm hungry" and is then fed, the child has made an operant response that influences when food will appear.

A **reinforcer** increases the probability that an operant behavior will occur again. There are two main types of reinforcers: positive and negative. **Positive reinforcers** are events that strengthen a response if they are experienced after that response occurs. They are roughly equivalent to rewards. The food given to a hungry pigeon after it pecks a key is a positive reinforcer; its presentation increases the pigeon's key pecking. Smiles, food, money, and many other desirable outcomes act as positive reinforcers for people. Presenting a positive reinforcer after a response is called *positive reinforcement*. **Negative reinforcers** are unpleasant stimuli such as pain, boredom, or a disapproving frown that strengthen a response if they are *removed* after the response occurs. For example, if the response of taking aspirin is followed by the removal of pain, aspirin taking is likely to occur when similar pain appears again. The process of strengthening behavior by following it with the removal of an aversive stimulus is called *negative reinforcement*. Note that whether it takes the form of presenting something pleasant or removing something aversive, reinforcement always *increases* the likelihood of the behavior that precedes it.

Escape and Avoidance Conditioning The effects of negative reinforcement can be studied through either escape conditioning or avoidance conditioning. **Escape conditioning** takes place when an organism learns to make a response in order to end an aversive stimulus, or negative reinforcer. Dogs learn to jump over the barrier in a shuttle box to escape shock (see Figure 8.10); parents often learn to give in to children's demands because doing so stops their whining. Now imagine that a signal—say, a buzzer or blinking light—occurs just a few seconds before the grid in one side of a shuttle box is electrified. If the animal jumps over the barrier very quickly after hearing or seeing the signal, it can avoid the shock altogether. When an animal or person responds to a signal in a way that avoids exposure to an aversive stimulus, **avoidance conditioning** has occurred.

This example illustrates that avoidance conditioning often represents a marriage of classical and instrumental conditioning. Because it predicts the shock, the buzzer or blinking light becomes a conditioned stimulus that, through classical conditioning, elicits a conditioned fear response. Like the shock itself, conditioned fear is an unpleasant internal sensation. The animal then acquires an instrumental response—jumping the barrier—which is reinforced because it terminates the unpleasant fear stimulus.

Along with positive reinforcement, avoidance conditioning is one of the most important influences on everyday behavior. Most people go to work or school even when they would rather stay in bed, and they stop at red lights even when they are in a hurry. Each of these behaviors reflects avoidance conditioning, because each behavior allows people to avoid a negative consequence, such as losing a job or getting a traffic ticket.

Avoidance is a very difficult habit to break (Solomon, Kamin & Wynne, 1953). Why? Partly because avoidance responses are often reinforced by fear reduction. Furthermore, avoidance responses prevent the opportunity to learn that the "rules" may have changed and that avoidance is no longer necessary. If you fear elevators and therefore avoid them, you will never discover that they are safe and comfortable. Unfortunately, avoidance conditioning may prevent people from learning new, more desirable behaviors. For example, fear of doing something embarrassing may cause people with limited social skills to learn to shy away from social situations.

Discriminative Stimuli and Stimulus Control Even if you have been reinforced for telling jokes at parties, you are not likely to do so at funerals.

Figure 8.10
A Shuttle Box
Studies of negative reinforcement frequently use a shuttle box. It has two compartments, usually separated by a barrier, and its floor is an electric grid. Shock can be administered through the grid to each compartment independently. In escape conditioning (the first panel), the animal can escape shock by jumping over the barrier to the next compartment. In avoidance conditioning (the middle panel), a buzzer signals the onset of shock; the animal can thus avoid the shock entirely if it jumps quickly enough after the buzzer sounds.

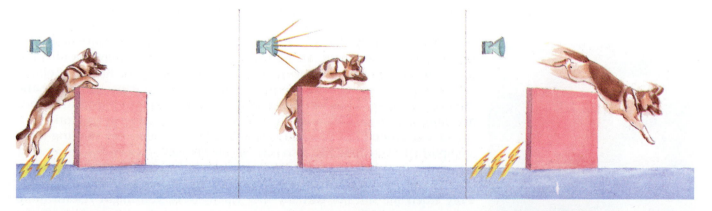

Source: From *The Psychology of Learning and Memory*, by Douglas L. Hintzman. Copyright © 1978 W. H. Freeman and Company. Reprinted with permission.

Figure 8.11
Stimulus Discrimination
In this experiment the rat could jump from the stand through any one of the three doors, but it was reinforced only if it jumped through the door that differed from the other two. As you can see, the rat learned to do this quite well. In the left-hand panel, for example, it learned to discriminate diagonal from horizontal stripes, and in the middle and right-hand panels, it learned to discriminate vertical from horizontal stripes.

Teaching new behavior patterns through operant conditioning is much easier when the teacher shapes the desired behavior by rewarding gradually improved versions rather than requiring perfect performance right away. Indeed, without shaping, that perfect performance might never occur, resulting in frustration for both teacher and learner.

Pigeons show similar wisdom. If they are reinforced for pecking a key when a red light is on but are not reinforced for pecking when a green light is on, they will eventually peck only when they see a red light. Their behavior demonstrates the effect of **discriminative stimuli,** which are stimuli that signal whether reinforcement is available if a certain response is made. When an organism learns to make a particular response in the presence of one stimulus but not another, *stimulus discrimination* has occurred (see Figure 8.11). Another way to say this is that the response is now under *stimulus control.* In general, stimulus discrimination allows people or animals to learn what is appropriate (reinforced) and inappropriate (not reinforced) in particular situations.

Stimulus generalization also occurs in operant conditioning; that is, organisms often perform a response in the presence of a stimulus that is similar, but not identical, to the one that previously signaled the availability of reinforcement. As in classical conditioning, the more similar the new stimulus is to the old, the more likely it is that the response will be performed. As an example, consider the student who got an A after engaging in lively dialogue with a friendly, informal instructor who encouraged discussion. The student will be more likely to repeat the same approach in future classes with other informal instructors than with those who appear more aloof and lecture oriented.

Forming and Strengthening Operant Behavior

Daily life is full of examples of operant conditioning. People go to movies, parties, classes, and jobs primarily because doing so brings reinforcement. What is the effect of the type or timing of the reinforcer? How are established behaviors eliminated? How can new responses be established through operant conditioning?

Shaping   Imagine that you want to train your dog, Moxie, to sit and to "shake hands." The basic method using positive reinforcement is obvious: every time Moxie sits and shakes hands, you give her a treat. But the problem is also obvious: smart as Moxie is, she may never spontaneously make the desired response, so you will never be able to give the reward. Instead of your teaching and Moxie's learning, the two of you will just stare at each other.

The way around this problem is to shape Moxie's behavior. **Shaping** is accomplished by reinforcing *successive approximations*—that is, responses that come successively closer to the desired response. For example, you might first give Moxie a dog treat whenever she sits down. Then you might reward her only when she sits and partially lifts a paw. Next, you might reward more complete paw lifting. Eventually, you would require that Moxie perform the entire sit-lift-shake sequence before giving the reward. Shaping is an extremely powerful, widely used tool. Animal trainers have used it to teach wild beasts to roller-skate and jump through hoops and to teach pigeons to play Ping-Pong (Breland & Breland, 1966).

Secondary Reinforcement   Often, operant conditioning begins with the use of **primary reinforcers**, events or stimuli—such as food—that are inherently rewarding. But Moxie's training will be somewhat disrupted if she must stop and eat every time she makes a correct response. Furthermore, once she gets full, food will no longer act as an effective reinforcer. To avoid these problems, animal trainers and others in the teaching business capitalize on the principle of secondary reinforcement.

A **secondary reinforcer** is a previously neutral stimulus that, if paired with a stimulus that is already reinforcing, will itself take on reinforcing properties. In other words, secondary reinforcers are rewards that people or animals learn to like. For example, if you say "Good girl!" just before feeding Moxie, the words will become reinforcing after a few such pairings and can then be used alone to reinforce Moxie's behavior (especially if they are paired with food now and then). Does this remind you of classical conditioning? It should, because the primary reinforcer (food) is a UCS; if the sound of "Good girl!" predictably precedes and thus signals food, it becomes a CS. This is why secondary reinforcers are sometimes called *conditioned reinforcers.*

Secondary reinforcement greatly expands the power of operant and instrumental conditioning (Schwartz & Reisberg, 1991). Money is the most obvious secondary reinforcer; some people will do anything for it, even though it tastes terrible. Its reinforcing power lies in its association with the many rewards it can buy. Smiles and other forms of social approval (like the words "Good job!") are also important secondary reinforcers for human beings. However, what becomes a secondary reinforcer can vary a great deal from person to person and culture to culture. For example, tickets to a rock concert may be an effective secondary reinforcer for some teenagers, but not all. A ceremony honoring outstanding job performance might be highly reinforcing to most employees in individualist cultures, but it might be embarrassing for those from cultures where collectivist values emphasize group cooperation rather than personal distinction. Still, when chosen carefully, secondary reinforcers can build or maintain behavior even when primary reinforcement is absent for long periods.

Delay and Size of Reinforcement   Much of human behavior is learned and maintained because it is regularly reinforced. But many people overeat, smoke, drink too much, or procrastinate, even though they know these behaviors are bad for them and even though they want to eliminate them. They just cannot seem to change; they seem to lack "self-control." If behavior is controlled by its consequences, why do people perform acts that are ultimately self-defeating?

An answer lies in the timing of reinforcers. The good feelings (positive reinforcers) that follow, say, drinking too much are immediate; hangovers and other negative consequences are usually delayed. Recall that in classical conditioning, increasing the delay between the conditioned stimulus and the unconditioned stimulus usually weakens the conditioned response. Similarly, operant conditioning is stronger when the delay in receiving a reinforcer is short (Kalish, 1981). Immediate consequences of a behavior affect the behavior more strongly than delayed consequences. Thus, under some conditions, delaying reward for even a few seconds can decrease the effectiveness of positive reinforcement. (An advantage of praise or other secondary reinforcers is that they can easily be delivered immediately after a desired response occurs.)

The size of a reinforcement is also important. In general, conditioning proceeds faster when the reinforcer is large than when it is small.

A touch, a smile, and a look of love are among the many social stimuli that can serve as positive reinforcers for humans.

Schedules of Reinforcement   So far, we have talked as if a reinforcer is delivered every time a particular response occurs. Sometimes it is, and this arrangement is called a **continuous reinforcement schedule**. Very often, however, reinforcement is administered only some of the time; the result is a **partial**, or **intermittent, reinforcement schedule**.

Most intermittent schedules can be classified according to (1) whether the delivery of reinforcers is determined by the number of responses made or by the time that has elapsed since the last reinforcer, and (2) whether the delivery schedule is fixed or variable. This way of classifying schedules produces four basic types of intermittent reinforcement.

1. **Fixed-ratio (FR) schedules** provide reinforcement following a fixed number of responses. A rat might receive food after every tenth bar press (FR 10) or after every twentieth one (FR 20); a factory worker might be paid ten dollars for every ten widgets he or she assembles.
2. **Variable-ratio (VR) schedules** also call for reinforcement after a given number of responses, but that number varies from one reinforcement to the next. On a VR 30 schedule, a rat might sometimes be reinforced after ten bar presses, sometimes after fifty bar presses, but an *average* of thirty responses would occur before reinforcement was given. Gambling also offers a variable-ratio schedule; a slot machine, for example, pays off only after a frustratingly unpredictable number of lever pulls.
3. **Fixed-interval (FI) schedules** provide reinforcement for the first response that occurs after some fixed time has passed since the last reward, regardless of how many responses have been made during that interval. For example, on an FI 60 schedule, the first response after sixty seconds have passed will be rewarded. Some radio stations use fixed-interval schedules to discourage "professional contestants" by stating that listeners cannot win a prize more than once every thirty days.
4. **Variable-interval (VI) schedules** reinforce the first response after some period of time, but the amount of time varies. In a VI 60 schedule, for example, the first response to occur after an *average* of one minute is reinforced, but the actual time between reinforcements might vary from, say, 1 second to 120 seconds. Teachers use VI schedules when they give "points"—at unpredictably varying intervals—to those children who are in their seats. A VI schedule has also been successfully used to encourage seat-belt use: during a ten-week test in Illinois, police stopped drivers at random and awarded prizes to those who were buckled up (Mortimer et al., 1988).

Different schedules of reinforcement produce different patterns of responding, as Figure 8.12 shows (Skinner, 1961). The figure illustrates two important points. First, both fixed- and variable-ratio schedules produce very high rates of behavior, because in both cases the frequency of reward depends directly on the rate of responding. Thus, manufacturers who want to maintain high production rates often use fixed-ratio schedules, paying factory workers on a *piecework* basis, according to the number of items they produce. Similarly, gamblers reinforced on a variable-ratio schedule for pulling the slot machine's handle tend to maintain a high rate of responding.

The second important aspect of Figure 8.12 involves the "scallops" shown in the FI schedule, which also occur to a lesser extent in the FR schedule. Under an FI schedule, it does not matter how many responses are made during the time between rewards. As a result, the rate of responding typically drops dramatically immediately after reinforcement and then increases as the time for another reward approaches. When teachers schedule quizzes on the same day each week, for example, most students will study just before each quiz and then almost cease studying immediately afterward. Behavior rewarded on vari-

Linkages: Factory workers at the Lincoln Electric Company, a welding equipment plant in Cleveland, Ohio, are paid for every unit they produce—in other words, on a fixed-ratio reinforcement schedule. The schedule results in very high production rates and in annual incomes of up to $85,000 for the workers. Most of the employees like the reward system, but they are not necessarily satisfied with their jobs. This may be because, as described in Chapter 12, on motivation and emotion, job satisfaction is usually based on factors other than high pay.

Figure 8.12
Schedules of Reinforcement
These curves show the patterns of
behavior that typically occur when
different types of schedules are in effect. The steepness of each curve indicates the rate of responding; the
thin diagonal lines crossing the
curves show when reinforcement
was given. In general, the rate of responding is higher under ratio
schedules than under interval
schedules.

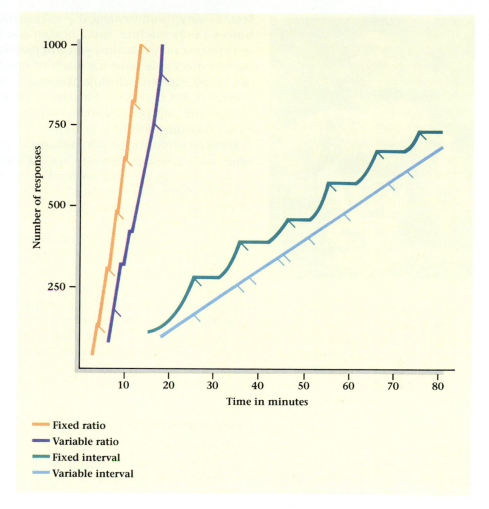

- Fixed ratio
- Variable ratio
- Fixed interval
- Variable interval

able-interval schedules looks quite different. The unpredictable timing of rewards typically generates slow but steady responding. Thus, if you know that
a "pop quiz" may occur any day, your studying is likely to be relatively steady
from day to day.

Schedules and Extinction   Just as breaking the link between a conditioned and an unconditioned stimulus weakens a classically conditioned response, ending the relationship between an operant response and its consequences weakens that response. In other words, failure to reinforce a response
extinguishes that response; the response occurs less often and eventually may
disappear. If bar pressing no longer brings food, a rat stops pressing; if repeated
phone calls to a friend bring nothing but ringing, you eventually stop phon-
ing. As in classical conditioning, extinction in operant conditioning does
not totally erase learned relationships. If a signaling stimulus reappears
some time after an operant response has been extinguished, that response
may recur (spontaneously recover) and, if again reinforced, it will be relearned
even faster.

In general, behaviors learned under a partial reinforcement schedule are far
more difficult to extinguish than those learned on a continuous reinforcement
schedule. This phenomenon—called the **partial reinforcement extinction ef-**

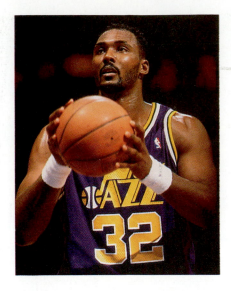

Partial reinforcement can create superstitious athletic rituals—such as performing a fixed sequence of actions prior to shooting a free-throw in basketball—which become so integral to success that performance will be disrupted if they are not performed. Thus superstitious behaviors may be maintained in a manner similar to avoidance conditioning; ritual acts are seen as preventing some negative consequence, and the person is too afraid of that consequence to find out if the ritual is really necessary.

Linkages: What events can act as rewards and motivate learning? (a link to Motivation and Emotion)

fect—is easy to understand if you imagine yourself in a hotel lobby with a broken candy machine and a broken slot machine. If you deposit money in the broken candy machine, you will probably extinguish (stop putting money in) very quickly. Because the machine usually delivers its goodies on a continuous reinforcement schedule, it is easy to tell that it is not going to provide a reinforcer. But because slot machines are known to offer rewards on an intermittent and unpredictable schedule, you might put in coin after coin, unsure of whether the machine is broken or is simply not paying off at the moment.

Behavior given partial reinforcement is resistant to extinction partially because such schedules actually reward unsuccessful as well as successful responses. That is, each time a reinforcement appears, it rewards not only the immediately preceding response but also, to a certain extent, the entire chain of previous responses that got no immediate reward, thus keeping the response sequence going.

Partial reinforcement also helps to explain why superstitious behavior is so resistant to extinction (Chance, 1988). Desirable events sometimes reinforce actions even if those actions had nothing to do with the event. The reward may follow the action through sheer luck, but this *accidental reinforcement* can function like a partial reinforcement schedule, strengthening the action that appeared to, but actually did not, cause the reward (Chance, 1988). Thus, someone who wins a lottery while wearing a particular shirt may begin wearing the "lucky shirt" more often. The laws of chance dictate that if you wear a "lucky shirt" often enough, a rewarding event will follow now and then, on a very sparse partial schedule.

Why Reinforcers Work

What makes primary reinforcers inherently reinforcing? One view is that primary reinforcers satisfy hunger, thirst, and other physiological needs basic to survival. This explanation is incomplete, however, because stimuli like saccharin, which have no nutritional value, can wield as much reinforcing power as sugar, which is nutritious. Other activities, like taking addictive drugs, are powerful reinforcers, despite their long-term threat to the health of the individual. Hence psychologists have sought other explanations for the mechanisms of reinforcement.

Activity Preference Some psychologists have argued that reinforcement is based, not on a stimulus itself, but on the opportunity to engage in an activity that involves the stimulus. According to David Premack (1965), for example, at any moment each person has a hierarchy of behavioral preferences, ranked from most to least desirable, like a kind of psychological Top 40. The higher on the hierarchy an activity is, the greater its power as a reinforcer, and any activity will serve as a reinforcer for any other activity that is less preferred at the moment. Thus, when parents use car keys to reward teenagers for studying or mowing the lawn, they are offering activities high on the teenagers' preference hierarchies to reinforce performance of activities lower on the hierarchy.

Preference hierarchies differ from one person to the next and from one occasion to the next. To a hungry person, eating will reinforce almost any behavior. But once hunger is satisfied, eating drops so low on the preference hierarchy that it temporarily loses virtually all power as a reinforcer. Because money can be exchanged for whatever a person finds reinforcing at the moment, it is almost always a powerful reinforcer.

As a result of such preference shifts, the opportunity to engage in a normally less preferred activity can sometimes reinforce performance of a more preferred activity *if* the person is prevented from carrying out the less preferred action (Timberlake & Farmer-Dougan, 1991). For example, even if a child prefers studying to participating in gym class, the opportunity to participate in gym may still reinforce studying, if the child is not allowed to engage in any gym activities for some time. When gym activity is held below its natural "baseline" level, its value as a reinforcer increases. Understanding activity preferences and the natural baseline distribution of activities over time can be very helpful in establishing effective reinforcers in "token economies" and other behavioral treatments (described in Chapter 16) for disruptive children or mentally disturbed adults (Timberlake & Farmer-Dougan, 1991).

Reinforcement in the Brain Whether reinforcement lies in specific stimuli or in particular activities, we still have not identified what it is that makes them pleasurable and thus reinforcing. Do all reinforcers exert a particular effect on the brain? This possibility was suggested in 1954, when James Olds and Peter Milner (1954) discovered that mild electrical stimulation of certain areas of the hypothalamus of rats can be such a powerful reinforcer that a hungry rat will ignore food in a Skinner box, preferring to press for hours a lever that stimulates these "pleasure centers" of its brain (see also Olds, 1973).

More recent evidence from brain stimulation research reveals that at least two different physiological processes may underlie reinforcement—one related to motivation and one to memory (White & Milner, 1992). The *motivational* properties of reinforcement—which prompt animals to approach activities previously associated with pleasure and to avoid those associated with discomfort—appear to involve stimulation of pathways in the striatum that use the neurotransmitter dopamine (White & Milner, 1992; Wise & Rompre, 1989). The process of solidifying *memories* about which stimuli have been associated with pleasure appears to involve stimulation of certain other dopaminergic regions of the brain, such as the lateral hypothalamus and the reticular formation. Thus, an association between a CS and a UCS, or between a response and its consequences, will be more permanently stored if the experience is followed by stimulation of these areas (Houston & Snyder, 1987). It is not yet clear whether these same physiological mechanisms form the basis for the power of all reinforcers, but evidence available thus far certainly suggests that they are important components of the process. As mentioned in Chapter 7, activation of dopaminergic systems is associated with the pleasure of many stimuli, including food, sex, and addictive drugs.

Punishment

Both positive and negative reinforcement *increase* the frequency of a response, either by presenting something pleasurable or by removing something unpleasant. In contrast to reinforcement, **punishment** involves the presentation of an aversive stimulus or the removal of a pleasant stimulus in order to *decrease* the frequency of the immediately preceding response. Shouting "No!" and swatting your dog when it begins chewing on the rug is punishment that presents a negative stimulus following a response. Confiscating a teenager's concert tickets because of rude behavior is punishment that removes a positive stimulus.

Punishment and negative reinforcement are often confused, but they are quite different. Reinforcement of any sort always *strengthens* behavior; punishment *weakens* it. If shock is *turned off* when a rat presses a lever, that is negative reinforcement; it increases the probability that the rat will press the lever when shock occurs again. But if shock is *turned on* when the rat presses the lever, that is punishment; the rat will be less likely to press the lever again.

Although punishment can change behavior, it has several drawbacks. First, like extinction, it does not "erase" an undesirable habit; it merely suppresses it. Children often repeat punished acts when they think they can avoid detection. Second, punishment often produces unwanted side effects. For example, if you punish a child for saying a vulgar word, the child may associate the punisher with the punishment and end up fearing you. Third, punishment is often ineffective, especially with animals or young children, unless it is given immediately after the response and each time the response is made. If a child gets into the cookie jar and enjoys a few cookies before being discovered and punished, the effect of punishment will be greatly reduced. If a child confesses to wrongdoing and is then punished, the punishment may discourage confession rather than eliminating undesirable behavior. Fourth, punishment is often an aggressive act, and children often learn through imitation. Hence, a punished child may learn to imitate the punishing behavior when relating to others. Finally, though punishment conveys information that inappropriate behavior occurred, by itself it does not specify correct alternatives. An "F" on a term paper says the assignment was poorly done but tells the student nothing about how to improve.

When used properly, however, punishment can work (see Figure 8.13). It is most effective when several guidelines are followed. First, to prevent development of a general fear of the punisher, he or she should specify why punishment is being given and that the behavior is being punished, not the person. Second, the punishment should be immediate and sufficiently severe to eliminate the undesirable response. Mild scolding may actually reinforce a child's pranks, because almost any attention is reinforcing to some children. Finally, more appropriate responses should be identified and positively reinforced. As the frequency of appropriate behavior increases through reinforcement, the frequency of the undesirable response (and the need for further punishment) drops.

When these guidelines are not followed, the beneficial effects of punishment may be wiped out or only temporary. American prisons provide one of the most obvious examples. Of 108,580 prisoners released from prisons in eleven states during 1983, 62.5 percent were arrested again within three years, and 41.4 percent were imprisoned again (Beck & Shipley, 1989).

Figure 8.13
The Uses of Punishment
This little boy suffered from chronic ruminative disorder, a relatively common condition in which an infant regurgitates all food. The picture on the left was taken when the boy was approximately one year old and had been vomiting for four months. The picture on the right is the same boy thirteen days after punishment with brief electric shocks had eliminated the vomiting response. His body weight increased 26 percent in two weeks. He was physically and psychologically healthy when tested six months, one year, and two years later (Lang & Melamed, 1969). When the danger of starvation is not so severe, electric shock may be replaced with some milder punishment, such as squirting lemon juice into an infant's mouth (Sajwaj, Libet & Agras, 1974).

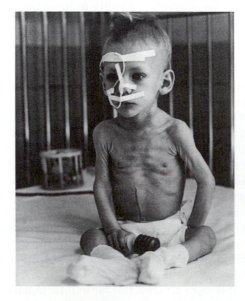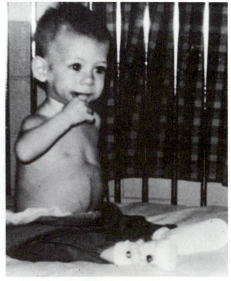

Source: Lang & Mealamed, 1969.

In Review: Reinforcement and Punishment

Concept	Description	Example or Comment
Positive reinforcement	Increasing the frequency of behavior by following it with the presentation of a positive reinforcer—a pleasant, positive stimulus or experience.	Saying "good job" after someone works hard to perform a task.
Negative reinforcement	Increasing the frequency of behavior by following it with the removal of a negative reinforcer—an unpleasant stimulus or experience.	Parents restore driving privileges to a teenager after a semester of improved grades.
Escape conditioning	A subject is conditioned to make a response that ends a negative reinforcer.	A little boy learns that crying will cut short the time that he must stay in his room.
Avoidance conditioning	A subject is conditioned to make a response that avoids a negative reinforcer.	You slow your car to the speed limit as soon as you spot a police car, thus avoiding arrest and reducing the fear of arrest. Very resistant to extinction.
Punishment	Decreasing the frequency of behavior (usually undesirable behavior) by either presenting an unpleasant stimulus or removing a pleasant one.	Swatting the dog after she steals food from the table. A number of cautions should be kept in mind before using punishment.

Operant Conditioning of Human Behavior

The principles of operant conditioning were originally worked out with animals in the laboratory, but they are valuable for understanding human behavior in an endless variety of everyday situations. ("In Review: Reinforcement and Punishment" summarizes some key concepts of operant conditioning.) The unscientific but very effective use of rewards and punishments by parents, teachers, and peers is vital to helping children learn what is and is not appropriate behavior at the dinner table, in the classroom, at a birthday party. Indeed, people learn how to be "civilized" in their own particular culture partly through positive ("Good!") and negative ("Stop that!") responses from others. As described in Chapter 3, differing patterns of rewards and punishments for boys and girls also underlie the development of behaviors that fit culturally approved *gender roles.*

The scientific study of operant conditioning has led to numerous treatment programs for altering problematic behavior. Behavioral programs that combine the use of rewards for appropriate actions and extinction (or carefully administered punishment) for inappropriate behaviors have helped countless mental patients, mentally retarded individuals, autistic children, and hard-to-manage children to develop the behavior patterns they need to live happier and more productive lives. Some of these procedures are discussed in Chapter 16, on treatment of psychological disorders. Many self-help books for people trying to lose weight, stop smoking, avoid procrastination, or reach other goals incorporate principles of positive reinforcement, recommending self-reward following each achievement in the program (Marx et al., 1992).

When people cannot do anything about the consequences of a behavior, discriminative stimuli may hold the key to changing the behavior. For example, people trying to quit smoking often find initial abstinence easier if they

Linkages: As described in Chapter 18 on social behavior and group influences, the prevalence of aggressive behavior varies considerably from culture to culture, in part because some cultures reward it more than others. For example, in some Eskimo cultures, aggressive behavior is actively discouraged and extremely rare (Oatley, 1993); it is much more common among the Yanomamo, a South American Indian group in which adult status (for males) is based on the ability to fight and even kill.

stay away from bars and other places that contain discriminative stimuli for smoking.   Stimulus control can also help insomniacs (Morawitz, 1989). Much more so than average, insomniacs tend to use their beds for nonsleeping activities such as watching television, writing letters, reading magazines, worrying, and so on. Soon the bedroom becomes a discriminative stimulus for so many activities that relaxation and sleep become less and less likely. But if insomniacs begin to use their beds only for sleeping, there is a good chance that their insomnia can be eliminated (Hill, 1982).

One of the most important things people learn through operant conditioning is that in most situations, they have at least some control over their environment. Babies learn that cries attract attention, children learn how to make the TV louder, adults learn what it takes to succeed in the workplace. In short, people learn to expect that certain actions on their part predict certain consequences. If this learning is disrupted or does not occur, problems may result. One is **learned helplessness**, a tendency to give up any effort to control the environment (Seligman, 1975).

An experiment with dogs provided one of the most powerful demonstrations of learned helplessness. Each dog stood in a harness over an electric grid. At random intervals, a strong electric shock was administered. The dogs in group A could turn off the shock by pushing a button with their nose, an example of escape conditioning. Each dog in group B was paired with one in group A. Group B animals could not control the shock; they had to wait until their partner shut it off. Thus, both groups received an identical amount of shock. The only difference was that those in group A could control it and those in group B could not.

An interesting thing happened when these dogs were moved to a new environment, a shuttle box similar to that in Figure 8.10. A signal was given and, after a ten-second interval, one side of the box was electrified. The dogs in group A quickly learned to jump over the barrier into the safe compartment. The dogs in group B at first barked and cried, but then they simply stood still and endured whatever shock was administered. Even though there was an obvious way to avoid the shock, these dogs never tried to find it. They had learned to be helpless (Mineka & Hendersen, 1985; Seligman & Maier, 1967).

Related studies suggest that lack of operant control over the environment can lead to helplessness in humans as well (Kofta & Sedek, 1989). In one experiment, people were given a set of problems to solve. There were no correct solutions, so no matter how hard they tried, these people were doomed to failure. Later, when these same people were given a new set of problems that could be solved quite easily, most of them failed again—this time because they did not *try* to find the correct solutions. Apparently they did not try because they believed that the task was beyond their abilities (Dweck & Repucci, 1973).

These results appear to reflect a general phenomenon. When people begin to *believe* that nothing they can do will change their lives or control their destiny, they generally stop trying to improve their lot (Dweck & Licht, 1980). Instead, they tend to endure painful situations passively and, at the cognitive level, attribute negative events to their own enduring and widespread shortcomings rather than to changeable external circumstances (Abramson, Metalsky & Alloy, 1989; Seligman, Klein & Miller, 1976). In both humans and animals, helplessness often results in severe depression and other stress-related problems, as described in Chapters 13 and 15 (Abramson, Metalsky & Alloy, 1989; Peterson, Seligman & Vaillant, 1988).

If learned helplessness arises from a perceived lack of control, then it should be possible to cure it by forcefully demonstrating the availability of control. Indeed, when dogs that had developed learned helplessness were helped over the barrier in the shuttle box where they showed passivity, they eventually learned to escape on their own (Seligman, Maier & Geer, 1968). Similarly, cognitive therapies for depression described in Chapter 16 often help people to deal with negative events in the hope that success at doing so will re-establish their sense of control, alter their attributions, and lift their spirits.

Cognitive Processes in Learning

As mentioned earlier, most North American psychologists of the first half of this century viewed the principles of classical and operant conditioning as the primary mechanisms responsible for all forms of learning, which took place, they thought, through the automatic, unthinking formation of simple associations. They argued further that, since both forms of conditioning depended upon observable responses, learning was directly tied to observable behavior. These assumptions have been strongly challenged over the years by evidence that *cognitive processes*—how people represent, store, and use information— play an important role in learning. This evidence includes research on latent learning, cognitive maps, insight, and observational learning.

Latent Learning and Cognitive Maps

Edward Tolman argued that much of learning involves *understanding and knowing*, cognitive processes that may not show up immediately in performance. When Tolman began his investigations in the 1920s, hundreds of experiments had been conducted in which rats were placed in mazes like the one shown in Figure 8.14. The rats' task was to go from the start box to the goal box, where they were rewarded with food. The rats typically took many wrong turns but over the course of many trials made successively fewer mistakes. The standard interpretation was that the rats learned a long chain of turning responses that were reinforced by the food. Tolman disagreed and offered evidence for an alternative interpretation.

Figure 8.14
Latent Learning
When rats are put in the same maze for several days, they make many wrong turns if no reinforcement is provided for correct turns. However, notice that the performance of group C improved dramatically the day after it first received reinforcement. The reinforcement, argued Edward Tolman, affected the rats' performance, but they must have learned the maze earlier, before receiving the reinforcement. Results like this led Tolman to conclude that animals develop a cognitive map of the maze even in the absence of reward (Tolman & Honzik, 1930).

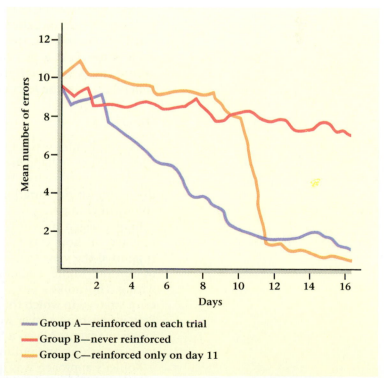

Group A—reinforced on each trial
Group B—never reinforced
Group C—reinforced only on day 11

In one of his studies, three groups of rats were placed in the same maze once a day for twelve consecutive days (Tolman & Honzik, 1930). For group A, food was placed in the goal box on each trial. These rats gradually improved their performance so that, by the end of the experiment, they made only one or two mistakes as they ran through the maze (see Figure 8.14). Group B also ran the maze once a day, but there was never any food in their goal box. These animals continued to make many errors throughout the experiment. Neither of these results is surprising, and each is consistent with a reinforcement view of learning.

The third group of rats, group C, was the critical one. For the first ten days, they received no reinforcement for running the maze and continued to make many mistakes. But on the eleventh day, food was placed in their goal box for the first time. Then a very surprising thing happened: on the day after receiving reinforcement, these rats made almost no mistakes. In fact, their performance was just as good as that of the rats who had been reinforced every day. In other words, the single reinforcement trial on day 11 produced a dramatic change in their performance the next day.

Tolman argued that these results supported two conclusions. First, notice that the rats in group C improved their performance the *first* time they ran the maze after being reinforced. The reinforcement on day 11 could not have significantly affected the rats' learning of the maze itself; it simply changed their subsequent performance. They must have learned the maze earlier. Therefore, the rats demonstrated **latent learning**—learning that is not evident when it first occurs. Second, because the rats' performance changed immediately after the first reinforcement trial, Tolman argued that the results he obtained could occur only if the rats had earlier developed a **cognitive map**—that is, a mental representation of the particular spatial arrangement, the maze.

Tolman concluded that cognitive maps are developed naturally through experience, even in the absence of any response or reinforcement. Research on learning in the natural environment has supported these views. Humans develop mental maps of shopping malls and city streets, even when they receive no direct reward for doing so (Tversky, 1991).

Thus, much as the Gestalt psychologists argued that the whole of a perception is different from the sum of its parts, cognitive views of learning hold that learning is more than the sum of reinforcement effects and stimulus-response associations. Just as perception may depend on the meaning attached to sensations, so, too, some forms of learning require higher mental processes and depend on how the learner attaches meaning to events.

Insight

Wolfgang Köhler was a Gestalt psychologist whose work on the cognitive aspects of learning happened almost by accident. A German, he was visiting the island of Tenerife when World War I broke out. The British confined Köhler to the island for the duration of the war, and he devoted his time to studying a colony of chimpanzees.

Köhler began his work only a decade or so after Thorndike published his research on how cats learn in a puzzle box. Recall that Thorndike's results supported the view that the gradual formation of associations is the bedrock of learning. Köhler and other Gestalt psychologists argued that Thorndike was wrong. Thorndike's puzzle box, Köhler said, forced animals to use a trial-and-error strategy in which they had to happen on an answer through associations. Perhaps pushing a lever would open the door, but how could the cat possibly know in advance? Even a Nobel laureate put in such a puzzle box would have to start pushing and pulling things until he or she discovered what worked.

Köhler's approach was quite different. He put a chimpanzee in a cage and placed a piece of fruit so that it was visible but out of the animal's reach. He sometimes hung the fruit from a string too high to reach, or on the ground too far outside the cage to be retrieved. Many of the chimps overcame these obstacles easily. For example, if the fruit was out of reach on the ground outside the cage, some chimps looked around the cage and, finding a long stick, used it to rake in the fruit. Surprised that the chimpanzees could solve these problems, Köhler tried more difficult tasks. Again, the chimps proved very adept, as Figure 8.15 illustrates.

Köhler claimed that the animals' behavior involved something more than automatic associations, and he buttressed his claim with three observations. First, once a chimpanzee solved a particular problem, it would immediately do the same thing in a similar situation. In other words, it acted as if it understood the problem. Second, Köhler's chimpanzees rarely tried a solution that did not work. Third, they often reached a solution quite suddenly. When confronted with a piece of fruit hanging from a string, for example, a chimp might jump for it several times. Then it would stop jumping, look up, and pace back and forth. Finally it would run over to a wooden crate, place it directly under the fruit, and climb on top of it to reach the fruit. Once, when there were no other objects in the room, a chimp went over to Köhler, dragged him by the arm until he stood beneath the fruit, and then started climbing up his back!

Köhler believed that the only explanation for these results was that the chimpanzees suddenly had **insight** into the problem as a whole, not just stimulus-response associations between its specific elements. In any case, Köhler's results showed that learning does not always proceed at the painfully slow pace dictated by trial and error.

Observational Learning: Learning by Imitation

Linkages: How can people learn from other people? (a link to Social Behavior and Group Influences)

Imagine that you are about to start a new job. How should you behave and dress? You will soon learn, partly by observing your co-workers, who act as *role models* for appropriate appearance and behavior on the job. The process of learning by watching others is called **observational learning**, also known as *social learning.*

Children are particularly influenced by the behavior of adult and peer role models. In one experiment, Albert Bandura showed nursery school children a film starring an adult and a large, inflatable, bottom-heavy "Bobo" doll (Bandura, 1965). The adult in the film punched the Bobo doll in the nose, kicked

Figure 8.15
Insight
Shown here are three examples of impressive problem solving by chimpanzees. (a) A chimpanzee has taken a fifteen-foot pole, fixed it in the ground, and climbed all the way to the top to grab the fruit. (b) After retrieving two wooden boxes from different areas of the compound, this chimp stacked them on top of one another, climbed to the top with a long pole, and then knocked down the fruit. (c) A chimp stacked three boxes on top of one another and climbed to the top of all three to reach the fruit.

(a)   (b)   (c)

Source: Köhler, 1976.

it, threw objects at it, and hit its head with a hammer while saying things like "Sockeroo!" There were different endings to the film. Some children saw an ending in which the aggressive adult was called a "champion" by a second adult and rewarded with candy and soft drinks. Some saw the aggressor scolded, spanked, and called a "bad person." Some saw a neutral ending in which there was neither reward nor punishment. After the film, each child was allowed to play alone with a Bobo doll. How the children played in this and similar studies led to some important conclusions about learning and about the role of cognitive factors in it.

Bandura found that children who saw the adult rewarded for aggression showed the most aggressive acts in play; they had received **vicarious conditioning**, a kind of observational learning in which one is influenced by seeing or hearing about the consequences of others' behavior. Those who had seen the adult punished for aggressive acts initially showed less aggression, but they still learned something. When later offered rewards for all the aggressive acts they could perform, these children displayed just as many as the children who had watched the rewarded adult. Observational learning can occur even when there are no vicarious consequences; many children in the neutral condition also imitated the model's aggression (see Figure 8.16).

The fact that people *can* learn by watching the behavior of others does not mean that they will. At one time or another, most people ignore the experience of others and must find out for themselves that it is not a good idea to wait until the last minute to study for an exam, to drink and drive, or to invest in get-rich-quick schemes. What determines whether observational learning will occur? According to Bandura, there are four requirements.

1. *Attention.* You cannot learn unless you pay reasonably close attention to what is happening around you.
2. *Retention.* You must not only attend to the observed behavior but also remember it at some later time.
3. *Ability to reproduce the behavior.* You must be capable of performing the act.
4. *Motivation.* In general, you will perform the act only if there is some motivation or reason to do so. People are most likely to imitate those whom they see *rewarded* for their behavior (as in the Bobo doll studies) and whom they *like.* Liking, in turn, tends to be enhanced if the model is similar to the observer in gender, age, or other characteristics or is attractive or powerful (Bandura, 1977). This is why advertisers use movie or sports stars, not street people, to endorse their products.

Observational learning seems to be a powerful source of the socialization discussed in the chapter on development. Experiments show, for example, that children are more willing to help and share after seeing a demonstration of helping by a warm, powerful model—even after some months have elapsed (Bryan, 1975; Mussen & Eisenberg-Berg, 1977).

Figure 8.16
Observational Learning
After children have observed a model, they often reproduce many of the model's acts precisely.

Bandura, Ross & Ross, 1963.

Thinking Critically

Does Watching Violence on Television Make People More Violent?

If observational learning is important, then surely television—and televised violence—must teach American children a great deal. It is estimated that the average child in the United States has spent more time watching television than attending school (Liebert & Sprafkin, 1988; Nielsen Media, 1990). It is further estimated that prime-time TV programs in the United States present an average of 5 violent acts per hour; some Saturday morning cartoons can include over 20 per hour (Gerbner et al., 1986; Radecki, 1990). By the time the average American child is fifteen years old, he or she will have watched approximately 24,000 televised shootings (Greene, 1985).

What is the effect of watching so much violence? Psychologists have speculated that watching televised violence might be emotionally arousing, making it more likely that viewers will react violently to frustration (Huston & Wright, 1989). Televised violence might also provide models that viewers imitate, particularly if the violence is carried out by attractive, powerful models—the "good guys," for example (Bandura, 1983). Finally, prolonged viewing of violent TV programs may "desensitize" viewers, making them less emotionally moved when they see others suffer and, as a result, less disturbed by inflicting pain on others (Cline, Croft & Courrier, 1973).

What am I being asked to believe or accept?

Many have argued that, through one or another of these mechanisms, watching violence on television causes violent behavior in viewers (Eron, 1987; Hearold, 1986). Indeed, in 1985 the American Psychological Association affirmed the conclusion of a National Institute of Mental Health study, which stated, "The consensus among most of the research community is that violence on television does lead to aggressive behavior by children and teenagers who watch the programs."

What evidence is available to support the assertion?

Three types of evidence back up the claim that watching violent television programs increases violent behavior. First, some evidence comes from anecdotes and case studies. Children have poked each other's eyes out after watching the Three Stooges appear to do so on television (Associated Press, 1984). And adults have claimed that watching TV shows prompted them to commit murders or other violent acts matching those seen on the shows.

Second, many correlational studies have found a strong link between watching violent television programs and later acts of aggression and violence. One study tracked people from the age of eight (in 1960) until thirty (in 1982). Those who watched more television violence as children were significantly more likely to be convicted of violent crimes as adults. These same people were also more likely to rely on physical punishment of their own children, and their children tended to be much more aggressive than average. These results were found in the United States, Israel, Australia, Poland, and the Netherlands. A significant positive correlation between television violence and violent behavior was even observed in countries such as Finland, where the number of violent shows is very small (Centerwall, 1989; Eron, 1987).

Finally, experiments have supported the view that TV violence increases aggression among viewers (Centerwall, 1989; Wood, Wong & Chachere, 1991). In one study, groups of boys watched violent or nonviolent programs in a controlled setting and then played floor hockey (Josephson, 1987). Boys who had watched the violent shows were more likely than those who had watched nonviolent programs to behave aggressively on the hockey floor.

Linkages: Can television teach children to be aggressive? (a link to Social Behavior and Group Influences)

Linkages: How can correlational research shed light on the influence of televised violence on aggression? (a link to Research in Psychology)

This effect was greatest for those boys who had the most aggressive tendencies to begin with. More extensive experiments in which children are exposed for long periods to carefully controlled types of television programs also suggest that exposure to large amounts of violent activity on television results in aggressive behavior (Huesmann, Laperspetz & Eron, 1984; Leyens et al., 1975; Parke et al., 1977). For example, compared with children who watched an equal number of nonviolent movies, children who were exposed to several violent movies became more aggressive in their interactions with other children (Leyens et al., 1975).

Are there alternative ways of interpreting the evidence?

Anecdotal reports and case studies are certainly open to different interpretations. If people face imprisonment or worse for their violent acts, how much credibility do you give to their claims that their actions were triggered by television programs? If anyone bothered to ask them, how many other people might say that the same programs made them *less* likely to be violent? Anecdotes alone do not provide a good basis for drawing solid scientific conclusions.

What about the correlational evidence? Recall from Chapter 2 that a correlation between two variables does not necessarily mean that one caused the other; both might be caused by a third factor. Why, for example, are certain people watching so much television violence in the first place? This question suggests two possible "third factors" that might account for the observed relationship between watching TV violence and acting aggressively.

For one thing, people who tend to be aggressive may prefer to watch more violent TV programs *and* behave aggressively toward others. Thus, personality traits or disposition, which we discuss in Chapter 14, may account for the observed correlations. Second, perhaps poverty, unemployment, or the effects of drugs and alcohol leave certain people both with more time to watch television *and* with frustration or other stressors that trigger aggressive behavior. One study tested this possibility by comparing the childhood television-viewing habits of forty-eight inmates imprisoned for violent crimes to those of forty-five noncriminals with similar socioeconomic backgrounds (Heath, Kruttschnitt & Ward, 1986). There was no significant difference between the groups' reported television watching as children, suggesting that early viewing habits did not create the difference in aggressiveness.

Finally, the results of controlled experiments on the effects of televised violence may lack generality (Freedman, 1988). Who is to say, for example, whether an increase in aggressive acts in a hockey game has any later bearing on a child's tendency to commit an act of violence?

What additional evidence would help to evaluate the alternatives?

By their nature, correlational studies of observed TV violence and violent behavior can never be conclusive because a third, unidentified causal variable might be responsible for the results. More important would be further evidence from controlled experiments (see, for example, Bryant, Carveth & Brown, 1981; Centerwall, 1990) in which equivalent groups of people are given different, long-term "doses" of TV violence and its effects on their subsequent behavior are observed. However, studies like this create a potential ethical dilemma. If watching violent television programs does cause violent behavior, are psychologists justified in creating conditions that might lead some people to be more violent? If such violence occurred, would the researchers be partly responsible to the victims and to society? If some subjects commit violent acts, should the researchers continue the experiment to establish a pattern, or should they terminate these subjects' participation? Difficulty in answering questions like these is partly responsible for the prevalence of short-term experiments and correlational research in this area and for some of the remaining uncertainty about the effects of television violence.

It would also be important to better understand how observed violence relates to other causes of aggressive behavior, some of which are discussed in Chapter 18.

What conclusions are most reasonable?

The preponderance of evidence collected so far makes it reasonable to conclude that watching TV violence may be one cause of violent behavior. But any cause-effect relationship between watching TV violence and acting violently is not an inevitable one, and there are many circumstances in which the effect does not occur (Widom, 1989). Parents, peers, and other environmental influences, along with personality factors, may dampen or amplify the effect of watching televised violence. Not every viewer cognitively interprets violence in the same way, and not every viewer is equally vulnerable (Wood, Wong & Chachere, 1991). Those most vulnerable may be those who are most aggressive or violence-prone in the first place, a trait that could well have been acquired by observing the behavior of parents or peers.

Cognition and Conditioning

Recognition of the role of cognitive factors in learning has profoundly changed psychologists' understanding of what is learned in classical and operant conditioning, and why. The associations and expectancies relating one event to another appear to be far more important in classical conditioning than the linkage of, say, a new stimulus to an old reflex (Rescorla, 1988; Turkkan, 1989). Cognitive factors can influence operant conditioning as well. Think back to our discussion of superstitious behavior. Why is it that winning the lottery can make the shirt worn that day "lucky" while having no effect on the status of the winner's shoes, socks, cologne, underwear, car, or dog? The answer lies partly in cognitive factors such as attention, memory, and expectancy. Perhaps because it was particularly distinctive (even ugly), the shirt was probably the item of clothing the person *attended to* and *remembered* best from that day; if a distinctive tie or scarf had been worn, it might have become "lucky" instead. No "lucky" car or dog was created, because people tend to expect that good or bad events will be related to things they *choose to do,* not to things they own. Furthermore, people focus more attention on (and remember better) occasions when rewards follow their actions than occasions when nothing significant occurs. In short, cognitive factors are often important in altering the impact of reinforcement.

Insights into the relationship between cognition and conditioning have made it possible to incorporate conditioning principles into explanations of cognitive activity. For example, the learning of *scripts* (that is, knowledge of how events typically unfold in a certain environment), *schemas* (organized or coherent sets of beliefs about a concept), and *mental models* (an understanding of how things work) can all be accounted for in terms of learning predictable relations between events, following the principles of classical conditioning. Accordingly, these cognitive features—discussed in more detail in Chapters 3 and 10—become less mysterious and more accessible to research.

Skill Learning

Cognitive factors are important in the development of all sorts of complex action sequences known as skills. Indeed, many of the skills that people learn to perform in everyday life—tying a shoe, opening doors, operating a computer, shooting a basketball, playing the piano, driving a car—can be learned, at least in part, without direct reinforcement or punishment. Instead, learning a skill depends mainly on imitation or on following instructions about what to do, plus a lot of practice. Some skills, like those of a basketball player or violinist, demand exceptional perceptual-motor coordination. Others, like those in scientific thinking, have a large cognitive component, requiring rapid understanding. In either case, the learning of skills usually involves automaticity, practice, and feedback.

The goal of many skill learners is to perform the skill *automatically*. As we discussed in the chapter on perception, automatic mental processing is characterized by high levels of speed and accuracy, along with a minimal demand for attention resources (Schneider, 1985; Dulany & Logan, 1992). Automatic processing seems to develop by replacing one kind of mental processing—a slow, serial computation—with the direct retrieval of the action or information from memory (Logan, 1992). For example, a young child may initially add 4 + 8 by using the serial process of counting. With greater skill development, however, the child answers automatically, by instantly retrieving from memory the association between the problem and the answer (Geary, Fan & Bow-Thomas, 1992).

The automaticity of skills can be acquired only through practice, but automatic behavior is learned most rapidly if the practice is *consistent*—that is, if the same stimuli are linked to the same responses on each trial. Thus, the computer operator will develop automatic processing more rapidly if practice occurs on machines whose keyboards are all the same.

Practice—the repeated performance of a skill—is the most critical component of skill learning. For perceptual-motor skills, both physical and mental practice are beneficial (Druckman & Bjork, 1992). For many cognitive skills, what counts most seems to be practice in *retrieving* relevant information from memory. Trying to recall and write down facts that you have read, for example, is a more effective learning tool than simply reading them a second time. (This point is elaborated in Chapter 9, on memory.)

How well you ultimately learn a skill depends less on how well you perform that skill during practice than on the effort that you expend in practice (Schmidt & Bjork, 1992). Large amounts of guidance may produce very good performance during practice, but too much of it may impair later performance (Wickens, 1992). Coaching students about correct responses in math, for example, may impair their ability later to retrieve the correct response from memory on their own. Independent practice at retrieving previously learned responses or information is more effortful, but is critical for skill development. Indeed, there is very little evidence for the effectiveness of "sleep learning" or similar schemes designed to make learning effortless (Phelps & Exum, 1992; Swets & Druckman, 1990). In short, "no pain, no gain."

So the most effective practice is carried out by learners who make independent choices and actions, but what if those choices are wrong? Suppose that a grade schooler starts "flailing" while practicing multiplication tables, coming up with essentially random answers. Clearly, in this case it is necessary to provide *feedback* about the correctness of the response. Our discussion of operant conditioning emphasized the importance for learning of prompt feedback in the form of reinforcement or punishment. But certain forms of feedback may not aid skill learning (Schmidt & Bjork, 1992). If feedback is given too soon after an action occurs or while it is still taking place, the feedback may divert the learner's attention from understanding how that action was achieved and what it felt like to perform it. Similarly, if feedback is so "rich" that detailed feedback occurs for virtually everything the learner does, it can have the same negative effects as too much guidance during practice. Overly rich feedback is often given to prevent the learner from making any mistakes, but learning to correct mistakes can be a key aspect of skill learning. If the learner comes to rely on the "crutch" of feedback, skill development may be impaired.

Forming Associations: The Role of Neural Networks

We have seen that much of learning—whether it involves linking conditioned stimuli and reflexes, responses and their consequences, or more complex understandings about how events predict other events—is based on the formation of *associations*. As a result of experience, some things remind us of other things, which remind us of still others, and so on. How are these associations actually stored? No one yet knows for sure, but the process probably involves a *network* of connections in the brain (Hintzman, 1991).

These associative networks can be very complex. Consider the word *dog*. As shown in Figure 8.17, each person's experience builds many associations to this word, and the strength of each association will reflect the frequency with which "dog" has been mentally linked to the other concepts in that person's life.

Using what they know about the laws of learning and about the way neurons communicate and alter their synaptic connections, psychologists have been trying to discover the principles governing how these associations are laid down. We discussed some of these efforts in Chapter 6 in terms of *neural networks* and *parallel distributed processing* models of how perception takes place. A key aspect of such models is the idea of *distributed memory* or *distributed knowledge* (see Chapter 9, on memory). These models say, for example, that the knowledge of "dog" does not lie in a single location, or *node*, within the brain. Instead, knowledge is distributed throughout the network of associations that connect the letters *D, O,* and *G,* along with other "doglike" experiences. In addition, as shown in Figure 8.17, each of the interconnected nodes that makes up your knowledge of "dog" are also connected to many other nodes. Thus, the letter *D* will be connected to "Daisy," "Danger," and a host of other things.

Neural network models of learning focus on how these connections are laid down as a function of experience (Hanson & Burr, 1990). For example, suppose you are learning a new word in a foreign language. Each time you read the word and associate it with its English equivalent, you strengthen the neural connections between the sight of the letters forming that word and all of the nodes activated when its English equivalent is brought to mind. Neural network or connectionist models of learning predict how much the strength of each linkage grows (in terms of the likelihood of neural communication between the two connected nodes) each time the two words are experienced together.

Figure 8.17
An Associative Network
Here is an example of a network of associations to the concept of dog. The knowledge associated with a dog does not lie exclusively in a small set of nodes, but is instead distributed across a network of associated nodes. All the associated nodes have some relationship to a dog, either through shared letters (for example, door and daisy) or associated meanings. The strength of some of these associations will grow as the person experiences their elements occurring together.

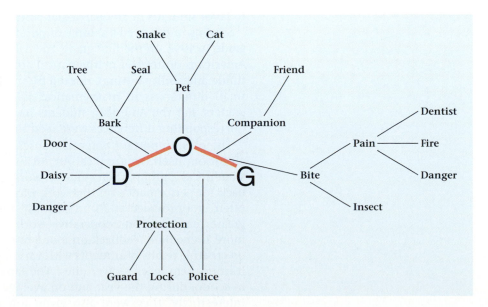

The details of various theories about how these connections grow are very complex (see Schwartz & Reisberg, 1991; Hanson & Burr, 1990), but a theme common to many is that the weaker the connection between two items, the greater the *increase* in connection strength when they are experienced together. Thus, in a simple classical conditioning experiment, the connections between the nodes characterizing the UCS and those characterizing the CS will show the greatest increase in strength during the first few learning trials. Notice that this prediction nicely matches the typical learning curve shown in Figure 8.3 (Rescorla & Wagner, 1972).

Few neural network models today can handle the learning of complex tasks, nor can they easily account for how people adapt when the "rules of the game" are suddenly changed and old habits must be unlearned and replaced (Hintzman, 1991). Still, a better understanding of what we mean by associations may very well lie in future research on neural network models.

Cultural Factors in Learning and Teaching

The study of how people learn is crucial to understanding how best to teach them (Glaser & Bassok, 1989). Teaching and training—explicit efforts to assist learners in mastering a specific skill or body of material—are a major aspect of socialization in virtually every culture. In the United States alone, there are some 97,000 primary and secondary schools and more than 3,500 colleges and universities (Cannon-Bowers et al., 1991; Chronicle of Higher Education, 1992). Many people believe these schools are not doing very well. The average performance of American students on tests of reading, math, and other basic academic skills has tended to fall short of that of youngsters in other countries, especially Asian countries (U.S. Department of Commerce, 1992; Stigler, 1992).

We discussed some possible reasons for these differences in academic performance in the chapter on development. For one thing, involvement in and support for education tend to be stronger in Asian cultures. Mothers in Japan, for example, have traditionally taken an extremely active role in their children's education (Fuson & Kwon, 1992). A more detailed picture of how American students and schools compare with others comes from a study by Harold Stevenson (1992) and his colleagues. They contrasted mathematical skills in typical U.S. urban schools (in Minneapolis and Chicago) with carefully matched samples in Taiwan and Sendai, Japan, using tests that were unlikely to favor students in any particular culture.

Stevenson followed a sample of pupils from first grade, in 1980, to eleventh grade in 1991. In the first grade, the Asian students scored no higher than the Americans on tests of mathematical aptitude (see Chapter 11 for more on aptitude and ability testing), nor did they enjoy math more. And there were only small differences in mathematical skills between American and Asian first graders. But the American students had fallen far behind by the fifth grade. Corresponding differences were seen in reading skills. Why?

The most important potential causes of these differences were found in the classroom itself. In a typical American classroom session, teachers talked to students as a group; then students worked at their desks independently. Feedback for performance on this work was usually delayed until the next day or, often, not provided at all. In contrast, the typical Japanese classroom placed greater emphasis on cooperative work between students. Teachers provided more immediate feedback on a one-to-one basis. And there was an emphasis on creating teams of students with varying abilities, a situation in which faster learners help teach slower ones. The Japanese children also spent more days in school during the year and on average spent more time doing homework. Interestingly, they were also given longer recesses than U.S. students and had more opportunities to get away from the classroom during a typical school day.

Do these cultural differences in classroom teaching styles by themselves explain the lagging scores of U.S. students? In fact, they do not tell the whole story. Stevenson's study also revealed differences in motivation and values. When he asked children to name a wish they would like to have granted by a "magical wizard," substantially more of the Asians than Americans made wishes associated with superior education and academic skill; most American children made wishes tied to money and other possessions. The Asian students also believed more strongly in the importance of hard work in academic success. The U.S. students, parents, and teachers were more inclined to believe that other factors—including ability, aptitude, and teachers' skill—were responsible. And compared with U.S. students and parents, the Japanese were less confident in how well they were doing and far less satisfied with the schools' ability to teach them.

Similar cultural differences in motivation and values show up among students within U.S. schools. Recent immigrants from Laos, Vietnam, and other southeast Asian nations typically perform extremely well compared with their native-born counterparts in the American school system, despite the fact that most of them spoke little or no English when they arrived (Steinberg, Dornbush & Brown, 1992). Interviews with these children revealed that compared with American students, far more children of the southeast Asian immigrants tended to reject goals of material pleasures and fun-seeking and to believe that hard work was important to success. Also, they received encouragement for and help with homework from older siblings as well as from parents (Caplan, Whitemore & Choy, 1989).

The significance of these cultural differences in learning and teaching is not altogether clear. Still, the educational community in the United States is paying attention to them. For example, Ann Brown and her colleagues (1992) have demonstrated the success of *reciprocal teaching*, in which children take turns actively teaching each other, a technique that closely parallels the cooperative arrangements characteristic of Japanese early education. More generally, psychologists and educators are considering how principles of learning can be applied to improve education (APA Monitor, 1992). For example, one study concluded that the most successful educational techniques apply basic principles of operant conditioning, offering positive reinforcement for correct performance and immediate corrective feedback following mistakes (Walberg, 1987).

Future Directions

Because learning is so basic to human life, it has been the subject of intense research for more than a hundred years. As a result, many important laws of learning have been discovered. Today, researchers seek to expand on this earlier work. Psychologists are working to determine the similarities and differences between the most automatic, stimulus-bound—often subconscious—learning and the learning that involves interpretation, reasoning, insight, and other cognitive processes.

There is renewed interest in classical conditioning, as psychologists recognize its importance in a range of experiences. The body's immune system, the activation of internal pain-control mechanisms, and even aspects of the understanding of language may be brought about when needed through classical conditioning. Indeed, as researchers recognize both the expanded role of classical conditioning in human behavior and the importance of cognitive processes in other animals, the principles of human and animal learning are drawing closer to each other (Roitblat & von Ferson, 1992; Terrace, 1991).

It is likely that the linkage of human and animal learning will be encouraged by the continued development of neural network models of learning, because the associations at the heart of these models are critical in both classical conditioning and cognitive learning. The development of computer-based artificial neural networks that can accurately imitate these forms of learning is a very exciting direction for future research. Other future work will focus on the role that brain chemical processes play in both the consolidation of learning and the operation of reinforcers (White & Milner, 1992).

Finally, psychologists and educators alike will continue to seek ways in which principles of learning identified in the researcher's laboratory can be applied to improving workers' job skills (Salas, 1991; Snow & Swanson, 1992) and teaching schoolchildren (Mayer, Tayika & Stanley, 1991; Vellutino, 1991; Weinstein, 1991). Some of these endeavors will focus on finding more effective applications of well-established learning principles (APA Task Force, 1992); others will take advantage of new technologies such as virtual reality, as discussed in Chapter 6 (Wickens, 1992).

To learn more about the field of learning, consider taking a course or two in the area. Some learning courses include laboratory sections that allow you to gain firsthand experience with the principles of human and animal learning.

Summary and Key Terms

Individuals adapt to changes in the environment through the process of *learning*, which is the modification through experience of pre-existing behavior and understanding.

Classical Conditioning: Learning Signals and Associations

Pavlov's Discovery

One form of learning is *classical conditioning*. It occurs when a *conditioned stimulus*, or *CS* (such as a tone), is repeatedly paired with an *unconditioned stimulus*, or *UCS* (such as meat powder on a dog's tongue), which naturally brings about an *unconditioned response*, or *UCR* (such as salivation). Eventually the conditioned stimulus will elicit a response, known as the *conditioned response*, or *CR*, even when the unconditioned stimulus is not presented.

Changing Conditioned Responses Over Time: Learning, Extinction, and Spontaneous Recovery

In general, the strength of a conditioned response grows as CS-UCS pairings continue. If the UCS is no longer paired with the CS, the conditioned response eventually disappears; this is *extinction*. After extinction, the conditioned response often reappears if the CS is presented after some time; this is *spontaneous recovery*. In addition, if the conditioned and unconditioned stimuli are paired once or twice after extinction, *reconditioning* occurs; that is, the conditioned response reverts to its original strength.

The Signaling of Significant Events

Classical conditioning involves learning that the CS is an event that predicts the occurrence of another event, the UCS. The conditioned response is not just an automatic reflex but a means through which animals and people develop mental models of the relation between events. The way stimuli are paired determines the speed and strength of conditioning. Classical conditioning works best when the conditioned stimulus precedes the unconditioned stimulus, an arrange-

ment known as forward conditioning. In general, a conditioned response develops best if the interval between the CS and UCS is no more than one-half to one second. Conditioning is also more likely when the CS reliably signals the UCS. In general, the strength of a conditioned response and the speed of conditioning increase as the intensity of the UCS—and the strength or salience of the CS—increase. The particular CS likely to be linked to a subsequent UCS depends in part on which stimulus was being attended to when the UCS occurred. Because of *stimulus generalization*, conditioned responses occur to stimuli that are similar but not identical to conditioned stimuli. Generalization is limited by *stimulus discrimination*, which prompts conditioned responses to some stimuli but not to others. *Second-order conditioning* occurs when a CS becomes powerful enough to make CSs out of stimuli associated with it.

Conditioning New Associations: Are All Signals Created Equal?

Some stimuli are easier to associate than others; organisms seem to be biologically prepared to learn certain associations, as exemplified by taste aversions.

Some Applications of Classical Conditioning

Research suggests that decreases in the body's immune response can be classically conditioned. Classical conditioning also plays a role in phobias and in behavioral treatments for them.

Linkages: Learning and Consciousness

People adapt, or become habituated, to events that are repeated often. According to Solomon's opponent-process theory, habituation is the result of a relatively automatic, involuntary A-Process—essentially an unconditioned response—and a conditioned B-Process that follows and counteracts the A-Process. This theory may help explain drug tolerance and some cases of drug overdose.

Instrumental and Operant Conditioning: Learning the Consequences of Behavior

Instrumental conditioning is a process through which responses are learned that help produce some rewarding or desired effect.

From the Puzzle Box to the Skinner Box

The *law of effect,* postulated by Edward Thorndike, holds that any response that produces a reward becomes more likely over time and any response that does not produce a reward becomes less likely over time. Skinner called this process *operant conditioning.* In operant conditioning the organism is free to respond at any time, and conditioning is measured by the rate of responding. In most respects, instrumental and operant conditioning are alike.

Basic Components of Operant Conditioning

An *operant* is a response that has some effect on the world. A *reinforcer* increases the probability that the operant preceding it will occur again; in other words, reinforcers strengthen behavior. There are two types of reinforcers: *positive reinforcers,* which strengthen a response if they are presented after that response occurs, and *negative reinforcers,* which strengthen a response if they are removed after it occurs. Both escape conditioning and avoidance conditioning are the result of negative reinforcement. *Escape conditioning* results when behavior terminates a negative reinforcer. *Avoidance conditioning* results when behavior avoids a negative reinforcer; it reflects both classical and operant conditioning. Behaviors learned through avoidance conditioning are very resistant to extinction. *Discriminative stimuli* indicate whether reinforcement is available for a particular behavior.

Forming and Strengthening Operant Behavior

Complex responses can be learned through *shaping,* which involves reinforcing successive approximations of the desired response. *Primary reinforcers* are inherently rewarding; *secondary reinforcers* are rewards that people or animals learn to like because of their association with primary reinforcers. In general, operant conditioning proceeds more quickly when the delay in receiving reinforcement is short than when it is long, and when the reinforcement is large than when it is small. Reinforcement may be delivered on a *continuous reinforcement schedule* or on one of four basic types of *partial,* or *intermittent, reinforcement schedules: fixed ratio* (FR), *variable ratio* (VR), *fixed interval* (FI), and *variable interval* (VI). Ratio schedules lead to a rapid rate of responding. Behavior learned through partial reinforcement, particularly through variable schedules, is very resistant to extinction; this phenomenon is called the *partial reinforcement extinction effect.* Partial reinforcement is involved in superstitious behavior, which results when a response is coincidentally followed by a reinforcer.

Why Reinforcers Work

Psychologists do not know for sure what makes reinforcers rewarding, but activity preference hierarchies and activity in the brain's pleasure centers are two possibilities.

Punishment

Punishment decreases the frequency of a behavior by following it with an unpleasant stimulus or removal of a pleasant one. Punishment modifies behavior but has several drawbacks. It only supresses behavior; fear of punishment may generalize to the person doing the punishing; it is ineffective when delayed; it can teach children to be aggressive; and it teaches only what not to do, not what should be done to obtain reward.

Operant Conditioning of Human Behavior

The principles of operant conditioning have been used in many spheres of life, from the teaching of everyday social skills to treatment of overeating and sleep disorders to classroom education. *Learned helplessness* appears to result when behavior has no influence over its consequences.

Cognitive Processes in Learning

Cognitive processes—how people represent, store, and use information—play an important role in learning.

Latent Learning and Cognitive Maps

Both animals and humans display *latent learning.* They also form *cognitive maps* of their environments, even in the absence of any reinforcement for doing so.

Insight

Experiments on *insight* also suggest that cognitive processes play an important role in learning, even by animals. Insights form suddenly and transfer to other problems.

Observational Learning: Learning by Imitation

The process of learning by watching others is called *observational learning,* or social learning. Some observational learning occurs through *vicarious conditioning,* in which one is influenced by seeing or hearing about the consequences of others' behavior. Observational learning is more likely to occur when the person observed is rewarded for the observed behavior. Observational learning is a powerful source of socialization.

Cognition and Conditioning

Classical and operant conditioning may be influenced by cognitive processes. In classical conditioning, an expectancy seems to be learned. A conditioned response is best formed when the conditioned stimulus is both a reliable and a useful predictor of the unconditioned stimulus. In operant conditioning, attention, memory, and expectations can all shape the impact of reinforcers. Insights into the relationship between cognition and conditioning have allowed psychologists to incorporate conditioning principles into explanations of cognitive activity.

Skill Learning

Observational learning, along with practice, plays an important role in the learning of skills. Learning a skill usually involves automaticity, a lot of practice, and corrective feedback.

Forming Associations: The Role of Neural Networks

According to neural network models, the associations so vital to learning are stored as a network of connections in the brain. These models emphasize that specific knowledge is distributed throughout an associative network of neural connections.

Cultural Factors in Learning and Teaching

Efficiently applying learning principles to the improvement of education and training requires not only understanding those principles but also attending to the role of cultural values and traditions in student performance.

Chapter 9

Memory

Outline

Memory is full of paradoxes. It is common, for example, for people to remember the name of their first-grade teacher but not the name of someone they met just a minute ago. And consider the case of Rajan Mahadevan, a man whom the *Guinness Book of World Records* listed as having the world's best memory after he memorized the first 31,811 places of *pi* (the ratio of the circumference of a circle to its diameter). He can memorize lists of 400 random digits and recall them without error. After studying a five-row by ten-column matrix of numbers for three minutes, he can recall perfectly any row, column, or quadrant of the matrix, in either forward or backward order (Thompson et al., 1991). But though Rajan has visited the psychology building at the University of Minnesota for more than fifteen years, he still has trouble recalling the location of the memory laboratory or the nearest restroom (Biederman et al., 1992). Like perception, memory is selective. While people retain a great deal of information, they also lose a great deal (Bjork & Vanhuele, 1992).

As the Linkages diagram suggests, memory is intimately tied to many other aspects of psychology. Without memory, you would not know how to shut off the alarm, take a shower, get dressed, or recognize objects. You would be unable to communicate with other people because you would not remember what words mean, or even what you had just said. You would be unaware of your own likes and dislikes (Vorauer & Ross, 1993), and you would have no idea of who you were in any meaningful sense (Kihlstrom, 1993). In this chapter we describe what is known about both memory and forgetting.

What Is Memory?

Mathematician John Griffith estimated that, over the course of the average person's lifetime, he or she will have stored roughly five hundred times as much information as can be found in all the volumes of the *Encyclopedia Britannica* (Hunt, 1982). The impressive capacity of human memory depends on the operation of a complex mental system. Our exploration of this system begins with a look at the kinds of information people remember. Then we describe the processes that are involved in remembering and forgetting.

Types of Memory

In which hand does the Statue of Liberty hold her torch? When was the last time you spent cash for something? What part of speech is used to modify a noun? Your attempt to answer the first question is likely to elicit a visual image; in order to answer the second, you must recall a particular event in your life; and the third question requires general knowledge that is unlikely to be tied to a specific event. Some theorists have argued that answering each of these questions requires a different type of memory (Brewer & Pani, 1984). How many types of memory are there? No one is sure, but most research suggests that there are at least three basic types. Each type of memory is named for the kind of information it handles: episodic, semantic, and procedural (Reed, 1992).

Any memory of a specific event that happened while you were present is an **episodic memory**—such as what you had for dinner yesterday, what you did last summer, or where you were last Friday night. **Semantic memory** contains generalized knowledge of the world that does not involve memory of a specific event. For example, you can answer a question like "Are wrenches pets or tools?" without remembering any specific episode in which you learned that wrenches are tools. As a general rule, people convey episodic memories by saying, "I remember when . . . ," whereas they convey semantic memories by saying, "I know that . . ." (Tulving, 1982). **Procedural memory**, which involves the *skill learning* discussed in Chapter 8, provides the memory for how to do things—how to ride a bicycle, read a map, or tie a shoelace, for example. Often, a procedural memory consists of a complicated sequence of movements that cannot be described adequately in words. For example, a gymnast might find it impossible to describe the exact motions in a particular routine.

Many activities require all three types of memory. Consider a game of tennis. Knowing the rules of the game or how many sets are needed to win a match involves semantic memory. Remembering which side served last requires episodic memory. Knowing how to lob or volley involves procedural memory.

Linkages

The questions in this diagram illustrate some of the relationships between the topic of this chapter, memory, and other chapter topics. A particularly interesting link occurs between the study of memory and the study of thought. How you think about something affects whether and how you remember it. At the same time, limitations on your memory affect what you can think about and thus how well you can solve problems and make decisions. Emotions, too, can affect what you remember; people who are happy and people who are sad are likely to do better at remembering different types of information, for example. The diagram shows just a sampling of the links between the study of memory and other aspects of psychology. The page numbers indicate where the questions in the diagram are discussed. ■

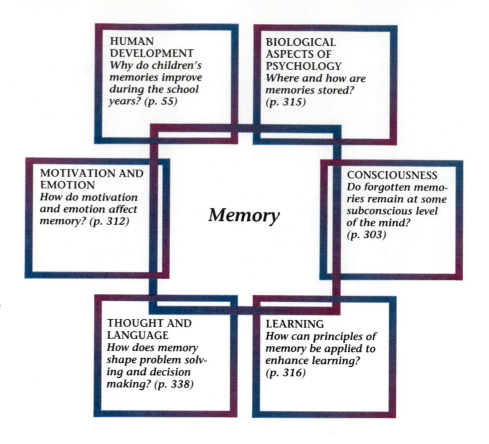

HUMAN DEVELOPMENT
Why do children's memories improve during the school years? (p. 55)

BIOLOGICAL ASPECTS OF PSYCHOLOGY
Where and how are memories stored? (p. 315)

MOTIVATION AND EMOTION
How do motivation and emotion affect memory? (p. 312)

Memory

CONSCIOUSNESS
Do forgotten memories remain at some subconscious level of the mind? (p. 303)

THOUGHT AND LANGUAGE
How does memory shape problem solving and decision making? (p. 338)

LEARNING
How can principles of memory be applied to enhance learning? (p. 316)

Procedural memories involve skills that can usually be learned only through repetition. This is why parents not only tell children how to tie a shoe but also show them the steps and then let them practice. Factors that enhance the learning of skills are described in Chapter 8.

Explicit and Implicit Memory

Until the last few years, psychologists interested in memory focused virtually all of their research on **explicit memory**, the processes through which people deliberately try to remember something (Masson & MacLeod, 1992; Nelson, Schreiber & McEvoy, 1992). If you try to remember where you went on your last vacation or tell someone where you were born, you will use explicit memory. In contrast, **implicit memory** is the unintentional recollection and influence of prior experiences (Nelson, Schreiber & McEvoy, 1992). While watching a movie involving a long car trip, for example, you may begin to feel anxious because you subconsciously recall the time you had engine trouble while driving across the country. Implicit memory operates automatically and requires no conscious effort.

It is not surprising that experience affects how people behave. What is surprising is that they are often not aware that their actions have been influenced by previous events. Because some influential events cannot be recalled even when people try to do so, implicit memory has been said to involve "retention without remembering" (Roediger, 1990). We gave some examples of this phenomenon in Chapters 6 and 7 in our discussion of subliminal perception and subconscious information processing.

The discovery of implicit memory processes and the fact that implicit and explicit memory sometimes follow very different principles are considered by some to be the major developments in memory theory over the past decade (Crowder, 1992). Imagine, for example, that people are asked to read a long list of words. After an hour they will forget some of the words, after a day they will forget most of the words, and after a week they will forget virtually all of them; their *explicit* memory for the words will have disappeared altogether. However, implicit memories remain because when the people are given word fragments such as *a-m—ill-*, and asked to complete the word (*armadillo*), they do better if the word had been on the "forgotten" list. In short, their previous exposure to the words continues to influence their performance, even though they cannot recall the words directly. Further, research with people in Eastern and Western cultures shows that they do just as well on this completion task after a week as they do after an hour (Komatsu & Naito, 1992; Mitchell, 1991). In cases like this, there is said to be a *dissociation* between explicit and implicit memory because a variable (the amount of time that has elapsed) affects one type of memory but not the other.

Researchers are studying the role of implicit memory (and dissociations between explicit and implicit memory) in many important psychological phenomena, including amnesia (Tulving, 1993), depression (Elliott & Greene, 1992), problem solving (Jacoby, Marriott & Collins, 1990), stereotyping (Smith, 1990), the development of self-concept in early childhood (Nelson, 1993), and the power of advertisements to associate comfort and familiarity with brand names (Duke & Carlson, 1993).

Basic Memory Processes

One of the authors sometimes drives to work and sometimes walks. On one occasion, he drove, forgot that he had driven, and walked home. When he failed to find his car in its normal spot the next morning, he reported the car stolen. After about twenty-four hours, the police called to say that "some college kids" had probably stolen the car because it was found on campus (next to the psychology building!). What went wrong? There are several possibilities, because memory depends on three basic processes—encoding, storage, and retrieval (see Figure 9.1).

First, information must be put into memory, a step that requires **encoding**. Just as incoming sensory information must be coded so that it can be communicated to the brain, information to be remembered must be put in a form that the memory system can accept and use. In the memory system, sensory information is put into various *memory codes,* which are mental representations of physical stimuli. For example, **acoustic codes** represent information as sequences of sounds. **Visual codes** represent stimuli as pictures. **Semantic codes** represent an experience by its general meaning. Thus, if you see a billboard that reads "Huey's Going Out of Business Sale—50% Off Everything in Stock," you might encode the sound of the words as if they had been spoken (acoustic coding), the image of the letters as they were arranged on the sign (visual coding), or the fact that you saw an ad for Huey's (semantic coding). The type of coding used can influence what is remembered. For example, semantic coding might allow you to remember that a car was parked in your neighbor's driveway just before their house was robbed. But if there was little or no other coding, you might not be able to remember the make, model, or color of the car (Anderson, 1990).

The second basic memory process is **storage**, which simply means maintaining information over time. Episodic, semantic, and procedural memories can all be stored for a very long time. When you find it possible to use a pogo stick

Figure 9.1
Basic Memory Processes
Remembering something requires three basic processes. First, the item must be encoded—put in a form that can be placed in memory. Second, it must be stored, or maintained, in memory. Finally, it must be retrieved, or recovered. If any of these processes fails to operate properly, forgetting will occur.

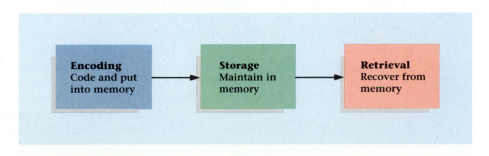

The human memory system allows people to encode, store, and retrieve a lifetime of experiences. Without it, you would have no sense of who you are.

or recall a vacation from many years ago, you are depending on the storage capacity of your memory.

The third process, **retrieval**, occurs when you find information stored in memory and bring it into consciousness. Retrieving stored information like your address or telephone number is usually so fast and effortless it seems automatic. Only when you try to retrieve other kinds of information—such as the answer to a quiz question that you know but cannot quite recall—do you become aware of the searching process.

Models of Memory

People remember some information far better and longer than other information. For example, suppose your friends throw a surprise party for you. On entering the room, you might barely notice, and later fail to recall, the flash from a camera. And you might forget in a few seconds the name of a person you met at the party. But if you live to be a hundred, you will never forget where the party took place or how surprised and pleased you were. Why do some stimuli leave no more than a fleeting impression and others remain in memory forever? In the following sections we examine four theoretical models of memory, each of which provides an explanation for this phenomenon.

Levels of Processing   The **levels-of-processing model** suggests that the most important determinant of memory is how extensively information is encoded or processed when it is first received. Consider situations in which a person intentionally tries to memorize something by *rehearsing* it—that is, by repeating it to themselves. There appear to be two basic types of mental rehearsal: maintenance and elaborative. **Maintenance rehearsal** involves simply repeating an item over and over. This method can be effective for remembering information for a short time. If you needed to look up a phone number, walk across the room, and then dial the number, maintenance rehearsal would work just fine. But what if you needed to remember something for hours or months or years? Far more effective in these cases is **elaborative rehearsal**, which involves thinking about how new material relates to information already stored in memory. For example, just repeating a new person's name to yourself is not a very effective strategy for memorizing it. Instead, if you have difficulty remembering new names, try thinking for a moment about how the new person's name is related to something you already know. If you are introduced to a man named Jim Crews, you might think, "He reminds me of my Uncle Jim, who always wears a crew cut."

Study after study has shown that memory is enhanced when people use elaborative rather than maintenance rehearsal (Anderson, 1990). The levels-of-processing model says that this enhancement occurs because of the degree or "depth" to which incoming information is mentally processed during elaborative rehearsal. The more you think about new information, organize it, and relate it to existing knowledge, the "deeper" the processing, and the better memory becomes.

Even when people are not trying to memorize information, their level of processing affects their memory. In several studies, for example, people were shown a long list of words but not asked to memorize them. Instead, some of the people were asked to indicate whether each word was printed in capital or small letters, a task that requires very shallow processing (the words do not even have to be read). After performing this task, these people showed very poor memory for the words on the list. Other people were asked whether each word rhymed with some other word, a task requiring a slightly deeper level of processing; these people showed better memory for the words. Finally, some people were asked to say whether each word described their own behavior. This task required a much deeper level of processing, and this group showed the best memory for the words (Bellezza, 1993).

The most important conclusion to be drawn from levels-of-processing research is that memory is much more strongly determined by internal factors, such as how people think about information and whether they relate it to existing knowledge, than by external factors, such as how the information is displayed.

Transfer-Appropriate Processing   The levels-of-processing model has inspired important lines of experimentation, but level of processing is not the only determinant of memory. Consider an experiment in which people were shown a long list of words and asked to answer one of two questions about each (Morris, Bransford & Franks, 1977). The questions were designed so that the subject would use either a semantic (meaning) code or a rhyming code (a version of acoustic coding). Thus, if the word was *house,* they would be asked either if "*house* is a type of building" or if "*house* rhymes with *mouse.*" Later, the subjects were asked to pick from a list those words they had been shown before.

Figure 9.2 shows the results. The subjects did much better at recognizing the words for which they had used a semantic code rather than a rhyming code. But when asked to pick out words that *rhymed* with the ones they had seen (for example, *grouse,* which rhymes with *house*), people did much better at identifying words that rhymed with words on which they used a rhyming code rather than a semantic code. Results like these inspired the concept of **transfer-appropriate processing**, which suggests that the critical determinant of memory is how the encoding process matches up with what is ultimately retrieved.

In another test of transfer-appropriate processing, half the students in a class were told that an exam would be multiple-choice, while the other half expected a series of essay questions. Only some of the students got the type of exam they expected, however. These students did much better on the exam than those who took an unexpected type of exam. Apparently, in studying for the exam the two groups used encoding strategies that were most appropriate to the type of exam they expected; those who tried to retrieve the information

Figure 9.2
The Match Between Encoding and Retrieval
Subjects who were asked to recognize words that the experimenter had shown them earlier did better if they had encoded the words on the basis of their meaning (semantic coding) rather than on the basis of what they rhymed with. But if asked to identify words that rhymed with those they had been shown, they did better on those that had been encoded using a rhyming code. These results support the transfer-appropriate model of memory.

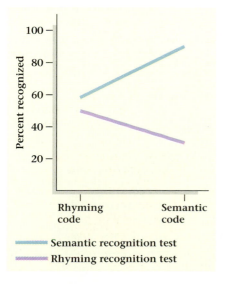

Semantic recognition test
Rhyming recognition test

in a way that did not match their encoding method had greater difficulty (d'Ydewalle & Rosselle, 1978). Results like these indicate that how well the encoding method transfers to the retrieval setting is just as important as the depth of processing.

Parallel Distributed Processing Models of Memory   Over the last thirty years, virtually all approaches to memory have conceptualized it as a system in which individual pieces of information are put in and taken out (Roediger, 1990). Today, some theorists are pursuing a new approach based on **parallel distributed processing** (or **PDP**) models of memory. These models suggest that new experiences don't just provide new facts that are later retrieved individually; they also change people's overall knowledge base, altering in a more general way their understanding of the world and how it operates. For example, if you compare your knowledge of college life today with what it was when you first arrived, chances are it has changed day by day in a way that is much more general than any single new fact you learned.

Because our understanding of neural network processing is still very limited, PDP memory theorists begin by asking how neural networks *might* provide a functional memory system (Anderson, 1990). We described the essential features of neural networks in Chapters 6 and 8, on perception and learning. In the case of memory, each unit of knowledge is ultimately connected to every other unit. The connections between units become stronger as they are experienced together more frequently. From this perspective, "knowledge" is distributed across a dense network of associations that allows people to quickly and efficiently draw inferences and generalizations. Just seeing the word *sofa*, for example, allows us to immediately gain access to knowledge about what a sofa looks like, what it is used for, where it tends to be located, who might buy one, and the like. PDP models of memory can account for this phenomenon very effectively.

Information Processing   The most influential and comprehensive theories of memory have historically been based on a general information-processing model, which we apply again in Chapter 10, on thought and language (Roediger, 1990). The **information-processing model** originally suggested that in order for information to become firmly embedded in memory, it must pass through three stages of mental processing: sensory memory, short-term memory, and long-term memory (Atkinson & Shiffrin, 1968).

Figure 9.3 outlines these stages. In the first stage, known as *sensory memory*, information from the senses—sights or sounds, for example—is held in *sensory registers* for a very brief period of time, often less than one second. Information in the sensory registers may be attended to, analyzed, and encoded as a meaningful pattern; this is the process of *perception* discussed in Chapter 6. If the information in sensory memory is perceived, it can enter the second processing stage, *short-term memory*. If nothing further is done, the information will

Figure 9.3
The Three Stages of Memory
One long-influential model of memory analyzes the memory system into three stages. The first stage captures information that the eyes, ears, and other sense organs pick up from the environment. In the second stage distinct patterns of energy, such as recognizable images or understandable words, are briefly held in consciousness. The third stage allows information to be retained for use hours, days, or even years later.

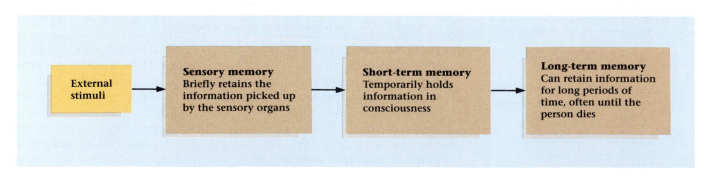

| External stimuli | → | **Sensory memory** Briefly retains the information picked up by the sensory organs | → | **Short-term memory** Temporarily holds information in consciousness | → | **Long-term memory** Can retain information for long periods of time, often until the person dies |

disappear in twenty seconds or so. But if the information in short-term memory is further processed, it may be encoded into *long-term memory,* where it may remain indefinitely.

Your reading of this sentence illustrates all three stages of memory processing. As you read, light energy reflected from the page is converted to neural activity and registered in sensory memory. If you pay attention to these stimuli, your perception of the patterns of light can be held in short-term memory. This stage of memory holds the early parts of the sentence so that they can be integrated and understood as you read the rest of the sentence. As you read, you are constantly recognizing words by matching your perceptions of them with the patterns and meanings you have stored in long-term memory. Thus, all three stages are necessary for you to understand a sentence.

Contemporary versions of the information-processing model emphasize the constant interactions among sensory, short-term, and long-term memory (Massaro & Cowan, 1993). For example, sensory memory can be thought of as that part of one's knowledge base (or long-term memory) that is momentarily activated by information sent to the brain via the sensory nerves. And short-term memory can be thought of as that part of one's knowledge base that is the focus of attention at any given moment. Like perception, memory is a very active process, and what is already in long-term memory influences how new information is encoded (Cowan, 1988). As a demonstration of this interaction, try the exercise in Figure 9.4.

How Do People Acquire New Memories?

Sensory, short-term, and long-term memory each provide a very different type of storage system. In the following sections we examine in more detail their unique characteristics and functions.

Sensory Memory

In order to recognize incoming stimuli, the brain must analyze and compare them to what is already stored in long-term memory. Although this process is very quick, it still takes time. The major function of **sensory memory** is to hold information long enough for it to be processed further (Stern, 1985). This maintenance is the job of the **sensory registers**, and there is a separate register for each of the five sensory modalities.

Memories held in the sensory registers are fleeting, but they last long enough for stimulus identification to begin (Ellis & Hunt, 1989). As you read a sentence, for example, you identify and interpret the first few words. At the

Figure 9.4
The Role of Memory in Comprehension
As a demonstration of the interaction between new information and information already in long-term memory, read the passage shown here, then turn away and try to recall as much of it as possible. Then read the footnote at the bottom of page 294 and reread the passage. During the second reading, the passage should make a lot more sense and be much easier to remember (Bransford & Johnson, 1972).

Reading the title of the passage allowed you to retrieve from long-term memory your knowledge about the topic. On the second reading, this knowledge created new expectations about the passage, which allowed you to process the passage more efficiently. In general, as you gain more knowledge in an area, it becomes easier and easier to remember new things about it.

The procedure is actually quite simple. First you arrange items into different groups. Of course one pile may be sufficient depending on how much there is to do. If you have to go somewhere else due to lack of facilities that is the next step; otherwise, you are pretty well set. It is important not to overdo things. That is, it is better to do too few things at once than too many. In the short run this may not seem important but complications can easily arise. A mistake can be expensive as well. At first, the whole procedure will seem complicated. Soon, however, it will become just another facet of life. It is difficult to foresee any end to the necessity for this task in the immediate future, but then, one never can tell. After the procedure is completed one arranges the materials into different groups again. Then they can be put into their appropriate places. Eventually they will be used once more and the whole cycle will then have to be repeated. However, that is part of life.

Source: Bransford & Johnson, 1972.

same time, subsequent words are being scanned, and these are maintained in your visual sensory register until you can process them as well.

In many ways, sensory memory brings coherence and continuity to the world. When you look slowly around, for example, it seems as if your eyes are moving smoothly, like a movie camera scanning a scene. In fact, they are not. As noted in Chapter 6, on perception, your eyes fixate at one point for about one-fourth of a second and then rapidly jump to a new position. The sensation of smoothness occurs because the scene is held in sensory memory until the eyes fixate again. Similarly, when you listen to someone speak, the auditory sensory register allows you to experience a smooth flow of information.

The fact that sensory memories quickly fade if they are not processed further is an adaptive characteristic of the memory system (Martindale, 1991). One simply cannot deal with all of the sights, sounds, odors, tastes, and tactile sensations that impinge on the sense organs at any given moment. As noted in Chapter 6, **selective attention**, the focusing of mental resources on only part of the stimulus field controls what information is processed further. Indeed, it is through perception that the elusive impressions of sensory memory are captured and transferred to short-term memory.

Short-Term, or Working, Memory

If you attend to and perceive a stimulus, a representation of the stimulus enters **short-term memory.** While the sensory registers typically store information for only a second or so, information in short-term memory is usually available for much longer. When you check *TV Guide* for the location of a show and then change to that channel, you are using short-term memory.

Material that is transferred to short-term memory from sensory or long-term memory can be consciously organized and thought about (Carpenter & Just, 1989). For this reason, many theorists prefer the term **working memory** to short-term memory; it is the system that enables people to do much of their mental work. Working memory has two major functions.

First, working memory allows you to construct and continually update a working model of the world and where you are in it. Imagine, for example, that you are walking down the street and see a man placing a large box into his car. If, a few seconds after you pass, he slams the door shut, you would not be startled because you would immediately recognize the source of the sound. In this sense, working memory is the representation of the present.

Second, working memory makes it possible for you to think and solve problems (Simon, 1989). It is the system that allows you to store, organize, and integrate facts. If a friend invites you to go dancing, your working-memory system allows you to mentally compare the prospect of going out with the knowledge that you have two chapters to read for tomorrow.

Encoding   Encoding of information in short-term memory is much more elaborative and varied than in the sensory registers (Brandimonte, Hitch & Bishop, 1992). Often, acoustic coding seems to dominate. One piece of evidence in support of this conclusion comes from an analysis of the mistakes people make when encoding information in short-term memory. These mistakes tend to be *acoustically related,* which means that they involve the substitution of similar sounds. For example, Robert Conrad (1964) showed people strings of letters and asked them to repeat the letters immediately. Their mistakes tended to involve replacing the correct letter—say, *C*—with another that sounded like it, such as *D, P,* or *T.* These mistakes occurred even though the letters were presented visually, without any sound.

Studies in several cultures have also shown that items are more difficult to remember if they are acoustically related rather than acoustically distinct. For

Note: The title of the passage on page 293 is "Washing Clothes."

example, American subjects perform much more poorly when they must remember a string of letters like *ECVTGB* (which all have similar sounds) rather than one like *KRLDQS* (which have distinct sounds). Similar results have been found in Chinese, which is written using characters that correspond roughly to English syllables. When Chinese students are shown a series of characters and then asked to write them, they get twice as many correct when the characters all have different sounds than when they all have the same sound (Zhang & Simon, 1985).

Notice, however, that the fact that the Chinese students remembered any of the acoustically identical characters suggests that they used some visual coding. Visual as well as acoustical codes are used in short-term memory. However, information that is coded visually tends to fade much more quickly (Cornoldi, DeBeni & Baldi, 1989).

Storage Capacity   You can easily determine the capacity of short-term memory by conducting the simple experiment, designed by Darlene Howard (1983), that is shown in Figure 9.5. The maximum number of items you can recall perfectly after one presentation is called the **immediate memory span.** If your memory span is like most people's, you can repeat about six or seven items from the test in this figure. The interesting thing is that you should come up with about the same number whether you estimate your immediate memory span with digits, letters, words, or virtually any type of unit (Hayes, 1952; Pollack, 1953). When George Miller (1956) noticed that studies of a wide variety of tasks showed the same limit on the ability to process information, he pointed out that the limit seems to be a "magic number" of seven plus or minus two. This is the capacity of short-term memory. The "magic number" applies, however, not to a certain number of discrete elements but to the number of meaningful *groupings* of information, called **chunks.**

Figure 9.5
Capacity of Short-Term Memory
These materials can be used to test your immediate, or short-term, memory span. Have a friend read the items in the top row at the rate of about one per second; then try to repeat them back in exactly the same order. If you are able to do this perfectly, have your friend read the next row. Each row contains one additional item. Continue until you make a mistake. Most people are perfect at this task until they reach six or seven items. The maximum number of items you can repeat back perfectly is your immediate memory span.

9	2	5								G	M	N						
8	6	4	2							S	L	R	R					
3	7	6	5	4						V	O	E	P	G				
6	2	7	4	1	8					X	W	D	X	Q	O			
0	4	0	1	4	7	3				E	P	H	H	J	A	E		
1	9	2	2	3	5	3	0			Z	D	O	F	W	D	S	V	
4	8	6	8	5	4	3	3	2		D	T	Y	N	R	H	E	H	Q
2	5	3	1	9	7	1	7	6	8	K	H	W	D	A	G	R	O	F	Z
8	5	1	2	9	6	1	9	4	5	0	U	D	F	F	W	H	D	Q	D	G	E
9	1	8	5	4	6	9	4	2	9	3	7	Q	M	R	H	X	Z	D	P	R	R	E	H

CAT BOAT RUG
RUN BEACH PLANT LIGHT
SUIT WATCH CUT STAIRS CAR
JUNK LONE GAME CALL WOOD HEART
FRAME PATCH CROSS DRUG DESK HORSE LAW
CLOTHES CHOOSE GIFT DRIVE BOOK TREE HAIR THIS
DRESS CLERK FILM BASE SPEND SERVE BOOK LOW TIME
STONE ALL NAIL DOOR HOPE EARL FEEL BUY COPE GRAPE
AGE SOFT FALL STORE PUT TRUE SMALL FREE CHECK MAIL LEAF
LOG DAY TIME CHESS LAKE CUT BIRD SHEET YOUR SEE STREET WHEEL

Source: Howard, 1983.

Those who provide simultaneous translation of a diplomat's speech must, among other things, store long, often complicated segments of speech in short-term memory while searching long-term memory for the equivalent second-language expressions. This complex task is made easier by grouping the speaker's words as phrases, sentences, and other large chunks.

To see the difference between discrete elements and chunks, read the following letters to a friend, pausing at each dash: *FB-ITW-AC-IAI-BMB-MW*. The chances are very good that your friend will not be able to repeat this string of letters perfectly. Why? There are fifteen letters, which is more than most people's immediate memory span. But if you read the letters so that they are grouped as *FBI-TWA-CIA-IBM-BMW,* the chances are very good that your friend will repeat the string easily (Bower, 1975). They are the same fifteen letters, yet they will be processed, *not* as fifteen separate letters, but as five meaningful chunks of information. The capacity of short-term memory is almost always between five and nine chunks.

The Power of Chunking   Chunks of information can become very complex. If someone read to you, "The boy in the red shirt kicked his mother in the shin," you could probably repeat the sentence very easily. Yet it contains twelve words and forty-three letters. How can you repeat the sentence so effortlessly? The answer is that people can build bigger and bigger chunks of information (Ericsson & Staszewski, 1989). In this case, you might represent "the boy in the red shirt" as one chunk of information rather than as six words or nineteen letters. Similarly, "kicked his mother" and "in the shin" represent separate chunks of information.

Learning to use bigger and bigger chunks of information can noticeably improve short-term memory. Children's memories improve in part because they gradually become able to hold as many as seven chunks in memory, but also because they become better able to group information into chunks (Servan-Schreiber & Anderson, 1990). Adults, too, can greatly increase the capacity of their short-term memory by more appropriate chunking (Waldrop, 1987); one man increased his immediate memory span to approximately one hundred items (Chase & Ericsson, 1981). In short, although the capacity of short-term memory is more or less constant—five to nine chunks of meaningful information—the size of those chunks can vary tremendously.

Notice that chunking demonstrates the interaction of short-term and long-term memory. You cannot come up with a meaningful grouping of information if you do no more than passively take it in. Chunking requires that you encode and organize the new information in terms of what you already know. Suppose you are buying something for 83 cents, so you go through your change and pick out two quarters, two dimes, two nickels, and three pennies. To do this you must remember the price, retrieve the rules of addition from

Information such as a new phone number is placed in short-term, or working, memory, where it tends to disappear rapidly unless we take steps to prevent its loss.

long-term memory, *and* keep a running count in short-term memory of how much change you have so far.

Duration   Imagine what life would be like if you kept remembering every phone number you ever dialed or every conversation you ever heard. This is unlikely because most people usually forget information in short-term memory quickly unless they continue repeating it to themselves (maintenance rehearsal). You may have experienced this adaptive (Bjork & Vanhuele, 1992), though sometimes inconvenient, phenomenon if you have ever been interrupted while repeating to yourself a new phone number you were about to dial, and then couldn't recall the number.

How long does unrehearsed information remain in short-term memory? To answer this question, John Brown (1958) and Lloyd and Margaret Peterson (1959) devised the **Brown-Peterson procedure**, which is a method for preventing rehearsal. A subject is presented with a group of three letters, such as *GRB*. Then the subject counts backward by threes from some number until a signal is given. Counting prevents the subject from rehearsing the letters. On the signal, the subject stops counting and tries to recall the letters. By varying the number of seconds that the subject counts backward, the experimenter can determine how much forgetting takes place over a certain amount of time. As you can see in Figure 9.6, information in short-term memory is forgotten gradually but rapidly: after eighteen seconds, subjects can remember almost nothing. Evidence from these and other experiments suggest that *unrehearsed* information can be maintained in short-term memory for no more than about twenty seconds.

Long-Term Memory

Short-term, or working, memory holds information so briefly that it is not what people usually have in mind when they talk about memory. Usually, they are thinking about **long-term memory**, whose encoding and storage processes we now consider.

Encoding   Some information is encoded into long-term memory automatically, without any conscious attempt to memorize it (Ellis, 1991). However, encoding information into long-term memory is often the result of a relatively deep level of conscious processing, which usually involves some degree of *semantic coding*. In other words, encoding in long-term memory often ignores details and instead encodes the general, underlying meaning of the information.

The dominance of semantic coding in long-term memory was demonstrated in a classic study by Jacqueline Sachs (1967). First, people listened to tape-recorded passages. Then Sachs gave them sentences and asked whether each exact sentence had been in the taped passage. People did very well when they were tested immediately (using mainly short-term memory). After only twenty-seven seconds, however, at which point the information had to be retrieved from long-term memory, they could not determine which of two sentences they had heard if both sentences expressed the same meaning. For example, they could not determine whether they had heard "He sent a letter about it to Galileo, the great Italian scientist" or "A letter about it was sent to Galileo, the great Italian scientist." In other words, they remembered the general meaning of what they had heard, but not the exact wording.

Counterfeiters depend on the fact that people encode the general meaning of visual stimuli rather than specific details. For example, most people from the United States shown the display in Figure 9.7 are unable to choose the

**Figure 9.6
Forgetting in
Short-Term Memory**
The graph shows the percentage of nonsense syllables recalled after various intervals during which rehearsal was prevented. Notice that there was virtually complete forgetting after a delay of eighteen seconds.

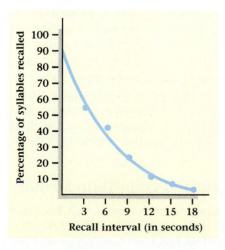

Source: Peterson & Peterson, 1959.

**Figure 9.7
Encoding into
Long-Term Memory**
Most subjects are unable to correctly identify the correct image of a penny. The answer is A.

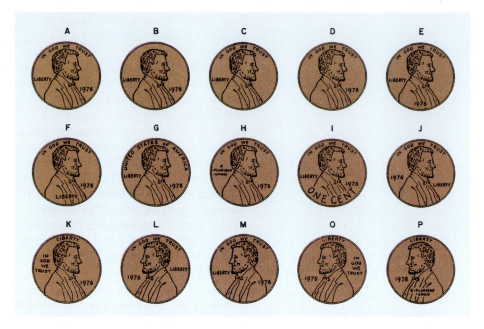

Source: Nickerson & Adams, 1979.

Compare the painting of an Italian village with a photo of the same scene. The painter is Franco Magnani, a village native who had not seen it in thirty years (Sacks, 1992). People with *eidetic imagery,* also called *photographic memory* have automatic, detailed, and vivid images of virtually everything they have seen. About 5 percent of children have eidetic imagery, but almost no adults do (Haber, 1979). Mr. Magnani's eidetic imagery was limited to the village of his birth.

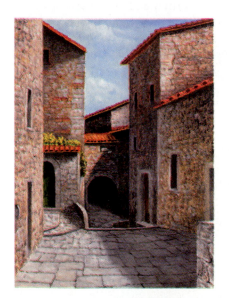

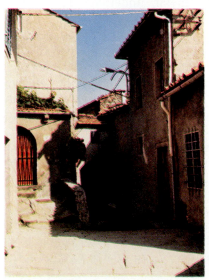

correct picture of a penny (Nickerson & Adams, 1979); people from Great Britain also do poorly at recognizing their country's coins (Jones, 1990).

Although long-term memory normally involves semantic coding, people can also use visual coding to process images into long-term memory. In one study, people viewed 2,500 pictures. Though it took sixteen hours just to present the stimuli, the subjects later correctly recognized more than 90 percent of the pictures tested (Standing, Conezio & Haber, 1970).

One reason pictures are remembered so well is that they have many distinctive features, which are likely to attract attention and thus to be perceived and encoded (Madigan, 1983). Another reason is that these stimuli may be represented in terms of both a visual code and a semantic code. *Dual coding theory* suggests that information is remembered better when it is represented in both codes rather than in only one (Paivio, 1986).

Storage Capacity   Whereas the capacity of short-term memory is limited, the capacity of long-term memory is extremely large; most theorists believe it is literally unlimited (Medin & Ross, 1992). It is impossible to prove this, but no one has ever been unable to learn something new because he or she had too much information stored in long-term memory. We do know for sure that people store vast quantities of information in long-term memory, and often remember it remarkably well for long periods of time. For example, people are amazingly accurate at recognizing the faces of their high school classmates after having not seen them for over twenty-five years (Bruck, Cavanagh & Ceci, 1991), and they do surprisingly well on tests of a foreign language or high school algebra fifty years after having formally studied these subjects (Bahrick, 1992; Bahrick & Hall, 1991).

Distinguishing Between Short-Term and Long-Term Memory

Earlier we noted that the levels-of-processing model suggests that how well something is remembered reflects a single dimension: the degree or depth to which incoming information is processed. Psychologists who adopt this perspective believe there is no need to distinguish between short-term and long-term memory: what people call short-term, or working, memory is simply that

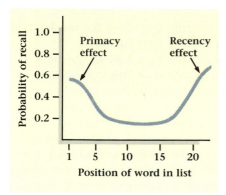

Figure 9.8
A Serial-Position Curve
The probability of recalling an item is plotted here as a function of its serial position in a list of items. Generally, the first several items are likely to be recalled (the primacy effect); items in the middle of the list are much less likely to be recalled; and the last several items are recalled very well (the recency effect).

Figure 9.9
Separating Short-Term from Long-Term Memory
Both a primacy and a recency effect occur when subjects must recall a list immediately after the last item is presented. But when subjects perform an arithmetic task after hearing the last item, the recency effect disappears. The arithmetic task apparently displaces the words in short-term memory, leaving only those in long-term memory available for retrieval. Thus it appears that the recency effect is based on retrieval of the last several items from short-term memory.

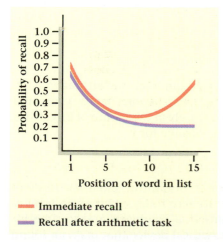

Source: Glanzer & Cunitz, 1966.

part of memory that they happen to be thinking about at any particular time, whereas long-term memory is the part of memory that they are not thinking about at any given moment. However, other psychologists argue that short-term and long-term memory are qualitatively different, that they obey different laws (Cowan, 1988). Determining whether short-term and long-term memory are qualitatively distinct has become one of the most important topics in the history of memory research (Bruce et al., 1992). Evidence that information is transferred from short-term memory to a very distinct storage system comes from experiments on recall and from the consequences of brain damage and drug use.

Experiments on Recall　Look at the following list of words for thirty seconds, then look away and try to recall as many words as you can, in any order: *bed, rest, quilt, dream, sheet, mattress, pillow, night, snore, pajamas.* Which words you recall depends in part on their *serial position*—that is, on where the words were in the list, as Figure 9.8 shows. This figure is a *serial-position curve,* a plot of the chances of recalling the words in each position in a list. For the first two or three words in a list, recall tends to be very good, a characteristic that is called the **primacy effect.** The probability of recall decreases for words in the middle of the list and then rises dramatically for the last few words. The ease of recalling words near the end of a list is called the **recency effect.**

The primacy effect occurs because the words at the beginning of a list are rehearsed much more often than any of the other words on the list (Koppenaal & Glanzer, 1990). But why does the recency effect occur? If short-term and long-term memory are indeed distinct, then one possibility is that when the test is given immediately after the list is read, the last four or five words in the list are still in short-term memory and thus are easily recalled. In contrast, the beginning and middle of the list must be retrieved from long-term memory.

To test this hypothesis, Murray Glanzer and Anita Cunitz (1966) gave a list of words to two groups of people. They asked one group to recall the list immediately after it was given. The second group was given a list, immediately performed a mental arithmetic task for thirty seconds, and then tried to recall as many words as possible. As Figure 9.9 shows, no recency effect occurred among those in the second group. Performing the arithmetic task before recalling the list displaced the last several words from short-term memory, making them no more likely to be recalled than those in the middle of the list. Since the performance of the two groups was otherwise very similar, the recency effect that usually occurs seems to be the result of keeping the last several words in short-term memory until the test is administered.

Results of Brain Damage and Drug Use　Evidence that information is transferred from short-term memory to another, distinct system also comes from observations of how certain brain injuries and drugs affect memory (Martinez, Schulteis & Weinberger, 1991). For example, damage to the hippocampus, which is part of the limbic system described in Chapter 4, often results in **anterograde amnesia,** a loss of memory for any event occurring after the injury.

A striking example is H.M., whose case was described in Figure 7.2 in the consciousness chapter (Milner, 1966). Part of his hippocampus had been removed in order to end severe epileptic seizures. Afterward, both his long-term memory and his short-term memory appeared normal, but he had a severe problem. He had the operation when he was twenty-seven years old. Two years later, he still believed that he was twenty-seven. When his family moved into a new house, H.M. could not remember the new address or even how to get there. When he was told that his uncle had died, he grieved in a normal way. But soon afterward, he began to ask why his uncle had not visited him. Each

A severe blow to the head can wipe out information held in short-term memory or prevent its transfer to long-term storage. Thus, after the fight, this boxer may not recall the punch that knocked him out.

time he was told of his uncle's death, H.M. became just as upset as when he was first told. In short, the surgery had apparently destroyed the mechanism that transfers information from short-term to long-term memory.

Another condition, **retrograde amnesia,** involves a loss of memory for events *prior* to some critical injury. Often, a person with this condition is unable to remember anything that took place in the months, or even years, before the injury. In most cases, the memories return gradually. The most distant events are recalled first, and the person gradually regains better and better memory for events leading up to the injury. Recovery is seldom complete, however, and the person may never remember the last few seconds before the injury. For example, one man received a severe blow to the head after being thrown from his motorcycle. After regaining consciousness, he claimed that he was eleven years old. Over the next three months, he gradually recalled more and more of his life. He remembered when he was twelve, thirteen, and so on—right up until the time he was riding his motorcycle the day of the accident. But he was never able to remember what happened just before the accident (Baddeley, 1982). Those final events must have been encoded into short-term memory, but apparently they were never successfully transferred into long-term memory. Drugs, such as marijuana, can also disrupt the transfer of new information from short-term to long-term memory, but may not affect retrieval of existing information from long-term memory (Darley et al., 1973).

The damage to memory in all these cases is consistent with the view that short-term and long-term memory are distinct systems; the problems are tied to an inability to transfer information from one system to the other. Psychologists do not yet know exactly how, physiologically, this transfer occurs. One view is that some physiological trace that codes the experience must be gradually transformed and stabilized, or *consolidated,* if the memory is to endure (Verfaellis & Cermak, 1991).

It seems likely that this consolidation depends primarily on the movement of electrochemical impulses within clusters of neurons in the brain (Berman, 1991). Events that suppress neural activity in the brain—physical blows to the head, anesthetics, carbon monoxide and other types of poisoning—all disrupt the transfer of information from short-term to long-term memory. Similarly, transfer of information from short-term to long-term memory is often disrupted by strong but random sets of electrical impulses, such as in the electroshock treatments described in Chapter 16, on the treatment of psychological disorders. The information being transferred from short-term to long-term memory seems to be particularly vulnerable to destruction during the first minute or so (Donegan & Thompson, 1991). Taken together, this research prompts most theorists to continue thinking of short-term and long-term memory as distinct systems (see, for example, Koppenaal & Glanzer, 1990).

Why Do People Forget?

The frustrations of forgetting—where you left your keys, the answer to a test question, an anniversary—are apparent to most people nearly every day (Neisser, 1991). In this section we look more closely at the nature of forgetting, and at some of the mechanisms that are responsible for it.

The Course of Forgetting

Hermann Ebbinghaus, a German psychologist, began the systematic study of memory and forgetting about a hundred years ago. Today, Ebbinghaus's methods seem rather quaint. He used only himself as a subject. And to time his experiments, he used a metronome, a mechanical device that makes a sound at constant intervals. His aim was to study memory in its "pure" form, uncon-

"Hey, good buddy! How you doin'?"

"Can't kick, big fella. What's shakin'?"

Source: Drawing by Lorenze; © 1988 The New Yorker Magazine Inc.

This man has not used a pogo stick since he was ten. Because his memory of how to do it is not entirely gone, he will take less time to relearn the skill than he needed to learn it initially. In other words, his memory will display some savings.

taminated by emotional reactions and other pre-existing associations between new material and what was already in memory. To eliminate such associations, Ebbinghaus created the *nonsense syllable,* a meaningless set of two consonants and a vowel, such as *POF, XEM,* and *QAL.* He read aloud, to the beat of the metronome, a list of nonsense syllables. Then he tried to recall the syllables.

To measure forgetting, Ebbinghaus devised the **method of savings,** which involves computing the difference between the number of repetitions needed to learn a list of words and the number of repetitions needed to relearn it after some time has elapsed. This difference is called the *savings.* If it took Ebbinghaus ten trials to learn a list and ten more trials to relearn it, there would be no savings, and forgetting would have been complete. If it took him ten trials to learn the list and only five trials to relearn it, there would be a savings of 50 percent.

As you can see in Figure 9.10, Ebbinghaus found that savings declines (and forgetting increases) as time passes. However, the most dramatic drop in what people retain in long-term memory occurs during the first nine hours, especially in the first hour. After this initial decline, the rate of forgetting slows down considerably. In Ebbinghaus's study, some savings existed even thirty-one days after the original learning.

Ebbinghaus's research had some important limitations, but it produced two lasting discoveries. One is the shape of the forgetting curve depicted in Figure 9.10. Psychologists have subsequently substituted words, sentences, and even stories for nonsense syllables. In virtually all cases the forgetting curve shows the same strong initial drop in memory, followed by a much more moderate decrease over time (Slamecka & McElree, 1983). Of course, people remember sensible stories better than nonsense syllables, but the *shape* of the curve is the same no matter what type of material is involved (Davis & Moore, 1935).

The second of Ebbinghaus's important discoveries is just how long lasting "savings" in long-term memory can be. Psychologists now know from the method of savings that information about everything from algebra to bike riding is often retained for decades (Medin & Ross, 1992). Thus, you may forget something you have learned if you do not use the information, but it is very easy to relearn the material if the need arises, indicating that the forgetting was not complete (MacLeod, 1988).

The Roles of Decay and Interference

Nothing we have said so far explains why forgetting occurs. In principle, either of two processes can be responsible (Reed, 1992). One process is **decay,** the

Figure 9.10
Ebbinghaus's Curve of Forgetting
Ebbinghaus found that most forgetting occurs during the first nine hours after learning, especially during the first hour. After that, forgetting continues, but at a much slower rate (Ebbinghaus, 1885).

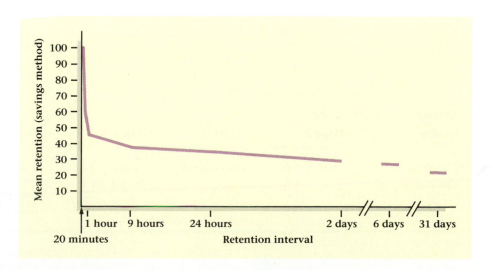

gradual disappearance of the mental representation of a stimulus, much as letters on a piece of steel are eaten away by rust and become less distinct over time. Forgetting might also occur because of **interference**, a process through which either the storage or retrieval of information is impaired by the presence of other information. Interference might occur either because one piece of information actually *displaces* other information, pushing it out of memory, or because one piece of information makes storing or recalling other information more difficult.

In the case of short-term memory, we noted that if an item is not rehearsed or thought about, memory for it decreases consistently over the course of twenty seconds or so. Thus decay appears to play a prominent role in forgetting information in short-term memory. But interference through displacement also produces forgetting from short-term memory. Like a workbench, short-term memory can hold only a limited number of items; when additional items are added, the old ones tend to "fall off" and are no longer available (Klatzky, 1980). Displacement is one reason why the phone number you just looked up is likely to drop out of short-term memory if you read another number before dialing. Rehearsal prevents displacement by continually re-entering the same information into short-term memory.

Analyzing the cause of forgetting from long-term memory is more complicated. In long-term memory there can be **retroactive interference**, in which learning new information can interfere with recall of older information, or **proactive interference**, in which old information interferes with learning or remembering new information. For example, retroactive interference would help explain why studying French vocabulary this term might make it more difficult to remember the Spanish words you learned last term. And because of proactive interference, the French words you are learning now might make it harder to learn German next term. Table 9.1 outlines the types of experiments used to study the influence of each form of interference in long-term memory.

Suppose a person learns something and then, when tested on it after various intervals, remembers less and less as the delay becomes longer. Is this forgetting due to decay or to interference? It is not easy to tell, because longer delays produce both more decay and more retroactive interference as the subject is exposed to further information while waiting. To separate the effects of decay

Table 9.1
Procedures for Studying Interference

Proactive interference occurs when previously learned material moves *forward* in time to interfere with the learning of new material. *Retroactive* interference occurs when learning new information inhibits the recall of information learned in the *past*.

Proactive Interference

Group	Time 1	Time 2	Time 3	Result
Experimental	Learn list A	Learn list B	Recall list B	The experimental group will suffer from proactive interference, and the control group will be able to recall more material from list B.
Control	—	Learn list B	Recall list B	

Retroactive Interference

Group	Time 1	Time 2	Time 3	Result
Experimental	Learn list A	Learn list B	Recall list A	The experimental group will suffer from retroactive interference, and the control group will be able to recall more of the material from list A.
Control	Learn list A	—	Recall list A	

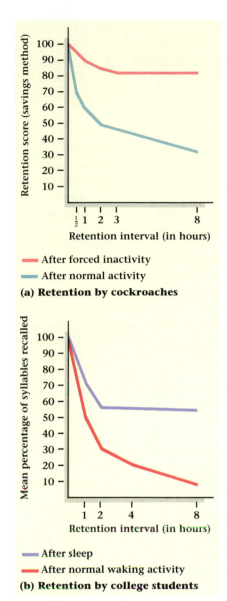

After forced inactivity

After normal activity

(a) Retention by cockroaches

After sleep

After normal waking activity

(b) Retention by college students

Source: Minimi & Dallenbach, 1946.

**Figure 9.11
Interference and Forgetting**
Forgetting is more rapid if (a) cockroaches or (b) college students engage in activity after learning than if they spend the time asleep. These results suggest that interference is more important than decay in forgetting information in long-term memory.

Linkages: Do forgotten memories remain at some subconscious level of the mind? (a link to Consciousness)

from those of interference, Karl Dallenbach sought to create situations in which time passed but there was no accompanying interference. Evidence of forgetting in such a situation would suggest that decay, not interference, was operating.

The subjects in one experiment were, of all things, cockroaches (Minimi & Dallenbach, 1946). Cockroaches normally avoid light, but the researchers conditioned them to avoid a dark area of their cage by shocking them there. After learning to stay in the light, some roaches were returned to their normal laboratory environment. Members of another group were placed individually in small cotton-lined boxes, in which they could breathe but not move. The researchers reasoned that this group would not experience the interference associated with normal physical activity. Later, each group of cockroaches was again taught to avoid the dark area. Figure 9.11(a) shows their savings score. As the delay in reconditioning lengthened, the difference between the groups grew. Savings declined only slightly for the immobilized cockroaches but dropped dramatically for those that had been normally active. These results strongly supported the notion that forgetting, at least in this situation, was due to interference, not to decay.

So much for cockroaches; what about humans? In another of Dallenbach's studies, college students learned a list of nonsense syllables and then either continued with their waking routine or were sheltered from interference by going to sleep. While the delay (and thus the potential for decay) was held constant for both groups, the greater interference associated with being awake produced much more forgetting, as Figure 9.11(b) shows (Jenkins & Dallenbach, 1924).

Results like these suggest that although it is possible that decay sometimes occurs, interference is the major cause of forgetting from long-term memory. But how does it work? Does interference push the forgotten information out of memory, or does it merely hinder the ability to retrieve it?

To find out, Endel Tulving and Joseph Psotka (1971) presented people with different numbers of word lists. Each list contained words from six semantic categories, such as types of buildings (*hut, cottage, tent, hotel*) or earth formations (*cliff, river, hill, volcano*). Some people learned a list and then recalled as many of the words as possible. Other groups learned the first list and then learned different numbers of other lists before trying to recall the first one.

The results were dramatic. As the number of intervening lists increased, the number of words that people could recall from the original list declined consistently. This finding reflected strong retroactive interference. Then the researchers gave a second test, in which they provided people with a clue by telling them the category of the words (such as types of buildings) to be recalled. Now the number of intervening lists had almost no effect on the number of words recalled from the original list, as Figure 9.12 shows. These results indicate that the words were still represented in long-term memory; they had not been pushed out, but the subjects had been unable to recall them without appropriate cues. In other words, the original forgetting was due to a failure in retrieval. Thus, putting more and more information in long-term memory may be like placing more and more marbles into a shoebox. Though none of the marbles disappears, it becomes increasingly difficult to find the specific one you are looking for.

Some theorists have concluded that all forgetting from long-term memory is due to some form of retrieval failure (Ratcliff & McKoon, 1989). Does this mean that everything in long-term memory remains there until death, even if people cannot always, or ever, recall it? Some theorists say yes, but others point out that the possibility of displacement cannot be dismissed entirely. No one yet knows for sure.

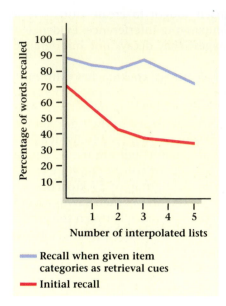

Recall when given item categories as retrieval cues

Initial recall

Source: Tulving & Psotka, 1971.

Figure 9.12
Retrieval Failures and Forgetting
These two curves show the results of the two stages in Tulving and Psotka's experiment. On the initial recall test, the ability to recall a list of items was strongly influenced by the number of other lists learned before the test, reflecting the effect of retroactive interference. On the second recall test, retrieval cues were provided, and the interfering effect of the intervening lists was negligible. In other words, information that could not be retrieved without cues could be recalled with cues.

Retrieving Memories

Have you ever been unable to recall the name of an old rock band or movie star, only to think of it the next day? Remembering something requires not only that it be appropriately coded and stored but also that you have the ability to bring it into consciousness—in other words, to *retrieve* it.

Retrieval Cues and Encoding Specificity

Stimuli that help people retrieve information from long-term memory, like the category information in the Tulving and Psotka (1971) experiment, are called **retrieval cues.** They allow people to recall things that were once forgotten and help them to recognize information stored in memory. In general, recognition tasks are easier than recall tasks because they contain more retrieval cues. For example, it is usually easier to recognize the correct alternative on a multiple-choice exam than to recall material on an essay test.

Which cues are most effective at aiding retrieval depends on the degree to which they tap into information that was encoded at the time of learning (Tulving, 1979; Tulving & Thomson, 1973). This rule, known as the **encoding specificity principle,** is consistent with the transfer-appropriate model of memory. Because long-term memories are often encoded semantically, cues that evoke the meaning of the stored information tend to work best. For example, imagine you have learned a long list of sentences, one of which is either (1) "The man lifted the piano" or (2) "The man tuned the piano." Having the cue "something heavy" during a recall test would probably help you remember the first sentence, because you probably encoded something about the weight of a piano, but "something heavy" would probably not help you recall the second sentence. The cue "makes nice sounds" would be likely to help you recall the second sentence, but not the first (Barclay et al., 1974).

Context and State Dependence

In general, people remember more when their efforts at recall take place in the same environment in which they learned, because they tend to encode features of the environment where the learning occurred (Bjork & Richardson-Klavehn, 1989). These features later act as retrieval cues.

Members of a university diving club provided one demonstration of this principle. They first learned lists of words while they were either on shore or submerged twenty feet underwater. They then tried to recall as many of the words as possible, again either on shore or underwater. Those who originally learned underwater scored much better when they were tested underwater than when they were tested on shore. Similarly, those who had learned the words on shore did better when tested on shore (Godden & Baddeley, 1975).

When memory can be helped or hindered by similarities in context, it is termed **context-dependent.** One study found that students remember better when tested in the classroom in which they learned the material than when tested in a different classroom (Smith, Glenberg & Bjork, 1978). This context-dependency effect is not always strong (Saufley, Otaka & Bavaresco, 1985; Smith, Vela & Williamson, 1988), but some students do find it helpful to study for a test in the classroom where the test will be given.

Like the external environment, the internal psychological environment can be encoded when people learn and thus can act as a retrieval cue. When a person's internal state can aid or impede retrieval, memory is called **state-dependent.** For example, if people learn new material while under the influence of marijuana, they tend to recall it better if they are also tested under the influence of marijuana (Eich et al., 1975). Similar effects have been found with alcohol (Overton, 1984), other drugs (Eich, 1989), and mood states. College

In Review: Factors Affecting Retrieval from Long-Term Memory

Process	Effect on Memory
Retroactive and proactive interference	Learning related information makes it more difficult to retrieve any specific fact. In proactive interference, old memories impair new learning; in retroactive interference, new memories impair retrieval of old ones.
Encoding specificity	Retrieval cues are effective only to the extent that they tap into information that was originally encoded.
Context dependence	Retrieval is most successful when it occurs in the same environment in which the information was originally learned.
State dependence	Retrieval is most successful when people are in the same psychological state as when they originally learned the information.

students remember more positive incidents from their diaries or from their earlier life when they are in a positive mood at the time of recall (Bower, 1981; Ehrlichman & Halpern, 1988). More negative events tend to be recalled when people are in a negative mood (Lewinsohn & Rosenbaum, 1987). These differences are strongest when people try to recall personally meaningful episodes, because these events were most likely to be colored by their own mood (Eich & Metcalfe, 1989). People who experience dramatic mood swings (such as those associated with bipolar disorder, as discussed in Chapter 15) tend to show very strong state-dependent memory effects.

Retrieval from Semantic Memory

All of the retrieval situations we have discussed so far are relevant to *episodic memory* ("In Review: Factors Affecting Retrieval from Long-Term Memory" summarizes this material). Obviously, *semantic memory,* which stores general knowledge about the world, is also important in everyday functioning. Researchers studying semantic memory typically ask subjects general-knowledge questions such as (1) Are fish minerals? (2) Is a beagle a dog? (3) Do birds fly? and (4) Does a car have legs? As you might imagine, most people virtually always respond correctly to such questions. By measuring the amount of time people take to answer the questions, however, psychologists gain important clues about how semantic memory is organized and how information is retrieved.

Semantic Networks   One of the most influential theories of semantic memory suggests that concepts are represented in a dense network of associations (Collins & Loftus, 1975). Figure 9.13 presents a fragment of what a *semantic memory network* might look like. In general, semantic network theories suggest that information is retrieved from memory through **spreading activation** (Medin & Ross, 1992). That is, whenever you think about some concept, it is activated in the network, and spreading activation (in the form of neural energy) begins to travel down all the paths related to it. For example, if a person is asked to say whether "A robin is a bird" is true or false, the concepts of both robin and bird will become activated and the spreading activation from each will intersect in the middle of the path.

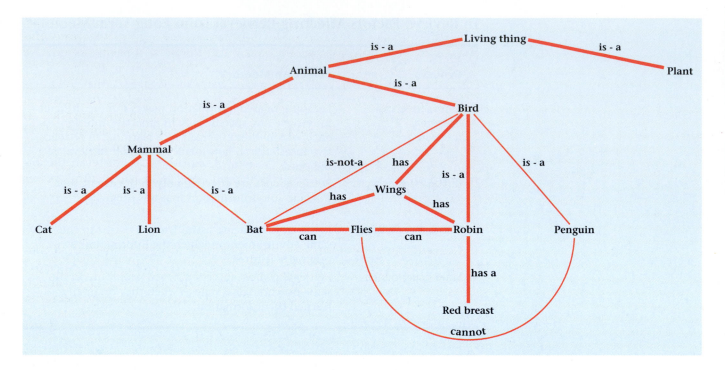

Figure 9.13
Semantic Networks
Here is a graphic representation of just a small part of a network of semantic associations. These networks allow people not only to retrieve specific pieces of previously learned information but also to make new inferences about concepts.

Some associations within the network are stronger than others. Differing strengths are depicted by the varying thickness of the lines in Figure 9.13; spreading activation travels more quickly along thick paths than along thin ones. For example, most people probably have a stronger association between "bat" and "can fly" or "has wings" than "is a mammal." Accordingly, most people respond more quickly to "Can a bat fly?" than to "Is a bat a mammal?"

Because of the tight organization of semantic networks and the speed at which activation spreads through the network, people gain access to an enormous body of knowledge about the world quickly and effortlessly. They retrieve not only facts that they have learned directly but also knowledge that allows them to infer or to compute other facts about the world (Medin & Ross, 1992). For example, imagine answering the following two questions: (1) Is a robin a bird? and (2) Is a robin a living thing? You can probably answer the first question "directly" because you probably learned this fact at some point in your life. However, you may never have consciously thought about the second question, so answering it requires some inference. Figure 9.13 illustrates the path to that inference. Because you know that a robin is a bird, a bird is an animal, and animals are living things, you infer that a robin must be a living thing. As you might expect, however, it takes slightly longer to answer the second question than the first.

Retrieving Incomplete Knowledge   Figure 9.13 also shows that concepts are represented in semantic memory as unique collections of features or attributes (concepts are discussed in more detail in Chapter 10, on thought and language). Often, people can retrieve some features but not enough to identify the whole concept. Thus, you might know that there is an animal that has wings, can fly, but is not a bird, and yet be unable to retrieve its name (Connor, Balota & Neely, 1992). In such cases you are said to be retrieving *incomplete knowledge.*

A very common example of incomplete knowledge is the *tip-of-the-tongue phenomenon.* In a typical experiment, dictionary definitions of particular words are read to people and they are asked to provide the name (Brown & McNeill, 1966). If they cannot recall a defined word, they are asked whether they can recall a particular feature of it. People are surprisingly good at this task, indicating that they are able to retrieve knowledge of the word, but knowledge that is incomplete (Brennen et al., 1990). Most people experience the tip-of-the-tongue phenomenon about once a week (Brown, 1991).

Another example of retrieving incomplete knowledge is the *feeling-of-knowing experience,* which is often studied by asking people trivia questions (Reder & Ritter, 1992). When they cannot answer a question, they are asked to estimate the probability that they could recognize the correct answer if they were given several options. Again, people are remarkably good at this task (Costermans, Lories & Ansay, 1992); even though they cannot recall the answer, people can retrieve enough knowledge to determine whether the answer is actually stored in memory.

Constructing Memories

The generalized knowledge about the world that each person has stored constantly affects memory (Harris, Sardarpoor-Bascom & Meyer, 1989). People use their existing knowledge to organize new information as they receive it and to fill in gaps in the information they encode and retrieve. In this way, memories are constructed.

To study this process, which is sometimes called *constructive memory,* Rebecca Sulin and D. James Dooling (1974) asked their subjects to read a long passage about a dictator. In one case, the dictator was a fictitious character named Gerald Martin; in another, Adolph Hitler. Later, subjects were asked if the passage contained the statement "He hated the Jews particularly and so persecuted them." This statement was not in the passage, but those who had been told that they were reading about Hitler "remembered" the statement more often than subjects who had read about Gerald Martin.

Another example of constructive memory comes from an experiment in which undergraduates waited for several minutes in the small, cluttered office of a graduate student (Brewer & Treyens, 1981). When later asked to recall everything that was in the office, most of the students mistakenly "remembered" that books were present, even though there were none. Apparently, the general knowledge that graduate students read many books influenced the subjects' memory of what was in the room.

Relating Semantic and Episodic Memory: PDP Models   Parallel distributed processing models offer one way of explaining how semantic and episodic information become integrated in constructive memories. As noted earlier, PDP models suggest that newly learned facts alter our general knowledge of what the world is like. Figure 9.14 shows a simple PDP network model of just a tiny part of someone's knowledge of the world (Martindale, 1991). At its center lie the intersections of several learned associations between specific facts, each of which is represented by an arrow. Thus, the network "knows" that Joe is a male European-American professor who likes Brie cheese and drives a Subaru. It also "knows" that Claudia is a female African-American professor who drives a Maserati. Notice that the network has never learned what type of cheese she prefers.

Suppose Figure 9.14 represents your memory and that you now think about Claudia. Because of the connections in the network, the facts that she is a female African-American professor who drives a Maserati would be activated; you would automatically remember these facts about Claudia. However, "likes Brie cheese" would also be activated because it is linked to other professors in the network. If the level of activation for Brie cheese is low, then the proposition that Claudia likes Brie cheese might be considered a hypothesis or an educated guess. But suppose *every other* professor you knew liked Brie. In that case, the connection between professors and "likes Brie cheese" would be

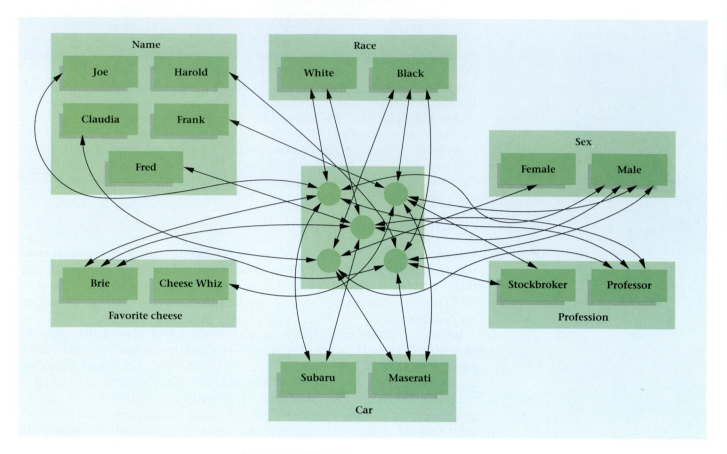

Figure 9.14
A Simple PDP Network Model
This simple parallel distributed processing network model represents with arrows what someone knows about how just six aspects of the world (shown in the ovals) are related (Martindale, 1991). Such network models are capable of accounting not only for what people know but also for the inferences and generalizations they tend to make. PDP models can become so complicated that researchers are still trying to understand all of their properties (Kruschke, 1992; Nosofsky, Kruschke & McKinley, 1992).

Source: Martindale, 1991.

strong, and the conclusion that Claudia likes Brie cheese would be held so confidently that it would take overwhelming evidence for you to change your mind (Rumelhart et al., 1986).

PDP networks also produce *spontaneous generalizations.* If your friend told you she just bought a new car, you would know without asking that—like all other cars you have experienced—it has four wheels. However, spontaneous generalizations can create significant errors if the network is based on limited or biased experience with a class of objects. For example, if the network in Figure 9.14 were asked what European-American males are like, it would think that all of them drive Japanese cars. Similarly, it would think that all African-American men are stockbrokers who drive fancy cars.

Ironically, researchers are encouraged by this prejudicial aspect of PDP networks because it is an accurate reflection of human thought and memory. As described in Chapter 17, on social cognition, virtually all people make spontaneous generalizations about males, females, European-Americans, African-Americans, and many other categories (Martindale, 1991). The only difference between the prejudiced and unprejudiced groups is that relatively unprejudiced people recognize that they are making the generalizations and consciously try to ignore or counteract them (Devine et al., 1991).

Schemas   PDP models also help us understand constructive memory by explaining the operation of the *schemas* that guide it. As described in the chapters on development and learning, schemas are mental representations of categories of objects, events, and people. For example, most Americans have a schema for *baseball game,* so that simply hearing these words is likely to activate whole clusters of information in long-term memory, including the rules of the game, images of players, bats, balls, a green field, summer days, and, perhaps, hot dogs and stadiums. The generalized knowledge contained in schemas provides a basis for making inferences about incoming information during the encoding stage. So if you hear that a baseball player was injured, your schema about baseball might prompt you to encode the player as a male, even though gender information was not mentioned. As a result, you are likely to recall the injury episode as involving a male player (see Figure 9.15 for another example).

As in the case of the students who falsely remembered books in a graduate student's office, people's schemas lead them to adjust their memories of events in accordance with what their prior experiences and cultural values tell them *probably* happened, or *should* have happened. The role of culture-specific schemas in constructive memory was demonstrated decades ago when Frederick Bartlett (1932) asked British university students to listen to a story about Native American culture called "The War of the Ghosts," in which spirit warriors take a young man with them into battle. When asked to retell the story from memory, the students tended to remember aspects that were in accord with the schemas of their own culture, and to forget aspects reflecting Native American schemas. One student, for example, retold the basics of the story, but left out the rather important fact that the warriors were ghosts!

Thinking Critically

Is the Memory of Eyewitnesses and Jurors Adequate to Produce Just Verdicts?

The courtroom is a place where memory processes play a vital role and where errors in memory can have tragic consequences. During a recent federal arson trial in Chicago, for example, a witness was asked if she could identify the man she saw running from a burning building. "Yeah, that's the guy," she said, looking toward one corner of the courtroom. To be sure there was no mistake, the judge asked her to single out the man—at which point she walked over and pointed at an assistant defense attorney (Gottesman, 1992).

There is a peculiar irony in the court system in the United States. Lawyers use notes to ask their questions in just the right way and in a particular order; judges use notes to deliver their instructions in an unbiased manner; and even defendants can use notes to aid in their own defense. But witnesses and jurors must often rely entirely on their own memories; many judges prohibit them from using any external memory aids, a tradition that most trial lawyers strongly support (Jacoby & Padgett, 1989).

What am I being asked to believe or accept?
The general assumption underlying court proceedings is that witnesses can accurately report what they have seen or heard; that jurors can accurately encode, store, and retrieve information about the evidence presented; and that jurors can then make a just decision.

What evidence is available to support the assertion?
There is actually very little scientific evidence to suggest that justice is most likely to prevail in a typical court proceeding. Judges and legislators rely instead on tradition and experience, interpreting the outcome of court proceedings as evidence that justice has been done in most cases. It is simply assumed that the motivation of witnesses and jurors to be accurate and to do

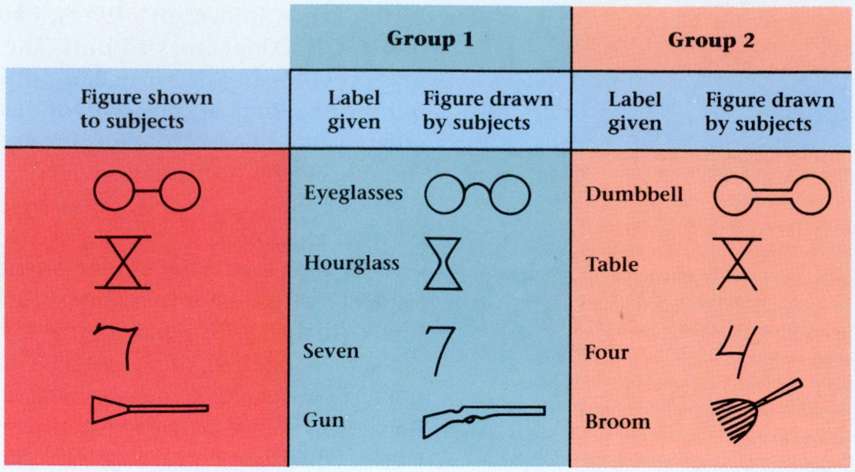

Figure 9.15
The Effect of Schemas on Recall
In one experiment, people were shown figures like these, along with labels that tended to activate certain schemas (Carmichael, Hogan & Walter, 1932). When showing the first figure, for example, the experimenter said either "This tends to resemble eyeglasses" or "This tends to resemble a dumbbell." When the subjects were later asked to reproduce the figures, their drawings were likely to resemble the items mentioned by the experimenter. In other words, the labels given to ambiguous items altered the subjects' memory of the items.

Figure shown to subjects	Group 1		Group 2	
	Label given	Figure drawn by subjects	Label given	Figure drawn by subjects
○—○	Eyeglasses	○○	Dumbbell	○—○
X	Hourglass	X	Table	X
7	Seven	7	Four	4
⊐—	Gun	⟋	Broom	🧹

the right thing renders them capable of playing their respective roles without significant error.

Are there alternative ways of interpreting the evidence?
The assumption that witnesses and jurors are highly motivated is probably a safe one; at least there is little evidence to suggest otherwise. But the outcomes that many interpret as evidence for the adequacy of the court system can also be viewed in less optimistic ways. There are many reasons to doubt that witnesses and jurors are capable of accurately remembering everything they see or hear, regardless of how motivated they may be.

Consider the jurors. Before they even think about the evidence presented, they need to remember the instructions given to them. Unfortunately, jurors appear to be very poor at this, probably because they do not fully understand all of the legal terms that judges use (Youngstrom, 1992). One researcher studied 238 people selected for jury duty in murder trials and found that 75 percent misunderstood key parts of the death penalty instructions (Hayes, 1992). Jurors in the first trial of the police officers who beat Rodney King (see Chapter 1) had to decide on five separate counts against the defendants, with separate criteria for each. Interviews after the trial showed that the jurors misremembered such things as whether "intent" had to be proved for all charges or only some of them (Deutsch, 1992).

Perhaps the most interesting research concerns the accuracy of eyewitnesses and how their testimony is interpreted (Loftus, 1993a). The most compelling evidence a lawyer can provide is that of eyewitnesses, but eyewitnesses make many mistakes (Loftus & Ketcham, 1991). Witnesses can remember only what is perceived, and they can perceive only what is attended to (Backman & Nilsson, 1991). The witnesses' task is to report as accurately as possible what they saw or heard; but no matter how highly motivated they are, there are limits to how faithful their reports can be (Kassin, Rigby & Castillo, 1991).

Even the form of a question can alter a witness's memory (Loftus, 1979). Experiments indicate that if a witness is asked, "How fast was the blue car going when it slammed into the truck?" he or she is likely to recall a higher speed than if asked "How fast was the blue car going when it hit the truck?" And when a situation is violent, the overall accuracy of eyewitness testimony is reduced (Burke, Heuer & Reisberg, 1992).

There is also evidence that an object mentioned after the fact is often mistakenly remembered as having been there in the first place (Dodson & Reisberg, 1991). For example, if a lawyer says that a screwdriver was lying on the ground (when it was not), witnesses often recall with great certainty having seen it (Ryan & Geiselman, 1991). Some theorists have suggested that witnesses are actually aware that they did not see the object themselves (Zaragoza & Koshmider, 1989), but this conclusion seems to be contradicted by more recent evidence (Lindsay, 1990). Other theorists have speculated that mentioning an object creates retroactive interference, making the original memory more difficult to retrieve (Tversky & Tuchin, 1989). However, there is now considerable evidence that, when objects are subsequently mentioned, they are integrated into the old memory representation and subsequently are not distinguished from what was originally seen (Loftus, 1992).

In judging the credibility of a witness, jurors often rely as much (or even more) on *how* the witness presents evidence as on the content or relevance of that evidence (Leippe, Manion & Romanczyk, 1992). Many jurors are impressed, for example, when a witness can recall a large number of details. In fact, extremely detailed testimony from prosecution witnesses is especially likely to lead to guilty verdicts, even when the details reported are irrelevant (Bell & Loftus, 1989). Apparently, when a witness gives very detailed testimony, jurors infer that the witness paid especially close attention or has a particularly accurate memory, and thus is highly credible. At first glance, these inferences might seem reasonable. However, as discussed in the chapter on perception, the ability to divide attention is limited. As a result, a witness might focus attention on the crime and the criminal or on the surrounding details, but probably not on both. Hence, witnesses who accurately remember unimportant details of a crime scene may not recall accurately the criminal's facial features or other identifying characteristics (Backman & Nilsson, 1991).

Even witnesses' confidence about their testimony is not always a reliable guide to their credibility. In several experiments, investigators have staged crimes for subjects who then report details of the crime and rate how confident they are about them. While witnesses' confidence tends to make jurors believe them (Leippe, Manion & Romanczyk, 1992), witness confidence ratings are frequently much higher than the accuracy of their reports. (Explanations for this overconfidence are discussed in Chapter 10, on thought and language.) In fact, a witness's asserted confidence is often unrelated to his or her accuracy (Kassin, Rigby & Castillo, 1991).

What additional evidence would help to evaluate the alternatives?
Several lines of evidence should be especially helpful to judges, legislators, and voters as they decide whether to alter the rules of judicial proceedings. Which jury instructions are easily remembered and which are not? What happens when a particular juror remembers something incorrectly? Do the other jurors correct the error during the deliberations? There is evidence that they may, but not always (Pennington & Hastie, 1983). Can careful instructions improve the memories of witnesses? Some recent research has indicated that when witnesses are told to think very carefully about the source of their memories, they can sometimes distinguish between whether they actually saw an object or someone else mentioned it to them at a later time (Lindsay & Johnson, 1989). If these types of warnings and instructions can be perfected, an important source of memory bias in the courtroom might be eliminated.

What conclusions are most reasonable?
Many safeguards are built into the U.S. judicial system to minimize the chances that an innocent person will be falsely convicted. Nevertheless, ex-

perimental evidence suggests that the system is far from perfect and might be improved by changes that take into account the limitations of human memory. Research on the role that memory plays in criminal proceedings may eventually lead to a court system that improves the protection of the rights and welfare of all citizens. ■

How do motivation and emotion affect memory?

Linkages: Motivation, Emotion, and Memory

As mentioned earlier, state-dependent memory reflects a match in a person's emotional state at two different times. The match between a person's emotional state at encoding and the content of the information acquired also affects memory (Mayer et al., 1990). When people in one study read a story that contained both happy and sad events, they recalled more happy incidents when they were feeling happy rather than sad (Bower, Gilligan & Monteiro, 1981). Their emotional state facilitated the processing of information that was similar in tone to that state. Evidence suggests that both the way information is encoded and the way it is retrieved are involved in this *mood congruency effect* (Lang, 1993).

The strength of the effect of emotions on memory depends on both the type of emotion and the information to be remembered (Clore et al., 1993). In general, positive emotions can do more than negative ones to facilitate memory. Negative emotions tend to interfere with memory (Ellis & Ashbrook, 1988), perhaps because they are often accompanied by angry or panicky thoughts that distract attention from retrieval. The impact of emotions on memory is greatest for information that does not have many links with what is already known (Hertel & Hardin, 1990). When there are few links, the emotion associated with the information may be one of the only cues available.

Work on relationships between emotion and memory has recently been applied to understanding aspects of clinical depression, which we discuss more fully in Chapter 15. Depressed individuals often report memory problems and difficulties in concentrating (Elliott & Greene, 1992). There is often a pronounced mood congruency effect: depressed subjects recall more negatively toned words than positively toned words, especially those negative words—such as *sad, tired,* or *confused*—that are associated with events related to depression (Denny & Hunt, 1992; Watkins et al., 1992). The opposite is true of nondepressed subjects. However, these differences between depressed and nondepressed subjects disappear when they are given an implicit memory test, such as the word-fragment completion task described earlier (Roediger & McDermott, 1992). It appears that clinically depressed individuals have very little cognitive capacity to devote to tasks for which difficult retrieval strategies are required (Hertel & Hardin, 1990). But implicit memory tasks do not require the same degree of conscious effort, so depressed individuals do just as well as nondepressed subjects on these tasks. These findings suggest that the cognitive disruptions often seen in clinical depression are specific to tasks requiring sustained mental effort (Weary & Edwards, 1994).

Very intense emotional experiences tend to produce memories that are unusually vivid, detailed, and long-lasting (Strongman & Kemp, 1991). In fact, they are called *flashbulb memories* because they preserve particular experiences in such great detail (Brown & Kulik, 1977; Heuer & Reisberg, 1990). People may recall many years later exactly where they were and what they were doing when they learned of a relative's death or when the 1991 Persian Gulf War started.

Based on both human and animal research, some theorists have suggested that there may be a special biological mechanism for flashbulb memories and that these memories are virtually perfect (LeDoux, Romanski & Xagoraris,

---

Linkages: When emotional reactions to an event are extreme, the defense mechanism of *repression* may occur, with the result that the person has no conscious memory of the event (see Chapter 14, on personality). Repression is relatively common among the victims, perpetrators, and witnesses of violent crimes (Loftus & Ketcham, 1991), and among those exposed to war and other traumatic events. Freud suggested that repression, like most other defense mechanisms, operates automatically and unconsciously.

Linkages: What chemicals and brain structures are involved when people form and store memories? (a link to Biological Aspects of Psychology)

1991; Mishkin & Appenzeller, 1987; Schmidt & Bohannon, 1988). However, the evidence on this question is mixed. For one thing, it appears that flashbulb memories occur primarily because the remembered event has many consequences for the person's life (McClosky, Wible & Cohen, 1988). When people get married or learn that a parent has died, they know that their life will change, often dramatically. As a result, they think about the event and form an elaborate network of associations with other areas of knowledge, thus making accurate retrieval of the event more likely (Cohen et al., 1990). In fact, flashbulb memories seem to be composed of three separate components: (1) information that is central to the critical event (for example, a close relative had a stroke and died), (2) peripheral details associated with critical event (such as who told you and how), and (3) personal circumstances (such as where you were). It may be that each of these components is forgotten at a different rate (Burke, Heuer & Reisberg, 1992; Pillemer, 1990).

Negative emotions can also have a very different effect on memory, motivating people *not* to recall particularly painful events, or to distort them in ways to make them less upsetting (Erdelyi, 1985). This phenomenon is known as *motivated forgetting.* In one study, for example, a subject kept a detailed record of daily events over a six-year period. When asked about them later, he recalled more than half of the positive events but only one-third of the negative ones (Wagenaar, 1986). Often people direct their attention away from upsetting situations (such as a severe accident), with the result that some of the details about them are never encoded. In general, people dwell on positive memories and make themselves feel better by trying to forget negative ones (Clore & Schwarz, 1994).

A report of motivated forgetting recently resulted in the conviction of George Franklin for the 1969 murder of his daughter's friend, Susan Kay Nason (Loftus, 1993b). Though Franklin's daughter Eileen witnessed the crime, she had no conscious recollection of the event for over twenty years. Then, while playing with her own daughter, Eileen remembered looking down at Susan just before she was murdered. She gradually recalled more details, many of which were verified by police records. Though motivated forgetting does occur, the validity of such reports must be carefully evaluated before they are accepted as fact (Loftus, 1993b).

Biological Bases of Memory

Psychologists who study memory tend to focus on the level of mental processing we have discussed in this chapter so far. However, some also consider the changes that take place in the brain when people encode, store, and retrieve information. Although our understanding is still quite limited, scientists are beginning to discover how and where brain cells change when memories are formed and stored.

Biochemical Mechanisms

Recall from Chapter 4 that communication between brain cells takes place at the synapses between axons and dendrites and that the communication depends on chemicals, called neurotransmitters, released at the synapses. There is evidence that new memories are associated with at least two kinds of changes in synapses.

First, new synapses may be formed, as we discussed in the Linkages section of Chapter 4. In animals that have been exposed to a complicated environment or required to learn a new motor task, neurons in certain parts of the brain develop more synapses, thus increasing communication both to and from other neurons (Black & Greenough, 1991; Crutcher, 1991). It is likely that these new synapses are involved in the storage of new memories.

Second, when a memory is stored, communication at existing synapses may be improved. The enhancement of existing synapses has been most clearly demonstrated in simple marine snails, such as *aplysia* and *hermissenda*. By studying individual synapses as a new memory is formed, researchers discovered that simultaneously activating two inputs to a synapse makes it easier for a signal from a single input to cross the synapse later (Goelet et al., 1986). Recent experiments indicate that similar strengthening, or **potentiation**, of synapses also occurs in other animals, including mammals (Brinton, 1991).

Because forming new synapses and strengthening existing ones require proteins, blocking the synthesis of new proteins blocks the formation of long-term memories (Matthies, 1989). As we described in Chapter 2, proteins are synthesized in accordance with instructions from the genes in the form of DNA sequences. Scientists are now studying the role of specific proteins in the formation of memories by altering the DNA sequences for those proteins in the genes of mouse embryos, then looking at the animals' memory capacity when these mutated mice mature. Some specific proteins have already been shown to affect learning ability by potentiating existing synapses (Silva et al., 1992; Grant et al., 1992), while others do so by aiding formation of new synaptic connections (Mayford et al., 1992; Qian et al., 1993).

In the hippocampus (see Figure 9.16), these changes appear to occur at synapses that use glutamate as a neurotransmitter. One type of glutamate receptor is initially activated only if the postsynaptic neuron is being stimulated by input from more than one neuron (Cotman, Monaghan & Ganong, 1988). After these multiple stimulations are repeated a number of times, this type of glutamate receptor appears to become sensitized so that input from just one neuron is sufficient to produce a response. Such a change in sensitivity could account for the development of conditioned responses, for example (see Chapter 8, on learning).

Figure 9.16
Some Brain Structures Involved in Memory
Neural activity in many different parts of the brain combine to allow us to encode, store, and retrieve memories. The complexity of the biological bases of these processes is underscored by recent research that shows, for example, that different aspects of a memory—such as the sights and sounds of some event—are stored in different parts of the cerebral cortex.

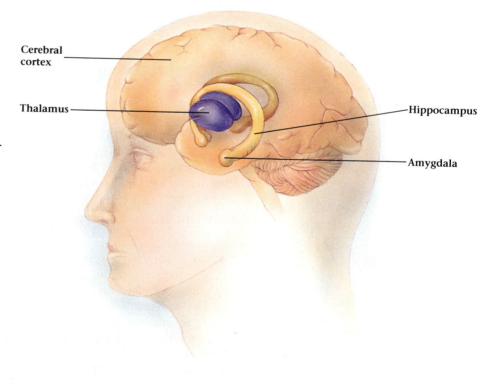

Acetylcholine also plays a prominent role in memory. The memory problems of Alzheimer's patients appear related to a deficiency in neurons that use acetylcholine and send fibers to the hippocampus and the cortex (Donegan & Thompson, 1991). Drugs that interfere with acetylcholine neurotransmission impair memory, and drugs or dietary supplements that increase the amount of acetylcholine in the brain sometimes improve memory in aging experimental animals and humans (Bartus et al., 1982). However, as mentioned in relation to "smart drugs" in Chapter 4, increasing acetylcholine levels is by no means a certain way to improve memory. Intense research is under way to better understand cholinergic systems and their relationship to memory (Martinez, Schulteis & Weinberger, 1991).

Brain Structures

Linkages: Where and how are memories stored? (a link to Biological Aspects of Psychology)

Where in the human brain do memory-related mechanisms occur? Do synapses develop and grow stronger only in special regions that store memories, or are memories distributed throughout the brain? It appears that memory involves both specialized regions for memory formation and widespread areas for storage (Zola-Morgan & Squire, 1990).

In the formation of new memories, several brain regions are vital (again, see Figure 9.16), including the hippocampus and nearby parts of the cortex and the thalamus (Squire, 1992). Damage to these areas results in anterograde amnesia (the inability to form new memories), as we described in the case of H.M., who had damage in the hippocampus and surrounding areas.

Interestingly, although patients cannot form new episodic memories following hippocampal damage, they can use their *procedural* memory. For example, H.M. was presented with a complicated puzzle on which mistakes are common and performance gradually improves with practice. Over several days his performance steadily improved, just as it does with normal people, and eventually he became virtually perfect. But each day on which he was given the puzzle, he insisted that he had never seen it before (Cohen & Corkin, 1981). Other researchers have also found intact procedural memories in patients who have anterograde amnesia for any new episodic material (Tulving, Hayman & Macdonald, 1991; Squire & McKee, 1992). Thus, while the hippocampus is crucial in the formation of new episodic memories, it appears that the procedural memory system may be governed by very distinct regions of the brain (Squire, 1992).

It is also clear that the hippocampus does not provide permanent long-term storage for memories. (If it did, H.M. would not have retained memories from the years before part of his hippocampus had been removed.) The hippocampus and thalamus send nerve fibers to the cerebral cortex, and it is in the cortex that memories are probably stored (Squire & Zola-Morgan, 1991). As described in Chapters 4 and 5, messages from different senses are represented in different regions of the cortex; specific aspects of an experience are probably stored near these regions. For example, memory for sounds is disrupted by damage to the auditory association cortex (Colombo et al., 1990). A memory, however, involves more than one sensory system. Even in the simple case of a rat remembering a maze, the experience of the maze involves visual experience, olfactory experience, specific movements, and the like. Thus, memories are both localized and distributed; certain brain areas store specific aspects of each remembered event, but many brain systems are involved in experiencing a whole event (Squire, 1986).

The more scientists learn about the physiology of memory, the more they see that no single explanation will account for all types of memory. No single brain structure or neurotransmitter is exclusively involved in memory formation or storage.

Improving Your Memory

In psychology, as in medicine, physics, and other sciences, practical progress does not always require theoretical certainty. Even though some basic questions about what memory is and how it works resist final answers, psychologists know a great deal about how people can improve their memories (Bellezza, 1981).

Classical Mnemonics

People with normal memory skills (Harris & Morris, 1984) as well as brain-damaged individuals (Wilson, 1987) can benefit from **mnemonics,** which are strategies for placing information into an organized context in order to remember it. For example, to remember the names of the Great Lakes, you might use the acronym HOMES (for Huron, Ontario, Michigan, Erie, and Superior). Verbal organization is the basis for many mnemonics. You can link items by weaving them into a story or a sentence or a rhyme. To help customers remember where they have parked their cars, some large garages have replaced section designations such as "A1" or "G8" with labels such as color names or months. Customers can then tie the location of their cars to information already in long-term memory—for example, "I parked in the month of my mother's birthday."

One simple but powerful method for remembering almost anything is the *peg-word system*. To use this method, first learn a list of words to serve as memory "pegs," such as "one is a bun, two is a shoe, three is a tree, four is a door, five is a hive, six is a stick, seven is heaven," and so on. Next, create an image or association between each item to be remembered and a peg word, as Figure 9.17 illustrates. In general, the more novel and vivid you make the images and the better they tie all of the objects together, the more effective they will be (Zoller, Workman & Kroll, 1989).

One of the authors was introduced to another popular mnemonic while he was an undergraduate. His roommate, who was known to brag a bit, said that he could remember any one hundred words if he had enough time to think about them. A bet of $100 was made, the words were read, and the author lost. The author's friend had used a powerful and ancient mnemonic called the *method of loci* (pronounced "low-sigh"), or the method of places. To use this method, first think about a set of familiar geographic locations. For example, if you use your home, you might imagine walking along the sidewalk, up the steps, through the front door, around all four corners of the living room, and through each of the other rooms. Next, imagine each item to be remembered in one of these locations. Whenever you want to remember a list, use the same locations, in the same order. As with the peg-word system, particularly vivid images seem to be particularly effective (Kline & Groninger, 1991). For example, tomatoes smashed against the front door or bananas hanging from the bedroom ceiling might be helpful in recalling items on a grocery list.

These and other mnemonic systems share one characteristic: each requires that you have a well-learned body of knowledge (such as peg words or locations) that can be used to provide a *context* for organizing incoming information (Hilton, 1986). The success of these strategies demonstrates again the importance of relating new information to knowledge already stored in memory.

Guidelines for More Effective Studying

Most of the procedures discussed so far were devised for remembering arbitrary lists. When you want to remember more organized material, such as a chapter in a textbook, the same principles apply (Palmisano & Hermann, 1991). Memory for text material is facilitated when people first create an over-

Linkages: How can principles of memory be applied to enhance learning? (a link to Learning)

Figure 9.17
The Peg-Word Technique
Gordon Bower (1973) suggested this example of the peg-word technique. Suppose you want to remember to pick up milk, bread, bananas, carrots, and coffee at the store. If you use this sample list of peg words, then the first word (number one) is bun. Since milk is the first item to be remembered, you might imagine milk being poured onto a bun. For the bread, you might imagine a shoe (number two) kicking a loaf of bread.

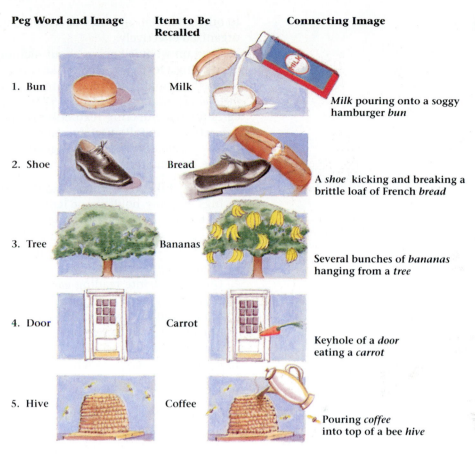

Peg Word and Image	Item to Be Recalled	Connecting Image
1. Bun	Milk	*Milk* pouring onto a soggy hamburger *bun*
2. Shoe	Bread	A *shoe* kicking and breaking a brittle loaf of French *bread*
3. Tree	Bananas	Several bunches of *bananas* hanging from a *tree*
4. Door	Carrot	Keyhole of a *door* eating a *carrot*
5. Hive	Coffee	Pouring *coffee* into top of a bee *hive*

Source: American Psychological Association, 1973.

all context for learning it, such as an outline (Glover et al., 1990). Resist the urge simply to read the material. Repetition may seem effective, because maintenance rehearsal keeps material in short-term memory; but it is not effective, no matter how much time you spend on it, for retaining information over long periods (Bjorklund & Green, 1992). Don't be subject to the "labor in vain effect" (Nelson & Leonesio, 1988). Instead, think about the material and elaborate it into an organized, meaningful context. What you learn will then be less subject to both proactive and retroactive interference (Anderson, 1990).

In addition, plan ahead and spend your time wisely. *Distributed practice* is much more effective than *massed practice* for learning new information. If you are going to spend ten hours studying for a test, you will be much better off studying for ten one-hour blocks (separated by periods of sleep and other activity) than "cramming" for one ten-hour block. By scheduling more study sessions, you will stay fresh and tend to think about the material from a new perspective each session. This method will help you elaborate the material and remember it.

Reading a Textbook More specific advice for remembering textbook material comes from a study that examined how successful and unsuccessful college students approach their reading (Whimbey, 1976). Unsuccessful students tend to read the material straight through; they do not slow down when they reach a difficult section; and they keep going even when they do not understand what they are reading. In contrast, successful college students monitor their understanding, reread difficult sections, and periodically stop to review what they have learned. In short, effective learners engage in a very deep level of processing. They are active learners, thinking of each new fact in relation to other material, and they develop a context in which many new facts can be organized effectively.

Based on what is known about memory, we suggest two specific guidelines for reading a textbook. First, make sure that you understand what you are reading before moving on (Hermann & Searleman, 1992). Second, use the *SQ3R method* (Thomas & Robinson, 1972), which is one of the most successful strategies for remembering textbook material (Anderson, 1990). SQ3R stands for five activities to follow when you read a chapter: survey, question, read, recite, review. These activities are designed to increase the depth to which you process the information you read.

1. *Survey* Take a few minutes to skim the chapter. Look at the section headings and any boldface or italicized terms. Obtain a general idea of what material will be discussed, how it is organized, and how its topics relate to one another and to what you already know. Some people find it useful to survey the entire chapter once and then survey each major section in a little more detail before reading it.
2. *Question* Before reading each section, ask yourself what content will be covered and what information should be extracted from it.
3. *Read* Read the text, but think about the material as you read. Are the questions you raised earlier being answered? Do you see the connections between the topics?
4. *Recite* At the end of each section, recite the major points. Resist the temptation to be passive by mumbling something like, "Oh, I remember that." Put the ideas into your own words.
5. *Review* Finally, at the end of the chapter, review all the material. You should see connections not only within a section but also among the sections. The objective is to see how the author has organized the material. Once you grasp the organization, the individual facts will be far easier to remember.

At the end, take a break. Relax. Approach each chapter fresh. Following these procedures will not only allow you to learn and remember the material better but also save you considerable time.

Lecture Notes Lectures are very common in colleges and universities, but they are far from an ideal method for conveying information. Important details in lectures are usually remembered no better than unimportant ones (Cohen, 1989). In fact, jokes and parenthetical remarks in a lecture seem to be remembered far better than major topic statements (Kintsch & Bates, 1977).

Taking notes does help people remember what was said in a lecture (Peper & Mayer, 1978). Unfortunately, effective note-taking is not an easily acquired skill. By using what you know about memory, however, you can devise some simple strategies for taking and using notes effectively. ("In Review: Improving Your Memory" summarizes these tips for studying.)

A first step is to realize that, in note-taking, more is not necessarily better; it may be worse. Taking detailed notes of everything requires that you pay close attention to everything that is said—the unimportant as well as the important—and leaves little time for thinking about the material. In fact, the thinking involved in note-taking is often more important than the writing, because it provides a framework for the facts. Notetakers who concentrate on expressing the major ideas in relatively few words remember more than those who try to catch every detail (Howe, 1970). In short, the best way to take notes is to think about what is being said, draw connections with other material in the lecture, and then summarize the major points clearly and concisely.

Once you have a set of lecture notes, what should you do with them? Review the notes as soon as possible after the lecture so that you can fill in missing

In Review: Improving Your Memory

Domain	Helpful Techniques
Lists of items	Use mnemonics: Look for meaningful acronyms. Try the peg-word technique. Use the method of loci.
Textbook material	Follow the SQ3R system. Allocate your time to allow for distributed practice. Read actively, not passively.
Lectures	Take notes, but record only the main points. Think about the overall organization of the material. Review your notes as soon after the lecture as possible in order to fill in missing points.
Studying for exams	Write a detailed outline of your lecture notes rather than passively reading them.

details and decipher your scribbles. (As discussed earlier, most forgetting from long-term memory occurs within the first few hours after learning.) When the time comes for serious study, resist the urge to read your notes passively. Use them actively, as if they were a chapter in a textbook. Write a detailed outline. Think about how various points are related. Once you have organized the material, the details will make more sense and will be much easier to remember.

Future Directions

Our understanding of memory has advanced considerably since Ebbinghaus began experimental investigations of it over a hundred years ago. During the 1990s, particularly spirited debates will center on exactly how many types of memory there are (Koppenaal & Glanzer, 1990), whether there are distinct biological structures devoted to each (Squire, 1992), the degree to which biological research into the chemical and anatomical substrates of memory can be integrated with the development of parallel distributed processing (PDP) models (Martindale, 1991), and the degree to which implicit memory processes affect consciousness (Nelson, Schreiber & McEvoy, 1992).

Researchers will also be studying the enormously elaborate autobiographical records that each individual retains over a lifetime. How people develop a representation of themselves in memory (Klein & Loftus, 1993a), how they relate this knowledge to memories of their early childhood (Nelson, 1993), and how they use knowledge about themselves as guides to choosing a mate or deciding on other actions (Vorauer & Ross, 1993) are all questions being vigorously pursued.

Expect the results of this and other research to challenge many traditional assumptions about such phenomena as clinical amnesia. Consider, for example, the case of K.C. While riding his motorcycle about ten years ago, he suffered a severe brain injury, which resulted in a dramatic personality change and one of the densest amnesias ever reported (Tulving, 1993). Although K.C. can read, write, speak, and understand others normally, he suffers from virtually complete retrograde *and* anterograde amnesia. Yet when K.C. is asked to "guess" at his personality, his descriptions of himself before and after the accident are different, and each corresponds very closely to what family members say he was, and is, like. In other words, although K.C. has no episodic memory for events, he has a great deal of self-knowledge. Theorists will be using cases like this to better understand how specific events become dissociated from more general knowledge of who we are, what we like, how we are motivated, and so on (Klein & Loftus, 1993b; Schneider, Roediger & Khan, 1993; Tulving, 1993).

There are, of course, many other as yet unanswered questions. Courses on learning and memory provide an excellent starting place for learning more about the latest research, as well as for studying the basic principles of memory in more detail. Other relevant courses include cognitive psychology and experimental psychology.

Summary and Key Terms

What Is Memory?
Human memory depends on a complex mental system.

Types of Memory
Most psychologists agree that there are at least three basic types of memory. *Episodic memory* contains information about specific events in a person's life. *Semantic memory* contains generalized knowledge about the world. *Procedural memory* (also called skill memory) contains information about how to do various things.

Explicit and Implicit Memory
Most research on memory has concerned *explicit memory,* the processes through which people deliberately try to remember something. Recently, however, psychologists have also begun to examine *implicit memory,* which refers to the unintentional recollection and influence of prior experiences.

Basic Memory Processes
There are three basic memory processes. *Encoding* transforms stimulus information into some type of mental representation. Encoding can be *acoustic* (by sound), *visual* (by appearance), or *semantic* (by meaning). *Storage* maintains information in the memory system over time. *Retrieval* is the process of gaining access to previously stored information.

Models of Memory
Four theoretical models of memory have guided most research. According to the *levels-of-processing* model, the most important determinant of memory is how extensively information is encoded or processed when it is first received. In general, *elaborative rehearsal* is much more effective than *maintenance rehearsal* in learning new information because it represents a deeper level of processing. According to the *transfer-appropriate processing* model, the critical determinant of memory is not how deeply information is encoded but whether the encoding process produces memory codes that are later accessed at the time of retrieval. *Parallel distributed processing* (or *PDP*) models of memory suggest that new experiences not only provide specific information but also become part of, and alter, a whole network of associations. The *information-processing* model suggests that, in order for information to become firmly embedded in memory, it must pass through three stages of processing: sensory memory, short-term memory, and long-term memory.

How Do People Acquire Memories?
Sensory Memory
Sensory memory maintains incoming stimulus information in the *sensory registers* for a very brief time. *Selective attention,* which is the process of focusing mental resources on only part of the stimulus field, controls what information in the sensory registers is actually perceived and transferred to short-term memory.

Short-Term, or Working, Memory
Short-term memory, which is also known as *working memory,* has two major functions: it constructs and updates an internal model of the environment, and it provides a system in which people can store, organize, and integrate facts and thereby solve problems and make decisions. Different memory codes can be used to encode information into short-term memory, but acoustic codes seem to be preferred in most verbal tasks. Studies of the *immediate memory span* indicate that the capacity of short-term memory is approximately seven *chunks,* or meaningful groupings of information. Studies using the *Brown-Peterson procedure* show that information in short-term memory is usually forgotten within about twenty seconds if it is not rehearsed.

Long-Term Memory
Long-term memory normally involves a semantic coding process, which means that people tend to encode the general meaning of incoming information, not specific details, into long-term memory. The capacity of long-term memory to store new information is extremely large, and most theorists believe it is literally unlimited.

Distinguishing Between Short-Term and Long-Term Memory
The levels-of-processing model holds that the distinction between short-term and long-term memory is unnecessary, but several pieces of evidence suggest that there are two distinct systems. For example, although serial-position curves show both a *primacy effect* and a *recency effect* after immediate recall, the recency effect is eliminated if a distracting task is administered just before recall. Further evidence that information is transferred from short-term to long-term memory comes from clinical cases of *anterograde* and *retrograde amnesia.*

Why Do People Forget?

The Course of Forgetting
Hermann Ebbinghaus began investigating long-term memory and forgetting about a hundred years ago and introduced the *method of savings.* He found that (1) the rate of forgetting from long-term memory is fastest during the first several hours after learning and then slows down considerably, and (2) savings can be extremely long lasting.

The Roles of Decay and Interference
Decay and *interference* offer two possible mechanisms for forgetting. While there is evidence of both decay and interference in short-term memory, it appears that most forgetting from long-term memory is due to either *retroactive interference* or *proactive interference.*

Retrieving Memories

Retrieval Cues and Encoding Specificity
Retrieval cues help people remember things that they would otherwise not be able to recall. The effectiveness of retrieval cues follows the *encoding specificity principle:* cues help retrieval only if they match some feature of the information that was originally encoded.

Context and State Dependence
All else being equal, memory is best when one attempts to retrieve information in the same environment in which it was learned; this is called *context-dependent* memory. When a person's internal state can aid or impede retrieval, memory is said to be *state-dependent.*

Retrieval from Semantic Memory
Retrieval from semantic memory is usually studied by examining how long it takes people to answer world knowledge questions. It appears that ideas are represented as associations in a dense semantic memory network, and the retrieval of information occurs by a process of *spreading activation.* Each concept in the network is represented as a unique collection of features or attributes. The tip-of-the-tongue phenomenon and the feeling-of-knowing experience represent the retrieval of incomplete knowledge.

Constructing Memories
In the process of constructive memory, people use their existing knowledge to fill in gaps in the information they encode and retrieve. PDP models provide one explanation of how people make spontaneous generalizations about the world. They also explain the schemas that shape the memories people construct.

Linkages: Motivation, Emotion, and Memory
Motivation and emotion affect memory in several ways. The mood congruency effect refers to the fact that memory is generally best when one's emotional state at the time of encoding matches the emotional tone of the information acquired. In addition, very intense emotional experiences tend to produce "flashbulb memories," which are unusually vivid, detailed, and long lasting. Motivated forgetting is the tendency not to recall particularly painful events, or to distort them in ways that make them less upsetting.

Biological Bases of Memory

Biochemical Mechanisms
Research has shown that memory can result from (1) new synapses being formed in the brain, and (2) communication at existing synapses being improved, a process called *potentiation.* Several neurotransmitters appear to be involved in the strengthening that occurs at synapses.

Brain Structures
The hippocampus and thalamus are among the brain regions known to play a role in the formation of memories. These structures send nerve fibers to the cerebral cortex, and it is there that memories are probably stored. Any single memory involves information from more than one sensory system, and messages from the different senses are represented in different regions of the cortex. Thus, memories appear to be both localized and distributed. Certain brain areas store specific aspects of each event, but several brain systems are involved in experiencing a whole event.

Improving Your Memory

Classical Mnemonics
Mnemonics are devices that are used to remember things better. Two of the simplest but most powerful mnemonics are the peg-word system and the method of loci. They are useful because they provide a context for organizing material more effectively.

Guidelines for More Effective Studying
The key to remembering textbook material is to read actively rather than passively. One of the most effective ways to do this is to follow the SQ3R method: survey, question, read, recite, and review. Similarly, to take lecture notes or to study them effectively, organize the points into a meaningful framework and think about how each main point relates to the others.

Chapter 10

Thought and Language

Outline

Dr. Joyce Wallace, a New York City internist, was having trouble figuring out what was the matter with "Laura McBride," a forty-three-year-old woman. Laura reported pains in her stomach and abdomen, aching muscles, irritability, occasional dizzy spells, and general tiredness (Rouéché, 1986). The doctor's initial hypothesis was iron-deficiency anemia, a condition in which the level of oxygen-carrying hemoglobin in the blood is too low. There was some evidence to support that hypothesis. A physical examination revealed that Laura's spleen was somewhat enlarged, and blood tests showed low hemoglobin and high production of red blood cells, suggesting that her body was attempting to compensate for the loss of hemoglobin. However, other tests revealed normal iron levels. Perhaps she was losing blood through internal bleeding, but a stool test ruled that out. Had Laura been vomiting blood? She said no. Blood in the urine? No. How about abnormally heavy menstrual flow? No. During the next week, as Dr. Wallace puzzled over the problem, Laura's condition worsened. She reported more intense pain, cramps, shortness of breath, and severe loss of energy. This woman's blood was becoming less and less capable of sustaining her. But if it was not actually being lost, what was happening to it? Finally, the doctor looked at a smear of Laura's blood on a microscope slide. What she saw indicated that some poison was destroying Laura's red blood cells. What could it be? Laura spent most of her time at home, but her teenage daughters, who lived with her, were not affected at all. Wallace asked herself, "What does Laura do that the girls do not?" Well, she works with paintings, repairing and restoring them. Paint. Lead! She might be suffering from lead poisoning! When the next blood test showed a lead level seven times higher than normal, Dr. Wallace knew she was right at last.

To solve this medical mystery, Dr. Wallace relied on her ability to think, solve problems, and make judgments and decisions. She used these higher mental processes to weigh the pros and cons of hypotheses and to reach decisions about what tests to order and how to interpret them. She also consulted with the patient and other physicians using that remarkable human ability known as language.

The work of a physician is but one example of the thinking, decision making, problem solving, and linguistic communication that occurs in an unending stream in human beings all the time. These processes are involved in everything from a restaurant customer's choice between shrimp and roast beef to a president's decisions about how to promote economic recovery. How good are human judgments and decisions? What factors influence them? How are thoughts transformed into language? Psychologists have been studying these questions for many years. In this chapter, we introduce some of their findings and highlight the importance of their research (see the Linkages diagram). We first examine a general framework for understanding human cognition and then look at specific cognitive processes.

Studying the Mind

If you think that Dr. Wallace had a difficult time diagnosing Laura's illness, consider the situation faced by the astronauts on *Apollo 13*. As they approached the moon on April 17, 1970, they heard an explosion. An oxygen tank had ruptured. Was the damage so extensive that the mission should be aborted? Which systems still operated normally? The crew needed to figure out how to survive with the depleted oxygen supply and how to navigate despite the damage. As it turned out, the moon landing had to be scrubbed, but ways were found to conserve enough oxygen to sustain the crew until they could get back to Earth.

The physician's task may appear far removed from the concerns of astronauts, but the mental processes involved are surprisingly similar. In both situations, people perceive a complex pattern of incoming stimuli, evaluate that pattern, and make decisions about it. Often these processes occur so quickly and appear so complicated that the task of analyzing them may seem like trying to nail Jell-O to a tree. To understand what happens between the presentation of stimuli and the execution of responses, many psychologists study people as if they were information-processing systems.

An **information-processing system** receives information, represents the information with symbols, and manipulates those representations. According to this model, information from a stimulus is passed

323

Linkages

The questions in this diagram illustrate a few of the relationships between the topics of this chapter, thought and language, and other chapter topics. For example, sensation, perception, consciousness, and memory—all examined in earlier chapters—provide the raw materials for thinking. In this chapter we see how these basic capacities are combined as people reason, imagine, judge, and talk. The page numbers indicate where the questions in the diagram are discussed. The diagram shows just a sampling of the linkages among topics; other linkages to the study of thought and language are shown in the diagrams in other chapters. All linkage questions are repeated in the margin near where they are discussed. ■

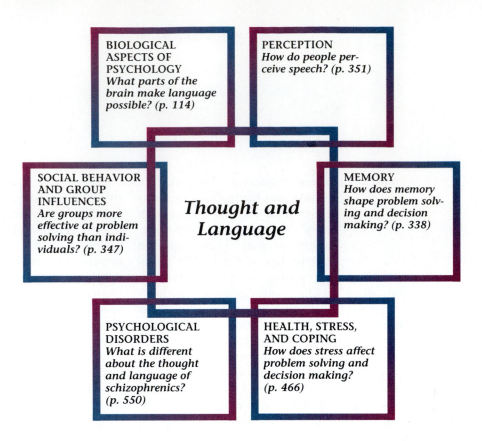

BIOLOGICAL ASPECTS OF PSYCHOLOGY
What parts of the brain make language possible? (p. 114)

PERCEPTION
How do people perceive speech? (p. 351)

SOCIAL BEHAVIOR AND GROUP INFLUENCES
Are groups more effective at problem solving than individuals? (p. 347)

Thought and Language

MEMORY
How does memory shape problem solving and decision making? (p. 338)

PSYCHOLOGICAL DISORDERS
What is different about the thought and language of schizophrenics? (p. 550)

HEALTH, STRESS, AND COPING
How does stress affect problem solving and decision making? (p. 466)

through several stages before a response is made, and at each stage, the information is transformed (Wickens, 1992). Figure 10.1 shows these stages.

In the first stage, information about the stimulus reaches the brain by way of the sensory receptors described in Chapter 5. This stage does not require attention. In the second stage, the information must be perceived and recognized, via perceptual processes detailed in Chapter 6. In the third stage, once the stimulus has been recognized, it is necessary to decide what to do with it. This stage demands more attention than does perception. The information may simply be stored in memory, as described in Chapter 9. If, however, the decision is made to take some action, a response must also be selected before the fourth stage—execution of the response—can occur. The response usually affects some part of the environment, providing new information that is "fed back" to the system to be processed.

Errors in Information Processing

When all goes well in the information-processing sequence, human behavior is a model of smooth efficiency. But errors can occur at various points, for various reasons. Sometimes errors result when a situation is misunderstood, as when you misread a test question or select the wrong approach to a problem. These errors, referred to as *mistakes* (Reason, 1990), result from failures during the early stages of information processing. Sometimes, errors occur later, during response selection and execution, as you intend to do one thing but let another action "slip" out. Perhaps you know the correct answer to a test question but mark the wrong spot on the answer sheet, or you intend to pour syrup on your pancakes but sleepily pour orange juice on them instead. Called *slips,* these errors in response selection and execution are particularly likely when performing well-practiced behaviors that occur more or less automatically without much conscious thought.

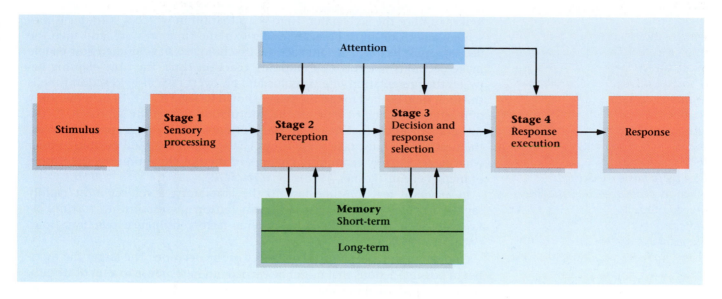

Figure 10.1
An Information-Processing Model
Information is transformed during each stage of information processing. Each stage requires some minimum amount of time for execution. Certain stages depend heavily on both short-term and long-term memory and require some attention—that limited supply of mental energy required for information processing to be carried out efficiently.

The information-processing model points to ways of preventing different kinds of errors (Reason, 1990; Wickens, 1992). For example, if a power plant is plagued by stage 1 mistakes because the amount of information coming from a vast array of instruments exceeds technicians' ability to correctly perceive all of it, the solution may be to reduce the information load by designing better displays. What if the problem involves stage 3 slips such as moving the wrong control handle? In that case the best course of action may be to redesign the instruments so that controls with different functions are located farther apart, have more distinctively shaped handles, or move in opposite directions (Norman, 1988).

Information-Processing Speed: Reaction Time

Imagine you are driving a little too fast and approach a green traffic light that suddenly turns yellow. In an instant you must decide whether to apply the

Linkages: The sensory-perceptual, response selection, and response execution stages of information processing sometimes take place so rapidly that people are not always aware of having completed them. This is especially true for skilled video-game players because, as described in Chapter 6, on perception, well-practiced tasks can be performed automatically.

brakes or floor the accelerator. Here is a situation in which a stimulus is presented, a decision must be made under extreme time pressure, and then the decision must be translated into action. Psychologists have studied how people make decisions like this by examining **reaction time**, the time elapsing between the presentation of a stimulus and an overt response. Reaction time is the total time needed for all the stages shown in Figure 10.1. In fact, the study of reaction time helped generate the information-processing approach. If cognition involves distinct stages, as the information-processing approach holds, then each stage must take some time. Therefore, one should be able to infer what stages exist by examining changes in **mental chronometry**, the timing of mental events (Posner, 1978).

In a typical reaction-time task in the laboratory, a subject must rapidly say a particular word or push a certain button in response to a stimulus. Even in such simple situations, several factors influence reaction times (Wickens, 1992).

One important factor is the *complexity* of the decision. The larger the number of possible actions that might be carried out in response to a set of stimuli, the longer the reaction time. The tennis player who knows that her opponent usually serves to the same spot on the court will have a simple decision to make when the serve is made and will react rapidly. In contrast, when she faces an opponent whose serve is less predictable, her reaction will be slower because a more complex decision about which way to move is now required.

Reaction time is also influenced by *stimulus-response compatibility*. If the spatial relationship between a set of possible stimuli and possible responses is a natural or compatible one, reaction time will be fast. If it is not, reaction time will be slower. Figure 10.2 illustrates compatible and incompatible relationships. Incompatible stimulus-response relationships are major culprits in causing slips in the use of all kinds of equipment (Norman, 1988).

Expectancy, too, affects reaction time. As noted in Chapter 6, expected stimuli are perceived more quickly than those that are surprising. Expectancy has the same effect on response time: people respond faster to stimuli that they anticipate and more slowly to those that surprise them. Similarly, responses people expect to make—such as hitting the brakes for a red light—occur more quickly than unexpected ones, such as warding off a purse-snatcher.

Finally, in any reaction-time task there is a *speed-accuracy tradeoff*. If you try to respond quickly, errors increase; if you try for an error-free performance, reaction time increases (Wickelgren, 1977). Sprinters who try too hard to anticipate the starting gun may have especially fast running times but may also have especially frequent false starts—errors—that disqualify them.

**Figure 10.2
Stimulus-Response Compatibility**

Suppose a cook is standing in front of an unfamiliar stove when a pot starts to boil over (a stimulus). The cook must rapidly adjust the appropriate dial to reduce the heat (the response). How fast the cook reacts may depend in part on the design of the stove. In the stove shown in (a), the dials are placed next to the burners, and a clear and visually compatible association determines which stimulus relates to which response. In (b), however, this compatibility does not exist, and reaction time will be much slower. Designers of automobiles, electronic equipment, photocopiers, and appliances pay a lot of attention to the relationship between buttons, levers, and dials and the actions that users want to accomplish with them.

(a) A compatible relationship   **(b) An incompatible relationship**

Picturing Information Processing: Evoked Brain Potentials

Research on reaction time has expanded understanding of decision making under time pressure, but reaction times cannot directly measure the details of what goes on between the presentation of a stimulus and the execution of a response. For example, reaction times alone cannot indicate how long it takes for response selection to begin, although there have been many ingenious efforts to make inferences about such things (Coles, 1989; Posner, 1978). To analyze mental events and their timing more directly, psychologists have turned to other methods, such as the electroencephalogram (EEG), to detect evoked brain potentials.

The **evoked brain potential** is a small, temporary change in voltage that occurs in response to discrete events. By recording a series of responses to the same event, researchers can determine the **average evoked potential.** Figure 10.3 shows an example. Each peak reflects the firing of large groups of neurons, within different regions of the brain, at different times during the information-processing sequence. Thus, the pattern of the peaks provides information that is more precise than overall reaction time.

For example, a large positive peak, called P300, occurs 300–500 milliseconds after a stimulus is presented. The exact timing of P300 is sensitive to factors that alter the speed of perceptual processes, like how hard it is to detect a stimulus. But the timing of the P300 is not affected by things that just alter the speed of response selection and execution, such as changes in stimulus-response compatibility (McCarthy & Donchin, 1979; Coles, 1989). Hence, the timing of a subject's P300 may provide an index of the duration of the first two stages shown in Figure 10.1.

Elements of Thought

Reaction times and evoked potentials yield clues about what is going on when you decide to stop or speed through that yellow traffic light, but they do not tell how you do it. Moreover, day after day you make decisions more complicated, more time consuming, and less well practiced than those made in reaction-time tasks. Like Dr. Joyce Wallace, the astronauts aboard *Apollo 13,* and millions of other people, you consider situations, imagine what might happen, daydream, and reminisce. In short, you think.

Figure 10.3
Average Evoked Potentials
Shown here is the average EEG tracing produced from several trials on which a subject's name was presented. Evoked potentials are averaged in this way so that the random variations in the EEG tracings are eliminated. The result is the appearance of a negative peak (N100) followed by a large positive peak (P300); by tradition, positive peaks are plotted as decreases while negative ones appear as increases on the tracings.

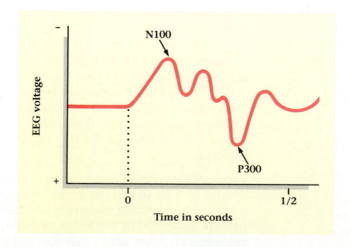

Decades ago, American behaviorist John Watson argued that thought is nothing more than covert speech. But if thought and speech are identical, why do people often have such a difficult time translating their thoughts into words? This intuitive case against Watson's view was bolstered in 1947 by a rather heroic experiment by Scott Smith (Smith et al., 1947). If Watson's view were correct, Smith reasoned, then paralyzing the speech muscles should disrupt thinking. Smith took a dose of curare, a potentially lethal drug that temporarily paralyzes the peripheral nervous system, including the vocal apparatus. The paralysis was so complete that Smith needed respirators to help him breathe. But despite the devastating effect of the drug on the speech system, Smith reported that he had lucid thoughts, could perform mental arithmetic, and understood what was going on around him just as well as before taking the drug. This and other experiments have made a convincing case that thought is more than covert speech.

Another way of looking at thought is to consider it as part of the information-processing model. In this view, cognitive processes involve a transformation and manipulation of information that has been encoded and stored in working memory and long-term memory. Thus, **thinking** can be defined as the manipulation of mental representations in order to form new representations.

What do people have in mind—what do they manipulate—when they think? What are the mental representations used in thought? A definitive answer has eluded both philosophers and psychologists. But as its definition suggests, thought depends on the memory processes discussed in the previous chapter. Indeed, because it occurs on a moment-to-moment basis, thought can be said to take place in working memory, where, like rehearsal, it requires attention and effort. But thought also depends on long-term memory for most of the information that it manipulates. This information may be organized in at least six ways—as concepts, propositions, mental models, schemas and scripts, words, and images. These provide the "raw material," or basic elements, of thought. People use these elements in different ways for various kinds of thinking—sometimes alone, and sometimes in combination. In the following sections we discuss these six elements and how people manipulate them in thought.

Concepts

Think about anything—dogs, happiness, sex, movies, fame, pizza—and you are manipulating concepts, one of the most basic ingredients of thought. **Concepts** are categories of objects, events, or ideas with common properties. Concepts may be concrete and visual, such as the concepts *round* or *red,* but they may also be abstract, such as the concepts *truth* and *justice.* To "have a concept" is to recognize the properties, relationships, or *features* that are shared by and define members of the category, and to ignore those that are not. For example, the concept *bird* includes such properties as having feathers, laying eggs, and being able to fly.

Concepts are vital to thought because they allow you to relate each object or event you encounter to a category that is already known. Concepts make logical thought possible. If you have the concepts *whale* and *bird,* you can decide whether a whale is a bird without having either creature in the room with you.

Types of Concepts   Some concepts (called **artificial concepts**) can be clearly defined by a set of rules or properties such that each member of the concept has all of the defining properties and no nonmember does. For example, the concept *square* can be defined as "a shape with four equal sides and four right-angle corners." Any object that does not contain all of these features simply is not a square. To study concept learning in the laboratory, psychologists often use artificial concepts because the members of the concept can be neatly defined (Trabasso & Bower, 1968).

In contrast, try to define the concept *home* or *game.* These are examples of **natural concepts,** concepts that have no fixed set of *defining* features but instead share a set of *characteristic* features. Members of a natural concept need not possess all of the characteristic features. One characteristic feature of the natural concept *bird,* for example, is the ability to fly; but an ostrich is a bird even though it cannot fly, because it possesses enough other characteristic features of bird (feathers, wings, and the like). Having just one bird property is not enough; snakes lay eggs and bats can fly, but neither are birds. It is usually the *combination* of properties that defines a concept. Outside the laboratory, most of the concepts people use seem to be natural rather than artificial.

The boundaries of a natural concept are fuzzy, and some members of the concept are better examples of the concept than others because they share more characteristic features of the concept (Rosch, 1975). A robin, a chicken, an ostrich, and a penguin are all birds. But a robin is a better example than the other three, because a robin can fly and is closer to the size and proportion of what most people, through experience, think of as a typical bird. A member of a natural concept that possesses all or most of its characteristic features is called a **prototype** or is said to be prototypical. Thus, the robin is a prototypical bird. As described in relation to network models of memory in Chapter 9, the more prototypical a member of a concept is, the more quickly people can decide if it is an example of the concept. Recall, for example, that people can decide more rapidly that "a robin is a bird" than that "a penguin is a bird."

Learning Concepts   Prototypes play a role in one of the most important cognitive tasks a child faces: learning the concepts he or she will need in order to think as an adult. Even adults continue to refine and elaborate concepts through experience. For example, the dimensions of the concepts *right* and *wrong* become more complex as moral development progresses. As we suggested in the chapter on development, people learn that it is sometimes wrong to follow orders and that disobedience in the face of injustice is sometimes right.

Some natural concepts are learned by identifying prototypes and then adding less typical examples as one learns more about the concept. This *prototype-matching strategy* is reflected in the illustrations in books for very young chil-

Both a space shuttle and a hot-air balloon are examples of the natural concept *aircraft,* but most people would probably think of the space shuttle, with its wings, as the better example. A prototype of the concept is probably an airplane.

The ease of concept learning can be predicted in part by the complexity of the concept and the kinds of rules involved in defining it (Bourne, 1967). The simplest classification rule is called the *one-feature rule,* in which only one attribute defines the concept. The next easiest classification rule to learn is the *conjunctive rule,* which is based on two or more attributes and requires that all of them be present. The slightly more difficult *disjunctive rule* holds that members of a concept must have one feature *or* another.

dren. The concept *house,* for example, is usually accompanied by a drawing of a square structure with windows and a chimney. An igloo is also a house, but it will take some time and experience for children who live in warm climates to learn that.

Children also learn concepts by forming and testing hypotheses about the rules defining them. For example, a child who sees a small, square grocery store might, on the basis of its size and shape, hypothesize that the grocery store is a house. This hypothesis will be disproved when he or she calls it a house and is corrected by a parent who explains the differences between houses and stores.

Representing and Combining Concepts

As thinking becomes more complex, concepts are often combined and represented in the other basic elements of thought.

Propositions   Thinking often involves relating concepts to one another, and these relationships are usually represented by propositions. A **proposition** is the smallest unit of knowledge that can stand as a separate assertion. Propositions, which usually take the form of sentences, may be true or false. They may represent the relationship between a concept and a property of that concept ("Birds have wings"), or they may relate two or more concepts to each other ("Dogs chase cats").

Mental Models   Especially when people think about physical processes and devices, the information manipulated may take the form of mental models (Medin & Ross, 1992). **Mental models** are clusters of propositions that represent people's understanding of how things (usually physical things) work; these models then guide their interaction with those things (Gentner & Stevens, 1983; Norman, 1988). For example, to understand the sequence of commands necessary to edit, save, and retrieve a computer file, people may use a mental model that consists of propositions such as "Each file must have its own name," "Pressing the F10 key stores the file in a place on the disk," and the like.

Sometimes, mental models are incorrect. For example, look at Figure 10.4. Which path do you think the marble will take after it leaves the tube? In one study, more than half of the college students tested incorrectly stated that it would follow the curved path rather than the straight one (McCloskie, 1983). The propositions that made up their mental model of how bodies move had the past motion of the ball influencing its current motion and denied one of Newton's basic laws of physics. When people hold incorrect mental models about physical illness and how it is cured, they may be less likely to follow prescribed medication or therapy regimens (Medin & Ross, 1992). Thus, those who fail to understand the persistent nature of viruses may stop taking medication when symptoms disappear, but well before the virus has been eliminated.

Schemas and Scripts   In Chapter 3, we defined *schemas* as basic units of knowledge, generalizations about the world that form through experience and serve as the building blocks of intellectual development. Schemas often embody the prototypes of concepts. Schemas about particular objects, events, and people also help us to understand, say, what cars are, how baseball is played, and how police officers usually dress. Like concepts, schemas serve as general representations of a large set of more specific examples. But as described in the memory chapter, schemas also generate *expectations* about objects, events, and people—that cars have four wheels, that baseball is played in the summer, that police arrest people.

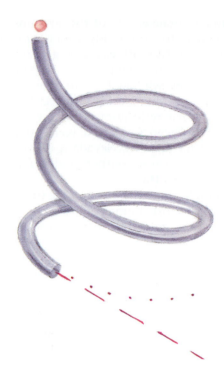

Schemas about familiar sequences of activities are called **scripts** (Shank & Abelson, 1977). If you have a mental script of the events that occur when you enter a restaurant to order dinner, mentally reviewing that script would help you think about what you should do in a particular situation. People also use scripts to interpret new information and events, putting them into the familiar framework of the script. Events that violate scripts may be misinterpreted or even ignored. You might, for example, step over a heart attack victim on the sidewalk because your script for walking down a city street tells you that someone lying on a sidewalk is drunk. Indeed, scripts are involved in the top-down processing (discussed in Chapter 6) that prompts people to recognize and react to expected events more quickly than to unexpected ones. If a bank customer pulls a gun and demands money, the script-violating aspect of the event—though attention getting—may slow observers' perception of the situation and interfere with decisions about a course of action.

Words   In the everyday process of thinking, people often translate concepts, propositions, mental models, and schemas and scripts into specific words. If you must figure out how long it would take three people to complete a job and you know how long it takes two people to finish it, you might find yourself silently restating the problem in words. Yet, although much of human thought seems to be language-bound, language is by no means necessary for thought to occur (Furth, 1964).

Images   Think about how an acquaintance would look in glasses. Did you conjure up a mental image? Often, thinking is based on the manipulation of visual images (Kosslyn, 1983). Research suggests that the manipulations performed on images are very similar to those that would be performed on the objects themselves (Kosslyn, 1983).

For example, Steven Kosslyn (1976) asked people to form a mental image of an object such as a cat and then asked questions about it, such as "Does it have a head?" and "Does it have claws?" The smaller the detail in question, the longer people took to answer the question, as if they were mentally zooming in on the detail necessary to answer the question. The finer the detail required by the question, the greater the zoom and the longer the response time.

Similarly, Roger Shepard and Jacqueline Metzler (1971) found evidence that people can imagine the rotation of objects like those shown in Figure 10.5. Their subjects' task was to decide if two objects were identical or mirror images of each other. Each addition to the difference in the angular orientation of the two objects added a constant amount to the time the subjects took to make the decision. Apparently, the subjects imagined the rotation of one of the objects at a constant rate until it was lined up in the same orientation as the other.

The need for mental rotation contributes to the problems people sometimes have if they are using a map and driving south in an unfamiliar city. Their visual image of the north-up map must be mentally rotated—like the objects in Shepard and Metzler's study—so that left and right on the map correspond with left and right as they look forward at the road. Designers of electronic maps for automobiles and aircraft are considering ways of allowing the map to rotate so that the direction one is heading is always "up" on the map (Aretz, 1991).

Even people who rarely use images in their thinking may employ them to navigate through a particular environment. Especially when that environment is new, people tend to imagine specific objects and landmarks as they try to go from one place to another. Eventually, as mentioned in the chapter on learning, after gaining a lot of experience with their environment, people acquire an overall *cognitive map* of it.

Figure 10.4
Applying a Mental Model
Subjects tried to imagine the path that the marble would follow as it exited the curved tube. Most subjects drew the incorrect (curved) path indicated by the dotted line, rather than the correct (straight) path, indicated by the dashed line (McCloskey, 1983).

Schemas, or learned generalizations about objects, events, and people, result in expectations about the world. People tend to be surprised when schema-based expectations are not met, as in the case of a motorcycle-riding dog or a three-wheeled automobile.

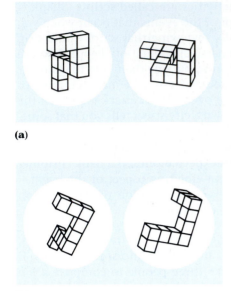

(a)

(b)

Source: Shepard & Metzler, 1971.

Figure 10.5
**Imagining the Rotation
of Objects**
Subjects were asked to decide if two
objects in pairs like these were identical or not. The time needed to decide about each pair increased with
the amount of rotation necessary to
put one object in the same orientation as the other. Apparently, to answer the question, the subjects imagined the rotation of the objects.
Here, the objects in (a) are identical;
those in (b) are different.

Useful as they are, cognitive maps are not accurate copies of the environment; they include systematic distortions. One distortion results from *rectangular bias,* a tendency to impose a rectangular north-south-east-west grid on
the environment (Wickens, 1992). For example, when asked to draw a map of
Paris, most Parisians straighten out the bends of the Seine River in an effort to
make it conform more closely to an east-west flow (Milgram & Jodelet, 1976).
The rectangular bias also distorts the sense of relative locations. If you were
asked where Reno, Nevada, is with respect to San Diego, California, you would
probably say northeast (Stevens & Coupe, 1978). After all, Nevada is east of
California, and Reno is north of San Diego. But because southern California
"bends" to the east, Reno is in fact northwest of San Diego.

In other words, people tend to simplify complex material. Most of the time,
this simplification is efficient and useful. But the costs humans must pay are
certain systematic biases, such as false perceptions guided by top-down processes and expectancies, distortions of memory, and distortions of spatial
thinking. As you will see in the next three sections, other forms of mental
simplification can distort reasoning, problem solving, and decision making.

Thinking Strategies

Whatever the elements of thought, the degree to which people achieve the
goals of thinking depends on how they manipulate those elements. If they
manipulate them to reach a valid conclusion, then these people are said to be
rational. If someone tells you that negotiating with terrorists only leads to
more terrorism, would you agree? To determine your response, you would
want to collect some evidence, but you would also need to exercise your powers of reasoning. **Reasoning** is the process by which people evaluate and generate arguments and reach conclusions. (The "Thinking Critically" section in
each chapter of this book is designed to highlight this vital process.)

Logical Reasoning: Deductive Logic

The mental procedures that yield a valid conclusion are known collectively as
logic. At the core of the study of logic lie the rules for evaluating **syllogisms,**
which are arguments made up of two propositions, called *premises,* and a conclusion based on those premises. For example, *All gun owners are people. All
criminals are people. Therefore, all gun owners are criminals.* Although the
premises are correct, the conclusion in this syllogism is false, because the
logic is faulty. If "All *A*'s are *B*" and "All *C*'s are *B*," it does *not* follow that "All
A's are *C.*"

Consider another example: *All psychologists are brilliant. The authors of this
text are psychologists. Therefore, the authors of this text are brilliant.* Do you agree?
The conclusion does follow logically from the premises, but the conclusion
might be at odds with your general knowledge of the world, because the first
premise is false. Obviously, reasoning depends on both knowledge of the
world and an understanding of what is logical. If premises are false, you should
reject a conclusion flowing from them as invalid, even if the logic of the argument is sound.

People are prone to make a number of errors in logical reasoning, which is
one reason why misleading advertisements can still attract sales and votes
(Solso, 1991). Psychologists have identified several sources of these errors.

1. *Bias about conclusions.* Consider the following syllogism: *America is a free
country. In a free country, all people have equal opportunity. Therefore, in America all people have equal opportunity.* People who agree with this conclusion

often do so because of their *prior belief* about the conclusion (McGuire, 1968). The same tendency often frustrates district attorneys prosecuting a member of the clergy or a harmless-looking senior citizen. Jurors may remain unpersuaded by logically sound arguments based on true premises simply because the logical conclusion (that a nice elderly woman poisoned her sister) is at odds with their schemas about such people and with their scripts about how the world operates. In other words, the conclusions that people reach are often based on both logical and wishful thinking (Evans, Barsten & Pollard, 1983).

2. *The conversion effect.* People often assume that premises are symmetrical— that if A implies B, then B implies A. This is wrong, of course: being a Democrat implies you are an American, but it does not follow that being an American implies you are a Democrat.

3. *Limits on working memory.* Solving syllogisms, particularly long ones, requires you to hold a lot of material in working memory while mentally manipulating it. This task is particularly difficult if elements in a syllogism involve negatives, as in "No dogs are nonanimals." If the amount of material to be manipulated exceeds the capacity of working memory, logical errors can easily result.

Cultural Differences in Logical Reasoning   Most of the time, logic and experience support the same conclusion. If they don't, the ideal option in most Western cultures is to rely on logic. But this ideal is not universal. In some cultures, direct experience is considered a surer guide than abstract logic.

As an example, consider the following syllogism-based question: *Ivan and Boris always eat together; Boris is eating; therefore, what is Ivan doing?* Most students in the United States would answer "eating," but a majority of Russian students say something like "I don't know. I wasn't there" (Solso, 1987). That answer is not incorrect; it is simply based on a qualitatively different line of reasoning, which argues that direct observation is the best, and perhaps only, way to establish the truth.

Alfred Bloom (1981) found that Chinese residents of Hong Kong showed a similar culturally based tendency to organize thought around known facts. His

No woman can be a combat pilot; this person is a woman, therefore, she should not be in combat. The logic of this syllogism is correct, but because the first premise is wrong, legislators and military policy makers who base their decisions on this logic alone will reach erroneous conclusions. Indeed, once excluded by law and regulation from military units likely to see combat, women's distinguished performance in dangerous close-support roles in Operation Desert Storm, for example, has led to recent changes that expand their role in combat.

subjects had a difficult time responding to questions such as "If the Hong Kong government were to pass a law requiring people to make weekly reports of their activities, how would you react?" Bloom's research indicated that the Chinese language does not allow easy expression of *counterfactual arguments,* which are arguments that consider hypothetical propositions that are not currently true. Such arguments are rarely found in Chinese newspapers.

So, although formal schooling tends to support logic-based formal operational thought (as mentioned in Chapter 3), the way people think is also shaped by the culture in which they learn to do it.

Inductive Reasoning: The Role of Heuristics in Forming Beliefs

In contrast to deductive reasoning, which involves determining the truth or falsity of conclusions on the basis of logical relations, inductive reasoning establishes a *degree of belief* in a hypothesis on the basis of many observations. This is just what scientists do as they collect evidence that can support or undermine a theory; it is what jurors do when weighing evidence for the guilt or innocence of a defendant.

People often make errors in inductive reasoning. A person might believe that a brand of car is terribly unreliable based only on the experience of one friend, or that a pain reliever works because a celebrity who has no expertise in medicine praised it in a commercial. Other errors in inductive reasoning are more subtle. Often these errors result from **heuristics,** which are "mental shortcuts" or "rules of thumb" by which people reach conclusions.

Suppose you are about to leave home but cannot find your watch. You might search for the watch in every possible location, room by room. This approach applies an **algorithm,** which is a systematic procedure that cannot fail to produce a solution. But to obtain the same outcome more quickly, you might instead use a heuristic: searching only in the places where your past experience suggests the watch might be. Similarly, in deciding which political candidates to vote for, your rule of thumb might be to support all those in a particular party—a heuristic—rather than researching the views of each individual.

Heuristics often guide judgments about what events are probable or what hypotheses are likely to be true. People use heuristics because they are easy and frequently work well. However, heuristics can also bias cognitive processes and cause errors. Amos Tversky and Daniel Kahneman have described three heuristics that people seem to use intuitively in making judgments (Tversky & Kahneman, 1974; Kahneman, Slovic & Tversky, 1982).

1. *The anchoring heuristic* People use the **anchoring heuristic** when they estimate the probability of an event, not by starting from scratch but by adjusting an earlier estimate. This strategy sounds reasonable, but the starting value biases the final estimate. Once people have fixed a starting point, their adjustments of the initial judgment tend to be insufficient. It is as if they drop a mental anchor at one hypothesis or estimate and then cannot move very far from that original judgment. Thus, if you thought that the probability of being mugged in New York is 90 percent and were then told that the figure is closer to 1 percent, you might reduce your estimate only to 80 percent. The anchoring heuristic presents a challenge for defense attorneys because, once affected by the prosecution's evidence (which is presented first), jurors' belief in a defendant's guilt may be difficult to alter (Hogarth & Einhorn, 1992). Similarly, as we discuss in Chapter 17, initial impressions are not easily shifted by later evidence.

2. *The representativeness heuristic* The **representativeness heuristic** involves basing your belief in a hypothesis or your conclusion that an example be-

longs to a certain class on the similarities between the example and a larger class of items, then determining whether the example represents essential features of the class. For example, suppose you encounter a man who is tidy, small in stature, wears glasses, speaks quietly, and is somewhat shy. If asked whether this person is likely to be a librarian or a farmer, what would you say? Tversky and Kahneman (1974) found that most of their subjects chose *librarian*. But the chances are that this answer would be wrong. It is true that the description is more similar to the prototypical librarian than to the prototypical farmer. But because there are many more farmers in the world than librarians, there are probably more farmers than librarians who match this description; therefore, a man matching this description is more likely to be a farmer than a librarian. In fact, almost any set of male physical features is more likely to belong to a farmer than a librarian.

Similarly, one study found that if a patient has symptoms that are similar to a common disease but are even more representative of a very rare one, physicians are likely to diagnose the rare disease (Christenssen-Szalanski & Bushyhead, 1981). On the basis of probability alone, it is more likely that the patient has the common disease, but the physicians used the representativeness heuristic in reaching a diagnosis. When using this heuristic, people ignore the overall probabilities and focus instead on what is representative or typical of the available evidence.

3. *The availability heuristic* Even when people use probability information to help them judge group membership or to assess a hypothesis, they may employ a third heuristic that can bias their thinking. The **availability heuristic** involves judging the probability that an event may occur or a hypothesis may be true by how easily the hypothesis or examples of the event can be brought to mind (Levi & Pryor, 1987). Thus, people tend to choose the hypothesis or alternative that is most mentally "available," much as you might choose which sweater to wear on the basis of which is on top in the drawer.

Like other heuristics, this shortcut tends to work well. After all, what people remember most easily *are* frequent events or hypotheses. However, the availability heuristic can lead to biased judgments, especially when mental availability and actual frequency fail to correspond. For example, television news reports showing the grisly aftermath of gang shootings and airline crashes may make these relatively rare events so memorable that people avoid certain cities or refuse to fly because they overestimate the frequency of crime or the probability of a crash (Slovic, 1984).

These three heuristics represent only some of the strategies that people use intuitively, and they create only some of the biases and limitations evident in human reasoning. (See "In Review: Tools of Thought" for a summary of the structures and transformations involved in thinking.) We discuss other biases and limitations in the following sections, as we take a closer look at two common goals of thinking: problem solving and decision making.

Problem Solving

If where you are is not where you would like to be, and the path to getting there is not obvious, then you have a *problem*. To solve a problem most efficiently, people should first diagnose it, then devise a plan to solve it, then execute the plan and, finally, evaluate the results (Bransford & Stein, 1993; Polya, 1957). However, the many unnecessarily replaced auto parts, unnecessary medical tests, and all-too-frequent misdiagnoses testify to the fact that people's problem-solving skills often leave much to be desired.

In Review: Tools of Thought

Tool	Definition	How It Is Used
Concepts	Categories of objects, events, or ideas with common properties	Concepts are related to one another through propositions.
Propositions	Smallest unit of knowledge that can stand as a separate assertion	Propositions are usually evaluated as to truth or falsity.
Syllogisms	Combination of two propositions (premises) and a conclusion	The conclusion is valid if it is logically consistent with correct premises.
Mental models	Clusters of propositions that represent people's understanding of how things work	Mental models guide people's interactions with things; they may be correct or biased.
Schemas and scripts	Generalizations about the world formed by experience; mental representations of a typical sequence of activity, usually involving people's behavior	Schemas represent a large set of specific examples and create expectations; scripts may be used to interpret what will happen or is happening in familiar situations—a component of top-down processing.
Words	Basic unit of langauge involved in much of our thinking	Words can be used to express concepts, propositions, syllogisms, mental models, and schemas and scripts.
Images	Visual mental representations of physical objects, events, and scenes	Images can be manipulated—rotated, expanded, and examined—to help thinking about spatial problems like those involved in navigation. Cognitive maps are images and may be biased.
Heuristics	Mental shortcuts or rules of thumb that help solve problems and reduce mental effort	Anchoring, representativeness, or availability heuristics can provide quick answers that are often correct, but may sometimes be biased.
Algorithms	Formal procedures that will eventually offer a solution to a problem if enough time and effort are spent	Algorithms are often avoided in thinking because they are inefficient.

Strategies for Problem Solving

When trying to get from a starting point to some goal, the best path may not necessarily be a straight line. In fact, obstacles may dictate starting in the opposite direction. So it is with problem solving. Sometimes, the best strategy is not to take mental steps aimed straight at your goal. Here are five strategies that may work better for some problems.

First, suppose a problem is so large that working memory cannot deal with all its elements at once. The best way to attack such a problem is through *decomposition:* divide it into smaller, more manageable subproblems. For instance, if you are working on a major paper, you might first construct an outline, then select the library materials most relevant to the outline, then summarize those materials, then begin writing a rough draft, and so on.

A second strategy is to *work backward.* Many problems are like a tree. The trunk is the information you are given; the solution is a twig on one of the limbs. If you work forward by taking the "givens" of the problem and trying to find the solution, it will be easy to branch off in the wrong direction. It may be more efficient to start at the end and work backward (Best, 1991). Consider, for example, the problem of planning a climb to the summit of Mount Everest (Bonington, 1976). The best strategy is to first figure out what equipment and supplies are needed at the highest camp on the night before the summit attempt, then how many people are needed to stock that camp the day before,

Linkages: Simply knowing about problem-solving strategies, such as decomposition, is not enough; as described in Chapter 12, on motivation and emotion, people must perceive the effort involved to be worth the rewards it is likely to bring.

Source: Drawing by Lorenze; © 1988 The New Yorker Magazine, Inc.

then how many people are needed to supply those who must stock the camp, and so on until the logistics of the entire expedition are established.

Third, find *analogies.* Many problems are similar to others you have encountered before. A supervisor may find, for example, that a seemingly hopeless impasse between co-workers may yield to the same compromise that worked last week in a family squabble. To take advantage of analogies, the problem solver needs first to recognize the similarities between current and previous problems, and then to recall the solution that worked before. Surprisingly, most people are not very good at drawing analogies from one problem to another (Medin & Ross, 1992). They tend to concentrate on the surface features that make problems appear different.

A fourth strategy to aid problem solving is to improve your *representation* of the "givens" of a problem. Often visualization is an important tool for representing these elements (Levine, 1988). The pictures shown in Figure 10.6, called *Venn diagrams,* are one example. To solve a syllogism, you can draw the Venn representation of the two premises and see whether the conclusion is consistent with both. Suppose you had to figure out the truth of the following syllogism: *All artists are beekeepers. Some beekeepers are chemists. Therefore, all artists are chemists.* Venn diagrams would show that this conclusion is false. More concrete images may also be used. Phillip Johnson-Laird and Mark Steedman (1978) found that subjects improved their performance on such problems by imagining sets of people who were dressed as beekeepers, artists, chemists, or some combination (for example, people wearing berets and holding a brush, with bees flying around them). Another study found that syllogisms were easier to solve if their premises involved concepts that could be visualized easily (like beekeepers) rather than those (like truth) that could not (Clemant & Falmagne, 1986).

Finally, for an especially difficult problem, allowing it to "incubate," by laying it aside for a while, is sometimes an effective strategy. A solution that once

Figure 10.6
Venn Diagrams
These diagrams represent three different but logically correct interpretations of the statement "Some *A*'s are not *B*'s." This statement is an equally valid description of *Some Democrats are not New Yorkers,* which is represented by (a); *Some federal employees are not senators,* which is represented by (b); or *Some Albanians are not Chinese,* which is represented by (c). Typically, however, people assume that only a diagram like (a) represents the statement and therefore assume that the statement also implies "Some *B*'s are not *A*'s."

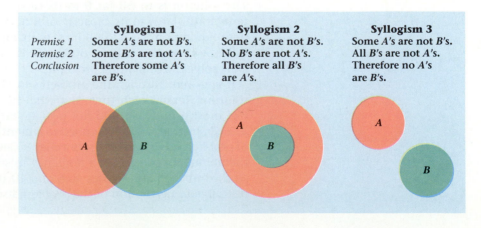

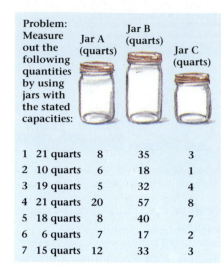

Problem: Measure out the following quantities by using jars with the stated capacities:	Jar A (quarts)	Jar B (quarts)	Jar C (quarts)
1 21 quarts	8	35	3
2 10 quarts	6	18	1
3 19 quarts	5	32	4
4 21 quarts	20	57	8
5 18 quarts	8	40	7
6 6 quarts	7	17	2
7 15 quarts	12	33	3

Figure 10.7
The Luchins Jar Problem
The problem is to obtain the volume of liquid shown in the first column by filling jars with the capacities shown in the next three columns. Each line represents a different problem. Such problems have been used to show that people often fall prey to mental sets that prevent them from using the most efficient solution.

Linkages: How does memory shape problem solving and decision making? (a link to Memory)

seemed out of reach may suddenly appear after a person engages in unrelated mental activity for a period of time (Silviera, 1971). Why? The benefits of incubation probably arise, not from subconscious processing, but from forgetting incorrect ideas that may have been blocking the path to a correct solution (Best, 1991).

Do these strategies work? They do. For example, Gary Bradshaw (1992) has studied how the Wright Brothers were able to solve the problem of heavier-than-air flight, when so many of their better-financed contemporaries failed. He concluded that the main factors were their ability to decompose the problem into its most important elements (stability, thrust, steering) and their selection of an appropriate analogy to represent the problem (the bird). These strategies led them to proceed from kites to gliders and then to the aircraft, rather than trying to develop air-propelled cars, as others did.

Problems in Diagnosis and Problem Solving

Many problem-solving difficulties occur at the start, during diagnosis, when a person forms and then tests hypotheses about the problem. In the following sections we describe four pitfalls to correctly diagnosing problems.

Multiple Hypotheses   Often, people begin to solve a problem with only a vague notion of which hypothesis to test. For example, there may be a dozen reasons why a car will not start. Which of these hypotheses should be tested and in what order?

People seem to have a difficult time entertaining more than two or three hypotheses at one time (Mehle, 1982). The limited capacity of working memory, discussed in Chapter 9, may be part of the reason. As a result, the correct hypothesis is often neglected. Which hypothesis a person considers may depend not on which is most likely but on the availability heuristic. In other words, the particular hypothesis considered may be one that is remembered most readily, which may not be the best hypothesis at all. Several characteristics might make one hypothesis easier to remember than others—for example, its simplicity, emotional content, and how recently it was experienced (Tversky & Kahneman, 1974). Thus, the auto mechanic troubleshooting your car might diagnose the problem as the same as one encountered the day before, simply because that hypothesis is most easily brought to mind.

Mental Sets   Sometimes people are so blinded by one hypothesis or strategy that they continue to apply it even when better alternatives should be obvious (a clear case of the anchoring heuristic at work). An example devised by Abraham Luchins (1942) is shown in Figure 10.7. The object of each problem in the figure is to use three jars with specified capacities to obtain a certain amount of liquid. For example, in the first problem you are to obtain 21 quarts by using three jars that have capacities of 8, 35, and 3 quarts, respectively. The solution is to fill Jar B to its capacity, 35 quarts, and then use its contents to fill Jar A to its capacity of 8 quarts, leaving 27 quarts in Jar B. Then pour liquid from Jar B to fill Jar C to its capacity twice, leaving 21 quarts in Jar B [$27 - (2 \times 3) = 21$]. In other words, the general solution is $B - A - 2C$. Now solve the remaining problems.

If you went through the problems in Figure 10.7, you found that a similar solution worked each time. But what happened with problem 7? If you are like most people, you did not notice that it has a simpler solution (namely, $A + C$). Instead, you succumbed to a **mental set,** the tendency for old patterns of problem solving to persist (Sweller & Gee, 1978). In the Luchins jar problem, the mental set consists of a tendency to stick with a strategy or solution that worked in the past. Figures 10.8 and 10.10 show that a mental set may also restrict your perception of the problem itself.

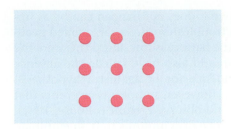

Figure 10.8
The Nine-Dot Problem
The task is to draw no more than four lines that run through all nine dots on the page without lifting your pencil from the paper. Figure 10.10 shows two ways of going beyond constraints to solve the problem.

Figure 10.9
An Example of Functional Fixedness
The task is to fasten together two strings that are hanging from the ceiling but are out of reach of each other. Several tools are available in the room. The solution is to take a tool, such as a pair of pliers, attach it to one of the strings, and swing it like a pendulum until that string can be reached while holding the other. The solution is not easily arrived at, however, because most people fixate on the usual function of the pliers as a hand tool rather than hypothesizing their role as a pendulum weight. People are more likely to use the pliers in this unusual way if the tools are scattered around the room rather than placed together in a tool box. Apparently, when the pliers are in a tool box, their function as a tool is emphasized, and the mental set becomes nearly impossible to break.

Yet another restriction on problem solving may come from experience with objects. Once people become accustomed to using an object for one type of function, they may be blinded to other ways of using it. Thus, experience may produce **functional fixedness**, a tendency to avoid using familiar objects in creative but useful ways. Figure 10.9 illustrates an example. An incubation strategy often helps to break mental sets.

The Confirmation Bias   Anyone who has suffered through a series of medical tests knows that diagnosis is not a one-shot decision. Instead, physicians choose an initial hypothesis on the basis of observed symptoms and then order further tests or evaluate additional symptoms to confirm or refute the hypothesis. This process may be distorted by the *confirmation bias:* humans have a strong bias to confirm rather than to refute the hypothesis they have chosen, even in the face of strong evidence against that hypothesis. In other words, people are quite willing to perceive and interpret data that support their hypothesis, but they tend to ignore information that is inconsistent with it (Ditto & Lopez, 1992; Levin, Kao & Wasserman, 1991). Thus, the confirmation bias may be seen as a form of the anchoring heuristic, in that it involves reluctance to abandon an initial hypothesis.

The 1979 accident at a nuclear power plant at Three Mile Island, in Pennsylvania, provides a dramatic example of confirmation bias (Adams, 1989; Rubinstein & Mason, 1979). A loss of coolant flowing to one of the reactors threatened to expose the radioactive fuel core and trigger a meltdown. The control-room operators could have formed either of two hypotheses about what was wrong inside the reactor. Either the water pressure in the reactor core was too high, creating the danger of an explosion, or it was too low, a condition that could lead to a meltdown. Several symptoms supported the correct hypothesis (the pressure was indeed low), but one defective meter indicated that the pressure was too high. During the first few minutes of the crisis, the operators paid attention only to the faulty indicator. Because they had used that meter to establish their original hypothesis of high pressure, they failed to appreciate symptoms of low pressure until after they had shut down an emergency pump that would have restored badly needed coolant. Their error made the situation far worse than it might have been (Adams, 1989; Rubinstein & Mason, 1979; Wickens, 1992).

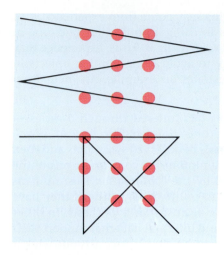

Figure 10.10
Two Creative Solutions to the Nine-Dot Problem
Many people find puzzles like this difficult because they fail to break out of mental sets that create artificial constraints on the range of solutions. Here, the mental sets involve the tendency to draw within the frame laid out by the dots and to draw through the middle of each dot. If you represented this problem in terms of the need to draw parallel and orthogonal lines, as the perceptual organization of the dots suggested, or to stay within the square, you were in trouble.

Ignoring Negative Evidence Often, what does *not* happen can be as important as what does. For example, when troubleshooting a car, a failed headlight might lead you to hypothesize that the battery is low. But if this were the case, other battery-powered equipment should also have failed. The absence of symptoms can provide important evidence for or against a hypothesis. Compared with symptoms that are *present,* however, symptoms or events that do not occur are less likely to be noticed and observed (Hunt & Rouse, 1981). People have a difficult time using the absence of symptoms to help eliminate hypotheses from consideration (Ashcraft, 1989).

Improving Problem-Solving Skills How can you improve your ability to solve problems? Perhaps the most obvious step you can take is to avoid errors in syllogistic reasoning. As mentioned earlier, Venn diagrams and vivid imagery can help. Other weaknesses in problem solving are more difficult to remedy. Psychologists have reasoned that it should be possible to train people not to fall prey to the biases that impair problem solving—to *debias* people, as Baruch Fischoff (1982) put it. Attempts to do this have produced some modest improvements in problem solving. For example, in one study, cautioning people against their tendency to anchor on a hypothesis reduced the magnitude of the confirmation bias and increased their openness to alternative evidence (Lopes, 1982).

Are there any easily taught techniques that will give you the problem-solving skill of an expert? Experts seem to avoid many of the pitfalls in problem solving. It is amazing how quickly a computer expert, for example, can find and solve a programming problem that has stumped a novice for hours. What do these experts bring to a situation that a novice does not? Knowledge based on experience, for one thing. Accordingly, experts frequently proceed by looking for analogies between current and past problems. More than novices, they can relate new information and new experiences to past experiences and existing knowledge (Larkin et al., 1981; Anderson, 1992; Bedard & Chi, 1992). The result is that experts can use existing knowledge to organize new information into chunks, as described in the chapter on memory.

By chunking many elements of information into a smaller number of more meaningful units, experts apparently can visualize problems more clearly and efficiently than novices. This efficiency is of critical importance for professional experts such as the fire chief who, arriving at the scene of a fire, must rapidly diagnose the nature of the fire and decide how best to attack it (Klein, 1989).

Experts can use their experience as a guide because they tend to perceive the similarity between new and old problems more deeply than novices (Chi, Feltovitch & Glaser, 1981; Hardimann, Dufresne & Mestre, 1989). Specifically, experts see the similarity of underlying principles, while novices perceive similarity only in superficial features. As a result, experts can more quickly and easily apply these principles to solve the new problem. In one study, for example, expert physicists and novice physics students sorted physics problems into groups (Chi, Feltovitch & Glaser, 1981). The novices grouped together problems that looked similar (such as those involving blocks lying on an inclined plane), while the experts grouped together problems that could be solved by the same principle (such as Newton's second law of motion).

Experience also gives experts a broader perspective on the problem domain, allowing them to perceive the whole problem "tree" so that they can work forward without error, thus avoiding the slower "working backward" strategy more suited to the novice (Bedard & Chi, 1992; Medin & Ross, 1992). Finally, successful problem solvers can explain each step in the solution, and can maintain awareness of precisely what is and is not understood along the way (Medin & Ross, 1992).

Are there shortcuts to achieving expertise? After carefully reviewing the literature, Richard Mayer (1983) concluded that claims of "instant" shortcuts to expertise must be viewed with some skepticism. The most important characteristic of any expert problem solver, he noted, is extensive knowledge in the problem area. Knowledge allows the expert to perceive the elements of a problem as a chunk, to understand the relations between problem elements, and to draw on past experience. In one study, teaching students to use general strategies, such as diagrams, did improve their ability to solve mathematical problems—but only after the students had mastered a good deal of mathematical knowledge (Schoenfeld, 1979). In short, there seems to be no substitute for putting in the hard work needed to acquire knowledge.

Although experts are often better problem solvers than novices, expertise also carries a danger: using past experience can lead to the traps of functional fixedness and mental sets. As a Zen proverb says, "In the mind of the beginner there are many possibilities; in the mind of the expert, few." The top-down, knowledge-driven processes described in the chapter on perception can bias you toward seeing what you expect or want to see. Thus, these processes can prevent you from seeing a problem in new ways. Indeed, there is a thin line between using past experience and being trapped by it.

These conclusions are supported by studies showing that, though experts may be more confident in their solutions (Payne, Bettman & Johnson, 1992), they are not always more accurate than novices in such areas as medical diagnosis, accounting, and pilot judgment (Bedard, 1989; Gard, 1989; Wickens et al., 1992).

The benefits of experience may also be limited by delay in the feedback about a solution (Brehmer, 1981; Dawes, Faust & Meehl, 1989). Often, experts receive information about the correctness of a proposed solution only long after they have forgotten how they came to it. As a result, they cannot use the feedback to improve problem-solving methods. Furthermore, confirmation bias may prevent experts from appreciating that a proposed solution was incorrect (Fischoff & Slovic, 1980); they may be less likely than novices to learn from mistakes (Hawkins & Hastie, 1990; Camerer & Johnson, 1991).

In short, experience alone does not ensure excellence at problem solving, and practice may not make perfect. Table 10.1 gives further reason for skepticism; it details some amazingly erroneous predictions by experts.

Problem Solving by Computer

In view of all of the weaknesses of human problem solving, some people hope that computers can take over some aspects of human thinking. (For a summary of our discussion of human problem solving, see "In Review: Solving Problems.") Scientists in the field of **artificial intelligence**, or **AI**, develop computer systems that imitate the products of human perception and thought. Even today, computers can, for example, beat all but the best chess masters (Solso, 1992). Indeed, there is good evidence that, for problems such as those involved in medical diagnosis, computers using fairly simple formulas can perform just as well as humans, if not better (Dawes, Faust & Meehl, 1989; Bradshaw & Shaw, 1992). Actually, a human-computer combination seems to work best, with humans establishing the presence and nature of the patient's symptoms and the computer *combining* this information to identify the most likely diagnosis. This conclusion also applies to the diagnosis of psychological problems (Nietzel, Bernstein & Milich, 1994). Scientists in AI have adopted two somewhat different approaches: symbolic reasoning and neural networks.

Symbolic Reasoning and Computer Logic   Early efforts at developing artificial intelligence focused on computers' enormous capabilities for logical,

Table 10.1
Some Expert Opinions

Experts typically have a large store of knowledge about their realm of expertise, but even confidently stated opinions based on this knowledge can turn out to be incorrect, as these examples from Christopher Cerf's *The Experts Speak* (1984) clearly show. The fallibility of such judgments was demonstrated again in 1993 when experts advising the FBI on its handling of a standoff with an armed religious cult in Texas predicted that cult leader David Koresh would not order his followers to kill themselves. When the FBI moved in, cult members set fire to their compound and all but nine of them died.

On the possibility of painless surgery through anesthesia:
"'Knife' and 'pain' are two words in surgery that must forever be associated. . . . To this compulsory combination we shall have to adjust ourselves." (Dr. Alfred Velpeau, professor of surgery, Paris Faculty of Medicine, 1839)

On the hazards of cigarette smoking:
"If excessive smoking actually plays a role in the production of lung cancer, it seems to be a minor one." (Dr. W. C. Heuper, National Cancer Institute, 1954)

On the stock market (one week before the disastrous 1929 crash that wiped out over $50 billion in investments):
"Stocks have reached what looks like a permanently high plateau." (Irving Fisher, professor of economics, Yale University, 1929)

On the prospects of war with Japan (three years before the December 1941 Japanese attack on Pearl Harbor):
"A Japanese attack on Pearl Harbor is a strategic impossibility." (Major George F. Eliot, military science writer, 1938)

On the value of personal computers:
"There is no reason for any individual to have a computer in their home." (Ken Olson, president, Digital Equipment Corporation, 1977)

On the concept of the airplane:
"Heavier-than-air flying machines are impossible." (Lord Kelvin, mathematician, physicist, and president of the British Royal Society, 1895)

syllogistic reasoning and symbol manipulation and on their abilities to follow general problem-solving strategies, such as working backward (Newell & Simon, 1972). This logic-based approach has been reasonably successful at addressing many problems through the development of expert systems. **Expert systems** are computer programs that solve problems in relatively restricted areas, like diagnosing infectious diseases, forecasting solar flares, or evaluating bank loan applications (Bradshaw & Shaw, 1992; Shortcliffe, 1983).

How do expert systems work? A problem-solving computer needs two basic elements: (1) an extensive knowledge base about the area in which problems are to be solved; and (2) an *inference engine,* a set of procedures for using the facts in the knowledge base to solve problems (Madni, 1988). The quality of these elements in expert systems depends largely on how well knowledge from human experts is captured and stored in computer code, a process known as *knowledge engineering.*

Valuable as it is, the logic-based approach to AI has important limitations. Expert systems, for example, are successful only in very narrowly defined fields. In spite of efforts to develop general problem-solving computers (Newell & Simon, 1972), the ability demonstrated in one domain (say, disease diagnosis) does not easily transfer to a different domain, such as locating mineral deposits. Success in each domain depends on a lot of "common-sense know-how" and on special heuristics that cannot be translated into general symbolic rules that the computer can shift from domain to domain. Specialized rules and information must be gathered from human experts in each domain (Chignell & Peterson, 1988). Thus "intelligent" computer reasoning seems to be very specific and narrow in scope.

Even within a domain, computers show limited ability. There are no ways of putting into computer code all aspects of the reasoning of human experts. Sometimes, the experts can only say, "I know it when I see it, but I can't put it into words" (Dreyfus & Dreyfus, 1988). Furthermore, computers still aren't very good at recognizing when standard rules don't apply or at realizing that a solution just doesn't make sense and that a new approach should be tried.

called *risky decisions* or *decisions under uncertainty.* Chance aside, psychologists have discovered many reasons why human decisions may lead to unsatisfactory outcomes, and we describe some of them here.

Evaluating Options

Suppose that you must choose between (1) an academic major that fascinates you but is unlikely to lead to a good job, or (2) a major that is less inherently interesting but virtually guarantees a high-paying career. Each option has both positive and negative features, or *attributes*—a fact that greatly complicates decision making. Deciding which car to buy, which college to attend, or even how to spend the evening are all examples of *multiattribute decision making* (Edwards, 1987). Often these decisions are complicated by difficulties in comparing the attributes and in estimating the probabilities of various outcomes.

Comparing Attributes   Multiattribute decisions can be difficult in part because the limited storage capacity of working memory does not permit people to easily keep in mind and compare all of the attributes of all of the options (Bettman, Johnson & Payne, 1990; Fischoff, Slovic & Lichtenstein, 1977). Instead, people tend to focus on the one attribute that is most important to them (Tversky, 1972). If, for instance, finishing a degree quickly is most important to you, then you might choose courses based mainly on curricular requirements, without giving much consideration to the reputations of the professors.

Furthermore, the attributes of the options involved in most important decisions cannot be measured in dollars or other relatively objective terms. Instead, people are forced to compare "apples and oranges." Psychologists use the term **utility** to describe the subjective, personal value of each attribute. In deciding on a major, for example, you would have to think about the positive and negative utilities of each attribute—such as the job prospects and intellectual stimulation—of each major. Then you must somehow weigh and combine these utilities. Will the positive utility of enjoying your courses be higher than the negative utility of risking unemployment?

Estimating Probabilities   Uncertainty adds other difficulties to the decision-making process: to make a good decision, you should take into account not only the attributes of the options but also the probabilities and risks of their possible outcomes. The economy could change by the time you graduate, closing many of today's job opportunities in one of the majors you are considering and perhaps opening opportunities in the other.

In studying risky decision making, psychologists begin by assuming that the best decision is the one that maximizes **expected value**, or the total amount of benefit you could expect to receive if the decision were repeated on several occasions. Suppose someone asks you to enter a raffle. You know that it costs $2 to enter and that the probability of winning the $100 prize is one in ten (.10). Should you enter? The expected value of entering is computed by multiplying the probability of gain (.10) by the size of the gain ($100); this is the average benefit you would receive if you entered the raffle many times. Next, from this product you would subtract the probability of loss, which is 1.0 (the entry fee is a certain loss), multiplied by the amount of the loss ($2). That is, $(0.10 \times \$100) - (1.0 \times \$2) = +\$8$. Since this eight-dollar expected value is greater than the expected value of not entering (which is zero), you should enter. However, if the odds of winning the raffle were one in a hundred (.01), then the expected value of entering would be $(.01 \times \$100) - (1.0 \times \$2) = -\$1$. In this case, since the expected value is negative, you should not enter the raffle.

Biases and Flaws in Decision Making

In fact, people do not always behave so as to maximize their expected values (Curim & Sarin, 1992), and it is important to consider some of the reasons why.

Gains, Losses, and Probabilities   For one thing, positive utilities are not mirror images of negative utilities. Instead, people generally feel worse about losing a certain amount than they feel good about gaining the same amount (Edwards, Lindman & Phillips, 1965), a phenomenon known as *loss aversion* (Tversky & Kahneman, 1991). Thus, they may be willing to expend more effort to try collecting a $100 debt than to try winning a $100 prize.

Further, large losses are seen as *disproportionately* more serious than small losses (Kahneman & Tversky, 1984). Though the prospect of losing $10,000 should, objectively, be seen as twice as bad as a $5,000 loss, people may do more than twice as much to avoid the larger loss. It is this reasoning in part that leads people to buy insurance—to avoid large losses, even though such losses are very unlikely.

It also appears that the utility of a specific gain depends not on the absolute increase in value but on what the starting point was. Suppose you can take some action to receive a coupon for a free dinner worth $10. Does this gain have the same utility as having an extra $10 added to a paycheck? The dollar amount is the same, but people tend to behave as if the difference in utility between $0 and $10 is much greater than the difference between $200 and $210. Thus, they may refuse to drive across town after work to earn a $10 bonus but would gladly make the same trip to pick up a $10 coupon. This tendency calls to mind Weber's law of psychophysics, discussed in Chapter 6, on perception. How much a difference in value means to you depends on how much you already have (Edwards, Lindman & Phillips, 1965); the more you have, the less it means.

Biases in the perception of probability are also a source of less than optimal decisions. Two such biases are especially interesting. The first is the tendency to overestimate rare probabilities—and to underestimate very frequent ones (Kahneman & Tversky, 1984). This bias helps explain not only why people buy insurance but also why they gamble and enter lotteries, even though the odds are against them and the decision to do so has a negative expected value. According to the formula for expected value, buying a $1 lottery ticket—when the probability of winning $4,000,000 is one in ten million—yields an expected value of −60 cents. But because people overestimate the probability of winning, they think there is a positive expected value. The tendency to overestimate the likelihood of unlikely events is amplified by the availability heuristic: vivid memories of rare gambling successes and the publicity given to lottery winners help people recall gains rather than losses when deciding about future gambles (Waagenaar, 1989). This same tendency can also be amplified by mood. People in a good mood tend to overestimate the probability that good things will happen to them, while those in a bad mood will exaggerate the likelihood of being mugged, losing a wallet, or other negative events (Wright & Bower, 1992).

Another bias relating to probability is called the *gambler's fallacy:* people believe that events in a random process will correct themselves. This belief is false. For example, if you flip a coin and it comes up heads ten times in a row, the chance that it will come up heads on the eleventh try is still 50 percent. Some gamblers, however, will continue feeding a slot machine that hasn't paid off much for hours, assuming it is "due." This assumption may be partly responsible for the resistance to extinction of intermittently reinforced behaviors, as described in Chapter 8.

Yet another factor underlying flaws in human decision making is the tendency for people to be unrealistically confident in the accuracy of their predictions. Baruch Fischoff and Donald MacGregor (1982) used an ingenious approach to study this bias. They asked people whether they believed that a certain event would occur—for example, that a certain sports team would win—and how confident they were about this prediction. After the events in question, the accuracy of the forecasts was computed and compared with the confidence assigned to the predictions. Sure enough, people's confidence in their predictions was consistently greater than their accuracy. This overconfidence operates even when people make predictions concerning the accuracy of their own memory (Fischoff, 1980).

Overconfidence about knowledge and judgments appears in many cultures, and in some more than others. In one study, students in China and the United States were asked to say how confident they were about their answers to general knowledge questions, such as "Do potatoes grow better in a cold or warm climate?" (Wright & Phillips, 1980). Both groups were overconfident, but the Chinese students were especially so. A study comparing Chinese, Japanese, and American students found the same result (Yates et al., 1989). Cultural differences in overconfidence may stem partly from culturally-based differences in how people think about their own judgments. For example, realistic evaluations of judgment accuracy requires thinking of reasons why you might be wrong as well as reasons why you might be right. Cultural traditions that strongly discourage Chinese students from challenging what they are told by teachers may also make them less likely than Americans to question what they tell themselves, and thus more likely to be overconfident. Indeed, compared to American and Japanese students, Chinese students were able to list the fewest arguments *against* their own judgments (Yates, Lee & Shinotsuka, 1992).

The moral of the story is to be wary when people in any culture express confidence that a forecast or decision is correct. They will be wrong more often than they think.

How Biased Are We?   Though the previous discussion suggests that human decision making is really quite flawed, psychologists are divided on the extent of the biases involved (Payne, Bettman & Johnson, 1992; Klein, 1989). While nearly everyone has made decisions they later regret, many human decisions are intended not to maximize expected value but to satisfy some other criterion, such as minimizing expected loss or producing acceptable outcomes with a minimum expenditure of time or mental effort (Bettman, Johnson & Payne, 1990). For example, it makes no sense to perform time-consuming mental gymnastics aimed at deciding what to wear each day.

It is also true that the "goodness" or "badness" of many decisions is difficult to assess, because so many of them depend on personal values (utilities), and these vary from person to person and from culture to culture. As suggested by our discussion of cultural factors in Chapter 2, people in individualist cultures may tend to assign high utilities to attributes that promote personal goals, whereas those in collectivist cultures might place greater value on attributes that bring group harmony and the approval of family and friends (Feather et al., 1992).

Are groups more effective at problem solving than individuals?

Linkages: Group Processes in Problem Solving and Decision Making

Problem solving and decision making are often done in groups. Couples, families, clubs, and all kinds of committees work on problems and decisions ranging from how to balance the budget to where to go on vacation. Labor and management teams hammer out contract agreements; juries deliberate the fate of defendants. Most dramatic, perhaps, is the work of groups in crisis, as exemplified by the air crew and ground personnel whose collective problem solving and decision making saved the lives of most of those on board a DC10 that crash-landed at Sioux City, Iowa, in 1989 (Predmore, 1991).

The processes that influence an individual's problem solving and decision making continue to operate when the individual is in a group, but group interactions also shape the outcome. For example, research by social psychologists reveals that the solution proposed by the most competent member is more likely to be adopted by the group if that member is initially supported by a second member (Laughlin & Ellis, 1986).

Typically, group discussions follow a consistent pattern (Hastie, Penrod & Pennington, 1984; Hoffman, 1979). First, various options are proposed and debated until the group sees that no one has strong objections to one option; that option becomes the minimally acceptable solution. From then on, the group criticizes any other proposal and argues more and more strongly for the first minimally acceptable solution, which is likely to become the group's decision (Hoffman & Maier, 1979). Thus the order in which options are considered can determine the outcome.

The outcome of group decisions is often more extreme—either riskier or more conservative—than the option that the average group member would have chosen (Kaplan, 1987); this tendency toward extreme decisions is called **group polarization.** For example, when groups bet on horses, they are more conservative than individuals (Knox & Safford, 1976). Two mechanisms apparently underlie group polarization. First, most arguments presented during the discussion favor the view of the majority, and most criticisms are directed at the minority view. Thus, it seems rational to those favoring the majority view to adopt an even stronger version of it (Isenberg, 1986). Second, as a group begins to agree that a particular decision is desirable, every member may try to establish himself or herself as being the most-committed group member; thus each individual may begin to advocate a more and more extreme position (Kaplan & Miller, 1987).

Are two, or even ten, heads better than one? Are people better at problem solving and decision making when they work in groups than on their own? If so, why? If not, why not? These are some of the questions about human thought studied by researchers in social psychology. In a typical experiment, a group of people is asked to solve a problem like the one in Figure 10.8 or to make a decision about, say, the guilt or innocence of a hypothetical defendant. Each person is asked to reach an individual answer and then to join with the others to try to reach a consensus. Such research indicates that a group's performance is higher than the average of its members working alone, but somewhat below the performance of its best members (Hastie, 1986; Faust, 1959; Sniezek, 1992).

Among the factors that improve or impair group performance are the following:

1. If the correct solution can be clearly demonstrated to the group, the "Eureka" phenomenon will probably occur, making it more likely that everyone in the group will accept the suggestion of the most competent member (who probably found the solution first). If the correct solution is not obvious, group performance will fall closer to the average of its members working alone.
2. Having more group members appears to increase the quality of group performance, but only up to a limit of about five. As group size increases beyond five, there is little improvement in performance (Davis, 1992). These results are important because they suggest that proposals to reduce the size

of trial juries from 12 to 6 would have little effect on the quality of decisions.

3. Group members who are confident or have high prestige or status are more likely than others to influence the group's deliberations; their opinions will probably be reflected in the group outcome (Hastie, Penrod & Pennington, 1984; Driskell & Salas, 1991). Whether these people will help or hurt the group's output depends on whether they express good ideas (Johnson & Torvicia, 1967). Ironically, there is little evidence that members with more competence (as opposed to status) always contribute more to group deliberations (Hastie, 1986).

4. The longer a group works together, and the more time it has to deal with its task, the closer group performance comes to the level of its most competent member. This is because, first, longer work periods give the group more opportunities to recognize and to be influenced by its most competent members (Laughlin, Vanderstoep & Hollingshead, 1991). Second, communication among the group members tends to improve with time. For example, airline crews do better at solving problems the longer they have worked together (Foushee & Helmreich, 1988).

Why do groups usually perform better on problem-solving tasks than the average of their members? Research on groups working on inductive reasoning problems, such as discovering the rule by which certain cards were grouped into a category (Laughlin, Vanderstoep & Hollingshead, 1991), has revealed three factors responsible for the superiority of group over individual performance. In a group it is more likely that (1) someone will identify the correct hypothesis from those that were plausible; (2) incorrect hypotheses will be rejected by someone; and (3) the information-processing load will be shared, so that relevant information lost from one person's working memory might be available in another's.

The quality of group problem solving and decision making will become even more important in future years as people increasingly use electronic mail, teleconferencing, and other high-tech equipment to interact as a group at a distance. It is not yet clear how "electronic groups" compare to their face-to-face counterparts. But there is some evidence that when group members communicate electronically, they tend to be more explicit and outspoken (a pattern dubbed "flaming"), and that their group solutions tend to be riskier and less conventional (Kiesler & Sproull, 1992).

Language

So far, our discussion of thinking has assumed that people have a crucial skill: the ability to use language. This ability provides both a vehicle for the mind's communication with itself and the most important means of communicating with others. Other animals can communicate, but none appears to have the means to do so with the systematic rules, precision, and infinite range of expression that human language allows. In this section we describe the elements that make up a language, how people use language to communicate, and how language is learned.

The Elements of Language

A **language** has two basic elements: symbols, such as words, and a set of rules, called **grammar,** for combining those symbols. These two components allow human language to be at once rule-bound and creative. With no more than 50,000 to 100,000 words (the vocabulary of the typical college student), humans can create and understand an infinite number of sentences. All of the sentences ever articulated are created from just a few dozen categories of sounds. The power of language comes from the way these rather unimpressive raw materials are organized according to rules. This organization occurs at several levels.

From Sounds to Sentences   Organization occurs first at the level of sounds. A **phoneme** is the smallest unit of sound that affects the meaning of speech. Changing a phoneme changes the meaning of a spoken word, much as changing a letter in a printed word changes its meaning. *Tea* has a meaning different from *sea,* and *sight* is different from *sit.*

Each spoken language consists of roughly thirty to fifty phonemes. English has twenty-six letters, but it has about forty phonemes. The *a* in *cat* and the *a* in *cake,* for example, are different English phonemes. Many of the letter sounds are phonemes (including *ell, aitch,* and *em*), but so are the sounds *th* and *sh.* Sounds that are considered one phoneme in English are different phonemes in other languages, and sounds that are different phonemes in English may be just one phoneme in another language. In Spanish, for example, *s* and *z* are considered the same phoneme.

Although changing a phoneme affects meaning, phonemes themselves are not meaningful. They are combined to form a higher level of organization: morphemes. A **morpheme** is the smallest unit of language that has meaning. Word stems like *dog* and *run* are morphemes, but so are prefixes like *un-* and suffixes like *-ed,* because they have meaning even though they cannot stand alone.

Words are made up of one or more morphemes. Words, in turn, are combined to form phrases and sentences according to a set of rules called **syntax.** For example, according to English syntax, a subject and a verb must be combined in a sentence, adjectives typically appear before the noun that they modify, and so forth. Compare the following sentences:

Fatal accidents deter careful drivers.

Snows sudden floods melting cause.

The first sentence makes sense, but the second sentence violates English syntax. If the words were reordered, however, they would produce the perfectly acceptable sentence "Melting snows cause sudden floods."

Even if you use English phonemes combined in proper ways to form morphemes strung together according to the laws of English syntax, you may not end up with an acceptable English sentence. Consider the sentence "Rapid bouquets deter sudden neighbors." It somehow sounds right, but it is nonsense. Why? It has syntax, but it ignores the set of rules, called **semantics,** that govern the meaning of words and sentences. For example, because of its meaning, the noun *bouquets* cannot be modified by the word *rapid.*

Surface Structure and Deep Structure   So far, we have discussed elements of language that are apparent in the sentences people produce. These elements were the focus of study for linguists for many decades. Then, in 1957, Noam Chomsky started a revolution in the study of language. He argued that if linguists studied only the language that people produce, they would never uncover the principles that account for all the sentences that people create. They could not explain, for example, how the sentence "This is my old friend" has more than one meaning. Nor could they account for the close relationship between the meanings of such sentences as "Don't give up just because things look bad" and "It ain't over 'til it's over."

To take these aspects of language into account, Chomsky proposed a more abstract level of analysis. Behind the word strings that people produce, called **surface structures,** there is, he said, a **deep structure,** an abstract representation of the relationships expressed in a sentence. For example, as Figure 10.11

Figure 10.11
Surface Structure and Deep
Structure
The listener on the right has interpreted the speaker's message in a way that differs from the speaker's intended deep structure. Obviously, identical surface structures can correspond to distinctly different deep structures.

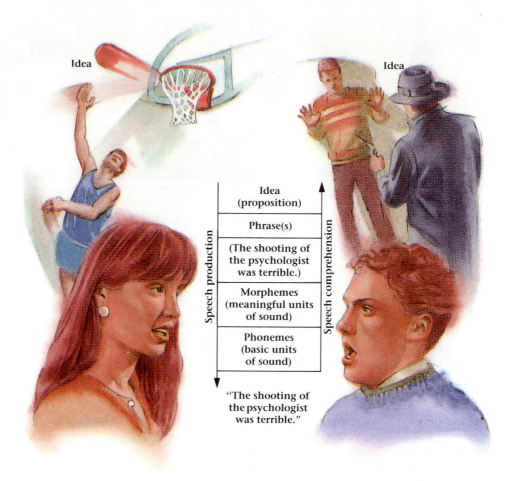

Idea

Idea

Speech production		Speech comprehension
	Idea (proposition)	
	Phrase(s)	
	(The shooting of the psychologist was terrible.)	
	Morphemes (meaningful units of sound)	
	Phonemes (basic units of sound)	

"The shooting of
the psychologist
was terrible."

illustrates, the surface structure "The shooting of the psychologist was terrible" may represent either of two deep structures: (1) that the psychologist had terrible aim, or (2) that it was terrible that someone shot the psychologist.

Chomsky also developed rules for transforming deep structures into surface structures and for relating sentences to one another. Since he proposed his first analysis of deep and surface structures, he and others have offered many revisions of those ideas. For our purposes, what is important about Chomsky's ideas is that they encouraged psychologists to analyze not just verbal behavior and grammatical rules but also mental representations.

Understanding Speech

When you listen to someone speak, your sensory, perceptual, and cognitive systems reconstruct the sounds into a representation of the speaker's idea. How? Like the perception of visual images discussed in Chapter 6, perception of speech depends not just on bottom-up processing of stimuli but also on top-down processing that uses knowledge, experience, and expectations to construct your own mental representation of what is said. This construction occurs at several levels.

Linkages: How do people perceive speech? (a link to Perception)

Perceiving Words and Sentences   When you listen to someone speak, you perceive the phonemes within a word as a continuous string, and you perceive a distinct pause between each word. In fact, as Figure 10.12 demonstrates, the pauses often actually occur *within* the words, not between them. You perceive breaks between the words because of the *top-down processing* discussed in Chapter 6. You know what the word should sound like, you recognize the sounds when they occur, and you perceive them as separate units, even if the physical stimuli are not separated.

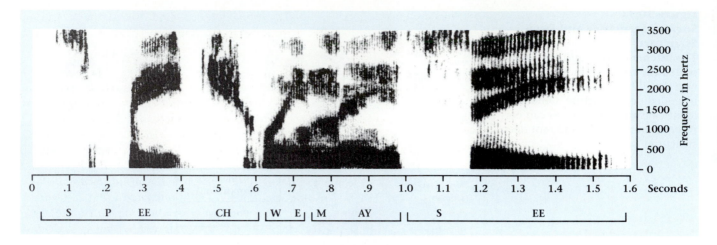

Source: Lachman, Lachman & Butterfield, 1979.

Figure 10.12
A Speech Spectrograph
This is a *speech spectrograph,* which represents the frequencies of speech sounds as they unfold over time. This spectrograph depicts the sounds of "Speech we may see." The vertical axis shows the frequencies of the speech sounds; the horizontal axis shows the passage of time. You would hear the phrase as four distinct words. Notice, however, that the pauses actually occur not between the words but between the *p* and *ee* in *speech* and again between *ee* and *ch* in the same word.

Linkages: Top-down perceptual processes, described in Chapter 6, help explain why speech in a language you do not understand sounds like a continuous stream that is spoken faster than your own language. Because your brain does not know where each unfamiliar word starts and stops, you do not perceive gaps between words—which, as shown in Figure 10.12, are often not physically there. Without these perceived gaps, speech sounds run together.

Similarly, when words are strung together as sentences, knowledge about both sentence structure and the world at large shapes the way they are processed. For example, people can remember the string "a haky deeb reciled the dison togently um flutests pav" more easily than the shorter string "Hak deem um flut recile pav togert disen," because the first is organized in a sentencelike structure (Epstein, 1961). And if you read the strings "Ruth eats fruit" and "Fruit eats Ruth" in a hurry, your mind will probably automatically reorganize the second string into another form, such as "The fruit was eaten by Ruth," so that it makes sense (Fillenbaum, 1974). In other words, people use their vast store of knowledge about grammatical structure, the meaning of words, and the world itself in order to process and understand language.

Using Context and Scripts   Suppose you have been able to program a computer with all the rules and knowledge discussed so far—with rules for combining spoken phonemes and written letters into words, with rules of syntax, a dictionary of the meanings of words, and an encyclopedia of knowledge of the world. Now you ask your unfortunate computer to make sense of the following conversation:

A: You goin' to the gym today to work out?
B: Well I *am* flabby, but only if I can hook a ride with Jim. It's a long way.
A: I'm afraid I heard his transmission's conked out, and it's at the shop.
B: Oh [pause], then I guess it won't work out.

The computer would be at a loss. For one thing, certain ambiguous terms have different meanings in different sentences (for example, *work out* in lines 1 and 4; *gym* versus *Jim* in lines 1 and 2). Because you understand the gist of the conversation, you understand the meaning of words or phrases like *hook, I'm afraid,* and *conked out,* and you know that the transmission is actually part of Jim's car, not a part of Jim. But these are things that the computer could not easily understand.

Difficulties in programming a computer to understand conversations arise first because the use of language relies on the *context* in which words are spoken or written. As noted in Chapter 6, people use context to interpret and impose meaning on stimuli—including language. A statement like "Wow, are you smart!" can be interpreted as "I think you're an idiot," depending on the context (and perhaps the tone of voice).

Individuals' personal histories—their educational and cultural backgrounds—also form part of the context that shapes their understanding of a communication. That background may determine the script that a listener uses to interpret ambiguous stimuli (Shank & Abelson, 1977). As an example, read the following:

Every Saturday night, four good friends get together. When Jerry, Mike, and Pat arrived, Karen was sitting in her living room writing some notes. She quickly gathered the cards and stood up to greet her friends at the door. They followed her into the living room but as usual they couldn't agree on exactly what to play. Jerry eventually took a stand and set things up. Finally, they began to play. Karen's recorder filled the room with soft and pleasant music. Early in the evening, Mike noticed Pat's hand and the many diamonds. As the night progressed the tempo of play increased. Finally, a lull in the activities occurred. Taking advantage of this, Jerry pondered the arrangement in front of him. Mike interrupted Jerry's reverie and said, "Let's hear the score." They listened carefully and commented on their performance. When the comments were all heard, exhausted but happy, Karen's friends went home. (Anderson et al., 1977)

In a laboratory study, music majors tended to interpret this passage as describing a music practice session; other students typically read it as the description of a card game (Anderson et al., 1977). The two groups used different scripts as a framework for interpreting ambiguous words like *stand* and *diamonds*. Building scripts into a computer's memory to resolve ambiguities is one of the greatest challenges in developing artificial intelligence systems for speech recognition (Shank & Hunter, 1985).

Conventions and Nonverbal Cues   Social *conventions,* commonly accepted practices and usage, also govern conversation. Though the words alone do not say so, "Will you join me in a cup of coffee?" conveys to most people an invitation to drink some coffee, not to climb into a giant cup. Similarly, someone who asks, "Do you know what time it is?" is not expecting a yes or no answer.

People are often also guided to an understanding of conversations by nonverbal cues. The frown, the enthusiastic nod, the bored yawn—all signal differences in understanding or interest that have an important bearing on the exchange of information. Thus it is not surprising that face-to-face conversations are more efficient than those in which speakers cannot see each other—a fact that should be considered when groups or teams must try to solve problems in separate locations, whether by telephone, electronic mail, or other means (Chapanis et al., 1977).

Learning to Speak: Stages of Language Development

Linkages: How do children learn to speak? (a link to Human Development)

Once people have learned to speak, they use the many rules of language naturally and automatically to generate correct sentences and to reject incorrect ones, even though most people would have a difficult time stating the rules. For example, in an instant you know that the words "Bei mir bist du schoen" are not English and that the string of words "Quickly peaches sheep deserve" is not an acceptable sentence. Children the world over learn language with impressive speed and regularity. Developmental psychologists have painstakingly detailed the steps in this process.

From Babblings to Words   **Babblings** are the first sounds infants make that resemble speech. These repetitions of syllables ("bababa," "mamama," "dadada") begin at about four months of age. Although meaningless to the baby, they are a delight to parents. During much of the first year, infants the world over make the same babbling sounds. At about nine months, however, babies who hear only English start to lose their German gutturals and French nasals. Beginning at this time, too, they begin to shorten some of their vocalizations to "da," "duh," and "ma." These sounds, which soon replace babbling, seem very much like language. Babies use them in specific contexts and with obvious purpose (Dore, 1978). Accompanied by appropriate gestures, they may be used to express joy ("oohwow") or anger ("uh-uh-uh"), to get something that is out of reach ("engh-engh"), or to point out something interesting ("dah!").

Ten- to twelve-month-olds can understand a few words—certainly more words than they can say (Huttenlocher, 1974). Proper names and object words are among the first words they understand. Often the very first word they understand is a pet's name.

Proper names and object words—words like *cookie, doggy, shoe, truck,* and *mama*—are also among the first words children are likely to say when, at around twelve to eighteen months of age, they begin to talk. Nouns for simple object categories (*dog, flower*) are acquired before more general nouns (*animal, plant*) or more specific names (*collie, rose*) (Rosch et al., 1976).

Of course, these early words do not sound exactly like adult language. Babies usually reduce them to a shorter, easier form, like "duh" for *duck* or "mih" for *milk.* Children make themselves understood, however, by using gestures, intonations, facial expressions, and interminable repetitions. If they have a word for an object, they "overextend" it to cover more ground. Thus, they might use *fly* for all insects and perhaps for other small things like raisins and M&Ms; they might use *dog* for cats, bears, and horses (Clark & Clark, 1977; Rosch, 1975). Children make these "errors" because their vocabularies are limited, not because they fail to notice the difference between dogs and cats or because they want to eat a fly (Fremgen & Fay, 1980; Rescorla, 1981).

Until they can say the conventional words for objects, children overextend the words they have, use all-purpose sounds (like "dat" or "dis"), and coin new words (like *pepping* for "shaking the pepper shaker"). This **one-word stage** of speech lasts for about six months. During this period, children build up their vocabularies a word at a time and tend to use words one at a time.

First Sentences   By eighteen to twenty-four months of age, children usually have a vocabulary of some fifty words. Then their language undergoes an explosion: they may learn several new words a day and begin to put words together. At first, children's sentences consist of two-word pairs. These two-word utterances are **telegraphic.** Brief and to the point, they leave out any word that is not absolutely essential. If she wants her mother to give her a book, the twenty-month-old might first say, "Give book," then, "Mommy give," and, if that does not work, "Mommy book." The child also uses rising intonation to indicate a question ("Go out?") and word stress to indicate location ("Play *park*") or new information ("*Big* car").

Three-word sentences come next in the development of language. They are still telegraphic, but more nearly complete: "Mommy give book." The child can now speak in sentences that have the usual subject-verb-object form of adult sentences. Other words and word endings begin appearing, too, such as the suffix *-ing,* the prepositions *in* and *on,* the plural *s,* and irregular past tenses ("It broke," "I ate") (Brown, 1973; Dale, 1976). Later, children learn to use the suffix *-ed* for the past tense ("I walked"). But once they have mastered the rule for using *-ed* to express past events, they overapply the rule to irregular verbs that they previously used correctly, saying, for example, "It breaked" or "It broked" or "I eated."

Children also expand their vocabularies with adjectives, although, at first, they do not always get the antonyms straight. For example, they are likely to use both *less* and *more* to mean "more" or *tall* and *short* to mean "tall" (Donaldson & Balfour, 1968). After acquiring some adjectives, children begin to use auxiliary verbs ("Adam is going") and to ask questions using *wh-* words (*what, where, whose, who, why, when,* in roughly this order). They begin to put ideas together in sentences ("Here's the ball I was looking for"). Until they are about five years old, however, children join events in the order in which they occur ("We went to the zoo and had ice cream") and understand sentences better if they follow this order (Clark, 1978; Kavanaugh & Jirkovsky, 1982). By age five, children have acquired most of the syntax of their native language.

How Is Language Acquired?

Despite all that has been learned in recent years about the steps children follow in learning language, mystery still surrounds the question of just how they learn it. Obviously, children pick up the specific content of language from the speech they hear around them; English children learn English, French children learn French. As parents and children share meals, playtime, and conversations, children learn that words refer to objects and actions and what the labels for them are. A recent study illustrated the influence of mothers' language training on their toddlers' vocabularies by comparing the language development of American and Japanese children (Tamis-LeMonda et al., 1992). American mothers were more likely than Japanese mothers to label and describe objects for their toddlers; their children, in turn, were more likely than Japanese children to understand and say these object words. But how do children learn syntax?

Linkages: Can the principles of conditioning explain how people learn to speak? (a link to Learning)

Conditioning, Imitation, and Rules   Our discussion of conditioning in Chapter 8, on learning, suggests one possibility: perhaps children learn syntax because of the way their parents reinforce them. In fact, however, parents usually are more concerned about *what* is said than about its form (Hirsch-Pasek, Treiman & Schneiderman, 1984). When the little boy with chocolate crumbs on his face says, "I not eat cookie," the mother is more likely to respond "Yes, you did eat it" rather than asking the child to say, "I did not eat the cookie," and then reinforcing him for using a grammatically correct form. Usually, adults do not give lessons on grammar. Observations suggest that reinforcement cannot fully explain the learning of syntax.

Modeling, or imitation, can help children learn syntax. They learn syntax most rapidly when adults offer simple revisions of their sentences, implicitly correcting their syntax, and then continue with the topic they are discussing. For example,

> *Child:* Mommy fix.
> *Mother:* Okay, Mommy will fix the truck.
> *Child:* It breaked.
> *Mother:* Yes, it broke.
> *Child:* Truck breaked.
> *Mother:* Let's see if we can fix it.

But if children learn syntax by imitation, why would they overgeneralize rules for plurals and past tenses? Why, for example, do children who at one time said "I went" later say "I goed"? Adults never use this form of speech. Its sudden appearance indicates that the child has mastered rules. In short, neither conditioning nor imitation seems entirely adequate to explain how children learn language. Children must still analyze for themselves the underlying patterns in the welter of language examples they hear around them.

A Critical Period for Language Acquisition   The ease with which children everywhere discover these patterns and learn language encourages some to argue that humans are "prewired," or biologically programmed, to learn language. This biological preparedness is reflected in the unique speech-generating properties of the human mouth and throat (Aitchison, 1983), as well as in brain regions discussed in Chapter 4, such as Broca's area and Wernicke's area (see Figure 4.17).

Chomsky (1957) has suggested that human beings possess an innate *language acquisition device—LAD* for short—that allows youngsters to gather ideas about the rules of language, without being aware of doing so. They then use these ideas to understand and construct their native language. This hypothesis is supported by the observation that children make up words like "goed," which shows that they understand language rules (in this case, the rule for forming past tense). It is also supported by the fact that there is some similarity in the syntax of all languages. Furthermore, children who are born deaf and never exposed to language make up gestural systems that have several properties of natural spoken language; for example, these systems place subjects before verbs and include agent-action-object sequences, such as "June saw Bob" (Goldin-Meadow & Feldman, 1977).

If there is a LAD, it does not guarantee that children will learn language. One unfortunate child was confined by her father to isolation and abuse in a small room until she was rescued at age thirteen and a half (Curtiss, 1977). Like the Wild Boy of Aveyron, whom we described in Chapter 3, she had not heard any language, and she could not speak at all when she was discovered. Even after six years of therapy and language training, she could not combine ideas into a single sentence. Such cases suggest that to acquire complex features of language, a person must be exposed to speech before a certain age. That is, there appears to be a *critical period* for learning language. In short, although genetic factors are largely responsible for the appearance and pace of language learning, certain environmental variables, such as delayed exposure to language, can alter the process significantly.

Bilingualism   Does trying to learn two languages at once, even before the critical period is over, impair the learning of either? Research suggests just the opposite. Children who are raised in a bilingual environment before the end of the critical period seem to show enhanced performance in each language (Hakuta & Garcia, 1989). There is also some evidence that *balanced bilinguals,* those who have roughly equal mastery of two languages, are superior to other children in cognitive flexibility, concept formation, and creativity (Padilla et

The existence of a critical period for language acquisition is supported by the fact that after the age of thirteen or fourteen, people learn a second language more slowly (Johnson & Newport, 1989) and virtually never learn to speak it without an accent (Lenneberg, 1967).

al., 1991). It is as if each language offers a slightly different perspective on thinking, and this dual perspective makes the brain more flexible.

The apparent benefits of bilingualism have important implications for U.S. school systems, where children from non-English speaking homes often receive instruction in their native language while taking classes in English. Although lack of control over school environments makes it difficult to perform true experiments on the effects of this practice, available evidence suggests that these bilingual programs facilitate educational achievement (Padilla et al., 1991). The evidence also suggests that rapid immersion in an English-only program may do considerable educational harm to children who enter school with no English-language background (Crawford, 1989).

Thinking Critically

Can Nonhumans Use Language?

Language, some say, is qualitatively different from all other forms of communication and sets humans apart from other creatures. Yet animals do use symbols to communicate. Bees dance in a way that indicates the direction and distance of sources of nectar; the grunts and gestures of chimpanzees signify various attitudes and emotions. The expressions of both creatures certainly qualify as communication, but they do not necessarily have the grammatical characteristics of language. Are any animals other than humans capable of learning language?

What am I being asked to believe or accept?

Over the last forty years, several researchers have asserted that nonhumans *can* master language. Chimpanzees and gorillas have been the most popular subjects, because at maturity they are estimated to have the intelligence of two- or three-year-old children, who are usually well on their way to learning language. Hence, if these animals are unable to learn language, their general intelligence cannot be blamed. Instead, failure would be attributed to the absence of a genetic makeup that permits language learning.

What evidence is available to support the assertion?

The question of whether nonhuman primates can learn to use language is not a simple one, for at least two reasons. First, language is more than just communication, but defining just when animals are exhibiting that "something more" is a source of debate. What seems to set human language apart from the gestures, grunts, chirps, or cries of other animals is grammar—as noted earlier, a set of formal rules for combining words. Using the rules of grammar, people can take a relatively small number of words and create with them an almost infinite number of unique sentences. Second, because of their muscular structures, nonhuman primates will never be able to "speak" in the same way that humans do (Aitchison, 1983). To test these animals' ability to learn language, investigators therefore must devise novel ways for them to communicate.

David and Ann Premack taught their chimp, Sarah, to communicate by placing different-shaped chips, symbolizing words, on a magnetic board (Premack, 1971). Lana, a chimpanzee studied by Duane Rumbaugh (1977), learned to communicate by pressing keys on a specially designed computer. American Sign Language (ASL), the language of the deaf that is based on hand gestures, has been used by Beatrice and Allen Gardner with the chimp Washoe, by Herbert Terrace with a chimp named Nim Chimsky (after Noam Chomsky), and by Penny Patterson with a gorilla named Koko. Kanzi, a bonobo or pygmy chimp studied by Sue Savage-Rumbaugh (1990), communicated through combinations of gestures and pointing to symbols on a board, while recognizing words spoken in human speech. Kanzi was a special case: he learned to communicate by listening to, watching, and "conversing" with his mother, then using what he had learned to interact with her trainers (Savage-Rumbaugh et al., 1986).

Studies of all six animals suggested that they could spontaneously use combinations of words to refer to things that were not present. Washoe, Lana, Sarah, Nim, Kanzi, and Koko all mastered from 130 up to 500 words. Their vocabulary included names for concrete objects, such as *apple* or *me;* verbs, such as *tickle* and *eat;* adjectives, such as *happy* and *big;* and adverbs, such as *again.* The animals combined the words in sentences, expressing wishes like "You tickle me" or "If Sarah good, then apple." Sometimes the sentences referred to things in the past. When an investigator called attention to a wound that Kanzi had received, the animal produced the sentence "Matata hurt," referring to the fact that Matata, his mother, had given him a disciplinary bite an hour earlier (Savage-Rumbaugh, 1990). Finally, all these animals seemed to enjoy their communication tools and used them spontaneously to interact with their caretakers, or other animals.

Of course, language also involves (1) combining words in a systematic way, according to the rules of a grammar, and (2) understanding or producing novel sentences. Most of the investigators mentioned here have argued that their animals have indeed mastered a crude grammar (Patterson, 1978; Premack, 1971; Greenfield & Savage-Rumbaugh, 1990). For example, if Washoe wanted to be tickled, she would gesture, "You tickle Washoe." But if she wanted to do the tickling, she would gesture, "Washoe tickle you." The correct placement of object and subject in these sentences suggested that Washoe was following a set of rules for word combination—in other words, a grammar (Gardner & Gardner, 1978). Furthermore, Savage-Rumbaugh observed several hundred instances in which Kanzi understood sentences he had never heard before. Once, for example, while his back was turned to the speaker, Kanzi heard the sentence "Jeanie hid the pine needles in her shirt." He turned around, approached Jeanie, and searched her shirt to find the pine needles. His actions would seem to indicate that he understood this new sentence the first time he heard it.

Are there alternative ways of interpreting the evidence?

Many of the early conclusions about primate language learning were challenged by Herbert Terrace and his colleagues in their investigation of Nim (Terrace et al., 1979). Terrace noticed many subtle characteristics of Nim's communications that seemed quite different from a child's use of language, and he argued that chimps in other studies demonstrated these same characteristics.

First, consider the size of sentences. Nim started with the ability to combine gestures into strings of two or three but never used longer strings that conveyed more sophisticated messages. Thus, the ape was never able to say anything equivalent to a three-year-old child's "I want to go to Wendy's for a hamburger, OK?"

Second, children use language spontaneously and creatively. They use it not only to communicate their wishes but also to express ideas and to guide their own activities. Terrace questioned whether the animals' use of language demonstrated these characteristics. Many of their sentences were requests for food, tickling, baths, pets, and other pleasurable objects and experiences. Is such behavior qualitatively different from the behavior of rats who run a maze to get food, or from that of the family dog, who learns to sit up and beg for table scraps? The apes are certainly intelligent, and their ability to string gestures together is impressive. However, argued Terrace, they lack the tendency to communicate in the spontaneous and expanding fashion of the

Several chimpanzees and gorillas have been taught to use American Sign Language (ASL). Here, Nim signs "play" upon seeing the teacher sign "out." Are these animals' remarkable accomplishments with ASL equivalent to human language acquisition?

Source: Courtesy of Professor H. S. Terrace, Columbia University.

two- or three-year-old child. Other researchers also concluded that chimps are not naturally predisposed to associate seen objects with heard words, as human infants are (Savage-Rumbaugh et al., 1983).

Finally, Terrace questioned whether experimenter bias influenced the reports of the chimps' communications. Consciously or not, experimenters who hope to conclude that chimps learn language might tend to ignore strings that violate grammatical order or to reinterpret ambiguous strings so that they make grammatical sense. If Nim sees someone holding a banana and signs, "Nim banana," the experimenter might assume the word order is correct and means "Nim wants the banana" rather than, for example, "That banana belongs to Nim," in which case the word order would be wrong.

What additional evidence would help to evaluate the alternatives?

Primate language studies are expensive and take many years. Accordingly, the amount of evidence in the area is small—just a handful of studies, each based mainly on a single subject. Obviously, more data are needed from more subjects exposed to a common methodology.

It is important, as well, to study the extent to which limits on the length of the primate's spontaneous sentences result from limits on working memory (Savage-Rumbaugh, 1990). If memory is indeed the main limiting factor, then the failure to produce progressively longer sentences does not necessarily reflect an inability to master language.

Research on how primates might spontaneously acquire language by listening to and imitating other primates, as Kanzi did, as well as naturalistic observations of communications among primates in their natural habitat, would also help scientists better understand their capacity to communicate.

What conclusions are most reasonable?

Psychologists are still not in full agreement about whether chimps can learn language. Two things are clear, however. First, whatever the chimp and gorilla do learn is a much more primitive and limited form of communication than that learned by children. Second, in chimps, unlike humans, the level of communication does not do justice to their overall intelligence; these animals are smarter than their "language" production suggests. Thus, the evidence to date favors the view that humans have language abilities that are unique but that under the right circumstances, and with the right tools, other primates can master many languagelike skills.

Knowledge, Language, and Culture

The language that people speak forms part of their knowledge of the world, and that knowledge, as noted in Chapter 6, guides perceptions. This relationship raises the question of whether differences among the languages of the world create differences in how people perceive and think about the world. We saw in Chapter 3, for example, that differences in the names for numbers in Korean and English may be partly responsible for differences between Korean and American children in mental arithmetic skills (Fusan & Kwon, 1992).

Benjamin Whorf claimed that language directly influences perception (Whorf, 1956). He noted, for example, that Eskimos have many more names for snow than do people in other cultures. Whorf proposed that this difference in language should lead to a greater perceptual ability at discriminating among varieties of snow. When the discrimination abilities of Eskimos and non-Eskimos are compared, there are indeed significant differences. However, these results leave another question unanswered: Are the differences in perception the *result* of differences in language?

One of the most interesting tests of Whorf's ideas was conducted by Eleanor Rosch (1975). She compared the perception of colors by Americans with that by members of the Dani tribe of New Guinea. In the language of the Dani, there are only two color names, one for dark, "cold" colors and one for lighter, "warm" ones. In contrast, English speakers have names for a vast number of different hues. Of these, it is possible to identify eleven *focal* colors; these are prototypes, the particular wavelengths of light that are the best examples of the eleven major color categories (red, yellow, green, blue, black, gray, white, purple, orange, pink, and brown). Thus, fire-engine red is the focal color for red. Rosch reasoned that, if Whorf's views were correct, then English speakers, who have verbal labels for focal colors, should recognize them better than nonfocal colors, but that for the Dani, the focal-nonfocal distinction should make no difference. In fact, however, Rosch found that both the Dani and the English-speaking Americans perceived focal colors more efficiently than nonfocal ones (Heider, 1972).

Thus, the fact that Eskimos have verbal labels for differences among snow textures that, say, Texans don't even perceive suggests a *correlation* between language and perception in various cultures. But it appears doubtful that language *causes* these differences in perception, as Whorf claimed. It seems far more likely that, beneath the differences in both language and perception, there is a third variable: frequency of use and the need for certain objects. Eskimos, for example, live in a snowy world. Their lives depend on making fine discriminations about the snow—between the snow bridge that is solid and the one that will collapse, for example. Hence, they learn to discriminate differences that are unimportant to people in warmer climates, and they attach names to those differences.

Future Directions

As some of the simpler, more easily observed phenomena associated with cognition yield their secrets, the challenge grows to understand the most complex

The Eskimo language has more names for various kinds of snow than does the English language. Eskimos are also far better than native English speakers at perceiving differing varieties of snow. Does this mean that language shapes perception? Or that environmental conditions and culturally based learning shape attention, perception, and the words used to describe important stimuli and events?

aspects of mental activity. For example, there are numerous questions about problem solving and decision making on the research agenda. How good or bad is human decision making? To what extent do decision-making heuristics save work and produce good results? What circumstances cause people to use particular strategies and heuristics in making decisions (Payne, Bettman & Johnson, 1992)? Does laboratory research on decision making by, say, mock juries have applications outside the laboratory? Can debiasing procedures be used to improve decision making outside the laboratory? What is the value of the products now on the market that are supposed to help people make decisions (Wickens, 1992)?

The information-processing approach will continue to promote a better understanding of the sources of human errors and of ways of preventing them (Norman, 1988; Reason, 1990). Researchers in the field of *cognitive engineering,* a discipline within engineering psychology (see Chapter 1), are applying knowledge about how people think to the design and display of complex systems related to aviation, industry, and computers (Vicente & Rasmussen, 1992). They are asking, for example, how computer menus or electronic databases should be organized to be most compatible with users' mental models of programs and data (Allen, 1991; Seidler & Wickens, 1992).

The study of artificial intelligence will continue to expand. Although many remain skeptical that computers will ever be able to match human mental abilities (Graubard, 1988), efforts to achieve this goal have helped scientists to learn more about the human mind and to design computer-based expert systems that can help solve problems. For example, verbal narratives spoken by expert problem solvers as they work are being used to help create computer programs that will solve new problems in the same way the experts do. And research on neural networks and connectionism has linked the psychological study of perception and cognition with studies of electrophysiology and computer science (Hinton, 1992). Psychologists' involvement in future research in this area will lead not only to more sophisticated computers but also to a fuller understanding of complex mental processes. This understanding will be enhanced by research using techniques such as brain-wave recording and cerebral blood flow measurement to provide insights into relations between specific language functions and activity in different regions of the cerebral cortex (Damasio & Damasio, 1992).

In short, cognitive psychology is rapidly becoming one of the most exciting areas in psychology. To learn more about the research explosion taking place in the areas of thought, decision making, problem solving, and language, consider taking courses in experimental psychology, cognitive psychology (sometimes called *higher processes* or *thinking*), psycholinguistics, or engineering psychology (sometimes called *human factors*).

Summary and Key Terms

Studying the Mind

The *information-processing system* approach offers a general model of human cognition. According to this model, between the presentation of a stimulus and the execution of a response, information is received, transformed, and manipulated through a series of stages.

Errors in Information Processing

Errors occur because of failures at different stages of information processing. Mistakes occur when perception or understanding is incorrect. Slips, which are often associated with highly practiced skills, occur when the wrong response is selected.

Information-Processing Speed: Reaction Time

The time elapsing between the presentation of a stimulus and an overt response is the *reaction time*. Among the factors affecting reaction times are the complexity of the choice of a response, stimulus-response compatibility, expectancy, and the tradeoff between speed and accuracy. *Mental chronometry* is the timing of the mental events occurring during reaction times.

Picturing Information Processing: Evoked Brain Potentials

Using methods such as the EEG, psychologists can also measure mental events as reflected in *evoked brain potentials* and *average evoked potentials*.

Elements of Thought

Thinking involves the manipulation of mental representations. These representations take at least six forms: concepts, propositions, mental models, schemas and scripts, words, and images.

Concepts

Concepts are categories of objects, events, or ideas with common properties. They may be natural or artificial. *Artificial concepts* are precisely defined by the presence or absence of certain features. *Natural concepts* are fuzzy; there is no fixed set of defining properties determining membership in a natural concept. Concepts are learned by building up a *prototype* or by testing hypotheses about what defines membership in them.

Representing and Combining Concepts

The raw material of thought may also take the form of *propositions,* which are assertions that state how two or more concepts are related. Propositions can be true or false. *Mental models* are essentially large clusters of propositions describing people's understanding (whether accurate or inaccurate) of physical devices or processes. Schemas serve as general representations of the world and also generate expectations about objects, events, and people. *Scripts* are schemas of fa-

miliar patterns or sequences, usually involving human activities; they help people think about those activities and interpret new events. People often mentally translate concepts, propositions, mental models, and scripts into words. *Images* may also be manipulated when people think. Mental images can be mentally inspected, expanded, and rotated. Mental representations of real environments are often distorted and simplified in systematic ways.

Thinking Strategies

Reasoning is the process by which people evaluate and generate arguments and reach conclusions.

Logical Reasoning: Deductive Logic

Syllogisms are sets of propositions that include premises and conclusions based on the premises. To reach a sound conclusion, people should consider both the empirical truth or falsity of the premises and the *logic* of the argument itself. People are prone to logical errors; their belief in a conclusion is often affected by the extent to which the conclusion is consistent with their attitudes as well as by other factors, including cultural background.

Inductive Reasoning: The Role of Heuristics in Forming Beliefs

Errors in reasoning also stem from using *heuristics,* mental shortcuts or rules of thumb, rather than *algorithms,* which are more time-consuming procedures that always produce a solution. Three important heuristics are the *anchoring heuristic* (estimating the probability of an event by adjusting a starting value), the *representativeness heuristic* (categorizing an event by how representative it is of a category of events, regardless of how probable the category is), and the *availability heuristic* (estimating probability by how available an event is in memory).

Problem Solving

Steps in problem solving include diagnosing the problem, then planning, executing, and evaluating a solution.

Strategies for Problem Solving

Especially when solutions are not obvious, problem solving can be aided by the use of strategies such as decomposition, working backward, finding analogies, finding better ways to represent the problem, and allowing for incubation.

Problems in Diagnosis and Problem Solving

Many of the difficulties that people experience in solving problems arise when dealing with hypotheses. People do not easily entertain multiple hypotheses. Because of *mental sets* they may persevere in applying one hypothesis even when it is unsuccessful and, through *functional fixedness,* may tend to miss opportunities to use familiar objects in unusual ways.

People are reluctant to revise or change hypotheses on the basis of new data. People also fail to use the absence of symptoms as evidence in solving problems.

Improving Problem-Solving Skills

Limitations in problem solving can be addressed in various ways. Pictures or Venn diagrams help solve syllogistic reasoning problems. Training can eliminate some biases. Experts are superior to novices in problem solving because of their knowledge and experience. They can draw on knowledge of similar problems, visualize related components of a problem as a single chunk, and perceive relations among problems in terms of underlying principles rather than surface features. There is no shortcut to obtaining the extensive knowledge that is the main component of expertise. However, expertise itself can prevent the expert from seeing problems in new ways.

Problem Solving by Computer

Some specific problems can be solved by computer programs known as *expert systems*. These systems are one application of *artificial intelligence (AI)*. There are two approaches to AI. One focuses on programming computers to imitate the logical manipulation of symbols that occurs in human thought; the other (involving connectionist, or neural network, models) attempts to imitate the connections among neurons in the human brain. Current problem-solving computer systems deal successfully only with specific domains. They cannot draw insight from different areas, and they do not exhibit common sense.

Decision Making

Evaluating Options

Decisions are sometimes difficult because there are too many alternatives and too many attributes of each alternative to consider at one time. Furthermore, decisions often involve comparisons of *utility,* not of simple objective value. Decision making is also complicated by the fact that the world is unpredictable, which makes decisions risky. People should act in ways that maximize the *expected value* of their decisions.

Biases and Flaws in Decision Making

People often fail to maximize expected value in their decisions because losses are perceived differently from gains of equal size and because they tend to overestimate the probability of rare events, underestimate the probability of very frequent events, and feel overconfident in the accuracy of their forecasts. The gambler's fallacy leads people to believe that outcomes in a random process are affected by previous outcomes. People make decisions aimed at goals other than maximization of expected value; these goals may be determined by personal and cultural factors.

Linkages: Group Processes in Problem Solving and Decision Making

Group decisions tend to show *group polarization,* the selection of more conservative or radical outcomes than would have been chosen by the average group member. Group-decision and problem-solving performance tends to fall below the per-

formance of the most competent member, but above that of the average of the members working alone. Group performance rises toward that of the most competent member if the correct solution is apparent, as group size increases (up to around five members), if high-status members of the group, who hold more influence, are also the most competent, and as groups work together for longer periods of time. Group performance may be different when groups communicate remotely instead of face to face.

Language

The Elements of Language

Language consists of *words* or word symbols and rules for their combination—a *grammar.* Spoken words are made up of *phonemes,* which are combined to make *morphemes.* Combinations of words must have both *syntax* (grammar) and *semantics* (meaning). Behind the word strings, or *surface structures,* is an underlying representation, or *deep structure,* that expresses the relationship among the ideas in a sentence. Ambiguous sentences occur when one surface structure reflects two or more deep structures.

Understanding Speech

When people listen to speech, the perceptual system allows them to perceive gaps between words, even when these gaps are not physically present in the stream of sound. Syntax and semantics also help people understand spoken messages. To understand language generally and conversations in particular, people use their knowledge of the context and of the world. This knowledge is often described through scripts. In addition, communication in conversations is guided by conventions and aided by nonverbal cues.

Learning to Speak: Stages of Language Development

Children develop grammar according to an orderly pattern. *Babblings* and the *one-word stage* of speech come first, then *telegraphic* two-word sentences. Next come three-word sentences and certain grammatical forms that appear in a somewhat predictable order. Once children learn certain regular verb forms and plural endings, they overgeneralize rules. Children acquire most of the syntax of their native language by the time they are five years old.

How Is Language Acquired?

Conditioning and imitation both play a role in a child's acquisition of language, but neither can provide a complete explanation of how children acquire syntax. Humans may be biologically programmed to learn language, perhaps through an inborn language acquisition device, or LAD. In any event, it appears that language must be learned during a certain critical period if normal language is to occur. The critical-period notion is supported by research on second-language acquisition.

Knowledge, Language, and Culture

Though it has been suggested that language shapes perceptions, it is more likely that environmental conditions and demands shape one's attention to and knowledge of the world and that language evolves to describe in more detail those aspects of the world that are especially important in one's culture.

Chapter 11

Mental Abilities

Outline

Consider the following brief sketches that describe four young college students and some of their varying abilities and interests. Do any of these descriptions remind you of anyone you know? Do any of them sound like you?

- Jack is always getting into trouble, but he's generally able to talk his way out of it somehow. However, his "street smarts" are not reflected in his grades, which are barely average. Still, if you were in trouble, you could count on him to find a solution.
- Deneace is on a full scholarship, earns A's in all her courses, and stars on the basketball team. Though she's only a sophomore, she is making plans for graduate study in mathematics.
- Ruthie doesn't know much about history or geography, except about the places she's traveled to, but she has a wide range of interests and can talk to anybody about almost anything. In so doing, she makes other people feel good about themselves.
- Sherman is a "computer nerd." He works at the university computing center and expresses his artistic talent by writing software to create portraits.

Each of these people is talented, but in different ways. How would you rank them in terms of **mental ability**—the capacity to reason, remember, understand, solve problems, and make decisions? In Chapters 9 and 10 we discussed similarities in the ways that people carry out these activities, whether they are plumbers in New York or physicists in Moscow. In contrast, we focus here on the ways in which people such as Jack and Deneace *differ* in their ability to perform these activities, and why. (The Linkages diagram shows relationships to other chapters.)

In Western cultures, mental ability tends to be thought of in terms of intelligence. Deneace might score highest on standard intelligence tests, with their emphasis on remembering, reasoning, and verbal and mathematical abilities. But would standard tests reflect Ruthie's social skills, Jack's "street smarts," or Shermond's artistic ability? And should they? If you were looking for an employee or evaluating a student, what characteristics would you want a test to tap?

These are among the questions we consider in this chapter. The answers matter in part because intelligence tests are often used as gatekeepers—determining who is allowed into a special class, an exceptional school, a lucrative career-track job—and as tools for diagnosis and research. After discussing the qualities that make any test good or bad, we look at some of the tests that psychologists have developed for measuring intelligence. We discuss what intelligence test scores mean and how they are used. Finally, we look beyond the tests to consider what intelligence is and how it is related to other mental abilities.

Assessing Mental Abilities: Principles of Testing

Unless you are very unusual, you have taken innumerable tests in your life—IQ tests, school examinations, the Scholastic Aptitude Test (SAT), tests for a driver's license, perhaps even some of the personality tests described in Chapter 14. Why are tests so widely used? Any **test** is a systematic procedure for observing behavior in a standard situation and describing it with the help of a numerical scale or a system of categories (Cronbach, 1970).

A test has three major advantages over interviews and other means of evaluation. First, the administration, scoring, and interpretation of tests are *standardized;* that is, the conditions are as similar as possible for everyone who takes the test. Standardization helps ensure that no matter who gives and scores the test, the results are comparable; it reduces the chance that extraneous factors will distort the results. Insofar as the biases of those giving the test do not influence the results, a test is said to be *objective.*

Second, tests use *quantifiable* terms—scores—to summarize the test taker's performance. This characteristic allows testers to calculate **norms**, which are descriptions of the frequency of particular scores. Norms tell test administrators, for example, what percentage of high school students obtained each possible score on a college entrance exam and whether a particular IQ score or entrance-exam score is above or below the average score.

Third, tests are *economical* and *efficient*. Once a test has been developed, it can often be given to many people in less time and for less money than other ways of obtaining information.

Linkages

This diagram illustrates some of the relationships between the topic of this chapter, mental abilities, and other chapter topics. In chapters so far we have examined processes and capabilities that are basic to human psychology. With this chapter we take up another perspective, one that emphasizes the differences among people.

Much of the research on mental abilities has involved attempts to measure and predict those abilities through tests. As a result, the research has helped spur procedures for determining whether tests give consistent, unbiased results and whether they measure what they are intended to measure. As you will see, these same procedures are critical in other areas of psychology, especially in attempts to understand differences in personality.

These and other topics that link the study of mental abilities and other aspects of psychology are discussed in this or other chapters of the text. The diagram shows just a sampling of these links. The numbers in parentheses indicate where the questions are discussed in the text. ■

Linkages: What measures are used to evaluate tests of mental ability? (a link to Research in Psychology)

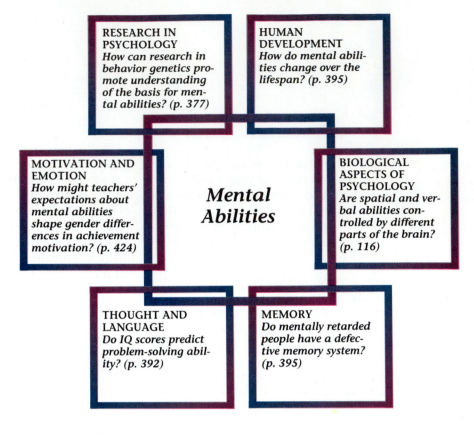

RESEARCH IN PSYCHOLOGY
How can research in behavior genetics promote understanding of the basis for mental abilities? (p. 377)

HUMAN DEVELOPMENT
How do mental abilities change over the lifespan? (p. 395)

MOTIVATION AND EMOTION
How might teachers' expectations about mental abilities shape gender differences in achievement motivation? (p. 424)

Mental Abilities

BIOLOGICAL ASPECTS OF PSYCHOLOGY
Are spatial and verbal abilities controlled by different parts of the brain? (p. 116)

THOUGHT AND LANGUAGE
Do IQ scores predict problem-solving ability? (p. 392)

MEMORY
Do mentally retarded people have a defective memory system? (p. 395)

Of course, some tests are better than others. Two characteristics are important in determining how good a test is: reliability and validity. Both are expressed in terms of a *correlation,* which is a measure of the relationship between two variables. For example, a high positive correlation between two variables, such as age and year in school, suggests that as one variable increases, so does the other. (Chapter 2 provides a fuller explanation of correlations.)

Reliability

If you stepped on a scale, checked your weight, stepped off, stepped back on, and found that your weight had increased by twenty pounds, you would be wise to try a different scale. A good scale, like a good test, must have **reliability**; in other words, the results must be repeatable or stable. If a person receives a very high score on a reasoning test the first time it is given but gets a very low score when the test is given again, the test is probably unreliable. The higher the reliability of a test, the less susceptible its scores are to insignificant or random changes in the test taker or the testing environment, such as the temperature of the room.

To estimate reliability, researchers obtain two sets of scores on the same test from the same people and compute the *correlation coefficient* between the scores. When the correlation is high and positive (usually above +.80 or so), the test is considered reliable. The two sets of scores can be obtained in several ways. The most obvious method is to give the same test to the same people on two occasions. This method is called *test-retest reliability.* Of course, the test-retest method can measure reliability only if the trait itself does not change during the time between the two tests. If a test measures short-term, or working, memory capacity and you learn how to chunk material in the period between the tests, your second score will be higher than the first, but not because the test is unreliable.

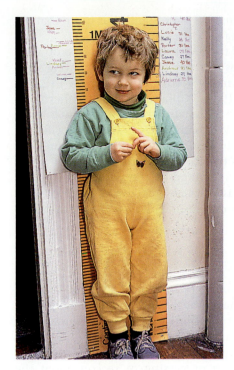

If a yardstick yields the same reading on two occasions on the same day, it is said to be a reliable measure of height. Tests that yield similar results on repeated occasions are also said to be reliable.

The test-retest method has an obvious problem: some people may benefit more than others from the experience of the first test, thus improving their scores on the second testing and making the test look unreliable. Other methods of calculating reliability alleviate this problem. One method uses an *alternate form* of the test on the second testing. Still another method is to use *split halves.* In this case, the test is given just one time, but when it is scored, the test is divided into two comparable halves. Each half is scored separately, and then the correlation between the two scores is calculated.

Validity

A test may be reliable and still not be valid. The **validity** of a test is the degree to which it measures what it is supposed to measure (Anastasi, 1976). No test has "high" or "low" validity in an absolute sense; its validity depends on how the test is being used. For example, a test that is excellent for measuring an individual's pain threshold would not be a valid measure of intelligence. In contrast, if people who score high on a test of creativity also produce award-winning artistic work, the test has high validity as a test of creativity. Thus, the extent to which scores on the SAT predict success in college is a measure of its validity.

Most forms of validity, as with reliability, can be measured with a correlation coefficient; but determining what the test scores should be correlated with may be troublesome. The answer depends on what the test is supposed to measure. There are three basic approaches.

One method is to analyze the degree to which the content of a test covers a representative sample of the domain to be measured; the resulting measure is called *content validity.* If an instructor spends only five minutes out of twenty lectures discussing the mating behavior of the tree frog and then devotes half of the midterm to this topic, you might want to question the content validity of the exam. Similarly, a test that measures only verbal fluency would not have acceptable content validity as an intelligence test. A content-valid test includes items relating to the entire area of interest, not just a narrow slice of it. Some researchers measure content validity by determining the percentage of experts who rate each item on a test as essential for measuring a particular trait or ability (Lawshe, 1975).

Another way of assessing validity measures *construct validity,* the extent to which scores on a test "behave" in accordance with a theory about whatever is being tested. For example, if your theory holds that intelligence is reflected in what you have learned and that people learn more as they get older, then older people should have higher scores on an intelligence test. If scores don't increase with age, the test has low construct validity with regard to this particular theory of intelligence.

A third approach is to measure *criterion-related validity,* the extent to which test scores correlate with another direct and independent measure of what the test is supposed to assess. This independent measure is called the *criterion.* To assess the criterion validity of a test of eye-hand coordination, for example, you might calculate its correlation with a test of skill at video games. When the goal is to predict future behavior, the criterion is some measure of future performance; criterion-related validity is then called *predictive validity.*

As an example, consider again the SAT. One way to measure its validity is to determine its ability to predict the grade-point average (GPA) of first-year college students. These grade-point averages, then, are the criteria, and the SAT is valid insofar as it is correlated with them. In fact, when the mathematical and verbal portions of the SAT are combined, its correlation with first-year college grade-point averages is about +.42 (Donlon, 1984). This figure is reasonably high, but in statistical terms it means that only about 18 percent of the variability in GPA is predictable from knowing SAT scores and that more than 80 percent of the variability in GPA is associated with other factors.

One reason the GPA-related validity of the SAT is not higher has to do with the criterion itself: the GPA. Certain areas of study have stricter grading standards than others; in other words, the mean grade-point averages in some courses are lower than in others (Ory, 1986; Williams, 1985). Furthermore, people with higher SAT scores tend to gravitate toward disciplines with tougher grading standards (Goldman & Widawski, 1976). Thus, the GPA for people in difficult courses is lower than it would be if uniform grading standards were applied, which in turn lowers the correlation of the GPA with SAT scores. In other words, criterion validity is limited by the stability of the criterion. If the criterion (in this case, GPA) is affected by factors other than what the test is supposed to measure, the test's criterion validity will be reduced.

Testing for Intelligence

Usually, it helps to begin the study of a concept by defining it, but defining intelligence has proved to be a difficult task. Psychologists do not agree on a single definition. Is intelligence the ability to think abstractly, or perhaps the ability to deal effectively with the environment? Robert Sternberg (1985) conceived of **intelligence** in terms of three characteristics: the possession of knowledge, the ability to use information processing to reason about the world, and the ability to employ that reasoning adaptively in different environments. On the other hand, E. G. Boring (1923) defined intelligence as "whatever an intelligence test measures." Pioneers in the study of intelligence focused on efforts to measure rather than define it, so we begin by examining those efforts.

A Brief History of IQ Tests

In the late 1800s Sir Francis Galton tried to test intellectual ability by measuring perceptual and motor abilities, such as how fast people responded to simple stimuli and how sensitive they were to pain. Other researchers soon concluded that these abilities had very little to do with intelligent behavior (Wissler, 1901). Alfred Binet, a French psychologist, took a different path; his test provided the model for today's intelligence tests.

In 1904 the French government commissioned Binet to find a way to identify children who might need special instruction. Two assumptions guided Binet when he created his set, or *battery,* of test items. First, he assumed that intelligence is involved in many reasoning, thinking, and problem-solving activities. Therefore, Binet looked for items that would highlight differences in children's ability to judge, reason, and solve problems (Binet & Simon, 1905). His test included tasks such as unwrapping a piece of candy, repeating numbers or sentences from memory, and identifying familiar objects (Frank, 1976). Second, Binet assumed that children's abilities increase with age. To select the items for his test, Binet administered potential questions to children of various ages and then categorized the questions according to the age at which the average child could answer them correctly. For example, a "six-year-old item" was one that a substantial majority of the six-year-olds could answer.

Thus, Binet's test included a series of *age-graded tasks.* By determining the number of items a child answered correctly at different age levels, the tester identified the child's *mental age.* Children whose mental age equaled their actual, or *chronological,* age were considered of "regular" intelligence (Reisman, 1976).

About a decade after Binet published his test, Lewis Terman at Stanford University developed an English version known as the **Stanford-Binet** (Terman,

Table 11.1
The Stanford-Binet

These are samples of the type of items included on the original Stanford-Binet test. In both Binet's original test and Terman's revision of it, an age level was assigned to each item.

Age	Task
2	Place geometric shapes into corresponding openings; identify body parts; stack blocks; identify common objects.
4	Name objects from memory; complete analogies (e.g., fire is hot; ice is _____); identify objects of similar shape; answer simple questions (e.g., "Why do we have schools?").
6	Define simple words; explain differences (e.g., between a fish and a horse); identify missing parts of a picture; count out objects.
8	Answer questions about a simple story; identify absurdities (e.g., in statements like "John had to walk on crutches because he hurt his arm"); explain similarities and differences among objects; tell how to handle certain situations (e.g., finding a stray puppy).
10	Define more difficult words; give explanations (e.g., about why people should be quiet in a library); list as many words as possible; repeat 6-digit numbers.
12	Identify more difficult verbal and pictured absurdities; repeat 5-digit numbers in reverse order; define abstract words (e.g., *sorrow*); fill in a missing word in a sentence.
14	Solve reasoning problems; identify relationships among points of the compass; find similarities in apparently opposite concepts (e.g., *high* and *low*); predict the number of holes that will appear when folded paper is cut and then opened.
Adult	Supply several missing words for incomplete sentences; repeat 6-digit numbers in reverse order; create a sentence using several unrelated words (e.g., *forest, businesslike,* and *dismayed*); describe similarities between concepts (e.g., *teaching* and *business*).

Source: Nietzel & Bernstein, 1987.

1916). Table 11.1 gives examples of the kinds of items included on the test. Terman added items to measure the intelligence of adults and, applying an idea suggested by William Stern, revised the method of scoring. A person's mental age was divided by his or her chronological age, and the quotient was multiplied by 100; the result was called the *intelligence quotient,* or *IQ.* Thus, a child whose mental age and chronological age were equal would have an IQ of 100, which is considered "average" intelligence. A ten-year-old child who scored at the mental age of a twelve-year-old would have an IQ of 12/10 × 100 = 120. From this method of scoring came the term **IQ test**, a name that is widely used for any test designed to measure intelligence on an objective, standardized scale.

The scoring method used with the Stanford-Binet allowed testers to rank everyone who took the test. This goal was important to Terman and others who popularized the test in the United States because, unlike Binet, they held that intelligence was a fixed and inherited entity; that different groups were favored with varying amounts of this thing called intelligence; and that IQ tests could pinpoint who did and who did not have the right genes to produce a suitable amount of intelligence. These beliefs led to some unfortunate outcomes, as enthusiasm for testing outpaced understanding of what was being tested.

Even before Terman developed the Stanford-Binet, psychologist Henry Goddard had translated Binet's test. In 1912 the U.S. immigration office asked Goddard to identify immigrants who were mentally defective. Goddard's test included questions that required familiarity not only with writing skills but also with U.S. culture, such as what a tennis court looks like. Today it is painfully obvious that the test was not a fair measure of the intelligence of immigrants or anyone else unfamiliar with the English language or with U.S. culture. But Goddard (1917) concluded from the test results that 83 percent of Jews, 80 percent of Hungarians, 87 percent of Russians, and 79 percent of Italians immigrating to America were "feeble-minded"!

The government used mental tests to deal with another problem as well: how to screen out army recruits of low mental ability and to assign appropriate jobs to new soldiers. When the United States entered World War I, a team of psychologists developed a test for these purposes. Again, the test favored people who were familiar with a particular culture. For example, one test item was "Five hundred is played with (*rackets, pins, cards, dice*)." Furthermore, the men were under stress and were tested in crowded rooms where instructions were not always audible. Forty-seven percent of those tested showed a mental age of thirteen or lower (Yerkes, 1921). From the test results C. C. Brigham (1923) incorrectly concluded that (1) from 1890 to 1915 the mental age of immigrants to America had declined and (2) the main source of this decline was the increase in immigration from Southern and Eastern Europe.

Brigham's conclusions, along with the results of Goddard's tests, became part of the "scientific" evidence that was used by the U.S. government in 1924 to limit immigration from various nations. Some people also used the test results to argue for segregation of African-Americans. And in some states people whose low IQ scores earned them the label of "imbecile" could be sterilized against their wishes or even without their knowledge (Gould, 1983).

In 1930 Brigham repudiated his statements about the army test results and acknowledged that much of what the tests measured was not innate intelligence but familiarity with American language and culture (Gould, 1983). Soon other psychologists recognized weaknesses in existing tests of mental abilities. Many concluded that intelligence could not be assessed by testing only verbal skills or, for that matter, by administering any one test.

A new test developed by David Wechsler (1949) addressed these concerns. Wechsler's test was made up of several subtests and improved on earlier tests in two key ways. First, some of Wechsler's subtests had little or no verbal content and reduced the extent to which answers depended on a particular culture. Second, the Wechsler test allowed the tester to develop a profile describ-

Comparison of verbal and performance scores on the Wechsler scales can provide useful information. For example, a high score on the performance scale and a low verbal score could mean that the child has a language deficiency that prevents the verbal scale from accurately measuring the child's mental abilities.

ing an individual's performance on each subtest and to compute more than one score. Thus, with Wechsler's approach a test can indicate a child's specific strengths *and* weaknesses. Wechsler's approach also acknowledged that describing intelligence by just one number is misleading.

IQ Tests Today

Modern editions of the Wechsler scales and the Stanford-Binet are the most widely used individually administered IQ tests in schools today. They are administered by specially trained people to one individual at a time.

The Wechsler test includes eleven subtests. Six require verbal skills and make up the **verbal scale** of the test. These include such items as remembering a series of digits, solving arithmetic problems, defining vocabulary words, and understanding and answering questions (for example, "What did Shakespeare do?"). The remaining five tests have little or no verbal content and make up the **performance scale.** They include tasks that require understanding the relations of objects in space and manipulation of materials—for example, assembling blocks, solving mazes, and completing pictures. Figure 11.1 gives examples of items from one section of the performance scale. The tester can compute a score for verbal IQ, performance IQ, and overall IQ. Different forms of the Wechsler test have been developed for different age ranges. For example, the *Wechsler Adult Intelligence Scale—Revised (WAIS-R)* is a test for adults, the

Figure 11.1
Sample Items from the Performance Section of WISC-III
Items like these tap aspects of intelligence but require little or no verbal ability.

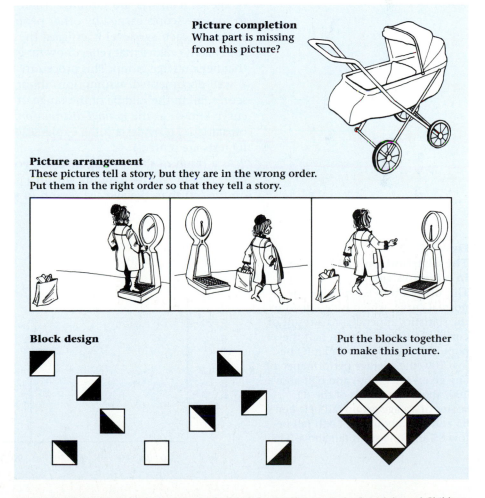

third revision of the *Wechsler Intelligence Scale for Children (WISC-III)* is for children five to fifteen, and the *Wechsler Preschool and Primary Scale of Intelligence—Revised (WPPSI-R)* is for preschoolers (Cohen, Swerdlik & Smith, 1992).

Like the Wechsler scales, the latest edition of the Stanford-Binet also uses subtests. It provides scores on verbal reasoning (for example, "What is similar about an orange, apple, and grape?"), quantitative reasoning (for example, math problems), abstract/visual reasoning (for example, explaining why one should wear a coat in winter), and working memory, along with a composite IQ (Thorndike, Hagan & Sattler, 1986).

Tests similar to the Stanford-Binet and Wechsler scales have been designed for administration to groups; examples include the Miller Analogies Test and the Wonderlic Personnel test. Group tests allow more data to be collected in less time, while also allowing test takers to work at their own pace. But group tests also have drawbacks. The tester has little chance to ensure that everyone is adequately motivated and has understood and followed instructions. These issues may be particularly important when testing children or anyone who is physically handicapped or emotionally disturbed (Aiken, 1987). Furthermore, compared with tests administered individually, group tests contain a larger proportion of multiple-choice questions and fewer questions that are performance based or open-ended. Thus, group tests generally sample a narrower range of behaviors.

IQ scores are no longer calculated by dividing mental age by chronological age. If you take an IQ test today, the points you earn for each correct subtest or age-level answer are summed. Then the summed raw scores are compared to the raw scores earned by other people. The average raw score obtained by people at each age level is *assigned* the IQ score of 100. Other raw scores are assigned IQ values that reflect how far each score deviates from the average for that person's age group. This procedure may sound arbitrary, but it is based on a well-documented assumption about many characteristics: most people's scores fall in the middle of the range of possible scores, creating a bell-shaped curve known as the *normal distribution,* shown in Figure 11.2. (The appendix on statistics provides a fuller explanation of the normal distribution and how IQ tests are scored.)

As a result of this scoring method, your **intelligence quotient**, or **IQ score**, reflects your *relative* standing within a population of your age. If you do better on the test than the average person in your age group, you will receive an IQ

Figure 11.2
The Distribution of IQ Scores in a Population

This distribution is typical of the normal curve, which is described in the statistics appendix. As a result of current scoring methods, half the population ends up with an IQ below 100 (the average performance of any given age group) and half above 100; about two-thirds of the IQ scores of an age group fall between 85 and 115; about one-sixth fall below 85 and one-sixth fall above 115.

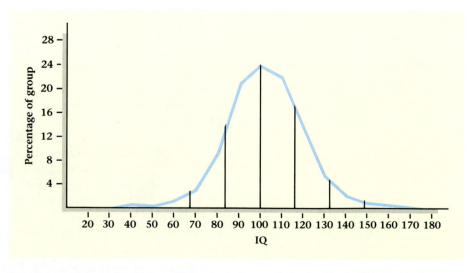

Note: Curve represents distribution of IQ scores in the standardized group for the 1937 version of the Stanford-Binet.

score above 100; how far above depends on how much better than average you do. Similarly, a person scoring below the age-group average will have an IQ below 100.

Evaluating IQ Tests

Our brief review of the history of IQ testing in the United States, and of its abuse in the service of prejudice, provides a warning: when considering a test score, proceed with caution. Understanding IQ scores requires first evaluating the tests from which they come and then interpreting the meaning of the scores themselves.

Are IQ Tests Reliable and Valid?

The measures of reliability and validity we discussed earlier provide a first step in judging the quality of IQ tests. How stable are scores on IQ tests? What do they predict?

How Reliable Are IQ Tests?   IQ scores obtained before the age of seven typically do not correlate very highly with scores on IQ tests given later, for two key reasons: Test items used with very young children are different from those used with older children; and, as discussed in Chapter 3, cognitive abilities change rapidly in the early years. During the school years, however, IQ scores tend to remain stable (Anastasi, 1988). The less time elapsing between two testings and the older the individuals are when first tested, the higher the test-retest correlations tend to be. For teenagers and adults, the reliability of IQ tests is high; split-half reliability correlations are generally about +.90.

Of course, a person's score may vary from one time to another if motivation or anxiety or similar factors change. The conditions of testing, as well as variations in motivation or anxiety, may produce misleading results. Still, compared with most tests, IQ tests usually provide consistent results.

How Valid Are IQ Tests?   Scores on various IQ tests correlate well with each other, but this does not necessarily mean they are measuring "intelligence." Because there is no independent measure of intelligence—recall that psychologists do not even agree on its definition—it is impossible to determine whether IQ tests are valid measures of intelligence.

Indeed, IQ tests assess only a narrow range of the qualities that might be considered aspects of intelligence (Sternberg, 1991). For example, the format of some IQ tests requires people to identify *one* correct answer (Jones, 1989), but, as discussed in Chapter 10, effective problem solving requires the ability to come up with multiple hypotheses.

IQ tests seem best at assessing aspects of intelligence related to schoolwork, such as abstract reasoning and verbal comprehension. Indeed, IQ tests are reasonably good at predicting success in school; the correlation of IQ with high school grades is about +.50 (Cronbach, 1970), which means that about one-fourth of the variability in grades is associated with variability in IQ scores.

Academic success, however, does not define all aspects of intelligent behavior. As children, Leonardo da Vinci and Thomas Edison had problems in reading, writing, or mathematics that would no doubt have resulted in low IQ scores. (Their problems were related to learning disabilities, which are mentioned in Chapter 15; see Table 15.2.) Can IQ tests predict anything besides academic success?

There is evidence that people who score high on tests of such cognitive abilities as verbal and arithmetic reasoning tend to perform better in the workplace than those who earned lower scores (Barrett & Depinet, 1991). The pre-

Many people who achieved great things in their lives did not always show childhood brilliance at academic tasks of the kind measured by intelligence tests. There is more to intelligence than IQ scores.

Linkages: What have psychologists done to make intelligence tests less culturally biased? (a link to Introducing Psychology)

dictive validity of IQ scores is especially good for managerial and other complex jobs (Hunter, 1986). High IQ scores apparently predict the ability to learn job-relevant information and to deal with unpredictable, changing aspects of the job environment (Hunter, 1986)—characteristics that are needed in complex jobs. Some research indicates that IQ scores are also highly correlated with performance on "real-life" tasks such as reading medicine labels, using the telephone book, and the like (Barrett & Depinet, 1991). One study that kept track of people for more than fifty years found that children with high IQs tended to grow up to be successful adults (Terman & Oden, 1947). However, the extent to which IQ tests predict job performance has recently been questioned. For example, Robert Sternberg argues that the most important aspects of performance are related to *tacit knowledge:* knowing what is and is not important on the job and how to allocate time and effort among different components of the job. He finds that measures of tacit knowledge are uncorrelated with IQ test scores (Sternberg, 1993).

Conclusions   By the standard measures for judging psychological tests, IQ tests have good reliability and reasonably good predictive validity for certain criteria, such as success in school. However, an IQ test score should not be taken as an infallible measure of "intelligence." IQ tests do not tap the full array of mental abilities, and a particular score may give a distorted view of an individual. For example, comfort and rapport with the tester sometimes affect performance on individually administered tests. If children are suspicious of strangers, are not used to prolonged one-to-one interactions with adults, or have not had a trusting relationship with adults, they may not exert maximum effort on the test (Jones, 1989).

Given our review of the history of intelligence testing in the United States, it is also important to ask if today's IQ tests are fair. Early IQ tests were biased against groups that were not familiar with the dominant culture of the day. (Figure 11.3 shows items from a test designed to illustrate cultural bias.) Some early IQ tests contained vocabulary items that would be unfamiliar to lower-income youths. For example, consider the question "Which is most similar to a xylophone? (*violin, tuba, drum, marimba, piano*)." No matter how intelligent children are, if they have never had a chance to see an orchestra or to have any experience with these instruments, they may easily miss the question.

Test makers today try to avoid obviously biased questions (Jones, 1989; Educational Testing Service, 1987). Furthermore, because IQ tests include more than one scale, areas that are most influenced by culture, such as vocabulary, can be assessed separately from dimensions that are less vulnerable to cultural bias. Still, controversy about the fairness of IQ tests continues.

Thinking Critically

Are IQ Tests Unfairly Biased Against Certain Groups?

Despite attempts to eliminate cultural bias from IQ tests, there are differences in the mean scores of various ethnic and cultural groups (Humphreys, 1988; Wainer, 1988; Chan & Lynn, 1989; Vincent, 1991; Taylor & Richards, 1991; Lynn, 1991; Geary, Fan & Bow-Thomas, 1992). Asian-Americans typically score highest, followed, in order, by European-Americans, Hispanic-Americans, and African-Americans. People have gone to court in an effort to halt the use of IQ tests as a guide for placing children in special-education classes (*Larry P.* v. *Riles,* 1975), for hiring (*Griggs* v. *Duke Power Company,* 1971), or for granting licenses to insurance agents. Plaintiffs in these cases argue that using IQ tests to make decisions about people unfairly deprives minorities of equal opportunities.

Figure 11.3
Items from the Black Intelligence Test of Cultural Homogeneity
Here are some items from a test in which success depends heavily on familiarity with words, terms, and expressions from African-American culture. Robert L. Williams of the Black Studies Program at Washington University constructed this test not to compete with standard tests of intellectual ability but to show that poor performance on a culture-bound test is probably due more to a lack of familiarity with the culture represented than to a lack of mental ability. (For each item, choose the correct definition or answer from the alternatives given.)

1. Black draught:
   (a) winter's cold wind
   (b) laxative
   (c) black soldier
   (d) dark beer

2. Clean:
   (a) just out of the bathtub
   (b) very well dressed
   (c) very religious
   (d) has a great deal

3. Crib:
   (a) an apartment
   (b) a game
   (c) a job
   (d) hot stuff

4. Do rag:
   (a) the hair
   (b) the shoes
   (c) washing
   (d) tablecloth

5. Four corners:
   (a) rapping
   (b) singing
   (c) the streets
   (d) dancing

6. Who wrote the Negro National Anthem?
   (a) Langston Hughes
   (b) Paul Lawrence Dunbar
   (c) James Weldon Johnson
   (d) Frederick Douglass

Answers:
1. B 3. A 5. D
2. B 4. A 6. C

Source: Williams, 1972.

What am I being asked to believe or accept?

Some critics of IQ tests argue that a disproportionately large number of people in some minority groups score low on IQ tests for reasons that are unrelated to intelligence, job potential, or other criteria that the tests are supposed to predict (Helms, 1992).

What evidence is available to support the assertion?

Research reveals several possible sources of bias in the tests. First, whatever the content of a test, noncognitive factors such as motivation and trust influence performance on IQ tests and may put certain groups at a disadvantage. Children from minority groups may be less likely than European-American children to be motivated to perform well on standardized tests and less likely to trust the adult tester (Bradley-Johnson, Graham & Johnson, 1986; Jones, 1989). Thus differences in IQ scores may reflect motivational differences among various groups, as described in the chapter on learning.

Second, many test items require vocabulary and experience drawn from the dominant middle-class culture in the United States. As a result, these tests often measure *achievement* in acquiring knowledge valued by that culture. But not all cultures value the same things (Serpell, 1994). A study of Cree Indians in northern Canada (Berry & Bennett, 1992) revealed that words and phrases synonymous with *competent* were *understands new things, pays attention, thinks carefully, good sense of direction,* and *accumulated knowledge.*

One phrase at the *incompetent* end of the scale was *lives like a white person.* "Culture-fair" tests that reduce, if not eliminate, dependence on knowledge of a specific culture do indeed produce smaller differences between majority and minority groups than more traditional measures. (See Figure 11.4.)

Third, IQ tests may reward those who *interpret* questions as expected by the test designer's culture. Conventional IQ tests have clearly defined "right" and "wrong" answers. Yet a person may interpret test questions in a manner that is "intelligent" or "correct" but that produces a "wrong" answer. The fact that you don't give the answer that the test designer was looking for does not mean that you can't. For example, when Liberian rice farmers were asked to sort objects such as a knife, machete, several kinds of vegetables, and the like, they grouped the knife with the vegetables. They said this was the clever way to do it: the knife goes with the vegetables because it is used to cut them. When the experimenter asked them to sort the objects the way a stupid person would do it, they grouped the cutting tools together, the vegetables together, and so on, much as most Americans would (Ciborowski, cited in Segall et al., 1990). What is "clever" in one culture can be seen as "stupid" in another. If various groups have ways of thinking about test items that differ from those of the test designer's culture, their scores will suffer.

Are there alternative ways of interpreting the evidence?

The evidence might be interpreted as showing that although IQ tests do *not* provide an unbiased measure of mental ability in general, they *do* provide a fair test of whether a person is likely to succeed in school or on the job. In short, they may be biased—but not in a way that unfairly discriminates among groups. Perhaps familiarity with the culture reflected in IQ tests is just as important for success at school or work in that culture as it is for success on the tests themselves. After all, the ranking among groups on measures of academic achievement is similar to the ranking for mean IQ scores (Sue & Okazaki, 1990). According to this view, it doesn't matter very much if IQ tests measure culture-related achievement as long as they are useful in predicting whatever criterion is of interest. In fact, "culture-fair" tests do not predict academic achievement as well as conventional IQ tests do (Aiken, 1987; Humphreys, 1988).

What additional evidence would help to evaluate the alternatives?

Evaluation of whether tests differentiate fairly or unfairly depends on whether the sources of test-score differences are relevant to predicting performance in the environment for which the test is intended. To take an extreme example, perhaps mean score differences between ethnic groups result entirely from certain test items that have nothing to do with how well the

Figure 11.4
Culture-Fair Tests
These are items from the Learning Potential Assessment Device (LPAD). The task here is to outline the square and two triangles embedded in patterns of dots, using each dot only once. The LPAD not only measures children's ability to deal with such problems but also allows them to try solving problems again after receiving some training. Thus a measure of baseline performance is supplemented by evidence of potential for learning.

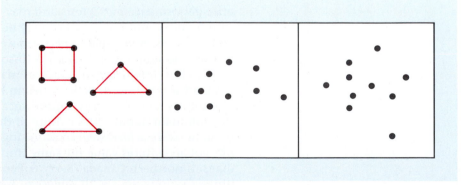

Source: Feuerstein, 1979.

test as a whole predicts academic success. It is important to conduct research on this possibility.

Alternative tests must also be explored, particularly those based on problem-solving skills and more open-ended questions (Jones & Appelbaum, 1989). These tests tap abilities not measured by most IQ tests. If new tests show less bias than traditional tests but equal or better predictive validity, many of the issues discussed in this section will have been resolved.

What conclusions are most reasonable?

The effort to reduce unfair cultural biases in tests is well founded, but "culture-fair" tests will be of little benefit if they fail to predict success as well as conventional tests do. Whether one considers it good or bad, fair or unfair, it is important to have information and skills that are valued by the culture that establishes criteria for educational and occupational achievement. As long as this is the case, it is reasonable that tests designed to predict success in these areas will measure a person's skills and access to the information valued by that culture.

Stopping at that conclusion, however, would mean freezing the status quo, whereby members of certain groups are denied many educational and economic benefits. As we discuss later, if attention were to be focused on altering poverty, poor schools, and inadequate nutrition and health care, many of the reasons for concern about test bias might be eliminated. ▪

Do IQ Scores Measure Innate Ability?

Linkages: How can research in behavior genetics promote understanding of the basis for mental abilities? (a link to Research in Psychology)

It is one thing to know that IQ tests predict academic or job success; it is something else to know what to make of particular test scores. How should teachers react if they are told that certain students have low IQ scores? If you receive a low IQ score, can you blame your parents' genes?

Years of research have led psychologists to conclude that both hereditary and environmental factors interact to influence mental abilities. For example, by asking many questions, bright children help generate an enriching environment for themselves; thus, innate abilities allow people to take better advantage of their environment (Scarr & Carter-Saltzman, 1982). In addition, the effects of heredity and environment are usually *confounded*. If bright parents give their children an environment favorable to the development of intelligence, their children are favored by both heredity and environment.

Correlational studies are one method psychologists use to try to untangle the influences of heredity and environment. But these studies must be interpreted with caution because, as noted in Chapter 2, correlation does not guarantee causation: finding significant *correlations* between IQ score differences and certain variables does not mean that those variables *caused* the IQ differences. With this caution in mind, psychologists have explored the influence of genetics on individual differences in IQ scores by comparing the scores of people who have different degrees of similarity in their genetic makeup and environment. For example, they have examined identical twins—pairs with exactly the same genetic makeup—who were separated when very young and reared in different environments. (You may want to review the Linkages section of Chapter 2, pages 34–38, which describes twin studies and other methods used in behavior genetics research to analyze hereditary and environmental influences.)

These correlational studies find, first, that hereditary factors are strongly related to IQ scores. When identical twins who were separated at birth and adopted by different families are tested many years later, the correlation between scores is usually high and positive, at least +.60 (Bouchard et al., 1990). If one twin receives a high IQ score, the other probably will too; if one is low, the other is likely to be low as well. However, studies of correlations between

378   Chapter 11 / *Mental Abilities*

IQ scores also highlight the importance of the environment (Capron & Duyme, 1989). Consider any two people—twins, siblings, or unrelated children—brought together in a foster home. No matter what the degree of genetic similarity in these pairs, the correlation between their IQ scores is higher if they share the same home than if they are raised in different environments, as Figure 11.5 shows (Scarr & Carter-Saltzman, 1982).

The strength of environmental influences is highlighted by studies that compare children's IQ scores before and after environmental changes such as adoption. Generally, studies of children from relatively impoverished backgrounds who were adopted into homes with more enriching intellectual environments—environments with interesting materials and experiences, as well as a supportive, responsive adult—find modest increases in the children's IQ scores (Weinberg, Scarr & Waldman, 1992).

A study of French children who were adopted soon after birth demonstrates the importance of both genetic and environmental influences. When these children were tested after years of living in their adopted homes, those whose biological parents were from higher socioeconomic groups (where superior IQs are most common) had higher IQ scores than those whose biological parents came from low socioeconomic groups, regardless of the socioeconomic status of the adopted homes (Capron & Duyme, 1989). These findings suggest that a genetic component of the children's mental abilities continued to exert an influence in the adopted environment. At the same time, the IQ scores of children from low socioeconomic backgrounds who were exposed to academically enriched environments through adoption rose by twelve to fifteen points (Capron & Duyme, 1989). Another study found that the IQ scores of adopted children were an average of fourteen points higher than those of siblings who remained with the biological parents in a poorer, less enriching environment (Schiff et al., 1978).

Some researchers have concluded that the influence of heredity and environment on mental abilities appears to be about equal (Loehlin, 1989; Plomin, 1990). It must be emphasized that such estimates of heritability—of the relative contributions of heredity and environment—apply only to groups, not to individuals. Thus, it would be inaccurate to say that 50 percent of *your* IQ score

Figure 11.5
Correlations of IQ Scores
The correlation between pairs increases as heredity or environmental similarity increases.

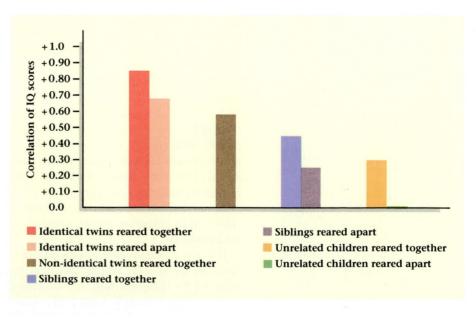

Source: Bouchard et al., 1981.

is inherited and 50 percent learned. It is far more accurate to say that about 50 percent of the *variation* in the IQ scores of a group of people is influenced by hereditary factors, and about 50 percent is influenced by the environment.

Even this last statement must be qualified because the relative contributions of heredity and environment are not fixed. Environmental influences, for example, seem to be greater at a younger age (Plomin, 1990) and tend to diminish over the years. Thus, a child's IQ will probably be affected more by the German measles that the mother contracted during pregnancy or by parental help with preschool reading than by, say, the courses available in junior high school.

One way to express the relationship of heredity and environment is to use the concept of **reaction range**. That is, genetics roughly define a potential range of ability, within which the effects of environment can push a child up or down. For any individual, however, the reaction range does not establish fixed, impenetrable boundaries; environmental factors might influence an individual's genetically based ability far more than would be expected for people in general (Platt & Sanislow, 1988; Zigler & Seitz, 1982).

What Causes Group Differences in IQ Scores?

Much of the controversy about differences in IQ scores is not over differences among individuals but over differences in the mean scores of groups such as poor people and rich people or Caucasian people and Asian people. To interpret these differences correctly and analyze their sources, we must avoid some pitfalls.

First, group scores are just that; they do not describe individuals. For example, although the mean score of Asian-Americans is higher than the mean score of European-Americans, large numbers of European-Americans score well above the mean score of Asian-Americans, and large numbers of Asian-Americans score below the mean level of European-Americans (see Figure 11.6).

Second, inherited characteristics are not necessarily fixed, and environmentally determined features are not necessarily changeable. A favorable environment may improve a child's performance, even if the inherited influences on that child's IQ are negative, and the effects of a harmful environment cannot always be corrected (Humphreys, 1984).

Figure 11.6
A Representation of Ethnic-Group Differences in IQ Scores
The average IQ score of Asian-Americans is typically four to six points higher than the average of European-Americans, who average twelve to fifteen points higher than African-Americans and Hispanic-Americans. However, the variation within groups is much greater than between groups.

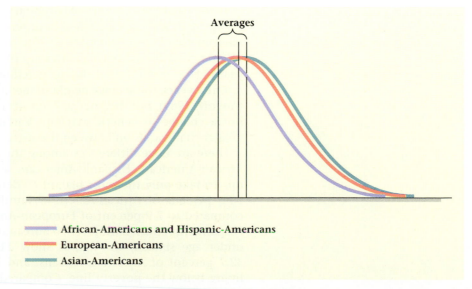

Socioeconomic Differences   Upper-class U.S. communities have shown mean IQ scores seventeen points higher than those of lower-class communities with the same ethnic makeup (Vane, 1972). The average IQ scores of children whose parents are of low socioeconomic status may be fourteen points below the average for children of middle socioeconomic status (Oakland & Glutting, 1990). IQ score differences associated with socioeconomic status also occur in other countries (Fergusson, Lloyd & Horwood, 1991; Murthy & Panda, 1987). Some data suggest that verbal tasks are more affected by socioeconomic status than are nonverbal tasks (Jordan, Huttenlocher & Levine, 1992). The size of the correlation between family income and children's IQ scores (+.30) indicates that about 9 percent of the variability in children's IQ scores is associated with variability in family income (Cleary et al., 1975). More than 90 percent is associated with other factors. But why should there be any relationship between IQ scores and family income?

Three factors seem to account for the correlation. First, parents' jobs and status depend on characteristics related to their own intelligence, and this intelligence is partly determined by a genetic component that in turn contributes to the child's IQ score. Second, the parents' income affects the child's environment in ways that can increase or decrease the child's IQ score (Cronbach, 1975; MacKenzie, 1984). Third, motivational differences may play a role. Upper- and middle-income families demonstrate greater motivation to succeed and excel in academic endeavors (Atkinson & Raynor, 1974). Perhaps these families instill in their children greater motivation to succeed on IQ tests. As a result, children from middle- and upper-class families perhaps make a greater effort and therefore obtain higher scores (Bradley-Johnson, Graham & Johnson, 1986; Zigler & Seitz, 1982).

Ethnic Differences   The mean IQ score of Asians, whether in North America or Asia, tends to be around five points higher than the mean score of Caucasians (Chan & Lynn, 1989; Lynn, 1991). And, as shown in Figure 11.6, the mean IQ score of African-Americans in the United States tends to be around fifteen points lower than the mean score of European-Americans, although this difference has been declining (Humphreys, 1988; Vincent, 1991). A similar difference has been found between the mean scores of Hispanic-Americans and European-Americans (Mercer, 1988). Why?

Some have argued that these differences are due mostly to inherited ability. In support of this view, Arthur Jensen (1969) noted that heredity makes an important contribution to the differences in IQ scores within groups. Note, however, that the existence of hereditary differences among individuals *within* groups does not indicate whether differences *between* groups result from similar genetic causes (Lewontin, 1976). Your genes shape your height, but the difference in height between a group of ten-year-olds and a group of fifteen-year-olds is certainly not due to hereditary factors alone. Similarly, over the last fifty years, the average height of Japanese males has increased by 3.5 inches (Angoff, 1989), but this increase reflects improved environmental conditions, not a change in genetic makeup. Variation within ethnic groups is much greater than variation between these groups (Zuckerman, 1990).

There are large differences among the environments in which the average African-American, Hispanic-American, and European-American child grows up. To take only the most blatant evidence, the latest figures available show 28.2 percent of African-American families living below the poverty level compared to 7.9 percent of European-American families and 28.7 percent of Hispanic-American families (U.S. Bureau of the Census, 1991). Among children under age sixteen, the figures show 11.3 percent of European-Americans, 32.7 percent of African-Americans, and 36.6 percent of Hispanic-Americans living below the poverty line. Compared with European-Americans, African-

Americans are more likely to have parents with poor educational backgrounds, as well as inferior nutrition, health care, and schools. All of these conditions are likely to pull down scores on IQ tests.

Evidence for the influence of environmental factors on the average black-white IQ difference comes from adoption studies. One such study involved African-American children from disadvantaged homes who were adopted by middle- to upper-class European-American families in the first years of their lives (Scarr & Weinberg, 1976). When measured a few years later, the mean IQ score of these children was 110. Using the scores of nonadopted children from similar backgrounds as a comparison suggests that adoption raised the children's IQ scores at least ten points. A ten-year follow-up study of these young-sters showed that their average IQ scores were still higher than the average scores of African-American children raised in disadvantaged homes (Weinberg, Scarr & Waldman, 1992).

As discussed in the chapters on human development and learning, cultural differences may also contribute to the variation in the mean scores of different ethnic groups. For example, the scores may in part reflect differences in motivation based on variations in the value placed on academic achievement. In one study of 15,000 African-American, Asian-American, Hispanic-American, and European-American high school students, parental and peer influences related to achievement tended to vary with ethnic group (Steinberg, Dornbusch & Brown, 1992). The Asian-American students had strong support for academic pursuits from both their parents and their peers. European-American students whose parents expected high academic achievement tended to associate with peers who also encouraged achievement, and they tended to achieve more academically than African-American and Hispanic-American students. The parents of the African-American students in the study supported academic achievement, but because their peers did not, performance may have suffered. The performance of the Hispanic-American students may have suffered from the fact that, in this study at least, they were more likely than the others to have authoritarian parents, whose emphasis on obedience (see Chapter 3) may have created conflicts with the schools' emphasis on independent learning.

In short, there appear to be important nongenetic factors working to decrease the mean score of African-American and Hispanic-American children. Indeed, the recently narrowing gap between African-American and European-American children on tests of mathematical aptitude and intelligence may be related to improved environmental conditions for many African-American children (Vincent, 1991). Whatever heredity might be contributing to children's performance, it may be possible for them to improve greatly, given the right conditions.

What Conditions Can Raise IQ Scores?

In the chapter on human development, we outlined some of the environmental conditions that help or deter cognitive development. For example, lack of caring attention or of normal intellectual stimulation can stymie a child's mental growth. Low test scores have been linked with poverty, chaos and noise in the home, poor schools, and inadequate nutrition and health care (Humphreys & Davey, 1988; Wachs & Gruen, 1982; Weinberg, 1989). Efforts to improve these conditions are part of a movement known as community psychology, which is discussed in Chapter 16.

Can the effect of bad environments be reversed? Not always, but efforts to intervene in the lives of children and enrich their environments have had some success. Conditions for improving children's performance include rewards for progress, encouragement of effort, and creation of expectations for success. Even in college, these conditions can be effective (Watkins, 1989).

There are differences in the average IQ scores of European-Americans and African-Americans, but those who attribute these differences primarily to hereditary factors are ignoring a number of environmental, social, and other nongenetic factors that are important in creating (and may now be narrowing) this IQ gap.

The best-known attempt to enrich children's environments in the United States is Project Head Start, a set of programs established by the federal government in the 1960s to help preschoolers from lower-income homes. In some of these programs, teachers visit the home and work with the child and parents on cognitive skills. In others, the children attend classes in nursery schools. Some programs emphasize health and nutrition. Head Start has brought measurable benefits to children's health as well as improvements in their academic and intellectual skills (Zigler & Seitz, 1982; Lee, Brooks-Gunn & Schnur, 1988). Closely related to Project Head Start are intervention programs for infants at risk because of low birth weight, low socioeconomic status, or low parental IQ scores. Such programs appear to enhance IQ scores by as much as nine points by the age of three; the effects appear especially strong for the infants of mothers with a high school education or less (Brooks-Gunn et al., 1992; Infant Health and Development Program, 1990; Ramey et al., 1992; Wasik et al., 1990).

In general, the most consistently effective programs for poor preschoolers provide a moderate degree of structure. They offer an orderly physical setting, a predictable schedule, high-quality educational materials, and teachers who try to provide regular opportunities for learning (Zigler & Seitz, 1982). Surprisingly, a review of 193 preschool programs found no difference in effectiveness between those in which parents did or did not play a role (White, Taylor & Moss, 1992).

Do the gains achieved by preschool enrichment programs last? Though program developers sometimes claim long-term benefits (Schweinhart & Weikart, 1991), such claims are disputed (see, for example, Spitz, 1991). The findings from more than 1,000 such programs are often contradictory, but the effect on IQ scores typically diminishes after a year or two (Woodhead, 1988). A study evaluating two of the better preschool programs concluded that they are at best only temporarily effective (Locurto, 1991a). One consistent, though very small, effect is that children who have taken part in enrichment programs are less likely to be held back in school or to need special-education programs (Palmer & Anderson, 1979; Locurto, 1991b). The fading of effects is probably due to reduced motivation, not loss of mental ability (Zigler & Seitz, 1982).

Project Head Start is designed to provide children from impoverished backgrounds with the preparation they will need to succeed in grade school. Such early-enrichment programs have resulted in IQ gains of from five to fifteen points (Lazar et al., 1982; Zigler & Seitz, 1982).

Children may lose motivation when they leave a special preschool program and enter the substandard schools that often serve poor children.

Martin Woodhead (1988) concluded that the primary benefits of early-enrichment programs probably lie in their effect on children's attitudes toward school. Especially in borderline cases, favorable attitudes toward school may help reduce the chances that children will be held back a grade or placed in special-education classes. Children who avoid these experiences may retain positive attitudes about school and enter a cycle in which gains due to early enrichment are maintained and amplified on a long-term basis (Woodhead, 1988).

IQ Scores in the Classroom

Obviously, IQ scores are neither a crystal ball into some predestined future nor a measure of some fixed quantity. Consider the case of Philip R., an African-American man now in his forties. When Philip was two, a physician labeled him mentally retarded, and he was sent to a state institution. His Stanford-Binet IQ score of 60 confirmed the doctor's label, and Philip remained in the institution for fifteen years. Because he communicated mainly with grunts and gestures, Philip received no formal training in academic subjects, but he did become highly proficient at daily living skills. At fifteen, Philip began to work with a local shoemaker, who was impressed with how rapidly the youngster mastered tasks that were demonstrated for him. Through this man's efforts, Philip began to speak a few words. At seventeen, Philip took an army physical; it revealed that he had a severe hearing loss in both ears. When surgery and dual hearing aids improved his hearing, Philip rapidly began to acquire expressive language. After learning basic academic skills from the shoemaker, Philip entered a public high school at the age of twenty-three. He graduated in three years, went to college, and completed medical school at the age of thirty-three. Today he is a successful orthopedic surgeon (DeStefano, 1986).

Using IQ scores or other labels to categorize people may also have more subtle effects on how they are treated and how they behave. In a controversial study, Robert Rosenthal and Lenore Jacobson (1968) found that labels create *expectancies*. Teachers were told that a test could indicate which grade-school students were about to enter a "blooming" period of rapid academic growth, and they were given the names of students who had supposedly scored high on the test. In fact, the experimenters *randomly* selected the "bloomers." But during the next year, the IQ scores of the bloomers dramatically increased; two-thirds showed an increase of at least twenty points. Only one-quarter of the children in the control group showed the same increase. Apparently, the teachers' expectancies about the children influenced them in ways that showed up on IQ tests.

Attempts to replicate Rosenthal and Jacobson's findings have not always been successful (Elashoff, 1979), and some researchers have found that the effect of inaccurate teacher expectancies, though statistically significant, is relatively small (Jussim, 1989). Still, it is important to ask how expectancies might become self-fulfilling prophecies. To find out, Alan Chaiken and his colleagues (1974) videotaped teacher-child interactions in a classroom in which teachers had been informed (falsely) that certain pupils were particularly bright. They found that the teachers favored the "brighter" students in several ways. They smiled at these students more often than at others, made more eye contact, and generally reacted more positively to their comments. Children receiving this extra social reinforcement not only get more intense teaching but are also more likely to enjoy school, to have their mistakes corrected, and to continue trying to improve. More recent research found that teachers provide a wider range of classroom activities for students for whom they have higher expectations, suggesting another way in which expectancies can influence outcomes (Blatchford et al., 1989). (In Chapter 12, on motivation and emotion, we describe how differential expectations about the academic potential of boys and girls can contribute to gender differences in performance and achievement motivation.)

These results suggest that the "rich get richer": those perceived to be blessed with high mental abilities are given better opportunities to improve those abilities. Is there also a "poor get poorer" effect? In fact, there is evidence that teachers tend to be less patient, less encouraging, and less likely to try teaching as much material to students whom they do not consider bright (Cooper, 1979; Luce & Hoge, 1978; Trujillo, 1986).

Whenever people try to "summarize" other people with a label, a test score, or a profile, they run the risk of oversimplifying reality and making errors. ("In Review: Influences on IQ Scores" lists the factors that can shape IQ scores.) But intelligence tests can also prevent errors. Boredom or lack of motivation at school can make a child appear mentally slow, even retarded. An IQ test conducted under the right circumstances is likely to reveal the child's abilities. The test can prevent the mistake of moving a bright child to a class for the mentally handicapped. And, as Alfred Binet had hoped, IQ tests have been enormously helpful in identifying children who do need special educational attention.

Furthermore, the alternatives to IQ tests may not be very attractive. Should teachers' judgments or some other subjective, potentially more biased assessment method replace testing (Weinberg, 1989)? Probably not. Objective mental abilities tests, despite their limitations, minimize the likelihood of assigning children to remedial work they don't need, or to advanced work they can't yet handle.

In Review: Influences on IQ Scores

Source of Effect	Description	Examples of Evidence for Effect
Genetic	Genes seem to establish an approximate range of performance on IQ tests.	The IQ scores of siblings who share no common environment are positively correlated. There is a greater correlation between scores of identical twins than between those of nonidentical twins.
Environmental	Environmental conditions push people up or down within the range of their potential. Nutrition, medical care, sensory and intellectual stimulation, interpersonal relations, and motivation are all significant features of the environment.	IQ scores have risen among children who are adopted into homes that offer a stimulating, enriching environment. Correlations between IQs of twins reared together are higher than for those reared apart.

Understanding Intelligence

The very existence of intelligence tests suggests that they are measuring something that people have to a greater or lesser degree. But is there actually a trait or set of traits that can be called *intelligence?* And do IQ tests measure all important aspects of it? We next consider several approaches to these questions about intelligence.

The Psychometric Approach

One method of studying intelligence, the **psychometric approach,** analyzes test scores in order to describe the structure of intelligence. Is intelligence one general ability, or is it a label for a bundle of abilities? If intelligence is a single characteristic, a potential employer might assume that someone with a low IQ could not do any mental task well. But if intelligence is composed of many independent abilities, a poor showing in one area—say, spatial abilities— would not rule out good performance in understanding information or solving word problems.

Spearman's g In the late 1920s, Charles Spearman, a statistician who helped develop methods for calculating the correlation coefficient, provided the cornerstone for recent debate about whether intelligence is a single, general characteristic. Spearman noted that scores on almost all tests of mental abilities were positively correlated (Spearman, 1927). That is, people who did well on one test tended to do better than average on all of the others. Spearman concluded that these correlations were created by a very general factor of mental ability, which he called **g,** or the **g-factor** of intelligence.

At first, Spearman held that people's scores on a test depended on just two things: the *g*-factor plus *s*-factors, which represented the specific information and skills needed for a particular test. Further examination of test scores, however, found correlations that could not be explained by either *g* or *s* and were called *group factors.* Spearman modified his theory to try to accommodate these factors, but he continued to maintain that *g* represented a controlling mental force (Gould, 1983).

L. L. Thurstone, in particular, disagreed with Spearman's theory. In 1938 he published a paper criticizing Spearman's mathematical methods and denying the significance of Spearman's *g.* Using a statistical technique called factor analysis, he analyzed the correlations among IQ tests. **Factor analysis** examines the correlations between all possible pairs of tests and identifies groups of tests that are more correlated with each other than they are with other tests. These differences in correlations may indicate that the tests within a group are all tapping one ability and that other groups of tests are measuring distinct abilities.

Instead of a dominating *g*-factor, Thurstone's factor analysis revealed several independent *primary mental abilities.* He identified these as numerical ability, reasoning, verbal fluency, spatial visualization, perceptual ability, memory, and verbal comprehension. Thurstone said that Spearman's *g*-factor contributed little to the correlation among scores. It was, he argued, secondary to the primary mental abilities.

Decades later, Raymond B. Cattell (1971) contested Thurstone's analysis, reanalyzed the data, and argued that *g* exists but that there are two kinds of *g,* which he labeled fluid and crystallized. **Fluid intelligence** is the basic power of reasoning and problem solving. It produces induction, deduction, and an understanding of relationships between ideas. **Crystallized intelligence,** in contrast, involves specific knowledge gained as a result of applying fluid intelligence. It produces, for example, a good vocabulary and familiarity with the multiplication tables. Since people with greater fluid intelligence are likely to gain more crystallized intelligence, measures of the two sorts of intelligence are positively correlated.

Conclusions   Who is right? After decades of research and debate, most psychologists today agree that there *is* a positive correlation between several tests of mental ability, a correlation that is due to one factor, labeled *g* (Carroll, 1991). However, the brain probably does not "contain" some unified "thing" corresponding to what people call intelligence, and *g* is likely to be a collection of subskills and mental abilities—such as reasoning ability, test-taking skill, reading ability, and so forth (Humphreys, 1984)—many of which are needed to succeed on any test of intelligence.

How important is *g*? Because *g* is the result of an analysis of correlations among scores, the answer depends on who is taking the tests. Any correlation coefficient is shaped by the range of data involved. Consider the correlation between height and weight. If you include all ages in the population—from infants to adults—the correlation between height and weight will be rather high, because infants are always much shorter and lighter than adults. But if you study only adults—a category that includes many short, heavy people and many tall, skinny people—the relationship between height and weight will be weaker and the correlation smaller. Similarly, if the range of mental abilities reflected by test scores is large, then there will generally be a positive correlation between most tests, and factor analysis will reveal the *g* factor. But when the range of ability is small, correlations decline, and factor analysis will give little evidence of the *g* factor.

In other words, the psychometric approach to the study of intelligence has important limitations (Fredericksen, 1986; Jones, 1989). The data it generates depend in part on which tests are used, which subjects take those tests and under what conditions, which methods of statistical analysis are chosen, and which labels are chosen to describe the factors that emerge. For these and other reasons, some scientists argue that the fundamental nature of mental abilities can be found only by turning to evidence other than the test scores used by the psychometric approach.

The Information-Processing Approach

IQ tests, the various analyses of *g*, and Thurstone's analysis of primary mental abilities all focus on the *products* of intelligence—the answers to a test. The **information-processing approach** looks instead at the *process* of intelligent behavior (Hunt, 1983; Sternberg, 1982, 1986; Vernon, 1987a; Sternberg & Gastel, 1989; Naglieri et al., 1991). It asks: What mental operations are necessary to answer the questions on an IQ test or to perform other intellectual tasks? What aspects of this performance depend on past learning, and what aspects depend on attention, working memory, and processing speed? In short, this approach relates the basic mental processes discussed in the chapters on perception, memory, and thought to research on IQ tests. Are there individual differences in basic mental processes that correlate with measures of intelligence? More specifically, are measures of intelligence related to differences in the attention available for basic mental processes or in the speed of these processes?

The notion that intelligence may be related to attention builds on the results of research by Earl Hunt and others (Eysenck, 1987; Hunt, 1980; Hunt & Lansman, 1983; Stankov, 1983). As discussed in the chapter on perception, attention represents a pool of resources or mental energy. When people perform difficult tasks or perform more than one task at a time, they must call on greater amounts of these resources. Does intelligent behavior depend on the amount of attention that can be mobilized (Eysenck, 1987; Weiss, 1986)? Early

Linkages: The information-processing model introduced in Chapter 10, on thought and language, suggests that human mental processes consist of an ongoing sequence of sensation, perception, decision making, and response selection and execution that allows us to recognize, think about, and respond to the world. Applying this model to intelligence might suggest that those with the most rapid information processors (the "fastest" brains) would do best on mental ability tests, including those required for college entrance. Research suggests, however, that this is true only to an extent and that there is more to intelligent behavior than sheer processing speed.

research by Hunt (1980) suggested that it does, that people with greater intellectual ability have more attentional resources available. There is also evidence for a positive correlation between IQ scores and performance on tasks requiring attention, such as mentally tallying the frequency of words in the "animal" category while reading a list of varied terms aloud (Stankov, 1989).

Another possible link between differences in information processing and differences in intelligence has been under study at least since Galton's work in the nineteenth century. Perhaps, suggested Galton, intelligent people have "faster brains" than other people—perhaps they carry out basic mental processes more quickly. When a task is complex, having a "fast brain" might decrease the chance that information will disappear from working memory before it can be used (Jensen, 1993; Vernon, 1987b; Larson & Saccuzzo, 1989). A "fast brain" might allow people to do a better job of mastering material in everyday life and therefore allow them to build up a good knowledge base (Vernon, 1983; Miller & Vernon, 1992).

These hypotheses sound reasonable, but research suggests that only about one-quarter of the variation in performance on tests of reasoning or general comprehension can be tied to differences in any one type of mechanistic information processing, such as the speed of access to long-term memory or the capacity of working memory (Lohman, 1989; Baker, Vernon & Ho, 1991; Miller & Vernon, 1992). This is a modest conclusion, and it suggests many other questions. For instance, are there "nonmechanistic" aspects of information processing that are correlated with performance on tests of reasoning? And how is information processing related to aspects of intelligence other than those measured by reasoning and comprehension tests? Robert Sternberg has integrated information-processing research into a broad theory of intelligence that addresses questions like these.

The Triarchical Theory of Intelligence

Sternberg's theory aims to explain a range of behavior that goes far beyond that measured by typical IQ tests. According to Sternberg (1988a), most theories of intelligence are incomplete, because a complete theory must deal with three aspects of intelligence: its internal components, the relation of these components to experience, and its external effects. Sternberg deals with each of these in his *triarchical theory* of intelligence.

First, says Sternberg, the internal aspect of intelligence consists of the processes involved in thinking. There are three sets of these internal processes, or *components:* performance components, knowledge-acquisition components, and metacomponents. *Performance components* are the processes of perceiving stimuli, holding information in working memory, comparing values, retrieving material from long-term memory, and calculating sums and differences. *Knowledge-acquisition components* involve the selective application of the processes used in gaining and storing new information. *Metacomponents* control the performance and knowledge-acquisition components; they are involved in organizing and setting up a problem. Metacomponents determine the problem-solving strategies people use—how they decide on the nature of a problem and know what performance components to use, what needs to be known before trying to solve a problem, and how to evaluate a proposed solution. According to Sternberg, the metacomponents hold the greatest importance in intelligent cognitive activities such as solving analogies (of the form "A is to B as C is to _____"). For example, Sternberg found that although people with better reasoning ability end up solving analogies faster and more accurately than people with lower reasoning ability, they devote *more time* to understanding the analogy—a metacomponent process—before coming up with the solution.

The second aspect of intelligence, says Sternberg, involves the relationship between the internal world of the components and the external world; it amounts to the ability to profit from experience by altering how the components are applied. According to Sternberg, intelligence involves being able both to deal with novelty and to make some processes automatic. Think of tourists in a foreign country, faced with unfamiliar customs, currency, and language. For more intelligent tourists, the process of converting menu prices from, say, Swiss francs into American dollars would become automatic, enabling them to devote more time to other novel aspects of the situation (such as how much to tip). When a task is familiar, good performance depends on the automatic manner in which performance components like encoding are carried out. But when a task is unfamiliar, good performance depends on the way that metacomponents aid reasoning and problem solving (Sternberg & Gastel, 1989).

Finally, in everyday life intelligence is manifested by adapting to or shaping environments or by selecting new environments. This aspect of intelligence might be thought of as "street smarts," as shown by Jack, one of the students described at the beginning of this chapter. Intelligent people can use performance components, knowledge-acquisition components, and metacomponents to achieve goals. Thus, intelligent behavior varies with the context. The kinds of knowledge and metacomponents that are appropriate for solving a physics problem in the laboratory are not the same as those needed for explaining your way out of an embarrassing situation, settling a family dispute, or getting the best price on a used car.

Because it is so broad, many parts of Sternberg's theory are difficult to test. Determining exactly how to measure "street smarts," for example, is a challenge that is now being addressed by researchers (Sternberg, 1993). Nevertheless, Sternberg's theory is important because it extends the concept of intelligence into areas that most psychologists traditionally did not examine and emphasizes what intelligence means in everyday life.

Multiple Intelligences

Many people whose IQ scores are only average have exceptional ability in one specific area. Even some mentally retarded people show incredible ability in narrowly defined skills (Treffert, 1988). One child whose IQ score was just 50 could correctly state the day of the week for any date between 1880 and 1950 (Scheerer, Rothmann & Goldstein, 1945). He could also play melodies on the piano by ear and sing Italian operatic pieces he had heard, although he had no understanding of what he was doing. He could also spell forward or backward any word spoken to him and memorize long speeches.

Cases of remarkable ability in one specific area constitute part of the evidence cited by Howard Gardner in support of his theory of *multiple intelligences* (Gardner, 1983). To study intelligence, Gardner focused on how people learn and use symbol systems such as language, mathematics, and music. He asked: Do these systems all require the same abilities and processes, the same "intelligence"? To find out, Gardner looked not just at test scores and information-processing experiments but also at the ways in which children develop, at the exceptional abilities of child prodigies and remarkable adults, at biological research, and at the values and traditions of various cultures.

According to Gardner, all people possess a small number of intellectual potentials, or "intelligences," each of which involves a set of skills that allows them to solve problems. Biology provides raw capacities unique to each of these intelligences; cultures provide symbolic systems such as language to mobilize the raw capacities. Although the intelligences normally interact, they can function with some independence, and individuals may develop certain intelligences further than others.

If only measuring the multifaceted concept of intelligence were this easy! To measure specific intelligences not tapped by standard IQ tests, Howard Gardner suggests options such as collecting samples of children's writing, assessing their ability to appreciate or produce music, and obtaining teacher reports of strength and weakness in athletic and social skills.

Source: Drawing by McCallister; © 1990 The New Yorker Magazine, Inc.

The specific intelligences that Gardner proposed are (1) linguistic intelligence; (2) logical-mathematical intelligence; (3) spatial intelligence; (4) musical intelligence; (5) body-kinesthetic intelligence, which is demonstrated by the skills of dancers, athletes, and neurosurgeons; and (6) personal intelligence, which refers to knowledge and understanding of oneself and of one's relations to others. Conventional IQ tests sample only the first three of these intelligences. Evidence for *g*, Gardner argued, comes from the fact that most IQ tests rely heavily on just linguistic and logical-mathematical intelligences. IQ tests predict academic success because schools value these particular intelligences. But conventional IQ tests, he claimed, fail to do justice to the diversity of intelligences. Accordingly, Gardner and his colleagues (Kornhaber, Krechevsky & Gardner, 1990) are working on the development of new means of assessing "multiple intelligences."

An Ecological Approach

Determination of the validity or usefulness of Gardner's theory of intelligence must await further research. The theory does, however, highlight aspects of mental ability that are not measured by IQ tests but that may be important in certain kinds of human activity. ("In Review: Analyzing Mental Abilities" summarizes Gardner's theory, along with the other views of intelligence we have discussed.) In a sense, we have come full circle, beginning with Galton's measures of sensory discrimination, through measures of *g*, to specific factors, multiple intelligences, and modern information-processing approaches (Sternberg, 1992). What comes next?

In Review: Analyzing Mental Abilities

Approach	Method	Key Findings or Propositions
Psychometric	Define the structure of intelligence by examining factor analysis of the correlations between scores on tests of mental abilities.	Performance on many tests of mental abilities is highly correlated, but this correlation, represented by *g*, reflects a bundle of abilities, not just one trait.
Information processing	Understand intelligence by examining the mental operations involved in intelligent behavior.	The speed of basic processes and the amount of attentional resources available make significant contributions to performance on IQ tests.
Sternberg's triarchical theory	Understand intelligence by examining the information processing involved in thinking, changes with experience, and effects in different environments.	Thinking involves three components. High intelligence is shown in the effective organization of these components, in altering their use to deal with novel or familiar problems, and in adapting problem-solving strategies to different environments.
Gardner's theory of multiple intelligences	Understand intelligence by examining test scores, information processing, biological and developmental research, the skills valued by different cultures, and exceptional people.	Biology provides the capacity for six distinct "intelligences" valued by society: linguistic, logical-mathematical, spatial, musical, body-kinesthetic, and personal.

As psychologists become more attuned to the effects of cultural factors on human behavior and mental processes, an *ecological approach* to intelligence—emphasizing the role of the environment in shaping intelligence—may become more prominent. This approach views intelligence as mental activity that allows people to select, shape, and adapt to those aspects of the environment most relevant to their lives (Greeno, 1991; Sternberg, 1985). In other words, the ecological approach suggests that, as mentioned earlier, intelligence is not the same in all environments. Thus, rather than working on the improvement of "culture-fair" tests designed to measure elements of intelligence that are shared by all cultures, the ecological approach would recognize that what is "intelligent" in one culture isn't necessarily the same as what is "intelligent" in another.

Diversity in Mental Abilities

Though psychologists still don't agree on what intelligence is, the study of IQ tests and intelligent behavior has yielded many insights into human mental abilities, and has highlighted the diversity of those abilities. It has shown that IQ tests do not measure all aspects of the abilities people have in mind when they talk about intelligence, and that some aspects of mental ability seem to be somewhat independent of intelligence as measured by traditional tests. In this section we briefly examine the diverse types and levels of mental abilities.

Creativity

In every area of human endeavor, there are people who demonstrate **creativity**; in other words, they can produce novel but effective solutions to challenges. Corporate executives and homemakers, scientists and artists, all may be more or less creative. To measure creativity, some psychologists have generated tests of **divergent thinking,** the ability to think along many paths to generate many solutions to a problem (Guilford & Hoepfner, 1971). The Consequences Test is an example. It asks questions like "Imagine all of the things that might possibly happen if all national and local laws were suddenly abolished" (Guilford, 1959). Divergent thinking tests are scored by counting the number of *different* but plausible responses that a person can list for each item or by assessing the extent to which a person's answers are different from those given by most test takers.

Of course, the ability to come up with different answers or different ways of looking at a situation does not guarantee that anything creative will be produced. Therisa Amabile has identified three components necessary for creativity (Amabile, 1989; Amabile, Hennessey & Grossman, 1986).

1. Expertise in the field of endeavor, which is directly tied to what a person has learned. For example, a painter or composer must know the paints, techniques, or instruments available.
2. A set of creative skills, including the ability to persist at problem solving, the use of divergent thinking, and the ability to break mental sets and take risks. Amabile believes that training can influence many of these skills, some of which are closely linked to the strategies for problem solving discussed in Chapter 10.
3. The motivation to pursue creative production for intrinsic (or internal) rewards such as satisfaction rather than for extrinsic (or external) rewards like prize money.

In fact, Amabile and her colleagues found that external rewards can deter creativity. They asked groups of children or adults to create artistic products such

Creative people may share certain personality traits, but being creative says little about one's IQ. Indeed, because traditional mental ability tests measure convergent thinking, while creativity requires divergent thinking, researchers have found relatively low correlations between IQ and creativity test scores.

as collages or stories. Some were asked only to work on the project. Others were told that the project was to be judged for its creativity and excellence and that rewards were to be given or winners announced. Experts, who had no idea which works were created by which group, judged work by those in the "reward" group to be significantly less creative.

What determines whether a person is creative? Two possibilities can be ruled out. First, creativity is not simply inherited. There is evidence that the environment influences creative behavior at least as much as it influences intelligence. For example, the correlation between the creativity scores of identical twins reared apart is lower than that between their IQ scores (Nichols, 1978). Second, one need not be "strange" or display a psychological disorder to be creative. There is some evidence, however, that creative people share traits of self-confidence, ambition, and perseverance. They are typically less conforming to societal and other norms, and more likely to take risks (Martindale, 1989).

Does creativity require a high IQ score? Correlations between people's scores on IQ tests and on tests of creativity are only modest, between +.10 and +.30 (Anastasi, 1971; Barron & Harrington, 1981; Dellas & Gaier, 1970; Rushton, 1990). This result is not surprising, because creativity requires divergent thinking, and traditional IQ tests test **convergent thinking**—the ability to apply logic and knowledge in order to narrow down the number of possible solutions to a problem. Thus, the questions on traditional IQ tests have only one or a small number of acceptable answers. The low correlation between IQ and creativity does not mean that the two are completely unrelated, however. Studies based on measures of creativity like the Consequences Test suggest that an average or above-average IQ is necessary (although not sufficient) for creative behavior to emerge (Barron & Harrington, 1981).

Creative behavior, in short, requires divergent thinking that is *appropriate* for a given situation or problem. To be productive rather than bizarre, a creative person must be firmly anchored to reality, understand society's needs, and learn from the experience and knowledge of others. These are qualities that require some degree of intelligence.

Intelligence, Problem Solving, and Cognitive Complexity

About twelve years ago, a certain "Mr. X" faced a lawsuit in Great Britain. He was accused of engaging in a number of complex but shady financial deals. In his defense, his lawyers claimed that because Mr. X had an IQ score of just 80 and minimal education, he simply could not have carried out the deals (Turnstall et al., 1982). That might sound reasonable, but there is evidence that a high IQ is not necessarily important for thinking through the kinds of financial problems that Mr. X was accused of handling.

Support for this argument comes from, of all places, the racetrack. Horse betting is, after all, a form of financial problem solving. To choose the winner consistently, a bettor needs a sophisticated mental model of all the variables that can influence how fast certain horses will run at a specific track—age, conditioning, weather, jockey, trainer, and the like —*and* how these variables will interact. A study of thirty avid racetrack bettors in Delaware revealed that some were clearly better bettors than others (Ceci & Liker, 1986). The good bettors, or "experts," predicted very accurately the final handicap that each horse was assigned at race time, a skill closely related to the ability to predict the winner. Most important, the expert and nonexpert bettors did not differ at all in the IQ scores they received on the WAIS. Both groups had received a mean IQ of around 100. At least one expert bettor had a WAIS IQ of only 82!

This study provides just one piece of the evidence that supports a general conclusion: IQ scores are not good predictors of problem-solving ability. Since IQ tests attempt to provide measures of ability free of knowledge about any particular domain, this result is not very surprising. As discussed in Chapter 10, effective problem solving requires knowledge about the domain associated with the problem. Furthermore, effective problem solving requires the ability to come up with multiple hypotheses and avoid mental sets or functional fixedness. In other words, good problem solving requires divergent thinking. As noted earlier, IQ tests stress convergent thinking.

If IQ scores do not predict problem-solving ability, are there other differences among individuals that do? Studies of mental abilities suggest two possible factors: cognitive complexity and the ability to devise a good strategy.

Cognitive complexity involves flexibility of thought and the ability to anticipate events and to alter a course of action based on unexpected happenings. Most important, cognitively complex people can think *multidimensionally;* in other words, they can interpret the consequences of their actions in a variety of ways and appreciate several aspects of a problem. In the study of Delaware bettors, expert and nonexpert bettors reached their predictions in different ways. The experts used a more cognitively complex mental model to integrate fifteen variables about each of the horses described in the official racing program. That is, in making their predictions, they considered more variables and relied more on the interactions among variables than did the nonexperts.

To measure cognitive complexity, Siegfried Streufert (1986) asked several business executives to play a game in which they managed a fictitious company, making decisions about investments, expansion, marketing, and so forth. Streufert rated the executives high on cognitive complexity if they simultaneously considered several factors and thought through the many implications of a decision. Two findings of Streufert's study were especially significant. First, cognitive complexity does not appear to be closely related to IQ scores. Second, cognitive complexity is *domain specific.* People who are cognitively complex in one domain, such as business decision making, may not

Linkages: Do IQ scores predict problem-solving ability? (a link to Thought and Language)

The outcome of a horse race depends on track conditions, temperature, the horses' training, the skill of the jockeys, and a multitude of other factors. People who display cognitive complexity—that is, who can keep in mind and mentally combine numerous interacting factors—tend to be especially successful at dealing with complicated situations, whether they involve betting, business decisions, or advanced scientific research.

show cognitive complexity in another area, such as family relations. An executive might react to a son or daughter in a rigid way, showing no appreciation for the child's point of view, even though the executive regularly considers all sides of business issues.

Other studies have highlighted the importance of strategies in distinguishing good from bad problem solvers. For example, Sternberg (1986) showed that differences in the ability to solve analogies can be traced to differences in problem-solving strategies. In Chapter 10 we discussed another example in which expert physicists used more sophisticated problem-solving methods than inexperienced students (Chi, Feltovitch & Glaser, 1981). The same results appeared in a study comparing problem solvers within a college physics class (Hardimann, Dufresne & Mestre, 1989). Poor problem solvers judged the similarity between physics problems in terms of surface features, such as whether the problems involved inclined planes; good problem solvers judged similarity in terms of underlying principles, such as whether problems could be solved using the same physical law. The differences were not related to underlying mathematical ability as measured by a typical IQ test.

If the everyday concept of "intelligence" means anything, it surely includes the ability to think and solve problems (Sternberg, 1991). But these results show that the relationship between scores on IQ tests and the capacity for intelligent thought is not necessarily strong or consistent. Good problem solvers in business, at home, or at the track depend to some extent on the mental abilities that IQ tests measure, but they also employ knowledge and processes that are not measured by traditional IQ tests (Ree & Earles, 1992; Sternberg, 1993).

Extremes of Mental Ability

Our understanding of mental abilities has also been advanced by studying people whose abilities fall outside the normal range of performance—the gifted and the mentally retarded.

Giftedness   Do all those with unusually high IQs become geniuses? Do their remarkable abilities mark them for social maladjustment? One of the most famous studies of the intellectually gifted was conducted by Louis Terman and his colleagues (Terman & Oden, 1947). This study began in 1922 with the identification of more than 1,500 children whose IQ scores were very high—most higher than 135 by age ten. Periodic interviews and tests over the next sixty years revealed that few if any became truly creative geniuses—such as world-famous inventors, authors, artists, or composers—but only 11 failed to graduate from high school, and more than two-thirds graduated from college. Ninety-seven earned Ph.D.s; 92, law degrees; and 57, medical degrees. In 1955 their median family income was well above the national average (Terman & Oden, 1959). In general, they were physically and mentally healthier than the nongifted.

Thus, as mentioned earlier, high IQ scores tend to predict success in life, but an extremely high IQ does not guarantee special distinction, even when students are placed into special "gifted" programs at school. Students in these programs tend to do no better on achievement tests than gifted students left in regular classes (Oakes, 1989), leading many psychologists and educators to question the programs' value. There is also concern that segregating gifted students for accelerated academic learning may make it harder for them to learn the social skills necessary for effective interaction with a diverse group of peers.

Mental Retardation   The label "mentally retarded" is applied to people whose measured IQ is less than about 70 *and* who fail to display the skill at

**Table 11.2
Categories of
Mental Retardation**

These are rough categories. Especially at the upper end of the scale, many retarded persons can be taught to handle tasks well beyond what their IQ score might suggest. Furthermore, IQ is not the only diagnostic criterion for retardation. Many people with IQs lower than 70 can function adequately in their everyday environment and hence would not be classified as mentally retarded.

Level of Retardation	IQ Scores	Characteristics
Mild	50–70	A majority of all the mentally retarded. Usually show no physical symptoms of abnormality. Individuals with higher IQs can marry, maintain a family, and work in unskilled jobs. Abstract reasoning is difficult for those with the lower IQs of this category. Capable of some academic learning to a sixth-grade level.
Moderate	35–49	Often lack physical coordination. Can be trained to take care of themselves and to acquire some reading and writing skills. Abilities of a 4- to 7-year-old. Capable of living outside an institution with their families.
Severe	20–34	Only a few can benefit from any schooling. Can communicate vocally after extensive training. Most require constant supervision.
Profound	Below 20	Mental age less than 3. Very limited communication. Require constant supervision. Can learn to walk, utter a few simple phrases, and feed themselves.

As the limitations and the potential of mentally retarded individuals become better understood, their opportunities and their role in society will continue to expand. This young man, the first retarded senatorial page, was hired by Senator John Chaffee, of Rhode Island, in 1985.

daily living, communication, and other tasks that is expected of those their age. They are sometimes referred to as "developmentally disabled" or "mentally challenged." People within this very broad category differ greatly in their mental abilities, and in their ability to function independently in daily life. Table 11.2 shows a classification that divides the range of low IQ scores into categories that reflect these differences.

Mental retardation sometimes has a clearly identifiable cause. The best-known example is *Down syndrome,* which is caused by an extra chromosome. Children with Down syndrome typically have IQ scores in the 40 to 55 range. Intelligence may also be limited by environmental conditions or traumas such as meningitis or encephalitis contracted during infancy, birth traumas resulting from an oversupply or undersupply of oxygen, and excessive use of drugs or alcohol by the mother during pregnancy.

In most cases, however, no genetic or environmental cause of retardation is directly observed. These are usually cases of mild retardation and are known as **familial retardation** for two reasons: (1) most people in this group come from families of lower socioeconomic status, and (2) they are more likely than those suffering from a genetic defect to have a relative who is also retarded (Plomin, 1989). These facts have led psychologists to conclude that familial retardation results from a complex interaction between heredity and environment.

Exactly *how* are the mentally retarded deficient in their cognitive skills? They are just as proficient as others at recognizing simple stimuli, and their rate of forgetting information from working memory is no more rapid (Belmont & Butterfield, 1971). But mildly retarded people do differ from other people in three important ways (Campione, Brown & Ferrara, 1982).

Linkages: Do mentally retarded people have a defective memory system? (a link to Memory)

1. They perform certain mental operations more slowly, such as retrieving information from long-term memory. When asked to repeat something they have learned, they are not as quick as a person of normal intelligence.
2. They simply know fewer facts about the world. It is likely that this deficiency is a consequence of a third problem.
3. They are not very good at using particular mental *strategies* that may be important in learning and problem solving. For example, they do not spontaneously rehearse material that must be held in working memory.

What are the reasons for this deficiency in using strategies? The differences between normal and retarded children in some ways resemble the differences between older and younger children discussed in Chapter 3. Both younger children and retarded children show deficiencies in *metamemory*—the knowledge of how their memory works. More generally, retarded children are deficient in **metacognition:** the knowledge of what strategies to apply, when to apply them, and how to deploy them in new situations so that new specific knowledge can be gained and different problems mastered (Ferretti & Butterfield, 1989).

It is their deficiencies in metacognition that most limit the intellectual performance of the mildly retarded. If retarded children are simply taught a strategy, they are not likely to use it again on their own or to transfer the strategy to a different task. Because of this characteristic, it is important to teach retarded children to evaluate the appropriateness of strategies (Wong, 1986) and to monitor the success of their strategies. Finally, like other children, retarded children should be shown that effort, combined with effective strategies, pays off (Borkowski, Weyhing & Turner, 1986).

Despite such difficulties, the intellectual abilities of the retarded can be raised. For example, one program emphasized positive parent-child communications and began when the children were as young as thirty months old. It helped children with Down syndrome to master reading skills at a second-grade level, providing the foundation for further achievement (Rynders & Horrobin, 1980; Turkington, 1987).

Designing effective programs for retarded children is complicated by the fact that the way people learn depends not just on cognitive skills but also on social and emotional factors. Much debate has focused on *mainstreaming,* the policy of teaching handicapped children, including those who are retarded, in regular classrooms with those who are not handicapped. Is mainstreaming good for retarded children? A number of studies of the cognitive and social skills of students who have been mainstreamed and those who were separated show few significant differences overall, though it appears that students at higher ability levels may gain more from being mainstreamed than their less mentally able peers (Cole et al., 1991).

How do mental abilities change over the life span?

Linkages: Mental Abilities and Aging

In the chapter on human development we described some of the ways in which mental abilities change over time. The findings regarding age-related changes depend to some extent on the method of study. One method, the **cross-sectional study,** compares data collected simultaneously from people of different ages. However, cross-sectional studies contain a major confounding variable: because older subjects were born in a different year than younger ones, they may have had very different educational, cultural, nutritional, and medical experiences. These differences, and not just younger age, might account for differences among older and younger people.

Changes associated with age can also be examined, as Terman and Oden did, through **longitudinal studies**, in which a group of people are repeatedly tested as they grow older. Longitudinal studies, however, may be marred by another problem. As people of the same age are tested through the years, fewer members of the group can be tested, because some die or become incapacitated. Those remaining are likely to be the healthiest in the group and may also have retained better mental powers than the dropouts (Botwinick, 1977). Hence, longitudinal studies may *underestimate* the degree to which abilities decline with age.

Despite their limitations, the general picture presented by both types of studies is reasonably consistent: IQ scores usually remain fairly constant from early adulthood until about sixty to seventy years of age. Then—excluding cases of senility, Alzheimer's disease, and other organic disorders—some components of intelligence, but not others, begin to fail. The chapter on development described some of these changes; our review of research on mental abilities and information processing now allows a more systematic look at them.

Crystallized intelligence, which depends on retrieving information and facts about the world from long-term memory, may continue to grow well into old age. *Fluid intelligence,* which involves rapid and flexible manipulations of ideas and symbols, remains stable during adulthood and then declines in later life (Hayslip & Sterns, 1979; Schaie, 1989). Among those over sixty-five or seventy, problems in several areas of information processing may impair problem-solving ability (Sullivan & Stankov, 1990). How and where does this decline show up?

1. *Working memory*   The ability to hold and organize material in working memory declines beyond age fifty or sixty, particularly when attention must be redirected (Parkin & Walter, 1991).
2. *Processing speed*   There is a general slowing of all mental processes (Lima, Hale & Myerson, 1991; Salthouse, Babcock & Shaw, 1991). Research has not yet isolated whether this slowing is due to reduced storage capacity, impaired processing efficiency, problems in coordinating simultaneous activities, or some combination of these factors (Salthouse, 1990; Babcock & Salthouse, 1990). For many tasks, this slowing does not create obstacles. But if a problem requires manipulating material in working memory, quick processing of information is critical (Rabbitt, 1977). To multiply two two-digit numbers mentally, for example, you must combine the subsums before they are forgotten.
3. *Organization*   Older people seem to be less likely to solve problems by adopting specific strategies, or heuristics (Young, 1966, 1971; Charness, 1987). For example, to locate a problem in the wiring of a circuit, you might perform a test that narrows down the regions where the problem might be. The tests carried out by older people tend to be more random and haphazard (Young, 1966, 1971). This result may occur partly because many older people are out of practice at solving such problems.
4. *Flexibility*   Older people tend to be less flexible in problem solving than their younger counterparts. They are less likely to consider alternative solutions (Salthouse & Prill, 1987), and they require more information before making a tentative decision (Rabbitt, 1977). Laboratory studies suggest that older people are also more likely than younger ones to choose conservative, risk-free options (Botwinick, 1966).
5. *Control of attention*   The ability to direct or control attention declines with age (Stankov, 1988; Wiegersma & Meertse, 1990). When required to switch their attention from one task to another, older subjects typically perform less well than younger subjects.

To summarize: In old age, as in earlier life, there is a gradual, continual accumulation of knowledge about the world; some systematic changes in the limits of mental processes; and qualitative changes in the way those processes are carried out.

Future Directions

The study and testing of mental abilities have far-reaching implications for education; for decisions as to who is hired, fired, or promoted; and for governmental policies for the disadvantaged. Because of this broad reach, these topics stir heated debates and biases that may have little to do with scientific findings. Yet some solid conclusions about intelligence and mental ability are emerging.

First, it is becoming clearer that different definitions of intelligence are needed to serve different purposes. Second, most psychologists agree that the brain does not contain some unified "thing" corresponding to intelligence and that the correlation between tests of mental ability, labeled *g,* is likely to reflect a bundle of abilities. Third, most psychologists agree that the mental abilities of a particular individual result from a complex interaction between heredity and environment.

Where is the field moving? There will be increasing effort to understand the information-processing operations that underlie intelligent behavior and how they are related to traditional measures of intelligence (Matarazzo, 1992). Further, we may see measures of intelligence that include processing speed, working memory capacity, and the like (West, Crook & Barron, 1992). Computerized testing, linked with research in cognitive psychology, may lead to more accurate estimates of ability than paper-and-pencil testing (Embretson, 1992). And research in cognitive psychology can be expected to lead to more measures of mental ability that directly assess the cognitive mechanisms identified by that research. One such measure, the Kaufman Assessment Battery for Children, or K-ABC, is already in use (Kaufman & Kaufman, 1983; Kaufman & Harrison, 1991). Many tests will likely go beyond traditional formats in an effort to tap divergent thinking (Sternberg, 1992).

It has been shown that scores on traditional intelligence tests such as the Stanford-Binet correlate with biological measures of brain functioning, including PET scans, nerve conduction velocity, reaction time, and glucose metabolism rate. Investigations into these "neural substrates of intelligence" are likely to become an important aspect of research on mental abilities in the next few decades (Matarazzo, 1992).

There will also be increased interest in an ecological approach to mental abilities, with its focus on investigating the impact of environmental and cultural factors on cognitive functioning. This approach is likely to be applied not only to studies of subcultural differences within countries, but also to studies of differences that appear from culture to culture (Embretson, 1992). At the same time, more sophisticated statistical analyses will produce a better understanding of the correlations between intelligence measures of different groups (Loehlin, 1989). These techniques may begin to overcome the fundamental limitation of correlations: they do not usually allow conclusions about what causes the correlation.

If you want to learn more about mental abilities, consider taking a course in tests and measurement, sometimes called psychometrics. Many courses in cognitive psychology also address the nature of individual differences in intelligent behavior. Advanced courses in behavioral genetics should also be of interest.

Summary and Key Terms

Mental ability refers to the capacity to perform the higher mental processes of reasoning, remembering, understanding, problem solving, and decision making.

Assessing Mental Abilities: Principles of Testing

Tests have three key advantages over other techniques of evaluation. They are standardized, so that the performances of different people can be compared; they produce scores that can be compared with *norms;* and they are economical and efficient.

Reliability

A good test must be *reliable,* which means that the results for each person are stable. Reliability can be measured by the test-retest, alternate-form, and split-halves methods.

Validity

A test is said to be *valid* if it measures what it is supposed to measure. Validity can be evaluated by measuring content validity, construct validity, or predictive validity; the last entails measurement of the correlation between the test score and another measure of the performance that the test is supposed to predict.

Testing for Intelligence

Psychologists have not reached a consensus on how best to define *intelligence.* Proposed definitions often focus on the role of intelligence in reasoning, problem solving, and dealing with the environment.

A Brief History of IQ Tests

Binet's pioneering test of intelligence included questions that required reasoning and problem solving of varying levels of difficulty, graded by age. Terman developed a revision of Binet's test that became known as the *Stanford-Binet;* it included items designed to assess the intelligence of adults as well as that of children and became the model for *IQ tests.* Early IQ tests in the United States required not just mental ability but also knowledge of U.S. culture, and the results were used to justify discrimination against certain groups. The Wechsler test remedied some of the deficiencies of the earlier IQ tests. Made up of subtests, some of which have little verbal content, this test allowed testers to generate scores for different parts of the test.

IQ Tests Today

In schools the Stanford-Binet and the Wechsler test are the most often used individually administered tests. Both include subtests and provide scores for parts of the test as well as an overall score. For example, Wechsler subtests that depend heavily on vocabulary are combined into a *verbal scale,* and the rest are combined into a *performance scale.* Currently, a person's *intelligence quotient,* or *IQ score,* reflects how far that person's performance on the test deviates from the average performance by people in his or her age group. An average performance produces an IQ of 100.

Evaluating IQ Tests

Are IQ Tests Reliable and Valid?

IQ tests are reasonably reliable, and they do a good job of predicting academic success. However, IQ tests assess only some of the abilities that might be considered aspects of intelligence, and they may favor those most familiar with middle-class culture. Nonetheless, this familiarity is also important for academic and occupational success.

Do IQ Scores Measure Innate Ability?

Both heredity and the environment influence IQ scores, and their effects interact. The influence of heredity is shown by the high correlation between IQ scores of identical twins raised in separate households and by the similarity in the IQ scores of children adopted at birth and their biological parents. The influence of the environment is revealed by the higher correlation of IQ between siblings who share the same environment than by those who do not and by the effects of environmental changes such as adoption. Some researchers have used the concept of *reaction range* to express the interaction between biological and environmental determinants of mental ability.

What Causes Group Differences in IQ Scores?

Different socioeconomic and ethnic groups have different mean IQ scores. These differences result from both environmental and genetic factors. Differences in motivation and environmental enrichment are major sources of differences in the mean IQ scores of these groups.

What Conditions Can Raise IQ Scores?

An enriched environment sometimes raises IQ scores. Initial large gains in cognitive performance that result from interventions like Project Head Start may decline over time, but the programs can produce lasting gains in other aspects of scholastic competence and may improve children's attitude toward school.

IQ Scores in the Classroom

Like any label, an IQ score can generate expectations that affect both how other people respond to a person and how that person behaves. Children labeled with low IQ scores may be offered fewer or lower-quality educational opportunities. On the other hand, IQ scores may help educators to identify a student's strengths and weaknesses and to offer the curriculum that will best serve that student.

Understanding Intelligence

The Psychometric Approach

The *psychometric approach* attempts to analyze the structure of intelligence by examining correlations between tests of mental ability. Because scores on almost all tests of mental abilities are positively correlated, Spearman concluded that all of these tests measure a general factor of mental ability, called *g* or the *g-factor* of intelligence. As a result of *factor analysis,* other researchers have concluded that intelligence is not a single trait. It seems likely that *g* reflects a collection of subskills and mental abilities needed to succeed on any test of intelligence. For example, Cattell distinguished between *fluid intelligence,* the basic power of reasoning and problem solving, and *crystallized intelligence,* the specific knowledge gained as a result of applying fluid intelligence. Because *g* is the result of an analysis of correlations, its importance varies with the test, the test takers, and the test interpreters.

The Information-Processing Approach

The *information-processing approach* to intelligence focuses on the processes by which intelligent behavior is produced. Small positive correlations have been found between IQ scores and measures of the flexibility and capacity of attention, and between IQ scores and measures of the speed of information processing.

The Triarchical Theory of Intelligence
According to Sternberg, intelligent thinking involves performance components, knowledge-acquisition components, and metacomponents. Sternberg's triarchical theory also holds that intelligence depends on the ability to profit from experience and to deal with the environment.

Multiple Intelligences
Gardner's approach to intelligence is based not only on mental tests and information-processing research but also on studies of prodigies, human development, biology, and various cultures. He holds that biology equips humans with the capacities for several intelligences that can function with some independence—specifically, linguistic, logical-mathematical, spatial, musical, body-kinesthetic, and personal intelligences.

An Ecological Approach
The ecological approach to intelligence highlights the role of the environment in shaping intellectual abilities that are functional for those in that environment. These abilities may differ somewhat from one culture to another.

Diversity in Mental Abilities
Creativity
Tests of *divergent thinking* are used to measure differences in *creativity.* In contrast, IQ tests require *convergent thinking.* Although creativity and IQ scores are not highly correlated, creative behavior requires a certain amount of intelligence, along with expertise in a creative field, skills at problem solv-

ing and divergent thinking, and motivation to pursue a creative endeavor for its own sake.

Intelligence, Problem Solving, and Cognitive Complexity
Because they emphasize convergent thinking and attempt to measure ability independent of knowledge in a domain, IQ tests are not good predictors of problem-solving ability. Effective problem-solving requires divergent thinking and knowledge about the domain associated with the problem.

Extremes of Mental Abilities
Knowledge about mental abilities has been expanded by research on giftedness and mental retardation. The latter term is applied to those with an IQ score below about 70 and whose communication and daily living skills are less than expected of people their age. In *familial retardation,* no genetic or environmental causes are evident. Compared to those of normal intelligence, retarded people process information more slowly, know fewer facts, and are deficient in *metacognition*—that is, at knowing and using strategies. Mentally retarded people can be taught strategies, but they must also be taught how and when to use those strategies.

Linkages: Mental Abilities and Aging
Studies of changes in mental abilities over time either examine a group of people of different ages (*cross-sectional studies*) or follow a group of people as they get older (*longitudinal studies*). Each technique has its limitations, but both reveal that crystallized intelligence increases well into old age, while fluid intelligence remains stable in adulthood, then declines in later life. More specifically, older people have reduced working memory capacity, slower processing speed, greater difficulty in organizing strategies, less flexibility in problem solving, and reduced control of attention.

Chapter 12

Motivation and Emotion

Outline

While one of the present authors was traveling halfway around the world to risk his life climbing Mt. Everest, one of our colleagues underwent an extremely painful medical procedure in hopes of increasing her chances of having children; another one spent that week driving around the Midwest in search of antique clocks to add to his collection. Why did they do these things? Why, for that matter, do people help others or ignore them, eat a lot or starve themselves, mow their lawns or let them grow wild, haunt art museums or sleazy bars, go to college or drop out of high school?

These are questions about motivation, about why people behave as they do. The word *motivation* comes from *movere,* the Latin word meaning "to move." Psychologists who study motivation focus on internal and external influences that might "move" a person. They ask questions such as: What starts a person acting in a particular way? What determines the direction, strength, and persistence of that action? In short, **motivation** refers to the influences that govern the initiation, direction, intensity, and persistence of behavior (Evans, 1989).

Like the question of how people behave and think, the puzzle of why they do so involves concepts and research from many areas of psychology (see the Linkages diagram). Part of the reason people behave as they do is that they are motivated to feel certain emotions, such as the joy of conquering a lofty peak or giving birth. Motivation can also affect emotions, as when your hunger makes you more likely to display anger toward someone who annoys you. In short, motivation and emotion are inextricably intertwined. In this chapter we provide an overview of concepts of motivation and look at research on some important examples of motivated behavior. We also examine the defining features of emotions and why they are valuable to human beings.

Concepts and Theories of Motivation

The concept of motivation helps psychologists to accomplish what Albert Einstein once said was the whole purpose of science: to discover unity in diversity. Suppose that a man holds down two jobs, consistently turns down invitations to the movies, wears old clothes, drives an old car, eats food left behind from other people's lunches, refuses to give to charity, and keeps his furnace set at sixty degrees in the dead of winter. Why? Possibly he does so because he likes to work hard, hates movies, fears new clothes and new cars, enjoys other people's cold leftovers, does not care about the poor, and likes cold air. This set of statements certainly covers all of this man's behaviors. But a far simpler way of accounting for those behaviors is to suggest that the man is trying to save as much money as possible. In other words, by suggesting a **motive,** a reason or purpose for behavior, you can find unity beneath the apparent diversity of many behaviors.

In more formal terms, motivation can be described as an **intervening variable,** which is a variable that is not observed directly but that helps to account for relationships between various stimuli and responses. In other words, environmental stimuli and behavioral responses to them are often related because of some motivational factor that intervenes, or comes between them. In the example shown in Figure 12.1, all the responses can be understood by viewing them as guided by the single unifying motive of thirst. As an intervening variable, motivation helps to explain why different stimuli can lead to the same response, and why the same stimulus can produce different responses.

Similarly, motivation provides a way to explain fluctuations in behavior over time. For example, many people cannot bring themselves to lose weight, quit smoking, or exercise until they actually experience a heart attack or other serious physical consequences of unhealthy lifestyles. Such consequences tend to make people feel more vulnerable to illness and, in accordance with the health-belief models discussed in Chapter 13, often motivate them to adopt a low-fat diet, give up tobacco, work out on a regular basis, and reduce the stress in their lives. In other words, particular stimuli—including eclairs, cigarettes, and health clubs—elicit different responses at different times. The idea that a person's motivation can change is useful in accounting for fluctuations in eating, drinking, smoking, or even the amount of effort people put into a marriage, a job, a tennis game, or other activities.

Linkages

The questions in this diagram illustrate some of the relationships between the topics of this chapter, motivation and emotion, and other chapter topics. The study of motivation and emotion is closely tied to biological psychology. To understand changes in sexual activity, for example, psychologists use information about how the brain and endocrine systems influence each other and how hormones influence behavior. Similarly, the bodily responses accompanying emotions provide a dimension that distinguishes emotions from other types of mental processes. Thus in this chapter we revisit a number of topics introduced in Chapter 4, including the central and autonomic nervous systems and the endocrine system. The diagram provides a sampling of additional linkages among motivation, emotion, and other aspects of psychology; the numbers in parentheses indicate where these linkages are discussed. ■

BIOLOGICAL ASPECTS OF PSYCHOLOGY
How does the brain affect eating? (p. 410)

SENSATION
Do people need a certain amount of sensory stimulation? (p. 169)

SOCIAL BEHAVIOR AND GROUP INFLUENCES
What motivates people to be aggressive? (p. 654)

Motivation and Emotion

MEMORY
How do motivation and emotion affect memory? (p. 312)

SOCIAL COGNITION
How are emotions influenced by the way people think about themselves? (p. 609)

HEALTH, STRESS, AND COPING
What motivational conflicts are tied to stress? (p. 427)

Sources of Motivation

The number of possible motives for human behavior seems endless. People are motivated to satisfy their need for food and water, of course, but they have many other needs as well. We mentioned in the preceding chapter, for example, that some people find the intrinsic (internal) rewards of creativity to be as motivating as the extrinsic (external) rewards of money or praise or power that motivate so many others. And as social animals, people are also influenced by motives to form emotional attachments to others, to become parents, and to affiliate in groups.

These and many other sources of human motivation fall into four general categories. First, human behavior is motivated by basic *biological factors,* particularly the need for food, water, sex, temperature regulation, and the like (Tinbergen, 1989). *Emotional factors* provide a second source of motivation (Petri, 1986). Panic, fear, anger, love, hatred, and many other emotions can be crucial to behavior ranging from selfless giving to brutal murder. Third, *cognitive factors* can motivate human behavior (Zimmerman & Schunk, 1989). People often behave in a certain way because of what they think is possible and because of how they anticipate others will respond. Fourth, motivation may stem from *social factors,* from reactions to parents, teachers, siblings, friends, television, and other sociocultural forces. The combined influence of these social factors in motivation has a profound effect on virtually every aspect of human behavior (Geen, Beatty & Arkin, 1984).

How do these sources of motivation act on behavior? Does one type dominate the others? Psychologists have incorporated these factors into theories designed to explain why humans behave as they do. No one theory provides a completely satisfactory explanation of all aspects of motivation, but each of the four most prominent—including instinct theory, drive-reduction theory, arousal theory, and incentive theory—offers an important perspective.

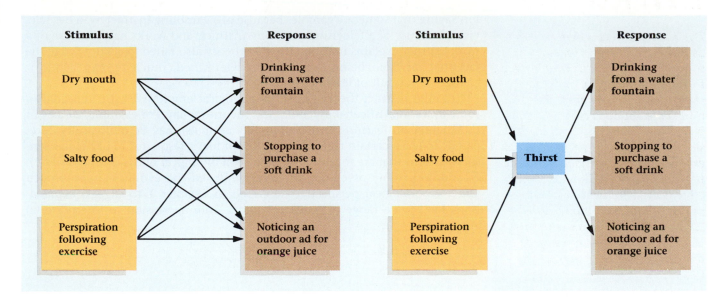

Figure 12.1
Motives as Intervening Variables
Motives can act as explanatory links between apparently unrelated stimuli and responses. In this example, seeing thirst as the common motive provides an explanation of why each stimulus elicits the responses shown.

Instinct Theory and Its Descendants

Early in this century many psychologists favored instinct theory. As described in Chapter 1, **instincts** are automatic, involuntary, and unlearned behavior patterns that are consistently "released" in the presence of particular stimuli (Tinbergen, 1989). For example, the male three-spined stickleback fish suddenly becomes aggressive when it spots the red underbelly of another male. This behavior is not learned and is often called a *fixed-action pattern.*

William McDougall (1908) postulated eighteen human instincts, including self-assertion, reproduction, pugnacity, and gregariousness. Within twenty years, the list of proposed human instincts had grown to 10,000; one critic suggested that his colleagues had "an instinct to produce instincts" (Bernard, 1924). Instincts had become meaningless labels that merely described behav-

The male greater frigate bird displays his red throat as part of a mating ritual. This behavior is instinctive; it does not have to be learned.

ior. Saying that someone gambles because of a gambling instinct, watches television because of a television-watching instinct, and works hard because of a work instinct explains nothing. Instinct theory also failed to acknowledge the fact that far from being rigid and predetermined, much human behavior changes as a result of learning.

Although instinct theory failed, its biological emphasis is still reflected in some more sophisticated psychological theories today. For example, we saw in the chapter on learning that people, like animals, may be biologically "prepared" to learn certain fears or aversions, or may "resonate" to particular sensory patterns that are meaningful because of biological needs (Shepard, 1984). In addition, some psychologists have employed the evolutionary approach and sociobiological perspective described in Chapter 1 to suggest explanations for a wide range of social behaviors from aggression to interpersonal attraction.

Thinking Critically

Does Evolution Explain How People Choose a Marriage Partner?

Some of those who take an evolutionary approach to psychology suggest that the choice of a marriage partner has a biological basis. Love and marriage, they say, are the result of an inborn desire to produce and nurture offspring so that one's own genes can survive in one's children and thus in generations to come. This sociobiological perspective focuses on the fact that males can father many children and can participate in conception from puberty until death, while females can have only a limited number of children and can conceive only between about the ages of fifteen and forty. According to this view, the limited number of offspring they can produce makes women more psychologically invested than men in the survival and development of each of their children. Males and females, therefore, will use different criteria for selecting an appropriate mate (see Figure 12.2).

What am I being asked to believe or accept?
According to the sociobiological perspective, males in all cultures should value most highly a female's *reproductive capacity* (as signified by youth, attractiveness, and good health), while females should value a male's capacity for *resource acquisition* (as signified by maturity, ambition, and earning capacity).

What evidence is available to support the assertion?
There certainly are data supporting an evolutionary view of love and marriage. In one study of more than 10,000 men and women in thirty-three countries on six continents and five isolated islands, males generally expressed a preference for youth and good health when looking for a prospective mate; females generally expressed a preference for male maturity and wealth (Buss, 1989, 1994). Moreover, in virtually every country younger women tended to marry older men. There is also evidence from an even wider array of cultures that women give more attention and other resources to each of their children than men do (Buss, 1991; Kenrick & Keefe, 1990).

Are there alternative ways of interpreting the evidence?
Much of the evidence cited in support of an evolutionary approach can also be interpreted to suggest that gender differences in mate-seeking (and many other social behaviors) are culturally learned, not biologically predetermined. For example, among the Zulu of South Africa, where women are expected to build houses, carry water, and perform other physically demanding

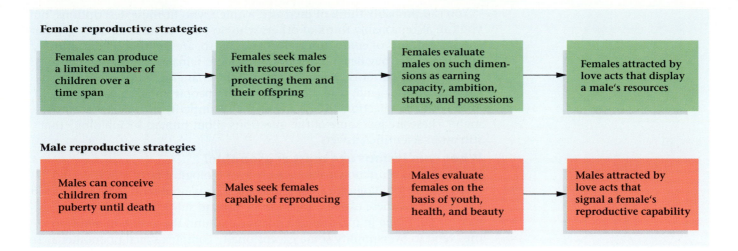

Figure 12.2
An Evolutionary Perspective on Love and Attraction
An evolutionary approach to partner selection in humans suggests that differing biological characteristics in males and females create priorities that motivate each gender to seek a differing set of characteristics in a potential marriage partner.

tasks, men value maturity and ambition in a prospective mate more than women do (Buss, 1989).

Further, the fact that women have been systematically denied economic and political power in many of the cultures studied may account for their tendency to rely on the security and economic power provided by men (Howard et al., 1987; Wallen, 1989). Females' mate-selection patterns may reflect widespread social and economic discrimination against them, not their innate biological needs.

What additional evidence would help to evaluate the alternatives?

These alternative explanations must be evaluated in light of additional information, especially from more intensive research on cultures in which traditional mate-selection criteria are and are not emphasized (Irons, 1989). For example, we do not yet know if, in cultures such as the Zulu, where men's preferences appear to emphasize women's maturity and ambition, men also have less economic opportunity and power than women. If so, this would strengthen the view that—for men and women alike—social factors play a strong role in influencing mate selection.

We also need to know more about courting behavior and its relationship to mate preferences in various cultures. For example, the evolutionary view of mating emphasizes *intrasexual competition,* in which males compete with other males for the most desirable females and females compete with one another for the most desirable males. If sociobiological mechanisms of mate selection operate in humans, we should see men and women competing for mates in different ways, each of which advertises the features most attractive to the opposite sex. Specifically, we would see males vying to display money, clothes, and other material resources that establish their status as "good providers." They would be less concerned with appearing youthful, attractive, and healthy. If they deceive, men would be most likely to exaggerate their status, earning power, or devotion to family life. Their criticisms of other men would focus on inferior income, immaturity, or lack of ambition. In contrast, women would be expected to compete in terms of reproductive capacity, not economic power or potential. They would try to appear as youthful, physically attractive, and healthy as possible and, if they deceive, it would be by understating their age, especially as they approach the end of their childbearing years. When criticizing other women, they would be expected to emphasize advancing age or unattractiveness.

You can probably think of men and women who fit these descriptions, but you can also probably think of others who do not. Are there actually gender-specific patterns of competition for mates? If so, are they consistent across cultures, or do they depend on what males and females in different cultures find ideal? Do patterns change to parallel the changing status of women in various cultures—and, if so, how quickly? Do people entering a culture with different mate-selection criteria adjust their competitive strategies accordingly? These are just some of the questions about human sociobiology that still await scientific answers.

What conclusions are most reasonable?

Given all that is unknown about the role of biological factors in love and marriage, sociobiological explanations must be viewed with extreme caution. For one thing, these explanations can be used to support the (often discriminatory) *status quo* in male-female relations around the world. In addition, they tend to oversimplify some exceptionally complex social phenomena. To take just the most obvious examples, many people fall in love and may marry but, for a variety of reasons, do not wish to become parents. Similarly, many people adopt, nurture, and love children who do not share, and thus cannot pass on, the adoptive parents' genes. And some people just will not compete in any way for the attention of a potential mate. Thus, although research on the evolutionary basis of love and marriage may broaden our understanding, sociobiological concepts alone are unlikely to fully account for what brings particular people together. Love and marriage, like many other aspects of psychology, appear to be shaped by a combination of biological and social factors, by nature and nurture. ▪

Drive Reduction Theory

Like instinct theory, drive reduction theory emphasizes the role of biological factors, but it is based on the concept of homeostasis. **Homeostasis** is the tendency for animals and humans to keep their physiological systems at a steady level, or equilibrium, by constantly adjusting themselves in response to change. We described a version of this concept in Chapter 4 when we discussed feedback loops that keep hormones at desirable levels.

According to **drive reduction theory**, an imbalance in homeostasis creates a **need**—a biological requirement for well-being. This need, in turn, creates a **drive**—a psychological state of arousal that prompts the organism to take action to restore the balance and, in the process, to reduce the drive (Hull, 1943). For example, if you have had no water for some time, the chemical balance of your body fluids is disturbed, creating a biological need for water. The psychological consequence of this need is a drive—thirst—that motivates you to find and drink water. After drinking, the need for water is satisfied, and the drive to drink is reduced. In other words, drives push people to satisfy needs, thus leading to drive reduction and a return to homeostasis (see Figure 12.3).

Drive reduction theory incorporates the influence of learning by distinguishing between primary and secondary drives. **Primary drives** are those that arise from basic biological needs, such as the need for food or water. (Recall from the chapter on learning that food, water, and other things that satisfy primary drives are known as *primary reinforcers*.) Neither basic biological needs nor the primary drives to satisfy them require any learning (Hull, 1951). However, through classical conditioning or other learning mechanisms, people acquire learned drives known as **secondary drives**. Once a secondary drive is acquired, it motivates people to act *as if* they have an unmet basic need. For example, as people learn to associate having money with the satisfaction of primary drives for food, shelter, and so on, having money may become a secondary drive. Having too little money (a condition most people feel they are

Figure 12.3
Drive Reduction Theory and Homeostasis
Internal homeostatic mechanisms, such as the regulation of body temperature or of food and water intake, are often compared to thermostats. If the temperature in a house drops below the thermostat setting, the heat comes on and brings the temperature up to that preset level, achieving homeostasis. When the temperature reaches or exceeds the preset point, the furnace shuts off.

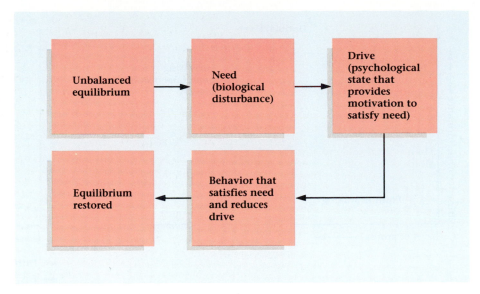

Figure 12.4
Curiosity
This monkey learned to perform a complicated task simply for the opportunity to look at a moving electric train.

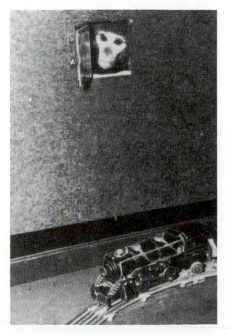

in most of the time) thus motivates a wide variety of behaviors—from hard work to thievery—designed to obtain more funds.

Drive reduction theory is able to account for far more behavior than instinct theory. But humans and animals go to great lengths to do things that do not obviously reduce any primary or secondary drive. Consider curiosity. Animals frequently explore and manipulate what is around them, even though these activities do not lead to drive reduction. When new objects are placed in the environment, most animals smell, touch, and manipulate them in countless ways. Rats will carefully explore every inch of a maze they have never seen, but the time they spend investigating a second maze depends on how similar it is to the first (Montgomery, 1953). Rats will also exert an extraordinary effort simply to enter a new environment, especially if it is complex and full of novel objects (Berlyne, 1960; Dember, Earl & Paradise, 1957; Myers & Miller, 1954). Monkeys are actually willing to "pay" for the opportunity to satisfy their curiosity (Bolles, 1975), as Figure 12.4 demonstrates. People are no less curious. Most find it difficult to resist checking out anything that is new or unusual. They go to the new mall or museum, read the newspaper, and travel around the world just to see what there is to see.

Arousal Theory

People also go out of their way to ride roller coasters, climb mountains, go to horror movies, and do countless other things that, like curiosity-motivated behaviors, fail to reduce any known drive (Csikszentmihalyi, 1975; Deci, 1980). Quite the opposite. These behaviors appear to *increase* people's levels of activation, or arousal. The realization that people are sometimes motivated to reduce arousal and sometimes seek to increase it (Smith & Dorfman, 1975) led to theories tying motivation to the regulation of arousal.

Most theorists think of **arousal** as a general level of activation reflected in the state of several physiological systems (Brehm & Self, 1989). Thus, one's level of arousal can be measured by electrical activity in the brain, by heart action, by muscle tension, and by the state of many other organ systems (Petri, 1986). Normally, arousal is lowest during deep, quiet sleep and highest during periods of panic or extreme excitement. Arousal is increased by hunger, thirst, or other biological drives. It is also elevated by very intense stimuli (bright lights or loud noises, for example), by unexpected or novel events, and by caffeine and other stimulant drugs.

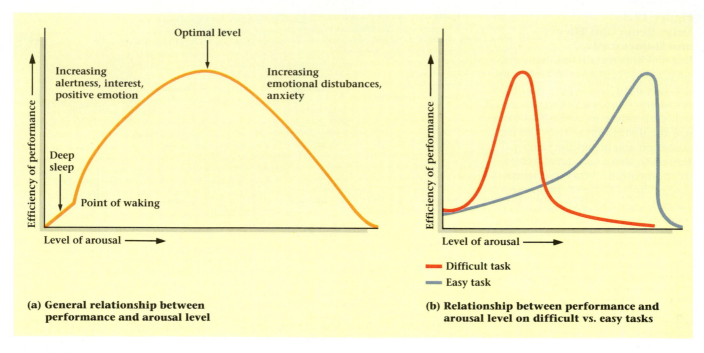

(a) **General relationship between performance and arousal level**

(b) **Relationship between performance and arousal level on difficult vs. easy tasks**

Source: Hebb, 1955.

Figure 12.5
The Arousal-Performance Relationship

Notice in part (a) that performance is very poor when arousal is very low *or* very high and that it is best when arousal is at some intermediate level. When you are nearly asleep, for example, it is difficult to process information efficiently or to organize verbal or physical responses. Overexcitement can also interfere with attention, perception, thinking, and the smooth coordination of physical actions. In general, optimal performance comes at a lower level of arousal on difficult or complex tasks and at a higher level of arousal on easy tasks, as shown in part (b). Thus, even a relatively small amount of overarousal can cause students to perform far below their potential on particularly difficult tests (Sarason, 1984). Because animal research early in this century by Robert Yerkes and his colleagues provided supportive evidence, this arousal-performance relationship is sometimes referred to as the Yerkes-Dodson law even though Yerkes never actually discussed performance as a function of arousal (Winton, 1987).

People perform best, and often feel best, when arousal is moderate. Figure 12.5 depicts the general relationship between level of arousal and efficiency of performance. Overarousal can be particularly detrimental to performance. For example, it has been estimated that because of overarousal, 75 to 85 percent of soldiers in battle sometimes "freeze" and are unable to fire their weapons (Marshall, 1947). Overarousal can also interfere with performance on intellectual tasks (Ford, Wright & Haythornthwaite, 1985); this lower level of performance is just one of the consequences of stress discussed in Chapter 13.

Arousal theories of motivation suggest that people are motivated to behave in ways that maintain what is, for them, an *optimal level* of arousal (Fiske & Maddi, 1961; Hebb, 1955). In general, people are motivated to increase their arousal level when it is too low and to decrease it when it is too high. They seek excitement when they are bored and relaxation when they have had too much excitement. After listening to lectures in the morning and studying all afternoon, for example, you might feel the urge to see an exciting movie that evening. But if your day was spent playing baseball, engaging in a fierce political debate, and helping a friend move, an evening of quiet relaxation might seem ideal. If you do not think so, it may be because you have a very high optimal level of arousal. Indeed, people differ substantially in the amount of arousal at which they are at their personal "peak" (Zuckerman, 1984).

Incentive Theory

Instinct, drive, and arousal theories of motivation all focus on internal processes that push people to behave in certain ways. Incentive theory, in contrast, emphasizes that environmental stimuli may motivate behavior by pulling people toward them. According to **incentive theory**, people act in order to attain positive incentives and avoid negative incentives. Differences in behavior from one person to another, or from one situation to another, can be traced to the incentives available and the value each person places on them at a given time. If a person *expects* a particular behavior to lead to an outcome that has high *value* to the person, he or she will be motivated to engage in that behav-

In Review: Theories of Motivation

Theory	Main Points
Instinct	Innate biological instincts guide behavior.
Drive reduction	Behavior is guided by biological needs and learned ways of reducing drives arising from those needs.
Arousal	People seek to maintain an optimal level of physiological arousal, which differs from person to person. Maximum performance occurs at optimal arousal levels.
Incentive	Behavior is guided by the lure of available rewards. Cognitive factors influence expectations of the value of various rewards and the likelihood of attaining them.

Linkages: People who characteristically enjoy high levels of arousal are likely to smoke, drink alcohol, engage in frequent sexual activity, listen to loud music, eat spicy foods, and do things that are novel and risky (Farley, 1986; Zuckerman, 1979). Those with a lower optimal arousal level tend to behave in ways that bring less intense stimulation and to take fewer risks. Most of the differences in optimal arousal have a strong biological basis and, as discussed in Chapter 14, may help shape broader differences in personality, such as introversion-extraversion.

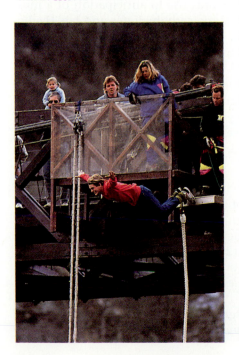

ior. The value of an incentive is influenced by biological as well as cognitive factors. For example, food is a more motivating incentive when you are hungry than when you are satiated (Logue, 1986).

Opponent Processes, Motivation, and Emotion   Both the changing value of incentives and the regulation of arousal play important roles in Richard Solomon's *opponent-process theory,* which we discussed in the Linkages section of Chapter 8, on learning (Solomon & Corbit, 1974). As noted there, this theory is based on two assumptions. The first is that any reaction to a stimulus is automatically followed by an opposite reaction, called the opponent process. For example, being startled by a sudden sound is typically followed by relaxation and relief. Second, after repeated exposure to the same stimulus, the initial reaction weakens, and the opponent process becomes quicker and stronger.

Research on opponent-process theory has revealed a predictable pattern of emotional changes that helps explain some people's motivation to repeatedly engage in arousing but dangerous activities such as skydiving or bungee-jumping. Prior to the first several episodes, people typically experience stark terror, followed by intense relief afterward. With further experience, however, the terror fades to mild anxiety, while what had been relief becomes a feeling of euphoria that eventually appears *during* the activity (Solomon, 1980). As a result, says Solomon, some people's motivation to pursue dangerous activity can become a virtual addiction.

The theoretical approaches we have outlined are complementary (see "In Review: Theories of Motivation"). Each emphasizes different sources of motivation, and each has helped to guide research into motivated behaviors such as eating, sex, and work, which we consider in the sections that follow.

Hunger and Eating

Hunger is deceptively simple; people get hungry when they do not eat. Much as a car needs gas, people need the fuel that food supplies. Is there a bodily mechanism that, like a car's gas gauge, signals your need for fuel? What causes hunger? What determines which foods you eat, and how do you know when to stop? The answers to these questions involve not only interactions between the brain and the rest of the body but also learning and social factors.

Biological Signals for Hunger

Folklore would tell you to look to the stomach as the source of cues about hunger and eating. After all, people say they feel "hunger pangs" in the stomach when it is "empty" and complain of having a "full stomach" after eating a large meal. The stomach does contract during hunger pangs, and filling the stomach with inert bulk reduces appetite (Cannon & Washburn, 1912; Janowitz & Grossman, 1949, 1951). But people who have had their stomachs removed because of illness still experience hunger when they do not eat and still eat normal amounts of food (Janowitz, 1967). Stomach cues operate mainly when people are very hungry or very full, and they are not necessary for knowing when to eat.

Linkages: How does the brain affect eating? (a link to Biological Aspects of Psychology)

If the body's "gas tank" does not by itself detect the amount of fuel available, how are hunger and eating regulated? It is the brain that more precisely assesses the body's fuel level, though not by directly monitoring what is in the stomach. Instead, the brain checks what is in the blood vessels. The brain's ability to "read" bloodborne signs of the body's need for fuel was established years ago when researchers deprived rats of food for long periods, then injected some of the deprived rats with the blood of rats that had just eaten. When given access to food, the injected rats ate very little, if anything (Davis et al., 1969).

The Signals: Nutrients and Hormones   What was it in the satiated animals' blood that told the hungry animals' brains that there was little need to eat? The brain detects both nutrients that are absorbed into the bloodstream from the stomach and hormones that are released into the bloodstream in response to those nutrients. These signals in the bloodstream can lead to hunger and eating or to **satiety**, the state of no longer wanting to eat.

The nutrients that the brain monitors include *glucose* (the main form of sugar used by the cells of the body), *fatty acids* (derived from fat), and *amino acids* (derived from protein). When the level of blood glucose drops, eating increases dramatically (Friedman & Stricker, 1976; Mogenson, 1976). When large doses of glucose are injected into the blood of a food-deprived animal, it refuses to eat.

The hormones that the brain monitors include *glucocorticoids, insulin,* and *cholecystokinin (CCK)*. Levels of glucocorticoids rise in anticipation of a meal and contribute to the motivation to consume carbohydrates and fats (Leibowitz, 1992). Insulin is released whenever glucose levels rise. Cholecystokinin is used as a neurotransmitter in the brain to signal satiety. It is also released from the stomach itself and is detected by the autonomic nervous system, which then signals the brain. During a meal, CCK is released from both the gut and from neurons in the hypothalamus (Schick, Yaksh & Go, 1986). When CCK is injected into animals' brains, they stop eating and show other signs of being satiated, such as grooming and sleeping (Smith & Gibbs, 1992). At high levels, cholecystokinin produces nausea, which partly explains the feelings that often accompany overeating.

Reading the Signals   Many parts of the brain contribute to the control of hunger and eating, but three regions of the hypothalamus play the primary role in reading and reacting to the signals of hunger. These regions of the hypothalamus are the ventromedial nucleus, the lateral hypothalamus, and the paraventricular nucleus (see Figure 12.6).

Within the *ventromedial nucleus,* neurons detect the blood levels of glucose. If the ventromedial nucleus of a rat is *destroyed,* the animal will eat far more than usual, increasing its weight up to threefold. Then the rat begins to eat enough food to maintain itself at this higher weight (Teitelbaum, 1961). If the ventromedial nucleus is electrically *stimulated,* the rat stops eating. Thus, the

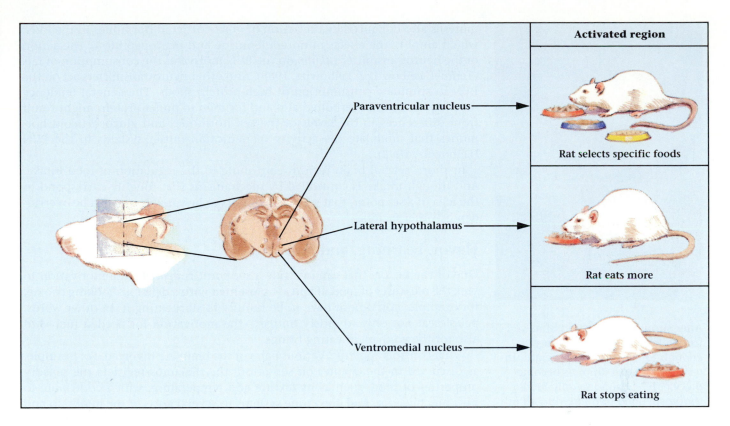

Activated region

Paraventricular nucleus

Rat selects specific foods

Lateral hypothalamus

Rat eats more

Ventromedial nucleus

Rat stops eating

Figure 12.6
The Hypothalamus and Hunger
Studies of the hypothalamus have concentrated on stimulating or destroying fibers that pass through the paraventricular nucleus, the lateral hypothalmus, and the ventromedial nucleus. Here are some of the results of this research.

ventromedial nucleus seems to act as a "stop-eating" center. Stimulate it and animals stop eating; destroy it and their tendency to stop eating is disrupted.

When fibers in the *lateral hypothalamus* are *destroyed,* rats stop eating almost entirely. Most resume eating eventually, but they consume only small amounts of their most preferred foods and maintain a much-reduced weight (Keesey & Powley, 1975). In contrast, if the lateral hypothalamus is electrically *stimulated,* rats begin to eat vast quantities, even if they have just consumed food. In short, the lateral hypothalamus seems to act as a "start-eating" center. When it is stimulated, it causes eating; when it is destroyed, the tendency to start eating is impaired.

One view of how these two regions interact uses the concept of a set point (Keesey & Powley, 1975; Nisbett, 1972; Powley & Keesey, 1970). It suggests that a mechanism in the brain establishes a level, or *set point,* based on body weight or a related metabolic signal. Normal animals eat until their set point is reached; then they stop eating and resume only when desirable intake falls below the set point. Destruction or stimulation of the lateral or ventromedial areas may alter the set point. For example, perhaps animals with damage to the ventromedial hypothalamus eat more and maintain a higher weight because their set points have been raised. Similarly, damage to the lateral hypothalamus may lower the set point, causing less eating and maintenance of a lower weight.

However, research on the *paraventricular nucleus* (PVN) indicates that the idea of simple "start-eating" and "stop-eating" centers does not do justice to the complexity of the brain's control of eating. Several neurotransmitters act on the PVN to selectively motivate the consumption of different types of food (Leibowitz, 1992). For example, the neurotransmitters *norepinephrine* and *neuropeptide Y* stimulate consumption of carbohydrates by acting on cells in the PVN. The neurotransmitter *serotonin* acts in the PVN to reduce carbohydrate consumption (Blundell, 1991). The motivation to consume carbohy-

After surgical destruction of its ventromedial nucleus, this rat ate enough to triple its body weight. Interestingly, such animals become picky eaters, choosing only foods that taste good and ignoring all others (Miller, Bailey & Stevenson, 1930; Teitelbaum, 1957).

drates is also enhanced by the action of glucocorticoid hormones in the PVN, which amplify the effects of norepinephrine and neuropeptide Y. The action of the neurotransmitter *galanin* on the PVN motivates the consumption of fats (Tempel, Leibowitz & Leibowitz, 1988). And other neurotransmitters act on the PVN to stimulate consumption of high-protein foods. The general tendency for women to prefer carbohydrates and for men to prefer protein might result from differences in the levels of the sex hormones and glucocorticoid hormones that modulate the activity of neurotransmitter systems in the PVN (Leibowitz, 1992).

In short, several brain regions contribute to the regulation of food intake. And though intake is controlled by mechanisms that roughly correspond to the idea of a set point, that set point appears to be variable and can be overridden by other factors.

Flavor, Learning, and Appetite

One of the factors that can override a set point is *appetite,* the motivation to seek the pleasures of food. If you are presented with a delicious-looking cookie, for example, you do not have to be hungry to start eating it. In other words, people eat not only to satisfy hunger—the motivation for needed fuel—but also for the enjoyment eating brings.

What controls appetite? Various parts of the brain are involved. For example, as discussed in the chapter on sensation, the thalamus registers the sensory properties of food, such as its texture and temperature, which contribute to how much we eat. And dopamine systems in several areas of the midbrain and forebrain are involved in the pleasurable feelings of eating. These feelings depend largely on the flavor of food and what people learn to associate with it.

Flavor Cues   In the chapter on sensation we note that taste and odor cues constitute flavor. In general, experiments confirm that flavor is particularly important in initiating eating (Blundell, 1991). Variety is also important. In one experiment, some animals were offered just one type of food while others were offered a succession of distinctly different-tasting foods. The group getting the varied menu ate nearly four times more than the one-food group. As each new food was introduced, the animals began to eat voraciously, regardless of how much they had already eaten (LeMagnen, 1971; Peck, 1978). Similar experiments with humans led to essentially the same conclusion (Cabanac, 1971). All things being equal, people consume more food during a multicourse meal than when only one type of food is served. Apparently, the taste of a particular food becomes less and less enjoyable as more of it is eaten (Woody et al., 1981).

Flavor motivates eating through its *hedonic value,* the pleasure arising from good tastes and smells (Cabanac, 1971). However, as suggested by incentive theory, hunger can modulate the hedonic value of flavor. For example, sweet tastes are inherently pleasurable, even to very young infants (Blass & Smith, 1992), but judgments about the pleasantness of sweet tastes are influenced by the presence of nutrients in the stomach. When glucose is infused into rats' stomachs, their facial expressions upon tasting sugar change from pleasure to disgust (Cabanac & Lafrance, 1992). Consuming a large amount of glucose makes the taste of sugar distinctly less pleasurable (Cabanac, 1971).

Learned Associations   As mentioned in the chapter on sensation, fat and protein have no inherent taste or odor. Why does eating these nutrients bring pleasure? In accordance with the classical conditioning principles described in Chapter 8, volatile odorants in these foods come to be associated with the nutritional value of their fat and protein content. This conditioning has been demonstrated in rats by infusing fat directly into the stomach, and pairing the infusion with the taste of either cherry or grape Kool-Aid (sweetened with non-nutritive saccharin). Rats soon prefer the flavor that was associated with the fat infusion (Lucas & Sclafani, 1989). Similarly, children come to prefer flavors that have been associated with high-fat ingredients (Johnson, McPhee, & Birch, 1991). It remains to be seen whether the new diet foods containing "fake fats" eventually lose their appeal because they do not contain the nutritive value normally associated with high-fat foods.

Conditioning contributes to the pleasure of eating in other ways as well. The tastes and odors associated with nutrients come to elicit conditioned physiological responses—such as secretion of saliva, gastric juices, and insulin—in anticipation of receiving those nutrients. These responses then augment appetite—by lowering blood glucose, for example—thus justifying the time-honored role of "appetizers." Just the sight of food can elicit these conditioned responses, which is part of why seeing a pizza on television may suddenly make you order one.

People learn not only to eat before they are in desperate need of fuel but also to stop eating before the nutrients from a meal that will eventually signal satiety have all been absorbed into the bloodstream. This is *conditioned satiation,* the tendency to stop eating because of the association of certain stimuli with satiety.

Social situations and other people provide some of the learned cues that stimulate an appetite for particular items. Eating popcorn at movies, pretzels with beer, and hot dogs at baseball games are just a few examples common in North American culture. Similarly, how much you eat may depend more on what others do than on what you need or want. Courtesy or custom might prompt you to consume less than normal, but in general the presence of other people tends to increase consumption. Most people eat 60 to 75 percent larger meals when they are with others than when eating alone (Redd & de Castro, 1992; de Castro & Brewer, 1992).

Eating Disorders

When something goes wrong in the mechanisms that regulate hunger and eating, a person may display an *eating disorder.* The most common and health-threatening eating disorders are obesity, anorexia nervosa, and bulimia nervosa.

Obesity According to the National Institutes of Health, 25 to 33 percent of all Americans are overweight (NIH, 1992). **Obesity** is a condition of severe overweight—often by as much as one hundred pounds—that threatens the health of millions of people by contributing to diabetes, high blood pressure, and increased risk of heart attack (Wilson, 1984).

Why do obese people gain so much weight? The body maintains a given weight through a combination of food intake and energy output (Keesey & Powley, 1986). To become obese, a person must consume more calories than the body can *metabolize,* or burn up; the excess calories are stored as fat. The body constantly metabolizes calories, and this metabolic level increases during activity. Because women tend to have a lower metabolic rate than men even when equally active, they tend to gain weight more rapidly than men when eating the same number of calories (Ferraro et al., 1992).

Does obesity result from consuming more food than normal or from abnormally low metabolic processes? Most obese people have normal resting metabolic rates and are not less active than lean people (Meijer et al., 1992). However, obese people usually eat more than those of normal weight. They are also finicky eaters; they eat larger-than-average amounts of foods they like and less-than-average amounts of less-preferred foods (Peck, 1978). When trying to restrict food intake, some obese people greatly underestimate how much they have eaten (Lichtman et al., 1992).

Inactivity during childhood is thought to contribute to weight gain, and television watching is a major cause of inactivity among overweight children (Dietz, 1991). Recent studies show that metabolic rates during television watching are even lower than during rest, and that the reduction while watching television may be even greater in obese children compared to those of normal weight (Klesges, Shelton & Klesges, 1993).

The fact that most obese people are fat because they eat more food does not mean that they are "morally lax." It has been suggested that deficits in the neurotransmitter serotonin increase obese people's craving for carbohydrates (Logue, 1991) or that obese people have a higher set point for body weight and therefore feel hungry more often than other people (Keesey, 1980; Nisbett, 1972). A higher set point could result both from genetics (Grilo & Pogue-Geile, 1991) and from early, even prenatal, nutrition that may have created particularly large and numerous fat cells (Foreyt & Kondo, 1984). The presence of especially large and numerous fat cells in obese individuals contributes to their tendency to accumulate fat (Hirsch & Knittle, 1970; Knittle et al., 1979).

Psychological explanations for obesity have also been proposed. Perhaps obese people fail to develop enough conditioned satiety following normal-sized meals to prevent overeating (Booth, 1980). Maladaptive reactions to stress may also be involved. Many people tend to eat more when under stress, and this reaction may be particularly extreme among those who become obese (Herman & Polivy, 1975; McKenna, 1972). However, obese people are no more likely than normal-weight people to display mental disorders (Stunkard & Wadden, 1992).

Losing weight and keeping it off for at least five years is extremely difficult (NIH, 1992). Why is it so hard for obese people to lose weight? Changes in the rate at which people metabolize food may contribute to the difficulty. If food intake is lowered, the metabolic rate also drops, conserving energy and curbing weight loss. This compensatory response makes evolutionary sense; it is highly adaptive for survival to conserve energy during times of famine, for example. But when obese people try to reduce to a normal weight, their metabolic rate tends to drop *below* a normal level. As a result, they begin to gain weight even while eating amounts that would maintain constant weight in others.

These facts suggest that long-term overeating can raise set points for weight (Keesey & Powley, 1986; Kolata, 1985). Thus, diet plans that focus on drastically reduced food intake can be counterproductive. In fact, animal studies suggest that losing and then regaining large amounts of weight, so-called cycling, can result in a slowly increasing average weight (Archambault et al., 1989; Brownell et al., 1986). Sometimes when dieting has proven ineffective, surgical interventions that modify the stomach and intestines and result in stronger satiety signals can be effective, but the results of surgery also depend on motivation to lose weight and on restrained eating (Kral, 1992).

To achieve gradual and permanent weight loss, increasing physical activity is important, because it burns calories without slowing the metabolic rate (Donahoe et al., 1984). The most effective weight-loss programs include reduced food intake, behavior modification to change attitudes and habits related to food, and an exercise program to increase energy expenditure (Safer, 1991).

Anorexia Nervosa The opposite of obesity is **anorexia nervosa**, an eating disorder characterized by self-starvation and dramatic weight loss. Anorexics often report strong hunger yet refuse to eat. Some anorexics are obsessed with food and its preparation but eat almost nothing. The self-starvation of anorexics creates serious, often irreversible, physical damage. Between 4 and 30 percent of these people actually starve themselves to death (Eisner et al., 1985; Szmukler & Russell, 1986). About 95 percent of the people who suffer from anorexia are female, and the worldwide incidence of the problem has increased greatly in the last few decades (Nielsen, 1990; Suematsu et al., 1985). As many as 1 percent of American women between the ages of fifteen and thirty are affected (Gilbert & DeBlassie, 1984).

The causes of anorexia are not known. (For a summary of the processes involved in hunger and the regulation of eating, see "In Review: Major Factors Controlling Hunger and Eating.") It has been speculated that anorexics have an abnormally low set point or some other physiological abnormality (Gwirtsman & Germer, 1981). Anorexics do have abnormal levels of several neurotransmitters, but this is probably a response to starvation rather than a cause, because the levels return to normal when weight is restored (Kaye et al.,

In Review: Major Factors Controlling Hunger and Eating

	Stimulate Eating	Inhibit Eating
Biological	Stomach contractions are associated with subjective feelings of hunger; taste becomes less enjoyable as more of a particular food is consumed, and thus varied tastes increase eating; the lateral area of the hypothalamus serves as a start-eating center by monitoring reductions in blood sugar.	The ventromedial nucleus of the hypothalamus serves as a stop-eating center by monitoring blood; CCK, a hormone, is released during a meal and "read" by the ventromedial nucleus.
Nonbiological factors	Sights and smells of particular foods elicit eating because of prior associations; family customs and social occasions often include norms for eating in particular ways; stress is often associated with eating more.	Contemporary American society values thinness, and thus can inhibit eating; conditioned satiation occurs when certain stimuli are associated with satiety.

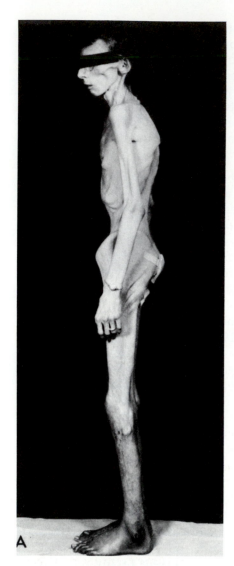

Some anorexics literally starve themselves to death. This woman weighed only forty-seven pounds when she began a treatment program that saved her life.

1989). However, neurotransmitter abnormalities may contribute to other symptoms associated with anorexia, including depression and infertility. Psychological factors that might contribute to the problem include an obsession with thinness and young people's concern with appearing attractive. In other words, anorexics appear to develop a fear of being fat, which they take to dangerous extremes (Achenbach, 1982). Many anorexics continue to view themselves as too fat or misshapen even as they are wasting away (Davis, 1986; Heilbrun & Witt, 1990).

Drugs, hospitalization, and psychotherapy are all used to treat anorexia. In about 70 percent of cases, some combination of treatment and the passage of time brings recovery and maintenance of normal weight (Hsu, 1980; Martin, 1985).

Bulimia Nervosa   Like anorexia, bulimia nervosa involves intense fear of being fat, but the victim may either be thin, normal in weight, or even overweight (Mitchell et al., 1990). **Bulimia nervosa** involves eating massive quantities of food (say, several boxes of cookies, a loaf of bread, a half gallon of ice cream, and a bucket of fried chicken) and then eliminating the food by self-induced vomiting or strong laxatives (Garfinkel, Moldofsky & Garner, 1980). These "binge-purge" episodes occur at least twice a week, sometimes twice a day (Fairburn, 1981; Mitchell & Pyle, 1985).

Like anorexics, bulimics are usually female; estimates of the frequency of anorexia and bulimia range from 1 to 10 percent of adolescent and college-age women (Haller, 1992). Their eating problems usually begin when they are about fifteen years old; and they are obsessed with being slender. However, bulimia and anorexia are separate disorders. Most bulimics realize that their eating habits are problematic, while most anorexics do not. Bulimia nervosa is usually not a life-threatening disorder (Hall et al., 1989; Schlesier-Stroop, 1984). There *are* consequences, however, including dehydration, nutritional imbalances, and intestinal damage. Many bulimics also develop dental problems and raw throats from frequent vomiting and from the objects they insert to induce vomiting. More generally, their preoccupation with eating and with avoiding weight gain prevents many bulimics from working productively (Herzog, 1982).

Bulimia nervosa appears to be caused by a combination of factors, including culturally encouraged overconcern with thinness and attractiveness, depression and other emotional problems, and as-yet undetermined biological abnormalities that might include defective satiety mechanisms (Johnson & Maddi, 1986; Rodin et al., 1990). Treatments for bulimia typically include individual or group therapy and, sometimes, antidepressant medication; these help about 80 percent of bulimic people to eat more normally (Herzog et al., 1990).

Sexual Behavior

Unlike food, sex is not necessary for individual survival. A species without a strong motivation for reproduction, however, would soon cease to exist. From one species to the next, the determinants of sexual motivation and behavior vary widely, but typically they include the individual's physiology, learned behavior, and the physical and social environment. For example, one species of bird that lives in the desert requires adequate sex hormones, a suitable mate, and a particular environment before it engages in sexual behavior. As long as the dry season lasts, it shows no interest in sex, but within ten minutes of the first rainfall the birds vigorously copulate.

What about people? Across cultures a consistent pattern of behavior leads up to copulation. Flirtatious behavior typically involves establishing eye contact and holding the gaze, talking with considerable animation about inconsequential things, gradually rotating to face each other, moving closer together, moistening the lips and smiling, displaying partially covered parts of the body, lightly touching each other as if by accident, and mirroring one another's postures and facial expressions (Perper, 1985).

What happens next? The first extensive laboratory research on human sexual behavior was conducted by William Masters and Virginia Johnson and reported in 1966 in *Human Sexual Response*. Their book contained detailed descriptions of the physical and psychological responses of more than six hundred males and females as they received natural or artificial sexual stimulation. Although their research examined sexual behavior in isolation from the contexts in which it normally occurs, it yielded important data about the **sexual response cycle**, which is the pattern of arousal during and after sexual activity (Masters & Johnson, 1966). As illustrated in Figure 12.7, the cycle is fundamentally similar in men and women, although women display more versions of it.

Once we look beyond the sexual response cycle, generalizations become more difficult. When do people become interested in sex, when do they choose to express these desires, and why? What determines their sexual preference? Biology provides the raw material for human sexual motivation, but learning and sociocultural factors can greatly modify how and when people express themselves sexually. In this section we take a brief look at just a few of these factors.

Hormones and Sexual Desire

The biological underpinnings of human sexual motivation are evident in the roles played by feminine and masculine hormones. The feminine hormones are **estrogens** and **progestins**; the main ones are **estradiol** and **progesterone**. The masculine hormones are **androgens**; the principal androgen is **testosterone**. Each of these hormones circulates in the bloodstream of members of *both* sexes, but relatively more androgens circulate in men and relatively more estrogens and progestins circulate in women. Figure 12.8 illustrates how feedback systems control the secretion of these hormones.

Figure 12.7
The Sexual Response Cycle
Men show one primary pattern of sexual response, which is depicted in part (a). Women display at least three different patterns from time to time; these are labeled A, B, and C in part (b). In both men and women, the first, or *excitement*, phase of the sexual response cycle occurs in response to sexually stimulating input, either from the environment or from one's own thoughts. If this stimulation continues, it leads to intensification of the excitement in the second, or *plateau*, phase. Sexual tension becomes extreme in this phase. If stimulation continues, the person reaches the third, or *orgasmic* stage, which, though it lasts only a few seconds, provides an intensely pleasurable release of physical and psychological tension. The *resolution* phase follows, during which the person returns to a state of relaxation. At this point, men enter a *refractory period* during which they are temporarily insensitive to sexual stimulation. Women are capable of immediately repeating the cycle if stimulation continues.

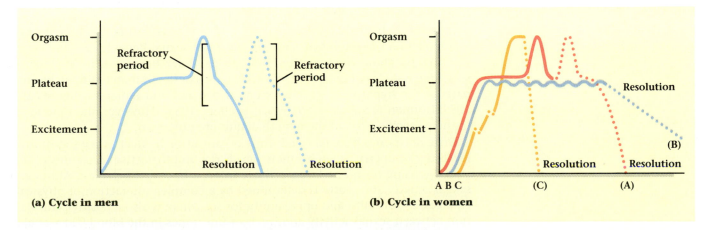

(a) Cycle in men

(b) Cycle in women

Source: Adapted from Masters & Johnson, 1966.

Figure 12.8
The Regulation of Sex Hormones
Feedback loops involving the hypothalamus and pituitary gland as well
as the ovaries or testes control the secretion of sex hormones. Leuteiniz-
ing hormone (LH) stimulates secretion of sex hormones in both males
and females. In males, high levels of
testosterone reduce activity in the
hypothalamus, which lowers secretion of LH, which causes less testosterone to be secreted. This negative
feedback system keeps the secretion
of testosterone within a fairly narrow range. In females, the feedback
loops are more complex, and produce a cyclic fluctuation of hormone
levels. During most of the menstrual
cycle, estrogen exerts a negative
feedback effect on LH. In addition, a
positive feedback effect occurs at the
middle of the menstrual cycle: estrogen increases hypothalamic activity,
causing more LH to be secreted,
which causes more estrogen to be secreted. A surge of LH is then released, which causes the ovary to release an egg. Androgens and
progestins also fluctuate across the
menstrual cycle.

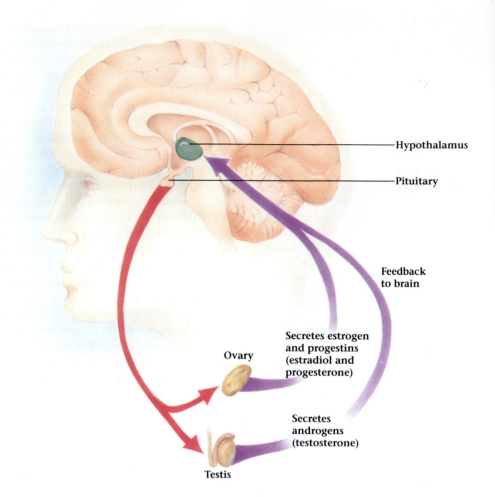

Hypothalamus

Pituitary

Feedback
to brain

Ovary

Secretes estrogen
and progestins
(estradiol and
progesterone)

Secretes
androgens
(testosterone)

Testis

Sex hormones have both organizational and activational effects (Phoenix et
al., 1959). The *organizational effects* are permanent changes in the brain that
change the way an individual thereafter responds to hormones. The *activational effects* are reversible changes in behavior that remain as long as the hormone levels are elevated.

In rats, the organizational effects of hormones occur right around the time
of birth, when either a "malelike" or a "femalelike" pattern of brain connections is laid down in particular brain regions. Because these regions, such as
the hypothalamus, differ in males and females, they are called *sexually dimorphic* regions. The male must be exposed to androgens during this time if normal male brain development and normal male sexual behavior are to occur.
Information about the organizational effects of sex hormones in humans is
sketchier. It is clear, however, that some regions of the human brain, including
parts of the hypothalamus, are different in males and females (Allen et al.,
1989; Hofman & Swaab, 1989; Swaab & Fliers, 1985). However, the functions
of these specific parts of the hypothalamus are unknown.

Once hormones have had their early organizational effects, they stay at low
levels until puberty, when hormone levels rise and the activational effects occur. The rising hormone levels activate interest in sexual behavior. Although
sexual activity at puberty is determined by a complex interaction of physical
changes, social skills, and opportunity for sex, there is also a positive correlation between sexual activity and levels of hormones in the blood (Udry et al.,
1985). Androgens clearly activate sexual interest in males (Davidson, Camargo
& Smith, 1979). And most studies show that estrogens stimulate sexual interest

in females (Sherwin, 1991; Wallen & Lovejoy, 1993). However, some research suggests that androgens motivate sexual interest in *both* sexes (Sherwin & Gelfand, 1987).

Further evidence of the activational effects of hormones comes from studies in which hormone levels have been altered for medical reasons. On the average, sexual motivation and behavior decline among people who have had their hormone-secreting ovaries or testes removed, although some individuals are apparently not affected (Sherwin, Gelfand & Brender, 1985). If appropriate hormonal treatments are given to people whose hormone levels have decreased as a result of surgical removal of the ovaries or testes, their sexual interest and behavior increase (Sherwin, Gelfand & Brender, 1985).

In analyzing the activational effects of hormones, it is important to distinguish between sexual desire and ability (Wallen & Lovejoy, 1993). In adult primates, human and nonhuman, the *ability* to copulate is independent of hormones. This fact may explain the failure of castration to prevent sex crimes by repeat offenders. Hormones affect sexual desire, but men whose testosterone levels are low because of medical conditions or castration still respond with erections to erotic stimuli (Kwan et al., 1983). Thus a sex offender treated with androgen antagonists or by castration would have less motivation to *seek out* sexual situations, but he would still show normal responsiveness to his preferred sexual stimulus (Wallen & Lovejoy, 1993).

Social Factors and Sexual Activity

Even in nonhuman primates, the expression of sexual desire is strongly influenced by social factors such as the presence of a sex partner (Wallen, 1990). Indeed, although hormones generally activate interest in sexual behavior among humans, the many forms this behavior takes are shaped more precisely by a lifetime of learning.

Children learn some sexual behaviors as part of the development of gender roles, as described in the chapter on human development. They may need particular kinds of early social experiences in order to develop normal sexual motivation and behavior. Psychologists cannot study this hypothesis experimentally in humans because it would require manipulating children's early social experiences. However, Harlow's research with monkeys, described in Chapter 3, suggests that contact with a nurturing adult is important for the development of normal sexual behavior (Harlow, 1958). Other studies show that the opportunity to engage in physical play before puberty is important. Animals that are denied play periods during development never learn to copulate successfully (Goldfoot, 1977).

Sexual behavior is also shaped by attitudes that change with changing cultural expectations. In a survey done in the 1920s, for example, most American husbands wanted more frequent sexual contact with their wives, whereas the wives wanted less (Davis, 1929). In a similar survey in the 1970s, only 2 percent of wives said that intercourse was too frequent, and 32 percent thought it was too infrequent (Bell & Bell, 1972). A desire for higher frequency of intercourse is also evident among unmarried women, especially those involved in a serious relationship (Sherwin & Sherry, 1985).

Sexual Dysfunctions   Social and psychological factors not only help shape human sexual behavior; they also contribute to **sexual dysfunction**, in which a person's desire for or ability to have satisfying sexual experiences is inhibited. For men, the most common sexual dysfunction is *erectile disorder* (once known as impotence), which is the inability to have or maintain an erection sufficient for intercourse. Most men experience erectile problems at some point in their lives; it is considered a sexual dysfunction only if erectile difficulties occur consistently enough to interfere with sexual functioning and a partner's satisfaction. Physical causes alone—such as fatigue, diabetes, hypertension, and the side effects of medication or excessive use of alcohol or other drugs—account for only a minority of cases. Psychological factors such as anxiety are seen as playing a significant causal role in as many as 95 percent of erectile disorder cases (Kaplan, 1974; LoPiccolo, 1991).

For women, the most common type of sexual dysfunction is probably *arousal disorder* (once known as frigidity), which involves infrequent orgasms or a lack of orgasms. Psychological factors such as self-consciousness (sometimes linked to parental or religious injunctions against sexual expression), a lack of self-confidence, or depression often contribute to their difficulties in experiencing orgasm. Problems reaching orgasm are also often associated with difficulties in the emotional qualities of the romantic relationship (Kaplan, 1979).

Sexual Orientation

Usually, human sexual activity is **heterosexual,** involving members of the opposite sex. When sexual behavior is directed toward a member of one's own sex, it is called **homosexual.** People who engage in such activities with partners of either sex are called **bisexual.** Whether you prefer to engage in sexual activities with members of your own or the opposite sex is one part of your *sexual orientation,* which has three components:

1. *Sexual identity* refers to whether you consider yourself male or female. Some people who have all of the physical characteristics of one sex nevertheless feel as though they are a member of the opposite sex. About 1 in 20,000 men consider their true identity to be female. About 1 in 50,000 women feel their true identity is male.
2. *Gender role* is a general pattern of work, appearance, and behavior associated with being a man or a woman. As discussed in Chapter 3, gender roles are strongly influenced by learning and cultural traditions.
3. *Sexual preference* refers to the gender to which one is sexually attracted, whether or not that attraction leads to sexual activity.

In many Western cultures, homosexuality was long considered a disease, a mental disorder, or a crime (Hooker, 1993). Attempts to alter the sexual orientation of homosexuals—using methods ranging from psychotherapy to brain surgery and electric shock—were ineffective (Burr, 1993). In 1973 the American Psychiatric Association dropped homosexuality from its *Diagnostic and Statistical Manual of Mental Disorders,* thus officially removing from this sexual orientation the stigma of psychopathology. However, many people still consider homosexuality to be both repugnant and immoral. Moral condemnations of homosexuality often assume that homosexual behaviors and preferences are a matter of choice, changeable by an act of will. However, there is increasing evidence that homosexuality in both men and women is largely determined by biological factors.

Biological Factors in Sexual Orientation   Early researchers looked for a biological cause of homosexuality in the levels of circulating hormones, but no differences between homosexuals and heterosexuals were found. More recent research has been based on the idea, established in animal studies, that during development hormones "masculinize" and "defeminize" the brain (Adkins-Regan, 1988). For example, women who were exposed to unusually high levels of androgens during fetal development are much more likely to become lesbians than their sisters who were not similarly exposed (Money, Schwartz & Lewis, 1984; Dittman et al., 1992). Following up on the discovery of sex differences in parts of the hypothalamus, researchers have studied the

Recent behavior genetic research employing the twin study approach (see Chapter 2) suggests that homosexuality might be genetically influenced. Richard Pillard, an author of one study of this issue, had personal reasons for suspecting this to be the case. He is gay, as are his brother and sister. He suspects that his father was gay, and one of his three daughters is bisexual (Burr, 1993).

hypothalamus of homosexual men. Two investigations have found anatomical differences in the hypothalamus of homosexual versus heterosexual men (Swaab & Hofman, 1990; LeVay, 1991).

Though provocative, these findings fall far short of explaining homosexuality. For one thing, they do not establish whether the brain differences are a cause or an effect of homosexuality. Furthermore, it is not known if these particular regions of the hypothalamus are related to sexual functions.

If sexual orientation is biologically determined, one might expect it to have a strong genetic component. Numerous studies of twins support this idea. One study examined 56 pairs of monozygotic male twins (whose genetic makeup is identical), 54 nonidentical twin pairs (whose genetic makeup is no more alike than that of other brothers), and 57 pairs of adopted brothers (who were genetically unrelated). At least one member of each pair was homosexual. Both brothers were homosexual or bisexual in 52 percent of the identical-twin pairs but in only 22 percent of the nonidentical pairs and just 11 percent of the adoptive pairs (Bailey & Pillard, 1991). Although there are fewer behavior genetic studies of female homosexuality, the available data are similar (Bailey & Benishay, 1993).

Psychological Factors in Sexual Orientation   However, there is also evidence that homosexuality may not be accounted for by biology alone. Unsatisfactory or disrupted family relationships, for example, might be related to homosexuality. Male homosexuals describe their fathers as being more rejecting and distant than do male heterosexuals (Siegelman, 1974). Only 23 percent of lesbian women but 83 percent of heterosexual women reported having a close relationship with their mothers. In one study 39 percent of lesbians—but only 5 percent of heterosexual women—had lost one or both parents, through divorce or death, before they were ten years old (Saghir & Robins, 1973).

Other evidence links homosexuality in adult males with certain reactions to gender roles during early childhood. Boys who do not fit gender-role stereotypes may be pressured into rejecting the role. In one survey, 67 percent of male homosexuals, as opposed to 3 percent of heterosexual males, considered themselves to be effeminate during preadolescence (Saghir & Robins, 1973). These males reported *gender nonconformity,* such as playing more with girls; as a result, they were called "sissies" by their male peers (Adams & Chioto, 1983; Bell, Weinberg & Hammersmith, 1983). Although these data are retrospective, their validity is strengthened by a study that followed males from early childhood to young adulthood. Of 44 extremely effeminate boys, 33, or 75 percent, became homosexual or bisexual; only one bisexual was identified in a comparison group of more masculine boys (Green, 1987). Still, many homosexual males (25 percent in Green's study) do not fit this developmental pattern.

Available evidence suggests that, just as heterosexuals are very diverse, so, too, are homosexuals. There is no evidence that all homosexuals share a common developmental pattern, family history, or biological predisposition. It appears that a homosexual orientation stems from the interaction of many family, sociosexual, and biological factors.

Success and Work

This sentence was written at 6 A.M. on a beautiful Sunday in June. Why would someone get up that early to work on a weekend? Why do people take their work seriously and do the best job they can? Most people work at least in part as the result of *extrinsic motivation,* the desire to receive external rewards such as financial compensation. But work and other forms of human behavior also reflect *intrinsic motivation,* the desire to work hard or perform well for the internal satisfaction it brings. Some of life's most pleasing rewards come from within.

The next time you visit someone's home or office, take a look at the mementos displayed there. There may be framed diplomas and certificates, trophies and ribbons, pictures of memorable personal events, and photographs of children and grandchildren. All of these are badges of worth, affirmations that the person deserves approval or admiration. That so many people proudly display such outward signs of their value serves as a reminder that much human behavior is motivated by the desire for approval, admiration, and other positive evaluations—in short, for *esteem*—from others and from themselves. In this section, we examine two of the most prominent avenues to esteem: achievement in general and a job in particular.

Achievement Motivation

Many athletes who hold world records continue to maintain rigorous training schedules; many people who have built small businesses into multimillion-dollar corporations continue to work eighty-hour weeks, overseeing every detail of the operation. What motivates such people?

A possible answer is **need achievement,** a specific motive first postulated by Henry Murray (1938). People with a high need for achievement are motivated to master tasks—be they sports, business operations, intellectual activities, artistic creations, hobbies, or virtually anything else—and they experience intense satisfaction from doing so. They expend considerable effort striving for excellence, they enjoy doing it, and they take great pride in achieving at a high level.

Figure 12.9
Assessment of Need Achievement
This picture is similar to those included in the Thematic Apperception Test, or TAT (Morgan & Murray, 1935). The strength of people's achievement motivation is inferred from the stories people tell about what has happened and will happen in TAT pictures. A response like "The young woman is hoping that she will be able to make her grandmother proud of her" would reflect clear achievement motivation.

Source: Murray, 1971.

Individual Differences   How do people with strong achievement motivation differ from other people? To find out, researchers gave children a test designed to measure their need for achievement (Figure 12.9 shows a test for adults) and then asked them to play a ring-toss game. Children who scored low on the test tended either to stand so close to the target that they never failed to score or so far away that it was impossible for them to succeed. In contrast, the children who scored high on the need-achievement test chose to stand at an intermediate distance from the target, making the game challenging but not impossible. These children were happy when they succeeded, and they saw the game as even more challenging when they failed (McClelland, 1958).

These and other experiments indicate that individuals with high achievement motivation tend to establish challenging and difficult—but realistic—goals. Perhaps most important, they actively pursue success and are willing to take risks in that pursuit. They experience intense satisfaction from success; in fact, one classic definition of high achievement motivation is the capacity to experience pride in success. But if they feel they have tried their best, individuals with high achievement motivation are not particularly bothered by failure. Those with low achievement motivation also prefer to succeed. For the most part, though, success brings them not joy but relief at having avoided failure (Atkinson & Birch, 1978).

In general, people who are very motivated to achieve tend to be preoccupied with their performance and level of ability. They prefer tasks that have clear outcomes, and they would rather receive feedback from a harsh but competent critic than from one who is friendlier but less competent (McClelland, 1985). They like to struggle with a problem rather than ask for help, they are able to delay gratification, and they make careful plans about the future (Raynor, 1970). In contrast, people less motivated to achieve do not enjoy or seek feedback, and they tend to respond to failure by quitting (Weiner, 1980).

Development of Achievement Motivation   Achievement motivation appears to be largely learned in early childhood, much of it through interactions with one's parents. For example, in one study young boys were given a very difficult task at which they were sure to fail. Fathers whose sons scored low on achievement motivation tests often became irritated, discouraged their boys from continuing to try, and often interfered or even completed the task themselves (Rosen & D'Andrade, 1959).

David McClelland (1985) has described the pattern of parenting that is typically associated with children who score high on achievement motivation tests. The parents of these children tend to (1) encourage the child to attempt difficult tasks, especially new ones; (2) offer praise and other rewards for success; (3) encourage the child to find ways to succeed, instead of merely complaining about failure; and (4) prompt the child to go on to the next, somewhat more difficult challenge.

Cultural influences also shape achievement motivation. In some cultures, advancing the goals of one's family or group represents a more highly valued achievement than attaining personal distinction. As measured by American tests, then, typical levels of achievement motivation can vary considerably from culture to culture (Markus & Kityama, 1991).

The written material used to teach children to read provides one source of cultural influence. Children receive subtle messages about what their culture values from the events and themes in stories. Is the hero or heroine someone who worked hard and overcame obstacles (thus modeling reinforcement of persistence and hard work) or someone who loafed and then won the lottery (suggesting that rewards come randomly and that commitment to achievement is irrelevant)? These are examples of differing achievement themes in children's stories; they are blueprints for the goals one should aspire to and how one reaches them.

Do these materials have an effect? One study found a strong positive correlation between the number of high-achievement themes in children's reading material and the industrial achievements (such as number of industrial patents issued) in these children's countries years later, when they became adults (de Charms & Moeller, 1962). However, there is no way to tell whether differences in reading material actually caused differences in achievement motivation.

Achievement motivation can be developed after childhood, even among people whose cultural backgrounds did not encourage it (McClelland, 1985). In one study, high school and college students with low achievement motivation were helped to develop fantasies about their own success. They imagined setting goals that were difficult but not impossible. Then they imagined themselves concentrating on breaking a complicated problem into smaller, more manageable steps. (You might recall from Chapter 10 that this decomposition strategy can be very useful in problem solving.) They fantasized about working intensely, failing but not being discouraged, continuing to work, and finally feeling elated at success. After the program, these students' grades and general academic performance improved, suggesting that their achievement motivation had been intensified (McClelland, 1985).

Achievement motivation may also be fostered by teaching children a long-term perspective in which they focus on constantly learning more (Elliott & Dweck, 1988). This perspective can motivate them to constantly improve and truly master the material. People who adopt this orientation toward mastery achieve at very high levels and experience intense pride in their accomplishments. This is true of both males and females (Bergen & Dweck, 1989).

Gender Differences in Achievement Motivation   The behavior of women with a high level of achievement motivation is much more variable than that of men equally motivated by achievement. In particular, women

*Linkages: How might teachers'
expectations about mental abilities
shape gender differences in
achievement motivation? (a link to
Mental Abilities)*

who are highly motivated to achieve do not always establish challenging goals for themselves when given a choice, and they do not always persist when confronted with failure (Dweck, 1986). In fact, some of them withdraw from and even avoid situations in which their achievement could be evaluated.

Gender differences in achievement motivation begin to appear at a very early age. The question of why they occur is the subject of considerable debate (Koestner, Zuckerman & Koestner, 1989). But it is clear that these differences are tied to the way boys and girls learn to think of themselves and their performance (Burns & Seligman, 1989). Females are much more likely than males to attribute failure on school-related tasks to a lack of ability, and they tend to begin doing so when they are quite young (Dweck & Gilliard, 1975). Many continue to see themselves as incompetent even in the face of objective evidence that they do better academically than their male counterparts (Licht & Dweck, 1984).

Girls' readiness to deprecate their own abilities in school may stem in part from classroom experiences (Kernis, Brockner & Frankel, 1989). For reasons that are not yet fully understood, elementary school teachers tend to use different styles of criticism for boys and girls. Girls are likely to be told what they did wrong and what they should do instead. Boys are also likely to hear this kind of criticism; but, in addition, boys are often told that they are not concentrating or are not being careful enough (Dweck et al., 1978). In other words, Carol Dweck suggests, the boys are encouraged to think that any failure was due only to lack of effort or some other aspect of the situation. In contrast, the feedback given to girls leads them to think that any failure is due to their incompetence.

Evidence for this interpretation comes from a study in which Dweck and her colleagues arranged for girls who were very motivated to achieve to receive the type of criticism normally directed toward boys. The girls' behavior became more like that of boys with high achievement motivation. The girls tended to adopt challenging goals, to try hard, and to persist in the face of failure (Dweck et al., 1978).

In many cultures, traditional gender-role stereotypes discourage a need for achievement among women. These stereotypes may portray the pursuit of excellence and mastery as "unfeminine" and threatening to men. As a result, some women may hide some of their successes or act in ways that undermine their chances of success—a pattern called "fear of success" (Horner, 1970). Other women may find satisfaction in the intrinsic rewards of a job well done, but limit their achievements by avoiding competition with men for power and authority (Offerman & Beil, 1992). Teachers as well as parents may communicate gender-role stereotypes about achievement, including information about "appropriate" areas of achievement for boys and girls. For example, many teachers expect boys to be better at math and girls to be better at reading, and thus often give more help and encouragement in math to boys compared to girls (Leinhardt et al., 1979). It is little wonder, then, that, by high school, girls don't do as well as boys in math (Hyde, Fennema & Lamon, 1990). Sadly, some of the same differential patterns in the treatment of males and females appear even among faculty at the college and graduate school levels (Hall & Sandler, 1982).

Jobs and Motivation

Employers are less likely to be interested in a worker's overall need to achieve than in whether their employees are motivated to work hard on the job. Intentionally or not, managers structure jobs in ways that reflect a theory about people and what motivates them (Riggio, 1989). Employers who see employees as basically lazy, untrustworthy, ambitionless creatures who work only for money tend to design jobs that are very structured and heavily supervised; they give employees very little say in deciding what to do and how to do it. These employers expect their workers to be satisfied if pay and benefits are good. But employees in these types of jobs tend *not* to be satisfied, and they show little motivation to perform at peak efficiency (Herzberg, 1968; Wexley & Yukl, 1984).

If good pay and benefits by themselves do not bring job satisfaction and motivation, what does? Edward Deci and his colleagues have suggested that poor motivation among workers arises largely from the feeling of having little or no control over the work environment (Deci, Connell & Ryan, 1987). Compared with those in rigidly structured jobs, workers tend to be more satisfied and productive if they are (1) encouraged to participate in decisions about how work should be done; (2) given problems to solve, without being told how to solve them; (3) taught more than one skill; (4) given lots of individual responsibility; and (5) given public recognition, not just money, for good performance. For example, instead of requiring factory workers to perform just one small task over and over on an assembly line, some employers have employees work in teams to discuss and solve problems and arrange for teams to produce a complete product. Workers in these "enhanced" jobs tend to be intrinsically as well as extrinsically motivated.

Allowing people to set and achieve clear goals is one way to increase their performance and satisfaction (Schneider, 1985). The goals that are most effective in maintaining work motivation have three characteristics (Katzell & Thompson, 1990). First, effective goals are personally meaningful. When employees are told in a memo from a faceless administrator that their goal should be an increase in production, they are likely to feel put upon and may not be motivated to meet the goal. Second, effective goals are specific and concrete. The goal of "doing better" is usually not a strong motivator. A particular target, such as increasing sales by 10 percent, makes a far more motivating goal. It is there for all to see, and whether the goal has been reached is easily determined. Finally, goals are likely to be effective if management supports goal setting by employees themselves, offers special rewards for reaching goals, and provides encouragement after failure.

In short, jobs that offer personal challenges, independence, and both intrinsic and extrinsic rewards are motivating jobs. They provide enough satisfaction for people to feel excitement and pleasure in continuing hard work. The

American companies have followed Japanese models in redesigning jobs to enhance responsibility and flexibility. The goal is to increase both employee productivity and job satisfaction by having employees work in teams that are responsible for solving production problems and making decisions about how best to do the job. Team members are publicly recognized for outstanding work, and part of their pay depends on the quality (not just the number) of their products and on the profitability of the whole company.

rewards for employers are potentially large as well. Increased job satisfaction leads to lower absenteeism and lower turnover (Ilgen & Klein, 1989).

Relations and Conflicts Among Motives

At any time, many motives might guide a person's behavior. What determines which ones will?

Maslow's Hierarchy

Abraham Maslow (1970) suggested that a hierarchy of five basic classes of needs, or motives, influence human behavior (see Figure 12.10). Needs at the lowest level of the hierarchy, he said, must be at least partially satisfied before people can be motivated by higher-level goals. From the bottom to the top of Maslow's hierarchy these five motives are as follows:

Linkages: What needs do others fulfill? (a link to Social Cognition)

1. *Biological,* such as food, water, oxygen, activity, and sleep.
2. *Safety,* such as being cared for as a child and having a secure income as an adult.
3. *Belongingness and love,* such as being part of various kinds of social groups and participating in affectionate sexual and nonsexual relationships.
4. *Esteem,* being respected as a useful, honorable individual.
5. *Self-actualization,* which means becoming all that one is capable of. People motivated by this need explore and enhance relationships with others, follow interests for intrinsic pleasure rather than status or esteem, and are concerned with issues affecting all people, not just themselves.

In general, research indicates that motives lower in Maslow's hierarchy do take precedence over those higher in the hierarchy, but Maslow's system has been criticized as too simplistic (Neher, 1991; Williams & Page, 1989). People do not always act according to his hierarchy; even when lower-level needs are unmet, some people continue to be motivated by higher levels in the hierarchy. The motivation of people deeply involved in political and moral causes, for example, appears to turn Maslow's hierarchy on its head; in 1981, Bobby Sand and eight others starved themselves to death in protest of British rule

Figure 12.10
Maslow's Hierarchy of Motives
According to Maslow, motives are organized in a hierarchy in which motives at lower levels take precedence over those at higher levels. Motives at lower levels must be at least partly satisfied before those above them can significantly influence an individual's behavior. Though Maslow viewed self-actualization as the essence of mental health, he recognized that very few people spend much time or effort seeking it. Only the rare individual, such as Mother Teresa or Dr. Martin Luther King, Jr., approaches full self-actualization, according to Maslow.

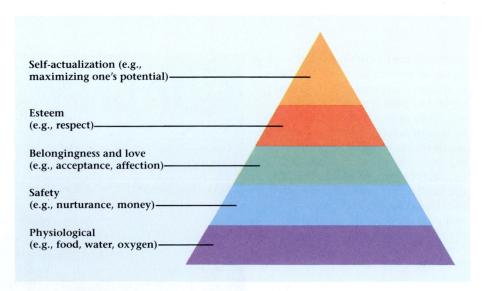

Self-actualization (e.g., maximizing one's potential)

Esteem (e.g., respect)

Belongingness and love (e.g., acceptance, affection)

Safety (e.g., nurturance, money)

Physiological (e.g., food, water, oxygen)

Source: Adapted from Maslow, 1943.

over Northern Ireland. Nevertheless, Maslow's classification is useful for thinking about the relationships among human motives.

Linkages: Conflicting Motives and Stress

What motivational conflicts are tied to stress?

Maslow's hierarchy makes it clear that differing motives can sometimes be in conflict. What is the result? Suppose you are alone and bored on a Saturday night, so you think about going to a convenience store for a snack. What are your motives? Hunger might play a role in sending you out, as might the prospect of the boredom-fighting stimulation (arousal) you will obtain from a trip to the store. Even sexual motivation might be involved, as you think about the possibility of meeting someone exciting in the frozen pizza aisle. But safety-related motives might make you hesitate. What if you should get mugged? And an esteem motive might prompt you to shrink from being seen alone on a Saturday night.

These are just a few of the motives that might be relevant to a trivial decision. When the decision is important, the number and strength of motivational pushes and pulls is likely to be greater, creating more internal conflict and acting as a source of stress. Neal Miller (1959) identified four basic types of motivational conflict:

1. *Approach-approach conflicts* When a person is motivated to engage in two desirable activities that cannot both be pursued, an *approach-approach conflict* exists. As the importance of the decision increases, so does the difficulty of making it.
2. *Avoidance-avoidance conflicts* An *avoidance-avoidance conflict* arises when avoidance of one unattractive situation forces exposure to another one. A woman with an unwanted pregnancy who is morally opposed to abortion faces an avoidance-avoidance conflict because neither having the baby nor terminating the pregnancy is desirable. Such conflicts are very difficult to resolve and create intense emotions.
3. *Approach-avoidance conflicts* When one event or activity has both attractive and unattractive features, an *approach-avoidance conflict* is created. Like avoidance-avoidance situations, approach-avoidance conflicts are difficult to resolve and often lead to prolonged periods of indecision.
4. *Multiple approach-avoidance conflicts* Suppose a person must choose between two jobs. One offers a high salary with a prestigious organization but requires long working hours and moving to a miserable climate. The other boasts plenty of opportunity for advancement and good fringe benefits, in a better climate, but offers lousy pay and an unpredictable schedule. This is an example of a *multiple approach-avoidance conflict,* which involves two or more alternatives, each of which has both positive and negative attributes. Multiple approach-avoidance conflicts are difficult to resolve partly because, as discussed in the decision-making section of Chapter 10, the attributes of each option are usually difficult to compare. For example, how many dollars a year are worth losing to live in a good climate?

Each of these types of conflict may create stress, a topic discussed in detail in Chapter 13. Most people in the midst of motivational conflicts tend to be tense, irritable, and more than usually vulnerable to physical and psychological problems. These reactions are especially likely when the correct choices are not obvious, when varying motives have approximately equal strength, and when a choice can bring frightening or irrevocable consequences (as in decisions to marry, to divorce, or to approve disconnection of a life-support system). Resolution of such conflicts may be a long time in coming or may be made impulsively and thoughtlessly, just to end the discomfort of uncertainty. Even after the conflict is resolved, stress responses may continue in the form of anxiety about the correctness of the decision or guilt over bad choices. Sometimes, these and other consequences of conflicting motives create depression and other serious disorders.

The fact that motivational conflicts are usually accompanied by anxiety and other strong emotional states provides another example of the close relationship between motivation and emotion in human life. Motivation can intensify emotion, as when a normally mild-mannered person's intense hunger results in an angry complaint about slow restaurant service. But emotions can also create motivation. Happiness, for example, is an emotion that most people want to experience, and they are motivated to engage in whatever behaviors— studying, artwork, beachcombing—they think will achieve it. Similarly, as an emotion that most people want to avoid, anxiety motivates all sorts of adaptive and maladaptive escape and avoidance behaviors, from leaving the scene of an accident to staying away from poisonous snakes. In the next part of this chapter, we take a closer look at emotions.

What Is Emotion?

Everyone seems to agree that joy, sorrow, anger, fear, anxiety, love, hate, mirth, and lust are emotions, but identifying the shared properties that make these experiences emotions—rather than, say, thoughts or impulses—is not easy. In fact, many cultures do not distinguish emotions from thoughts. The Chewong of Malaysia, for example, consider the liver the seat of both what we call thoughts and feelings (Russell, 1991). Several of psychology's best theorists have highlighted the features of emotion that we describe here (Averill, 1980; Frijda, 1986; James, 1890; Lazarus, 1991; Oatley & Jenkins, 1992; Ortony, Clore & Collins, 1988; Izard, 1991).

Defining Characteristics

In the most general terms, emotions are organized psychological and physiological reactions that occur when your relationship to the world changes. These reactions are partly subjective experiences and partly objective patterns of behavior and physiological arousal. The subjective experience of emotion has several characteristics:

1. Emotion is *transitory;* it tends to have a relatively clear beginning and end. In contrast, moods tend to be longer-lasting.
2. Emotional experience has *valence,* which means it is either positive or negative.
3. Emotional experience is elicited in part by a *cognitive appraisal* of a situation with respect to your goals. Winning a scholarship, which is perceived as consistent with one's goals, elicits positive emotions. Events inconsistent with your goals—such as failing an exam—elicit negative emotions. The same event can elicit dramatically different emotions depending on what the event means to an individual.
4. Emotional experience *alters thought processes,* often by directing attention toward some things and away from others. The anguish of parents whose child is killed by a drunken driver, for example, may prompt them to alter their perception of the importance of drunk-driving laws.
5. Emotional experience *elicits an action tendency,* the motivation to behave in certain ways. The grieving parents' anger, for example, may generate impulses to harm the drunken driver or the motivation to work for stronger penalties for driving while intoxicated.

Emotional experiences depend in part on our interpretation of situations and how those situations relate to our goals. The stimulus for these drastically different emotional reactions was the same—namely, the announcement of the winners of a cheerleading contest. Each woman's emotional experience following this stimulus depended on whether she perceived the situation as making her a winner or a loser.

6. Emotional experiences are *passions* that happen to you, not actions you initiate. You exert some control over your emotions because they are partly determined by how you interpret situations, including your own emotional experience as it develops. If you interpret an emotional experience as fear, for example, you may amplify your experience of fear. Still, you cannot decide to experience joy or sorrow; instead, you "fall in love" or are "overcome by grief." In other words, emotional experiences have a different relation to the self than conscious cognitions.

The subjective aspects of emotions are, therefore, experiences that are both triggered by the thinking self and experienced by the self as happening to the self. They reveal the individual as both agent and object, as both I and me, both the controller of thoughts and the recipient of passions. The extent to which you are a "victim" of your passions versus a rational designer of your emotions is one of the central dilemmas of human existence, and a subject of literature as much as of psychology.

The objective aspects of emotion consist of both learned and innate *expressive displays* and *internal bodily responses*. The expressive displays—a smile, a frown—communicate feelings to other people. The internal bodily responses—changes in heart rate, for example—provide the physiological adjustments needed in order for you to perform the action tendencies generated by emotional experience. If you throw a temper tantrum at the object of your anger, for example, your heart must deliver additional oxygen and fuel to your muscles.

Both the subjective and the objective aspects of emotions can vary in intensity, from the quiet satisfaction of a person watching a beautiful sunset to the raging fury of a wronged lover. As discussed earlier in this chapter, too much or too little emotional arousal can cause problems. For example, too little emotion may impair social interactions, whereas an overly emotional person may be unable to concentrate or to coordinate thoughts and actions efficiently.

In summary, an **emotion** is a transitory, valenced experience that is felt with some intensity as happening to the self, generated in part by a cognitive appraisal of situations, and accompanied by both learned and innate physical responses. Through emotion, people communicate their internal states and intentions to others, but emotion also functions to direct and energize a person's own thoughts and actions. Emotion often disrupts thought and behavior, but it also triggers and guides cognitions and organizes, motivates, and sustains behavior and social relations.

Emotions and the Autonomic Nervous System

The autonomic nervous system is responsible for most of the physiological changes that accompany emotional reactions. If you get red in the face when you are angry or embarrassed, it is because the autonomic nervous system has increased the flow of blood to your face. As noted in Chapter 4, the *autonomic nervous system,* or *ANS,* is the part of the peripheral nervous system that carries information between the brain and all organs of the body except the striated muscles (such as the arm and leg muscles). The ANS affects all of the organs—the heart and blood vessels, the digestive system, and so on. Each of these organs has ongoing activity independent of the autonomic nervous system, but input from the autonomic system *modulates* this activity, increasing or decreasing it. For example, your heart continues to beat even without input from the ANS, but that input may increase or decrease its rate.

By modulating the activity of organs, the autonomic nervous system coordinates their functioning to meet the needs of the whole organism and prepares the body for changes. If you are aroused to increased activity—to run to catch a bus, for instance—more glucose is needed to fuel your muscles. The autonomic nervous system provides the needed energy by stimulating secretion of glucose-generating hormones and by promoting blood flow to the muscles.

Organization of the Autonomic Nervous System   Figure 12.11 shows that the autonomic nervous system is organized into two divisions: the sympathetic nervous system and the parasympathetic nervous system. The **parasympathetic nervous system** typically influences activity related to the protection, nourishment, and growth of the body. Digestion is one example. The parasympathetic system increases movement of the intestinal system, allowing more nutrients to be extracted from food. The **sympathetic nervous system** usually prepares the organism for vigorous activity. When one part of the sympathetic system is stimulated, other parts are stimulated "in sympathy" with it (Gellhorn & Loofbourrow, 1963). Activation of the sympathetic nervous system usually produces increased heart rate and blood pressure, rapid or irregular breathing, dilated pupils, perspiration, dry mouth, increased blood sugar, piloerection ("goose bumps"), trembling, and other changes. You have probably experienced these reactions after a near-accident. They are sometimes called the **fight-or-flight syndrome,** because they prepare the body to combat or to run from a threatening situation. Either branch of the autonomic nervous system can be activated during an emotion. For example, the sympathetic nervous system increases your heart rate when you are angry; the parasympathetic nervous system causes tears to flow when you are grieving.

In both the parasympathetic and sympathetic systems, there is a relay station called a *ganglion* between the central nervous system (CNS) and target organs. In the parasympathetic system, the neurotransmitter at the target organ is acetylcholine (see Figure 12.11), but in the sympathetic system the neurotransmitter at the target organ is almost always norepinephrine (also known as noradrenaline). Very often, the same organ is innervated by fibers of both the sympathetic and the parasympathetic system, each of which may produce opposite effects. For example, norepinephrine released by the sympathetic nerves on the heart speeds up the heart, whereas acetylcholine released by parasympathetic nerves slows it down.

These skydivers are likely to show notable changes in autonomic arousal just before a jump, but it would probably be unclear from their physiological activity alone whether the emotion they experience is fear or excitement.

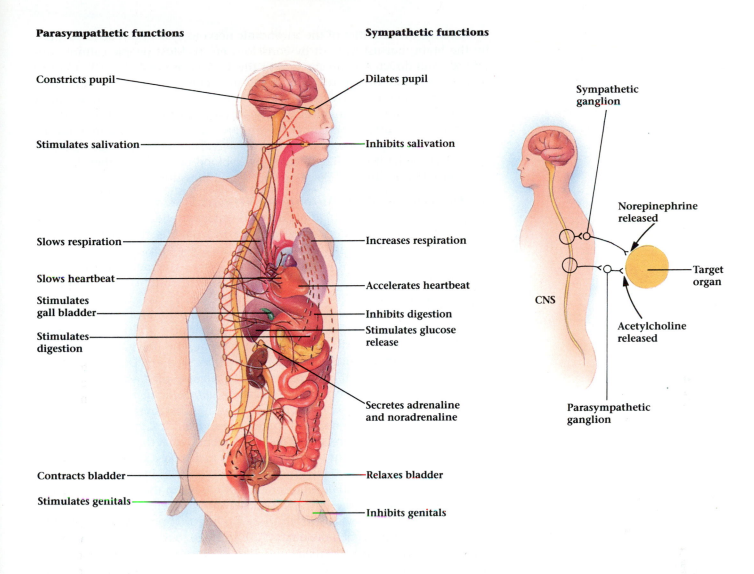

Parasympathetic functions

- Constricts pupil
- Stimulates salivation
- Slows respiration
- Slows heartbeat
- Stimulates gall bladder
- Stimulates digestion
- Contracts bladder
- Stimulates genitals

Sympathetic functions

- Dilates pupil
- Inhibits salivation
- Increases respiration
- Accelerates heartbeat
- Inhibits digestion
- Stimulates glucose release
- Secretes adrenaline and noradrenaline
- Relaxes bladder
- Inhibits genitals

Sympathetic ganglion

Norepinephrine released

Target organ

CNS

Acetylcholine released

Parasympathetic ganglion

Figure 12.11
The Autonomic Nervous System
Emotional responses involve activation of the autonomic nervous system, which includes sympathetic and parasympathetic subsystems. Which of the bodily responses depicted do you associate with emotional experiences?

One part of the sympathetic nervous system deserves special mention: the **adrenal glands.** There are two adrenal glands, one on each side of the body just above the kidney. Each adrenal gland has two parts, both of which participate in emotional responses. The outer *adrenal cortex* is part of the endocrine system; the inner *adrenal medulla* is part of the sympathetic nervous system. The adrenal cortex releases cortisol, a hormone whose important role in the body's reactions to stress is discussed in Chapter 13. The adrenal medulla acts as a ganglion of the sympathetic system, since it links the brain and various sympathetic target organs. Like other ganglia, the adrenal medulla receives stimulation from the central nervous system. Unlike other ganglia, however, the cells of the adrenal gland do not have axons that travel to a target organ. Instead, its cells simply dump noradrenaline and adrenaline into the bloodstream, thereby activating all target organs of the sympathetic system.

The Autonomic Nervous System and Consciousness The autonomic nervous system and the parts of the brain involved in consciousness are connected, but only indirectly. The ANS does provide direct feedback to sensory areas of the brain (Cechetto & Saper, 1988), but these areas do not appear to participate directly in consciousness. Thus, you are not aware that your stomach has secreted gastric juices, but you may hear your stomach grumbling.

Similarly, the activities of the autonomic nervous system can be influenced by the brain, but usually not by conscious effort. Most people cannot consciously and directly create changes in the activity of the ANS, such as a rise in blood pressure or sweating, but they can decide to do certain things that will, in turn, alter the activities of the ANS. To arouse autonomic innervation of your sex organs, you might imagine yourself in an erotic situation. To raise your blood pressure, you might hold your breath and strain your muscles. To lower your blood pressure, you might use *biofeedback* techniques (see Chapter 13) to learn what it feels like to have lower blood pressure and then learn to reproduce that feeling and decrease your blood pressure.

Lie Detection and the Autonomic Nervous System   The normally involuntary nature of the autonomic nervous system provides the basis for using polygraphs as lie detectors. *Polygraphs* are instruments that record several types of physiological activity. For lie detection, polygraphs record physiological responses governed by the autonomic nervous system—usually heart rate, breathing, and skin resistance (which is affected by slight changes in perspiration).

Use of the polygraph as a lie detector is based on the idea that emotional responses usually accompany lies, because people feel guilty or fear being found out. To identify the perpetrator of a crime, the polygraph tester asks questions that are specifically related to the crime, such as, "Did you stab anyone on October 23, 1993?" Responses to such *relevant questions* are then compared to responses to general inquiries, called *control questions,* such as, "Have you ever tried to hurt someone?" The assumption is that most innocent people may have tried to hurt someone at some time and will feel guilty when asked, but they should have no reason to feel guilty about what they did on October 23, 1993. Thus, an innocent person is expected to display a stronger emotional response to control than to relevant questions (Raskin & Podlesny, 1979).

Most people do have some emotional response when they lie, but statistics about the accuracy of the polygraph in detecting deception are difficult to obtain. Estimates vary widely, from those finding that polygraphs can detect 90 percent of guilty, lying individuals (Raskin, 1986) to those saying that truthful, innocent persons are deemed guilty liars as often as 40 percent of the time (Ben-Shakhar & Furedy, 1990).

The wide variance in the evidence suggests that the results reflect factors other than the alleged link between lying and emotion—in particular, cognitive interpretations. A person who believes that lying is acceptable and that fooling the polygraph is possible would not generate a fear response while lying on the test. However, an innocent person convinced that "everything always goes wrong" might show a large fear response, which would wrongly suggest guilt.

For a polygraph test to be effective, the person being tested must believe that the machine is infallible in its ability to detect lies. Since this is not true, using the polygraph requires lying to the person being tested. Even the most favorable evidence regarding the effectiveness of the lie detector has another damaging interpretation. In a situation involving few liars and many innocent people, even if polygraph tests caught 90 percent of the liars and exonerated 90 percent of the innocent, they would still falsely accuse a large number of people of lying.

Polygraph testing can catch some liars, but most researchers think that a guilty person can "fool" a polygraph lie detector. In fact, the American Psychological Association expressed "great reservations about the use of polygraph tests to detect deception" (Abeles, 1985). Alternative lie-detecting devices are now under development. One of these measures the brain waves emitted during certain cognitive operations (Farwell & Donchin, 1991). Another takes advantage of the fact that people show different patterns of involuntary eye movements when scanning familiar versus unfamiliar objects (Cohen et al., 1994). Preliminary studies indicate that, when subjects are asked to lie about which items in a sequence of stimuli they have seen before, researchers are able to accurately detect the lies by noting when the verbal report and the eye-movement pattern do not match. Such devices may someday prove to be more accurate than polygraph tests because they do not depend on a connection between making false statements and emotional responses.

Where Is Emotion: In the Heart or in the Head?

No other psychological process produces the kinds of bodily responses that emotions produce. Most thoughts do not arouse noticeable physiological changes, but all emotions prompt some type of physical response. How do these responses fit into the experience of emotion? This question has been the center of one of the major controversies in the study of emotion.

William James's Theory

Suppose you are walking in the woods and come upon a mean-looking bear. The encounter scares the daylights out of you, and you begin to run for dear life. Do you run because you are afraid, or are you afraid because you run? The example and the question come from the work of William James, one of the first psychologists to propose a formal answer to questions about how physiological responses are related to the experience of emotion. James argued that you are afraid because you run. Your running and other physiological responses, he said, follow directly from the perception of the bear. Without some form of these responses, you would feel no fear.

Presented like this, in its simplest form, James's theory may sound preposterous. It goes against common sense, which says that it would be silly to run from something unless you are already afraid of it. How did James come to conclude otherwise? James's main method was to scrutinize his own mental processes. He decided that after stripping away all physiological responses, there was nothing left of the experience of an emotion (James, 1890). Because a similar view was presented by Carle Lange, a Danish physician, James's formulation is sometimes called the *James-Lange theory* of emotion.

Observing Peripheral Responses Figure 12.12 outlines the components of emotional experience, including those emphasized by James. First, a perception affects the cerebral cortex, said James;

then quick as a flash, reflex currents pass down through their pre-ordained channels, alter the condition of muscle, skin, and viscus; and these alterations, perceived, like the original object, in as many portions of the cortex, combine with it in consciousness and transform it from an object-simply-apprehended into an object-emotionally-felt. (James, 1890, p. 759)

In other words, the brain interprets a situation in such a way that physiological responses are called for, but the interpretation is not necessarily conscious until the physical responses occur. This subsequent perception of peripheral responses, according to James, constitutes the experience of emotion. *Peripheral responses* are bodily responses—such as a palpitating heart, sinking stomach, facial grimace, and perspiration—rather than neural responses confined to the central nervous system. Thus, James's theory holds that reflexive peripheral responses precede the experience of emotion. The conscious aspect of emotion arises later, when the brain observes these responses.

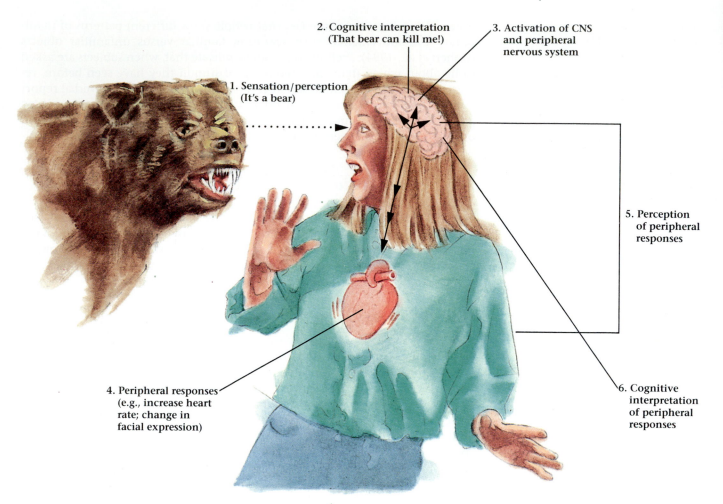

2. Cognitive interpretation
(That bear can kill me!)

3. Activation of CNS
and peripheral
nervous system

1. Sensation/perception
(It's a bear)

5. Perception
of peripheral
responses

4. Peripheral responses
(e.g., increase heart
rate; change in
facial expression)

6. Cognitive
interpretation
of peripheral
responses

Figure 12.12
Components of Emotion
Emotion entails numerous components, including activity in the
central nervous system (the brain
and spinal cord) and peripheral responses. Emotion theorists have argued about which of these components are essential for emotion.
William James emphasized #5, the
perception of peripheral responses,
such as changes in heart rate, while
Stanley Schachter emphasized #6,
the cognitive interpretation and labeling of those peripheral responses.
Walter Cannon believed that #3 was
sufficient, and that emotion could
occur wholly in the central nervous
system.

Notice that, according to James's view, there is no emotion generated solely
by activity of the central nervous system. There is no direct central experience
of emotion in a special "brain center." This theory, therefore, suggests one
reason why you may have difficulty knowing your true feelings: you must
interpret your feelings from your responses; there is no direct access to feelings
from one part of the brain to another.

Evaluating James's Theory   There are more than 500 different labels for
emotions in the English language (Averill, 1980). Is physiological feedback sufficiently varied to generate all of these emotions? According to James's theory,
since the perception of peripheral physiological responses constitutes emotion, each shade of emotion should stem from distinguishable patterns of
physiological arousal. For example, fear should be tied to one pattern of bodily
responses, and anger should arise from a different pattern. According to
James's theory, if two patterns of responses are not different, then they cannot
be distinguished as two emotions.

Contemporary research shows that the pattern of autonomic changes does
vary with different emotional states. For example, Figure 12.13 shows that anger and fear both cause heart rate to rise; but anger increases blood flow to the
hands and feet, whereas fear reduces blood flow to the hands and feet (Ekman,
Levenson & Friesen, 1983; Levenson, Ekman & Friesen, 1990). Thus, fear produces "cold feet"; anger does not. Disgust is distinguished from other negative
emotions in that it causes an increase in muscle activity but no increase in
heart rate. Also, when people mentally "relive" different emotional experiences, they show different patterns of autonomic activity (Ekman, Levenson
& Friesen, 1983).

**Figure 12.13
Patterns of Physiological
Change Associated with
Different Emotions**

In one experiment, movements of the face characteristic of different emotions produced different patterns of change in (a) heart rate; (b) peripheral blood flow, as indexed by finger temperature; (c) skin conductance; and (d) muscle activity (Levenson, Ekman & Friesen, 1990). For example, making an angry face caused heart rate and finger temperature to rise, whereas making a fearful face (as in Figure 12.14) raised heart rate but lowered finger temperature.

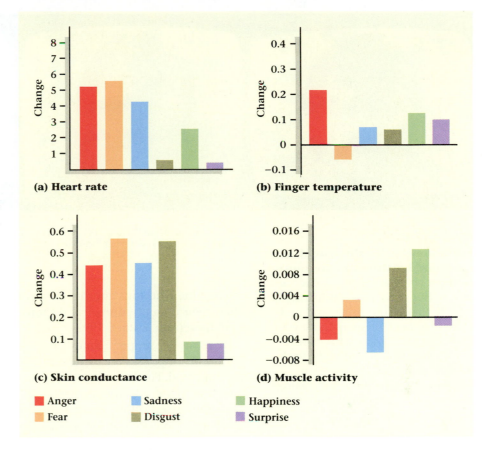

Source: Figure 3 from "Voluntary Facial Action Generates Emotion-Specific Autonomic Nervous System Activity," by R. W. Levenson, P. Ekman, and W. V. Friesen, *Psychophysiology*, 1990, *27*, 363–384. Copyright 1990 The Society for Psychophysiological Research. Reprinted with permission of the author and the publisher from Levenson, Ekman, and Friesen, 1990.

Furthermore, different patterns of autonomic activity are intimately associated with specific emotional facial expressions, and vice versa (Ekman, 1993). When Paul Ekman and his colleagues (Ekman, Levenson & Friesen, 1983) instructed professional actors to move specific facial muscles or parts of the face, various facial configurations produced autonomic responses like those normally accompanying emotion (see Figure 12.14). A similar experiment used nonactors as subjects (Levenson, Ekman & Friesen, 1990). The patterns of autonomic activity produced when they made expressions of fear, anger, disgust, and sadness could be differentiated from one another and from happiness. Also, a large majority of the subjects reported feeling the emotion associated with the expression they had created, even though they could not see their own expressions and did not realize that this specific emotion was being modeled.

Edgar Allan Poe noted this relationship between facial expressions and feelings more than a hundred years ago:

When I wish to find out how wise or how stupid or how good or how wicked is anyone, or what are his thoughts at the moment, I fashion the expression of my face, as accurately as possible, in accordance with the expression of his, and then wait to see what thoughts or sentiments arise in my mind or heart, as if to match or correspond with the expression. (Quoted in Levenson, Ekman & Friesen, 1990)

Mimicking the face of a person you are talking with may elicit in you the same feelings that person is having, including the autonomic responses, and may thus contribute to empathy. When subjects are asked to empathize with and

Source: Copyright, Paul Ekman, 1983. Photos of actor Tom Harrison, from Ekman, P., Levenson, R. W. & Friesen, W. V. (1983). Autonomic nervous system distinguishes among emotions, *Science*, 221, 1208–1210.

Figure 12.14
Voluntary Facial Movements and Emotional Autonomic Responses
Without being asked to experience an emotion, this man was instructed to (left) "raise your brows and pull them together"; (center) "raise your upper eyelids"; and (right) "also stretch your lips horizontally, back toward your ears." Carrying out these instructions produced changes in heart rate characteristic of fear and the experience of fear.

describe the emotions another person is experiencing, they are most accurate when their own physiological responses match those of the person they observe (Levenson & Ruef, 1992).

These results support James's theory because they indicate that peripheral autonomic responses are sufficiently varied that at least basic emotions can be discriminated. Further, when people voluntarily produce peripheral responses (by contracting appropriate facial muscles), the emotions associated with those responses follow. James's theory correctly predicted that subjects who voluntarily produce the physiological responses associated with fear will feel fear even though there is nothing in the environment to be afraid of.

James's theory also implies that if a person cannot experience physiological changes in the body's periphery, he or she should not experience emotions. One approach to testing this prediction is to evaluate the emotional effects of drugs that modify the physiological responses produced during emotions. Indeed, drugs that reduce physiological arousal can reduce the intensity of emotional experience. When propranolol, a drug that blocks sympathetic responses, was given to music students at a recital, it reduced their experience of anxiety—and improved their piano playing (Brantigan, Brantigan & Joseph, 1978).

Another test of this prediction has come from studying people with spinal cord injuries. George Hohmann (1966) reasoned that if peripheral feedback is important to the experience of emotion, then people with spinal cord injuries that reduce peripheral responses should have less intense experience of emotions. This is just what Hohmann found, but his work was conducted in the 1960s, when treatment for spinal cord injuries emphasized passive resignation to disability; thus these people may have withdrawn from emotional situations (Chwalisz, Diener & Gallagher, 1988). More recent studies of individuals with spinal cord injuries who were actively coping and maintained important life goals showed that they experienced the full range of emotions, including as much happiness as noninjured people (Chwalisz, Diener & Gallagher, 1988; Bermond et al., 1991). Further, they reported no reduction in the intensity of emotional experiences before and after their injuries, even though they did notice reductions in the physical accompaniments to the emotions.

These data appear to contradict James's theory, but spinal cord injuries do not usually affect facial expressions, and James included facial expressions in the bodily responses that are interpreted as emotions. Accordingly, some researchers have argued for a variant of James theory called the *facial feedback hypothesis,* which says that movements of the face can provide sufficient peripheral information to fuel the experience of emotion (Izard, 1971, 1990; Laird, 1984). Thus, if you find yourself frowning, you must be unhappy. The facial movement is involuntary, and the feedback from that movement directs further emotional responses.

Schachter's Cognitive Labeling Theory

Contemporary theorists such as Stanley Schachter have elaborated on James's emphasis on the interpretation of physiological arousal. In Schachter's theory, physiological feedback need not be sufficiently varied by itself to generate subtle emotional differences. Instead, Schachter proposed that emotions are produced by *both* feedback from peripheral responses and a cognitive appraisal of what caused those responses (Schachter & Singer, 1962). Thus, cognitive interpretation comes into play twice: once when you perceive the situation that leads to bodily responses and again when you identify feedback from those responses as a particular emotion (see Figure 12.12).

The Labeling of Arousal   Because of his collaboration with Jerome Singer, Schachter's theory is often called the *Schachter-Singer theory* of emotion. Schachter agreed with James that the first step in emotion is the perception of a situation, followed by bodily responses. However, whereas James said that the brain perceives these responses as a particular emotion solely on the basis of the feedback, Schachter argued that the brain may interpret a particular pattern of feedback in many ways and give it many labels. He said that the cognitive act of *labeling* an originally undifferentiated pattern of physiological arousal constitutes the core of emotion (Schachter & Singer, 1962).

The labeling of arousal depends on an **attribution,** which is the process of identifying the cause of some event. People may attribute their physiological arousal to different emotions depending on the information that is available about the situation. For example, if you are watching the final seconds of a close football game, you might attribute your racing heart, rapid breathing, and perspiration to excitement; but you might attribute the same physiological reactions to anxiety if you are waiting for an important exam to begin. Thus, the emotion you experience upon seeing a bear in the woods might be fear, excitement, astonishment, or surprise, depending on how you label your reaction.

Evaluating Schachter's Theory   Schachter's refinement of James's theory predicts that if emotional arousal is attributed to a *nonemotional* cause, the intensity of emotional experience should be reduced. So if you notice your heart pounding before an exam but say to yourself, "Sure my heart's pounding, but I'm not nervous—I just drank five cups of coffee!" then you should feel "wired" from caffeine rather than afraid or worried. This prediction has received some support (Schachter & Singer, 1962).

Schachter's theory also predicts that if arousal is artificially induced—by drugs, for example—emotion will be experienced if there is a situation to which the drug-induced arousal can reasonably be attributed. This prediction was supported by Schachter's early work (Schachter & Singer, 1962), but the magnitude of the effect was small. Indeed, some investigators have been unable to replicate Schachter's results (Leventhal & Tomarken, 1986; Marshall & Zimbardo, 1979; Maslach, 1979).

Physiological arousal from nonemotional sources can *intensify* emotional experience, however (Zillmann, 1984). For example, people who have been aroused by physical exercise show greater anger when provoked than people who have been physically less active. The person attributes the exercise-produced arousal to anger, thus intensifying the emotion. Similarly, compared with a person at rest, exercise-aroused people experience stronger feelings of

Linkages: Schachter's theory of emotion predicts that these sports fans would attribute their physiological arousal to the game they are watching and label their emotion "excitement." Further, in line with the information-processing model described in Chapter 10, the emotions people experience also depend partly on their cognitive interpretation of situations (Lazarus & Folkman, 1984). Those who see a team's defeat as a disaster will experience more negative emotions than those who think of it as a challenge to improve.

attraction or dislike when they meet an attractive or unattractive member of the opposite sex (White, Fishbein & Rutstein, 1981).

Transfer of Excitation   When arousal from one experience carries over to an independent situation, it is called **transferred excitation** (Reisenzein, 1983). People remain physiologically aroused longer than they think they do, which helps explain transfer of excitation. For the transfer to occur, there must be a period during which the overt signs of arousal subside but the sympathetic nervous system is still active. If the person still felt aroused, he or she would accurately attribute the arousal to exercise (Zillmann, 1978a). The transfer of excitation is especially likely when the pattern of arousal from the nonemotional source is similar to the pattern associated with a particular emotion. Thus, a person is more likely to mistake the pounding heart, increased respiration, and facial redness created by exercise for anger rather than contentment.

Arousal created by one emotion can also transfer to intensify another. For example, arousal from fear, like arousal from exercise, can enhance sexual feelings. One study of this transfer took place in British Columbia over a deep gorge filled with roaring rapids. The gorge could be crossed either by a precarious swinging bridge or by a safe wooden structure across a quiet part of the river. A female experimenter asked men who had just crossed each bridge to fill out a questionnaire that included a measure of sexual imagery. The men who met the woman after crossing the dangerous bridge had much higher sexual imagery scores than the men who had crossed the safe bridge. Furthermore, they were more likely to rate her as attractive (Dutton & Aron, 1974). When the person giving out the questionnaire was a male, however, the type of bridge crossed had no impact on sexual imagery.

One interpretation of these results is that excitement from crossing the bridge was transferred to the men's interaction with the woman. However, your critical thinking skills might lead you to consider another possibility: perhaps the men who crossed the dangerous bridge were simply more adventurous in both bridge crossing and sexual encounters. This possibility was tested by repeating the experiment, with one change. This time, the woman approached the men farther down the trail, long after the arousal from crossing the bridge had subsided. In this case, the apparently adventurous men were no more likely than others to rate the woman as attractive or to call her for a date, suggesting that it was indeed transfer of excitation, not just adventurousness, that produced the original difference between groups.

Walter Cannon's Theory

Could the activation of any part of the central nervous system produce an experience of emotion in the absence of facial or internal bodily responses? Walter Cannon thought so, and he suggested an alternative to James's theory. In his view, you feel fear at the sight of a wild bear without ever taking a step. The responses of the autonomic nervous system, he said, do not help generate emotion (Cannon, 1927). Instead, Cannon proposed that the experience of emotion originates in the central nervous system—specifically, in the thalamus, the structure in the brain that relays information from most sense organs to the cortex.

According to Cannon's theory of emotion (known as the *Cannon-Bard theory*, in recognition of Philip Bard's contribution), the brain interprets an emotional situation through the thalamus, which sends signals simultaneously to the autonomic nervous system and to the cerebral cortex, where the emotion becomes conscious. So when you see a bear, the brain receives sensory information about it, interprets that information as a bear, and *directly* creates the experience of fear while *at the same time* sending messages to the heart, lungs, and legs to initiate a rapid departure. According to Cannon's theory, there is a direct, central nervous system experience of emotion, with or without feedback about peripheral responses (see Figure 12.12).

Updating Cannon's Theory Subsequent work suggests that the thalamus does not produce the direct central experience of emotion, as Cannon had theorized. Do other parts of the brain perhaps create this experience? Recent research points to several possibilities. Work with animals indicates that for one basic emotion, fear, connections from the thalamus go directly to the amygdala (see Figure 12.15), which generates the emotional responses (LeDoux, Romanski & Xagoraris, 1989). According to this evidence, strong emotions can sometimes bypass the cortex and do not require conscious thought to activate them. This may explain why people find it so difficult to overcome a strong fear, or phobia, even though they may consciously know the fear is irrational.

Another updated version of Cannon's theory suggests that specific parts of the brain produce the feelings of pleasure or pain in emotion. This notion came about when scientists discovered by accident that electrical stimulation of certain parts of the brain is reinforcing. (These are the "pleasure centers" discussed in Chapter 8, on learning.) The scientists noticed that rats with stimulating electrodes in their brains kept returning to the place in the cage where they received the stimulation. The investigators thought this was bizarre behavior, but they had the insight to revise the apparatus so the animals could control delivery of the stimulation by pressing a bar. Amazingly, rats pressed the bar incessantly to receive this electrical stimulation, even to the point of neglecting needs for food and water (Olds & Milner, 1954).

The brain areas in which stimulation is experienced as pleasurable include the locus coeruleus and other areas associated with the autonomic nervous

Figure 12.15
Parts of the Brain Involved in the Experience of Emotion
Sensory information comes into the brain to alert the individual to an emotion-evoking situation. Most sensory information goes through the thalamus; the cingulate cortex and hippocampus are involved in the interpretation of this sensory input. Output from these areas goes to the amygdala and hypothalamus, which control the autonomic nervous system via brainstem connections. There are also connections from the thalamus directly to the amygdala. The locus coeruleus is one area of the brainstem that causes both widespread arousal of cortical areas and changes in autonomic activity.

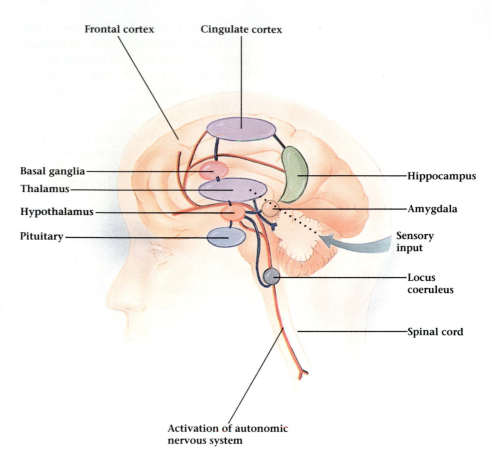

system, as well as the dopaminergic systems, described in Chapter 7, which are activated by drugs of abuse (Segal & Bloom, 1976; Wise, 1988). In contrast, there are other brain regions whose stimulation is so aversive that animals will work hard to avoid it. Presumably, part of the direct central experience of emotions involves areas of the brain whose activity is experienced as either reinforcing or aversive. The areas of the brain activated by the kind of events that elicit emotion in humans have widespread outputs throughout the brain. Thus, the central nervous system experience of emotion may be widely distributed rather than narrowly localized (Derryberry & Tucker, 1992).

Some of the brain regions where stimulation is reinforcing appear to form a kind of "autonomic nervous system" within the brain (Hartman et al., 1986). Just as the autonomic nervous system modulates the activity of organs that can function without input from the ANS, several neurotransmitter systems in the brain appear to modulate the activity of other brain cells. Noradrenergic cells in the locus coeruleus play this "autonomic" role, releasing noradrenaline and modulating the activity of other brain cells, as well as sending signals to the autonomic nervous system in the periphery (Olpe, Steinmann & Jones, 1985).

Data suggesting that the brain contains its own "autonomic nervous system" suggest a variation on Cannon's theory that unifies the picture of emotional responses. The same cells that project fibers down the spinal cord to activate the traditional autonomic nervous system also appear to send fibers into the rest of the brain, activating cells in areas such as the hypothalamus and the limbic system. Thus, an emotional situation energizes the entire body, including parts of the brain, creating changes in the central nervous system that are part of the same response that produces a racing heart or other symptoms of emotion in the peripheral autonomic system. A common neural system could

In Review: Theories of Emotion

Theory	Source of Emotions	Evidence for Theory
James-Lange	The CNS generates specific physical responses; observation of the physical responses constitutes emotion.	Different emotions are associated with different physical responses.
Schachter-Singer	The CNS generates nonspecific physical responses; interpretation of the physical responses in light of the situation constitutes emotions.	Excitation generated by physical activity can transfer to increase emotional intensity.
Cannon-Bard	Parts of the CNS directly generate emotions; physical responses are not necessary.	People with spinal cord damage experience a full range of emotions without feedback from peripheral responses.

arouse the brain *and* activate emotional facial expressions and autonomic visceral responses (Levenson, Ekman & Friesen, 1990).

Thus, there is increasing evidence for the main thrust of Cannon's theory: that emotion occurs through the activation of specific parts of the central nervous system. However, different parts of the central nervous system may be activated for different emotions and for different aspects of the total emotional experience.

Conclusions "In Review: Theories of Emotion" summarizes key elements of the three theories we have discussed. It appears that both peripheral autonomic responses (including facial responses) and the cognitive interpretation of those responses play a role in the experience of emotion. In addition, there appears to be some direct experiencing of emotion by the central nervous system, independent of physiological arousal. So emotion is probably both in the heart and in the head (including the face). The most basic emotions probably occur directly within the central nervous system, and the many shades of discernible emotions probably arise from attributions, including evaluations of physiological responses. No theory has completely resolved the issue of which, if any, component of emotion is primary. However, the theories we have discussed have helped psychologists better understand how these components interact to produce emotional experience.

How Do People Communicate Emotions?

Imagine a woman sitting down to watch television. You can see her face, but you cannot see what she is watching. She might be involved in complex patterns of thought, perhaps comparing her investments with those of the experts on "Wall Street Week." Equally plausibly, her mind might be attaining the consistency of mashed potatoes as she watches reruns of "Gilligan's Island." There is very little you can observe that indicates the nature of her thought patterns. However, if the television program creates an emotional experience, you could make a reasonably accurate guess about what kind of emotion it is by watching her face (Patrick, Craig & Prkachin, 1986; Wagner, MacDonald & Manstead, 1986). Why should an emotional experience cause the muscles of the face to contract in a distinct pattern? So far, we have described emotion from the inside, as people experience their own emotions. In this section, we examine the communication of emotion—in other words, how people express and recognize emotions.

Different species have evolved a variety of ways to communicate emotions. For people, even movement and body positioning can convey a certain amount of emotional information. In conversation between members of the opposite sex, for example, leaning toward and looking directly at one another usually indicate liking and possibly even sexual interest; leaning back and looking away tend to suggest boredom or hostility. Such cues, however, are often complex and subtle. Contrary to the claims of popular books and articles on body language, there is no fixed set of body movements or postures that always conveys a specific set of emotional messages (Goleman, 1986).

Indeed, in humans, facial movement and expression play the primary role in communicating emotions, and we focus our attention on them. The human face can generate thousands of different expressions (Izard, 1971). Observers can discriminate very small changes in facial patterns; a twitch of the mouth can carry a lot of information. Are facial expressions of emotion innate, or are they learned? And how are they controlled? How are they used in communicating emotion?

Innate Expressions of Emotion

Charles Darwin observed that certain facial expressions seem to be universal. He proposed that these expressions are biologically determined, passed on genetically from one generation to the next. The facial expressions seen today, Darwin argued, are those that have been most effective at telling others something about how a person is feeling and what he or she is about to do. If someone is red in the face and scowling, for example, you will probably assume that he or she is angry, and you will be unlikely to choose that particular moment to ask for a loan.

Darwin's theory about facial expressions is not entirely accurate, because some facial expressions that express emotions are learned, not inborn. However, two types of evidence indicate that, as Darwin proposed, the basic facial expressions of emotions are innate.

One source of evidence comes from infants. They do not need to be taught to grimace in pain or to smile in pleasure; they exhibit facial movements that are appropriately correlated with their well-being. Even blind infants, who

The innate origin of some emotional expressions is supported by the fact that the facial movement pattern we call a smile is related to happiness, pleasure, and other positive emotions in human cultures throughout the world.

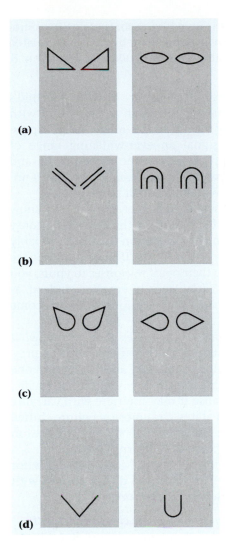

Source: Aronoff, Barclay & Stevenson, 1988.

Figure 12.16
Elements of Ceremonial Facial Masks That Convey Threat
Certain geometrical elements are common to the threatening ceremonial masks of many cultures. People in various cultures were asked which member of each pair was more threatening. In these displays the triangular and diagonal elements in the left-hand member of each pair convey threat most clearly. Note that Halloween pumpkins carved to look "scary" tend to have these threatening elements as well.

cannot see adults in order to imitate them, show the same emotional expressions as do sighted infants (Goodenough, 1932).

A second line of evidence for innate facial expressions comes from research showing that, for the most basic emotions, people of all cultures show similar facial responses to similar emotional stimuli (Ekman, 1984, 1993; Ekman & Friesen, 1986). Studies that demonstrate the universality of emotional expressions ask people to look at photographs of faces and then pick what emotion the person in the photo is feeling. The pattern of facial movements we call a smile, for example, is universally related to positive emotions. Sadness is almost always accompanied by slackened muscle tone and a "long" face. Likewise, in almost all cultures, people contort their faces in a similar way when presented with something disgusting. And a furrowed brow is frequently associated with frustration or unpleasantness (Smith, 1989).

Anger is also associated with a facial expression that is recognized by almost all cultures. One study on the expression of anger and threat examined the artwork—particularly ceremonial masks—of various Western and non-Western cultures (Aronoff, Barclay & Stevenson, 1988). The threatening masks of all eighteen cultures under examination contained similar elements, such as triangular eyes and diagonal lines on the cheeks. In particular, angular and diagonal elements carry the impression of threat (see Figure 12.16).

Social and Cultural Aspects of Emotional Expression

Although some basic emotional expressions are innate, many other expressions are neither innate nor universal (Ekman, 1993). And though there seems to be a core of emotional responses that is recognized by all cultures, there is also a certain amount of cultural variation in recognizing some emotions. In one study, for example, Japanese subjects agreed with American subjects about which facial expressions communicated happiness, surprise, and sadness, but they frequently disagreed with Americans about which faces represented anger, disgust, and fear (Matsumoto & Ekman, 1989). Members of preliterate cultures such as the Fore of New Guinea agree even less with people in Western cultures on the labeling of facial expressions (Russell, 1991). Similarly, there are also variations in how cultures interpret emotions expressed by tone of voice (Mesquita & Frijda, 1992). For some emotions, voice cues are recognized more accurately in some cultures than in others. In one study, for example, Taiwanese subjects were best at recognizing sad voices, whereas Dutch subjects were best at recognizing happy tones (Van Bezooijen, Otto & Heenan, 1983).

People learn how to express certain emotions in particular ways, as specified by cultural rules. Suppose you say, "I just bought a new car," and all your friends stick their tongues out at you. In North America, this probably would mean that they feel jealous or resentful. In China, this response would express surprise.

Even smiles can vary as people learn to use them to communicate certain feelings. Ekman and his colleagues categorized seventeen types of smiles, including "false smiles," which are aimed at convincing another person that enjoyment is occurring; "masking smiles," which hide unhappiness; and "miserable smiles," which indicate a willingness to endure unpleasantness. They called the smile that occurs with genuine happiness the *Duchenne smile,* after the French investigator who more than a hundred years ago first noticed the difference between spontaneous, happy smiles and posed smiles. A genuine, Duchenne smile includes contractions of the muscles around the eyes (which creates a distinctive wrinkling of the skin around the eyes) as well as of the muscles that raise the lips and cheeks. Very few people can voluntarily contract the muscles around the eyes when they pose a fake smile, so this feature can often be used to discern "lying smiles" from genuine smiles (Ekman, Friesen & O'Sullivan, 1988). In a study of people watching films by themselves, the

Duchenne smile was highly correlated with subjective reports of positive emotions, as well as with EEG recordings of a pattern of brain waves related to positive emotions. Other types of smiles were not (Ekman, Davidson & Friesen, 1990).

Learning About Emotions   The effects of learning are evident in a child's expanding repertoire of emotional expressions. Although infants begin with an innate set of emotional responses, they soon learn to imitate facial expressions and to use facial expressions to signal an ever-widening range of emotions. As they grow older, these expressions become more precise and somewhat more individualized, so that a particular expression conveys an unmistakable emotional message to anyone who knows that person well.

If facial expressions become too idiosyncratic, however, no one will know what the expressions mean, and they will fail to elicit the desired response from others. Operant shaping, described in the chapter on learning, probably helps keep emotional expressions within certain limits. If you could not see other people's facial expressions or observe their overt responses to yours, you might show fewer, or at least less intense, facial signs of emotion. Indeed, as congenitally blind people grow older, their facial expressions tend to become less animated (Izard, 1977).

As children grow, they learn an *emotion culture*—rules that govern what emotions are appropriate in what circumstances and what emotional expressions are allowed. These rules vary from culture to culture and also within one culture over time. For example, the people of Ifaluk, a tiny island in the Pacific, condemn the expression of happiness because it may interfere with carrying out one's duties (Lutz, 1987). In the United States, the emotion culture shifted from relative unconcern with anger in the last century to stricter suppression of the expression of anger in this century (Stearns & Stearns, 1986).

The emotion culture can also change within a lifetime. Medical students, for example, must learn new rules about expressing emotions during contact with human bodies. As one medical student described the process:

How do I set aside 25 years of living? Experience which made close contact with someone's body a sensual event? Maybe it's attraction, maybe disgust. But it isn't supposed to be part of what I feel when I touch a patient. I feel some of those things, and I want to learn not to. (Quoted in Smith & Kleinman, 1989)

The extent to which control of emotional expression is expected varies from one culture to another. This was illustrated in a study of Japanese and American students who were shown movies that contained distressing scenes. When the subjects viewed the movie with a group of peers, the Japanese students showed little facial expressiveness compared with the American students. But, as pictured here, when they viewed the movie by themselves, Japanese and American students showed the same facial expressions (Ekman, Friesen, and Ellsworth, 1972).

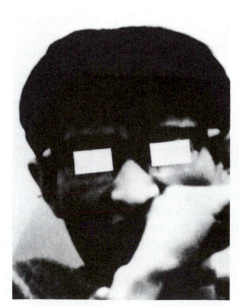 

Thus, relearning the rules of emotion is part of an unofficial curriculum at medical school; by observing doctors, students learn how to modify and control these feelings (Smith & Kleinman, 1989).

Emotion cultures also influence how people describe and categorize their feelings, producing both commonalities and differences across cultures (Russell, 1991). At least five of the seven basic emotions listed in an ancient Chinese book called the *Li Chi*—joy, anger, sadness, fear, love, disliking, and liking (Chai & Chai, 1885/1967)—are considered primary emotions by most Western theorists. But despite the fact that English has more than five hundred emotion-related words, some emotion words in other languages have no English equivalent. According to Milan Kundera, the Czech word *litost* has no exact translation: "It designates a feeling as infinite as an open accordion, a feeling that is the synthesis of many others: grief, sympathy, remorse, and an indefinable longing. . . . *Litost* is a state of torment caused by a sudden insight into one's own miserable self" (quoted in Russell, 1991). The Japanese word *ijirashii* also has no English counterpart; it refers to the feeling of seeing someone praiseworthy overcoming an obstacle (Russell, 1991).

Similarly, other cultures have no equivalent for some English emotion words. Many cultures do not distinguish between anger and sadness, for example. The Ilongot, a head-hunting group in the Philippine Islands, have only one word, *liget,* for both anger and grief (Rosaldo, quoted in Russell, 1991). There is no word for sadness in Tahitian and, apparently, no concept of it. One Westerner described a Tahitian man as sad over separation from his wife and child, but the man himself felt *pe'a pe'a*—a generic word for feeling ill, troubled, or fatigued—and did not attribute it to the separation (Levy, 1973). Tahitians also have no word for anything like guilt, but they have 46 terms for different types of anger.

Communicating Through Emotional Expressions The communicative value of emotional expressions depends on context. One of the most interesting examples is **social referencing** (Campos & Stenberg, 1981). In an uncertain situation, other people provide a *reference* that reduces uncertainty. People may look to the facial expressions, tone of voice, and bodily gestures of others for guidance about how to proceed. A novice chess player, for instance, might reach out to move the queen, catch sight of a spectator's grimace, and infer that another move would be better. The person providing the facial cues may or may not intend to communicate information. If a situation has no ambiguities, people may not pay attention even if the cues are present.

For infants, the visual-cliff experiments described in the chapter on perception provide an example of an uncertain situation. To reach its mother, an infant in these experiments must cross the visual cliff (see Figure 6.29). If there is no apparent dropoff or if the drop is very dramatic, there is no ambiguity, and a one-year-old knows what to do. It crawls across in the first case and stays put in the second case. However, if the apparent dropoff is shallow enough to create uncertainty (say, two feet), then the infant looks to its mother's emotional expressions to resolve the uncertainty. In one study, mothers were asked to display either a fearful or a joyful face. When the mothers made a fearful face, no infant crossed the glass floor. But when they posed a joyful face, fifteen out of nineteen infants crossed (Sorce et al., 1981). Infants who cannot yet understand spoken language depend to a large degree on adults' emotional expressions for information (Campos & Barrett, 1984).

Communication through emotional expression may explain some behaviors that many have considered biologically "wired in." For example, mothers' emotional expressions influence infants' fear of strangers. If a stranger enters the room and the mother abruptly says "Hello" and frowns, an eight-month-old infant will have an increased heart rate and show distress when the stranger approaches. But if the mother says a cheery "Hello," the infant's heart rate actually slows down, and it shows less distress (Sorce et al., 1981). Thus, the emotional expression of one person can communicate values and shape the behavior of another person.

Facial Expressions and the Brain

A posed, social smile and a smile that reflects real happiness not only look somewhat different but also are controlled by different neurons in the brain (Rinn, 1984). Voluntary facial movements are controlled by a part of the motor cortex known as the *pyramidal motor system.* Involuntary facial movements accompanying emotions are governed by the *extrapyramidal motor system,* which is controlled by subcortical areas such as the basal ganglia (see Figure 12.15). People can partially suppress emotion-driven facial expressions because the pyramidal system can control the extrapyramidal system.

Neurological damage can disrupt these control systems, as Figures 12.17 and 12.18 illustrate. The man shown in Figure 12.17 can smile reflexively when he is happy, but he cannot force himself to smile. The woman shown in Figure 12.18 laughs uncontrollably, but she feels no mirth (Peck, 1969).

Studies of people with different kinds of brain damage have revealed another characteristic of emotional expression. As noted in the chapter on biological aspects of psychology, although the cerebral hemispheres normally operate together, they play somewhat different roles in functions such as language. Similarly, the perception, experience, and expression of emotion are not controlled equally by each hemisphere. For example, some people with damage to the left hemisphere no longer laugh at jokes, even though they can still understand the meaning of the words, the logic (or illogic) underlying them, and the punch lines. And compared with normal individuals, depressed people show greater electrical activity in the right frontal cortex (Schaffer, Davidson & Saron, 1983).

There is some controversy about hemispheric asymmetries and emotion, however. In general, the right frontal hemisphere is activated during emotions (Borod, 1992), and there is agreement that negative emotions are related to right hemisphere activity. Some investigators argue, though, that the left hemisphere is more active than the right in positive emotions. For example, EEG recordings indicate that occurrence of the Duchenne smile (which accompanies positive emotions) is correlated with activation of the left frontal cortex (Davidson et al., 1990). This asymmetry of EEG activity during smiling is found even in infants (Davidson, 1984).

However, for facial expressions in general, the right hemisphere contributes more than the left to activation of facial muscles (Sackeim, Gur & Saucy, 1978). Because the nerves controlling muscles cross over the midline, the contribution of the right hemisphere is observed in the left side of the face. Thus the left side of the face is more expressive than the right.

Future Directions

We have seen that both biological and social factors play important roles in shaping emotional expressions. Further research is needed to clarify how these factors interact in emotional experience and expression (Ekman, 1993).

In fact, psychologists have still not determined exactly how emotional experiences are produced. Current knowledge suggests, however, that future studies will find that thinking and feeling cannot be as neatly separated as psychologists in the past might have wished. Those working in the field of artificial intelligence have even begun to attempt computer simulations of human thinking that include emotions. Future research is likely to emphasize

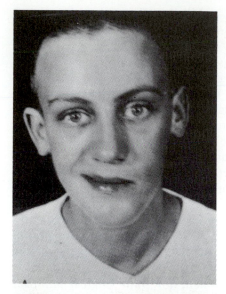

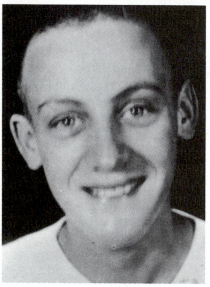

Source: From *The Neurological Examination* by R. N. DeJong. New York: Lippincott/Harper & Row, 1967.

Figure 12.17
Control of Voluntary and Emotional Facial Movements
This man has a tumor in the motor cortex that prevents him from voluntarily moving the muscles on the left side of his face to form a smile. In the top photograph he is trying to smile in response to a command from the examiner. Even though he cannot smile on command, he is perfectly capable of smiling with genuine happiness, as the bottom photograph shows, because these movements are controlled by the extrapyramidal motor system.

**Figure 12.18
Separation of Emotional
Experience from
Emotional Expression**
This woman has a neurological disease (amyotrophic lateral sclerosis)
that causes involuntary nonemotional laughing. She reported that
the laughter was painful and that she
was struggling to suppress it.

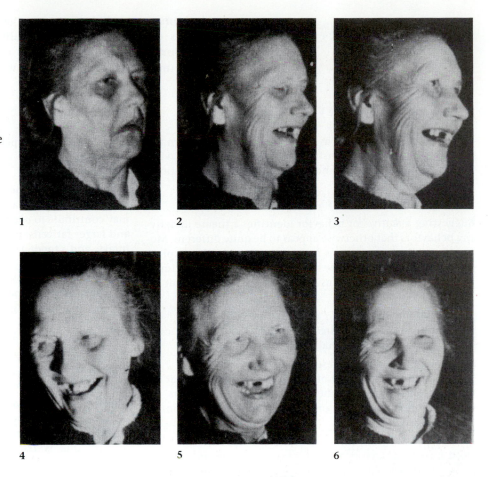

Source: From "Pathophysiology of emotional disorders associated with brain damage" by K. Poeck, in
P. J. Vinken and G. W. Bruyn (eds.) *Handbook of Clinical Neurology*, vol. 3. New York: American Elsevier,
1969.

the adaptive functions of emotions, instead of portraying them as disruptions
to smooth functioning.

As PET scans, MRI, EEG recordings, and other techniques for monitoring
brain activity are refined, researchers may be able to observe brain activity
more precisely and to relate that activity to subjective emotional experience.
Determining the areas of the brain that generate emotions may also clarify
how emotions and motivational systems interact.

Meanwhile, motivational research, which in the past was concerned with
short-term motives, has been shifting toward attention to motives that are
pursued over the long term. Personality, clinical, social, developmental, and
biological psychologists are all contributing to this effort. One recent trend,
for example, is to examine *personal strivings*, long-term goals that people pursue over a long period and try to achieve through their everyday actions. Personal strivings might include developing a coherent philosophy of life, becoming a respected scholar in a certain area, contributing to a successful and happy
family, or becoming a world-class chess player. People who report high levels
of life satisfaction tend to be committed to at least one long-term life objective
(Emmons, 1993).

If you wish to study the topics discussed in this chapter in more detail, consider taking a course in motivation and emotion. Most courses in biological
psychology also deal with the physiological and anatomical bases of motivation and emotion. A course on health psychology or stress and coping may
offer valuable coverage of the negative effects of emotional overarousal, and

courses in human sexuality deal extensively with the motivational and emotional aspects of sexual behavior. Finally, consider courses in personality or industrial-organizational psychology as sources of more information on achievement motivation in general and workplace behavior in particular.

Summary and Key Terms

Motivation can be defined as those processes that govern the initiation, direction, intensity, and persistence of behavior. Emotions both influence and are influenced by motivation.

Concepts and Theories of Motivation

Suggesting a *motive* for behavior identifies a theme underlying behaviors that otherwise appear to be quite different. Motivational concepts serve as *intervening variables* that explain both why one response may be given to very different stimuli and why the same stimulus may produce very different responses over time.

Sources of Motivation

Motivation has many sources, but they fall into four categories: biological, emotional, cognitive, and social.

Instinct Theory and Its Descendants

In animals *instincts* are innate, fixed-action patterns that are automatically elicited by the presence of some stimulus. Instinct theory has failed to provide a general explanation for human motivation.

Drive Reduction Theory

Both biological factors and learning are important in *drive reduction theory*. This theory holds that when *homeostasis* is upset, a *need* is created, which produces a *drive* to restore homeostasis. Biology creates the *primary drives,* but people are also motivated by *secondary drives,* which are learned.

Arousal Theory

According to *arousal theory,* people are motivated to maintain an optimal level of *arousal.* People generally feel best and perform best when they are at their own optimal level.

Incentive Theory

The role of environmental incentives is highlighted by *incentive theory.* In general, people are motivated to perform behaviors when they expect those behaviors to have outcomes that they value highly.

Hunger and Eating

Hunger and eating are complex processes controlled by biological, social, and psychological factors.

Biological Signals for Hunger

Cues from the stomach play a part in regulating hunger, but the role of the brain appears central. The brain monitors glucose, insulin, and other substances in the blood. Levels of these substances signal the need for food or indicate *satiety.* Through the hypothalamus (the lateral hypothalamus, the ventromedial nucleus, and the paraventricular nucleus), the brain acts to start and stop eating. These mechanisms function as if they were maintaining a set point of body weight.

Flavor, Learning, and Appetite

Eating is also influenced by the taste and smell (flavor) of food, and by people's experience with food. Conditioned satiety, conditioned appetite, and cues from others can all alter eating.

Eating Disorders

Obesity, anorexia nervosa, and bulimia nervosa are all health-threatening eating disorders. Among the factors that may contribute to *obesity* are body type, gender, having more and larger fat cells, a higher-than-average set point for food intake, and a tendency to cope with stress by eating. *Anorexia nervosa* is marked by self-starvation, sometimes leading to death. *Bulimia nervosa* is characterized by consumption of large quantities of food and then purging with laxatives or self-induced vomiting.

Sexual Behavior

Though not essential for individual survival, sexual motivation is very strong in human beings. The *sexual response cycle* is similar for men and women.

Hormones and Sexual Desire

Hormones have important organizational and activational effects. The masculine hormones are called *androgens;* the primary one is *testosterone.* The feminine hormones are called *estrogens* and *progestins;* the two primary ones are *estradiol* and *progesterone.* The role of hormones in human sexual behavior is less well understood than it is in animals.

Social Factors and Sexual Activity

Social and cultural factors, including gender roles, as well as attitudes toward sex often outweigh biological determinants of human sexual behavior. These factors also play a significant role in the appearance of *sexual dysfunctions* such as erectile disorder (in men) and arousal disorder (in women).

Sexual Orientation

Sexual activity may be *heterosexual, homosexual,* or *bisexual.* Sexual orientation has three components—identity, roles, and preferences. Recent evidence indicates that sexual orientation may be largely, though not entirely, determined by biological factors.

Success and Work

Most people's work results from extrinsic and intrinsic motivation.

Achievement Motivation

Need achievement is reflected in the capacity to experience pride in success. Individuals with high achievement motivation strive to achieve excellence, persist in the face of failure, and establish challenging but realistic goals. Gender differences in achievement behavior are pronounced and often appear at a young age. These differences appear to reflect early learning experiences.

Jobs and Motivation

Workers are most satisfied when they are working toward their own goals and get concrete feedback. Jobs that offer clear and specific goals, a variety of tasks, individual responsibility, and other intrinsic rewards are the most motivating.

Relations and Conflicts Among Motives

Maslow's Hierarchy

Maslow proposed a hierarchy of five classes of human motives, from meeting basic biological needs to attaining self-actualization. Maslow said motives at the lowest levels must be at least partially satisfied before people can be motivated by higher-level goals.

Linkages: Conflicting Motives and Stress

Four basic types of motivational conflict have been identified: approach-approach, avoidance-avoidance, approach-avoidance, and multiple approach-avoidance conflicts. Such conflicts act as stressors, and people caught in them often experience physical and psychological problems. Motivational conflicts also highlight the intimate relationships between motivation and emotion.

What Is Emotion?

Defining Characteristics

An *emotion* is a transitory, valenced experience that is felt with some intensity as happening to the self, is generated in part by a cognitive appraisal of a situation, and is accompanied by both learned and reflexive responses.

Emotions and the Autonomic Nervous System

The visceral responses that are part of emotional experiences are produced by the autonomic nervous system (ANS). This system modulates the activity of all the body's organs, allowing the body to respond to demands from the environment in a coordinated fashion. The autonomic nervous system has two divisions: the *sympathetic* system, which usually prepares the body for vigorous action, and the *parasympathetic* system, which is involved mainly in the protection, nourishment, and growth of the body. The *adrenal glands,* acting as specialized cells of the sympathetic nervous system, contribute to the *fight-or-flight syndrome* by releasing adrenaline into the bloodstream. Activity of the autonomic nervous system does not reach consciousness directly but can be detected indirectly, such as through biofeedback. Because of the involuntary nature of the autonomic responses that often accompany feelings of guilt, polygraphs have been used as lie detectors, but they are far from perfect.

Where Is Emotion: In the Heart or in the Head?

William James's Theory

James's theory of emotion holds that peripheral responses are the primary source of emotion and that self-observation of these responses constitutes the emotional experience. James's theory is supported by evidence that, at least for several basic emotions, physiological responses are distinguishable enough for emotions to be generated in this way. Distinct facial expressions are linked to particular patterns of physiological change. Studies of people with spinal cord damage do not support an important role for autonomic activity in parts of the body beyond the face.

Schachter's Cognitive Labeling Theory

Schachter's refinement of James's theory of emotion suggests that peripheral responses are primary sources of emotion but that cognitive interpretations of the eliciting situation are required to label the emotion, a process that depends on *attribution.* Attributing arousal from one situation to stimuli in another situation can produce *transferred excitation,* intensifying the emotion experienced in the second situation.

Walter Cannon's Theory

Cannon's theory of emotion proposes that emotional experience occurs independent of peripheral responses and that there is a direct experience of emotion based on activity of the central nervous system. Updated versions of this theory suggest that various parts of the central nervous system may be involved in different emotions and different aspects of emotional experience. Some pathways in the brain, such as that from the thalamus to the amygdala, allow strong emotions to occur before conscious thought can take place. Specific parts of the brain appear to be responsible for the feelings of pleasure or pain in emotion. One updated version of Cannon's theory suggests that emotion depends on pathways in the brain, including those from the locus coeruleus, that constitute a kind of "autonomic nervous system" within the brain, modulating the activity of other areas of the brain.

How Do People Communicate Emotions?

In humans, facial movement, voice tones, and bodily movements are all involved in communicating emotions.

Innate Expressions of Emotion

Darwin suggested that certain facial expressions of emotion are innate and universal and that these expressions evolved because they communicate an animal's emotional condition to other animals. Some facial expressions of basic emotions do appear to be innate. Even blind infants smile when happy and frown when experiencing discomfort. And certain facial movements are universally associated with certain emotions. The link between the Duchenne smile and enjoyment is one example.

Social and Cultural Aspects of Emotional Expression

Many expressions of emotion are learned. As a result, the same emotion may be expressed facially in different ways in different cultures. Especially in ambiguous situations, other people's facial expressions of emotion may be vital sources of information about what to do or what not to do, a phenomenon called *social referencing.* As children grow up, they learn an emotion culture, the rules of emotional expression appropriate to their culture.

Facial Expressions and the Brain

Voluntary facial movements and involuntary facial expressions are controlled by different parts of the brain. The right and left cerebral hemispheres play somewhat different roles in emotional expression. The right frontal areas are activated in negative emotions. The right hemisphere also plays the dominant role in facial expressions of emotion (the left side of the face shows more expressiveness) and the perception of both positive and negative emotion. However, left frontal areas are activated in some positive emotional expressions such as the Duchenne smile.

Chapter 13

Health, Stress, and Coping

Outline

In trying to make elderly people happy and healthy, most nursing homes protect them from the bothersome details of life. A reliable schedule is established for them. Nutritionally balanced meals are planned for them and served at the same time each day in a particular room. Even decisions about bedroom furniture are taken care of so that the residents have little to worry about. Why, then, are nursing home residents often unhappy, unhealthy, and much more likely to die than elderly people who must cope with all of life's daily hassles?

According to some psychologists, these problems appear partly because of the efforts made on behalf of residents. In one nursing home, some residents were allowed more control over what they ate, how their rooms were arranged, and whether their personal telephones were turned on or off. During the next eighteen months, these people were more active and alert, happier and healthier, and had a death rate 50 percent lower than residents who received equal attention from the staff but whose decision-making power was unchanged (Rodin, 1986a). Even among elderly people outside of nursing homes or other institutions, a sense of personal control and an optimistic outlook have been associated with resistance to disease (Rodin, 1986b). Attempts to protect the elderly from daily decision making may create a sense of lost control that is stressful—and as we discuss in this chapter, stress can make people more vulnerable to illness.

The impact of perceived control over daily life on the health and longevity of the elderly illustrates one dimension of **health psychology**, "a field within psychology devoted to understanding psychological influences on how people stay healthy, why they become ill, and how they respond when they do get ill" (Taylor, 1991, p. 6). As the Linkages diagram suggests, health psychologists use knowledge from many subfields of psychology to enhance understanding of the psychological and behavioral processes associated with health and illness (Matarazzo, 1984; Taylor, 1991). In this chapter we describe some of the ways in which health is related to psychological, social, and behavioral factors as well as what health psychologists are doing to understand these relationships and to apply their research to prevent illness and promote

better health. We examine in particular how stress affects health, how psychological factors affect the processes underlying physical disorders, and what techniques are effective for coping with stress and for changing health-endangering behaviors.

Health Psychology

Though its name is relatively new, the concepts underlying health psychology are ancient. For thousands of years people in many cultures around the world have believed that people's mental state, their behavior, and their health are linked (Matarazzo, 1984). Today, scientific evidence for this belief has been documented (Landrine & Klonoff, 1992). We know, for example, that through their impact on psychological and physical processes, the stresses of life can influence physical health. Researchers have also associated anger, hostility, pessimism, depression, and hopelessness with the appearance of physical illnesses. Similarly, poor health has been linked to such behaviors as lack of exercise, inadequate diet, smoking, and alcohol and drug abuse.

Health psychology is related to a broader interdisciplinary field called **behavioral medicine,** whose goals are essentially the same as those of health psychology: using knowledge from the behavioral sciences to promote scientific understanding of health and illness. Researchers and practitioners come to behavioral medicine from many sciences—including psychology, medicine, medical sociology, medical anthropology, and health education. Together they have mounted a formidable effort to expand research and education about behavioral factors associated with health and illness, and to promote preventive and treatment efforts to reduce the prevalence of illness and minimize its effects (Blanchard, 1992a; Matarazzo, 1980).

Health psychology and behavioral medicine have become increasingly prominent in the United States in part because of changing patterns of illness. Until the middle of the twentieth century, the major causes of illness and death in the United States were acute infectious diseases such as influenza, tuberculosis, and pneumonia. With these killers now tamed,

Linkages

The questions in this diagram illustrate a few of the relationships between the topics of this chapter—health, stress, and coping—and other chapter topics. Emotional, cognitive, biological, and behavioral factors all have an impact on health, and through their effects on these factors, so do the stressors you encounter every day. As you can see, many aspects of psychology contribute to and are illuminated by an understanding of the relationships among psychology, behavior, and health. The diagram shows just a sampling of the links among health, stress, and various areas of psychology; the page numbers in parentheses indicate where the questions in the diagram are discussed. ■

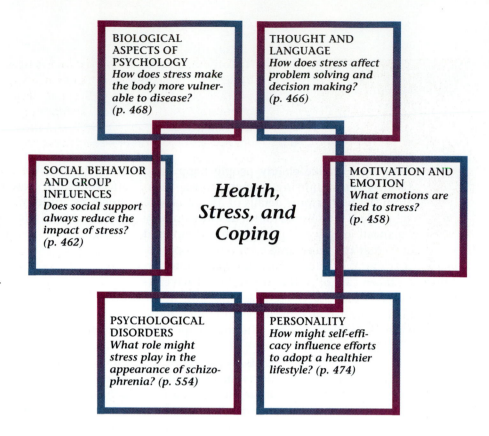

BIOLOGICAL ASPECTS OF PSYCHOLOGY
How does stress make the body more vulnerable to disease? (p. 468)

THOUGHT AND LANGUAGE
How does stress affect problem solving and decision making? (p. 466)

SOCIAL BEHAVIOR AND GROUP INFLUENCES
Does social support always reduce the impact of stress? (p. 462)

Health, Stress, and Coping

MOTIVATION AND EMOTION
What emotions are tied to stress? (p. 458)

PSYCHOLOGICAL DISORDERS
What role might stress play in the appearance of schizophrenia? (p. 554)

PERSONALITY
How might self-efficacy influence efforts to adopt a healthier lifestyle? (p. 474)

chronic illness—such as cancer, diabetes, and diseases of the heart, lungs, and vascular system—have become the leading causes of disability and death. Compared with acute diseases, these chronic diseases develop more slowly and are more heavily influenced by psychological, lifestyle, and environmental factors (Taylor, 1991). As Table 13.1 shows, lifestyle choices such as whether to smoke affect the risk for the five leading causes of death in the United States. Further, the psychological and behavioral factors that contribute to these illnesses can be altered by psychological methods. Indeed, in 1990 the Secretary of the U.S. Department of Health and Human Services (USDHHS) stated that as many as 50 percent of deaths in the United States were due to potentially preventable lifestyle behaviors (USDHHS, 1990).

One goal of health psychology and behavioral medicine is to help people understand the role they can play in controlling their own health and longev-

Table 13.1
Lifestyle Behaviors That Affect the Leading Causes of Death in the United States

This table shows five of the leading causes of death in the United States today, along with behaviors that contribute to their development. Health psychologists and researchers in related disciplines recognize that our physical health is intimately related not only to inherited characteristics and the dangers of the physical environment but also to behavior patterns and the cultural, social, and psychological environment.

	Alcohol	Smoking	Diet	Exercise	Stress
Heart disease	x	x	x	x	x
Cancer	x	x	x		?
Accidents and injury	x	x			
Stroke	x	x	x	?	?
Lung disease		x			

Source: Adapted from USDHEW (1979); USDHHS (1990); Matarazzo (1984).

Health psychologists have made important contributions by developing programs to help people stop smoking, increase exercise, eat healthier diets, and make other lifestyle changes that lower their risk of illness and death.

Figure 13.1
The Process of Stress
Stressful events, a person's reactions to those events, and interactions between the person and the situation are all important components of stress. The interactions are stress mediators; they moderate or intensify the impact of a stressful situation. For example, just one or two minor stressors might create extreme stress reactions if they are not controllable and are the latest of dozens of hassles in the life of a stress-prone individual with few coping skills. The same circumstances might not have much effect if that individual is more skilled or has more support from family or friends. Note the two-way relationships in the stress process. For example, as effective coping skills minimize stress responses, the experience of having milder stress responses will solidify those skills. And as coping skills (such as refusing unreasonable demands) improve, some stressors (such as a boss's unreasonable demands) may decrease.

ity. For example, health psychologists have facilitated early detection of disease by educating people about signs of cancer, heart disease, and other serious illnesses and encouraging them to seek medical attention while life-saving treatment is still possible. Encouraging women to perform breast self-examinations (Rakowski et al., 1992) and men to do testicular exams (Taylor, 1991) are just two examples of health psychology programs that can save thousands of lives each year. Health psychologists have also studied why some people fail to follow the treatment regimes that are vital to the control of diseases such as diabetes, heart disease, and high blood pressure. Discovering these factors and devising procedures that encourage greater compliance could speed recovery, prevent unnecessary suffering, and save many lives.

Health psychologists have also been instrumental in studying, and helping people understand, the role played by stress in physical health and illness. In the next section, we explore several dimensions of the stress process and consider its effects on physical and psychological well-being.

Understanding Stress

You have probably heard that death and taxes are the only two things you can be sure of in life. If there is a third, it must surely be stress. Stress is basic to life—no matter how wealthy, powerful, attractive, or happy you might be. It comes in many forms—a difficult exam, an automobile accident, waiting in a long line, a day on which everything goes wrong. Mild stress can be stimulating, motivating, and sometimes desirable. But as it becomes more severe, stress can bring on physical, psychological, and behavioral problems.

Stress is the process that occurs as individuals adjust to or deal with environmental circumstances that disrupt, or threaten to disrupt, their physical or psychological functioning (Lazarus & Folkman, 1984; Taylor, 1991). Thus stress involves a transaction between people and their environments. The environmental circumstances (such as exams or accidents) that cause people to make adjustments are called **stressors**. **Stress reactions** are the physical, psychological, and behavioral responses (such as nausea, nervousness, and fatigue) that people display in the face of stressors.

Interestingly, some people are more strongly affected by stressors than other people, or may be more affected on one occasion or another. Why? The answer appears to lie in *mediating factors* that influence the transaction between people and their environments. Mediating factors include variables such as the extent to which people can predict and control their stressors, how they interpret the threat involved, the social support they get, and their stress-coping skills. These mediating factors dampen or amplify a stressor's impact. Thus, as shown in Figure 13.1, stress is not a specific event but a process in which the

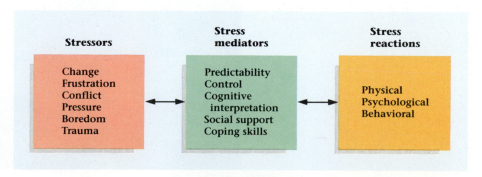

Stressors	Stress mediators	Stress reactions
Change Frustration Conflict Pressure Boredom Trauma	Predictability Control Cognitive interpretation Social support Coping skills	Physical Psychological Behavioral

nature and intensity of stress responses depend to a large degree on how stressors are mediated by factors such as the way people think about them and the skills they have to cope with them.

Stressors

For humans most stressors have both physical and psychological components. Athletes, for example, are challenged by the demands of physical exertion, as well as by the pressure of competition. Here, we focus on psychological stressors.

Psychological Stressors   Even very pleasant events can be stressors (Brown & McGill, 1989). For example, the increased salary and status associated with a promotion may be desirable, but the upgrade usually brings new pressures as well. Similarly, people often feel exhausted after a vacation. Still, the events and situations most likely to be associated with stress are unpleasant ones— those involving daily hassles and frustrations, negative life changes and strains, and catastrophies (DeLongis, Folkman & Lazarus, 1988; Gatchel, Baum & Krantz, 1989).

Daily hassles are minor irritations, pressures, and annoyances that, if experienced only occasionally, would not be significant stressors. But when experienced more regularly, hassles can have cumulative effects (Bolger et al., 1989). For example, research in the United States and Britain shows that noise associated with living near large airports has adverse affects on children and adults (Cohen, 1980; Kryter, 1990; Scattarella, 1992).

Life changes and strains can be major stressors, particularly if the changes are negative and if they force a person to make adjustments. Divorce, illness in the family, unemployment, difficulties at work, and moving to a new city are just a few examples of changes and strains that create demands to which people must adjust (Cohen & Williamson, 1991; Cohen, Tyrrell & Smith, 1991; Price, 1992). Being unable to earn a decent living because of adverse economic conditions or job discrimination consititutes another long-term strain that acts as a stressor.

Catastrophic events are shocking, potentially life-threatening experiences. Examples include traumas such as physical or sexual assault, military combat, fire, tornadoes, torture, or accidents involving loved ones (see, for example,

Commuting to and from work on trains or freeways includes both noise and crowding. For those who experience these hassles on a daily basis, the effect can be greater than that coming from larger problems (see, for example, Weinberger et al., 1987).

Bartone et al., 1992). Catastrophic events can lead to serious psychological disorders, as discussed later.

Measuring Stressors   Which stressors are most harmful? Are major changes worse than daily hassles? In order to study stress more precisely, psychologists have tried to measure the impact of particular stressors.

In 1967 Thomas Holmes and Richard Rahe made a pioneering effort to find a standard way of measuring the stress in a person's life. Working on the assumption that all change, positive or negative, is stressful, they asked a large number of people to rate—in terms of *life-change units,* or *LCUs*—the amount of change and demand for adjustment represented by a list of events such as divorcing, being fired, retiring, losing a loved one, becoming pregnant. (Getting married, the event against which raters were told to compare all other stressors, was rated as slightly more stressful than losing one's job.) On the basis of these ratings, Holmes and Rahe created the Social Readjustment Rating Scale, or SRRS. People taking the SRRS receive a stress score equal to the sum of the LCUs for the items they have recently experienced.

Numerous studies show that people scoring high on the SRRS and other life-change scales are more likely to suffer physical illness, mental disorder, or other problems than those with lower scores (De Benedittis, Lornenzetti & Pieri, 1990; Dohrenwend & Dohrenwend, 1978; Monroe, Thase & Simons, 1992). Still, questions have been raised about whether measuring life change alone tells the whole stress story (see, for example, Birnbaum & Sotoodeh, 1991). Accordingly, investigators have developed scales such as the Life Experiences Survey, or LES (Sarason, Johnson & Siegal, 1978), that go beyond the SRRS to measure not just what life events have occurred but also the respondents' *perception*—on a scale of -3 to $+3$—of how intensely positive or negative the events were. As you might expect, scales like the LES generally show that negative events have a stronger negative impact on health than positive events do (De Benedittis, Lornenzetti & Pieri, 1991; Sarason et al., 1985).

The LES also gives respondents the opportunity to write in and rate any stressors they have experienced that are not on the printed list. This personalized approach is particularly valuable for capturing the differing impact and meaning that experiences may have for men and women and for individuals from different cultural or subcultural groups (Nicassio, 1985). Divorce, for example, may have very different meanings to people of different religious or cultural backgrounds. Similarly, members of certain ethnic groups are likely to experience stressors—such as prejudice and discrimination—that are not felt by other groups (Castro & Magana, 1991; Lopez & Takemoto-Chock, 1992).

Other researchers have developed questionnaires to assess daily hassles and uplifts (DeLongis, Folkman & Lazarus, 1988; Kanner et al., 1981). Table 13.2 shows several items from one of these scales. Research suggests that predictions about the severity of disorder may be improved when they are based on consideration of daily hassles (but not uplifts) as well as major stressors (Brantley et al., 1987; DeLongis, Folkman & Lazarus, 1988; Garrett et al., 1991). In fact, some research has shown that daily hassles are more predictive of future illness than are major life events (Garrett et al., 1991; Weinberger, Hiner & Tierney, 1987). However, much more information will be needed about the mediating influences shown in Figure 13.1 before accurate predictions about individuals can be made.

Stress Responses

Physical, psychological, and behavioral stress reactions often occur together, especially as stressors become more intense. Furthermore, one type of stress response can set off a stress response in another dimension. For example, a

Table 13.2
Daily Hassles and Uplifts

Here are some items from the Daily Hassles and Uplifts Scale. The respondent is asked to make bedtime ratings (on a 0–4 scale) of the degree to which each item was a hassle or an uplift that day. Ratings over several days or weeks can give a detailed picture of a person's stressors and pleasures. This information has helped researchers appreciate the role of daily hassles in stress-related disorders.

How Much of a Hassle Was This Item for You Today?						How Much of an Uplift Was This Item for You Today?				
0	1	2	3	4	Your child(ren)	0	1	2	3	4
0	1	2	3	4	Time with family	0	1	2	3	4
0	1	2	3	4	Sex	0	1	2	3	4
0	1	2	3	4	Fellow workers	0	1	2	3	4
0	1	2	3	4	Your workload	0	1	2	3	4
0	1	2	3	4	Meeting deadlines	0	1	2	3	4
0	1	2	3	4	Having enough money	0	1	2	3	4
0	1	2	3	4	Your physical appearance	0	1	2	3	4
0	1	2	3	4	The weather	0	1	2	3	4
0	1	2	3	4	Your neighborhood	0	1	2	3	4
0	1	2	3	4	Cooking	0	1	2	3	4
0	1	2	3	4	Home entertainment	0	1	2	3	4
0	1	2	3	4	Amount of free time	0	1	2	3	4

Source: DeLongis, Folkman & Lazarus, 1988.

physical stress reaction such as mild chest pains may lead to the psychological stress response of worrying about a heart attack. Still, it is useful to analyze separately each category of stress responses.

Physical Stress Responses: The GAS   Anyone who has experienced a near accident or some other sudden, very frightening event knows that the physical responses to stress include rapid breathing, increased heartbeat, sweating, and, a little later, shakiness. These reactions are part of a general pattern, or *syndrome,* known as the fight-or-flight syndrome. As we discussed in Chapters 4 and 12, this syndrome prepares the body to face or to flee an immediate threat. When the danger is past, fight-or-flight responses subside. However, when stressors are long-lasting, these responses are only the beginning of a sequence of reactions.

Careful observation of animals and humans led Hans Selye (pronounced "sell-yay") to suggest that the sequence of physical responses to stress occurs

Figure 13.2
The General Adaptation Syndrome

Hans Selye's research suggested that physical reactions to stress occur in three phases: the alarm reaction, the stage of resistance, and the stage of exhaustion. During the alarm reaction, the body's resistance temporarily drops below its normal, ongoing level as it absorbs the initial impact of the stressor. However, the resistance soon increases dramatically, leveling off in the resistance stage, but ultimately declining if the exhaustion stage is reached. More recent approaches suggest that this sequence of events is not always as consistent and predictable as Selye suggested.

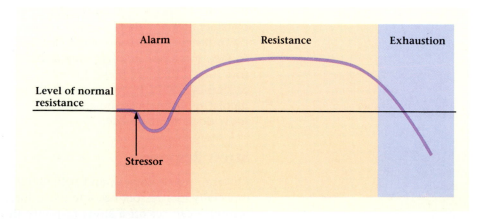

Source: Adapted from Selye, 1974.

in a consistent pattern and is triggered by the effort to adapt to any stressor. Selye called this sequence the **general adaptation syndrome,** or GAS (Selye, 1956, 1976). The GAS has three stages, as Figure 13.2 shows.

The first stage is the *alarm reaction,* which involves some version of the fight-or-flight syndrome. In the face of a mild stressor such as a hot room, the reaction may simply involve changes in heart rate, respiration, and perspiration that help the body regulate its temperature. More severe stressors prompt more dramatic alarm reactions, rapidly mobilizing the body's adaptive energy, much as a burglar alarm alerts the police and mobilizes them to take action (Selye, 1956).

How do alarm reactions occur? They are controlled by the sympathetic branch of the autonomic nervous system through organs and glands that make up the *sympatho-adreno-medullary (SAM)* system. As shown on the right side of Figure 13.3, stressors prompt the brain's hypothalamus to activate the sympathetic branch of the ANS, which stimulates the medulla (inner part) of the adrenal gland. The adrenal gland, in turn, secretes *catecholamines*—especially adrenaline and noradrenaline—which circulate in the blood stream, activating various organs including the liver, the kidneys, the heart, and the lungs. The

Figure 13.3
**Organ Systems Involved
in the GAS**
Stressors produce a wide variety of physiological responses that begin in the brain and spread to many organs throughout the body. For example, catecholamines from the medulla of the adrenal glands cause the kidneys to raise blood pressure. The pituitary gland triggers release of endogenous opiates, the body's natural pain-killers. It also stimulates release of corticosteroids, which help resist stress but, as we describe later, also tend to suppress the immune system, making the body more vulnerable to infection.

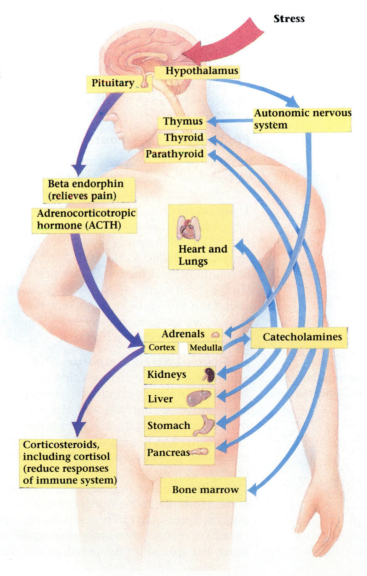

Linkages: Emotional stress responses can be severe, but they usually subside with time. However, people plagued with numerous stressful events in quick succession may experience increasingly intense feelings of fatigue, depression, and helplessness. These reactions can sometimes become so severe as to be considered symptoms of major depressive disorder, generalized anxiety disorder, or other stress-related mental disorders discussed in Chapter 15.

Linkages: What emotions are tied to stress? (a link to Motivation and Emotion)

results are increased blood pressure, enhanced muscle tension, increased blood sugar, and other physical changes needed to cope with stressors.

If the stressor persists, the *resistance* stage of the GAS begins. Here, obvious signs of the initial alarm reaction diminish as the body settles in to resist the stressor on a long-term basis. The drain on adaptive energy is slower during the resistance stage than it was during the alarm reaction, but the body is working very hard as a second stress response pattern—involving the *pituitary-adreno-cortical (PAC)* system—comes into play. As shown on the left side of Figure 13.3, the hypothalamus activates the PAC system by stimulating the pituitary gland in the brain. The pituitary, in turn, secretes hormones such as adrenocorticotropic hormone (ACTH). Among other things, ACTH stimulates the adrenal gland's cortex (outer surface) to secrete *corticosteroids;* these hormones release the body's energy supplies and fight inflammation.

The overall effect of these stress systems is to generate emergency energy to meet stressors. The more stressors there are and the longer they last, the longer the body must expend resources in an effort to resist them. This continued campaign of biochemical resistance is costly. It slowly but surely uses up the body's reserves of adaptive energy until the capacity to resist is gone. The body enters the third GAS stage, known as *exhaustion.* In extreme cases, such as prolonged exposure to freezing temperatures, the result is death. More commonly, the exhaustion stage brings signs of physical wear and tear, especially in organ systems that were weak in the first place or heavily involved in the resistance process. For example, if adrenaline and cortisol, which help fight stressors during the resistance stage, remain at high levels for an extended time, they can damage the heart and blood vessels, suppress the functioning of the body's disease-fighting immune system, and thus promote illnesses ranging from heart disease, high blood pressure, and arthritis to colds and flu (Cohen, Tyrrell & Smith, 1991; Cohen & Williamson, 1991; Cohen et al., 1992). Selye referred to illnesses that are caused or promoted by stressors as **diseases of adaptation.**

Selye's model has been very influential, but it has also been criticized for underestimating the role of psychological factors in stress, such as a person's emotional state or the way a person thinks about stressors (Appley & Trumbull, 1986; Lazarus & Folkman, 1984). These criticisms have led to the development of *psychobiological models,* which are models that emphasize the importance of psychological as well as biological variables in regulating and producing stress responses (DePue & Monroe, 1986; Smith & Anderson, 1986). According to psychobiological models, psychological variables, such as whether a person thinks about a stressor as an uncontrollable threat or a controllable challenge, shape the impact of stressors. Furthermore, threat, conflict, frustration, and other psychological stressors can stimulate some of the same responses as physical danger (Frankenhaeuser et al., 1971; Rozanski et al., 1988).

Emotional Stress Responses   The physical stress responses we have described are usually accompanied by emotional stress responses. If someone shows a gun and demands your money, you will no doubt experience the GAS alarm reaction, but you will also feel some strong emotion, probably fear, maybe anger. In fact, when people describe stress, they are more likely to say, "I got upset and felt angry and frustrated!" than "My heart rate increased and my blood pressure went up." In other words, they are likely to mention changes in how they feel.

In most cases, emotional stress reactions subside soon after the stressors are gone. However, if stressors continue for a long time or come in a tight sequence, emotional stress reactions may persist. When people do not have a chance to recover their emotional equilibrium, they commonly report feeling tense, irritable, short-tempered, or anxious more and more of the time.

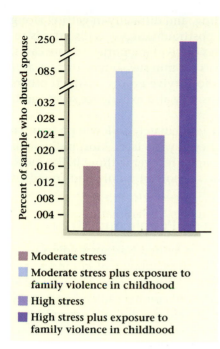

Legend:
- Moderate stress
- Moderate stress plus exposure to family violence in childhood
- High stress
- High stress plus exposure to family violence in childhood

Figure 13.4
Stress and Violence
Many researchers have found that unemployment, inadequate pay, job dissatisfaction, and other stressors are associated with increases in the rate and severity of domestic violence (Mason & Blankenship, 1987; Ponzetti, Cate & Koval, 1982). One aspect of this relationship was examined in an interview study of 1,436 married people (about half female); the graph illustrates the findings. Though the vast majority of these married people did not abuse their spouses, the more stressors they faced, the more likely they were to be physically aggressive. Aggression was especially likely among those who, as children, saw their own parents react to stressors with violence toward one another or toward them (Seltzer & Kalmuss, 1988).

Linkages: How might environmental stress make psychological disorders more likely? (a link to Psychological Disorders)

Cognitive Stress Responses   Reductions in the ability to concentrate, to think clearly, or to remember accurately are typical cognitive stress responses. One of the most common cognitive stress responses is **catastrophizing**, which means dwelling on and overemphasizing the potential consequences of negative events (Sarason et al., 1986). For example, during examinations, test-anxious college students are likely to say to themselves, "I'm falling behind" or "Everyone else is doing better than I am" (Sarason, 1984). These reactions are especially likely in people of moderate ability and those most uncertain about how well they will do (Spielberger, 1979). By dividing attention and thus reducing information-processing ability, catastrophizing can interfere directly with cognitive functioning; in turn, arousal is intensified, adding to the total stress response and further hampering performance (Darke, 1988; Geen, 1985). In other words, worrying too much about failure can make failure more likely.

Behavioral Stress Responses   Clues about people's physical and emotional stress reactions come from changes in how they look, act, or talk. Strained facial expressions, a shaky voice, tremors or spasms, and jumpiness are common behavioral stress responses. Posture can also convey information about stress, a fact observed by skilled interviewers.

Even more obvious behavioral stress responses appear as people attempt to escape or avoid stressors. Some people quit their jobs, drop out of school, turn to alcohol, or even attempt suicide. Unfortunately, as discussed in the chapter on learning, escape and avoidance tactics deprive people of the opportunity to learn more adaptive ways of coping with stressful environments, including college (Cooper et al., 1992).

Aggression is another common behavioral response to stressors. All too often, as Figure 13.4 indicates, this aggressiveness is directed at members of one's own family (Hepworth & West, 1988; MacEwan & Barling, 1988). In the months after Hurricane Andrew hit south Florida in 1992, for example, the rate of domestic violence reports in the devastated area doubled. As discussed in Chapter 18, stressors are just one of many factors that underlie human aggression.

Burnout and Posttraumatic Stress Disorder   Physical, psychological, and behavioral stress responses sometimes appear together in patterns known as burnout and posttraumatic stress disorder. **Burnout** (also called *gradual mental stress*) is an increasingly intense pattern of physical, psychological, and behavioral dysfunction in response to a continuous flow of stressors (Glass, McKnight & Valdimarsdottir, 1993; Maslach & Jackson, 1982; Sauter, Murphy & Hurrell, 1990). As burnout approaches, previously reliable workers or once-attentive spouses may become indifferent, disengaged, impulsive, or accident prone. They may miss work frequently, oversleep, perform their jobs poorly, abuse alcohol or other drugs, and become irritable, suspicious, withdrawn, depressed, and unwilling to talk about stress or anything else (Taylor, 1991). Burnout now accounts for some 11 percent of occupational disease claims by U.S. workers (Sauter, Murphy & Hurrell, 1990).

A different pattern of severe stress reactions is illustrated by the case of Mary, a thirty-three-year-old nurse who was raped at knifepoint by an intruder in her apartment (Spitzer et al., 1983). In the weeks following the attack, she became afraid of being alone and was preoccupied with the attack and with fear that it might happen again. She had additional locks installed on doors and windows but had difficulty concentrating and could not immediately return to work. She was repelled by the thought of sex.

Mary suffered from **posttraumatic stress disorder** (PTSD), a pattern of adverse reactions following a traumatic event. Among the characteristic reactions are anxiety, irritability, jumpiness, inability to concentrate or work pro-

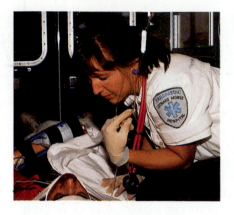

Burnout on the job is especially likely when people face unrelenting pressure brought on by a heavy workload and the need to make split-second, life-and-death decisions. Air-traffic control typifies such occupations, but burnout is also a problem in law enforcement, medicine, nursing, and many other fields.

ductively, sexual dysfunction, a lack of feeling, and difficulty in getting along with others. The most common feature of posttraumatic stress disorder is re-experiencing the trauma through nightmares or vivid memories. In rare cases, *flashbacks* occur in which the person behaves for minutes, hours, or days as if the trauma were occurring again. People who survive events in which others perished or who feel blame for others' deaths may also experience severe guilt or depression.

Posttraumatic stress disorder may appear immediately following a trauma, or it may not occur until weeks, months, or even years later. Most individuals require professional help, although some seem to recover without it. For most, improvement takes time; for nearly all, the support of family and friends is vital to recovery (Solomon, Mikulincer & Avitzur, 1988).

Stress Mediators: Interactions Between People and Stressors

During the 1991 Persian Gulf War, a number of United Nations soldiers were killed by "friendly fire" when pilots flying in close support of ground forces mistakenly identified them as the enemy. Many of these tragic errors in decision making were probably a result of the stress of combat (Adler, 1993). Why did stress disrupt the performance of some individuals and not others? More generally, why is it that one individual survives, even thrives, under the same circumstances that lead another to break down, give up, and burn out? As mentioned earlier, a number of mediating factors help determine how much impact a given stressor will have (see Figure 13.1).

Predictability and Control Knowing that a particular stressor *might* occur but being uncertain whether it *will* tends to increase the impact of the stressor. For example, wives of American men missing in action in the Vietnam War showed poorer physical and emotional health than those who knew that their spouses had been killed in action or were being held as prisoners of war (Hunter, 1979).

In other words, predictable stressors tend to have less impact than those that are unpredictable (Lazarus & Folkman, 1984), especially when the stressors are intense and occur for relatively short periods (Abbott, Schoen & Badia, 1984). For example, rats given a reliable warning signal every time they are to receive a shock show less severe physiological responses and more normal eating and

Stress responses do not always cease when the stressors that created them are gone. A pattern of lingering problems known as posttraumatic stress disorder is especially likely following such catastrophic events as rape.

drinking habits than animals given no warnings (Weinberg & Levine, 1980). Among humans, men and women whose spouses had died suddenly displayed more immediate disbelief, anxiety, and depression than those who had weeks or months to prepare for the loss (Parkes & Brown, 1972). This is not to say that predictability provides total protection against stressors. Laboratory research with animals has shown that predictable stressors, even if relatively mild, can be more damaging than unpredictable ones if they occur over long periods of time (Abbott, Schoen & Badia, 1984).

Perceptions of control can also mediate the effects of stressors. If people believe they can exert some control over them, stressors usually have less impact. For example, Albert Bandura and his colleagues found that as snake phobic clients developed a sense of control through treatment, their physical stress responses—such as secretion of adrenaline, cortisol, and endogenous opiates—were reduced and their immune system functioning improved (Bandura et al., 1985, 1988; Wiedenfeld et al., 1990).

Simply believing that a stressor is controllable, even if it isn't, can reduce its impact. In one study that examined the cause of panic attacks, panic-disorder clients inhaled a mixture of carbon dioxide and oxygen that typically causes such clients to have panic attacks (Sanderson, Barlow, & Rapee, 1988). Half the clients were led to believe that they could control the concentration of the mixture. Compared to those who believed they had no control, significantly fewer of those who believed they had control experienced full-blown panic attacks during the session, and their panic symptoms were fewer and less severe.

Indeed, people who feel they have no control over negative events appear especially prone to develop physical and psychological problems. They often experience feelings of helplessness and hopelessness that may promote depression or other mental disorders (Alloy & Clements, 1992). Similarly, studies have shown that breast cancer patients who harbor a sense of helplessness about their disease have a lower survival rate than those who have a greater sense of control (Jensen, 1987; Rodin & Salovey, 1989).

How Stressors Are Interpreted   The effects of perceived control on responses to stress are just part of a more general relationship between how people think about stressors and the impact of stressors. As discussed in Chapter 6, perceptions of the world depend on which things people attend to and how they interpret them. A person might see a bright light as glaring or glowing and a broad smile as warm or phony. Similarly, in Chapter 12 we noted that emotional reactions to events can depend on how people think of them. A given stressor, be it a hot elevator or a deskful of work, usually has more negative impact on those who perceive it as an uncontrollable threat rather than as a controllable challenge (Ganellen & Blaney, 1984; Rhodewalt & Zone, 1989).

Evidence for the effects of cognition on stress responses comes from both laboratory experiments and surveys. Figure 13.5 shows the results of a classic experiment that demonstrated these effects. In this case, the intensity of physiological arousal during a film depended on how the viewers were instructed to think about the film (Lazarus et al., 1965). Similarly, noise-related distress among people living near airports appears to have more to do with how they evaluate the airport (for example, as a nuisance or as a source of employment) than with how much noise they must endure (Tracor, Inc., 1971).

The influence of cognitive factors weakens somewhat as stressors become more extreme. For example, chronic pain patients tend to show higher levels of physical activity if they feel a sense of control over their pain, but this effect does not hold for those whose pain is severe (Jensen & Karoly, 1991). Still, even the impact of natural disasters or major stressors such as divorce may be

Figure 13.5
Cognition and Stress
In a classic experiment, Richard Lazarus and his colleagues showed three groups of students a stressful film containing graphic scenes of bloody industrial accidents and gave the groups different instructions regarding what to think about during the film. There were clear differences in the physiological arousal of the groups during the film, as measured by sweat-gland activity. Those who were instructed to remain detached from the bloody scenes (the intellectualizers) or to think of them as unreal (the denial group) were less upset than those in an unprepared control group. These results exemplify the fact that the way in which people think about stressors can affect their responses to those stressors.

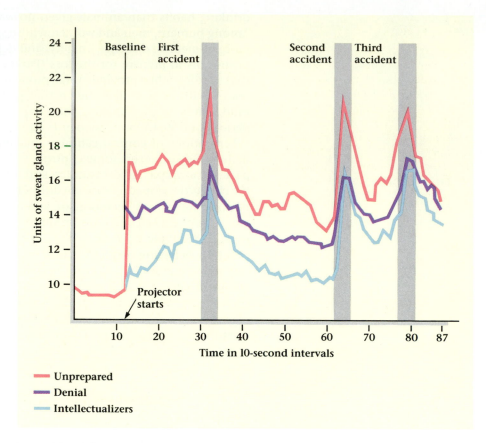

Source: Adapted from Lazarus et al., 1965.

less severe for those who think of them as challenges to be overcome. In short, many stressful events are not inherently stressful; their impact depends on such cognitive factors as perceived controllability and danger (Wiedenfeld et al., 1990).

Coping Skills and Social Support   Just as a football player in a sturdy helmet and protective pads is far less likely to be hurt in a game than someone wearing a T-shirt and cutoffs, people usually suffer fewer ill effects from a stressor if they are well equipped to cope with it (Aldwin & Revenson, 1987). There are numerous ways of coping. Most can be categorized as either *problem-focused,* which means trying to alter or eliminate a source of stress, or *emotion-focused,* which means attempting to regulate the negative emotional consequences of the stressor (Folkman et al., 1986). These two forms of coping sometimes work together. For example, you might deal with the problem of noise from a nearby airport by forming a community action group to push for tougher noise abatement regulations and, at the same time, calm your anger when the noise occurs by mentally focusing on the group's efforts to improve the situation. Susan Folkman and Richard Lazarus (1988) have devised a widely used scale to assess the specific ways that people cope with stressors; Table 13.3 shows some examples from their scale.

If you have ever appreciated the comforting presence of a good friend during troubled times, you can probably vouch for the importance of social support in tempering the impact of stressful events. Social support consists of resources provided by other persons; friends and social contacts on whom you can depend for support form your **social support network** (Cohen & Syme, 1985; Gottlieb, 1981). The support may take many forms, from eliminating the stressor (such as helping with car trouble) to buffering its impact by pro-

Linkages: Does social support always reduce the impact of stress? (a link to Social Behavior and Group Influences)

Table 13.3
Ways of Coping

Coping is defined as one's cognitive and behavioral efforts to manage specific demands that are appraised as taxing one's resources (Folkman et al., 1986). This table illustrates two major approaches to coping: problem-focused, in which one attempts to alter the source of the problem, and emotion-focused, in which one attempts to manage stress-related emotions.

Coping Skills	Example
Problem-focused coping skills	
Confronting	"I stood my ground and fought for what I wanted."
Seeking social support	"I talked to someone to find out more about the situation."
Planful problem solving	"I made a plan of action and I followed it."
Emotion-focused coping skills	
Self-controlling	"I tried to keep my feelings to myself."
Distancing	"I didn't let it get to me; I tried not to think about it too much."
Positive reappraisal	"I changed my mind about myself."
Accepting responsibility	"I realized I brought the problem on myself."
Escape/avoidance (wishful thinking)	"I wished that the situation would go away or somehow be over with."

Source: Adapted from Folkman et al., 1986; Taylor, 1991.

viding companionship, ideas for coping, or reassurance that one is cared about and valued and that everything will be all right (Rook, 1987; Sarason & Sarason, 1985). Even when social support cannot eliminate stressors, it can help people to feel less anxious, more optimistic, more capable of control, and more willing to try new ways of dealing with stressors.

The stress-reducing effects of social support have been documented for a wide range of stressors including cancer (Baron et al., 1990), crowding (Lepore, Evans & Schneider, 1991), military combat (Bartone et al., 1992), natural disasters (Kaniasty & Norris, 1993), and AIDS (Hays, Turner & Coates, 1992). These effects were well illustrated in a pair of studies on undergraduate and graduate students (Goplerud, 1980; Jemmott & Magloire, 1988). Those with the least adequate social support networks suffered more emotional distress and were more vulnerable to upper respiratory infections during times of high academic stress compared with classmates who were part of a supportive network. Indeed, one team of researchers concluded that having inadequate social support is as dangerous as smoking cigarettes because it nearly doubles a person's risk of dying from disease, suicide, or other causes (House, Landis & Umberson, 1988).

But perhaps you've noticed a problem here. The quality of social support may influence a person's ability to cope with stress, but the relationship may also work the other way around: people's ability to cope may determine the quality of social support they receive (Billings & Moos, 1981; Dunkel-Schetter, Folkman & Lazarus, 1987). For example, people who complain endlessly about stressors but never try to do anything about them may discourage social support, while those with an optimistic, action-oriented approach may attract reliable support. Further, an important aspect of social support is cognitive: the recognition that others care and will help (Pierce, Sarason & Sarason, 1991; Lakey & Cassady, 1990).

Obviously, the relationship between social support and the impact of stressors is not a simple one. Having too much support or support of the wrong kind can be as bad as not having enough. When friends and family overprotect a person, he or she may put *less* energy into coping efforts. Thus, an overprotective family might actually lengthen the time it takes for a worker who was

The AIDS memorial quilt provides a tangible reminder of the important role of social support in helping people cope with stressors of all kinds. To some extent, however, the effect of social support depends on a person's ability to perceive it, an ability that may be related to dispositional optimism. A clear perception of support, in turn, may help people to make more effective use of their coping skills.

Linkages: Are there stress-prone or disease-prone personalities? (a link to Personality)

The role of stress mediators was evident during and after the 1991 Persian Gulf War. Of the nearly 3 percent of U.S. soldiers who developed posttraumatic stress disorder, most were individuals who had the greatest exposure to combat, the least stress-resistant personalities, and the lowest levels of social support from other soldiers (Bartone et al., 1992).

disabled by an accident or illness to return to work (Garrity, 1973; Hyman, 1971; Wortman, 1984). Similarly, people living in crowded conditions might initially perceive the situation as providing lots of social support, but these conditions may eventually become an added source of stress (Lepore, Evans & Schneider, 1991). Thus, there are circumstances under which the efforts of a social support network can become annoying, disruptive, or interfering, and may increase stress and intensify psychological problems (Pagel, Erdley & Becker, 1987).

Stress and Personality   Some of the stress-mediating factors we have discussed reflect enduring cognitive habits, individual differences in how people think about stressors and the world in general. Cognitive habits often seen as part of *hardy personalities* appear to help insulate people from the ill effects of stress, while others, often seen in *disease-prone personalities,* may leave people especially vulnerable to those effects (Alloy & Clements, 1992; Eysenck, 1988; Freidman & Booth-Kewley, 1987a; Watson & Pennebaker, 1989).

One component of hardy personality seems to be *dispositional optimism,* the belief or expectancy that things will work out positively (Scheier & Carver, 1987). Optimistic students, for example, experience fewer physical symptoms at the end of the academic term, and optimistic coronary bypass surgery patients have been shown to heal faster than pessimists (Scheier et al., 1989; Taylor, 1991) and to perceive their quality of life following coronary surgery to be higher than those with less optimistic outlooks (Fitzgerald et al., 1993).

Optimism might provide a stress-buffering effect. Among HIV-positive gay men, for example, dispositional optimism has been associated with lower psychological distress, fewer worries, and lower perceived risk of acquiring full-blown AIDS (Taylor et al., 1992). These effects appear due in part to optimists' tendency to use challenge-oriented, problem-focused coping strategies that attack stressors directly, whereas pessimists use emotion-focused coping such as denial and avoidance (Scheier, Weintraub & Carver, 1986). Another study of HIV-positive gay men showed that active coping strategies are associated with improved functioning of the immune system (Goodkin et al., 1992).

Do more optimistic people live longer overall? The results we described would suggest just that, but a seventy-year longitudinal study found that children who were optimistic in childhood actually tended to die younger than their more pessimistic age-mates (Friedman et al., in press). The measures of optimism used in that study were different from those used today, so this result should be interpreted with caution. Still, it suggests that factors in addition to optimism are probably important in surviving the effects of life's stressors.

People who tend to think of stressors as temporary and who do not always blame themselves for the onset of stressors appear to be harmed less by them. This cognitive stance can be quite adaptive, especially when combined with a challenge orientation. Its benefits can also be seen, however, among many devout people whose religious beliefs prompt them to think of poverty, disease, and other objective stressors, not as challenges to be overcome, but as temporary conditions to be endured until their suffering is rewarded.

There is also a flip side to these relationships between cognitive patterns and vulnerability to stress. That is, stress-related health problems tend to be more common among people who persist at mentally evading stressors; who perceive them as long-term, catastrophic threats that they brought on themselves; and who are pessimistic about their ability to overcome the stressors (see, for example, Bandura, 1989; DeAngelis, 1992; Miller, Brody & Summerton, 1988; Peterson, Seligman & Vaillant, 1988; Scheier & Carver, 1987). In short, individual differences in how stressors are perceived and interpreted can combine

In Review: Stress Responses and Stress Mediators

Category	Examples
Responses	
Physical	Fight-or-flight syndrome (increased heart rate, respiration, and muscle tension, sweating, pupillary dilation); release of adrenaline and other chemicals. Eventual breakdown of organ systems involved in prolonged resistance to stressors.
Psychological	Anger, anxiety, depression, and other emotional states; inability to concentrate or think logically; catastrophic thinking.
Behavioral	Aggression and escape/avoidance tactics (including suicide attempts).
Mediators	
Predictability	A tornado that strikes without warning may have a more devastating emotional impact than a long-predicted hurricane.
Control	Repairing a disabled spacecraft may be less stressful for the astronauts doing the work than for their loved ones on Earth, who can do nothing to help.
Interpretation	Thinking of a difficult new job as a challenge will create less discomfort than focusing on the threat of failure.
Coping skills	Having no effective way to relax after a hard day may prolong tension and other stress responses.
Social support	Having no one to talk to about a rape or other trauma may amplify the negative impact of the experience.

with emotional and other factors to increase or decrease vulnerability to mental and physical problems.

Our review of personality and other factors that can alter the impact of stressors should make it obvious that what is stressful for a given individual is not determined simply by predispositions, coping styles, or situations. (See "In Review: Stress Responses and Stress Mediators.") What seems most important are interactions between the person and the situation, the mixture of each individual's resources and the specific characteristics of the situations encountered (Smith, 1993).

Linkages: Thinking Under Stress

How does stress affect problem solving and decision making?

The potentially fatal impact of stressors lies primarily in their ability to alter physiological arousal. As mentioned in the chapter on motivation and emotion, a moderate level of arousal may improve a person's ability to perform a task, but overarousal or underarousal can interfere with the efficient processing of information and with performance (see Figure 12.5). For example, if boredom produces enough underarousal that inattention results, a railroad worker may fail to throw a crucial switch, thus causing a train wreck.

Overarousal is also dangerous because, as arousal increases above a moderate level, it is the performance of complex and difficult tasks—such as dealing with aircraft emergencies—that is most likely to be disrupted. Why? One reason is that increased arousal strengthens the tendency to perform behaviors that are most *dominant,* the ones a person knows best. This reaction may aid performance of an easy, familiar task like riding a bike; but on more difficult or unfamiliar tasks, the well-learned behaviors elicited by overarousal may not be the right ones. For example, when overaroused by frustration or time pressure, American tourists in countries where cars are driven on the left side of the road, such as Britain or Japan, tend to revert to their old habit of entering the right-hand lane as they make right turns. This tendency causes numerous head-on collisions each year.

Linkages: How does stress affect the ability to attend to various stimuli? (a link to Perception)

Overarousal created by stressors also impairs performance on difficult tasks by interfering with people's ability to think clearly about complex material. For one thing, it tends to narrow the range of attention. The consequent inability to scan a wide range of creative solutions may add to the time needed to solve problems or reason efficiently (Darke, 1988; Keinan, Friedland & Ben-Porath, 1987). Stress-narrowed attention may intensify difficulties with problem solving that were discussed in Chapter 10, on thought and language. For example, stress can accentuate the tendency to cling to *mental sets,* which are well established, though possibly inefficient, approaches to problems. More specifically, stress can intensify *functional fixedness,* which is the tendency to use objects for only one purpose. People in hotel fires, for example, sometimes die trapped in their rooms because in the stress of the moment it

Moderate arousal can facilitate performance, but overarousal can interfere with it.

The effects of stress on thinking are often displayed by participants on "Jeopardy!" and other game shows. Under the intense pressure of time, competition, and the knowledge that millions of people are watching, contestants sometimes miss questions that seem ridiculously easy to those calmly recalling the answers at home.

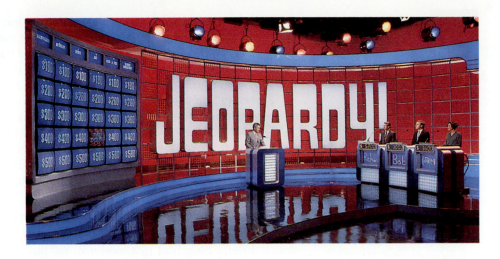

did not occur to them to use the telephone or a piece of furniture to break a window.

Decision making may also suffer when people face stressors. People who normally consider carefully all aspects of a situation before making a decision may, under stress, act impulsively and sometimes foolishly (Keinan, Friedland & Ben-Porath, 1987). Couples whose dating relationships have been full of conflict may suddenly decide to break up and then, just as suddenly, get married. High-pressure salespeople try to take advantage of people's tendency to act impulsively when under the influence of stressors by creating artificially time-limited offers or by telling customers that others are waiting to buy the item they are considering (Cialdini, 1988).

Research on the links among stress, thinking, and performance has helped to highlight the importance of reducing the stress under which people perform complex tasks. For years, commercial pilots have been limited in the number of hours they may fly per day, and air-traffic controllers are encouraged to take breaks every two hours. But sometimes, as when an engine is on fire or a nuclear reactor malfunctions, extreme stress is inevitable. The Federal Aviation Administration, commercial airlines, and other organizations have instituted new research and training programs designed to increase the likelihood that people will cooperate effectively during a crisis, consider all their options, and pay attention to all information that might avert a tragedy (Adler, 1989, 1993).

The Physiology and Psychology of Health and Illness

Several studies mentioned so far have suggested that stress shapes the development of physical illness by affecting cognitive, physiological, and behavioral processes. Those studies are part of a much larger body of research in health psychology and behavioral medicine that sheds light on the relationship between stress and illness as well as on how people can behave in ways that preserve their health. In this section, we focus more specifically on how stress can, directly or indirectly, lead to physical illnesses. One of the most important connections between stress and illness occurs through the immune system.

Stress, the Immune System, and Illness

The role of physiological stress responses in reducing the body's ability to fight disease was demonstrated more than a century ago. On March 19, 1878, at a

Linkages: How does stress make the body more vulnerable to disease? (a link to Biological Aspects of Psychology)

A patrolling immune system cell sends out an extension known as a *pseudopod* to engulf and destroy a bacterial cell before alerting more defenders. Psychological stressors can alter immune system functions through a number of mechanisms. They can activate neural connections between the sympathetic nervous system and organs of the immune system through response systems that have direct suppressant effects on immune function. These suppressant effects are due largely to the release of cortisol and other corticosteroid hormones from the adrenal cortex (see Figure 13.3). Adrenaline secreted from the adrenal medulla under stress can also suppress immune cells, as do endogenous opiates (endorphins), which also ease pain.

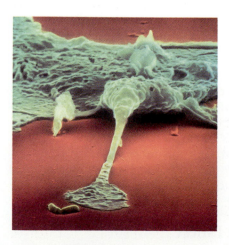

Source: Lennart Nilsson © Boehringer Ingelheim International GMBH.

seminar before the Académie de Médécine de Paris, Louis Pasteur showed his distinguished audience three chickens. One healthy bird, the control chicken, had been raised normally. A second bird had been intentionally infected with bacteria but given no other treatment; it was also healthy. The third chicken Pasteur presented was dead. It had been infected with the same bacteria as the second bird, but it had also been physically stressed by being exposed to cold temperatures (Kelley, 1985); as a result, the bacteria killed it.

Research conducted since Pasteur's time has greatly expanded knowledge about how stressors affect the body's reaction to disease. **Psychoneuroimmunology** is the field that examines the interaction of psychological and physiological processes that affect the body's ability to defend itself against disease.

The Immune System and Illness   The body's first line of defense against invading substances and microorganisms is the **immune system**, which we briefly discussed in Chapter 4, on biological aspects of psychology. Components of the immune system kill or inactivate foreign or harmful substances in the body such as viruses, bacteria, and cancer cells. If the immune system is impaired—by stressors, for example—a person is left more vulnerable to colds, mononucleosis, and many other infectious diseases (Cohen & Williamson, 1991; Cohen, Tyrrell & Smith, 1991; Jemmott & Magloire, 1988; Kiecolt-Glaser & Glaser, 1992). Disabling of the immune system is the process by which the human immunodeficiency virus (HIV) leads to AIDS and leaves the HIV-infected person defenseless against infections or cancers.

There are many facets to the human immune system. One important component is the action of immune system cells, especially white blood cells, called *leukocytes,* which are formed in the bone marrow and serve as the body's mobile defense units. Leukocytes are called into action when foreign substances are detected. Among the varied types of leukocytes are *B-cells,* which mature in the bone marrow, and *T-cells,* which mature in the thymus. Generally, T-cells kill other cells, and B-cells produce *antibodies,* which are circulating proteins that bind to specific foreign toxins and initiate their inactivation. Another type of leukocyte, *natural killer cells,* destroy a wide variety of foreign organisms, but they have particularly important anti-viral and anti-tumor functions.

Yet another type of immune system cell is the *macrophage.* Macrophages engulf foreign cells and digest them in a process called *phagocytosis* (eating cells). These scavengers are able to squeeze out of the blood stream and enter organs where they engulf foreign cells.

The activity of immune system cells can be either strengthened or inhibited by a number of systems, including the endocrine system and the central and autonomic nervous systems. It is through these connections that stress-related psychological and emotional factors can affect the functioning of the immune system (see Figure 4.24). The precise mechanisms by which the nervous system affects the immune system are not yet fully understood. But there is evidence that the brain can influence the immune system indirectly by altering the secretion of hormones that modify circulating T-cells and B-cells and directly by making connections with the immune organs, such as the thymus, where T-cells and B-cells are stored (Felten et al., 1991).

The Immune System and Stress   Researchers have shown convincingly that people under stress are more likely than their less stressed counterparts to develop infectious diseases and to experience reactivation of latent viruses responsible for oral herpes (cold sores) or genital herpes (Cohen & Williamson, 1991; Kiecolt-Glaser & Glaser, 1992). For example, Sheldon Cohen and colleagues in the United Kingdom (Cohen, Tyrrell & Smith, 1991) exposed 394 healthy adult volunteers to one of five respiratory viruses or a placebo. After being quarantined, the subjects were asked about the number and severity of life stresses they had experienced in the previous year. After controlling for factors such as prior history of colds, exposure to other viruses, and health practices, the researchers found that the more stress the subjects had experienced, the greater was the likelihood that their exposure to a virus would result in colds and respiratory infections.

These findings are supported by other research showing more directly that a variety of stressors lead to suppression of the immune system. For example, one group of researchers compared activity of natural killer cells in medical students one month before final exams and on the first day of the exams; natural killer cell activity was significantly lower at the stressful time of the exams (Kiecolt-Glaser et al., 1984; Glaser et al., 1987). Similarly, decrements in natural killer cell activity have been observed in both males and females following the death of their spouses (Irwin et al., 1987), and a variety of immune system impairments have been found in people suffering the effects of separation, divorce, lack of social support, and loneliness (Kiecolt-Glaser & Glaser, 1992). Each of these stressors has been associated with depression, which is itself associated with reductions in immune system activity (Petitto et al., 1992).

The relationship between stress and the immune system is especially important in persons who are HIV-positive but do not yet have AIDS. Their immune systems are already seriously compromised, so further stress-related decrements could be life threatening (Kiecolt-Glaser & Glaser, 1992). Recent research indicates that psychological stressors are associated with the progression of HIV-related illnesses (Ickovics & Rodin, 1992). Unfortunately, people with HIV (and AIDS) face a particularly heavy load of immune-suppressing psychological stressors, including bereavement, unemployment, uncertainty about the future, and daily reminders of serious illness. A lack of perceived control and resulting depression can further amplify their stress responses.

Moderators of Immune Function   The effects of social support and other stress-moderating factors can be seen in the activity of the immune system. For example, immune system functioning among students who can get emotional help from friends while facing stressors appears better than among those with less adequate social support (Jemmott & Magloire, 1988).

James Pennebaker (1985, 1990) has suggested that social support helps prevent illness mainly by providing the person under stress with an opportunity to express pent-up thoughts and emotions. Keeping important things to oneself, says Pennebaker, is itself a form of stress (Pennebaker, Colder & Sharp, 1990). In the laboratory, for example, subjects who were asked to try to deceive an experimenter displayed elevated physiological arousal (Pennebaker & Chew, 1985; Waid & Orne, 1981). Further, the spouses of suicide or accidental death victims who do not or cannot confide their feelings to others are most likely to develop physical illnesses during the year following the death (Pennebaker & O'Heeron, 1984). Disclosing the stresses and traumas one has experienced, even if done anonymously, has been associated with enhanced immune functioning and decreased use of health services among students (Greenberg & Stone, 1992; Pennebaker et al., 1988; Pennebaker & Beall, 1986). Future research in psychoneuroimmunology promises to reveal vital links in the complex chain of mental and physical events that determine whether people become ill or stay healthy.

Heart Disease and Behavior Patterns

Stress responses have also been linked to coronary heart disease. Research on this relationship began years ago, when two cardiologists, Meyer Friedman and Ray Rosenman (1959, 1974), noticed that the front edges of their waiting room

The Type A behavior pattern involves far more than just working hard. Type A individuals are much more interested in their achievements in the world of work than in social relationships. They often display selfishness, a strong fear of failure, and considerable hostility toward those whom they feel stand in the way of their success.

chairs were being worn out especially fast. It was as if patients with heart disease were always on the edge of their seats. Interviews revealed that, indeed, many of the patients displayed a pattern of behavior that Friedman and Rosenman ultimately called Type A. People who display the **Type A** pattern tend to be impatient, intensely competitive, and aggressive, nonstop workers. They constantly attempt to do more and more in less and less time. They need to control events and tend to become very upset if they feel they cannot do so (Glass, 1977). Some are also quite hostile. **Type Bs**, on the other hand, are more easygoing, mild mannered, less concerned with time, and less hostile.

In 1981 the National Heart, Lung, and Blood Institute convened a panel of experts to evaluate the Type A behavior pattern as an independent risk factor for coronary heart disease (CHD) and myocardial infarction (MI), or heart attack. The panel concluded that Type A behavior *does* pose a risk for CHD that is greater than the risks associated with age, hypertension, serum cholesterol, and smoking (Review Panel, 1981). This conclusion was based on numerous studies showing that people who display the Type A pattern are more than twice as likely to suffer heart disease than their Type B peers (Review Panel, 1981; Matthews, 1982; Siegel, 1984). Although several studies failed to find this relationship between Type A and CHD (see, for example, Hearn, Murray & Luepker, 1989), many others did (examples include Almada et al., 1991; Barefoot et al., 1989; Smith, 1992; Williams et al., 1988). Further, most recent studies indicate that it is not the Type A pattern as a whole but some of its components that increase a person's risk for coronary heart disease. In particular, these studies implicate hostility as the "toxic" agent most responsible for the increased risk of CHD (Matthews, 1988; Smith, 1992; Williams et al., 1988).

Thinking Critically

Does the Hostile Type A Behavior Pattern Increase the Risk of Heart Disease?

What am I being asked to believe or accept?

Many researchers contend that individuals displaying the Type A behavior pattern, particularly those who also display hostility, are at increased risk for coronary heart disease and heart attack. This risk, they say, is independent of coexisting risk factors such as heredity, diet, smoking, and drinking.

What evidence is available to support the assertion?

The precise mechanism underlying the relationship between Type A and illness is not clear (Smith, 1992). According to one theory, the increased risk of CHD and MI is thought to result from the tendency of hostile Type A's to be particularly reactive to stressors, especially when challenged. For example, when forced to rapidly solve arithmetic problems, Type A's show an increased heart rate and/or increased blood pressure (see, for example, Lundberg et al., 1989; Smith & Brown, 1991). Like a driver who damages a car by simultaneously flooring the accelerator and applying the brakes, these "hot reactors" may create excessive wear and tear on the arteries in the heart as their increased heart rate pushes blood through constricted vessels (Contrada, 1989; Elliot & Buell, 1983). Increases in sympathetic nervous system activation not only stress the coronary arteries but also are accompanied by surges of stress-related hormones from the adrenal glands: the catecholamines (adrenaline and noradrenaline) and cortisol (Lundberg et al., 1989; Williams et al., 1991; Suarez et al., 1991). High levels of these hormones, in turn, are associated with increased fatty substances such as blood cholesterol that is deposited in arteries and contribute to atherosclerosis (hardening of the arteries) and CHD. Plasma lipids such as cholesterol and triglycerides also tend to be elevated in hostile people (Dujovne & Houston, 1991).

Are there alternative ways of interpreting the evidence?

The studies cited in support of the relationship between the hostile Type A pattern and CHD are not the kind of true experiments described in Chapter 2. Researchers cannot manipulate the independent variable by creating Type A patterns in people, nor can they create experimental conditions in which groups of individuals who differ *only* in terms of the hostile Type A pattern are compared on heart disease, the dependent variable. Accordingly, it is difficult to reach unambiguous conclusions about cause-effect relationships in this and many other areas of health psychology and behavioral medicine.

Some researchers suggest that higher CHD/MI rates among hostile Type A's are due not to the impact of the hostile Type A pattern on autonomic reactivity and hormone surges, but to a third variable that causes both. It may be that genetically determined autonomic reactivity makes both a hostile Type A pattern *and* heart disease more likely (Krantz et al., 1988).

Supporting this alternative interpretation is evidence that, while undergoing surgical stress under general anesthesia, hostile Type A individuals show unusually strong autonomic reactivity (Krantz & Durel, 1983). Since they are not conscious, it is more likely that oversensitivity to stressors, not hostile thoughts, are causing this exaggerated response. Other data suggest that there is a genetic contribution to the development of hostility (see, for example, Smith et al., 1991). Thus, it is at least plausible that some individuals are biologically predisposed to exaggerated autonomic reactivity *and* to hostile Type A behavior, each of which is independent of the other.

What additional evidence would help to evaluate the alternatives?

Several lines of evidence could assist in evaluating these two interpretations of the relationship between hostile Type A behavior and CHD/MI. One approach would be to examine the relationship among hostility, CHD, and social and cultural factors (Thoreson & Powell, 1992). If the strength of the relationship between hostility and CHD varies across social or cultural groups, then the theory of biological determination would be less tenable.

John Barefoot and his colleagues (1991) examined part of this issue in a large sample of 2,500 adults. They found that the hostility scores of African-Americans were much higher than those of European-Americans and that, among the African-Americans, hostility scores were highest for those in lower income and education groups. The relationship between hostility and income was not present among European-Americans. Further, African-Americans have been found to react to stressors with greater blood pressure increases than European-Americans (Durel et al., 1989). Of course, elevations in hostility and blood pressure reactivity do not necessarily translate directly into CHD. Overall, African-Americans do not differ much from European-Americans in CHD death rates. Moreover, when income level is controlled for, African-American death rates from CHD are *lower* than those of European-Americans, despite higher hostility scores (USDHHS, 1990).

What conclusions are most reasonable?

Although there is some inconsistency, most studies continue to find that hostile Type A individuals have a greater risk of heart disease and heart attacks than their nonhostile counterparts (Smith, 1992). That is, the bulk of the evidence indicates that hostility is the most toxic component of the Type A pattern. But the causal relationships are probably more complex than any current theory suggests; it appears that many factors underlie the relationship between hostility and CHD.

A more elaborate model may be required—one that takes into account (1) that some individuals may be biologically predisposed to react to stress and challenge with hostility and increased cardiovascular activity, which in turn can contribute to heart disease; (2) that hostile people amplify and perpetuate their stress reactions through aggressive thoughts and actions, which in turn provoke others and elicit additional stressors; and (3) that those high in hostility also tend to harm their health more than less hostile people by smoking, drinking, overeating, not exercising, and engaging in other high-risk behaviors (Houston & Vavac, 1991; Smith, 1992).

It is also important to keep in mind that the relationship between CHD/MI and the Type A pattern seen in European-American men may not be universal. There is some evidence that this relationship may also hold for women and for individuals representing other ethnic and cultural groups (see, for example, Koskenvuo et al., 1988; Sprafka et al., 1990; Weidner et al., 1987), but we do not know for sure whether the relationship between hostility and CHD, for example, is the same (Landrine & Klonoff, 1992; Smith, 1992; Thoresen & Powell, 1992). Final conclusions must await research that examines in greater detail the relationships among Type A behavior, hostility, and CHD in women and in individuals from various cultural and ethnic groups.

Risking Your Life: Health-Endangering Behaviors

Though the role of the hostile Type A pattern in heart disease is not entirely clear, we have seen that many of today's major health problems are caused or amplified by preventable behaviors such as those listed in Table 13.1 (USDHHS, 1990).

Smoking   Smoking is the single most preventable cause of death in the United States (USDHHS, 1990). It has been estimated that, if people did not smoke cigarettes, 400,000 fewer U.S. citizens would die in the next twelve months; 25 percent of all cancer deaths and thousands of heart attacks would never occur (Lichtenstein & Glasgow, 1992; USDHHS, 1990). Cigarette smoking accounts for more deaths than do all other drugs, car accidents, suicides, homicides, and fires *combined* (Grunberg, 1992). Further, nonsmokers who in-

The Type A pattern has been detected in people as young as eleven, and general predispositions for Type A behavior may appear much earlier (MacEvoy et al., 1988; Matthews & Siegel, 1983). However, the pattern usually emerges most clearly in adolescence or early adulthood (Steinberger, 1986; Wright, 1988).

"Mrs. Davis, I think I have to slow down."

Source: Drawing by Weber; © 1990 The New Yorker Magazine, Inc.

hale "second-hand" smoke face an elevated risk for lung cancer and other respiratory diseases (Bauman, Koch & Fisher, 1989; USDHHS, 1990), a fact that has fueled a militant nonsmokers' rights movement in North America.

Overall, smoking is declining in the United States—about 26 percent of adults now smoke—but it has been increasing in certain segments of the population, especially among young women (Centers for Disease Control, 1993). Poorer, less educated people are particularly likely to smoke. High smoking rates are also found among certain Native American tribes in the northern plains, among Hispanic-American males, and among African-Americans. Some Native American tribes in the Southwest and most Asian groups are less likely than other groups to smoke (Gritz & St. Jeor, 1992; USDHHS, 1990). In many other countries, especially Third World countries, smoking is still the rule rather than the exception.

Alcohol Like tobacco, alcohol is a potentially addicting substance that can lead to major health problems. In addition to its association with most other leading causes of death including heart disease, stroke, cancer, and liver disease, alcohol abuse contributes to irreversible damage to brain tissue and to gastrointestinal illnesses, among many others. Both male and female alcohol abusers may experience disruption of their reproductive functions, such as early menopause in women and erectile disorder in men. As noted in the chapter on human development, alcohol consumption by pregnant women is the most preventable cause of birth defects. The economic costs of alcohol abuse total $70 billion a year (USDHHS, 1990); about 15 percent of U.S. health care costs are for alcoholism. We discuss alcohol abuse further in Chapter 15, on psychological disorders.

Unsafe Sex The threat of AIDS has become a fact of life around the world. In just the past decade, over one-quarter of a million Americans have been diagnosed as having AIDS and as many as two million more have been infected with HIV, the virus that leads to AIDS. An estimated 75,000 of these Americans are adolescents (St. Lawrence, 1993). Currently, the majority of those affected in the United States are male, but the rate for females is doubling every year or two (Ickovics & Rodin, 1992).

Unsafe sex—especially having sex without using a condom—greatly increases the risk of contracting HIV, yet many American adolescents and adults continue this dangerous practice (Catania et al., 1992). Like smoking and many other health-threatening behaviors, unprotected sex is disproportionately common among low-income individuals, many of whom are members of ethnic minority groups (St. Lawrence, 1993). Among African-American men the risk of contracting AIDS is three times greater than for European-American men; the risk for African-American women is fifteen times higher than for European-American women (USDHHS, 1990).

As described in the next section, health psychologists are deeply involved in the fight against the spread of HIV and AIDS (Kiecolt-Glaser & Glaser, 1992; Kelly & Murphy, 1992).

Promoting Healthy Behavior

The process of altering or eliminating behaviors that pose risks to health and at the same time fostering healthy behavior patterns is called **health promotion** (Taylor, 1991). In their health promotion efforts, many health psychologists conduct and apply research on the cognitive factors associated with the development and alteration of health-related behaviors. They aim to better understand the thought processes that lead people to health-endangering behaviors and to tailor intervention programs that alter or take those those processes into account.

Health Beliefs and Health Behaviors

The cognitive approach to health psychology is embodied in various *health-belief models,* one of the most influential of which was developed by Irwin Rosenstock and his colleagues (1974). This model has been extensively tested (see, for example, Aspinwall et al., 1991) and is based on the assumption that people's decisions about health-related behaviors (such as smoking) are guided by four main factors:

1. A perception of *personal* threat or susceptibility to contracting a specific illness. (Do you believe that *you* will get lung cancer from smoking?)
2. A perception of the seriousness of the illness and the severity of the consequences of having it. (How serious do you think lung cancer is, and what will happen to you if you get it?)
3. The belief that a particular practice will reduce the threat. (Will *your* stopping smoking prevent *you* from getting lung cancer?)
4. The decisional balance between the perceived costs of enacting the health practice and the benefits expected from this practice. (Will the reduced chance of getting cancer in the future be worth the discomfort and loss of pleasure associated with stopping smoking?)

Using this health-belief model, one would expect that the person most likely to quit smoking would be someone who believed that he or she was susceptible to getting cancer from smoking, that cancer was serious and life-threatening, and that the benefits of preventing cancer clearly outweighed the difficulties associated with quitting.

Other belief factors not included in Rosenstock's model may be important as well. For example, people are not likely to try to quit smoking unless they believe they can. Thus, *self-efficacy,* the belief that one is able to perform some behavior (see Chapter 14, on personality), is an additional determinant of decisions about health behaviors (Aspinwall et al., 1991; Bandura, 1986; Taylor, 1991).

Health-belief models have been useful in predicting a variety of health behaviors, including safe-sex practices among gay men at risk for AIDS (Aspinwall et al., 1991), adherence to medical regimes among diabetic adolescents (Bond, Aiken & Somerville, 1992), and having mammograms to screen for breast cancer (Rakowski et al., 1992).

Linkages: How might self-efficacy influence efforts to adopt a healthier lifestyle? (a link to Personality)

Changing Health Behaviors: Stages of Readiness

Knowing who is most likely to change their health-related behaviors is important, but health psychologists have also sought to understand the entire process of change. According to James Prochaska and his colleagues, successful change involves five stages (Prochaska, DiClemente & Norcross, 1992). Prochaska describes these five stages as follows:

1. *Precontemplation*   The person does not perceive that he or she has a problem and has no intention of changing in the foreseeable future.
2. *Contemplation*   The person is aware of a problem behavior that should be changed and is seriously thinking about changing it. People often get stuck here. Cigarette smokers, for example, have been known to contemplate quitting for years.
3. *Preparation*   The person has a strong intention to change, has specific plans to do so, and may already have taken preliminary steps, such as cutting down on smoking.
4. *Action*   The person at this stage is engaging successfully in behavior change. Because relapse is so prevalent in health-related behaviors, people in this stage must remain successful for up to six months before they officially reach the next stage.

Figure 13.6
Stages of Readiness to
Change Health Behaviors
Prochaska's theory that readiness to change health behaviors progresses through predictable stages has guided decisions by many health psychologists about whether to encourage a person to start a program for changing health behaviors. These decisions are guided as well by an exploration of the person's history of progress through the stages, and by an understanding of the stage in which the person seems to be at the moment.

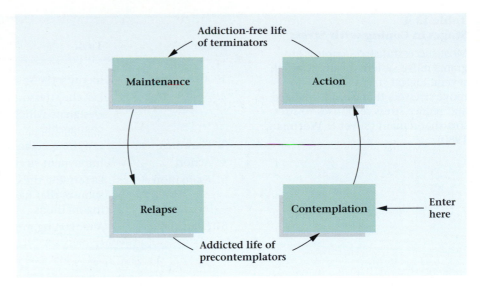

Source: Prochaska, DiClemente & Norcross, 1992.

5. *Maintenance*   The person uses skills learned along the way to continue the healthy behavior and to prevent relapse.

The path from precontemplation through maintenance is not a smooth one. Usually, people relapse and go through the stages again until they finally achieve stability in the healthy behavior they desire (see Figure 13.6). For example, smokers typically require three to four cycles through the stages and up to seven years before they finally reach the maintenance stage (Prochaska et al., 1992).

What factors contribute to movement from one stage to the next? Prochaska and his colleagues found that the factors facilitating progress at one stage may be different from those most important at another. However, *decisional balance,* the outcome of weighing the pros and cons of changing, is important for predicting progress at any stage (Prochaska, 1992). This finding applies to many health-related behaviors, including getting mammograms (Rakowski et al., 1992), participating in exercise programs (Marcus, Rakowski & Rossi, 1992), and quitting smoking, among others (Prochaska & DiClemente, 1992).

Programs for Stress-Coping and Health Promotion

Helping people to tip the decisional balance in favor of healthy change is but one strategy that health psychologists apply to improve people's stress-coping skills and promote healthier lifestyles. Let's consider a few specific procedures and programs used in this wide-ranging effort.

Linkages: Can stress-management programs help alleviate psychological disorders? (a link to Treatment of Psychological Disorders)

Planning Stress-Coping Programs   Just as people with extra money in the bank can weather a financial crisis, those with stress-coping skills may escape the harmful effects of intense stress. Like family money, the ability to handle stress appears to come naturally to some people, but coping can also be learned.

The first step in learning to cope with stress is to make a systematic assessment of the degree to which stress is disrupting one's life. This assessment involves (1) identifying events and situations that contain conflict, change, and other stressors; and (2) noting the physical effects of stress, such as headaches, lack of concentration, or excessive smoking or drinking.

Table 13.4 lists the other steps in a stress-coping program. Notice that the second step is to select an appropriate goal. Should you try to eliminate stressors or to alter your response to them? Knowing the difference between

Table 13.4
Stages in Coping with Stress
Most successful stress-coping programs move systematically through several logical stages and aim to remove stressors that can be changed and reduce stress responses to stressors that remain (Silver & Wortman, 1980).

Stage	Task
1. Assessment	Identify the sources and effects of stress.
2. Goal setting	List the stressors and stress responses to be addressed. Designate which stressors are and are not changeable.
3. Planning	List the specific steps to be taken to cope with stress.
4. Action	Implement stress-coping plans.
5. Evaluation	Determine the changes in stressors and stress responses that have occurred as a result of stress-coping methods.
6. Adjustment	Alter coping methods to improve results, if necessary.

changeable and unchangeable stressors is important. If your current major has become a source of severe stress, you might change your major; but simply skipping stressful exams would not be wise. Stress-related problems appear especially prevalent among people who either exhaust themselves trying to change stressors that cannot be changed or miss opportunities to change those stressors that can be changed (Folkman, 1984).

No one method of coping with stressors is universally successful. For example, denying the existence of an uncontrollable stressor may be fine in the short run but may lead to problems if no other coping method is used (Suls & Fletcher, 1985). Similarly, people who rely exclusively on an active problem-solving approach may handle controllable stressors well but find themselves nearly helpless in the face of uncontrollable ones (Rodin & Salovey, 1989). Individuals most successful at stress management may be those best able to adjust their coping methods to the demands of changing situations and differing stressors (Carver, Scheier & Weintraub, 1989; Costa & McCrae, 1989; Folkman et al., 1986; House, Umberson & Landis, 1988).

Developing Coping Strategies   Like stress responses, strategies for coping with stress can be emotional, cognitive, behavioral, or physical. *Cognitive coping strategies* change how people interpret stressors; help people think more calmly, rationally, and constructively in the face of stress; and may generate a more hopeful emotional state. For example, students with heavy course loads may experience anxiety, confusion, discouragement, lack of motivation, and the desire to run away from it all. Frightening, catastrophic thoughts about these stressors (for example, "What if I fail?") can amplify stress responses. Cognitive coping strategies replace catastrophic thinking with thoughts in which stressors are viewed as challenges rather than threats (Ellis & Bernard, 1985). This substitution process is often called **cognitive restructuring** (Lazarus, 1971; Meichenbaum, 1977). It can be done by practicing constructive thoughts such as "All I can do is the best I can." Cognitive coping does not eliminate stressors, but it can make them less threatening and disruptive.

Seeking and obtaining social support from others are effective *emotional coping strategies*. The perception that you have emotional support, are cared for, and valued by others tends to be an effective buffer against the ill effects of many stressors (Taylor, 1991). With emotional support comes feedback from others, and advice on how to approach stressors. Having enhanced emotional resources has been associated with increased survival time in cancer patients (Anderson, 1992), enhanced immune function (Kiecolt-Glaser & Glaser, 1992), and more rapid recovery from illness (Taylor, 1991).

Relaxation can be used to ease a variety of health-related problems. For example, one study of the side effects of cancer treatment found that progressive relaxation training resulted in significant reductions in anxiety, physiological arousal, and nausea following chemotherapy (Burish & Jenkins, 1992).

Behavioral coping strategies involve rearranging behavior patterns in ways that minimize the impact of stressors. Time management is one example. You might keep track of your time for a week and start a time-management plan. The first step is to set out a schedule that shows how time is now typically spent; then decide how to allocate your time in the future. A time-management plan can help control catastrophizing thoughts by providing reassurance that there is enough time for everything and a plan for handling it all.

Behavioral, emotional, and cognitive skills often interact closely. Discussing stressors and seeking feedback from others helps you think more rationally and calmly, and makes it easier to develop and use sensible plans for behavioral coping. When behavioral coping eliminates or minimizes stressors, people find it easier to think and feel better about themselves.

Physical coping strategies are aimed at directly altering one's physical responses before, during, or after stressors occur. The most common physical coping strategy is some form of drug use. Prescription medications are sometimes an appropriate aid for coping with stress, especially when stressors are severe and acute, such as at the sudden death of one's child. But if people depend on prescriptions or other drugs, including alcohol, to help them face stressors, they often attribute any success to the drug, not to their own skill. Furthermore, the drug effects that blunt stress responses may also interfere with the ability to apply coping strategies. And if the drug is abused, it can become a stressor itself. The resulting loss of perceived control over stressors may make those stressors even more threatening and disruptive.

Nonchemical methods of reducing physical stress reactions include progressive relaxation training, physical exercise, biofeedback training, and meditation, among others (Carrington, 1984; Dubbert, 1992; Tarler-Benlolo, 1978). Meditation is described in Chapter 7; here, we consider two other procedures.

In **biofeedback training**, special equipment records stress-related physiological activity, such as heart rate, blood pressure, and muscle tension, and then feeds this information to a person through a changing tone or meter reading. With practice, some people develop strategies that control these physiological processes and then use these strategies to reduce stress responses (Budzynski & Stoyva, 1984). Biofeedback has been useful in treating a variety of illnesses including asthma (Lehrer, Sargonaraj & Hochron, 1992) and tension headache (Blanchard, 1992b). Whether biofeedback can have significant and enduring effects on severe stress-related problems such as high blood pressure and migraine headache is less certain (Gatchel, Baum & Krantz, 1989).

Progressive relaxation training is one of the most popular physical methods for coping with stress. Edmund Jacobson developed the technique during

Teams of psychologists and other mental health personnel provide on-the-spot stress-management programs to people affected by hurricanes, tornadoes, mass murders, airplane crashes, and other sudden traumas. Organized by groups such as NOVA (the National Organization for Victim Assistance), these programs help victims, their families, and disaster-relief workers to manage immediate emotional reactions. They also offer weeks of follow-up sessions, as needed, in an effort to prevent later psychological problems.

the 1930s (Jacobson, 1938). Today, progressive relaxation is learned by tensing a group of muscles (such as the hand and lower arm) for a few seconds, then releasing the tension and focusing on the resulting feelings of relaxation. This procedure is repeated for each of sixteen muscle groups throughout the body (Bernstein & Borkovec, 1973). Once some skill at relaxation is developed, it can be used to calm down anywhere and anytime, often without lying down (Blanchard & Andrasik, 1985; Wolpe, 1982). ("In Review: Methods for Coping with Stress" summarizes our discussion of stress-coping methods.)

Linkages: How have psychologists in biological and personality psychology helped to prevent heart disease? (a link to Introducing Psychology)

Changing Type A Behavior

To reduce the health risks faced by hostile Type A individuals, researchers have developed programs to help these people to alter their frantic lifestyles and the intensity of their stress reactions. In one study, the goal was to prevent second heart attacks in Type A individuals who had already had one (Friedman et al., 1986). Over a thousand of these heart attack patients received either (1) routine post–heart attack counseling (such as advice about diet and exercise), (2) routine counseling plus a Type A modification program, or (3) no treatment. The modification program included progressive relaxation training, group discussion of the reasons for Type A behavior and its dangers, making changes (such as saying no to overtime assignments) designed to reduce stressors, and slowing the pace of life by eating more slowly and taking time out to do nothing. After five years, recurrence of heart attacks was significantly lower among people who received counseling plus the Type A modification program than among groups that received either routine counseling or no treatment (see Figure 13.7).

Similar programs have altered the behavior of healthy Type A people (Levenkron et al., 1983; Roskies et al., 1986), but it is still not known whether the interventions actually prevent first heart attacks. Research that analyzes the value of stress-management programs for healthy Type A's is difficult because these people are usually in the "precontemplation stage": most are unwilling to take time out to learn to slow down.

Preventing or Coping with AIDS

The spread of AIDS has spurred efforts by health psychologists both to change sexual behavior that transmits the infection and to minimize stressors among those who have been infected with HIV (Antoni et al., 1991; Kelly & Murphy, 1992).

Jeffrey Kelly and his colleagues, for example, have designed programs that have reduced sex-related AIDS risks in gay men (Kelly & Murphy, 1992). The programs include role-playing to teach strategies to resist pressure for high-risk sex (for example, unprotected sex with strangers). Compared to those in nonparticipating control groups, program participants displayed better knowl-

In Review: Methods for Coping with Stress

Type of Coping Method	Examples
Cognitive	Thinking of stressors as challenges rather than as threats; avoiding perfectionism.
Behavioral	Implementing a time-management plan; where possible, making life changes to eliminate stressors.
Physical	Progressive relaxation training, exercise, biofeedback, meditation.

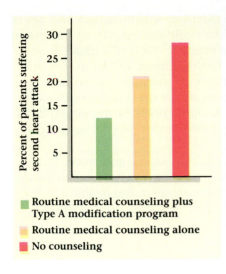

Source: Friedman et al., 1986.

Figure 13.7
Results of a Stress-Management Program
Meyer Friedman and his colleagues (1986) found that Type A heart attack victims were significantly less likely to suffer second attacks if they received help in altering their Type A behavior in addition to routine medical counseling. This bodes especially well for these people's health because there is evidence that even Type A heart patients who receive no such help are already less likely to die of recurring heart attacks than Type B heart attack patients, who are less competitive and hostile (Ragland & Brand, 1988). The reasons for this difference in long-term survival rates are not entirely clear. One possibility is that heart attacks in Type A's are brought on more by the intensity of their stress reactions than by an overall deterioration in their hearts (Brackett & Powell, 1988; Matthews, 1988). Thus the hearts of Type A's may be in better condition after an attack than those of Type B's. Whatever the case, the success of Friedman's program underscores the importance of stress-coping programs in cardiac rehabilitation.

edge about AIDS, greater skill at demanding safe sex, decreases in risky sexual behavior, and increased condom use during the sixteen months following the program. Several such programs are now in operation.

Michael Antoni and his colleagues (1991) have demonstrated significant stress reduction and enhanced immune function in a group of gay men awaiting the outcome of HIV tests. These changes were attributed to a five-week course in stress-coping strategies that included progressive relaxation training, cognitive restructuring, instruction in self-monitoring of stressors, and use of social support. The changes were especially significant because they were maintained even by men who learned that they were infected with HIV.

Health psychologists are also working on methods for lowering the risk for AIDS among adolescents. This is an important target group because many sexually active adolescents hold health beliefs that make them feel invulnerable to AIDS and thus cause them to greatly underestimate the risk of contracting the disease through unprotected sex (Abraham et al., 1992; Gladis et al., 1992; St. Lawrence, 1993). Adolescent-oriented AIDS prevention efforts focus on safe-sex media campaigns and studies of the cognitive and emotional factors that can enhance their effectiveness. Their impact is still being evaluated.

Future Directions

Health psychology and behavioral medicine will likely become increasingly important in future health-promotion and illness-prevention efforts. This is because they work. Following the antismoking programs of recent decades, for example, there has been a steady decline in the overall percentage of smokers in the U.S. population. Although much more work needs to be done, we can expect decreased rates of lung cancer and other smoking-related diseases due to these health-promotion efforts (USDHHS, 1990). Expect to see research aimed at isolating more precisely the toxic components of the Type A pattern and at developing more effective methods for changing the pattern (Thoresen & Powell, 1992; Smith, 1992). There will also be new culturally tailored health psychology programs for preventing the spread of HIV/AIDS (Kalichman et al., 1993). For example, a five-city U.S. government-sponsored AIDS Community Intervention Demonstration Project is mobilizing the principles of learning, social psychology, and related concepts to teach and motivate intravenous drug users (and their partners), prostitutes, homeless children, and people in other high-risk groups to protect themselves from the disease (O'Reilly & Higgins, 1991; USDHHS, 1992).

In the foreseeable future we can expect to discover much more about the extent to which psychological processes affect changes in immunity (Cohen, Tyrrell & Smith, 1991; Kiecolt-Glaser & Glaser, 1992) and the degree to which people can alter these processes at will. In their efforts to understand stress and its impact, researchers are likely to focus on how people and situations reciprocally influence one another over time. Research on coping and social support is turning toward questions such as how particular coping styles attract or repel support and the role of expectation and perception in buffering or amplifying stressors (Pierce, Sarason & Sarason, 1992).

Of interest as well will be questions about how coping skills develop and the degree to which they can be strengthened through formal training programs. There may also be research on adjusting environments to match individuals' coping styles. It has been suggested, for example, that hospitals should routinely assess patients' preferences for focusing on or avoiding stressors, and then adjust accordingly the information given to each patient about his or her illness or treatment (Ludwick-Rosenthal & Neufeld, 1993).

Future research will surely explore the extent to which current findings in health psychology and stress generalize across cultural and subcultural groups (Lonner & Malpass, 1994). It is likely, for example, that individuals from diverse cultural backgrounds conceptualize health, illness, and treatment in different ways (Beardsley, 1994; Manson, 1994). Accordingly, individuals with varying belief systems may respond differently to stress-reduction or other health-promotion programs (Landrine & Klonoff, 1992). Such cultural differences will be given increasing attention as new health psychology programs are developed for specific groups of people.

For a more detailed look at health psychology, stress, and stress management, consider taking courses in health psychology, behavioral medicine, stress and coping, or other stress-related topics. Most courses in abnormal psychology and some in personality also examine the relationships among stress, health, mental disorder, and individual characteristics.

Summary and Key Terms

Health Psychology

Recognition of the link between stress and illness, as well as the role of behaviors such as smoking in elevating the risk of illness, prompted the development of *health psychology* and *behavioral medicine.* Researchers in these related fields seek to understand how psychological factors are related to physical disease and to use behavioral sciences, including psychology, to help people behave in ways that prevent or minimize disease and promote health.

Understanding Stress

The term *stress* refers in part to *stressors,* which are events and situations to which people must react. The term is also used to refer to *stress reactions.* Most generally, however, stress is viewed as an ongoing, interactive process that takes place as people adjust to and cope with their environment.

Stressors

Stressors may be physical or psychological. Psychological stressors range from daily hassles, to life changes and strains, to catastrophic events. Stressors can be measured by tests like the SRRS, the LES, and the Daily Hassles Scale, but scores on such tests provide only a partial picture of the stress in a given individual's life.

Stress Responses

Responses to stressors can be physical, psychological, and behavioral. These stress responses can occur alone or in combination, and the appearance of one can often stimulate the others.

Physical stress responses include changes in heart rate, respiration, and many other processes that are part of a pattern known as the *general adaptation syndrome,* or *GAS.* The GAS has three stages: the alarm reaction, resistance, and exhaustion. The GAS helps people resist stress but, if present too long, can lead to depletion of immune system functions and to physical illnesses, which Selye called *diseases of adaptation.*

Psychological stress responses include emotional and cognitive reactions. Anxiety, anger, and depression are among the most common emotional stress reactions. Cognitive stress reactions include *catastrophizing* and disruptions in the ability to think clearly, remember accurately, and solve problems efficiently.

Behavioral stress responses include specific changes in posture and coordination as well as facial expressions, tremors, or jumpiness, which reflect physical tension or emotional stress reactions. More global behavioral stress responses include everything from irritability to absenteeism or even suicide attempts. Patterns of behavioral response to severe, long-lasting stressors or to trauma have been identified as *burnout* and *posttraumatic stress disorder.*

Stress Mediators: Interactions Between People and Stressors

The key to understanding stress appears to lie in understanding the interaction of specific stressors with particular people. Stressors are likely to have greater impact if they are unpredictable, uncontrollable, or involve a continuous parade of daily problems. The people most likely to react strongly to a stressor are those who perceive stressors as uncontrollable threats, who have an inadequate *social support network,* or who have few stress-coping skills.

Linkages: Thinking Under Stress

Stressors can disrupt thinking through their effects on physiological arousal. Underarousal can lead to boredom and inattention, while overarousal impairs the ability to think clearly and to perform complex tasks effectively. The effects of stress on arousal can lead to errors and accidents.

The Physiology and Psychology of Health and Illness

Stress, the Immune System, and Illness

Under stress, some of the hormones released from the adrenal gland, such as cortisol, reduce the effectiveness of the cells of the *immune system* (T-cells, B-cells, natural killer cells, macrophages) in combatting foreign invaders such as viruses and cancer cells. *Psychoneuroimmunology* is the field that examines the interaction of psychological and physiological processes that affect the body's ability to defend itself against disease.

Heart Disease and Behavior Patterns

People who live hostile, competitive, *Type A* lifestyles are more likely to suffer heart disease than their more relaxed *Type B* peers. The hostility and reactivity of Type A's are thought to somehow damage the cardiovascular system.

Risking Your Life: Health-Endangering Behaviors

Most of the major health problems in Western cultures are related to preventable behaviors such as smoking and drinking alcohol. Having unsafe sex is a major risk factor for contracting HIV.

Promoting Healthy Behavior

The process of altering or eliminating health-risky behaviors and fostering healthy behavior patterns is called *health promotion.*

Health Beliefs and Health Behaviors

People's health-related behaviors are partly guided by their beliefs about health risks and what they can do about them.

Changing Health Behaviors: Stages of Readiness

The process of changing health-related behaviors appears to involve several stages, including precontemplation, contemplation, preparation, action, and maintenance. Understanding which stage people are in, and helping them move through these stages is an important task in health psychology.

Programs for Stress-Coping and Health Promotion

In order to cope with stress, a person must recognize stressors, establish goals, and develop a stress-management plan for coping. Important coping skills include *cognitive restructuring,* acting to minimize the number or intensity of stressors, and using *biofeedback training, progressive relaxation training,* and other techniques for reducing physical stress reactions. These stress-coping procedures are often part of health psychologists' programs for altering Type A behavior or controlling stress reactions among HIV-infected people. Other health psychologists are involved in developing and implementing programs aimed at reducing the spread of HIV and AIDS.

Chapter 14

Personality

Outline

During World War II, the U.S. government needed spies, assassins, and other specialists for secret operations behind enemy lines. Applicants for these jobs were given special psychological tests, including one in which the candidate was permitted just a few minutes to instruct and supervise two enlisted men—"Buster" and "Kippy"—in the construction of a five-foot, cube-shaped wooden frame. What the candidate did not know was that the men were psychologists whose job was to frustrate and enrage him. Buster and Kippy were so good at acting lazy, stupid, and hostile that the cube was never built in the allotted time.

Did the government think that its spies would someday need to build giant Tinker Toy cubes in Nazi Germany? No, but the government did need to assess how well a person could perform under dangerous and stressful working conditions. The test was supposed to measure candidates' skill, ingenuity, endurance, and resistance to stress. The testers assumed that if a candidate did well on the test, then these characteristics were part of his personality and would come to the fore when needed.

This process of investigating people's personality as a means of predicting how they might react in the future is very similar to what most people do when they meet someone new. They observe how the person behaves, form impressions, and make predictions of how that person will act at other times or under other circumstances. In this sense, we are all personality theorists. Psychologists follow similar procedures in studying personality, but they do so in a more systematic and scientific fashion. Although there is no universally accepted definition, psychologists generally view **personality** as the unique pattern of enduring psychological and behavioral characteristics by which each person can be compared and contrasted with other people. Personality research, in turn, focuses on understanding the consistent patterns of cognition, emotion, and behavior that make people differ from and resemble one another. With such a large agenda, personality researchers must incorporate information from virtually all other areas of psychology (see the Linkages diagram).

Indeed, personality has been said to lie at the crossroads of all psychological research (Mischel, 1981); it is the coalescence in a particular individual of all the psychological, behavioral, and biological processes discussed in the other chapters of this book. To gain a comprehensive understanding of just one individual's personality, for example, one must know about developmental experiences (including cultural influences), genetic and other biological characteristics, perceptual and other information-processing habits and biases, and social skills as well as typical patterns of emotional expression. Searching for general principles underlying the formation and expression of personality requires integration of information at least as diverse.

The search leads psychologists to address a wide variety of questions about personality, such as how people's personalities develop across the course of their lifespan, why some people tend to be optimistic whereas others are usually pessimists, how much personality changes over a person's lifetime, and the degree to which behavior is consistent or variable from one situation to the next.

The specific questions psychologists ask about personality, and the approach they take to studying it, can vary considerably—depending in large measure on which of the theoretical approaches to psychology they prefer (see Chapter 1 and Figure 14.1). In this chapter we describe four basic theoretical approaches to the study of personality and some of the ways in which personality theory and research are being applied. We begin by presenting the psychodynamic approach, which was developed in the late nineteenth century by Sigmund Freud and subsequently modified by a number of those he influenced. Next, we describe the dispositional approach, which focuses on patterns of characteristic traits and types that form individual personalities. Then we describe the cognitive-behavioral approach, which explores the roles of learning and cognition in shaping human behavior and personality. Finally, we consider the phenomenological approach, with its emphasis on the importance of each person's unique view of the world in shaping his or her personality. Our overview of these varying approaches is followed by a description of some of the tests that psychologists have developed to measure and compare people's personalities, along with some examples of how these instruments are being used in personality research and in other ways as well.

Linkages

The questions in this diagram illustrate just a few of the many relationships between the topic of this chapter, personality, and other chapter topics. (The numbers in parentheses indicate where the questions in the diagram are discussed.) In exploring research on personality, we revisit, for example, the general theoretical approaches to psychology outlined in Chapter 1, and we take a closer look at some of the issues—such as infants' relationships with their parents—outlined in Chapter 3, on human development. The theories of personality described in this chapter are also linked closely to ideas about the likely causes of the psychological disorders presented in Chapter 15, and to the treatment of those disorders (Chapter 16). ■

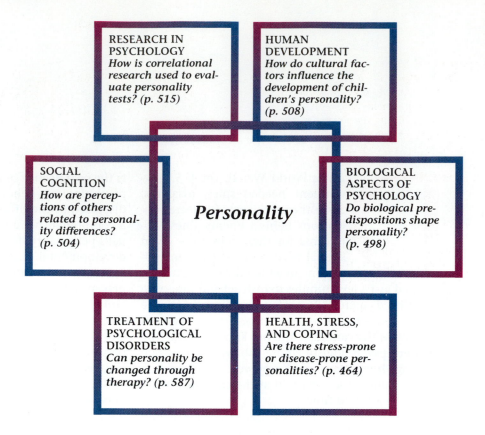

RESEARCH IN PSYCHOLOGY
How is correlational research used to evaluate personality tests? (p. 515)

HUMAN DEVELOPMENT
How do cultural factors influence the development of children's personality? (p. 508)

SOCIAL COGNITION
How are perceptions of others related to personality differences? (p. 504)

Personality

BIOLOGICAL ASPECTS OF PSYCHOLOGY
Do biological predispositions shape personality? (p. 498)

TREATMENT OF PSYCHOLOGICAL DISORDERS
Can personality be changed through therapy? (p. 587)

HEALTH, STRESS, AND COPING
Are there stress-prone or disease-prone personalities? (p. 464)

The Psychodynamic Approach

Some people think personality is clearly reflected in behavior. A person with an "obnoxious personality," for example, shows it by acting obnoxiously. But is that all there is to personality? Not according to Sigmund Freud, who likened personality to an iceberg whose tip is clearly visible but whose bulk is hidden underwater.

As a physician during the 1890s, Freud specialized in treating "neurotic" disorders, such as blindness or paralysis for which there was no physical cause. His patients did not appear to be faking, but their symptoms could often be made to disappear under hypnosis. These cases led Freud to believe in *psychic determinism*, the idea that personality and behavior are determined more by psychological factors like old resentments than by biological conditions or current events. He proposed, further, that people may not know why they feel, think, or act the way they do, because these activities are partly controlled by the *unconscious* portion of the personality—the part of which people are not normally aware.

From these ideas Freud created the **psychodynamic approach** to personality, which holds that the interplay of various unconscious psychological processes determines thoughts, feelings, and behavior. Understanding personality therefore requires exploring the unconscious, and Freud developed several methods for doing so. For example, Freud believed that **free association**, which involves saying whatever comes to mind, discloses thoughts, feelings, and impulses that are normally unconscious. The nature and content of a person's dreams and various aspects of everyday behavior also provide data for personality assessment. These methods became part of Freud's theory of personality, his approach to research, and his therapy techniques, which are collectively known as **psychoanalysis.**

Figure 14.1
A Phrenological Map
The approach one takes to personality helps determine what questions one asks about it. For example, the eighteenth-century anatomist Franz Gall took an anatomical approach. He believed that each of thirty-five faculties (such as sense of humor or hostility) was localized in a specific part of the brain. He claimed that bumps on the skull reflected better-developed faculties and, thus, a stronger tendency to think or act in some particular way. Gall's approach—called phrenology—could not withstand scientific evaluation, but it illustrates that all approaches to personality, even unsuccessful ones, contain a set of assumptions that forms a personality theory, ways of measuring or assessing personality (Gall used physical examination of the skull), and methods to evaluate the theory (Gall tried to relate bumps to behavior). Most approaches to personality also suggest methods for helping people change, usually involving psychotherapy.

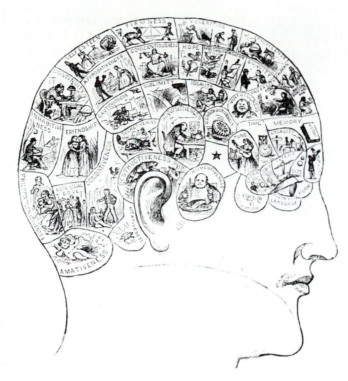

The Structure and Development of Personality

According to Freud, people are born with basic instincts or needs—not only for food, water, and air but also for sex and aggression. He believed that needs for love, knowledge, security, and the like are derived from these more fundamental desires. Each person faces the task of figuring out how to meet his or her needs in a world that often frustrates these efforts. According to Freud, personality develops out of each person's struggle with this task and is reflected in the ways he or she goes about satisfying a range of needs.

Id, Ego, and Superego As Figure 14.2 illustrates, Freud described the personality as having three major components: the id, the ego, and the superego.

Freud saw the **id** as the inborn, unconscious portion of the personality where two types of instincts reside. The life instincts, which he called *Eros,* promote positive, constructive behavior and reflect a source of energy (sometimes called psychic energy) known as **libido.** Life instincts motivate behaviors that satisfy basic needs for food, water, and sex, but they can also engender loftier and more uniquely human acts, including musical or artistic creativity. Freud saw a second class of instincts, called *Thanatos,* or death instinct, as responsible for aggressive and destructive acts.

The id seeks immediate satisfaction of both kinds of instincts, regardless of society's rules or the rights or feelings of others. In other words, the id operates on the **pleasure principle**, which guides people toward whatever feels good. The hungry person who snatches food from someone's plate while passing an outdoor café is satisfying an Eros-driven id impulse. What others might think of this act is of no concern to the id because it is not based in reality; in fact, the id does not distinguish fantasy from reality. According to Freud, merely fantasizing about an aggressive or sexual act can satisfy instinctual impulses.

As children grow they learn that doing whatever they want is not always acceptable. Drawing with Mom's lipstick on the living room wall might be fun, but it might also lead to a scolding. As parents, teachers, and others place

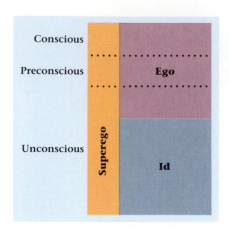

Source: Adapted from Liebert & Spiegler, 1987.

Figure 14.2
Freud's Conception of the Personality Structure
This theoretical organization consists of the primitive, impulsive id; the stern, demanding superego (which includes the conscience); and the reality-oriented ego, which must work out compromises between internal demands and the limitations imposed by the external world. Notice that parts of the personality are conscious, parts unconscious. Further, Freud recognized that between these levels is the preconscious—a region discussed in Chapter 7 as the location of memories and other material not usually in awareness but that can be brought into consciousness with little or no effort.

more restrictions on the expression of id impulses, a second part of the personality—the **ego** (or "self")—evolves from the id. The ego is responsible for organizing ways to get what a person wants in the world. It operates on the **reality principle**, making compromises between the id's unreasoning demands for immediate satisfaction and the practical constraints of the real world. The ego is the "executive" of the personality because it tries to get needs met while protecting people from the harm that might result if they became aware of, let alone immediately acted out, their id impulses.

The more experience people have with the rules and morals of society, the more they tend to adopt them. As a result, children learn that certain behaviors are wrong and will even scold themselves for doing bad things. **Introjection** is the term Freud used for this process of *internalizing* parental and societal values into the personality. Introjected values, "shoulds" and "should nots," form the third component of personality: the **superego**. "Should nots," the things people come to believe are wrong, make up the part of the superego known as the *conscience*. Pressure to conform to "shoulds," the ideal behaviors that people believe are right, comes from a second part of the superego, known as the *ego ideal*. The superego might be thought of as operating on the *morality principle*, since violating either category of its rules results in guilt. The superego is just as relentless and unreasonable as the id in its demands to be obeyed. And like the id, the superego does not clearly distinguish between thought and action; to the superego, thinking "bad" thoughts is as punishable as doing bad things (Pervin, 1989).

Conflicts and Defenses Freud saw that basic needs (id), reason (ego), morality (superego), and the demands of the environment are often at odds. He called the inner turmoil among personality components *intrapsychic* or *psychodynamic conflict*, and he believed that the number, nature, and outcome of these conflicts shape each individual's personality.

Most of what is in the unconscious, Freud said, is frightening or socially taboo. Therefore, for self-protection, people's egos try to keep this material out of awareness. They feel irrational, or *neurotic*, anxiety when unconscious id impulses (such as the desire to harm a parent) threaten to reach consciousness. *Moral anxiety*, experienced as guilt or shame, occurs over behavior that the superego has condemned (Phares, 1991). (These contrast with *realistic anxiety*, which is felt in the face of real danger in the outside world.)

One of the most important functions of the ego is to defend against neurotic and moral anxiety. Often it does so by organizing realistic actions, as when a person seeks help because of impulses to abuse a child. However, the ego may also control anxiety or guilt by resorting to **defense mechanisms**, which are unconscious tactics that either keep threatening material from surfacing or disguise it when it does (see Table 14.1).

To illustrate, suppose you find yourself physically attracted to your best friend's lover. The most primitive unconscious impulse might be to kill your friend, but becoming consciously aware of this impulse would bring a flood of anxiety and guilt. To prevent this, your ego might use the defense mechanism of repression. Unlike suppression, in which you consciously push unacceptable feelings out of awareness, **repression** does so unconsciously, leaving you unaware that you had the taboo desires in the first place. Keeping strong feelings under wraps involves a distortion of reality that takes tremendous effort, like trying to hold an inflated beach ball under water. Thus, although everyone uses defense mechanisms at one time or another to reduce stress and temporarily ease tensions, overreliance on them can lead to psychological problems, as described in Chapter 15.

**Table 14.1
Psychodynamic
Defense Mechanisms**

According to Freud, defense mechanisms employ various forms of self-deception to keep people from seeing themselves in a negative light. These defenses do help in the short run by deflecting anxiety or guilt, but they sap energy. They also prevent people from dealing directly with the source of their problems and are thus maladaptive in the long run. If they are used too extensively, one's self-image and view of others can become distorted and lead to various symptoms of psychological disorder, especially to what Freud called neurosis.

Repression	Unconsciously pushing threatening memories, urges, or ideas from conscious awareness: A person may experience loss of memory for traumatic or threatening events such as witnessing a horrible crime.
Rationalization	Attempts to make actions or mistakes seem reasonable: The reasons or excuses given (e.g., "I spank my children because it is good for them") have a rational ring to them, but they are not the real reasons for the behavior.
Projection	Unconsciously attributing one's own unacceptable thoughts or impulses to another person: Instead of recognizing that "I hate him," a person may feel that "He hates me."
Reaction formation	Defending against unacceptable impulses by acting opposite to them: Sexual interest in a married friend might appear as strong dislike instead.
Sublimation	Converting unacceptable impulses into socially acceptable actions, and perhaps symbolically expressing them: Sexual or aggressive desires may appear as artistic creativity or devotion to athletic excellence.
Displacement	Deflecting an impulse from its original target to a less threatening one: Anger at one's boss may be expressed through hostility toward the mail clerk, a family member, or even the dog.
Denial	Simply discounting the existence of threatening impulses: A person may vehemently deny ever having had even the slightest degree of physical attraction to a person of the same sex.
Compensation	Striving to make up for unconscious impulses or fears: A business executive's extreme competitiveness might be aimed at compensating for unconscious feelings of inferiority.

Stages in Personality Development   Freud proposed that personality develops during childhood in several stages. He called these **psychosexual stages** because at each stage a particular part of the body, called an *erogenous zone,* becomes the main source of sensual pleasure. Failure to resolve the unique problems and conflicts that arise at a given stage, said Freud, can leave a person *fixated*—that is, overly attached to or unconsciously preoccupied with the area of pleasure associated with that stage. Fixation occurs to some extent for everyone, he said, leaving each person with certain personality characteristics as adults.

According to Freud, a child's first year or so is called the **oral stage**, because the mouth is the center of pleasure. The infant uses its mouth to eat and to explore. If oral needs are either neglected or overindulged, perhaps through very early weaning or very late weaning, fixation at the oral stage might occur. This fixation might produce adult characteristics ranging from overeating or alcoholism to the use of "biting" sarcasm or desperate dependence on others.

The second psychosexual stage—the **anal stage**—occurs during the second year, when the focus of pleasure and conflict shifts from the mouth to the anus

Freud called the first year or so of life the oral stage because, during this time, children use their mouths not only for eating but for exploring their world. Children in the oral stage put into their mouths anything they can get their hands on.

as the child faces the demand for toilet training. It is at this stage that Freud believed the child's ego evolves to mediate between the id's desires—for the pleasures of bowel movements at will, for example—and parental demands, especially for socially appropriate toilet behavior. Toilet training that is too harsh, or that begins too early or too late, can lead to fixation. Adult characteristics associated with fixation at the anal stage might range from being stingy and extremely organized (thus symbolically withholding feces) to being sloppy, disorganized, or impulsive (symbolically expelling feces at will).

By the age of three or so and for about two years thereafter, the focus of pleasure shifts to the genital area. Emphasizing the psychosexual development of boys, Freud called this period the **phallic stage.** During this stage the boy experiences sexual desire for the mother and a desire to eliminate, even kill, the father, with whom the boy competes for the mother's affection. Freud called this constellation of impulses the **Oedipus complex,** because it parallels the plot of the Greek tragedy *Oedipus Rex.* The boy's hostile fantasies about his father create a fear of retaliation, including fear of being castrated. This fear, called *castration anxiety,* becomes so strong that the ego represses the incestuous desires, and the boy seeks to identify with and imitate his father, including taking on his father's moral values as the basis for his developing superego.

According to Freud, the female child begins with a strong attachment to her mother; but as she realizes that boys have penises and girls do not, the child begins to hate her mother, perhaps blaming her for the missing anatomy, and develops *penis envy.* She then transfers her love to her father. But because the girl must still avoid her mother's disapproval, she identifies with and imitates her mother.

Freud believed that most people are fixated to some degree at the phallic stage. Unresolved conflicts of this stage might produce adult characteristics ranging from difficulties in relationships with those in authority to problems in maintaining a stable love relationship to the appearance of disordered or socially disapproved sexual behavior.

As the phallic stage draws to a close, its conflicts are repressed or otherwise quieted by the ego. An interval of peace known as the **latency period** ensues, during which sexual impulses lie dormant. During adolescence, sexual impulses reappear at the conscious level, and the genitals again become the focus of pleasure. Thus begins what Freud called the **genital stage**, a period that spans the rest of life.

Variations on Freud's Personality Theory

Freud's ideas—especially those about the Oedipus complex and the role of infantile sexuality—created instant controversy in public and professional circles alike. Nowhere was the debate more lively than among members of the Vienna Psycho-Analytic Society, a group of Freud's followers—mostly young Viennese psychiatrists.

Eventually, many of his followers found themselves disagreeing with Freud over such critical issues as the importance of instinctual sexual impulses in shaping personality, the role of social experiences in personality development, and whether adult personality is essentially fixed in the first six years of life, as psychoanalytic theory suggests. Freud's intolerance of those who disagreed with him led a number of former followers to part company with him and many of his orthodox psychoanalytic views. These dissenters have been called *neo-Freudians* because they maintained many of the basic tenets of Freud's theory as they developed their own.

Alfred Adler's Individual Psychology   The first major dissenter was Alfred Adler, who split with Freud in 1911 over Adler's emphasis on the role of social rather than sexual urges in personality development. Adler (1927) began with the assumption that each person is born helpless and dependent, which creates unpleasant feelings of inferiority. These negative feelings, combined with an innate desire to become a full-fledged member of the social world, provide the impetus for the development of personality. Adler referred to this process as *striving for superiority*, by which he meant a drive for fulfillment as a person, not just a desire to best others. If feelings of inferiority are intense, they drive a person to compensate for perceived inferiority. When the individual's personality revolves around trying to make up for some perceived deficit, the pattern is sometimes called an *inferiority complex.*

According to Adler, the ways each person tries to reach fulfillment constitute personality or, as he called it, **style of life.** Adler suggested that the style of life is directed not just by the unconscious but by what he called guiding fictions, which are conscious ideas, goals, and beliefs that arise primarily from experiences within the family. For example, a child who is pampered and protected may believe that he or she is "special" and exempt from society's rules. This guiding fiction that "I'm special" is likely to lead to a selfish style of life in which personal fulfillment comes at the expense of others. In contrast, "There is good in everyone" and "Tomorrow will be better than today" are guiding fictions that, whether true or not, are likely to create positive, upbeat styles of life.

Carl Jung's Analytic Psychology   In 1914, Carl Jung (pronounced "yoong") became the second major figure to leave the Psycho-Analytic Society. Although he agreed with much of what Freud had said, Jung (1916) argued that libido was not based solely on sexual and aggressive instincts. He saw it instead as a more general life force of the kind described by Eastern religions for centuries. For Jung, the life force includes an innate drive for creativity, for growth-oriented resolution of conflicts, and for the productive blending of basic impulses with real-world demands.

Jung also believed that everyone has both a personal unconscious (containing individual memories and impulses) and a **collective unconscious,** a kind of memory that stores all the images and ideas that humans have accumulated during eons of evolution. Some of these images are called **archetypes,** because they consist of classic images or concepts. *Mother,* for instance, is an archetype; everyone is born with a shared readiness to see and react to certain people as mother figures. More ominous is the *shadow* archetype (similar to the id). It contains basic instincts harking back to prehuman centuries and, according to Jung, is embodied in notions like sin and the devil.

Jung did not identify specific stages in personality development. He suggested instead that people develop, over time, differing degrees of *introversion* (a tendency to reflect on one's own experiences) or *extraversion* (a tendency to focus on the social world) and differing tendencies to rely on specific psychological functions, such as thinking versus feeling. The combination of these tendencies, said Jung (1933), creates personalities that display distinctive and predictable patterns of behavior.

Other Neo-Freudians A number of other neo-Freudian and post-Freudian theorists followed Adler's lead by focusing on the ways other people help shape an individual's personality. Several prominent psychoanalysts, including Erich Fromm (1941), Karen Horney (pronounced "horn-eye") (1937), and Harry Stack Sullivan (1953), argued that once biological needs are met, the attempt to meet social needs (to feel protected, secure, and accepted, for example) is most influential in forming personality. The strategies people use to meet these needs, such as dominating other people or being dependent on them, become the personality. (Note the similarity to Adler's concept of a style of life.)

Harry Stack Sullivan went so far as to say that "personality" is simply a name for each person's pattern of interpersonal behaviors. To understand personality he looked to the pattern of what a person did with others, said to others, and believed about others. For Sullivan, a person's self (the rough equivalent of Freud's ego) develops not to mediate unconscious conflict but to preserve feelings of security in an interpersonal world in which anxiety is the major threat. The self acts like a benevolent authority figure, guiding the development of personality, trying to maintain security with other people, seeking prestige, and protecting against anxiety through maneuvers similar to Freud's ego defense mechanisms. When anxiety becomes too severe, these maneuvers become so extreme or so rigid that disturbed interpersonal relationships result.

The emphasis on social factors in personality development is also reflected in the influential work of Erik Erikson (1963, 1968). As described in Chapter 3, on human development, Erikson proposed eight *psychosocial* stages as an alternative to Freud's psychosexual stages. As shown in Table 3.2 (page 67), the most important developments at each stage involve social, not sexual, crises.

The importance of social over instinctual factors in personality has recurred as a major theme in the development of psychodynamic theories. For example, *ego psychologists,* including Freud's daughter, Anna, have described the ego as more than a mediator in conflicts among id, superego, and environment; in their view the ego begins to develop as a creative, adaptive force in its own right even before the anal stage (A. Freud, 1946; Fraiberg, 1987). It is responsible for language development, perception, attention, planning, learning, and many other psychological functions (Hartmann, 1939).

Contemporary Psychodynamic Theories

As the evolution of psychodynamic approaches to personality continues, some of its most influential variants have come to focus on the importance of *object relations,* a person's relationships with significant objects, which include people. For example, self-psychologists and object relations theorists such as Melanie Klein (1975), Otto Kernberg (1976), and Heinz Kohut (1984) point to the critical importance of early attachments between infants and their love objects, usually the mother and other primary caregivers. They study how pri-

While Freud believed that personality problems involved conflicts among the structures of personality, contemporary self-psychology and object relations theorists believe that problems arise from arrested personality development due to early (pre-Oedipal) relationships and object attachments (Eagle & Wolinzky, 1985).

mary caregivers provide protection, acceptance, and recognition, and otherwise meet the infant's needs (Bacal & Newman, 1990; Blatt & Lerner, 1983). These object relations have a significant impact on personality development. From these early relationship experiences, a child develops its sense of self, its security, and its identity. Ideally, development follows a sequence (discussed in Chapter 3) in which the child forms a secure early bond to the mother or other caregiver, tolerates gradual separation from the object of attachment, and finally develops the ability to relate to others as an independent, secure individual (Ainsworth, 1989). Distorted object relations can lead to inadequate self-esteem, difficulties in trusting or making commitments to others, or more serious mental disorders (Eagle, 1984).

Evaluation of the Psychodynamic Approach

Sigmund Freud developed the most comprehensive and influential personality theory ever proposed. His views influenced modern Western thinking about psychology, medicine, literature, religion, sociology, and anthropology. His ideas have also been applied in psychotherapy, which is the attempt to alleviate mental disorder through psychological means. Psychodynamic therapies—discussed in detail in Chapter 16—aim to help people become aware of previously unconscious aspects of personality so that they can resolve old conflicts. Freud's concepts also stimulated development of personality assessments, including the projective tests we describe later in this chapter.

Still, Freud's psychodynamic theory has several weaknesses. For one thing, it was based on observations of an unrepresentative sample of humankind: a small number of upper-class Viennese patients, mostly women, who not only had mental problems but were raised in a society that considered discussion of sex to be uncivilized. Moreover, Freud's thinking about personality and its development reflects West European and North American social and cultural values, which may or may not be helpful in understanding people in other cultures (Landrine & Klonoff, 1992). For example, the concepts of ego and self that are so central to Freud's personality theory (as well as to those of his followers) are based on the self-oriented values of individualist cultures, but may be less central to personality development in the more collectivist cultures of Asia, Africa, and Latin America, for example (Markus & Kitayama, 1991).

Freud's conclusions may have been distorted by other biases as well, such as his refusal to believe his patients' accounts of sexual abuse by parents and other adults. He interpreted their reports as fantasies and wish fulfillment, not as memories—an interpretation that has become more questionable as the reality of child sexual abuse has become clearer (Masson, 1983). Freud's focus on male psychosexual development and his bias toward male anatomy as something to be envied by women have also caused both male and female feminists to reject some or all of his ideas (Chesler, 1972).

In addition, Freud's definitions of concepts such as id, ego, and unconscious conflict lack the precision required for scientific measurement and testing (Smith & Vetter, 1991). For example, suppose a psychologist suspects that a man harbors strong, unconscious aggressive impulses. The suspicion would be confirmed if the man is often angry and hostile. But if he is unusually even-tempered, this calm could be seen as a defense against aggressive impulses. Occasional angry outbursts might be viewed as wavering ego control. In short, there is almost nothing the man might do that could not be interpreted as reflecting unconscious aggression.

Finally, Freud's belief that human beings are driven mainly by unconscious instinctual desires ignores evidence that much human behavior goes beyond instinct gratification. The conscious drive to attain personal, social, and spiritual goals is also an important determinant of behavior, as is learning from others.

Some of the weaknesses in Freudian theory have been addressed by ego psychologists and others who have altered some of Freud's concepts and devoted more attention to social influences on personality. Still, the psychodynamic approach is better known for generating hypotheses about personality than for testing them scientifically (Eagle & Wolinzky, 1985). A few investigators have attempted to investigate scientifically the existence and operation of psychodynamic constructs (see, for example, Silverman, 1985; Silverman & Weinberger, 1985), but flaws in the research have prevented general acceptance of the results (Balay & Shevrin, 1988; Eagle & Wolinzky, 1985). Research on psychodynamic theory *is* becoming more sophisticated and increasingly reflects a genuine interest in subjecting psychodynamic principles to empirical evaluation (Hardaway, 1990; Wallerstein, 1989). Nevertheless, the psychodynamic approach to personality is less popular among psychologists now than it had been in past decades (Conway, 1988; Smith, 1982). Indeed, the popularity of other approaches has been fueled by the desire to measure personality more precisely, by concern that even contemporary psychodynamic theories underestimate the importance of learning and conscious intent, and by interest in building theories that are more applicable to non-Western cultures (Zook & Walton, 1989).

The Dispositional Approach: Types and Traits

If you were to ask a friend to describe the personality of someone you both know, he or she could probably do it without too much trouble. The personality sketch would probably be organized into a small number of descriptive categories. For example:

She is a truly caring person, a real extrovert. She is generous with her time, and she works very hard at everything she does. Yet, sometimes I think she also lacks self-confidence. She is submissive to other people's demands because she needs to be accepted by them.

In other words, most people describe others by referring to the type of people they are ("extrovert"), to their most notable traits ("caring," "lacks confidence"), or to their needs ("needs to be accepted"). Together, these statements describe a person's dispositions, the inclinations or tendencies that help to direct how he or she usually thinks and behaves (Phares, 1991). This dispositional approach to personality is the oldest of all.

The dispositional approach (also called the type-trait approach) makes three basic assumptions:

1. Each person's personality characteristics are relatively stable and therefore predictable over time. Thus, a gentle person tends to stay that way day after day, year after year.
2. These dispositions are relatively stable across diverse situations, and they explain why people act in predictable ways in many different settings. A person who is fiercely competitive at work will probably be competitive on the tennis court or at a party.
3. Each person has a different set of dispositions, or at least a set of dispositions of varying strengths that assume a unique pattern. The result is an endless variety of unique human personalities.

Thus, the **dispositional approach** views personality as a combination of stable internal characteristics that define who people are and that motivate them to behave in certain ways (Murray, 1962; Allport, 1961). We will describe two examples of the dispositional approach: one that focuses on broad personality types, and one that focuses on traits and their combinations.

Personality Types

When you hear someone say, "He's not my type" or "I'm not that type of person," you are hearing echoes of an age-old dream: to be able to classify people into a few basic types. This attempt goes back at least as far as Hippocrates, a physician of ancient Greece. He suggested that a certain temperament, or basic behavioral tendency, is associated with each of four bodily fluids, or humors: blood, phlegm, black bile, and yellow bile. Personality type, said Hippocrates, depends on how much of each humor a person has. The terms for these personality types—sanguine (optimistic), phlegmatic, (slow, lethargic), melancholic (sad, depressive), and choleric (angry, irritable)—still survive.

Other dispositional theorists have tried to relate people's physical appearance to the type of personality they develop (Williams, 1967). This notion has great appeal; people tend to maintain mental schemas telling them that certain types of people have a certain "look." In Chapters 10 and 17, on thought and social cognition, we describe how such schemas guide people's assumptions about, and impressions of, the people they meet (Warner & Sugarman, 1986).

The study of the relationship between personality and the physical characteristics of the face or body is called *physiognomy* and goes back to Gall's phrenology (see Figure 14.1). Modern physiognomy was promoted in the 1940s by William Sheldon, an American physician and psychologist who believed that certain body builds were associated with different temperaments. However, research has not supported the validity of compressing human personality into a few types based on facial or bodily characteristics alone.

Personality Traits

A personality *type* is a discrete category. When people are "typed," they belong to one class or another such as male or female. Traits, in contrast, are continuous qualities that individuals possess in different amounts. A person can possess a lot or a little of some trait or fall anywhere in between on a measure of that trait. Thus, according to the trait approach, each personality can be described in terms of how strong it is on various traits, such as hostility, sociability, and the like (see Figure 14.3).

Allport's Trait Theory Gordon Allport (1961) spent thirty years studying how traits combine to form the normal personality. He reported at least 18,000 traits. He also found that many of the labels for these traits refer to the same thing ("hostile," "nasty," and "mean" all convey a similar meaning), so that when people are asked to give a personality sketch, they can usually do the job using only about seven trait labels. Of course, for each person described, those seven labels might be very different. Allport believed that such a set of labels represents a person's *central traits,* those that are usually apparent to others and comprise characteristics that organize and control behavior in many different situations. Central traits are roughly equivalent to the descriptive terms used in letters of recommendation ("reliable" or "distractable," for example) that are meant to convey what can be expected from a person most of the time (Phares, 1991). Allport also found what he called *secondary traits,* those that are more specific to certain situations and control far less behavior. "Hates salad bars" is an example of a secondary trait. In a few people, Allport found *cardinal traits*—dispositions that are so pervasive as to resemble passions that govern virtually everything a person does. Albert Schweitzer and Mother Teresa, for example, illustrate the cardinal trait of humanitarianism.

In his research, Allport often took a *nomothetic* approach; that is, he carefully compared many individuals in terms of the personality traits commonly found in most people to some degree. Still, Allport never lost sight of the importance of studying the patterns of traits that appear in unique combination in an

Figure 14.3
Two Personality Profiles
From the trait perspective, personality is like a fabric of many different-colored threads, some bright, some dull, some thick, some thin, which are never woven together in exactly the same combination twice. Personality traits can occur at different strengths in different people. Here are trait profiles for Rodney, an inner-city social worker, and James, a sales clerk in a department store. Compared to James, Rodney is equally industrious, more generous, and less nervous, extraverted, and aggressive. Allport suggested that personality profiles describing only about seven central traits can give a fair picture of what you might expect if you met these individuals. Still, each of us is to some extent different from everyone else in the world.

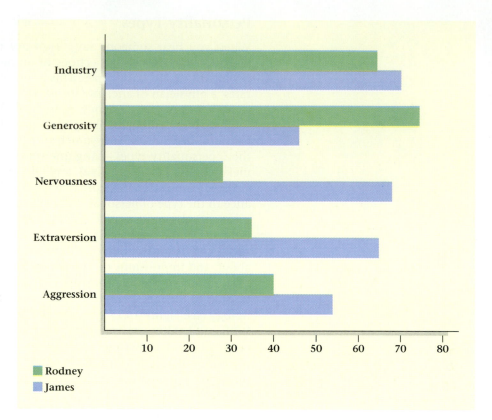

individual (the *idiographic* approach). His work in both areas provided an important part of the foundation for modern research on personality traits.

Factor-Analytic Methods   Suppose that everyone has one hundred common traits but each person possesses them in different strengths. If you want to compare the personalities of two people, you would have to measure all hundred traits. It would be more convenient to know whether some of those hundred traits are correlated with others, so that if someone is strong on, say, optimism, that person is also going to be strong on happiness, friendliness, and hopefulness. If you knew these correlations, you could compare personalities by measuring just a few specific traits. It would be even better if, after identifying "trait clusters," you could determine why they appear together. Perhaps each cluster belongs to a more basic dimension of personality, so that a personality can be fully described by finding a person's position on just a handful of basic dimensions. In fact, this strategy is followed by some personality researchers. Using a mathematical method known as *factor analysis,* they identify groups of traits that are correlated with one another but uncorrelated with other groups. They then give each group of traits a label that describes the personality dimension that underlies it. This, in essence, was the approach used by British psychologist Hans Eysenck.

Using factor analysis, Eysenck concluded that one's personality can be described in terms of three basic factors (Eysenck, 1970, 1981):

1. *Psychoticism*—People high on psychoticism show such traits as cruelty, hostility, coldness, oddness, and rejection of social customs. Those low on psychoticism do not show these traits.
2. *Introversion-extraversion*—Extraverts are sociable and outgoing, enjoy parties and other social activities, take risks, and love excitement and change. Introverts tend to be quiet, thoughtful, and reserved, enjoying solitary pursuits and avoiding excitement and social involvement.

3. *Emotionality-stability*—At one extreme of emotionality-stability (also called *neuroticism*) are traits such as moodiness, restlessness, worry, anxiety, and other negative emotions. People at the opposite end of this dimension are calm, even-tempered, relaxed, and emotionally stable.

Figure 14.4 illustrates traits that, according to Eysenck, result from various combinations of introversion-extraversion and emotionality-stability. Eysenck claimed that a number of key characteristics about people can be predicted from their scores on paper-and-pencil tests such as the Eysenck Personality Inventory, which is designed to measure Eysenck's three personality factors. Indeed, one research review (Pervin, 1989) showed, for example, that compared to extraverts, introverts are more sensitive to pain, more easily fatigued, and more susceptible to having their performance disrupted by excitement. Introverts also tend to do better in school, prefer more solitary vocations, and have less need for novelty. Extraverts are more sexually active, enjoy sexual and aggressive humor more, and are more suggestible than introverts.

Eysenck also found that people with behavior disorders show characteristic scores on the dimensions shown in Figure 14.4. Criminals, for example, are more likely to be in the "choleric" quadrant and tend to display restless, aggressive, and impulsive behavior. People with anxiety disorders tend to be in the "melancholic" quadrant.

A Biological Basis for Traits   Eysenck argued that a person's position on these dimensions is determined largely by biological variables. In particular, he tied differences in extraversion-introversion to characteristic variations in cortical arousal. If a person inherits a nervous system with a low level of arousal, said Eysenck, he or she will be relatively insensitive to the effects of rewards and punishments, and will therefore not very easily develop conditioned responses, including conditioned fears. If they do not develop such fears, they will not easily learn to play by the rules. As we discussed in the chapter on motivation and emotion, low levels of arousal may lead a person to look constantly for excitement and change in order to increase arousal. In

Linkages: How do differences in sensitivity to stimulation shape personality? (a link to Sensation)

Figure 14.4
Eysenck's Major
Personality Dimensions
According to Eysenck, combining varying degrees of emotionality-stability and introversion-extra-version produces characteristic combinations of traits. For example, an introverted but stable person is likely to be controlled and reliable, whereas an introverted but emotional person is likely to be rigid and anxious. This figure also illustrates the rather amazing fact that the traits appearing in the four quadrants created by crossing these two of Eysenck's personality dimensions correspond roughly to Hippocrates' four temperaments. A third personality dimension, psychoticism, also plays a part in Eysenck's system.

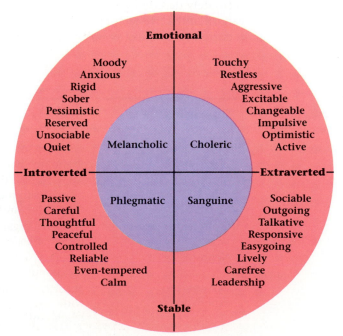

Source: Eysenck & Rachman, 1965.

short, the person will be extraverted. In contrast, if a person inherits a sensitive, "overaroused" nervous system, Eysenck's theory predicts that he or she is likely to be strongly affected by rewards and punishments, to readily develop conditioned responses such as fears and oversensitivities, and to avoid excessive stimulation; in other words, he or she will be an introvert.

The "Big Five" Model of Personality

Eysenck's analysis has considerable research support (Eysenck, 1982), and it remains influential. However, it did not end the search for the cluster of basic factors or traits that could most completely describe human personality. More recent factor-analytic research has led many trait theorists to believe that five factors, not three, best define the organization of human personality (McCrae & John, 1992).

The components of this so-called **big five**, or **five-factor model** of personality are neuroticism, extraversion, openness, agreeableness, and conscientiousness (see Table 14.2 for a list of the adjectives that define each dimension). Paul Costa and Robert McCrae (1989) developed a test called the NEO Personality Inventory (described later) to measure the strength of these five factors. The importance of the "big five" is underscored by the fact that different investigators find these factors (or a set very similar to them) when they factor-analyze data from numerous sources, including personality inventories, peer ratings of personality characteristics, and checklists of descriptive adjectives (see, for example, McCrae & John, 1992; Tupes & Christal, 1961). These five factors even emerged from people's ratings of how well drawings of people in social and solitary situations described their own personality (Paunonen et al., 1992).

If the "big five" factors are basic components of human personality, they should also appear in cultures other than the one in which they were first discovered. Indeed, there is increasing evidence that some version of these five factors reliably appears in samples of people in Canada, Germany, Finland, Poland, China, and Japan (Bond, Nakazato & Shiraishi, 1975; Paunonen et al., 1992; Yang & Bond, 1990). The value of these five factors for efficiently and accurately describing personality around the world is not yet clear, but some variant of the five-factor model—and the trait approach from which it came— is currently the most popular among personality researchers.

Table 14.2
Descriptors of the Big Five Personality Dimensions

Dimension	Defining Descriptors
Extraversion	Active, assertive, energetic, outgoing, talkative, gesturally expressive, and gregarious
Agreeableness	Appreciative, forgiving, generous, kind, trusting, noncritical, warm, compassionate, considerate, straightforward
Conscientiousness	Efficient, organized, planful, reliable, thorough, dependable, ethical, productive
Neuroticism	Anxious, self-pitying, tense, emotionally unstable, impulsive, vulnerable, touchy, worrying
Openness to experience	Artistic, curious, imaginative, insightful, original, wide interests, unusual thought processes, intellectual interests

Source: Adapted from McCrae & John, 1992.

Thinking Critically

Are Personality Traits Inherited?

Where do the "big five" factors or other personality traits come from? Could genes play a role? One study described a pair of twins who had been separated at five weeks of age and did not meet for thirty-nine years. Both men drove Chevrolets, chain-smoked the same brand of cigarettes, had divorced a woman named Linda, were remarried to a woman named Betty, had sons named James Allan, had dogs named Toy, enjoyed similar hobbies, and had served as sheriff's deputies (Tellegen et al., 1988).

What am I being asked to believe or accept?

Cases like this, as well as biologically based theories such as Eysenck's, have helped focus the attention of behavior geneticists on the possibility that some core aspects of personality might be partly inherited (Goldsmith, 1983; Heath et al., 1992; Plomin, 1989).

What evidence is available to support the assertion?

The evidence and the arguments regarding this assertion are much like those presented in Chapter 11, where we discussed the origins of differences in mental abilities. Anecdotes about children who seem to "have" their parents' or grandparents' bad temper, generosity, or shyness are often presented in support of the heritability of personality. Indeed, resemblances in personality among family members do provide one important source of evidence. Several studies have found moderate but significant correlations between children's personality test scores and those of their parents and siblings (Dixon & Johnson, 1980; Loehlin, Horn & Willerman, 1981; Scarr et al., 1981).

Stronger evidence comes from twin studies in Europe and the United States that compared identical twins raised together, identical twins raised apart, nonidentical twins raised together, and nonidentical twins raised apart (Pedersen et al., 1988; Tellegen et al., 1988). They found that identical twins (who have exactly the same genes) are more alike in personality than are nonidentical twins (whose genes are no more similar than other siblings), regardless of whether they are raised apart or together. And among identical twins themselves, being raised together or apart also makes little difference; they still show consistent patterns of similarity in personality. Finally, research consistently shows that identical twins are more alike than nonidentical twins in their activity level, sociability, anxiety, and emotionality, all of which appear among the "big five" traits (Plomin, 1989). One study that reviewed research on some 30,000 twin pairs from four countries concluded that there was about a 50 percent heritability for extraversion and stability (Loehlin, 1989). Other investigators argue that 30 percent may be more accurate (Plomin, 1990). However, traits such as aggression and distractibility do not show as strong a genetic component (Plomin & Foch, 1980), and characteristics such as political attitudes and religious beliefs show no genetic relationships at all (Plomin, 1989, 1990).

Are there alternative ways of interpreting the evidence?

Family resemblances in personality could reflect inheritance or social influence. An obvious alternative interpretation of this evidence might be that parent-child similarities come not from a child's genes but from the environment, especially from the modeling that parents and siblings provide. Children learn many rules, skills, and behaviors by watching those around them; perhaps they learn their personalities as well. Further, the fact that nontwin siblings are less alike than twins may well result from what is called *non-shared environments*. A child's place in the family birth order, differences in the way parents treat each of their children, and accidents and illnesses that alter a particular child's life or health are examples of nonshared factors that can have a differential impact on each individual. Compared to twins, especially identical twins, nontwins tend to be affected by more nonshared environmental factors.

What additional evidence would help to evaluate the alternatives?

One way to evaluate the degree to which personality is inherited would be to study people in infancy, before the environment has had a chance to exert its influence. If the environment were entirely responsible for personality, newborn infants should be essentially alike. However, as discussed in Chapter 3, on human development, newborns do show differences in temperament—varying markedly in amount of activity, sensitivity to the environment, tendency to cry, and interest in new stimuli (Kagan, 1989; Kagan & Snidman, 1991; Korner, 1971). These differences suggest biological and perhaps genetic influences.

To evaluate the relative contributions of nature and nurture beyond infancy, psychologists have examined characteristics of adopted children. The influence of heredity in personality is supported if adopted children are more like their biological than their adoptive parents. If they are more like their adoptive family, a strong role for environmental factors in personality would be suggested. In actuality, adopted children's personalities tend to resemble the personalities of their biological parents and siblings more than those of the families in which they are raised (Loehlin, Willerman & Horn, 1985; Scarr et al., 1981).

However, further research is needed to determine more clearly what aspects of the environment are most important in shaping personality. Thus far, most investigators conclude that the shared environment—factors such as socioeconomic status that equally affect all children in the same family—appear to have little influence on personality variation. As noted above, however, nonshared environmental influences appear to be very important in personality development (Hoffman, 1991; Plomin & Daniels, 1987). The exact impact on personality development of nonshared environmental factors that may be different for twins and nontwin siblings has not yet been fully or systematically examined. Additional research on the role of nonshared factors in personality development and how these might differentially affect twin and nontwin siblings' development is obviously vital. Indeed, lack of attention to the role of nonshared environmental factors in twin studies may be leading researchers to overestimate genetic influences on personality and to underestimate the impact of the environment in sibling similarities (Hoffman, 1991).

What conclusions are most reasonable?

As noted in previous chapters, the influences of heredity and environment are so intimately intertwined as to be inseparable except in theoretical terms. In relation to personality, as with mental abilities, some observers go so far as to say that any attempt to separate the effects of nature and nurture is meaningless since genetic inheritance always emerges within an environment that exerts simultaneous influences. Eysenck noted that asking about their separate effects is as illogical as asking which is more important in melting metal: the heat of the flame or the nature of the metal (Pervin, 1989). With these cautions in mind, it seems wisest to draw rather tentative conclusions about the sources of personality.

The evidence available so far suggests that genetic influences do appear to contribute significantly to the variation in many personality traits. However, understanding the nature and implications of such a statement is important. First, there is no evidence of a specific gene for any specific personality trait.

Linkages: Do biological predispositions shape personality? (a link to Biological Aspects of Psychology)

The genetic contribution to personality most likely comes in the form of physical characteristics and general predispositions toward certain levels of activity, emotionality, and sociability (Eysenck, 1981; Kagan, Reznick & Snidman, 1988; Kagan & Snidman, 1991; Tellegen et al., 1988; Plomin, 1989, 1990). These physical features and predispositions then interact with environmental factors such as family experiences to produce specific personality features. Thus, children who inherit a frail body may be especially likely targets for aggression by other children. These experiences, in turn, might help create a tendency to avoid social interaction and thus encourage development of an introverted personality, characterized by self-consciousness and a preference for privacy. If the slender child has also inherited a predisposition toward social shyness or introversion, the development of the child's personality in this direction would be even more pronounced. Of course, genetic predisposition toward particular personality characteristics may or may not appear in behavior, depending on whether the environment supports or suppresses it. Changes in biologically predisposed traits are not only possible; they may actually be quite common as children develop (Kagan & Snidman, 1991). Even the personalities of identical twins become less similar over time as they are exposed to differing environmental experiences (McCartney, Harris & Bernieri, 1990). It appears that rather than inheriting specific personality traits, people inherit raw materials out of which personality is shaped by the world. ◼

Evaluation of the Dispositional Approach

In Chapter 3, on human development, we mentioned that many aspects of people's thought and action remain relatively stable over their lifespan (Costa & McCrae, 1992; McCrae & John, 1992; McAdams, 1992; Woodall & Matthews, 1993). The dispositional, or type-trait, approach to personality has gained wide acceptance among those who seek to explore and explain this stability on the basis of interacting genetic and environmental factors. However, there are some problems and weaknesses associated with the dispositional approach.

For one thing, dispositional theories seem better at describing people than at understanding them. You might say, for example, that Michelle is nasty to others because she has a strong hostility trait; but other factors, such as how people treat her, could just as easily be responsible. It is important to go beyond merely inventing trait names to describe behavior. Eysenck and others have tried to do so by isolating a few trait dimensions that can be used to predict how people will behave in a wide range of situations. It is in making such predictions that trait theory may be most useful (Epstein & O'Brien, 1985).

Second, the descriptions produced by dispositional approaches may not say much about a person that is unique. Consider how you might react to the following personality sketch:

You have a strong need for other people to like and admire you. You have a tendency to be critical of yourself. You have a great deal of unused capacity, which you have not turned to your advantage. . . . Disciplined and controlled on the outside, you tend to be worrisome and insecure inside. . . . At times you are extroverted, affable, and sociable; at other times, you are introverted, wary, and reserved. . . .

Does this description sound familiar? Does it describe anyone you know? Don't be surprised if it sounds like you. When psychology professors gave a longer version of this sketch to students who had just taken a personality test, nearly all of them said it was a "good" or even "excellent" description of their own personality (Ulrich, Stachnik & Stainton, 1963). At their worst, disposi-

The dispositional approach to personality is highlighted in the courtroom, where defense attorneys try to show that their clients are not the type of people who would commit certain acts and where lawyers on both sides seek to disqualify jurors who display traits suggesting that they might be unsympathetic to their case. Though most people tend to think about other people in dispositional terms, critics of this approach to personality point out that it does not always result in accurate predictions of human behavior.

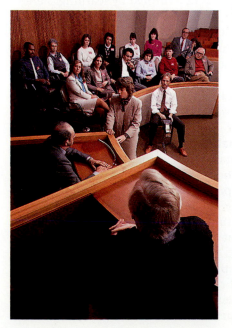

tional descriptions may be general enough to apply to most people, somewhat like the horoscopes printed each day in the newspapers.

The dispositional approach has also been faulted for offering a short list of traits of varying strengths that provides, at best, a static and superficial description of personality, one that fails to capture how traits combine to form a complex and dynamic individual (McAdams, 1992; Pervin, 1989). Nor do trait theories pay enough attention, critics say, to the interaction of stable traits with varying situations. Are people high on extraversion always gregarious, or does the expression of gregariousness depend on the situation in which they find themselves? The importance of person-situation interactions is emphasized by the cognitive-behavioral approach to personality, to which we now turn.

The Cognitive-Behavioral Approach

According to the psychodynamic and dispositional approaches, personality consists of inner dynamics or traits that guide thinking and outward behavior. In contrast, those taking a **cognitive-behavioral approach** view personality mainly as the array of behaviors that people acquire through learning and display in particular situations. Some aspects of this approach reflect a traditional behavioral assumption—namely, that all behavior is learned through classical and operant conditioning. However, we shall see that the cognitive-behavioral approach expands that original scope by emphasizing (1) the role of *learned patterns of thought* in guiding our actions and (2) the fact that much of personality is learned in *social situations* through observing the behavior of other people, including family members (Phares, 1991; Rotter, 1990). Accordingly, the cognitive-behavioral approach is sometimes called the *social-learning* approach to personality.

Roots of the Cognitive-Behavioral Approach

Elements of the cognitive-behavioral approach can be traced back to the radical behaviorism of John B. Watson. As noted in Chapter 1, Watson (1924) used research on classical conditioning to support his claim that all human behavior, from mental disorder to scientific skill, is determined by learning. Behavioral theorists eventually recognized that Watson's view was limited. Subsequently, as described in Chapter 8, on learning, B. F. Skinner widened the behavioral approach by emphasizing the importance of operant conditioning in learning. Among his contributions was the careful analysis of *functional relationships*—that is, how overt behavior is learned in relation to observable environmental events such as rewards and punishments. Skinner saw people's behavior—their personalities, in essence—as largely controlled by stimuli that come to signal reward or punishment.

Through what he called **functional analysis,** Skinner sought to understand behavior in terms of its function in obtaining rewards or avoiding punishment. For example, if observation of a schoolboy's aggressive behavior reveals that it occurs mainly when a teacher is present to break up fights, it may be that the aggression is being rewarded by the extra teacher attention. Rather than describing personality traits, then, functional analysis summarizes what people find rewarding or punishing, what they are capable of, and what skills they lack.

Once the hallmark of the behavioral approach to personality, classical and operant conditioning principles are still considered vitally important in the development of behavior. However, much as Freud's followers challenged some of his original ideas, many proponents of the behavioral approach became dissatisfied with what they saw as its too-narrow focus on observable behaviors and its corresponding de-emphasis of the role of thoughts in guiding behavior. The cognitive-behavioral approach to personality resulted from their efforts over the last two decades to address these perceived deficiencies.

Proponents of this very popular approach to personality seek to assess and understand how learned patterns of thought contribute to behavior and how behavior and its consequences alter cognitive activity as well as future actions. In dealing with the aggressive schoolboy, for example, cognitive behaviorists would want to know not only how and what he has learned to do under particular circumstances but also what he thinks about himself, his teachers, and his behavior—and his expectations about each. Among the most influential of the cognitive-behavioral or social-learning theorists are Julian Rotter, Albert Bandura, and Walter Mischel.

Rotter's Expectancy Theory

Rotter (1954) argued that learning creates cognitive expectancies that guide behavior. Specifically, he suggested that any behavior is determined by (1) what a person expects to happen following the behavior, and (2) the value the person places on the outcome. For example, people spend a lot of money on clothes to be worn at a job interview because (1) past learning leads them to expect that doing so will help get them the job, and (2) they place a high value on having the job. To Rotter, then, behavior is determined not only by the rewarding consequences Skinner emphasized but also by a cognitive *expectation* that a particular behavior will obtain that reward (Phares, 1991).

Rotter also suggested that people learn general ways of thinking about the world, especially about how life's rewards and punishments are controlled. Some people (*internals*) are likely to expect events to be controlled by their own efforts. That is, what they achieve and the reinforcements they obtain are due to efforts they make themselves. Others (*externals*) tend to expect events to be determined by external forces over which they have no control. If an external succeeds, he or she will be likely to believe that success was due to chance or luck.

Linkages: As noted in Chapter 12, incentive theories of motivation emphasize the role of paychecks, good grades, and other desirable external goals in explaining a wide range of behavior, from physical labor to diligent studying. Incentives lie at the heart of Rotter's expectancy theory, a cognitive-behavioral theory of personality that views people's behavior as guided by learned expectations about the consequences of their actions and the perceived value of those consequences.

"You know, we're just not reaching that guy."

An internal locus of control and dispositional optimism are aspects of the so-called stress-resistant, or hardy, personality (Kobasa, 1982). As noted in Chapter 13, dispositional optimism may be beneficial because it promotes active coping with stressors, which, in turn, may enhance the immune system's ability to resist disease.

Figure 14.5
Reciprocal Determinism
Bandura suggests that the way people think, the way they behave, and the nature of their environment are all determined by one another. For example, hostile thinking can lead to hostile behavior (line a), which in turn can intensify hostile thoughts (line c). At the same time, all that hostility is likely to offend others and create an environment of anger (line b), which calls forth even more negative thoughts and actions (lines d and e). These negative thoughts then alter perceptions, making the environment seem more threatening (line f).

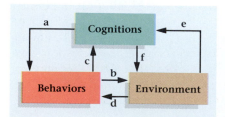

Rotter developed a personality test, called the *Internal-External Locus of Control Scale,* or *I-E,* to measure these beliefs. Numerous studies have shown that people's scores on the test do correlate with differences in their behavior (Rotter, 1990). For example, internals do better at jobs in which they can set their own pace, whereas externals work better when a machine controls the pace (Eskew & Riche, 1982; Phares, 1991). Internals are also more health conscious than externals, more likely to seek medical treatment when they need it (Strickland, 1989), and generally less prone to stress-related illness.

Albert Bandura and Reciprocal Determinism

Albert Bandura has emphasized the complex and constant interaction among cognitive patterns, the environment, and behavior. He points out that whether people learn through direct experience with rewards and punishments or through the cognitively mediated processes of observational learning described in Chapter 8, their behavior tends to affect their environment, which in turn may affect cognitions, which then may affect behavior, and so on. In short, according to Bandura (1978), personality is shaped by what he called *reciprocal determinism* (see Figure 14.5).

One cognitive element in this web of influence is especially important in Bandura's view: **self-efficacy,** which is the learned expectation of success, the belief that you can successfully perform a behavior regardless of past failures or current obstacles. Bandura says that overt behavior is largely controlled by individuals' expectations of their ability to perform, their self-efficacy. The higher a person's self-efficacy regarding a particular situation, the greater will be the actual accomplishments in that situation. Thus, going to a party with the belief that you have the skills necessary to be a social success may create that success and blunt the impact of minor failures.

According to Bandura, self-efficacy interacts with expectancies about the outcome of behavior in general, and the result of this interplay helps to shape a person's psychological well-being (Bandura, 1982a). Figure 14.6 shows how different interactions among these cognitions may produce different emotions and behaviors. If, for example, a person has little self-efficacy and also expects that nothing anyone does has much effect on the world, apathy may result. But if a person with low self-efficacy believes that other people do enjoy the benefits of their efforts, the result is likely to be self-disparagement and depression.

Mischel's Person-Situation Theory

Cognitive-behavioral theorists see learned beliefs or expectancies as characterizing each individual and differentiating one from another. While dispositional theorists might refer to such beliefs or expectancies as traits, social-learning theorist Walter Mischel (1986) calls them *person variables,* the cognitive variables that he believes outline the important dimensions along which individuals differ.

The most important person variables, according to Mischel, are (1) competencies (the thoughts and actions the person can perform); (2) perceptions (how the person perceives the environment); (3) expectations (what the person expects to follow from various behaviors and what the person believes he or she is capable of doing—again, a matter of self-efficacy); (4) subjective values (the person's ideals and goals); and (5) self-regulation and plans (the person's standards for self-reward and plans for reaching goals).

Mischel made the distinction between traits and person variables on the basis of evidence that information about personality traits may not be helpful in predicting a person's behavior; people often behave differently in different

	Outcome expectation	
	-	+
Self-efficacy judgment +	Social activism Protest Grievance Milieu change	Assured opportune action
-	Resignation Apathy	Self-devaluation Despondency

Source: Bandura, 1982a.

Figure 14.6
Self-efficacy, Outcome
Expectancies, and
Psychological Well-Being
According to Bandura, a person's emotions and behavior reflect the interaction of self-efficacy and outcome expectancies. Thus, a person who has learned to believe that his or her efforts lead to success (high self-efficacy), but who perceives the environment to be unresponsive to those efforts, may become resentful and socially active. Combining that same level of self-efficacy with perceptions that the environment is responsive would lead, in this model, to a person who is both active and self-assured.

situations. To predict how a person might behave, said Mischel, we also need to know about the situation in which the behavior will occur. Mischel's views sparked a "person-situation" debate between cognitive-behavioral and trait theorists about whether personality traits or situational factors were more influential in guiding behavior. As in most debates, this one produced no clear winners. However, the controversy has helped to clarify the interaction of personal and situational variables under various conditions. Many of the conclusions that have emerged (Kenrick & Funder, 1988) are consistent with Bandura's concept of reciprocal determinism:

1. Traits influence behavior only in relevant situations. The trait of anxiousness, for example, may be predictive of anxiety, but only in situations where the person feels threatened.
2. Traits can lead to behaviors that alter situations that, in turn, promote other behaviors. Thus, a hostile child can elicit aggression in others and, in turn, precipitate a fight.
3. People choose to be in situations that are in accord with their traits. Introverts, for instance, are more likely to choose quiet environments, while extraverts tend to seek out livelier, more social circumstances.
4. Traits are more influential in some situations than in others. In ambiguous or unconstrained situations—a picnic, for example—people's behavior may be predicted from their personality traits (extraverts will probably play games and socialize while introverts will watch). However, in socially constrained situations such as a funeral, personality traits will not differentiate one person from another; all are likely to be quiet and somber.

Today, cognitive-behavioral and social-learning theorists devote much of their research to examining how person variables develop, how they are related to stress and health, and how they interact with situational variables.

Evaluation of the Cognitive-Behavioral Approach

The traditional behavioral perspective on personality holds many attractions. It offers an objective, experimentally oriented approach that defines its concepts operationally, relies on empirical data for its basic principles, and bases its applications on the results of empirical research (Pervin, 1989; Phares, 1991). Evolution of the cognitive-behavioral approach has expanded the utility and explanatory scope of learning principles in such socially important areas as aggression, the effects of mass media on children, and the development of self-regulatory processes that enhance personal control over behavior. The popularity of the cognitive-behavioral approach also stems from the ease with which its principles can be translated into treatment procedures for many types of psychological disorders (see Chapter 16).

Yet, attractive as they may be to some, behavioral approaches have not escaped criticism. Behavioral theories that emphasize classical and operant conditioning are accused of reducing human beings to a set of acquired responses derived solely from relationships with the environment. This view, critics say, is too narrow, minimizes the importance of subjective experience, fails to consider unconscious processes, neglects the contribution of emotion to personality, and tends to exclude genetic, physiological, and other influences not based on learning. Cognitive-behavioral theories have addressed some of these criticisms through their emphasis on expectancies, self-efficacy, and person variables, but they are criticized by some for not going far enough in that direction (Phares, 1991). For many, a far more palatable alternative is provided by the phenomenological approach to personality, to which we now turn.

Linkages: How are perceptions of others related to personality differences? (a link to Social Cognition)

The Phenomenological Approach

Suppose you and a friend meet someone new at a party. Comparing notes later, you discover a major discrepancy in your reactions. You thought the new person was entertaining and humorous and showed a genuine interest in others. Your friend saw the same person as a "phony" who hid behind a humorous style and merely pretended to be interested. How can two people draw such opposite conclusions from the same conversation? Perhaps it was not the same conversation. Just as each person sees something different in a cloud formation, each of you perceived a different reality, a different conversation, and a different person.

This interpretation reflects the **phenomenological approach** to personality, which maintains that the way people perceive and interpret the world forms their personalities and guides their behavior. Proponents of this view emphasize the fact that, as noted in Chapter 6, on perception, each individual perceives reality somewhat differently, and they assert that these differences—rather than instincts, traits, or learning experiences—are central to understanding human personality. From this perspective, no one can understand another person without somehow perceiving the world through that person's eyes. All behavior, even if it looks bizarre, is meaningful to the person displaying it. Unlike theories that emphasize the instincts and learning processes that humans and lower animals seem to have in common, the phenomenological approach focuses on mental qualities that set humans apart: self-awareness, creativity, planning, decision making, and responsibility. For this reason, the phenomenological approach is also called the *humanistic* view of personality.

This approach to personality is rooted in philosophy as well as psychology. (In the language of philosophy, the mental experiencing of the world is called a *phenomenon,* and the study of how each person experiences reality is *phenomenology.*) The idea that each person experiences a unique version of reality derives from existential philosophers such as Kierkegaard and Sartre. The idea that people actively shape that reality stems in part from the Gestalt psychologists, whose work is described in Chapter 6. The phenomenological approach also grew partly out of revisions of Freud's ideas—out of the work of Adler and Jung, who emphasized positive aspects of human nature, and of ego analysts, who highlighted the ego's direction of efforts toward growth.

In short, phenomenological theorists emphasize that each person actively constructs his or her own world. Humans, they say, are not merely passive carriers of traits, crucibles of intrapsychic conflict, or behavioral clay that is molded by learning. Instead, according to the phenomenological approach, the primary human motivator is an innate drive toward growth that prompts people to fulfill their unique and natural potential. Like the planted seed that naturally becomes a flower, people are inclined toward goodness, creativity, love, and joy.

George Kelly (1955), an experimental psychologist-turned-therapist, tried to blend some of these phenomenological concepts in a theory that also contained cognitive-behavioral features. Kelly emphasized that people's view of reality is important in guiding their behavior, but he suggested that this view is shaped by learned expectations. Expectations, said Kelly, form *personal constructs,* which are generalized ways of anticipating the world. According to Kelly, the nature of each person's unique constructs determines personality and influences behavior; personality development stems from the search for constructs that will allow people to predict and understand themselves and others. Perhaps because of its hybrid nature or its complexity, Kelly's theory has received far less attention than the more purely phenomenological theories of personality offered by Carl Rogers and Abraham Maslow.

Linkages: What is reality? Everyone present probably has somewhat differing perceptions about what actually happened on the play that started this argument. Their disagreement reflects the phenomenological view that each person's unique perceptions of the world shape personality and guide behavior. As described in Chapter 6, these perceptions are often influenced by factors associated with top-down processing; in this case, expectations and motivation stemming from differing team loyalties are likely to influence reality for each side's players, coaches, and fans.

The Self Theory of Carl Rogers

The name of Carl Rogers is almost synonymous with the phenomenological approach (Rogers, 1942, 1951, 1961, 1970, 1980). Rogers assumed that each person responds as an organized whole to reality as he or she perceives it. He emphasized **self-actualization**, which he described as an innate tendency toward growth that motivates all human behavior. To Rogers, personality is the expression of each individual's self-actualizing tendency as it unfolds in that individual's uniquely perceived reality. To learn about personality, Rogers relied heavily on unstructured interviews in which those being interviewed decided what they wanted to talk about. Given sufficient freedom and encouragement, said Rogers, people eventually and spontaneously reveal whatever is important about their personalities.

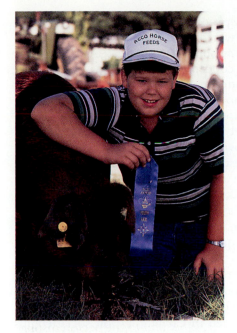

According to Carl Rogers's self theory of personality, people who are clearly aware of their likes and dislikes, skills and shortcomings, will be more likely to become fulfilled, or self-actualized, than people who habitually alter their thoughts, feelings, and actions in an effort to please others. From the look on his face, this prize winner appears to be enjoying genuine satisfaction.

The Concept of Self   Central to Rogers's theory is the *self,* the part of experience that a person identifies as "I" or "me." According to Rogers, those who accurately experience the self—with all its preferences, abilities, fantasies, shortcomings, and desires—are on the road to self-actualization. The progress of those whose experiences of the self become distorted, however, is likely to be slowed or even stopped.

How can self-experiences become distorted? Rogers suggested that people have a natural tendency to evaluate experiences as positive if these experiences enhance self-actualization and as negative if they impede it. People also have a natural tendency to seek positive experiences and to avoid negative ones, simply on the basis of their genuine, or organismic, reaction to them. A child would probably say, "I like ice cream," because it tastes good, or "I hate cough syrup," because it tastes bad. The child is aware of these self-experiences and is comfortable saying, essentially, "I like what feels good." In Rogers's terms, the child's organismic experience and self-experience are consistent, or *congruent.*

Very early in life, however, children learn to need the approval of others, which Rogers called *positive regard.* As a result, evaluations by parents, teachers, and others begin to affect children's evaluations. When the evaluations by others concur with a child's own evaluation (as when the pleasure of finger painting is enhanced by a parent's approval), the child not only feels the other's positive regard but also evaluates the self as "good" for having earned approval. The result is a clearly identified and positively evaluated experience of the self ("I like to paint") that the child gladly acknowledges. This self-experience becomes part of the **self-concept**, which is the way one thinks of oneself. Unfortunately, things do not always go so smoothly. If a pleasurable self-experience is evaluated negatively by others, you must either do without their positive regard or re-evaluate the experience. Rogers argued that people often choose to suppress their genuine feelings in order to get approval. Thus, a little boy who is chided by his parents for enjoying doll play might adopt a distorted self-experience ("I don't like dolls" or "Feeling good is bad").

In other words, personality is shaped partly by the self-actualizing tendency and partly by others' evaluations. In this way, people come to like what they are "supposed" to like and to behave as they are "supposed" to behave. To an extent, this process is adaptive, allowing people to get along in society. However, it often requires that they stifle the self-actualizing tendency and distort experience. Rogers argued that psychological discomfort, anxiety, or mental disorder can result when the feelings people let themselves experience or express are inconsistent, or *incongruent,* with their true feelings.

Conditions of Worth   Incongruence is likely when parents and teachers create **conditions of worth**—that is, when they lead a child to believe that his or her worth as a person depends on displaying the "right" attitudes, behaviors, and values. Although conditions of worth are first set up by external pressure, they eventually become part of the person's internal makeup. (Notice the similarity between this idea and Freud's concept of superego.)

Conditions of worth are created whenever *people* are evaluated instead of their behavior. For example, parents who find their child smearing Jell-O on the kitchen floor are unlikely to say, "I love you, but I do not approve of this particular behavior." They are more likely to shout, "Bad boy!" or "Bad girl!" thus suggesting that the child can be loved and considered worthwhile only by being well behaved. As a result, the child's self-experience is not "I like smearing Jell-O, but Mom and Dad don't approve," but "Playing with Jell-O is bad, and I am bad if I like it, so I don't like it," or "I like it, so I must be bad." The child may eventually come to display very neat and tidy behaviors that do not belong to the real self but, rather, are part of the ideal self dictated by the parents. Or the child may become quite naughty, in line with the new belief that he or she is "bad."

Thus, from Rogers's perspective, rewards and punishments may shape or condition behavior, but their real importance for personality development lies in their potential for creating conditions of worth and, in turn, distorted self-perceptions and incongruence. As discussed in Chapter 17, on social cognition, research by cognitive psychologists tends to support Rogers's view that self-perception plays an important role in personality and that congruence may indeed be important for psychological well-being.

Maslow's Humanistic Psychology

Like Rogers, Abraham Maslow (1954, 1962, 1971) saw personality as the expression of a basic human tendency toward growth and self-actualization. Maslow believed that self-actualization is not just a human capacity but a human need. In fact, as noted in Chapter 12, Maslow described it as the highest need in a hierarchy of needs. According to Maslow, people may be distracted from self-actualization by preoccupation with other needs.

According to Maslow's humanistic theory of personality, most people are preoccupied with what they do not have. The key to personal fulfillment, he said, lies in focusing on what we *do* have, not only in terms of material possessions but also in terms of skills and experiences.

Most people, said Maslow, are controlled by a **deficiency orientation**, a preoccupation with meeting perceived needs for material things. This orientation produces perceptions that life is a meaningless exercise in disappointment and boredom. People holding these perceptions are likely to behave in problematic ways. For example, in an attempt to satisfy the need for love and belongingness, people may focus on what love can give them (security), not on what they can give to another. According to Maslow, this deficiency orientation may lead a person to be jealous of a partner and to focus on what is missing; as a result, the person will never truly experience love and security.

In contrast, people with a **growth orientation** do not focus on what is missing but draw satisfaction from what they have, what they are, and what they can do. This orientation opens the door to what Maslow called *peak experiences,* in which one feels joy, even ecstasy, in the mere fact of being alive, being human, and knowing that one is utilizing one's fullest potential.

Evaluation of the Phenomenological Approach

The phenomenological approach coincides with the way many people view themselves. It gives a central role to each person's immediate experience and emphasizes the uniqueness of each individual. It is an optimistic approach that places faith in a person's ability to fulfill his or her ultimate capacities.

The best-known applications of the phenomenological approach to personality are the client-centered therapy of Carl Rogers and the Gestalt therapy of Fritz Perls. These methods are discussed in Chapter 16. The phenomenological approach also inspired short-term group experiences, such as sensitivity training and encounter groups, designed to help people to become more aware of themselves and the way they relate to others. And a course called *Parent Effectiveness Training,* or *PET* (Gordon, 1970) applies Rogers's self theory to help parents avoid creating conditions of worth while maximizing their children's potential.

Yet to its critics, the phenomenological view is naive, romantic, and unrealistic. Are people all as inherently good and "growthful" as this approach suggests? Phenomenologists have also been chided for slighting the importance of inherited characteristics, biological processes, learning, situational influences, and unconscious motivation in shaping personality. The idea that everyone is directed only by an innate growth potential is viewed by critics as an oversimplification. So, too, is the phenomenological assumption that all human problems stem from blocked self-actualization; this view, critics claim, may lead to therapy in which everyone is treated basically the same.

Like the dispositional approach, phenomenological theories have been faulted for doing a better job of describing personality than explaining it. Saying that people behave as they do because of their perceptions, constructs, or actualizing tendencies does not deal with important underlying questions. Where does the actualizing tendency come from? How do perceptions develop? General notions that personality simply unfolds are unsatisfying to those interested in understanding personality development in more detail.

Many phenomenological concepts, like many psychodynamic variables, are too vague to be tested empirically. Self-actualization and peak experience are two examples. Although phenomenologists like Rogers devoted years to systematic research on the relationship between people's self-perceptions and their behavior problems, and on the changes in self-perception that occur during therapy, many others have actively avoided the scientific approach. They believe that people can understand themselves only through personal experience, not through experiments. This point of view has made the phenomenological approach unacceptable to those who favor experimental research as a means of learning about personality.

In Review: Major Approaches to Personality

Approach	Basic Assumptions About Behavior	Typical Research Methods
Psychodynamic	Determined by largely unconscious intrapsychic conflicts	Case reports
Dispositional	Determined by types, traits, or needs	Analysis of tests for basic personality dimensions
Cognitive-behavioral	Determined by learning, cognitive factors, and specific situations	Analysis of interactions between people and situations
Phenomenological	Determined by unique perception of reality	Studies of relationships between perceptions and behavior

Finally, the phenomenological emphasis on the development and enhancement of the self—even the postulation of an innate drive toward self-actualization—reflects culture-specific ideas. Just as psychodynamic conceptions of ego may be culture-bound, Rogers's portrayal of the independent, autonomous self as an entity that is based on one's achievement, that creates a sense of differentiation from others, and whose full expression and actualization are prerequisites for mental health may not apply outside of North America and other Western cultures. In Japan, Africa, and parts of Latin America, for example, the self is defined mainly in relation to others, especially within the family (Markus & Kitayama, 1991). Thus, as described in the next section, the foundations of phenomenological self theories are in direct conflict with the values of cultures that prize being indirect with others, working to help other people and groups to achieve their goals, and avoiding personal recognition. So although the concept of self is found universally in some form, it can vary enough across cultures that a personality theory based on only one culture's conception of it will be severely limited in its ability to explain human behavior. ("In Review: Major Approaches to Personality" summarizes key features of the phenomenological approach, along with those of the other approaches we have described.)

Linkages: Personality, Culture, and Human Development

How do cultural factors influence the development of children's personality?

In many Western cultures, it is common to hear people encourage others to "stand up for yourself" or to "blow your own horn" in order to "get what you have coming to you." We should keep after what we want, they say, because "the squeaky wheel gets the grease." In middle-class America, for example, the value of self-promotion and personal distinction is taught to children, particularly male children, very early in life (Markus & Katayama, 1991; Josephs, Markus & Tafarodi, 1992). As exemplified by TV's enormously influential "Mr. Rogers' Neighborhood" show, for example, American children are encouraged to feel special, to want self-esteem, and to feel good about themselves. Those who learn and display these values tend to receive praise and encouragement for doing so.

As a result of such cultural training, many people in North American and European cultures develop personalities that are largely based on a sense of high self-worth. In a study by Hazel Markus and Shinobu Kitayama (1991), for example, 70 percent of a sample of U.S. students believed they were superior to their peers and 60 percent believed they were in the top 10 percent on a wide variety of personal attributes! This tendency toward self-enhancement is evident as early as age four.

A sense of independence, uniqueness, and self-esteem is seen by some to be a fundamental aspect of being human (Kitayama & Markus, 1992; Maslow, 1962; Rogers, 1961). We mentioned in Chapter 3, for example, that Erik Erikson saw personal identity and self-esteem as parts of normal psychosocial development. Thus, middle-class Americans who fail to value and strive for independence, self-promotion, and unique personal achievement may be seen as displaying a personality disorder, some form of depression, or other psychological problems described in Chapter 15.

Do these ideas reflect universal truths about personality development or, rather, the influence of the cultures that generated them? It is certainly clear that people in many non-Western cultures develop very different personal orientations. In Asian cultures such as China and Japan, for example, developing an independent, unique self is not emphasized. In fact, children there are encouraged to develop and maintain harmonious relations with others and *not* to stand out from the crowd, lest they diminish someone else. In contrast to America's "squeaky wheel gets the grease" principle, in Japan one commonly hears that "The nail that sticks out gets pounded down." In Japanese, the word for "different" (*tigau*) also means "wrong" (Markus & Kitayama, 1991; Kitayama & Markus, 1992). Japanese children are taught to be self-effacing, to diminish the value of personal contributions. One of their developmental tasks is to fit into the larger social and group matrix; as young as two and a half, they are actively taught the joy and value of group work. When they paint, for example, they are likely to do it as a group project (Kitayama & Markus, 1992).

In contrast to the *independent* self-system common in Western cultures, then, this more collectivist orientation promotes an *interdependent* self-system through which people see themselves as a fraction of a whole, as an entity that has little or no meaningful definition without reference to the group (see Figure 14.7).

These contrasting cultural definitions of the self tend to exert effects on the development of personality in collectivist (interdependent) and individualist (independent) cultures. Kitayama and his colleagues (1992) examined some of these cultural effects, as reflected in feelings about the self. They asked university students in Japan to rate the frequency with which they experienced certain emotions, and to identify the source of those emotions. They found that positive moods or feelings, such as calmness or elation, were strongly associated with positive *inter*personal connections. However, there was no relationship between positive feelings and *personal* accomplishments; personal achievements were actually associated with generally negative emotions. For American students, opposite results appeared: positive feelings were most associated with personal achievement (Kitayama & Markus, 1992).

Recognition of the role of cultural factors in establishing ideals of personality development requires that various approaches to personality be evaluated in terms of the extent to which they apply to cultures different from the one in which they were developed. Their applicability to males and females must also be considered. Recent research has demonstrated, for example, that even

Figure 14.7
Independent and Interdependent Self-Systems
The large circles represent the "self" and the small circles represent specific others. Boldface Xs indicate those aspects of self given most attention and elaboration. In (a), the independent view of self, the person is self-contained and defined independently of others. Others are important, but not for self-definition. In (b), the interdependent self-system, the focus is the self intersecting with others, and it is through this intersection that the self finds definition.

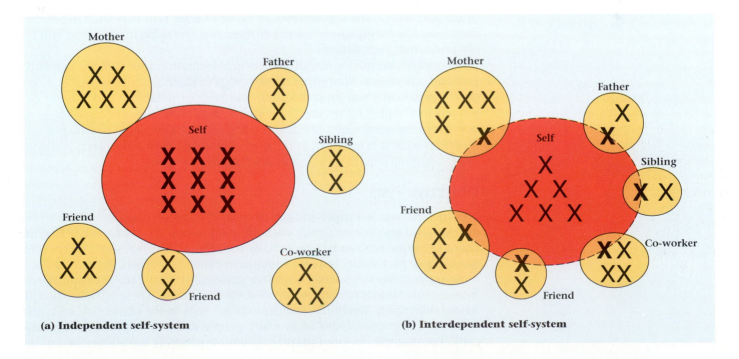

(a) Independent self-system

(b) Interdependent self-system

within North American cultures, gender differences are evident in the development of self-esteem. Females tend to achieve their sense of self and self-esteem from attachments to important others, in keeping with the interdependent self-system, while males' self-esteem tends to develop more in relation to personal achievement, in a manner more like that described for the independent self-system (Josephs, Markus & Tafarodi, 1992). Cross-gender and cross-cultural differences in the nature and determinants of a sense of self underscore the pervasive effects of gender and culture on the development of many aspects of human personality. These factors can also influence the accuracy of some of the personality assessment procedures described in the next section.

Assessing Personality

Suppose you are a psychologist whose task it is to select big-city police officers for undercover work. How would you go about deciding which candidates had the personality characteristics necessary for the job? There are three basic tools used for assessing and describing personality: observations, interviews, and tests. Information generated by these tools is often used in personnel selection, in the diagnosis of psychological disorders, in making predictions about a convict's or mental patient's dangerousness, and in other risky decision situations (Bartol, 1991; Matarazzo, 1992).

In Chapter 2, we introduced the use of *observational* methods in psychological research. Observation allows direct assessment of many aspects of personality, including how often a specific behavior occurs, how well is it performed, and how consistent a person's behavior is in different situations. Psychologists have developed elaborate systems for coding and quantifying observations of behavior from which personality statements might be inferred (see, for example, Funder & Sneed, 1993). *Interviews* provide a way to gather information from the person's own point of view. They can be open-ended and tailored to the intellectual level, emotional state, and special needs of the person being assessed. Interviews can also be *structured,* aimed at gathering information about specific topics without spending much time on other issues. Structured interviews such as the one outlined in Table 14.3 are routinely used in personality research; their planned nature ensures that the same information will be obtained from each person.

Personality tests offer a way of gathering information that is more standardized and economical than either observations or interviews. To be useful, however, a personality test must meet the standards of reliability and validity described in Chapter 11, on mental abilities. *Reliability* refers to how stable or consistent the results of a test are; *validity* reflects the degree to which a test measures what it is intended to measure. The many personality tests available today are traditionally classified as *objective* or *projective.*

Objective Tests

An **objective test** is a paper-and-pencil form containing questions ("Have you ever worried about your family without good reason?"), statements ("I think about sex more than most people"), or concepts ("My ideal self"). Responses to objective personality tests are sometimes called *self-reports*. Because of their standardized, written format, objective personality tests can be administered by nonprofessionals to many subjects at the same time. These tests can also be scored objectively, much like multiple-choice tests in the classroom. And, just as in the classroom, results from many people can be compared mathematically. For example, before interpreting your apparently high score on an ob-

Table 14.3
Sample Questions from the Anxiety Disorders Interview Schedule—Revised (ADIS-R)

Structured interviews, such as this one for diagnosing panic disorder (described in Chapter 15), help ensure that each interviewer asks the same questions in the same way. This consistency increases reliability, making it more likely that information obtained from several clients can be meaningfully compared.

1. Have you had times when you have felt a sudden rush of intense fear or anxiety or feeling of impending doom?

   Yes ____ No ____

2. (a) In what situation(s) have you had these feelings?

   _____

   _____

   (b) Have you had these feelings come "from out of the blue," or while you are at home alone, or in situations where you did not expect them to occur?

   Yes ____ No ____

   (c) When you are faced with (phobic situation), does the anxiety come on as soon as you enter it, or is it sometimes delayed, or unexpected?

   Delayed: Yes ____ No ____

3. How long does it take for the rush of anxiety to become intense?

   ____ minutes

4. How long does the anxiety usually last at its peak level?

   ____ minutes

Source: Di Nardo & Barlow, 1989.

jective test of anxiety, a psychologist would compare the score with *norms,* or average scores from others of your age and gender. Only if you were well above these averages would you be considered unusually anxious.

Some objective tests focus on one aspect of personality, such as anger or anxiety (Spielberger, 1983, 1988). Others measure several personality characteristics in order to assess patterns of normal functioning or to identify psychological problems.

The most widely used objective test for diagnosing psychological disorders is the *Minnesota Multiphasic Personality Inventory,* better known as the *MMPI* (Dahlstrom, 1992). This 566-item true-false test was developed during the 1930s at the University of Minnesota by Starke Hathaway and J. C. McKinley. The MMPI can be given in its original form, in a second edition called MMPI-2, and in a newer version designed specifically for adolescents called MMPI-A (NCS, 1992).

All versions of the MMPI are organized into ten *clinical scales,* which are groups of items that—in previous research—had elicited a characteristic pattern of responses from people who displayed particular psychological disorders or personality characteristics (see Figure 14.8). The MMPI and MMPI-2 also contain four *validity scales* (seven in the MMPI-A), which are item groups designed to detect whether respondents distorted their answers, misunderstood the items, or were uncooperative. For example, someone who responds "true" to items such as "I never get angry" or "Criticism doesn't bother me" may not be giving honest answers to the test as a whole. Interpretation of the person's responses to the clinical scales are made in light of the potential problems or distortions suggested by validity-scale scores.

Consistent with the nature of the clinical scales, interpreting the MMPI is largely a matter of comparing respondents' profiles—such as those shown in Figure 14.8—to those of persons already known to display certain personality characteristics. Respondents are generally presumed to share characteristics with the group whose profile theirs most closely resembles. So while a very high score on one scale, such as depression, for example, might indicate a problem in the dimension measured by that scale, MMPI interpretation usually focuses on the overall *pattern* in the clinical scales—particularly on the combination of two or three scales on which a person has unusually high scores. Scoring and interpretation is often speeded by computers that have been programmed to compare a respondent's profile to thousands of others and to summarize the characteristics associated with the profile it matches best.

There is considerable evidence for the reliability and validity of MMPI scales, but even the latest editions of the test are far from perfect measurement tools

Figure 14.8
The MMPI: Clinical Scales and Sample Profile
A score of 50 on the clinical scales is average. Scores at or above 65 on the MMPI-2 mean that the person's responses on that scale are more extreme than at least 95 percent of the normal population. The red line represents the profile of Kenneth Bianchi, the infamous "Hillside Strangler" who murdered thirteen Los Angeles women in the late 1970s. His profile would be interpreted as characteristic of a shallow person with poor self-control and little personal insight who is sexually preoccupied and unable to reveal himself to others. The profile in green comes from a more normal man, but it is characteristic of someone who is self-centered, passive, unwilling to accept personal responsibility for his behavior, and, when under stress, complains of numerous vague physical symptoms.

The clinical scales abbreviated in the figure are as follows:

1. Hypochondriasis (Hs) (concern with bodily functions and symptoms)
2. Depression (D) (pessimism, hopelessness, slowed thinking)
3. Hysteria (Hy) (use of physical or mental symptoms to avoid problems)
4. Psychopathic deviate (Pd) (disregard for social customs, emotional shallowness)
5. Masculinity/femininity (Mf) (interests associated with a particular gender)
6. Paranoia (Pa) (delusions, suspiciousness)
7. Psychasthenia (Pt) (worry, guilt, anxiety)
8. Schizophrenia (Sc) (bizarre thoughts and perceptions)
9. Hypomania (Ma) (overactivity, excitement, impulsiveness)
10. Social introversion (Si) (shy, insecure)

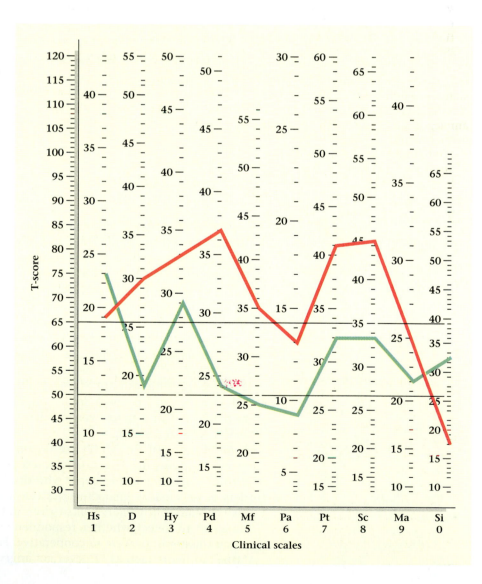

(Helmes & Reddon, 1993). The validity of MMPI interpretations may be particularly suspect when—because of cultural factors—the perceptions, values, and experiences of the respondent are very different from those of the test developers and the people to whom the respondent's results will be compared. Thus, a profile that looks typical of people with a certain disorder might reflect the culture-specific way the respondent interpreted the test items, not a mental problem (Dana, 1988; Greene, 1991). Even though MMPI-2 uses comparison norms that represent a more culturally diverse population than those of the original MMPI, psychologists must remain cautious when interpreting profiles of people who identify with minority subcultures. Computer-based interpretations must also be treated with caution. Though highly objective, they should not be automatically accepted at face value. Like most personality test data, computer analyses of various MMPI tests are most useful when supplemented and confirmed by interviews and/or observations.

There are a number of objective tests designed to measure a broad range of personality variables in normal populations. One increasingly popular example is the *Neuroticism Extraversion Openness Personality Inventory, Revised* or *NEO-PI-R*, which was developed specifically to measure the "big five" traits described earlier (Costa & McCrae, 1992). Table 14.4 shows how the test's results are presented. One innovative feature of the NEO-PI-R is its "private" and "public" versions. The first asks for the respondent's self-assessment; the second asks a person who knows the respondent to rate him or her on various dimensions. Personality descriptions derived from the two versions are often quite similar, but discrepancies may indicate problems. For example, if a person's self-ratings are substantially different from those of a spouse, marital problems may be indicated; in addition, the nature of the discrepancies could suggest a focus for marital therapy.

Table 14.4
Sample Summary of Results from the NEO-PI-R Personality Inventory

The NEO-PI-R assesses each of five main personality dimensions, as well as six subdimensions that make up the main dimensions. In this example of the results that a respondent might receive, the five factors scored are, from the top row to the bottom row, neuroticism, extraversion, openness, agreeableness, and conscientiousness. Costa and McCrae (1989) argue that the NEO-PI-R can be used to aid in the diagnosis of personality disorders and to understand how psychotherapy might affect different types of clients. For example, people who score high on the extraversion factor might prefer group to individual therapy, whereas introverts might do better in individual treatment.

Compared with the responses of other people, your responses suggest that you can be described as:

- [ ] Sensitive, emotional, and prone to experience feelings that are upsetting.
- [x] Generally calm and able to deal with stress, but you sometimes experience feelings of guilt, anger, or sadness.
- [ ] Secure, hardy, and generally relaxed even under stressful conditions.

- [ ] Extraverted, outgoing, active, and high-spirited. You prefer to be around people most of the time.
- [ ] Moderate in activity and enthusiasm. You enjoy the company of others but you also value privacy.
- [x] Introverted, reserved, and serious. You prefer to be alone or with a few close friends.

- [ ] Open to new experiences. You have broad interests and are very imaginative.
- [ ] Practical but willing to consider new ways of doing things. You seek a balance between the old and the new.
- [x] Down-to-earth, practical, traditional, and pretty much set in your ways.

- [ ] Compassionate, good-natured, and eager to cooperate and avoid conflict.
- [x] Generally warm, trusting, and agreeable, but you can sometimes be stubborn and competitive.
- [ ] Hardheaded, skeptical, proud, and competitive. You tend to express your anger directly.

- [x] Conscientious and well organized. You have high standards and always strive to achieve your goals.
- [ ] Dependable and moderately well organized. You generally have clear goals but are able to set your work aside.
- [ ] Easygoing, not very well organized, and sometimes careless. You prefer not to make plans.

Table 14.5
Some Scales from the
Personality Research Form

Notice the difference between these traits and the disordered characteristics measured by the MMPI. The PRF scales were derived from a list of psychological needs proposed by Henry Murray.

Scale	Description of High Scorer
Achievement	Aspires to accomplish difficult tasks; maintains high standards and is willing to work toward distant goals; responds positively to competition; willing to put forth effort to attain excellence.
Affiliation	Enjoys being with friends and people in general; accepts people readily; makes efforts to win friendships and maintain associations with people.
Autonomy	Tries to break away from restraints, confinement, or restrictions of any kind; enjoys being unattached, free, not tied to people, places, or obligations; may be rebellious when faced with restraints.
Change	Likes new and different experiences; dislikes routine and avoids it; may readily change opinions or values in different circumstances; adapts readily to changes in environment.
Dominance	Attempts to control environment, and to influence or direct other people; expresses opinions forcefully; enjoys the role of leader and may assume it spontaneously.
Endurance	Willing to work long hours; doesn't give up quickly on a problem; persevering, even in the face of great difficulty; patient and unrelenting in work habits.
Exhibition	Wants to be the center of attention; enjoys having an audience; engages in behavior that wins the notice of others; may enjoy being dramatic or witty.

Source: Jackson, 1974.

Figure 14.9
Interpretations Based on a
Draw-a-Person Test

These drawings were made by an eighteen-year-old male who had been caught stealing a television set. Using a psychodynamic approach, a psychologist interpreted the muscular figure as the young man's attempt to boast of masculine prowess, but also saw the muscles as overinflated into a "puffy softness," suggesting feelings of inadequacy. The drawing of the babylike figure was seen to reveal feelings of vulnerability, dependency, and a desire for affection. Appealing as these interpretations may be, the use of projective tests in personality assessment is not generally supported by research. In most cases, the results of projective tests have low predictive validity or add little information beyond what the psychologist might have inferred from other existing information. In fact, even untrained observers are able to make relatively accurate judgments about a person's personality characteristics simply by watching a sample of the person's behavior on videotape (Funder & Colvin, 1988).

Source: Hammer, 1968.

Another popular personality test is the *Personality Research Form,* or *PRF* (Jackson, 1967, 1984; Paunonen et al., 1992). As with the NEO-PI-R, the PRF's items are grouped into scales, but PRF scales are designed to measure several basic needs (see Table 14.5). As is true of many other personality tests, factor analysis of PRF results typically reveals the "big five" personality dimensions (Paunonen et al., 1992).

Projective Tests

Unlike objective tests, **projective tests** contain relatively unstructured stimuli, such as inkblots, which can be perceived in many ways. Indeed, in accordance with the psychodynamic theory behind projective tests (sometimes called projective techniques), they provide ambiguous stimuli that can be perceptually organized in so many ways that responses are guided not so much by the stimuli as by the individual's unconscious needs, motives, fantasies, conflicts, thought patterns, and other hidden aspects of personality. Some projective tests ask people to draw items such as a house, a person, or a tree (see Figure 14.9), to fill in the missing parts of incomplete pictures or sentences, or to say what they associate with a particular word.

In one widely used projective test, the *Thematic Apperception Test,* or *TAT,* the person looks at drawings and constructs a story about what is going on in the picture. (We described the TAT in the discussion of need for achievement in Chapter 12, but it is also used to assess personality more generally.) The test was developed by Henry Murray, who argued that personality develops as peo-

Figure 14.10
The Rorschach Inkblot Test
Here is an inkblot similar to those included in the Rorschach test, which contains a set of ten patterns, some in color, others in black and white. The subject is asked to tell what the blot might be and then to explain why. What do you see? Most scoring methods pay attention to (1) what part of the blot the person responds to; (2) what particular features (such as small details or color) appear to determine each response; (3) the content of responses (for example, animals, knives, blood, maps, body parts); and (4) the popularity or commonness of the subject's responses compared to those of others who have taken the test. Several researchers have developed systems designed to guide the scoring and interpretation of Rorschach responses and to make the process more objective (Erdberg, 1990; Exner, 1985).

Linkages: How is correlational research used to evaluate personality tests? (a link to Research in Psychology)

ple find ways to meet their needs, some of which are unconscious and thus measurable only through projective methods. For example, if a person's stories about TAT pictures all contain a central character who feels abandoned and unloved, this might indicate that the person has a strong need for security and acceptance. Another well-known projective test, the *Rorschach,* asks people to say what they see in a series of inkblots (see Figure 14.10).

Compared with the answers to objective tests, the stories, drawings, associations, and other responses to projective tests are difficult to translate reliably into numerical scores. In an effort to reduce the subjectivity involved in projective test interpretation, some psychologists have developed more structured—and thus potentially more reliable—scoring systems for instruments like the Rorschach (Erdberg, 1990; Exner, 1985). Nonetheless, projective personality tests have generally lower reliability and validity than objective tests (Acklin, McDowell & Orndoff, 1992; Anastasi, 1988; Lanyon, 1984). Yet projective tests continue to be used by many practicing psychologists and researchers. Why? For one thing, projective tests make it difficult for respondents to detect what is being measured and what the "best" answers would be. Projective testers argue, therefore, that their tests can measure aggressive and sexual impulses and other personality features that people might otherwise be able to hide. The ambiguous stimuli in projective tests may also capture how people respond to the uncertainty that they confront in daily life. Proponents also point to specific instances—as in studies assessing achievement motivation via the TAT—where projectives show acceptable reliability and validity (Spangler, 1992).

("In Review: Personality Tests" summarizes the characteristics of objective and projective tests, along with some of their advantages and disadvantages.)

Using Personality Tests

Objective personality tests are often used to help select people for jobs ranging from office workers to emergency medical technicians. How good is the predictive validity of such tests? One study evaluated the validity of the MMPI as a predictor of job performance among law enforcement officers in small towns in Vermont (Bartol, 1991). The researchers had access to the MMPI profiles of 600 officers hired over a twelve-year period. They compared the profiles of

In Review: Personality Tests

Type of Test	Characteristics	Advantages	Disadvantages
Objective	Paper-and-pencil format; quantitatively scored	Efficiency, standardization	Subject to deliberate distortion
Projective	Unstructured stimuli create maximum freedom of response; scoring is subjective, though some objective methods exist	"Correct" answers not obvious; designed to tap unconscious impulses; flexible use	Reliability and validity lower than that of objective tests

those who did well in their jobs with those who were fired or forced to resign due to problems such as excessive use of force, inappropriate use of firearms, or poor performance in crisis situations.

An "immaturity index" was created by combining scores on several MMPI scales, including the Lie scale (a validity scale designed to measure a tendency to put oneself in an unrealistically positive light), K scale (a validity scale designed to measure defensiveness), Pd scale (antisocial behavior), Ma scale (high activity and impulsiveness), and Hy scale (related to denial of problems). The immaturity index correctly classified 80 percent of the performance outcomes for these officers. Had this index been used in the initial hiring decisions, only a small fraction of the ultimately unacceptable candidates would have been hired, thus avoiding the majority of costly hiring mistakes.

Although retrospective results such as these are common, conclusions about the value of a personality test in personnel selection depends on how well it predicts the performance of potential employees. In this case, the immaturity index was found to predict the quality of first-year job performance in 86 percent of a group of newly hired officers. Promising as these results are, this MMPI-based index must be further cross-validated on additional samples in other locations, including big-city police forces. It must also be recognized that, like most such indexes, this one is not perfect; if it had been used as the only selection criterion, it would have kept about 17 percent of ultimately successful applicants from being hired. As described in Chapter 11, decisions about how many errors of this type are acceptable are difficult to make; often they are made on social and political, rather than scientific, grounds. Lawsuits against using personality tests in hiring decisions have become more frequent in recent years and, because many consider such tests to constitute an invasion of privacy, their use has been banned in the hiring of federal employees in the United States.

The privacy issue is a thorny one; the question of who owns personality test scores and what can be done with them is fraught with ethical and legal problems. In most situations, people have the right to review their own test results, but who else should have access to them? Many people worry that if test results are kept in their personnel files, potential employers or others who might review them could get the wrong impression. Just because an MMPI profile indicates that someone is unlikely to be successful as a small-town police officer, for example, it does not mean that the person won't be good at any number of other occupations. The gravity of such issues has led the American Psychological Association to publish ethical standards relating to procedures for the development, dissemination, and use of psychological tests, including personality tests (APA, 1974, 1981, 1992). The goal is not only to improve the reliability and validity of tests but also to ensure that their results are properly used and do not infringe on individuals' rights.

Future Directions

There are many approaches to the concept of personality. In spite of differences among those approaches, there are also important similarities. All recognize that personality development begins in childhood and that much of personality develops through experience. All focus on the fundamental struggle each person faces in adapting to the world, even though the various approaches describe that adaptation differently, in terms of dealing with intrapsychic conflicts, developing traits, learning responses, or growing toward self-actualization. Finally, because thoughts can affect (and be affected by) behaviors and emotions, all of the current approaches deal with cognitive processes in personality.

Continued progress toward a fuller understanding of human personality will be aided by a growing tendency to integrate the most scientifically validated aspects of all these approaches, as well as by the growth of research on the many ways in which cultural factors affect personality development. This research will focus on differences not only among geographically separate cultures (North American, African, and Asian, for example) but also among people who are born and raised in diverse subcultures within a single country such as the United States. By looking at similarities as well as differences, this research will help clarify whether or not basic dimensions such as the "big five" are culture-general (that is, universal), culture-specific, or somewhere in between (Paunonen et al., 1992; Yang & Bond, 1990).

The biological bases of personality dimensions will also receive intense attention. Researchers will work to understand which traits or temperaments are inborn, how stable they are over time, and how these are altered and shaped by specific developmental and cultural experiences (Woodall & Matthews, 1993). New conceptualizations of personality will examine personality from an evolutionary perspective, focusing on the adaptive nature of personality traits and how they have served to maintain the human species (Buss, 1991).

Objective personality assessment will become more sophisticated as it comes to rely less exclusively on self-report measures and incorporates peer observations as well (Funder & Sneed, 1993). This broader approach to assessment appears not only in the NEO-PI-R but also in a nonverbal version of the Personality Research Form, called the Nonverbal Personality Questionnaire, or NPQ (Paunonen et al., 1992). Ideally, these new testing approaches will decrease the problems of subjective bias that can cloud interpretations of some self-report personality measures.

Consistent with the emphasis on cognitive factors in all aspects of psychology, research on personality differences will continue to focus on such variables as how different people perceive and process information about themselves and their environment, what attributions they make about themselves and other people's behavior and personality, and how their emotions and thoughts interact to influence their attitudes and behavior.

If you want to learn more about personality and the latest research in the area, consider taking a basic course in personality psychology and perhaps a laboratory in personality research methods.

Summary and Key Terms

Personality refers to the pattern of psychological and behavioral characteristics that distinguishes each person from everyone else. To understand personality, researchers study many aspects of a person, usually emphasizing a particular point of view. The four main approaches to personality are the psychodynamic, the dispositional, the cognitive-behavioral, and the phenomenological. Each approach contains basic assumptions about and methods for measuring personality.

The Psychodynamic Approach

The *psychodynamic approach,* founded by Freud, assumes that personality is formed out of conflicts between basic needs and the demands of the real world. Most of these conflicts occur at an unconscious level, but their effects can be seen in everyday behavior, as well as in *free association* and other methods used in *psychoanalysis.*

The Structure and Development of Personality

Freud believed that personality has three components—the *id,* which is a reservoir of *libido* and operates on the *pleasure principle;* the *ego,* which operates according to the *reality principle;* and the *superego,* which *introjects* society's rules and values. These structures are often in unconscious conflict. Various ego *defense mechanisms,* such as *repression,* keep these conflicts from becoming conscious. Freud proposed that the focus of conflict changes as personality develops through *psychosexual stages* he called the *oral stage,* the *anal stage,* the *phallic stage* (with its *Oedipus complex*), the *latency period,* and the *genital stage.*

Variations on Freud's Personality Theory

Numerous psychodynamic theories have been based on Freud's original formulations. Prominent theorists include Adler, who held that a person's *style of life* constitutes personality; Jung, who argued that each person has both a personal and a *collective unconscious,* which stores *archetypes;* and Erikson, who proposed that personality develops through psychosocial, not psychosexual, stages. These and other psychodynamic variations tend to downplay the role of instincts and the unconscious, emphasizing instead the importance of conscious processes, ego functions, and social and cultural factors.

Contemporary Psychodynamic Theories

Current psychodynamic theories derive from the neo-Freudians' emphasis on family and social relationships. According to self-psychology and object relations theories, personality development depends mainly on the nature of early interactions between the individual (self) and one's caregivers (objects).

Evaluation of the Psychodynamic Approach

The psychodynamic approach is reflected in many forms of psychotherapy. Critics fault the approach—especially Freud's orthodox version—for its lack of a scientific base, for the vagueness of its concepts, and for its view of humans as driven by instincts.

The Dispositional Approach: Types and Traits

The *dispositional approach* assumes that personality is made up of a set of stable internal characteristics that guide behavior. These characteristics have sometimes been described as personality types but more often as traits.

Personality Types

For centuries, people have tried to place other people into a small number of personality types, but this effort has not generally been successful.

Personality Traits

Personality traits are seen by many as the building blocks out of which personality is created. These traits can appear at varying strengths in each person. Factor analysis of the results of personality tests is one method of isolating underlying personality dimensions. Recently, personality researchers have isolated five such dimensions, referred to as the *big five* or the *five-factor model.* Personality traits may be derived from inherited tendencies that provide the raw materials out of which experience molds each personality.

Evaluation of the Dispositional Approach

Dispositional theories have been criticized for being better at describing personality than at explaining it and for offering overly general descriptions of individuals. Inadequate emphasis on person-situation interactions has also raised questions about dispositional theories.

The Cognitive-Behavioral Approach

The *cognitive-behavioral approach* to personality assumes that personality is a label that summarizes the unique patterns of thinking and behavior that a person learns. Often called the social-learning approach, it expanded on traditional behavioral approaches by emphasizing the role of cognitive factors, including observational learning, in personality development.

Roots of the Cognitive-Behavioral Approach

John Watson argued that personality can be understood in terms of patterns of classically conditioned responses. B. F. Skinner emphasized the *functional analysis of behavior,* which examines how behavior has been rewarded or punished.

Rotter's Expectancy Theory

Julian Rotter noted that learning creates cognitive expectancies that guide behavior. These expectancies can include a general belief that rewards come about through either personal efforts (internal locus of control) or chance (external locus of control).

Albert Bandura and Reciprocal Determinism

Bandura believes that personality develops largely through cognitively mediated learning, including observational learning. He sees personality as reciprocally determined by interactions among cognition, environmental stimuli, and behavior. One's *self-efficacy* reflects belief in one's ability to accomplish a given task and is an important determinant of what behaviors are displayed.

Mischel's Person-Situation Theory

Mischel believes that person variables are responsible for the ways different people respond in different situations. He says that person variables interact with situational variables to determine behavior. Mischel described how the varying importance of person and situation variables may account for consistencies and inconsistencies in behavior.

Evaluation of the Cognitive-Behavioral Approach
The cognitive-behavioral approach has led to new forms of psychological treatment and many other applications. Critics of the approach see even its latest forms as too mechanistic and incapable of capturing what most psychologists mean by personality, including beliefs, intentions, and values.

The Phenomenological Approach

The *phenomenological approach,* which is also called the humanistic approach, is based on the assumption that personality is determined by the unique ways in which each individual views the world. These perceptions form a personal version of reality and guide behavior as people strive to reach their fullest human potential.

The Self Theory of Carl Rogers
Rogers believed that personality development is driven by an innate tendency toward *self-actualization,* but that one's *self-concept* is shaped also by social evaluations. He proposed that when people are free from the effects of *conditions of worth,* they will be psychologically healthy.

Maslow's Humanistic Psychology
Maslow saw self-actualization as the highest need in a hierarchy of needs. Personality development is most natural, he said, when people adopt a *growth orientation* rather than a *deficiency orientation.*

Evaluation of the Phenomenological Approach
Applications of the phenomenological approach include certain forms of psychotherapy, special group experiences designed to enhance personal growth, and Parent Effectiveness Training. Although the phenomenological approach has a large following, it has been faulted for being too idealistic, for failing to explain personality development, and for being vague and unscientific.

Linkages: Personality, Culture, and Human Development

Many people in individualist cultures of North America and Europe are taught to believe in the importance of self-worth and personal distinction. This independent self-system contrasts with the interdependent self-system often fostered in collectivist cultures, where the self is defined mainly in relation to family or other groups. Contrasting definitions of the self in different cultures, and for males and females, tend to exert differing influences on the development of personality.

Assessing Personality

Personality is usually assessed through some combination of observations, interviews, and tests.

Objective Tests
Objective tests present true-false or other written items and result in scores that can easily be compared to group norms. The MMPI and the NEO-PI-R are prominent examples of objective tests.

Projective Tests
Based on psychodynamic theories, *projective tests* present ambiguous stimuli in an attempt to reveal unconscious personality characteristics.

Using Personality Tests
Personality tests, especially the objective variety, have been employed in an effort to identify people suited for certain occupations. They can be helpful in this regard, but their use raises a number of legal and ethical questions.

Chapter 15

Psychological Disorders

Outline

During his freshman year at college, Mark decided to take a blood test for HIV, the virus that causes AIDS. Although Mark's test revealed no HIV infection, he was not as relieved as he thought he would be. He began to think of what he had done since the testing. "What if I contracted the virus after the test?" The thought that he might have HIV obsessed him all the more when he discovered that HIV is not detectable for about six months after exposure to it. He had another test, also negative, but he still worried. He decided that sexual abstinence and absolute cleanliness were the only ways to ensure safety. Mark's thoughts turned to the places in which he might contract HIV. A call to the Center for Disease Control AIDS hotline and extensive reading in the library revealed that the AIDS virus can live outside of the human body for anywhere from ten minutes to several hours or even days; no one really knows for sure.

Mark concluded from this uncertainty that HIV could live indefinitely outside of the body and could therefore be anywhere and everywhere. He began to scrub himself whenever he touched people's hands, money, door knobs, walls and floors, anything. People with AIDS, he thought, could have touched these things, or they might have bled on the street and he might have tracked their infected blood into his car and house and bathroom. Eventually he felt he had to scrub everything around him up to 40 times in each direction; it took him several exhausting hours simply to shower and dress. He washed himself and the shower knobs before touching them, and, once in the shower, he felt he had to wash his body in cycles of 13 strokes. If his feet touched the bare floor, he had to wash them again before putting on his underwear to ensure that his feet would not contaminate the fabric and then his genitals. He was sure his hands, rubbed raw from constant washing, were especially susceptible to infection so he wore gloves at all times except in the summer, when he wrapped his fingers in flesh-colored bandages. The process of protecting himself from HIV—which eventually included repeatedly cleaning his room, car, clothes, books, magazines, and videos—was wearing him out and severely restricting his activities; he could not go anywhere without first considering the risk of infection.

Obviously, Mark has psychological problems. In fact, professionals diagnosed him as displaying a form of mental disorder, also known as psychological disorder, or psychopathology. **Psychopathology** involves patterns of thought, emotion, and behavior that are maladaptive, disruptive, or uncomfortable either for the person affected or for others. Psychopathology is a social as well as a personal matter, and it has attracted the attention of psychologists in many subfields (see the Linkages diagram).

For centuries, psychopathology has fascinated people, in part because its appearance is difficult to predict. Sometime in their lives, most people encounter tragedy or trauma—a death, the loss of a job, a financial disaster—but somehow they adjust and go on. For some people, however, a single crisis can be psychologically shattering. Other individuals suffer mental disorders even though there is no apparent trauma.

Surveys have found that in any one-year period 28.1 percent of the adult population in the United States alone shows mild to severe mental disorder and that nearly one-third have experienced a disorder sometime in their lives (Meyers et al., 1984; Regier et al., 1993; Robins et al., 1984). More than 22 percent of American children display significant mental disorder in any given year (Costello et al., 1988). These overall rates of mental disorder are found, with only minor variations, in all segments of American society (see Figure 15.1), including males and females in all ethnic groups (Burnham et al., 1987; Canino et al., 1987; Peterson et al., 1993). What determines who will "break down" and who will not? Is it a matter of will power, genetics, neurotransmitters, learned skills, sheer luck, or something else? In this chapter we describe major categories of psychological disorders, discuss some of their possible causes, and examine critical issues surrounding the nature of psychopathology.

Understanding Psychological Disorders: Some Basic Issues

Most people agree that psychological disorders are typically signaled by *abnormal* behavior or mental processes, but there is less agreement, across cultures and even within cultures, about exactly what be-

Linkages

The questions in this diagram illustrate some of the relationships between the topic of this chapter, psychological disorders, and the topics of other chapters. In their efforts to describe and explain psychological disorders, psychologists rely heavily on concepts and data from many areas of psychology, as well as from other sciences. Remember that the questions shown in this diagram are only a sample of these links; stay alert for others as you read. The page numbers indicate where the questions in the diagram are discussed. ∎

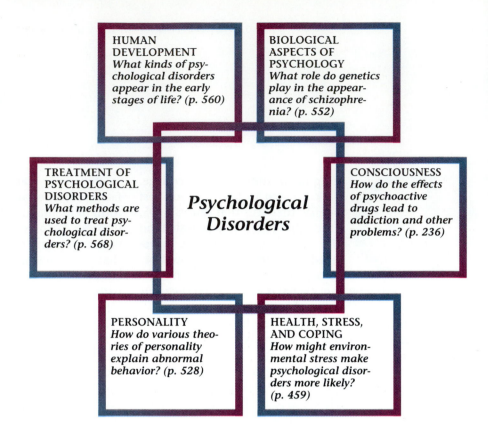

HUMAN DEVELOPMENT
What kinds of psychological disorders appear in the early stages of life? (p. 560)

BIOLOGICAL ASPECTS OF PSYCHOLOGY
What role do genetics play in the appearance of schizophrenia? (p. 552)

TREATMENT OF PSYCHOLOGICAL DISORDERS
What methods are used to treat psychological disorders? (p. 568)

Psychological Disorders

CONSCIOUSNESS
How do the effects of psychoactive drugs lead to addiction and other problems? (p. 236)

PERSONALITY
How do various theories of personality explain abnormal behavior? (p. 528)

HEALTH, STRESS, AND COPING
How might environmental stress make psychological disorders more likely? (p. 459)

This individual is surely unusual, but whether he will be labeled "abnormal" and perhaps required to have treatment for psychological disorder depends on a number of factors, the most important of which is how abnormality is defined by those he most immediately affects and by the larger culture in which he lives.

haviors or mental processes should be considered abnormal and just when treatment is required. Everyday decisions about these issues depend upon a combination of formal laws, social rules, and cultural traditions that shape the way a culture reacts to its members. If you live in a tolerant culture and do not upset other people too much, you can behave in unusual ways and still not be formally diagnosed or treated for psychopathology. Our collection of news clippings includes a story about a man in Long Beach, California, who moved out of his apartment and left behind sixty thousand pounds of rocks, chunks of concrete, and slabs of cement neatly boxed and stacked in every room. In a less tolerant time or place he might be taken into custody for treatment. We begin our exploration of psychopathology by considering some factors that determine what is considered normal and abnormal in various cultures today.

What Is Abnormal?

Most people would agree that it is abnormal for a person to attempt suicide every time he or she is upset with the way a romantic partner is behaving. On the other hand, very few people would label as "abnormal" someone who wears long-sleeved shirts in the summer. It is the vast range of behaviors between these extremes that causes debate over what is normal, what is merely odd, and what is abnormal. Here are three typical approaches to defining abnormality.

The Statistical Approach One straightforward way of deciding whether behavior is abnormal is to ask how common it is. From this perspective, whatever occurs frequently or is close to the behavior of the average person is considered normal. Thus, the **statistical approach** defines normal behavior in terms of what is most common, what the average person does. Abnormality is then defined as deviance from what is seen in the greatest number of people, or in the average person. For example, most people probably become angry

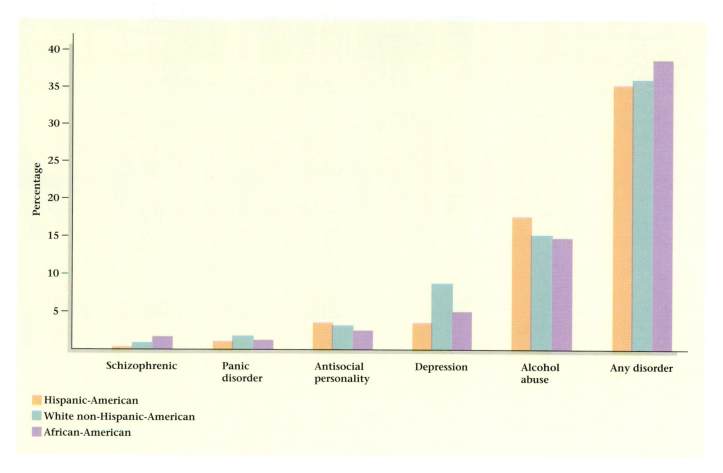

Figure 15.1
Lifetime Prevalence of Mental Disorders
Diagnostic surveys of 18,000 adults in five U.S. cities revealed that nearly one-third experienced some form of mental disorder at some time in their lives. Here are the prevalence data from these studies for several mental disorders among Hispanic-Americans, non-Hispanic-American whites, and African-Americans. Note that the size of the differences between these groups varies across disorders, but that all differences are relatively small and none are statistically significant.

Source: Data from Karno et al., 1987 and Robbins et al., 1984.

Linkages: How do norms help define abnormality? (a link to Social Behavior and Group Influences)

with a co-worker at some point over something the co-worker has done, and occasional anger is not usually considered abnormal. But if a person acts angrily toward almost everyone, almost every day, you might label this behavior abnormal, in part because it represents a large departure from what is expected from the average person.

The statistical point of view provides an apparently clear criterion for abnormality, but it presents some difficulties. For example, should people who score significantly above average on IQ tests be considered abnormal? The statistical approach does not take into account the fact that some "deviant" behaviors, such as the ability to speak twelve languages, are valuable and desirable. Another problem with the statistical view is that it equates normality with *conformity*. But nonconformists are often creative thinkers. If everyone behaved the same, the research that led to computers, organ transplants, and space exploration might never have been done.

The Valuative Approach   An alternative to the statistical view of abnormality is the **valuative approach**: it says that behavior is abnormal if a person acts in ways that are not valued, no matter how many other people also behave that way. This criterion is sometimes called a *sociocultural standard* because it equates abnormality with violations of social rules and cultural norms. The valuative approach gets around the problem of calling geniuses and other socially valued nonconformists "abnormal." Valuative criteria mean that abnormality will be defined *relative* to prevailing social or cultural standards. Thus, unusual behavior might be ignored by this definition if it does not violate

Abuse of the valuative approach to abnormality can lead to persecution of people who oppose those in power. Mental hospitals in the former Soviet Union were notorious as warehouses for political dissidents who were labeled mentally ill because they challenged the prevailing social order.

prevailing standards in a specific culture or if it is particularly valued in that culture.

Is every devalued behavior truly abnormal, even if it is prevalent? If a society's answer is yes, very few people will be considered normal because there are so many ways of being abnormal and because most people probably display at least one of them at some time or another. Valuative criteria can be overly restrictive. Further, stress resulting from constant efforts to conform to all of a society's valuative criteria might itself promote anxiety and other psychological problems. And valuative criteria can be perverted to serve the goals of those in power. In the early 1800s, for example, a mental disorder called *drapetomania* was said to afflict American slaves. Its sole symptom was running away from one's owner (Landrine, 1991).

The valuative definition of abnormality is inherently variable because social rules and values differ from culture to culture, within different subcultures, and from generation to generation. What is normal in one culture may be abnormal in another. On one Pacific island, gifts of food are assumed to be poisoned, and a poor crop is attributed to magical theft of nutrients from the soil. Anyone who is friendly is considered crazy (MacAndrew & Edgerton, 1969). Even within a culture, different groups—violent street gangs and state legislators, for example—may define normality in significantly different ways. The effect of time on definitions of abnormality can be seen in America's changing views of homosexuality. Once widely condemned as sinful, illegal, and a form of mental disorder, the status of homosexuality in civilian and military life is now hotly debated as many segments of society accept it as an alternative lifestyle to be legally protected from discrimination.

The Practical Approach   In reality, no single definition of abnormality is fully satisfactory. Therefore, mental health professionals, courts, and the public tend to use a combination of the statistical and valuative views. In this **practical approach,** judgments about abnormality and about who should receive treatment depend on (1) the *content* of behavior (what a person does), (2) the *context* of behavior (where and when the person does it and its effect on others and their rights), and (3) the *subjective consequences* of the behavior for the person (how much suffering and distress the person feels).

With regard to *content,* behavior is likely to be judged abnormal by a culture if it (1) is maladaptive or disabling, (2) appears bizarre or irrational, or (3) is unpredictable and uncontrolled. Still, people will tolerate a considerable amount of bizarre and unpredictable behavior in themselves and others if the behavior is not frequent or disruptive enough to interfere with the conduct of everyday life. This *dysfunction* or *disability criterion* is probably the most fundamental aspect of judgments about the content of behavior. One successful businessman lined all his clothes with newspaper to protect himself against harmful radiation from alien spacecraft. Everyone at the office thought this was bizarre, but because he did his job efficiently, his behavior did not lead to formal diagnosis or treatment.

The second dimension of the practical approach relates to *context*—where and when behavior occurs. How would you feel if you were asked to enter an elevator and stare directly at another passenger during the ride? Or to tell jokes at a funeral? If you would hesitate, it is probably because you recognize that these actions would be inappropriate to the situation. Behaviors may be labeled abnormal if people use poor judgment about where they display them, thereby making others uncomfortable. At the same time, the practical approach to abnormality says that people can perform all sorts of unconventional activities as long as they do not create too much discomfort for others and as long as they confine these activities to private places or to situations where everyone present approves. In short, decisions about whether the content of behavior is abnormal are often modified in light of its context.

The third dimension of the practical approach—the *subjective consequences* of behavior—recognizes that even behavior that does not directly interfere with everyday functioning or disturb anyone else may cause the person to suffer. Subjective distress is not a necessary feature of abnormality. But when—as in the case of Mark, which opened this chapter—suffering is prolonged and unusually intense, it may be sufficient for a judgment of abnormality.

In most Western cultures, nudity is not considered abnormal when in private or even on a designated nude beach. But it is not considered acceptable in most public situations, including on campus. When this University of California at Berkeley student—shown "dressed" for a court appearance—attended classes nude for several months to protest "social repression," complaints from other students led to his dismissal.

In summary, it is difficult to identify behaviors that are universally considered abnormal. The practical approach defines as *abnormal* statistically frequent or infrequent behavior that makes the person uncomfortable, that disables daily functioning, or that harms, significantly disrupts the lives, or violates the rights and values of others (Wakefield, 1992).

Explaining Psychological Disorders

Many explanations for psychological disorders have been advanced over the centuries. In the Western world, the **demonological** or **supernatural model** was dominant until about the fourth century B.C. and then again during the Middle Ages (from about the fifth to about the fifteenth century A.D.). According to this model, mental disorder is the work of supernatural forces. In medieval Europe a great deal of deviant behavior was tolerated and even encouraged if it was attributed to devotion to God. Thus, whipping oneself for one's sins was generally viewed as godly (Kroll, 1973). During the late Middle Ages, heresy (disbelief in established religious doctrine) and other unusual behaviors were viewed as the work of the devil and his witches; heretics were burned at the stake and exorcisms were performed to rid people of controlling demons.

Although supernatural causes of abnormality are not emphasized in Western cultures today, many other cultures around the world—as well as certain ethnic and religious subcultures in North America—employ supernatural (especially demonic) explanations of disordered thinking and behavior. For example, the Khmer peoples of Cambodia (many of whom now live in the United States) have a concept, known as *cku ʒt,* that encompasses a wide range of mental and behavioral problems. These problems begin when major life disruptions—such as being caught in or displaced from a war zone—throw the brain and body out of balance, and disturb relationships with past lives, with destiny, and one's ancestors. As a result, say the Khmer, affected people are left vulnerable to brain collapse, vengeance by ancestors, and interference from evil spirits and sorcerers (Eisenbruch, 1992). As immigration patterns increase cultural diversity in the populations of many Western countries, awareness of *cku ʒt* and other non-Western conceptions of disorder is increasing as well. In the next chapter we discuss efforts made by Western mental health professionals to meet the needs of clients from diverse cultural backgrounds.

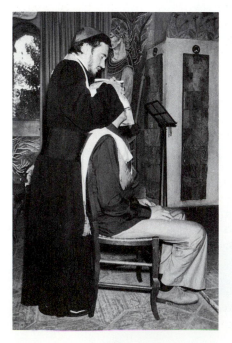

Though no longer dominant in Western culture, supernatural explanations of mental disorder and supernaturally oriented cures, such as this exorcism, remain a part of many cultures and subcultures around the world.

The Medical Model and Mental Illness   Alternatives to the supernatural model of disorder appeared as early as the fourth century B.C., when the ancient Greek physician Hippocrates introduced a **medical model** of abnormality. He said that disorders such as depression were the result of physical problems, not supernatural causes. Later Greek and Roman physicians expanded on or revised Hippocrates' views, giving rise to the notion of *mental illness.* As the Middle Ages drew to a close, the medical model regained prominence in Western cultures, and specialized hospitals or *asylums* for the insane began to appear throughout Europe. Medical doctors again took over responsibility for those considered mentally ill.

The medical model, also known today as the **biological model,** focuses on biological disturbances in the brain and continues to shape the ways that people in Western cultures think about and treat psychological disorders. People tend to refer to psychological disorders as mental illness, and they commonly turn to medical doctors and hospitals for treatment. Neuroscientists and others who investigate these disorders typically approach them as they would approach any physical illness, seeing problematic symptoms stemming from an underlying illness that can be diagnosed, treated, and cured.

The enduring influence of the medical model is based partly on the fact that there are forms of abnormality that have a definite biological cause (Spitzer et al., 1992). They include disorders such as **dementia,** which is characterized by

Hogarth's eighteenth-century portrayal of "Bedlam," the colloquial name for London's St. Mary's of Bethleham hospital. Most early mental hospitals were little more than prisons where the public could buy tickets to gawk at the patients, much as people go to the zoo today.

a loss of intellectual functions. Common symptoms include disturbances in memory, personality changes, and **delirium** (a clouded state of consciousness in which the person's thinking is confused and disjointed). The most frequent causes of dementia are progressive deterioration of the brain as a result of aging or long-term alcohol abuse; acute diseases and disorders such as encephalitis, brain tumors, or head injury; and drug intoxication. In severe cases of dementia, such as Alzheimer's disease, the person may eventually become unable to recognize family members or to recall his or her name, address, or occupation.

Research in neuroscience and behavior genetics has also implicated biological factors in a number of other psychological disorders to be described later, including schizophrenia, depression, and some forms of anxiety disorder. This research suggests that such disorders are related to abnormalities in the various brain structures and/or neurotransmitters described in Chapter 4 as being important for mental functioning.

But are all psychological disorders wholly physical illnesses? Not necessarily. Most psychological disorders cannot be fully explained by biological factors alone. For example, as mentioned in Chapter 2, family studies, twin studies, and other behavior genetics investigations have found the risk of developing schizophrenia to be higher in those most closely related to schizophrenics. But we will see that, unlike eye color, people do not directly inherit schizophrenia or most other psychological disorders. Instead, they inherit brain structures and other biological characteristics that may create behavioral tendencies that predispose people to develop certain disorders under certain conditions.

Is it appropriate to consider people "sick" even when they display disorders for which no clear physical basis has been found? Traditionalists in psychiatry and psychology say yes, either because a physical cause is suspected or because psychological disorders resemble physical illness. Others say no. The most prominent and vocal of these critics is psychiatrist Thomas Szasz (pronounced "zaws"), who believes that the concept of mental illness is not only inappro-

Thomas Szasz and others have called the concept of mental illness a myth that encourages the use of drugs and hospitalization to try to solve "problems in living" that may have nothing to do with physical illness (Szasz, 1960, 1974, 1987). This approach, they say, deemphasizes the value of treatments provided by psychologists and other nonmedical professionals, and also tends to place mental patients in an undesirable, inferior social role in which they are to wait passively for a physician's "cure" rather than trying to improve on their own.

priate but harmful (Szasz, 1960, 1987). Szasz and others believe that labeling people as mentally ill affects what others think and expect of them, perhaps leading the labeled people to continue deviant behavior because others expect it of them. Further, he believes that calling people "sick patients" puts all the power and responsibility for cure in the hands of medical authorities. The implication is that patients need take no responsibility for their condition or their treatment, other than to follow doctors' orders.

Szasz prefers to think of mental disorders that do not have a clear, specific physical cause as "problems in living." His objections to the concept of mental illness have stimulated a great deal of debate. They have also prompted increasing recognition of the value of nonmedical concepts of abnormal behavior and (as described in Chapter 16) an expansion of the legal rights of those who receive treatment for mental disorder. However, thinking of psychological disorders as merely "problems in living" creates some problems of its own. Doing so risks trivializing the suffering of many of those who experience intense personal distress, and it may discourage some people from seeking professional help. In other words, there is danger in replacing one extreme position ("all disorder is illness") with another ("no disorder is illness").

Linkages: Psychological Disorders and Approaches to Personality

How do various theories of personality explain abnormal behavior?

Sigmund Freud began to question a different aspect of the medical model late in the 1800s, long before Szasz came on the scene. Freud did not quarrel with its mental illness analogy, but he challenged its presumption that psychological disorders had only physical causes. In doing so, he created the first influential *psychological* model of mental disorders. Freud's explanations of these disorders came as part of his more general psychodynamic approach to personality, which we described in Chapter 14. As also noted in that chapter, cognitive-behavioral and phenomenological approaches to personality suggest their own psychological explanations for mental disorders.

Freud's *psychodynamic approach* views psychological disorders as the result of unresolved, mostly unconscious clashes between instinctual desires of the id and the demands of the environment and society. These conflicts, he said, begin early in childhood and may create severe anxiety. Various forms of disordered thought and behavior may result from the ego's attempts to prevent anxiety from reaching consciousness.

Contemporary versions of the psychodynamic model also explain disorders in terms of early childhood experiences and unconscious processes, but they focus less on instinctual urges and more on the role of early interpersonal relationships. For example, we saw in Chapter 14 that *object relations* theorists see the lack of appropriate early attachment to, or bonding with, primary caregivers as resulting in distorted relationships that set the stage for interpersonal difficulties, low self-esteem, and a confused identity later in life.

According to the *cognitive-behavioral approach* to personality, most psychological disorders are caused by problematic learning experiences and current situations. Behavioral theorists suggest that people learn disordered behaviors in the same way that they learn any other behaviors. Just as you learned to avoid hot barbecue grills after being burned, a person who is terrified of crossing bridges probably learned this fear through negative experiences on a bridge. Thus, while biological factors might create predispositions for disorder, behaviorists say the appearance of disordered behavior mainly depends on learning. The cognitive-behavioral approach suggests that those who violate a culture's expectations for normal behavior need not be seen as sick but, rather, as having learned maladaptive ways of thinking and behaving (Kanfer, 1992). Thus, a person's *behavior* can be labeled abnormal without labeling as abnormal the person displaying it.

As described in the personality chapter, those who take a cognitive-behavioral approach emphasize as well how observational learning, expectancies, and other thought processes affect (and are affected by) people's interactions with the world (Kanfer, 1992). From this perspective, a person's depression, for example, would be seen as stemming not only from external events, such as the loss of a job, but also from learned patterns of distressing thoughts about events, such as "I never do anything right."

The *phenomenological approach* to personality sees human behavior as guided by the way each person perceives the world. If all goes well, the person naturally develops his or her unique potential. However, if self-actualization is blocked, psychological growth stops and psychological disorder may appear as a signal of the blockage. Growth is usually obstructed by a failure to be in touch with and express one's true feelings. When this happens, the person's perceptions of reality begin to be distorted. The greater the perceptual distortion and the less the emotional contact with one's feelings, the more serious the psychological disorder. Phenomenologists assume that abnormal behavior, no matter how unusual or seemingly irrational, is a reasonable reaction to the world, as the person perceives it.

Psychodynamic, behavioral, and phenomenological approaches to personality all provide logical explanations for psychological disorders. However, as is the case with biological factors, psychological approaches alone have proven inadequate to explain all forms of abnormality. This is partly because many disorders have both biological and psychological causes, but psychological explanations are also limited to the extent that their conceptions of disorder reflect the experiences and assumptions characteristic of Western cultures. Thus, they may not apply as well to people from other cultural backgrounds.

Sociocultural Factors in Psychological Disorders

A complete account of psychological disorders must include attention to the social and cultural factors that influence people's behavior and mental processes. We have already seen that values, norms, and beliefs are among the sociocultural factors that influence which behaviors are considered abnormal in a given time and place.

Sociocultural factors also influence the form that disorders take, their severity or duration, and the ways in which they tend to be dealt with (Carson & Butcher, 1992).

In the United States, for example, women are two to three times more likely than men to experience depression. This gender difference holds for European-Americans, Hispanic-Americans, and African-Americans and also appears in many other countries from Kenya to Iceland (Matlin, 1993; Nolen-Hoeksma, 1990). Some investigators have suggested that hormonal differences might account for this gender difference, but Margaret Matlin and others argue instead that it is largely due to the impact of sociocultural attitudes and values that demean women, limit their opportunities, and create gender roles that lead women to react to stressful events with feelings of helplessness and depression (Matlin, 1993). In accordance with *their* gender roles, says Matlin, men in these cultures are especially likely to react to stressors with aggressiveness and increased alcohol consumption, and are thus more likely to display drug abuse disorders, for example, rather than depression (Matlin, 1993; Nolen-Hoeksma, 1990).

According to one sociocultural analysis, *culture-general* psychological disorders are found in virtually all cultures, while *culture-specific* disorders are seen only in certain cultures (Brislin, 1993). This distinction is not cut-and-dried, however, because the sources and manifestations of even culture-general disorders tend to be related to the beliefs, values, and traditions of particular cultures. Again consider depression, for example. Depression appears in virtually all cultures, but its causes and symptoms vary from culture to culture (Manson, 1994). Feelings of guilt are common in depressed people in North America and Europe, but not in Nigeria. Similarly, concern with bodily functioning is a major component of depression in China and some other cultures, but is far less prominent elsewhere (Brislin, 1993).

The role of sociocultural factors is especially clear in culture-specific disorders. In Southeast Asia, Southern China, and Malaysia, for example, one encounters a condition called *Koro*. Primarily a male condition, the victim fears that his penis will shrivel, retract into the body, and cause him to die (in females, the fear relates to a shriveling of the breasts). *Koro* appears only in cultures holding the specific supernatural beliefs that explain it, but epidemics of *Koro* are often triggered by economic hard times (Tseng et al., 1992).

In short, sociocultural factors can play a major role in creating unusual forms of mental disorder and in shaping the specific symptoms of those more commonly seen around the world. And because sociocultural factors almost always lead to differential treatment of people on the basis of their gender or ethnicity, and thus to differing roles and stressors, explanations of psychological disorders must always take these factors into account.

Diathesis-Stress as an Integrative Approach   Research on psychological disorders suggests that most of them arise from a varying combination of sources, including biological imbalances, hereditary characteristics, brain damage, enduring psychological characteristics, socioculturally mediated learning experiences, and stressful life events. These multiple causes are taken into account by the **diathesis-stress approach**, which suggests that people's inherited biological characteristics and early learning experiences can create a predisposition (or *diathesis*) toward development of a psychological disorder, but that the actual appearance of that disorder depends on what stressors they encounter in life.

For example, a person may have inherited a tendency toward sadness or may have learned depressing patterns of thinking about events, but expression of these predispositions may appear as a depressive disorder only under particularly stressful circumstances, such as a financial crisis. If few severely stressful

Table 15.1
Five Ways of Explaining Psychopathology

José is a married fifty-five-year-old electronics technician and the healthy and vigorous father of two adult children. He was recently forced to go on medical leave because of a series of unexpected, uncontrollable panic attacks in which he experienced dizziness, heart palpitations, sweating, and fear of impending death. These attacks have also prevented him from engaging in his favorite pastime, scuba diving, for fear that a panic attack under water would be fatal. However, he has been able to maintain a part-time computer business out of his home. (Panic disorder is discussed in more detail later in this chapter; the outcome of this case is described in Chapter 16).

Approach	Possible Cause	Possible Treatment
Medical/biological	Organic disorder (brain tumor?); endocrine (e.g., thyroid) disorder	Drugs, surgery
Psychodynamic	Unconscious conflicts and desires; instinctual impulses breaking through ego defenses into consciousness, causing panic.	Psychotherapy to gain insight into unconscious
Cognitive-behavioral	Bodily stress symptoms interpreted as signs of serious illness or impending death. Receives reward in the form of relief from work stress and opportunity to work at home.	Develop cognitive coping techniques such as relaxation and noncatastrophic thinking
Phenomenological	Failure to recognize genuine feelings about work and his place in life. Fear of expressing himself.	Therapy to put him in touch with feelings about life and work
Diathesis-stress	Biologically predisposed to be overly responsive to stressors. Stress of work and extra activity exceeds capacity to cope and triggers panic as stress response.	Learn to monitor stress level, learn new stress-coping techniques, and change lifestyle as needed

situations occur, or if the person has skills adequate for coping with them, depression may not occur, or may be less intense. You will encounter the diathesis-stress approach repeatedly in discussions of the causes of a number of psychological disorders described in this chapter. Table 15.1 provides an example of how this approach, and the other explanatory approaches we have described, might view and treat a particular case of psychopathology.

Classifying Psychological Disorders

In spite of differing definitions of abnormality within and across cultures, there does seem to be a set of behavior patterns that roughly defines the range of most abnormality in most cultures. It has long been the goal of those who study abnormal behavior to establish a system of classifying these patterns in order to understand and deal with them. *Psychodiagnosis* is the traditional term for the process of classifying patients' mental disorders. (Proponents of the cognitive-behavioral and phenomenological models favor the term *assessment*, which they feel reflects their emphasis on describing clients in more detail than diagnostic labels can provide.)

In 1917 the American Psychiatric Association began publishing what has become the "official" diagnostic classification system, the *Diagnostic and Statistical Manual of Mental Disorders (DSM)*. Each subsequent edition of the DSM has included more categories. The latest edition, DSM-IV, contains more than three hundred specific diagnostic labels. (A less extensive listing of mental disorders appears as one section of the World Health Organization's *International Classification of Diseases,* now in its tenth edition, ICD–10).

A Classification System: DSM-IV

DSM-IV describes the abnormal patterns of thinking and behavior that define various mental disorders. For each disorder, DSM-IV provides specific criteria outlining the conditions that must be present before a person is given that diagnostic label. A diagnostician using DSM-IV can evaluate a person on five dimensions, or *axes,* which together provide a broad picture of a person's problems and their context. On Axis I the diagnostician records major mental disorders such as schizophrenia or major depressive disorder; Table 15.2 lists these major disorder categories. Axis II includes personality disorders. Any medical conditions that might be important in understanding a person's mental or behavioral problems are listed on Axis III. On Axis IV the diagnostician notes psychosocial and environmental problems (such as loss of a loved one, physical or sexual abuse, discrimination, unemployment, poverty, homelessness, inadequate health care) that are important for understanding a person's psychological problems. Finally, a rating (from 100 down to 1) of the person's current level of psychological, social, and occupational functioning appears on Axis V. Here is a sample of a complete DSM-IV diagnosis.

Axis I Major depressive disorder, single episode; alcohol abuse.

Axis II Dependent personality disorder.

Axis III Alcoholic cirrhosis of the liver.

Axis IV Problems with primary support group (death of spouse).

Axis V Global assessment of functioning = 50.

Because they had become too vague, two time-honored terms—neurosis and psychosis—no longer appear as major categories in the DSM. **Neurosis** referred to conditions in which some form of anxiety was the major characteristic. **Psychosis** referred to conditions involving more extreme problems that left the patient "out of touch with reality" or unable to function on a daily basis. The disorders once gathered under these headings now appear in various Axis I categories in DSM-IV.

Purposes and Problems of Psychodiagnosis   A major goal of psychodiagnosis is to determine the nature of clients' problems so that the most appropriate treatment can be given. Diagnoses are also important for research on the causes of mental disorders. If researchers can accurately and reliably place patients into groups with similar disorders, they will have a better chance of spotting commonalities in genetic features, biological abnormalities, and environmental experiences that might differentiate people in one disorder group from those in other groups, thereby providing clues to how the conditions began.

Diagnosis must be done with care, however, because it can have unintended but disastrous effects. For example, while a Chinese immigrant named David Tom was being treated for tuberculosis in an American hospital, a diagnostician failed to realize that his "odd language" was actually an unusual Chinese dialect and labeled him severely mentally ill. Tom was kept in mental institutions for more than thirty years. When the error was finally discovered in 1983, he was released, but his physical and mental condition had deteriorated so much during his hospital stay that he would spend the rest of his life in a group home for former mental patients.

The potential for misdiagnosis, and for the biasing effects of diagnostic labels, was highlighted by a study in which David Rosenhan (1973) and eight

Table 15.2
The Diagnostic and Statistical Manual (DSM) of the American Psychiatric Association

Axis I of the fourth edition (DSM-IV) lists the major categories of mental disorders. Axis II contains personality disorders.

Axis I (Clinical Syndromes)

1. *Disorders usually first diagnosed in infancy, childhood, or adolescence* Problems such as hyperactivity, childhood fears, abnormal aggressiveness or other notable misconduct, frequent bedwetting or soiling, and other problems in normal social and behavioral development. Mental retardation and autistic disorder (severe impairment in social and behavioral development), as well as other problems in the development of skill in reading, speaking, mathematics, or English.

2. *Delirium, dementia, amnestic, and other cognitive disorders* Problems caused by physical deterioration of the brain due to aging, disease, drugs or other chemicals, or other possibly unknown causes. These problems can appear as an inability to "think straight" (delirium) or as loss of memory and other intellectual functions (dementia).

3. *Substance-related disorders* Psychological, behavioral, physical, social, or legal problems caused by dependence on or abuse of a variety of chemical substances, including alcohol, heroin, cocaine, amphetamines, hallucinogens, PCP, marijuana, and tobacco.

4. *Schizophrenia and other psychotic disorders* Severe conditions characterized by abnormalities in thinking, perception, emotion, movement, and motivation that greatly interfere with daily functioning. Problems involving false beliefs (delusions) about such things as being loved by some high-status person, having inflated worth or power, or being persecuted, spied on, cheated on, followed, harassed, or kept from reaching important goals. Serious mental problems that are similar to but not as intense as schizophrenic or delusional disorders.

5. *Mood disorders* (also called *affective disorders*) Severe disturbances of mood, especially depression, overexcitement (mania), or alternating episodes of each extreme (as in bipolar disorder).

6. *Anxiety disorders* Specific fears (phobias), panic attacks, generalized feelings of dread, rituals of thought and action (obsessive-compulsive behavior) aimed at controlling anxiety, and problems caused by traumatic events, such as rape or miliary combat (see Chapter 13 for more on posttraumatic stress disorder).

7. *Somatoform disorders* Physical symptoms, such as paralysis and blindness, that have no physical cause. Unusual preoccupation with physical health or with nonexistent or elusive physical problems (hypochondriasis, somatization disorder, pain disorder).

8. *Factitious disorders* False mental disorders, which are intentionally produced to satisfy some psychological need.

9. *Dissociative disorders* Psychologically caused problems of consciousness and self-identification, including loss of memory (amnesia) or the development of more than one identity (multiple personality).

10. *Sexual and gender identity disorders* Problems of (a) finding sexual arousal through unusual objects or situations (like baby shoes or exposing oneself), (b) unsatisfactory sexual activity (sexual dysfunction; see Chapter 12), or (c) identifying with the opposite gender.

11. *Eating disorders* Problems associated with eating too little (anorexia nervosa) or binge eating followed by self-induced vomiting (bulimia nervosa). (See Chapter 12).

12. *Sleep disorders* Severe problems involving the sleep-wake cycle, especially an inability to sleep well at night or to stay awake during the day. (See Chapter 7.)

(Continued)

13. *Impulse control disorders*   Compulsive gambling, stealing, or fire setting.
14. *Adjustment disorders*   Failure to adjust to or deal well with such stressors as divorce, financial problems, family discord, or other unhappy life events.

Axis II (Personality Disorders)

Personality disorders   Diagnostic labels given to individuals who may or may not receive an Axis I diagnosis but who show lifelong behavior patterns that are unsatisfactory to them or that disturb other people. The problematic features of their personality may involve unusual suspiciousness, unusual ways of thinking, self-centeredness, shyness, overdependency, excessive concern with neatness and detail, or overemotionality, among others.

associates presented themselves at different psychiatric hospitals. Each person complained of the same faked symptoms: hearing a voice that said "empty," "hollow," and "thud." Otherwise, they reported only truthful facts about their very normal lives. All were admitted to the hospitals as patients, most with a diagnosis of schizophrenia, a serious disorder. Once in the hospital, these "patients" behaved normally and reported no voices or other symptoms. However, they were not detected as frauds by the staff (only by actual patients on the same wards). The staff interpreted actions such as taking notes about their experiences as symptoms that confirmed the original diagnoses. Why? Interpretations vary, but the main reason is probably that, as discussed in Chapter 6, on perception, people tend to see what they expect to see. Hospital staff expect to see disorders, thus making it more likely that whatever the volunteers said or did would be interpreted as abnormal. In addition, because of the anchoring heuristic and confirmation bias (discussed in Chapter 10), the diagnosticians tended to stick to their original hypothesis that these people were mentally ill, keeping them in the hospital for an average of 19 days (some stayed as long as 52 days) before the study ended.

Cases such as these have fueled decades of debate over the pros and cons of psychodiagnosis. One major concern is *interrater reliability,* which is the degree to which different diagnosticians give the same diagnostic label to the same person. Agreement on many diagnoses has improved since about 1980, when DSM-III introduced specific criteria for assigning each diagnosis. Some studies indicate interrater agreement as high as 83 percent on schizophrenia and mood disorder, and agreement for many other Axis I categories in the high 70s (Corty, Lehman & Myers, 1993; Grove, 1987; Matarazzo, 1983). However, there are also instances of much lower reliability figures on Axis I disorders such as phobia (Mannuzza, Martin & Gallops, 1989). Reliability tends to be lower for diagnosis of the Axis II personality disorders (Mellsop et al., 1982) and for childhood disorders (Bemporad & Schwab, 1986). In one study at a New York psychiatric hospital, very different diagnoses were given to the same patients by different clinicians in as many as 75 percent of 131 randomly chosen cases (Lipton & Simon, 1985).

A second important question about psychodiagnosis concerns its *validity;* that is, do diagnostic labels give accurate information about the person? This is a difficult question because it is hard to find a fully acceptable standard for accuracy. Should the diagnosis be compared to the judgments of experts? Or should it be tested against the course of the patient's disorder? Despite these problems, there is evidence supporting the validity of some DSM criteria (Drake & Vaillant, 1985; Robins & Helzer, 1986), even though the validity for many categories remains too low. Of course, no shorthand label can specify exactly what each person's problems are or exactly how that person will behave in the future. All that can be reasonably expected of a diagnostic system is that it allows informative, general descriptions of the types of problems displayed by people who have been placed in different categories.

Thinking Critically

Is Psychodiagnosis Biased?

Some researchers and clinicians suggest that bias among diagnosticians contributes to problems with the reliability and validity of diagnostic labels. Like other people, diagnosticians hold expectations and stereotypes about certain groups of people, and these cognitive biases could color their judgments about how to label the behavior displayed by members of these groups.

What am I being asked to believe or accept?

It has been alleged that a woman will be given a different, probably more severe, diagnosis than a man who presents similar symptoms, and that simply because they are members of a particular ethnic group, some people are diagnosed as suffering certain disorders more often than those in other groups. Gender is indeed an important variable—some disorders occur more often in men, others in women—but significant gender bias in diagnosis has not been found even though it has been studied a great deal (Matlin, 1993; Mowbray, Herman & Hazel, 1992; Nolen-Hoeksma, 1990). Here, we focus on ethnicity as a possible biasing factor. It is of special interest not only because it has been studied extensively but also because there is evidence that ethnicity, like social class and gender, is an important variable in the development of mental illness. Thus the argument to be considered here is that clinicians in the United States base their diagnoses partly on the ethnic group to which their clients belong and, more specifically, that there is bias against African-Americans.

What evidence is available to support the assertion?

Several facts suggest the possibility of ethnic bias in psychodiagnosis. For example, African-American people receive the diagnosis of schizophrenia more frequently than European-Americans do (Manderscheid & Barrett, 1987). Further, relative to their presence in the general population, African-Americans are overrepresented in public mental hospitals, where the most serious forms of disorder are seen, and underrepresented in private hospitals and outpatient clinics, where less severe problems are treated (Lindsey & Paul, 1989; Snowden & Cheung, 1990).

Are there alternative ways of interpreting the evidence?

Differences in diagnosis or treatment between ethnic groups do not automatically point to bias based on ethnicity. Perhaps there are real differences in psychological functioning associated with different ethnic groups. For example, if, on the average, African-Americans are exposed to more major stressors such as poverty and violence, they could be more vulnerable to more serious forms of mental disorder. Poverty, not diagnostic bias, could also be responsible for the fact that African-Americans seek help more often at less expensive public hospitals rather than at more expensive private ones.

What additional evidence would help to evaluate the alternatives?

Do African-Americans actually display more signs of mental disorder, or do diagnosticians just perceive them as more disordered? One way of approaching this question would be to conduct experiments in which diagnosticians assign labels to clients on the basis of case histories, test scores, and the like. Unknown to the diagnosticians, the cases would be selected so that pairs of clients show about the same objective amount of disorder, but one member of the pair is identified as European-American, the other as African-American. Bias among the clinicians would be suggested if the African-American member of each pair more often received a diagnosis or a more severe diagnosis. However, studies like this are difficult to conduct in clinical settings.

A strategy that has been used with real clinical populations has clinicians conduct extensive, detailed interviews with patients and then reach a diagnosis and a judgment of the severity of the symptoms. These diagnoses and judgments are then statistically analyzed in equations that examine which variables predict the actual diagnoses the patients received when admitted to the hospital. If, after controlling for the type and severity of symptoms, a researcher discovers that African-Americans are still diagnosed with a certain disorder more often than European-Americans, evidence for bias is rather strong. In studies that seek to control for the amount and severity of symptoms reported by African-American and European-American patients, African-Americans are indeed more frequently diagnosed as schizophrenic (Pavkov, Lewis & Lyons, 1989). In contrast, a large-scale study of mental disorder found that when people were interviewed and diagnosed in their own homes, the diagnosis of schizophrenia was given only slightly more often to African-Americans than to European-Americans (Snowden & Cheung, 1990; Robins et al., 1984). In other words, there is little evidence that schizophrenia is more common among African-Americans in the community, but they appear more likely to receive this diagnosis when entering a hospital. Thus the presence of ethnic bias is suggested, at least in some diagnoses.

What conclusions are most reasonable?

Just as DSM-IV is imperfect, so are those who use it. Bias does not necessarily reflect deliberate discrimination, however; it may be unintentional. Chapters 10 and 17, on thinking and social cognition respectively, discuss how cognitive biases and stereotypes shape human thought in matters large and small. No matter how precisely researchers specify the ideal criteria for assigning diagnostic labels, it is always possible that biases and stereotypes can interfere with the objective application of those criteria.

Recognizing the imperfections of the human information-processing system, clinical researchers seek the best ways to blend their judgments with those of computers that have been programmed to weigh and combine test scores and other information in an unbiased fashion (Nietzel, Bernstein & Milich, 1994). However, our discussion in Chapter 10 of the limitations of artificial intelligence suggests that humans will always play a role in diagnosis. As long as they do, some bias is likely to remain.

Bringing the effects of that bias to some irreducible minimum requires a better understanding of it. For example, clinicians whose ethnic or socioeconomic background is different from that of their clients may not understand that, while a certain behavior, such as averting one's gaze during conversation, may be abnormal in their own cultural group, it may be quite normal in the client's subculture. Steven Lopez (1989) emphasizes the need to recognize and understand the limitations in information processing that affect clinicians, while Hope Landrine (1991) stresses the need for understanding the sociocultural bases of our concepts of normality and abnormality. Research on memory, problem solving, decision making, social attributions, and other aspects of culture and cognition may turn out to be key ingredients in reducing bias in the diagnosis of psychological disorders. ■

DSM-IV provides a convenient framework for our description of psychological disorders. We do not have the space to cover all the DSM-IV categories, so we will sample several of the most prevalent, socially significant, or unusual examples.

As you read, try not to catch "medical student's disease." Just as medical students often think they have the symptoms of every illness they read about, psychology students frequently worry that their behavior (or that of a relative or friend) signals some type of mental disorder. This is usually not the case; it is just that everyone has some problems, some of the time. It might be a good idea to review the criteria of the practical approach to abnormality and consider how frequently a problem occurs before deciding whether you or someone you know needs psychological help.

Anxiety Disorders

If you have ever been tense before an exam or a date or a visit to the dentist, you have a good idea of what anxiety feels like. Increased heart rate, sweating, rapid breathing, a dry mouth, and a sense of dread are common components of anxiety. Brief episodes of moderate anxiety are a normal part of life for most people. For others, anxiety is so intense, long standing, or disruptive to their daily lives that it is called an **anxiety disorder**.

Types of Anxiety Disorders

We discuss four types of anxiety disorders: phobia, generalized anxiety disorder, panic disorder, and obsessive-compulsive disorder. Another type, called posttraumatic stress disorder, is described in Chapter 13, on health, stress, and coping. Together, these are the most common psychological disorders in the United States.

Phobia   An intense, irrational fear of an object or situation that is not likely to be dangerous is called a **phobia**. The phobic person usually realizes that the fear makes no sense but cannot keep it from interfering with daily life. Most objects or situations are potential fear stimuli; thousands of phobias have been described (see Table 15.3).

DSM-IV classifies phobias into specific, social, and agoraphobia subtypes. **Specific phobias** involve fear and avoidance of heights, blood, animals, automobile or air travel, and other specific stimuli and situations. They are the most prevalent of the anxiety disorders, affecting some 7 to 10 percent of American adults and children (Burnham et al., 1987; Costello et al., 1988; Robins et al., 1984). Here is an example from one of the authors' files.

Mr. L. was a fifty-one-year-old office worker who became terrified whenever he had to drive over a bridge. For years, he avoided bridges by taking roundabout ways to

Table 15.3
Common Phobias

Phobias are traditionally named by identifying the Greek word for the feared object or situation, then attaching the word *phobia* to the end. Phobia is the Greek word for morbid fear, after the lesser Greek god, Phobos. Here are a few common phobias, along with their Greek names.

Name	Feared Stimulus	Name	Feared Stimulus
Acrophobia	Heights	Aerophobia	Flying
Claustrophobia	Enclosed places	Entomophobia	Insects
Hematophobia	Blood	Gamophobia	Marriage
Gephyrophobia	Crossing a bridge	Ophidiophobia	Snakes
Kenophobia	Empty rooms	Xenophobia	Strangers
Cynophobia	Dogs	Melissophobia	Bees

THE FAR SIDE   By GARY LARSON

Luposlipaphobia: The fear of being pursued by timber wolves around a kitchen table while wearing socks on a newly waxed floor.

Specific phobias are, as their name implies, usually focused on specific objects or situations and can sometimes be unusual enough to create grist for the humor mill. The discomfort and dysfunction caused by severe phobias of any kind, however, are no laughing matter.

and from work, and he refused to be a passenger in anyone else's car, lest they use a bridge. Even this very inconvenient adjustment was shattered when Mr. L. was transferred to a position requiring frequent automobile trips, many of which were over bridges. He refused the transfer and was fired.

Social phobias involve intense, persistent anxiety about being negatively evaluated by others or publicly embarrassed by doing something impulsive or humiliating. The anxiety is so great that the person's normal functioning is impaired. Common social phobias are fear of public speaking, "stage fright," fear of eating or writing in front of others, and using public rest rooms. When social phobia involves virtually all social situations in a person's life, it is referred to as "generalized social phobia."

Agoraphobia is a strong fear of being separated from a safe place like home or from a safe person, such as a spouse or close friend, or of being trapped in a place from which escape might be difficult. Attempts to leave home lead to intense anxiety and terror, so that severe agoraphobics seldom even try to go out alone. Crowded public places like theaters, shopping malls, or public transportation are particularly avoided because the person fears becoming helpless and incapacitated by some calamity such as experiencing intense anxiety or panic.

Like other phobias, agoraphobia is more often reported by women, many of whom are totally housebound by the time they seek help. Although agoraphobia occurs less frequently than specific phobias (affecting about 2.5 percent of the U.S. population), it is the phobia that most often leads people to seek treatment, mainly because it so severely disrupts everyday life (Barlow, 1988; Chambliss & Goldstein, 1980).

Generalized Anxiety Disorder   Excessive and long-lasting anxiety that is not focused on any particular object or situation marks **generalized anxiety disorder**. Because the problem occurs in virtually all situations and because the person cannot pinpoint its source, this type of anxiety is sometimes called *free-floating anxiety*. For weeks at a time, the person feels anxious and worried, sure that some disaster is imminent. The person becomes jumpy and irritable; sound sleep is impossible. Fatigue, inability to concentrate, and physiological signs of anxiety are also common (Borkovec & Inz, 1990).

Panic Disorder   For some people, anxiety takes the form of **panic disorder**. Like the man described in Table 15.1, people suffering from panic disorder experience terrifying *panic attacks* that often come without warning or obvious cause and are marked by intense heart palpitations, pressure or pain in the chest, dizziness or unsteadiness, sweating, and feeling faint; victims often believe they are having a fatal heart attack. They may worry constantly about having future panic episodes, and thus curtail activities to avoid possible embarrassment. In fact, it is often the fear of experiencing another panic attack that leads to agoraphobia (Barlow, 1988); the person begins to fear and avoid places where help won't be available should panic recur. As many as 30 percent of the U.S. population have experienced at least one panic attack within the past year, though in most cases this does not lead to full-blown panic disorder (Norton, Cox & Malan, 1992). Here is a case that did.

Geri, a 32-year-old nurse, had her first panic attack while driving on a freeway. Afterward, she could not force herself to drive on the freeway again. Her next attack occurred while she was with a patient and a doctor in a small examining room. A sense of impending doom flooded over her and she burst out of the office and into the parking lot, where she felt immediate relief. From then on, her fear of another attack made it impossible for her to tolerate any close quarters, including crowded shopping malls. She eventually quit her job because of terror of the examining rooms.

The form that a social phobia takes depends in part on sociocultural factors. In Japan, for example, where cultural values emphasize collectivism (group-oriented values and goals, as discussed in Chapter 1), a common social phobia is *Tai-jin Kyofu Sho,* fear of embarrassing those around you (Takahashi, 1989; Tanouye, 1992).

Linkages: Excessive hand washing is a classic feature of obsessive-compulsive disorder. Though learning and environmental stress appear to play the major role in shaping and triggering this and other anxiety disorders, biological factors—including genetically inherited characteristics and deficiencies in certain neurotransmitters (see Chapter 4)—may result in an oversensitive nervous system and a predisposition toward anxiety.

Obsessive-Compulsive Disorder   Anxiety is also the root of **obsessive-compulsive disorder (OCD)**. As in the case of Mark, described at the opening of this chapter, people displaying obsessive-compulsive disorder are plagued by persistent, upsetting, and unwanted thoughts called *obsessions* (Mark's obsessions centered on infection by HIV). These obsessive thoughts may then motivate repetitive, uncontrollable behaviors, called *compulsions,* that the person feels will neutralize the fears associated with those thoughts (Mark's compulsions included incessant cleaning). If the person tries to interrupt the obsessive thoughts or cease the compulsive behavior, severe agitation and anxiety usually result. This pattern is similar to, but much more intense than, the occasional experience of having a repetitive, unwanted thought or tune running on "in the back of our mind" or rechecking to see that a door is locked. In OCD, the obsessions and compulsions are intense, disturbing, and often bizarre intrusions that can severely impair daily activities.

Typical obsessive thoughts revolve around the possibility of harming someone or becoming infected. Compulsive behaviors often take the form of repetitive rituals, such as counting things, arranging objects "just so," or repeated washing.

Causes of Anxiety Disorders

As with all the forms of psychopathology we will consider, the exact causes of anxiety disorders are a matter of debate. All theoretical approaches offer explanations. Research suggests that biological factors, distortions in thinking, and learning are particularly important (Barlow, 1988; Rachman, 1989).

Biological Factors   Their genes may predispose some people to anxiety disorders. Research indicates, for example, that if one identical twin has an anxiety disorder, his or her co-twin is more likely also to have an anxiety disorder than is the case between pairs of nonidentical twins (Torgersen, 1983). Most anxiety disorders, particularly panic disorder, appear to run in families (Crowe et al., 1983; Kendler et al., 1986). Perhaps, then, anxiety disorders develop out of a physiological predisposition to react with anxiety to a wide range of situations, which results, in part, from inheriting an autonomic system that is oversensitive to stress (see, for example, Barlow, 1988).

The predisposition to anxiety disorders may be based on abnormalities in neurotransmitter systems. Excessive activity of norepinephrine in certain parts of the brain has been linked with panic disorder, and excessive serotonin has been associated with obsessive-compulsive disorder (Gorman et al., 1989; Rapoport, 1989). There is also evidence that anxiety-generating neural impulses may run unchecked when the neurotransmitter GABA is prevented from exerting its normal inhibitory influence in certain neural pathways (Friedman, Clark & Gershon, 1992; Zorumski & Isenberg, 1991).

There may also be something physically wrong in people with panic disorder (Gorman et al., 1989). Unlike normal subjects, many of these individuals have a panic episode after receiving an injection of lactate or caffeine, inhaling carbon dioxide, or taking yohimbine (a drug that blocks one type of norepinephrine receptor). Because these substances all stimulate brainstem areas that control the autonomic nervous system, one hypothesis is that panic-disorder patients have hypersensitive brainstem mechanisms and are therefore especially prone to fear responses (Gorman et al., 1989).

Although biological predispositions may set the stage for anxiety disorders, most researchers agree that environmental stressors and psychological factors, including cognitive processes and learning, bring about most anxiety disorders (Barlow, 1988).

Cognitive Factors   Persons suffering from an anxiety disorder may exaggerate the danger associated with their environment, thereby creating an unrealistic expectation that bad events are going to happen (Mogg et al., 1993; Tomarken, Mineka & Cook, 1989). In addition, they tend to underestimate their own capacity for dealing with threatening events, resulting in anxiety and desperation when feared events do occur (Beck & Emery, 1985; Reiss & McNally, 1985; Telch et al., 1989).

As an example, consider the development of a panic attack. Though the appearance of unexplained symptoms of physical arousal may set the stage for a panic attack, the person's cognitive interpretation of those symptoms can determine whether or not the attack actually develops. In one study of panic attacks induced by breathing air rich in carbon dioxide, some subjects were told that they could control the amount of carbon dioxide they were inhaling by turning a dial on a control panel. Others were told they could not control it. In fact the dial had no effect for either group, but subjects who had the illusion of control were far less likely to have a full-blown panic attack (Sanderson, Rapee & Barlow, 1989). Thus, if catastrophic thoughts about embarrassment or death occur in response to initial symptoms, and the person believes that he or she has no control over the symptoms, they may set off a snowball effect in which fear continues to grow into panic.

The Role of Learning   Upsetting thoughts—about money or illness, for example—are often difficult to dismiss, especially when people are under a lot of stress or feel incapable of dealing effectively with the problems they are worried about. As the thoughts become more persistent, they engender increased anxiety. If an action such as cleaning temporarily relieves the anxiety, that action may be strengthened through the process of negative reinforcement discussed in Chapter 8. But such actions do nothing to eliminate the obsessive thoughts and so become compulsive, endlessly repeated rituals that keep the person trapped in a vicious circle of anxiety (Barlow, 1988; Rachman & Hodgson, 1980). Thus, according to the cognitive-behavioral approach, obsessive-compulsive disorder might be a pattern that is sparked by distressing thoughts and maintained by operant conditioning.

Phobias may also be explained in part by the principles of classical conditioning described in Chapter 8. The object of the phobia becomes an aversive conditioned stimulus through association with a traumatic event that acts as an unconditioned stimulus (see, for example, Öst, 1992). Fear of dogs, for example, may result from a dog attack. Observing or hearing about other people's bad experiences can produce the same result; most people who fear flying have never been in a plane crash. Once the fear is learned, avoidance of the feared object prevents the person from finding out that there is no need to be afraid. This cycle of avoidance helps explain why many fears do not simply extinguish, or disappear, on their own.

Why are phobias about snakes and spiders so common even though people are seldom harmed by them? And why are there so few cases of electrical-outlet phobia when people are frequently shocked by them? As we discussed in the chapter on learning, the answer may be that people are *biologically prepared* to learn associations between certain stimuli and certain responses. In other words, certain stimuli and certain responses appear to be especially easy to link through conditioning (Hamm, Vaitl & Lang, 1989). People may be biologically prepared to learn to fear and to avoid stimuli that had the potential to harm their evolutionary ancestors (Seligman, 1971).

Some laboratory evidence supports the notion that people are biologically prepared to learn certain phobias. A group of Swedish psychologists attempted to classically condition people to fear certain stimuli by associating the stimuli with electric shocks (Öhman, Dimberg & Öst, 1985; Öhman, Erixon & Lofberg, 1975). The subjects developed about equal conditioned anxiety reactions to slides of houses, human faces, and snakes. Later, however, when they were

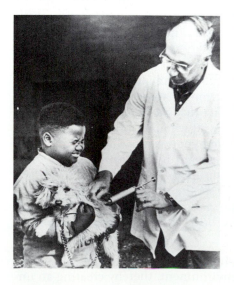

Many phobias, including those of needles, blood, and medically related situations, are acquired vicariously. Fears developed through observational learning can be as strong as those learned through direct experience (Kleinknecht, 1991), although direct conditioning is the more common pathway to phobia (Merckelbach et al., 1989; Öst, 1992).

A biological preparedness to learn to fear snakes and other potentially dangerous stimuli makes sense from an evolutionary point of view. There would be a distinct adaptive advantage for animals (and humans) to rapidly learn a fearful response to objects or situations that are seen to frighten their parents or peers. Those who do so are more likely to survive and to pass on their genes to the next generation.

tested without shock, the reaction to snakes remained long after the houses and faces had failed to elicit a fear response. It has been suggested that the preparedness effect may not be as strong as once thought (Hugdahl & Johnson, 1989; McNally, 1987; Zafiropoulou & McPherson, 1986), but a series of investigations with animals has supported preparedness theory (Cook & Mineka, 1990). If a monkey sees another monkey behaving fearfully in the presence of a live or toy snake, it quickly develops a strong and persistent fear of snakes. Interestingly, if the snake is entwined in flowers, the observer monkeys come to fear only the snake, not the flowers (Cook & Mineka, 1987). Thus the fear conditioning was selective, focusing only on potentially dangerous creatures such as snakes or crocodiles (Zinbarg & Mineka, 1991), not on harmless stimuli. Data like these suggest that anxiety disorders probably arise through the combined effects of genetic predispositions and learning.

Somatoform Disorders

Sometimes people show symptoms of a *somatic,* or physical, disorder, even though there is no physical cause. Because these are psychological problems that take somatic form, these conditions are called **somatoform disorders.** The classic example is **conversion disorder,** a condition in which a person appears to be, but is not, blind, deaf, paralyzed, or insensitive to pain in various parts of the body. (An earlier term for this disorder was *hysteria.*) Conversion disorders are rare, accounting for only about 2 percent of psychiatric diagnoses. Although they can occur at any point in life, they usually appear in adolescence or early adulthood.

Conversion disorders differ from true physical disabilities in several ways. First, they tend to appear when a person is under severe stress. Second, they often help reduce that stress by enabling the person to avoid unpleasant situations. Third, the person may show remarkably little concern about what is apparently a rather serious problem. Finally, the symptoms may be organically impossible or improbable, as Figure 15.2 illustrates. One university student, for example, experienced visual impairment that began each Sunday evening and became total blindness by Monday morning. Her vision would begin to return on Friday evenings and was fully restored in time for weekend football

Figure 15.2
Glove Anesthesia
In this conversion disorder, the person's insensitivity stops abruptly at the wrist (b). But as shown in (a) the nerves of the hand and arm blend, so if they were actually impaired, part of the arm would also lose sensitivity. Other neurologically impossible symptoms seen in conversion disorder include sleepwalking at night on legs that are "paralyzed" during the day.

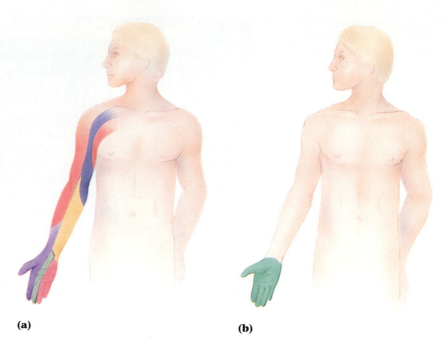

(a)   (b)

games and other social activities. She expressed no undue concern over her condition (Holmes, 1991).

Can people with a conversion disorder see and hear, even though they act as though they cannot? Experiments show that they can (Grosz & Zimmerman, 1970), but this does not necessarily mean that they are malingering, or lying. Research described in Chapter 7, on consciousness, suggests that people can use sensory input even when they are not consciously aware of doing so (Bargh, 1982; Schacter, Chiu & Ochsner, 1993). Rather than destroying visual or auditory ability, the conversion process may prevent the person from being aware of information that the brain is still processing.

Another form of somatoform disorder is **hypochondriasis**, a strong, unjustified fear that one has, or might get, cancer, heart disease, AIDS, or other serious physical problems. The fear prompts frequent visits to physicians and reports of numerous symptoms. Their bodily preoccupation often leads hypochondriacs to become "experts" on their most feared diseases. In a related condition called **somatization disorder**, individuals make dramatic but often vague reports about a multitude of physical problems rather than any specific illness. **Pain disorder** is marked by complaints of severe, often constant pain (typically in the neck, chest, or back) with no physical cause.

Traditional explanations of somatoform disorders focus on conversion disorder. Freud believed that it results when anxiety related to unconscious conflict is converted into physical symptoms. (This belief is, in fact, the source of the term *conversion*.) In explaining somatoform disorders, behavioral as well as psychodynamic theorists point out that somatoform disorders can produce benefits by relieving sufferers of unpleasant responsibilities. Sociocultural factors may be at work in shaping some of these disorders. Cross-cultural psychologists point out that it is common in many Asian, Latin American, and African cultures for people to channel psychological or interpersonal conflicts into physical symptoms such as headaches or stomachaches, while in North America, these conflicts are more likely to result in anxiety or depression (Brislin, 1993). Genetic factors do not seem to be important in somatoform disorders.

Dissociative Disorders

A sudden and usually temporary disruption in a person's memory, consciousness, or identity characterizes **dissociative disorders.** Temporary dissociative states are familiar to most people, as when, for example, after many hours of highway driving they suddenly realize they have little or no recollection of what happened during the last half-hour. Dissociative disorders are more intense and long lasting, as in the case of John, a thirty-year-old computer manufacturing executive. John was a meek person who was dependent on his wife for companionship and support. It came as a jolt when she announced that she was leaving him to live with his younger brother, an act she justified by saying, "This time I'm gonna try it before I buy it." John did not go to work the next day. In fact, nothing was heard from him for two weeks. Then he was arrested for public drunkenness and assault in a city more than three hundred miles from his home. The police discovered that during those two weeks John lived under another name at a cheap hotel and worked selling tickets at a pornographic movie theater. When he was interviewed, John did not know his real name or his real home, could not explain how he reached his present location, and could not remember much about the previous two weeks.

John's case illustrates the dissociative disorder known as **dissociative fugue,** which is characterized by a sudden loss of personal memory and the assumption of a new identity in a new locale. Another dissociative disorder, **dissociative amnesia,** also involves sudden memory loss. As in fugue, all personal identifying information may be forgotten, but the person does not leave home or create a new identity. These are rare, usually brief conditions, lasting only hours or days in most cases, but they tend to attract intense publicity because they are so perplexing.

The most famous dissociative disorder is *dissociative identity disorder,* or **multiple personality disorder,** a condition in which a person has more than one identity, each of which speaks, acts, and writes in a very different way. Each personality seems to have its own memories, wishes, and (often conflicting) impulses. Here is a case example:

A 42-year-old woman was brought to a psychiatrist by her husband, who complained that during arguments about money or other matters, she would suddenly either change into uncharacteristically flamboyant clothes and go to a nearby bar to flirt with strangers, or curl up on the floor and talk as if she were a young child. She refused to discuss these episodes with her husband, but an interview conducted under hypnosis revealed that during these times she experienced being "Frieda," the girlfriend of a Russian soldier who had been sexually molested in her native Poland after World War II. Once hypnosis was terminated, she had no memory of "Frieda." (Spitzer et al., 1989)

How do dissociative disorders develop? Psychodynamic theorists see massive repression of unwanted impulses or memories as the basis for creating a "new person" who acts out otherwise unacceptable impulses or recalls otherwise unbearable memories. Behavioral theorists focus on the fact that everyone is capable of behaving in different ways depending on circumstances (for example, boisterous in a bar, quiet in a museum) and that, in rare cases, this variation can become so extreme that a person feels and is perceived by others as a "different person." Further, an individual may be rewarded for a sudden memory loss or unusual behavior by escaping stressful situations, responsibilities, or punishment for misdeeds.

Evaluating these hypotheses has been difficult in part because of the rarity of dissociative disorders. However, multiple personality seems to be more fre-

Chris Sizemore's multiple personality disorder inspired the book and movie entitled *The Three Faces of Eve.* Dramatizations of her story and others, such as *Sybil,* focus on behavioral changes across personalities, but there seem to be distinct biological differences as well. Heart rate and blood pressure may differ from one personality to the next; and in some women, the different personalities are on different menstrual cycles (Putnam, Zahn & Post, 1990). Some personalities may be aware of the existence of the others; some may not. Shifts among personalities are sudden, dramatic, and often stress related. Ms. Sizemore, an artist, no longer displays mutiple personality disorder.

quent recently; clinicians are either looking for it more carefully or the conditions leading to it are more prevalent. One study in Canada suggested that between 5 and 10 percent of the adult population may suffer from some form of dissociative disorder (Ross, Joshi & Currie, 1990). Newly available data suggest three conclusions. First, many people displaying multiple personalities have experienced events they would like to forget or avoid. The vast majority (some clinicians believe all) have suffered severe, unavoidable, persistent abuse in childhood (Ross et al., 1990). Second, most of them appear to be skilled at self-hypnosis, through which they can induce a trancelike state. Third, most found that they could escape the trauma of abuse at least temporarily by creating "new personalities" to deal with the stress (Bliss, 1980; Kluft, 1987; Ross et al., 1990).

Though sustained physical or sexual abuse may be a primary culprit in the development of multiple personality, not all abused children display multiple personality. Thus, researchers still have the task of understanding the specific combination of personal characteristics and environmental conditions that leads to this disorder. ("In Review: Anxiety, Somatoform, and Dissociative Disorders" presents a summary of our discussion of these topics.)

Mood Disorders

Everyone's feelings, or *affect,* tend to rise and fall from time to time. However, when people experience extremes of mood—wild elation or deep depression—for long periods, when they shift from one extreme to another, and especially when their moods are not consistent with the events around them, they are said to show a **mood disorder** (also known as *affective disorder*). We will describe two main types: depressive and bipolar disorders.

Depressive Disorders

Depression plays a central role in most mood disorders. It can range from occasional "down" periods to episodes severe enough to require hospitalization. A person suffering **major depressive disorder** feels sad and hopeless for weeks or months, often losing interest in all activities and taking pleasure in nothing. Feelings of inadequacy, worthlessness, or guilt are common. Everything, from

In Review: Anxiety, Somatoform, and Dissociative Disorders

Disorder	Subtypes	Major Symptoms
Anxiety disorders	Phobias	Intense, irrational fear of objectively nondangerous situations or things, leading to disruptions of behavior.
	Generalized anxiety disorder	Excessive anxiety not focused on a specific situation or object; free-floating anxiety.
	Panic disorder	Terrifying, repeated attacks of intense fear involving physical symptoms such as faintness, dizziness, and nausea.
	Obsessive-compulsive disorder	Persistent ideas or worries accompanied by ritualistic behaviors performed to neutralize the anxiety-driven thoughts.
Somatoform disorders	Conversion disorder	A loss of physical ability (e.g., sight, hearing) that is related to psychological factors.
	Hypochondriasis	Preoccupation with or belief that one has serious illness in the absence of any physical evidence.
	Pain disorder	Preoccupation with pain in the absence of physical reasons for the pain.
Dissociative disorders	Amnesia/fugue	Sudden, unexpected loss of memory, which may result in relocation and the assumption of a new identity.
	Multiple personality disorder (dissociative identity disorder)	Appearance within same person of two or more distinct personalities, each with a unique way of thinking and behaving.

This figurine from pre-Columbian Mexico helps to illustrate the long history and pervasiveness of depression in virtually all cultures of the world (World Health Organization, 1973).

conversation to bathing, is an unbearable, exhausting effort. Changes in eating habits resulting in weight loss or, sometimes, weight gain often accompany major depressive disorder, as does sleep disturbance or, less often, excessive sleeping. Problems in concentrating, making decisions, and thinking clearly are also common. In extreme cases, depressed people may express false beliefs, or **delusions**—worrying, for example, that the government is planning to punish them. Major depressive disorder may come on suddenly or gradually. It may consist of a single episode or, more commonly, an irregular, sometimes lifelong pattern of depressive periods. Here is one case example:

Mr. J. was a fifty-one-year-old industrial engineer. . . . Since the death of his wife five years earlier, he had been suffering from continuing episodes of depression marked by extreme social withdrawal and occasional thoughts of suicide. . . . He drank, and when thoroughly intoxicated would plead to his deceased wife for forgiveness. He lost all capacity for joy. . . . Once a gourmet, he now had no interest in food and good wine . . . [he] could barely manage to engage in small talk. As might be expected, his work record deteriorated markedly. Appointments were missed and projects haphazardly started and left unfinished. (From Davison & Neale, 1990, p. 221)

Many cases of depression do not become this extreme. A less severe pattern of depression is called **dysthymic disorder**, in which the person shows the sad mood, lack of interest, and loss of pleasure associated with major depression, but less intensely and for a longer period. (The duration must be at least two years for the diagnosis of dysthymic disorder to be made.) Mental and behavioral disruption are also less severe; most people exhibiting dysthymic disorder do not require hospitalization.

Somewhere between 240,000 and 600,000 people in the United States and Canada attempt suicide each year; more than 30,000 succeed (McIntosh, 1991; National Center for Health Statistics, 1988). Worldwide, the annual death toll from suicide is 120,000. Suicide is usually associated mainly with depression; in fact, people who suffer major depressive disorder are often hospitalized as a precaution. But suicide is also related to other disorders, especially alcoholism, schizophrenia, and panic disorder (Fawcett et al., 1990; Johnson, Weissman & Klerman, 1990; National Institute of Mental Health, 1986).

Suicide and Depression   Virtually all of the factors related to depression are also associated with suicide. These include interpersonal crises, such as divorce; financial failure; sudden death in the family; intense feelings of frustration, anger, hopelessness, or self-hatred; and an absence of long-term or meaningful life goals (Garland & Zigler, 1993; Paykel, Prusoff & Myers, 1975; Slater & DePue, 1981). Constant stress often leads to depression, so it is not surprising that people whose lives are particularly stress-filled show significantly higher suicide rates than the general population.

Among students, the suicide rate increases dramatically at the beginning of each school year and at the end of each term (Klagsbrun, 1976). It also rises after the breakup of an engagement or other romantic relationship (Hendlin, 1975; Miller, 1975). Suicide is the third leading cause of death among adolescents (Garland & Zigler, 1993) and the second leading cause of death among college students; about ten thousand try to kill themselves each year, and about one thousand succeed. This rate is much higher than for eighteen- to twenty-four-year-olds in general, but much lower than for the elderly (National Institute of Mental Health, 1986; Blazer, Bacher & Manton, 1986). One recent study of university students found that about 25 percent had contemplated suicide in the previous year and 10 percent had attempted suicide at some time in their lives. However, only 4.6 percent reported having actually injured themselves in their attempts (Meehan et al., 1992).

Knowing who will and who will not attempt suicide is difficult, but there are some guidelines. Attempts tend to be associated with some form of significant psychological pain and with a tendency to seek instant escape from problems. Female attempters outnumber males three to one, but males—especially those over forty-five, divorced, and living alone—succeed twice as often, perhaps because they are more intent on dying and thus tend to choose more lethal means.

There are significant differences in suicide rates among different ethnic and cultural groups in the United States. For example, although there is considerable variation from tribe to tribe, the overall rate for Native Americans is 13.6 per 100,000 people, compared to 12.9 for European-Americans, 9.1 for Asian-Americans, 7.5 for Hispanic-Americans, and 5.7 for African-Americans (Garland & Zigler, 1993; Howard-Pitney et al., 1992; McIntosh, 1992). One study revealed that 30 percent of Zuni adolescents had actively attempted suicide and that 70 percent of these attempters had tried two or more times (Howard-Pitney et al., 1992). For all groups, previous attempts suggest that future ones are likely (Garland & Zigler, 1993), especially when the person has made a specific plan and given away possessions (Clark et al., 1989).

One myth about suicide is that people who talk about it will never try it. On the contrary, those who say they are thinking of suicide are much more likely to try suicide than people from the general population. In fact, according to Edwin Shneidman (1987), 80 percent of suicides are preceded by some kind of warning, whether direct ("I think I'm going to kill myself") or vague ("Sometimes I wonder if life is worth living"). Though not everyone who threatens suicide follows through, if you suspect that someone you know is thinking about suicide, encourage the person to contact a mental health professional or a crisis hotline. If the danger is imminent, make the contact yourself and ask for advice about how to respond.

Bipolar Disorder

The alternating appearance of two emotional extremes, or poles, characterizes **bipolar disorder.** We have already described one emotional pole: depression. The other is **mania,** which is an elated, very active emotional state. People in a manic state tend to be totally optimistic, boundlessly energetic, certain of having extraordinary powers and abilities, and bursting with all sorts of ideas. They become irritated with anyone who tries to reason with them or "slow them down." During manic episodes the person may make impulsive and unwise decisions, including spending their life savings on foolish schemes.

In bipolar disorder, manic episodes may alternate every few days, weeks, or years with periods of deep depression (sometimes, periods of relatively normal mood separate these extremes). This pattern has also been called *manic depression.* Compared with major depressive disorder, bipolar disorder is rare; it occurs in only about 1 percent of adults. Slightly more common is a pattern of less extreme mood swings known as *cyclothymic disorder,* the bipolar equivalent of dysthymia.

Causes of Mood Disorders

Psychological Theories   Traditional psychodynamic theory suggests that depression is most likely among people with strong dependency needs. These needs leave the person vulnerable to exaggerated grief over interpersonal rejection or the death of a loved one. Because the lost loved one has been incorporated as part of the person's identity, anger and resentment over being abandoned that should be directed at others are turned inward as feelings of worthlessness and blame.

Cognitive-behavioral theories about mood disorders are currently more influential than psychodynamic ones. Like psychodynamic theorists, behaviorists recognize that people can become depressed in response to a wide variety of negative events, especially the death of a loved one, the end of an intimate relationship, or the loss of a job (Monroe & Simons, 1991). However, the behavioral perspective sees these events as resulting in the loss of important sources of reward, which can lead to depression in a number of ways. For example, the depressed mood resulting from loss often leads to a reduction in pleasant activities. This loss of pleasure creates more depression, which may then be maintained by the reinforcing effects of the attention and sympathy it attracts from others (Lewinsohn, 1974).

Another possible path to depression is through *learned helplessness,* which we described in the chapter on learning. When animals have no control over shock or other aversive events, they begin to appear depressed and become inactive. Interestingly, people who temporarily learn this helplessness in the laboratory deal with laboratory tasks in ways similar to truly depressed individuals (Hiroto & Seligman, 1975; Klein & Seligman, 1976). Thus, lack of control over one's life, especially over its rewards and stressors, may be an important factor in depression. As suggested earlier, the extent to which women have less control over their lives may help explain why about twice as many women as men in many cultures become depressed (Matlin, 1993; Radloff, 1975; Strickland, 1992).

Linkages: How might a person's perceptual style influence the development of mental disorder? (a link to Perception)

Many people, however, have limited control; why aren't they all depressed? How people think about themselves, their world, and their future also seems important (Lewinsohn, 1988). Aaron Beck's (1967, 1991) cognitive theory of depression suggests that depressed people develop mental habits of (1) blaming themselves when things go wrong, (2) focusing on and exaggerating the dark side of events, and (3) jumping to overly generalized pessimistic conclusions. These cognitive habits, says Beck, are errors that lead to depressing thoughts and other symptoms of depression.

Depressed people do hold more negative beliefs about themselves and their lives than other people, but the exact significance of these beliefs is not yet clear (Gara et al., 1993; Haaga, Dyck & Ernst, 1991). First of all, pessimistic beliefs may be a symptom of depression rather than a cause of it. Second, research indicates that the negative beliefs of depressed persons may not be errors at all; they may be very accurate (Snyder & Higgins, 1988; Taylor & Brown, 1988). In fact, their beliefs may be more accurate than those of non-depressed people, a difference that has been termed the "sadder-but-wiser" effect (Alloy & Abramson, 1979).

The way people tend to explain the world, their *attributional style,* may also be a key cognitive factor in depression. Some researchers suggest that severe, long-lasting depression is far more likely among people who attribute their lack of control to a permanent, generalized lack of personal competence rather than to "the way things are" (Abramson, Seligman & Teasdale, 1978; Seligman et al., 1988; Sweeney, Anderson & Bailey, 1986). Thus, people may be prone to depression when they blame negative events on themselves and believe they will always be incapable of doing better. A newer version of attributional theory postulates *hopelessness* as a subtype of depression. Here, depression follows from the belief that a highly valued event will not occur, or that an aversive outcome will occur. This negative anticipation, coupled with a negative attributional style ("I'll never be able to change the situation"), leads to hopeless depression (Abramson, Metalsky & Alloy, 1989; Metalsky et al., 1993).

Notice that cognitive-behavioral explanations of depression are consistent with diathesis-stress theory. They suggest that certain cognitive styles constitute a predisposition (or diathesis) that makes a person vulnerable to depression (Peterson & Seligman, 1984), which is more likely to appear in the face of significant stress. The cognitive-behavioral perspective also suggests that whether depression continues, or worsens, depends in part on how people respond when they start to feel depressed. Those who ruminate about negative events, about why they occur, and even about feeling depressed are likely to feel more and more depressed. According to Susan Nolen-Hoeksma (1990), this *ruminative style* is especially characteristic of women and may help explain gender differences in the frequency of depression. When men start to feel sad, she says, they tend to use a *distracting style,* engaging in activity that helps bring them out of their depressed mood (Nolen-Hoeksma, 1990; Nolen-Hoeksma, Morrow & Fredrickson, 1993).

Biological Factors   When animals learn helplessness in the laboratory, they also show changes in the neurotransmitters norepinephrine and serotonin (Hughes, et al., 1984). As we discussed in Chapter 4, on biological aspects of psychology, these neurotransmitters are important in the regulation of moods. Can malfunctioning of these or other neurotransmitter systems help explain mood disorders?

Linkages: Is depression caused by a chemical imbalance in the brain? (a link to Biological Aspects of Psychology)

Norepinephrine and serotonin systems may well be malfunctioning in depression because, for one thing, many of the drugs that relieve depression alter norepinephrine and serotonin systems in the brain. The nature of the malfunction is neither simple nor clear, however. It once appeared that depression was associated with abnormally low levels of norepinephrine and/or serotonin (see, for example, Garver & Davis, 1979), but this is not always the case (Gold, Goodwin & Chrousos, 1988). According to one alternative theory, depression may result from a dysregulation of norepinephrine and serotonin, such that their levels and effects cannot be kept within the normal range (Siever & Davis, 1985). Other researchers suspect that depression is related to abnormalities in the sensitivity of receptors for these neurotransmitters, not in the level of the chemicals themselves (McNeal & Cimbolic, 1986).

There is also some evidence that these neurotransmitter systems, and the hormone systems related to them, are overly responsive to stressors in depressed people (Lickey & Gordon, 1991). For example, simply standing up quickly enough to produce slight dizziness causes depressed people to secrete more norepinephrine than nondepressed people (Rudorfer et al., 1985). Many depressed people also oversecrete hormones such as corticotropin releasing factor, a substance that leads to the release of the stress-related hormone cortisol (Lickey & Gordon, 1991; Nemeroff et al., 1989; Siever & Davis, 1985). Abnormally high cortisol levels have been found in about 70 percent of people diagnosed with major depressive disorder (Carroll, 1982; Poland et al., 1987). Finally, a synthetic hormone that *suppresses* the secretion of cortisol in normal people leads to *higher* levels of cortisol in depressed people (Kathol et al., 1989). Findings such as these might help explain the relationship between depression and stressful events.

The cyclical nature of many mood disorders suggests that abnormalities in biological rhythms play a role in these disorders. For example, people with bipolar disorder sometimes become depressed every few months, regardless of whether life is going well or not. Similarly, during the shorter-daylight months of the year, people suffering from *seasonal affective disorder,* or *SAD,* slip into severe depression, accompanied by irritability, excessive sleeping, intense carbohydrate craving, and consequent weight gain (Blehar & Rosenthal, 1989). Their depression tends to ease as daylight hours get longer (Kasper et al., 1989). Treatment by exposure to full spectrum light for as little as a couple of hours a day relieves this form of depression in many cases (Blehar & Rosenthal, 1989). Disruption of biological rhythms is also suggested by the fact that many depressed people tend to have trouble sleeping; in most cases, they wake up abnormally early. Part of the reason some depressed people feel as they do may be that their biological clocks tell them that they are trying to function in the middle of the night. Resetting biological rhythms through methods such as sleep deprivation has relieved depression in some cases (Kuhs & Tolle, 1991). Evidence for disrupted biological rhythms in mood disorders may actually support neurotransmitter theories of causation because the disruptions may be traceable to abnormalities in norepinephrine, serotonin, dopamine, and other neurotransmitters that regulate the body's internal clock (Wehr et al., 1983).

Whatever their primary biological basis, there is evidence that genetics influence a person's chances of developing a mood disorder. The evidence is especially strong for bipolar disorder. One review of research with twins found that if one member of an identical-twin pair developed bipolar disorder, 72 percent of the other members showed the same disorder; this happened in only 14 percent of nonidentical pairs (Allen, 1976). Other studies have found similar results (Egeland et al., 1987; Nurnberger & Gershon, 1984; Winder et al., 1986). The search continues for the specific gene or genes involved in the transmission of elevated risk for bipolar disorder (Barinaga, 1989; Hodgkinson, Mullan & Gurling, 1990). The children of parents who show major depressive disorder are more likely to develop depression themselves, but the evidence for inheritability of major depressive disorder is not as strong as for bipolar disorder (Andreasen et al., 1987).

Indeed, there may be several types of depression and several types of bipolar disorder, each caused by different combinations of genetic and environmental factors. This possibility is supported by data from studies showing that young people the world over face an increasing risk of becoming depressed (Cross-National Collaborative Group, 1992). Since these people's gene pools are so diverse, the kind of depression seen in this international trend may be due to increasingly stressful environmental conditions, ranging from air pollution and crowding to unemployment and political unrest.

The number and complexity of causal factors in mood disorders makes a diathesis-stress model—which recognizes the interaction of predispositions and life stresses—an especially appropriate guide for future research.

Schizophrenia

Here is part of a letter that arrived in the mail a few months ago:

Dear Sirs:
Pertaining to our continuing failure to prosecute violations of minor's rights to sovereign equality which are occurring in gestations being compromised by the ingestation of controlled substances, . . . the skewing of androgyny which continues in female juveniles even after separation from their mother's has occurred, and as a means of promulflagitating my paying Governor Hickel of Alaska for my employees to have personal services endorsements and controlled substance endorsements, . . . the Iraqi oil being released by the United Nations being identifed as Kurdistanian oil, and the July, 1991 issue of the Siberian Review spells President Eltsin's name without a letter y.

The author of this letter would probably be diagnosed as schizophrenic. **Schizophrenia** is a pattern of symptoms involving severely disturbed thinking, emotion, perception, and behavior; usually it seriously impairs the person's ability to communicate and disrupts most aspects of daily functioning.

Schizophrenia is one of the most serious and disabling of all mental disorders, and its core symptoms are seen in virtually all parts of the world (World Health Organization, 1979). It occurs in about 1 percent of the population in the United States, in about equal numbers of men and women, and it tends to develop in adolescence or early adulthood. Those diagnosed as schizophrenic usually require hospitalization, sometimes for weeks or months, sometimes for many years. At any specific time, this diagnostic group occupies about half the beds in mental hospitals. In the United States, about three or four million of these individuals are permanently unemployed and often unemployable. Some recover. One study of persons labeled schizophrenic in nine different countries found that, when reassessed after two years, as many as 75 percent in some countries, such as India, no longer displayed schizophrenic symptoms (Draguns, 1990; Dube, Kumar & Dube, 1984; World Health Organization, 1979). In other countries, including the United States, the prospects are much less encouraging, but this may be due to use of more stringent diagnostic criteria.

Symptoms of Schizophrenia

Disorders of Thought   Schizophrenics display problems in both how they think and what they think. In fact, it was the apparent loosening of bonds among thoughts that prompted nineteenth-century psychiatrist Eugen Bleuler to coin the word *schizophrenia,* or "split mind" (see Neale, Oltmanns & Winters, 1983). Contrary to popular belief, *schizophrenia* does *not* mean "split personality," as in multiple personality disorder but, rather, refers to a splitting up of normally integrated mental processes, such as thoughts and feelings. Thus, a schizophrenic may giggle while claiming to feel sad.

The *form* of schizophrenic thought is often incoherent. *Neologisms* ("new words" that have meaning only to the person speaking them) are common; the word "promulflagitating" in the letter above is one example. That letter also illustrates *loose associations,* the tendency for one thought to be logically unconnected, or only superficially connected, to the next. Sometimes the associations are based on double meanings or on the way words sound (*clang associations*). For example, "My true family name is Abel or A Bell. We descended from the clan of Abel, who originated the bell of rights, which we now call the bill of rights." In the most severe cases, thought becomes just a jumble of words known as *word salad.* For example, "Upon the advisability of held keeping, environment of the seabeach gathering, to the forest stream,

Linkages: What is different about the thought and language of schizophrenics? (a link to Thought and Language)

reinstatement to be placed, poling the paddleboat, of the swamp morass, to the forest compensation of the dunce" (Lehman, 1967, p. 627).

The *content* of schizophrenic thinking is also disturbed. Often it includes a bewildering assortment of delusions, especially delusions of persecution. The person may think that space aliens are trying to steal his or her thoughts and may interpret everything from radio programs to hand gestures as part of the plot. Delusions that common events are somehow related to oneself are called *ideas of reference.* Delusions of grandeur may also be present; one young schizophrenic was convinced that the president of United States was trying to contact him for advice. Other types of delusions include *thought broadcasting,* in which the person believes that his or her thoughts can be heard by others; *thought blocking* or *withdrawal,* the belief that someone is either preventing thoughts or "stealing" them as they appear; and *thought insertion,* the belief that other people's thoughts are appearing in one's mind. Some schizophrenics believe that, like puppets, their behavior is controlled by others.

Other Symptoms of Schizophrenia   Schizophrenics often report that they cannot focus their attention. They may feel overwhelmed as they try to attend to everything at once. Various perceptual disorders may appear. The person may feel detached from the real world; other people may seem to be flat cutouts. The body may feel like a machine, or parts of it may seem to be dead or rotting.

In a nine-nation study, about 75 percent of those diagnosed as schizophrenic reported **hallucinations,** or false perceptions, usually of voices (Sartorius, Shapiro & Jablensky, 1974). These voices may sound like an overheard conversation, or they may urge the person to do or not to do things; sometimes they comment on or narrate the person's actions.

Unlike people suffering from mood disorders, schizophrenics usually do not experience extreme emotions. In fact, they may experience "flat" affect, showing little or no emotion even in the context of happy or sad events. Indeed, the classic picture of the chronic schizophrenic includes lack of interest in anything, total preoccupation with an inner world (a condition known as *autism*), and loss of the sense of self. Schizophrenics who do display emotion often do so inappropriately—crying for no apparent reason, or flying into a rage in response to a simple question.

Some schizophrenics appear very agitated, ceaselessly moving their limbs, making facial grimaces, or pacing the floor in highly ritualistic sequences. Others become so withdrawn that they move very little. Lack of motivation and social skills, deteriorating personal hygiene, and an inability to function day to day are other common characteristics of schizophrenia. Although these problems can develop suddenly, more often they appear gradually. They can become totally incapacitating.

Types of Schizophrenia

DSM-IV lists five major subtypes of schizophrenia. A **residual schizophrenia** subtype applies to persons who have had a prior episode of schizophrenia but currently are not displaying delusions, hallucinations, or other symptoms. Specific patterns of symptoms characterize the other four subtypes—disorganized, catatonic, paranoid, and undifferentiated.

The main features of **disorganized schizophrenia** are unrelated delusions and hallucinations. Speech may be incoherent. Strange facial grimaces and ritualistic movements are common. Affect is flat, though there may be inappropriate laughter or giggling. Personal hygiene is neglected, and the person may lose bowel and bladder control. Though often seen on urban streets, only about 5 percent of schizophrenics fall into this category.

The symptoms of schizophrenia often occur in characteristic patterns. This woman displays the inactivity and odd posturing associated with catatonic schizophrenia.

The most significant characteristic of **catatonic schizophrenia** is disorder of movement. The individual alternates between total immobility or stupor and wild excitement. Especially during stupor, the person may not speak, ignoring all attempts at communication, and either becomes rigid or shows a "waxy flexibility," which allows the person to be "posed" in virtually any posture. This subtype is also rare, occurring in only about 8 percent of all cases (McGlashan & Fenton, 1991).

About 40 percent of all schizophrenics appear in the **paranoid schizophrenia** subtype. Its most prominent features are delusions of persecution or grandeur accompanied by anxiety, anger, argumentativeness, or jealousy. Sometimes these feelings lead to violence. Compared with the other subtypes, paranoid schizophrenia tends to appear later in life, typically after the age of twenty-five or thirty; the onset is often sudden; and there is much less obvious impairment (Fenton & McGlashan, 1991). In most cases, the person is able to complete an education, hold a job, and even have a family before problems become severe. Here is a description of one case with a particularly late onset:

Mr. S. was first admitted to the hospital at the age of forty-eight. Some weeks earlier, he had taken to sealing the cracks under doors and in window sashes with the metal from empty toothpaste tubes to "keep out radio waves" that were being directed at him by agents of "the Tsar Nicholas." He lost his job around this time because of similar behavior at work, but he attributed his dismissal to the machinations of enemies and unnamed fellow workers. On the hospital ward he was condescending to the other patients, demanding many privileges for himself and giving lengthy accounts of the importance attached to him by both the Russians and the White House. He spent many hours perusing newspapers to see if his movements were reported there. (Summarized from Maher, 1966, p. 308)

Finally, as the name implies, **undifferentiated schizophrenia** is marked by patterns of disordered behavior, thought, and emotion that cannot be placed easily in any of the other subtypes. About 40 percent of diagnosed schizophrenics fall into this category (Fenton & McGlashan, 1991).

In addition to identifying these subtypes, researchers have classified schizophrenic symptoms as positive or negative (Nicholson & Neufeld, 1993). *Positive symptoms* include the *presence* of hallucinations, bizarre movements, and other unusual thoughts or behaviors. *Negative symptoms,* such as apathy, lack of emotion, or immobility, are defined by an *absence* of normal thoughts or actions. Many patients exhibit both positive and negative symptoms, though most do not display all identified schizophrenic symptoms. As we will see, some researchers believe that forms of schizophrenia dominated by positive or negative symptoms may stem from different causes.

The Search for Causes

There has probably been more research on the causes of schizophrenia than on the causes of any other form of psychological disorder. One thing is certain: no single theory can adequately account for all forms of schizophrenia.

Biological Factors Schizophrenia runs in families (see, Figure 2.5; Gottesman, 1991; Kennedy et al., 1988). The children and siblings of schizophrenics are, overall, about ten times more likely than other people to develop schizophrenia. Among twins where one is identified as suffering from schizophrenia, identical twins are much more likely to share schizophrenia than are nonidentical twins. Further, children of schizophrenics who are adopted by normal parents display schizophrenia more often than the general population (Allen, Cohen & Pollin, 1972; Kety et al., 1975). Still, most people with schizophrenic relatives are not schizophrenic. What may be inherited is a *predisposition,* or diathesis, toward schizophrenia.

Linkages: What role do genetics play in the appearance of schizophrenia? (a link to Biological Aspects of Psychology)

Part of this predisposition may have to do with biochemistry. Several lines of research support the hypothesis that neurotransmitters, especially dopamine, play a role in causing or at least intensifying schizophrenic thought and behavior. For example, there is a high positive correlation between the effectiveness of drugs used to treat schizophrenia and their ability to block the action of dopamine in the brain (Seeman & Lee, 1975). Further, as described in Chapter 7, heavy use of amphetamines is tied both to the stimulation of dopamine systems in the brain and to schizophrenia-like symptoms (Snyder, 1978). Indeed, giving amphetamines to schizophrenics makes their problems worse (Angrist, Lee & Gershon, 1974). Finally, paranoid suspiciousness can be induced by cocaine, a drug that also stimulates dopamine neurotransmitter systems (Sherer et al., 1988). All of these findings support the idea that excess dopamine or oversensitivity to dopamine (perhaps because of an abnormally high number of dopamine receptors) may be responsible either for some forms of schizophrenia or for the intensity of its symptoms, especially positive symptoms (Davis, 1978; Davis et al., 1991; Meltzer & Stahl, 1976; Seidman, 1990; Wong et al., 1986).

Some of the symptoms of schizophrenia have also been linked to abnormalities in areas of the brain involved in integrating attention, perception, emotion, and thought (Suddath et al., 1990). Data from autopsies, x-rays, PET scans, and MRIs suggest a possible tie between schizophrenia and many structural abnormalities. These abnormalities include shrinking or deterioration of cells in the cerebral cortex or cerebellum, resulting—as brain cells die—in enlargement of the brain's fluid-filled *ventricles* (see Figure 15.3); disorganization of cells in the hippocampus (an area involved with the expression of emotion); reduced blood flow in certain parts of the brain, especially the frontal lobes (Andreasen et al., 1990; Weinberger, Berman & Zec, 1986; Wolkin et al., 1992); and abnormalities in *brain lateralization* (the pattern of dominance of one cerebral hemisphere over the other), and in the way the hemispheres communicate with each other (Crow et al., 1989; Newlin, Carpenter & Golden, 1981).

But not all schizophrenics display such physical abnormalities—and some normal people do. As researchers have gathered more and more evidence, they have found interesting but unexplained variations. For one thing, enlarged lateral ventricles may be found in male but not female schizophrenics (Andreasen et al., 1990).

Figure 15.3
Brain Abnormalities in Schizophrenia

Here is a magnetic resonance imaging (MRI) comparison of the brains of a pair of identical twins, one of whom (on the right) was diagnosed as schizophrenic. The schizophrenic twin has greatly enlarged ventricles (the fluid-filled cavities indicated by arrows) and correspondingly less brain tissue, including that in the hippocampal area, a region involved in memory and emotion. The same results appeared in fourteen other identical-twin pairs; in some cases, the schizophrenic twin also had smaller temporal lobes. No significant differences appeared between members of a seven-pair control group of normal identical twins (Suddath et al., 1990). These results add support for the idea that brain abnormalities are associated with schizophrenia. Because identical twins have the exact same genes, the abnormalities appear to stem from nongenetic factors. What these may be is unclear; viral infections during critical periods of brain development, head injury, and oxygen deprivation at birth are among the possibilities (Andreasen et al., 1990).

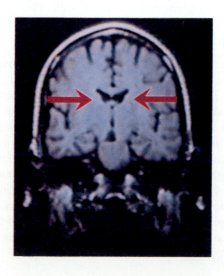 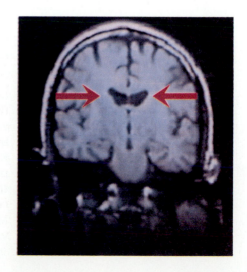

The nature of abnormalities in neurotransmitter systems and brain structures may be related to the person's symptoms. Excessive dopamine activity seems tied most closely to delusions and other positive symptoms of schizophrenia; dopamine-blocking drugs tend to blunt those symptoms. Negative symptoms, such as withdrawal, are associated with decreased dopamine activity, especially in prefrontal brain areas (Cohen & Servan-Schreiber, 1992; Davis et al., 1991). Negative symptoms have also been associated with abnormal brain structures such as enlarged lateral ventricles; schizophrenics with positive symptoms tend to have comparatively normal-looking brains (Andreasen et al., 1990; Crow, 1980). Firm conclusions about the meaning of all these correlational data await further research.

Psychological Factors   Psychodynamic theorists suggest that schizophrenic symptoms represent regression to early childhood, an extreme reaction to anxiety about expressing or becoming aware of unacceptable unconscious impulses (Freud, 1924). Psychoanalytic views of schizophrenia lack strong research support, however.

Behavioral theories suggest that the problematic thoughts and behaviors of people labeled as schizophrenic reflect their learned, though maladaptive, ways of trying to cope with anxiety (Mednick, 1958, 1970). Problems may also stem from patterns of reinforcement and punishment early in life: unfortunate learning experiences may have extinguished normal processes and inadvertently rewarded maladaptive behaviors and thoughts (Ullmann & Krasner, 1975).

On the assumption that the experiences that lead to schizophrenia occur in childhood, several theorists have looked for its psychological origins in the families of schizophrenics. They have focused especially on the effects of conflict, coldness, and poor communication in the family (see, for example, Fromm-Reichmann, 1948; Goldstein & Strachan, 1987; Roff & Knight, 1981). Even in a wildly disturbed family, however, only one child out of several may become schizophrenic. Further, the same conditions associated with schizophrenia in one person's family background may be associated with less severe disorders or no disorder at all in someone else's.

There is evidence for higher rates of relapse among recovered schizophrenics whose families show a chronically high level of emotional overinvolvement or criticism, termed *expressed emotion* (Jenkins & Karno, 1992). But so far, research has not supported the idea that family conditions alone cause schizophrenia. Indeed, faulty communication in the families of schizophrenics might be one of the *effects* of having a schizophrenic person disrupt the family (Asarnow & Horton, 1990). Thus it is important to be cautious about invoking family theories of schizophrenia. The guilt and anguish of family members who feel blamed for their relative's devastation can, itself, be devastating (Johnson, 1989).

Linkages: What role might stress play in the appearance of schizophrenia? (a link to Health, Stress, and Coping)

The Vulnerability Model: An Integrative View   This discussion brings us back to the diathesis-stress approach, which currently seems to offer the best perspective from which to view research on the causes of schizophrenia (Fowles, 1992). ("In Review: Schizophrenia" summarizes causal theories as well as the symptoms and subtypes of schizophrenia.) This approach is embodied in the *vulnerability model* of schizophrenia (Cornblatt & Erlenmeyer-Kimling, 1985; Zubin & Spring, 1977). This model suggests that (1) different people have differing degrees of vulnerability (diatheses) to schizophrenia; (2) this vulnerability is partly genetic, or may result from early prenatal or birth complications including maternal illness and malnutrition (Barr, Mednick & Munk-Jorgensen, 1990; Susser & Lin, 1992); and (3) the vulnerability may involve psychological components, such as a history of poor parenting, as well

In Review: Schizophrenia

Aspect	Key Features
Common Symptoms	
Disorders of thought	Disturbed *content,* including delusions; and disturbed *form,* such as loose associations, neologisms, and word salad.
Disorders of perception	Hallucinations or false perceptions; poorly focused attention.
Disorders of emotion	Flat affect; or inappropriate tears, laughter, or anger.
Subtypes	
Disorganized	Unrelated delusions and hallucinations most prominent; flat affect; incoherence and disorganized behavior.
Catatonic	Disorders of movement most prominent, including stupor, bizarre postures, and excitement.
Paranoid	Delusions most prominent; later onset than other subtypes.
Undifferentiated	Schizophrenic symptoms that do not fit any of the other subtypes.
Possible Causes	
Biological	Genetics; excess of dopamine or dopamine receptors (especially where positive symptoms prevail); abnormalities in brain structure (especially where negative symptoms prevail).
Psychological	Learned maladaptive behavior; disturbed patterns of family communication.

Figure 15.4
The Vulnerability Model of Schizophrenia
In this model, a person can cross the threshold into schizophrenia through many combinations of predisposition and stress. It can happen as the result of, for example, a strong predisposition for schizophrenia and little environmental stress (point D), a weak predisposition and a great deal of stress (point C), or any other sufficiently potent combination.

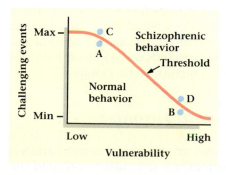

Source: Zubin & Spring, 1977.

as biological components. Many different blendings of vulnerability and stress can lead to schizophrenia, as Figure 15.4 illustrates. Persons whose genetic characteristics or prenatal experiences leave them vulnerable to develop schizophrenia may be especially likely to do so if they are later exposed to learning experiences or family conflicts and other stressors that draw out and maintain schizophrenic patterns of thought and action. Those same experiences and stressors would not be expected to lead to schizophrenia in people who are less vulnerable to developing the disorder. Clearly, schizophrenia is a highly complex disorder (probably more than one disorder), whose origins appear to lie in numerous biological and psychological domains, some of which are yet to be discovered (Heinrichs, 1993).

Personality Disorders

People labeled as having personality disorders are as disturbing to others as they are disturbed themselves. **Personality disorders** are long-standing, inflexible ways of behaving that are not so much severe mental disorders as styles of life, which, from childhood or adolescence, create problems for those who display them and for others (Millon, 1981). As mentioned in Chapter 14, some psychologists view personality disorders as interpersonal strategies or as the expression of extreme, rigid, and maladaptive personality traits (see, for example, Widiger & Kelso, 1983).

Several personality disorders are listed on Axis II of DSM-IV. Some of them seem to be less severe but chronic versions of other disorders appearing on Axis I (Widiger & Shea, 1991). For example, the person diagnosed as **schizotypal personality disorder** displays some of the peculiarities seen in schizophrenia but is not disturbed enough to be diagnosed as schizophrenic. Rather than hallucinating, the person may report "illusions" of people or objects. He or she may also exhibit "magical thinking," including odd superstitions or beliefs (for example, that salt under the mattress will prevent insomnia). **Avoidant personality disorder** is akin to social phobia in the sense that the person tends to be a "loner" with a long-standing pattern of avoiding social situations and of being particularly sensitive to criticism or rejection by others. The person wants to be with others but is too inhibited. The main characteristics of **narcissistic personality disorder** are an exaggerated sense of self-importance, extreme sensitivity to criticism, constant need for attention, and a tendency to arrogantly overestimate personal abilities and achievements. This person wants to be seen with the "right people" but has few, if any, friends.

From the perspective of public welfare and safety, the most serious, as well as the most widely studied personality disorder, is **antisocial personality.** It is marked by a long-term pattern of irresponsible, impulsive, unscrupulous, even criminal behavior, beginning in childhood or early adolescence. In the nineteenth century, the pattern was called *moral insanity,* because such persons appeared to have no morals or common decency; later, people in this category were called *psychopaths* or *sociopaths.* The current "antisocial personality" label more accurately portrays them as troublesome, but not "insane" by the legal standards we will discuss shortly. About 3 percent of men and about 1 percent of women in the United States fall into this diagnostic category.

At their least troublesome, these people are a nuisance to others. They are often charming, intelligent, glib talkers who borrow money and fail to return it; they are arrogant and self-centered manipulators who "con" others into doing things for them, usually by lying and taking advantage of the decency and trust of others. A hallmark of those displaying antisocial personality is a lack of anxiety, remorse, or guilt, whether they have wrecked a borrowed car or killed an innocent person (Hare, 1991; Hare, Hart & Harpur, 1991; Harpur, Hare & Hakstian, 1989).

There are numerous theories about the causes of antisocial personality. Some research suggests a genetic predisposition, possibly in the form of chronic underarousal of both the autonomic and central nervous systems (Caderet, 1985; Patrick, Bradley & Lang, 1993; Raine, Venables & Williams, 1990). This underarousal may render these people less sensitive to punishment than is normally the case (Eysenck, 1960; Fenz, 1971; Newman & Kosson, 1986). From psychological and social perspectives, broken homes, rejection by parents, lack of good parental models, lack of attachment to early caretakers, conflict-filled childhoods, and living in poverty have all been suggested as stressors that contribute to the problem. However, biological underarousal and psychosocial stressors also appear in the backgrounds of people who do not develop antisocial personalities, so the causal picture is still cloudy.

A Sampling of Other Psychological Disorders

The disorders described so far represent some of the most prevalent and socially disruptive psychological problems encountered in cultures around the world. Several others were mentioned in other chapters. In Chapter 7, for example, we discussed insomnia, night terrors, and other sleep disorders; mental

Serial killings by Ted Bundy, pictured here several months before his execution, and the violent crime sprees documented in Truman Capote's *In Cold Blood* and Norman Mailer's *The Executioner's Song,* represent the antisocial personality at its worst. At present there is no successful method for permanently altering the behavior of people displaying antisocial personality (American Psychiatric Association, 1989), but they seem to become less active and dangerous after the age of forty (Hare, McPherson & Forth, 1988).

retardation was covered in Chapter 10; sexual dysfunctions were mentioned in Chapter 12; and posttraumatic stress disorder was described in Chapter 13. We now consider two other significant psychological problems: substance-related disorders and some disorders of childhood.

Substance-Related Disorders

The use of alcohol and other psychoactive drugs has created major political, economic, social, and health problems worldwide. When people use psychoactive drugs for months or years in ways that harm themselves or others, they show what is called, in DSM-IV, a **substance-related disorder.** The substances involved most often are alcohol and other depressants, such as barbiturates and Quaaludes; opiates, such as heroin; stimulants, such as cocaine or amphetamines; and psychedelics, such as LSD.

As mentioned in Chapter 7, on consciousness, one effect of using some substances (including alcohol, heroin, and amphetamines) is **addiction,** a physical need for the substance. DSM-IV calls addiction *physiological substance dependence.* Usually, addiction is evident when the person begins to need more and more of a substance to achieve the desired state; this is called *building a tolerance.* When addicted people stop using the substance, they experience painful, often terrifying and potentially dangerous *withdrawal symptoms* as the body tries to readjust to a substance-free state. Even when use of a drug does not create physical addiction, some people may overuse, or *abuse,* it because it gives them temporary self-confidence, enjoyment, or relief from tension. DSM-IV defines *substance abuse* as a pattern of use that causes serious social, legal, or interpersonal problems. Thus, people can become *psychologically* dependent on psychoactive drugs without becoming physically addicted to them. We described these drugs and their impact on consciousness in Chapter 7; here we focus on the causes and broader consequences of their use.

Alcoholism More than 13 percent of American adults—in excess of 20 million people—display *alcohol dependence or abuse,* a pattern of continuous or intermittent drinking that may lead to addiction and almost always causes severe social, physical, and other problems (Canino et al., 1987; Robins et al., 1984). Males exceed females in this category by a ratio of about 6 to 1, though

The effects of alcohol dependence and abuse extend far beyond the individual who drinks to excess. It is estimated that some 43 percent of U.S. adults have had contact with an alcoholic in their families (Sullivan, 1991; NCHS, 1991; NIAAA, 1991). Children growing up in families in which one or both parents abuse alcohol are at increased risk for developing a host of mental disorders, including substance-related disorders (Sher et al., 1991). And, as described in Chapter 3, children of mothers who abused alcohol during pregnancy may be born with fetal alcohol syndrome.

the problem is on the rise among women and among teenagers of both genders. Prolonged overuse of alcohol can result in life-threatening liver damage, reduced cognitive abilities, vitamin deficiencies that can lead to an irreversible brain disorder called *Korsakoff's psychosis* (severe memory loss), and a host of other physical ailments. Alcohol dependence or abuse, commonly referred to as alcoholism, has been implicated in half of all the traffic fatalities, homicides, and suicides that occur each year; alcoholism also figures prominently in rape and child abuse (Alcohol and Health Report, 1984; ADAMHA, 1987), as well as in elevated rates of hospitalization and absenteeism from work (Julien, 1992).

The psychoanalytic approach suggests that dependence on alcohol, or on other psychoactive drugs, results from dependency needs that were never satisfied in infancy (Shedler & Block, 1990). Research on this hypothesis, however, also shows many other personality traits to be correlated with the appearance of alcoholism, so the role of inordinate dependency, let alone its causal impact, has not been established. One behavioral theory suggests that people learn to use alcohol because it helps them cope more comfortably with stressors. But use can become abuse, often addiction (see Table 15.4), if drinking is a person's main coping strategy (Walters, 1992). The stress-reduction theory of alcoholism has been supported by studies showing that alcohol can reduce animals' learned fear of a particular location and that animals in a stressful conflict situation will choose to drink alcohol if it is available (Conger, 1951; Freed, 1971). The stress-reducing effects of alcohol have also been shown in humans (Sher & Levenson, 1982), but not consistently (Steele & Josephs, 1988).

The importance of learning is also suggested by evidence that alcoholism is more common in ethnic and cultural groups (such as the Irish and English) where frequent drinking tends to be socially reinforced than in groups (such as the Jews, Italians, and Chinese) where all but moderate drinking tends to be discouraged (Frankel & Whitehead, 1981). Further, differing social support for drinking can result in differing drinking patterns within a cultural group. For example, one study found significantly more drinking among Japanese men living in Japan (where social norms for males' drinking are most permissive)

Table 15.4
Social Drinking Versus Alcoholism

Social drinking differs markedly from alcoholism, but it is all too easy for people to drift from social to alcoholic drinking patterns. Alcoholism can include heavy drinking on a daily basis, on weekends only, or in isolated binges lasting weeks or months.

Social Drinkers	Alcoholics
Sip drinks.	Gulp drinks.
Usually drink in moderation and can control the amount consumed.	Drink increasing quantities (develop tolerance). Sometimes drink until blacking out. May not recall events that occur while drinking.
Usually drink to enhance the pleasure of social situations.	Drink for the chemical effect, often to relieve tension or face problems; often drink alone, including in the morning to reduce hangover or to face the day.
Do not usually think about or talk about drinking in nondrinking situations.	Become preoccupied with getting next drink, often sneaking drinks during working hours or at home.
Do not experience physical, social, or occupational problems caused by drinking.	Suffer physical disorders, damaged social relationships, and impaired capacity to work because of drinking.

compared to those living in Hawaii or California, where excessive drinking is less strongly supported (Kitano et al., 1992). Learning would also help explain why the prevalence of alcoholism is higher than average among people working as bartenders and cocktail servers, and in other jobs where alcohol is available and drinking is socially reinforced, even expected (Fillmore & Caetano, 1980). (It is also possible, however, that it was attraction to alcohol that led some of these people into such jobs in the first place.)

Although excessive drinking may be partially explained by learning, heredity may also play a part, especially in males. The sons of alcoholics are more likely than others to become alcoholic themselves; if the sons are identical twins, both are at increased risk for alcoholism, even when they are raised apart (Cloninger, 1987; Goodwin, Crane & Guze, 1973; McGue, Pickens & Svikis, 1992). The role of genetics appears to be greatest among males who begin their alcoholic drinking pattern at an early age and display other conduct problems as teenagers (McGue, Pickens & Svikis, 1992). For females, and for males whose problem drinking appears later in life, the evidence for genetic causes is much less compelling. For these people, it may be that any genetic predisposition is too weak to result in alcoholism unless it is amplified by social and cultural family influences that promote drinking (McGue, Pickens & Svikis, 1992). Indeed, recent reanalysis of the evidence suggests that the genetic component of alcoholism may not be as strong overall as once believed (Gelernter, Goldman & Risch, 1993); it is certainly not clear just what might be inherited or what genes are involved.

Heroin and Cocaine Dependence

Like alcoholics, heroin and cocaine addicts suffer many serious health problems, as a result both of the drug itself and of the poor eating and health habits it engenders. The danger of death from an overdose, contaminated drugs, or AIDS (contracted through blood in shared needles), as well as suicide, is always present as well.

Continued use or overdoses of cocaine can cause problems ranging from nausea and hyperactivity to paranoid thinking, sudden depressive "crashes," and even death. An estimated one million Americans have become dependent on cocaine, and millions more use it on occasion (National Institute on Drug Abuse, 1991). The widespread availability of crack, a powerful and relatively cheap form of cocaine, has made it one of the most dangerous and addicting drugs in existence. Pregnant women who use cocaine are much more likely than nonusers to lose their babies through spontaneous abortions, placental detachments, early fetal death, or stillbirths. The more than 50,000 "crack babies" born each year to cocaine-using mothers are at risk for numerous physical and mental birth defects (Julien, 1992).

Although addiction to substances like heroin is largely understood to be a biological process brought about by the physical effects of the drugs, explaining why people first use them is more complicated. The causes of initial drug abuse are even less well established than the reasons for alcohol abuse. One current line of theorizing suggests that there might be a genetic tendency toward behavioral disregulation or compulsions that predisposes some people to abuse many kinds of drugs, including alcohol (Smith et al., 1992; Holden, 1991).

Psychological factors, such as the need to reduce stress, emulation of drug-using peers, thrill seeking, and social maladjustment, have all been proposed as initial causes of substance abuse. The desire to gain social status appears to be partially responsible for the increased use and abuse of cocaine in recent years. Research has still not yet established why drugs become a problem for some people and not for others, but, again, it is likely that some predisposition sets the stage on which specific psychological processes and stressors play out their roles.

Linkages: What kinds of psychological disorders appear in the early stages of life? (a link to Human Development)

Psychological Disorders of Childhood

As we described in Chapter 3, childhood is a period of rapid physical, cognitive, emotional, and social changes. These changes and the stress associated with them can create or worsen disorders in children. Stress can do the same in adults, but childhood disorders are not just miniature versions of adult psychopathology. Because children's development is still incomplete and because their capacity to cope with stress is limited in important ways, children are often vulnerable to special types of disorders. Two broad categories encompass the majority of childhood behavior problems: externalizing and internalizing disorders (Quay, 1979).

The *externalizing,* or *undercontrolled,* category includes behaviors that are aversive to people in the child's environment. Lack of control, especially in boys, shows up in *conduct disorders* characterized by aggression, disobedience, destructiveness, and other obnoxious behaviors. Often these behaviors involve criminal activity. A genetic predisposition toward conduct disorders is highly likely, but it is also clear that environmental and parenting factors influence the antisocial behavior of these children (Rutter & Giller, 1983). Recall that this pattern is consistent with antisocial personality disorder in adults.

Another kind of externalizing problem is *attention-deficit hyperactivity disorder (ADHD).* This label is given to children who are impulsive and unable to concentrate on an activity as well as other children their age can (Schachar & Logan, 1990). Many of these children are *hyperactive;* they have great difficulty sitting still or otherwise controlling their physical activity. Their impulsiveness and lack of self-control contribute to an astonishing ability to annoy and exhaust those around them and to create numerous problems, especially at school (Henker & Whalen, 1989). Genetic predisposition, the occurrence of brain damage, dietary problems, poisoning from lead or other household substances, and ineffective parenting have all been proposed as possible causes of hyperactivity, but the role played by each of these factors is still uncertain (Hauser et al., 1993; Marshall, 1989). Also uncertain is exactly what constitutes hyperactivity. Cultural standards about acceptable activity levels in children vary, so a "hyperactive" child in one culture might be considered merely "active" in another. Indeed, when mental health professionals from four cultures used the same rating scales to judge the presence and severity of hyperactivity in a videotaped sample of childrens' behavior, the Chinese and Indonesians rated the children as significantly more hyperactive than did their American and Japanese colleagues (Mann et al., 1992). Such findings remind us again that sociocultural standards can be important determinants of what is acceptable, and hence what is abnormal, in various parts of the world.

The second broad category of child behavior problems involves *internalizing,* or *overcontrol.* Children in this category experience internal distress, especially depression and anxiety, and may be socially withdrawn. In *separation anxiety disorder,* for example, the child constantly worries that he or she will be lost, kidnapped, or injured or that some harm may come to a parent (usually the mother). The child clings desperately to the parent and becomes upset or sick at the prospect of any separation. Refusal to go to school (sometimes called "school phobia") is often the result.

A few childhood disorders do not fall in either the externalizing or internalizing category. An example is *autistic disorder,* a severe and puzzling condition, usually identified within the first thirty months of life, in which babies show no sign of attachment to their mothers, fathers, or anyone else. Autistic babies do not smile, laugh, or make eye contact with their parents. They will not tolerate being held and cuddled; they seem unable to enter the social realm. As years go by, they ignore others and instead rock themselves repetitively or play endlessly, it seems, with ashtrays, keys, or other inanimate objects. Language development is seriously disrupted in these children. Half never learn to speak at all. Autistic disorder occurs in fewer than five children per ten thousand births; but, with few exceptions (Lovaas, 1987), it leads to a life of marginal adjustment, often within an institution.

Possible biological roots of autistic disorder include oversensitivity to stimulation (Zentall & Zentall, 1983) or abnormally high levels of natural opiates (discussed in Chapters 4 and 5), which may make autistic children less needful of comfort and other social interaction (Herman et al., 1986). Autistic children may also have problems with cell communication in the language areas of the brain (Minshew, Payton & Sclabassi, 1986). The specific causes of autistic disorder remain unknown.

Disorders of childhood differ from adult disorders not only because the patterns of behavior are distinct but also because their early onset renders childhood disorders especially capable of disrupting development. To take one example, children whose avoidance of school causes spotty attendance may not only fall behind academically but also fail to form the relationships with other children that promote normal social development. Some children never make up for this deficit. They may drop out of school and risk a life of poverty, crime, and violence. For some, the long-term result may be adult forms of mental disorder.

Mental Illness and the Law

As promised, we have reviewed some of the main forms of psychological disorder. We have also seen that, in accordance with the medical model predominating in many Western cultures, people displaying these disorders tend to be seen as "mentally ill." This label usually implies that the person needs help, but what does it say about the person's responsibilities as a citizen? For example, if "mentally ill" people commit a crime, should they be prosecuted and punished, given treatment, or both? Consider the following case:

Cheryl was barely twenty when she married Glen, a graduate student in biology. They moved into a large apartment complex near the university and within three years had two sons. Cheryl's friends had always been impressed by the attention and affection she showered on her boys; she seemed to be the ideal mother. She and Glen had serious marital problems, however, and she felt trapped and unhappy. One day Glen came home to find that Cheryl had stabbed both children to death. At her murder trial, she was found not guilty by reason of insanity and was placed in a state mental institution.

This verdict reflected laws and rules that protect severely disordered persons in the United States when they are accused of crimes. The protection takes two forms.

First, under certain conditions the mentally ill may be protected from prosecution. If, at the time of their trial, individuals accused of a crime are unable to understand the proceedings and charges against them or to assist in their own defense, they are declared to be *mentally incompetent* and therefore not eligible for trial. In such cases, the defendant is sent to a mental institution until he or she becomes mentally competent. If still not competent after a court-specified period, two years in most cases, the defendant may be permanently ineligible for trial and either committed in civil court to a mental institution or released. This is a rare outcome, however, because competency to stand trial requires only minimal mental abilities. If drugs can produce even temporary mental competence, the defendant will usually go to trial.

Second, the mentally ill may be protected from punishment. In most U.S. states, defendants may be judged not guilty by reason of insanity if, *at the time of the crime,* mental illness prevented them from (1) understanding what they were doing, (2) knowing that what they were doing was wrong, or (3) resisting the impulse to do wrong. The first two of these criteria—understanding the nature or wrongfulness of an act—are known as the *M'Naughton rule.* This rule stems from an 1843 English case in which a man named Daniel M'Naughton, upon hearing "instructions from God," tried to kill Prime Minister Robert Peel; he was found not guilty by reason of insanity and put into a mental institution for life. The third criterion is known as the *irresistible impulse test.* All three criteria are combined in a rule proposed by the American Law Institute (ALI) in 1962 and now followed in most U.S. states:

A person is not responsible for criminal conduct if at the time of such conduct as a result of mental disease or defect he lacks substantial capacity either to appreciate the criminality (wrongfulness) of his conduct or to conform his conduct to the requirements of law. (ALI, 1962, p. 66)

This rule was the basis for Cheryl's defense, and the jury accepted it. If defendants are judged to be insane and dangerous to themselves or others at the time of trial, they are usually required to receive treatment, typically through commitment to a hospital, until judged to be cured or no longer dangerous.

Insanity rules have several problems. First, Thomas Szasz and others whose opposition to the mental illness concept we discussed earlier, disagree with the protective purpose of the rules. They argue that everyone, even those who meet legal criteria for insanity, should be held responsible for their actions and punished for their crimes. In addition, there are significant problems with the implementation of rules about insanity. Different experts often give conflicting, highly technical testimony about a defendant's sanity at the time of the crime. (One expert said Cheryl was sane; the other concluded she was insane.) The jury of nonexperts is left in the almost impossible position of deciding which expert to believe. Furthermore, in some cases, a defendant found not guilty by reason of insanity may spend more time in a mental hospital than if he or she had been convicted of the crime and sentenced to prison. This happens very rarely, but it does illustrate how well-intentioned laws can produce a miscarriage of justice.

What can be done about these problems? Three U.S. states have abolished the insanity defense. Three other less extreme reforms have also been attempted. First, several states now permit a verdict of *guilty but mentally ill.* Defendants found guilty but mentally ill still serve a sentence but are supposed to receive treatment while in a prison or special institution. Critics object that this verdict is a compromise that ensures neither proper treatment nor proper verdicts since mentally ill prisoners should receive treatment anyway. For federal courts, a second reform (embodied in the Insanity Defense Reform Act) eliminated the irresistible-impulse criterion from the definition of insanity. Third, the federal courts and some states now require the *defendant* to prove that he or she was insane at the time of the crime, rather than requiring the prosecution to prove that the defendant was sane.

Clearly, no generally satisfactory solution for the dilemmas surrounding mental disorder and criminal behavior has yet been found. Note, however, that the intensity of the arguments is disproportionately high given the frequency of the problem. The insanity plea is raised in only 1 to 2 percent of the felony cases that go to trial, and it is successful in only a tiny fraction of those cases.

Future Directions

There have been many ideas over the years about what constitutes abnormality. Even today the criteria for calling someone "crazy" differ from one culture or subculture to the next. Mental health professionals are expanding the practical approach to consider the content and consequences of behavior within its sociocultural context. Future years are likely to see a continued trend, begun with DSM-IV, toward basing diagnoses not only on what a person does but also on what values and traditions the behavior reflects, where and when it occurs, and who, if anyone, suffers (Rogler, 1992; Fabrega, 1992). Ideally, DSM's continuing evolution toward ever more specific criteria for assessing disorders should leave less room for bias based on ethnicity, gender, and other sociocultural variables. Further, researchers and clinicians are more aware than ever that when psychological differences between men and women are seen, male behavior and mental processes do not necessarily define normality (Riger, 1992).

Will there ultimately be separate rules for assessing disorders in men and women or in European-, African-, Asian-, Native-, and Hispanic-Americans? Probably not. Instead, there will likely be a growing recognition that gender and other sociocultural variables may endow people with differing characteristics and, more certainly, expose them to different experiences, conflicts, responsibilities, resources, and values. Diagnosticians will become more sensitive to the fact that these differences may influence different groups to deal with the world in ways that are not necessarily familiar, but not necessarily pathological either (Fabrega, 1992; Landrine, 1991).

Research into the causes of mental disorders will reflect continued attention to biological explanations. The focus will not be entirely biological, however. Adopting a diathesis-stress approach, researchers will be looking for multiple rather than single causes for disorders. They will examine how a variety of interacting factors—biological, psychological, environmental, and sociocultural—may or may not produce abnormality, depending on how these factors are combined. For example, researchers who study depression are trying to identify not only which specific cognitive patterns are associated with depression (Metalsky et al., 1993) but also how these patterns are related to other personality characteristics (Nietzel & Harris, 1990) and how the patterns interact with negative life events (Monroe & Simons, 1992). Because it seems clear that no single perspective is capable of explaining all mental disorders, we expect the future will see more and more cooperation among researchers from many perspectives.

Researchers will also be trying to refine the classification of mental disorders by identifying subtypes and variants that may have differing causes. This trend is exemplified by research suggesting that different biological factors may be associated with different subtypes of schizophrenia.

We have offered only a glimpse of the problems, issues, and theories that characterize the study of psychological disorders. For more detailed coverage, enroll in a course in abnormal psychology.

Summary and Key Terms

Psychopathology involves patterns of thinking, feeling, and behaving that are maladaptive, disruptive, or distressing either for the person affected or for others.

Understanding Psychological Disorders: Some Basic Issues

Abnormal behavior is defined largely by the culture in which the behavior takes place.

What Is Abnormal?

Exactly what is abnormal can be defined by the *statistical approach,* a comparison to what most people do, or by the *evaluative approach,* which is guided by what society values. Each view has problems. The *practical approach* looks at the content, context, and consequences of behavior. From the practical perspective, abnormal behavior makes a person uncomfortable, disables daily functioning, or interferes substantially with the lives of others.

Explaining Psychological Disorders

Abnormal behavior has been attributed, at one time or another, to the action of gods or the devil (the *demonological* or *supernatural model*) and to physical disease (the *medical* or *biological model*). The medical model, which suggests that all mental disorder results from physical illness, is very influential in most Western cultures, but some form of the supernatural model is employed in some Western subcultures and many non-Western cultures. The influence of the Western medical model is strengthened by disorders such as *dementia* and *delirium,* that have a definite biological cause.

Szasz has argued that mental illness is just a term for people's problems in living and that viewing all of them as illnesses deprives people of their rights. Szasz's critics suggest that his position is too extreme and may create new injustices, including depriving people of needed treatment.

Linkages: Psychological Disorders and Approaches to Personality

Each of the approaches to personality described in Chapter 14 suggests a different set of psychological causes of mental disorder. The psychodynamic approach focuses on unconscious conflicts and early interpersonal relations. Cognitive-behavioral approaches emphasize learned maladaptive actions and thoughts. And the phenomenological approach sees disorders as resulting from blocked self-actualization.

Sociocultural factors help define abnormality and influence the form that disorders take in different parts of the world. No single model can adequately explain all psychological disorders. However, the *diathesis-stress approach* takes all of them into account by highlighting interactions among inherited predispositions, acquired psychological characteristics, and the stress of life.

Classifying Psychological Disorders

There seems to be a set of behavior patterns that roughly defines abnormality in most cultures.

A Classification System: DSM-IV

The dominant system for classifying abnormal behavior is the Diagnostic and Statistical Manual (DSM-IV) of the American Psychiatric Association. It includes more than three hundred specific categories of mental disorder that can be described using five dimensions, or axes. Some psychologists question the DSM's reliability, validity, and vulnerability to biased use.

Anxiety Disorders

Long-standing and disruptive patterns of anxiety characterize *anxiety disorders.*

Types of Anxiety Disorders

The most prevalent type of anxiety disorder are the *phobias,* which include *specific phobia, social phobia,* and *agoraphobia.* Other anxiety disorders include *generalized anxiety disorder,* which involves nonspecific anxiety; *panic disorder,* which brings unpredictable attacks of intense anxiety; and *obsessive-compulsive disorder (OCD),* in which uncontrollable repetitive thoughts and ritualistic actions occur.

Causes of Anxiety Disorders

The most influential explanations of anxiety disorders suggest that they may develop as a result of a combination of biological predisposition for strong anxiety reactions and the impact of fear-enhancing thought patterns and learned anxiety responses.

Somatoform Disorders

Somatoform disorders include *conversion disorder,* which involves physical problems that have no apparent physical cause; *hypochondriasis,* an unjustified concern over being or becoming ill; *somatization disorder,* in which the person complains of numerous, unconfirmed physical complaints; and *pain disorder,* in which pain is felt in the absence of a physical cause.

Dissociative Disorders

Dissociative disorders involve such rare conditions as *dissociative fugue, dissociative amnesia,* and dissociative identity disorder *(multiple personality disorder),* in which a person suffers sudden memory loss or develops two or more separate identities. The experience of abuse in childhood may be a causal factor in multiple personality disorder.

Mood Disorders

Mood disorders, also known as affective disorders, are quite common and involve extreme moods that may be inconsistent with events.

Depressive Disorders

Major depressive disorder is marked by feelings of inadequacy, worthlessness, and guilt; in extreme cases, *delusions* may also occur. Also seen is *dysthymic disorder,* which includes similar but less severe symptoms persisting for a long period. Suicide is often related to these disorders, as well as to panic disorder and other problems.

Bipolar Disorder

Alternating periods of depression and *mania* characterize *bipolar disorder,* which is also known as manic depression. Cyclothymic disorder, an alternating pattern of less extreme mood swings, is more common.

Causes of Mood Disorders

Mood disorders have been attributed to dependency needs, loss of significant sources of reward, pessimistic patterns of thinking, disruptions in neurotransmitter systems, and irregularities in daily biological rhythms. A predisposition toward some of these problems may be inherited, though their appearance may be determined by a diathesis-stress process.

Schizophrenia

Symptoms of Schizophrenia

Schizophrenia is perhaps the most severe and puzzling disorder of all. Among its symptoms are problems in thinking, perception (often including *hallucinations*), attention, emotion, movement, motivation, and daily functioning.

Types of Schizophrenia

Five subtypes of schizophrenia have been identified, including *residual, disorganized, catatonic, paranoid,* and *undifferentiated.* Positive symptoms of schizophrenia include the presence of such features as hallucinations or disordered speech; behavioral withdrawal, immobility, and the absence of affect are examples of negative symptoms.

The Search for Causes

Genetic factors, neurotransmitter problems, brain abnormalities, regression to infancy, unfortunate learning experiences, and disturbed family interactions have all been implicated as possible causes of schizophrenia. The diathesis-stress approach, often described in terms of the vulnerability model, remains a promising framework for research into the multiple causes of schizophrenia.

Personality Disorders

Personality disorders are long-term patterns of behavior that are not as severe as other mental disorders and are not always associated with personal discomfort, although they may be disturbing to others. Examples include *schizotypal, avoidant, narcissistic,* and *antisocial personality disorders.*

A Sampling of Other Psychological Disorders

Substance-Related Disorders

Substance-related disorders involving alcohol and other drugs affect millions of people. *Addiction* to and psychological dependence on these substances contribute to disastrous personal and social problems, including physical illnesses, accidents, and crime. Genetic factors may create a predisposition for *alcoholism,* but learning, cultural traditions, and other nonbiological processes are also important. For addiction to heroin and cocaine, stress reduction, imitation, thrill seeking, and social maladjustment may be more important factors than genetics; but the exact causes of initial use of these drugs are unknown.

Psychological Disorders of Childhood

Childhood disorders can be categorized as externalizing conditions, such as conduct disorders or attention hyperactivity deficit disorders, and as internalizing disorders, in which children show overcontrol, experiencing internal distress as in separation anxiety disorder. The most severe childhood disorder is autistic disorder, in which the child shows no concern for or attachment to others.

Mental Illness and the Law

Current rules protect people accused of crimes from prosecution or punishment if they are mentally incompetent at the time of their trial or if they were legally insane at the time of their crime. But difficulty in establishing the mental state of defendants and other knotty problems have created dissatisfaction with those rules and prompted a number of reforms, including the "guilty but mentally ill" verdict.

Chapter 16

Treatment of Psychological Disorders

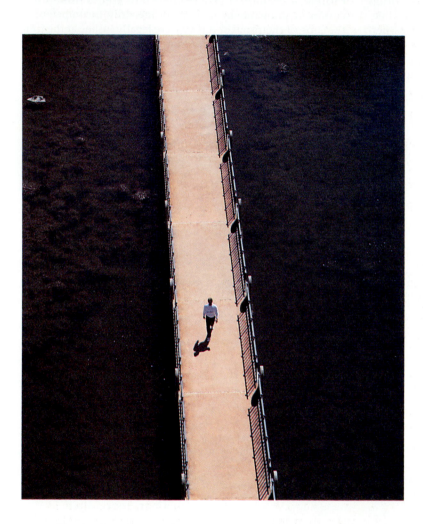

Outline

In the last chapter, we described José, a fifty-five-year-old electronics technician who had to take medical leave from his job after he suddenly began to experience frequent and severe panic attacks (see Table 15.1). Though four months of diagnostic testing turned up no physical problems, José spent most of his time sitting at home, worrying. His physician referred him to a psychologist, but José resisted, saying that his condition was not "just in his head." Eventually, he received psychological treatment for panic disorder, a condition described in Chapter 15. Within a few weeks, his panic attacks had ceased, and José was back to all his old activities. After the psychologist helped him to reconsider his workload, José decided to retire from his industrial job in order to pursue more satisfying work at his home-based computer business.

At some time in their lives, about one of every ten people in the United States receives treatment for a psychological disorder (Klerman, 1983), and during any one-year period, 14.7 percent receive some form of mental health services (Regier et al., 1993). Often, the problems involve the disorders described in Chapters 13 and 15, but they may also be relatively mild difficulties, such as shyness or lack of self-confidence. In this chapter, we examine methods for treating and preventing a wide range of psychological disorders. The bases for most of these methods lie in the theories of stress-coping, personality, and psychological disorder reviewed in Chapters 13, 14, and 15. By spelling out proposed explanations for what can go wrong in the development of personality and behavior, and the role of stress in both, those theories provide important guidelines for treatment (see the Linkages diagram).

After first examining some basic features of the treatment of psychological disorders, we discuss psychodynamic, phenomenological, and behavioral approaches to treatment. These approaches rely on **psychotherapy**, the treatment of psychological disorders through psychological methods, such as talking about problems and exploring new ways of thinking and acting. We then consider the biological approach to treatment, which depends mainly on drugs and other physical therapies. Although we discuss different approaches in separate sections, keep in mind that the majority of mental health professionals see themselves as *eclectic therapists;* in other words, they might lean toward one treatment approach, but, in working with particular clients or particular problems, they borrow methods from other types of therapy as well (Jensen, Bergin & Greaves, 1990). It is also common nowadays for clients to receive psychoactive medication during the course of psychological treatment (Lickey & Gordon, 1991).

Essentials of Treatment

All treatments for psychological disorders share certain basic features—not only with one another but also with efforts to help the physically ill (Frank, 1973, 1978). These common features include a *client* or patient, a *therapist* or helper who is accepted as capable of helping the client, and a special relationship between the client and therapist (Grencavage & Norcross, 1991). In addition, all forms of treatment are based on some *theory* about the causes of the client's problems. The theories may presume causes ranging from magic spells to infections and everything in between (Frank, 1973). From theories flow *procedures* for dealing with the client's problems. Traditional healers combat supernatural forces with ceremonies and prayers, medical doctors treat chemical imbalances with drugs, and psychologists seek to alter psychological processes through psychotherapy.

People receiving psychotherapy may be classified into three categories. *Inpatients* are treated in a hospital or other residential institution; in public hospitals, many are older adult males from lower social class backgrounds. *Outpatients* receive psychotherapy while living in the community; they tend to be younger than the average inpatient, more often female than male, and typically come from the middle or upper classes. A final category is made up of people who come to therapy not because of major problems but to seek personal growth; they are usually young to middle-aged adults who have the intellectual curiosity, financial resources, and leisure time to devote to the exploration of their personal relationships and their potential as human beings.

Linkages

The questions in this diagram illustrate a few of the relationships between the topic of this chapter, the treatment of psychological disorders, and other chapter topics. Many treatment techniques covered in this chapter grew out of the theories of personality reviewed in Chapter 14. For example, the behavioral approach to personality, with its emphasis on learning principles, inspired the learning-based methods of behavior therapy that focus on teaching disturbed people how to act in more adaptive ways. Modern methods of treatment also owe much to biological psychology. In particular, research on neurotransmitters contributed greatly to the development of drugs that can be used in the treatment of psychological disorders.

These and other links—a sampling of which is shown in the diagram—are discussed in the text. The page numbers indicate where in the text each question is explored. ■

RESEARCH IN PSYCHOLOGY
What research methods have been used to evaluate treatment for psychological disorders? (p. 586)

BIOLOGICAL ASPECTS OF PSYCHOLOGY
What biological mechanisms underlie drug treatment of psychological disorders? (p. 600)

HEALTH, STRESS, AND COPING
Can stress-management programs help alleviate psychological disorders? (p. 475)

Treatment of Psychological Disorders

CONSCIOUSNESS
Can meditation help people deal with psychological problems? (p. 233)

THOUGHT AND LANGUAGE
How can therapists help people alter maladaptive thought patterns? (p. 582)

LEARNING
What principles of learning can help people change maladaptive behaviors? (p. 577)

Linkages: What methods are used to treat psychological disorders? (a link to Psychological Disorders)

Providers of psychological treatment are also a diverse group. **Psychiatrists** are medical doctors who complete specialty training in the treatment of mental disorders. **Psychologists** who do psychotherapy have completed a masters or doctoral degree in clinical or counseling psychology, often followed by additional specialized training. Unlike psychiatrists, psychologists are not authorized to prescribe drugs, though if a recent and very controversial proposal were to be adopted, prescription privileges would be extended to clinical psychologists who have been specially trained for this function (DeLeon, Fox & Graham, 1991). *Psychiatric social workers* typically hold a master's degree from a school of social work and provide therapy in a hospital or clinic, though many also enter private practice. *Psychiatric nurses, occupational therapists,* and *recreational therapists* also provide various forms of therapy, most often as part of a hospital treatment team.

These therapists' most general goal is to help troubled people change their thinking, feelings, and behavior so that they will be happier and more productive. The specific methods employed in pursuit of this goal can take many forms. Among the methods available are those aimed at promoting insight into the hidden causes of problems, those designed to promote personal growth through more genuine self-expression, and those which help clients learn and practice new ways of thinking and acting. The particular methods employed depend on several factors. The problems, preferences, and financial circumstances of the client often shape the treatment sought and the methods used, as do the time available for treatment and the therapist's theoretical leanings and methodological preferences. There are many methods from which to choose. Over the last century, hundreds of specific methods of psychotherapy have been identified (see, for example, Corsini, 1989; Parloff, 1987), though most of them fall into one of three categories: psychodynamic, phenomenological, and behavioral.

The methods used to treat abnormality are related to the presumed cause of the problems. In the days when gods or demons were blamed for behavior disorders, magical-religious practitioners tried to make the victim's body an uncomfortable place for an evil spirit. Here, an afflicted person's head is placed in an oven, resulting in the departure of numerous evil spirits.

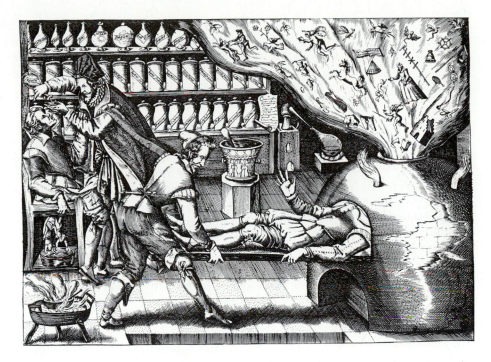

Psychodynamic Psychotherapy

The field of formal psychotherapy began in the late nineteenth century when Sigmund Freud established the psychodynamic approach to personality and disorder described in Chapters 14 and 15. Central to his approach, and to modern revisions of it, is the assumption that personality and behavior reflect the efforts of the ego to referee conflicts, usually unconscious, among various components of the personality. Freud's method of treatment, **psychoanalysis**, offers a set of psychological procedures for understanding unconscious conflicts and working through their effects. His one-to-one method of studying and treating people, his systematic search for relationships between an individual's life history and current problems, his emphasis on thoughts and emo-

The image of therapy that comes quickest to many people's minds is of someone lying on a couch describing dreams to a bearded, pipe-smoking therapist. To be sure, some therapy is done this way. But no single image can capture the many forms of modern treatment. It is offered to individuals, families, and groups in hospitals, community mental health centers, private clinics, and halfway houses (in which former hospital residents and other clients live while receiving therapy, supervision, and support). Treatment is also provided in prisons, military bases, drug and alcoholism treatment centers, and other places.

tions in treatment, and his focus on the client-therapist relationship reappear in almost all forms of psychotherapy. We will describe Freud's classical psychoanalytic methods first, then consider some more recently developed treatments that are rooted in his psychodynamic approach.

Classical Psychoanalysis

Classical psychoanalysis developed mainly out of Freud's medical practice. He was puzzled by patients who suffered from hysterical ailments—blindness, paralysis, or other symptoms that had no physical cause. (As mentioned in Chapter 15, these are now called conversion disorders in DSM-IV.) Freud tried to cure these patients through hypnotic suggestion, but he found it only partially and temporarily successful. Later, he and a colleague named Joseph Breuer began asking hypnotized patients to recall events that might have caused their symptoms. Eventually, Freud stopped using hypnosis and merely had the patient relax on a couch and report the memories that came to mind.

The results of this "talking cure" were surprising. Freud and Breuer were struck by how many patients reported childhood memories of sexual abuse, usually by a parent or other close relative. Either child abuse was rampant in Vienna at the time or his patients' reports were distorted by psychological factors. Freud ultimately concluded that his patients' memories of childhood seduction might in fact reflect childhood fantasies (a conclusion that has come under attack, as discussed in the chapter on personality). This reasoning focused classical psychoanalysis on the exploration of unconscious wishes and conflicts. His patients' hysterical symptoms, Freud concluded, developed out of conflicts about those wishes and fantasies.

Classical psychoanalytic treatment aims to help clients gain insight by recognizing and dealing with unconscious thoughts and emotions and to help them work through the many ways in which those unconscious elements affect everyday life. For example, a man might be hostile toward his boss, an older co-worker, and all other "parent figures" in his life because he is unconsciously re-enacting childhood conflicts with an overprotective parent. The psychoanalyst would help the client recognize his hidden, pent-up anger toward the parent, experience it, and trace how this unconscious source of continuing anger and the defenses around it have been creating problems.

Classical psychoanalytic treatment may require as many as three to five sessions per week, usually over several years. Generally, the psychoanalyst aims to maintain a compassionate neutrality during treatment so that the client can, with the therapist's guidance, slowly develop insight into how past conflicts determine current problems. To provide this guidance the therapist uses several techniques.

Free Association   Freud believed that many clues to the unconscious lie in the constant stream of thoughts, feelings, memories, and images experienced by all people. These clues can be uncovered and understood, he said, if the client relaxes defenses that block or distort the stream of consciousness. Thus, one of most basic techniques of classical psychoanalysis is **free association**, in which the client relaxes, often lying on a couch, and reports everything that comes to mind as soon as it occurs, no matter how trivial, bizarre, or embarrassing it may seem.

Clues to the unconscious may appear in the way thoughts are linked rather than in the thoughts themselves. Consider this example from the free association of a middle-aged male:

My Dad called long distance last night. He seemed upset. . . . (Long silence.) I almost fell asleep there for a minute. I used to do that a lot in college. Once I woke up and saw the professor standing over me. He was shaking me and the whole class was laughing.

Notice that after talking about his father, the client fell silent. When clients stop talking or claim that their minds are blank, the psychoanalyst may suspect that unconscious defense mechanisms are keeping threatening material out of consciousness. In this case, after having first thought about his father, the client remembered receiving punishment from an authority figure. This sequence might be a clue that unconscious conflicts with his father have not yet been resolved.

The Interpretation of Dreams   As discussed in the chapter on consciousness, dreams may be a by-product of brain activity during sleep, but their content may also reflect the dreamer's emotional state or psychological concerns. Psychoanalysts believe that dreams express wishes, impulses, and fantasies that the dreamer's defenses keep unconscious during waking hours. Even in dreams, however, defenses usually disguise threatening material so that the dream does not frighten (and awaken) the dreamer. In classical psychoanalysis, considerable time is devoted to helping the client search for the unconscious meaning of dreams.

For example, suppose a woman reports a dream in which the president of the United States is fighting with a waiter in an Italian restaurant. The client's description of the dream provides its *manifest content.* Manifest content often contains unimportant features and events from the day or reflects temporary needs. In this case, perhaps the dreamer had just seen the president on television. According to psychoanalytic theory, however, a dream also has *latent content,* which is its unconscious meaning, expressed by the dream's symbolism. Perhaps the restaurant represents an Italian friend, and the fight between president and waiter symbolizes the dreamer's conflict about wanting to be wealthy and powerful (the president) but also wanting to be of service to ("wait on") others. To explore latent content, the analyst may suggest an interpretation or ask the client to free-associate to parts of the dream.

Giving Interpretations   The classical analyst offers **interpretations**, or alternative ways of looking at the client's thoughts and behaviors, to help the client become more aware of all aspects of his or her personality, including

According to Freud, human actions are determined by a combination of conscious intentions and unconscious influences. Even apparently trivial or accidental behavior may hold important messages from the unconscious. Thus, in classical psychoanalysis, forgetting the content of a dream or the time of a therapy appointment might reflect a client's unconscious resistance to treatment. Even accidents may be meaningful. The waiter who spills hot soup on an elderly male customer might be acting out unconscious aggressive impulses against a father figure.

defenses and the unconscious material behind them. Here is an example of a classical analytic interpretation.

Client: I'm sorry I'm late, but my brother-in-law called just as I was leaving. He told me my sister is sick again and asked if I had any extra cash to help with her medical bills. I said I did, but I don't know how I can help them and keep coming to see you. Sometimes, everything falls on me at once.

Therapist: You know, last session, we began to see that you have some very negative feelings toward your parents. That was difficult for you to accept. Today, you start off by saying that, through no fault of your own, you may not be able to continue therapy. Could it be that whenever you are threatened by what you are learning about yourself here, you use something beyond your control to divert our attention? I wonder, because you told me you used to get out of trouble this way as a child. When your parents got angry with you, you always blamed your mistakes on someone else who kept you from doing what you should. What do you think?

The psychoanalyst's basic strategy is to construct increasingly accurate and empathic accounts of what has happened to the client (but has been "forgotten") and what is happening to the client (but is not understood). The analyst gradually shares these accounts with the client through interpretations.

Analysis of the Transference   Classical psychoanalysts believe that if they reveal nothing about themselves to a client, a transference relationship will develop. In **transference** the client unconsciously re-enacts, toward the therapist, many of the feelings, attitudes, reactions, and conflicts experienced in childhood with parents and other significant people. A "new edition" of the client's problems—a recapitulation of childhood conflicts—appears in this transference. The transference may take many forms, including falling in love with the therapist, becoming dependent, or being hostile. Classical psychoanalysts believe that focusing on and analyzing the transference allow clients to see how old conflicts continue to haunt their lives and to resolve these problems from the past.

Contemporary Variations on Psychoanalysis

Though classical psychoanalysis is still practiced (Fonagy & Moran, 1990), it is not as prevalent as it was several decades ago (Jensen, Bergin & Greaves, 1990). The decline is due partly to disenchantment with Freud's instinct-based personality theory, to the fact that classical psychoanalysis is so expensive and time consuming, to its limitations for use with children, and to the availability of many alternative forms of treatment, including variations on classical psychoanalysis.

Many of the variations were developed by the neo-Freudian theorists discussed in Chapter 14. As noted there, some give less emphasis than Freud did to the past and to biologically based drives stemming from the id and unconscious. They tend to stress the client's current problems and how the power of the ego can be harnessed to solve them. Some have been designed for use with children (Klein, 1960; A. Freud, 1946). Examples of these variations include *ego analysis* (Hartmann, 1958; Klein, 1960), *interpersonal therapy* (Sullivan, 1954), and *individual analysis* (Adler, 1963). A particularly popular contemporary psychodynamic approach is known as *object relations therapy* (Bacal & Newman, 1990; Cashdan, 1988; Greenberg & Mitchell, 1983; Kohut, 1983).

Object relations analysts believe that personality, and the conflicts among its components, derive from the need for supportive human relationships. The mother-child relationship—and the attachment patterns described in Chapter 3, on development—form the prototype for these relationships (Kohut, 1971;

Contemporary variants of psychoanalytic treatment include fantasy play and other techniques that make the approach more useful with children. A child's behavior and comments while playing with puppets representing family members, for example, allows a form of free association that the therapist hopes will reveal important unconscious material (such as fear of abandonment). Therapeutic play also offers an opportunity for the child to reexperience and reconsider—in a safe environment—troubling events of the past and to begin to develop better ways of dealing with them.

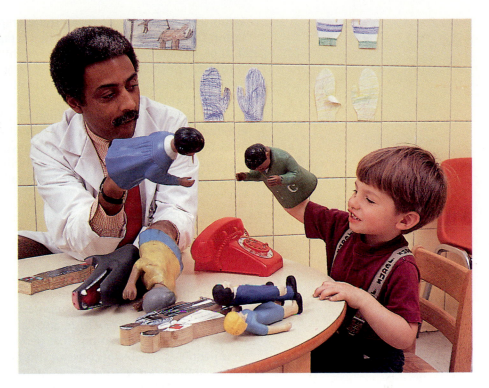

Cashdan, 1988). (The term *object* refers to anything, from symbols to people, that can have emotional significance for a person.) The powerful need for human contact takes center stage in object relations therapy, since most of the difficulties that bring clients to treatment involve their relationships with others.

Psychoanalysts who adopt an object relations perspective take a much more active role than classical analysts do. The object relations analyst works to develop a nurturing relationship with the client, providing a sort of "second chance" for the client to receive the support that might have been absent in infancy and to counteract some of the consequences of maladaptive early attachment patterns (see, for example, Lieberman & Pawl, 1988). The analyst seeks to demonstrate that the client will not be abandoned:

Beth: "Does it pay for me to keep coming?"

Therapist: "I'll be here next week . . . same time, same place."

Beth: "I'm not sure I'll be coming."

Therapist: "You decide what's best. Just remember, this time is yours. I'll be here no matter what you decide." (Cashdan, 1973, p. 89)

Therapy focuses not only on the transference but also on analysis of the therapist's feelings toward the client, called *countertransference*. For example, if transference leads a client to treat the therapist as a mother, the therapist might, because of countertransference, unintentionally begin treating the client as her child. Ideally, the development and analysis of this emotionally intimate relationship serves as a stepping stone for the client to develop healthier, more satisfying relationships with others.

Other variations on psychoanalysis retain more of Freud's ideas but alter the format of treatment so that it is less intense, less expensive, and appropriate for a broader range of clients. For example, *psychoanalytically oriented psychotherapy* (Alexander, 1963) and *time-limited dynamic psychotherapy* use basic psychoanalytic methods, but flexibly (Davanloo, 1978; Sifneos, 1979; Strupp,

1989). The client may sit facing the therapist and spend more time in conversation than in free association. The therapist may be more active than a classical psychoanalyst in directing the client's attention to evidence of particular conflicts. The goal of treatment may range from giving psychological support to achieving basic changes in personality, and therapy may be completed in fewer than thirty sessions.

With their focus on interpersonal relationships rather than instincts, their emphasis on clients' potential for self-directed problem solving, and their reassurance and emotional supportiveness, contemporary variants on classical psychoanalysis have helped the psychodynamic approach to retain its influence among mental health professionals (Cashdan, 1988; Jensen, Bergin & Greaves, 1990).

Phenomenological Psychotherapy

While some therapists who were trained in classical psychoanalysis sought to revise or modernize Freud's approach, others developed radical new therapies based on a phenomenological approach to personality. As discussed in Chapters 14 and 15, *phenomenologists,* also called *humanistic psychologists,* emphasize the subjective interpretations that people place on events. Phenomenologists view people as capable of consciously controlling their own actions and taking responsibility for their decisions. Many phenomenological therapists believe that human behavior is motivated not by sexual or aggressive instincts but by an innate drive toward growth that is guided from moment to moment by the way people interpret the world. Disordered behavior reflects a blockage of natural growth, brought on by distorted perceptions or lack of awareness about feelings. Thus, phenomenological therapists operate on the following assumptions:

1. Treatment is a human encounter between equals, not a cure given by an expert. It is a way to help clients restart their natural growth and to feel and behave as they really are.
2. Clients will improve on their own, given the right conditions. These ideal conditions promote clients' awareness, acceptance, and expression of their feelings and perceptions. Thus, as in psychodynamic approaches, therapy promotes insight. Phenomenological therapy, however, seeks insight into current feelings and perceptions, not into unconscious childhood conflicts.
3. Ideal conditions in therapy can best be established within a relationship in which the client feels totally accepted and supported. It is the client's experience of this relationship that brings beneficial changes. (As noted earlier, this assumption is also important in object relations therapy.)
4. Clients must remain responsible for choosing how they will think and behave.

There are many forms of phenomenological treatment. We will consider just two, those of Carl Rogers and Frederick S. Perls.

Client-Centered Therapy

Carl Rogers was trained in psychodynamic methods during the 1930s, but he soon began to question their value. He especially disliked being a detached, expert observer who "figured out" the client. He became convinced that a less formal approach would be more effective for the client and more comfortable for the therapist. As a result, Rogers developed *nondirective therapy,* which depends on the client's own drive toward growth or self-actualization. Rogers allowed his clients to decide what to talk about and when, without direction, judgment, or interpretation from the therapist. This approach, now called **client-centered**—or **person-centered**—**therapy**, relies on the creation of a relationship that reflects three intertwined therapist attitudes: unconditional positive regard, empathy, and congruence.

Unconditional Positive Regard The attitude Rogers called **unconditional positive regard** consists of nothing more or less than treating the client as a valued person, no matter what. This attitude is communicated through the therapist's willingness to listen, without interrupting, and to accept what is said without evaluating it. The therapist need not *approve* of everything the client says, just accept it as reflecting a part of the person who said it. Because they trust clients to solve their own problems, Rogerian therapists do not give advice. To do so, said Rogers, carries the subtle message that clients are incompetent, making them less confident and more dependent on help.

Empathy Rogerian therapists try to appreciate how the world looks from the client's point of view. This involves far more than saying "I know what you mean." The client-centered therapist tries to replace an *external frame of reference*—looking at the client from the outside—with an *internal frame of reference* characterized by **empathy,** which involves an emotional understanding of what the client might be thinking and feeling. Client-centered therapists convey empathy by showing that they are actively listening to the client. Like other skillful interviewers, they make eye contact with the client, nod in recognition as the client speaks, and give other signs of careful attention. They also use **reflection,** a paraphrased summary of the client's words and the feelings that appear to accompany them; reflection confirms the communication, shows the therapist's interest, and helps the client to perceive thoughts and feelings. Here is an example:

Client: This has been such a bad day. I've felt ready to cry any minute and I'm not even sure what's wrong!

Therapist: You really do feel so bad. The tears just seem to well up inside, and it must be a little scary to not even know why you feel this way.

Notice that by paraphrasing what the client said, the therapist reflected back not only the obvious feelings of sadness but also the fear in the client's voice. Most clients respond to empathic reflection by elaborating on their feelings.

Carl Rogers' client-centered therapy can take place individually or in groups. Rogers believed that, as successful treatment progresses, clients become more self-confident, more aware of their feelings, more accepting of themselves, more comfortable and genuine with other people, more reliant on self-evaluation than on the judgments of others, and more effective and relaxed.

In this example, the client went on to say, "It *is* scary, because I don't like to feel in the dark about myself. I have always prided myself on being in control."

By communicating the desire to listen and understand, the therapist can bring important material into the open without asking disruptive questions. Even in everyday situations, people who are thought of as easy to talk to tend to be "good listeners" who reflect back the important messages they hear from others. In therapy, an empathic listener makes clients feel valued and worthy; thus, they are more likely to be confident and motivated to solve their problems.

Congruence Sometimes called *genuineness,* **congruence** refers to a consistency between the way the therapist feels and acts toward the client. The therapist's unconditional positive regard and empathy must be genuine. Experiencing the therapist's congruence allows the client to see that relationships can be built on openness and honesty. This experience is thought to help the client become more congruent in other relationships.

Here is an excerpt that illustrates the therapeutic attitudes just described.

Client: . . . I cannot be the kind of person I want to be. I guess maybe I haven't the guts or the strength to kill myself and if someone else would relieve me of the responsibility or I would be in an accident I, I . . . just don't want to live.

Therapist: At the present time things look so black that you can't see much point in living. [Note the use of empathic reflection and the absence of any criticism.]

Client: Yes. I wish I'd never started this therapy. I was happy when I was living in my dream world. There I could be the kind of person I wanted to be. But now there is such a wide, wide gap between my ideal and what I am. . . . [Notice how the client responds to reflection by giving more information.]

Therapist: It's really a tough struggle digging into this like you are and at times the shelter of your dream world looks more attractive and comfortable. [Reflection]

Client: My dream world or suicide. . . . So I don't see why I should waste your time—coming in twice a week—I'm not worth it—What do you think?

Therapist: It's up to you. . . . It isn't wasting my time. I'd be glad to see you whenever you come but it's how you feel about it. . . . [Note the congruence in stating an honest desire to see the client and the unconditional positive regard in trusting her capacity and responsibility for choice.]

Client: You're not going to suggest that I come in oftener? You're not alarmed and think I ought to come in every day until I get out of this?

Therapist: I believe you are able to make your own decision. I'll see you whenever you want to come. [Positive regard]

Client: (*Note of awe in her voice*) I don't believe you are alarmed about—I see—I may be afraid of myself but you aren't afraid for me. [She experiences the therapist's confidence in her.]

Therapist: You say you may be afraid of yourself and are wondering why I don't seem to be afraid for you? [Reflection]

Client: You have more confidence in me than I have. I'll see you next week . . . maybe. (Rogers, 1951, p. 49)

The client was right. At that point, the therapist did have more confidence in her than she had in herself. (She did not kill herself, by the way.)

Gestalt Therapy

Another form of phenomenological treatment was developed by Frederick S. (Fritz) Perls, a European psychoanalyst who was also trained in Gestalt psy-

Gestalt therapists pay particular attention to clients' "body language," especially when it conflicts with what they are saying. If this client had just said that she is looking forward to starting her new job, the therapist would probably challenge that statement in an effort to make the client more aware of her ambivalence.

Linkages: What principles of learning can help people change maladaptive behaviors? (a link to Learning)

chology. We noted in the chapter on perception that the term *gestalt* ("organized whole") refers to perceptual principles through which people actively organize stimuli into meaningful patterns. Accordingly, Perls emphasized that the reality each person experiences depends on how he or she organizes and perceives the world (Perls, Hefferline & Goodman, 1951). Perls believed that psychological growth continues naturally as long as people perceive, remain aware of, and act on their true feelings. If people are blind to some aspects of themselves, their perceptions and behavior are not unified. Growth stops, and symptoms appear.

Like client-centered therapy, **Gestalt therapy** seeks to create conditions in which clients can become more unified, self-aware and self-accepting, and thus ready to grow again. However, Gestalt therapists use more direct and dramatic methods than do Rogerians. Often working in group settings, Gestalt therapists prod clients to become aware of feelings and impulses that they have denied or disowned and to discard foreign feelings, ideas, and values. For example, incongruities between what clients say and how they behave are pointed out, often quite directly, either by the therapist or by other group members. Any attempts to escape present reality by talking about the past or the future are also confronted as the Gestalt therapist works to keep clients' attention focused on thoughts and feelings in the "here and now." In addition, Gestalt therapists may ask clients to engage in imaginary dialogues with other people, with parts of their own personalities, and even with objects. Like a shy person who can be socially outgoing only while in a Halloween costume, clients often find that these dialogues help to get them in touch with, and express, their feelings.

Behavior Therapies

The psychodynamic and phenomenological approaches assume that if clients gain insight into underlying problems, the symptoms created by those problems will disappear. Behavior therapists emphasize a different kind of insight. They try to help clients see their problems as learned behaviors that can be changed, without searching for hidden meanings or unconscious causes.

Suppose that you are the person described at the beginning of this chapter. You have a panic attack almost every time you leave home and find relief only when you return. Making excuses when friends invite you out temporarily eases your anxiety but does nothing to solve the problem. Could you reduce your fear without looking for unconscious causes? By helping you to understand the learning and conditioning principles that maintain your fear and then to learn new responses in feared situations, behavior therapies offer just such an alternative.

This approach is the logical outcome of the assumptions of the behavioral view. As discussed in Chapters 14 and 15, the behavioral approach sees learning as the basis of normal personality, and of most behavior disorders. According to this perspective, disordered behavior and thinking are samples of the maladaptive thoughts and actions that the client has learned. Fear of leaving home (agoraphobia), for example, is seen by behaviorists as developing through classical conditioning as people associate panic attacks with events that mostly occur away from home. The problem is maintained in part through operant conditioning; staying home, and making excuses for doing so, is rewarded by reduced anxiety. Therapists who adopt a behavioral approach argue that if past learning experiences can produce problems, systematic new learning experiences might help alleviate them. Even if the learning that led to phobias and other problems began in childhood, behaviorists focus on solving today's problems through new experiences based on the principles of learning discussed in Chapter 8. (You may find it helpful to look again at the summaries of these principles on pages 249 to 257 and pages 259 to 273.)

Behavioral approaches to treatment were foreshadowed in the 1920s by the work of Watson, Pavlov, and others who studied the learned nature of fear. In the late 1950s and early 1960s, researchers began using classical and operant conditioning principles to alter disordered human behavior (Kazdin, 1978). By 1970, behavioral treatment had become a very popular alternative to psychodynamic and phenomenological methods. Behavioral treatments that rely mainly on classical conditioning principles are usually referred to as **behavior therapy.** Those that focus on operant conditioning methods are often referred to as **behavior modification.** Behavioral treatment that focuses on changing thinking patterns as well as overt behaviors is called **cognitive-behavior therapy.** Some of the most notable features of behavioral treatment include:

1. Development of a good therapist-client relationship. As in other therapies, this relationship enhances clients' confidence that change is possible and makes it easier for them to speak freely and to cooperate in the treatment.
2. Careful listing of the behaviors and thoughts to be changed. This assessment and the establishment of specific goals sometimes replace the formal psychodiagnosis used in other approaches. Thus, instead of treating "depression" or "schizophrenia," behavior therapists work to change the specific thoughts, behaviors, and emotional reactions that cause people to be given these labels.
3. A therapist who acts as a kind of teacher/assistant by providing learning-based treatments, giving "homework" assignments, and helping the client make specific plans for dealing with problems.
4. Continuous monitoring and evaluation of treatment along with constant adjustments to any procedures that do not seem to be effective.

Behavioral treatment takes many forms. We first describe techniques that emphasize changes in overt behavior and then discuss cognitive behavior therapy, which concentrates on modifying thinking patterns as well.

Techniques for Modifying Behavior

Some of the most important and commonly used behavioral treatment techniques are systematic desensitization, modeling, positive reinforcement, extinction, aversive conditioning, and punishment.

Systematic Desensitization   A behavioral treatment often used to help clients deal with phobias and other forms of irrational anxiety was developed by Joseph Wolpe (1958). Called **systematic desensitization,** it is a method for reducing intense anxiety by visualizing a graduated series of anxiety-provoking stimuli while maintaining a state of relaxation. Wolpe believed that this process so weakens the learned association between anxiety and the feared object that the fear disappears.

Wolpe first arranged for clients to do something incompatible with being afraid. Since it is hard to be tense and deeply relaxed at the same time, Wolpe used a technique called *progressive relaxation training* (described in Chapter 13) to prevent anxiety. Next the client relaxes while imagining an item from an *anxiety hierarchy,* a sequence of increasingly fear-provoking situations (see Table 16.1). The client works through the hierarchy gradually, imagining a more difficult scene only after being able to tolerate the previous one without distress. Once clients can calmly imagine being in feared situations, they are better able to deal with them. Desensitization may be especially effective if the client can work on a hierarchy *in vivo,* or in real life (Chambliss, 1990).

Exactly why systematic desensitization works is not clear. Most clinicians believe that change occurs either through classical conditioning of a new,

Linkages: How do therapists use learning principles to treat psychological disorders? (a link to Learning)

**Table 16.1
A Sample
Desensitization Hierarchy**

Desensitization hierarchies contain increasingly fear-provoking stimuli, which the client visualizes while using relaxation techniques to remain calm. This hierarchy contains sample scenes from the top and bottom sections of a hierarchy that was used to desensitize a client's fear of flying.

1. You are reading a newspaper and notice an ad for an airline.
2. You are watching a television program that shows a group of people boarding a plane.
3. Your boss tells you that you need to take a business trip by air.
4. You are in your bedroom packing your suitcase for your trip.
   .
   .
   .
12. Your plane begins to move as you hear the flight attendant say "be sure your seat belt is securely fastened."
13. You look at the runway as the plane is ready for takeoff.
14. You look out the window as the plane rolls down the runway.
15. You look out the window as the plane leaves the ground.

**Figure 16.1
Participant Modeling**

The benefits of participant modeling were first convincingly demonstrated in a study comparing the effects of this treatment to those of symbolic modeling (watching filmed models), systematic desensitization, and no treatment (control) in the treatment of snake phobia. As the graph illustrates, all three behavioral methods produced more interaction with snakes than no treatment, but participant modeling was clearly the best; 92 percent of the subjects in that group were virtually free of any fear. The power of participant modeling has been repeatedly confirmed over the years (see, for example, Öst, Salkovskis & Hellström, 1991).

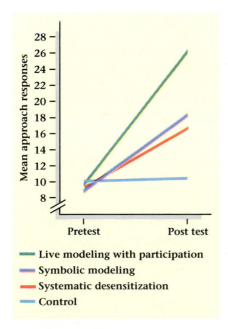

- ■ Live modeling with participation
- ■ Symbolic modeling
- ■ Systematic desensitization
- ■ Control

Source: Bandura, Blanchard & Ritter, 1969.

calmer response to the fear-provoking stimulus or through extinction, as the object or situation that had been a conditioned fear stimulus repeatedly occurs without being paired with pain or any other unconditioned stimulus (Rachman, 1990).

Modeling   Therapists often teach clients desirable behaviors by demonstrating those behaviors. In **modeling**, the client watches other people perform desired behaviors, thus vicariously learning skills without going through a lengthy trial-and-error process. In fear treatment, modeling can teach the client how to respond in a nonfearful way, and it can vicariously extinguish conditioned fear responses. For example, one therapist showed a twenty-four-year-old student with a severe spider phobia how to kill spiders with a fly swatter and had her practice this skill at home with rubber spiders (MacDonald & Bernstein, 1974). The combination of live modeling with gradual practice is called *participant modeling;* it is one of the most powerful treatments for fear (see Figure 16.1).

Modeling is also a major part of **assertiveness and social skills training**, a way of teaching clients how to interact with people more comfortably and effectively. The goal of social skills training may be anything from helping college students with social phobias learn to make conversation on dates to rebuilding mental patients' ability to interact normally with people outside the hospital (Benton & Schroeder, 1990; Corrigan, 1991; Wallace et al., 1992; Wong et al., 1993). In assertiveness training, the therapist helps clients learn to be more direct and expressive in social situations. Note that *assertiveness* does not mean aggressiveness; it means clearly and directly expressing both positive and negative feelings and standing up for one's rights while respecting the rights of others (Alberti & Emmons, 1986). Assertiveness training is often done in groups and involves both modeling and role playing of specific situations. For example, in one program, group assertiveness training helped wheelchair-bound adults more comfortably handle the socially awkward situations in which they often find themselves (Gleuckauf & Quittner, 1992).

Positive Reinforcement   Behavior therapists also use systematic **positive reinforcement**, or rewards, to alter problematic behaviors and to teach new skills in cases ranging from childhood tantrums and juvenile delinquency to schizophrenia and self-starvation. Following the operant conditioning principles described in Chapter 8, they set up contingencies, or rules, that specify the behaviors to be strengthened through rewards. In one study, autistic children, who, as described in Chapter 15, use very little language, were rewarded with grapes, popcorn, or other items for saying "please," "thank you," and "you're welcome" while exchanging crayons and blocks with a therapist. The therapist initially modeled the behavior by saying the appropriate words. The children almost immediately began to utter the phrases spontaneously. The effects generalized to situations involving other toys, and, as indicated in Figure 16.2, the new skills were still evident six months later (Matson et al., 1990).

For severely retarded or disturbed clients in institutions, some behavior therapists establish a **token economy**, a system of rewarding desirable behaviors with tokens, which are items such as poker chips that can be exchanged for snacks, access to television, or other rewards (Ayllon & Azrin, 1968; Kazdin, 1982). The goal is to shape behavior patterns that will persist outside the institution. Although token economies can be very effective, their use is limited mainly to situations in which tight control over all sources of reinforcement is possible (see, for example, Menditto et al., 1991).

Extinction   Just as reinforcement can be used to strengthen desirable behaviors, other behavioral techniques can weaken undesirable behaviors. In operant conditioning, **extinction** is the process of removing the reinforcers that normally follow a particular response. If you have ever given up telephoning someone whose line is busy, you know how extinction works: when a behavior does not "pay off," people usually stop it. Though extinction changes behavior rather slowly, it has been a popular way of treating children and retarded or seriously disturbed adults, because it provides a gentle way to eliminate undesirable behaviors.

Another application of extinction is **flooding**, a procedure that keeps people in a feared but harmless situation, depriving them of their normally rewarding

Figure 16.2
Results of a Positive Reinforcement Program for an Autistic Child
Note that during baseline (before reinforcement), the child rarely said "please," "thank you," or "you're welcome." But the girl increased her spontaneous verbalizations over the three reinforcement phases. Saying "please" approached 100 percent by session 15, at which point she also began receiving reinforcement for saying "thank you" when she was given a toy. Finally, after session 25, reinforcement for saying "you're welcome" increased that behavior to the 100% level. At a 6-month follow-up session, she performed all three target phrases 100 percent of the time.

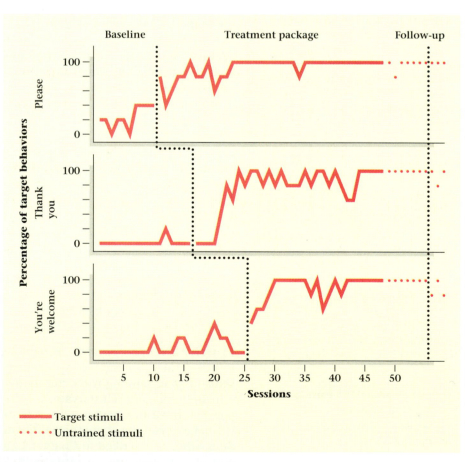

Source: Matson et al., 1990.

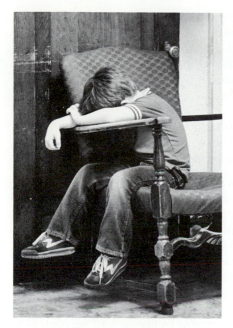

If undesirable behavior cannot be ignored or is being rewarded by on-lookers (as when a child gets laughs by rapping on a classmate's head), the client may be placed in a boring place for a few minutes. This "time out" from positive reinforcement interrupts the reward process.

escape pattern. (Flooding, and related methods based on the extinction of classically conditioned fear responses, are also called *exposure techniques*.) When someone is kept in contact with a fear-eliciting conditioned stimulus (CS), without experiencing a severe unconditioned stimulus (UCS), the fear-eliciting power of the CS eventually diminishes and the fear response extinguishes. In one recent study, clients who feared injections were given continuous *in vivo* exposure to needle stimuli, including mild finger pricks, harmless subcutaneous injections, and venipuncture—that is, having blood drawn (Öst, Hellström & Kåver, 1992). After a single, approximately two-hour session, 19 of 20 clients were able to have their blood drawn without significant anxiety. These effects were maintained at a one-year follow-up assessment.

Though often highly effective, flooding is equivalent to immediately exposing a fearful client to the most distressing item on a desensitization hierarchy. Accordingly, some therapists and clients prefer more gradual exposure methods, especially for treating agoraphobia and other problems in which a client's fear is not focused on a specific stimulus (Foa, Rothbaum & Kozak, 1989). In such cases, exposure involves escorting the client away from home for increasing periods, eventually venturing into shopping malls and other previously avoided places (Kleinknecht, 1991).

Aversive Conditioning   Many unwanted behaviors are so habitual and temporarily rewarding that they must be made less attractive if the client is to have any chance of learning alternatives. Methods for lessening the appeal of once-desirable stimuli are known as **aversive conditioning**, because they employ classical conditioning principles to associate physical or psychological discomfort with behaviors, thoughts, or situations the client wishes to stop or avoid. For example, alcoholics might be allowed to drink after taking a nausea-producing drug, so that the taste and smell of alcohol are associated with nausea rather than with the usual pleasurable feelings (Cannon & Baker, 1981).

A form of aversive conditioning called *covert sensitization* is, in a sense, the opposite of systematic desensitization. The client first thinks of the inappropriately attractive stimulus or situation and is then exposed to tape-recorded depictions of frightening or disgusting stimuli. For example, covert sensitiza-

Linkages: Flooding is designed to extinguish severe anxiety by allowing it to occur without reinforcement. By the end of his airplane flight, this fearful client was far less anxious than he had been at the beginning. Like other behavioral treatments, flooding stems from the behavioral approach to personality described in Chapter 14. A fundamental assumption of that approach is that behavior disorders, like normal behaviors, are learned and can thus be "unlearned."

tion was used to treat a man who had been repeatedly arrested for making obscene phone calls. While imagining making an obscene call, the client heard vivid descriptions of his greatest fears: snakes, vomiting, and choking. Finally, he imagined his mother walking in on him during a call. After a month of treatment he was no longer sexually aroused by thoughts of obscene calls, and he had made no such calls even two years later (Moergen, Merkel & Brown, 1990).

Still, aversive conditioning is unpleasant and uncomfortable, and its effects are often temporary. Many therapists thus avoid this method or use it only long enough to allow the client to learn alternative behaviors.

Punishment   Sometimes the only way to eliminate a dangerous or disruptive behavior is to punish it with an unpleasant but not harmful stimulus, such as a shouted "No!" or a mild electric shock. Unlike aversive conditioning, in which the unpleasant stimulus occurs along with the behavior to be eliminated (a classical conditioning approach), **punishment** is an operant conditioning technique; it presents the unpleasant stimulus *after* the undesirable response occurs. (Though technically distinct, the two methods may overlap.) As discussed in the chapter on learning, most therapists prefer using punishment mainly as a last resort, such as when a client's life is in danger or all other methods have failed. Just such a case is illustrated in Figure 8.13 on page 270.

Cognitive-Behavior Therapy

Linkages: How can therapists help people alter maladaptive thought patterns? (a link to Thought and Language)

Psychodynamic and phenomenological therapists have long recognized that problematic thought patterns may lead to depression, anger, or anxiety. Behavior therapists have also attacked these problems, using methods known collectively as cognitive behavior therapy. In simplest terms, *cognitive-behavior therapy* helps clients change the way they think as well as the way they behave. For example, some clients already know *how* to be assertive in social situations but need to identify the habitual thoughts (such as "I shouldn't draw attention to myself") that get in the way of self-expression. Once these cognitive obstacles are brought to light, the therapist encourages the client to try new ways of thinking. The therapist may also help clients learn to say things to themselves that promote desirable behavior and prevent a relapse into undesirable behavior (Marlatt & Gordon, 1985).

Rational-Emotive Therapy and Cognitive Restructuring   One prominent form of cognitive behavior therapy is **rational-emotive therapy (RET)**. Developed by Albert Ellis (1962, 1973, 1993; Ellis & Dryden, 1987), RET is based on the principle that anxiety, guilt, depression, and other psychological problems are caused by how people think about events. RET aims first at identifying self-defeating, problem-causing thoughts such as: "I must be loved or approved by everyone," "I must be perfectly competent, adequate, and achieving to be worthwhile," or "There is always a right or a perfect solution to every problem, and it must be found or the results will be catastrophic." After the client learns to recognize thoughts like these and see how they cause problems, the therapist uses modeling, encouragement, and logic to help the client replace these thoughts with more realistic and beneficial ones. Here is part of an RET session with a thirty-nine-year-old woman who suffered from panic attacks. She has just said that it would be "terrible" if she had an attack in a restaurant and that people "should be able to handle themselves!"

Therapist: . . . The reality is that . . . "shoulds" and "musts" are the rules that other people hand down to us, and we grow up accepting them as if they are the absolute truth, which they most assuredly aren't.

Client: You mean it is perfectly okay to, you know, pass out in a restaurant?

Therapist: Sure!

Albert Ellis developed rational emotive therapy (RET), a treatment method focused on altering the self-defeating thoughts that he sees as underlying clients' problems. Ellis says, for example, that you get upset not because you fail a test but because you believe failure to be a disaster that indicates you are no good. Many of Ellis's ideas have been incorporated into various forms of cognitive-behavior therapy.

Client: But . . . I know I wouldn't like it to happen.

Therapist: I can certainly understand that. It would be unpleasant, awkward, inconvenient. But it is illogical to think that it would be terrible, or . . . that it somehow bears on your worth as a person.

Client: What do you mean?

Therapist: Well, suppose one of your friends calls you up and invites you back to that restaurant. If you start telling yourself, "I might panic and pass out and people might make fun of me and that would be terrible," you are going to make yourself uptight. And you might find you are dreading going to the restaurant, and you probably won't enjoy the meal very much.

Client: Well, that is what usually happens.

Therapist: But it doesn't have to be that way. . . . The way you feel, your reaction . . . depends on what you choose to believe or think, or say to yourself. . . . (Masters et al., 1987)

Cognitive-behavior therapists use many techniques related to RET to help clients learn to think in more adaptive ways, thus allowing them to begin practicing new behaviors that irrational thoughts once prevented. Behavioral techniques aimed at replacing upsetting thoughts with alternative thinking patterns were originally described as *cognitive restructuring* (Lazarus, 1971). These methods help clients learn calming thoughts to use in anxiety-provoking situations, such as tests or unpleasant conversations. These thoughts might take the form of "OK, stay calm, you can handle this if you just focus on the task and don't worry about being perfect" (Meichenbaum, 1977). These methods are sometimes expanded into *stress inoculation training,* in which the therapist asks the client to imagine being in a stressful situation so that he or she can practice new cognitive skills to reduce stress (Meichenbaum, 1985).

Beck's Cognitive Therapy   Especially in cases of depression or anxiety disorders, behavior therapists often use Aaron Beck's **cognitive therapy**, which contains another type of cognitive restructuring (Beck, 1976, 1993; Beck et al., 1992). As described in Chapter 15, Beck bases his approach on the idea that negative cognitive patterns are maintained by errors in logic and erroneous beliefs such as "I can't do anything right," or (if something is accomplished) by value-minimizing thoughts such as "Anyone could do that." These thoughts and beliefs, in turn, lead to low self-esteem, depression, and anxiety.

Cognitive therapy is an organized problem-solving approach in which the therapist actively collaborates with clients to help them notice how certain negative thoughts precede anxiety and depression. Then, much as in the five-step critical thinking system illustrated throughout this book, these thoughts and beliefs are considered as hypotheses to be tested rather than as assertions to be uncritically accepted. Accordingly, therapist and client take the role of "investigators" and develop ways to test beliefs such as "I can never do anything right." For example, they might agree on tasks that the client will attempt as "homework"—such as completing a long-overdue household project or making the acquaintance of a new neighbor. Success at accomplishing these structured behavioral tasks provides concrete evidence to challenge the erroneous beliefs that are viewed as underlying anxiety and depression, thus helping to alleviate these problems (Beck et al., 1979, 1992). The following example illustrates how Beck's hypothesis-testing approach challenged a dysfunctional belief system in a depressed fifty-one-year-old man.

Therapist: I understand that you haven't been out of your bed for a year. Why is that?

Patient: I can't walk.

Therapist: What would happen if you tried?

Aaron Beck's cognitive therapy aims to help depressed clients identify, challenge, and correct logical errors in thinking, including unrealistic pessimism born of the tendency to dwell on their shortcomings and the negative events in their lives.

Patient: I'd fall on my face, I guess.

Therapist: How about testing that out?

Patient: I *know* I can't walk.

Therapist: Suppose I hold your arm. [The patient then took a few steps supported by the therapist. He continued to walk . . . without further assistance.]

Therapist: You did better than you expected.

Patient: I guess so. [From Beck, 1976, pp. 284–285]

As mentioned in Chapter 15, however, depressed peoples' specific thoughts may not be in error; depression may be associated with a general cognitive style in which people attribute negative events to their own general and enduring incompetence rather than, say, to bad luck or a temporary lack of effort (Peterson & Seligman, 1984). Accordingly, cognitive-behavior therapists also help depressed clients develop more optimistic ways of thinking and reduce their tendency to blame themselves for negative outcomes (Taylor, 1989).

Group and Family Therapies

Much psychotherapy is conducted in individual interviews, but it can also be done with groups of clients or with family units.

Group therapy refers to the simultaneous treatment of several clients under the guidance of a therapist who tries to facilitate helpful interactions among group members. Psychodynamic, behavioral, and phenomenological treatment can all be adapted for use in groups. Many groups are organized around one type of problem (such as alcoholism) or one type of client (such as adolescents or single parents). In most cases, six to twelve clients meet with their therapist at least once a week for about two hours. All group members agree to hold confidential everything that occurs within group sessions.

Group therapy offers features not found in individual treatment (Yalom, 1985). First, group therapy allows the therapist to observe clients interacting with one another. Second, clients often feel less alone as they listen to others and recognize that many people struggle with difficulties similar to or even more severe than their own. This recognition tends to raise each client's expectations for improvement, a factor important in all forms of treatment. Third, group members can bolster one another's self-confidence and self-acceptance as they come to trust and value one another and develop group cohesiveness. Fourth, clients learn from one another. They share ideas for solving problems and give one another honest feedback about how each member "comes across." Fifth, the group experience, perhaps through mutual modeling, may make clients more willing to share their feelings and to be more sensitive to other people's needs, motives, and messages. Finally, group therapy allows clients to try out new skills in a safe environment.

Some of the advantages of group therapy are also put to use in *self-help, or mutual help, organizations.* Self-help groups are made up of people who share some problematic experience—ranging from drug addiction, childhood sexual abuse, or cancer to overeating, compulsive gambling, or schizophrenia—and who meet to help one another (Zimmerman et al., 1991). The explosive growth of the self-help movement during the last two decades in North America and around the world (Gidron, Chesler & Chesney, 1991) has been fueled partly by troubled people who prefer to seek help from friends, teachers, physicians, or other "unofficial" helpers before turning to mental health practitioners, and partly by those who have been dissatisfied with professional treatment. Often following the lead of groups like Alcoholics Anonymous (AA), dozens of self-help organizations operate today through hundreds of thousands of local

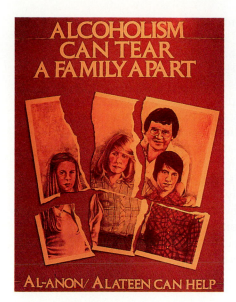

The self-help movement is part of a rapidly growing network of mental health and anti-addiction services offered by volunteer helpers, including friends and relatives of troubled people. The services provided by these nonprofessional groups have come to comprise some 21 percent of the total mental health and anti-addiction services offered in the United States (Regier et al., 1993). While some welcome this trend, many professionals are doubtful about the effectiveness of these groups.

chapters, enrolling 10 to 15 million participants in the United States and about half a million in Canada (Gottlieb & Peters, 1991; Jacobs & Goodman, 1989; Powell, 1990). Though most welcome all comers, some groups are organized by and for disabled persons, people with particular ethnic backgrounds, or other specific populations (Gutierrez, Ortega & Suarez, 1990; Kurtz, 1990; Neighbors, Elliot, & Gant, 1990). Lack of reliable data makes it difficult to assess the value of many self-help groups, but available information suggests that active members may obtain some moderate improvement in their lives (Nietzel, Guthrie & Susman, 1990).

As its name implies, **family therapy** involves treatment of two or more individuals from the same "family system," one of whom—often a troubled adolescent or child—is the initially identified client. The term *family system* highlights the idea that the problems displayed by one family member often reflect problems in the entire family's functioning as a group (Nugent, 1994). Ultimately, then, the whole family becomes the client, and treatment involves as many members as possible. Indeed, the goal of family therapy is not just to alleviate the identified client's problems but to create harmony and balance within the family by helping each member understand the family's interactions and the problems they create (Gurman, Kniskern & Pinsoff, 1986).

Family therapy developed from several sources: (1) the psychodynamic theory that psychological disorders are rooted in early family relationships and conflicts; (2) clinical observations that clients who are stabilized in a mental hospital often relapse when they return to their families; and (3) a recognition that few, if any, problems occur in a vacuum and, hence, must be dealt with in the family setting that maintains them. As in group therapy, the family format gives the therapist an excellent view of how the initially identified client interacts with others. It also provides a forum for discussing issues important to the family's life.

Family therapy can be adapted to many theoretical approaches. For example, family therapists who emphasize object relations theory point out that if parents have not worked out conflicts with their own parents, these conflicts will surface in relationships with their spouses and children. Accordingly, their family therapy sessions might focus on the parents' problems with their own

Family therapy—conducted here with a single parent and his children—initially focuses on the most troubled, or troublesome, individual. Eventually, however, treatment explores the role each family member plays in the problems of the "family system."

parents and, when possible, include members of the older generation (Framo, 1982; Nugent, 1994; Skynner, 1981). Another popular approach, called *structural family therapy,* concentrates on communication patterns among family members (Minuchin & Fishman, 1981). It focuses on changing the rigid patterns and rituals that create alliances (such as mother and child against father), which perpetuate conflict and prevent the communication of love, support, or even anger. Structural family therapists argue that when dysfunctional communication structures are eliminated, problematic behaviors decrease because they are no longer necessary for survival in the family system.

Virginia Satir, a well-known family therapist (Satir, 1967, 1982), examines and teaches family communication skills. She draws from phenomenological theory in that she believes that family members' symptoms result from blocked emotional growth and that removing these blocks frees people to take advantage of innate resources. Her version of family therapy aims not only to improve communication patterns but also to promote self-esteem (Nugent, 1994). Here is an excerpt from one of her sessions:

Mother: His pleasure is doing things he knows will get me up in the air. Every minute he's in the house . . . constantly.

Therapist: There's no pleasure to that, my dear.

Mother: Well, there is to him.

Therapist: No, you can't see his thoughts. You can't get inside his skin. All you can talk about is what you see and hear. You can say it *looks* as though it's for pleasure.

Mother: All right. Well, it looks as though, and that's just what it looks like constantly.

Therapist: He could be trying to keep your attention, you know. It is very important to Johnny what Mother thinks.

Behavior therapists have also employed the family therapy format, using their sessions as meetings at which family members can discuss and agree on behavioral "contracts." Often based on operant conditioning principles, these contracts establish rules and reinforcement contingencies that help parents encourage their children's desirable behaviors (and discourage undesirable ones) and help spouses become more supportive of one another (Behrens, Sanders & Halford, 1990; Tiedemann & Johnston, 1992).

Evaluating Psychotherapy

Linkages: What research methods have been used to evaluate treatment for psychological disorders? (a link to Research in Psychology)

Psychotherapy has been available for nearly a hundred years, and still people are asking if it works. The question lingers because although most psychotherapists and their clients testify to psychotherapy's effectiveness, confirming its effectiveness through experimental research has proved to be challenging and controversial (Dawes, 1992).

The value of psychotherapy was first widely questioned in 1952 when British psychologist Hans Eysenck reviewed several studies that compared the effects of traditional psychodynamic therapy with the results of routine medical care or no treatment for thousands of clients. To the surprise and dismay of many therapists, Eysenck (1952) concluded that traditional psychodynamic therapy did not increase the rate of improvement. In fact, he claimed that more untreated than treated clients recovered. Eysenck (1961, 1966) later supported his conclusions with additional evidence. Critics, however, argued that Eysenck was wrong (de Charms, Levy & Wertheimer, 1954; Luborsky, 1954, 1972). They claimed that he ignored studies supporting the value of psychotherapy and misinterpreted his data. They pointed out, for example, that untreated clients may have been less disturbed than those in treatment; that untreated clients may have received informal treatment from their doctors; and that physicians who judged untreated clients' progress might have used more lenient criteria than the psychotherapists who rated their own clients.

Indeed, studies of a wide range of treatments have yielded consistently more optimistic results than Eysenck found. For example, psychotherapy clients did better than no-treatment controls in 20 of 33 studies reviewed by Lester Luborsky, Barton Singer, and Lise Luborsky (1975); the other 13 studies were interpreted as "ties." Other researchers have used a mathematical technique called *meta-analysis* to quantify and summarize the outcomes of many different studies in a way that allows their results to be combined as if they came from a single study. One meta-analysis of 475 psychotherapy outcome studies found that the average therapy client is better off after therapy than 80 percent of clients who do not receive therapy (Smith, Glass & Miller, 1980). Other meta-analyses have supported this assertion (Brown, 1987) and have produced the following additional conclusions about the effects of psychotherapy:

1. In general, better-designed studies yield larger estimates of the success of psychotherapy (Landman & Dawes, 1982).
2. Improvement is reasonably lasting, at least as measured up to eighteen months after the end of treatment (Nicholson & Berman, 1983).
3. Only a few clients (perhaps 10 percent) are worse off after psychotherapy (Lambert, Shapiro & Bergin, 1986; Smith, Glass & Miller, 1980).

Though meta-analytic research suggests that therapy works in general, important questions remain. For example, not all therapists agree on the definition of "success" in therapy. Some look for changes in unconscious conflicts while others focus on alterations in overt behavior. In the outcome studies analyzed, a different set of observers using different standards might have made less optimistic judgments about the success of treatment (Strupp & Hadley, 1977). Further, though the improvements reported are statistically significant (that is, greater than would be expected by chance), they are not necessarily clinically significant. *Clinically significant* changes are not just measurable; they must also be substantial enough to make important differences in the person's life, as Figure 16.3 illustrates. For example, a reduction in scores on an anxiety test might be *statistically* significant in a group of treated clients; but if those clients do not feel and act noticeably less anxious in daily life, the change may not be clinically significant. The need to demonstrate the clinical significance of treatment effects is now clearer than ever (Dawes, 1992).

Linkages: How do statistical analyses help summarize the effects of psychotherapy? (a link to Research in Psychology)

Linkages: Can personality be changed through therapy? (a link to Personality)

Figure 16.3
Clinical Significance
Research on psychological treatment must consider whether its effects are clinically as well as statistically significant. Here, the shaded area shows the range of deviant behaviors per minute displayed by normal boys in their homes. The solid line shows the average deviant behavior for a group of boys being treated for severe behavior problems using operant reinforcement for appropriate behavior. The boys' improvement was not only significant in comparison to their pretreatment baselines but also reflected a change that was clinically significant because it placed them in the range of behavior seen in normal children.

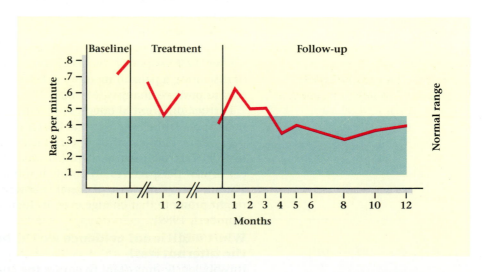

Source: Patterson, 1974.

Thinking Critically

Is One Approach to Psychotherapy Better Than the Others?

General trends aside, most clients want to know which approach to psychotherapy is most likely to result in clinically significant improvements in *their* problems. Each approach has been successfully used to deal with a wide range of problems, from mild anxiety to severe depression and schizophrenia. Further, although most therapists believe that their own particular brand of treatment is superior to others (see, for example, Giles, 1990), the popularity of an eclectic approach suggests that most therapists also believe that no single approach to treatment is always the best one. Does this mean that all approaches are equally effective?

What am I being asked to believe or accept?

Some researchers argue that theoretical models of behavior disorder and the specific treatment methods based on them are irrelevant to the success of psychotherapy: all approaches, they say, are equally effective. This has been called the "Dodo Bird Verdict," after the *Alice in Wonderland* creature who, when called upon to judge who had won a race, answered, "Everybody has won and all must have prizes" (Luborsky, Singer & Luborsky, 1975).

What evidence is available to support the assertion?

Some evidence does suggest that there are no significant differences in the overall effectiveness of the psychodynamic, phenomenological, and behavioral approaches to therapy. Studies comparing the effects of these treatment approaches in the same experiment have failed to show that one approach is notably superior to another (Cross, Sheehan & Kahn, 1982; Olson et al., 1981; Sloane et al., 1975; Snyder & Wills, 1989; Stiles, Shapiro & Elliott, 1986).

Are there alternative ways of interpreting the evidence?

One possibility is that the evidence for the Dodo Bird Verdict is based on methods that simply cannot detect genuine differences among treatments. For example, consider how the success of psychotherapy is measured. The client's condition before and after treatment is often determined through personality tests, interviews, or self-ratings. Behaviorally oriented researchers in particular argue that these assessments are too vague and global to capture specific and important changes in behavior and thus obscure potentially important differences among therapies (Rachman & Wilson, 1980).

It may also be that some specific techniques are more successful than others, but that because therapies are usually grouped by theoretical orientation (psychodynamic, phenomenological, behavioral) rather than by the specific procedures employed, the impact of those procedures is not detected (Giles, 1990). In other words, it may be the *good moments* in therapy (Mahrer & Nadler, 1986)—specific events or interactions such as trying a new behavior or disclosing a painful memory—that can occur as part of *any* treatment that lead to positive changes (Marmar, 1990).

Further, differential effects of specific procedures might be obscured by the beneficial features shared by almost all forms of therapy—such as the support of the therapist, the hope and expectancy for improvement that therapy instills, the trust that develops between client and therapist, and the discovery of new perspectives on problem solving (Grencavage & Norcross, 1991). Thus, a therapist whose personal characteristics motivate a client to change might promote that change even if the formal methods used are mediocre (Lambert, 1989).

What additional evidence would help to evaluate the alternatives?

It is obviously important to ensure the continuation of research on "good moments," common features, and other factors that might explain similarities in the effects of different approaches to treatment. However, the Dodo Bird Verdict may actually be the right answer to the wrong question about psychotherapy. Instead of looking for one "best" approach, researchers need to explore what Gordon Paul called the "ultimate question" about psychotherapy: "What treatment, by whom, is most effective for this individual with that specific problem, under what set of circumstances?" (Paul, 1969a, p. 44).

What conclusions are most reasonable?
This analysis suggests caution in drawing conclusions about the relative value of different approaches to therapy. Further, as described in the next section, troubled people or their relatives should carefully consider several factors when choosing a treatment approach and therapist most likely to be best for them.

Addressing the "Ultimate Question"

Much more research is needed to discover the combinations of therapists, clients, and treatments that are ideally suited to remedying particular psychological problems (Talley, Strupp & Morey, 1990). These combinations have not yet been mapped out, but when differences do show up in meta-analyses or comparative studies, they tend to reveal a small to moderate advantage for behavioral and cognitive-behavioral methods, especially in the treatment of the anxiety disorders (Andrews & Harvey, 1981; Borkovec et al., 1991; Giles, 1990; Kazdin & Wilson, 1978; Lambert, Shapiro & Bergin, 1986; Rachman & Wilson, 1980; Searles, 1985). ("In Review: Approaches to Psychological Treatment" summarizes key features of the main approaches to treatment.)

Regardless of the theoretical approach involved, the client-therapist relationship seems to play a role in the success of treatment. Certain people seem to be particularly effective in forming productive human relationships. Even without formal training, these people can sometimes be as helpful as professional therapists because of personal qualities that are inspiring, healing, and soothing to others (Berman & Norton, 1985). Their presence in self-help groups may well underlie some of the success of those groups and, among professionals, may help account for the apparent equivalence of differing treatments. If, as Carl Rogers argued, approach-free factors, especially those associated with the client-therapist relationship, hold the key to successful treatment, it might be wiser to teach new therapists how to exploit those factors rather than how to use specific techniques.

Even in light of the apparently equivalent effects of different treatments, the choice of a specific form of treatment, like the choice of a particular therapist, should not be made randomly. Careful consideration should be given to (1) what treatment approach, methods, and goals the client finds comfortable and appealing, (2) information about the potential therapist's "track record" of clinically significant success with a particular method for treating problems like those the client faces, and (3) the likelihood of forming a productive relationship with the therapist. This last consideration assumes special importance when client and therapist do not share similar cultural backgrounds.

Cultural Factors in Psychotherapy

Imagine that you have become very depressed after moving into a different culture in order to pursue your education or occupation. One of your new friends refers you to a therapist who specializes in such problems. During your first session the therapist stares at you intently, touches your head for a moment, and says, "You have taken in a spirit from the river and it is trying to get out. I will help." The therapist then begins chanting softly and appears to go into a trance.

In Review: Approaches to Psychological Treatment

Dimension	Classical Psychoanalytic	Contemporary Psychodynamic	Phenomenological	Behavioral
Nature of the human being	Driven by sexual and aggressive urges	Driven by the need for human relationships	Has free will, choice, and capacity for self-actualization	A product of social learning and conditioning; behaves on the basis of past experience
Therapist's role	Neutral; helps client explore meaning of free associations and other material from the unconscious	Active; develops relationship with client as a model for other relationships	Facilitates client's growth; some are active, some nondirective	Teacher/trainer who helps client replace undesirable thoughts and behaviors; active, action-oriented
Time frame	Emphasizes unresolved unconscious conflicts from the distant past	Understanding the past, but focusing on current relationships	Here and now; focuses on immediate experience	Current behavior and thoughts; may not need to know original causes in order to create change
Goals	Psychosexual maturity through insight; strengthening of ego functions	Correction of effects of failures of early attachment; development of satisfying intimate relationships	Expanded awareness, fulfillment of potential; self-acceptance	Changes in thinking and behaving in particular classes of situations; better self-management
Typical methods	Free association; dream analysis, analysis of transference; interpretations	Interpretations; analysis of transference and countertransference	Reflection-oriented interviews designed to convey unconditional positive regard, empathy, congruence, exercises to promote self-awareness	Systematic desensitization, modeling, assertiveness and social skills training, positive reinforcement, aversive conditioning, punishment, extinction, cognitive restructuring

What would you think? Would you return for a second visit? If you are like most people in Western cultures, you might decide not to seek further help unless you could find someone with whom you shared certain beliefs and expectations about what is wrong with you and what should be done about it.

Though not always so extreme, a similar culture clash may occur when some members of minority groups, especially recent immigrants from non-Western cultures, come in contact with mental health professionals who do not share their background or worldview. This clash may be partly to blame for the underuse of, or withdrawal from, mental health services among African-Americans, Asian-Americans, Hispanic-Americans, Native Americans, and other minority populations (Cheung & Snowden, 1990; Price & McNeill, 1992; Spencer & Hemmer, 1993; D. W. Sue, 1990). Often, the problem lies in mismatched goals. A therapist raised to believe that one should confront and overcome life's problems may encounter a client who believes that one should work at calmly accepting the vicissitudes of life (Draguns, 1989; Sundberg & Sue, 1989). The result may be much like two people singing a duet using the same music but different lyrics.

Major efforts are under way to ensure that cultural differences between clients and therapists do not impede the delivery of treatment to anyone who wants or needs it (Pederson et al., 1989; Pederson, 1994). Virtually every mental health training program in North America is seeking to recruit higher percentages of students from traditionally underserved minority groups in order to make it easier to match clients with therapists from similar cultural backgrounds (see, for example, Hammond & Yung, 1993). In the meantime, researchers are examining the value of matching therapeutic *techniques* with clients' culturally based expectations and preferences (Sue, 1992). For example, a therapist who emphasizes individualist goals, such as being independent and taking responsibility for the direction of change, might prefer nondirective techniques. But many clients from collectivist cultures—where there is emphasis on subjugating personal wishes to the expectations of family and friends—might expect to receive direct instructions about how to overcome problems.

David Sue and his students have investigated the hypothesis that the collectivist values of Asian cultures would lead Asians and Asian-Americans to prefer a directive, problem-solving approach, such as behavior therapy, over nondirective, client-centered methods. Sue (1992) found that a preference for directive treatment was highest among foreign-born Asians compared to American-born Asians and European-Americans. However, there are always individual differences; two clients from the same culture may react very differently to a treatment that group research suggests should be ideal for both of them. In Sue's (1992) study, for example, more than a third of the foreign-born Asians preferred the nondirective approach and 28 percent of the European-Americans preferred the directive approach.

Graduate training programs and continuing-education efforts are informing today's psychotherapists about the nuances of intercultural communication and the cultural values of particular groups (LaFromboise & Foster, 1989; LaFromboise, 1992). This training helps clinicians appreciate, for example, that it is considered impolite in some cultures to make eye contact with a stranger and, hence, that clients from those cultures are not necessarily depressed, lacking in self-esteem, or inappropriately deferent just because they fix their eyes on the floor during an interview (see, for example, Ibrahim, 1991). By providing a cultural extension of Carl Rogers' concept of empathy, cultural sensitivity training helps therapists to appreciate the way the client's culture interprets and interacts with the world and thus to set goals that are in harmony with that view (Ibrahim, 1991; Pederson, 1994). Minimizing the chances of cultural misunderstanding and miscommunication is one of the many obligations that therapists assume whenever they see a client.

Linkages: How have clinical psychologists become more sensitive to culturally diverse clients? (a link to Introducing Psychology)

Rules and Rights in the Therapeutic Relationship

Psychological treatment can be an intensely emotional experience, and the relationship established with a therapist can profoundly affect the client's life. Professional ethics and common sense require the therapist to ensure that this relationship does not harm the client. For example, the American Psychological Association's *Ethical Principles for Psychologists and Code of Conduct* forbid a sexual relationship between therapist and client because of the severe harm it can cause the client (APA, 1992; Williams, 1992). These standards also require therapists, with a few exceptions, to keep everything a client says in therapy strictly confidential.

Confidentiality is one of the most important features of a successful therapeutic relationship because it allows the client to discuss unpleasant or embarrassing feelings, behaviors, or events without fear that the therapist might disclose these secrets to others. Professionals may consult with one another about a client, but each is required not to reveal information to outsiders (including members of the client's family) without the client's consent.

Professional rules about confidentiality are backed up in most states by laws recognizing that information revealed in therapy—like information given to a priest, a lawyer, or a physician—is privileged communication. This means that a therapist can refuse, even in court, to answer questions about a client or to provide personal notes or tape recordings from therapy sessions. However, under some special circumstances the law may require a therapist to violate confidentiality. Among these circumstances are when (1) the client is so severely disturbed or suicidal that hospitalization is needed, (2) the client uses his or her mental condition and history of therapy as part of his or her defense in a civil or criminal trial, (3) the therapist must defend against the client's charge of malpractice, and (4) the therapist believes the client may commit a violent act against others.

This last condition poses a dilemma. Suppose a client says, "Someday I'm going to kill that brother of mine!" Should the therapist consider this a serious threat and warn the brother? In most cases, the danger is not real, but there have been tragic exceptions. A famous example occurred in 1969. A graduate student receiving therapy at the University of California at Berkeley revealed his intention to kill Tatiana Tarasoff, a young woman whom he had dated the previous year but who had since rejected him. The therapist took the threat seriously and consulted his supervisor and the campus police. It was decided that there was no real danger, so neither Tatiana nor her parents were warned. After terminating therapy, the client killed Ms. Tarasoff. Her parents sued the university, the campus police, and the therapist. The parents won their case, thus setting an important precedent. Several states now have laws that make a therapist liable for failing to take steps to protect those who are threatened with violence by the therapist's clients (Monahan, 1993).

Clients are also protected from being casually committed to mental hospitals. According to decisions by federal courts, a person threatened with commitment can expect written notice; an opportunity to prepare a defense with the help of an attorney; a court hearing, with a jury if desired; and the right to take the Fifth Amendment to avoid self-incrimination. Furthermore, before a person can be forcibly committed, the state must provide "clear and convincing" evidence that he or she not only is mentally ill but also gravely disabled or poses an "imminent danger" to himself or herself or to others. Most states now require a periodic review of every committed person's records to determine whether he or she should be released. The person also has the right to receive treatment while hospitalized. Finally, people have the right to refuse certain forms of treatment and to be subjected to as little restriction of their freedom as possible.

Larry Hogue, a fifty-two-year old homeless crack cocaine addict, has been arrested or sent to mental hospitals more than thirty times since 1985 for threatening people on the streets of New York City. However, laws protecting the rights of the mentally ill—and the fact that he has not committed any serious crimes—have prevented him from being committed to a hospital against his will. The frustration local authorities feel over his case highlights the difficulties inherent in balancing the rights of mental patients and those of the public.

Rules regarding hospitalized mental patients help protect them from abuse, neglect, coercion, and exploitation, but they create some difficulties as well. Staff members at mental health facilities worry that they might be sued if they keep patients unnecessarily confined or if they release a patient who then harms someone. Thus the dilemma: to find a way to balance the legal rights of the patient against those of the public.

Biological Treatments

Hippocrates, a physician of ancient Greece, was among the first to propose that psychological problems have physical causes. He prescribed rest, special diets, laxatives, and abstinence from alcohol or sex as treatments for psychological disorders. In the mental hospitals of Europe and America during the sixteenth through eighteenth centuries, treatment of psychological disorders was based in part on Hippocrates' formulations and consisted mainly of physical restraints, laxative purges, bleeding of "excess" blood, and induced vomiting. Cold baths, hunger, and other physical discomforts were also used in efforts to shock patients back to normality. Today, biological treatments for psychological problems are more sophisticated and include electroconvulsive therapy, psychosurgery, and, especially, psychoactive drugs.

Electroconvulsive Therapy

In the 1930s, a Hungarian physician named Von Meduna used a drug to induce convulsions in schizophrenics. He believed—incorrectly—that, since schizophrenia and epilepsy rarely occurred in the same person, epileptic-like seizures might combat schizophrenia. In 1938, Italian physicians Ugo Cerletti and Lucio Bini created seizures more easily by passing an electric current through schizophrenics' brains. During the next twenty years or so, this procedure, called **electroconvulsive therapy** (ECT), became a routine treatment for schizophrenia, depression, and, sometimes, mania. Upon awakening after an

This crib was used in the nineteenth century to restrain unmanageable mental patients. The device was gentle compared with some of the methods endorsed in the late 1700s by Benjamin Rush, who is known as the "father" of American psychiatry. He advocated curing patients by frightening or disorienting them—for example, by placing them in a coffinlike box that was then briefly immersed in water.

ECT session, the patient typically remembered nothing about the events just preceding the shock and experienced confusion. Although many patients improved, they often relapsed. ECT's benefits also had to be weighed against such side effects as varying degrees of memory loss, speech disorders, and, in some cases, death due to cardiac arrest (Lickey & Gordon, 1991).

Recent modifications in ECT procedures—such as applying shock to only one hemisphere, using different electrical wave forms, ensuring that patients have sufficient oxygen, and inducing profound muscle relaxation—have made modern ECT less hazardous. When ECT is used in combination with other forms of treatment, its relapse rate is significantly diminished as well (Lickey & Gordon, 1991; Janicak et al., 1985; Janicak et al., 1991; NIMH, 1985). About 100,000 people a year receive ECT in the United States; about twice that number, in Great Britain (Julien, 1992; Squire, 1987). ECT is used primarily for patients whose depression is severe, who cannot tolerate or do not respond to antidepressant drugs, or who are at high risk for suicide. ECT is also occasionally used with manic patients (Janicak et al., 1991; Julien, 1992; Lickey & Gordon, 1991). Contrary to Von Meduna's early claims, however, ECT is not an effective treatment for schizophrenia unless the patient is also severely depressed.

No one knows for sure how ECT works, though it is clear that the convulsion, not the shock, is important. It may be that convulsions somehow improve neurotransmitter function and thereby alter mood (Chiodo & Antelman, 1980; Julien, 1992). Another view is that the neurotransmitters that help the brain recover from convulsions also reduce activity in areas of the brain associated with depression, thus relieving it (Sackeim, 1985). These are promising leads, but since shock affects many aspects of brain function, identifying the specific mechanisms underlying ECT's effects on depression is exceedingly difficult (Julien, 1992; Sackeim, 1988).

Because of its dramatic and potentially dangerous nature, ECT remains a controversial method of treatment for serious depression. Critics want it outlawed; proponents perceive its benefits as outweighing its potential costs in most cases (Lickey & Gordon, 1991; Small, Small & Milstein, 1986).

Psychosurgery

In 1937, Egas Moniz introduced a surgical technique called **prefrontal lobotomy** for the treatment of mental disorder. In this form of **psychosurgery**, small holes were drilled in the skull and a sharp instrument was inserted and moved from side to side to destroy brain tissue (Freeman & Watts, 1942). The theory was that emotional reactions become exaggerated in disturbed people by neural processes in the frontal lobes and that the lobotomy disrupts these processes. During the 1940s and 1950s, psychosurgery was almost routine in

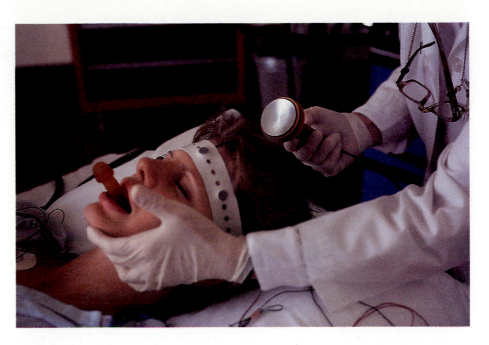

To make electroconvulsive therapy (ECT) safer, patients today are given an anesthetic to make them unconscious before the shock is delivered and a muscle relaxant to prevent bone fractures during the convulsions. Also, the duration of the shock is now only about a half a second and, in contrast to the dozens or even hundreds of treatments administered decades ago, patients now receive a total of only about six to twelve shocks, one approximately every two days. Finally, to minimize undesirable side effects, particularly memory loss, some doctors place both electrodes on the nondominant side of the patient's head instead of passing current through both cerebral hemispheres.

the treatment of schizophrenia, depression, anxiety, aggressiveness, and obsessive-compulsive disorder (Valenstein, 1980). Unfortunately, brain surgery is risky, sometimes fatal; its benefits are uncertain; and its side effects and complications, including epilepsy, are irreversible. Today, psychosurgery is done only in rare cases where all else has failed, and it focuses on only small amounts of brain tissue (Jenike et al., 1991; Sachdev, Hay & Cumming, 1992).

Psychoactive Drugs

The use of ECT and psychosurgery declined after the 1950s not only because of their complications and general distastefulness but also because they have been largely supplanted by psychoactive drugs. In Chapters 4 and 7, we discussed how psychoactive drugs affect neurotransmitter systems and consciousness. Here, we will describe how drugs are used to combat anxiety, depression, mania, and schizophrenia. Table 16.2 lists a few of these drugs, along with their uses, effects, and side effects.

Neuroleptics (Antipsychotics) The early 1950s saw the discovery of a group of drugs that revolutionized the treatment of severe mental disorder. Called **neuroleptics**, or **antipsychotics**, these drugs dramatically reduced the intensity of such psychotic symptoms as hallucinations, delusions, paranoid suspiciousness, disordered thinking, and incoherence in many mental patients, especially schizophrenics. As a result of taking these drugs, many mental patients became better able to care for themselves and more responsive to their environments. Thousands were able to leave their hospitals. For those who remained, straightjackets, padded cells, and other once-common restraints were no longer needed.

The most widely used of the antipsychotic drugs are the *phenothiazines*, of which the first, chlorpromazine (Thorazine), has been especially popular. Another neuroleptic called haloperidol (Haldol) is comparable to the phenothiazines in overall effectiveness, but it creates less sedation (Julien, 1992). Patients who do not respond to one of these neuroleptics may respond to the other. Between 60 and 70 percent of patients receiving these drugs show improvement, though fewer than 30 percent respond well enough to live entirely on their own.

Table 16.2
A Sampling of Psychoactive
Drugs Used for Treating
Psychological Disorders

For Schizophrenia: Neuroleptics (Antipsychotics)

Chemical Name	Trade Name	Effects and Side Effects
Chlorpromazine Haloperidol	Thorazine Haldol	Reduces hallucinations, delusions, incoherence, jumbled thought processes Causes movement-disorder side effects, including tardive dyskinesia
Clozapine	Clozaril	Reduces psychotic symptoms; causes no movement disorders, but raises risk of serious blood disease

For Mood Disorders: Antidepressants and Mood Elevators
Tricyclics

Imiprimine Amitriptyline	Tofranil Elavil, Amitid	Acts as antidepressant, but also has antipanic action; causes sleepiness and other moderate side effects; potentially dangerous if taken with alcohol

Other Antidepressants

Fluoxetine	Prozac	Has both antidepressant and anti-obsessive action
Clomipramine	Anafranil	Blocks reuptake of serotonin; has anti-obsessive action

Other Drugs

Lithium	Lithium carbonate	Calms mania; reduces mood swings of bipolar disorder; overdose harmful, potentially deadly

For Anxiety Disorders: Anxiolytics
Benzodiazepines

Chlordiazepoxide Diazepam	Librium Valium	Acts as potent anxiolytic for generalized anxiety, panic, stress; extended use may cause physical dependence and withdrawal syndrome if abruptly discontinued
Alprazolam	Xanax	Also has antidepressant effects; often used in agoraphobia (has high dependence potential)

Other Anti-anxiety Agents

Buspirone	BuSpar	Has slow-acting anti-anxiety action; no known dependence problems

These neuroleptics do have problematic side effects, the mildest of which include dry mouth, blurred vision, urinary retention, dizziness, and skin pigmentation problems. More serious side effects include symptoms similar to those of Parkinson's disease, such as muscle rigidity, restlessness, tremor, and slowed movement. Some of these side effects can be treated with medication; but the most serious, *tardive dyskinesia (TD),* is an irreversible disorder of the motor system that appears only after years of neuroleptic use. Affecting at least 25 percent of patients who take chlorpromazine or haloperidol, TD involves grotesque, uncontrollable, repetitive movements of the body, often including ticlike movements of the face and thrusting of the tongue. Sometimes the person's arms or legs flail unpredictably. Indeed, TD can be far worse than the mental disorder that led to treatment.

Clozapine (Clozaril) has effects like those of the phenothiazines, but it does not cause movement disorders. Though no more effective overall than the phenothiazines, clozapine has helped many patients who did not respond to the phenothiazines or haloperidol (Pickar et al., 1992). Unfortunately, for about 2 percent of those who take it, clozapine greatly increases the risk of developing a fatal blood disease called *agranulocytosis,* which is marked by the loss of white blood cells and consequent susceptibility to infectious disease. Weekly blood tests are required to detect early signs of this disease, thus greatly increasing the cost of clozapine treatment (Lickey & Gordon, 1991).

Antidepressants   Soon after antipsychotic drugs appeared, they were joined by **antidepressants**, which, as their name suggests, are medications designed to relieve symptoms of depression. About 60 to 70 percent of patients who take these drugs show improved mood, greater physical activity, increased appetite, and more deep (stage 4) sleep. Curiously, though these drugs have almost immediate effects on neurotransmitters (usually increasing serotonin or norepinephrine availability), their effects on depressive symptoms do not occur until a week or two after dosage begins; maximum effects take even longer. The mechanism underlying these drugs' effects is consistent with some theories about the biology of depression discussed in Chapter 15, but the time lag suggests that the effects occur through some sort of long-term compensatory process in the nervous system.

There are several classes of antidepressant drugs. The *monoamine oxidase inhibitors* (MAO-I) are effective in many cases of depression, and in some cases of panic disorder; but they can produce severe hypertension if mixed with foods containing "tyramine," a substance found in aged cheeses, red wine, and chicken livers (Julien, 1992). Fortunately, a new class of MAO-I drugs is now available that does not risk this side effect (Julien, 1992).

Another popular class of antidepressant is the *tricyclic antidepressants* (TCAs). The TCAs have been prescribed more frequently than MAO-I drugs because they seem to work somewhat better. They also have fewer side effects, though some patients stop taking TCAs because of the sleepiness, dry mouth, dizziness, blurred vision, hypotension, constipation, and urinary retention they can cause. Further, taking TCAs and drinking alcohol can increase the effects of both, with potentially fatal results. Still, if side effects are controlled, TCAs can help many depressed patients and, like the MAO-I drugs, can also reduce the severity and frequency of panic attacks in some panic disorder patients.

A "second generation" of antidepressants affects serotonin rather than norepinephrine (Julien, 1992). The major drug in this group is called *fluoxetine* (Prozac). Fluoxetine is now the most widely prescribed antidepressant in the United States, mainly because it is at least as effective as the TCAs (about 60 to 80 percent of depressed people who take it find significant relief), but it has milder side effects. Fluoxetine and other serotonin-related drugs, such as clomipramine (Anafranil), are also effective in treating obsessive-compulsive disorder.

Lithium   Around 1970 the mineral salt *lithium* was found to calm manic patients and, if taken regularly, to prevent both the depression and the mania associated with bipolar disorder (Berger, 1978; Coppen, Metcalf & Wood, 1982). Administered as lithium carbonate, lithium is effective in about 80 percent of manic patients. Without lithium, the typical bipolar patient has a manic episode about every 14 months and a depressive episode about every 17 months (Lickey & Gordon, 1991). With lithium, attacks of mania occur as rarely as every nine years. The lithium dosage, however, must be exact and carefully controlled; taking too much can cause vomiting, nausea, tremor, fatigue, slurred speech, and, with severe overdoses, coma or death. Further, lithium is not useful for treating a manic episode in progress because, like antidepressants, it takes a week or two of regular use before its effects are seen. So, as with the antidepressants, lithium's effects probably occur through some form of long-term adaptation as the nervous system adjusts to the presence of the drug.

Anxiolytics   During the 1950s, a new class of drugs called **tranquilizers** was shown to reduce mental and physical tension and the symptoms of anxiety. The first of these drugs, called meprobamate (Miltown or Equanil), acts somewhat like barbiturates (see Chapter 7), meaning that overdoses can cause sleep and even death. Because they do not pose this danger, the *benzodiazepines,* particularly chlordiazepoxide (Librium) and diazepam (Valium), became the worldwide drug treatment of choice for anxiety (Blackwell, 1973). Today, these and other anti-anxiety drugs, now called **anxiolytics,** continue to be the most widely prescribed and used of all legal drugs. They have an immediate calming effect on anxiety and are quite useful in treating the symptoms of generalized anxiety and posttraumatic stress disorder. One of the newest of the benzodiazepines, alprazolam (Xanax), has also become especially popular for the treatment of panic disorder and agoraphobia (Klosko et al., 1990).

Benzodiazepines can have bothersome side effects such as sedation, lightheadedness, and impaired psychomotor and mental functioning. Combining these drugs with alcohol can have fatal consequences, and continued use of anxiolytics can lead to tolerance and physical dependence. After heavy or long-term use, attempts to stop taking these drugs, particularly if the change is abrupt, can result in severe withdrawal symptoms, including seizures and a return of anxiety more intense than the patient had initially experienced (Julien, 1992; Rickels et al., 1993).

An anxiolytic called buspirone (BuSpar) provides an alternative anxiety treatment that eliminates some of these problems, but it acts more slowly. Like the antidepressants, buspirone's effects do not occur for days or weeks after treatment begins; in fact, many patients quit taking it because they think it has no effect other than dizziness, headache, and nervousness (Lickey & Gordon, 1991). Yet buspirone can ultimately equal diazepam in reducing generalized anxiety (Feighner, Merideth & Hendrickson, 1982). Further, it does not seem to promote dependence, causes less cognitive and psychomotor impairment than the benzodiazepines, and does not interact negatively with alcohol.

Human Diversity and Drug Treatment   So far, we have talked about drug treatment effects in general, but there can be significant differences between members of various ethnic groups and between men and women in terms of the psychoactive drug dose necessary to produce clinical effects. For example, Keh-Ming Lin, director of the Center on the Psychobiology of Ethnicity at UCLA, has demonstrated that, compared to Asians, Caucasians need significantly higher doses of the benzodiazepines, haloperidol, lithium, and possibly the tricyclic antidepressants in order to obtain equally beneficial effects (Lin et al., 1991). In addition, African-Americans may show a faster response to TCAs than European-Americans and respond to lower doses of lithium (Strickland, 1991). Whether Hispanics differ from other ethnic groups is not yet clear (Mendoza et al., 1991). Some of these ethnic differences are thought to be a function of genetically regulated differences in drug metabolism, while others may be due to dietary practices.

Gender differences in drug response are also coming under investigation. Recent studies suggest that females may maintain higher plasma levels of therapeutic psychoactive drugs, show better response to neuroleptics, but experience more adverse effects such as tardive dyskinesia (Yonkers et al., 1992). It is believed that hormonal and body-composition differences (such as the ratio of body fat to muscle), among other factors, may be the sources of gender differences in drug response (Dawkins & Potter, 1991; Yonkers et al., 1992). Continued research on these and other dimensions of human diversity will undoubtedly lead to more effective, and safer, drug treatments for psychological disorders.

Evaluating Biological Treatments

"In Review: Biological Treatments for Psychological Disorders" summarizes our discussion of biological treatment methods; our comments here focus on the most dominant of these, the psychoactive drugs. In spite of their widespread success in the treatment of psychological disorders, critics point out three major problems with their use.

First, even if a disorder has physical components, drugs may mask the problem without curing it. This masking effect is desirable in treating otherwise incurable physical conditions such as diabetes, but it may divert attention from potentially effective nondrug approaches to psychological problems. Anxiolytics, for example, do not teach people to cope with the source of their anxiety. Second, abuse of some drugs (such as the benzodiazepines) can result in physical or psychological dependence. Third, side effects present a problem. Some are merely annoying, such as the thirst and dry mouth produced by some antidepressants. Other side effects, like tardive dyskinesia, are far more serious. Although these side effects occur in a minority of patients, some are irreversible, and it is impossible to predict in advance who will develop them.

Still, research on psychoactive drugs holds the promise of creating better medications, a fuller understanding of the origin and nature of some psychological disorders, and more informed medication practices. For example, advances in research on individual variations in the structure of the genes that create different types of dopamine receptors may explain why some patients

In Review: Biological Treatments for Psychological Disorders

Method	Typical Disorders Treated	Possible Side Effects	Mechanism of Action
Electroconvulsive therapy (ECT)	Severe depression	Temporary confusion, memory loss	Uncertain
Psychosurgery	Schizophrenia, severe depression, obsessive-compulsive disorder	Listlessness, overemotionality, epilepsy	Uncertain
Psychoactive drugs	Anxiety disorders, depression, obsessive-compulsive disorder, mania, schizophrenia	Variable, depending on drug used: movement disorders, physical dependence	Alteration of neurotransmitters in the brain

respond to phenothiazines that bind primarily to one type of dopamine receptor while other patients respond only to clozapine, which has a preference for another type of dopamine receptor (Van Tol et al., 1992). This research may guide the development of new drugs matched to specific receptors, so that the symptoms of schizophrenia can be alleviated without the risk of movement disorders posed by the phenothiazines or the potentially lethal side effects of clozapine. Similarly, research on anxiolytics promises to reveal information about the chemical aspects of anxiety.

Drugs and Psychotherapy

We have seen that both drugs and psychotherapy can be effective in treating psychological disorders. Is one better than the other? Can they be effectively combined? Considerable research is being conducted to address these questions.

So far, although the occasional study does show one approach or the other to be more effective, there is no clear consensus; overall, neither form of therapy is clearly superior for treating problems such as the anxiety disorders and major depressive disorder. For example, one large-scale study on the treatment of depression found that, in general, two forms of psychotherapy (cognitive-behavior therapy and interpersonal therapy) were equally effective and that neither differed from treatment with imipramine, a tricyclic antidepressant drug (Elkins et al., 1989). There was some indication that imipramine was more effective than psychotherapy in the most severe cases of depression, however. Similarly, a study on the treatment of panic disorder found no significant differences between groups receiving behavior therapy or the anxiolytic drug alprazolam (Xanax) (Klosko et al., 1990).

Studies that have examined the joint use of drugs and psychotherapy have found surprisingly little advantage in their combination (Hollon, Shelton & Loosen, 1991; Lickey & Gordon, 1991). Thus, it has been suggested that the most conservative strategy for treating anxiety and depression is, at least, to begin with some form of psychotherapy (which has no major negative side effects) and then to add or switch to drug treatment only if the psychotherapeutic approach is ineffective. Often, clients who do not respond to one method will be helped by the other.

Linkages: Biological Aspects of Psychology and the Treatment of Psychological Disorders

What biological mechanisms underlie drug treatment of psychological disorders?

As noted in Chapter 4, all sensing, perceiving, thinking, feeling, and behaving, whether normal or abnormal, is ultimately mediated by biological processes, especially those in the brain, and most especially those involving neurotransmitters. Alterations in the availability of these neurotransmitters, and thus in the activity of the neural circuits they influence, affects the ebb and flow of neural communication, the integration of information in the brain and, ultimately, behavior and mental processes. Because different neurotransmitters are especially active in particular brain regions or circuits (see Figure 4.14), altering the functioning of particular neurotransmitter systems will have relatively specific psychological and behavioral effects.

Some of the drugs we have described for the treatment of psychological disorders were developed specifically to alter a neurotransmitter system that biological theories suggest might be involved in particular types of disorder; in other cases, causal theories evolved from (often accidental) findings that drugs known to affect certain neurotransmitters help patients who display some disorder.

Let's consider in a little more detail some of the ways in which therapeutic psychoactive drugs affect neurotransmitters. Recall from Chapter 4 that a given neuron can receive excitatory ("fire") or inhibitory ("don't fire") signals via neurotransmitters that facilitate or inhibit firing. Some therapeutic drugs amplify excitatory signals, while others increase inhibition. For example, the benzodiazepines (Valium, Xanax) exert their anti-anxiety effects by helping the inhibitory neurotransmitter GABA to bind to postsynaptic receptors and, thus, suppress neuronal firing. This enhanced inhibitory effect acts as a sort of braking system that slows the activity of GABA-nergic neurons involved in the experience of anxiety. However, benzodiazepines also slow the action of all GABA-nergic neural systems, including those associated with motor activity and mental processing, which are spread throughout the brain. The result is the decreased psychomotor coordination and reduced clarity of thinking that appear as benzodiazepine side effects.

Other therapeutic drugs reduce postsynaptic activity by serving as *receptor antagonists* (see Figure 7.13), acting to block the receptor site normally used by a particular neurotransmitter. Some neuroleptics, the phenothiazines and haloperidol, for example, exert their antipsychotic effects by blocking receptors for dopamine, a neurotransmitter that, as described in Chapter 4, is important for movement. Thus, these drugs compete with dopamine, blocking the firing of dopaminergic neurons. The fact that dopamine blockage seems to normalize the jumbled thinking processes of many schizophrenics suggests that, as discussed in Chapter 15, schizophrenia may be partly due to excess dopamine activity. Unfortunately, reducing this activity can create severe disorders in the movement systems that are also controlled by dopamine.

Another mechanism through which psychoactive drugs exert their therapeutic influence is increasing the amount of a neurotransmitter available at the receptors, thus maximizing its effects. This enhanced availability can be accomplished either by stimulating production of the neurotransmitter or, as is more common in therapeutic drugs, by keeping it in circulation in the synapse. Normally, after a neurotransmitter has been released, it flows back to the presynaptic terminal where it is stored for later use. If this *reuptake* process is blocked, the neurotransmitter remains in the synapse, ready to work. The tricyclic antidepressants, for example, operate by blocking the reuptake of norepinephrine, while fluoxetine and clomipramine block reuptake of serotonin. Again, these effects are consistent with biological theories suggesting that some cases of depression are traceable to faulty norepinephrine or serotonin systems.

Community Psychology: From Treatment to Prevention

It has been argued for decades that even if psychologists knew exactly how to treat every psychological problem, there would never be enough mental health professionals to help everyone who needs it (Albee, 1968). This view fostered the rise of **community psychology,** a movement that aims both to treat troubled people in their home communities and to promote social and environmental changes that would minimize or prevent psychological disorders.

One aspect of community psychology, the *community mental health movement,* arose during the 1960s as an attempt to make treatment available to people in their own communities. Thanks to the availability of antipsychotic drugs, as well as concern that mental hospitals were little more than warehouses for patients, thousands of people were released from mental institu-

Professional and nonprofessional staff members at community mental health centers provide traditional therapy and mental health education, along with walk-in facilities or "hotlines" for people who are suicidal or in crises related to rape or domestic violence. They also offer day treatment to former mental patients, many of whom are homeless. Indeed, the presence of thousands of homeless mentally disturbed people on the streets of American cities has fueled criticism that community mental health programs have failed to provide necessary treatment to former mental patients and others in need of long-term care.

tions. It was expected that they would receive low-cost mental health services in newly funded community mental health centers. In fact, far fewer centers opened than expected. The *deinstitutionalization* process did spare patients the oppressive tedium of the hospital environment, but the mental health services available in the community never matched the need for them. As a result, former mental patients have swelled the ranks of the homeless who risk the dangers of life on city streets (Kelly et al., 1992); community mental health centers and other agencies continue trying to meet their social, physical, and mental health needs (Freiberg, 1992).

Community psychology also attempts to prevent psychological problems (Albee, 1985). Many of these problems—especially those leading to child abuse, marital strife, failure in school, alcoholism, drug abuse, and suicide—occur in generation after generation. Trying to deal with these problems after they appear is like trying to rescue one person after another from a rushing river. Eventually, someone must go upstream and do something about whatever is causing all those people to fall in the river (Rappaport, 1977). Accordingly, some community psychologists seek to head off the stress-producing effects of unemployment, poverty, and overcrowded, substandard housing. Do something about social problems causing stress, say community psychologists, and you will reduce more stress and prevent more psychological problems than a battalion of psychotherapists could.

Less ambitious, but perhaps even more significant, are efforts to detect psychological problems in their earliest stages and keep them from becoming worse, and to minimize the long-term effects of psychological disorders and prevent their recurrence. Examples include suicide prevention (Garland & Zigler, 1993); programs that train teachers to identify early signs of child abuse; programs that help emotionally disturbed or mentally retarded individuals develop the skills necessary for semi-independent living in the community (Wallace et al., 1992); and programs, including Project Head Start, that help preschoolers whose backgrounds decrease their chances of doing well in school and put them at risk for delinquency (Zigler, Taussig & Black, 1992).

Future Directions

Though still far from its ultimate goals, community psychology will continue to reach out to those in need and to pursue the ideal of preventing psychological disorders (Shore, 1992). There are indications that helping people learn how to control stress, to develop new competencies, and to help one another may make it possible to prevent or minimize the impact of certain social-psychological problems (see, for example, Markman et al., 1993; Zimmerman et al., 1991). As research illuminates more of the social and cultural causes and cures of psychological disorder, community psychology will become even more valuable.

The self-help movement is also likely to continue growing, and to expand to deal with new areas of human distress. The relationship between self-help groups and mental health professionals has been characterized by a certain amount of mutual suspicion and conflict (Humphreys, 1993). Some professionals are concerned, for example, that self-help groups are not capable of dealing with some problems and, worse, are diverting people from the more formal help they need. Though they have offered little in the way of outcome research, self-help group organizers feel their programs offer benefits that professionals can't. Both approaches are likely to flourish, especially if professionals and nonprofessionals can reach a clearer understanding of what the other can contribute to the task of helping distressed people (Salzer, McFadden & Rappaport, in press).

As in the recent past, formal psychotherapy is likely to reflect eclecticism as therapists of all theoretical preferences borrow techniques from one another. This openmindedness will also appear in research on such new techniques as eye movement desensitization and reprocessing, or EMD/R (Kleinknecht & Morgan, 1992), as discussed in Chapter 2. Researchers will also surely focus more than ever on demonstrating the clinical, not just the statistical, significance of treatments (Jacobson & Truax, 1991; Moses-Zirkes, 1993; Speer, 1992).

Future years will also see the discovery of new psychoactive drugs, perhaps drugs without serious side effects. Just as important, the results of research on differences in drug effects that are related to gender and ethnicity will inform prescription practices. This information, along with therapists' increased sensitivity to the importance of cultural differences, will make therapeutic services more palatable to, and more effective with, increasingly diverse populations (Pederson, 1994; Snowden & Hines, 1994).

Indeed, though various treatments for psychological disorders relieve the suffering of thousands of clients each year, the goal is always to do better. A vital route to improved treatment lies in mapping out the specific methods most likely to be most effective for each client's problems. Research aimed at this goal will focus on answering the "ultimate question" that we mentioned earlier: "What treatment, by whom, is most effective for this individual with that specific problem, under which set of circumstances?" (Paul, 1969a, p. 44). Research on this question and on how how various treatments produce their effects will occupy researchers for many years to come.

Several courses can help you learn more about the treatment of psychological disorders. In particular, we suggest that you take courses in psychotherapy, counseling, behavior modification, psychopharmacology, and community psychology.

Summary and Key Terms

Psychotherapy for psychological disorders is usually based on psychodynamic, phenomenological, or behavioral theories of personality and behavior disorder. Most therapists combine features of these theories in an eclectic approach. The biological approach is reflected in the use of drugs and other physical treatment methods.

Essentials of Treatment

All forms of treatment include (1) a client, (2) a therapist, (3) an underlying theory of behavior disorder, (4) a set of treatment procedures, which the underlying theory says should help, and (5) a special relationship between the client and therapist, which may make it easier for improvement to occur. Therapy may be offered to inpatients and outpatients in many different settings by *psychologists, psychiatrists,* and other mental health professionals. The goal of treatment is to help people change their thinking, feelings, and behavior so that they will be happier and more productive. This goal may be pursued by promoting insight into the hidden causes of behavior problems, fostering personal growth through genuine self-expression, or helping clients learn new ways of thinking and acting.

Psychodynamic Psychotherapy

Psychodynamic psychotherapy began with Freud's *psychoanalysis* and seeks to help clients gain insight into unconscious conflicts and impulses and then to explore how those factors have created disorders.

Classical Psychoanalysis

Exploration of the unconscious is aided by the use of *free association,* dream interpretation, and analysis of *transference.* The therapist often gives *interpretations* of what the client says and does, in order to help examine unconscious meanings.

Contemporary Variations on Psychoanalysis

Some variations on psychoanalysis focus less on the id, the unconscious, and the past and more on helping clients to harness the ego to solve problems in the present. Other forms retain most of Freud's principles but use a more flexible format. Object relations therapy, a newer form of psychoanalysis, examines the effects of early family relationships on current ones, and seeks to improve the latter.

Phenomenological Psychotherapy

Phenomenological psychotherapy helps clients to become more aware of discrepancies between their feelings and their behavior. These discrepancies are seen to be at the root of behavior disorders and, according to the phenomenological approach, can be resolved by the client once they are brought to light in the context of a genuine, trusting relationship with the therapist.

Client-Centered Therapy

Carl Rogers's *client-centered therapy,* also known as *person-centered therapy,* is the most prominent form of phenomenological treatment. Rogerian therapists help mainly by adopting attitudes toward the client that express *unconditional positive regard, empathy,* and *congruence.* These attitudes create a nonjudgmental atmosphere in which it is easier for the client to be honest with the therapist, with himself or herself, and with others. *Reflection* provides one way of creating this atmosphere.

Gestalt Therapy

Therapists employing the *Gestalt therapy* of Fritz Perls use more active techniques than Rogerian therapists, often confronting and challenging clients with evidence of their defensiveness, game playing, and other efforts to escape self-exploration.

Behavior Therapies

Behavior therapy, behavior modification, and *cognitive-behavior therapy* apply laboratory-based principles of learning to eliminate undesirable patterns of thought and behavior and to strengthen more desirable alternatives.

Techniques for Modifying Behavior

Common behavioral treatments include *systematic desensitization, modeling,* and *assertiveness and social skills training.* More generally, behavioral therapists use *positive reinforcement* (sometimes in a *token economy*), techniques based on *extinction* (such as *flooding*), *aversive conditioning,* and *punishment* to strengthen desirable behaviors or weaken problematic behaviors.

Cognitive-Behavior Therapy

Many behavior therapists also employ cognitive behavior therapy to help clients alter the way they think as well as how they behave. Among the specific cognitive-behavioral methods are *rational-emotive therapy (RET),* cognitive restructuring, stress inoculation training, and *cognitive therapy.*

Group and Family Therapies

Therapists of all theoretical persuasions offer *group therapy* and *family therapy.* These forms of treatment take advantage of the group or family setting to enhance the effects of treatment. The group format is also adopted in many self-help or mutual help organizations.

Evaluating Psychotherapy

There is little agreement about exactly how to measure improvement following psychotherapy and how best to assure that observed improvement was actually due to the treatment itself and not to some other factor. One prominent method for outcome research is meta-analysis. Most current observers conclude that clients who receive psychotherapy are better off than most clients who receive no treatment but that no single approach is uniformly better than all others for all clients and problems.

Addressing the "Ultimate Question"

No single treatment approach appears consistently superior to all the others, and research is needed to discover the combinations of therapists, clients, and treatments ideally suited to treating particular psychological problems. Several factors, including personal preferences, must be considered when choosing a form of treatment and a therapist.

Cultural Factors in Psychotherapy

The effects of cultural differences in values and goals between therapist and client have attracted increasing attention. Efforts are under way to minimize the problems these differences can create.

Rules and Rights in the Therapeutic Relationship

Whatever the specific form of treatment, the client has, among other rights, the right to confidentiality and protection from unjustified confinement in a mental hospital.

Biological Treatments

Biological treatment methods seek to relieve psychological disorder by physical rather than psychological means.

Electroconvulsive Therapy

Electroconvulsive therapy (ECT) involves passing an electric current through the patient's brain, usually in an effort to relieve severe depression.

Psychosurgery

Psychosurgery procedures such as *prefrontal lobotomy* are used, usually as a last resort, in an attempt to disrupt neural connections in the brain thought to be associated with mental disorder.

Psychoactive Drugs

Today the most prominent form of biological treatment involves psychoactive drugs, including those with *antipsychotic (neuroleptic), antidepressant,* or *tranquilizing (anxiolytic)* effects.

There appear to be significant differences between members of various ethnic groups, and between men and women, in terms of the amount of a psychoactive drug necessary to produce clinical effects.

Evaluating Biological Treatments

Psychoactive drugs have proven impressively effective in many cases, but critics point out a number of undesirable side effects associated with these drugs, the risks of abuse, and the dangers of over-reliance on chemical approaches to human problems that might have other solutions.

Drugs and Psychotherapy

So far, neither psychotherapy or drug treatment has been found clearly superior overall for treating problems such as anxiety or depression.

Linkages: Biological Aspects of Psychology and the Treatment of Psychological Disorders

The biological basis for the effects of psychoactive drug treatment lies in the drugs' effects on neurotransmitter systems. These effects include enhancing or blocking the action of neurotransmitters.

Community Psychology: From Treatment to Prevention

Concern about the effectiveness of individual treatment and the realization that there will never be enough therapists to treat all who need help prompted the development of *community psychology.* Community mental health programs and efforts to prevent mental disorders are the two main elements of community psychology. Community mental health centers came into being in the 1960s and, in spite of the fact that government funding never reached anticipated levels, the staff of the facilities are trying, against overwhelming odds, to meet former mental patients' social, physical and mental health needs. At the same time, community psychologists seek to head off the stress-producing factors that promote psychological disorders.

Chapter 17

Social Cognition

Outline

It is often said that the newspapers carry only bad news. Reports abound of people being murdered, raped, and robbed, of stores being burned, of corporate secrets being stolen, and of all sorts of other antisocial acts. In the midst of this, it is easy to forget how generous and helpful people can be. For example, each year around Thanksgiving, when the *New York Times* prints descriptions of the neediest families in the city, hundreds of thousands of dollars pour in from donors who have never met those they are helping, and who ask for nothing in return.

Aggression and aiding, cheating and charity are among the topics studied in **social psychology**, the specialty concerned with all the ways a person's behavior and mental processes are influenced by other people. No aspect of life escapes this influence, as the Linkages diagram suggests. In the next chapter we focus on patterns of group and interpersonal behavior such as conformity, aggression, and cooperation. In this chapter, we begin our coverage of social psychology by examining **social cognition**, the mental processes associated with how people perceive and react to other individuals and groups. We look at how processes examined in previous chapters—perception, learning, memory, thought, and feeling—occur when their objects are other people and at how other people influence these processes. In doing so, we consider how people think about themselves and others, how they form impressions of others, how they form and change attitudes, and how and why they use stereotypes to judge other people, sometimes in prejudiced ways.

Social Construction of the Self

Each of us lives in both a personal and social world. You experience your thoughts and feelings as personal, but they are products of the social and cultural environment, influenced by others in important ways. In the chapters on human development and on personality, we described how each individual develops within a cultural context. We explored how collectivist and individualist cultures emphasize different core values and encourage contrasting definitions of the self. Most European and North American cultures, for example, tend toward an individualistic emphasis in which each person is taught to be independent and self-sufficient. In contrast, most cultures in places such as Asia and South America tend toward collectivist values, which encourage people to think of themselves as interdependent parts of a larger network (DeAngelis, 1992). In this section we look more closely at how people think about themselves in the social context provided by other people.

Social Comparison

People spend a good amount of time thinking about themselves, trying to evaluate their own perceptions, opinions, values, abilities, and so on. Decades ago, Leon Festinger (1954) noted that self-evaluation involves two distinct types of questions: those that can be answered by taking a simple objective measurement and those that cannot. You can determine your height or weight by measuring it, but for other types of questions—about mental ability or athletic prowess, for example—there are no objective criteria. In these cases, according to Festinger's theory of **social comparison**, people use other people as a basis of comparison. Research shows that when you wonder how intelligent (Butler, 1992), interesting (Wheeler & Miyake, 1992), or attractive (Brown et al., 1992) you are, you use *social* rather than objective criteria.

Whom do you use as a basis of comparison? Festinger said that people look to people who are similar to themselves. If you are curious about how good a singer you are, you are likely to compare yourself not with opera stars like Kathleen Battle or Luciano Pavarotti, but with singers at your own level of experience and ability (Kruglanski & Mayseless, 1990). The categories of people to which you see yourself as belonging and to which you habitually compare yourself are called **reference groups.**

Which reference groups you use can shape your satisfaction with life (Taylor, Buunk & Aspinwall, 1990). Consider people from a lower-class background who work their way up to a middle-class life. Along with new jobs and more responsibilities comes a higher income, but also new reference groups. As such people begin to move up in an organization, they begin to associate with others who have an even higher standard of living. If they use these people as a basis for comparison, they begin to experience **relative depri-**

Linkages

The questions in this diagram illustrate some of the relationships between the topic of this chapter, social cognition, and other chapter topics. (The page numbers indicate where the questions are discussed.) We will see, for example, that the basic principles discussed in the chapter on perception apply to social cognition as well. Thus, when you meet a new neighbor, your first impression will reflect the influence of top-down processing discussed in Chapter 6. Research on social cognition, however, provides a more detailed view of why your first impression is likely to be a lasting impression. We will also see that the cognitive biases and mental shortcuts discussed in the chapter on thought and language help explain how people think about themselves and others. ■

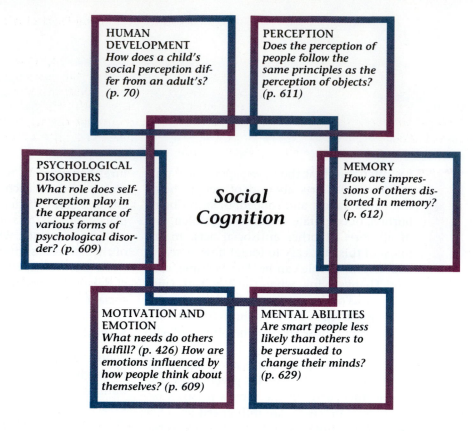

HUMAN DEVELOPMENT
How does a child's social perception differ from an adult's? (p. 70)

PERCEPTION
Does the perception of people follow the same principles as the perception of objects? (p. 611)

PSYCHOLOGICAL DISORDERS
What role does self-perception play in the appearance of various forms of psychological disorder? (p. 609)

Social Cognition

MEMORY
How are impressions of others distorted in memory? (p. 612)

MOTIVATION AND EMOTION
What needs do others fulfill? (p. 426) How are emotions influenced by how people think about themselves? (p. 609)

MENTAL ABILITIES
Are smart people less likely than others to be persuaded to change their minds? (p. 629)

vation—the sense that, compared with those in a reference group, they are not doing well. Thus, moving from the lower to the middle or from the middle to the upper class is often an uncomfortable and frustrating experience (Crosby & Gonzalez-Intal, 1982). Similarly, when teenagers move from the relatively high status of being a senior in high school to the relatively low status of being a first-year college student, the sudden change in reference group and relative standing often creates disorientation, anxiety, and self-doubt, at least temporarily. Chronic use of extreme reference groups—such as the rich or famous—can create depression and anxiety for the average person (Taylor & Lobel, 1989). The cognitive-behavioral therapies described in Chapter 16 often help overly self-critical people develop more positive self-evaluations by encouraging them to use more realistic reference groups.

Social Identity Theory

Social comparison also plays an important part in the formation of an **identity,** a person's mental representation of who he or she is. According to **social identity theory,** one's identity results from a fundamental tension between the need to be like others and a corresponding need to feel unique. Thus, social identity theorists suggest that people search for an optimal level of distinctiveness when thinking about themselves in relation to others (Brewer, 1991). People form not only a *personal identity,* which corresponds to all those characteristics that make the individual unique, but also a *group identity,* in which the self gains meaning from associations with similar others.

A group identity permits people to feel part of a larger whole. Its importance is seen in the pride people feel when a member of their family graduates from college or when a local team wins a big game (Hogg & Hardie, 1991). In wars between national, ethnic, or religious groups, individuals sacrifice and sometimes die for the sake of their group identity. A group identity is also one reason people donate money to those in need, support friends in a crisis, and

Linkages: Are there significant cultural differences in the development of a sense of self? (a link to Human Development)

display other helping behaviors. At the same time, however, defining ourselves in terms of a group identity can foster an "us versus them" orientation that sets the stage for prejudice, discrimination, and intergroup conflict.

Of course, people have both personal and group identities no matter what their cultural background, but the relative emphasis given to each differs in individualistic and collectivist cultures. In individualistic cultures, one's personal identity tends to be detailed, concrete, and salient. In collectivist cultures, it is the group identity that tends to be more salient. Thus, when people are asked to describe themselves, those from individualistic cultures tend to respond with statements like "I am assertive and athletic" or "I am shy and creative." In contrast, those from collectivist cultures tend to respond with statements such as "I am the third son" or "I help on the family farm."

Cultural influences on the self are subtle, but powerful. In fact, recent research suggests that those who align themselves with the dominant values of their culture tend to have greater self-esteem and satisfaction with life than those who are not so aligned (Markus & Kitayama, 1991).

Linkages: Social Cognition and Psychological Disorders

What role does self-perception play in the appearance of various forms of psychological disorder?

The mental representations that people form of themselves, their **self-schemas,** differ not only in a general way from culture to culture but also more specifically from person to person within a culture (Showers, 1992). In the chapter on human development we described how an identity is formed from childhood through adolescence, but a person's identity may be refined and changed throughout life. How people think about themselves can influence not only self-esteem and life satisfaction but also mental health.

Patricia Linville (1982) identified one significant characteristic of self-schemas. She distinguished between unified and differentiated self-schemas. People with a *unified self-schema* think of themselves as having more or less the same characteristics or attributes in every situation (at home, at a party, and so on) and in every role (as a student, friend, or romantic partner). In contrast, people with *differentiated self-schemas* think of themselves as having different attributes in different roles or situations (Dixon & Baumeister, 1991).

Linkages: How are emotions influenced by how people think about themselves? (a link to Motivation and Emotion)

These differences in the way people think about themselves have a strong impact on their emotional experiences (Clark, 1994). Imagine a student who fails an exam. No one is happy about that experience. But those with a unified self-schema tend to have a much stronger emotional reaction to it because they tend to interpret failure in this one area as implying incompetence in all areas (Niedenthal, Setterlund & Wherry, 1992). After failing, they are likely to think less of themselves not only as students but also as romantic partners, as sons or daughters, and so on. In contrast, people with a differentiated self-schema may think less of themselves as students, but failing an exam will have fewer implications for how they think of themselves in their other social roles (Kihlstrom & Klein, 1994). As described in Chapter 15, a tendency to see oneself as generally and permanently inadequate rather than as merely being prone to specific or temporary weaknesses may form the cognitive basis for depression and other psychological disorders.

Self-schemas contain information not only about what a person is (the *actual self*) but also about what a person wants to be (the *ideal self*) and what moral training tells a person he or she should be (the *ought self*). Discrepancies between the actual and ideal selves or between the actual and ought selves create emotional reactions as early as the preschool years (Wells & Higgins,

The way people think about themselves—their self-schema—can have a major impact on how they react emotionally to other people and to events. If, for example, you think of your value or competence in one situation as representing your value in all situations, then depression over a broken relationship might leave you feeling depressed about life in general. People who recognize that failure in one area does not mean they are utterly worthless may suffer less devastating emotional reactions to a particular unpleasant event.

1989). For most people, thinking about the discrepancy between the actual self and the ideal self produces emotions such as sadness, disappointment, and dissatisfaction (Higgins, 1987). In more extreme cases, however, people begin to ruminate about such matters, and this can result in symptoms of depression (Scott & O'hara, 1993; Weary & Edwards, 1994). Discrepancies between the actual self and the ought self usually produce emotions such as guilt and fear of rejection, but in some cases they result in anxiety-related disorders (Higgins, 1989; Scott & O'hara, 1993). People often feel that they must do something to reduce the discrepancy, and they may try to do so by somehow punishing themselves (Higgins, 1989). Effective treatment of depression and anxiety disorders often requires a careful analysis of why and how people think about such discrepancies (Weary & Edwards, 1994).

Social Perception

There is a story about a company president who was having lunch with a man being considered for an executive position. When the man salted his food without first tasting it, the president decided not to hire him. The reason, she explained, was that the company would never hire a person who acted before collecting all relevant information. The candidate lost his chance because of the president's **social perception**, which refers to the processes through which people interpret information about others, draw inferences about people, and develop mental representations of them. Social perception influences whether you see a person as hostile or friendly, repugnant or likable. It also helps to determine how you explain why people act as they do.

First Impressions

Conventional wisdom says that first impressions of other people are very important, and research confirms their significance (Ross & Jackson, 1991). First impressions are easily formed, difficult to change, and typically have a long-lasting influence on how one person reacts to another. How do people form impressions of people? And why are they so resistant to change?

Schemas   The perception of people follows many of the same laws as the perception of objects, including the Gestalt principles discussed in Chapter 6. Consider Figure 17.1. As suggested by Gestalt principles, most people would not say that it is composed of eight separate straight lines; they are more likely to describe it as "a square with a notch in one side" (Woodworth & Schlosberg, 1954). Robert Woodworth suggested that this tendency is based on a **schema-plus-correction process.** In this case the mental representation, or schema, is "a square"; the correction is the notch. People use the schemas they already have to perceive and interpret new information.

The perception of people, like the perception of objects, involves the use of pre-existing schemas to integrate individual bits of information (Wyer & Carlston, 1994). Your schema about grandmothers, for example, probably leads you to expect them to be elderly, sweet, gentle, kind, and conservative dressers. When you are introduced to a grandmother, you may perceive those characteristics that are a part of your schema of grandmothers, even if the particular grandmother you meet does not display them. Schemas allow you to skip the task of perceiving each element of a stimulus separately, to look instead at meaningful configurations, and to fill in missing information by using knowledge stored in long-term memory. It may take a very unusual grandmother (perhaps one who is forty-five years old, wears tight jeans, and rides a motorcycle) to focus your perceptions on her actual attributes (Hamilton & Sherman, 1994).

Forming Impressions   Schemas help create the tendency for people to infer a great deal about a person automatically, on the basis of limited information, and thus to form impressions quickly (Brewer, 1988). Suppose you attend a party where you are introduced to a woman who appears to be in her mid-thirties and is wearing a long black dress with a pearl necklace. You are told that she has just finished writing her third novel. After five minutes of conversation, you might infer that she is articulate, intelligent, educated, wealthy, witty, and much more interesting than anyone you have met in the past ten years. It is typical for people to take a few isolated bits of verbal and nonverbal behavior and infer from them all sorts of things about a person's life and personality. Some of them may be true, others not.

Two general tendencies influence whether a first impression is positive or negative. First, all else being equal, people tend to give others the benefit of the doubt and form positive impressions of them. In the absence of contradictory information, people assume that others are similar to themselves (Srull & Gaelick, 1983). Since most people tend to have a positive evaluation of themselves, they are predisposed toward liking other people as well.

The second principle is that negative information tends to carry more weight than positive information (Klein, 1991). Why? People may act positively for any number of reasons: because they are nice, because they like you, because they are polite, or because they want to sell you insurance. However, it is assumed that negative acts come about only because the person is unfriendly or has some other undesirable characteristic (Coovert & Reeder, 1990). As a result, people are particularly attentive to negative acts and tend to weigh them heavily when forming impressions.

Lasting Impressions   In addition to being formed easily, first impressions tend to be difficult to change and thus to have a long-lasting influence (O'Sullivan & Durso, 1984). There are at least four reasons for the stability of first impressions.

Linkages: Does the perception of people follow the same principles as the perception of objects? (a link to Perception)

Figure 17.1
A Schema-Plus-Correction
Mental representations known as schemas create coherent, organized sets of beliefs and expectations (Medin & Ross, 1992). People who see an object like this tend to use pre-existing knowledge (their schema of a square) and then correct or modify it in some way (here, with a notch). However, they will probably remember seeing only a square because, over time, people tend to forget corrections and remember only schemas.

Linkages: How are impressions of others distorted in memory? (a link to Memory)

This particular grandmother probably does not fulfill your schema— your mental representation—of how grandmothers in general are supposed to look and act. Schemas help us to quickly categorize and respond appropriately to the people we meet, but they can also create narrowmindedness and, as we shall see later, prejudice.

First, as discussed in the chapter on thought and language, people tend to be very confident, often overconfident, about their judgments. This confidence leads them to feel certain that they are correct and that they understand another person, even when they have little objective information about that person (Fiske & Ruscher, 1989).

Second, people tend to interpret new information and events in ways that are consistent with an original impression. If you immediately like someone and he or she compliments you, you are likely to interpret the compliment as sincere praise. If, however, the compliment comes from someone you dislike, you will probably interpret it as insincere and begin looking for an ulterior motive. Similarly, self-assured behavior tends to be interpreted as "confidence" in those one likes, but as arrogance or conceit in those one dislikes. In short, the meaning given to new social information is shaped by what is already known or believed about a person (Ditto & Lopez, 1992).

Third, people remember their general impression or schema of another person better than any correction that is later added (Stangor & McMillan, 1992). Imagine that you form an impression of someone as honest. Then one day you see the person receive too much change from a cashier and keep it. You may temporarily think of the person as someone who is basically honest but who occasionally commits a dishonest act. However, over time you will tend to forget the dishonest deed while vividly remembering your positive impression of the person as honest (Graesser et al., 1980). In contrast, if you have a negative impression of someone, you will tend to forget positive things the person has done (Srull & Wyer, 1983).

Finally, people often act in ways that elicit from another person behavior that is consistent with their overall impression of that person (Harris et al., 1992). This important tendency is worth a closer look.

Self-Fulfilling Prophecies   Suppose you hear a man say something at a party that sounds boastful. This initial impression may prompt you to ask the man more about his accomplishments. As he lists them, you become convinced that he is boastful indeed (Jussim, 1989). Similarly, if the staff in a mental institution believes and acts as if patients diagnosed as schizophrenic are unable to bathe themselves, eat properly, and so on, those patients may become less and less likely to try to take care of themselves. In short, an initial impression, belief, or hypothesis can constitute a **self-fulfilling prophecy** (Merton, 1948), because it elicits behavior that ultimately confirms it (Wyer, Strack & Fuhrman, 1988).

The power of self-fulfilling prophecies was illustrated by a study in which men and women participated in a "get acquainted" conversation over an intercom system. Before the conversations took place, the men were shown photographs and told, falsely, that they were pictures of their partners. Some saw photographs of very attractive women, while others saw pictures that led them to believe their partner was somewhat unattractive. In fact, none of the photographs bore any relationship to the women's actual attractiveness. Independent judges listened to the ensuing conversations (but saw neither participant) and rated the women's behavior and personality. The women whom the men thought were attractive were judged as more articulate, lively, interesting, exciting, and fun to be with. Apparently, when the men thought their partners were physically attractive, they were more friendly and engaging themselves, and this behavior, in turn, elicited more positive reactions from the women. In contrast, men who thought their partners were unattractive behaved in a way that drew comparatively dull responses (Snyder, Tanke & Berscheid, 1977).

Self-fulfilling prophecies also help maintain judgments about groups. If you assume that members of a certain ethnic group are pushy or aggressive, for example, you might display defensiveness or even hostility toward them.

"You are fair, compassionate, and intelligent, but you are perceived as biased, callous, and dumb."

Faced with this behavior, members of the group might become frustrated and angry. Their reactions fulfill your prophecy and perpetuate the impressions that created it (Ross & Jackson, 1991).

Explaining Behavior: Attribution

So far, we have examined how people form impressions about the characteristics of other people. But perceptions of others include another key element: explanations of behavior. People tend to form *implicit theories* about why people (including themselves) behave as they do and about what behavior to expect in the future (Cheng & Novick, 1992). Psychologists use the term **attribution** to describe the process people go through to explain the causes of behavior (including their own).

As an example, suppose a friend failed to return borrowed books on time. You could attribute the behavior to many causes, from an unanticipated emergency to simple selfishness. Which of these alternatives you choose is important because it would help you to *understand* your friend's behavior, *predict* what will happen if your friend asks to borrow something in the future, and decide how to *control* the situation should it arise again. Similarly, whether a person attributes a spouse's nagging to stress-induced irritability or lack of love can influence whether that person will work on the marriage or work to dissolve it (Clark, 1994).

People tend to attribute behavior in a particular situation to either mainly internal causes—characteristics of the person—or mainly external (situational) causes. For example, if you attribute your friend's failure to return books to internal causes, you might decide your friend is inconsiderate, disorganized, lazy, or forgetful. If you look for mainly external causes, you might start to worry about the accident or sudden illness your friend must have suffered. Similarly, if you were to fail an exam, you might explain it by concluding that you're not very smart or that your schedule left you too little time to study. The attribution, in turn, might determine how much you study for the next exam or even whether you decide to stay in school. As discussed in the chapter

Linkages: As discussed in Chapter 11, on mental abilities, a teacher's first impression of a student's intelligence can create self-fulfilling prophecies. Teachers may inadvertently or consciously deprive children who impressed them as "dull" of the learning opportunities enjoyed by those who appeared "bright." This differential treatment may result in lowered academic performance, thus fulfilling the initial expectation.

on motivation and emotion, males and females tend to make different kinds of attributions in this type of situation. Partly as a result of feedback from teachers, males are more likely than females to attribute failure to inadequate study time or other external causes; females tend to attribute failure to a lack of ability (Burns & Seligman, 1989). These attributional differences may help males, and impair females, in maintaining self-confidence and persistence in the face of failure, especially in academic situations.

Criteria for Attributions   The decision to attribute behavior to internal or to external causes depends on three key characteristics of the behavior: consensus, consistency, and distinctiveness (Kelley, 1973). For example, suppose your father intensely dislikes your friend Ralph. Does the problem lie within your father? To decide how to explain the behavior, you would use three criteria:

1. *Consensus* is the degree to which other people's behavior is similar to that of the person in question—in this case, your father. If everyone you know thinks Ralph is a jerk, your father's behavior has a high degree of consensus, and you would attribute his reaction to something external to him, something in the situation (probably something about Ralph). However, if everyone else thinks Ralph is the sweetest guy on earth, your father's negative response would have low consensus, and you would probably attribute it to something about your father, such as his being a grouch.

2. *Consistency* is the degree to which the behavior occurs repeatedly in a particular situation. If your father sometimes warmly invites Ralph to dinner and sometimes throws him out of the house, the consistency of his behavior is low. This low consistency suggests that your father's behavior is attributable to the external situation—probably something that Ralph sometimes does. If the hostile behavior occurs every time Ralph is around, it has high consistency. But is your father's consistent behavior attributable to a stable internal cause (his consistent grouchiness) or to a stable external cause (a consistently jerky friend)? This question is difficult to answer without information about the third characteristic, distinctiveness.

3. *Distinctiveness* depends on the predictability of behavior in various situations. If your father is nasty to all your friends, no matter how they behave, his behavior toward Ralph has little distinctiveness. Low distinctiveness suggests that his reactions are attributable to his own internal characteristics. However, if he gets along with everyone except Ralph, your attribution about the cause of his behavior is likely to shift toward a cause that resides outside your father's personality, such as how Ralph acts.

In short, an internal attribution is most likely when there is low consensus, high consistency, and low distinctiveness. Thus, if you observe a coworker insulting customers (low consensus; most employees are polite to customers) every day (high consistency) no matter what the customers do (low distinctiveness), you would probably attribute this behavior to the coworker's personality rather than to the weather, the customers, or some other external cause. On the other hand, if you saw the same coworker on just one day (low consistency) being rude (low consensus) to one particular customer (high distinctiveness), you would be more likely to attribute the incident to the customer's behavior or some other external factor. External attributions are often made in response to other information patterns as well, as Figure 17.2 illustrates.

The Fundamental Attribution Error   Many experiments have supported the principles outlined in Figure 17.2 (Brown, 1986). These experiments suggest that, for the most part, people are logical in the way they go about

Figure 17.2
Causal Attribution
Here are the most common patterns of consensus, consistency, and distinctiveness that lead people to attribute other people's behavior to internal or external causes.

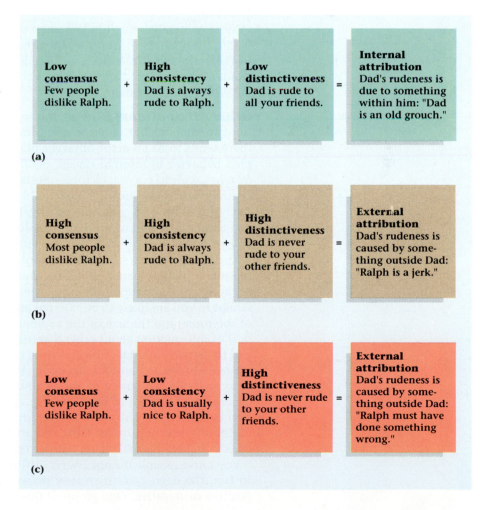

making causal attributions (Trope, Cohen & Alfieri, 1991). However, people also have cognitive biases. These show up not only in the systematic problem-solving and decision-making errors described in the chapter on thought and language, but also in inferences about the causes of people's actions (Kunda, 1990). Psychological shortcuts sometimes create **attributional biases**, which are tendencies to systematically distort one's view of behavior.

One prominent example is the **fundamental attribution error**, which is a general, widespread tendency to attribute the behavior of others to internal factors (Burger, 1991). Imagine that you hear another student give an incorrect answer in class. You will probably attribute the behavior to an internal cause and infer that the person is not very smart. In doing so, however, you will fail to take into account many other factors (for example, lack of adequate study time) that might be relevant.

The fundamental attribution error has some significant consequences. For one thing, it may generate great confidence about impressions of other people. It also leads to underestimates of the variability in another person's behavior created by external causes (Sande, Goethals & Radloff, 1988). Imagine a student who goes home every year at spring break to read and help around the house. The student's parents may believe this behavior occurs because the student is quiet, responsible, and serious. Because they make these internal attributions, they may not realize how differently their child acts at parties or football games or in other situations (Baxter & Goldberg, 1987). In general, people see other people in only a small set of situations, but it is only when you see them in many settings that the true variability in their behavior becomes apparent. This fact helps explain why dating is so fascinating, and can be so frustrating.

More generally, the fundamental attribution error may lead people to blame the victims of unfortunate circumstances (Ryan, 1977). Unemployed workers are sometimes seen as lazy, and homeless people as irresponsible; women who are raped are sometimes accused of having been seductive (Wyer, Bodenhausen & Gorman, 1985).

Other Attributional Biases   It is interesting that people usually avoid the fundamental attribution error when they explain their own behavior. In fact, there tends to be an **actor-observer bias;** that is, while attributing other people's behavior to internal causes, people are biased toward attributing their own behavior to *external* factors, especially when the behavior is inappropriate or involves failure (Brown & Rogers, 1991). When you drive slowly and tentatively, it is because you are looking for a particular address, not because you are a dimwitted ninny, like that slowpoke who crawled along in front of you yesterday.

The actor-observer bias results mainly from differences in the social information available when considering your own and others' behavior. When *you* are acting in a situation—giving a speech, perhaps—the stimuli that are most salient to you are likely to be external and situational, such as the temperature of the room and the size of the audience. Further, you have access to a great deal of information about other external factors, such as how much time you had to prepare your talk, the upsetting conversation you had this morning, or the speech course you took last term. Whatever the outcome of your efforts, you can easily attribute it to one or all of these external causes. But when you observe the behavior of someone else, the most salient stimulus in the situation is *that person*. Since you do not know what happened to the person last night, this morning, or last term, you are likely to attribute whatever he or she does to stable, internal characteristics (Fletcher, Reedes & Bull, 1990).

Of course, people do not always attribute their behavior to external forces. In fact, the degree to which they do so depends on whether the outcome is positive or negative. One group of researchers assessed attributions made by introductory psychology students about their performance on a midterm examination (Smith & Ellsworth, 1987). Students who did well perceived the test as being fair and attributed their performance to their ability. But students who performed poorly believed that the test was unfair, and they attributed their performance to a picky instructor. These students showed a **self-serving bias**, the tendency to take credit for success (attributing it to one's personal characteristics or efforts) but to blame external causes for failure.

The Self-Protective Functions of Social Cognition

The self-serving bias occurs, in part, because people are motivated not to think about negative information. If you just failed an exam, it is painful to admit that it was fair. Moreover, to attribute failure to an internal characteristic is likely to be threatening to self-esteem. In fact, people are often motivated to think about such things in ways that protect them from threatening conclusions (Brown & Rogers, 1991).

Unrealistic optimism is one example. When asked to estimate the likelihood of various events, people tend to believe that positive events (such as traveling or having a gifted child) are more likely to happen to themselves than to others, and that negative events (such as being in an accident or having cancer) are more likely to happen to others than to themselves (Weinstein, 1989). This unrealistic optimism persists even when there is evidence against it. For example, though unrealistic optimism initially declined among victims of the severe earthquake that shook California in 1989, it returned to its normal level after three months (Burger & Palmer, 1992).

Why does everyone seem to think that he or she is better off than average? One reason is a feeling of *unique invulnerability* to negative events. For example, people judge unprotected sexual intercourse with multiple partners *by other people* to create a high risk for unwanted pregnancy (Whitley & Hern, 1991) and sexually transmitted diseases (Taylor et al., 1992), yet they believe that they themselves are at low risk and often fail to take precautions (Catania et al., 1992; Chase, 1992). One mechanism that can create feelings of invulnerability is an *illusion of control* over what are, in fact, uncontrollable events (Langer, 1989). For example, people estimate their chances of winning a lottery as higher when they can choose their own number than when a number is given to them (Langer, 1978).

When people *are* responsible for some outcome, they may use other methods of maintaining self-esteem (Baumeister & Cairns, 1992). For example, people show a pronounced tendency to believe that their own traits and abilities are both unique (Agostinelli et al., 1992) and valuable (Dunning & Cohen, 1992). When people anticipate a loss of self-esteem, they often adopt a *self-handicapping strategy* in which they arrange for failure to be attributed to an external cause (Luginbuhl & Palmer, 1991). They may procrastinate, take drugs or alcohol, get too little sleep, or reduce their level of effort—actions that make the cause of their subsequent performance ambiguous (Hirt, Deppe & Gordon, 1991). These self-defeating actions can then be used to "explain" failure in a way that does not reflect internal characteristics, and thus protects self-esteem (Tice, 1991). This strategy is used primarily when people have succeeded in the past but doubt whether they can maintain similar success (Tice & Baumeister, 1990).

In the short run, each of the biases we have discussed allows escape from something painful; but each can also set the stage for a distorted view of reality and, in the long run, can create problems. ("In Review: Some Biases in Social Perception" summarizes the common cognitive biases discussed here.) Feelings of invulnerability and illusions of control—like the defense mechanisms described in Chapter 14, on personality—may temporarily decrease anxiety, but they may also prevent people from taking the rational steps necessary for

In Review: Some Biases in Social Perception

Bias	Description
Importance of first impression	Ambiguous information is interpreted in line with a first impression, and the initial schema is recalled better and more vividly than any later correction to it. Actions based on this impression may elicit behavior that confirms it.
Fundamental attribution error	The general tendency to attribute the behavior of others to internal factors.
Actor-observer bias	The tendency for actors to attribute their own behavior to external causes and for observers to attribute the behavior of others to internal factors.
Self-serving bias	The tendency to attribute one's successes to internal factors and one's failures to external factors.
Unrealistic optimism	The tendency to assume that positive events are more likely and negative events are less likely to occur to oneself than to others.
Illusion of control	The general tendency to assume that one has control over events even when this is not true.

long-term protection. Because people believe they are "hardy," they may not quit smoking; because they believe they live in a secure building, they may not lock their doors (Gollwitzer & Kinney, 1989). Self-handicapping strategies protect self-esteem in the short run, but in the long run they prevent achievements and eliminate the possibility of receiving useful information about one's strengths and weaknesses. As we discussed in Chapter 14, a certain amount of self-deception may help people deal with stress, but overreliance on distortions of reality can, in the long term, complicate the task of coping with negative events.

Interpersonal Attraction

One fascinating aspect of social perception is the question of whether the people you think about attract you or repel you. From childhood onward, people find that they like some people and dislike others. Why? Folklore says that "opposites attract," but it also says that "birds of a feather flock together." Like most instances of folk wisdom, each of these statements has some validity, but each needs to be qualified in important ways. To examine interpersonal attraction, we begin by looking at factors that lead to an initial attraction between people. We then examine how liking sometimes develops into more intimate relationships.

Keys to Attraction

What is it that makes you like some people and not others? For attraction, as for the attribution of causes, characteristics of both the environment and the person play a role.

In general, the more often people make contact with someone, the more they tend to like that person. This is one reason why next-door neighbors are much more likely to become friends than people who live farther from one another.

Linkages: How can mental processes occuring outside of awareness alter our liking for other people? (a link to Consciousness)

The Environment When thinking about why one person becomes attracted to another, it is easy to overlook the obvious. One of the most important determinants of attraction is simple physical proximity, or *propinquity*. In apartment complexes, for example, many more friendships are formed among people who live on the same floor than among people who live on different floors (Nahemow & Lawton, 1975). Similarly, the likelihood that coworkers will form friendships increases when they have a lot of contact with each other (Segal, 1974).

Propinquity is important because it breeds familiarity (Moreland & Zajonc, 1982). As long as you are neutral or like a person even slightly at the beginning, you will tend to like the person more as you have additional contact (Bornstein, 1989). You will become more comfortable, less apprehensive, and feel as if you have a better understanding of the person.

The situation in which people first meet also influences attraction. The effect of the situation reflects the principles of conditioning discussed in the chapter on learning. If you meet a stranger under comfortable physical conditions, you are much more likely to be attracted to that person than if the meeting occurs when you are hot or otherwise uncomfortable (Griffitt & Veitch, 1971). Similarly, receiving a reward in the presence of a stranger increases the chances that you will like the stranger (Lott & Lott, 1974). Association with rewards may generate attraction even if the other person is not responsible for providing the reward. In one study, an experimenter evaluated the creativity of a subject while another person watched. Compared with those who received a negative evaluation, subjects receiving a positive evaluation tended to like both the experimenter and the observer more, even though the observer did not provide any reinforcement (Griffitt & Guay, 1969). Thus, at least among people who are initially strangers, liking can occur because a person is associated with something pleasant.

Similarity of Attitudes People tend to like those whom they perceive as similar to themselves more than those whom they perceive as dissimilar (Grover & Brockner, 1989). In fact, there is a strong, direct relationship between the proportion of attitudes or opinions shared by two people and how

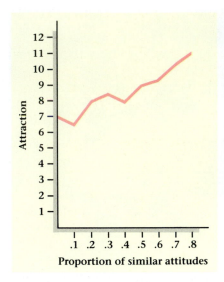

Source: Adapted from Byrne & Nelson, 1965.

Figure 17.3
Interpersonal Attraction and Attitudes
This graph shows the results of a study in which people first learned about the attitudes of another person. Their liking of the person was strongly influenced by the proportion of attitudes the person expressed that were similar to their own.

much one likes the other, as Figure 17.3 illustrates. This is true of children, college students, adult workers, and senior citizens (Clore, 1975).

Among the most influential similarities are attitudes toward people in the same social network. Imagine that John likes Tim. Then John meets Terry. John will be more attracted to Terry if Terry also likes Tim than if he does not. Now imagine a new scenario in which John dislikes Terry. Under these conditions, John will be more attracted to Tim if Tim also dislikes Terry. All else being equal, it appears that "the enemy of my enemy is my friend" (Aronson & Cope, 1968). In fact, when two people like each other, they seem to develop a norm by which they agree to like and dislike the same people (Jellison & Oliver, 1983).

More generally, people greatly prefer *balanced* over *imbalanced* relationships. As Figure 17.4 illustrates, if John likes Tim, the relationship is balanced as long as they agree on their evaluation of a third person, regardless of whether they like or dislike that person. However, the relationship will be imbalanced if John and Tim disagree on their evaluation of a third person.

One reason for the link between similar attitudes and attraction is that people who share the same opinions confirm or validate each other's view of the world (Swann, Stein-Seroussi & Giesler, 1992). But the relationship is not a simple one-way street, from similarity to attraction. When people interact for some time, *reciprocal causality* may occur: in other words, attraction may both affect and be affected by attitude similarity (Clark & Reis, 1988). Once you begin to develop a close bond with someone, your attitudes might become more similar to those of the other person, or you might change your perceptions of the other person's attitudes to make them more similar to your own. In one study, subjects were led to believe that another person either liked or disliked them (Curtis & Miller, 1986). When they thought the other person liked them, they saw that other person as warmer, friendlier, more open, a better listener, more trustworthy, and more similar to themselves. And when they interacted with a person perceived as liking them, the subjects themselves acted friendlier than if the person was said not to like them.

Thus, whereas theorists once believed that the proportion of similar attitudes has a direct causal influence on how much two people like each other (Byrne, 1971), research now shows that attraction also influences attitudes. Furthermore, the original conception ignored the possibility that repulsion between people with dissimilar attitudes might be more important than attraction between people with similar attitudes (Rosenbaum, 1986). If someone disagrees with you on even one or two important issues, you may develop an immediate and strong dislike for that person. Recent research indicates that disagreements on key issues do decrease attraction (Palmer & Kalin, 1991). But there is still a strong and direct relationship between the number of similar attitudes and the degree to which two people like each other (Smeaton, Byrne & Murnen, 1989).

Personality Styles   Yet another characteristic that influences attraction is *personality style*. Figure 17.5 summarizes the most often studied personality styles (Gurtman, 1992). In general, people are attracted to others who have a personality style that *complements* their own. Sometimes this involves being attracted to people who are very similar to oneself, and sometimes it involves being attracted to people who are opposite along key dimensions (Wiggins, Phillips & Trapnell, 1989). As Figure 17.5 shows, for characteristics related to control, opposite styles are complementary. Thus people who are dominant, competitive, and assured tend to be attracted to, and get along best with, those who are submissive, deferent, and unassured (and vice versa). But for characteristics related to affiliation, similar styles are complementary. Thus people who are sociable and warm tend to prefer others who are sociable and warm (Bluhm, Widiger & Miele, 1990). From their first contacts, people who share

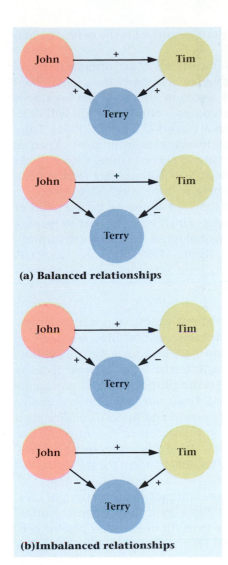

(a) Balanced relationships

(b) Imbalanced relationships

complementary personality styles talk more and become psychologically closer more quickly (Nowicki & Manheim, 1991).

Physical Attractiveness There is no doubt that physical attractiveness is another important factor in attraction, particularly in determining whether friendships are initiated (Feingold, 1992). Even among members of the same sex, physical attractiveness is a key to popularity. This relationship is seen in grade school (Cavior & Dokecki, 1969) and continues into adulthood (Hatfield, 1986).

In the initial stages of a relationship, it appears that "more is better" as far as physical attractiveness is concerned; people enjoy their interactions much more with those who are very attractive than with those who are not (Garcia et al., 1991). However, people who are dating steadily, engaged, or married tend to be very similar in their level of physical attractiveness (Kalick, 1988). According to the **matching hypothesis**, people are more likely to be romantically attracted to someone who is similar in physical attractiveness to themselves (Folkes, 1982). It is also possible, however, that people are always attracted to those with the most physical beauty, but since the most physically attractive people are in greatest demand, each person must balance the benefits of having a physically attractive partner against the possibility of rejection. Thus, it may be compromise, not preference, that leads people to pair off with those who are roughly equivalent to themselves in physical attractiveness (Carli, Ganley & Pierce-Otay, 1991).

Intimate Relationships and Love

Over time, people who are attracted to each other may become *interdependent,* which means that the thoughts, emotions, and behaviors of one person affect the thoughts, emotions, and behaviors of the other (Clark, 1994). Put another way, two people are interdependent to the degree that the events in one person's life affect both of them simultaneously. Interdependence occurs in large measure as the thoughts and values of one person become part of the self-

Figure 17.4
Balanced and Imbalanced Relationships
These are the most common balanced and imbalanced patterns of relationships among three people. The plus and minus signs refer to liking and disliking, respectively. Balanced relationships are comfortable and harmonious; imbalanced ones are often full of conflict and friction.

Figure 17.5
Personality Style and Interpersonal Attraction
The vertical line represents a control variable; research suggests that it is on this dimension that opposites attract. The horizontal line represents an affiliation variable; on this dimension, people tend to be attracted to those similar to themselves.

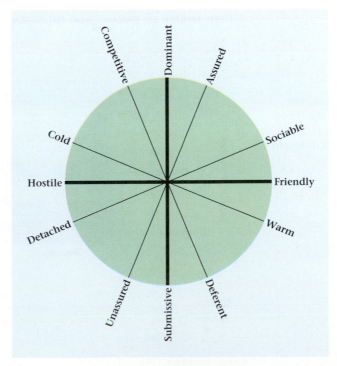

Though passion need never die, the basis for long-term intimate relationships tends to shift over the years from passionate love to companionate love, which is characterized by mutual self-disclosure, shared interests, and reciprocal caring.

concept of the other (Aron et al., 1991). Interdependence is the defining characteristic of intimate relationships.

When people are asked to name the key ingredients of an intimate relationship, the most common responses are *affection* and *emotional expressiveness* (Helgeson, Shaver & Dyer, 1987). Signs of affection are important because if one person perceives the other to be uninterested, communication will deteriorate and the person will begin to withdraw (Sayers & Baucom, 1991). Emotional expressiveness is important because it enhances feelings of closeness and commitment and because it is comforting to express strong emotions. As noted in Chapter 13, being able to disclose strong feelings may reduce stress and the risk of stress-related illness (Greenberg & Stone, 1992; Rice, 1992).

Other key components of intimate relationships appear to be the *result* of intimacy (Clark & Reis, 1988). One is *support,* which refers in part to helping with the daily hassles of life but also to psychological support, such as propping up a friend's confidence (Manne & Zautra, 1989). Intimacy also frequently brings *cohesiveness,* which refers to joint activities such as taking a vacation together, and *sexuality* (Clark, 1994).

Analyzing Love Affection, emotional expressiveness, support, cohesiveness, sexuality—these characteristics of intimate relationships are likely to bring something else to mind: love. Yet intimacy and love are not synonymous. Most theorists agree that there are different types of love (Fehr & Russell, 1991). One widely accepted view distinguishes between passionate love and companionate love (Hatfield, 1988). *Passionate love* is intense, arousing, and marked by both strong physical attraction and intense emotional attachment. Sexual feelings are very strong and thoughts of the other intrude on a person's awareness frequently. *Companionate love* is less arousing but psychologically more intimate. It is marked by mutual concern for the welfare of the other (Hendrick & Hendrick, 1986).

Robert Sternberg (1988b) has offered a more comprehensive analysis of love. According to his *triangular theory,* love has three basic components: *passion, intimacy,* and *commitment.* Variations in the strength of each component generate qualitatively different types of love, as Figure 17.6 illustrates. According to this analysis, passionate love (which Sternberg calls *romantic love*) involves a high degree of passion and intimacy, but it lacks a meaningful degree of

Figure 17.6
A Typology of Love
According to Sternberg, different types of love result when the three basic components in his triangular theory of love combine in different strengths.

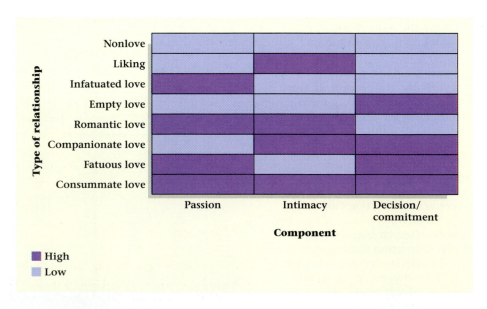

Source: Sternberg, 1986.

commitment to the other person. *Companionate love* is marked by a great deal of intimacy and commitment but little passion. As Figure 17.6 shows, other types of love are also possible, the most complete and satisfying of which, according to Sternberg, is *consummate love.* It is the most complete because it includes a high level of all three components. It is the most satisfying because the relationship is more likely to fulfill many of the needs of each partner.

Cultural factors have a strong influence on the value people place on love. In the United States, love is idealized in the popular media and 87 percent of all Americans believe that love is crucial to a satisfying marriage (Baron & Byrne, 1991). In India, however, it is only in the last fifteen years that movies have shown people who choose their spouses based on love rather than through prearranged matches made by their parents (Kaufman, 1980). In the former Soviet Union, only 40 percent of the people say that they married because of love; the majority marry because of loneliness, shared interests, or an unplanned pregnancy (Baron & Byrne, 1991).

Strong and Weak Marriages   Whatever their basis, satisfying marriages are associated with both physical and psychological health, while unsatisfying marriages are associated with increased health problems (Burman & Margolin, 1992). In Western cultures, communication appears to be a key in determining marital satisfaction. In fact, the mutual sharing of interests, beliefs, opinions, and the like is often more important than sex (Sternberg & Grajek, 1984). In general, women—but not men—tend to be more satisfied with their marriage when the partners talk a lot about the relationship itself (Acitelli, 1992).

The perception that a relationship is equitable also enhances marital satisfaction (Clark, 1994). After the birth of a first child, for example, many wives find that they have much more work than they expected. If their husbands do not share this work to the degree they expected, wives' marital satisfaction tends to decrease (Hackel & Ruble, 1992).

Another important determinant of long-term marital satisfaction is how the couple deals with the conflict and anger that occur in virtually all marriages. In both happy and unhappy marriages, men tend to respond to their spouse's anger with anger of their own. But in happy marriages, the cycle of angry reactions is ultimately broken, usually by the wife, allowing the couple to deal with the problem at hand during moments of calm (Rusbult et al., 1991). In unhappy marriages, both the husband and wife trade increasingly angry and hurtful remarks until communication breaks down (Gottman & Levenson, 1992). When these episodes become frequent, couples begin to attribute any negative behavior of the spouse to an internal cause (such as lack of concern) and any positive behavior to an external cause, such as the proximity of a holiday (Bradbury & Fincham, 1992; Fincham & Bradbury, 1993). Thus, even if one spouse tries to improve the marriage, his or her efforts are dismissed by the other as insincere or unimportant.

How important is monogamy to marital satisfaction? The answer depends to some extent on cultural factors. Jealousy can be a major threat to marriage in the United States (White & Mullen, 1990), where disapproval of extramarital sex ranges from 80 to 90 percent. It may be of less concern elsewhere; for example, only 50 percent of those living in Belgium and 10 percent of those living in Denmark view extramarital sex negatively (Lawson, 1988).

Attitudes

People's views on extramarital sex reflect their attitudes. An **attitude** is a predisposition to respond cognitively, emotionally, or behaviorally to a particular object in a particular way (Rajecki, 1990). The object can be anything—from inanimate things such as nuclear power plants, to specific individuals or groups, to actions such as having an abortion. Attitudes play an important role in guiding how people react to other people, what causes they support, what politicians they vote for, which brands they buy, and countless other daily decisions.

Components of Attitudes

Most theorists agree that an attitude has three components, as illustrated in Figure 17.7 (Breckler & Wiggins, 1989). The *cognitive* component is a set of beliefs, such as that whales are endangered and about to become extinct. The emotional, or *affective,* component consists of an evaluation: a like or dislike of the object of the attitude. Finally, the *behavioral* component involves a way of acting toward the attitude object. For example, if your attitude toward whales includes the belief that they are on the verge of extinction and the feeling that this state of affairs is very sad, you might donate money to the Save the Whales fund (McGuire, 1989).

If the cognitive, emotional, and behavioral components of attitudes were always in harmony, such that evaluations and actions always reflected what people believed, psychologists could measure all aspects of an attitude by measuring any one component. In fact, however, discrepancies among the components often arise, for several reasons (Eagly & Chaiken, 1993). First, there are always competing motives and competing attitudes (Rajecki, 1990). You might think about donating to the Save the Whales fund but then realize that your father's birthday is coming up. As a result, you might end up spending the money on a gift, even though the cognitive and affective components of your attitude toward whales remain positive. Second, an attitude can be expressed in many ways. One person might donate money, another might display a bumper sticker, another might fire off angry letters to members of Congress, and still another might picket whaling companies (Ronis, Yates & Kirscht, 1989). It is often difficult to predict what action a person will take. Third, social pressure may cause a person to suppress the behavioral aspects of an attitude while retaining the other components (Ajzen, 1989). Thus, someone who believes that the rights of homosexuals should be protected might not campaign for this cause because doing so would upset family members or coworkers who hold strong antihomosexual attitudes.

What determines whether people's behavior will be consistent with the cognitive and affective components of their attitudes? Five factors are important.

Figure 17.7
Three Components of an Attitude
The three components of an attitude can be measured separately and through different assessment channels. For example, the cognitive component of an attitude is typically assessed through surveys, interviews, and other self-report methods. The affective component might be monitored by physiological recordings taken while a person watches a film about a topic relevant to the attitude. Measurement of the behavioral component could entail observing what a person does in relation to the attitude object.

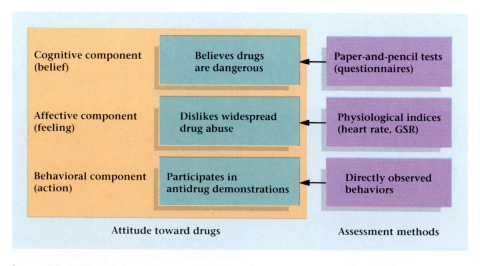

Source: Adapted from Kahn, 1984.

First, consistency is most likely when the behavior in question matches a *subjective norm,* or what people believe other important people in their life think they should do. As already mentioned, attitude-consistent behavior is most likely to be suppressed when people believe that others would disapprove (Eagly & Chaiken, 1993). Second, people must have *perceived control*—the belief that they can actually perform the attitude-consistent behavior (Beck & Ajzen, 1991). You may hold a positive attitude about becoming a famous opera star, but if you don't believe it is possible, you are not likely to even try. (Note the linkage with Bandura's concept of self-efficacy, discussed in the chapter on personality.) Third, consistency is most likely when people are consciously *aware* of the cognitive and affective components of their attitudes (Fazio, Herr & Powell, 1992). Fourth, *direct experience* with the attitude object increases the likelihood of attitude-consistent behavior (Eagly, 1992). For example, if your positive attitude toward champagne is based on having actually tasted it, you are more likely to buy it than if your attitude stems solely from its image. Finally, people who *monitor* their own behavior closely are more likely to behave in accordance with the cognitive and affective components of their attitudes (Koestner, Bernieri & Zuckerman, 1992).

Does it matter to people if their behavior does not conform to their feelings or beliefs, or if several attitudes are in conflict? What happens when the components of an attitude are inconsistent? Two theories—cognitive dissonance theory and self-perception theory—have suggested answers to these questions.

Cognitive Dissonance Theory   The relationship between behavior and attitudes, and what occurs when they are inconsistent, was addressed by Leon Festinger's (1957) classic **cognitive dissonance theory.** This theory holds that people prefer their many cognitions, including those about their own behavior, to be consistent with one another. When their cognitions are inconsistent, or *dissonant,* people feel uneasy and are motivated to make them more consistent. If you hold the cognitions "I smoke" and "Smoking is bad," you should be motivated to reduce the resulting dissonance. One way to reduce dissonance is to alter the inconsistent cognition or attitude.

Festinger and Merrill Carlsmith (1959) conducted one of the earliest studies of dissonance. First, they asked people to turn pegs on a board, a very dull task. Later, some of these people were asked to persuade a waiting subject that the task was "exciting and fun." Some were told that they would be paid $1 to tell this lie; the rest were promised $20. After they had talked to the waiting subject, their attitudes toward the dull task were measured.

Figure 17.8 shows the results. It might seem reasonable that those who were paid $20 would like the dull task better than those paid just $1, but just the reverse occurred. Why? Festinger and Carlsmith (1959) argued that telling another person that a boring task is enjoyable will produce dissonance (between the thoughts "I think the task is boring" and "I am saying it is fun"). To reduce this dissonance, the people who were paid just $1 adopted a more favorable attitude toward the task, making their cognitions consistent: "I think the task is fun" and "I am saying it is fun." But if a person has adequate justification for the behavior, any dissonance will automatically be reduced simply by thinking about the justification. When subjects were paid $20, they had adequate justification for lying and so did not need to change their attitudes toward the task.

Literally hundreds of other experiments have also found that people often reduce dissonance by changing their attitudes (Aronson, 1988). In one of these demonstrations, people were asked to eat fried grasshoppers (Zimbardo et al., 1965). In some cases, the experimenter made this request in a very friendly and apologetic way, explaining that the grasshoppers had been shipped prematurely and had to be consumed before they spoiled. In other cases, the ex-

Figure 17.8
Cognitive Dissonance and Attitude Change

People were paid by an experimenter to say that a boring task was enjoyable. According to cognitive dissonance theory, those paid $20 had clear justification for lying and should have experienced little dissonance between what they said and what they felt about the task; in fact, their attitude toward the task did not change very much. However, subjects who received just $1 had little justification to lie and could reduce their dissonance mainly by displaying a more positive attitude toward the task, which they did.

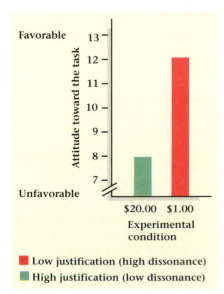

Source: Festinger & Carlsmith, 1959.

perimenter was rude and unfriendly, complaining that the subjects were late and were wasting his time. According to cognitive dissonance theory, those who were asked to eat grasshoppers by the friendly experimenter could easily justify their actions: "I don't like the idea of eating grasshoppers," but "I'm eating them to please this nice person." Like the subjects who were paid $20 to lie, these subjects did not change their attitude toward grasshoppers, reporting them to be very distasteful. However, subjects approached by a rude experimenter could reduce the dissonance brought on by their agreement to eat something distasteful only by changing their attitude toward it. As expected by dissonance theory, these subjects said the grasshoppers tasted good.

Self-Perception Theory   Cognitive dissonance theory assumes that an inconsistency among a person's thoughts results in a state of tension, but Daryl Bem (1967) suggested an alternative explanation of attitude change that does not presuppose internal tension. According to Bem's **self-perception theory**, situations often arise in which people are not quite sure about their attitudes. When this happens, Bem says, people look back to their behavior, consider it in light of the circumstances, and then *infer* what their attitude about it must have been. That is, you say, "If I did that under those circumstances, my attitude about it must be this." This process requires no tension to drive it.

Consider again the grasshopper experiment. According to Bem, the subjects' attitudes were determined not by dissonance reduction but by their inferences about their actions. Subjects in the nice-experimenter condition may have thought, "Well, if I ate grasshoppers, I must have done it because the experimenter was so nice about it, but they really tasted terrible." This kind of thinking would leave these subjects' distaste for grasshoppers intact. Subjects in the other condition may have thought, "I ate the grasshoppers, but that experimenter was such a jerk that I never would have done it if they hadn't tasted good."

Obviously self-perception theory and cognitive dissonance theory often make the same predictions. Indeed, both may be correct to some extent. Self-perception theory seems to apply best when people hold no prior attitude or when that attitude is weak and ill-defined, as in the case of never-tasted foods (Olson, 1992). But when an attitude is strong and clearly defined, and especially when holding it is important for a person's self-concept, dissonance creates a very uncomfortable psychological state (Thibodeau & Aronson, 1992). Dissonance theory suggests that, especially in individualistic cultures, this state is so uncomfortable that people are motivated to change their attitude so that all of the cognitions are brought back into a consonant relationship (Losch & Cacioppo, 1990). In collectivist cultures, which emphasize group rather than individual values, behaving at variance with one's personal beliefs may create less discomfort—and thus less motivation for attitude change—because those beliefs tend to be seen as less important for self-esteem than acting in socially acceptable ways (Berry et al., 1992; Bharati, 1985).

Forming Attitudes

People are not born with attitudes, but from early childhood onward, they continue to form attitudes about new objects. The advertising industry recognizes, and capitalizes on, the process of attitude formation. Advertisers spend nearly $100 billion each year to place their messages virtually everywhere, from the inside of the New York Metropolitan Opera program to the rear end of city buses. They do it because sales figures suggest that it works. How are attitudes formed?

Virtually all of the principles discussed in the chapter on learning play a role in the formation of new attitudes. In childhood, modeling and other forms of social learning are especially important. Children learn from parents not only what objects are but also what they should believe and feel about them and how they should act toward them. For example, children may learn from their parents' words not only that snakes are reptiles but also that snakes should be feared and avoided. Thus, as the process of concept learning described in Chapter 10 proceeds, there appears to be a parallel process of learning attitudes about those same concepts (Tourangeau & Rasinski, 1988). Some theorists view attitudes as complex knowledge structures that are stored in long-term memory and used just like any other information (Judd et al., 1991; Tourangeau, Rasinski & D'Andrade, 1991).

Classical conditioning can also produce positive or negative attitudes (Krosnick et al., 1992). Advertisers have found, for example, that people are more likely to form a positive attitude toward a product when it is repeatedly paired with enjoyable music (Gorn, 1982), soothing colors (Middlestadt, 1990), or other stimuli that elicit good feelings (Aaker & Stayman, 1989). Attitudes are also influenced by operant conditioning, as when parents reward a child for stating particular views or acting in particular ways.

Of course, attitudes are also formed on the basis of direct experience with objects. One interesting result of experience is the *mere exposure effect.* All else being equal, attitudes toward an object—a drink, a clothing style, a politician, and so on—tend to become more positive as people are exposed to it more often (Bornstein, Kale & Cornell, 1990). It is common, for example, for people to like a song only after they have heard it several times.

Changing Attitudes: The Role of Persuasive Communications

How many times has someone who disagrees with you tried to change your attitude? It happens all the time in relation to religion, politics, sports, fashion, and nearly everything else. Whether a communication succeeds in changing an attitude depends on a number of factors, including characteristics of (1) the communicator, (2) the message, and (3) the audience (Petty & Cacioppo, 1981).

The Communicator   Various characteristics of the communicator influence whether a message will change the audience's attitude:

1. Sources perceived as *credible,* or knowledgeable about the topic, are more effective at changing attitudes than are low-credibility sources (Cooper & Croyle, 1984).

In a political campaign, each candidate uses persuasive communications designed to strengthen the positive attitudes of supporters and to change the attitudes of those who are undecided, or even negative, about his or her candidacy. Ideally, positive attitudes will be translated into votes.

2. Listeners are more likely to be persuaded if a communicator is perceived to be *trustworthy*. For this reason, people's attitudes are more likely to be influenced by a message that is accidentally overheard than by a presentation obviously intended to persuade (Walster & Festinger, 1962). To exploit this fact, advertisers often use testimonials from apparently unpaid consumers, who are supposedly unaware of being photographed.

3. As the *similarity* between the communicator and the audience increases, the communicator tends to be more effective in changing attitudes (Cialdini, Petty & Cacioppo, 1981). There appear to be two reasons for this effect. First, people perceive communicators who are similar to themselves as more trustworthy than those who are less similar. Second, all else being equal, people tend to like others who are similar to themselves more than those who are perceived as dissimilar.

The Message   Imagine that your school is considering a 50 percent increase in tuition. Most of the administrators favor the proposal, but most of the students are against it. Suppose you wish to promote opposition to the proposal. What should you say to persuade people to your point of view?

Whether it is best to present one or two sides of an issue depends on the prior attitudes of the audience (Cialdini, Petty & Cacioppo, 1981). Thus, if you are speaking to students, an already sympathetic audience, the most effective communication would contain only arguments against the tuition increase. This one-sided communication would bolster the audience's prior beliefs and reinforce its members' tendency to oppose the proposal. Contrary arguments can only sow the seeds of doubt. However, in talking to an audience that opposes your point of view, it is usually better to present both sides of the issue. In this way, you show respect for the audience's attitudes, recognize the validity of those attitudes, but also provide arguments for changing them. In short, a one-sided message is more effective when the audience is predisposed toward the speaker's point of view; a two-sided message is more effective when the attitude of the audience is contrary to that of the speaker (McGuire, 1985).

The amount of attitude change is greatest when a persuasive message states explicit conclusions; for example, "It is therefore obvious that increasing tuition 50 percent will prevent many people from attending college." This principle applies with people of all intelligence levels (McGuire, 1969). But how mild or extreme should the conclusions be? An answer is suggested by a study in which students first rated the quality of several poems and then heard a message purportedly stating the "real" quality of the poems. Some students heard a message that supposedly came from a high-credibility source (a famous poet); others, from a low-credibility source (an uninformed undergraduate from an obscure school). When the students rated the poems again, their attitudes tended to change in the direction suggested by the message they had heard, and the amount of change was always greater for the high-credibility source (see Figure 17.9). However, the amount of change depended on both the credibility of the speaker and the amount of discrepancy between the speaker's message and the students' original ratings. For the high-credibility speaker, the greater the discrepancy between the message and the students' ratings, the larger the attitude change. For the low-credibility speaker, the most attitude change occurred when the discrepancy between the message and the students' original ratings was moderate (Aronson, Turner & Carlsmith, 1963).

Sometimes communicators try to change attitudes by instilling fear in the audience. A commercial aimed at persuading people not to drive after drinking alcohol, for example, might show a violent car crash. **Fear appeals** can change attitudes, but they have important limitations. Even when fear produces lasting effects on the *cognitive* component of an attitude, the effects on behavior

Figure 17.9
Communicator Credibility and Persuasion
In general, highly credible sources produce more attitude change as the discrepancy between the speaker's arguments and the audience's attitudes increases. Low-credibility sources are most effective when arguing for moderate amounts of attitude change.

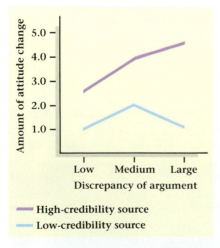

Source: Aronson, Turner & Carlsmith, 1963.

often fade after several weeks or months (Rotfeld, 1989). More often than not, when fear has provoked efforts to quit smoking, for example, people eventually start smoking again (Glasgow & Bernstein, 1981). Further, fear appeals are most effective when they are not *too* frightening and when they are accompanied by information about how to avoid the fearful consequences. If nothing but extremely frightening information is given, many people block out the message (Beck & Frankel, 1981).

Linkages: Are smart people less likely than others to be persuaded to change their minds? (a link to Mental Abilities)

The Audience   Whoever is communicating and whatever the message, some people in the audience change their attitudes and others do not (Petty, Priester & Wegener, 1994). What factors are important in determining who changes and who does not?

One possibility is intelligence. Perhaps intelligent people, because they can better comprehend arguments, change their attitudes more easily than less intelligent people. Or perhaps intelligent people are better able to detect logical flaws in the arguments presented, are more likely to think of counterarguments, and are therefore *less* likely to be persuaded to change their attitudes. In fact, research shows that both of these processes occur. Very intelligent people comprehend persuasive arguments better than less intelligent people, but they are also better able to refute them. As a result, there is no overall relationship between intelligence and susceptibility to persuasion (Rhodes & Wood, 1992).

Susceptibility to persuasion does seem related to self-esteem, however. William McGuire (1969) suggested that individuals with low self-esteem are not confident about the correctness of their attitudes and thus often change them in response to persuasive messages. However, people with low self-esteem also tend to be inattentive and to have little interest in the events that surround them. As a result, although individuals with low self-esteem are prone to accept the arguments of others, they may not focus enough attention on those arguments to receive and think about them (see Figure 17.10, a and b). Individuals high in self-esteem do pay attention to what others think, but they are so self-confident that they are seldom swayed. Consequently, both groups show little attitude change (see Figure 17.10c). In contrast, those with moderate levels of self-esteem pay a reasonable amount of attention to what others say; they are also sufficiently unsure of their own attitudes to be persuaded. Thus, these individuals tend to change their attitudes the most (Rhodes & Wood, 1992).

Possibly the most important audience characteristic in attitude change is *psychological involvement:* how important the topic or issue is to the listener. High involvement motivates the person to think carefully about the message. If strong arguments are provided, high involvement leads to greater attitude change; but if the arguments are weak, high involvement leads to less attitude change regardless of how attractive or credible the speaker is (Petty, Priester & Wegener, 1994).

Two Routes to Attitude Change   This discussion suggests two different routes to attitude change. Sometimes people change their attitude through what is called a *peripheral route,* which involves responding to relatively superficial *persuasion cues* such as the speaker's attractiveness or the length and detail of the argument. Impressive as they are, such persuasion cues say nothing about the logic or validity of the message. In contrast, people may also change an attitude through a *central route,* following steps like those outlined in the Thinking Critically sections of this book. They think carefully about the message and the validity of its claims, about whether it leaves out pertinent information, about alternative interpretations of evidence, and so on.

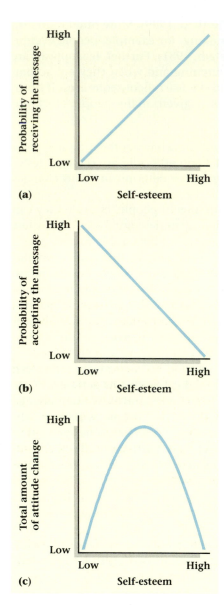

(a)

(b)

(c)

Source: Adapted from McGuire, 1968.

Figure 17.10
Self-Esteem and Attitude Change
People with high self-esteem pay attention to and understand a persuasive message but are usually so confident in their own beliefs that they reject it. Those with low self-esteem would be likely to accept the arguments presented; but because they seldom notice the message, they do not usually change their attitudes. People with moderate levels of self-esteem tend to show the greatest susceptibility to a persuasive message, because they not only notice and understand it but also tend to be uncertain of the correctness of their own beliefs.

In Review: Forming and Changing Attitudes

Type of Influence	Description
Modeling and conditioning	Attitudes are sometimes formed and changed through classical and operant conditioning processes or by observing the way others behave and speak about the attitude object.
Cognitions and behavior	When cognitions are inconsistent, they can lead to a change in attitude. For example, people who believe smoking is unhealthy and yet continue to smoke may come to think less negatively about smoking.
Communicator	Attitudes are most likely to be changed when people hear arguments presented by a communicator who is perceived as credible, trustworthy, and similar to themselves.
Message	When hearing a message that is inconsistent with their attitude, people are most likely to change their attitude when both sides of the issue are presented. Messages that arouse fear can also be effective if they include specific information about how to avoid the fearful consequences.
Audience	Attitude change is most likely among those with moderate levels of self-esteem. High personal involvement can also foster attitude change, but only if the argument for change is strong.

Both of these routes to persuasion are recognized in the **elaboration likelihood model** of attitude change (see Figure 17.11). This model suggests that when people have both the motivation and the ability to carefully process an argument, they tend to take a central route, elaborating on the argument by thinking of information that may support or disconfirm it (Cacioppo, Petty & Crites, 1993). However, when either the ability or motivation to process an argument is low, people tend to take a peripheral route; they do not elaborate on the message very much and overrely on various (often irrelevant) persuasion cues. ("In Review: Forming and Changing Attitudes" summarizes some of the major processes through which attitudes are formed and changed.)

Prejudice and Stereotypes

All of the principles underlying impression formation, attribution, attraction, and attitudes come together in prejudice and stereotypes (Hamilton & Sherman, 1994). **Stereotypes** are impressions or schemas of entire groups of people. They are more powerful and more dangerous than individual impressions because they involve the false assumption that all members of a group share the same characteristics. Although the characteristics that make up the

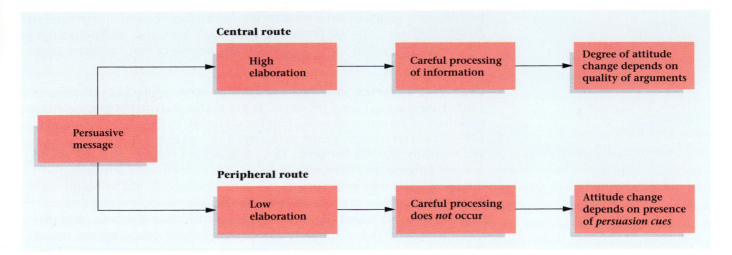

Figure 17.11
The Elaboration Likelihood Model of Attitude Change
This model suggests that people change their attitudes either by carefully processing and evaluating evidence that may support or undermine an argument (the central route), or by relying on persuasion cues such as the physical attractiveness of the person making the argument (the peripheral route). Such cues may be irrelevant to the validity of the argument but, for people who are unmotivated or unable to take a central route, can be very influential (Cacioppo, Petty & Crites, 1993).

stereotype may be positive, they are usually negative. The most prevalent and powerful stereotypes focus on observable personal attributes, particularly ethnicity, gender, and age (Brewer, 1988).

Stereotyping often leads to **prejudice**, which is a positive or negative attitude toward an individual based simply on his or her membership in some group (Fiske & Von Hend, 1992). *Prejudice* means literally "to prejudge." Like other attitudes, prejudice has cognitive, affective, and behavioral components. Indeed, stereotyped thinking is the cognitive component of prejudicial attitudes. The hatred, admiration, anger, and other feelings people have about stereotyped groups constitute the affective component. The behavioral component of prejudice often results in **discrimination**, which is differential treatment of individuals who belong to different groups.

Theories of Prejudice

Not all prejudice and stereotyping occur for the same reason (Duckitt, 1992). We describe three theories, each of which has empirical support and accounts for some, but not all, instances of stereotyping and prejudice.

Motivational Theories   One approach to prejudice looks at personality structure for an explanation. T. W. Adorno and his colleagues found that prejudice is most likely among people whose parents used punishment or harsh words to instill the belief that they must defer to and obey all those with a higher status than themselves (Adorno et al., 1950). This kind of upbringing was described in Chapter 3 as authoritarian parenting and, according to Adorno, encourages the development of a cluster of traits called the **authoritarian personality.** People with an authoritarian personality view the world as a strict social hierarchy. They feel they have the right to demand deference and cooperation from all those who have lower status. In order to know whom to obey and from whom to demand obedience, authoritarian people are motivated to identify other people's status in relation to themselves. This sets the stage for the development of negative stereotypes of those perceived as occupying a lower status, and for prejudice and discrimination against them.

One piece of evidence supporting the concept of authoritarian personality is that people who are prejudiced against one group also tend to be prejudiced against other groups (Ehrlich, 1973). This pattern suggests that stereotypes and prejudice may serve some psychological need to derogate others. According to psychodynamic theorists, authoritarian personalities may be displacing the hostility they originally felt toward their punitive parents onto the stereotyped group. They may also be projecting their own fears and weaknesses onto the stereotyped group, thereby convincing themselves that the other group is inferior.

Cognitive Theories   A second approach to stereotyping and prejudice examines them as cognitive processes. It holds that stereotypes are inevitable responses to an extraordinarily complex social world (Hamilton & Sherman, 1994). There are so many people, so many situations in which one meets them, and so many possible behaviors that they might perform, that one cannot possibly attend to and remember them all. The most effective way to deal with this complexity is to group people into social categories. Just as people form categories for chairs, boats, shoes, and so on, rather than remembering every detail about every object they have ever encountered, people also form categories for people (Devine & Baker, 1991). They create categories and mental lists of associated characteristics for teachers, athletes, strangers, politicians, criminals, and so on. The characteristics associated with these categories represent stereotypes. As mentioned in Chapter 9, parallel distributed processing (PDP) models of memory suggest that stereotypes are examples of incorrect *spontaneous generalizations* arising from the network of associations about the world that people hold in their long-term memories.

How do people categorize other people? As we noted earlier, people often focus on age, gender, ethnicity, and other detectable distinctions (Brewer, 1988). They use these characteristics as the basis for creating ingroups and outgroups (Wilder & Shapiro, 1991). An **ingroup** is any category of which people see themselves as a member. If you are African-American, African-Americans probably form your ingroup; if you are an African-American student, African-American students may form an even more specific ingroup. An **outgroup** is any group of which people do not see themselves as a member. People tend to see ingroup members as more physically attractive than outgroup members, and they assume that ingroup members have more desirable personality characteristics and engage in more socially accepted forms of be-

According to learning theory, negative attitudes about members of ethnic groups, for example, are based on negative personal experiences or the negative experiences and attitudes people hear about from others. New and more positive experiences can alter these negative attitudes.

havior (Beike & Sherman, 1994). As might be expected, people tend to give preferential treatment to ingroup members (Hamilton & Sherman, 1994).

Learning Theories   People often hold negative attitudes toward groups with whom they have had little or no contact. This fact supports another approach to prejudice, which emphasizes that prejudices, like other attitudes, are learned. Children can learn prejudices even without any experience with particular groups just by watching and listening to the words and deeds of parents, peers, and others (Karlins, Coffman & Walter, 1969). Movies and television programs may portray ethnic or other groups in ways that teach stereotypes and prejudice. Children may also be directly reinforced for stereotypes and prejudices.

Are the processes underlying stereotyping and prejudice spontaneous reactions, as PDP models of learning and memory suggest? Patricia Devine (1989a) has argued that many stereotypes are learned at a very early age and are known equally well by less prejudiced and more prejudiced individuals. In fact, if European-Americans are asked to describe the common stereotype of an African-American, the responses of less and more prejudiced people are almost identical (Devine, 1989b). In many situations, people automatically become aware of the stereotype when in the presence of a person from the stereotyped group. However, less prejudiced individuals make a strong distinction between their knowledge of the stereotype and their personal beliefs, and they think carefully about the difference between the two (Devine, 1989b). This leads them to treat people more as individuals and less as members of a stereotyped group. Because stereotypes are common and learned at an early age, however, it seems that most people cannot help but think about them—even if they do not believe them and show few signs of discrimination in their overt behavior (Devine et al., 1991).

Thinking Critically

Does Contact with a Group Decrease Prejudice Against It?

One implication of learning theories of prejudice and stereotyping is that these phenomena are primarily due to ignorance or misinformation about members of unfamiliar groups (Miller & Davidson-Podgorny, 1987). With increasing contact, each group should receive information that is inconsistent with the prior stereotype. In addition, the contact should show members of different groups that they are more similar than they expected and that members of the other group are not all the same. According to this line of reasoning, stereotypes and prejudice should weaken as a result.

What am I being asked to believe or accept?
The **contact hypothesis** states that stereotypes and prejudices about a group will be reduced as contact with the group increases.

What evidence is available to support the assertion?
A natural test of the contact hypothesis occurred during the 1960s and 1970s, when desegregation laws prompted many schools across the United States to admit African-American students for the first time. Early results did not provide much support for the contact hypothesis. A few studies found a decrease in prejudice, but most found either no change or an increase in prejudice following desegregation (Rogers & Miller, 1981).

Negative results may mean that a hypothesis is overly simplistic or too broad, not utterly incorrect. Theorists recognized this possibility and began to refine the contact hypothesis. They asked whether intergroup contact

Certain kinds of contact between members of different ethnic groups can reduce their prejudice toward one another. In one study of summer campers, children who had the most contact with members of another ethnic group showed much less prejudice at the end of the camp than those with less contact (Eaton & Clore, 1975).

might lead to more positive attitudes for certain people or in certain situations.

Specifically, it was suggested that intergroup contact would have more positive effects for younger children (whose learned prejudices have not had as much time to solidify) than for older children (who have had more "practice" at prejudice). In fact, researchers found evidence for this interaction between contact and age. When first brought together in school, older children were very sensitive to intergroup differences in academic achievement, social interaction styles, athletic abilities, and the like. These perceived differences created considerable antagonism between African-Americans and European-Americans (Miller, Rogers & Hennigan, 1983). Such problems were much less severe for children whose schooling began in an integrated environment.

In addition to age, the school environment shaped the effect of contact (Miller & Brewer, 1984). Intergroup contact reduced prejudice and stereotyping only under specific conditions (Cook, 1985). First, members of the two groups had to have roughly equal social and economic status. Second, the school situation had to foster cooperation and interdependence. When white and black students worked together on group projects and had to rely on one another's cooperation, attitudes toward one another improved. Third, the contact between group members had to occur on a one-on-one basis; it was only when one *individual* got to know another *individual* that the errors contained in stereotypes became apparent. Finally, it was important that members of each group were seen as typical and not unusual in any significant way. When these four conditions were met, both white and black children's attitudes toward one another became more positive. Unfortunately, in the vast majority of schools, these conditions were not met (Miller & Brewer, 1984).

Are there alternative ways of interpreting the evidence?

There are several problems with drawing conclusions about the contact hypothesis on the basis of observed consequences of naturally occurring situations such as desegregation. For one thing, the situations in which the observations took place were not, by their very nature, under experimental control. So, for example, the fact that contact with other ethnic groups at a younger age is associated with less prejudice could be due to the early contact itself or to numerous uncontrolled factors, such as growing up in a more tolerant era, having a particularly enlightened teacher, or the like. In short, perhaps the young children would have been less prejudiced than the older ones even without the contact.

What additional evidence would help to evaluate the alternatives?

Data from naturalistic observations must be supplemented by evidence from experimental studies aimed at determining more precisely if, when, and how intergroup contact leads to reductions in prejudice and stereotyping. So far, several experimentally created classroom situations have been tested for their effects on children's prejudice (Aronson, 1990). The most effective create cooperative learning, such as giving each child a piece of a puzzle that the multi-ethnic group must solve together (Slavin, 1985). Even with adults, friendly, cooperative contact in which two people work jointly toward a common goal tends to result in mutual respect and liking (Cook, 1984). Competition has the opposite effect, perhaps because a competitor's actions, even when benign, are often attributed to self-serving motives, and negative attitudes toward the competitor often result, especially if he or she is very competent (Wilder & Shapiro, 1989). In contrast, cooperative settings elicit empathic reactions. Successes lead to joint pride, and even mistakes or failures by the partner are often tolerated. In short, the other person is seen as someone who is similar to oneself, someone who tries hard and often succeeds, but also someone who sometimes makes mistakes (Lanzetta & Englis, 1989).

Additional studies like these, in the classroom and in the laboratory, will be valuable not only for evaluating the contact hypothesis but also as a guide to sculpting environments that foster greater interpersonal tolerance and understanding.

What conclusions are most reasonable?

Based on the evidence available so far, it appears that stereotyping and prejudice are often based on ignorance or misunderstanding born of unfamiliarity with other groups. It also appears that stereotyping and prejudice can be reduced through contact with members of the other group. However, contact alone is clearly not sufficient. Members of each group must perceive themselves to be of equal status, to be interdependent, and to share many of the same concerns. They must perceive others as individuals rather than merely as members of one group or another. Significant reductions in prejudice cannot be expected as long as there are obvious status differences in the larger society (Foster & Finchilescu, 1986). Because ethnic differences in status and opportunity continue to exist, contact can provide only part of the solution to the problems of stereotyping, prejudice, and discrimination. ■

Future Directions

Social cognition is a dynamic and exciting aspect of social psychology. Each year new discoveries are reported, novel theories are proposed, and researchers examine the intricacies of social interaction at a finer level of detail (Wyer & Srull, 1994). There is no doubt that this trend will continue.

One issue that cuts across all of the areas discussed in this chapter is the degree to which social cognition occurs automatically during social interactions (Smith, 1994). More and more research is showing that social thought is often spontaneous, automatic, and sometimes even beyond conscious control (Bargh, 1994).

As an example, consider attributions. One group of researchers took advantage of the encoding specificity principle to study how and when attributions are made (Newman & Uleman, 1990). As noted in Chapter 9, on memory, a retrieval cue is effective only when it taps into information that was originally encoded; this principle can be used to identify those situations in which people spontaneously make trait attributions (Bassili, 1989a). In one study, subjects read a series of statements such as "The secretary solves the mystery halfway through the book." After reading many sentences, the subjects were asked to recall them and were given certain retrieval cues to help. For the preceding sentence, the cue *smart* (a trait attribution) was much more effective than the cues *typewriter* and *detective* (both of which are semantically related to the topic of the sentence). But this difference in cue effectiveness would occur only if subjects spontaneously inferred that the secretary must be smart when they first read the sentence. Interestingly, subjects had no recollection of having made this inference (Newman & Uleman, 1989). Such spontaneous attributions do not always occur, but they are very likely when one person is trying to form an impression of another (Bassili, 1989b).

Investigating how and what people think in their natural social environment is difficult, but researchers have shown enormous creativity in designing studies of these issues (Carlston, 1994). If you are interested in learning more about such studies, consider taking an introductory social psychology course. Many psychology departments also offer more advanced courses in this subfield, including a course on attitudes.

Summary and Key Terms

Social psychology examines how a person's behavior and mental processes are influenced by other people. One aspect of this study is *social cognition,* the mental processes by which people perceive and react to others.

Social Construction of the Self

People are products of the social and cultural environment.

Social Comparison

When people have no objective criteria by which to judge themselves, they turn to *social comparison,* using others as criteria against which to judge themselves. Categories of people that are habitually used for social comparison are known as *reference groups.* Comparison to reference groups sometimes produces *relative deprivation.*

Social Identity Theory

According to *social identity theory,* one's *identity* results from a fundamental tension between the need to be like others and a corresponding need to feel unique. This leads to a personal identity that corresponds to all those characteristics that make one unique and to a group identity in which the self gains meaning from one's association with similar others. People in individualistic cultures tend to have stronger and more salient personal identities, while those from collectivist cultures tend to have stronger and more salient group identities.

Linkages: Social Cognition and Psychological Disorders

People's mental representations of themselves, their *self-schemas,* differ from culture to culture and from person to person within a culture. People with unified self-schemas tend to think of themselves as more or less the same all the time, while people with differentiated self-schemas tend to think of themselves as having different attributes in different roles or situations. People with unified self-schemas may have more intense emotional reactions to unpleasant situations, and may be more prone to depression or anxiety.

Social Perception

Social perception guides impressions of others and interpretations of the reasons for their behavior.

First Impressions

First impressions are formed easily and quickly, in part because people use existing schemas when they perceive others. Often they apply a *schema-plus-correction process.* First impressions are difficult to change because people (1) are confident of their impressions of others, (2) tend to interpret new information so that it is consistent with the original impression, (3) tend to remember their general impression or schema better than any correction that is later added, and (4) often act in ways that elicit confirming information, a process known as *self-fulfilling prophecy.*

Explaining Behavior: Attribution

Attribution is the process of explaining the causes of people's behavior, including one's own. People tend to attribute behavior to causes that are either internal or external to the actor. In general, people do this by applying three criteria to the behavior: consensus, consistency, and distinctiveness. Attributions are also shaped by *attributional biases,* which are tendencies to distort one's view of behavior systematically. The most common are the *fundamental attribution error,* the *actor-observer bias,* and the *self-serving bias.*

The Self-Protective Functions of Social Cognition

People often protect themselves from admitting something threatening (especially about themselves) through unrealistic optimism, a general illusion of control, and self-handicapping strategies.

Interpersonal Attraction

Keys to Attraction

Interpersonal attraction is a function of many variables. Propinquity is important because it allows for familiarity. The situation in which people first meet is important because positive or negative aspects of the situation tend to be associated with the other person. Obviously, characteristics of the other person are also important. Initially, attraction is strongest to those who are most physically attractive. But for long-term relationships, the *matching hypothesis* applies: people tend to choose others who have about the same level of physical attractiveness. Attraction is also greatest when two people share many similar attitudes.

Intimate Relationships and Love

The defining characteristic of an intimate relationship is interdependence. The most important components of an intimate relationship are affection and emotional expressiveness; these often lead to feelings of support, cohesiveness, and sexuality. Sternberg's triangular theory suggests that love is a function of three components: passion, intimacy, and commitment. Depending on the relative strengths of the three components, there are qualitatively different types of love. Marital satisfaction depends on communication, the perception that the relationship is equitable, and the ability to deal effectively with conflict and anger.

Attitudes

An *attitude* is a predisposition to respond to a particular object in a particular way.

Components of Attitudes

Most theorists agree that attitudes have three components: the cognitive, affective, and behavioral. However, the three components are not always consistent, and it is often difficult to predict a specific behavior from what a person believes or feels about an object. *Cognitive dissonance theory* postulates that an inconsistency between cognitions (as in attitude-behavior discrepancies) creates discomfort that often results in tension-reducing attitude change. *Self-perception theory* holds that attitudes can sometimes follow one's behavior rather than cause it.

Forming Attitudes

Attitudes are often viewed as knowledge structures that are stored in long-term memory. Attitudes can be learned through modeling and classical or operant conditioning. They are also subject to the mere exposure effect: all else being equal, people develop greater liking for a new object as they are exposed to it more often.

Changing Attitudes: The Role of Persuasive Communications

Attitude change is most likely when the source of a communication is perceived as credible, trustworthy, and similar to oneself. In general, a one-sided message is more effective when the audience is sympathetic to the speaker's point of view, while a two-sided message is more effective when the attitude of the audience is contrary to that of the speaker. Attitude change is also greatest when the speaker states explicit conclusions. *Fear appeals* can be highly effective—but only if they are not too frightening and are accompanied by specific guidelines for how to avoid the fearful consequences. Attitude change is greatest among individuals who have moderate levels of self-esteem. A high level of psychological involvement may encourage or discourage attitude change. If involvement is high and strong arguments are presented, attitude change is likely. The *elaborative likelihood model* suggests that attitude change can follow different routes depending on a person's ability and motivation to carefully consider an argument.

Prejudice and Stereotypes

Stereotypes often lead to *prejudice* and *discrimination*.

Theories of Prejudice

One motivational theory suggests that prejudice and stereotyping are most common among people with an *authoritarian personality* because they feel a need to derogate others. Cognitive theories suggest that people categorize others into groups in order to reduce social complexity. The most common way to categorize is to place others into an *ingroup* or an *outgroup*. Outgroup members are often discriminated against. Another approach notes that stereotypes, prejudice, and discriminatory behaviors can be learned from parents, peers, or the popular culture. In line with the *contact hypothesis,* intergroup contact can lead to a reduction of prejudice and more favorable attitudes toward the stereotyped group—but only if it occurs under specific conditions, such as where members of different groups have equal status.

Chapter 18

Social Behavior and Group Influences

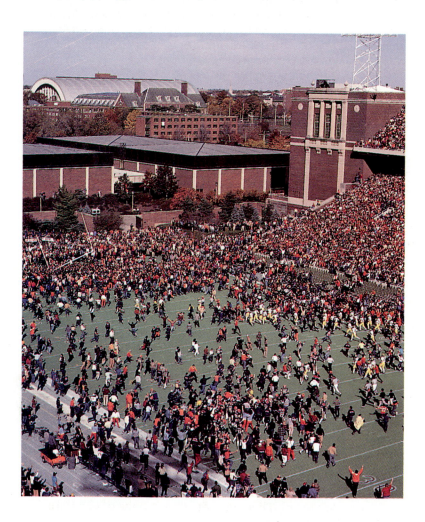

Outline

LOS ANGELES, AUG. 24, 1992. (Reuters) Twenty-two people were killed in Los Angeles over the weekend, the worst period of violence in the city since it was ravaged by riots earlier this year, the police said today.

Twenty-four others were wounded by gunfire or stabbings, including a 19-year old woman in a wheelchair who was shot in the back when she failed to respond to a motorist who asked for directions in south Los Angeles.

"The guy stuck a gun out of the window and just fired at her," said a police spokesman, Lieut. David Rock. The woman was later described as being in stable condition.

Among those who died was an off-duty officer . . . a 14-year old girl killed in a fight between rival gangs . . . and a Little League baseball coach who had argued with the father of a boy he was coaching.

News stories like these can be depressing, but they reflect an undeniable aspect of human social life. In fact, skyrocketing crime statistics are probably underestimates; one study found that in 1990 Americans reported to the police only about 38 percent of all crimes, and only 48 percent of all violent crimes. Some have speculated that in the United States antisocial acts are so commonplace that they are increasingly being seen as normal, not deviant (Moynihan, 1993).

In the previous chapter we focused primarily on how people think about themselves and others. Now we extend this analysis by examining *social behavior*—how people behave with and toward others—and how it is influenced by others. This influence occurs in many ways (see the Linkages diagram), some more obvious than others. We begin by examining some of the more subtle forms of social influence, including the mere presence of others.

Social Influence

The presence of other people often affects the way you think, feel, and act, even when people do not specifically ask you to do anything (Goodwin, 1992). Probably the most pervasive yet subtle way in which the social world influences people is through norms.

Norms are learned, socially based rules that prescribe what people should or should not do in various situations. They are transmitted by parents, teachers, clergy, peers, and other agents of culture. Even when they cannot be verbalized explicitly (they are seldom written as laws), norms are so powerful that people often follow them automatically. At a movie, for example, norms tell you that you should get in line to buy a ticket rather than push people out of the way; they also give you the expectation that others will do the same. By telling people what is expected of them and others, norms make social situations less ambiguous and more comfortable.

Social norms can be classified into two types: descriptive and injunctive (Cialdini, Reno & Kallgren, 1990). *Descriptive norms* indicate what most other people do and thereby provide pressure or permission to do the same. In one study, for example, visitors to an amusement park were given a handbill that read "DON'T MISS TONIGHT'S SHOW" just before they entered a narrow walkway. Figure 18.1 shows that 40 percent of the people threw the handbill on the sidewalk when they saw sixteen discarded handbills already on the ground; in contrast, only 10 percent of the people littered when they saw only a single handbill on the ground.

Injunctive norms provide more specific information about what others approve or disapprove. One very powerful injunctive norm is *reciprocity,* the tendency to respond to others as they have acted toward you (Cialdini, 1984). When an investigator sent Christmas cards to strangers, most responded with a card of their own; some even scribbled a personal note of good cheer (Kunz & Woolcott, 1976). During the 1970s and 1980s, members of the Hare Krishna Society tried a strategy based on the reciprocity norm. Instead of simply asking people in public places for a donation, they first gave people a small gift, such as a flower. Then they asked for money but told people they could keep the flower whether or not they made a donation. This procedure was hugely successful (Cialdini, 1984).

Norms are neither universal nor unchanging (Kagitcibasi & Berry, 1989). In some Near Eastern cultures, people put their faces only inches away from the person they are talking with, displaying a norm that violates the greater distance westerners usually observe. In certain American subcultures, youngsters are revered by peers for skill and daring at committing crimes. Social roles and status also affect which norms influence particular people in particular situ-

Linkages

The questions in this diagram illustrate some of the relationships between the topics of this chapter, social behavior and group influences, and other chapter topics. Only a small sample of these relationships is included here; indeed, all of the mental and behavioral processes described in earlier chapters may be influenced by other people. Research by social psychologists goes beyond showing how other people affect the individual; it also explores patterns of behavior among people, such as aggression and altruism. To study these behaviors, social psychologists draw on research from virtually all other subfields of psychology. To examine aggression, for example, they have investigated the roles of biological factors, emotion, learning, and other processes. The page numbers in the diagram indicate where the listed linkages are discussed in the text. ■

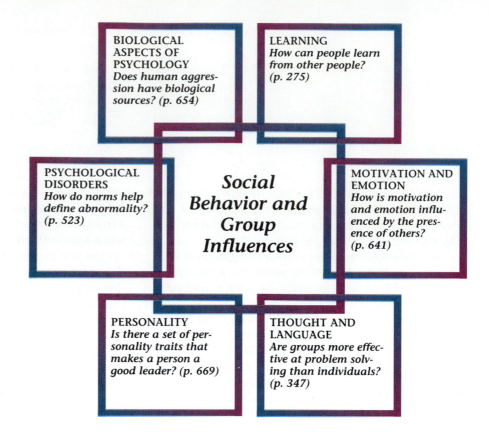

BIOLOGICAL ASPECTS OF PSYCHOLOGY
Does human aggression have biological sources? (p. 654)

LEARNING
How can people learn from other people? (p. 275)

PSYCHOLOGICAL DISORDERS
How do norms help define abnormality? (p. 523)

Social Behavior and Group Influences

MOTIVATION AND EMOTION
How is motivation and emotion influenced by the presence of others? (p. 641)

PERSONALITY
Is there a set of personality traits that makes a person a good leader? (p. 669)

THOUGHT AND LANGUAGE
Are groups more effective at problem solving than individuals? (p. 347)

ations. Imagine yourself in a professor's office. The professor may lean back and put his or her feet up on the desk. But if you put your feet on the professor's desk, you would be breaking a norm.

The social influence exerted by norms creates orderly social behavior. But social influence can also lead to a breakdown in order. For example, **deindividuation** is a hypothesized psychological state in which a person becomes "submerged in the group" and loses the sense of individuality (Diener, 1979). When people experience deindividuation, they appear to undergo heightened emotional arousal and an intense feeling of cohesiveness with the group; they appear to become part of the "herd," and they may perform acts that they would not do otherwise.

Deindividuation appears to be caused by two factors (Prentice-Dunn & Rogers, 1989). First, normal cues to accountability are diminished. The person

Linkages: The social norms that guide how people dress and what they should do and should not do in various situations are a major aspect of the culturally determined socialization process, which, as described in the chapter on human development, begins in infancy. The process is the same the world over—parents, teachers, peers, religious leaders, and others communicate their culture's social norms to children—but differences in those norms result in quite different behaviors from culture to culture.

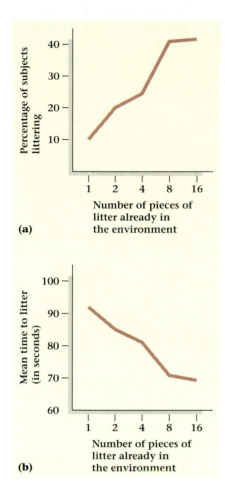

(a)

(b)

Figure 18.1
Descriptive Norms
As shown in part (a), four times as many people threw a handbill on the sidewalk when they saw many handbills apparently discarded by others as when only one discarded handbill was visible. Part (b) shows that people littered more quickly when the ground was already covered with litter than when it was relatively litter-free (Cialdini, Reno & Kallgren, 1990).

How is motivation and emotion influenced by the presence of others?

no longer thinks that he or she can be held personally accountable for what happens. Second, attention shifts away from internal thoughts and standards and toward the external environment. Having members of the group sing in unison or wear unusual uniforms (such as Ku Klux Klan robes and hoods) fosters this shift of attention.

The effects of deindividuation may be desirable, as when a military unit completes a daring rescue by engaging in dangerous activities that each individual might not perform alone (Diener, 1980). More often, however, deindividuation results in antisocial acts, and the emotional arousal that is generated makes such behavior difficult to stop (Prentice-Dunn & Rogers, 1989). Fans at rock concerts and athletic events have trampled one another to death in their frenzy to get the best seats; normally mild-mannered adults have thrown rocks or fire bombs at police during political protests; and Adolf Hitler and Charles Manson, for example, influenced groups of their followers to commit murderous ethnic atrocities and ritual murders. Deindividuation is one example of how, given the right circumstances, quite normal people can engage in destructive, even violent behavior.

Linkages: Motivation and the Presence of Others

In Chapter 12 we noted that social factors such as parental attitudes toward achievement often affect motivation. A person's current motivational state is also affected by the presence of other people. To illustrate, consider the very first experiment in social psychology, conducted by Norman Triplett in 1897.

Triplett noticed that bicyclists tended to race faster when a competitor was near than when all competitors were out of sight. Did seeing one another remind the riders of the need to go faster to win? To test this possibility, Triplett arranged for bicyclists to complete a twenty-five-mile course under three conditions: riding alone and racing against the clock; riding with another cyclist, but not in competition; or competing directly with another rider. The cyclists went much faster when another rider was present than when they were simply racing against the clock, whether or not they were competing against the other person. Something about the presence of the other person, rather than competition, produced increased speed.

The term **social facilitation** describes circumstances in which the mere presence of other people improves performance. This improvement does not always occur, however. The presence of other people sometimes *impairs* performance, a process known as **social interference**. For decades these results seemed contradictory; then Robert Zajonc (pronounced "zye-onze") suggested that both could be explained by one process: arousal.

The presence of other people, said Zajonc, increases a person's general level of arousal or motivation (Zajonc, 1965). As we discussed in Chapter 13, on health, stress, and coping, arousal increases the tendency to perform those behaviors that are most *dominant*—the ones you know best—and this tendency may either help or hinder performance. When you are performing a familiar task such as riding a bike, increased arousal due to the presence of others should allow you to ride even faster than normal. But when a task is unfamiliar, complex, or difficult, performing the most dominant responses may be detrimental. If you try to perform a recently learned dance in the arousal-producing presence of others, old dance moves may appear, making your performance look awkward. In other words, according to Zajonc, other people's presence can help or hinder performance depending on whether the most likely behavior in the situation is beneficial or harmful to that performance.

What is there about the presence of others that leads to arousal? Research evidence suggests two factors (Geen, 1989). First, people expect other people to evaluate their performance; therefore, they feel apprehensive about what others will think, whether those others are actually judging them or not (Sanna & Shotland, 1990). Second, the presence of others may create arousal by intensifying self-evaluation. Self-evaluation generally facilitates performance when the task is easy but impairs performance when the task is difficult (Jackson, Buglione & Glenwick, 1988).

So far we have discussed situations in which an individual's motivation on a task is altered by the mere presence of others. If these other people are also working on the same task, however, their impact changes slightly (Sanna, 1992). When a group performs a task, it is not always possible to identify each individual's contributions. In these situations, people often exert less effort than when performing alone, a phenomenon termed **social loafing** (Williams & Karav, 1991). Whether the task is pulling on a rope, clapping as loudly as possible, or trying to solve intellectual puzzles, people tend to work harder when performing alone than with others (Ingham et al., 1974; Kravitz & Martin, 1986; Wedon & Gargano, 1988).

Where, when, and why does social loafing happen? Social loafing has been observed in Western and non-Western cultures alike (Gabrenya, Latané & Wang, 1983) and occurs only when people are able to "hide in the crowd"— that is, when their own individual level of performance cannot be identified (Seta, Seta & Donaldson, 1991). Under these conditions, a person's level of arousal appears to decrease in the presence of others, as does apprehension over being negatively evaluated (Harkins, 1987). Anyone who has played in a large band or sung in a big chorus knows the temptation to skip the hardest part of a piece, on the assumption that no one will know the difference. When people can be lazy and exert less effort with no one knowing, they usually take advantage of the situation.

Social loafing can be seen in all sorts of groups, from volunteer committees to search parties. In business, social loafing can reduce productivity. Thus it is important for managers to develop ways of evaluating the efforts of every individual in a work group, not just the overall output of a team (Ilgen & Klein, 1989; Shepperd, 1993).

Conformity and Compliance

Suppose you are with three friends. One says that Franklin Roosevelt was the greatest president in the history of the United States. You think that the greatest president was Abraham Lincoln, but before you can say anything, another friend agrees that it was Roosevelt, and then the other one does as well. What would you do? Disagree with all three? Maintain your opinion but keep quiet? Change your mind?

When people change their behavior or beliefs to match those of other members of a group, they are said to conform. **Conformity** occurs as a result of real or imagined, though *unspoken*, group pressure (Levine, 1989). When everyone around you stands up to applaud a performance you thought was mediocre, you may conform by standing as well. No one tells you to do this; the group's behavior simply creates a silent but influential pressure to follow suit. **Compliance**, in contrast, occurs when people adjust their behavior because of a direct request. If the last holdout for acquittal on a jury finally succumbs to the other jurors' browbeating, he or she has complied with overt social pressure.

The Role of Norms

Conformity and compliance are usually generated by a group's spoken or unspoken norms. Muzafer Sherif (1937) managed to chart the formation of a

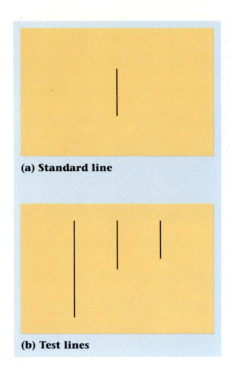

(a) Standard line

(b) Test lines

Source: Asch, 1955.

Figure 18.2
Types of Stimulus Lines Used
in Experiments by Asch
Subjects in Asch's experiments saw a
new set of lines on each of eighteen
trials. Such experiments demonstrate
that people often conform to the
views of others in a group.

Linkages: How do pressures for
conformity to differing cultural
values shape developmental
patterns? (a link to Human
Development)

group norm by taking advantage of a perceptual illusion called the *autokinetic*
phenomenon. If you are placed in a completely dark room and shown a small,
stationary point of light, the light will appear to move. (*Autokinetic* means
"self-movement.") Some people tend to see a lot of movement; others report
only a little. Each person's estimates of the apparent movement tend to stay
within a small, characteristic range, such as from one to two inches or from
five to six inches. Sherif put several people together in a dark room, switched
on a point of light, and asked each person to report aloud how far the light
had moved on repeated exposures. Eventually, the subjects' estimates tended
to fall within a common *group* range; they had established a group norm. Even
more important, when the individuals in the group were later tested alone,
they continued to follow this norm.

The subjects in Sherif's experiment began by disagreeing with one another
about an ambiguous situation and only slowly developed a group norm.
Solomon Asch (1956) examined how people would respond when they faced
a norm that already existed but that was obviously wrong. He showed subjects
a standard line like the one in Figure 18.2(a); then they saw a display like that
in Figure 18.2(b). Their task was to pick out the line in the display that was the
same length as the line they had been shown first.

Each subject performed the task as part of a small group, but in reality all of
the other participants were confederates of the experimenter. There were two
conditions. In the control condition, the subject responded before any of the
other participants. In the experimental condition, the subject did not respond
until after the confederates did. The confederates chose the obviously correct
response on six trials, but on the other twelve trials they all gave the same,
obviously incorrect response. Thus, on twelve trials, each subject was confronted with a "social reality" created by the group norm that conflicted with
the physical reality created by what the person could clearly see. Only 5 percent of the subjects in the control condition ever made a mistake on this easy
perceptual task. However, among subjects who heard the confederates' responses before giving their own, about 70 percent made at least one error by
conforming to the group norm.

Why Do People Conform?

Why did the people in Asch's experiment give so many incorrect responses
when they were capable of near-perfect performance? One possibility, called
public conformity, is that they did not really change their minds. Instead, perhaps they gave an answer they did not believe simply because it was the socially desirable thing to do. Another possibility is called *private acceptance:* perhaps the subjects used the confederates' responses as legitimate evidence about
reality, were convinced that their own perceptions were wrong, and so
changed their minds. Morton Deutsch and Harold Gerard (1955) reasoned that
if conformity disappeared when people gave their responses in private with
complete anonymity, then Asch's findings must reflect public conformity, not
private acceptance. In fact, conformity does decrease when people respond
anonymously instead of publicly, but it is not eliminated (Deutsch & Gerard,
1955). People sometimes publicly produce responses that they do not believe,
but hearing other people's responses also influences their private beliefs
(Moscovici, 1985).

Why do group norms wield such power? Research suggests three influential
factors (Levine, 1989). First, people are motivated to be correct (Insko et al.,
1985), and norms provide information about what is right and wrong. Second,
people are motivated to be liked by other members of the group (Insko et al.,
1983). Finally, norms guide the dispensation of social reinforcement and punishment (Levine, 1989). From childhood on, people in many cultures learn
that going along with group norms is good and earns rewards. (These positive

These worshipers at Mecca exemplify the power of religion and other social forces to produce conformity to group norms.

outcomes presumably help compensate for not always saying or doing exactly what one pleases.) People also learn that breaking a norm may bring punishments ranging from scoldings for small violations to imprisonment for nonconformity with norms that have been translated into laws.

Consider what life would be like if there were no conformity to group norms—if, for example, no one paid attention to norms about taking turns when speaking, knocking before opening a closed door, or respecting people's rights to their own property. At best, life would be chaotic and unpredictable; at worst, the fabric of society would begin to disintegrate. Conversely, if everyone conformed all the time and in exactly the same way, the world might be a rather boring place, bereft of the variety, eccentricity, and even strangeness that make human beings so fascinating. Thus, members of human social groups constantly search for the delicate balance that will ensure group survival without squelching the individuality that many cultures value (Goethals, 1986).

When Do People Conform?

Clearly, people do not always conform to group influence. In the Asch studies, for example, nearly 30 percent of the subjects did not go along with the confederates' obviously erroneous judgments. Countless experiments have probed the question of what combinations of people and circumstances do and do not lead to conformity.

Ambiguity of the Situation   Ambiguity is very important in determining how much conformity will occur. As the physical reality of a situation becomes less clear, people rely more and more on others' opinions (Shaw, Rothschild & Strickland, 1957), and conformity to a group norm becomes more likely.

You can demonstrate conformity on any street corner. First, create an ambiguous situation by having several people look up at the top of a building or high in the sky. When people ask what is going on, be sure everyone excitedly reports seeing something vague but interesting—perhaps a tiny, shiny object or a faint, mysterious light. (The hint of a flying saucer sighting will help.) If the alleged stimulus is fleeting or difficult to see, people are likely to perceive your group as providing valid information about the world. If you are especially successful, conforming newcomers will begin persuading other passers-by that there is something fascinating to be seen.

Unanimity and Size of the Majority   If ambiguity contributes so much to conformity, why did so many of Asch's subjects conform to a judgment that was unambiguously wrong? The answer has to do with the unanimity of the group's judgment and the number of people expressing it.

Specifically, people experience great pressure to conform as long as the majority is unanimous. If even one other person in the group disagrees with the majority view, conformity drops greatly. For example, when Asch (1951) arranged for just one confederate to disagree with the others, fewer than 10 percent of the subjects conformed. Once unanimity is broken, it becomes much easier to disagree with the majority, even if the other nonconformist does not agree with the person's own view (Nemeth & Chiles, 1988).

Conformity also depends on the size of the group. Asch (1955) examined this relationship by varying the number of confederates in the group from one to fifteen. Conformity to incorrect norms grew as the number of people in the group increased, but most of the growth in conformity occurred as the size of the majority rose from one to about three or four members; further additions to the size of the majority had little effect. Other experimenters found different results, however. Under certain circumstances, conformity increased significantly as the size of the majority exceeded three or four (Gerard, Wilhelmy & Connolley, 1968; Milgram, Bickman & Berkowitz, 1969).

The key to these apparently contradictory results seems to lie in how people *perceive* the opinions of the majority (Tanford & Penrod, 1984). In other words, the majority may have an actual size and a psychological size. The *psychological size* equals the number of members whose assessments are perceived as independent, as reflecting each individual's carefully considered judgment. If everyone in a large group gives the same spoken answer to a question, one after the other, you might consider only the first three or four responses to be independent assessments. After that, you might perceive the rest of the people as giving answers just to be compatible, and their answers may have little effect on you. Only the first few answers, which you perceive as independent, determine the psychological size of the majority.

Personal Characteristics   In nearly any situation some people will conform more than others. One important determinant of conformity is familiarity with the task; social status is another. People who are unfamiliar with a situation or have relatively low status in a group are the ones most likely to conform (Buss et al., 1987).

Familiarity and status help predict conformity, but they may also be responsible for erroneous beliefs, such as that women conform more than men (Crutchfield, 1955). Early research showed this gender difference, but the tasks used in those experiments were often more familiar to men than to women. Subsequent research using materials that are equally familiar to both sexes found no male-female differences in conformity (Eagly & Carli, 1981). Why do some people still perceive women as more conforming than men in spite of evidence to the contrary? Part of the answer may lie in their perception of the relative social status of males and females. Those who think of women as having lower social status than men in most social situations are most likely to see females as easier to influence, even though men and women conform equally often (Eagly, 1987).

Attraction to a group also influences conformity. People are more likely to conform when they like the members of a group than when there is little or no attraction (Forsyth, 1983). Attraction may increase conformity because people tend to trust the judgment of those they like or because they want the approval of people to whom they are attracted. Conformity based on the desire for approval from attractive group members appears to be particularly likely among those with low self-esteem (Stang, 1972).

Another personal characteristic that may shape conformity is the degree to which people are concerned with being liked or with being correct. People who are preoccupied with being liked are likely to conform, particularly when they are also attracted to the others in the group. In contrast, people who are preoccupied with being right are less likely to conform, no matter how much or how little they are attracted to others in the group (Insko et al., 1985). Individuals from collectivist cultures may be particularly likely to conform so as not to cause disharmony in the group (Berry et al., 1992).

Inducing Compliance

In the experiments just described, the subjects experienced psychological pressure to conform to the views or actions of others, even though no one specifically asked them to do so. In contrast, *compliance* involves changing what you say or do because of a direct request from someone who has no authority over you.

How is compliance brought about? Many people believe that the direct approach is always best: if you want something, ask for it. But salespeople, political strategists, social psychologists, and other experts on the subject have learned that often the best way to get something is to ask for something else. This strategy usually takes one of three forms: the foot-in-the-door technique, the door-in-the-face procedure, or the low-ball approach.

The *foot-in-the-door technique* consists of beginning with small requests and working up to larger ones. Its name comes from an experiment in which homeowners in a wealthy California neighborhood were approached in one of two ways. In some cases, the experimenter claimed to represent a group concerned with reducing traffic accidents in the community and asked the homeowners if a large and unattractive "Drive Carefully" sign could be placed on their front lawn. Approximately 17 percent of the people approached in this way complied with the request. In the foot-in-the-door condition, homeowners were first asked only to sign a petition urging their legislators to work toward decreasing the number of accidents in the community. Several weeks later, a different experimenter asked these same people to place the "Drive Carefully" sign on their lawn. In this case, 55 percent of the people complied (Freedman & Fraser, 1966).

Subsequent research has confirmed the compliance-inducing effect of preceding a large request with a smaller one (Beaman et al., 1983). Why should this be so? First, people are usually far more likely to comply with a request whose cost in time, money, effort, or inconvenience is low rather than high. Second, complying with a small request makes people think of themselves as being committed to the cause or issue. This occurs through the self-perception and cognitive dissonance processes discussed in Chapter 17. For example, in the study just described, subjects might think something like, "If I signed this petition, I must care enough about traffic safety to do something about it." Compliance with the higher-cost request (displaying the sign) was thus increased because doing so was consistent with these people's self-perceptions and past actions (Eisenberg et al., 1987).

People take advantage of the foot-in-the-door technique all the time. For example, some companies first ask prospective customers to respond to a mail survey about their product and then ask to visit to explain how it works (with no obligation, of course). Only then is the customer asked to buy the product. In some cases, the initial request requires only that the prospective customer

The door-in-the-face strategy is the heart and soul of most bargaining situations. Whether negotiations are between political groups or labor and management, each side usually begins by proposing plans that are obviously unacceptable to the other side. But neither side expects the initial proposal to be accepted; it is only the first and most extreme request, compared to which later proposals will appear to be a compromise.

In 1989 Chinese students were joined by thousands of other civilians in demonstrating for democracy in Beijing's Tiananmen Square. When the demonstration became too large, government leaders ordered Chinese troops to fire on the civilians. Many of the demonstrators were killed. When authority figures deliver orders, they are often obeyed—in spite of the consequences (Hans, 1992).

accept a free gift. Agreeing to fill out the forms necessary to receive the gift constitutes the first, low level of compliance, to be followed, the company hopes, by compliance with a later request to buy something. Free gifts not only constitute a foot in the door but are likely to invoke the reciprocity norm: once they accept something, many people feel obligated to reciprocate by buying something.

The opposite approach, known as the *door-in-the-face procedure,* can also be effective in obtaining compliance (Cann, Sherman & Elkes, 1975). This strategy begins with a very large request that is likely to be denied. Then the person making the original request concedes that it was rather extreme and substitutes a lesser alternative, which is what the requester wanted in the first place. Because the new request now seems so modest in contrast with the first one, it is more likely to be granted.

A third technique for "getting X by asking for Y" is called the *low-ball approach* (Cialdini et al., 1978). The first step is to obtain a verbal commitment from someone to do something. The second step is to show that only a higher-cost version of the initial request will do any good. Finally, that higher-cost request is made. The low-ball approach differs from the foot-in-the-door technique because the initial request is escalated after it is agreed to but before it can be fulfilled. For example, a student we know got a ride to campus every day in time for an 8:00 A.M. class from a friend whose first class was not until 10:00. She did it by first asking the friend if she could hitch a ride every day. Only after he had said yes did she tell him that she had to be picked up by 7:30. Apparently the low-ball approach works because once the initial request is granted, the person feels committed to help even if a later version of the request is larger (Burger & Petty, 1981).

Low-ball methods are often used in *bait-and-switch* sales schemes. For example, after a customer agrees to buy a microwave oven at a special sale price, the salesperson may come back from the storeroom to say that none of those models is left but that they do have an even better model at a "slightly" higher price. Experts at this tactic use it so skillfully that customers may end up spending two or three times what they had planned.

Obedience

Compliance involves a change in behavior in response to a request. In contrast, **obedience** involves complying with an explicit *demand,* typically from an acknowledged authority figure (Kelman & Hamilton, 1989).

Obedience in the Laboratory   In the 1960s Stanley Milgram realized that psychologists knew little about obedience and so developed a laboratory procedure to study it. Through an ad in local newspapers, he recruited forty male volunteers between the ages of twenty and fifty for his first experiment. Among the subjects were professionals, white-collar businessmen, and un-skilled workers (Milgram, 1963).

Imagine you are one of the people who answered the ad. When you arrive for the experiment, you join a fifty-year-old gentleman who has also volun-teered and has been scheduled for the same session. The experimenter explains that the purpose of the experiment is to examine the effects of punishment on learning. One of you—the "teacher"—will help the learner remember a list of words by administering electric shock whenever he makes a mistake. Then the experimenter turns to you and asks you to draw one of two cards out of a hat. The one you draw says "TEACHER." You think to yourself that this must be your lucky day.

Now the learner is taken into another room and strapped into a chair, as shown in Figure 18.3. Electrodes are attached to his arms. You are shown a shock generator with thirty switches. The experimenter explains that the switch on the far left administers a very mild, 15-volt shock and that each succeeding switch increases the shock by 15 volts; the one on the far right delivers 450 volts. You also notice several labels on the shock generator. The far left section is labeled "Slight shock." Looking across the panel, you see "Moderate shock," "Very strong shock," and, at the far right, "Danger—severe shock." The last two switches are ominously labeled "XXX." The experimenter explains that you, the teacher, will begin by reading a list of word pairs to the learner. Then you will go through the list again, presenting just one word of each pair; the learner should indicate which word went with it. After the first mistake, you are to throw the switch to deliver 15 volts of shock. Each time the learner makes another mistake, you are to increase the shock by 15 volts.

You begin, following the experimenter's instructions. But after the learner makes his fifth mistake and you throw the switch to give him 75 volts, you hear a loud moan. At 90 volts, the learner cries out in pain. At 150 volts, he screams and asks to be let out of the experiment. You look to the experimenter, who says, "Proceed with the next question."

**Figure 18.3
Studying Obedience
in the Laboratory**
In this photograph from Milgram's original experiment, a man is being strapped into a chair with electrodes on his arm. Although subjects in the experiment do not know it, the man is actually a confederate of the exper-imenter and receives no shock.

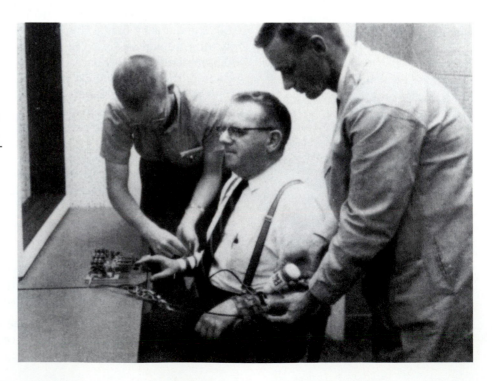

What do you do? In fact, no shock was delivered in Milgram's experiments. The "learner" was always a confederate of the experimenter, and the moans and other signs of pain were an act. But you do not know that. What would you do in this situation? Suppose you continue and eventually deliver 180 volts. The learner screams that he cannot stand the pain any longer and starts banging on the wall. The experimenter says, "You have no other choice; you must go on." Would you continue? Would you keep going even when the learner begged to be let out of the experiment and then fell silent? Would you administer 450 volts of potentially deadly shock to a perfect stranger just because an experimenter demands that you do so?

Figure 18.4 shows what the subjects in Milgram's experiment did. Only five subjects stopped before 300 volts. Of the forty subjects in the experiment, twenty-six (or 65 percent) went all the way to the 450-volt level. The decision to continue was difficult and stressful for the subjects. Many protested repeatedly; but each time the experimenter told them to continue, they did so. Here is a partial transcript of what a typical subject said.

[After throwing the 180-volt switch]: *He can't stand it. I'm not going to kill that man in there. Do you hear him hollering? He's hollering. He can't stand it. What if something happens to him? I'm not going to get that man sick in there. He's hollering in there. Do you know what I mean? I mean, I refuse to take responsibility. He's getting hurt in there. . . . Too many left here. Geez, if he gets them wrong. There are too many of them left. I mean, who is going to take responsibility if anything happens to that gentleman?*

[After the experimenter accepts responsibility]: *All right. . . .*

[After administering 240 volts]: *Oh, no, you mean I've got to keep going up the scale? No sir, I'm not going to kill that man. I'm not going to give him 450 volts.*

[After the experimenter says, "The experiment requires that you go on"]: *I know it does, but that man is hollering in there, sir.*

This subject administered shock up to 450 volts. (Milgram, 1974)

Factors Affecting Obedience

Milgram had not expected so many subjects to deliver such apparently intense shocks. Was there something about his procedure that produced such high

Figure 18.4
Results of Milgram's Obedience Experiment
Note that 65 percent of the subjects tested gave the maximum amount of shock available. When Milgram asked a group of undergraduates how the subjects in the experiment would respond, they estimated that fewer than 2 percent of the people would go all the way to 450 volts. He then asked a group of psychiatrists, who gave similar predictions.

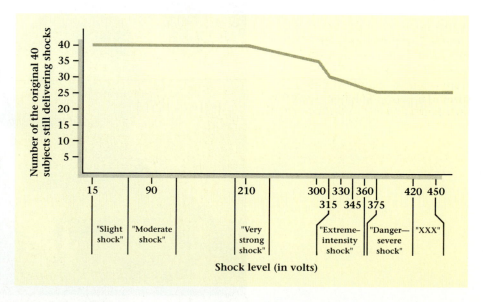

Source: Milgram, 1963.

levels of obedience? To find out, Milgram and other researchers varied the original procedure in numerous ways. The overall level of obedience to an authority figure was nearly always quite high, but the degree of obedience was affected by several characteristics of the situation and procedure.

Prestige   One possibility is that the status and legitimacy of the experimenter helped produce high levels of obedience in Milgram's original experiment. After all, that study was conducted at Yale University, and the newspaper ad had stated that the experimenter was a professor at Yale. To test the effects of status and prestige, Milgram rented a deserted office building in Bridgeport, Connecticut. He then placed an ad in the local newspaper that made no mention of Yale and instead said the research was sponsored by a private firm. In all other ways, the experimental procedure was identical to the original.

Under these less prestigious circumstances, the level of obedience dropped, but to a smaller extent than Milgram expected; 48 percent of the subjects continued to the maximum level of shock, compared with 65 percent in the original study. Milgram concluded that people were willing to do great harm to another even if the authority figure was not "particularly reputable or distinguished."

Proximity   In another variation on Milgram's original design, the extent of contact between the subject and the authority figure—the experimenter—was varied. For example, when the authority figure gave the instructions by phone, only 20 percent of the subjects gave the maximum shock; many other subjects lied, saying that they were continuing to administer higher levels of shock when they were not (Rada & Rogers, 1973). However, obedience remained quite high if the authority figure gave the instructions in person and then left the room (Rada & Rogers, 1973). In other words, the ability to obtain obedience apparently depended on some personal contact. Once the experimenter was established as an authority in the subject's mind, the contact did not need to be maintained. As proximity to the authority figure declined, however, obedience tended to drop as well.

Proximity between subject and victim also had an effect, as Figure 18.5 shows. As proximity to the victim increased, the level of obedience decreased

Milgram's research suggested that the close proximity of an authority figure enhances obedience to authority. This principle is clearly employed in military organizations, where no member is ever far away from a source of authority in the form of a person of higher rank.

Figure 18.5
Obedience as a Function of Proximity to the Victim
The more feedback the subject received from the victim, the less shock he or she administered. In the remote condition, the subject and learner were in different rooms, and the subject could neither see nor hear the learner. In the voice feedback condition, the subject could hear the learner but not see him. In the proximity condition, subject and learner were in the same room, so that the learner could be seen and heard. In the touch proximity condition, the subject had to press the learner's hand onto a metal dish in order to administer the shock.

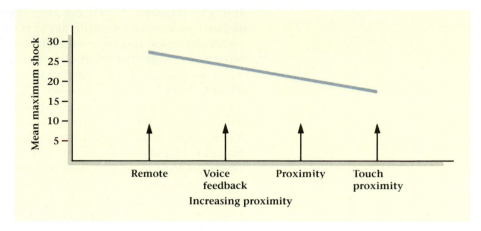

Source: Milgram, 1972.

substantially (Milgram, 1965). These results are consistent with the belief that it is easier for soldiers to follow orders to kill other people by long-range shooting or high-altitude bombing than by, say, stabbing.

Presence of Others Who Disobey   These studies may lead you to wonder (as Milgram did) how the presence of other people might affect obedience. Milgram (1965) created a situation in which there were three teachers. Teacher 1 (who was a confederate of the experimenter) read the words to the learner. Teacher 2 (who was also a confederate) indicated whether the learner had made a correct or incorrect response. Then it was up to Teacher 3 (the actual subject) to deliver the shock when a mistake was made. At 150 volts, the learner began to complain bitterly that the shock was too painful. At this point, Teacher 1 (a confederate) refused to participate any longer and left the room. The experimenter asked him to come back, but he refused. The experimenter then instructed Teachers 2 and 3 to continue by themselves. The experiment continued for several more trials. However, at 210 volts, Teacher 2 said that the learner was suffering too much pain and also refused to participate. The experimenter then told Teacher 3 (the actual subject) to continue the procedure. In this case, only 10 percent of the subjects (compared with 65 percent in the original study) continued to deliver shock all the way up to 450 volts. Thus, as the research on conformity would suggest, it appears that the presence of others who disobey is the most powerful factor reducing subjects' obedience.

Evaluating Milgram's Studies

Nearly all social scientists agree that Milgram's studies were telling experiments. For the first time, here was evidence that a person did not have to be sadistic or in any way abnormal to inflict pain—or even death—on another person (Saks, 1992). Given the right circumstances, it appeared that nearly everyone is capable of such acts. Nevertheless the meaning and ethics of Milgram's work continues to be debated (Ross, 1988).

Linkages: How do ethical concerns limit research on human obedience? (a link to Research in Psychology)

Ethical Questions   Although the "learners" in Milgram's experiment suffered no pain, the subjects did. Milgram himself (1963) observed subjects "sweat, stutter, tremble, groan, bite their lips, and dig their fingernails into their flesh. Full-blown uncontrollable seizures were observed for three subjects" (p. 375). Against the potential harm inflicted by Milgram's experiments stands the potential gains. For example, people who learn about Milgram's work often take his findings into account when deciding how to react in social situations (Sherman, 1980). But even if social value has come from Milgram's studies, was it ethical for Milgram to treat his subjects as he did?

Milgram made several arguments in defense of his experiments. First, he noted that he expected nearly all of the subjects to stop at some point, certainly before they reached the "danger" level. Second, Milgram argued that his debriefing of the subjects prevented the experiment from doing any lasting harm. At the conclusion of the experiment, each subject was told that most people went all the way to the 450-volt level and that the learner did not experience any shock at all. Then the learner was brought into the room and chatted with the subject in a friendly fashion. Milgram claimed that this procedure helped the subjects understand that their behavior in the experiment was not unusual. Third, when Milgram later sent his subjects a questionnaire, 84 percent indicated they were glad that they had participated in the study. They felt that they had learned something important about themselves and that the experience had been worthwhile. Thus, Milgram argued, the experience was actually a positive one.

Ethical questions are difficult ones. The dialogue between Milgram and his critics has helped push investigators to consider further the ethical implications of their research. Today, committees evaluate proposals for experiments and are charged with protecting human subjects, balancing subjects' welfare against the gains that might result from an experiment. It is unlikely that these committees would approve Milgram's study if he proposed it today, and less controversial ways to study obedience have now been developed (Sackoff & Weinstein, 1988).

Questions of Meaning   Milgram's results were dramatic, but do they mean that most people are putty in the hands of authority figures? (For a summary of those results, plus the results of studies on conformity and compliance, see "In Review: Types of Social Influence.") Under the right circumstances, do people blindly follow inhumane orders from their leaders? Would you and your neighbors obey orders to incinerate people, as many Nazis and their collaborators did during World War II?

Some people interpret Milgram's data in just that fashion, and they may be right. However, drawing broad conclusions about human behavior in general on the basis of Milgram's results may be a mistake. The results of Milgram's experiments might, in large measure, reflect subjects' willingness to go along with an experimenter's charade, not obedience to dangerous demands. Martin Orne argued, for example, that many of Milgram's subjects must have realized that an experimenter would not actually endanger the life of another human being merely in order to study learning. Some subjects might also have noticed that, since the experimenter could have acted as the "teacher" himself, it must be their own behavior, not the learner's, that was under study (Orne & Holland, 1968).

If Orne is right, Milgram's ingenious research may have generated overly pessimistic conclusions about human beings. However, news reports provide daily evidence of cruelty by people obeying the authority of military, terrorist, and cult leaders. Soldiers of every army in history, including U.S. soldiers, appear to have followed orders that resulted in inhumane acts against civilians as well as against enemy soldiers. Although many people routinely question and overtly oppose authority figures when they feel it is important to do so, most people do what authorities tell them to do, even when they have doubts.

The truth about the extent of human obedience and the circumstances under which it will be displayed remains to be discovered, but it may be less flattering than one might wish. We say this partly because much inhumanity occurs even without pressure for obedience. For example, a good deal of peo-

In Review: Types of Social Influence

Type	Definition	Key Findings
Conformity	A change in behavior or beliefs to match those of others in a group	In cases of ambiguity, people slowly develop a group norm and then adhere to it.
		Conformity occurs because people want to be right, because they want to be liked by others, and because conformity to group norms is usually reinforced.
		Conformity usually increases as the ambiguity of the situation, the psychological size of the majority, and the attractiveness of the group increases. Nonconformity is most likely among members who enjoy high status within the group.
Compliance	A change in behavior or beliefs because of a direct request	Compliance increases with the foot-in-the-door technique, which begins with a small request and works up to a larger one.
		The door-in-the-face procedure can also be used. After making a large request that is denied, the speaker substitutes a less extreme alternative that was desired all along.
		The low-ball approach also elicits compliance. A verbal commitment for something minor is first obtained; then the person claims that only a higher-cost version of the original request will suffice.
Obedience	A change in behavior to match an explicit demand, typically from an acknowledged authority figure	People may inflict great harm on others as long as an authority demands that they do so.
		Even when people obey orders to harm another person, they often agonize over the decision. The psychological stress involved can be extremely intense.
		People are most likely to disobey orders to harm another person when they have close proximity to the victim or see another person disobey.

ple's aggressiveness toward other people appears to come from within. In the next section, we consider human aggressiveness and some of the circumstances that influence its expression.

Aggression

Carl Panzram proclaimed with perverse pride that virtually his entire life was spent trying to figure out ways to make people suffer. In the late 1920s he decided he would build a bomb designed to explode on contact and place it on a train track in the middle of a long tunnel. After the explosion, and before the passengers could escape from the train, Panzram planned to pump poisonous gas into the tunnel and, wearing a gas mask, go in and rob all of the bodies. He estimated that he could kill nearly four hundred people and collect up to $100,000, which he planned to use to finance additional acts of terrorism. Fortunately, Panzram's technical expertise was not sufficient to carry out his plans in full, but he did manage to kill twenty-five people before being caught, tried, and executed (Harrison, 1976).

Linkages: What motivates people to be aggressive? (a link to Motivation and Emotion)

Linkages: How do differing approaches to psychology explain aggression? (a link to Introducing Psychology)

Linkages: Does human aggression have biological sources? (a link to Biological Aspects of Psychology)

Aggression occurs whenever an act is intended to harm another person (Baron & Richardson, 1992). Under the right circumstances, even the most peaceable person can lash out aggressively in anger (Berkowitz, 1993). For example, over 70 percent of parents in the United States report that they have slapped their child in anger, and one-fifth of all parents have hit their children with objects such as sticks or leather belts. About one-third of U.S. husbands and wives have hit their spouse in anger, and life-threatening attacks with guns or knives occur in about one out of twenty marriages (Straus, Gelles & Steinmetz, 1980). Violent crimes now occur at the rate of 1.5 million per year in the United States alone, including more than 90,000 rapes and 20,000 murders (Saks, 1992).

Why Are People Aggressive?

Psychologists once believed that aggression stems from a single underlying cause—namely, an instinct for aggression. Freud proposed that aggression is innate, inevitable, and universal. Specifically, he suggested that aggression is an instinctive biological urge that gradually builds up and at some point must be released. Sometimes it is released in the form of physical or verbal abuse against another person. At other times the aggressive impulse is turned inward and produces self-punitive actions, even suicide.

A slightly more complicated view is offered by *sociobiology*, which, as described in Chapter 1, is the study of the relationship between a species' evolutionary heritage and its social behaviors. From this perspective, aggression once helped people compete for mates, thus ensuring survival of their genes in the next generation. Through the principles of natural selection, then, aggressive tendencies were passed on through successive generations.

But Freudian and sociobiological theories seem too simplistic to fully account for human aggressiveness. For one thing, there are large differences in aggression from culture to culture (Averill, 1993), thus suggesting that, even if aggressive *impulses* are universal, the appearance of aggressive *behavior* reflects an interplay of nature and nurture (Lore & Schultz, 1993). No equation can predict when people will be aggressive, but years of research have revealed a number of important biological, learning, emotional, and environmental factors that combine in various ways to produce aggression in various situations.

Biological Mechanisms   The evidence for some genetic influence on aggression is strong, especially in animals (Cairns, Gariepy & Hood, 1990). In one study, the most aggressive members of a large group of mice were interbred; then the most aggressive of their offspring were also interbred. After this procedure was followed for twenty-five generations, the resulting animals would immediately attack any mouse put in their cage. Continuous inbreeding of the least aggressive members of the original group produced animals that were so nonaggressive that they would refuse to fight even when attacked (Lagerspetz & Lagerspetz, 1983). Research on human twins reared together or apart suggests that there is a genetic component to aggression in people as well (Rushton et al., 1986; Tellegen et al., 1988). As mentioned in the chapter on personality, however, the genetic component of aggressiveness is smaller than it is in traits such as sociability or anxiety (Plomin & Foch, 1980).

Numerous areas of the brain influence aggression (Albert & Walsh, 1984). In mice, rats, cats, dogs, and humans, lesions of the septum, the hypothalamus, and related areas (see Figure 4.15) are followed by *defensive aggression*, which is heightened aggressive responsiveness to stimuli that are not ordinarily threatening. Stimulating different parts of the hypothalamus in cats produces two different types of aggression: intense rage, in which the cats arch their backs, hiss violently, and attack anything that moves, or a slower, more gradual attack that resembles the normal predatory behavior of cats (Flynn et

Freud saw human aggression as instinctual, inevitable, and requiring some kind of expression. The best that can be hoped for, according to psychoanalytic theory, is that aggression will be released through socially acceptable activities, such as playing football or other aggressive games, "beating" an opponent in chess, or "destroying" the enemy in a video arcade game.

al., 1970). When surgical lesions are made in the same hypothalamic regions in cats, aggressive behaviors often cease altogether. In most animal studies, lesions in the amygdala also decrease aggression. Indeed, small lesions in the human amygdala have been used to reduce aggression in people suffering from hyperaggressiveness brought on by epilepsy (Albert & Walsh, 1984).

Many people who exhibit sudden and extreme forms of aggression are suffering from some type of brain disorder (Mednick, Gabrielli & Hutchings, 1984). Consider the case of Charles Whitman, a former altar boy and Eagle Scout, who was a student at the University of Texas when he began experiencing episodes of intense anxiety. He got into several fights, assaulted his wife, and in conversations with psychiatrists revealed impulses toward extremely violent behavior. Shortly thereafter, he murdered his wife and his mother, and then took a high-powered rifle to the top of a campus observation tower and for two hours shot at everyone he saw before the police killed him. An autopsy on Whitman revealed a tumor the size of a walnut in the amygdala.

Hormones also play an important role in aggression. As described in the chapter on development, male humans tend to be more aggressive than females; the same is true in nonhuman animals (Eagly & Steffen, 1986). One possibility is that aggression is related to the amount of the masculine hormone *testosterone* present in each sex (Olweus, 1986). Experiments have shown that aggressive behavior increases or decreases dramatically with the amount of testosterone in an animal's body (Frank et al., 1991), and violent criminals have been found to have abnormally high levels (Dabbs et al., 1987). Among normal men, variations in testosterone show a small but statistically significant correlation with aggressiveness (Gray, Jackson & McKinley, 1991).

In Norway, 224 men who had been convicted of aggressive sex crimes were castrated, which dramatically lowered their testosterone levels, their sex drive, and their sexually related aggressiveness. But these men still behaved aggressively in situations unrelated to sex (Bremer, 1959). This result suggests that testosterone has its greatest and most durable influence, not through day-to-day effects, but through its impact on early brain development. One natural test of this hypothesis occurred when pregnant women were given testosterone in an attempt to prevent miscarriages. Accordingly, their children were exposed to high doses of testosterone during prenatal development. Figure

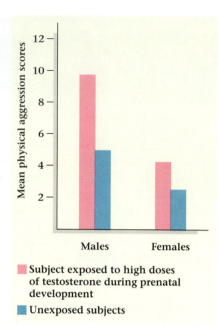

Figure 18.6
Testosterone and Aggression
A study of women who received testosterone during pregnancy to prevent miscarriage found that their children became more aggressive than the mothers' other same sex children who had not been exposed to testosterone during prenatal development. This effect held for both males and females (Reinisch, Ziemba-Davis & Sanders, 1991).

Learning to express aggression is especially easy for children living in war zones, where aggressive acts are modeled daily.

18.6 shows that these children grew up to be more aggressive than their same-sex siblings who were not exposed to testosterone during prenatal development (Reinisch, Ziemba-Davis & Sanders, 1991).

Learning and Cultural Mechanisms   Although biological factors may increase or decrease the likelihood of aggression, cross-cultural research makes it clear that learning also plays a role. Aggressive behavior is much more common in individualistic than in collectivist cultures, for example (Oatley, 1993), and major differences appear even within individualistic cultures. There are nearly five times as many homicides annually in the United States as in Scotland, the second most violent industrialized nation (DeAngelis, 1992). Cultural differences in the expression of aggression appear to stem in part from differing cultural values. For the Arapesh of New Guinea there are strong norms for cooperation and peaceful coexistence, and aggressive behavior is extremely rare (Mead, 1963). For the Utku—an Eskimo culture—aggression in any form is interpreted as a sign of social incompetence. In fact, the Utku use the same word to mean "aggressive" and "childish" (Oatley, 1993). The effects of culture on aggression can also be seen in the fact that the incidence of aggression in a given culture changes over time as cultural values change (Baron & Richardson, 1992).

People learn many aggressive responses by watching others (Baron & Richardson, 1992). The most obvious example is copycat crime, in which one person's well-publicized act of aggression (such as poisoning food or medicine in stores) is duplicated within days by other people. More generally, children learn and perform many novel aggressive responses that they see modeled by others (Bandura, 1983). Bandura's "Bobo doll" experiments, which are described in the chapter on learning, provide impressive demonstrations of the power of observational learning. Its significance is also highlighted by studies of the effects of televised violence, also discussed in Chapter 8. For example, the amount of violent content watched on television by eight-year-olds predicts aggressiveness in these children even ten years later (Centerwell, 1989; Eron, 1987). Of course, individual differences in temperament, the modeling of nonaggressive behaviors by parents, and other factors can temper the effects of violent television; not everyone who sees aggression becomes aggressive. Nevertheless, observational learning does play a significant role in the development and display of aggressive behavior (Baron & Richardson, 1992).

Immediate reward or punishment can also alter the frequency of aggressive acts. For example, people become increasingly aggressive when they are positively reinforced for aggressiveness. Figure 18.7 illustrates one example. Other research indicates that people become less aggressive if they are punished for aggressive acts (Donnerstein & Donnerstein, 1976). In short, a person's accumulated experiences—including culturally transmitted teachings—combine with the rewards and punishments operating daily within the environment to influence whether, when, and how aggressive acts occur (Baron & Richardson, 1992).

When Are People Aggressive?

In general, people are more likely to be aggressive when they are both physiologically aroused and experiencing strong emotion such as anger (Lang, 1993). People tend either to lash out at those who make them angry or to displace their anger onto defenseless targets such as children or pets. However, aggression can also be made more likely by other forms of emotional arousal, especially *frustration,* a condition that occurs when obstacles block the fulfillment of goals.

Frustration and Aggression   Suppose that a friend interrupts your studying for an exam by coming over unannounced to borrow a book. If things

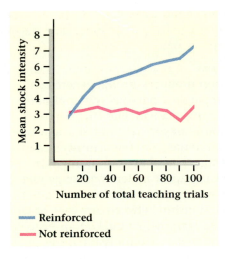

Source: Geen & Stonner, 1971.

Figure 18.7
Reinforcement and Aggression
In this experiment, people were asked to teach a person new material. They had the opportunity to administer electric shock as punishment for any errors that occurred. Some subjects were reinforced by the experimenter with praise when they delivered the shock. Other subjects were given no reinforcement for delivering shock. People who were reinforced for giving shock clearly became more aggressive over the course of the experiment.

have been going well that day and you are feeling happy and confident about the exam, you are likely to be friendly and accommodating. But what if you are feeling frustrated? What if you are behind in your preparations, and your friend's visit represents the fifth interruption in the last hour? Under these emotional circumstances, you may react aggressively, perhaps berating your startled visitor for not calling ahead (Berkowitz, 1993).

Your aggressiveness in this situation conforms to the predictions of the **frustration-aggression hypothesis**, which was developed by John Dollard and his colleagues (Dollard et al., 1939). They proposed that "the occurrence of aggressive behavior always presupposes the existence of frustration, and contrawise . . . the existence of frustration always leads to some form of aggression" (p. 1). This hypothesis generated hundreds of experiments, many of which indicated that the hypothesis was too simple and too general. Frustration does not always produce aggression (Gentry, 1970). Sometimes it produces depression and withdrawal (Seligman, 1991). In addition, not all aggression is preceded by frustration. In many of the experiments described earlier, for example, the subjects were not frustrated, but they still made aggressive responses.

After many years of research, Leonard Berkowitz modified the frustration-aggression hypothesis in two ways. First, he suggested that frustration produces not aggression but a readiness to respond aggressively (Berkowitz, 1981). Once this readiness exists, cues in the environment that are associated with aggression will often lead a frustrated person to behave aggressively. Such cues could include objects such as guns or knives, television scenes of people arguing, and the like. Neither the frustration alone nor the cues alone are sufficient to set off aggression. When combined, however, they often do. Support for this aspect of Berkowitz's theory has been quite strong (Carlson, Marcus-Newhall & Miller, 1990).

Second, Berkowitz proposed that frustration creates a readiness to respond aggressively to the degree that it produces a negative emotion (Berkowitz, 1989). For example, unexpected failure at some task tends to create a more intense negative reaction than a failure that is expected (Berkowitz, 1988). For this reason, aggression is more likely to occur following an unexpected failure than after one that was expected. A number of experiments have supported this aspect of Berkowitz's theory as well (Finman & Berkowitz, 1989).

Generalized Arousal   Imagine you have just jogged two miles. You are hot, sweaty, and out of breath, but you are not angry. Still, the physiological arousal caused by jogging increases the probability that you will become aggressive if, say, a passer-by shouts an insult (Zillmann, 1983). Why? The answer lies in a phenomenon described in the chapter on motivation and emotion: arousal from one experience may carry over to an independent situation, producing what is called *transferred excitation*. Thus, the physiological arousal caused by jogging may intensify your reaction to an insult (Sapolsky, 1984).

By itself, however, generalized arousal does not lead to aggression. It is most likely to produce aggression when the situation contains some reason, opportunity, or target for aggression (Zillmann, 1988). In one study, for example, people engaged in two minutes of vigorous exercise. Then they had the opportunity to deliver electric shock to another person. The exercise increased the level of shock delivered only if the subjects were first insulted (Zillmann, Katcher & Milavsky, 1972). Apparently, the arousal resulting from the exercise made aggression more likely; the insult "released" it. These findings are in keeping with the notion suggested by learning theorists (and by Berkowitz's revision of the frustration-aggression hypothesis) that aggression occurs not merely as a function of internal impulses *or* particular situations but as a result of the interaction of individual characteristics and particular environmental circumstances.

Thinking Critically

Does Pornography Cause Aggression?

In both men and women, sexual stimulation produces strong, generalized physiological arousal, especially in the sympathetic nervous system. Heart rate increases, adrenaline is released, breathing changes, and there is an experience of excitement and pleasure. If arousal in general can make a person more likely to be aggressive (given a reason, target, and opportunity), then the question arises whether stimuli that create sexual excitation might be dangerous. In particular, does viewing pornographic material make people more likely to be aggressive? Over the years, numerous scholars concluded that there is no evidence for an overall relationship between any type of antisocial behavior and mere exposure to pornographic material (Donnerstein, 1984). However, in 1986 the U.S. Attorney General's Commission on Pornography re-examined the question and after a year of study concluded that pornography is dangerous.

What am I being asked to believe or accept?

Specifically, the commission said that there is a causal link between viewing erotic material and several forms of antisocial behavior, including sexually related crimes.

What evidence is available to support the assertion?

The commission cited several types of evidence in support of its conclusion. First, there was the testimony of men convicted of sexually related crimes. Rapists, for example, are unusually heavy consumers of pornography, and they often say that they were aroused by erotic material immediately before committing a rape (Silbert & Pines, 1984). Similarly, child molesters often use pornography involving young children immediately before committing their crimes (Marshall, 1989).

In addition, the commission cited experimental evidence that men who are most aroused by aggressive themes in pornography are also the most potentially sexually aggressive. For example, compared with most men, convicted rapists become much more sexually aroused by scenes of rape and less aroused by scenes of mutually consenting sex (Abel, Blanchard & Barlow, 1981).

Perhaps the most compelling evidence cited by the commission, however, came from transferred-excitation studies. In a typical study of this type, subjects are told that another subject in a separate room (actually a confederate of the experimenter) will be performing a learning task and that they are to administer an electric shock every time the person makes a mistake. The subject can vary the intensity of the shock (none actually reaches the confederate), but they are told that changing the intensity will not affect the speed of learning. So the shock intensity (and presumed pain) that they choose to administer is taken as an index of aggressive behavior. Some subjects watch a sexually explicit film before beginning the learning trials. The arousal created by the film appears to transfer into aggression, especially when the arousal is experienced in a negative way. For example, after watching a film in which several men have sex with the same woman, the subjects became aroused but tended to label the experience as somewhat unpleasant. In this condition, their aggressiveness during the learning experiment was greater than after watching no film at all (Donnerstein, 1984).

Are there alternative ways of interpreting the evidence?

The commission's interpretation of evidence was quickly criticized, on several counts. First, critics argued that some of the evidence should be given little weight. In particular, how credible is the testimony of convicted sex offenders? It may reflect self-serving attempts to lay the blame for their crimes on pornography. These reports cannot establish that exposure to pornography causes aggression. Indeed, it may be that pornography partially *satisfies* sex offenders' aggressive impulses rather than creating them (Byrne & Kelley, 1989). Similarly, the fact that rapists are most aroused by rape-oriented material can show only that they prefer violence-oriented pornography, not that such materials created their impulse to rape.

What about the evidence from transferred-excitation studies? To interpret these studies, you need to know that the pornography that led to increased aggression contained violence as well as sex; the sexual activity depicted was painful for or unwanted by the woman. Thus, the subsequent increase in aggression could have been due either to transfer of sexual arousal or to the effects of observing violent behavior.

In fact, several careful experiments have found that even highly arousing sexual themes do not, in and of themselves, produce aggression. When men in transferred-excitation studies experience *pleasant* arousal by viewing a film depicting nudity or joyous, mutually consenting sexual activity, their subsequent aggression is actually less than when they viewed no film or a neutral film (Donnerstein, Linz & Penrod, 1987). In short, the transferred-excitation studies might be interpreted as demonstrating not that sexually arousing material causes aggression but that portrayals of violence influence aggressiveness.

What additional evidence would help to evaluate the alternatives?

Two types of evidence are needed to understand more clearly the effects of pornography on aggression. First, since pornography can include sexual acts, aggressive acts, or both, the effects of each of these components must be more carefully examined (Hall & Hirschman, 1991). Second, factors affecting males' reactions to pornography, particularly pornography that involves violence, must be more clearly understood (Malamuth et al., 1991). Work has already begun on each of these fronts.

Aggressive themes—whether specifically paired with sexual activity or not—do appear to increase subsequent aggression (Linz, Donnerstein & Penrod, 1988). Research has focused on *aggressive pornography,* which contains sexual themes but also scenes of violence against women (Check & Guloien, 1989). In laboratory experiments, males often administer larger amounts of shock to females after viewing aggressive pornographic films as compared to neutral films. There is no parallel increase in aggression against other males, indicating that the films create not a generalized increase in aggression but an increase in aggressiveness directed toward women (Zillmann & Weaver, 1989). Similarly, viewing aggressive pornography that depicts the *rape myth*—in which the victim of sexual violence appears to be aroused by the aggression—usually leads males to become less sympathetic toward the rape victim and more tolerant of aggressive acts toward women (Linz & Donnerstein, 1989). Sexually explicit films that contain no violence have no effects on attitudes toward rape (Linz, Donnerstein & Penrod, 1988).

In one study, 35 percent of all college men reported having been exposed to aggressive pornography within the past twelve months (Demare, Briere & Lips, 1988), and the figure may be even higher in the general population. Are all these men equally likely to become rapists? The evidence available so far suggests that the answer is no. Whether aggressive pornography alters men's behavior and attitudes toward women depends to some extent on the men. For example, compared to most men, convicted rapists report a much greater need to dominate and control women, and they show high levels of generalized anger toward women (Marshall, 1989). The men who appear most prone to acting out the scenes of violence against women that they see in aggressive pornography appear to be those who hold positive attitudes toward the domination of women and feel anger toward women in general (Malamuth, 1988).

What conclusions are most reasonable?

The attorney general's commission seemed to ignore numerous studies showing that the relationship between sexual arousal and aggression is neither consistent nor simple (Kelley et al., 1989). Analysis of this relationship reveals the importance of distinguishing between pornography in general and aggressive pornography in particular. The best evidence suggests that portrayals of violence—including aggressive pornography—affect attitudes toward aggression, and that they may make sexual violence more likely in some viewers (Wood, Wong & Chachere, 1991).

In general, however, the evidence offers no mandate for associating sexual arousal created by nonaggressive pornography with aggressive behavior. Indeed, for most people, sexual arousal and aggression remain quite separate. Even when the two are linked in particular people, there is evidence that the association is learned and can sometimes be changed. In one study, for example, sexually aggressive males underwent therapy in which they masturbated while viewing films of nonviolent, mutually enjoyable intercourse. They became sexually responsive to such scenes and less sexually responsive to depictions of violence (Abel, Blanchard & Becker, 1976). The use of nonaggressive erotic materials has also become an effective part of other, similar therapies (Kelley et al., 1989). ■

Figure 18.8
Effects of Temperature on Aggression
Research on police reports has revealed that rapes, assaults, family disturbances, and violent uprisings such as street riots are most likely to occur during the hottest days of the year.

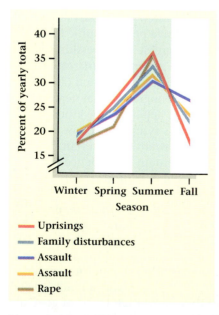

Source: Anderson, 1989.

Environmental Influences on Aggression   The link between physiological arousal and the likelihood of aggressive behavior points to another possibility—namely, that stressful environmental conditions can create enough arousal to make aggressive behavior more likely (Bell, 1992). This issue is one of the research topics of **environmental psychology**, the study of the relationship between people's physical environment and their behavior (Paulus & Nagar, 1989). One particularly important aspect of the environment is the weather. High temperatures, for example, are a source of stress; as Figure 18.8 indicates, aggression and violence are most likely to occur during the hottest days of summer (Anderson, 1989).

Air pollution and noise—usually defined as any unwanted sound (Kryter, 1970)—are also sources of stress, and they, too, can influence whether a person displays aggression (Holahan, 1986). For example, people tend to become more aggressive when breathing air that contains ethyl mercapton, a mildly unpleasant-smelling pollutant common in urban areas (Rotton et al., 1979). A study conducted in Dayton, Ohio, found that the frequency of aggressive family disturbances increased along with the ozone level in the air (Rotton & Frey, 1985). And in laboratory studies, nonsmokers are more likely to become aggressive when breathing smoke-filled rather than clear air (Zillmann, Baron & Tamborini, 1981). Noise also tends to make people more likely to display aggression, especially if the noise is unpredictable and irregular (Ward, 1974).

Living arrangements also influence aggressiveness. Compared with the tenants in high-rise apartment buildings, those in buildings with fewer floors are less likely to behave aggressively (Fisher, Bell & Baum, 1984). This difference appears to be due in part to how people feel when they are crowded. Crowding tends to create physiological arousal and to make people tense, uncomfortable, and more likely to report negative feelings (Epstein, Woolfolk & Lehrer, 1981). This arousal and tension can influence people to like one another less and to be more aggressive. One study of juvenile delinquents found that the number of behavior problems they displayed (including aggressiveness) was directly related to how crowded their living conditions had become (Ray et al., 1982).

Studies of prisons have also found that as crowding increases, so does the incidence of overt aggression (Paulus, 1988). One result of this research is that psychologists are working with architects to develop settings that are psychologically comfortable. Because the architectural layout of prisons affects the physical health of the inmates (Schaeffer et al., 1988) as well as the incidence of violent aggression, a psychologically comfortable facility—although it might cost more to build—may speed rehabilitation and reduce the time and money needed to contend with aggressiveness, uncooperativeness, and damage stemming from violence (Wener, Frazier & Farbstein, 1987).

Altruism and Helping Behavior

On a winter day several years ago, an airliner crashed into the ice-filled Potomac River in Washington, D.C. Many of the survivors were thrown, injured or unconscious, into the water and were in danger of drowning or freezing to death. A bystander named Lenny Skutnik dove into the river and helped several people to shore before exhaustion and the frigid temperatures nearly killed him. Skutnik acted as he did, not for money or any other material benefit, but simply to help other human beings.

Skutnik's actions provide a dramatic example of a common situation: people helping one another by doing everything from picking up dropped packages to donating kidneys. **Helping behavior** is defined as any act that is intended to benefit another person. Closely related to it is **altruism**, an unselfish concern for another's welfare (Batson, 1987). In the following sections we examine some of the reasons for altruism and helping, along with some of the conditions in which people are most likely to help others.

Why Do People Help?

The tendency to help others begins early. Young children often begin to help others as a form of self-punishment (Kenrick, 1989). They try to "make up" for a bad deed by doing a good deed. As they grow older, children use helping behavior to gain social approval, and their efforts at helping become more elaborate (Zahn-Waxler, Iannotti & Chapman, 1982). Often they follow examples set by people around them; their helping behaviors are shaped by the norms established by their families and the broader culture. Further, children are praised and given other rewards for helpfulness, but scolded for selfishness. Eventually children come to believe that being helpful is good and that they are good when they are helpful.

By the late teens, people often help others even when no one is watching and no one will know that they did so (Cialdini, Baumann & Kendrick, 1981). Why? There are three major theories of why people help even when they cannot expect others to reward them for doing so.

According to the **negative state relief model**, helping aids in eliminating negative moods and unpleasant feelings (Cialdini & Fultz, 1990). Indeed, there is evidence that people in a bad mood are more likely than those in a neutral mood to help others (Carlson & Miller, 1987), and people usually report feeling much better after having helped someone (Millar, Millar & Tesser, 1988). It appears that people learn to reward themselves after acts of good will by saying to themselves something like "I'm a good person for having done that." According to the negative state relief model, then, people help for essentially selfish reasons: to eliminate their own unpleasant emotional state or to make themselves feel good.

Even before their second birthday, some children begin to offer help to those who are hurt or crying by snuggling, patting, or offering food or even their own teddy bears.

However, some research on helping is not explained by the negative state relief model. For one thing, negative moods do not always lead to helping (Miller & Carlson, 1990); feeling depressed, for example, often leads to withdrawal. And people in a positive mood are often more likely to help than those in a negative mood (Cunningham et al., 1990). There appear to be two reasons for this. First, people in a positive mood are motivated to maintain their pleasant mood state (Clore & Schwarz, 1994), and rejecting a plea for help might jeopardize that state. Second, people in a positive mood feel unusually confident and capable of producing social good (Cunningham et al., 1990).

The second major theory of helping, the **empathy-altruism model**, holds that unselfish helping can occur as a result of empathy with another person (Batson et al., 1989). As mentioned in the chapter on treatment, *empathy* involves understanding or experiencing another person's emotional state (Dovidio, Allen & Schroeder, 1990). People are much more likely to help when they empathize with the other person. In fact, experiments have shown that people will help others even when their own personal distress is prolonged or increased (Eisenberg, 1991). People are most likely to help when the helpful behavior is relatively easy and painless, but several studies suggest that truly unselfish forms of altruism do exist, even when the cost is high (Batson, 1990). It appears that although people sometimes help others in order to reduce their own unpleasant emotional state, empathizing with another person can also lead to unselfish helping.

The third major theory of helping comes from sociobiology (Simon, 1990). It might seem that helping others at the risk of your own welfare would not be adaptive behavior, and that the genes of individuals who help others would have long ago disappeared. But people, like other animal species, do help one another, often at great personal risk; some even die protecting their family or home (Ridley & Dawkins, 1981). One sociobiological hypothesis holds that altruistic behavior survives in a species because it protects an individual's *genes* even when it endangers the individual. By helping or even dying for a cousin, a sibling, or, most of all, one's own child, the person increases the likelihood that at least some of his or her genetic characteristics will be passed on to the next generation through the beneficiary's future reproduction (Knauft, 1989). Another proposal holds that people help because, in the long run, they are helping themselves (Caporael et al., 1989). Although there may be an immediate personal cost for helping others, doing so perpetuates a culture in which helping is the norm (Simon, 1990). This ensures that we ourselves will obtain help when we need it.

Although sociobiology may predict the behavior of a species or a group, it does not appear to be very good at predicting the behavior of specific individuals (Tooby & Cosmides, 1989). Any behavior—including helping—has many causes and can be explained at many levels. To say there is a genetic contribution is part of the story, but it is not the whole story. Ultimately, any decision to help is based on a recognition that the other person needs help, on a weighing of the relative costs and benefits, on a judgment of whether one is capable of providing help, and so on. It is these more proximate causes that sociobiology has yet to address (Rushton, 1988).

When Are People Most Likely to Help?

Deeply rooted and well learned as they are, human altruism and helping behaviors are neither automatic nor invariable. This fact was dramatically demonstrated in New York City in 1964, when a woman named Kitty Genovese was repeatedly attacked and ultimately killed by a man with a knife, in full view and hearing of dozens of her neighbors. The tragic episode took more than thirty minutes to unfold, but no one physically intervened, and no one called the police until it was too late.

Public dismay and disbelief followed. Psychologists wondered whether something about the situation that night had deterred people from helping. Numerous studies of helping behavior followed; many of them led to important insights about the characteristics of situations that promote or inhibit helping. Among the most important of these characteristics are the clarity of the need for help, the attractiveness of the person in need, the familiarity of the situation, and the number of people available to help (Baron & Byrne, 1991).

Is the Need Recognized? The clarity of someone's need for help has a major impact on whether others provide help (Clark & Word, 1974). In one study, undergraduate students waiting alone in a campus building observed what appeared to be an accident involving a window washer. The man screamed as he and his ladder fell to the ground; then he began to clutch his ankle and groan in pain. All of the students looked out of the window to see what had happened, but only 29 percent of them did anything to help. Other students experienced the same situation, with one important difference: the man said he was hurt and needed help. In this case, more than 80 percent of the subjects came to his aid (Yakimovich & Saltz, 1971). Apparently, this one additional cue eliminated any ambiguity in the situation and led the vast majority of people to offer their help. In a similar experiment, 100 percent of the observers responded to a direct request for help (Clark & Word, 1972).

The Attractiveness of the Person in Need People are much more likely to help those they find attractive or likable. In one study, people with a large birthmark were less likely to receive help than those without such a mark (Piliavin, Piliavin & Rodin, 1975). Similarly, stranded motorists are more likely to receive help if they are dressed neatly than if their clothes are dirty and their hair is messy (Graf & Riddell, 1972; Morgan, 1973). Males are also more likely to help female rather than male motorists stranded by car trouble (West et al., 1975), and they are more likely to assist physically attractive rather than unattractive females (West & Brown, 1975).

Familiarity with the Surroundings The probability that people will offer help also increases if they are in a familiar situation. This relationship was demonstrated in an experiment that set up an apparent emergency in a New York City subway station (where most of the observers were commuters who had come to the station many times) and in New York's LaGuardia Airport (where many of the travelers had never been before). A man with a bandaged leg and crutches hobbled along until he came upon a person sitting alone. Then he tripped, fell to the ground, and grasped his knee as if in pain (Latané & Darley, 1970). More than twice as many people helped in the subway station than in the airport. Further, habitual subway users were much more likely to help than those who used the subway infrequently.

The Presence of Others The tendency to help is strongly influenced by the number of other people present. Somewhat surprisingly, however, the presence of others *inhibits* helping behavior (Miller & McFarland, 1987). This phenomenon was true in the Genovese case, and it has been demonstrated time and time again in everyday life, as well as in controlled experiments (Latané & Darley, 1968).

One explanation for this inhibiting effect is that each person thinks that someone else will help the victim. The tendency to deny any personal responsibility for responding when others are present is known as **diffusion of responsibility** (Mynatt & Sherman, 1975).

The degree to which the presence of other people will inhibit helping may depend on who those other people are. When they are strangers, perhaps poor communication inhibits helping. People have difficulty speaking to strangers,

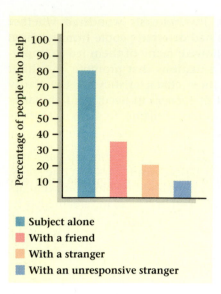

- ■ Subject alone
- ■ With a friend
- ■ With a stranger
- ■ With an unresponsive stranger

Source: Latané & Rodin, 1969.

**Figure 18.9
Helping in the Presence
of Friends or Strangers**
People are more likely to help when
they are alone than in a group. However, diffusion of responsibility is
lessened when the members of the
group know one another.

particularly in an emergency, and without speaking, it is difficult to know what the others intend to do. According to this logic, if people are with friends rather than strangers, they should be less embarrassed, more willing to discuss the problem, and thus more likely to help.

In one experiment designed to test this idea, a female experimenter led the subject to a room where he or she was to wait either alone, with a friend, with a stranger, or with a stranger who was a confederate of the experimenter (Latané & Rodin, 1969). The experimenter then stepped behind a curtain into an office. For nearly five minutes, she could be heard doing normal chores—opening and closing the drawers of her desk, shuffling papers, and so on. Then she climbed up on a chair. Soon there was a loud crash, and she screamed, "Oh, my god. . . . My foot, I . . . I can't move it. Oh, my ankle. . . . I can't get this . . . thing off me." Then the subject heard her groan and cry.

Would the subject go behind the curtain to help? Once again, as you can see in Figure 18.9, people were most likely to help if they were alone. When one other person was present, subjects were more likely both to communicate with one another and to offer help if they were friends than if they were strangers. When the stranger was the experimenter's confederate (who had been instructed not to help the woman in distress), very few subjects offered to help. Other studies have confirmed that bystanders' tendency to help increases when they are coworkers or members of the same club, or know each other in some other way (Rutkowski, Gruder & Romer, 1983).

Conclusions Whether helping and altruism are displayed depends on an interaction between the people involved and the situation. (See "In Review: Helping Behavior" for a summary of the major reasons why people help and the conditions under which they are most likely to do so.) Understanding the complexities underlying helping and altruism is of practical as well as theoretical importance. Indeed, the tendency to interpret emergency situations as emergencies and to take responsibility for doing something about them appears to be strengthened by an understanding of the social psychology of helping. For example, when confronted with a contrived emergency under circumstances unlikely to promote helping, students who had recently learned about diffusion of responsibility offered help nearly twice as often as those who had not received that information (Beaman et al., 1978). There is also a lesson here for the victims of mishaps. Especially if a number of people are present, it

In Review: Helping Behavior

Possible Reasons Why People Help	When People Are Most Likely to Help
Helping eliminates negative moods and justifies positive self-reinforcement.	The need of the other person is recognized.
Helping is triggered by empathy with those in need.	The other person is attractive.
Unselfish altruism.	The potential helper is familiar with the surrounding environment.
Our genetic heritage predisposes people to help.	Few others are present.
	The others present are friends or acquaintances of the potential helper.

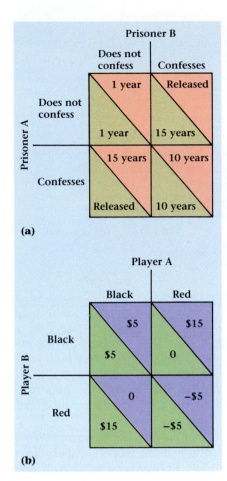

Prisoner B

	Does not confess	Confesses
Does not confess	1 year / 1 year	Released / 15 years
Confesses	15 years / 15 years	10 years / 10 years

(a)

Player A

	Black	Red
Black	$5 / $5	$15 / 0
Red	0 / $15	−$5 / −$5

(b)

Figure 18.10
The Prisoner's Dilemma
In many cases, mutual cooperation is beneficial to two parties and mutual competition is harmful to both, but one party can exploit the cooperativeness of the other. The prisoner's dilemma provides a model for such situations. These diagrams show the potential payoffs in (a) the prisoner's dilemma and in (b) the prisoner's dilemma game described in the text. Each player's payoff is a function of how both people respond.

is important not only to ask for help but to tell a specific onlooker to take some specific action (for example, "You, in the yellow shirt, please call an ambulance!").

Cooperation, Competition, and Conflict

Helping is one of the many ways in which people cooperate in order to accomplish their goals, but people also compete with others for limited resources. For example, several law students might form a study group to help one another pass the bar exam. The same students might then compete with one another for a single job opening at a prestigious law firm.

Cooperation is any type of behavior in which people work together to attain a goal. **Competition** exists whenever individuals try to attain a goal for themselves while denying that goal to others. Of course, many activities fall somewhere between cooperation and competition or combine elements of both. For example, in team sports, people cooperate with their teammates but compete with members of the opposing team. When do people choose to cooperate, and when do they choose to compete?

The Prisoner's Dilemma

Suppose two people are separated immediately after being arrested for a serious crime. The district attorney believes they are guilty but does not have the evidence to convict them. Each prisoner can either confess or not. If they both refuse to confess, they will each be convicted of a minor offense and will be jailed for just one year. If they both confess, the district attorney will recommend a ten-year sentence. However, if one prisoner remains silent and one confesses, the district attorney will allow the confessing prisoner to go free, while the other will serve the maximum fifteen-year sentence.

Each prisoner faces a dilemma. Figure 18.10(a) outlines the possible outcomes. Obviously, the strategy that will guarantee the best *mutual* outcome—short sentences for both prisoners—is cooperation: both should remain silent. But the prisoner who remains silent runs the risk of receiving a very long sentence if the other prisoner confesses, and the prisoner who talks has the chance of gaining individually if the other prisoner does not talk. Thus, each prisoner has an incentive to compete for freedom by confessing. But if they *both* compete and confess, each will end up going to jail for longer than if nothing was said.

By setting up analogous situations in the laboratory, psychologists create what is called a **prisoner's dilemma game** (Schopler et al., 1991). In a typical example, two people sit before separate control panels. Each subject has a red button and a black button, one of which is to be pushed on each of many trials. If, on a given trial, both subjects press their black buttons, each wins five dollars. If both press the red button, each loses five dollars. However, if player A presses the red button and player B presses the black button, A will win fifteen dollars and B will win nothing. Thus, pressing the black button is a cooperative response, allowing both players to gain; pressing the red button is a competitive response.

Figure 18.10(b) shows the possible outcomes for each trial. Over the course of the experiment, the combined winnings of the players are greatest if each presses the black button—that is, if they cooperate. By pressing the black button, however, one player becomes open to exploitation, because on any trial the other can take all the winnings and deny that person any gain by pressing the red button. Indeed, each player stands to benefit the most individually by pressing the red button occasionally.

Competition and cooperation are deeply interwoven components of human behavior. Each of these farmers is competing with others for maximum yields and profits, but when an accident or illness incapacitates one grower, neighbors usually pitch in to harvest the crop.

What happens when people play the game? Overall, there is a strong tendency for people to exploit each other (Rosenbaum, 1980). People tend to respond competitively (Komorita, Sweeney & Kravitz, 1980) and find it difficult to resist the competitive choice on any given trial. This choice wins them more money on that trial, but in the long run they gain less than they would have gained through cooperation.

The prisoner's dilemma game parallels numerous real-life dilemmas. When competing companies establish advertising budgets or when competing nations plan military budgets, each side could save enormous sums if both sides would cut their spending in half. But neither side is certain that the other will in fact cooperate. Fearing that the other side will instead spend enough to pull ahead, they continue to compete. This cycle dominated political life for nearly fifty years of Cold War between the United States and the former Soviet Union.

If acting competitively leads to smaller rewards in the long run, why do people persist in being competitive? There seem to be two reasons (Komorita, 1984). First, winning more than an opponent seems to be rewarding in itself. In the prisoner's dilemma game, many people want to outscore an opponent even if the result is that they win less money overall. Second, and more important, once several competitive responses are made, the competition seems to feed on itself (Insko et al., 1990). Each person becomes distrustful of the other, and cooperation becomes increasingly difficult. The more competitive one person acts, the more competitive the other becomes (Axelrod, 1984).

Fostering Cooperation

Is there any way to overcome the strong tendency to act competitively? Communication can make a difference (Bornstein et al., 1989). Usually, experimenters do not permit communication between the players in the prisoner's dilemma game. But in one study, the more visual and auditory communication was possible, the more cooperation occurred (Wichman, 1970). In another study, cooperation increased when one player communicated an intent to cooperate and then immediately followed it up with a cooperative response (Brickman, Becker & Castle, 1979).

Unfortunately, not all communication increases cooperation, just as not all contact between ethnic groups reduces prejudice. If the communication takes the form of a threat, people apparently interpret the threat itself as a competitive response and are likely to respond competitively (van de Kragt et al.,

1986). Furthermore, the communication must be relevant. In one study, co-operation increased only when people spoke openly about the game and how they would be rewarded for various responses. Praising each other for past cooperation was most beneficial (Orbell, van de Kragt & Dawes, 1988).

People can also communicate implicitly, through the strategy they use. We have already noted that being competitive makes the other person less coop-erative. It is possible to break this circle by adopting the *reformed sinner strat-egy:* respond very competitively at first but then consistently give a cooperative response. Once the cooperative responses begin and are recognized as consis-tent, the other person usually reciprocates by cooperating (Axelrod, 1984).

Now imagine that one player consistently acts in a cooperative fashion no matter how the other person responds. This consistent cooperation has a pow-erful effect, especially if it occurs early in the game, before competitiveness has surfaced (Gruder & Duslak, 1973). The other person usually adopts the same strategy and begins cooperating as well. Sometimes, however, people view consistent cooperativeness as an invitation to take advantage of the other player (Hamner & Yukl, 1977). If a player is very competitive or doubts the cooperative player's motives, a cooperative strategy may lead to exploitation (Cotterell, Eisenberger & Spelcher, 1992).

Of all possible strategies, the most effective for producing long-term coop-eration is to use basic learning principles and play *tit-for-tat,* rewarding coop-erative responses with cooperation and punishing exploitation by generating exploitative strategies of one's own. Cooperating after a cooperative response and competing after a competitive response produces a high degree of coop-eration over time (Komorita, Parks & Hulbert, 1992). Apparently, the players learn that the only way to come out ahead is to cooperate.

Interpersonal Conflict

The prisoner's dilemma represents a situation in which cooperative behavior ultimately leads to a greater payoff for each individual. But in situations called *zero-sum games,* one person can win only at the other's expense. In these situ-ations, because the rewards are finite, when one person wins more, there are fewer resources left for the other person. Election campaigns, lawsuits over division of a deceased relative's estate, and competition among children for a coveted toy are all examples of zero-sum games. These situations lead to **inter-personal conflict,** a process of social dispute in which one person believes that another stands in the way of something of value.

Causes of Conflict   There are four major causes of interpersonal conflict (Baron & Byrne, 1991). One is competition for scarce resources. If a business has only five offices with windows, for example, employees will compete for them. Some managers report spending as much as 20 percent of their time dealing with interpersonal conflicts based on such competition (Thomas & Schmidt, 1976).

A second major cause of interpersonal conflict is revenge. The reciprocity norm discussed earlier applies not only to positive acts such as sending greet-ing cards but also to negative actions. Some people who feel exploited or de-prived or otherwise aggrieved spend months or even years plotting ways of getting back at those they hold responsible (Baron & Richardson, 1992).

Interpersonal conflict may also arise because people attribute unfriendly motives to others. If people attribute a compliment to an attempt to patronize them or if they explain a failure to notice them as a deliberate snub, they may become angry enough to confront the offending person (Baron, 1988). Some-times these attributions are accurate, but often conflict results from the attri-butional errors discussed in the chapter on social cognition, especially the fun-

Revenge against organizations by employees who feel wronged can re-sult in theft, disclosure of company secrets, and other troublesome acts (Wall Street Journal, 1992). In ex-treme cases, fired employees have returned to murder the supervisors they blame for perceived injustices against them.

damental attribution error. It is easy, for example, to attribute a coworker's silence to an internal cause such as resentment toward you when it might actually reflect the person's preoccupation with a sick relative or some other external event.

Attributional errors are related to a final source of interpersonal conflict: faulty communication. A comment intended as a compliment is sometimes interpreted as a snide remark; constructive criticism is sometimes perceived as a personal attack. Such miscommunication may start a cycle of increasingly provocative actions, in which each person believes the other is being aggressive and unfair (Baumeister, Stillwell & Wotman, 1991).

Managing Conflict   Interpersonal conflict can damage relationships between people and impair the effectiveness of organizations, but it can also lead to beneficial changes. Industrial-organizational psychologists have found that it is much better to manage conflict effectively than to try to eliminate it.

The most common way of managing organizational conflict is *bargaining.* Each side—labor and management, for example—produces a series of offers and counteroffers until a solution that is acceptable to both emerges. At its best, bargaining can produce a win-win situation in which each side receives what is most important and gives up what is less important. Even when this ideal is not possible, however, the bargaining process helps each side to better understand the other side and to appreciate compromise (Thompson, 1990).

If bargaining fails, *third-party interventions* are often useful. Like a therapist working with a couple, an outside mediator can often help the two sides to focus on important issues, defuse emotions, clarify positions and proposals, and make suggestions that allow each side to compromise without losing face (Carnevale & Pruitt, 1992).

Other techniques for managing conflict involve the *introduction of superordinate goals.* Suppose a manager is planning to select one person in a department for a promotion. To alleviate the resulting conflict, the manager might establish a bonus pool that all workers will share if they increase productivity by a specified amount. With this incentive, increased productivity should become a superordinate goal for all of the workers. Such goals can focus everyone's attention on what they have in common and strengthen bonds within the group (Pruitt et al., 1991).

In short, although interpersonal conflict can be very harmful if left unchecked, it can also be managed in a way that benefits the group. Much as psychotherapy can help people resolve personal conflict in a way that leads to growth, interpersonal conflict within an organization can be handled in a way that leads to innovations, increased loyalty and motivation, and other valuable changes.

Group Processes

In the past few years United States government officials decided to send U.S. troops to Somalia and the Persian Gulf, leaders in the United Nations decided to place peacekeeping forces in several African and Eastern European trouble spots, debates raged among politicians in Canada, Mexico, and the United States about a new trade agreement, and many corporations decided to reorganize. In the chapter on thought and language we described some of the factors—such as group size, the status of various members, and the order in which options are considered—that influence the nature and quality of decisions made by groups like these. Here, we consider some of the social psychological processes that often occur in groups to alter the behavior of their members and the quality of their collective efforts.

Group Leadership

A good leader can greatly aid a group in pursuing its tasks, and a poor one can impede a group's functioning. What makes a good leader? Marvin Shaw (1981) reviewed thirty years of research on the personality of leaders and suggested that only three generalizations can be made. First, leaders tend to score very high on whatever skills are crucial to the group. Often they are intelligent, creative, and have good verbal skills. Second, leaders tend to have good social skills. They may have the ability to make others feel important, listened to, and cared for; they certainly can make others like them. Finally, leaders tend to be ambitious. They show initiative and self-confidence, and they enjoy being in a position of leadership.

Shaw also discovered that having these traits is not sufficient to ensure that a person will lead well. People who are effective leaders in one situation may not be effective in another (Hollander, 1985). It appears that there is no single type of good leader. Instead, good leadership depends on a person's traits, on the situation, and on the person's style of handling it.

Two main styles of leadership have been identified. The first style is **task-oriented** (Shaw, 1981). These leaders provide very close supervision, lead by giving directives, and generally discourage group discussion. Their style may not endear them to group members. Other leaders tend to adopt a **socio-emotional** style. They provide loose supervision, ask for members' ideas, and are generally concerned with subordinates' feelings (Shaw, 1981). They are usually well liked by the group, even when they must reprimand someone (Boyatzis, 1982).

The "best" leaders seem to be those whose style matches the circumstances and demands of the group's task (Sorrentino & Field, 1986). Task-oriented leaders are most effective when the group is working under time pressure, when the task is unstructured, and when circumstances make it unclear as to what needs to be done first and how the duties should be divided. People stranded in an elevator in a burning building, for example, need a task-oriented leader. On the other hand, socioemotional leaders are most effective when the task is structured and there are no severe time limitations (Chemers, 1987). These people would be particularly effective, for example, in managing an office in which the workers know their jobs very well.

Studies of leadership in Western cultures have revealed some interesting gender differences. In general, women tend to be more democratic leaders than men (Eagly & Johnson, 1990). In unstructured groups, men tend to emerge as leaders when the group is task-oriented; women tend to become leaders when socioemotional factors are most important. One interpretation of these observations is that the gender-role learning processes described in

Linkages: Is there a set of personality traits that makes a person a good leader? (a link to Personality)

Today, management training programs are designed to help leaders become more aware of leader-situation interactions (Ancona, 1987), and also to alert women and other minorities to the unique pressures they are likely to face (Morrison & Von Glinow, 1990). In many corporations, high-level executives are trained to select lower-level leaders whose style matches the situation in which they will be operating (Leary et al., 1986). Research suggests that these programs can help leaders perform more effectively (Organ & Bateman, 1991).

Chapter 3 lead males to "specialize" in behaviors that are task-oriented while females tend to "specialize" in behaviors that create and maintain social harmony (Eagly & Karav, 1991). However, studies have found that while women and men are evaluated equally favorably when they adopt a socioemotional style, women are evaluated less favorably than men when they act as task-oriented leaders (Eagly, Makhijani & Klonsky, 1992). Furthermore, the difference occurs even when the male and female leaders' behaviors are identical! Thus there appears to be a bias against women who behave in stereotypically male, task-oriented ways. This bias is particularly strong in the judgments made by male members of the group (Eagly, Makhijani & Klonsky, 1992).

Groupthink

Especially in small, close-knit groups, decisions may be distorted by **groupthink,** a process that renders group members unable to evaluate new options and decisions realistically (Janis, 1985). The decision of NASA to launch the space shuttle *Challenger* in 1986 appears to have been an example of groupthink. Although several engineers from outside of NASA expressed serious reservations about the design of the rocket and the wisdom of blasting off when temperatures were in the thirties, the small group responsible for launch control ignored their warnings. In fact, the *Challenger* exploded seventy-three seconds after liftoff, killing all aboard.

Groupthink is particularly likely when three conditions exist (Janis, 1985): (1) the group is very cohesive and feels isolated from outside forces; (2) the group is experiencing intense stressors, especially time pressure (Worchel & Shackelford, 1991); and (3) the leader is not impartial. This last condition appeared to play a crucial role in President Kennedy's decision to invade Cuba at the Bay of Pigs in 1961. Before the final decision was made, several advisors were told that the president had made up his mind and that it was time to "close ranks with the president." This created enormous pressures for conformity (McCauley, 1989).

When these three conditions are met, groups tend to become very close-minded and to rationalize their decision as the only reasonable one. They dismiss other options and quickly suppress any dissenting voices. As a result, the group becomes more and more certain that its decision cannot possibly be wrong.

The development of groupthink, combined with pressure for obedience to their leader, appears to have been responsible for violent behavior against law enforcement officials by members of a religious cult near Waco, Texas, in February 1993. Cut off from the outside world, and convinced by self-styled Christ figure Vernon Howell (also known as David Koresh) that it was either "us or them," cult members shot at federal agents who were executing a search warrant for illegal weapons at the cult's "Apocalypse Ranch" compound; four agents were killed. Groupthink appeared to influence later decisions by both sides. After a fifty-one-day standoff, the FBI saw no alternative but to batter holes in the compound and pump in tear gas; in response to Koresh's orders, cult members set their buildings afire. All but nine of about eighty cult members, including twenty-five children, died in the suicidal inferno.

Though some researchers have recently questioned the prevalence and dangers of groupthink (Aldag & Fuller, 1993), many others have worked on developing techniques to help groups avoid it. One is to designate someone to play "devil's advocate," constantly challenging the group's emerging consensus and offering alternatives (Janis, 1985). Another is to encourage the expression of diverse opinions by making them anonymous. The group members might sit at separate computer terminals and type all the options that occur to them. Each option is displayed for all to see, but no one knows who suggested what. The group then discusses each option via computer mail so that, again, no one can tell who is saying what. Research on this procedure suggests that it is effective in stimulating logical debate and making people less inhibited about disagreeing with the group (O'Brien, 1991).

Social Dilemmas

Logical debate and even rational thinking may fail in the face of **social dilemmas.** These are situations—usually occurring in large community groups—in which an action that is most rewarding for each individual will, if adopted by all, become catastrophic for everyone. For instance, it might be in a factory owner's self-interest to dump toxic waste into a river; but if all factories do the same, the environment will eventually become uninhabitable for everyone. Similarly, you will be financially better off by refusing to donate to the public broadcasting system; but if everyone refuses to donate, no one will have access to its programs. The same kinds of dilemmas exist in group and international relations. For example, a country might feel more secure when it obtains nuclear warfare capabilities; but the more countries that have nuclear weapons, the more everyone's security is threatened (Kramer, 1989).

Social dilemmas reflect inherent conflicts between the interests of the individual and those of the group and between short-term and long-term interests. A number of psychological processes, including the cognitive biases discussed in Chapter 10, on thought and language, may deter efforts to alleviate these conflicts. The psychological basis of arms races, for example, is being studied intensely (Kramer, Meyerson & Davis, 1990). In Chapter 10 we described how eyewitnesses, jurors, investors, and people in general tend to be overconfident about their judgments. Politicians, too, may become overcommitted to prior decisions and therefore reassert their support for the retention of weapons even after a military threat has passed (Staw & Ross, 1989). Similarly, the tendency (discussed in Chapters 10 and 17) to interpret new data in a manner consistent with prior beliefs can keep nations trapped in old policies. Nearly any action on the part of a country that has been an enemy is likely to be seen as aggressive and potentially threatening. This tendency makes an arms race very difficult to stop (Staw & Ross, 1989).

From a psychological perspective, the key to slowing or stopping international conflict seems to lie in shifting from escalating competition to escalating cooperation. One method for doing so may be to frame decisions differently. For example, in the past, the United States and Russia each compared its own military strength to that of the other in order to determine its military needs. Reframing the decision to compare the cost of security needs to the cost of other internal needs, or to include in both countries' equations the benefits of reducing their arsenals, gives competitive considerations less weight. This reframing process appears to be highly effective in accelerating the current process of nuclear disarmament (Kramer, Meyerson & Davis, 1990).

Future Directions

The influence of other people is diverse and multifaceted. You influence others, and they influence you. People help you and hurt you, cooperate with you and compete against you. Laboratory and field research in social psychology has helped to illuminate each of these processes and will continue to do so.

One focus of this research is likely to be intercultural contact. As communication technologies make the world ever smaller, as immigration and emigration increase, and as multinational corporations expand into more and more countries, interaction among people from very different cultural backgrounds will continue to grow. As work groups become more culturally diverse, they gain mental and cultural resources (Jackson, 1991) and protection against groupthink (Adler, 1990). Compared with homogenous groups, they tend to explore many more options and think about a problem from more—and more distinct—points of view. But members of culturally diverse groups may also experience less interpersonal attraction (Triandis, Kurowski & Gelfand, 1993) and more difficulty in communicating, especially during the initial stages of interaction (Samovar & Porter, 1988). Entire concepts such as incentive plans may be foreign to some members of a culturally diverse group (Argyle, 1988). Compared with people in homogenous groups, those in heterogenous groups often experience more stress and mutual mistrust and spend less time developing group solidarity (Adler, 1990).

With problems like these in mind, social psychologists will continue to study ways to help culturally diverse groups to perform more effectively (Triandis, Kurowski & Gelfand, 1993). Already, many corporations are building on social psychological research as they develop employee training programs (Lublin, 1992). These programs now tend to emphasize the importance of learning more about the values, norms, and interaction styles of coworkers and clients from other cultures. As each group member becomes more comfortable interacting with people from diverse backgrounds, stress tends to ease, group cohesion tends to grow, and everyone's creativity tends to increase as they begin to incorporate diverse perspectives into their thinking (Triandis, Kurowski & Gelfand, 1993).

There is still a great deal to be learned. In the years ahead, social psychologists will continue to examine the role of culture and the impact of intercultural experience on human behavior and mental processes. Their research on cultural diversity will be balanced by the study of the similarities of people of every culture. Social psychologists will also continue efforts to apply their research in the service of reducing aggression, preventing world conflict, and promoting world peace (Deutsch, 1993; Lore & Schultz, 1993). As noted in the previous chapter, liking, cooperation, and mutual understanding are enhanced as people learn, through contact and other means, to perceive members of outgroups as more similar to themselves. Psychologists will be working on ways to foster this perception of similarity. In fact, psychologists from numerous countries have formed an organization called Psychologists for Social Responsibility. Its members are dedicated to studying issues such as group conflict as well as to providing workshops to find international solutions to the conflicts and social dilemmas that the people of the world must face and resolve together.

Summary and Key Terms

Social Influence

Norms establish the rules for what should and should not be done in a particular situation. Descriptive norms indicate what most other people do and thereby create pressure to do the same. Injunctive norms provide more specific information about what others approve or disapprove. *Deindividuation* is a hypothesized psychological state in which people temporarily lose their individuality in a group situation. As a result, their normal inhibitions are relaxed, and they may perform aggressive or illegal acts that they would not do otherwise. Deindividuation is most likely to occur when normal accountability cues are diminished and a person's attention is focused away from internal thoughts and toward the external environment.

Linkages: Motivation and the Presence of Others

A person's current motivational state is affected by the presence of other people. By enhancing one's most likely behavior in a situation, other people sometimes create *social facilitation,* which improves performance, and sometimes create *social interference,* which impairs it. When people work together in groups, they often exert less effort than when alone, a phenomenon termed *social loafing.*

Conformity and Compliance

People often display *conformity* and *compliance* in social situations.

The Role of Norms
People tend to follow the normative responses of others, and groups create norms when none already exist.

Why Do People Conform?
People sometimes publicly produce responses that they do not believe, but at other times the responses of others have a genuine impact on private beliefs. People conform because they want to be right, because they want to be liked, and because they are generally rewarded for doing so.

When Do People Conform?
People are most likely to conform when they have low status, the situation is ambiguous, and others in the group are unanimous in their evaluation. Also, conformity generally increases with increasing attraction to the group and with increased psychological size of the faction holding the majority view.

Inducing Compliance
Effective techniques for inducing compliance include the foot-in-the-door technique, the door-in-the-face procedure, and the low-ball approach.

Obedience

Obedience involves complying with an explicit demand, typically from an authority.

Obedience in the Laboratory
Milgram's research indicates that levels of obedience are high even when obeying an authority's commands appears to result in pain and suffering for another person. Laboratory studies of obedience make it clear, however, that people experience considerable turmoil when inflicting pain on another person.

Factors Affecting Obedience
Obedience declines as the status of the authority figure declines, as the authority figure becomes more distant, as proximity to the victim increases, and when others are observed disobeying the authority figure.

Evaluating Milgram's Studies
Milgram's studies suggested that people do not have to be sadistic or otherwise abnormal to inflict pain on another person. However, because the subjects in these studies suffered such stress, the studies have been questioned on ethical grounds. Milgram was careful to debrief his subjects and have them later interact with the confederate in a friendly fashion. After the experiment, the vast majority of the subjects felt that the experience had been worthwhile.

Aggression

Aggression is an act intended to harm another person.

Why Are People Aggressive?
Aggression can occur for many reasons. Biological factors include genetics, brain tumors, and hormonal influences. Learning is also important, however, because people learn to aggress both from watching others and from being rewarded for being aggressive. There are wide cultural differences in the incidence of aggression.

When Are People Aggressive?
A variety of emotional factors play a role in aggression. The *frustration-aggression hypothesis* suggests that frustration can lead to aggression, particularly if cues that invite or promote aggression are present. Arousal from sources completely unrelated to aggression, such as exercise, can also make aggressive responses more likely, especially if aggression is already a dominant response in that situation. There is no evidence that sexual arousal, in and of itself, produces aggression. However, exposure to aggressive pornography results in men becoming more accepting of aggressive acts toward women. Environmental factors such as high temperature, air pollution, noise, and crowding appear to increase the likelihood of aggressive behavior, especially when people are already angry. Because of this, research in *environmental psychology* is being applied to design more psychologically comfortable places to live and work.

Altruism and Helping Behavior

Human behavior is also characterized by *altruism* and *helping behavior.*

Why Do People Help?
There are three major theories of why people help others. According to the *negative state relief model,* people help for essentially selfish reasons—to make themselves feel better and to eliminate negative moods and unpleasant feelings. There is also evidence, however, that people sometimes help even when their own distress is prolonged or increased. This finding has led to the *empathy-altruism model,* which suggests that some helping is truly unselfish and altruistic. Finally, sociobiology theory suggests that humans have a genetic predisposition to help.

When Are People Most Likely to Help?
Helping behavior is most likely when the need for help is clear, when the person who needs help is attractive, when the helpers are familiar with the surroundings, and when *diffusion of responsibility* is not created by the presence of other people.

Cooperation, Competition, and Conflict

Cooperation is behavior in which people work together to attain a goal; *competition* exists when individuals try to attain a goal while denying that goal to others.

The Prisoner's Dilemma
When given a choice between cooperation and competition, people often compete with one another. This is true even when, as in the *prisoner's dilemma game,* they receive fewer rewards for competing than for cooperating.

Fostering Cooperation

Communication between competing parties generally leads to an increase in cooperation, especially if the communication is nonthreatening and relevant to the situation. One of the most effective strategies for producing long-term cooperation is playing tit-for-tat—that is, rewarding cooperative responses with cooperation and punishing exploitation by generating exploitative strategies of one's own.

Interpersonal Conflict

Interpersonal conflict begins when one person believes that another may stand between that person and something of value. Competition for scarce resources, revenge, attributing another's behavior to unfriendly motives, and faulty communication are frequent sources of interpersonal conflict. Bargaining, third-party interventions, and the introduction of superordinate goals are helpful procedures for managing conflict.

Group Processes

Group Leadership

There is no single personality type or behavioral style that always results in good leadership. *Task-oriented* leaders are most effective when the task is unstructured and the group is working under time pressure. *Socioemotional* leaders are most effective when the task is structured and there are no severe time limitations.

Groupthink

The pattern of thinking called *groupthink* is most likely to occur when a group is cohesive and feels isolated from outside forces, when it lacks a truly impartial leader, and when its decisions are made under stress.

Social Dilemmas

Social dilemmas are situations in which the option that is most rewarding for each individual will, if adopted by all, become catastrophic for everyone.

Appendix

Statistics in Psychological Research

Understanding and interpreting the results of psychological research depends on *statistical analyses,* which are methods for describing and drawing conclusions from data. Chapter 2 introduced some terms and concepts associated with *descriptive statistics*—the numbers that psychologists use to describe and present their data—and with *inferential statistics*—the mathematical procedures used to draw conclusions from data and to make inferences about what they mean. Here, we present more details about these statistical analyses that will help you to evaluate research results.

Describing Data

To illustrate our discussion, consider a hypothetical experiment on the effects of incentives on performance. The experimenter presents a simple list of mathematics problems to two groups of subjects. Each group must solve the problems within a fixed time, but for each correct answer, the low-incentive group is paid ten cents, while the high-incentive group gets one dollar. The hypothesis to be tested is the **null hypothesis,** the assertion that the independent variable manipulated by the experimenter will have no effect on the dependent variable measured by the experimenter. In this case, the null hypothesis holds that the size of the incentive (the independent variable) will not affect performance on the mathematics task (the dependent variable).

Assume that the experimenter has obtained a random sample of subjects, assigned them randomly to the two groups, and done everything possible to avoid the confounds and other research problems discussed in Chapter 2. The experiment has been run, and the psychologist now has the data: a list of the number of correct answers given by each subject in each group. Now comes the first task of statistical analysis: describing the data in a way that makes them easy to understand.

The Frequency Histogram

The simplest way to describe the data is to draw up something like Table A.1, in which all the numbers are simply listed. After examining the table, you might discern that the high-incentive group seems to have done better than the low-incentive group, but the difference is not immediately obvious. It might be even harder to see if more subjects had been involved and if the scores included three-digit numbers. A picture is worth a thousand words, so a more satisfactory way of presenting the same data is in a picturelike graphic known as a **frequency histogram** (see Figure A.1).

Table A.1
A Simple Data Set
Here are the test scores obtained by thirteen subjects performing under low-incentive conditions and thirteen subjects performing under high-incentive conditions.

Low Incentive	High Incentive
4	6
6	4
2	10
7	10
6	7
8	10
3	6
5	7
2	5
3	9
5	9
9	3
5	8

Construction of a histogram is simple. First, divide the scale for measuring the dependent variable (in this case, the number of correct solutions) into a number of categories, or "bins." The bins in our example are 1–2, 3–4, 5–6, 7–8, and 9–10. Next, sort the raw data into the appropriate bin. (For example, the score of a subject who had 5 correct answers would go into the 5–6 bin, a score of 8 would go into the 7–8 bin, and so on.) Finally, for each bin, count the number of scores in that bin and draw a bar up to the height of that number on the vertical axis of a graph. The set of bars makes up the frequency histogram.

Because we are interested in comparing the scores of two groups, there are separate histograms in Figure A.1: one for the high-incentive group and one for the low-incentive group. Now the difference between groups that was difficult to see in Table A.1 becomes clearly visible: more people in the high-incentive group obtained high scores than in the low-incentive group.

Histograms and other pictures of data are useful for visualizing and better understanding the "shape" of research data, but in order to analyze data statistically, the data making up these graphic presentations must be handled in other ways. For example, before we can tell whether two histograms are different statistically or just visually, the data they represent must be summarized using descriptive statistics.

Figure A.1
Frequency Histograms
The height of each bar of a histogram represents the number of scores falling within each range of score values. The pattern formed by these bars gives a visual image of how research results are distributed.

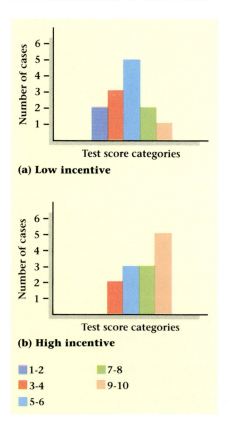

(a) Low incentive

(b) High incentive

■ 1-2   ■ 7-8
■ 3-4   ■ 9-10
■ 5-6

Descriptive Statistics

The four basic categories of descriptive statistics (1) measure the number of observations made; (2) summarize the typical value of a set of data; (3) summarize the spread, or variability, in a set of data; and (4) express the correlation between two sets of data.

N The easiest statistic to compute, abbreviated as N, simply describes the number of observations that make up the data set. In Table A.1, for example, $N = 13$ for each group, or 26 for the entire data set. Simple as it is, N plays a very important role in more sophisticated statistical analyses.

Measures of Central Tendency It is apparent in the histograms in Figure A.1 that there is a difference in the pattern of scores between the two groups. But how much of a difference? What is the typical value, the *central tendency*, that represents each group's performance? As described in Chapter 2, there are three measures that capture this typical value: the mode, the median, and the mean. Recall that the *mode* is the value or score that occurs most frequently in the data set. The *median* is the halfway point in a set of data: half the scores fall above the median, half fall below it. The *mean* is the arithmetic average. To find the mean, add the values of all the scores and divide by the number of scores.

Measures of Variability The variability, or spread, or dispersion of a set of data is often just as important as its central tendency. This variability can be quantified by measures known as the *range* and the *standard deviation*.

As described in Chapter 2, the range is simply the difference between the highest and the lowest value in a data set. For the data in Table A.1, the range for the low-incentive group is $9 - 2 = 7$; for the high-incentive group, the range is $10 - 3 = 7$.

The standard deviation, or SD, measures the average difference between each score and the mean of the data set. To see how the standard deviation is calculated, consider the data in Table A.2. The first step is to compute the mean of the set—in this case, $20/5 = 4$. Second, calculate the difference, or *deviation* (*D*), of each score from the mean by subtracting the mean from each score, as in column 2 of Table A.2. Third, find the average of these deviations. However, if you calculated the average by finding the arithmetic mean, you would sum the deviations and find that the negative deviations exactly balance the positive ones, resulting in a mean difference of 0. Obviously there is more than zero variation around the mean in the data set. So, instead of employing the arithmetic mean, we compute the standard deviation by first squaring the deviations (which removes any negative values), summing these squared deviations, dividing by *N*, and then taking the square root of the result. These simple steps are outlined in more detail in Table A.2.

The Normal Distribution Now that we have described histograms and reviewed some descriptive statistics, we will re-examine how these methods of representing research data relate to some of the concepts discussed elsewhere in the book.

In most subareas in psychology, when researchers collect many measurements and plot their data in histograms, the pattern that results often resembles that shown for the low-incentive group in Figure A.1. That is, the majority

**Table A.2
Calculating the
Standard Deviation**

The standard deviation of a set of scores reflects the average degree to which those scores differ from the mean of the set.

Raw Data	Difference from Mean = D		D^2
2	$2 - 4$	$= -2$	4
2	$2 - 4$	$= -2$	4
3	$3 - 4$	$= -1$	1
4	$4 - 4$	$= 0$	0
9	$9 - 4$	$= 5$	25
Mean = 20/5 = 4			$\Sigma D^2 = 34$

$$\text{Standard deviation} = \sqrt{\frac{\Sigma D^2}{N}} = \sqrt{\frac{34}{5}} = \sqrt{6.8} = 2.6$$

Note: Σ means "the sum of."

Figure A.2
The Normal Distribution
Many kinds of research data approximate the symmetrical shape of the
normal curve, in which most scores
fall toward the center of the range.

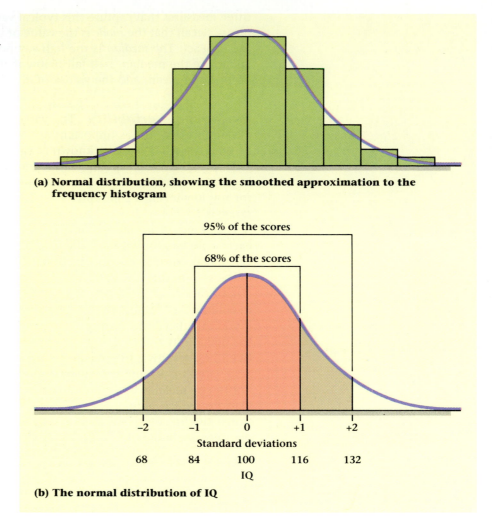

(a) Normal distribution, showing the smoothed approximation to the frequency histogram

(b) The normal distribution of IQ

of scores tend to fall in the middle of the distribution, with fewer and fewer occurring as one moves toward the extremes. As more and more data are collected, and as smaller and smaller bins are used (perhaps containing only one value each), the histograms tend to smooth out, until they resemble the bell-shaped curve known as the **normal distribution**, or *normal curve*, which is shown in Figure A.2a. When a distribution of scores follows a truly normal curve, its mean, median, and mode all have the same value. Furthermore, if the curve is normal, we can use its standard deviation to describe how any particular score stands in relation to the rest of the distribution.

IQ scores provide an example. They are distributed in a normal curve, with a mean, median, and mode of 100 and an SD of 16 (see Figure A.2b). In such a distribution, half of the population will have an IQ above 100, and half will be below 100. The shape of the true normal curve is such that 68 percent of the area under it lies within one standard deviation above and below the mean. In terms of IQ, this means that 68 percent of the population has an IQ somewhere between 84 (100 minus 16) and 116 (100 plus 16). Of the remaining 32 percent of the population, half falls more than 1 SD above the mean, and half falls more than 1 SD below the mean. Thus, 16 percent of the population has an IQ above 116, and 16 percent scores below 84.

The normal curve is also the basis for percentiles. A **percentile score** indicates the percentage of people or observations that fall below a given score in a normal distribution. In Figure A.2b, for example, the mean score (which is also the median) lies at a point below which 50 percent of the scores fall. Thus, the mean of a normal distribution is at the 50th percentile. What does this mean for IQ? If you score 1 SD above the mean, your score is at a point above which only 16 percent of the population falls. This means that 84 percent of the population (100 percent minus 16 percent) must be below that score; so this IQ score is at the 84th percentile. A score at 2 SDs above the mean is at the 97.5 percentile, because only 2.5 percent of the scores are above it in a normal distribution.

Scores may also be expressed in terms of their distance in standard deviations from the mean, producing what are called **standard scores**. A standard score of 1.5, for example, is 1.5 standard deviations from the mean.

Correlation Histograms and measures of central tendency and variability describe certain characteristics of one dependent variable at a time. However, psychologists are often concerned with describing the *relationship* between two variables. Measures of correlation are often used for this purpose. We discussed the interpretation of the *correlation coefficient* in Chapter 2; here we describe how to calculate it.

Recall that correlations are based on the relationship between two numbers associated with each subject or observation. The numbers may represent, say, a person's height and weight or the IQ of a parent and child. Table A.3 contains this kind of data for four subjects from our incentives study who took the test twice. (As you may recall from Chapter 11, the correlation between their scores would be a measure of *test-retest reliability*.) The formula for computing the Pearson product-moment correlation, or *r*, is as follows:

$$r = \frac{\Sigma(x - M_x)\,(y - M_y)}{\sqrt{\Sigma(x - M_x)^2\,\Sigma(y - M_y)^2}}$$

where:

x = each score on variable 1 (in this case, test 1)
y = each score on variable 2 (in this case, test 2)
M_x = the mean of the scores on variable 1
M_y = the mean of the scores on variable 2

The main function of the denominator in this formula is to ensure that the coefficient ranges from +1.00 to −1.00, no matter how large or small the values of the variables being correlated. The "action element" of this formula is the numerator. It is the result of multiplying the amounts by which each of

Table A.3
Calculating the Correlation Coefficient

Though it appears complex, calculation of the correlation coefficient is quite simple. The resulting *r* reflects the degree to which two sets of scores tend to be related, or to co-vary.

Subject	Test 1	Test 2	$(x - M_x)(y - M_y)$ [b]
A	1	3	$(1 - 3)(3 - 4) = (-2)(-1) = +2$
B	1	3	$(1 - 3)(3 - 4) = (-2)(-1) = +2$
C	4	5	$(4 - 3)(5 - 4) = (1)(1)\ \ \ = +1$
D	6	5	$(6 - 3)(5 - 4) = (3)(1)\ \ \ = +3$
	[a] $M_x = 3$	$M_y = 4$	$\Sigma(x - M_x)(y - M_y)\ \ \ = +8$

[c] $\Sigma(x - M_x)^2 = 4 + 4 + 1 + 9 = 18$
[d] $\Sigma(y - M_y)^2 = 1 + 1 + 1 + 1 = 4$

[e] $r = \dfrac{\Sigma(x - M_x)(y - M_y)}{\sqrt{\Sigma(x - M_x)^2\,\Sigma(y - M_y)^2}} = \dfrac{8}{\sqrt{18 \times 4}} = \dfrac{8}{\sqrt{72}} = \dfrac{8}{8.48} = +.94$

two observations (x and y) differ from the means of their respective distributions (M_x and M_y). Notice that, if the two variables "go together" (so that, if one is large, the other is also large, and if one is small, the other is also small), then either both will tend to be above the mean of their distribution or both will tend to be below the mean of their distribution. When this is the case, $x - M_x$ and $y - M_y$ will both be positive, or they will both be negative. In either case, their product will always be positive, and the correlation coefficient will also be positive. If, on the other hand, the two variables go opposite to one another, such that, when one is large, the other is small, one of them is likely to be smaller than the mean of its distribution, so that either $x - M_x$ or $y - M_y$ will have a negative sign, and the other will have a positive sign. Multiplying these differences together will always result in a product with a negative sign, and r will be negative as well.

Now compute the correlation coefficient for the data presented in Table A.3. The first step (step a in the table) is to compute the mean (M) for each variable. M_x turns out to be 3 and M_y is 4. Next, calculate the numerator by finding the differences between each x and y value and its respective mean and by multiplying them (as in step b of Table A.3). Notice that, in this example, the differences in each pair have like signs, so the correlation coefficient will be positive. The next step is to calculate the terms in the denominator; in this case, as shown in steps c and d in Table A.3, they have values of 18 and 4. Finally, place all the terms in the formula and carry out the arithmetic (step e). The result in this case is an r of +.94, a high and positive correlation suggesting that performances on repeated tests are very closely related. A subject doing well the first time is very likely to do well again; a person doing poorly at first will probably do no better the second time.

Inferential Statistics

The descriptive statistics from the incentives experiment tell the experimenter that the performances of the high- and low-incentive groups differ. But there is some uncertainty. Is the difference large enough to be important? Does it represent a stable effect or a fluke? The researcher would like to have some *measure of confidence* that the difference between groups is genuine and reflects the effect of incentive on mental tasks in the real world, rather than the effect of the particular subjects used, the phase of the moon, or other random or uncontrolled factors. One way of determining confidence would be to run the experiment again with a new group of subjects. Confidence that incentives produced differences in performance would grow stronger if the same or a larger between-group difference occurs again. In reality, psychologists rarely have the opportunity to repeat, or *replicate,* their experiments in exactly the same way three or four times. But *inferential statistics* provide a measure of how likely it was that results came about by chance. They put a precise mathematical value on the confidence or probability that rerunning the same experiment would yield similar (or even stronger) results.

Differences Between Means: The t Test   One of the most important tools of inferential statistics is the *t* test. It allows the researcher to ask how likely it is that the difference between two means occurred by chance rather than as a function of the effect of the independent variable. When the *t* test or other inferential statistic says that the probability of chance effects is small enough (usually less than 5 percent), the results are said to be *statistically significant.* Conducting a *t* test of statistical significance requires the use of three descriptive statistics.

The first component of the t test is the size of the observed effect, the difference between the means. Recall that the mean is calculated by summing a group's scores and dividing by the number of scores. In the example shown in Table A.1, the mean of the high-incentive group is 94/13, or 7.23, and the mean of the low-incentive group is 65/13, or 5. Thus, the difference between the means for the high- and low-incentive groups is $7.23 - 5 = 2.23$.

Second, the standard deviation of scores in each group must be known. If the scores in a group are quite variable, the standard deviation will be large, indicating that chance may have played a large role in producing the results. The next replication of the study might generate a very different set of group scores. If the scores in a group are all very similar, however, the standard deviation will be small, which suggests that the same result would probably occur for that group if the study were repeated. Thus, the *difference* between groups is more likely to be significant when each group's standard deviation is small. If variability is high enough that the scores of two groups overlap (in Table A.1, for example, some people in the low-incentive group actually did better on the math test than some in the high-incentive group), the mean difference, though large, may not be statistically significant.

Third, we need to take the sample size, N, into account. The larger the number of subjects or observations, the more likely it is that a given difference between means is significant. This is so because, with larger samples, random factors within a group—the unusual performance of a few people who were sleepy or anxious or hostile, for example—are more likely to be canceled out by the majority, who better represent people in general. The same effect of sample size can be seen in coin tossing. If you toss a quarter five times, you might not be too surprised if heads comes up 80 percent of the time. If you get 80 percent heads after one hundred tosses, however, you might begin to suspect that this is probably not due to chance alone and that some other effect, perhaps some bias in the coin, is significant in producing the results. (For the same reason, a relatively small correlation coefficient—between diet and grades, say—might be statistically significant if it was based on 50,000 students. As the number of subjects increases, it becomes less likely that the correlation reflects the influence of a few oddball cases.)

To summarize, as the differences between the means get larger, as N increases, and as standard deviations get smaller, t increases. This increase in t raises the researcher's confidence in the significance of the difference between means.

Now we will calculate the t statistic and show how it is interpreted. The formula for t is:

$$t = \frac{(M_1 - M_2)}{\sqrt{\dfrac{(N_1 - 1)S_1^2 + (N_2 - 1)S_2^2}{N_1 + N_2 - 2}\left(\dfrac{N_1 + N_2}{N_1 N_2}\right)}}$$

where:

M_1 = mean of group 1
M_2 = mean of group 2
N_1 = number of scores or observations for group 1
N_2 = number of scores or observations for group 2
S_1 = standard deviation of group 1 scores
S_2 = standard deviation of group 2 scores

Despite appearances, this formula is quite simple. In the numerator is the difference between the two group means; t will get larger as this difference gets larger. The denominator contains an estimate of the standard deviation of the *differences* between group means; in other words, it suggests how much the difference between group means would vary if the experiment were repeated many times. Since this estimate is in the denominator, the value of t will get smaller as the standard deviation of group differences gets larger. For the data in Table A.1,

$$t = \frac{M_1 - M_2}{\sqrt{\frac{(N_1 - 1)S_1^2 + (N_2 - 1)S_2^2)}{N_1 + N_2 - 2}\left(\frac{N_1 + N_2}{N_1 N_2}\right)}}$$

$$= \frac{7.23 - 5}{\sqrt{\frac{(12)\,(5.09) + (12)\,(4.46)}{24}\left(\frac{26}{169}\right)}}$$

$$= \frac{2.23}{\sqrt{.735}} = 2.60 \text{ with 24 df}$$

To determine what a particular t means, we must use the value of N and a special statistical table called, appropriately enough, the *t table*. We have reproduced part of the t table in Table A.4.

First, find the computed value of t in the row corresponding to the **degrees of freedom**, or **df**, associated with the experiment. In this case, degrees of freedom are simply $N_1 + N_2 - 2$ (or two less than the total sample size or number of scores). Since our experiment had 13 subjects per group, df = $13 + 13 - 2 = 24$. In the row for 24 df in Table A.4, you will find increasing values of t in each column. These columns correspond to decreasing p values, the probabilities that the difference between means occurred by chance. If an obtained t value is equal to or larger than one of the values in the t table (on the correct df line), then the difference between means that generated that t is said to be significant at the .10, .05, or .01 level of probability. Suppose, for example, that an obtained t (with 19 df) was 2.00. Looking along the 19 df row, you find that 2.00 is larger than the value in the .05 column. This allows you to say that the probability that the difference between means occurred by chance was no greater than .05, or 5 in 100. If the t had been less than the value in the .05 column, the probability of a chance result would have been greater than .05. As noted earlier, when an obtained t is not large enough to exceed t table values at the .05 level, at least, it is not usually considered statistically significant.

The t value from our experiment was 2.60, with 24 df. Because 2.60 is greater than all the values in the 24 df row, the difference between the high- and low-incentive groups would have occurred by chance less than 1 time in 100. In other words, the difference is statistically significant.

Table A.4
The *t* Table

This table allows the researcher to determine whether an obtained t value is statistically significant. If the t value is larger than the one in the appropriate row in the .05 column, the difference between means that generated that t score is usually considered statistically significant.

df	*p Value* .10 (10%)	.05 (5%)	.01 (1%)
4	1.53	2.13	3.75
9	1.38	1.83	2.82
14	1.34	1.76	2.62
19	1.33	1.73	2.54
22	1.32	1.71	2.50
24	1.32	1.71	2.49

Beyond the* t Test   Many experiments in psychology are considerably more complex than simple comparisons between two groups. They often involve three or more experimental and control groups. Some experiments also include more than one independent variable. For example, suppose we had been interested not only in the effect of incentive size on performance but also in the effect of problem difficulty. We might then create six groups whose subjects would perform easy, moderate, or difficult problems with low or high incentives.

In an experiment like this, the results might be due to the incentive, the problem difficulty, or the combined effects (known as the *interaction*) of the two. Analyzing the size and source of these effects is typically accomplished through procedures known as *analysis of variance*. The details of analysis of variance are beyond the scope of this book; for now, note that the statistical significance of each effect is influenced by differences between means, standard deviation, and sample size in much the same way as described for the *t* test.

For more detailed information about how analysis of variance and other inferential statistics are used to understand and interpret the results of psychological research, consider taking courses in research methods and statistical or quantitative methods.

Summary and Key Terms

Psychological research generates large quantities of data. Statistics are methods for describing and drawing conclusions from data.

Describing Data

Researchers often test the *null hypothesis,* which is the assertion that the independent variable will have no effect on the dependent variable.

The Frequency Histogram

Graphic representations such as *frequency histograms* provide visual descriptions of data, making the data easier to understand.

Descriptive Statistics

Numbers that summarize a set of data are called descriptive statistics. The easiest statistic to compute is N, which gives the number of observations made. A set of scores can be described by giving two other types of descriptive statistic: a measure of central tendency, which describes the typical value of a set of data, and a measure of variability. Measures of central tendency include the mean, median, and mode; variability is typically measured by the range and by the standard deviation. Sets of data often follow a *normal distribution,* which means that most scores fall in the middle of the range, with fewer and fewer scores occurring as one moves toward the extremes. In a truly normal distribution the mean, median, and mode are identical. When a set of data shows a normal distribution, a data point can be cited in terms of a *percentile score,* which indicates the percentage of people or observations falling below a certain score, and in terms of *standard scores,* which indicate the distance, in standard deviations, that a score is located from the mean. Another type of descriptive statistic, a correlation coefficient, is used to measure the correlation between sets of scores.

Inferential Statistics

Researchers use inferential statistics to quantify the probability that conducting the same experiment again would yield similar results.

Differences Between Means: The t Test

One inferential statistic, the *t test,* assesses the likelihood that differences between two means occurred by chance or reflect the effect of an independent variable. Performing a *t* test requires using the difference between the means of two sets of data, the standard deviation of scores in each set, and the number of observations or subjects. Interpreting a *t* test requires that *degrees of freedom* also be taken into account. When the *t* test indicates that the experimental results had a low probability of occurring by chance, the results are said to be statistically significant.

Beyond the t Test

When more than two groups must be compared, researchers typically rely on analysis of variance in order to interpret the results of an experiment.

Glossary

Absolute threshold The minimum amount of stimulus energy that can be detected 50 percent of the time. (See also *internal noise* and *response bias*.) (*p. 179*)

Accessory structure A structure, such as the lens of the eye, that modifies a stimulus. In some sensory systems, this modification is the first step in sensation. (*p. 131*)

Accommodation (1) The ability of the lens to change its shape and bend light rays so that objects are in focus. (*p. 142*) (2) The process of modifying schemas as an infant tries out familiar schemas on objects that do not fit them. (*p. 50*)

Acoustic code A mental representation of information as a sequence of sounds. (*p. 289*)

Action potential An impulse that travels down an axon when the neuron becomes depolarized and sodium rushes into the cell. This kind of nerve communication is "all or none": the cell either fires at full strength or does not fire at all. (*p. 97*)

Active sleep (also called *REM sleep*) A stage of sleep during which the EEG resembles that of someone who is active and awake; the heart rate, respiration, blood pressure, and other physiological patterns are also very much like those occurring during the day. At the same time, the sleeper begins rapid eye movements beneath closed lids, and muscle tone decreases to the point of paralysis. (*p. 223*)

Actor-observer bias The tendency to attribute other people's behavior to internal causes while attributing one's own behavior (especially our errors and failures) to external causes. (*p. 616*)

Acuity Visual resolution or clarity, which is greatest in the fovea because of its large concentration of cones. (*p. 144*)

Adaptation The process through which responsiveness to an unchanging stimulus decreases over time. (*p. 132*)

Adaptive reading A skill in which a reader speeds up and slows down according to the information content of the material and the level of comprehension that it requires. (*p. 208*)

Addiction Development of a physical need for a psychoactive drug. (*p. 236 and p. 557*)

Adrenal gland A part of the sympathetic nervous system that affects target organs by releasing adrenaline and noradrenalin into the bloodstream. The adrenal medulla facilitates communication between the brain and various target organs; the adrenal cortex is involved in stress reactions. The release of adrenaline is responsible for the fight-or-flight syndrome. (See also *fight-or-flight syndrome*.) (*p. 431*)

Affective disorder See *mood disorder*.

Age regression A phenomenon displayed by some hypnotized people that involves recalling and re-enacting behaviors from childhood. (*p. 230*)

Aggression An act that is intended to cause harm or damage to another person. (*p. 654*)

Agonists Drugs that bind to a receptor and mimic the effects of the neurotransmitter that normally fits that receptor. (*p. 235*)

Agoraphobia A strong fear of being alone or away from the security of home. (*p. 538*)

Alcoholism A pattern of continuous or intermittent drinking that may lead to addiction and almost always causes severe social, physical, and other problems. (*p. 558*)

Algorithm A systematic procedure that cannot fail to produce a solution to a problem. It is not usually the most efficient way to produce a solution. (See also *heuristic*.) (*p. 334*)

Altered state of consciousness (also called *alternate state of consciousness*) A condition that exists when quantitative and qualitative changes in mental processes are extensive enough that the person or objective observers notice significant differences in psychological and behavioral functioning. (*p. 221*)

Altruism An unselfish concern with another's welfare. (*p. 661*)

Amplitude The difference between the peak and the baseline of a waveform. (*p. 135*)

Amygdala A structure in the forebrain that, among other things, associates features of stimuli from two sensory modalities, such as linking the shape and feel of objects in memory. (*p. 109*)

Analgesia The absence of the sensation of pain in the presence of a normally painful stimulus. The brain appears to use serotonin and endorphins to block painful stimuli. (*p. 166*)

Anal stage The second of Freud's psychosexual stages, usually occurring during the second year of life, in which the focus of pleasure and conflict shifts from the mouth to the anus. The demand for toilet training conflicts with the child's instinctual pleasure in having bowel movements at will. (*p. 487*)

Anchoring heuristic A shortcut in the thought process that involves adding new information to existing information to reach a judgment. (*p. 334*)

Androgens Masculine hormones that circulate in the bloodstream and regulate sexual motivation in both sexes. The principal androgen is testosterone, and relatively more androgens circulate in men than in women. (See also *testosterone*.) (*p. 417*)

Anorexia nervosa An eating disorder characterized by self-starvation and dramatic weight loss. (*p. 415*)

ANS See *autonomic nervous system*.

Antagonists Drugs that bind to a receptor and prevent the normal neurotransmitter from binding. (*p. 235*)

Anterograde amnesia A loss of memory for any event that occurs after a brain injury. (See also *retrograde amnesia*.) (*p. 299*)

Antidepressant A drug that relieves depression. (*p. 597*)

Antipsychotic A drug that alleviates the symptoms of schizophrenia or other severe forms of psychological disorder. (*p. 595*)

Antisocial personality A personality disorder involving a long-term, persistent pattern of impulsive, selfish, unscrupulous, even criminal behavior. (*p. 556*)

Anxiety disorder A condition in which intense feelings of apprehension are long-standing or disruptive. (See also *generalized anxiety disorder, panic disorder, phobia,* and *obsessive-compulsive disorder.*) (*p. 537*)

Anxiolytic A drug that reduces feelings of tension and anxiety. (see also *tranquilizer.*) (*p. 598*)

Archetype According to Jung, a classic image or concept that is part of the collective unconscious. One archetype is the idea of mother; everyone is born with a kind of predisposition toward seeing and reacting to certain people as mother figures. (*p. 489*)

Arousal A general level of activation that is reflected in several physiological systems and can be measured by electrical activity in the brain, heart action, muscle tension, and the state of many other organ systems. (*p. 407*)

Arousal theory A theory of motivation stating that people are motivated to behave in ways that maintain what is, for them, an optimal level of arousal. (*p. 408*)

Artificial concept Concepts that can be clearly defined by a set of rules or properties, so that each member of the concept has all of the defining properties and no nonmember does. (See also *natural concept.*) (*p. 328*)

Artificial intelligence The field that studies how to program computers to imitate the products of human perception, understanding, and thought. (*p. 341*)

Assertiveness and social skills training A set of methods for teaching clients who are anxious or unproductive in social situations how to interact with others more comfortably and effectively. (*p. 579*)

Assimilation The process of taking in new information about objects by trying out existing schemas on objects that fit those schemas. (*p. 49*)

Association cortex Those parts of the cerebral cortex that receive information from more than one sense or combine sensory and motor information to perform such complex cognitive tasks as associating words with images or abstract thought. (*p. 114*)

Attachment A deep, affectionate, close, and enduring relationship with the single person with whom a baby has shared many experiences. (*p. 61*)

Attention The process of directing and focusing certain psychological resources, usually by voluntary control, to enhance information processing, performance, and mental experience. (*p. 204*)

Attitude A predisposition toward a particular cognitive, emotional, or behavioral reaction to an object, individual, group, situation, or action. (*p. 623*)

Attribution The process of explaining the causes of people's behavior, including one's own. (See also *attributional bias.*) (*p. 437 and p. 613*)

Attributional bias A tendency to distort one's view of behavior. (See also *fundamental attribution error.*) (*p. 616*)

Auditory nerve The bundle of axons that carries stimuli from the hair cells of the cochlea to the brain to facilitate hearing. (*p. 137*)

Authoritarian parent A firm, punitive, and unsympathetic parent who values obedience from the child and authority for himself or herself, does not encourage independence, is detached, and seldom praises the child. The result of this parenting style is often an unfriendly, distrustful, and withdrawn child. (*p. 68*)

Authoritarian personality The traits exhibited by people who view the world as a strict social hierarchy and feel they have the right to demand deference and cooperation from all those who have lower status. (*p. 631*)

Authoritative parent A parent who reasons with the child, encourages give and take, is firm but understanding, and gives the child more responsibility as he or she gets older. Children of this type of parent are usually friendly, cooperative, self-reliant, and socially responsible. (*p. 68*)

Autoimmune disorders Disorders in which the immune system attacks parts of the body it should not attack. (*p. 125*)

Autonomic nervous system (ANS) A subsystem of the peripheral nervous system that carries messages between the central nervous system and the heart, lungs, and other organs and glands in the body. The ANS regulates the activity of these organs and glands to meet varying demands placed upon the body and also provides information to the brain about that activity. (*p. 103*)

Availability heuristic A shortcut in the thought process that involves judging the frequency or probability of an event or hypothesis by how easily the hypothesis or examples of the event can be brought to mind. Thus, people tend to choose the hypothesis or alternative that is most mentally "available." (*p. 335*)

Average evoked potential A series of evoked brain potentials made in response to the same stimuli. The recording of average evoked potentials reflects the firing of large groups of neurons, within different regions of the brain, at different times during the sequence of information processing. The pattern of peaks provides information about mental chronometry that is more precise than overall reaction time. (See also *evoked potential.*) (*p. 327*)

Aversive conditioning A method for reducing unwanted behaviors by using classical conditioning principles to create a negative response to some stimulus. (*p. 581*)

Avoidance conditioning A type of learning in which an organism responds to a signal in a way that avoids exposure to an aversive stimulus. (*p. 263*)

Avoidant personality disorder Personality disorder characterized by avoidance of social situations and extreme sensitivity to criticism or rejection by others. (*p. 556*)

Axon The fiber that carries signals from the body of a neuron out to where communication occurs with other neurons. Each neuron generally has only one axon leaving the cell body, but that one axon may have many branches. (*p. 96*)

Babblings Repetitions of syllables; the first sounds infants make that resemble speech. (*p. 353*)

Basilar membrane The floor of the fluid-filled duct that runs through the cochlea. Waves passing through the fluid in the duct move the basilar membrane, and this movement deforms hair cells that touch the membrane. (See also *cochlea.*) (*p. 137*)

Behavioral approach (also called *behavioral model*) Personality theories based on the assumption that human behavior is determined mainly by what a person has learned in life, especially by the rewards and punishments a person has experienced in interacting with other people. According to this approach, the consistency of people's learning histories, not an inner personality structure, produces characteristic behavior patterns. (*p. 7*)

Behavioral medicine A broad-based movement focused on how behavior and illness are linked. Medical doctors, psychologists, dentists, nurses, health educators, social workers, and other health-related professionals work together to find ways to use behavioral science to aid in the prevention, detection, treatment, and cure of physical disease. (*p. 451*)

Behavior genetics The study of the effect of genes on behavior. (*p. 36*)

Behavior modification Treatments that use operant conditioning methods to change behavior by helping, often literally teaching, clients to act differently. (*p. 578*)

Behavior therapy Treatments that use classical conditioning principles to change behavior by helping, often literally teaching, clients to act differently. (*p. 578*)

Biased sample A group of research subjects selected from a population each of whose members did not have an equal chance of being chosen for study. (*p. 29*)

Big five The five traits found in many factor-analytic studies of personality that have been proposed as the basic components of human personality: neuroticism, extroversion, openness to experience, agreeableness, and conscientiousness. (*p. 496*)

Binocular disparity A depth cue based on the difference between the two retinal images. It exists because each eye receives a slightly different view of the world. This difference, which decreases with distance, is measured by the brain, which combines the two images to create the perception of a single image located at a particular distance. (*p. 190*)

Biofeedback training Training methods whereby people can monitor and attempt to control normally unconscious physiological processes such as blood pressure, skin conductance, and muscle tension. (*p. 477*)

Biological approach (also called *biological model*) A view in which behavior and behavior disorders are seen as the result of physical processes, especially those relating to the brain and to hormones and other chemicals. (*p. 4 and p. 526*)

Biological psychologist (also called *physiological psychologist*) A psychologist who analyzes the biological factors influencing behavior and mental processes. (*p. 3*)

Biological psychology (also called *physiological psychology*) The psychological specialty that researches the physical and chemical changes that cause and occur in response to behavior and mental processes. (*p. 93*)

Bipolar cells Cells through which a visual stimulus passes after going to the photoreceptor cells and before going to the ganglion cells. (*p. 145*)

Bipolar disorder A condition in which a person alternates between the two emotional extremes of depression and mania. (*p. 546*)

Bisexual People who engage in sexual activities with partners of both sexes. (*p. 420*)

Blind spot The point at which the axons from all of the ganglion cells converge and exit the eyeball. This exit point has no photoreceptors and is therefore insensitive to light. (*p. 152*)

Blood-brain barrier The aspect of the structure of blood vessels supplying the brain that allows only certain substances to leave the blood and interact with brain tissue. (*p. 234*)

Bottom-up processing Aspects of recognition that depend first on the information about the stimulus that comes "up" to the brain from the sensory receptors. (See also top-down processing.) (*p. 196*)

Brightness The overall intensity of all of the wavelengths that make up light. (*p. 148*)

Brown-Peterson procedure A method for determining how long unrehearsed information remains in short-term memory. It involves presenting a stimulus to individuals, preventing them from rehearsing it by having them perform a counting task, and then testing recall of the stimulus. (*p. 297*)

Bulimia nervosa An eating disorder that involves eating massive quantities of food and then eliminating the food by self-induced vomiting or strong laxatives. (*p. 416*)

Burnout A gradually intensifying pattern of physical, psychological, and behavioral dysfunctions in response to a continuous flow of stressors. (*p. 459*)

Case study A research method involving the intensive examination of some phenomenon in a particular individual, group, or situation. It is especially useful for studying complex or relatively rare phenomena. (*p. 23*)

Catastrophizing Dwelling on and overemphasizing the consequences of negative events; one of the most common cognitive stress responses. (*p. 459*)

Catatonic schizophrenia A type of schizophrenia characterized by a movement disorder in which the individual may alternate between total immobility or stupor (sometimes holding bizarre, uncomfortable poses for long periods) and wild excitement. (*p. 552*)

Central nervous system (CNS) The part of the nervous system encased in bone, including the brain and the spinal cord, whose primary function is to process information provided by the sensory systems and decide on an appropriate course of action for the motor system. (*p. 101*)

Cerebellum The part of the hindbrain whose function is to control finely coordinated movements and to store learned associations that involve movement, such as those movements required in dancing or athletics. (*p. 107*)

Cerebral cortex The outer surface of the cerebrum, consisting of two cerebral hemispheres. It is physically divided into four areas, called the frontal, parietal, occipital, and temporal lobes. It is divided functionally into the sensory cortex, the motor cortex, and the association cortex. (*p. 112*)

Cerebral hemisphere One-half, either right or left, of the round, almost spherical, outermost part of the cerebrum. (*p. 112*)

Cerebrum (also called the *telencephalon*) The largest part of the forebrain; it is divided into the right and left cerebral hemispheres and contains the striatum and the limbic system. (*p. 109*)

Chromosome A long, thin structure in every biological cell that contains genetic information in the form of more than a thousand genes strung out like a chain. (*p. 34*)

Chunk Stimuli that are perceived as one unit or a meaningful grouping of information. Most people can hold five to nine (seven plus or minus two) chunks of information in short-term memory. (*p. 295*)

Circadian rhythm A cycle, such as waking and sleeping, that repeats about once a day. (*p. 226*)

Classical conditioning A procedure in which a neutral stimulus is paired with a stimulus that elicits a reflex or other response until the neutral stimulus alone comes to elicit a similar response. (*p. 251*)

Client-centered therapy (also called *person-centered therapy*) A type of therapy in which the client decides what to talk about and when, without direction, judgment, or interpretation from the therapist. This type of treatment is characterized by three important and interrelated therapist attitudes: unconditional positive regard, empathy, and congruence. (See also *congruence, empathy,* and *unconditional positive regard.*) (*p. 575*)

Clinical psychologist A psychologist who seeks to assess, understand, and correct abnormal behavior. (*p. 4*)

Closure A Gestalt grouping principle stating that people tend to fill in missing contours to form a complete object. (*p. 185*)

CNS See *central nervous system.*

Cochlea A fluid-filled spiral structure in the ear in which auditory transduction occurs. (*p. 137*)

Coding Translation of the physical properties of a stimulus into a pattern of neural activity that specifically identifies those physical properties. (*p. 133*)

Cognitive approach A way of looking at human behavior that emphasizes research on how the brain takes in information, creates perceptions, forms and retrieves memories, processes information, and generates integrated patterns of action. (*p. 8*)

Cognitive-behavioral approach An approach to personality that sees personality as a label summarizing the unique patterns of thinking and behavior that a person learns. (*p. 510 and p. 529*)

Cognitive-behavior therapy Treatment methods that help clients change the way they think as well as the way they behave. Cognitive obstacles are brought to light, and the therapist encourages the client to try new ways of thinking. (*p. 578*)

Cognitive dissonance theory A theory that proposes that uneasiness results when people's cognitions about themselves or the world are inconsistent with one another. Dissonance motivates people to take some action to make the cognitions consistent. (*p. 625*)

Cognitive map A mental representation, or picture, of the environment. (*p. 274*)

Cognitive psychologist A psychologist whose research focus is on analysis of the mental processes underlying judgment,

decision making, problem solving, imagining, and other aspects of human thought or cognition. (*p. 3*)

Cognitive restructuring A therapy technique or process for coping with stress that involves replacing stress-provoking thoughts with more constructive thoughts in order to make stressors less threatening and disruptive. (*p. 476*)

Cognitive therapy An organized problem-solving approach in which the therapist actively collaborates with clients to help them notice how certain negative thoughts precede anxiety and depression. (*p. 583*)

Collective unconscious According to Jung, a kind of memory bank in which are stored all the images and ideas the human race has accumulated since its evolution from lower forms of life. (See also *archetype.*) (*p. 489*)

Common fate A Gestalt grouping principle stating that objects moving in the same direction and at the same speed are perceived as belonging together. (*p. 186*)

Community psychology A movement whose goal is to minimize or prevent psychological disorders through promoting changes in social systems and through community mental health programs designed to make treatment methods more accessible to the poor and others who are unserved or underserved by mental health professionals. (*p. 601*)

Competition Any type of behavior in which individuals try to attain a goal for themselves while denying that goal to others. (*p. 665*)

Complementary colors Colors that result in gray when lights of those two colors are mixed. Complementary colors are roughly opposite each other on the color circle. (*p. 150*)

Compliance Adjusting one's behavior to match that of a group because of directly expressed social influence. (*p. 642*)

Computational view An approach to perception that focuses on how perception occurs; it tries to explain how computations by the nervous system translate raw sensory stimulation into an experience of reality. (*p. 177*)

Concept A class or category of objects, events, or ideas that have common properties. (See also *artificial concept* and *natural concept.*) (*p. 328*)

Concrete operations According to Piaget, the third stage of cognitive development, during which children can learn to count, measure, add, and subtract; their thinking is no longer dominated by visual appearances. (*p. 53*)

Conditioned response (CR) In classical conditioning, the response that the conditioned stimulus elicits. (*p. 251*)

Conditioned stimulus (CS) In classical conditioning, the originally neutral stimulus that, through pairing with the unconditioned stimulus, comes to elicit a conditioned response. (*p. 251*)

Conditions of worth According to Rogers, the feelings an individual experiences when the entire person, instead of a specific behavior, is evaluated. The person may feel that his or her worth as a person depends on displaying the right attitudes, behaviors, and values. (*p. 505*)

Cones Photoreceptors in the retina that use one of three varieties of iodopsin, a color-sensitive photopigment, to distinguish colors. (See also *rods.*) (*p. 144*)

Conformity Changing one's behavior or beliefs to match

those of other group members, generally as a result of real or imagined, though unspoken, group pressure. (*p. 642*)

Confounding variable In an experiment, any factor that affects the dependent variable along with or instead of the independent variable. Confounding variables include random variables, the placebo effect, and experimenter bias. (*p. 26*)

Congruence In client-centered therapy, a consistency between the way therapists feel and the way they act toward the client; therapists' unconditional positive regard and empathy must be real, not manufactured. (*p. 576*)

Conscious level The level at which mental activities that we are aware of from moment to moment occur. (See also *preconscious level.*) (*p. 219*)

Consciousness The awareness of external stimuli and our own mental activity. (*p. 213*)

Conservation The ability to recognize that the important properties of a substance, such as number, volume, or weight, remain constant despite changes in shape, length, or position. (*p. 53*)

Constructionist view A view of perception taken by those who argue that the perceptual system uses fragments of sensory information to construct an image of reality. (See also *ecological view.*) (*p. 176*)

Context-dependent memory Memories that can be helped or hindered by similarities or differences between the context in which they are learned and that in which they are recalled. (*p. 304*)

Continuity A Gestalt grouping principle stating that sensations that appear to create a continuous form are perceived as belonging together. (*p. 185*)

Continuous reinforcement schedule In operant conditioning, a pattern in which a reinforcer is delivered every time a particular response occurs. (*p. 266*)

Control group In an experiment, the group that receives no treatment or provides some other base line against which to compare the performance or response of the experimental group. (*p. 26*)

Conventional moral reasoning Reasoning that reflects a concern about other people as well as the belief that morality consists of following rules and conventions. (*p. 78*)

Convergence (1) The receiving of information by one bipolar cell from many photoreceptors. Convergence allows bipolar cells to compare the amount of light on larger regions of the retina and increases the sensation of contrast. (*p. 145*) (2) A depth cue involving the rotation of the eyes to project the image of an object on each retina. The closer an object is, the more "cross-eyed" the viewer must become to achieve a focused image of it. (*p. 190*)

Convergent thinking The ability to apply the rules of logic and what one knows about the world in order to narrow down the number of possible solutions to a problem or perform some other complex cognitive task. (*p. 391*)

Conversion disorder A somatoform disorder in which a person appears to be, but actually is not, blind, deaf, paralyzed, insensitive to pain in various parts of the body, or even pregnant. (See also *somatoform disorder.*) (*p. 541*)

Cooperation Any type of behavior in which several people work together to attain a goal. (*p. 665*)

Cornea The curved, transparent, protective layer through which light rays enter the eye. (*p. 141*)

Corpus callosum A massive bundle of fibers that connects the right and left cerebral hemispheres and allows them to communicate with each other. Severing the corpus callosum causes difficulty in performing tasks that require information from both hemispheres, such as recognizing and naming objects. (*p. 115*)

Correlation In research, the degree to which one variable is related to another; the strength and direction of the relationship is measured by a correlation coefficient. Correlation does not guarantee causation. (*p. 24*)

Correlation coefficient A statistic, *r*, that summarizes the strength and direction of a relationship between two variables. Correlation coefficients vary from 0.00 to ±1.00. The plus or minus sign indicates the direction, positive or negative, of a relationship. An *r* of +1.00 or -1.00 indicates a perfect correlation, which means that if you know the value of one variable, you can predict with certainty the value of the other variable. (*p. 30*)

Counseling psychologist See *clinical psychologist.*

Creativity The capacity to produce original solutions or novel compositions. (*p. 390*)

Critical period An interval during which certain kinds of growth must occur if development is to proceed normally. (*p. 46*)

Critical thinking The process of assessing claims and making judgments on the basis of well-supported evidence. (*p. 19*)

Cross-sectional study A research method in which data collected simultaneously from people of different ages are compared. (*p. 395*)

Crystallized intelligence The specific knowledge gained as a result of applying fluid intelligence. It produces verbal comprehension and skill at manipulating numbers. (See also *fluid intelligence.*) (*p. 385*)

Culture The accumulation of values, rules of behavior, forms of expression, religious beliefs, occupational choices, and the like, for a group of people who share a common language and environment. (*p. 13*)

Cytokines Chemicals released by immune cells into the bloodstream, which regulate other immune processes and influence brain activity. (*p. 125*)

Dark adaptation The increasing ability to see in the dark as time passes, due to the synthesis of more photopigments by the photoreceptors. (*p. 143*)

Data Numbers that represent research findings and provide the basis for research conclusions. (*p. 30*)

Decay The gradual disappearance of the mental representation of a stimulus. (*p. 301*)

Deep structure An abstract representation of the relationships expressed in a sentence; the various underlying meanings of a given sentence. (*p. 350*)

Defense mechanism A psychological response that helps protect a person from anxiety and the other negative emotions accompanying stress; it does little or nothing to eliminate the source of stress. (*p. 486*)

Deficiency orientation According to Maslow, a preoccupation with meeting perceived needs for material things a person does not have that can lead to perceiving life as a meaningless exercise in disappointment and boredom. (*p. 504*)

Degrees of freedom   The total sample size or number of scores in a data set, less the number of experimental groups. (*p. A-8*)

Deindividuation   A hypothesized psychological state occurring in group members that results in loss of individuality and a tendency to do things not normally done when alone. (*p. 640*)

Delirium   An organic mental disorder that involves a clouded state of consciousness. The person has trouble "thinking straight," may be unable to focus on a conversation or other environmental events, and may appear confused. Symptoms may also include delusions, hallucinations, and disruption of the normal sleep-waking cycle. (*p. 527*)

Delusion   A false belief, such as those experienced by people suffering from schizophrenia or extreme depression. (*p. 545*)

Dementia   An organic mental disorder that involves a loss of intellectual functions. It may occur alone or in combination with delirium. The most common symptoms involve loss of memory-related functions. (See also *delirium*.) (*p. 526*)

Demonological model   An explanation of abnormal behavior as the work of the devil or other supernatural forces. (*p. 526*)

Dendrite   In a neuron, the fiber that receives signals from the axons of other neurons and carries that signal to the cell body. A neuron can have up to several hundred dendrites. (*p. 96*)

Deoxyribonucleic acid (DNA)   The molecular structure of a gene that provides the genetic code. Each DNA molecule consists of two strands of sugar, phosphate, and nitrogen-containing molecules twisted around each other in a double spiral. (*p. 34*)

Dependent variable   In an experiment, the factor affected by the independent variable. (*p. 25*)

Depressant   A psychoactive drug that inhibits the functioning of the central nervous system. (*p. 237*)

Depth perception   Perception of distance, one of the most important factors underlying size and shape constancy. Depth perception allows us to experience the world in three-dimensional depth, not as a two-dimensional movie. (*p. 188*)

Descriptive statistics   Numbers that summarize a set of research data. (*p. A-2*)

Developmental psychologist   A psychologist who seeks to understand, describe, and explore how behavior and mental processes change over the course of a lifetime. (*p. 4*)

Developmental psychology   The psychological specialty that documents the course of people's social, emotional, moral, and intellectual development over the life span and explores how development in different domains fits together, is affected by experience, and relates to other areas of psychology. (*p. 41*)

Diathesis-stress approach   An integrative approach to psychological disorders that recognizes that each person inher-

its certain physical predispositions that leave him or her vulnerable to problems that may or may not appear, depending on what kinds of situations that person confronts. People who must deal with particular stressors may or may not develop psychopathology, depending on their predisposition and ability to cope with those stressors. (*p. 530*)

Difference threshold   See *just-noticeable difference.*

Diffusion of responsibility   The process through which a person tends not to take personal responsibility for helping someone in trouble when others are present. (*p. 663*)

Discrimination   Differential treatment of various groups; the behavioral component of prejudice. (See also *prejudice*.) (*p. 631*)

Discriminative stimuli   Stimuli that signal whether reinforcement is available if a certain response is made. (*p. 264*)

Diseases of adaptation   Illnesses that are caused or promoted by stressors. (*p. 458*)

Disorganized schizophrenia   A rare type of schizophrenia characterized by a variety of jumbled and unrelated delusions and hallucinations. The person may display incoherent speech, strange facial grimaces, and meaningless ritual movements and may neglect personal hygiene and lose bowel and bladder control. (*p. 551*)

Dispositional approach   A personality theory based on the assumptions that (1) each person has stable, long-lasting dispositions toward displaying certain behaviors, attitudes, and emotions; (2) these dispositions are general in that they appear in diverse situations; and (3) each person has a different set of dispositions, or at least a set of dispositions that assume a unique pattern. (*p. 492*)

Dissociation theory   A theory that defines hypnosis as a condition in which people relax central control of mental processes and share some of that control with the hypnotist, who is allowed to determine what the person will experience and do. According to this theory, hypnosis is a socially agreed-upon opportunity to display one's ability to let mental functions become dissociated. (See also *role theory* and *state theory*.) (*p. 231*)

Dissociative amnesia   A psychological disorder marked by a sudden loss of memory, which results in the inability to recall one's own name, occupation, or other identifying information. (*p. 543*)

Dissociative disorder   A rare condition that involves a sudden and usually temporary disruption in a person's memory, consciousness, or identity. (*p. 543*)

Dissociative fugue   A sudden loss of memory and the assumption of a new identity in a new locale. (*p. 543*)

Divergent thinking   The ability to think along many alternative paths to generate many different solutions to a problem. (*p. 390*)

DNA   See *deoxyribonucleic acid.*

Double-blind design   A research design in which neither the experimenter nor the subjects know who is in the experimental group and who is in the control group. This design helps prevent experimenter bias (a confounding variable). (*p. 27*)

Dream   A storylike sequence of images, sensations, and perception that lasts anywhere from several seconds to many minutes and occurs mainly during REM sleep (though it may take place at other times). (*p. 228*)

Drive In drive theory, a psychological state of arousal, created by an imbalance in homeostasis that prompts an organism to take action to restore the balance and, in the process, reduce the drive. (See also *need, primary drive,* and *secondary drive.*) (*p. 406*)

Drive reduction theory A theory of motivation stating that much motivation arises from constant imbalances in homeostasis. (See also *drive* and *homeostasis.*) (*p. 406*)

Drug abuse The self-administration of drugs in ways that deviate from a culture's medical or social norms. (*p. 235*)

Dyslexia A condition in which a person who shows normal intelligence and full comprehension of spoken words has difficulty understanding written words. (*p. 209*)

Dysthymia A pattern of depression in which the person shows the sad mood, lack of interest, and loss of pleasure associated with major depressive disorder, but to a lesser degree. (See also *major depressive disorders.*) (*p. 545*)

Ecological view An approach to perception that states that humans and other species are so well adapted to their natural environment that many aspects of the world are perceived automatically and at the sensory level, without requiring higher-level analysis and inferences. (See also *constructionist.*) (*p. 176*)

ECT See *electroconvulsive therapy.*

Ego In psychodynamic theory, that part of the personality that makes compromises and mediates conflicts between and among the demands of the id, the superego, and the real world; the ego operates according to the reality principle. (See also *id* and *reality principle.*) (*p. 486*)

Elaboration likelihood model A model of attitude change suggesting that people who have the motivation and ability to carefully evaluate an argument change their attitudes by considering the argument's content (the central route), while those with less motivation or ability tend to take a peripheral route and overrely on various (often irrelevant) persuasion cues. (*p. 630*)

Elaborative rehearsal A memorization method that involves thinking about how new information relates to information already stored in long-term memory. (*p. 290*)

Electroconvulsive therapy (ECT) A brief electric shock administered to the brain, usually to reduce profound depression that does not respond to drug treatments. (*p. 593*)

Embryo The developing individual from the fourteenth day after fertilization until the third month after fertilization. (*p. 45*)

Emotion A transitory, valenced experience that is felt as happening to the self, is generated, in part, by the cognitive appraisal of a situation, and is accompanied by both learned and reflexive physical responses. (*p. 429*)

Empathy In client-centered therapy, the therapist's attempt to appreciate how the world looks from the client's point of view. Empathy requires an internal perspective, a focus on what the client might be thinking and feeling. (*p. 575*)

Empathy-altruism model A theory that suggests that people help others because of empathy with their needs. (*p. 662*)

Encoding The process of putting information into a form that the memory system can accept and use; the process of constructing mental representations of physical stimuli. (*p. 289*)

Encoding specificity principle A retrieval principle stating that the ability of a cue to aid retrieval effectively depends on the degree to which it taps into information that was encoded at the time of the original learning. (*p. 304*)

Endocrine systems Cells that form organs called glands and communicate with one another by secreting chemicals called hormones. (*p. 123*)

Endorphin One of a class of neurotransmitters that can bind to the same receptors that opiates, such as morphine and heroin, bind to and that produces the same behavioral effects of pain relief, euphoria, and, in high doses, sleep. (*p. 100*)

Environmental psychology The study of the effects of the general physical environment on people's behavior and mental processes. (*p. 660*)

Episodic memory A person's recall of a specific event that happened while he or she was present. (*p. 287*)

Escape conditioning A type of learning in which an organism learns to make a particular response in order to terminate an aversive stimulus. (*p. 263*)

Estradiol A feminine hormone; the main estrogen. (*p. 417*)

Estrogens Feminine hormones that circulate in the bloodstream of both men and women; relatively more estrogens circulate in women. One of the main estrogens is estradiol. (See also *estradiol, progesterone,* and *progestins.*) (*p. 417*)

Ethologist A scientist who studies animals in their natural environment to observe how environmental cues affect behavior. (*p. 6*)

Evoked brain potential A small, temporary change in EEG voltage that is evoked by some stimulus. One such change is the P300, a positive swing in electrical voltage that occurs about 300 milliseconds after a stimulus. It can be used to determine if a stimulus distracts a person's attention from a given task. (*p. 327*)

Evolutionary approach An approach to psychology that emphasizes the inherited, adaptive aspects of behavior and mental processes. (*p. 6*)

Excitatory postsynaptic potential (EPSP) A postsynaptic potential that depolarizes the neuronal membrane, bringing the cell closer to threshold for firing an action potential. (*p. 99*)

Expected value The total benefit to be expected if a decision, though not always correct, were repeated several times. (*p. 345*)

Experiment A situation in which the researcher manipulates one variable and then observes the effect of that manipulation on another variable, while holding all other variables constant. (*p. 25*)

Experimental group In an experiment, the group that receives the experimental treatment; its performance or response is compared with that of one or more control groups. (*p. 26*)

Experimental psychologist A psychologist who conducts experiments aimed at understanding learning, memory, perception, and other basic behavioral and mental processes. (*p. 3*)

Experimenter bias A confounding variable that occurs when an experimenter unintentionally encourages subjects to respond in a way that supports the hypothesis. (*p. 27*)

Expert system A computer program that helps people solve problems in a fairly restricted, specific area, such as the diagnosis of diseases. (*p. 342*)

Explicit memory The process through which people deliberately try to remember something. (*p. 288*)

Extinction The gradual disappearance of a conditioned response or operant behavior due to elimination either of the association between conditioned and unconditioned stimuli or of rewards for certain behaviors. (*p. 252 and p. 580*)

Factor analysis A statistical technique that involves computing correlations between large numbers of variables. Factor analysis is commonly used in the study of intelligence and intelligence tests. (*p. 385*)

Familial retardation Cases of mild retardation for which no environmental or genetic cause can be found. Most of the people in this group come from families in the lower socioeconomic classes and are more likely than those suffering from a genetic defect to have a relative who is also retarded. (*p. 394*)

Family therapy A type of treatment inspired by the psychodynamic theory that many psychological disorders are rooted in family conflicts. It involves two or more individuals from the same family, one of whose problems make him or her the initially identified client, although the family itself ultimately becomes the client. (*p. 585*)

Fear appeal A method of changing attitudes that involves instilling fear in the audience; it may produce lasting effects on the cognitive component of an attitude but does not usually have a lasting influence on behavior. (*p. 628*)

Feature detector A cell in the cortex that responds to a specific feature of an object. (*p. 154*)

Fetal alcohol syndrome A pattern of defects found in babies born to alcoholic women that includes physical malformations of the face and mental retardation. (*p. 46*)

Fetus The developing individual from the third month after conception until birth. (*p. 45*)

FI See *fixed interval schedule*.

Fiber tract Axons that travel together in bundles. They are also known as *pathways*. (p. 104)

Fight-or-flight syndrome The physical reactions initiated by the sympathetic nervous system that prepare the body to fight or to run from a threatening situation. These reactions include increased heart rate and blood pressure, rapid or irregular breathing, dilated pupils, perspiration, dry mouth, increased blood sugar, decreased gastrointestinal motility, and other changes. (See also *adrenal gland* and *sympathetic nervous system*.) (*p. 124 and p. 430*)

Figure That part of the visual field that has meaning, stands in front of the rest, and always seems to include the contours or borders that separate it from the relatively meaningless background. (See also *ground*.) (*p. 184*)

Five-factor model See *big five*.

Fixed interval (FI) schedule In operant conditioning, a type of partial reinforcement schedule that provides reinforcement for the first response that occurs after some fixed time has passed since the last reward. (*p. 266*)

Fixed ratio (FR) schedule In operant conditioning, a type of partial reinforcement schedule that provides reinforcement following a fixed number of responses. (*p. 266*)

Flooding A procedure for reducing anxiety that involves keeping a person in a feared, but harmless, situation. Once deprived of his or her normally rewarding escape pattern, the client has no reason for continued anxiety. (*p. 580*)

Fluid intelligence The basic power of reasoning and problem solving. Fluid intelligence produces induction, deduction, reasoning, and understanding of relationships between different ideas. (See also *crystallized intelligence*.) (*p. 385*)

Forebrain The most highly developed part of the brain; it is responsible for the most complex aspects of behavior and mental life. (*p. 108*)

Formal operational period According to Piaget, the fourth stage in cognitive development, usually beginning around age eleven. It is characterized by the ability to engage in hypothetical thinking, including the imagining of logical consequences and the ability to think and reason about abstract concepts. (*p. 76*)

Fovea A region in the center of the retina where cones are highly concentrated. (*p. 144*)

FR See *fixed ratio schedule*.

Free association A psychoanalytic method that requires the client to report everything that comes to mind as soon as it occurs, no matter how trivial, senseless, or embarrassing it may seem. (*p. 484 and p. 570*)

Free-floating anxiety See *generalized anxiety disorder*.

Frequency The number of complete waveforms, or cycles, that pass by a given point in space every second. For sound waves, the unit of measure is called a hertz (Hz); one hertz is one cycle per second. (*p. 135*)

Frequency histogram A graphic presentation of data that consists of a set of bars, each of which represents how frequently different values of variables occur in a data set. (*p. A-1*)

Frequency matching (also called the *volley theory*) A theory of hearing that explains how frequency is coded: the firing rate of a neuron matches the frequency of a sound wave. For example, one neuron might fire at every peak of a wave; so a 20 hertz sound could be coded by a neuron that fires twenty times per second. (*p. 139*)

Frustration-aggression hypothesis A proposition that the existence of frustration always leads to some form of aggressive behavior. (*p. 657*)

Functional analysis of behavior A method of understanding behavior (and thus the person) that involves analyzing exactly what responses occur under what conditions. This approach emphasizes the role of operant conditioning. (See also *operant conditioning*.) (*p. 510*)

Functional fixedness A tendency to think about familiar objects in familiar ways that may prevent using them in other, more creative ways. (*p. 339*)

Fundamental attribution error The tendency to be more aware of the influence of situational factors on one's own behavior than on the behavior of others. (*p. 616*)

Ganglion cells The cells in the retina that generate action potentials. They're stimulated by bipolar cells; their axons extend out of the retina and travel to the brain. (*p. 146*)

GAS See *general adaptation syndrome.*

Gate control theory A theory of pain suggesting a functional "gate" in the spinal cord that either lets pain impulses travel upward to the brain or blocks their progress. (*p. 165*)

Gender role General patterns of work, appearance, and behavior that a society associates with being male or female. (*p. 71*)

Gene The biological instructions inherited from both parents and located on the chromosomes that provide the blueprint for physical development throughout the life span. (See also *deoxyribonucleic acid, genotype,* and *phenotype.*) (*p.34*)

General adaptation syndrome (GAS) A consistent and very general pattern of responses triggered by the effort to adapt to any stressor. The syndrome consists of three stages: alarm reaction, resistance, and exhaustion. (*p. 457*)

Generalized anxiety disorder A condition that involves relatively mild but long-lasting anxiety that is not focused on any particular object or situation. (*p. 538*)

Generativity The concern of adults in their thirties with producing or generating something. (*p. 84*)

Genetics The biology of inheritance. (*p. 34*)

Genital stage The fifth and last of Freud's psychosexual stages, which begins during adolescence when the person begins to mature physically and sexual impulses begin to appear at the conscious level. The young person begins to seek out relationships through which sexual impulses can be gratified. This stage spans the rest of life. (*p. 489*)

Genotype The full set of genes, inherited from both parents, contained in twenty-three pairs of chromosomes. (*p. 36*)

Gestalt psychologists A group of psychologists who suggested, among other things, that there are six principles or properties behind the grouping of stimuli that lead the human perceptual system to "glue" raw sensations together in particular ways, organizing stimuli into a world of shapes and patterns. (See also *closure, continuity, proximity, similarity,* and *simplicity.*) (*p. 185*)

Gestalt therapy A form of treatment based on the assumption that clients' problems arise when people behave in accordance with other people's expectations rather than on the basis of their own true feelings. Gestalt therapy seeks to create conditions in which clients can become more unified, more self-aware, and more self-accepting. (*p. 577*)

g-factor A general intelligence factor that Charles Spearman postulated as accounting for positive correlations between people's scores on all sorts of mental ability tests. (*p. 385*)

Glands Organs that secrete hormones into the bloodstream. (*p. 123*)

Gradient A continuous change across the visual field. (See also *movement gradient* and *textural gradient.*) (*p. 189*)

Grammar A set of rules for combining the symbols, such as words, used in a given language. (See also *language.*) (*p. 349*)

Ground The meaningless, contourless part of the visual field; the background. (See also *figure.*) (*p. 184*)

Group polarization The tendency for groups to make decisions that are more extreme than the decision an individual group member would make. (*p. 348*)

Group therapy Psychotherapy involving five to ten individuals. Clients can be observed interacting with one another; they can feel relieved and less alone as they listen to others who have similar difficulties, which tends to raise each client's hope and expectations for improvement; and they can learn from one another. (*p. 584*)

Groupthink A pattern of thinking that, over time, renders group members unable to evaluate realistically the wisdom of various options and decisions. (*p. 670*)

Growth orientation According to Maslow, drawing satisfaction from what is available in life, rather than focusing on what is missing. (*p. 504*)

Gustation The sense that detects chemicals in solutions that come into contact with receptors inside the mouth; the sense of taste. (*p. 160*)

Health promotion The process of altering or eliminating behaviors that pose risks to health and at the same time fostering healthy behavior patterns. (*p. 473*)

Health psychology A field in which psychologists conduct and apply research aimed at promoting human health and preventing illness. (*p. 451*)

Height in the visual field A depth cue whereby more distant objects are higher in the visual field than those nearby. (*p. 188*)

Helping behavior Any act that is intended to benefit another person. (*p. 661*)

Heterosexual Sexual motivation that is focused on members of the opposite sex. (*p. 420*)

Heuristic A mental shortcut or rule of thumb. (See also *anchoring heuristic, availability heuristic,* and *representativeness heuristic.*) (*p. 334*)

Hindbrain An extension of the spinal cord contained inside the skull. Nuclei in the hindbrain, especially in the medulla, control blood pressure, heart rate, breathing, and other vital functions. (*p. 106*)

Hippocampus A structure in the forebrain associated with the formation of new memories. (*p. 109*)

Homeostasis The tendency for organisms to keep their physiological systems at a stable, steady level by constantly adjusting themselves in response to change. (*p. 406*)

Homosexual Sexual motivation that is focused on members of a person's own sex. (*p. 420*)

Hormone A chemical that is secreted by a gland into the bloodstream, which carries it throughout the body, enabling the gland to stimulate remote cells with which it has no direct connection. (*p. 123*)

Hue The essential "color" determined by the dominant wavelength of a light. Black, white, and gray are not considered hues because they have no predominant wavelength. (*p. 148*)

Humanistic approach An approach to psychology that views behavior as controlled by the decisions that people make about their lives based on their perceptions of the world. (See *phenomenological approach.*) (*p. 9*)

Hypnosis An altered state of consciousness brought on by special induction techniques and characterized by varying degrees of responsiveness to suggestions for changes in experience and behavior. (*p. 229*)

Hypnotic susceptibility The degree to which people respond to hypnotic suggestions. (*p. 230*)

Hypochondriasis A strong, unjustified fear of physical illness. (*p. 542*)

Hypothalamus A structure in the forebrain that regulates hunger, thirst, and sex drives; it has many connections to and from the autonomic nervous system and to other parts of the brain. (*p. 108*)

Hypothesis In scientific research, a prediction stated as a specific, testable proposition about a phenomenon. (*p. 20*)

Id In psychodynamic theory, a personality component containing a reservoir of unconscious psychic energy (sometimes called *libido*) that includes the basic instincts, desires, and impulses with which all people are born. The id operates according to the pleasure principle, seeking immediate satisfaction, regardless of society's rules or the rights or feelings of others. (See also *pleasure principle*.) (*p. 485*)

Identity A person's mental representation of who he or she is. (*p. 608*)

Identity crisis A phase during which an adolescent attempts to develop an integrated image of himself or herself as a unique person by pulling together self-knowledge acquired during childhood. (*p. 75*)

Immediate memory span The maximum number of items a person can recall perfectly after one presentation of the items, usually six or seven items. (See also *chunk*.) (*p. 295*)

Immune system The body's first line of defense against invading substances and microorganisms. The immune system includes T-cells, which attack virally infected cells; B-cells, which form antibodies against foreign substances; and natural killer cells, which kill invaders like tumor cells and virally infected cells. (*p. 125 and p. 468*)

Implicit memory The unintentional recollection and influence of prior experiences. (*p. 288*)

Incentive theory A theory of motivation stating that behavior is goal directed; actions are directed toward attaining desirable stimuli, called positive incentives, and toward avoiding unwanted stimuli, called negative incentives. (*p. 408*)

Independent variable The variable manipulated by the researcher in an experiment. (*p. 25*)

Inferential statistics A set of procedures that provides a measure of how likely it is that research results came about by chance. These procedures put a precise mathematical value on the confidence or probability that rerunning the same experiment would yield similar (or even stronger) results. (*p. 32*)

Information processing The process of taking in, remembering or forgetting, and using information. It is one model for understanding people's cognitive abilities. (*p. 55*)

Information-processing approach An approach to the study of intelligence that focuses on mental operations, such as attention and memory, that underlie intelligent behavior. (*p. 386*)

Information-processing model A model of memory in which information must pass through sensory memory, short-term memory, and long-term memory in order to become firmly embedded in memory. (*p. 292*)

Information-processing system The procedures for receiving information, representing information with symbols, and manipulating those representations so that the brain can interpret and respond to the information. (*p. 323*)

Ingroup Any category of which people see themselves as a member. Characteristics such as age, sex, race, occupation, and other detectable distinctions form the basis of the categories. (See also *outgroup*.) (*p. 632*)

Inhibitory postsynaptic potential (IPSP) A postsynaptic potential that hyperpolarizes the neuronal membrane, taking the cell farther from the threshold for firing an action potential. (*p. 99*)

Insight In problem solving, a sudden understanding about what is required to produce a desired effect. (*p. 274*)

Insomnia The most common sleeping problem, in which a person feels tired during the day because of trouble falling asleep or staying asleep at night. (*p. 224*)

Instinct An innate, automatic disposition toward responding in a particular way when confronted with a specific stimulus; instincts produce behavior over which an animal has no control. (*p. 403*)

Instrumental conditioning A process through which responses are learned that help produce some rewarding or desired effect. (*p. 260*)

Intellectualization In psychodynamic theory, a defense mechanism that minimizes anxiety by viewing threatening issues in cold, abstract terms. (*p. 487*)

Intelligence Those attributes that center around reasoning skills, knowledge of one's culture, and the ability to arrive at innovative solutions to problems. (*p. 368*)

Intelligence quotient An index of intelligence once calculated by dividing one's tested mental age by one's chronological age and multiplying by 100. Today, IQ is a number that reflects the degree to which a person's score on an intelligence test deviates from the average score of others in his or her age group. (*p. 372*)

Interference The process through which either the storage or the retrieval of information is impaired by the presence of other information. (See also *proactive interference* and *retroactive interference*.) (*p. 302*)

Intermittent reinforcement schedule See *partial reinforcement schedule*.

Internal noise The spontaneous, random firing of nerve cells that occurs because the nervous system is always active. Variations in internal noise can cause absolute thresholds to vary. (*p. 179*)

Interneurons Cells in the retina through which photoreceptor cells make connections to other types of cells in the retina. (*p. 146*)

Interpersonal conflict A process of social dispute in which one person believes that another stands in the way of something of value. (*p. 667*)

Interposition A depth cue whereby closer objects block one's view of things farther away. (*p. 189*)

Interpretations In classical psychoanalysis, alternative ways of looking at the client's thoughts and behaviors in order to help the client become more aware of all aspects of his or her personality, including defenses and the unconscious material behind them. (*p. 571*)

Intervening variable A variable that is not observed directly but that helps to account for a relationship between stimuli and responses. (*p. 401*)

Introjection   In psychodynamic theory, the process of incorporating, or internalizing, parental and societal values into the personality. (*p. 486*)

Ions   Molecules that carry a positive or negative electrical charge. (*p. 96*)

IQ score   See *intelligence quotient.*

IQ test   A test designed to measure intelligence on an objective, standardized scale. (*p. 369*)

Iris   The part of the eye that gives it its color and adjusts the amount of light entering it by constricting to reduce the size of the pupil or relaxing to enlarge it. (*p. 141*)

Jet lag   A syndrome of fatigue, irritability, inattention, and sleeping problems caused by air travel across several time zones. (*p. 226*)

JND   See *just-noticeable difference.*

Just-noticeable difference (JND)   (also called *difference threshold*) The smallest detectable difference in stimulus energy. (See also *Weber's law.*) (*p. 181*)

Kinesthesia   The sense that tells you where the parts of your body are with respect to one another. (*p. 168*)

Language   Symbols and a set of rules for combining them that provides a vehicle for the mind's communication with itself and the most important means of communicating with others. (*p. 349*)

Latency period   The fourth of Freud's psychosexual stages, usually beginning during the fifth year of life, in which sexual impulses lie dormant and the child focuses attention on education and other matters. (*p. 488*)

Latent learning   Learning that is not demonstrated at the time it occurs. (*p. 274*)

Lateral geniculate nucleus (LGN)   A region of the thalamus in which the axons from most of the ganglion cells in the retina finally end and form synapses. (*p. 153*)

Lateral inhibition   The enhancement of the sensation of contrast that occurs when greater response to light in one photoreceptor cell suppresses the response of a neighboring cell. (*p. 146*)

Lateralization   The tendency for one cerebral hemisphere to excel at a particular function or skill compared to the other hemisphere. (*p. 116*)

Law of effect   A law stating that if a response made in the presence of a particular stimulus is followed by a reward, that same response is more likely to be made the next time the stimulus is encountered. Responses that are not rewarded are less likely to be performed again. (*p. 261*)

Learned helplessness   A phenomenon that occurs when an organism has or believes that it has no control over its environment. The typical result of this situation or belief is to stop trying to exert control. (*p. 272*)

Learning   The modification through experience of pre-existing behavior and understanding. (*p. 249*)

Lens   The part of the eye directly behind the pupil. Like the lens in a camera, the lens of the eye is curved so that it bends light rays, focusing them on the retina, at the back of the eye. (*p. 142*)

Levels-of-processing model   A view stating that differences in how well something is remembered reflect the degree or depth to which incoming information is mentally processed. How long the information stays in memory depends on how elaborate the mental processing and encoding becomes. (*p. 290*)

LGN   See *lateral geniculate nucleus.*

Libido   See *id.*

Light and shadow   A feature of visual stimuli that contributes to depth perception. (*p. 189*)

Light intensity   A physical dimension of light waves that refers to how much energy the light contains; it determines the brightness of light. (See also *light wavelength.*) (*p. 141*)

Light wavelength   A physical dimension of light waves that refers to their length. At a given intensity, different light wavelengths produce sensations of different colors. (See also *light intensity.*) (*p. 141*)

Limbic system   A set of brain structures that play important roles in regulating emotion and memory. The limbic system is a "system" because its components have major interconnections and influence related functions. (*p. 109*)

Linear perspective   A depth cue whereby the closer together two converging lines are, the greater the perceived distance. (*p. 189*)

Locus coeruleus   A small nucleus in the brainstem that contains most of the cell bodies of neurons that use norepinephrine in the brain. (*p. 107*)

Logic   The mental procedures that yield a valid conclusion during the reasoning process. (See also *reasoning.*) (*p. 332*)

Longitudinal study   A research method in which a group of people is repeatedly tested as they grow older. (*p. 396*)

Long-term memory   The stage of memory in which semantic encoding dominates, and for which the capacity to store new information is believed to be unlimited. (*p. 297*)

Looming   A motion cue involving a rapid expansion in the size of an image so that it fills the available space on the retina. People tend to perceive a looming object as an approaching stimulus, not as an expanding object viewed at a constant distance. (*p. 191*)

Loudness   A psychological dimension of sound determined by the amplitude of a sound wave; waves with greater amplitude produce sensations of louder sounds. Loudness is described in units called decibels. (*p. 136*)

Lucid dreaming   The awareness that a dream is a dream while it is happening. This phenomenon is evidence that sleep does not involve a total loss of consciousness or mental functioning. (*p. 228*)

Magnetic resonance imaging (MRI)   A highly advanced technique that detects naturally occurring magnetic fields surrounding atoms in brain tissue to create exceptionally clear pictures of the structures of the brain. (*p. 106*)

Maintenance rehearsal   Repeating information over and over to keep it active in short-term memory. This method is ineffective for encoding information into long-term memory. (See also *elaborative rehearsal.*) (*p. 290*)

Major depressive disorder   A condition in which a person feels sad and hopeless for weeks or months, often losing interest in all activities and taking pleasure in nothing. Weight loss and lack of sleep or, in some cases, overeating and excessive sleeping are frequent accompaniments, as are problems in concentrating, making decisions, and thinking clearly. (*p. 544*)

Mania An elated, very active emotional state. (*p. 546*)

Matching hypothesis A hypothesis that people are most likely to be attracted to others who are similar to themselves in physical attractiveness. (*p. 621*)

Maturation Natural growth or change, triggered by biological factors, that unfolds in a fixed sequence relatively independent of the environment. (*p. 42*)

Mean A measure of central tendency that is the arithmetic average of the scores in a set of data; the sum of the values of all the scores divided by the total number of scores. (*p. 31*)

Median A measure of central tendency that is the halfway point in a set of data: half the scores fall above the median, half fall below it. (*p. 31*)

Medical model See *biological approach.*

Meditation A set of techniques designed to create an altered state of consciousness characterized by inner peace, calmness, and tranquillity. (*p. 232*)

Medulla An area in the hindbrain that controls blood pressure, heart rate, breathing, and other vital functions through the use of reflexes and feedback systems. (*p. 106*)

Menopause The point in middle adulthood when a woman stops menstruating. (*p. 81*)

Mental ability A capacity to perform the higher mental processes of reasoning, remembering, understanding, problem solving, and decision making. (*p. 365*)

Mental chronometry The timing of mental events that allows researchers to infer what stages exist during cognition. (See also *average evoked potential, evoked brain potential,* and *information-processing system.*) (*p. 326*)

Mental model A cluster of propositions that represents people's understanding of how things work and guides their interaction with those things. (*p. 330*)

Mental set The tendency for old patterns of problem solving to persist, even when they might not be the most efficient method for solving a given problem. (*p. 338*)

Metacognition The knowledge of what strategies to apply, when to apply them, and how to deploy them in new situations so that new specific knowledge can be gained and different problems mastered. (*p. 395*)

Method of savings A method for measuring forgetting by computing the difference between the number of repetitions needed to learn, say, a list of words and the number of repetitions needed to relearn it after some time has elapsed. (*p. 301*)

Midbrain A small structure that lies between the hindbrain and the forebrain. The midbrain relays information from the eyes, ears, and skin, and controls certain types of automatic behaviors in response to information received through those structures. (*p. 108*)

Midlife transition A point at around age forty when adults take stock of their lives, reappraise their priorities, and, sometimes, modify their lives and relationships. (*p. 84*)

Mnemonics Strategies for placing information in an organized context in order to remember it. Two powerful methods are the peg-word system and the method of loci. (*p. 316*)

Mode A measure of central tendency that is the value or score that occurs most frequently in a data set. (*p. 31*)

Modeling A method of therapy in which desirable behaviors are demonstrated as a way of teaching them to clients. (*p. 579*)

Mood disorder (also called *affective disorder*) A condition in which a person experiences extremes of mood for long periods, shifts from one mood extreme to another, and experiences moods that are inconsistent with the happy or sad events around them. (*p. 544*)

Morpheme The smallest unit of language that has meaning. (See also *phoneme.*) (*p. 350*)

Motivation The influences that account for the initiation, direction, intensity, and persistence of behavior. (*p. 401*)

Motive A reason or purpose for behavior. (*p. 401*)

Motor cortex The part of the cerebral cortex whose neurons control voluntary movements in specific parts of the body. Some neurons control movement of the hand; others stimulate movement of the foot, the knee, the head, and so on. (*p. 113*)

Motor systems The parts of the nervous system that influence muscles and other organs to respond to the environment in some way. (*p. 101*)

Movement gradient The graduated difference in the apparent movement of objects across the visual field. Faster relative movement across the visual field indicates closer distance. (*p. 190*)

Multiple personality disorder The most famous and least commonly seen dissociative disorder, in which a person reports having more than one identity, and sometimes several, each of which speaks, acts, and writes in a very different way. (See also *dissociative disorder.*) (*p. 543*)

Myelin A fatty substance that wraps around some axons and increases the speed of action potentials. (*p. 97*)

Narcissistic personality disorder A personality disorder characterized by an exaggerated sense of self-importance combined with self-doubt. (*p. 556*)

Narcolepsy A daytime sleep disorder in which a person switches abruptly and without warning from an active, often emotional waking state into several minutes of REM sleep. In most cases the muscle paralysis associated with REM causes the person to collapse on the spot and to remain briefly immobilized even after awakening. (*p. 224*)

Narcotic A psychoactive drug, such as opium, morphine, or heroin, that has the ability to produce both sleep-inducing and pain-relieving effects. (*p. 241*)

Natural concept Concepts that have no fixed set of defining features but instead share a set of characteristic features. Members of a natural concept need not possess all of the characteristic features. (*p. 329*)

Naturalistic observation The process of watching without interfering as a phenomenon occurs in the natural environment. (*p. 23*)

Need In drive reduction theory, a biological requirement for well-being that is created by an imbalance in homeostasis. (See also *drive, primary drive,* and *secondary drive.*) (*p. 406*)

Need achievement A motive influenced by the degree to which a person establishes specific goals, cares about meeting those goals, and experiences feelings of satisfaction by doing so; it is often measured by the Thematic Appercep- tion Test. (*p. 422*)

Negative feedback system An arrangement in which the output of a system is monitored, such that output above a certain level will terminate further output until activity returns to an acceptable level. (*p. 124*)

Negative reinforcer An unpleasant stimulus, such as pain. The removal of a negative reinforcer following some response is likely to strengthen the probability of that response recurring. The process of strengthening behavior by following it with the removal of a negative reinforcer is called negative reinforcement. (See also *positive reinforcer.*) (*p. 262*)

Negative state relief model A theory suggesting that people help others because doing so reduces their own negative moods and unpleasant feelings. (*p. 661*)

Nervous system A complex combination of cells whose primary function is to allow an organism to gain information about what is going on inside and outside the body and to respond appropriately. (*p. 93*)

Neuroleptic See *antipsychotic.*

Neuromodulators Neurotransmitters that in some circumstances modify the response to other neurotransmitters at a synapse. (*p. 98*)

Neuron The fundamental unit of the nervous system; a nerve cell. Neurons have the ability to communicate with one another. (*p. 95*)

Neurosis A condition in which a person is uncomfortable (usually anxious) but can still function. (*p. 532*)

Neurotransmitter A chemical that assists in the transfer of signals from the axon of one neuron (presynaptic cell) across the synapse to the receptors on the dendrite of another neuron (postsynaptic cell). (*p. 98*)

Neurotransmitter system A group of neurons that communicates by using the same neurotransmitter, such as acetylcholine or dopamine. (*p. 234*)

Nightmare A frightening, sometimes recurring dream that takes place during REM sleep. (*p. 225*)

Night terrors A rapid awakening from stage 4 sleep, often accompanied by a horrific dream that causes the dreamer to sit up staring, let out a bloodcurdling scream, and experience a state of intense fear that may last up to thirty minutes. This phenomenon is especially common in children, but milder versions occur among adults. (*p. 225*)

Nonconscious level A segment of mental activity devoted to those processes that are totally inaccessible to conscious awareness, such as blood flowing through veins and arteries, the removal of impurities from the blood, and the measuring of blood sugar by the hypothalamus. (*p. 219*)

Norm (1) A description of the frequency at which a particular score occurs, which allows scores to be compared statistically. (*p. 365*) (2) A learned, socially based rule that prescribes what people should or should not do in various situations. (*p. 639*)

Normal distribution A dispersion of scores such that the mean, median, and mode all have the same value. When a distribution has this property, the standard deviation can be used to describe how any particular score stands in relation to the rest of the distribution. (*p. A-4*)

Nuclei Collections of nerve cell bodies in the central nervous system. (*p. 104*)

Null hypothesis The assertion that the independent variable manipulated by the experimenter will have no effect on the dependent variable measured by the experimenter. (*p. A-1*)

Obedience A form of compliance in which people comply with a demand, rather than with a request, because they think they must or should do so; obedience can be thought of as submissive compliance. (See also *compliance.*) (*p. 647*)

Obesity A condition in which a person is severely overweight, often by as much as one hundred pounds. (*p. 413*)

Objective test A paper-and-pencil form containing clear, specific questions, statements, or concepts to which the respondent is asked to give yes-no, true-false, or multiple-choice answers. (*p. 500*)

Object permanence The knowledge, resulting from an ability to form mental representations of objects, that objects exist even when they are not in view. (*p. 52*)

Observational learning Learning how to perform new behaviors by watching the behavior of others. (*p. 274*)

Obsessive-compulsive disorder An anxiety disorder in which a person becomes obsessed with certain thoughts or images or feels a compulsion to do certain things. If the person tries to interrupt obsessive thinking or compulsions, severe agitation and anxiety usually result. (*p. 539*)

Oedipus complex According to psychodynamic theory, during the phallic stage a boy's id impulses involve sexual desire for the mother and the desire to eliminate, even kill, the father, who is competition for the mother's affection. The hostile impulses create a fear of retaliation so strong that the ego represses the incestuous desires. Then the boy identifies with the father and begins to learn male sex-role behaviors. (See also *phallic stage.*) (*p. 488*)

Olfaction The sense that detects chemicals that are airborne, or volatile; the sense of smell. (*p. 157*)

Olfactory bulb The brain structure that receives messages regarding olfaction, or the sense of smell. (*p. 159*)

One-word stage A stage of language development during which children build their vocabularies one word at a time, tend to use one word at a time, and tend to overextend the use of a single word. (*p. 354*)

Operant A response that has some effect on the world; it is a response that operates on the environment in some way. (See also *operant conditioning.*) (*p. 262*)

Operant conditioning A virtual synonym for instrumental conditioning; a process studied by B. F. Skinner in which an organism learns to respond to the environment in a way that helps produce some desired effect. Skinner's primary aim was to analyze how behavior is changed by its consequences. (*p. 261*)

Operational definitions Statements that define variables describing the exact operations or methods used in research. (*p. 20*)

Opponent-process theory (1) A theory of color vision stating that the visual elements sensitive to color are grouped into three pairs: a red-green element, a blue-yellow element, and a black-white element. Each element signals one color or the other—red or green, for example—but never both. (*p. 150*) (2) A theory of motivation based on the assumptions that, first, any reaction to a stimulus is automatically followed by an opposite reaction, called the opponent process; and that, second, after repeated exposure to the same stimulus, the initial reaction weakens, and the opponent process becomes stronger. (*p. 409*)

Optic chiasm Part of the bottom surface of the brain where half of the optic nerve fibers cross over to the opposite side of the brain; beyond the chiasm the fibers ascend into the brain itself. (*p. 152*)

Optic nerve A bundle of fibers composed of axons from ganglion cells that carries visual information to the brain. (*p. 152*)

Oral stage The first of Freud's psychosexual stages, occurring during the first year of life, in which the mouth is the center of pleasure. (*p. 487*)

Otolith A small crystal in the fluid-filled vestibular sacs of the inner ear that, when shifted by gravity, stimulates nerve cells that inform the brain of the position of the head relative to the earth. (*p. 169*)

Outgroup Any group of which people do not see themselves as a member. (See also *ingroup.*) (*p. 632*)

Pain disorder A somatoform disorder marked by complaints of severe often constant pain with no physical cause. (*p. 542*)

Panic disorder Anxiety in the form of terrifying panic attacks that come without warning or obvious cause. These attacks last for a few minutes and are marked by heart palpitations, pressure or pain in the chest, dizziness or unsteadiness, sweating, and faintness. They may be accompanied by feeling detached from one's body or feeling that people and events are not real. The person may think he or she is about to die or "go crazy." (*p. 538*)

Papillae Structures that contain groups of taste receptors; the taste buds. (*p. 160*)

Parallel distributed processing (PDP) models An approach to understanding object recognition in which various elements of the object are thought to be simultaneously analyzed by a number of widely distributed but connected neural units in the brain. When applied to memory, these models suggest that new experiences don't just provide new facts that are later retrieved individually; they also change people's overall knowledge base, altering in a more general way their understanding of the world and how it operates. (*p. 201 and p. 292*)

Paranoid schizophrenia A type of schizophrenia characterized by delusions of persecution or grandeur accompanied by anxiety, anger, superiority, argumentativeness, or jealousy; these feelings sometimes lead to violence. (*p. 552*)

Parasympathetic nervous system The subsystem of the autonomic nervous system that typically influences activity related to the protection, nourishment, and growth of the body. (See also *autonomic nervous system.*) (*p. 430*)

Partial reinforcement extinction effect A phenomenon in which behaviors learned under a partial reinforcement schedule are far more difficult to extinguish than those learned on a continuous reinforcement schedule. Individuals on a partial reinforcement schedule usually are not immediately aware that their behavior is no longer being reinforced; they are used to not being rewarded for every response. However, individuals on a continuous reinforcement schedule are accustomed to being reinforced for each response and are more sensitive to the lack of reward. (*p. 267*)

Partial reinforcement schedule (also called *intermittent reinforcement schedule*) In operant conditioning, a pattern of reinforcement in which a reinforcer is administered only some of the time after a particular response occurs. (See also *fixed interval schedule, fixed ratio schedule, variable interval schedule,* and *variable ratio schedule.*) (*p. 266*)

Pathway See *fiber tract.*

Percentile score The percentage of people or observations that fall below a given score in a normal distribution. (*p. A-4*)

Perception The process through which people take raw sensations from the environment and interpret them, using knowledge, experience, and understanding of the world, so that the sensations become meaningful experiences. (*p. 175*)

Perceptual constancy The perception of objects as constant in size, shape, color, and other properties despite changes in their retinal image. (*p. 187*)

Performance scale Five subtests in the Wechsler scales that include tasks that require spatial ability and the ability to manipulate materials; these subtests provide a performance IQ. (See also *verbal scale.*) (*p. 371*)

Peripheral nervous system All of the nervous system that is not housed in bone. It has two main subsystems: the somatic nervous system and the autonomic nervous system. (*p. 101*)

Permissive parent A parent who gives his or her child complete freedom and whose discipline is lax. Children of this type of parent are often immature, dependent, and unhappy, lack self-reliance and self-control, and seek parental help for even the slightest problems. (*p. 68*)

Personality The pattern of psychological and behavioral characteristics by which each person can be compared and contrasted with other people; the unique pattern of characteristics that emerges from the blending of inherited and acquired tendencies to make each person an identifiable individual. (*p. 483*)

Personality disorder Long-standing, inflexible ways of behaving that are not so much severe mental disorders as styles of life, which, from childhood or adolescence, create problems—usually for others. (*p. 555*)

Personality psychologist A psychologist who focuses on the unique characteristics that determine individuals' behavior. (*p. 4*)

Person-centered therapy See *client-centered therapy.*

Phallic stage The third of Freud's psychosexual stages, lasting from approximately ages three to five, in which the focus of pleasure shifts to the genital area; the Oedipus complex occurs during this stage. (See also *Oedipus complex.*) (*p. 488*)

Phenomenological approach (also called *phenomenological model*) A view of personality based on the assumption that each personality is created out of each person's unique way of perceiving and interpreting the world. Proponents of this view believe that one's personal perception of reality shapes and controls behavior from moment to moment. (*p. 506*)

Phenotype How an individual looks and acts, which depends on how a person's inherited characteristics interact with the environment. (*p. 36*)

Pheromones Chemicals that are released by one animal and detected by another, and then shape that second animal's behavior or physiology. Often, though not always, the pheromone is detected by the olfactory system. (*p. 159*)

Phobia An anxiety disorder that involves a strong, irrational fear of an object or situation that does not objectively justify such a reaction. The phobic individual usually realizes that the fear makes no sense but cannot keep it from interfering with daily life. (*p. 537*)

Phoneme The smallest unit of sound that affects the meaning of speech. (See also *morpheme.*) (*p. 350*)

Photopigment A chemical contained in photoreceptors that responds to light and assists in changing light into neural activity. (*p. 142*)

Photoreceptor A nerve cell in the retina that codes light energy into neural activity. (See also *rods* and *cones.*) (*p. 142*)

Physical dependence See *addiction.*

Physiological psychologist See *biological psychologist.*

Physiological psychology See *biological psychology.*

Pinna The crumpled, oddly shaped part of the outer ear that collects sound waves. (*p. 137*)

Pitch How high or low a tone sounds; the psychological dimension determined by the frequency of sound waves. High-frequency waves are sensed as sounds of high pitch. (*p. 136*)

Placebo A physical or psychological treatment that contains no active ingredient but produces an effect because the person receiving it believes it will. In an experiment, the placebo effect (a confounding variable) occurs when the subject responds to the belief that the independent variable will have an effect, rather than to the actual effect of the independent variable. (*p. 27*)

Place theory (also called the *traveling wave theory*) A theory of hearing stating that hair cells at a particular place on the basilar membrane respond most to a particular frequency of sound. High-frequency sounds produce a wave that peaks soon after it starts down the basilar membrane. Lower-frequency sounds produce a wave that peaks farther along the basilar membrane. (*p. 139*)

Pleasure principle In psychodynamic theory, the operating principle of the id, which guides people toward whatever feels good. (See also *id.*) (*p. 485*)

Polygenic Describing characteristics that are determined by more than one gene or pair of genes. (*p. 36*)

Positive reinforcement See *positive reinforcer.*

Positive reinforcer A stimulus that strengthens a response if it follows that response. It is roughly equivalent to a reward. Presenting a positive reinforcer after a response is called positive reinforcement. (See also *negative reinforcer.*) (*p. 262*)

Positron emission tomography (PET scanning) A technique that detects—and creates a visual image of—activity in various parts of the brain. (*p. 106*)

Postconventional moral reasoning Reasoning that reflects moral judgments based on personal standards or universal principles of justice, equality, and respect for human life. (*p. 78*)

Posthypnotic amnesia The inability of hypnotic subjects to recall what happened during hypnosis. For some, recall fails even when they are told what went on. (*p. 230*)

Posthypnotic suggestion Instructions about experiences or behavior to take place after hypnosis has been terminated. (*p. 230*)

Postsynaptic potential The change in the membrane potential of a neuron that has received stimulation from another neuron. (*p. 99*)

Posttraumatic stress disorder A pattern of adverse and disruptive reactions following a traumatic event. One of its most common features is re-experiencing the original trauma through nightmares or vivid memories. (*p. 459*)

Practical approach Defines normal versus abnormal behavior in terms of its content, the context in which is occurs, and the subjective consequences it brings about. (*p. 524*)

Preconscious level A segment of mental activity devoted to sensations and everything else that is not currently conscious, but of which people can easily become conscious at will. The amount of material at this level far surpasses what is present at the conscious level at any given moment. (See also *conscious level, nonconscious level, subconscious level,* and *unconscious level.*) (*p. 219*)

Preconventional moral reasoning Reasoning that is not based on the conventions or rules that guide social interactions in society. (*p. 78*)

Prefrontal lobotomy A form of psychosurgery in which a sharp instrument is inserted into the brain and used to destroy brain tissue. (*p. 594*)

Prejudice A positive or negative attitude toward an entire group of people. (See also *discrimination.*) (*p. 631*)

Preoperational period According to Piaget, the second stage of cognitive development, during which children begin to understand, create, and use symbols to represent things that are not present. (*p. 52*)

Primacy effect A characteristic of recall in which recall for the first two or three items in a list is particularly good. (See also *recency effect.*) (*p. 299*)

Primary cortex See *primary visual cortex.*

Primary drive A drive that arises from basic biological needs. (See also *drive, need,* and *secondary drive.*) (*p. 406*)

Primary reinforcer Something that meets an organism's most basic needs, such as food, water, air, and moderate temperatures. A primary reinforcer does not depend on learning to exert its influence. (See also *secondary reinforcer.*) (*p. 265*)

Primary visual cortex An area in the occipital lobe, at the back of the brain, to which neurons in the lateral geniculate nucleus relay visual input. (*p. 153*)

Prisoner's dilemma game A research situation in which mutual cooperation guarantees the best mutual outcome; mixed cooperative and competitive responses by each person guarantee a favorable outcome for one person and an unfavorable outcome for the other; and mutual competition guarantees the worst mutual outcome. (*p. 665*)

Proactive interference A cause of forgetting in which previously learned information, now residing in long-term memory, interferes with the ability to remember new information. (See also *retroactive interference.*) (*p. 302*)

Procedural memory (also called *skill memory*) A type of memory that contains information about how to do things. (*p. 287*)

Progesterone A feminine hormone; the main progestin. (*p. 417*)

Progestins Feminine hormones that circulate in the bloodstream of both men and women; relatively more progestins circulate in women. One of the main progestins is progesterone. (See also *estradiol, estrogen,* and *progesterone.*) (*p. 417*)

Progressive relaxation training A procedure for learning to relax that involves tensing a group of muscles for a few seconds, then releasing that tension and focusing attention on the resulting feelings of relaxation; the procedure is repeated at least once for each of sixteen muscle groups throughout the body. Progressive relaxation training is a popular physiological method for coping with stress and an important part of systematic desensitization, a method for treating phobias. (*p. 477*)

Projective test Personality tests made up of relatively unstructured stimuli, such as inkblots, which can be perceived and responded to in many ways; particular responses are seen as reflecting the individual's needs, fantasies, conflicts, thought patterns, and other aspects of personality. (*p. 514*)

Proposition The smallest unit of knowledge that can stand as a separate assertion, may be true or false, and may represent a relationship between a concept and a property of that concept or between two or more concepts. (*p. 330*)

Proprioceptive The sensory systems that allow us to know about where we are and what each part of our body is doing. (See also *kinesthesia* and *vestibular sense.*) (*p. 168*)

Prototype A member of a natural concept that possesses all or most of its characteristic features. (*p. 329*)

Proximity A Gestalt grouping principle stating that the closer objects are to one another, the more likely they are to be perceived as belonging together. (*p. 185*)

Psychedelic Psychoactive drugs, such as LSD, PCP, and marijuana, that alter consciousness by producing a temporary loss of contact with reality and changes in emotion, perception, and thought. (*p. 242*)

Psychiatrist A medical doctor who has completed special training in the treatment of mental disorder. Psychiatrists can prescribe drugs. (*p. 568*)

Psychoactive drug A chemical substance that acts on the brain to create some psychological effect. (*p. 233*)

Psychoanalysis A method of psychotherapy that seeks to help clients gain insight by recognizing, understanding, and dealing with unconscious thoughts and emotions presumed to cause their problems and work through the many ways in which those unconscious causes appear in everyday behavior and social relationships. (*p. 484 and p. 569*)

Psychodynamic approach (also called *psychodynamic model*) A view developed by Freud that emphasizes the interplay of unconscious mental processes in determining human thought, feelings, and behavior. (*p. 6 and p. 484*)

Psychological dependence A condition in which a person continues drug use despite adverse effects, needs the drug for a sense of well-being, and becomes preoccupied with obtaining the drug if it becomes unavailable. (*p. 236*)

Psychologist In the realm of treatment, a therapist whose education includes completion of a masters or doctoral degree in clinical or counseling psychology, often followed by additional specialized training. Unlike psychiatrists, psychologists are not authorized to prescribe drugs. (*p. 568*)

Psychology The science of behavior and mental processes. (*p. 3*)

Psychometric approach A way of studying intelligence that emphasizes the analysis of the "products" of intelligence, especially scores on intelligence tests. (*p. 385*)

Psychoneuroimmunology The field that examines the interaction of psychological and physiological processes that affect the ability of the body to defend itself against disease. (*p. 468*)

Psychopathology Patterns of thinking and behaving that are maladaptive, disruptive, or uncomfortable for the person affected or for those with whom he or she comes in contact. (*p. 521*)

Psychopharmacology The study of psychoactive drugs and their effects. (*p. 233*)

Psychophysics An area of research that focuses on the relationship between the physical characteristics of environmental stimuli and the conscious psychological experience those stimuli produce. Psychophysical researchers seek to understand how people make contact with and become conscious of the world. (*p. 178*)

Psychosexual stage In psychodynamic theory, a period of personality development in which internal and external conflicts focus on particular issues. There are five stages during which pleasure is derived from different areas of the body. (See also *anal stage, genital stage, latency period, oral stage,* and *phallic stage.*) (*p. 487*)

Psychosis A condition involving a loss of contact with reality or an inability to function on a daily basis. (*p. 532*)

Psychosurgery Procedures that destroy various regions of the brain in an effort to alleviate psychological disorders; this surgery is done infrequently and only as a last resort. (*p. 594*)

Psychotherapy The treatment of psychological disorders through psychological methods, such as analyzing problems, talking about possible solutions, and encouraging more adaptive ways of thinking and acting. (*p. 567*)

Puberty The condition of being able for the first time to reproduce; it occurs during adolescence and is characterized by fuller breasts and rounder curves in females and by broad shoulders and narrow hips in males. Facial, underarm, and pubic hair grows. Voices deepen, and acne may appear. (*p. 73*)

Punishment The presentation of an aversive stimulus or the removal of a pleasant stimulus; punishment decreases the frequency of the immediately preceding response. (*p. 269 and p. 582*)

Pupil An opening in the eye, just behind the cornea, through which light passes. (The pupil appears black because there is no light source inside the eyeball and very little light is reflected out of the eye.) (*p. 141*)

Quasi-experiments Research studies whose designs approximate the control of a true experiment (*quasi-* means "resembling") but may not include manipulation of the independent variable, random assignment of subjects to groups, or other elements of experimental control. (*p. 28*)

Quiet sleep (also called *slow-wave sleep*) Sleep stages 1 through 4, which are accompanied by slow, deep breathing; a calm, regular heartbeat; and reduced blood pressure. (*p. 222*)

Random sample A group of research subjects selected from a population each of whose members had an equal chance of being chosen for study. (*p. 28*)

Random variable In an experiment, a confounding variable in which an uncontrolled or uncontrollable factor affects the dependent variable along with or instead of the independent variable. Random variables can include factors such as differences in the subjects' backgrounds, personalities, and physical health, as well as differences in experimental conditions. (*p. 26*)

Range A measure of variability that is the difference between the highest and the lowest value in the data set. (*p. 32*)

Rational-emotive therapy (RET) A treatment that involves identifying self-defeating, problem-causing thoughts that clients have learned and using modeling, encouragement, and logic to help the client replace these maladaptive thought patterns with more realistic and beneficial ones. (*p. 582*)

Reaction range A roughly defined area of genetically determined potential for mental ability within which environmental factors operate to increase or decrease a person's demonstrated mental ability. Reaction range is a theoretical concept, not a fixed set of boundaries on mental ability. (*p. 379*)

Reaction time The elapsed time between the presentation of a stimulus and an overt response to it. (*p. 326*)

Reality principle According to psychodynamic theory, the operating principle of the ego that involves, for example, compromises between the unreasoning demands of the id to do whatever feels good and the demands of the real world to do what is acceptable. (See also *ego.*) (*p. 486*)

Reasoning The process by which people evaluate and generate arguments and reach conclusions. (See also *logic.*) (*p. 332*)

Recency effect A characteristic of recall in which recall is particularly good for the last few items on a list. (See also *primacy effect.*) (*p. 299*)

Receptive field The portion of the world that affects a given neuron. For example, in the auditory system, one neuron might respond only to sounds of a particular pitch; that pitch is its receptive field. (*p. 147*)

Receptor (1) A site on the surface of the postsynaptic cell that allows only one type of neurotransmitter to fit into it and thus trigger the chemical response that may lead to an action potential. (*p. 98*) (2) A cell that is specialized to detect certain types of energy and convert it into neural activity. This conversion process is called transduction. (*p. 131*)

Reconditioning The relearning of a conditioned response following extinction. Because reconditioning takes much less time than the original conditioning, some change in the organism must persist even after extinction. (*p. 252*)

Reduced clarity A depth cue whereby an object whose retinal image is unclear is perceived as being farther away. (*p. 189*)

Reference group A category of people to which people compare themselves. (*p. 607*)

Reflection Restating or paraphrasing what the client has said, which shows that the therapist is actively listening and helps make the client aware of the thoughts and feelings he or she is experiencing. (*p. 575*)

Reflexes Involuntary, unlearned reactions in the form of swift, automatic, and finely coordinated movements in response to external stimuli. Reflexes are organized completely within the spinal cord. (*p. 48 and p. 105*)

Refractory period A short rest period between action potentials; it is so short that a neuron can send action potentials down its axon at rates of up to one thousand per second. (*p. 97*)

Reinforcer A stimulus event that increases the probability that the response that immediately preceded it will occur again. (See also *positive reinforcer* and *negative reinforcer.*) (*p. 262*)

Relative deprivation The sense that a person is not doing as well as others in the same reference group. (*p. 607*)

Relative size A depth cue whereby larger objects are perceived as closer than smaller ones. (*p. 188*)

Reliability The degree to which a test can be repeated with the same results. Tests with high reliability yield scores that are less susceptible to insignificant or random changes in the test taker or the testing environment. (*p. 366*)

REM behavior disorder A sleep disorder in which a person fails to show the decreased muscle tone normally seen in REM sleep, thus allowing the sleeper to act out dreams, sometimes with dangerous results. (*p. 226*)

REM sleep See *active sleep.*

Representativeness heuristic A shortcut in the thought process that involves judging the probability that a hypothesis is true or that an example belongs to a certain class of items by first focusing on the similarities between the example and a larger class of events or items and then determining whether the particular example represents essential features of the larger class. (*p. 334*)

Repression In psychodynamic theory, a defense mechanism that involves unconsciously forcing unacceptable impulses out of awareness, leaving the person unaware that he or she had the taboo desires in the first place. (*p. 486*)

Residual schizophrenia The designation for persons who have displayed symptoms of schizophrenia in the past, but not in the present. (*p. 551*)

Response criterion The internal rule a person uses to decide whether or not to report a stimulus; it reflects the person's motivation and expectations. (*p. 179*)

RET See *rational-emotive therapy.*

Reticular formation A network of nuclei and fibers threaded throughout the hindbrain and midbrain. This network alters the activity of the rest of the brain. (*p. 106*)

Retina The surface at the back of the eye onto which the lens focuses light rays. (*p. 142*)

Retrieval The process of recalling information stored in memory and bringing it into consciousness. (*p. 290*)

Retrieval cues Stimuli that allow people to recall things that were once forgotten and help them to recognize information stored in memory. (*p. 304*)

Retroactive interference A cause of forgetting in which new information placed in memory interferes with the ability to recall information already in memory. (*p. 302*)

Retrograde amnesia A loss of memory for events prior to some critical brain injury. Often, a person will be unable to remember anything that occurred in the months, or even years, before the injury. In most cases, the memories return gradually, but recovery is seldom complete. (See also *anterograde amnesia.*) (*p. 300*)

Rods Photoreceptors in the retina that allow sight even in dim light because their photopigment contains rhodopsin, a light-sensitive chemical. Rods cannot discriminate colors. (See also *cones.*) (*p. 144*)

Role theory A theory that states that hypnotized subjects act in accordance with a special social role, which demands compliance. According to this theory, the procedures for inducing hypnosis provide a socially acceptable reason to follow the hypnotist's suggestions. (See also *dissociation theory* and *state theory.*) (*p. 231*)

Sampling The process of selecting subjects who are members of the population that the researcher wishes to study. (*p. 28*)

Satiety The condition of no longer wanting to eat. (*p. 410*)

Saturation The purity of a color. A color is more pure, more saturated, if a single wavelength is relatively more intense—contains more energy—than other wavelengths. (*p. 148*)

Schema A basic unit of knowledge; a generalization based on experience of the world. Schemas organize past experience and provide a framework for understanding future experience; a coherent, organized set of beliefs and expectations that can influence the perception of others and objects. (*p. 49*)

Schema-plus-correction process An impression to which a change has been added. In social perception, the initial impression of a person is remembered better than is the change. (*p. 611*)

Schizophrenia A pattern of severely disturbed thinking, emotion, perception, and behavior that constitutes one of the most serious and disabling of all mental disorders. (*p. 550*)

Schizotypal personality disorder A pattern of emotional and behavior disorder that is similar to, but significantly less intense than, schizophrenia. (*p. 556*)

Script A mental representation of a familiar sequence of activity, usually involving people's behavior. (*p. 56*)

SD See *standard deviation.*

Secondary drive A stimulus that acquires the motivational properties of a primary drive through classical conditioning or other learning mechanisms. (See also *drive, need,* and *primary drive.*) (*p. 406*)

Secondary reinforcer A reward that people or animals learn to like. Secondary reinforcers gain their reinforcing properties through association with primary reinforcers. (*p. 265*)

Second-order conditioning A phenomenon in learning when a conditioned stimulus acts like a UCS, creating conditioned stimuli out of events associated with it. (*p. 255*)

Selective attention The focusing of mental resources on only part of the stimulus field. (*p. 294*)

Self-actualization According to Rogers, an innate tendency toward growth that motivates all people to seek the full realization of their highest potential. (*p. 505*)

Self-concept The way one thinks of oneself. (*p. 507*)

Self-efficacy According to Bandura, learned expectations about the probability of success in given situations; a person's expectation of success in a given situation may be enough to create that success and even to blunt the impact of minor failures. (*p. 508*)

Self-fulfilling prophecy An impression-formation process in which an initial impression elicits behavior in another that confirms the impression. (*p. 612*)

Self-perception theory A theory that holds that when people are unsure of their attitude in a situation, they consider their behavior in light of the circumstances and then infer what their attitude must have been. (*p. 626*)

Self-schemas Mental representations that people form of themselves. (*p. 609*)

Self-serving bias The cognitive tendency to attribute one's successes to internal characteristics while blaming one's failures on external causes. (*p. 617*)

Semantic code A mental representation of an experience by its general meaning. (*p. 289*)

Semantic memory A type of memory containing generalized knowledge of the world that does not involve memory of specific events. (*p. 287*)

Semantics In language, the rules that govern the meaning of words and sentences. (See also *syntax.*) (*p. 350*)

Semicircular canal An arc-shaped tube in the inner ear containing fluid that, when shifted by head movements, stimulates nerve cells that provide information to the brain about the rate and direction of those movements. (*p. 169*)

Sensation A message from a sense, which comprises the raw information that affects many kinds of behavior and mental processes. (*p. 131*)

Sense A system that translates data from outside the nervous system into neural activity, giving the nervous system, especially the brain, information about the world. (*p. 131*)

Sensitivity The ability to detect a stimulus; sensitivity is influenced by neural noise, the intensity of the stimulus, and the capacity of the sensory system. (*p. 180*)

Sensorimotor period The first in Piaget's stages of cognitive development, when the infant's mental activity is confined to sensory perception and motor skills. (*p. 51*)

Sensory cortex The part of the cerebral cortex located in the parietal, occipital, and temporal lobes that receives stimulus information from the skin, eyes, and ears, respectively. (*p. 113*)

Sensory memory A type of memory that is very primitive and very brief, but lasts long enough to connect one impression to the next, so that people experience a smooth flow of information. (See also *sensory register.*) (*p. 293*)

Sensory register A memory system that holds incoming information long enough for it to be processed further. (See also *sensory memory.*) (*p. 293*)

Sensory systems The parts of the nervous system that provide information about the environment; the senses. (*p. 101*)

Sexual dysfunction Problems with sex that involve sexual motivation, arousal, or orgasmic response. (*p. 419*)

Sexual response cycle The pattern of arousal during and after sexual activity. (*p. 417*)

Shaping In operant conditioning, a procedure that involves reinforcing responses that come successively closer to the desired response. (*p. 264*)

Short-term memory (also called *working memory*) A stage of memory in which information can last less than half a minute unless rehearsed. (*p. 294*)

Signal-detection theory A formal mathematical model of what determines a person's report that a near-threshold stimulus has or has not occurred. (*p. 179*)

Similarity A Gestalt grouping principle stating that similar elements are perceived to be part of a group. (*p. 185*)

Simplicity A Gestalt grouping principle stating that people tend to group stimulus features in a way that provides the simplest interpretation of the world. (*p. 185*)

Sleep apnea A sleep disorder in which people briefly but repeatedly stop breathing during the night. (*p. 224*)

Sleepwalking A phenomenon that starts primarily in non-REM sleep, especially in stage 4, and involves walking while one is asleep. It is most common during childhood. In the morning sleepwalkers usually have no memory of their travels. (*p. 226*)

Slow-wave sleep See *quiet sleep.*

Social clock Particular age ranges during which certain milestones that mark a person's progress through life, such as completing school, leaving home, and getting married, are expected to occur. (*p. 83*)

Social cognition Mental processes associated with people's perceptions of and reactions to other people. (*p. 607*)

Social comparison Using other people as a basis of comparison for evaluating oneself. (*p. 607*)

Social dilemma A situation in which the short-term decisions of individuals become irrational in combination and create long-term, clearly predictable damage for a group. (*p. 671*)

Social facilitation A phenomenon in which the mere presence of other people improves a person's performance on a given task. (*p. 641*)

Social identity theory A theory that states that one's identity results from a fundamental tension between the need to be like others and a corresponding need to feel unique. (*p. 608*)

Social interference The impairment of human performance by the presence of other people. (*p. 641*)

Socialization The process by which parents, teachers, and others teach children the skills and social norms necessary to be well-functioning members of society. (*p. 67*)

Social loafing Exerting less effort when performing a group task (in which one's contribution cannot be identified) than when performing the same task alone. (*p. 642*)

Social perception The processes through which people interpret information about others, draw inferences about them, and develop mental representations of them. (*p. 610*)

Social phobia A strong, irrational fear relating to social situations. Common examples include fear of being negatively evaluated by others or publicly embarrassed by doing something impulsive, outrageous, or humiliating. (*p. 538*)

Social psychologist A psychologist who studies how people influence one another's behavior and attitudes, especially in groups. (*p. 4*)

Social psychology The psychological subfield that explores the effects of the social world on the behavior and mental processes of individuals, pairs, and groups. (*p. 607*)

Social referencing A phenomenon in which other people's facial expressions, tone of voice, and bodily gestures serve as guidelines for how to proceed in uncertain situations. (*p. 445*)

Social support network The friends and social contacts on whom one can depend for help and support. (*p. 462*)

Sociobiology The study of the relationship between a species' evolutionary heritage and its social behaviors, such as aggression, cooperation, child care, and sexual behavior. (*p. 6*)

Socioemotional leadership A leadership style in which the leader provides loose supervision, asks for group members' ideas, and is generally concerned with subordinates' feelings. (*p. 669*)

Somatic nervous system The subsystem of the peripheral nervous system that transmits information from the senses to the central nervous system and carries signals from the CNS to the muscles that move the skeleton. (*p. 102*)

Somatic sense (also called *somatosensory system*) A sense that is spread throughout the body, not located in a specific organ. Somatic senses include touch, temperature, pain (the skin senses), and kinesthesia. (*p. 161*)

Somatization disorder A somatoform disorder in which the person has numerous physical complaints without verifiable physical illness. (*p. 542*)

Somatoform disorder A psychological problem in which a person shows the symptoms of some physical (somatic) disorder, even though there is no physical cause. (See also *conversion disorder.*) (*p. 541*)

Somatosensory system See *somatic sense.*

Sound A repetitive fluctuation in the pressure of a medium like air. (*p. 134*)

Spatial codes In the sensory systems, coding attributes of a stimulus in terms of the location of firing neurons relative to their neighbors. (*p. 133*)

Specific nerve energies A doctrine that states that stimulation of a particular sensory nerve provides codes for that one sense, no matter how the stimulation takes place. (*p. 133*)

Specific phobias Phobias that involve fear and avoidance of heights, blood, animals, and other specific stimuli and situations. (*p. 537*)

Spinal cord The part of the central nervous system contained within the spinal column that receives signals from peripheral senses (such as touch and pain) and relays them to the brain. It also conveys messages from the brain to the rest of the body. (*p. 105*)

Spontaneous recovery The reappearance of the conditioned response after extinction and without further pairings of the conditioned and unconditioned stimuli. (*p. 252*)

Spreading activation A principle that, in semantic network theories of memory, explains how information is retrieved. (*p. 305*)

Standard deviation (SD) A measure of variability that is the average difference between each score and the mean of the data set. (*p. 32*)

Standard score A value that indicates the distance, in standard deviations, between a given score and the mean of all the scores in a data set. (*p. A-5*)

Stanford-Binet A test for determining a person's intelligence quotient, or IQ. (*p. 368*)

State-dependent memory Memories that are aided or impeded by a person's internal state. (*p. 304*)

State of consciousness The characteristics of consciousness at any particular moment—for example, what reaches awareness, what levels of mental activity are most prominent, and how efficiently a person is functioning. (*p. 221*)

State theory A theory that proposes that hypnosis does indeed create an altered state of consciousness. (See also *dissociation theory* and *role theory*.) (*p. 231*)

Statistical approach Defines normal versus abnormal behavior in terms of what is most common, what the average person does. (*p. 522*)

Statistically significant In statistical analysis, a term used to describe the results of an experiment when the outcome of a statistical test indicates that the probability of those results occurring by chance is small (less than 5 percent). (*p. 33*)

Stereotype An impression or schema of an entire group of people that involves the false assumption that all members of the group share the same characteristics. (*p. 630*)

Stimulant A psychoactive drug that has the ability to increase behavioral and mental activity. Amphetamines and cocaine do so primarily by augmenting the action of the neurotransmitters dopamine and norepinephrine. (*p. 239*)

Stimulus discrimination A process through which individuals learn to differentiate among similar stimuli and respond appropriately to each one. (See also *stimulus generalization*.) (*p. 255*)

Stimulus generalization A phenomenon in which a conditioned response is elicited by stimuli that are similar but not identical to the conditioned stimulus. The greater the similarity between a stimulus and the conditioned stimulus, the stronger the conditioned response will be. (*p. 255*)

Storage The process of maintaining information in the memory system over time. (*p. 289*)

Stress The process of adjusting to circumstances that disrupt, or threaten to disrupt, a person's equilibrium. (*p. 453*)

Stressor An event or situation to which people must adjust. (*p. 453*)

Stress reaction The physical, psychological, and behavioral responses people display in the face of stressors. (*p. 453*)

Striatum A structure within the forebrain that is involved in the smooth initiation of movement. (*p. 108*)

Style of life According to Adler, the ways in which each person goes about trying to reach personal and social fulfillment. (*p. 489*)

Subconscious level The term used to designate the mental level at which important but normally inaccessible mental processes take place. (See also *unconscious level*.) (*p. 219*)

Substance-related disorder A problem that involves use of psychoactive drugs for months or years in ways that harm the user or others. (*p. 557*)

Substantia nigra An area of the midbrain involved in the smooth initiation of movement. (*p. 108*)

Sudden infant death syndrome (SIDS) A disorder in which a sleeping baby stops breathing but does not awaken and suffocates. (*p. 225*)

Superego According to psychodynamic theory, the component of personality that tells people what they should and should not do. Its two subdivisions are the conscience, which dictates what behaviors are wrong, and the ego ideal, which sets perfectionistic standards for desirable behaviors. (*p. 486*)

Supernatural model See *demonological model*.

Suprachiasmatic nuclei Nuclei in the hypothalamus that generate biological rhythms. (*p. 109*)

Surface structure The strings of words that people produce; the order in which words are arranged. (*p. 350*)

Survey A research method that involves giving people questionnaires or special interviews designed to obtain descriptions of their attitudes, beliefs, opinions, and intentions. (*p. 24*)

Syllogism In the reasoning process, an argument made up of two propositions, called premises, and a conclusion based on those premises. (See also *proposition*.) (*p. 332*)

Sympathetic nervous system The subsystem of the autonomic nervous system that usually prepares the organism for vigorous activity, including the fight-or-flight syndrome. (See also *autonomic nervous system* and *fight-or-flight syndrome*.) (*p. 430*)

Synapse The tiny gap between neurons across which the neurons communicate. (*p. 96*)

Synaptic plasticity The ability to create synapses and to change the strength of synapses. (*p. 118*)

Syntax In language, the set of rules that govern the formation of phrases and sentences. (See also *semantics*.) (*p. 350*)

Task-oriented leadership A leadership style in which the leader provides close supervision, leads by giving directives, and generally discourages group discussion. (*p. 669*)

Telegraphic speech Utterances that are brief and to the point and that leave out any word not absolutely essential to the meaning the speaker wishes to convey; children's first sentences, consisting of two-word utterances. (*p. 354*)

Temperament An individual's basic, natural disposition; the beginning of an individual's identity or personality, which is evident from infancy. (*p. 60*)

Temporal codes In the sensory systems, coding attributes of a stimulus in terms of changes in the timing of neural firing. (*p. 133*)

Teratogen A harmful substance, such as alcohol and other drugs, that can cause birth defects. (*p. 46*)

Terminal drop A sharp decline in mental functioning that tends to occur in late adulthood, a few years or months before death. (*p. 86*)

Test A systematic procedure for observing behavior in a standard situation and describing it with the help of a numerical scale or a category system. (*p. 365*)

Testosterone A masculine hormone, the principal androgen. (See also *androgens.*) (*p. 417*)

Textural gradient A graduated change in the texture, or "grain," of the visual field, whereby changes in texture across the retinal image are perceived as changes in distance; objects with finer, less detailed textures are perceived as more distant. (*p. 189*)

Texture A Gestalt grouping principle stating that when features of stimuli have the same texture (such as the orientation of certain elements) they tend to be grouped together. (*p. 185*)

Thalamus A structure in the forebrain that relays signals from the eyes and other sense organs to higher levels in the brain and plays an important role in processing and making sense out of this information. (*p. 108*)

Theory An integrated set of propositions that can be used to account for, predict, and even control certain phenomena. (*p. 21*)

Thinking The manipulation of mental representations, performed in order to form new representations. (*p. 328*)

Timbre The quality of sound that identifies it, so that, for example, a middle C played on the piano is clearly distinguishable from a middle C played on a trumpet. The timbre depends on the mixture of frequencies and amplitudes that make up the sound. (*p. 136*)

Token economy A system for improving the behavior of severely disturbed or mentally retarded clients in institutions that involves rewarding desirable behaviors with tokens that can be exchanged for snacks, field trips, access to television, or other privileges. (*p. 580*)

Tolerance A condition in which increasingly larger drug doses are needed to produce a given effect. (*p. 236*)

Top-down processing Those aspects of recognition that are guided by higher-level cognitive processes and psychological factors like expectations. (See also *bottom-up processing.*) (*p. 196*)

Topographical representation A map of each sense, contained in the primary cortex. Any two points that are next to each other in the stimulus will be represented next to each other in the brain. (*p. 135*)

Tranquilizer A class of drugs used to reduce mental and physical tension and symptoms of anxiety. (See also *anxiolytic.*) (*p. 598*)

Transduction The second step in sensation, which is the process of converting incoming energy into neural activity through receptors. (*p. 131*)

Transfer-appropriate processing A model of memory that suggests that a critical determinant of memory is how the encoding process matches up with what is ultimately retrieved. (*p. 291*)

Transference A phenomenon in which a client transfers to the therapist many of the feelings, attitudes, reactions, and conflicts experienced in childhood toward parents, siblings, and other significant people. (*p. 572*)

Transferred excitation The process of carrying over arousal from one experience to an independent situation, which is especially likely to occur when the arousal pattern from the

nonemotional source is similar to the pattern associated with a particular emotion. (*p. 438*)

Trichromatic theory The theory postulated by Young and Helmholtz that there are three types of visual elements, each of which is most sensitive to different wavelengths, and that information from these three elements combines to produce the sensation of color. (*p. 149*)

Tympanic membrane A tightly stretched membrane (also known as the eardrum) in the middle ear that generates vibrations that match the sound waves striking it. (*p. 137*)

Type A A personality type characterized by nonstop working, intense competitiveness, aggressiveness, and impatience, accompanied by an especially strong need to control events. (See also *Type B.*) (*p. 470*)

Type B A personality type characterized by a more relaxed and easygoing attitude than that associated with the Type A personality. (See also *Type A.*) (*p. 470*)

Type-trait approach See *dispositional approach.*

Unconditional positive regard In client-centered therapy, the therapist's attitude that expresses caring for and acceptance of the client as a valued person. (*p. 575*)

Unconditioned response (UCR) In classical conditioning, the automatic or unlearned reaction to a stimulus. (See also *conditioned response.*) (*p. 251*)

Unconditioned stimulus (UCS) In classical conditioning, the stimulus that elicits a response without conditioning. (See also *conditioned stimulus.*) (*p. 251*)

Unconscious level A segment of mental activity proposed by Freud that contains sexual, aggressive, and other impulses, as well as once-conscious but unacceptable thoughts and feelings of which an individual is completely unaware. (See also *conscious level, nonconscious level, preconscious level, and subconscious level.*) (*p. 219*)

Undifferentiated schizophrenia Patterns of disordered thought, behavior, and emotions that are characteristic of schizophrenia but that cannot easily be placed in any specific schizophrenic subtype. (*p. 552*)

Utility In rational decision making, any subjective measure of value. (*p. 345*)

Validity The degree to which a test measures what it is supposed to measure. (*p. 367*)

Valuative approach Defines normal versus abnormal behavior relative to prevailing social or cultural standards. (*p. 523*)

Variable interval (VI) schedule In operant conditioning, a type of partial reinforcement schedule that provides reinforcement for the first response after some varying period of time. For example, in a VI 60 schedule the first response to occur after an average of one minute would be reinforced, but the actual time between reinforcements could vary from, say, 1 second to 120 seconds. (*p. 266*)

Variable ratio (VR) schedule A type of partial reinforcement schedule that provides reinforcement after a varying number of responses. For example, on a VR 30 schedule, a rat might sometimes be reinforced after ten bar presses, sometimes after fifty bar presses, but an average of thirty responses would occur before reinforcement is given. (*p. 266*)

Variables Specific factors or characteristics that can take on different values in research. (*p. 21*)

Verbal scale Six subtests in the Wechsler scales that measure verbal skills as part of a measure of overall intelligence. (See also *performance scale*.) (*p. 371*)

Vestibular sacs Organs in the inner ear that connect the semicircular canals and the cochlea, and contribute to the body's sense of balance. (*p. 169*)

Vestibular sense The proprioceptive sense that provides information about the position of the body in space and about its general movements. It is often thought of as the sense of balance. (*p. 169*)

VI See *variable interval schedule*.

Vicarious conditioning Learning the relationship between a response and its consequences (either reinforcement or punishment) or the association between a conditioned stimulus and a conditioned response by watching others. (*p. 276*)

Visible light Electromagnetic radiation that has a wavelength from about 400 nanometers to about 750 nanometers. (A nanometer is one-billionth of a meter.) (*p. 141*)

Visual code A mental representation of stimuli as pictures. (*p. 289*)

Volley theory See *frequency matching*.

Vomeronasal organ A portion of the mammalian olfactory system that is sensitive to nonvolatile pheromones. (*p. 160*)

Vulnerability model A view of schizophrenia that suggests that different people have differing degrees of vulnerability to schizophrenia; this vulnerability may not be entirely inherited; and it may involve psychological and biological components. (See also *stress*.) (*p. 554*)

Wavelength The distance from one peak to the next in a waveform. (*p. 135*)

Weber's law A law stating that the smallest detectable difference in stimulus energy, the just-noticeable difference (JND), is a constant fraction, K, of the intensity of the stimulus, I. The constant varies for each sensory system and for different aspects of sensation within those systems. In algebraic terms, Weber's law is JND = KI. (See also *just-noticeable difference*.) (*p. 181*)

Withdrawal syndrome A complex of symptoms associated with the termination of administration of a habit-forming substance. (*p. 236*)

Word A unit of language composed of one or more morphemes. (See also *morpheme*.) (*p. 350*)

Working memory See *short-term memory*.

References

Aaker, D. A., & Stayman, D. M. (1989). What mediates the emotional response to advertising? The case of warmth. In P. Cafferata & A. Tybout (Eds.), *Cognitive and affective responses to advertising.* Lexington, MA: Lexington Books.

Abbott, B. B., Schoen, L. S., & Badia, P. (1984). Predictable and unpredictable shock: Behavioral measures of aversion and physiological measures of stress. *Psychological Bulletin, 96,* 45–71.

Abel, G. G., Blanchard, E. B., & Barlow, D. H. (1981). Measurement of sexual arousal in several paraphilias: The effects of stimulus modality, instrumental set, and stimulus content on the objective. *Behavior Research and Therapy, 19,* 25–33.

Abel, G. G., Blanchard, E. B., & Becker, J. V. (1976). Psychological treatment of rapists. In M. Walker & S. Brodsky (Eds.), *Sexual assault: The victim and the rapist.* Lexington, MA: Lexington Books.

Abeles, N. (1985). Proceedings of the American Psychological Association, 1985. *American Psychologist, 41,* 633–663.

Abernethy, B. (1988). Visual search in sport and ergonomics: Its relationship to sport and perform expertise. *Human Performance, 1,* 205–235.

Abraham, C., Sheeran, P., Spears, R., & Abrams, D. (1992). Health beliefs and promotion of HIV-preventive intentions among teenages: A Scottish perspective. *Health Psychology, 11,* 363–370.

Abraham, F. D., Abraham, R. H., & Shaw, C. D. (1991). *A visual introduction to dynamical systems theory for psychology.* Santa Cruz, CA: Aerial Press.

Abraham, G. E. (1983). Nutritional factors in the etiology of the premenstrual tension syndromes. *Journal of Reproductive Medicine, 28,* 446–464.

Abraham, H. D., & Wolf, E. (1988). Visual function in past users of LSD: Psychophysical findings. *Journal of Abnormal Psychology, 97,* 443–447.

Abrams, R., Taylor, M., Faber, R., Ts'o, T., Williams, R., & Almy, G. (1983). Bilateral vs. unilateral electronconvulsive therapy: Efficacy and melancholia. *American Journal of Psychiatry, 140,* 463–465.

Abramson, L. Y., Metalsky, G. I., & Alloy, L. B. (1989). Hopelessness depression: A theory-based subtype. *Psychological Review, 96,* 358–372.

Abramson, L. Y., Seligman, M. E. P., & Teasdale, J. D. (1978). Learned helplessness in humans: Critique and reformulation. *Journal of Abnormal Psychology, 87,* 49–74.

Achenbach, T. M. (1982). *Developmental psychopathology* (2nd ed.). New York: Wiley.

Acitelli, L. K. (1992). Gender differences in relationship awareness and marital satisfaction among young married couples. *Personality and Social Psychology Bulletin, 18,* 102–110.

Acklin, M., McDowell, C., II, & Orndoff, S. (1992). Statistical power and Rorschach: 1975–1991. *Journal of Personality Assessment, 59,* 366–379.

Adam, K., & Oswald, I. (1977). Sleep is for tissue restoration. *Journal of the Royal College of Physicians, 11,* 376–388.

Adams, G. R., & Jones, R. M. (1983). Female adolescents' identity development: Age comparisons and perceived child-rearing experience. *Developmental Psychology, 19,* 249–256.

Adams, H. E., & Chioto, J. (1983). Sexual deviations. In H. E. Adams & P. B. Sutker (Eds.), *Comprehensive handbook of psychopathology.* New York: Plenum Press.

Adams, J. A. (1989). *Human factors engineering.* New York: Macmillan.

Adams, M. J. (1990). *Beginning to read.* Cambridge, MA: MIT Press.

Adams, R., Maurer, D., & Davis, M. (1986). Newborns' discrimination of chromatic from achromatic stimuli. *Journal of Experimental Child Psychology, 41,* 267–281.

Ader, R., & Cohen, N. (1982). Behaviorally conditioned immunosuppression and murine systemic lupus erythematosus. *Science, 215,* 1534–1536.

Ader, R., & Cohen, N. (1985). CNS-immune system interactions: Conditioning phenomena. *Behavior and Brain Sciences, 8,* 379–394.

Ader, R., Felten, D., & Cohen, N. (1990). Interactions between the brain and the immune system. *Annual Review of Pharmacology and Toxicology, 30,* 561–602.

Adkins-Regan, E. (1988). Sex hormones and sexual orientation in animals. *Psychobiology, 16,* 335–347.

Adler, A. (1963). *The practice and theory of individual psychology* (original work published 1927). Paterson, NJ: Littlefield Adams.

Adler, N. J. (1990). *International dimensions of organizational behavior* (2nd ed.). Boston: Kent.

Adler, T. (1989, March). FAA establishes unit to study human error. *APA Monitor.*

Adler, T. (1993). Bad mix: Combat stress, decisions. *APA Monitor,* March, p. 1.

Adorno, T. W., Frenkel-Brunswik, E., Levinson, D. J., & Sanford, R. N. (1950). *The authoritarian personality.* New York: Harper & Row.

Agostinelli, G., Sherman, S. J., Presson, C. C., & Chassin, L. (1992). Self-protection and self-enhancement biases in estimates of population prevalence. *Personality and Social Psychology Bulletin, 18,* 631–642.

Aiken, L. R. (1987). *Assessment of intellectual functioning.* Boston, MA: Allyn & Bacon.

Ainsworth, M. D. S. (1973). The development of infant-mother attachment. In B. M. Caldwell & H. N. Ricciuti (Eds.), *Review of child development research: Vol. 3.* Chicago: University of Chicago Press.

Ainsworth, M. D. S. (1989). Attachments beyond infancy. *American Psychologist, 44,* 709–716.

Ainsworth, M. D. S., Blehar, M. D., Waters, E., & Wall, S. (1978). *Patterns of attachment: A psychological study of the Strange Situation.* Hillsdale, NJ: Lawrence Erlbaum Associates.

Aitchison, J. (1983). *The articulate mammal: An introduction to psycholinguistics* (2nd ed.). New York: Universe.

Ajzen, I. (1989). Attitude structure and behavior. In A. R. Pratkanis, S. J. Breckler, & A. G. Greenwald (Eds.), *Attitude structure and function.* Hillsdale, NJ: Lawrence Erlbaum Associates.

Alan Guttmacher Institute (1981). *Teenage pregnancy: The problem that hasn't gone away.* New York: Alan Guttmacher Institute.

Albee, G. (1968). Conceptual models and manpower requirements in psychology. *American Psychologist, 23,* 317–320.

Albee, G. (1985, February). The answer is prevention. *Psychology Today.*

Albert, D. J., & Walsh, M. L. (1984). Neural systems and the inhibitory modulation of agnostic behavior: A comparison of mammalian species. *Neuroscience and Biobehavioral Reviews, 8,* 5–24.

Albert, R. D. (1988). The place of culture in modern psychology. In P. Bronstein & K. Quina (Eds.), *Teaching a psychology of people.* Washington, DC: American Psychological Association.

Alberti, R. E., & Emmons, M. L. (1986). *Your perfect right: A guide to assertive living* (5th ed.). San Luis Obispo, CA: Impact Publishers.

Alcantara, A. A., Chaney, K. A., Pazdera, T. M., Woziwodzkia, P. K., & Greenough, W. T. (1993). CFOS expression in learning—associated areas of rat cerebellum during initial acquisition of a motor learning task. *Behavioral and Neural Biology.*

Alcock, J. E. (1987). Parapsychology: Science of the anomalous or search for the soul? *Brain and Behavior Science, 10,* 553–643.

Alcohol and health: Report to the U.S. Congress. (1984). Rockville, MD: Department of Health and Human Services.

Alcohol, Drug Abuse, and Mental Health Administration (ADAMHA). (1987). *Update: Facts from the sixth special report to Congress on alcohol and health.* Washington, DC: ADAMHA.

Aldag, R. J., & Fuller, S. R. (1993). Beyond fiasco: A reappraisal of the groupthink phenomenon and a new model of group decision processes. *Psychological Bulletin, 113,* 533–552.

Aldwin, C. M., & Revenson, T. A. (1987). Does coping help? A reexamination of the relation between coping and mental health. *Journal of Personality and Social Psychology, 53,* 337–348.

Alexander, C. N., Rainforth, M. V., & Gelderloos, P. (1991). Transcendental meditation, self-actualization, and psychological health: A conceptual overview and statistical meta-analysis. *Journal of Social Behavior and Personality, 6,* 189–247.

Alexander, F. M. (1963). *Fundamentals of psychoanalysis.* New York: W. W. Norton.

Allen, B. L. (1991). Cognitive research in information science: Implications for design. In M. Williams (Ed.), *Annual Review of Information Science and Technology, 26,* 3–37.

Allen, G. J. (1977). *Understanding psychotherapy.* Champaign, IL: Research Press.

Allen, J. P., & Turner, E. (1990). Where diversity reigns. *American Demographics, 12,* 34–38.

Allen, K. E., Hart, B. M., Buell, J. S., Harris, F. R., & Wolf, M. M. (1964). Effects of social reinforcement on isolate behavior of a nursery school child. In L. P. Ullmann & L. Krasner (Eds.), *Case studies in behavior modification.* New York: Holt, Rinehart and Winston.

Allen, L. S., Hines, M., Shryne, J. E., & Gorski, R. A. (1989). Two sexually dimorphic cell groups in the human brain. *Journal of Neuroscience, 9,* 497–506.

Allen, M. G. (1976). Twin studies of affective illness. *Archives of General Psychiatry, 33,* 1476–1478.

Allen, M. G., Cohen, S., & Pollin, W. (1972). Schizophrenia in veteran twins: A diagnostic review. *American Journal of Psychiatry, 128,* 939–947.

Alloy, L. B., & Abramson, L. Y. (1979). Judgment of contingency in depressed and nondepressed students: Sadder but wiser? *Journal of Experimental Psychology: General, 108,* 441–485.

Alloy, L., & Clements, C. (1992). Illusion of control: Invulnerability to negative affect and depressive symptoms after laboratory and natural stressors. *Journal of Abnormal Psychology, 101,* 234–245.

Allport, G. W. (1961). *Pattern and growth in personality.* New York: Holt, Rinehart & Winston.

Allred, K. D., & Smith, T. W. (1989). The hardy personality: Cognitive and physiological responses to evaluative threat. *Journal of Personality and Social Psychology, 56,* 257–266.

Almada, S., Zonderman, A., Shekelle, R., Dyer, A., Daviglus, M.,

Costa, L., & Stamler, J. (1991). Neuroticism and cynicism and risk of death in middle-aged men: The Western Electric study. *Psychosomatic Medicine, 53,* 165–175.

Amabile, T. (1989). *Growing up creative.* New York: Random House.

Amabile, T. M., Hennessey, B. A., & Grossman, B. S. (1986). Social influences on creativity: The effects of contracted-for reward. *Journal of Personality & Social Psychology, 50,* 14–23.

Amato, P. R. & Keith, B. (1991). Parental divorce and the well-being of children: A meta-analysis. *Psychological Bulletin, 110,* 26–46.

Ambrosini, M. V., Langella, M., Gironi-Carnivale, U. A., & Giuditta, A. (1992). The sequential hypothesis of sleep function: III. The structure of postacquisition sleep in learning and non-learnring rats. *Physiology and Behavior, 51,* 217–226.

American Law Institute. (1962). *Model penal code: Proposed offical draft.* Philadelphia: Author.

American Psychiatric Association. (1989). *Treatments of psychiatric disorders.* Washington, DC: American Psychiatric Association.

American Psychological Association. (1974). *Standards for educational and psychological test and manuals.* Washington, DC: Author.

American Psychological Association. (1981). Ethical principles of psychologists. *American Psychologist, 36,* 633–638.

American Psychological Association. (1981/1989). Ethical principles of psychologists. *American Psychologist, 36,* 633–638. (Amended June 2, 1989)

American Psychological Association. (1984). *Behavioral research with animals.* Washington, DC: American Psychological Association.

American Psychological Association. (1987). *Casebook on ethical principles of psychologists.* Washington, DC: American Psychological Association.

American Psychological Association. (1989). *Membership directory.* Washington, DC: APA.

American Psychological Association. (1990). Ethical principles of psychologists (Amended June 2, 1989). *American Psychologist, 45,* 390–395.

American Psychological Association. (1992a). APA continues to refine its ethics code. *APA Monitor,* May.

American Psychological Association. (1992b). Ethical principles of psychologists and code of conduct. *American Psychologist, 47,* 1597–1611.

Anastasi, A. (1971). Note on the concepts of creativity and intelligence. *Journal of Creative Behavior, 5,* 113–116.

Anastasi, A. (1976). *Psychological testing* (4th ed.) New York: Macmillan.

Anastasi, A. (1982). *Psychological testing* (5th ed.). New York: Collier Macmillan.

Anastasi, A. (1988). *Psychological testing* (6th ed.). New York: Macmillan.

Ancona, D. G. (1987). Groups in organizations: Extending laboratory models. In C. Hendrick (Ed.), *Group processes and intergroup relations.* Newbury Park, CA: Sage.

Andersen, G. J. (1986). The perception of self motion: Psychological and computational approach. *Journal of Experimental Psychology: Perception & Human Performance, 11,* 122–132.

Anderson, B. L. (1992). Psychological interventions for cancer patients to enhance the quality of life. *Journal of Consulting and Clinical Psychology, 60,* 569–575.

Anderson, C. A. (1989). Temperature and aggression: Ubiquitous effects of heat on occurrence of human violence. *Psychological Bulletin, 106,* 74–96.

Anderson, J. A. (1992). Problem solving and learning. *American Psychologist, 48,* 35–44.

Anderson, J. R. (1979). *Cognitive psychology.* New York: Academic Press.

Anderson, J. R. (1989). A rational analysis of human memory. In H. L. Roediger & F. I. M. Craik (Eds.), *Varieties of memory and consciousness.* Hillsdale, NJ: Lawrence Erlbaum Associates.

Anderson, J. R. (1990). *Cognitive psychology and its implications* (3rd ed.). New York: W. H. Freeman

Anderson, J. R. (1992). Problem solving and learning. *American Psychologist, 48,* 35–44.

Anderson, N. B. (1989). Racial differences in stress-induced cardiovascular reactivity and hypertension: Current status and substantive issues. *Psychological Bulletin, 105,* 89–105.

Anderson, N. H. (1989). Functional memory and on-line attribution. In J. N. Bassili (Ed.), *On-line cognition in person perception.* Hillsdale, NJ: Lawrence Erlbaum Associates.

Anderson, R. C., Reynolds, R. E., Schallert, D. L., & Goetz, E. T. (1977). Frameworks for comprehending discourse. *American Educational Research Journal, 14,* 367–382.

Anderson, T. H. (1978). *Another look at the self-questioning study technique* (Technical Ed. Rep. No. 6). Champaign: University of Illinois, Center for the Study of Reading.

Andreasen, N. C., Olson, S. A., Dennert, J. W., & Smith, M. R. (1982). Ventricular enlargement in schizophrenia: Relationship to positive and negative symptoms. *American Journal of Psychiatry, 139,* 297–302.

Andreasen, N. C., Rice, J., Endicott, J., Coryell, W., Grove, W. W., & Reich, T. (1987). Familial rates of affective disorder. *Archives of General Psychiatry, 44,* 461–472.

Andreasen, N., Ehrhardt, J., Swayze, V., Alliger, R., Yuh, T., Cohen, G., & Ziebell, S. (1990). Magnetic resonance imaging of the brain in schizophrenia. *Archives of General Psychiatry, 47,* 35–44.

Andrews, G., & Harvey, R. (1981). Does psychotherapy benefit neurotic patients? *Archives of General Psychiatry, 138,* 1203–1208.

Andrews, J. D. W. (1989). Integrating vision of reality: Interpersonal diagnosis and the existential vision. *American Psychologist, 44,* 803–817.

Angoff, W. H. (1989). The nature-nurture debate, aptitudes, and group differences. *American Psychologist, 43,* 713–720.

Angrist, B., Lee, H. K., & Gershon, S. (1974). The antagonism of amphetamine-induced symptomatology by a neuroleptic. *American Journal of Psychiatry, 131,* 817–819.

Annual Review of Neuroscience, 15, 1–29.

Anrep, G. V. (1920). Pitch discrimination in the dog. *Journal of Physiology, 53,* 367–385.

Anshel, M. W., & Wrisberg, C. A. (1988). The effect of arousal and focused attention on warmup decrement. *Journal of Sport Behavior, 11,* 18–31.

Antoni, M. H., Baggett, L., Ironson, G., LaPerriere, A., August, S., Klimas, N., Schneiderman, N., & Fletcher, M. A. (1991). Cognitive-behavioral stress management interventions buffer distress responses and immunologic changes following notification of HIV-1 seropositive. *Journal of Consulting and Clinical Psychology, 59,* 906–915.

APA Task Force. (1992, January/February). APA task force emphasizes psychology's contributions to education. *The Psychology Teacher Network, 2*(1), 1–10.

Appley, M. H., & Trumbull, R. (Eds.) (1986). *Dynamics of stress: Physiological, psychological, and social perspectives.* New York: Plenum Press.

Archambault, C. M., Czyzewski, D., Cordua y Cruz, G. D., Foreyt, F. P., & Mariotto, M. J. (1989). Effects of weight cycling in female rats. *Physiology and Behavior, 46,* 417–421.

Archer, J. (1991). The influence of testosterone on human aggression. *British Journal of Psychiatry, 82,* 1–28.

Archer, J., & Lloyd, B. (1985). *Sex and gender.* Cambridge: Cambridge University Press.

Arenberg, D. (1982). Changes with age in problem solving. In F. I. M. Craik & S. Trehub (Eds.), *Aging and cognitive processes* (pp. 221–236). New York: Plenum.

Aretz, A. J. (1991). The design of electronic map displays. *Human Factors, 33*(1), 85–101.

Argyle, M. (1988). *Bodily communication.* London: Methuen.

Arkin, R. M., & Baumgardner, A. H. (1985). Self-handicapping. In J. H. Harvey & G. Weary (Eds.), *Attribution: Basic issues and applications.* New York: Academic Press.

Arlin, P. K. (1980, June). *Adolescent and adult thought: A search for structures.* Paper presented at the meeting of the Jean Piaget Society, Philadelphia, PA.

Arnheim, R. (1969). *Visual thinking.* Berkeley: University of California Press.

Aron, A., Aron, E. N., Tudor, M., & Nelson, G. (1991). Close relationships as including others in the self. *Journal of Personality and Social Psychology, 60,* 241–253.

Aronoff, J., Barclay, A. M., & Stevenson, L. A. (1988). The recognition of threatening stimuli. *Journal of Personality and Social Psychology, 54,* 647–655.

Aronson, E. (1988). *The social animal* (5th ed.). San Francisco: W. H. Freeman.

Aronson, E. (1990). Applying social psychology to desegregation and energy conservation. *Personality and Social Psychology Bulletin, 16,* 118–132.

Aronson, E., & Cope, V. (1968). My enemy's enemy is my friend. *Journal of Personality and Social Psychology, 8,* 8–12.

Aronson, E., Brewer, M., & Carlsmith, J. M. (1963). Experimentation in social psychology. In G. Lindzey & E. Aronson (Eds.), *The handbook of social psychology: Vol. 1* (3rd ed.). New York: Random House.

Aronson, E., Turner, J. A., & Carlsmith, J. M. (1963). Communicator credibility and communication discrepancy as a determinant of opinion change. *Journal of Abnormal and Social Psychology, 67,* 31–36.

Artiberry, M., Yonas, A., & Bensen, A. S. (1989). Self-produced locomotion and development of responsiveness to textural gradients. *Developmental Psychology, 25,* 976–982.

Asarnow, J. R., & Horton, A. A. (1990). Coping and stress in families of child psychiatric inpatients: Parents of children with depressive and schizophrenic spectrum disorders. *Child Psychiatry and Human Development, 21,* 145–157.

Asch, S. E. (1951). Effects of group pressure upon the modification and distortion of judgments. In H. Guetzkow (Ed.), *Groups, leadership, and men.* Pittsburgh: Carnegie Press.

Asch, S. E. (1955). Opinions and social pressure. *Scientific American, 193,* 31–35.

Asch, S. E. (1956). Studies of independence and conformity: A minority of one against a unanimous majority. *Psychological Monographs, 70,* 1–70.

Aserinsky, E., & Kleitman, N. (1953). Regularly occurring periods of eye motility and concomitant phenomena during sleep. *Science, 118,* 273.

Ashcraft, M. H. (1989). *Human memory and cognition.* Glenview, IL: Scott, Foresman.

Ashmead, D. H., & Perlmutter, M. (1980). Infant memory in everyday life. In M. Perlmutter (Ed.), *New directions in child development: Children's memory.* San Francisco: Jossey-Bass.

Aslin, R. N., Pisoni, D. B., & Jusczyk, P. W. (1983). Auditory development and speech perception in infancy. In P. H. Mussen (Ed.), *Handbook of child psychology: Vol. 2.* New York: Wiley.

Aspinwall, L., Kemeny, M., Taylor, S., Schneider, S., & Dudley, J. (1991). Psychosocial predictors of gay men's AIDS risk-reduction behavior. *Health Psychology, 10,* 432–444.

Associated Press. (1984). *Man sets wife afire after watching TV movie.*

Associated Press. (1986). *Media general poll.*

Associated Press. (1989, August 20). Think you have a great memory? Forget it. *Chicago Tribune*, sec. 2, p. 1.

Associated Press. (1992). *Rape survey raises count.* April 23.

Aston-Jones, G., Chiang, C., & Alexinsky, T. (1991b). Discharge of noradrenergic locus coeruleus neurons in behaving rats and monkeys suggests a role in vigilance. *Progress in Brain Research, 88*, 501–520.

Aston-Jones, G., Shipley, M.T., Chouvet, G., Ennis, M., van Bockstaele, E., Pieribone, V., Shiekhattar, R., Akaoka, H., Drolet, G., Astier, B., Charlety, P., Valentino, R. J., & Williams, J. T. (1991a). Afferent regulation of locus coeruleus neurons: Anatomy, physiology and pharmacology. *Progress in Brain Research, 88*, 47–75.

Atkinson, J. W., & Birch, D. (1978). *Introduction to motivation* (2nd ed.). New York: D. Van Nostrand.

Atkinson, J. W., & Raynor, J. O. (1974). *Personality, motivation, and achievment.* Washington, DC: Hemisphere.

Atkinson, R. C., & Shiffrin, R. M. (1968). Human memory: A proposed system and its control processes. In K. Spence (Ed.), *The psychology of learning and motivation: Vol. 2.* New York: Academic Press.

Atkinson, R. L., Fuchs, A., Pastors, J. G., & Saunders, J. T. (1992). Combination of very-low-calorie diet and behavior modification in the treatment of obesity. *American Journal of Clinical Nutrition, 56*, 199S-202S.

Austin, J. T., & Hanisch, K. A. (1990). Occupational attainment as a function of abilities and interests: A longitudinal analysis using Project TALENT data. *Journal of Applied Psychology, 75*, 77–86.

Averill, J. R. (1993). Putting the social in social cognition, with special reference to emotion. In R. S. Wyer & T. K. Srull (Eds.), *Toward a general theory of anger and emotional aggression: Advances in social cognition, Vol. VI.* Hillsdale, NJ: Lawrence Erlbaum Associates.

Averill, J. S. (1980). On the paucity of positive emotions. In K. R. Blankstein, P. Pliner, & J. Polivy (Eds.), *Advances in the study of communication and affect: Vol. 6. Assessment and modification of emotional behavior.* New York: Plenum Press.

Axelrod, R. (1984). *The evolution of cooperation.* New York: Basic Books.

Axelrod, R., & Dion, D. (1988). The further evolution of cooperation. *Science, 242*, 1385–1390.

Axsom, D. (1989). Cognitive dissonance and behavior change in psychotherapy. *Journal of Experimental Social Psychology, 25*, 234–252.

Ayllon, T., & Azrin, N. H. (1968). *The token economy: A motivational system for therapy and rehabilitation.* New York: Appleton-Century-Crofts.

Babad, E., Bernieri, F., & Rosenthal, R. (1989). Nonverbal communication and leakage in the behavior of biased and unbiased teachers. *Journal of Personality and Social Psychology, 56*, 89–94.

Babcock, R., & Salthouse, T. (1990). Effects of increased processing demands on age differences in working memory. *Psychology and Aging, 5*, 421–428.

Bacal, H. A., & Newman, K. M. (1990). *Theories of object relations: Bridges to self psychology.* New York: Columbia University Press.

Bach, S., & Klein, G. S. (1957). The effects of prolonged subliminal exposure of words. *American Psychologist, 12*, 397–398.

Backman, L., & Nilsson, L. (1991). Effects of divided attention on free and cued recall of verbal events and action events. *Bulletin of the Psychonomic Society, 29*, 51–54.

Backstrom, T., & Carstensen, H. (1974). Estrogen and progesterone in plasma in relation to premenstrual tension. *Journal of Steroid Biochemistry, 5*, 257–260.

Baddeley, A. (1982). *Your memory: A user's guide.* New York: Macmillan.

Bahr, S. J., Chappell, C. G., & Leigh, G. K. (1983). Age at marriage, role enactment, role consensus, and marital satisfaction. *Journal of Marriage and the Family, 45*, 795–803.

Bahrick, H. P. (1984). Semantic memory content in permastore: Fifty years of memory for Spanish learned in school. *Journal of Experimental Psychology: General, 113*, 1–29.

Bahrick, H. P. (1992). Stabilized memory of unrehearsed knowledge. *Journal of Experimental Psychology: General, 121*, 112–113.

Bahrick, H. P., & Boucher, B. (1968). Retention of visual and verbal codes of the same stimuli. *Journal of Experimental Psychology, 78*, 417–422.

Bahrick, H. P., & Hall, L. K. (1991). Lifetime maintenance of high school mathematics content. *Journal of Experimental Psychology: General, 120*, 20–33.

Bailey, J. M., & Benishay, D. S. (1993). Familial aggregation of female sexual orientation. *American Journal of Psychiatry, 150*, 272–277.

Bailey, J. M., & Pillard, R. C. (1991). A genetic study of male sexual orientation. *Archives of General Psychiatry, 48*, 1089–1096.

Baillargeon, R. (1987). Object permanence in 3 1/2 and 4 1/2 month-old infants. *Developmental Psychology, 23*, 655–664.

Baillargeon, R. (1992). The object concept revisited: New directions in the investigation of infants' physical knowledge. In C. E. Granrud (Ed.), *Visual perception and cognition in infancy: Carnegie-Mellon Symposia on Cognition* (Vol. 23). Hillsdale, NJ: Lawrence Erlbaum Associates.

Baillargeon, R., Graber, M., Devos, J., & Black, J. (1990). Why do young infants fail to search for hidden objects? *Cognition, 36*, 255–284.

Baker, L. T., Vernon, P. A., & Ho, H. (1991). The genetic correlation between intelligence and speed of information processing. *Behavior Genetics, 21*, 351–367.

Baker, T. B., & Tiffany, S. T. (1985). Morphine tolerance as habituation. *Psychological Review, 92*, 78–108.

Bakker, D. J. (1990). *Neuropsychological treatment of dyslexia.* New York: Oxford University Press.

Balay, J., & Shevrin, H. (1988). The subliminal psychodynamic activation method: A critical review. *American Psychologist, 43*, 161–174.

Bales, J. (1988, December). Vincennes: Findings could have helped avert tragedy, scientists tell Hill panel. *APA Monitor*, pp. 10–11.

Balestreri, R., Fontana, L., & Astengo, F. (1987). A double-blind placebo-controlled evaluation of the safety and efficacy of vinpocetine in the treatment of patients with chronic vascular senile cerebral dysfunction. *Journal of the American Geriatric Society, 35*, 425–430.

Balota, D. A. (1983). Automatic semantic activation and episodic memory encoding. *Journal of Verbal Learning and Verbal Behavior, 22*, 88–104.

Bandura, A. (1965). Influence of a model's reinforcement contingencies on the acquisition of imitative responses. *Journal of Personality and Social Psychology, 1*, 589–595.

Bandura, A. (1969). *Principles of behavior modification.* New York: Holt, Rinehart and Winston.

Bandura, A. (1977). *Social learning theory* (original work published 1971). Englewood Cliffs, NJ: Prentice-Hall.

Bandura, A. (1978). The self system in reciprocal determinism. *American Psychologist, 33*, 344–358.

Bandura, A. (1982a). The assessment and predictive generality of self-percepts of efficacy. *Journal of Behavior Therapy and Experimental Psychiatry, 13*, 195–199.

Bandura, A. (1982b). Self-efficacy mechanism in human agency. *American Psychologist, 37*, 122–147.

Bandura, A. (1983). Psychological measurement of aggression. In R. G. Green and C. I. Donnerstein (Eds.), *Aggression: Theoretical and empirical reviews* (Vol. 1). New York: Academic Press.

Bandura, A. (1986). *Social foundations of thought and action: A social cognitive theory.* Englewood Cliffs, NJ: Prentice-Hall.

Bandura, A. (1989). Self-efficacy mechanism in physiological activation and health-promoting behavior. In J. Madden IV, S. Matthysse, & J. Barchas (Eds.), *Adaptation, learning, and affect.* New York: Raven Press.

Bandura, A., Blanchard, E. B., & Ritter, B. (1969). The relative efficacy of desensitization and modeling approaches for inducing behavioral, affective, and attitudinal changes. *Journal of Personality and Social Psychology, 13,* 173–199.

Bandura, A., Cioffi, D., Taylor, C. B., & Brouillard, M. E. (1988). Perceived self-efficacy in coping with cognitive stressors and opioid activation. *Journal of Personality and Social Psychology, 55,* 479–488.

Bandura, A., O'Leary, A., Taylor, C. B., Gauthier, J., & Gossard, D. (1987). Perceived self-efficacy and pain control: Opioid and nonopioid mechanisms. *Journal of Personality and Social Psychology, 53,* 563–571.

Bandura, A., Ross, D., & Ross, S. A. (1963). Imitation of film-mediated aggressive models. *Journal of Abnormal and Social Psychology, 66,* 3–11.

Bandura, A., Taylor, C., Williams, S., Mefford, I., & Barchas, J. (1985). Catecholamine secretion as a function of perceived coping self-efficacy. *Journal of Personality and Social Psychology, 53,* 406–414.

Bank, S., & Kahn, M. D. (1975). Sisterhood-brotherhood is powerful: Sibling subsystems and family therapy. *Family Process, 14,* 311–337.

Banks, M. S., & Salapatek, P. (1983). Infant visual perception. In P. H. Mussen (Ed.), *Handbook of child psychology: Vol. 2. Infancy and developmental psychobiology.* New York: Wiley.

Banks, W. P., & Krajicek, D. (1991). Perception. *Annual Review of Psychology, 42,* 305–332.

Barbaro, N. M. (1988). Studies of PAG/PVG stimulation for pain relief in humans. *Progress in Brain Research, 77,* 165–173.

Barber, T. X. (1969). *Hypnosis: A scientific approach.* New York: Van Nostrand Reinhold.

Barclay, J. R., Bransford, J. D., Franks, J. J., McCarrell, N. S., & Nitsch, K. (1974). Comprehension and semantic flexibility. *Journal of Verbal Learning and Verbal Behavior, 13,* 471–481.

Barefoot, J., Dodge, K., Peterson, B., Dalhstrom, G., & Williams, R. (1991). The Cook-Medley Hostility Scale: Item content and ability to predict survival. *Psychosomatic Medicine, 51,* 46–57.

Barefoot, J., Peterson, B., Dalhstrom, G., Siegler, I., Anderson, N., & Williams, R. (1989). Hostility patterns and health implications: Correlates of Cook-Medley Hostility Scale scores in a national survey. *Health Psychology, 10,* 18–24.

Barenboim, C. (1981). The development of person perception in childhood and adolescence: From behavioral comparisons to psychological constructs to psychological comparisons. *Child Development, 52,* 129–144.

Bargh, J. A. (1982). Attention and automaticity in the processing of self-relevant information. *Journal of Personality and Social Psychology, 43,* 425–436.

Bargh, J. A. (1994). The four horsemen of automaticity: Awareness, intention, efficiency, and control in social psychology. In R. S. Wyer & T. K. Srull (Eds.), *Handbook of social cognition* (2nd ed.). Hillsdale, NJ: Lawrence Erlbaum Associates.

Barinaga, M. (1989). Manic depression gene put in limbo. *Science, 246,* 886–887.

Barlow, D. (1988). *Anxiety and its disorders.* New York: Guilford.

Barlow, D., Rapee, R., & Brown, T. (1992). Behavioral treatment of generalized anxiety disorder. *Behavior Therapy, 23,* 551–570.

Barnett, B. J. (1989). Information processing components and knowledge representation: An individual differences approach to modeling pilot judgment. *Proceedings of the 33rd Annual Meeting of the Human Factors Society.* Santa Monica, CA: Human Factors Society.

Barnett, P. A., & Gotlieb, I. H. (1988). Psychosocial functioning and depression: Distinguishing among antecedents, concomitants, and consequences. *Psychological Bulletin, 104,* 97–126.

Baron, J. (1989). Why a theory of social intelligence needs a theory of character. In R. S. Wyer & T. K. Srull (Eds.), *Advances in social cognition: Vol. 2. Social intelligence and cognitive assessments of personality.* Hillsdale, NJ: Lawrence Erlbaum Associates.

Baron, R. A. (1988). Attributions and organizational conflict: The mediating role of apparent sincerity. *Organizational Behavior and Human Decision Processes, 41,* 111–127.

Baron, R. A., & Byrne, D. (1991). *Social psychology: Understanding human interaction* (6th ed.). Boston: Allyn & Bacon.

Baron, R. A., & Richardson, D. R. (1992). *Human aggression* (2nd ed.). New York: Plenum.

Baron, R., Cutuona, C., Hicklin, D., Russell, & Lubaroff, D. (1990). Social support and immune function among spouses of cancer patients. *Journal of Personality and Social Psychology, 59,* 344–352.

Barr, C., Mednick, S., & Munk-Jorgensen, P. (1990). Exposure to influenza epidemics during gestation and adult schizophrenia: A 40-year study. *Archives of General Psychiatry, 47,* 869–874.

Barrett, C. J. (1978). Effectiveness of widows' groups in facilitating change. *Journal of Consulting and Clinical Psychology, 46,* 20–31.

Barrett, G. V., & Depinet, R. L. (1991). A reconsideration of testing for competence rather than for intelligence. *American Psychologist, 46,* 1012–1024.

Barrett, J. E. (Ed.). (1979). *Stress and mental disorder.* New York: Raven.

Barron, F., & Harrington, D. M. (1981). Creativity, intelligence, and personality. *Annual Review of Psychology, 52,* 439–476.

Bartholomew, K., & Horowitz, L. M. (1991). Attachment styles among young adults: A test of a four-category model. *Journal of Personality and Social Psychology, 61,* 226–244.

Bartol, C. (1991). Predictive validation of the MMPI for small-town police officers who fail. *Professional Psychology: Research and Practice, 22,* 127–132.

Bartone, P., Gifford, R., Wright, K., Marlowe, D., & Martin, J. (1992). U.S. soldiers remain healthy under Gulf War stress. Paper presented at the 4th annual convention of the American Psychological Society, San Diego.

Bartoshuk, L. M. (1990). Distinctions between taste and smell relevant to the role of experience. In E. D. Capaldi, E. D. & T. L. Powley (Eds.), *Taste, experience, and feeding.* Washington, DC: American Psychological Association.

Bartoshuk, L. M. (1991). Taste, smell, and pleasure. In R. C. Bollef (Ed.), *The hedonics of taste.* Hillsdale, NJ: Lawrence Erlbaum Associates.

Bartoshuk, L. M., & Wolfe, J. M. (1990). Conditioned taste aversion in humans: Are there olfactory versions? *Chemical Senses, 15,* 551.

Bartoshuk, L. M., Gentile, R. L., Moskowitz, H. R., & Meiselman, H. L. (1974). Sweet taste induced by miracle fruit (Synsephalum dulcificum). *Physiology and Behavior, 12,* 449–456.

Bartus, R. T., Dean, R. L., III, Beer, B., and Lippa, A. S. (1982). The cholinergic hypothesis of geriatric memory dysfunction. *Science, 217,* 408–417.

Basgall, J. A., & Snyder, C. R. (1988). Excuses in waiting: External locus of control and reactions to success-failure feedback. *Journal of Personality and Social Psychology, 54,* 656–662.

Bassili, J. N. (1989a). Trait encoding in behavior identification and dispositional inference. *Personality and Social Psychology Bulletin, 15,* 285–296.

Bassili, J. N. (1989b). Traits as action categories versus traits as person attributes in social cognition. In J. N. Bassili (Ed.), *Online cognition in person perception.* Hillsdale, NJ: Lawrence Erlbaum Associates.

Bates, E. (1976). *Language and context: The acquisition of pragmatics.* New York: Academic Press.

Bates, J. E. (1980). The concept of difficult temperament. *Merrill-Palmer Quarterly, 25,* 299–319.

Batson, C. D. (1987). Prosocial motivation: Is it ever truly altruistic? In L. Berkowitz (Ed.), *Advances in experimental social psychology* (Vol. 20). Orlando, FL: Academic Press.

Batson, C. D. (1990). How social an animal? The human capacity for caring. *American Psychologist, 45,* 336–346.

Batson, C. D., Batson, J. G., Griffitt, C. A., Barrientos, S., Brandt, J. R., Sprengelmeyer, P., & Bayly, M. J. (1989). Negative-state relief and the empathy-altuism hypothesis. *Journal of Personality and Social Psychology, 56,* 922–933.

Battaglia, G., Yeh, S. Y., & De Souza, E. B. (1988). MDMA-induced neurotoxicity: Parameters of degeneration and recovery of brain serotonin neurons. *Pharmacology, Biochemistry and Behavior, 29,* 269–274.

Baucom, D. H., & Epstein, N. (1990). *Cognitive-behavioral marital therapy.* New York: Brunner/Mazel.

Baucom, D. H., Sayers, S. L., & Duhe, A. (1989). Attributional style and attributional patterns among married couples. *Journal of Personality and Social Psychology, 56,* 596–607.

Bauman, K., Koch, G., & Fisher, L. (1989). Family cigarette smoking and test performance by adolescents. *Health Psychology, 8,* 97–106.

Baumeister, R. F. (1984). Choking under pressure: Self-consciousness and paradoxical effects of incentives on skillful performance. *Journal of Personality and Social Psychology, 46*(3), 610–620.

Baumeister, R. F. (1989). Social intelligence and the construction of meaning in life. In R. S. Wyer & T. K. Srull (Eds.), *Advances in social cognition: Vol. 2. Social intelligence and cognitive assessments of personality.* Hillsdale, NJ: Lawrence Erlbaum Associates.

Baumeister, R. F., & Cairns, K. J. (1992). Repression and self-presentation: When audiences interfere with self-deceptive strategies. *Journal of Personality and Social Psychology, 62,* 851–862.

Baumeister, R. F., Stillwell, A., & Wotman, S. R. (1991). Victim and perpetrator accounts of interpersonal conflict: Autobiographical narratives about anger. *Journal of Personality and Social Psychology, 60,* 156–174.

Baumgardner, A. H., & Arkin, R. M. (1987). Coping with the prospect of social disapproval: Strategies and sequelae. In C. R. Snyder & C. Ford (Eds.), *Clinical and social psychological perspectives on negative life events.* New York: Plenum.

Baumgardner, A. H., Kaufman, C. M., & Levy, P. E. (1989). Regulating affect interpersonally: When low self-esteem leads to greater enhancement. *Journal of Personality and Social Psychology, 56,* 907–921.

Baumrind, D. (1971). Current patterns of parental authority. *Developmental Psychology Monographs, 4*(1, part 2).

Baumrind, D. (1975). Early socialization and adolescent competence. In S. E. Dragastin & G. H. Elder (Eds.), *Adolescence in the life cycle.* New York: Wiley.

Baumrind, D. (1985). Research using intentional deception: Ethical issues revisited. *American Psychologist, 40,* 165–174.

Baumrind, D. (1986). Familial antecedents of social competence in middle childhood. Unpublished monograph, Institute of Human Development, University of California, Berkeley.

Baumrind, D. (1989, April). Sex-differentiated socialization effects in childhood and adolescence in divorced and intact families. Paper presented at the meeting of the Society for Research in Child Development, Kansas City, MO.

Baumrind, D. (1991). Effective parenting during the early adolescent transition. In P. A. Cowan & E. M. Hetherington (Eds.), *Family transition* (pp. 111–163). Hillsdale, NJ: Lawrence Erlbaum Associates.

Baxter, L. R., Schwartz, J. M., Bergman, K. S., Szuba, M. P., Guze, B. H., Mazziotta, J. C., Alazraki, A., Selin, C. E., Ferng, H. K., Munford, P., & Phelps, M. E. (1992). Caudate glucose metabolic rate changes with both drug and behavior therapy for obsessive-compulsive disorder. *Archives of General Psychiatry, 49,* 681–689.

Baxter, L.R., et al. (1985). Can lithium carbonate prolong the antidepressant effect of sleep deprivation? *Archives of General Psychiatry, 42,* 631.

Baxter, T. L., & Goldberg, L. R. (1987). Perceived behavioral consistency underlying trait attributions to oneself and another: An extension of the actor-observer effect. *Personality and Social Psychology Bulletin, 13,* 437–447.

Baylis, G. C., & Driver, J. (1992). Visual parsing and response competition: The effect of grouping factors. *Perception and Psychophysics, 51,* 145–162.

Beaman, A. L., Barnes, P. J., Klentz, B., & McQuirk, B. (1978). Increasing helping rates through information dissemination: Teaching pays. *Personality and Social Psychology Bulletin, 4,* 406–411.

Beaman, A. L., Cole, C. M., Preston, M., Klentz, B., & Steblay, N. M. (1983). Fifteen years of foot-in-the-door research: A meta-analysis. *Personality and Social Psychology Bulletin, 9,* 181–196.

Beardsley, L. M. (1994). Medical diagnosis and treatment across culture. In W. J. Lonner and R. S. Malpass (Eds.), *Psychology and Culture.* New York: Allyn & Bacon.

Beatty, J. (1982). Task evoked pupillary responses, processing load, and the structure of processing resources. *Psychological Bulletin, 91,* 276–292.

Beatty, W. W. (1985). Assessing remote memory for space: The Fargo Map Test. *Journal of Experimental and Clinical Neuropsychology, 7,* 640.

Beatty, W. W., & Spangenberger, M. (1988). Persistence of geographic memories in adults. *Bulletin of the Psychonomic Society, 26,* 104–105.

Beck, A. (1976). *Cognitive therapy and the emotional disorders.* New York: International Universities Press, Inc.

Beck, A. J., & Shipley, B. E. (1989). *Special report: Recidivism of prisoners released in 1983.* Washington, DC: U.S. Department of Justice, Bureau of Justice Statistics.

Beck, A. T. (1967). *Depression: Clinical, experimental and theoretical aspects.* New York: Harper & Row.

Beck, A. T. (1987). Cognitive model of depression. *Journal of Cognitive Psychotherapy, 1,* 2–27.

Beck, A. T. (1991). Cognitive therapy: A thirty-year retrospective. *American Psychologist, 46,* 368–375.

Beck, A. T. (1993). Cognitive therapy: Past, present, and future. *Journal of Consulting and Clinical Psychology, 61,* 194–198.

Beck, A. T., & Emery, G. (1985). *Anxiety disorders and phobias: A cognitive perspective.* New York: Basic Books.

Beck, A. T., Rush, A. J., Shaw, B. F., & Emery, G. (1979). *Cognitive therapy of depression.* New York: Guilford Press.

Beck, A., Sokol, L., Clark, D., Berchick, R., & Wright, F. (1992). A crossover study of focused cognitive therapy for panic disorder. *American Journal of Psychiatry, 149,* 778–783.

Beck, J. (1966). Perceptual grouping produced by changes in orientation and shape. *Science, 154,* 538–563.

Beck, K. H., & Frankel, A. (1981). A conceptualization of threat communications and protective health behavior. *Social Psychology Quarterly, 3,* 204–217.

Beck, L., & Ajzen, I. (1991). Predicting dishonest actions using the theory of planned behavior. *Journal of Research in Personality, 25,* 285–301.

Becker, S., & Hinton, G. E. (1992). Self-organizing neural network that discovers surfaces in random-dot stereograms. *Nature, 355,* 161–163.

Bedard, J. (1989). Expertise in auditing: Myth or reality? *Accounting, Organizations and Society, 14,* 113–131.

Bedard, J., & Chi, M. T. H. (1992). Expertise. *Current Directions in Psychological Science, 1,* 135–139.

Begault, D. R., & Wenzel, E. M. (1992). Techniques and applications for binaural sound manipulation in human-machine interfaces. *International Journal of Aviation Psychology, 2,* 1–22.

Begg, I., & Denny, J. P. (1969). Empirical reconsideration of atmosphere and conversion interpretations of syllogistic reasoning errors. *Journal of Experimental Psychology, 81,* 351–354.

Behrens, B. C., Sanders, M. R., & Halford, W. K. (1990). Behavioral marital therapy: An evaluation of treatment effects across high- and low-risk settings. *Behavior Therapy, 21,* 423–433.

Beike, D. R., & Sherman, S. J. (1994). Social inference: Inductions, deductions, and analogies. In R. S. Wyer & T. K. Srull (Eds.), *Handbook of social cognition* (2nd ed.). Hillsdale, NJ: Lawrence Erlbaum Associates.

Beilin, H. (1992). Piaget's enduring contribution to developmental psychology. *Developmental Psychology, 28,* 191–204.

Bell, A., Weinberg, M. S., & Hammersmith, S. K. (1983). *Sexual preference development in men and women.* Bloomington: Indiana University Press.

Bell, B. E., & Loftus, E. F. (1989). Trivial persuasion in the courtroom: The power of (a few) minor details. *Journal of Personality and Social Psychology, 56,* 669–679.

Bell, P. A. (1992). In defense of the negative affect escape model of heat and aggression. *Psychological Bulletin, 111,* 342–346.

Bell, R. R., & Bell, P. L. (1972). Sexual satisfaction among married women. *Medical Aspects of Human Sexuality, 6,* 136–144.

Bellezza, F. S. (1981). Mnemonic devices: Classification, characteristics, and criteria. *Review of Educational Research, 51,* 247–275.

Bellezza, F. S. (1993). Does "perplexing" describe the self-reference effect? Yes! In T. K. Srull & R. S. Wyer (Eds.), *The mental representation of trait and autobiographical knowledge about the self: Advances in social cognition: Vol. V.* Hillsdale, NJ: Lawrence Erlbaum Associates.

Belli, R.F. (1989). Influences of misleading postevent information: Misinformation interference and acceptance. *Journal of Experimental Psychology: General, 118,* 72–85.

Belliveau, J. W., Kwong, K. K., Kennedy, D. N., Baker, J. R., Stern, C. E., Benson, R., Chesler, D. A., Weisskoff, R. M., Cohen, M. S., Tootell, R. B. H., Fox, P. T., Brady, T. J., & Rosen, B. R. (1992). Magnetic resonance imaging mapping of brain function: Human visual cortex. *Investigative Radiology, 27,* 59–65.

Belmont, J. M., & Butterfield, E. C. (1971). Learning strategies as determinants of memory deficiencies. *Cognitive Psychology, 2,* 411–420.

Belsky, J. (1988). The "effects" of infant day care reconsidered. *Early Childhood Research Quarterly, 3,* 235–272.

Belsky, J. (1992). Consequences of child care for children's development: A deconstructionist view. In A. Booth (Ed.), *Child care in the 1990s: Trends and consequences.* Hillsdale, NJ: Lawrence Erlbaum Associates.

Bem, D. J. (1967). Self-perception: An alternative interpretation of cognitive dissonance phenomena. *Psychological Review, 74,* 183–200.

Bem, D. J., & Allen, A. (1974). On predicting some of the people some of the time: The search for cross-situational consistencies in behavior. *Psychological Review, 81,* 506–520.

Bem, S. L. (1987). Masculinity and femininity exist only in the mind of the perceiver. In J. M. Reinisch, L. A. Rosenbaum, & S. A. Sanders (Eds.), *Masculinity/femininity: Basic perspectives.* New York: Oxford University Press.

Bemis, K. M. (1978). Current approaches to the etiology and treatment of anorexia nervosa. *Psychological Bulletin, 85,* 593–617.

Bemporad, J. R., & Schwab, M. E. (1986). The DSM-III and clinical child psychiatry. In T. Millon & G. L. Klerman (Eds.), *Contemporary directions in psychopathology: Toward the DSM-IV* (pp. 135–150). New York: Guilford Press.

Ben-Shakhar, G. & Furedy, J. J. (1990). *Theories and applications in the detection of deception: A psychophysiological and international perspective.* New York: Springer-Verlag.

Benca, R. M., Obermeyer, W. H., Thisted, R. A., & Gillin, J. C. (1992). Sleep and psychiatric disorders. A meta-analysis. *Archives of General Psychiatry, 49,* 651–658.

Bennett, H. L., Giannini, J. A., & Davis, H. S. (1985). Nonverbal response to intraoperational conversation. *British Journal of Anaesthesia, 57,* 174–179.

Benson, H. (1975). *The relaxation response.* New York: Morrow.

Benton, M., & Schroeder, H. (1990). Social skills training with schizophrenics: A meta-analytic evaluation. *Journal of Consulting and Clinical Psychology, 58,* 741–747.

Berbaum, K., Bevert, T., & Chung, C. (1983) Light source position in the perception of object shape. *Perception, 12,* 411–416.

Berenbaum, S. A., & Hines, M. (1992). Early androgens are related to childhood sex-typed toy preferences. *Psychological Science, 3,* 203–206.

Bergen, J. R., & Adelson, E. H. (1988). Early vision and texture perception. *Nature, 333,* 363–364.

Bergen, R. S., & Dweck, C. S. (1989). The functions of personality theories. In R. S. Wyer & T. K. Srull (Eds.), *Advances in social cognition: Vol. 2: Social intelligence and cognitive assessments of personality.* Hillsdale, NJ: Lawrence Erlbaum Associates.

Berger, P. A. (1978). Medical treatment of mental illness. *Science, 200,* 974–981.

Berkman, L., & Syme, S. L. (1979). Social networks, host resistance, and mortality: A nine-year follow-up study of Alameda County residents. *American Journal of Epidemiology, 109,* 186–204.

Berkowitz, B. (1965). Changes in intellect with age: IV. Changes in achievement and survival in older people. *Journal of Genetic Psychology, 107,* 3–14.

Berkowitz, L. (1981). Aversive conditions as stimuli for aggression. In L. Berkowitz (Ed.), *Advances in experimental social psychology: Vol. 15.* New York: Academic Press.

Berkowitz, L. (1984). Some effects of thought on anti- and pro-social influences of media events: A cognitive-neoassociation analysis. *Psychological Bulletin, 95,* 410–427.

Berkowitz, L. (1988). Frustrations, appraisals, and aversively stimulated aggression. *Aggressive Behavior, 14,* 3–11.

Berkowitz, L. (1989). Frustration-aggression hypothesis: Examination and reformulation. *Psychological Bulletin, 106,* 59–73.

Berkowitz, L. (1993). Toward a general theory of anger and emotional aggression. In R. S. Wyer & T. K. Srull (Eds.), *Toward a general theory of anger and emotional aggression: Advances in social cognition, Vol. VI.* Hillsdale, NJ: Lawrence Erlbaum Associates.

Berkowitz, L., & Heimer, K. (1989). On the construction of the anger experience: Aversive events and negative priming in the formation of feelings. In L. Berkowitz (Ed.), *Advances in experimental social psychology* (Vol. 22). New York: Academic Press.

Berkun, M. M. (1964). Performance decrement under psychological stress. *Human Factors, 6,* 21–30.

Berlyne, D. E. (1960). *Conflict, arousal, and curiosity.* New York: McGraw-Hill.

Berman, J. S., & Norton, N. C. (1985). Does professional training make a therapist more effective? *Psychological Bulletin, 98,* 401–407.

Berman, R. F. (1991). Electrical brain stimulation used to study mechanisms and models of memory. In J. L. Martinez & R. P. Kesner (Eds.), *Learning and memory: A biological view* (2nd ed.). San Diego: Academic Press.

Bermond, B., Fasotti, L., Nieuwenhuyse, B., & Schuerman, J. (1991). Spinal cord lesions, peripheral feedback and intensities of emotional feelings. *Cognition and Emotion, 5,* 201–220.

Bernard, L. L. (1924). *Instinct.* New York: Holt, Rinehart & Winston.

Berndt, T. J. (1978a, August). *Children's conceptions of friendship and the behavior expected of friends.* Paper presented at the annual meeting of the American Psychological Association, Toronto, Ontario.

Berndt, T. J. (1978b, August). *Developmental changes on conformity to parents and peers.* Paper presented at the annual meeting of the American Psychological Association, Toronto, Ontario.

Berndt, T. J., & Hawkins, J. A. (1987). *The contribution of supportive friendships to adjustment after the transition to junior high school.* Unpublished manuscript, Department of Psychological Sciences, Purdue University.

Bernstein, D. A. (1970). The modification of smoking behavior: A search for effective variables. *Behaviour Research and Therapy, 8,* 133–146.

Bernstein, D. A., & Borkovec, T. D. (1973). *Progressive relaxation training: A manual for the helping professions.* Champaign, IL: Research Press.

Bernstein, I. H., Bissonnette, V., Vyas, A., & Barclay, P. (1989). Semantic priming: Subliminal perception or context? *Perception and Psychophysics, 45,* 153–161.

Bernstein, I. L. (1978). Learned taste aversions in children receiving chemotherapy. *Science, 200,* 1302–1303.

Berry, J. W., & Bennett, J. A. (1992). Cree conceptions of cognitive competence. *International Journal of Psychology, 27,* 73–88.

Berry, J. W., Poortinga, Y. A., Segall, M. H., & Dasen, P. R. (1992). *Cross-cultural psychology: Research and applications.* New York: Cambridge University Press.

Berscheid, E., Snyder, M., & Omoto, A. M. (1989). Issues in studying close relationships: Conceptualizing and measuring closeness. In C. Hendrick (Ed.), *Review of personality and social psychology* (Vol. 10). Newbury Park, CA: Sage.

Best, C. T., & Queen, H. F. (1989). Baby, it's in your smile: Right hemiface bias in infant emotional expressions. *Developmental Psychology 25,* 264–276.

Best, D. (1992). Cross-cultural themes in developmental psychology. Paper presented at workshop on crosscultural aspects of psychology. Western Washington University, Bellingham, June.

Best, J. B. (1989). *Cognitive psychology.* St. Paul, MN: West Publishing Co.

Best, J. B. (1992). *Cognitive psychology* (3rd ed.). St. Paul, MN: West Publishing.

Bettman, J. R., Johnson, E. J., & Payne, J. W. (1990). A componential analysis of cognitive effort in choice. *Organizational Behavior and Human Decision Processes, 45,* 111–139.

Bettman, J. R., Payne, J. W., & Staelin, R. (1986). Cognitive considerations in designing effective labels for presenting risk information. *Journal of Marketing and Public Policy, 5,* 1–28.

Bexton, W. H. (1953). *Some effects of perceptual isolation in human beings.* Unpublished doctoral dissertation, McGill University, Montreal.

Bexton, W. H., Heron, W., & Scott, T. H. (1954). Effects of decreased variation in the sensory environment. *Canadian Journal of Psychology, 8,* 70–76.

Bharati, A. (1985). The self in Hindu thought and action. In A. J. Marsella, G. de Vos, & F. L. K. Hsu (Eds.), *Culture and the self.* New York: Tavistock Publications.

Bharucha, J. J. (1984). Anchoring effects in music: The resolution of dissonance. *Cognitive Psychology, 16,* 485–518.

Biederman, I. (1987). Recognition by components. *Psychological Review, 94,* 115–147.

Biederman, I., Cooper, E. E., Fox, P. W., & Mahadevan, R. S. (1992). Unexceptional spatial memory in an exceptional memorist. *Journal of Experimental Psychology: Learning, Memory, and Cognition, 18,* 654–657.

Biederman, I., Mezzanotte, R. J., Rabinowitz, J. C., Franeolin, C. M., & Plude, D. (1981). Detecting the unexpected in photointerpretation. *Human Factors, 23,* 153–163.

Bies, R. J., Shapiro, D. L., & Cummings, L. L. (1990). Causal accounts and managing organizational conflict: Is it enough to say it's not my fault? *Communication Research, 5,* 381–399.

Bijou, S. W., & Baer, P. M. (1961). *Child development: Vol. 1. A systematic and empirical theory.* New York: Appleton-Century-Crofts.

Billings, A. G., & Moos, R. H. (1981). The role of coping responses and social resources in attentuating the impact of stressful life events. *Journal of Behavioral Medicine, 4,* 139–157.

Billings, A. G., & Moos, R. H. (1984). Coping, stress, and social resources among adults with unipolar depression. *Journal of Personality and Social Psychology, 46*(4), 877–891.

Billings, A. G., & Moos, R. H. (1985). Life stressors and social resources affect posttreatment outcomes among depressed patients. *Journal of Abnormal Psychology, 94*(2), 140–153.

Binet, A., & Simon, T. (1905). Methodes nouvelles pour le diagnostic du niveau intellectuel des anormaux. *L'Annee Psychologique, 11,* 191–244.

Birnbaum, M. H., & Sotoodeh, Y. (1991). Measurement of stress: Scaling the magnitudes of life changes. *Psychological Science, 2,* 236–243.

Bjork, R. A., & Vanhuele, M. (1992). Retrieval inhibition and related adaptive peculiarities of human memory. *Advances in Consumer Research, 19,* 155–160.

Bjorklund, D. F., & Green, B. L. (1992). The adaptive nature of cognitive immaturity. *American Psychologist, 47,* 46–54.

Black, J. E., & Greenough, W. T. (1991). Developmental approaches to the memory process. In J. L. Martinez & R. P. Kesner (Eds.), *Learning and memory: A biological view* (2nd ed.). San Diego: Academic Press.

Black, J., Carroll, J., & McGuigan, S. (1987). What kind of minimal instruction manual is the most effective? In J. Carroll & P. Tanner (Eds.), *Human factors in computing systems and graphic interface.* Toronto, Canada: Computer-Human Interaction and Graphics Interface.

Blackwell, B. (1973). Psychotropic drugs in use today. *Journal of the American Medical Association, 225,* 1637–1641.

Blakemore, C., & Van Slayters, R. C. (1974). Reversal of the physiological effects of monocular deprivation in kittens: Further evidence for a sensitive period. *Journal of Physiology, 206,* 419–436.

Blalock, J. E. (1989). A molecular basis for bidirectional communication between the immune and neuroendocrine system. *Physiology Review, 69,* 1–32.

Blanchard, E. (1990). Elevated basal levels of cardiovascular responses in Vietnam veterans with PTSD: A health problem in the making? *Journal of Anxiety Disorders, 4,* 233–237.

Blanchard, E. (1992a). Introduction to the special issue on behavioral medicine: An update for the 1990s. *Journal of Consulting and Clinical Psychology, 60,* 491–492.

Blanchard, E. (1992b). Psychological treatment of benign headache disorders. *Journal of Consulting and Clinical Psychology, 60,* 537–551.

Blanchard, E. B., & Andrasik, F. (1985). *Management of chronic headaches: A psychological approach.* New York: Pergamon Press.

Blass, E. M., & Smith, B. A. (1992). Differential effects of sucrose, fructose, glucose, and lactose on crying in 1-day-old to 3-day-old human infants: Qualitative and quantitative considerations. *Developmental Psychology, 28,* 804–810.

Blatchford, P., Burke, J., Farquhar, C., & Plewis, I. (1989). Teacher expectations in infant school: Associations with attainment and progress, curriculum coverage and classroom interaction. *British Journal of Educational Psychology, 59,* 19–30.

Blatt, S. J., & Lerner, H. (1983). Psychodynamic perspectives on personality theory. In M. Hersen, A. E. Kazdin, & A. S. Bellack (Eds.), *The clinical psychology handbook* (pp. 61–68). New York: Pergamon Press.

Blazer, D. G., Bacher, J. R., & Manton, K. G. (1986). Suicide in late life: Review and commentary. *Journal of the American Geriatrics Society, 34,* 519–525.

Blehar, M., & Rosenthal, N. (1989). Seasonal affective disorders and phototherapy. *Archives of General Psychiatry, 46,* 469–474.

Bliss, E. L. (1980). Multiple personalities: Report of fourteen cases with implications for schizophrenia and hysteria. *Archives of General Psychiatry, 37,* 1388–1397.

Block, J. (1971). *Lives through time.* Berkeley: Bancroft Books.

Block, J. H. (1980). Another look at sex differentiation in the socialization behavior of mothers and fathers. In F. Denmark & J. Sherman (Eds.), *Psychology of women: Future directions of research.* New York: Psychological Dimensions.

Block, J. H. (1983). Differential premises arising from differential socialization of the sexes: Some conjectures. *Child Development, 54,* 1335–1354.

Block, J. R., & Yuker, H. E. (1989). *Can you believe your eyes?* New York: Gardner Press, Inc.

Block, V., Hennevin, E., & LeConte, P. (1977). Interaction between post-trial reticular stimulation and subsequent paradoxical sleep in memory consolidation processes. In R. R. Drucker-Colin & J. L. McGaugh (Eds.), *Neurobiology of sleep and memory.* New York: Academic Press.

Bloom, A. H. (1981). *The linguistic shaping of thought: A study of the impact of language on thinking in China and the West.* Hillsdale, NJ: Lawrence Erlbaum Associates.

Bluhm, C., Widiger, T. A., & Miele, G. M. (1990). Interpersonal complementarity and individual differences. *Journal of Personality and Social Psychology, 58,* 464–471.

Blum, K., Noble, E., Sheridan, P., Montgomery, A., Ritchie, T., Jagadeeswaran, P., Nogami, H., Briggs, A., & Cohn, J. (1990). Allelic association of human dopamine D2 receptor gene in alcoholism. *Journal of the American Medical Association, 263,* 2055–2060.

Blurton-Jones, N. (1972). Categories of child-child interaction. In N. Blurton-Jones (Ed.), *Ethological studies of child behaviour.* Cambridge: Cambridge University Press.

Bolger, N., DeLongis, A., Kessler, R., & Schilling, E. (1989). Effects of daily stress on negative mood. *Journal of Personality and Social Psychology, 57,* 808–818.

Bolles, R. C. (1975). *Theory of motivation* (2nd ed.). New York: Harper & Row.

Bond, G., Aiken, L., & Somerville, S. (1992). The Health Beliefs Model and adolescents with insulin-dependent diabetes mellitus. *Health Psychology, 11,* 190–198.

Bond, M., Nakazato, H., & Shiraishi, D. (1975). Universality and distinctiveness in dimensions of Japanese person perception. *Journal of Cross-Cultural Psychology, 6,* 346–357.

Bonica, J. (1984). Interview quoted in C. Wallis, Unlocking pain's secrets. *Time,* pp. 58–66.

Bonica, J. J. (1992). Importance of the problem. In G. M. Aronoff (Ed.), *Evaluation and treatment of chronic pain.* Baltimore: Williams & Wilkins.

Bonington, C. (1976). *Everest the hard way.* New York: Random House.

Bonnet, M. H., & Arand, D. L. (1989). Sleep loss in aging. *Clinics in Geriatric Medicine, 5,* 405–420.

Booth, D. A. (1980). Acquired behavior controlling energy intake and output. In A. J. Stunkard (Ed.), *Obesity.* Philadelphia: W. B. Saunders.

Bootzin, R. R., & Nicassio, P. M. (1978). Behavioral treatments for insomnia. In M. Herson, R. Eisler, & P. M. Miller (Eds.), *Progress in behavior modification: Vol. 6.* New York: Academic Press.

Boring, E. G. (1923). Intelligence as the tests test it. *New Republic, 35,* 35–37.

Boring, E. G. (1930). A new ambiguous figure. *American Journal of Psychology, 42,* 444–445.

Borkovec, T. D., & Bauer, R. M. (1982). Experimental design in group outcome research. In A. Bellack & M. Hersen (Eds.), *International handbook of behavior modification and therapy.* New York: Plenum.

Borkovec, T. D., Hopkins, M., Lyonfields, J., Lytle, R., Possa, S., Roemer, L., & Shadick, R. (1991). Efficacy of nondirective therapy, applied relaxation, and combined cognitive behavioral therapy for generalized anxiety disorder. Paper presented at the meeting of the Association for the Advancement of Behavior Therapy, New York, November.

Borkovec, T. D., & Inz, J. (1990). The nature of worry in generalized anxiety disorder: A predominence of thought activity. *Behaviour Research and Therapy, 28,* 153–158.

Borkovec, T. D., & Mathews, A. M. (1988). Treatment of non-phobic anxiety disorders: A comparison of non-directive, cognitive, and coping desensitization therapy. *Journal of Consulting and Clinical Psychology, 56,* 877–884.

Borkowski, J. G., Weyhing, R. S., & Turner, L. A. (1986). Attributional retraining and the teaching of strategies. *Exceptional Children, 53,* 130–137.

Bornstein, G., Rapoport, A., Kerpel, L., & Katz, T. (1989). Within- and between-group communication in intergroup competition for public goods. *Journal of Experimental Social Psychology, 25,* 422–436.

Bornstein, R. F. (1989). Exposure and affect: Overview and meta-analysis of research, 1968–1987. *Psychological Bulletin, 106,* 265–289.

Bornstein, R. F., Kale, A. R., & Cornell, K. R. (1990). Boredom as a limiting condition on the mere exposure effect. *Journal of Personality and Social Psychology, 58,* 791–800.

Borod, J. C. (1992). Interhemispheric and intrahemispheric control of emotion: A focus on unilateral brain damage. *Journal of Consulting and Clinical Psychology, 60,* 339–348.

Borrie, R. A. (1991). The use of restricted environmental stimulation therapy in treating addictive behaviors. *International Journal of the Addictions, 25,* 995–1015.

Botwinick, J. (1966). Cautiousness in advanced age. *Journal of Gerontology, 21,* 347–353.

Botwinick, J. (1977). Intellectual abilities. In J. E. Birren & K. W. Schaie (Eds.), *Handbook of the psychology of aging.* New York: Van Nostrand Reinhold.

Bouchard, T. J., & McGue, M. (1981). Familial studies of intelligence: A review. *Science, 212,* 1055–1059.

Bouchard, T. J., Jr., Lykken, D. T., McGue, M., Segal, N. L., & Tellegen, A. (1990). Sources of human psychological differences: The Minnesota study of twins reared apart. *Science, 250,* 223–228.

Boudewyns, P. A., Stwertka, S. A., Hyer, L. A., Albrecht, J. W., & Sperr, E. V. (1993). Eye movement desensitization for PTSD of combat: A treatment outcome pilot study. *The Behavior Therapist, 16,* 29–33.

Bourne, L. E. (1967) Learning and utilization of conceptual rules. In B. Kleinmuntz (Ed.), *Concepts and the structure of memory.* New York: Wiley.

Bovard, E. W. (1985). Brain mechanisms in effects of social support on viability. In R. B. Williams (Ed.), *Perspectives on behavioral medicine.* New York: Academic Press.

Bowen, G. L., & Orthner, D. K. (1983). Sex-role congruency and marital quality. *Journal of Marriage and the Family, 45,* 223–230.

Bower, G. H. (1970). Organizational factors in memory. *Cognitive Psychology, 1,* 18–46.

Bower, G. H. (1973). How to . . . uh . . . remember! *Psychology Today,* pp. 62–67.

Bower, G. H. (1975). Cognitive psychology: An introduction. In W. K. Estes (Ed.), *Handbook of learning and cognitive processes: Vol. 1.* Hillsdale, NJ: Lawrence Erlbaum Associates.

Bower, G. H. (1981). Mood and memory. *American Psychologist, 36,* 129–148.

Bower, G. H., Gilligan, S. G., & Monteiro, K. P. (1981). Selectivity of learning caused by affective states. *Journal of Experimental Psychology: General, 110,* 451–473.

Bower, T. G. R., & Wishart, J. G. (1972). The effects of motor skill on object permanence. *Cognition, 1,* 165–172.

Bowerman, C. E., & Kinch, J. W. (1956). Changes in family and peer orientation of children between the fourth and tenth grades. *Social Forces, 37,* 206–211.

Bowlby, J. (1951). *Maternal care and mental health.* World Health Organization Monograph 2. Geneva: World Health Organization.

Bowlby, J. (1973). *Attachment and loss: Vol. 2. Separation.* New York: Basic Books.

Bowlby, J. (1989). *A secure base: Parent-child attachment and healthy human development.* New York: Basic Books.

Boyatzis, R. E. (1982). *The competent manager.* New York: Wiley.

Bozarth, M. A., & Wise, R. A. (1984). Anatomically distinct opiate receptor fields mediate reward and physical dependence. *Science, 224,* 516–518.

Bozarth, M. A., & Wise, R. A. (1985). Toxicity associated with long-term intravenous heroin and cocaine self-administration in the rat. *Journal of the American Medical Association, 254,* 81–83.

Brackett, C. D., & Powell, L. (1988). Psychosocial and physiological predictors of sudden cardiac death after healing of acute myocardial infarction. *American Journal of Cardiology, 61,* 979–983.

Bradbury, T. N., & Fincham, F. D. (1988). Individual difference variables in close relationships: A contextual model of marriage as an integrative framework. *Journal of Personality and Social Psychology, 54,* 713–721.

Bradbury, T. N., & Fincham, F. D. (1992). Attributions and behavior in marital interaction. *Journal of Personality and Social Psychology, 63,* 613–628.

Bradley-Johnson, S., Graham, D. P., & Johnson, C. M. (1986). Token reinforcement on WISC-R performance for white, low-socioeconomic, upper and lower elementary-school-age students. *Journal of School Psychology, 24,* 73–79.

Bradshaw, G. (1992). The airplane and the logic of invention. In R. N. Giere (Ed.), *Minnesota Studies in the Philosophy of Science* (pp. 239–250). Minneapolis, MN: University of Minnesota Press.

Bradshaw, G. (in press). Beyond animal language. In H. L. Roitblat, L. M. Herman, & P. Nachtigall (Eds.), *Language and communication: Comparative perspectives.* Hillsdale, NJ: Lawrence Erlbaum Associates.

Bradshaw, G. L., & Shaw, D. (1992). Forecasting solar flares: Experts and artificial systems. *Organizational Behavior and Human Decision Performance, 53,* 135–157.

Braginsky, B. M., Grosse, M., & Ring, K. (1966). Controlling outcomes through impression management: An experimental study of the manipulative tactics of mental patients. *Journal of Consulting Psychology, 30,* 295–300.

Brandimonte, M. A., Hitch, G. J., & Bishop, D. V. M. (1992). Influence of short-term memory codes on visual image processing: Evidence from image transformation tasks. *Journal of Experimental Psychology: Learning, Memory, and Cognition, 18,* 157–165.

Bransford, J. D., & Johnson, M. K. (1972). Contextual prerequisites for understanding: Some investigations of comprehension and recall. *Journal of Verbal Learning and Verbal Behavior, 11,* 717–726.

Bransford, J. D., & Stein, B. S. (1993). *The ideal problem solver* (2nd ed.). New York: W. H. Freeman.

Bransford, J. D., Nitsch, K. E., & Franks, J. J. (1977). Schooling and the facilitation of knowing. In R. C. Anderson, R. J. Spiro, & W. E. Montague (Eds.), *Schooling and the acquisition of knowledge.* Hillsdale, NJ: Lawrence Erlbaum Associates.

Brantigan, T. A., Brantigan, C. O., & Joseph, N. H. (1978). Beta blockage and musical performance. *Lancet, 896,* ii.

Brantley, P. J., Dietz, L. S., McKnight, G. T., Jones, G. N., & Tulley, R. (1988). Convergence between daily stress inventory and endocrine measures of stress. *Journal of Consulting and Clinical Psychology, 56,* 549–551.

Brantley, P., Waggoner, C., Jopnes, G., & Rappaport, N. (1987). A daily stress inventory: Development, reliability, and validity. *Journal of Behavioral Medicine, 10,* 61–71.

Braunstein, M. (1990). Structure from motion. In J. Elkind, S. Card, J. Hochberg, & B. Huey (Eds.), *Human performance models for computer-aided engineering.* Orlando, FL: Academic Press.

Brazelton, T. B., & Tronick, E. (1983). Preverbal communication between mothers and infants. In W. Damon (Ed.), *Social and personality development.* New York: W. W. Norton.

Breckler, S. J., & Wiggins, E. C. (1989). On defining attitude and attiude theory: Once more with feeling. In A. R. Pratkanis, S. J. Breckler, & A. G. Greenwald (Eds.), *Attitude structure and function.* Hillsdale, NJ: Lawrence Erlbaum Associates.

Breggin, P. R. (1979). *Electroshock: Its brain-disabling effects.* New York: Halsted Press.

Brehm, J. (1972). *Responses to loss of freedom: A theory of psychological reactance.* Morristown, NJ: General Learning Press.

Brehm, J. W. (1989). Psychological reactance: Theory and applications. *Advances in Consumer Research, 16,* 72–75.

Brehm, J. W., & Self, E. A. (1989). The intensity of motivation. *Annual Review of Psychology, 40,* 109–131.

Brehm, S. S., & Smith, T. W. (1986). Social psychological approaches to psychotherapy and behavior change. In S. L. Garfield & A. E. Bergin (Eds.), *Handbook of psychotherapy and behavior change* (3rd ed.). New York: Wiley.

Brehmer, B. (1981). Models of diagnostic judgment. In J. Rasmussen & W. Rouse (Eds.), *Human detection and diagnosis of systems failures.* New York: Plenum Press.

Breier, A., Charney, D. S., & Heninger, G. R. (1986). Agoraphobia with panic attacks: Development, diagnostic stability and course of illness. *Archives of General Psychiatry, 43,* 1029–1036.

Breland, K., & Breland, M. (1966). *Animal behavior.* New York: Macmillan.

Bremer, J. (1959). *Asexualization.* New York: Macmillan.

Brennen, T., Baguley, T., Bright, J., & Bruce, V. (1990). Resolving semantically induced tip-of-the-tongue states for proper nouns. *Memory & Cognition, 18,* 339–347.

Breuer, J., & Freud, S. (1966). *Studies on hysteria* (original work published 1896). New York: Avon.

Brewer, M. B. (1988). A dual process model of impression formation. In T. K. Srull & R. S. Wyer (Eds.), *Advances in social cognition: Vol. 1. A dual process model of impression formation.* Hillsdale, NJ: Lawrence Erlbaum Associates.

Brewer, M. B. (1991). The social self: On being the same and different at the same time. *Personality and Social Psychology Bulletin, 17,* 475–482.

Brewer, W. F., & Nakamura, G. V. (1984). The nature and functions of schemas. In R. S. Wyer & T. K. Srull (Eds.), *Handbook of social cognition: Vol. 1.* Hillsdale, NJ: Lawrence Erlbaum Associates.

Brewer, W. F., & Pani, J. R. (1984). The structure of human memory. In G. H. Bower (Ed.), *The psychology of learning and motivation: Vol. 17.* New York: Academic Press.

Brewer, W. F., & Treyens, J. C. (1981). Role of schemata in memory for places. *Cognitive Psychology, 13,* 207–230.

Brickman, P., Becker, L. J., & Castle, S. (1979). Making trust easier and harder through two forms of sequential interaction. *Journal of Personality and Social Psychology, 37,* 515–521.

Brigham, C. C. (1923). *A study of American intelligence.* Princeton, NJ: Princeton University Press.

Brinton, R. E. (1991). Biochemical correlates of learning and memory. In J. L. Martinez & R. P. Kesner (Eds.), *Learning and memory: A biological view* (2nd ed.). San Diego: Academic Press.

Brislin, R., (1993). *Understanding culture's influence on behavior.* Fort Worth: Harcourt, Brace, Jovanovich.

Brody, E. B., & Brody, N. (1976). *Intelligence: Nature, determinants, and consequences.* New York: Academic Press.

Brody, J. E. (1983, December 13). Divorce's stress exacts long-term health toll. *New York Times,* p. 17

Brody, N. (1990). Behavior therapy versus placebo: Comment on Bowers and Clum's meta-analysis. *Psychological Bulletin, 107,* 106–109.

Bronstein, B., & Quina, K. (1988). Perspectives on gender balance and cultural diversity in the teaching of psychology. In P. Bronstein & K. Quina (Eds.), *Teaching a psychology of people.* Washington, DC: American Psychological Association.

Brooks-Gunn, J. (1988). Antecedents and consequences of variations in girls' maturational timing. *Journal of Adolescent Health Care, 9*(5), 1–9.

Brooks-Gunn, J., & Furstenberg, F. F. (1989). Adolescent sexual behavior. *American Psychologist, 44,* 249–257.

Brooks-Gunn, J., Gross, R. T., Kraemer, H. C., Spiker, D., & Shapiro, S. (1992). Enhancing the cognitive outcomes of low birth weight, premature infants: For whom is the intervention most effective? *Pediatrics, 89,* 1209–1215.

Brown, A. L. (1975). The development of memory: Knowing, knowing about knowing, and knowing how to know it. In H. W. Reese (Ed.), *Advances in child development and behavior: Vol. 10.* New York: Academic Press.

Brown, A. L., Campione, J. C., Webber, L. S., & McGilly, K. (1992). Interactive learning environments: A new look at assessment and instruction. In B. Gifford & M. C. O'Connor (Eds.), *Changing assessments: Alternative views of aptitude, achievement, and instruction.* Boston: Kluever.

Brown, A. S. (1991). A review of the tip-of-the-tongue experience. *Psychological Bulletin, 109,* 204–233.

Brown, H., Adams, R. G., & Kellam, S. G. (1981). A longitudinal study of teenage motherhood and symptoms of distress: Woodlawn Community Epidemiological Project. In R. Simmons (Ed.), *Research in community and mental health: Vol. 2.* Greenwich, CT: JAI Press.

Brown, J. (1958). Some tests of the decay theory of immediate memory. *Quarterly Journal of Experimental Psychology, 10,* 12–21.

Brown, J. (1987). A review of meta-analyses conducted on psychotherapy outcome research. *Clinical Psychology Review, 7,* 1–23.

Brown, J. D., & McGill, K. L. (1989). The cost of good fortune: When positive life events produce negative health consequences. *Journal of Personality and Social Psychology, 57,* 1103–1110.

Brown, J. D., & Rogers, R. J. (1991). Self-serving attributions: The role of physiological arousal. *Personality and Social Psychology Bulletin, 17,* 501–506.

Brown, J. D., Novick, N. J., Lord, K. A., & Richards, J. M. (1992). When Gulliver travels: Social context, psychological closeness, and self-appraisals. *Journal of Personality and Social Psychology, 62,* 717–727.

Brown, R. (1986). *Social psychology: The second edition.* New York: The Free Press.

Brown, R. A. (1973). *First language.* Cambridge: Harvard University Press.

Brown, R., & Kulik, J. (1977). Flashbulb memories. *Cognition, 5,* 73–99.

Brown, R., & McNeill, D. (1966). The "tip-of-the-tongue" phenomenon. *Journal of Verbal Learning and Verbal Behavior, 5,* 325–337.

Brownell, K. D., Greenwood, M. R. C., Stellar, E., & Shrager, E. E. (1986). The effects of repeated cycles of weight loss and regain in rats. *Physiology and Behavior, 38,* 459–464.

Bruce, D., & Bahrick, H. P. (1992). Perceptions of past research. *American Psychologist, 47,* 319–328.

Bruce, H. M. (1969). Pheromones and behavior in mice. *Acta Neurologica Belgica, 69,* 529–538.

Bruck, M., Cavanagh, P., & Ceci, S. J. (1991). Fortysomething: Recognizing faces at one's 25th reunion. *Memory & Cognition, 19,* 221–228.

Brundin, P., Nilsson, O. G., Gage, F. H., & Bjorkland, A. (1985). Cyclosporin A increases survival of cross-species intrastriatal grafts of embryonic dopamone-containing neurons. *Brain Research, 60,* 204–208.

Bruner, J. (1964). The course of cognitive growth. *American Psychologist, 19,* 1–55.

Bruner, J. (1992). Another look at new look 1. *American Psychologist, 47*(6), 780–783.

Bruton, C. J., Crow, T. J., Frith, C. D., Johnstone, E. C., Owens, D. G. C., & Roberts, G. W. (1990). Schizophrenia and the brain: A prospective cliniconeuropathological study. *Psychological Medicine, 20,* 285–304.

Bryan, J. H. (1975). Children's cooperation and helping behaviors. In E. M. Hetherington (Ed.), *Review of child development research: Vol. 5.* Chicago: University of Chicago Press.

Bryan, J. H., & Luria, Z. (1978). Sex-role learning: A test of the selective attention hypothesis. *Child Development, 49,* 13–23.

Bryant, J., Carveth, R. A., & Brown, D. (1981). Television viewing and anxiety: An experimental examination. *Journal of Communication, 31,* 106–119.

Bryant, R. A., & McConkey, K. M. (1989). Hypnotic blindness: A behavioral and experiential analysis. *Journal of Abnormal Psychology, 98,* 71–77.

Buchsbaum, M. S., Ingvar, D. H., Kessler, R., Waters, R. N., Cappelletti, J., van Kammen, D. P., King, A. C., Johnson, J. L., Manning, R. G., Flynn, R. W., Mann, L. S., Bunney, W. E., & Sokoloff, L. (1982). Cerebral glucography with positron tomography: Use in normal subjects and patients with schizophrenia. *Archives of General Psychiatry, 39,* 251–259.

Buck, L., & Axel, R. (1991). A novel multigene family may encode odorant receptors: A molecular basis for odor recognition. *Cell, 65,* 175–181.

Budzynski, T. H., & Stoyva, J. M. (1984). Biofeedback methods in the treatment of anxiety and stress. In R. L. Woolfolk & P. M. Lehrer (Eds.), *Principles and practice of stress management.* New York: Guilford Press.

Bunney, W. E., Jr., Goodwin, F. K., & Murphy, D. L. (1972). The "switch process" in manic-depressive illness: 3. Theoretical implications. *Archives of General Psychiatry, 27,* 312–317.

Burchfield, S. R. (1979). The stress response: A new perspective. *Psychosomatic Medicine, 41,* 661–672.

Burger, J. M. (1991). Changes in attributions over time: The ephemeral fundamental attribution error. *Social Cognition, 9,* 182–193.

Burger, J. M., & Burns, L. (1988). The illusion of unique invulnerability and the use of effective contraception. *Personality and Social Psychology Bulletin, 14,* 264–270.

Burger, J. M., & Palmer, M. L. (1992). Changes in and generalization of unrealistic optimism following experiences with stressful events: Reactions to the 1989 California earthquake. *Personality and Social Psychology Bulletin, 18,* 39–43.

Burger, J. M., & Petty, R. E. (1981). The low-ball compliance technique: Task or person commitment? *Journal of Personality and Social Psychology, 40,* 492–500.

Burish, T., & Jenkins, R. (1992). Effectiveness of biofeedback and relaxation training in reducing the side effects of cancer chemotherapy. *Health Psychology, 11,* 17–23.

Burke, A., Heuer, F., & Reisberg, D. (1992). Remembering emotional events. *Memory & Cognition, 20,* 277–290.

Burman, B., & Margolin, G. (1992). Analysis of the association between marital relationships and health problems: An interactional perspective. *Psychological Bulletin, 112,* 39–63.

Burnam, M., Hough, R., Escobar, J., Karno, M., Timbers, D., Telles, C., & Locke, B. (1987). Six-month prevalence of specific psychiatric disorders among Mexican Americans and non-Hispanic whites in Los Angeles. *Archives of General Psychiatry, 44,* 687–694.

Burns, M. O., & Seligman, M. E. P. (1989). Explanatory style across the life span: Evidence for stability over 52 years. *Journal of Personality and Social Psychology, 56,* 471–477.

Burr, C. (1993). Homosexuality and biology. *Atlantic Monthly, 271,* 47–65.

Buske-Kirschbaum, A., Kirschbaum, C., Stierle, H., Lehnert, H., & Hellhammer, D. (1992). Conditioned increase of natural killer cell activity (NKCA) in humans. *Psychosomatic Medicine, 54,* 123–132.

Buss, A. H. (1989). Personality as traits. *American Psychologist, 44,* 1378–1388.

Buss, D. (1991). Evolutionary personality psychology. *Annual Review of Psychology, 42,* 459–491.

Buss, D. M. (1981). Predicting parent-child interactions from children's activity level. *Developmental Psychology, 17,* 59–65.

Buss, D. M. (1989). Sex differences in human mate preferences: Evolutionary hypotheses tested in 37 cultures. *Behavioral and Brain Sciences, 12,* 1–49.

Buss, D. M. (1991). Evolutionary personality psychology. *Annual Review of Psychology.* Palo Alto, CA: Annual Reviews.

Buss, D. M. (1994). Mate preferences in 37 cultures. In W. J. Lonner & R. S. Malpass (Eds.), *Psychology and culture.* Boston: Allyn & Bacon.

Buss, D. M., Gomes, M., Higgins, D. S., & Lauterbach, K. (1987). Tactics of manipulation. *Journal of Personality and Social Psychology, 52,* 1219–1229.

Butcher, J. N. (1979). Use of the MMPI in personnel selection. In J. N. Butcher (Ed.), *New developments in the use of the MMPI.* Minneapolis: University of Minnesota Press.

Butcher, J. N. (Ed.) (1987). *Computerized psychological assessment: A practitioner's guide.* New York: Basic Books.

Butcher, J. N., & Hatcher, C. (1988). The neglected entity in air disaster planning: Psychological services. *American Psychologist, 43,* 724–729.

Butcher, J. N., Dahlstrom, W. G., Graham, J. R., Tellegen, A., & Kaemmer, B. (1989). *Manual for administration and scoring of the MMPI-2.* Minneapolis: University of Minnesota Press.

Butler, R. (1992). What young people want to know when: Effects of mastery and ability goals on interest in different kinds of social comparisons. *Journal of Personality and Social Psychology, 62,* 934–943.

Butler, R. N. (1963). The life review: An interpretation of reminiscence in the aged. *Psychiatry, 26,* 65–76.

Butler, R. N. (1975). *Why survive? Being old in America.* New York: Harper & Row.

Byrne, D. (1971). *The attraction paradigm.* New York: Academic Press.

Byrne, D. (1977). Social psychology and the study of sexual behavior. *Personality and Social Psychology Bulletin, 3,* 3–30.

Byrne, D., & Kelley, K. (1989). Basing legislative action on research data: Prejudice, prudence, and empirical limitations. In D. Zillmann & J. Bryant (Eds.), *Pornography: Research advances and policy considerations.* Hillsdale, NJ: Lawrence Erlbaum Associates.

Byrne, D., & Nelson, D. (1965). Attraction as a linear function of proportion of positive reinforcements. *Journal of Personality and Social Psychology, 1,* 659–663.

Byrne, D., Clore, G. L., & Smeaton, G. (1986). The attraction hypothesis: Do similar attitudes affect anything? *Journal of Personality and Social Psychology, 51,* 1167–1170.

Byrne, D., London, O., & Reeves, K. (1968). The effects of physical attractiveness, sex, and attitude similarity on interpersonal attraction. *Journal of Personality, 36,* 259–271.

Cabanac, M. (1971). The physiological role of pleasure. *Science, 173,* 1103–1107.

Cabanac, M., & Lafrance, L. (1992). Ingestive/aversive response of rats to sweet stimuli: Influence of glucose, oil, and casein hydrolyzate gastric loads. *Physiology and Behavior, 51,* 139–143.

Caci1oppo, J. T., & Berntson, G. G. (1992). Social psychological contributions to the decade of the brain. *American Psychologist, 47,* 1019–1028.

Cacioppo, J. T., Petty, R. E., & Crites, S. L. (1993). Attitude change. In V. S. Ramachandran (Ed.), *Encyclopedia of human behavior.* San Diego, CA: Academic Press.

Cairns, R. B., Gariepy, J., & Hood, K. E. (1990). Development, microevolution, and social behavior. *Psychological Review, 97,* 49–65.

Calder, B. J., & Gruder, C. L. (1989). Emotional advertising appeals. In P. Cafferata & A. Tybout (Eds.), *Cognitive and affective responses to advertising.* Lexington, MA: Lexington Books.

Camerer, C., & Johnson, E. J. (1991). The process-performance paradox in expert judgment: How can experts know so much and predict so badly? In K. M. Ericsson & J. Smith (Eds.), *Toward a theory of expertise: Prospects and limits.* Cambridge: Cambridge University Press.

Campbell, B. A., & Kraeling, D. (1953). Response strength as a function of drive level and amount of drive reduction. *Journal of Experimental Psychology, 45,* 97–101.

Campbell, D. T., & Stanley, J. C. (1966). *Experimental and quasi-experimental designs for research.* Chicago: Rand McNally.

Campbell, J. P., Daft, R. L., & Hulin, C. L. (1982). *What to study: Generating and developing research questions.* Beverly Hills, CA: Sage.

Campione, J. C., Brown, A. L., & Ferrara, R. A. (1982). Mental retardation and intelligence. In R. J. Sternberg (Ed.), *Handbook of human intelligence.* Cambridge: Cambridge University Press.

Campos, J., Langer, A., & Krowitz, A. (1970). Cardiac responses on the visual cliff in prelocomotor human infants. *Science, 170,* 196–197.

Camras, L. A. (1977). Facial expressions used by children in a conflict situation. *Child Development, 48,* 1431–1435.

Canino, G., Bird, H., Shrout, P., Rubio-Stipec, M., Bravo, M., Martinez, R., Sesman, M., & Guevara, L. (1987). The prevalence of specific psychiatric disorders in Puerto Rico. *Archives of General Psychiatry, 44,* 727–735.

Cann, A., Sherman, S. J., & Elkes, R. (1975). Effects of initial request size and timing of a second request on compliance: The foot-in-the-door and the door-in-the-face. *Journal of Personality and Social Psychology, 32,* 774–782.

Cannon, D. S., & Baker, T. B. (1981). Emetic and electric shock alcohol aversion therapy: Assessment of conditioning. *Journal of Consulting and Clinical Psychology, 49,* 20–33.

Cannon, W. B. (1927). The James-Lange theory of emotions: A critical examination and an alternative. *American Journal of Psychology, 39,* 106–124.

Cannon, W. B., & Washburn, A. L. (1912). An explanation of hunger. *American Journal of Physiology, 29,* 444–454.

Cannon-Bowers, J. A., Salas, E., & Converse, S. A. (1990, December). Cognitive psychology and team training: Training shared mental models of complex systems. *Human Factors Bulletin, 33*(12), 1–4.

Cannon-Bowers, J. A., Tannenbaum, S. I., Salas, E., & Converse, S. A. (1991). Toward an integration of training theory and technique. *Human Factors, 33*(3), 281–292.

Cantor, N., & Kihlstrom, J. F. (1989). Social intelligence and cognitive assessments of personality. In R. S. Wyer & T. K. Srull (Eds.), *Advances in social cognition: Vol. 2: Social intelligence and cognitive assessments of personality.* Hillsdale, NJ: Lawrence Erlbaum Associates.

Cantor, N., & Langston, C. A. (1989). Ups and downs of life tasks in a life transition. In L.A. Pervin (Ed.), *Goal concepts in personality and social psychology.* Hillsdale, NJ: Lawrence Erlbaum Associates.

Caplan, G. (1964). *Principles of preventive psychiatry.* New York: Basic Books.

Caplan, N., Whitemore, J. K., & Choy, M. H. (1989). *The boat people and achievement in America: A study of family life, hard work, and cultural values.* Ann Arbor: University of Michigan Press.

Caporael, L. R., Dawes, R. M., Orbell, J. M., & van de Kragt, A. J. C. (1989). Selfishness examined: Cooperation in the absence of egoistic incentives. *Behavioral and Brain Sciences, 12,* 683–739.

Capron, C., & Duyme, M. (1989). Assessment of effects of socioeconomic status on IQ in a full cross-fostering study. *Nature, 340,* 552–553.

Caramazza, A., & Hillis, A. E. (1991). Lexical organization of nouns and verbs in the brain. *Nature, 349,* 788–790.

Carey, M. P., & Burish, T. G. (1988). Etiology and treatment of the psychological side effects associated with cancer chemotherapy: A critical review and discussion. *Psychological Bulletin, 104,* 307–325.

Cargan, L., & Melko, M. (1982). *Singles: Myths and realities.* Beverly Hills, CA: Sage.

Carli, L. L., Ganley, R., & Pierce-Otay, A. (1991). Similarity and satisfaction in romantic relationships. *Personality and Social Psychology Bulletin, 17,* 419–426.

Carlson, C. R., & Masters, J. C. (1986). Inoculation by emotion: Effects of positive emotional states on children's reactions to social comparison. *Developmental Psychology, 22,* 760–765.

Carlson, J. S., Jensen, C. M., & Widaman, K. F. (1983). Reaction time, intelligence and attention. *Intelligence, 7,* 329–344.

Carlson, M., & Miller, N. (1987). Explanation of the relation between negative mood and helping. *Psychological Bulletin, 102,* 91–108.

Carlson, M., Marcus-Newhall, A., & Miller, N. (1990). Effects of situational aggression cues: A quantitative review. *Journal of Personality and Social Psychology, 58,* 622–633.

Carlston, D. (1994). An information processing theory of social experience. In T. K. Srull & R. S. Wyer (Eds.), *An information processing theory of social experience: Advances in social cognition, Vol. VII.* Hillsdale, NJ: Lawrence Erlbaum Associates.

Carmichael, L. L., Hogan, H. P., & Walter, A. A. (1932). An experimental study of the effect of language on the reproduction of visually perceived form. *Journal of Experimental Psychology, 15,* 73–86.

Carnevale, P. J., & Pruitt, D. G. (1992). Negotiation and mediation. *Annual Review of Psychology, 43,* 531–582.

Carpenter, P. A., & Just, M. A. (1989). The role of working memory in language comprehension. In D. Klahr & K. Kotovsky (Eds.), *Complex information processing.* Hillsdale, NJ: Lawrence Erlbaum Associates.

Carraher, T., Schliemann, A. D., & Carraher, D. W. (1988). Mathematical concepts in everyday life. In C. G. Saxe & M. Gearhart (Eds.), *Children's mathematics: Vol. 41. New directions for child development* (pp. 71–87). San Francisco: Jossey-Bass.

Carrington, P. (1984). Modern forms of meditation. In R. L. Woolfolk & P. M. Lehrer (Eds.), *Principles and practice of stress management.* New York: Guilford Press.

Carrington, P. (1986). Meditation as an access to altered states of consciousness. In B. B. Wolman & M. Ullman (Eds.), *Handbook of states of consciousness.* New York: Van Nostrand Reinhold.

Carroll, J. B. (1982). The measurement of intelligence. In R. J. Sternberg (Ed.), *Handbook of human intelligence.* Cambridge: Cambridge University Press.

Carroll, J. B. (1991). No demonstration that g is not unitary. *Intelligence, 15,* 423–436.

Carroll, J. M., & Carrithers, C. (1984). Blocking learner error states in a training-wheels system. *Human Factors, 26,* 377–390.

Carson, R. C., & Butcher, J. (1992). *Abnormal psychology and modern life* (9th ed.). Boston: HarperCollins.

Carson, R. C., Butcher, J. N., & Coleman, J. C. (1988). *Abnormal psychology and modern life* (8th ed.). Glenview, IL: Scott, Foresman.

Cartwright, R. D. (1974). The influence of a conscious wish on dreams: A methodological study of dream meaning and function. *Journal of Abnormal Psychology, 83,* 387–393.

Cartwright, R. D. (1978). *A primer on sleep and dreaming.* Reading, MA: Addison-Wesley.

Cartwright, R. D., Lloyd, S., Knight, S., & Trenholme, I. (1984). Broken dreams: A study of the effects of divorce and depression on dream content. *Psychiatry, 47,* 251–259.

Carver, C. S., Scheier, M. F., & Weintraub, J. K. (1989). Assessing coping strategies: A theoretically based approach. *Journal of Personality and Social Psychology, 56,* 267–283.

Carver, C., Coleman, A., & Glass, D. (1976). The coronary-prone behavior pattern and suppression of fatigue on a treadmill task. *Journal of Personality and Social Psychology, 33,* 460–466.

Case, R., Kurland, M., & Goldberg, J. (1982). Operational efficiency and the growth of short-term memory span. *Journal of Experimental Child Psychology, 33,* 386–404.

Cashdan, S. (1973). *Interactional psychotherapy: Stages and strategies in behavioral change.* New York: Grune & Stratton.

Cashdan, S. (1988). *Object relations therapy: Using the relationship.* New York: W. W. Norton.

Casper, R. C., Eckhert, E. D., Halmi, K. A., Goldberg, S. C., & Davis, J. M. (1980). Bulimia: Its incidence and clinical importance in patients with anorexia nervosa. *Archives of General Psychiatry, 37,* 1030–1035.

Caspi, A., Elder, G. H., & Bem, D. J. (1988). Moving away from the world: Life-course patterns of shy children. *Developmental Psychology, 24,* 824–831.

Castro, F., & Magaña, D. (1991). A course in health promotion in ethnic minority populations. In P. Bronstein & K. Quina (Eds.), *Teaching a psychology of people.* Washington, DC: American Psychological Association.

Catania, J. A., Coates, T. J., Stall, R., Turner, H., Peterson, J., Hearst, N., Dolcini, M. M., Hudes, E., Gagnon, J., Wiley, J., & Groves, R. (1992). Prevalence of AIDS-related risk factors and condom use in the United States. *Science, 258,* 1101–1106.

Cattell, R. B. (1971). *Abilities: Their structure, growth and action.* Boston: Houghton Mifflin.

Cattell, R. B., & Eber, H. W. (1962). *Manual for forms A and B of the Sixteen Personality Factor Questionnaire.* Champaign, IL: Institute for Personality and Ability Testing.

Cavanaugh, J. C. (1988). The place of awareness in memory development across adulthood. In L. W. Poon, D. C. Rubin, & B. A. Wilson (Eds.), *Everyday cognition in adulthood and later life.* Cambridge: Cambridge University Press.

Cavior, N., & Dokecki, P. R. (1969). *Physical attractiveness and popularity among fifth-grade boys.* Paper presented at the annual convention of the Southwestern Psychological Association.

Cechetto, D. F., & Saper, C. B. (1990). Role of the cerebral cortex in autonomic function. In A. D. Loewy & K. M. Spyer (Eds.), *Central regulation of autonomic functions.* New York: Oxford University Press.

Ceci, S. J., & Liker, J. K. (1986). A day at the races: A study of IQ, expertise and cognitive complexity. *Journal of Experimental Psychology: General, 115,* 255–266.

Centers for Disease Control (1993). *Morbidity, mortality weekly report, 42,* 230–233.

Centerwall, L. (1990). Controlled TV viewing and suicide in countries: Young adult suicide and exposure to television. *Social Psychiatry and Social Epidemiology, 25,* 149–153.

Centerwell, B. S. (1989). Exposure to television as a cause of violence. In G. Comstock (Ed.), *Public communication and behavior* (Vol. 2). San Diego: Academic Press.

Cerf, C. (1984). *The experts speak.* New York: Pantheon.

Cermak, L. S. (1989). Synergistic ecphory and the amnesic patient. In H. L. Roediger & F. I. M. Craik (Eds.), *Varieties of memory and consciousness.* Hillsdale, NJ: Erlbaum.

Chaiken, A. L., Sigler, E., & Derlega, V. J. (1974). Nonverbal mediators of teacher expectancy effects. *Journal of Personality and Social Psychology, 30,* 144–149.

Chamberlain, L. (1990). Chaos and the butterfly effect. *Network, 8,* 11–12.

Chambliss, D. L. (1990). Spacing of exposure sessions in the treatment of agoraphobia and simple phobia. *Behavior Therapy, 21,* 217–229.

Chambliss, D., & Goldstein, A. (1980). The treatment of agoraphobia. In A. Goldstein & E. Poa (Eds.), *Handbook of behavioral interventions.* New York: Wiley.

Chan, J., & Lynn, R. (1989). The intelligence of six-year-olds in Hong Kong. *Journal of Biosocial Science, 21,* 461–464.

Chance, P. (1988, April). *Knock wood.* Psychology Today.

Chapanis, A., Parrish, R., Ockman, R. B., & Weeks, G. D. (1977). Studies in interactive communications: II. *Human Factors, 19,* 101–126.

Chapman, C. R., Benedetti, C., Colpitts, Y. H., & Gerlach, R. (1983). Naloxone fails to reverse pain threshold elevated by acupuncture: Acupuncture analgesia reconsidered. *Pain, 16,* 13–31.

Charness, N. (1987). Component processes in bridge bidding and novel problem-solving tasks. *Canadian Journal of Psychology, 41,* 223–243.

Chase, G. (1986). Visual information processing. In K. Boff, L. Kaufman, & J. Thomas (Eds.), *Handbook of perception and human performance* (Vol. 2). New York: Wiley.

Chase, M. (1992). Low condom use by heterosexuals is found in survey. *Wall Street Journal,* November 13.

Chase, W. G., & Ericsson, K. A. (1979, November). *A mnemonic system for digit span: One year later.* Paper presented at the meeting of the Psychonomic Society, Phoenix, AZ.

Chase, W. G., & Ericsson, K. A. (1981). Skilled memory. In J. R. Anderson (Ed.), *Cognitive skills and their acquisition.* Hillsdale, NJ: Lawrence Erlbaum Associates.

Check, J. V. P., & Guloien, T. H. (1989). Reported proclivity for coercive sex following repeated exposure to sexually violent pornography, nonviolent dehumanizing pornography, and erotica. In D. Zillmann & J. Bryant (Eds.), *Pornography: Research advances and policy considerations.* Hillsdale, NJ: Lawrence Erlbaum Associates.

Chemers, M. M. (1987). Leadership processes: Intrapersonal, interpersonal, and societal influences. In C. Hendrick (Ed.), *Group processes.* Newbury Park, CA: Sage.

Cheng, P. W., & Novick, L. R. (1992). Covariation in natural causal induction. *Psychological Review, 99,* 365–382.

Cherry, C. (1953). Some experiments on the reception of speech with one and two ears. *Journal of the Acoustical Society of America, 25,* 975–979.

Chesler, P. (1972). *Women and madness.* New York: Doubleday.

Chesnic, M., Menyuk, P., Liebergott, J., Ferrier, L., & Strand, K. (1983, April). *Who leads whom?* Paper presented at the meeting of the Society for Research in Child Development, Detroit, MI.

Cheung, F., & Snowden, L. (1990). Community mental health and ethnic minority populations. *Community Mental Health Journal, 26,* 277–291.

Chi, M. (1978). Knowledge structures and memory development. In R. S. Siegler (Eds.), *Children's thinking: What develops?* Hillsdale, NJ: Lawrence Erlbaum Associates.

Chi, M. T. H., Glaser, R., & Farr, M. J. (Eds.) (1988). *The nature of expertise.* Hillsdale, NJ: Lawrence Erlbaum Associates.

Chi, M. T., Feltovitch, P. J., & Glaser, R. (1981). Representation of physics knowledge by novices and experts. *Cognitive Science, 5,* 121–152.

Chidester, T. R. (1990). *Human factors research: Narrowing the extremes of flight crew performance.* Washington, DC: Federation of Behavioral, Psychological and Cognitive Sciences.

Chignell, B., & Peterson, J. G. (1988). Strategic issues in knowledge engineering. *Human Factors, 30,* 381–394.

Chiodo, L. A., & Antelman, S. M. (1980). Electroconvulsive shock: Progressive dopamine autoreceptor subsensitivity independent of repeated treatment. *Science, 210,* 799–801.

Chomsky, N. (1957). *Syntactic structures.* The Hague: Mouton.

Chorover, L. (1965). Discussion of the effects of electroconvulsive shock on performance and memory. In D. P. Kimble (Ed.), *The anatomy of memory.* Palo Alto, CA: Science & Behavior Books.

Christensen, L. (1988). Deception in psychological research: When is its use justified? *Personality and Social Psychology Bulletin, 14,* 664–675.

Christenssen-Szalanski, J. J., & Bushyhead, J. B. (1981). Physicians' use of probabilistic information in a real clinical setting. *Journal of Experimental Psychology: Human Perception and Performance, 7,* 928–936.

Christianson, S. (1989). Flashbulb memories: Special, but not so special. *Memory & Cognition, 17,* 435–443.

Chronicle of Higher Education. (1992). *Almanac.* Washington, DC.

Chugani, H. T., & Phelps, M. E. (1986). Maturational changes in cerebral function in infants determined by 18FDG positron emission tomography. *Science, 231,* 840–843.

Churchland, P. M., & Churchland, P. S. (1990). Could a machine think? *Scientific American,* January, 32–37.

Churchland, P. S., & Sejnowski, T. J. (1992). *The computational brain.* Cambridge, MA: MIT Press/Bradford Books.

Chwalisz, K., Diener, E., & Gallagher, D. (1988). Autonomic arousal feedback and emotional experience: Evidence from the spinal cord injured. *Journal of Personality and Social Psychology, 54,* 820–828.

Cialdini, R. B. (1984). *Influence: The new psychology of modern persuasion.* New York: Quill.

Cialdini, R. B. (1988). *Influence: Science and practice.* Glenview, IL: Scott, Foresman.

Cialdini, R. B., & Fultz, J. (1990). Interpreting the negative mood-helping literature via "mega"-analysis: A contrary view. *Psychological Bulletin, 107,* 210–214.

Cialdini, R. B., Baumann, D. J., & Kenrick, D. T. (1981). Insights from sadness: A three-step model of the development of altruism as hedonism. *Developmental Review, 1,* 207–223.

Cialdini, R. B., Cacioppo, J. T., Bassett, R., & Miller, J. A. (1978). Low-ball procedure for producing compliance: Commitment then cost. *Journal of Personality and Social Psychology, 36,* 463–476.

Cialdini, R. B., Petty, R. E., & Cacioppo, J. T. (1981). Attitude and attitude change. *Annual Review of Psychology, 32,* 357–404.

Cialdini, R. B., Reno, R. R., & Kallgren, C. A. (1990). A focus theory of normative conduct: Recycling the concept of norms to reduce littering in public places. *Journal of Personality and Social Psychology, 58,* 1015–1026.

Cialdini, R. B., Schaller, M., Houlihan, D., Arps, K., Fultz, J., & Beaman, A. L. (1987). Empathy-based helping: Is it selflessly or selfishly motivated? *Journal of Personality and Social Psychology, 52,* 749–758.

Clark, D. A., & Beck, A. T. (1989). Cognitive theory and therapy of anxiety and depression. In P. C. Kendall & D. Watson (Eds.), *Anxiety and depression: Distinctive and overlapping features* (pp. 379–412). New York: Academic Press.

Clark, D. C., Gibbons, R. D., Fawcett, J., & Scheftner, W. A. (1989). What is the mechanism by which suicide attempts predispose to later suicide attempts? A mathematical model. *Journal of Abnormal Psychology, 98,* 42–49.

Clark, D., Solkovski, P., Hackman, A., & Gelder, M. (1991). Long-term outcome of cognitive therapy for panic disorder. Paper presented at the 25th annual meeting of the Association for the Advancement of Behavior Therapy. New York, November.

Clark, E. (1978). Strategies for communicating. *Child Development, 49,* 953–959.

Clark, H., & Clark, E. (1977). *Psychology and language: An introduction to psycholinguistics.* New York: Harcourt Brace Jovanovich.

Clark, L. A,. & Watson, D. (1991). Tripartite model of anxiety and depression: Psychometric evidence and taxonomic implications. *Journal of Abnormal Psychology, 100,* 316–336.

Clark, L. F. (1994). Social cognition and health psychology. In R. S. Wyer & T. K. Srull (Eds.), *Handbook of social cognition* (2nd ed.). Hillsdale, NJ: Lawrence Erlbaum Associates.

Clark, M. (1994). Close relationships. In R. S. Wyer & T. K. Srull (Eds.), *Handbook of social cognition* (2nd ed.). Hillsdale, NJ: Lawrence Erlbaum Associates.

Clark, M. S. (1984). Record keeping in two kinds of relationships. *Journal of Personality and Social Psychology, 47,* 549–557.

Clark, M. S., & Isen, A. M. (1982). Toward understanding the relationship between feeling states and social behavior. In A. H. Hastorf & A. M. Isen (Eds.), *Cognitive social psychology.* New York: Elsevier.

Clark, M. S., & Reis, H. T. (1988). Interpersonal processes in close relationships. *Annual Review of Psychology, 39,* 609–672.

Clark, R. D., & Word, L. E. (1972). Why don't bystanders help? Because of ambiguity? *Journal of Personality and Social Psychology, 24,* 392–400.

Clark, R. D., & Word, L. E. (1974). Where is the apathetic bystander? Situational characteristics of the emergency. *Journal of Personality and Social Psychology, 29,* 279–287.

Clarke, A. M., & Clarke, A. D. B. (1976a). Some continued experiments. In A. M. Clarke & A. D. B. Clarke (Eds.), *Early experience: Myth and evidence.* New York: Free Press.

Clarke, A. M., & Clarke, A. D. B. (Eds.) (1976b). *Early experience: Myth and evidence.* London: Open Books.

Clarke-Stewart, K. A. (1973). Interactions between mothers and their young children: Characteristics and consequences. *Monographs of the Society for Research in Child Development, 38*(6–7, Serial No. 153).

Clarke-Stewart, K. A. (1978). And daddy makes three: The father's impact on mother and young child. *Child Development, 49,* 466–478.

Clarke-Stewart, K. A. (1980). The father's contribution to child development. In F. A. Pedersen (Ed.), *The father-infant relationship: Observational studies in a family context.* New York: Praeger Special Studies.

Clarke-Stewart, K. A. (1988a). Parents' effects on children's development: A decade of progress? *Journal of Applied Developmental Psychology, 9,* 41–84.

Clarke-Stewart, K. A. (1988b). What does research say about the effects of day care? In L. J. Schweinhart & L. de Pietro (Eds.), *Shaping the future for early childhood programs* (pp. 23–27). Ypsilanti, MI: High/Scope Press.

Clarke-Stewart, K. A. (1989a). Infant day care: Maligned or malignant? *American Psychologist, 44,* 266–273.

Clarke-Stewart, K. A. (1989b). Risks for children when parents divorce. *NEA Today: Issues '89,* Vol. 7(6).

Clarke-Stewart, K. A., & Fein, G. G. (1983). Early childhood programs. In P. H. Mussen (Ed.), *Handbook of child psychology: Vol. 2. Infancy and developmental psychobiology.* New York: Wiley.

Clarke-Stewart, K. A., & Hevey, C. M. (1981). Longitudinal relations in repeated observations of mother-child interaction from 1 to 2–1/2 years. *Developmental Psychology, 17,* 127–145.

Clarkson-Smith, L., & Hartley, A. (1989a). Relationships between physical exercise and cognitive abilities in older adults. *Psychology and Aging, 4,* 183–189.

Clarkson-Smith, L., & Hartley, A. (1989b). Structural equation models of relationships between exercise and cognitive abilities. *Psychology and Aging, 5,* 437–446.

Claus, J. J., Ludwig, C., Mohr, E., Giuffra, M., Blin, J., & Chase, T. N. (1991). Nootropic drugs in Alzheimer's disease—symptomatic treatment with pramiracetam. *Neurology, 41,* 570–574.

Clausen, J., Sersen, E., & Lidsky, A. (1974). Variability of sleep measures in normal subjects. *Psychophysiology, 11,* 509–516.

Clayton, P., Grove, W., Coryell, W., Keller, M., Hirshfeld, R., & Fawcett, J. (1991). Follow-up and family study of anxious depression. *American Journal of Psychiatry, 148,* 1512–1517.

Cleary, T. A., Humphreys, L. G., Kendrick, S. A., & Wesman, A. (1975). Educational use of tests with disadvantaged students. *American Psychologist, 30,* 15–41.

Cleckley, H. (1976). *The mask of sanity* (5th ed.). St. Louis: Mosby.

Clemant, C., & Falmagne, R. C. (1986). Logical reasoning, world knowledge, and mental imagery. *Memory & Cognition, 14,* 299–307.

Clifford, B. R., & Hollin, C. R. (1981). Effects of the type of incident and number of perpetrators on eyewitness testimony. *Journal of Applied Psychology, 67,* 364–370.

Cline, V. B., Croft, R. G., & Courrier, S. (1973). Desensitization of children to television violence. *Journal of Personality and Social Psychology, 27,* 360–365.

Cloninger, C. (1987). Neurogenic adaptive mechanisms in alcoholism. *Science, 236,* 410–416.

Clore, G. L. (1975). *Interpersonal attraction: An overview.* Morristown, NJ: General Learning Press.

Clore, G. L., & Schwarz, N. (1994a). Affect and cognition. In R. S. Wyer & T. K. Srull (Eds.), *Handbook of social cognition* (2nd ed.). Hillsdale, NJ: Lawrence Erlbaum Associates.

Clore, G. L., & Schwarz, N. (1994b). Affect and emotion. In R. S. Wyer & T. K. Srull (Eds.), *Handbook of social cognition* (2nd ed.). Hillsdale, NJ: Lawrence Erlbaum Associates.

Clore, G. L., Ortony, A. Dienes, B., & Fujita, F. (1993). Where does anger dwell? In R. S. Wyer & T. K. Srull (Eds.), *Towards a general theory of anger and emotional aggression: Implications of the cognitive-neoassociationistic perspective for the analysis of anger and other emotions.* Hillsdale, NJ: Lawrence Erlbaum Associates.

Coates, R. A., Soskoline, C. L., Calzavara, L., Read, S. E., Fanning, M. M., Shephard, F. A., Klein, M. M., & Johnson, J. K. (1987). The reliability of sexual histories in AIDS-related research: Evaluation of an interview administered questionnaire. *Canadian Journal of Public Health, 77,* 343–348.

Coates, T. J. (1990). Strategies for modifying sexual behavior for primary and secondary prevention of HIV disease. *Journal of Consulting and Clinical Psychology, 58,* 57–69.

Coates, T. J., & Thoreson, C. E. (1977). *How to sleep better.* Englewood Cliffs, NJ: Prentice-Hall.

Cofer, L. F., Grice, J., Palmer, D., Sethre-Hofstad, L., & Zimmermann, K. (1992). Evidence for developmental continuity of individual differences in morningness-eveningness. Paper presented at the annual meeting of the American Psychological Society, San Diego, California, June 20–22.

Cohen, F., & Lazarus, R. S. (1979). Coping with the stresses of illness. In G. C. Stone, F. Cohen, & N. E. Adler (Eds.), *Health psychology: A handbook.* San Francisco: Jossey-Bass.

Cohen, G. (1989). *Memory in the real world.* Hillsdale, NJ: Lawrence Erlbaum Associates.

Cohen, J., & Servan-Schreiber, D. (1992). Context, cortex, and dopamine: A connectionist approach to behavior and biology in schizophrenia. *Psychological Review, 99,* 45–77.

Cohen, L. (Ed.) (1987). *Research on stressful life events: Theoretical and methodological issues.* Beverly Hills, CA: Sage.

Cohen, N. J., & Corkin, S. (1981). The amnesic patient H.M.: Learning and retention of a cognitive skill. *Neuroscience Abstracts, 7,* 235.

Cohen, N. J., & Eichenbaum, H. (1993). *Memory, amnesia, and the hippocampal system.* Cambridge, MA: MIT Press.

Cohen, N. J., McCloskey, M., & Wible, C. B. (1988). There is still no case for a flashbulb-memory mechanism: Reply to Schmidt and Bohannon. *Journal of Experimental Psychology: General, 117,* 336–338.

Cohen, N. J., McCloskey, M., & Wible, C. G. (1990). Flashbulb memories and underlying cognitive mechanisms: Reply to Pillemer. *Journal of Experimental Psychology: General, 119,* 97–100.

Cohen, N., & Ader, R. (1988). Immunomodulation by classical conditioning. *Advances in Biochemical Psychopharmacology, 44,* 199–202.

Cohen, R. J., Swerdlik, M. E., & Smith, D. E. (1992). *Psychological testing and assessment.* Mountain View, CA: Mayfield.

Cohen, S. (1980). Aftereffects of stress on human performance and social behavior. A review of research and theory. *Psychological Bulletin, 88,* 82–108.

Cohen, S., & Hoberman, H. M. (1983). Positive events and social supports as buffers of life change stress. *Journal of Applied Social Psychology, 13,* 99–125.

Cohen, S., & Syme, S. L. (1985). Issues in the study and application of social support. In S. Cohen & S.L. Syme (Eds.), *Social support and health.* New York: Academic Press.

Cohen, S., & Williamson, G. (1991). Stress and infectious disease. *Psychological Bulletin, 109,* 5–24.

Cohen, S., & Wills, T. A. (1985). Stress, social support, and the buffering hypothesis. *Psychological Bulletin, 98,* 310–357.

Cohen, S., Kaplan, J. R., Cunnick, J. E., Manuck, S. B., & Rabin, B. S. (1992). Chronic social stress, affiliation, and cellular immune response in nonhuman primates. *Psychological Science, 3,* 301–304.

Cohen, S., Tyrrell, D., & Smith, A. (1991). Psychological stress and susceptibility to the common cold. *The New England Journal of Medicine, 325,* 606–612.

Cohn, J. F., & Tronick, E. Z. (1983). Three-month-old infants' reaction to simulated maternal depression. *Child Development, 54,* 185–193.

Cohn, J. F., Campbell, S. B., Matias, R., & Hopkins, J. (1990). Face-to-face interactions of post-partum depressed and nondepressed mother-infant pairs at 2 months. *Developmental Psychology, 26,* 15–23.

Cohn, J., & Tronick, E. Z. (1989). Specificity of infants' response to mothers' affective behavior. *Journal of the American Academy of Child and Adolescent Psychiatry, 28,* 242–248.

Cohn, L. D. (1991). Sex differences in the course of personality development: A meta-analysis. *Psychological Bulletin, 109,* 252–266.

Cohn, N. B., & Strassberg, D. S. (1983). Self-disclosure reciprocity among preadolescents. *Personality and Social Psychology Bulletin, 9,* 97–102.

Coile, D. C., & Miller, N. E. (1984). How radical animal activists try to mislead humane people. *American Psychologist, 39,* 700–701.

Colby, A., Kohlberg, L., Gibbs, J., & Lieberman, M. (1983). A longitudinal study of moral judgment. *Monographs of the Society for Reserach in Child Development, 48*(1, Serial No. 200).

Cole, K. N., Mills, P. E., Dale, P. S., & Jenkins, J. R. (1991). Effects of preschool integration for children with disabilities. *Exceptional Children, 58,* 36–45.

Coleman, D. (1992). Why do I feel so tired? Too little, too late. *American Health, 11*(4), 43–46.

Coleman, D. J., & Kaplan, M. S. (1990). Effects of pretherapy videotape preparation on child therapy outcomes. *Professional Psychology: Research and Practice, 21,* 199–203.

Coles, M. (1989). Modern mind-brain reading: Psychophysiology, physiology & cognition. *Psychophysiology, 26,* 251–269.

Colletta, N. D. (1979). Support systems after divorce: Incidence and impact. *Journal of Marriage and the Family, 41,* 837–846.

Collins, A. M., & Loftus, E. F. (1975). A spreading activation theory of semantic processing. *Psychological Review, 82,* 407–428.

Collins, D. L., Baum, A., & Singer, J. E. (1983). Coping with chronic stress at Three Mile Island: Psychological and biochemical evidence. *Health Psychology, 2,* 149–166.

Colombo, M., D'Amato, M. R., Rodman, H. R., & Gross, C. G. (1990). Auditory association cortex lesions impair auditory short-term memory in monkeys. *Science, 247,* 336–338.

Colrain, I. M., Mangan, G. L., Pellett, O. L., & Bates, T. C. (1992). Effects of post-learning smoking on memory consolidation. *Psychopharmacology, 108,* 448–451.

Commission of Inquiry into the Non-medical Use of Drugs. (1970, 1972, 1973). *Interim Report.* Ottawa: Queen's Printer for Canada.

Condry, J., & Condry, S. (1976). Sex differences: A study in the eye of the beholder. *Child Development, 47,* 812–819.

Condry, J., & Siman, M. L. (1974). Characteristics of peer adult-oriented children. *Journal of Marriage and the Family, 36,* 543–554.

Conger, J. J. (1951). The effects of alcohol on conflict behavior in the albino rat. *Quarterly Journal of Studies on Alcohol, 12,* 1–29.

Connelly, J. C. (1980). Alcoholism as indirect self-destructive behavior. In N. L. Farberow (Ed.), *The many faces of suicide: Indirect self-destructive behavior*. New York: McGraw-Hill.

Connor, L. T., Balota, D. A., & Neely, J. H. (1992). On the relation between feeling of knowing and lexical decision: Persistent subthreshold activation of topic familiarity? *Journal of Experimental Psychology: Learning, Memory, and Cognition, 18,* 544–554.

Conrad, R. (1964). Acoustic confusions in immediate memory. *British Journal of Psychology, 55,* 75–84.

Contrada, R. J. (1989). Type A behavior, personality hardiness, and cardiovascular responses to stress. *Journal of Personality and Social Psychology, 57,* 895–903.

Conway, J. B. (1988). Differences among clinical psychologists: Scientists, practitioners, and scientist-practitioners. *Professional Psychology: Research and Practice, 19,* 642–655.

Cook, S. W. (1984). The 1954 social science statement and school desegregation: A reply to Gerard. *American Psychologist, 39,* 819–832.

Cook, S. W. (1985). Experimenting on social issues: The case of school desegregation. *American Psychologist, 40,* 452–460.

Cook, T., & Mineka, S. (1987). Second-order conditioning and overshadowing in the observational conditioning of fear in monkeys. *Behaviour Research and Therapy, 25,* 349–364.

Cook, T., & Mineka, S. (1990). Selective association in the observational conditioning of fear in rhesus monkeys. *Journal of Experimental Psychology: Animal Behavior Processes, 16,* 372–389.

Cooper, C. L. (1985). *Psychosocial stress and cancer*. New York: Wiley.

Cooper, G. D., Adams, H. B, & Scott, J. C. (1988). Studies in REST: I. Reduced environmental stimulation therapy (REST) and reduced alcohol consumption. *Journal of Substance Abuse Treatment, 5,* 61–68.

Cooper, H. (1979). Pygmalion grows up: A model for teacher expectation communication and performance influence. *Review of Educational Research, 49,* 389–410.

Cooper, J. R. (1991). Drug treatment in Alzheimer's disease. *Archives of Internal Medicine, 151,* 245–249.

Cooper, J., & Croyle, R. T. (1984). Attitudes and attitude change. *Annual Review of Psychology, 35,* 395–426.

Cooper, J., & Fazio, R. (1984). A new look at dissonance theory. In L. Berkowitz (Ed.), *Advances in experimental social psychology* (Vol. 17). Orlando: Academic Press.

Cooper, L. A., Schacter, D. L., Ballesteros, S., & Moore, C. (1992). Priming and recognition of transformed three-dimensional objects: Effects of size and reflection. *Journal of Experimental Psychology: Learning, Memory, and Cognition, 18,* 43–57.

Cooper, M., Russell, M., Skinner, J., Frone, M., & Mudar, P. (1992). Stress and alcohol use: Moderating effects of gender, coping and alcohol expectancies. *Journal of Abnormal Psychology, 101,* 139–152.

Cooper, R. M., & Zubek, J. P. (1958). Effects of enriched and restricted early environments on the learning ability of bright and dull rats. *Canadian Journal of Psychology, 12,* 159–164.

Coovert, M. D., & Reeder, G. D. (1990). Negativity effects in impression formation: The role of unit formation and schematic expectations. *Journal of Experimental Social Psychology, 26,* 49–62.

Coppen, A., Metcalf, M., & Wood, K. (1982). Lithium. In E. S. Paykel (Ed.), *Handbook of affective disorders*. New York: Guilford Press.

Corbetta, M., Miezin, F. M., Dobmeyer, S., Shulman, G. L., & Petersen, S. E. (1991). Selective and divided attention during visual discriminations of shape, color, and speed: Functional anatomy by positron emission tomography. *Journal of Neuroscience, 11,* 2383–2402.

Corby, N., & Solnick, R. L. (1980). Psychosocial and physiological influences on sexuality in the older adult. In J. E. Birren & R. B. Sloane (Eds.), *Handbook of mental health and aging* (pp. 893–921). Englewood Cliffs, NJ: Prentice-Hall.

Cordes, C. (1985, April). A step back. *APA Monitor,* 12–14.

Coren, S., & Aks, D. J. (1990). Moon illusion is observed in pictures. *Journal of Experimental Psychology: Human Perception and Performance, 16,* 365–380.

Coren, S., & Girgus, J. (1978). *Seeing is deceiving: The psychology of visual illusions*. Hillsdale, NJ: Lawrence Erlbaum Associates.

Corina, D. P., Vaid, J., & Bellugi, U. (1992). The linguistic basis of left hemisphere specialization. *Science, 255,* 1258–1260.

Cork, R. C., Kihlstrom, J. F., & Hameroff, S. R. (1992). Explicit and implicit memory dissociated by anesthetic technique. *Society for Neuroscience Abstracts, 22,* 523.

Cornblatt, B., & Erlenmeyer-Kimling, L. E. (1985). Global attentional deviance in children at risk for schizophrenia: Specificity and predictive validity. *Journal of Abnormal Psychology, 94,* 470–486.

Cornell-Bell, A. H., Finkbeiner, S. M., Cooper, M. S., & Smith, S. J. (1990). Glutamate induces calcium waves in cultured astrocytes: Long-range glial signaling. *Science, 247,* 470–473.

Cornoldi, C., & DeBeni, R., & Baldi, A. P. (1989). Generation and retrieval of general, specific, and autobiographical images representing concrete nouns. *Acta Psychologica, 72,* 25–39.

Corrigan, P. (1991). Social skills training in adult psychiatric populations: A meta-analysis. *Journal of Behavior Therapy and Experimental Psychiatry, 22,* 203–210.

Corsini, R. (Ed.) (1981). *Handbook of innovative psychology*. New York: Wiley.

Corsini, R. J. (1989). *Current psychotherapies* (4th ed.). Itasca, IL: Peacock.

Corter, C. M., Zucker, K. J., & Galligan, R. F. (1980). Patterns in infants' search for mother during brief separation. *Developmental Psychology, 16,* 62–70.

Corty, E., Lehman, A. F., & Myers, C. P. (1993). Influence of psychoactive substance use on the reliability of psychiatric diagnosis. *Journal of Consulting and Clinical Psychology, 61,* 165–170.

Corwin, J. T. (1992). Regeneration in the auditory system. *Experimental Neurology, 115,* 7–12.

Corwin, J. T., & Cotanche, D. A. (1988). Regeneration of sensory hair cells after acoustic trauma. *Science, 240,* 1772–1774.

Costa, P. T. (1992). Set like plaster? Evidence for the stability of adult personality. Paper presented at the American Psychological Association Convention, Washington, DC.

Costa, P. T., Jr., & McCrae, R. R. (1988). Personality in adulthood: A six-year longitudinal study of self-reports and spouse ratings on the NEO personality inventory. *Journal of Personality and Social Psychology, 54,* 853–863.

Costa, P. T., Jr., & McCrae, R. R. (1989). Personality, stress, and coping: Some lessons from a decade of research. In K. S. Markides & C. L. Cooper (Eds.), *Aging, stress, social support, and health*. New York: Wiley.

Costa, P. T., Jr., Zonderman, A. B., McCrae, R. R., Cornoni-Huntley, J., Locke, B. Z., & Barbano, H. E. (1987). Longitudinal analyses of psychological well-being in a national sample: Stability of mean levels. *Journal of Gerontology, 42,* 50–55.

Costa, P., & McCrae, R. (1978, 1985, 1989, 1991). *NEO Personality Inventory*. Odessa, FL: Psychological Assessment Resources, Inc.

Costa, P., & McCrae, R. (1992). *Revised NEO Personality Inventory: NEO PI and NEO Five-Factor Inventory (NEO FFI: Professional Manual)*. Odessa, FL: Psychological Assessment Resources, Inc.

Costello, E., Costello, A., Edelbrock, C., Burns, B., Dulcan, M., Brent, D., & Janiszewski, S. (1988). Psychiatric disorders in pediatric primary care. *Archives of General Psychiatry, 45,* 1107–1116.

Costermans, J., Lories, G., & Ansay, C. (1992). Confidence level and feeling of knowing in question answering: The weight of inferential processes. *Journal of Experimental Psychology: Learning, Memory, and Cognition, 18,* 142–150.

Cotman, C. W., Monaghan, D. T., & Ganong, A. H. (1988). Excitatory amino acid neurotransmission: NMDA receptors and Hebb-type synaptic plasticity. *Annual Review of Neuroscience 11,* 61–80.

Cotterell, N., Eisenberger, R., & Speicher, H. (1992). Inhibiting effects of reciprocation wariness on interpersonal relationships. *Journal of Personality and Social Psychology, 62,* 658–668.

Cowan, N. (1988). Evolving concepts of memory storage, selective attention, and their mutual constraints within the human information-processing system. *Psychological Bulletin, 104,* 163–191.

Cowan, W. M. (1979). The development of the brain. *Scientific American, 241,* 112–133.

Coward, W. M., & Sackett, P. R. (1990). Linearity of ability-performance relationships: A reconfirmation. *Journal of Applied Psychology, 75,* 297–300.

Cowen, E. L. (1982). Help is where you find it: Four informal helping groups. *American Psychologist, 37,* 385–395.

Cowen, E. L. (1983). Primary prevention: Past, present, and future. In R. D. Felner, L. A. Jason, J. N. Moritsugu, & S. S. Faber (Eds.), *Preventive psychology: Theory, research and practice.* New York: Pergamon Press.

Cowen, G., & Sharp, D. (1988). Neural nets and artificial intelligence. In S. R. Graubard (Ed.), *The artificial intelligence debate.* Cambridge, MA: MIT Press.

Cowey, A., & Stoerig, P. (1992). Reflections on blindsight. In A. D. Milner & M. D. Rugg (Eds.), *The neuropsychology of consciousness.* San Diego, CA: Academic Press.

Cowles, J. T. (1937). Food-tokens as incentives for learning by chimpanzees. *Comparative Psychology Monographs 14*(5, Serial No. 71).

Cox, T. (1984). Stress: A psychophysiological approach to cancer. In C. L. Cooper (Ed.), *Psychosocial stress and cancer.* New York: Wiley.

Coyle, J. T., Price, D. L., & DeLong, M. R. (1983). Alzheimer's disease: A disorder of cortical cholinergic innervation. *Science, 219,* 1184–1190.

Craighead, L. W. (1984). Sequencing of behavior therapy and pharmacotherapy for obesity. *Journal of Consulting and Clinical Psychology, 52,* 190–199.

Craik, F. I. M., & Lockhart, R. S. (1972). Levels of processing: A framework for memory research. *Journal of Verbal Learning and Verbal Behavior, 11,* 671–684.

Craik, F. I. M., & Rabinowitz, J. C. (1984). Age differences in the acquisition and use of verbal information. In H. Bouma & D. G. Bouwhuis (Eds.), *Attention and performance: Vol. 10.* Hillsdale, NJ: Lawrence Erlbaum Associates.

Craik, K. H. (1986). Psychological perspectives on technology as societal option, source of hazard, and generator of environmental impacts. In V. Covello & J. Mumpower (Eds.), *Technology assessment, environmental impact assessment, and risk analysis.* New York: Springer-Verlag.

Crandall, C. S. (1988). Social contagion of binge eating. *Journal of Personality and Social Psychology, 55,* 588–598.

Crawford, C., Smith, M., & Krebs, D. (Eds.) (1987). *Sociobiology and psychology: Ideas, issues, and applications.* Hillsdale, NJ: Lawrence Erlbaum Associates.

Crawford, J. (1989). *Bilingual education: History, politics, theory, and practice.* New York: Crane.

Crawford, M., & Marecek, J. (1989). Psychology reconstructs the female. *Psychology of Women Quarterly, 13,* 147–165.

Crick, F., & Mitchison, G. (1983). The function of dream sleep. *Nature, 304,* 111–114.

Cronbach, L. J. (1970). *Essentials of psychological testing* (3rd ed.). New York: Harper & Row.

Cronbach, L. J. (1975). Five decades of public controversy over mental testing. *American Psychologist, 30,* 1–14.

Crosby, F. J. (1991). *Juggling: The unexpected advantages of balancing career and home for women and their families.* New York: The Free Press.

Crosby, F., & Gonzalez-Intal, A. M. (1982). Relative deprivation and equity theories: A comparative analysis of approaches to felt injustice. In R. Folger (Ed.), *The sense of injustice: Social psychological perspectives.* New York: Plenum Press.

Cross, D. G., Sheehan, O. W., & Kahn, J. A. (1982). Short- and long-term follow-up of clients receiving insight-oriented therapy and behavior therapy. *Journal of Consulting and Clinical Psychology, 50,* 103–112.

Cross-National Collaborative Group. (1992). The changing rate of major depression: Cross-national comparisons. *Journal of the American Medical Association, 268,* 3089–3105.

Crow, T. J. (1980). Molecular pathology of schizophrenia: More than one disease process? *British Medical Journal, 280,* 66–68.

Crow, T. J., Ball, Bloom, S. R., Brown, R., Bruton, C. J., Colter, N., Frith, C. D., Johnstone, E. C., Owens, D. G. C., & Roberts, G. W. (1989). Schizophrenia as an anomaly of development of cerebral asymmetry: A postmortem study and a proposal concerning the genetic basis of the disease. *Archives of General Psychiatry, 46,* 1145–1150.

Crow, T. J., Cross, A. J., Cooper, S. J., Deakin, J. F., Ferrier, I. N., Johnson, J. A., Joseph, M. H., Owen, F., Poulter, M., Lofthouse, R., et al. (1984). Neurotransmitter receptors and monoamine metabolites in the brains of patients with Alzheimer-type dementia and depression, and suicides. *Neuropharmacology, 12,* 1561–1569.

Crow, T., Ball, J., Bloom, S., Brown, R., Bruton, C., Colter, N., Frith, C., Johnstone, E., Owens, D., & Roberts, G. (1989). Schizophrenia as an anomaly of development of cerebral asymmetry: A postmortem study and a proposal concerning the generic basis of the disease. *Archives of General Psychiatry, 46,* 1145–1150.

Crowder, R. G. (1989). Modularity and dissociations in memory systems. In H. L. Roediger & F. I. M. Craik (Eds.), *Varieties of memory and consciousness.* Hillsdale, NJ: Lawrence Erlbaum Associates.

Crowder, R. G. (1992). Adaptation and communication as models for learning and memory. *Contemporary Psychology, 37,* 139–142.

Crutcher, K. A. (1991). Anatomical correlates of neuronal plasticity. In J. L. Martinez & R. P. Kesner (Eds.), *Learning and memory: A biological view* (2nd ed.). San Diego: Academic Press.

Crutchfield, R. A. (1955). Conformity and character. *American Psychologist, 10,* 191–198.

Csikszentmihalyi, M., & Larson, R. (1984). *Being adolescent: Conflict and growth in the teenage years.* New York: Basic Books.

Culebras, A. (1992). Update on disorders of sleep and the sleep-wake cycle. *Psychiatric Clinics of North America, 15,* 467–489.

Culp, R. E., Cook, A. S., & Housley, P. C. (1983). A comparison of observed and reported adult-infant interactions: Effects of perceived sex. *Sex Roles, 9,* 475–479.

Cunningham, M. R., Shaffer, D. R., Barbee, A. P., Wolff, P. L., & Kelley, D. J. (1990). Separate processes in the relation of elation and depression to helping: Social versus personal concerns. *Journal of Experimental Social Psychology, 26,* 13–33.

Curcio, C. A., Sloan, D. R., Jr., Packer, O., Hendrickson, A. E., & Kalina, R. E. (1987). Distribution of cones in human and monkey retina: Individual variability and radial asymmetry. *Science, 236,* 579–582.

Curran, J. P., & Lippold, S. (1975). The effects of physical attraction and attitude similarity on attraction in dating dyads. *Journal of Personality, 43,* 528–539.

Curran, J. P., & Monti, P. M. (1982). *Social skills training: A practical handbook for assessment and treatment.* New York: Guilford Press.

Currim, I. S., & Sarin, R. K. (1992). Robustness of expected utility model in predicting individual choices. *Organizational Behavior and Human Decision Processes, 52,* 544–568.

Curtis, R. C., & Miller, K. (1986). Believing another likes or dislikes you: Behaviors making the beliefs come true. *Journal of Personality and Social Psychology, 51,* 284–290.

Curtiss, S. (1977). *Genie: A psycholinguistic study of a modern-day wild child.* New York: Academic Press.

Cutting, J. (1987). Perception and information. *Annual Review of Psychology, 38,* 61–90.

Czeisler, C. A. (1988). *Final report on the Philadelhia Police Department shift rescheduling program.* Boston: Center for Design of Industrial Schedules.

Czeisler, C. A., Johnson, M. P., Duffy, J. F., Brown, E. N., Ronda, J. M., & Kronauer, R. E. (1990). Exposure to bright light and darkness to treat physiologic maladaptation to night work. *New England Journal of Medicine, 322,* 1253–1259.

Czeisler, C. A., Kronauer, R. E., Allan, J. S., Duffy, J. F., Jewett, M. E., Brown, E. N., & Ronda, J. M. (1989). Bright light induction of strong (Type 0) resetting of the human circadian pacemaker. *Science, 244,* 1328–1333.

d'Yclewalle, G., & Rosselle, H. (1978). Text expectations in text learning. In M. M. Gruneberg, P. E. Morris, & R. N. Sykes (Eds.), *Practical aspects of memory.* Orlando, FL: Academic Press.

Dabbs, J. M., Jr., Frady, R. L., Caur, T. S., & Besch, N. F. (1987). Saliva testosterone and criminal violence in young prison inmates. *Psychosomatic Medicine, 49,* 174–182.

Dahlstrom, W. G. (1992). The growth in acceptance of the MMPI. *Professional Psychology: Research and Practice, 23,* 345–348.

Dahlstrom, W. G., Lachar, D., & Dahlstrom, L. E. (1986). *MMPI patterns of American minorities.* Minneapolis: University of Minnesota Press.

Dale, P. S. (1976). *Language and the development of structure and function.* New York: Holt, Rinehart and Winston.

Daly, M., & Wilson, M. (1988). *Homicide.* New York: Aldine de Gruyter.

Damasio, A. R., & Damasio, H. (1992, September). Brain and language. *Scientific American, 267,* 88–109.

Damasio, A. R., Damasio, H., & Van Hoesen, G. (1982). Prosopagnosia: Anatomic basis and behavioral mechanisms. *Neurology, 32,* 331–341.

Damon, W., & Hart, D. (1982). The development of self-understanding from infancy through adolescence. *Child Development, 53,* 841–864.

Damos, D. (1992). *Multiple task performance.* London: Taylor & Francis.

Dana, R. H. (1988). Culturally diverse groups and MMPI interpretation. *Professional Psychology: Research and Practice, 19,* 490–495.

Daniel, W. F., & Crovitz, H. F. (1983). Acute memory impairment following electroconvulsive therapy: 1. Effects of electrical stimulus and number of treatments. *Acta Psychiatrica Scandinavica, 67,* 57–68.

Darke, S. (1988). Effects of anxiety on inferential reasoning task performance. *Journal of Personality and Social Psychology, 55,* 499–505.

Darley, C. F., Tinklenberg, J. R., Hollister, L. E., & Atkinson, R. C. (1973a). Marijuana and retrieval from short-term memory. *Psychopharmacologica, 29,* 231–238.

Darley, C. F., Tinklenberg, J. R., Roth, W. T., Hollister, L. E., & Atkinson, R. C. (1973b). Influence of marijuana on storage and retrieval processes in memory. *Memory & Cognition, 1,* 196–200.

Davanloo, J. (Ed.) (1978). *Basic principles and techniques in short-term dynamic psychotherapy.* New York: Spectrum.

Davidson, A. D. (1979, Spring). Coping with stress reactions in rescue workers: A program that worked. *Police Stress.*

Davidson, A. R., Jaccard, J. J., Triandis, H. C., Morales, M. L., & Diaz-Guerrero, R. (1976). Cross-cultural model testing: Toward a solution of the etic-emic dilemma. *International Journal of Psychology, 11,* 1–13.

Davidson, J. M., Camargo, C. A., & Smith, E. R. (1979). Effects of androgen on sexual behavior in hypogonadal men. *Journal of Clinical Endocrinological Metabolism, 48,* 955–958.

Davidson, J. M., Kwan, M., & Greenleaf, W. J. (1982). Hormonal replacement and sexuality in men. *Clinics in Endocrinology and Metabolism, 11,* 599–623.

Davidson, R. J. (1980). Consciousness and information processing: A biocognitive perspective. In J. M. Davidson & R. J. Davidson (Eds.), *The psychology of consciousness.* New York: Plenum.

Davidson, R. J. (1984). Affect, cognition, and hemispheric specialization. In C. E. Izard, J. Kagan, & R. B. Zajonc (Eds.), *Emotions, cognition, and behavior.* Cambridge: Cambridge University Press.

Davidson, R. J., Ekman, P., Saron, C., Senulis, J., & Friesen, W. V. (1990). Approach-withdrawal and cerebral asymmetry: Emotional expression and brain physiology: I. *Journal of Personality and Social Psychology, 58,* 330–341.

Davis, J. D., Gallagher, R. J., Ladove, R. F., & Turansky, A. J. (1989). Inhibition of food intake by a humoral factor. *Journal of Comparative and Physiological Psychology, 67,* 407–414.

Davis, J. H. (1992). Some compelling intuitions about group consensus decisions, theoretical and empirical research, and interpersonal aggregation phenomena: Selected examples, 1950–1990. *Organizational Behavior and Human Decision Processes, 52,* 3–38.

Davis, J. M. (1978). Dopamine theory of schizophrenia: A two-factor theory. In L. C. Wynne, R. L. Cromwell, & S. Matthysse (Eds.), *The nature of schizophrenia: New approaches to research and treatment* (pp. 105–115). New York: Wiley.

Davis, K. B., (1929). *Factors in the sex life of twenty-two hundred women.* New York: Harper & Brothers.

Davis, K., Kahn, R., Ko, G., & Davidson, M. (1991). Dopamine in schizophrenia: A review and reconceptualization. *American Journal of Psychiatry, 148,* 1474–1486.

Davis, R. (1986). Assessing the eating disorders. *The Clinical Psychologist, 39,* 33–36.

Davis, R. A., & Moore, C. C. (1935). Methods of measuring retention. *Journal of General Psychology, 12,* 144–155.

Davison, G. C., & Neale, J. M. (1990). *Abnormal psychology* (5th ed.). New York: Wiley.

Dawes, R. (1992). *Psychology and psychotherapy: The myth of professional expertise.* New York: The Free Press.

Dawes, R., Faust, D., & Meehl, P. E. (1989). Clinical versus actuarial judgment. *Science, 243,* 1668–1674.

Dawkins, K., & Potter, W. (1991). Gender differences in pharmacokinetics and pharmacodynamics of psychotropics: Focus on women. *Psychopharmacology Bulletin, 27,* 417–426.

De Benedittis, G., Lornenzetti, A., & Pieri, A. (1990). The role of stressful life events in the onset of chronic primary headache. *Pain, 40,* 65–75.

de Castro, J. M., & Brewer, E. M. (1992). The amount eaten in meals by humans is a power function of the number of people present. *Physiology and Behavior, 51,* 121–125.

de Charms, R., & Moeller, G. H. (1962). Values expressed in American children's readers: 1800–1950. *Journal of Abnormal and Social Psychology, 64,* 136–142.

de Charms, R., Levy, J., & Wertheimer, M. (1954). A note on attempted evaluations of psychotherapy. *Journal of Clinical Psychology, 10,* 233–235.

De La Fuente, J-R., & Alarcon-Segovia, D. (1980). Depression as expressed in precolumbian Mexican art. *American Journal of Psychiatry, 137,* 1095–1098.

de Lacoste-Utamsing, C. & Holloway, R. L. (1982). Sexual dimorphism in the human corpus callosum. *Science, 216,* 1431–1432.

De Rios, M. D. (1992). Power and hallucinogenic states of consciousnes among the Moche: An ancient Peruvian society. In C. A. Ward (Ed.), *Altered states of consciousness and mental health: A cross-cultural perspective.* Newbury Park, CA: Sage.

De Robertis, E., Pena, C., Paladini, C., & Medine, J. H. (1988). New developments on the search for the endogenous ligand(s) of central benzodiazepine receptors. *Neurochemistry International, 13,* 1–11.

De Silva, P., Rachman, S., & Seligman, M. E. P. (1977). Prepared phobias and obsessions: Therapeutic outcome. *Behaviour Research and Therapy, 15,* 65–77.

Dean, W., & Morganthaler, J. (1990). *Smart drugs and nutrients.* Santa Cruz, CA: B&J Publications.

DeAngelis, T. (1989, November). NIMH fails to reach its prevention goals. *APA Monitor,* p. 29.

DeAngelis, T. (1992a). Illness linked with repressive coping style. *APA Monitor, 23,* 14–15.

DeAngelis, T. (1992b). Senate seeks answers to rising tide of violence. *APA Monitor,* May, p. 11.

DeAngelis, T. (1992c). The "Who am I" question wears a cloak of culture. *American Psychological Association Monitor,* October.

Deci, E. L. (1980). *The psychology of self-determination.* Lexington, MA: D. C. Heath.

Deci, E. L., Connell, J. P., & Ryan, M. (1987). *Self-determination in a work organization.* Unpublished manuscript, University of Rochester, Rochester, NY.

Defares, P. B., Grossman, P., & de Swart, H. C. G. (1983). Test anxiety, cognitive primitivation, and hyperventilation. In H. M. van der Ploeg, R. Schwarzer, & C. D. Sprilberger (Eds.), *Advances in test anxiety research: Vol. 2.* Hillsdale, NJ: Lawrence Erlbaum Associates.

Deikman, A. J. (1982). *The observing self.* Boston: Boston Press.

DeJong, R. N. (1967). *The neurological examination.* New York: Lippincott/Harper & Row.

DeKay, W. T., & Buss, D. M. (1992). Human nature, individual differences, and the importance of context: Perspectives from evolutionary psychology. *Current Directions in Psychological Science, 1,* 184–189.

DeLeon, M. J., McRae, T., Tsai, J. R., George, A. E., Marcus, D. L., Freeman, M., Wolf, A. P., & McEwen, B. S. (1988). Abnormal cortisol response in Alzheimer's disease linked to hippocampal atrophy. *The Lancet, 2*(8607), 391–392.

DeLeon, P., Fox, R., & Graham, S. (1991). Prescription privileges: Psychology's next frontier. *American Psychologist, 46,* 384–393.

Dellas, M., & Gaier, E. C. (1970). Identification of creativity: The individual. *Psychological Bulletin, 73,* 55–73.

DeLoache, J. S. (1987). Rapid change in the symbolic functioning of very young children. *Science, 238,* 1556–1557.

DeLongis, A., Folkman, S., & Lazarus, R. S. (1988). The impact of daily stress on health and mood: Psychological and social resources as mediators. *Journal of Personality and Social Psychology, 54,* 486–495.

Demare, D., Briere, J., & Lips, H. M. (1988). Violent pornography and self-reported likelihood of sexual aggression. *Journal of Research in Personality, 22,* 140–153.

Dember, W. N., Earl, R. W., & Paradise, N. (1957). Response by rats to differential stimulus complexity. *Journal of Comparative and Physiological Psychology, 50,* 514–518.

Dembroski, T. M., & Williams, R. B. (1989). Definition and assessment of coronary-prone behavior. In N. Schneiderman, P. Kauf-

mann, & S. M. Wiess (Eds.), *Handbook of research methods in cardiovascular behavioral medicine.* New York: Plenum.

Dement, W. (1960). The effect of dream deprivation. *Science, 131,* 1705–1707.

Dement, W., & Kleitman, N. (1957). Cyclic variations in EEG during sleep and their relation to eye movements, body motility and dreaming. *Electroencephalography and Clinical Neurophysiology, 9,* 673–690.

Dement, W., Guilleminault, C., & Zarcone, V. (1975). The pathologies of sleep: A case series approach. In D. B. Tower (Ed.), *The nervous system: Vol. 2. The clinical neurosciences.* New York: Raven Press.

Dempster, F. N. (1988). The spacing effect: A case study in the failure to apply the results of psychological research. *American Psychologist, 43,* 627–634.

Denmark, F., Russo, N. F., Frieze, I. H, & Sechzer, J. A. (1988). Guidelines for avoiding sexism in psychological research. *American Psychologist, 43,* 582–585.

Dennerstein, L., Spencer, G. C., Gotts, G., Brown, J. B., Smith, M. A., & Burrows, G. D. (1985). Progesterone and the premenstrual syndrome: a double-blind crossover trial. *British Medical Journal, 290,* 1617–1621.

Dennet, D. C., & Kinsbourne, M. (1992). Time and the observer: The where and when of consciousness in the brain. *Behavioral and Brain Sciences, 15,* 183–247.

Dennett, D. C. (1991). *Consciousness explained.* Boston: Little, Brown.

Dennis, W. (1960). Causes of retardation among institutional children: Iran. *Journal of Genetic Psychology, 96,* 47–59.

Dennis, W. (1973). *Children of the creche.* New York: Appleton-Century-Crofts.

Denny, E. R., & Hunt, R. R. (1992). Affective valence and memory in depression: Dissociation of recall and fragment completion. *Journal of Abnormal Psychology, 101,* 575–580.

Denton, G. (1980). The influence of visual pattern on perceived speed. *Perception, 9,* 393–402.

Denton, K., & Krebs, D. (1990). From the scene to the crime: The effect of alcohol and social context on moral judgment. *Journal of Personality and Social Psychology, 59,* 242–248.

DePue, R. A., & Monroe, S. M. (1986). Conceptualization and measurement of human disorder in life stress research: The problem of chronic disturbance. *Psychological Bulletin, 99,* 36–51.

Derlega, V. J., Winstead, B. A., Wong, P. T. P., & Greenspan, M. (1987). Self-disclosure and relationship development: An attributional analysis. In M. E. Roloff & G. R. Miller (Eds.), *Interpersonal processes: New directions in communication research.* Newbury Park, CA: Sage.

Derogowski, J. B. (1989). Real space and represented space: Cross cultural perspectives. *Behavior and Brain Sciences, 12,* 51–73.

Derryberry, D., & Tucker, D. M. (1992). Neural mechanisms of emotion. *Journal of Consulting and Clinical Psychology, 60,* 329–338.

DeStefano, L. (1986). *Personal communication.* University of Illinois.

Deutsch, D. (1992). Paradoxes of musical pitch. *Scientific American, 267,* 88–95.

Deutsch, J. A., Young, W. G., & Kalogeris, T. J. (1978). The stomach signals satiety. *Science, 201,* 165–167.

Deutsch, L. (1992). Bias, confusion, emotion led to verdict, responses show. *Champaign-Urbana News-Gazette,* May 10.

Deutsch, M. (1993). Educating for a peaceful world. *American Psychologist, 48,* 510–517.

Deutsch, M., & Gerard, H. B. (1955). A study of normative and informative social influences on individual judgments. *Journal of Abnormal and Social Psychology, 51,* 629–636.

Devane, W. A., Dysarz, F. A., III, Johnson, M. R., Melvin, L. S., &

Howlett, A. C. (1988). Determination and characterization of a cannabinoid receptor in rat brain. *Molecular Pharmacology, 34,* 605–613.

Devane, W. A., Hanus, L., Breuer, A., Pertwee, R. G., Stevenson, L. S., Griffin, G., Gibson, D., Mandelbaum, A., Etinger, A., & Mechoulam, R. (1992). Isolation and structure of a brain constituent that binds to the cannabinoid receptor. *Science, 258,* 1946–1949.

Devine, P. G. (1989a). Automatic and controlled processes in prejudice: The role of stereotypes and personal beliefs. In A. R. Pratkanis, S. J. Breckler, & A. G. Greenwald (Eds.), *Attitude structure and function.* Hillsdale, NJ: Lawrence Erlbaum Associates.

Devine, P. G. (1989b). Stereotypes and prejudice: Their automatic and controlled components. *Journal of Personality and Social Psychology, 56,* 5–18.

Devine, P. G., & Baker, S. M. (1991). Measurement of racial stereotype subtyping. *Personality and Social Psychology Bulletin, 17,* 44–50.

Devine, P. G., Monteith, M. J., Zuwerink, J. R., & Elliot, A. J. (1991). Prejudice with and without compunction. *Journal of Personality and Social Psychology, 60,* 817–830.

DeVries, R. (1969). Constancy of generic identity in the years three to six. *Monographs of the Society for Research in Child Development, 34*(3, Serial No. 127).

DeWitt, L. A., & Samuel, A. G. (1990). The role of knowledge based function in music perception. *Journal of Experimental Psychology: General, 119,* 123–144.

Dhar, V., & Murphy, B. E. (1990). Double-blind randomized crossover trial of luteal phase estrogens (Premarin) in premenstrual syndrome (PMS). *Psychoneuroendocrinology, 15,* 489–493.

Dhar, V., & Murphy, B. E. (1991). The premenstrual syndrome and its treatment. *Journal of Steroid Biochemistry and Molecular Biology, 39,* 275–281.

Diamond, A. (1985). Development of the ability to use recall to guide action, as indicated by infants' performance on AB. *Child Development, 56,* 868–883.

Dickinson, A., & Mackintosh, N. J. (1978). Classical conditioning in animals. *Annual Review of Psychology, 29,* 587–612.

Diener, E. (1979). Deindividuation, self-awareness, and disinhibition. *Journal of Personality and Social Psychology, 37,* 1160–1171.

Diener, E. (1980). Deindividuation: The absence of self-awareness and self-regulation in group members. In P.B. Paulus (Ed.), *The psychology of group influence.* Hillsdale, NJ: Lawrence Erlbaum Associates.

Dietz, W. (1991). Physical activity and childhood obesity. *Nutrition, 7,* 295–296.

DiLollo, V., Hanson, D., & McIntyre, J. S. (1983). Initial stages of visual information processing in dyslexia. *Journal of Experimental Psychology: Human Perception and Performance, 9,* 923–935.

Dimsdale, J. E. (1988). A perspective on type A behavior and coronary disease. *New England Journal of Medicine, 318,* 110–112.

DiPietro, J. A. (1981). Rough and tumble play: A function of gender. *Developmental Psychology, 17,* 50–58.

Dittman, R. W., Kappes, M. E., & Kappes, M. H. (1992). Sexual behavior in adolescent and adult females with congenital adrenal hyperplasia. *Psychoneuroendocrinology, 17,* 153–170.

Ditto, P. H., & Lopez, D. F. (1992). Motivated skepticism: Use of differential decision criteria for preferred and nonpreferred conclusions. *Journal of Personality and Social Psychology, 63,* 568–584.

Dixon, L. K., & Johnson, R. C. (1980). *The roots of individuality.* Monterey, CA: Brooks/Cole.

Dixon, M., Brunet, A., & Laurence, J.-R. (1990). Hypnotizability and automaticity: Toward a parallel distributed processing model of hypnotic responding. *Journal of Abnormal Psychology, 99,* 336–343.

Dixon, T. M., & Baumeister, R. F. (1991). Escaping the self: The moderating effect of self-complexity. *Personality and Social Psychology Bulletin, 17,* 363–368.

Dobson, K. S. (1989). A meta-analysis of the efficacy of cognitive therapy for depression. *Journal of Consulting and Clinical Psychology, 57,* 414–419.

Dodd, D. K. (1985). Robbers in the classroom: A deindividuation exercise. *Teaching of Psychology, 12,* 89–91.

Dodson, C., & Reisberg, D. (1991). Indirect testing of eye witness memory: The (non)effect of misinformation. *Bulletin of the Psychonomic Society, 29,* 333–336.

Dohrenwend, B. S., & Dohrenwend, B. P. (1978). Some issues in research on stressful life events. *Journal of Nervous and Mental Disease, 166,* 7–15.

Dohrenwend, B. S., & Dohrenwend, B. P. (1984). Life stress and illness: Fomulations of the issues. In B. S. Dohrenwend & B. P. Dohrenwend (Eds.), *Stressful life events and their contexts.* New Brunswick, NJ: Rutgers University Press.

Doise, W., Csepeli, G., Cann, H. D., Gouge, C., Larson, K., & Ostell, A. (1972). An experimental investigation into the formation of intergroup representations. *European Journal of Social Psychology, 2,* 202–204.

Dollard, J., Doob, L., Miller, N., Mowrer, O. H., & Sears, R. R. (1939). *Frustration and aggression.* New Haven: Yale University Press.

Domjan, M., & Wilson, N. E. (1972). Specificity of cue to consequence in aversion learning in the rat. *Psychonomic Science, 26,* 143–145.

Donaldson, M., & Balfour, G. (1968). Less is more: A study of language comprehension in children. *British Journal of Psychology, 59,* 461–471.

Donchin, E. (1981). Surprise! . . . Surprise? *Psychophysiology, 18,* 493–513.

Donchin, E., Kramer, A. F., & Wickens, C. D. (1986). Applications of brain event-related potentials to problems in engineering psychology. In M. G. H. Coles, E. Donchin, & S. Porges (Eds.), *Psychophysiology: Systems, processes, and applications* (pp. 702–718). New York: Guilford Press.

Donegan, N. H., & Thompson, R. F. (1991). The search for the engram. In J. L. Martinez & R. P. Kesner (Eds.), *Learning and memory: A biological view* (2nd ed.). San Diego: Academic Press.

Donlon, T. F. (Ed.). (1984). *College board technical handbook for the SAT.* New York: College Entrance Examination Board.

Donnerstein, E. (1984a). Aggression. In A. S. Kahn (Ed.), *Social psychology.* Dubuque, IA: William C. Brown.

Donnerstein, E. (1984b). Pornography: Its effects on violence against women. In N. M. Malamuth & E. Donnerstein (Eds.), *Pornography and sexual aggression.* New York: Academic Press.

Donnerstein, E., & Donnerstein, M. (1976). Research in the control of interracial aggression. In R. G. Geen & E. C. O'Neal (Eds.), *Perspectives on aggression.* New York: Academic Press.

Donnerstein, E., Linz, D., & Penrod, S. (1987). *The question of pornography.* New York: Free Press.

Donovan, W. L., Leavitt, L. A., & Balling, J. D. (1978). Maternal physiological response to infant signals. *Psychophysiology, 15,* 68–74.

Dore, J. (1978). Conditions for the acquisition of speech acts. In I. Markova (Ed.), *The social context of language.* New York: Wiley.

Dornbusch, S. M., Ritter, P. L., Leiderman, P. H., Roberts, D. F., & Fraleigh, M. J. (1987). The relation of parenting style to adolescent school performance. *Child Development, 58,* 1244–1257.

Doty, R. L. (1981). Olfactory communication in humans. *Chemical Senses, 6,* 351–376.

Dovidio, J. F., Allen, J. L., & Schroeder, D. A. (1990). Specificity of empathy-induced helping: Evidence for altruistic motivation. *Journal of Personality and Social Psychology, 59,* 249–260.

Downing, J. (1986). The psychological and physiological effects of MDMA on normal volunteers. *Journal of Psychoactive Drugs, 18,* 335–340.

Dowson, D. I., Lewith, G. T., & Machin, D. (1985). The effects of acupuncture versus placebo in the treatment of headache. *Pain, 21,* 35–42.

Draguns, J. (1989). Dilemmas and choices in cross-cultural counseling: Universal versus culturally distinctive. In P. Pederson, J. Draguns, W. Lonner, & J. Trimble (Eds.), *Counseling across cultures.* (3rd ed.). Honolulu: University of Hawaii Press.

Drake, R. E., & Vaillant, G. E. (1985). A validity study of Axis II of DSM-III. *American Journal of Psychiatry, 142,* 553–558.

Dreyfus, H. L., & Dreyfus, S. E. (1987). *Mind over machine.* New York: The Free Press.

Dreyfus, H. L., & Dreyfus, S. E. (1988). Making a mind versus modeling the brain: Intelligence back at a branchpoint. In S. R. Graubard (Ed.), *The artificial intelligence debate.* Cambridge, MA: MIT Press.

Dreyfus, H., & Dreyfus, S. (1986). Why computers may never think like people. *Technology Review, 89,* 41–61.

Driskell, J. E., & Salas, E. (1991). Group decision making under stress. *Journal of Applied Psychology, 76*(3), 473–478.

Drucker-Colin, R. R., & McGaugh, J. L. (Eds.) (1977). *Neurobiology of sleep and memory.* San Diego: Academic Press.

Druckman, D., & Bjork, R. A. (Eds.) (1991). *In the mind's eye: Enhancing human performance.* Washington, DC: National Academy Press.

Druckman, D., & Swets, J. A. (1988). *Enhancing human performance: Issues, theories, and techniques.* Washington, DC: National Academy Press.

Dubbert, P. (1992). Exercise in behavioral medicine. *Journal of Consulting and Clinical Psychology, 60,* 613–618.

Dube, K., Kumar, N., & Dube, S. (1984). Long-term course and outcome of the Agra cases in the International Pilot Study of Schizophrenia. *Acta Psychiatria Scandinavica, 70,* 170–179.

DuBois, D. L., & Hirsch, B. J. (1990, August). Peer support and adolescent adjustment: A two-year longitudinal analysis. Paper presented at the 98th annual meeting of the American Psychological Association, Boston.

DuBois, D. L., Felner, R. D., Brand, S., Adan, A. M., & Evans, E. G. (1992). A prospective study of life stress, social support, and adaptation in early adolescence. *Child Development, 63,* 542–557.

Dubow, E. F., Huesmann, L. R., & Eron, L. D. (1987). Childhood correlates of adult ego development. *Child Development, 58,* 859–869.

Duckitt, J. (1992). Psychology and prejudice: A historical analysis and integrative framework. *American Psychologist, 47,* 1182–1193.

Dujovne, V., & Houston, B. (1991). Hostility-related variables and plasma lipid levels. *Journal of Behavioral Medicine, 14,* 555–564.

Duke, C. R., & Carlson, L. (in press). Applying implicit memory measures: Word fragment completion in advertising tests. *Journal of Consumer Psychology.*

Duke, P. M., Carlsmith, J. M., Jennings, D., Martin, J. A., Dornbusch, S. M., Gross, R. T., & Siegel-Gorelick, B. (1982). Educational correlates of early and late sexual maturation in adolescence. *Journal of Pediatrics, 100,* 633–637.

Dulany, D., & Logan, G. (Eds.). (1992). Special issue: Views and varieties of automaticity. *American Journal of Psychology, 105.*

Dunkel-Schetter, C., Folkman, S., & Lazarus, R. S. (1987). Correlates of social support receipt. *Journal of Personality and Social Psychology, 53,* 71–80.

Dunn, A. J. (1989). Psychoneuroimmunology for the psychoneuroendocrinologist: A review of animal studies of nervous system-immune system interactions. *Psychoneuroendocrinology, 14,* 251–274.

Dunn, J. (1992). Siblings and development. *Current Directions in Psychological Science, 1*(1), 6–9.

Dunn, J., Brown, H., Slomkowski, C., Tesla, C., & Youngblade, L. (1991). Young children's understanding of other people's feelings and beliefs: Individual differences and their antecedents. *Child Development, 62,* 1352–1366.

Dunning, D., & Cohen, G. L. (1992). Egocentric definitions of traits and abilities in social judgment. *Journal of Personality and Social Psychology, 63,* 341–355.

Duplessis, Y. (1979). Current directions in European parapsychology. In W. G. Roll (Ed.), *Research in parapsychology* (1979). Metuchen, NJ: Scarecrow Press.

Durel, L. A., Carver, C., Spitzer, S., Llabre, M. M., Weintraub, G. J., Saab, P. G., & Schneiderman, N. (1989). Association of blood pressure with self-report measures of anger and hostility among black and white men and women. *Health Psychology, 8,* 557–576.

Dusek, J. B., & Flaherty, J. F. (1981). The development of the self-concept during the adolescent years. *Monographs of the Society for Research in Child Development, 46*(4, Serial No. 191).

Dush, D. M., Hirt, M. L., & Schroeder, H. (1983). Self-statement modification with adults: A meta-analysis. *Psychological Bulletin, 94,* 408–422.

Dustman, R., Emmerson, R., Ruhling, R., Shearer, D., Steinhaus, L., Johnson, S., Bonekat, H., & Shigeoka, J. (1990). Age and fitness effects on EEG, ERPs, visual sensitivity, and cognition. *Neurobiology of Aging, 11,* 193–200.

Dutton, D. G., & Aron, A. P. (1974). Some evidence for heightened sexual attraction under conditions of high anxiety. *Journal of Personality and Social Psychology, 30,* 510–517.

Dweck, C. S., & Gilliard, D. (1975). Expectancy statements as determinants of reactions to failure: Sex differences in persistence and expectancy change. *Journal of Personality and Social Psychology, 32,* 1077–1084.

Dweck, C. S., & Licht, B. G. (1980). Learned helplessness and intellectual achievement. In M. E. P. Seligman & J. Garber (Eds.), *Human helplessness: Theory and application.* New York: Academic Press.

Dweck, C. S., & Repucci, N. D. (1973). Learned helplessness and reinforcement responsibility in children. *Journal of Personality and Social Psychology, 25,* 109–116.

Dweck, C. S., Davidson, W., Nelson, S., & Enna, B. (1978). Sex differences in learned helplessness: II. The contingencies of evaluative feedback in the classroom, and III. An experimental analysis. *Developmental Psychology, 14,* 268–276.

Eagle, M. (1984). *Recent developments in psychoanalysis: A critical evaluation.* New York: McGraw-Hill.

Eagle, M. N., & Wolinzky, D. L. (1985). The current status of psychoanalysis. *Clinical Psychology Review, 5,* 259–269.

Eagly, A. H. (1987). *Sex differences in social behavior: A social-role interpretation.* Hillsdale, NJ: Lawrence Erlbaum Associates.

Eagly, A. H. (1992). Uneven progress: Social psychology and the study of attitudes. *Journal of Personality and Social Psychology, 63,* 693–710.

Eagly, A. H., & Carli, G. (1981). Sex of researchers and sex-typed communications as determinants of sex differences in influenceability: A meta-analysis of social influence studies. *Psychological Bulletin, 90,* 1–20.

Eagly, A. H., & Chaiken, S. (1993). *The psychology of attitudes.* Fort Worth, TX: Harcourt Brace Jovanovich.

Eagly, A. H., & Johnson, B. T. (1990). Gender and leadership style: A meta-analysis. *Psychological Bulletin, 108,* 233–256.

Eagly, A. H., & Karav, S. J. (1991). Gender and the emergence of leaders: A meta-analysis. *Journal of Personality and Social Psychology, 60,* 685–710.

Eagly, A. H., & Steffen, V. J. (1986). Gender and aggressive behavior: A meta-analytic review of the social psychology literature. *Psychological Bulletin, 100,* 309–330.

Eagly, A. H., Makhijani, M. G., & Klonsky, B. G. (1992). Gender and the evaluation of leaders: A meta-analysis. *Psychological Bulletin, 111,* 3–22.

Easterbrook, J. A. (1959). The effect of emotion on cue utilization and the organization of behavior. *Psychological Review, 66,* 183–207.

Eaton, W. O., & Clore, G. L. (1975). Interracial imitation at a summer camp. *Journal of Personality and Social Psychology, 32,* 1099–1105.

Ebbinghaus, H. (1885). *Memory: A contribution to experimental psychology* (H. A. Roger & C. E. Bussenius, Trans., 1913). New York: Columbia University Press.

Eberts, R., & MacMillan, A. C. (1985). Misperception of small cars. In R. Eberts & C. Eberts (Eds.), *Trends in ergonomics/human factors III.* Amsterdam: Elsevier.

Eckert, E. D., Bouchard, T. J., Bohlen, J., & Heston, L. L. (1986). Homosexuality in monozygotic twins reared apart. *British Journal of Psychiatry, 148,* 421–425.

Edelstein, B. A., & Michelson, L. (Eds.) (1986). *Handbook of prevention.* New York & London: Plenum Press.

Educational Testing Service (1987). *ETS sensitivity review process.* Princeton, NJ: ETS.

Edwards, A. E., & Acker, L. E. (1972). A demonstration of the long-term retention of a conditioned GSR. *Psychosomatic Science, 26,* 27–28.

Edwards, W. (1987). Decision making. In G. Salvendy (Ed.), *Handbook of human factors.* New York: Wiley.

Edwards, W., Lindman, H., & Phillips, L. D. (1965). Emerging technologies for making decisions, In T. M. Newcomb (Ed.), *New directions in psychology II.* New York: Holt, Rinehart and Winston.

Efron, A. (1992). Residual asymmetrical dualism: A theory of mind-body relations. *Journal of Mind and Behavior, 13,* 113–136.

Egeland, B., Jacobvitz, D., & Sroufe, L. A. (1988). Breaking the cycle of abuse. *Child Development, 59,* 1080–1088.

Egeland, J. A., Gerhard, D. S., Pauls, D. L., Sussex, J. N., Kidd, K. K., Allen, C. R., Hostetter, A. M., & Housman, D. E. (1987). Bipolar affective disorders linked to DNA markers on chromosome II. *Nature, 325,* 783–787.

Ehrlich, H. J. (1973). *The social psychology of prejudice.* New York: Wiley.

Ehrlichman, H., & Halpern, J. N. (1988). Affect and memory: Effects of pleasant and unpleasant odors on retrieval of happy and unhappy memories. *Journal of Personality and Social Psychology, 55,* 769–779.

Eich, E. (1989). Theoretical issues in state dependent memory. In H. L. Roediger & F. I. M. Craik (Eds.), *Varieties of memory and consciousness.* Hillsdale, NJ: Lawrence Erlbaum Associates.

Eich, E., & Metcalfe, J. (1989). Mood dependent memory for internal versus external events. *Journal of Experimental Psychology: Learning, Memory, and Cognition, 15,* 443–455.

Eich, J. E., Weingartner, H., Stillman, R. C., & Gillin, J. C. (1975). State dependent accessibility of retrieval cues in the retention of a categorized list. *Journal of Verbal Learning and Verbal Behavior, 14,* 408–417.

Eichorn, D. H., Clausen, J. A., Haan, N., Honzik, M. P., & Mussen, P. H. (1981). *Present and past in middle life.* New York: Academic Press.

Eikelboom, R., & Stewart, J. (1982). Conditioning of drug-induced physiological responses. *Psychological Review, 89,* 507–528.

Einhorn, H., & Hogarth, R. (1982). Prediction, diagnosis and causal thinking in forecasting. *Journal of Forecasting, 1,* 23–36.

Eisenberg, N. (1991). Meta-analytic contributions to the literature on prosocial behavior. *Personality and Social Psychology Bulletin, 17,* 273–282.

Eisenberg, N., & Miller, P. A. (1987). The relation of empathy to prosocial and unrelated behaviors. *Psychological Bulletin, 101,* 91–119.

Eisenberg, N., & Strayer, J. (1987). Critical issues in the study of empathy. In N. Eisenberg & J. Strayer (Eds.), *Empathy and its development.* Cambridge, Eng., Cambridge University Press.

Eisenberg, N., Cialdini, R. B., McCreath, H., & Shell, R. (1987). Consistency-based compliance: When and why do children become vulnerable? *Journal of Personality and Social Psychology, 52,* 1174–1181.

Eisenbruch, M. (1992). Toward a culturally sensitive DSM: Cultural bereavement in Cambodian refugees and the traditional healer as taxonomist. *Journal of Nervous and Mental Disease, 180,* 8–10.

Eisner, J., Roberts, W., Heymsfield, S., & Yager, J. (1985). Anorexia nervosa and sudden death. *Annals of Internal Medicine, 102,* 49–52.

Ekman, P. (1980). Biological and cultural contributions to body and facial movement in the expression of emotions. In A. Rorty (Ed.), *Explaining emotions.* Berkeley: University of California Press.

Ekman, P. (1984). Expression and the nature of emotion. In K. Sherer & P. Ekman (Eds.), *Approaches to emotion.* Hillsdale, NJ: Lawrence Erlbaum Associates.

Ekman, P. (1993). Facial expression and emotion. *American Psychologist, 48,* 384–392.

Ekman, P., & Friesen, W. V. (1986). A new pan-cultural facial expression of emotion. *Motivation and Emotion, 10,* 159–168.

Ekman, P., Davidson, R. J., & Friesen, W. V. (1990). The Duchenne smile: Emotional expression and brain physiology II. *Journal of Personality and Social Psychology, 58,* 342–353.

Ekman, P., Friesen, W. V., & Ellsworth, P. (1972). *Emotion in the human face: Guidelines for research and a review of findings.* New York: Pergamon Press.

Ekman, P., Friesen, W. V., & O'Sullivan, M. (1988). Smiles when lying. *Journal of Personality and Social Psychology, 54,* 414–420.

Ekman, P., Levenson, R. W., & Friesen, W. V. (1983). Autonomic nervous system activity distinguishes among emotions. *Science, 221,* 1208–1210.

Elashoff, J. D. (1979). Box scores are for baseball. *Brain and Behavioral Sciences, 3,* 392.

Eldridge, J. C., Murphy, L. L., & Landfield, P. W. (1991). Cannaboids and the hippocampal glucocorticoid receptor: Recent findings and possible significance. *Steroids, 56,* 226–231.

Elicker, J., & Sroufe, L. A. (1992/3). Predicting peer competence and peer relationships in childhood from early parent-child relationships. In R. Parke & G. Ladd (Eds.), *Family-peer relationships: Modes of linkage.* Hillsdale, NJ: Lawrence Erlbaum Associates.

Elkins, I., Shea, T., Watkins, J., Imber, S., Sotsky, S., Collins, J., Glass, D., Pilkonis, P., Leber, W., Docherty, J., Fiester, S., & Perloff, M. (1989). National Institute of Mental Health treatment of depression collaborative research program. *Archives of General Psychiatry, 46,* 971–982.

Elliot, R. S., & Buell, J. C. (1983). The role of the central nervous system in sudden cardiac death. In T.M. Dembroski, T. Schmidt, & G. Blunchen (Eds.), *Biobehavioral bases of coronary-prone behavior.* New York: Karger.

Elliott, C. L., & Greene, R. L. (1992). Clinical depression and implicit memory. *Journal of Abnormal Psychology, 101,* 572–574.

Elliott, E. S., & Dweck, C. S. (1988). Goals: An approach to motivation and achievement. *Journal of Personality and Social Psychology, 54,* 5–12.

Ellis, A. (1962). *Reason and emotion in psychotherapy.* New York: Lyle Stuart.

Ellis, A. (1973). Rational-emotive therapy. In R. Corsini (Ed.), *Current psychotherapies*. Itasca, IL: Peacock.

Ellis, A. (1993). Reflections on rational-emotive therapy. *Journal of Consulting and Clinical Psychology, 61,* 199–201.

Ellis, A., & Bernard, M. E. (1985). *Clinical applications of rational-emotive therapy.* New York: Plenum Press.

Ellis, A., & Dryden, W. (1987). *The practice of rational-emotive therapy.* New York: Springer-Verlag.

Ellis, H. C., & Ashbrook, P. W. (1988). Resource allocation model of the effects of depressed mood states on memory. In K. Fiedler & J. Forgas (Eds.), *Affect, cognition, and social behavior.* Toronto: Hogrefe.

Ellis, H. C., & Hunt, R. R. (1983). *Fundamentals of human memory and cognition* (3rd ed.). Dubuque, IA: William C. Brown.

Ellis, H. C., & Hunt, R. R. (1989). *Fundamentals of human memory and cognition* (4th ed.). Dubuque, IA: William C. Brown.

Ellis, L., & Ames, M. A. (1987). Neurohormonal functioning and sexual orientation: A theory of homosexuality-heterosexuality. *Psychological Bulletin, 101,* 233–258.

Ellis, N. R. (1991). Automatic and effortful processes in memory for spatial location. *Bulletin of the Psychonomic Society, 29,* 28–30.

Ellis, S. R. (1991). Nature and origins of virtual environments: A bibliographical essay. *Computing Systems in Engineering, 2,* 321–347.

Ellison, K. W., & Buckhout, R. (1981). *Psychology and criminal justice.* New York: Harper & Row.

Elton, D., Burrows, G. D., & Stanley, G. V. (1980). Chronic pain and hypnosis. In G. D. Burrows & L. Dennerstein (Eds.), *Handbook of hypnosis and psychosomatic medicine.* Amsterdam: Elsevier.

Embretson, S. E. (1992). Computerized adaptive testing: Its potential substantive contributions to psychological research and assessment. *Current Directions in Psychological Science, 1,* 129–131.

Emmons, R. A. (1993). Motives and life goals. In S. Briggs, R. Hogan, & W. Jones (Eds.), *Handbook of personality psychology.* Orlando: Academic Press.

Emmons, R. A., & King, L. A. (1988). Conflict among personal strivings: Immediate and long-term implications for psychological and physical well-being. *Journal of Personality and Social Psychology, 54,* 1040–1048.

Emmons, R. A., & King, L. A. (1989). Personal striving differentiation and affective reactivity. *Journal of Personality and Social Psychology, 56,* 478–484.

Endler, N. S., & Parker, J. D. A. (1990). Multidimensional assessment of coping: A critical evaluation. *Journal of Personality and Social Psychology, 58,* 844–854.

Engel, A. K., Konig, P., Kreiter, A. K., Schillen, T. B., & Singer, W. (1992). Temporal coding in the visual cortex: New vistas on integration in the nervous system. *Trends in Neuroscience, 15,* 218–226.

Engen, T. (1987). Remembering odors and their names. *American Scientist, 75,* 497–502.

Engen, T., Gilmore, M. M., & Mair, R. G. (1991). Odor memory. In T. V. Getchell et al. (Eds.), *Taste and smell in health and disease.* New York: Raven Press.

Engs, R. C., Slawinska, J. B., & Hanson, D. J. (1991). The drinking patterns of American and Polish university students: A cross-nation study. *Drug and Alcohol Dependence, 27,* 167–175.

Enright, R. D., Lapsley, D. K., & Levy, V. M., Jr. (1983). Moral education strategies. In M. Pressley & J. R. Levin (Eds.), *Cognitive strategy research: Educational application.* New York: Springer-Verlag.

Eppley, K. R., Abrams, A. I., & Shear, J. (1989). Differential effects of relaxation techniques on trait anxiety: A meta-analysis. *Journal of Clinical Psychology, 45,* 957–974.

Epstein, S., & O'Brien, E. J. (1985). The person-situation debate in historical and current perspective. *Psychological Bulletin, 98,* 513–537.

Epstein, W. (1961). The influence of syntactical structure on learning. *American Journal of Psychology, 74,* 80–85.

Epstein, Y. M., Woolfolk, R. L., & Lehrer, P. M. (1981). Physiological, cognitive, and nonverbal responses to repeated experiences of crowding. *Journal of Applied Social Psychology, 11,* 1–13.

Erdberg, P. (1990). Rorschach assessment. In G. Goldstein & M. Hersen (Eds.), *Psychological Assessment* (2nd ed.). New York: Pergamon Press.

Erdelyi, M. H. (1985). *Psychoanalysis: Freud's cognitive psychology.* San Francisco: W. H. Freeman.

Erdelyi, M. H. (1992). Psychodynamics and the unconscious. *American Psychologist, 47*(6), 784–787.

Erdelyi, M. H., & Goldberg, B. (1979). Let's not sweep repression under the rug: Toward a cognitive psychology of repression. In J. F. Kihlstrom & F. J. Evans (Eds.), *Functional disorders of memory.* Hillsdale, NJ: Lawrence Erlbaum Associates.

Ericsson, K. A., & Polson, P. G. (1988). An experimental analysis of the mechanisms of a memory skill. *Journal of Experimental Psychology: Learning, Memory, and Cognition, 14,* 305–316.

Ericsson, K. A., Chase, W. G., & Faloon, S. (1980). Acquisition of a memory skill. *Science, 208,* 1181–1182.

Eriksen, C., & Yeh, Y. Y. (1985). Allocation of attention in the visual field. *Journal of Experimental Psychology: Human Perception & Performance, 11,* 583–597.

Erikson, E. H. (1963). *Childhood and society.* New York: W. W. Norton.

Erikson, E. H. (1968). *Identity: Youth and crisis.* New York: W. W. Norton.

Eron, L. D. (1987). The development of aggressive behavior from the perspective of a developing behaviorism. *American Psychologist, 42,* 435–442.

Eron, L. D., Huesmann, R., Brice, P., Fischer, P., & Mermelstein, R. (1983). Age trends in the development of aggression, sex typing, and related television habits. *Developmental Psychology, 19,* 71–77.

Eskew, R. T., & Riche, C. V. (1982). Pacing and locus of control in quality control inspection. *Human Factors, 24,* 411–415.

Evans, C. (1983). *Landscapes of the night: How and why we dream.* New York: Viking Press.

Evans, D. A., Funkenstein, H., Alber, M. S., Scherr, P. A., Cook, N. R., Chown, M. J., Hebert, L. E., Hennekens, C. H., & Taylor, J. O. (1989). Prevalence of Alzheimer's disease in a community population of older persons. *Journal of the American Medical Association, 262,* 2551–2556.

Evans, J., Barsten, J., & Pollard, P. (1983). On the conflict between logic and belief in syllogistic reasoning. *Memory and Cognition, 11,* 295–306.

Evans, P. (1989). *Motivation and emotion.* New York: Routledge.

Evans, S. M., & Griffiths, R. R. (1992). Caffeine tolerance and choice in humans. *Psychopharmacology, 108,* 51–59.

Exner, J. E. (1985). *The Rorschach: A comprehensive system* (Vol. 1, 2nd ed.). New York: Wiley.

Eysenck, H. J. (1952). The effects of psychotherapy: An evaluation. *Journal of Consulting Psychology, 16,* 319–324.

Eysenck, H. J. (1960). *Behavior therapy and the neuroses.* London: Pergamon Press.

Eysenck, H. J. (1961). The effects of psychotherapy. In H. J. Eysenck (Ed.), *Handbook of abnormal psychology.* New York: Basic Books.

Eysenck, H. J. (1966). *The effects of psychotherapy.* New York: International Science Press.

Eysenck, H. J. (1970). *The structure of human personality* (3rd ed.). London: Methuen.

Eysenck, H. J. (1980). *The causes and effects of smoking.* Beverly Hills, CA: Sage.

Eysenck, H. J. (1982). Development of a theory. In C. D. Spielberger (Ed.), *Personality, genetics, and behavior.* New York: Praeger.

Eysenck, H. J. (1987). Speed of information processing, reaction time, and the theory of intelligence. In P. A. Vernon (Ed.), *Speed of information-processing and intelligence* (pp. 21–67). Norwood, NJ: Ablex.

Eysenck, H. J. (1988, December). Health's character. *Psychology Today,* pp. 27–35.

Eysenck, H. J. (Ed.). (1981). *A model for personality.* New York: Springer-Verlag.

Eysenck, H. J., & Eysenck, M. W. (1985). *Personality and individual differences.* New York: Plenum.

Eysenck, H. J., & Rachman, S. (1965). *The causes and cures of neurosis: An introduction to modern behavior therapy based on learning theory and the principle of conditioning.* San Diego: Knapp.

Fabrega, H. (1992). Diagnosis interminable: Toward a culturally sensitive DSM-IV. *Journal of Nervous and Mental Disease, 180,* 5–7.

Fabricius, W. V., & Wellman, H. M. (1983). Children's understanding of retrieval cue utilization. *Developmental Psychology, 19,* 15–21.

Facchinetti, F., Centini, G., Parrini, D., Petroglia, F., D'Antona, N., Cosmi, E. V., & Genazzani, A. R. (1982). Opioid plasma levels during labor. *Gynecology & Obstetrics Investigations, 13,* 155–163.

Facchinetti, F., Martignoni, E., Petraglia, F., Sances, M. G., Nappi, G., & Genazzani, A. R. (1987). Premenstrual fall of plasma beta-endorphin in patients with premenstrual syndrome. *Fertility and Sterility, 47,* 570–573.

Faden, A. I., Demediuk, P., Panter, S. S., & Vink, R. (1989). The role of excitatory amino acids and NMDA receptors in traumatic brain injury. *Science, 244,* 798–800.

Fairburn, C. (1981). A cognitive behavioral approach to the treatment of bulimia. *Psychological Medicine, 11,* 707–711.

Faraone, S. V., & Tsuang, M. T. (1985). Quantitative models of the genetic transmission of schizophrenia. *Psychological Bulletin, 98,* 41–66.

Farber, B. (Ed.) (1983). *Stress and burnout in human service professions.* New York: Pergamon Press.

Farberow, N. L., & Litman, R. E. (1958–1970). *A comprehensive suicide prevention program.* (Unpublished final report DHEW NIMH Grants No. MH 14946 & MH 00128.) Los Angeles, CA: Suicide Prevention Center.

Farberow, N. L., Shneidman, E. S., & Leonard, C. (1963, February 25). *Suicide among general medical and surgical hospital patients with malignant neoplasms.* (Medical Bulletin MB-9, pp. 1–11). Washington, DC: Veterans Administration, Department of Medicine and Surgery.

Farkas, G., Grobe, R., & Shuan, Y. (1990). Cultural differences and school success: Gender, ethnicity, and poverty groups within an urban school district. *American Sociological Review, 55,* 127–142.

Farley, F. (1986, May). *The big T in personality.* Psychology Today.

Farley, J., & Alkon, D. L. (1985). Cellular mechanisms of learning, memory, and information storage. *Annual Review of Psychology, 36,* 419–494.

Farwell, L. A., & Donchin, E. (1989). Detection of guilty knowledge with ERPs. *Society for Psychophysiology Abstracts, 26,* S8.

Farwell, L. A., & Donchin, E. (1991). The truth will out: Interrogative polygraphy ("lie detection") with event-related potentials. *Psychophysiology, 28,* 531–547.

Faust, W. L. (1959). Group vs. individual problem-solving. *Journal of Abnormal and Social Psychology, 59,* 68–72.

Fawcett, J., Scheftner, W., Fogg, L., & Clark, D. (1990). Time-related predictors of suicide in major affective disorder. *American Journal of Psychiatry, 147,* 1189–1194.

Fazio, R. H., Herr, P. M., & Powell, M. C. (1992). On the development and strength of category-brand associations in memory: The case of mystery ads. *Journal of Consumer Psychology, 1,* 1–13.

Feather, N. T., & Volkmer, R. E. (1988). Preference for situations involving effort, time pressure, and feedback in relation to Type A behavior, locus of control, and test anxiety. *Journal of Personality and Social Psychology, 55,* 266–271.

Fechter, L. D., Young, J. S., Carlisle, L. (1988). Potentiation of noise induced threshold shifts and hair cell loss by carbon monoxide. *Hearing Research, 34,* 1, 39–48.

Fehr, B., & Russell, J. A. (1991). The concept of love viewed from a prototype perspective. *Journal of Personality and Social Psychology, 60,* 425–438.

Feighner, J., Merideth, C., & Hendrickson, G. (1982). A double blind comparison of buspirone and diazepam in outpatients with generalized anxiety disorder. *Journal of Clinical Psychiatry, 43,* 103–107.

Feingold, A. (1988). Cognitive gender differences are disappearing. *American Psychologist, 43,* 95–103.

Feingold, A. (1992). Good-looking people are not what we think. *Psychological Bulletin, 111,* 304–341.

Felner, R. D., & Adan, A. M. (1988). The school transitional environment project: An ecological intervention and evaluation. In R. H. Price (Ed.), *Fourteen ounces of prevention: A casebook for practitioners.* Washington, DC: American Psychological Association.

Felten, D. L., Cohen, N., Ader, R., Felten, S. Y., Carlson, S. L., & Roszman, T. L. (1991). Central neural circuits involved in neural-immune interactions. In R. Ader (Ed.), *Psychoneuroimmunology* (2nd ed.). New York: Academic Press.

Fenton, W., & McGlashan, T. (1991). Natural history of schizophrenia subtypes: I. Longitudinal study of paranoid, hebephrenic, and undifferentiated schizophrenia. *Archives of General Psychiatry, 48,* 969–977.

Fenz, W. D. (1971). Heart rate responses to a stressor: A comparison between primary and secondary psychopaths and normal controls. *Journal of Experimental Research in Personality, 5,* 7–13.

Fergusson, D. M., Lloyd, M., & Horwood, L. J. (1991). Family ethnicity, social background and scholastic achievement: An eleven-year longitudinal study. *New Zealand Journal of Educational Studies, 26,* 49–63.

Fernald, A. (1981, April). *Four-month-olds prefer to listen to "motherese."* Paper presented at the meeting of the Society for Research in Child Development, Boston, MA.

Fernald, A. (1990, December). Cited by T. Adler, "Melody is the message" of infant-directed speech. *APA Monitor,* p. 9.

Ferraro, P., Conti-Tronconi, B., & Guidotti, A. (1986). DBI, an anxiogenic neuropeptide found in human brain. *Advances in Biochemistry and Psychopharmacology, 41,* 177–185.

Ferraro, R., Lillioja, S., Fontvieille, A. M., Rising, R., Bogardus, C., & Ravussin, E. (1992). Lower sedentary metabolic rate in women compared with men. *Journal of Clinical Investigation, 90,* 780–784.

Ferretti, R. P., & Butterfield, E. C. (1989). Intelligence as a correlate of children's problem solving. *American Journal of Mental Retardation, 93,* 424–433.

Festinger, L. (1954). A theory of social comparison processes. *Human Relations, 7,* 117–140.

Festinger, L. (1957). *A theory of cognitive dissonance.* Evanston, IL: Row, Petersen.

Festinger, L., & Carlsmith, J. M. (1959). Cognitive consequences of forced compliance. *Journal of Abnormal and Social Psychology, 58,* 203–210.

Festinger, L., Pepitone, A., & Newcomb, T. M. (1952). Some consequences of deindividuation in a group. *Journal of Abnormal and Social Psychology, 47,* 383–389.

Feuerstein, R. (1980). *Instrumental enrichment: An intervention program for cognitive modifiability.* Baltimore: University Park Press.

Fiandaca, M. S., Kordower, J. H., Hansen, J. T., Jiao, S. S., & Gash, D. M. (1988). Adrenal medullary autografts into the basal ganglia of cebus monkeys: Injury-induced regeneration. *Experimental Neurology, 102,* 76–91.

Field, T., Woodson, R., Cohen, D., Garcia, R., & Greenberg, R. (1983). Discrimination and imitation of facial expressions by term and preterm neonates. *Infant Behavior and Development, 6,* 485–490.

Fillenbaum, S. (1974). Pragmatic normalization: Further results for some conjunctive and disjunctive sentences. *Journal of Experimental Psychology, 103,* 913–921.

Fillmore, K. M., & Caetano, R. (1980, May 22). *Epidemiology of occupational alcoholism.* Paper presented at the National Institute on Alcohol Abuse and Alcoholism's Workshop on Alcoholism in the Workplace, Reston, VA.

Fincham, F. D., & Bradbury, T. N. (1993). Marital satisfaction, depression, and attributions: A longitudinal analysis. *Journal of Personality and Social Psychology, 64,* 442–452.

Fine, T. H., & Turner, J. W. (1982). The effect of brief restricted environmental stimulation therapy in the treatment of essential hypertension. *Behaviour Research and Therapy, 20,* 567–570.

Finer, B. (1980). Hypnosis and anesthesia. In G. D. Burrows & L. Dennerstein (Eds.), *Handbook of hypnosis and psychosomatic medicine.* Amsterdam: Elsevier.

Fink, M. (1979). *Convulsive therapy: Therapy and practice.* New York: Raven.

Fink, M. (1988). The use of ECT in the United States. *American Journal of Psychiatry, 145,* 133–134.

Finman, R., & Berkowitz, L. (1989). Some factors influencing the effects of depressed mood on anger and overt hostility toward another. *Journal of Research in Personality, 23,* 70–84.

Finn, P. R., Zeitouni, N. C., & Pihl, R. O. (1990). Effects of alcohol on psychophysiological hyperreactivity to nonaversive stimuli in men at high risk for alcoholism. *Journal of Abnormal Psychology, 99,* 79–85.

Fiore, J., Becker, J., & Coppel, D. (1983). Social network interactions: A buffer or a stress. *American Journal of Community Psychology, 11,* 423–439.

Firestein, S., & Werblin, F. (1989). Odor-induced membrane currents in vertebrate-olfactory receptor neurons. *Science, 244,* 79–82.

Fischer, E., Haines, R., & Price, T. (1980). *Cognitive issues in head up displays.* (NASA Technical Paper 1711). Washington, DC: NASA.

Fischoff, B. (1977). Perceived informativeness of facts. *Journal of Experimental Psychology: Human perception and performance, 3,* 349–358.

Fischoff, B. (1980). A little learning: Confidence in multicue judgment tasks. In R. Nickerson (Ed.), *Attention and performance VIII.* Hillsdale, NJ: Lawrence Erlbaum Associates.

Fischoff, B. (1982). Debiasing. In D. Kahneman, P. Slovic, & A. Tversky (Eds.), *Judgment under uncertainty: Heuristics and biases.* New York: Cambridge University Press.

Fischoff, B., & MacGregor, D. (1982). Subjective confidence in forecasts. *Journal of Forecasting, 1,* 155–172.

Fischoff, B., & Slovic, P. (1980). A little learning . . . confidence in multicue judgment tasks. In R. Nickerson (Ed.), *Attention and performance: VIII.* Hillsdale, NJ: Lawrence Erlbaum Associates.

Fischoff, B., Slovic, P., & Lichtenstein, S. (1977). Knowing with certainty: The appropriateness of extreme confidence. *Journal of Experimental Psychology: Human Perception and Performance, 3,* 552–564.

Fisher, J. D., Bell, P. A., & Baum, A. (1984). *Environmental psychology* (2nd ed.). New York: Holt, Rinehart and Winston.

Fisher, S., & Greenberg, R. P. (1977). *The scientific credibility of Freud's theories and therapy.* New York: Basic Books.

Fishman, S. M., & Sheehan, D. V. (1985, April). Anxiety and panic: Their cause and treatment. *Psychology Today,* pp. 26–32.

Fiske, D. W., & Maddi, S. R. (1961). *Functions of varied experience.* Homewood, IL: Dorsey Press.

Fiske, M. (1980). Tasks and crises of the second half of life: The interrelationship of commitment, coping, and adaptation. In J. E. Birren & R. B. Sloane (Eds.), *Handbook of mental health and aging.* Englewood Cliffs, NJ: Prentice-Hall.

Fiske, S. T. (1989). Examining the role of intent: Toward understanding its role in stereotyping and prejudice. In J. S. Uleman & J. A. Bargh (Eds.), *Unintended thought.* New York: Guilford Press.

Fiske, S. T., & Pavelchak, M. A. (1986). Category-based versus piecemeal-based affective responses: Developments in schema-triggered affect. In R. M. Sorrentino & E. T. Higgins (Eds.), *Handbook of motivation and cognition.* New York: Guilford Press.

Fiske, S. T., & Ruscher, J. B. (1989). On-line processes in category-based and individuating impressions: Some basic principles and methodological reflections. In J. N. Bassili (Ed.), *On-line cognition in person perception.* Hillsdale, NJ: Lawrence Erlbaum Associates.

Fiske, S. T., & Von Hend, H. M. (1992). Personality feedback and situational norms can control stereotyping processes. *Journal of Personality and Social Psychology, 62,* 577–596.

Fitch, N., Becker, R., & Heller, A. (1988). The inheritance of Alzheimer's disease: A new interpretation. *Annals of Neurology, 23,* 14–19.

Fitzgerald, T. E., Tennen, H., Afflect, G. S., & Pransky, G. (1993). The relative importance of dispositional optimism and control appraisals in quality of life after coronary artery bypass surgery. *Journal of Behavioral Medicine. 16,* 25–43.

Fixen, D. L., Phillips, E. L., Phillips, E. A., & Wolf, M. M. (1976). The teaching-family model of group home treatment. In W. E. Craighead, A. E. Kazdin, & M. J. Mahoney (Eds.), *Behavior modification: Principles, issues, and applications.* Boston: Houghton Mifflin.

Flaherty, C. F., Uzwiak, A. J., Levine, J., Smith, M., Hall, P., & Schuler, R. (1980). Apparent hyperglycemic and hypoglycemic conditional responses with exogenous insulin as the unconditioned stimulus. *Animal Learning and Behavior, 8,* 382–386.

Flavell, J. H. (1985). *Cognitive development* (2nd ed.). Englewood Cliffs, NJ: Prentice-Hall.

Flavell, J. H., & Wellman, H. M. (1977). Metamemory. In R. V. Kail & J. W. Hagen (Eds.), *Perspectives on the development of memory and cognition.* Hillsdale, NJ: Lawrence Erlbaum Associates.

Flavell, J. H., Beach, D. H., & Chinsky, J. M. (1966). Spontaneous verbal rehearsal in a memory task as a function of age. *Child Development, 37,* 283–299.

Flavell, J. H., Friedrichs, A. G., & Hoyt, J. D. (1970). Developmental changes in memorization processes. *Cognitive Psychology, 1,* 324–340.

Fleming, I., Baum, A., & Weiss, L. (1987). Social density and perceived control as mediators of crowding stress in high density residential neighborhoods. *Journal of Personality and Social Psychology, 52,* 899–906.

Fletcher, G. J. O., Reedes, G. D., & Bull, V. (1990). Bias and accuracy in attitude attribution: The role of attributional complexity. *Journal of Experimental Social Psychology, 26,* 275–288.

Flynn, J., Vanegas, H., Foote, W., & Edwards, S. (1970). Neural mechanisms involved in a cat's attack on a rat. In M. Whelan, R. F. Thompson, M. Verzeano, & N. Weinberger (Eds.), *The neural control of behavior.* New York: Academic Press.

Foa, E. B., Rothbaum, B. O., & Kozak, M. J. (1989). Behavioral treatments for anxiety and depression. In P. C. Kendall & D. Watson (Eds.), *Anxiety and depression: Distinctive and overlapping features* (pp. 413–454). San Diego: CA: Academic Press.

Fodor, J. A., Bever, T. G., & Garrett, M. F. (1974). *The psychology of language.* New York: McGraw-Hill.

Foenander, G., & Burrows, G. D. (1980). Phenomena of hypnosis: 1. Age regression. In G. D. Burrows & L. Dennerstein (Eds.), *Handbook of hypnosis and psychosomatic medicine.* Amsterdam: Elsevier.

Foley, K. M., & Macaluso, C. (1992). Adjuvant analgesic drugs in cancer pain management. In G. M. Aronoff (Ed.), *Evaluation and treatment of chronic pain.* Baltimore: Williams & Wilkins.

Folkes, V. S. (1982). Communicating the reasons for social rejection. *Journal of Experimental Social Psychology, 18,* 235–252.

Folkman, S. (1984). Personal control and stress and coping processes: A theoretical analysis. *Journal of Personality and Social Psychology, 46,* 839–852.

Folkman, S., & Lazarus, R. (1988). *Manual for the ways of coping questionnaire.* Palo Alto, CA: Consulting Psychologists Press.

Folkman, S., & Lazarus, R. S. (1980). An analysis of coping in a middle-aged community sample. *Journal of Health and Social Behavior, 21,* 219–239.

Folkman, S., & Lazarus, R. S. (1985). If it changes, it must be a process: A study of emotion and coping during three stages of a college examination. *Journal of Personality and Social Psychology, 48,* 150–170.

Folkman, S., Chesney, M., Pollack, & Phillips, C. (1992). Stress, coping, and high-risk sexual behavior. *Health Psychology, 11,* 218–222.

Folkman, S., Lazarus, R. S., Gruen, R. J., & DeLongis, A. (1986). Appraisal, coping, health status, and psychological symptoms. *Journal of Personality and Social Psychology, 50,* 571–579.

Folkman, S., Lazarus, R., Dunkel-Shetteer, DeLongis, A., & Gruen, R. (1986). Dynamics of a stressful encounter: Cognitive appraisal, coping, and encounter outcomes. *Journal of Personality and Social Psychology, 50,* 992–1003.

Fonagy, P., & Moran, S. (1990). Studies on the efficacy of child psychoanalysis. *Journal of Consulting and Clinical Psychology, 58,* 684–695.

Foote, S. L., Bloom, F. E., & Aston-Jones, G. (1983). Nucleus locus coeruleus: New evidence of anatomical and physiological specificity. *Physiology Review, 63,* 844–914.

Ford, C. E., Wright, R. A., & Haythornthwaite, J. (1985). Task performance and magnitude of goal valence. *Journal of Research in Personality, 19,* 253–260.

Ford, D. E., & Kamerow, D. B. (1989). Epidemiological study of sleep disturbances and psychiatric disorders: An opportunity for prevention? *Journal of the American Medical Association, 262,* 1479–1484.

Forehand, R., & McMahon, R. J. (1981). *Helping the non-compliant child: A clinician's guide to parent training.* New York: Guilford.

Foreyt, J. P., & Kondo, A. T. (1984). Advances in behavioral treatment of obesity. In M. Hersen, R. M. Eisler, & P. M. Miller (Eds.), *Progress in behavior modification: Vol. 16.* New York: Academic Press.

Forsyth, D. R. (1983). *An introduction to group dynamics.* Monterey, CA: Brooks/Cole.

Foss, D. J., & Spence, J. T. (1992). Do you believe in miracles? *American Psychological Society Observer,* February.

Foster, D., & Finchilescu, G. (1986). Contact in a "non-contact" society: The case of South Africa. In M. Hewstone & R. Brown (Eds.), *Contact and conflict in intergroup encounters.* New York: Blackwell.

Foulke, E. (1991). Braille. In M. A. Heller & W. Shiff (Eds.), *The psychology of touch.* Hillsdale, NJ: Lawrence Erlbaum Associates.

Foulkes, D., & Fleisher, S. (1975). Mental activity in relaxed wakefulness. *Journal of Abnormal Psychology, 84,* 66–75.

Foushee, H. C. (1984). Dyads and triads at 35,000 feet: Factors affecting group process and aircrew performance. *American Psychology, 39,* 885–893.

Foushee, H. C., & Helmreich, R. L. (1988). Group interaction and flightcrew performance. In E. Wiener & D. Nagel (Eds.), *Human factors in aviation.* San Diego, CA: Academic Press.

Fowles, D. (1992). Schizophrenia: Diathesis-stress revisited. (1992). *Annual Review of Psychology, 43,* 303–336.

Foxx, R. M., Faw, G. D., & Weber, G. (1991). Producing generalization of inpatient adolescents' social skills with significant adults in a natural environment. *Behavior Therapy, 22,* 85–99.

Foxx, R. M., McMorrow, M. J., Davis, L. A., & Bittle, R. G. (1988). Replacing a chronic schizophrenic man's delusional speech with stimulus-appropriate response. *Journal of Behavior Therapy and Experimental Psychiatry, 19,* 43–50.

Fozard, J. L. (1980). The time for remembering. In L. W. Poon (Ed.), *Aging in the 1980s: Psychological issues.* Washington, DC: American Psychological Association.

Fozard, J., Wolf, E., Bell, B., Farland, R., & Podolsky, S. (1977). Visual perception and communication. In J. Birren & K. Schaie (Eds.), *Handbook of the psychology of aging.* New York: Van Nostrand Reinhold.

Fraiberg, S. (1987). Pathological defenses in infancy. In L. Fraiberg (Ed.), *Selected writings of Selma Fraiberg.* Columbus, OH: Ohio State University Press.

Framo, J. L. (1982). *Explorations in marital and family therapy.* New York: Springer-Verlag.

Frank, G. (1976). Measures of intelligence and critical thinking. In I. B. Weiner (Ed.), *Clinical methods in psychology.* New York: Wiley.

Frank, J. S. (1973). *Persuasion and healing* (rev. ed.). Baltimore: Johns Hopkins University Press.

Frank, J. S. (1978). *Psychotherapy and the human predicament.* New York: Schocken Books.

Frank, L. G., Glickman, S. E., & Licht, P. (1991). Fatal sibling aggression, precocial development, and androgens in neonatal spotted hyenas. *Science, 252,* 702–704.

Frankel, B. G., & Whitehead, P. C. (1981). *Drinking and damage: Theoretical advantages and implications for prevention* (Monograph 14). New Brunswick, NJ: Rutgers Center of Alcohol Studies.

Frankel, F. H. (1984). Electroconvulsive therapies. In T. B. Karasu (Ed.), *The psychiatric therapies.* Washington, DC: American Psychological Association.

Frankenberg, W. K., & Dodds, J. B. (1967). The Denver developmental screening test. *Journal of Pediatrics, 71,* 181–191.

Frankenhaeuser, M., Nordheden, B., Myrsten, A., & Post, B. (1971). Psychophysiological reactions to understimulation and overstimulation. *Acta Psychologica, 35,* 298–308.

Frankmann, S. P., & Green, B. G. (1987). Differential effects of cooling on the intensity of taste. *Annals of the New York Academy of Science, 510,* 300–303.

Frase, L. T. (1975). Prose processing. In G. H. Bower (Ed.), *The psychology of learning and motivation: Vol. 9.* New York: Academic Press.

Fredericksen, N. (1986). Toward a broader conception of human intelligence. *American Psychologist, 41,* 445–452.

Freed, E. X. (1971). Anxiety and conflict: Role of drug-dependent learning in the rat. *Quarterly Journal of Studies on Alcohol, 32,* 13–29.

Freedman, J. L. (1988). Television violence and aggression: What the evidence shows. In S. Oskamp (Ed.), *Television as a social issue.* Newbury Park, CA: Sage.

Freedman, J. L., & Fraser, S. C. (1966). Compliance without pressure: The foot-in-the-door technique. *Journal of Personality and Social Psychology, 4,* 195–202.

Freeman, A., Simon, K. M., Beutler, L. E., & Arkowitz, H. (1989). *Comprehensive handbook of cognitive therapy.* New York: Plenum.

Freeman, E., Rickels, K., Sondheimer, S. J., & Polansky, M. (1990). Ineffectiveness of progesterone suppository treatment for premenstrual syndrome. *Journal of the American Medical Association, 264,* 349–353.

Freeman, W., & Watts, J. W. (1942). *Psychosurgery.* Springfield, IL: Charles C. Thomas.

Freiberg, P. (1992). Steps outlined to help homeless mentally ill. *APA Monitor,* August, p. 57.

Fremgen, A., & Fay, D. (1980). Overextensions in production and comprehension: A methodological clarification. *Journal of Child Language, 7,* 205–211.

Freud, A. (1946). *The ego and the mechanisms of defense.* New York: International Universities Press.

Freud, S. (1900). The interpretation of dreams. In J. Strachey (Ed.), *The standard edition of the complete psychological works of Sigmund Freud: Vol. 8.* London: Hogarth Press.

Freud, S. (1914). *The psychopathology of everyday life.* New York: Macmillan.

Freud, S. (1924). The loss of reality in neurosis and psychosis. *Collected papers, 2,* 277–282.

Freud, S. (1930). *Three contributions of the theory of sex.* New York: Nervous and Mental Disease Publishing.

Frezza, M., Di Padova, C., Pozzato, G., Terpin, M., Baraona, E., & Lieber, C. S. (1990). High blood alcohol levels in women: The role of decreased gastric alcohol dehydrogenase activity and first-pass metabolism. *New England Journal of Medicine, 322,* 95–99.

Fride, E., & Mechoulam, R. (1993). Pharmacological activity of the cannabinoid receptor agonist, anandamide, a brain constituent. *European Journal of Pharmacology, 231,* 313–314.

Friedman, E., Clark, D., & Gershon, S. (1992). Stress, anxiety, and depression: Review of biological, diagnostic, and nosologic issues. *Journal of Anxiety Disorders, 6,* 337–363.

Friedman, H. S., & Booth-Kewley, S. (1987a). The "disease-prone personality": A meta-analytic view of the construct. *American Psychologist, 42,* 539–555.

Friedman, H. S., & Booth-Kewley, S. (1987b). Personality, Type A behavior, and coronary heart disease: The role of emotional expression. *Journal of Personality and Social Psychology, 53,* 783–792.

Friedman, H. S., & Booth-Kewley, S. (1988). Validity of the Type A construct: A reprise. *Psychological Bulletin, 104,* 381–384.

Friedman, H., & Booth-Kewley, S. (1987). The "disease-prone personality": A meta-analytic view of the construct. American Psychologist. 42, 539–555.

Friedman, H., Tucker, J., Tomlinson-Keasey, C., Schwartz, J., Wingard, & Criqui, M. (in press). Does childhood personality predict longevity? *Journal of Personality and Social Psychology.*

Friedman, M. I., & Stricker, E. M. (1976). The physiological psychology of hunger: A physiological perspective. *Psychological Review, 83,* 409–431.

Friedman, M., & Rosenman, R. H. (1959). Association of specific overt behavior patterns with blood and cardiovascular findings: Blood cholesterol level, blood clotting time, incidence of arcus senilis, and clinical coronary artery disease. *Journal of the American Medical Association, 169,* 1286–1296.

Friedman, M., & Rosenman, R. H. (1974). *Type A behavior and your heart.* New York: Knopf.

Friedman, M., Thoresen, C., Gill, J., Ulmer, D., Powell, L., Price, V., Brown, B., Thompson, L., Rabin, D., Breall, W., Bourg, E., Levy, R., & Dixon, T. (1986). Alteration of type A behavior and its effects on cardiac recurrences in post myocardial infarction patients: Summary results of the recurrent coronary prevention project. *American Heart Journal, 112,* 653–665.

Friedmann, T. (1989). Progress toward human gene therapy. *Science, 244,* 1275–1281.

Frijda, N. H. (1986). *The emotions.* Cambridge: Cambridge University Press.

Frisch, H. L. (1977). Sex stereotypes in adult-infant play. *Child Development, 48,* 1671–1675.

Frodi, A. M., Lamb, M. E., Leavitt, L. A., & Donovan, W. L. (1978). Fathers' and mothers' responses to infant smiles and cries. *Infant Behavior and Development, 1,* 187–198.

Fromm, E. (1941). *Escape from freedom.* New York: Rinehart.

Fromm-Reichmann, F. (1948). Notes on the development of treatment of schizophrenics by psychoanalytic psychotherapy. *Psychiatry, 11,* 263–273.

Funder, D., & Colvin, C. (1988). Friends and strangers: Acquaintanceship, agreement, and the accuracy of personality judgement. *Journal of Personality and Social Psychology, 55,* 149–158.

Funder, D., & Sneed, C. D. (1993). Behavioral manifestations of personality: An ecological approach to judgmental accuracy. *Journal of Personality and Social Psychology, 64,* 479–490.

Furstenberg, F. F. (1982). Conjugal succession: Reentering marriage after divorce. In P. B. Baltes & O. G. Brim, Jr. (Eds.), *Lifespan development and behavior: Vol. 4* (pp. 107–146). New York: Academic Press.

Furstenberg, F. F., Brooks-Gunn, J., & Chase-Lansdale, L. (1989). Teenaged pregnancy and childbearing. *American Psychologist, 44,* 313–320.

Furstenberg, F. F., Jr., and Cherlin, A. J. (1991). *Divided families: What happens to children when parents part.* Cambridge, MA: Harvard University Press.

Furth, H. (1964). Research with the deaf: Implications for language and cognition. *Psychological Bulletin, 62,* 145–164.

Fuson, K. C., & Kwon, Y. (1992a). Effects on children's addition and subtraction of the system of number words and other cultural tools. In J. Bideaud & C. Meljac (Eds.), *Pathways to number.* Villeneueve d'asq, France: University de Lille.

Fuson, K. C., & Kwon, Y. (1992b). Korean children's understanding of multidigit addition and subtraction. *Child Development, 63,* 491–506.

Gabrenya, W. K., Jr., Latané, B., & Wang, Y. E. (1983). Social loafing in cross cultural perspective. *Journal of Cross-Cultural Psychology, 14,* 368–384.

Gaddis, T. E., & Long, J. O. (1970). *Killer: A journal of murder.* New York: Macmillan.

Gagnon, J. H., & Simon, W. (1973). *Sexual conduct: The social sources of human sexuality.* Chicago: Aldine.

Galin, D. (1974). Implications for psychiatry of left and right cerebral specialization. *Archives of General Psychiatry, 31,* 572–583.

Gallup, G. G., McClure, M. K., Hill, S. D., & Bundy, R. A. (1971). Capacity for self-recognition in differentially reared chimpanzees. *Psychological Record, 21,* 69–74.

Gallup, G. H., Jr., & Newport, F. (1991). Belief in paranormal phenomena among adult Americans. *Skeptical Inquirer, 15,* 137–146.

Ganchrow, J. R., Steiner, J. E., & Daher, M. (1983). Neonatal facial expressions in response to different qualities and intensities of gustatory stimuli. *Infant Behavior and Development, 6,* 189–200.

Ganellen, R. J., & Blaney, P. H. (1984). Hardiness and social support as moderators of the effects of life stress. *Journal of Personality and Social Psychology, 47,* 156–163.

Gara, M. A., Woolfolk, R. L., Cohen, B. D., Goldston, R. B., Allen, L. A., & Novalany, J. (1993). Perception of self and other in major depression. *Journal of Abnormal Psychology, 102,* 93–100.

Garber, R. J. (1992). Long-term effects of divorce on the self-esteem of young adults. *Journal of Divorce and Remarriage, 17,* 131–138.

Garcia Coll, C. T., Oh, W., & Hoffman, J. The social ecology: Early parenting of Caucasian American mothers. *Child Development, 58,* 955–963.

Garcia, J., & Koelling, R. A. (1966). Relation of cue to consequences in avoidance learning. *Psychonomic Science, 4,* 123–124.

Garcia, J., Hankins, W. G., & Rusiniak, K. W. (1974). Behavioral regulation of the milieu interne in man and rat. *Science, 185,* 824–831.

Garcia, J., Kimeldorf, D. J., Hunt, E. L., & Davies, B. P. (1956). Food and water consumption of rats during exposure to gamma radiation. *Radiation Research, 4,* 33–41.

Garcia, J., Rusiniak, K. W., & Brett, L. P. (1977). Conditioning food-illness aversions in wild animals: Caveat Canonici. In H. Davis & H. M. B. Hurwitz (Eds.), *Operant-Pavlovian interactions.* Hillsdale, NJ: Lawrence Erlbaum Associates.

Garcia, S., Stinson, L., Ickes, W., Bissonnette, V., & Briggs, S. R. (1991). Shyness and physical attractiveness in mixed-sex dyads. *Journal of Personality and Social Psychology, 61,* 35–49.

Gardner, H. (1983). *Frames of mind: The theory of multiple intelligences.* New York: Basic Books.

Gardner, R. A., & Gardner, B. T. (1978). Comparative psychology and language acquisition. *Annals of the New York Academy of Science, 309,* 37–76.

Garfield, S. L. (1982). Eclecticism and integration in psychotherapy. *Behavior Therapy, 13,* 610–623.

Garfinkel, P. E., Moldofsky, H., & Garner, D. M. (1980). The heterogeneity of anorexia nervosa. *Archives of General Psychiatry, 37,* 1036–1040.

Garland, A. F., & Zigler, E. (1993). Adolescent suicide prevention: Current research and social policy implications. *American Psychologist, 48,* 169–182.

Garmezy, N. (1988, April). *From adult schizophrenia to children resilient under stress.* Paper presented at the annual meeting of the Midwestern Psychological Association, Chicago, IL.

Garrett, V., Brantley, P., Jones, G., & McNight, G. (1991). The relation between daily stress and Crohn's Disease. *Journal of Behavioral Medicine, 14,* 187–196.

Garrity, T. F. (1973). Vocational adjustment after first myocardial infarction: Comparative assessment of several variables suggested in the literature. *Social Science and Medicine, 7,* 705–717.

Garrity, T. F. (1975). Morbidity, mortality, and rehabilitation. In W. D. Gentry & R. B. Williams, Jr. (Eds.), *Psychological aspects of myocardial infarction and coronary care.* St. Louis: Mosby.

Garvey, C. (1975). Requests and responses in children's speech. *Journal of Child Language, 2,* 41–63.

Gatchel, R. J., Baum, A., & Krantz, D. S. (1989). *An introduction to health psychology* (2nd ed.). New York: Random House.

Gaver, D. L., & Davis, J. M. (1979). Biogenic amine hypotheses of affective disorders. *Life Sciences, 24,* 383–394.

Gawin, F. H. (1991). Cocaine addiction: Psychology and neurophysiology. *Science, 251,* 1580–1586.

Gawin, F. H., & Ellinwood, E. H., Jr. (1988). Cocaine and other stimulants: Actions, abuse, and treatment. *New England Journal of Medicine, 318,* 1173–1182.

Gazzaniga, M. S. (1989). Organization of the human brain. *Science, 245,* 947–952.

Gazzaniga, M. S., & LeDoux, J. E. (1978). *The integrated mind.* New York: Plenum Press.

Geary, D. C., Fan, L., & Bow-Thomas, C. C. (1992). Numerical cognition: Loci of ability differences comparing children from China and the United States. *Psychological Sciences, 3,* 180–185.

Gebhardt, D. L., & Crump, C. E. (1990). Employee fitness and wellness programs in the workplace. *American Psychologist, 45,* 262–272.

Geen, R. G. (1985). Test anxiety and visual vigilance. *Journal of Personality and Social Psychology, 49,* 963–970.

Geen, R. G. (1989). Alternative conceptions of social facilitation. In P. B. Paulus (Ed.), *Psychology of group influence* (2nd ed.). Hillsdale, NJ: Lawrence Erlbaum Associates.

Geen, R. G., & Donnerstein, E. I. (Eds.) (1983). *Aggression: Theoretical and empirical reviews.* New York: Academic Press.

Geen, R. G., Beatty, W. W., & Arkin, R. M. (1984). *Human motivation.* Boston: Allyn & Bacon.

Geer, J. H., Davison, G. C., & Gatchel, R. I. (1970). Reduction of stress in humans through nonveridical perceived control of aversive stimulation. *Journal of Personality and Social Psychology, 16,* 731–738.

Gelderloos, P., Frid, M. J., Goddard, P. H., Xue, X., & Loliger, S. A. (1988). Creating world peace through the collective practice of the Maharishi Technology of the Unified Field: Improved U.S.-Soviet relations. *Social Science Perspectives Journal, 2,* 80–94.

Gelernter, J., Goldman, D., & Risch, N. (1993). The A1 allele at the D_2 dopamine receptor gene and alcoholism: A reappraisal. *Journal of the American Medical Association, 269,* 1673–1677.

Gellhorn, E., & Loofbourrow, G. N. (1963). *Emotions and emotional disorders.* New York: Harper & Row.

Gelman, R. (1969). Conservation acquisition: A problem of learning to attend to relevant attributes. *Journal of Experimental Child Psychology, 7,* 167–187.

Gelman, R., & Baillargeon, R. (1983). A review of some Piagetian concepts. In P. H. Mussen (Ed.), *Handbook of child psychology* (Vol. 3). New York: Wiley.

Gentner, D. (1983). Structure mapping: A theoretical framework for analogy. *Cognitive Science, 7,* 155–170.

Gentner, D., & Stevens, A. L. (1983). *Mental models.* Hillsdale, NJ: Lawrence Erlbaum Associates.

Gentry, W. D. (1970). Effects of frustration, attack, and prior aggressive training on overt aggression and vascular processes. *Journal of Personality and Social Psychology, 16,* 718–725.

Gerard, H. B., Wilhelmy, R. A., & Connolley, E. S. (1968). Conformity and group size. *Journal of Personality and Social Psychology, 8,* 79–82.

Gerbner, G., Gross, L., Morgan, M., & Signorielli, N. (1986). Living with television: The dynamics of the cultivation process. In J. Bryant & D. Zillmann (Eds.), *Perspectives on media effects.* Hillsdale, NJ: Lawrence Erlbaum Associates.

Gergen, K. J., & Bauer, R. A. (1967). Interactive effects of self-esteem and task difficulty on social conformity. *Journal of Personality and Social Psychology, 6,* 16–21.

Gerschman, J. A., Reade, P. C., & Burrows, G. D. (1980). Hypnosis and dentistry. In G. D. Burrows & L. Dennerstein (Eds.), *Handbook of hypnosis and psychosomatic medicine.* Amsterdam: Elsevier.

Geschwind, N. (1979). Specializations of the human brain. *Scientific American, 241,* 180–199.

Geschwind, N., & Galaburda, A. M. (1985). Cerebral lateralization: Biological mechanisms, associations and pathology: I. A hypothesis and a program for research. *Archives of Neurology, 42,* 428–459.

Gewirtz, J. L. (1972). *Attachment and dependency.* Washington, DC: Winston.

Gfeller, J. D., Lynn, S. J., & Pribble, W. E. (1987). Enhancing hypnotic susceptibility: Interpersonal and rapport factors. *Journal of Personality and Social Psychology, 52,* 595–596.

Ghiselli, E. E. (1973). The validity of aptitude tests in personnel selection. *Personnel Psychology, 26,* 461–477.

Gibbard, A. (1989). Selfish genes and ingroup altruism. *Behavioral and Brain Sciences, 12,* 706–707.

Gibson, E. J., & Walk, R. D. (1960). *The visual cliff.* Scientific American, 202, 64–71.

Gibson, J. J. (1979). *The ecological approach to visual perception.* Boston: Houghton Mifflin.

Gidron, B., Chesler, M. A., & Chesney, B. K. (1991). Cross-cultural perspectives on self-help groups: Comparisons between participants and nonparticipants in Israel and the United States. *American Journal of Community Psychology, 19,* 667–681.

Gifford, R. (1987). *Environmental psychology: Principles and practice.* Boston: Allyn & Bacon.

Gil, D. G. (Ed.) (1979). *Child abuse and violence.* New York: AMS Press.

Gilbert, C. D. (1992). Horizontal integration and cortical dynamics. *Neuron, 9,* 1–13.

Gilbert, E., & DeBlassie, R. (1984). Anorexia nervosa: Adolescent starvation by choice. *Adolescence, 19,* 840–846.

Gilbert, R. M. (1984). Caffeine consumption. In G. A. Spiller (Ed.), *The methylxanthine beverages and foods: Chemistry, consumption, and health effects.* New York: Liss.

Giles, T. R. (1983). Probable superiority of behavioral interventions: II. Empirical status of the equivalence of therapies hypothesis. *Journal of Behavior Therapy & Experimental Psychiatry, 14,* 189–196.

Giles, T. R. (1990). Bias against behavior therapy in outcome reviews: Who speaks for the patient? *The Behavior Therapist, 13,* 86–90.

Gill, M. M., & Brenman, M. (1959). *Hypnosis and related states.* New York: International Universities Press.

Gill, M. M., & Hoffman, I. Z. (1982). A method of studying the analysis of aspects of the patient's experience of the relationship in psychoanalysis and psychotherapy. *Journal of the American Psychoanalytic Association, 30,* 137–167.

Gillette, M. U. (1986). The suprachiasmatic nuclei: Circadian phase-shifts induced at the time of hypothalamic slice preparation are preserved in vitro. *Brain Research, 379,* 176–181.

Gilligan, C. (1982). *In a different voice: Psychological theory and women's development.* Cambridge: Harvard University Press.

Gilligan, C., & Wiggins, G. (1987). The origins of morality in early childhood relationships. In J. Kagan & S. Lamb (Eds.), *The emergence of morality.* Chicago: University of Chicago Press.

Gilman, A. G., Goodman, L. S., Rall, T. W., & Murad, F. (1985). *Goodman and Gilman's the pharmacological basis of therapeutics* (7th ed.). New York: Macmillan.

Gilmore, J. B. (1989). Randomness and the search for psi. *International Journal of Parapsychology, 53,* 309–340.

Gladis, M. M., Michela, J. L., Walter, H., & Vaughan, R. (1992). High school students' perceptions of AIDS risk: Realistic appraisal or motivated denial? *Health Psychology, 11,* 307–316.

Glanzer, M., & Cunitz, A. (1966). Two storage mechanisms in free recall. *Journal of Verbal Learning and Verbal Behavior, 5,* 351–360.

Glaser, R. (1990). The reemergence of learning theory within instructional research. *American Psychologist, 45,* 29–39.

Glaser, R., & Bassok, M. (1989). Learning theory and the study of instruction. *Annual Review of Psychology, 40,* 631–666.

Glaser, R., Rice, J., Sheridan, J., Fertel, R., Stout, J. C., Speicher, C., Pinsky, D., Kotur, M., Post, A., Beck, M., & Kiecolt-Glaser, J. (1987). Stress-related immune suppression: Health implications. *Brain, Behavior, and Immunity, 1,* 7–20.

Glasgow, R. E., & Bernstein, D. A. (1981). Behavioral treatment of smoking behavior. In L. A. Bradley & C. K. Prokop (Eds.), *Medical psychology: A new perspective.* New York: Academic Press.

Glass, D. C. (1977). Behavior patterns, stress, and coronary disease. Hillsdale, NJ: Lawrence Erlbaum Associates.

Glass, D., McKnight, D., & Valdimarsdottir, H. (1993). Depression, control, and burnout in hospital nurses. *Journal of Consulting and Clinical Psychology, 61,* 147–155.

Gleitman, L. R., Newport, E. L., & Gleitman, H. (1984). The current status of the motherese hypothesis. *Journal of Child Language, 11,* 43–79.

Glenn, S. M., & Cunningham, C. C. (1983). What do babies listen to most? A developmental study of auditory preferences in non-handicapped infants and infants with Down's syndrome. *Developmental Psychology, 19,* 332–337.

Glick, P. C. (1980). Remarriage: Some recent changes and variations. *Journal of Family Issues, 1,* 455–478.

Glover, J. A., Krug, D., Dietzer, M., George, B. W., & Hannon, M. (1990). "Advance" advance organizers. *Bulletin of the Psychonomic Society, 28,* 4–6.

Glowinski, J. (1981). In vivo release of transmitters in the cat basal ganglia. *Federation Proceedings, 40,* 135–141.

Glueckauf, R., & Quittner, A. (1992). Assertiveness training for disabled adults in wheelchairs: Self-report, role-play, and activity pattern outcomes. *Journal of Consulting and Clinical Psychology, 60,* 419–425.

Gnepp, J. (1983). Children's social sensitivity: Inferring emotions from conflicting cues. *Developmental Psychology, 19,* 805–814.

Goddard, H. H. (1917). Mental tests and the immigrant. *Journal of Delinquency, 2,* 243–277.

Godden, D. R., & Baddeley, A. D. (1975). Context-dependent memory in two natural environments: On land and underwater. *British Journal of Psychology, 66,* 325–331.

Goelet, P., Castellucci, V. F., Schacher, S. & Kandel, E. R. (1986). The long and the short of long-term memory: A molecular framework. *Nature, 322,* 419–422.

Goethals, G. R. (1986). Fabricating and ignoring social reality: Self-serving estimates of consensus. In J. M. Olson, C. P. Herman, & M. P. Zanna (Eds.), *Relative deprivation and social comparison.* Hillsdale, NJ: Lawrence Erlbaum Associates.

Goetz, C. G., Stebbins, G. T., Klawans, H. L., Koller, W. C., Grossman, R. G., Bakay, R. A., & Penn, R. D. (1991). United Parkinson Foundation Neurotransplantation Registry on adrenal medullary transplants: Presurgical, and 1- and 2-year follow-up. *Neurology, 41,* 1719–1722.

Gogel, W. C. (1990). A theory of phenomenal geometry and its applications. *Perception and Psychophysics, 48,* 105–123.

Gold, D. R., Rogacz, S., Bock, N., Tosteson, T. D., Baum, T. M., Speizer, F. E., & Czeiler, C. A. (1992). Rotating shift work, sleep, and accidents related to sleepiness in hospital nurses. *American Journal of Public Health, 82,* 1011–1014.

Gold, L. H., Hubner, C. B., & Koob, G. F. (1989). A role for the mesolimbic dopamine system in the psychostimulant actions of MDMA. *Psychopharmacology, 99,* 40–47.

Gold, P. W., Goodwin, F. K., & Chrousos, G. P. (1988). Clinical and biochemical manifestations of depression: relation to the neurobiology of stress. *New England Journal of Medicine, 319,* 348–353.

Goldberger, L. (1982). Sensory deprivation and overload. In L.

Goldberger & S. Breznitz (Eds.), *Handbook of stress: Theoretical and clinical aspects.* New York: Free Press.

Golden, C. J., Moses, J. A., Fishburne, F. J., Engum, E., Lewis, G. P., Wisniewski, A. M., Conley, F. K., Berg, R. A., & Graber, B. (1981). Cross-validation of the Luria-Nebraska Neuropsychological Battery for the presence, lateralization, and location of brain damage. *Journal of Consulting Clinical Psychology, 50,* 87–95.

Goldenberg, H. (1983). *Contemporary clinical psychology* (2nd ed.). Monterey, CA: Brooks/Cole.

Goldenberg, I., & Goldenberg, H. (1980). *Family therapy: An overview.* Monterey, CA: Brooks/Cole.

Goldfoot, D. A. (1977). Sociosexual behaviors of nonhuman primates during development and maturity: Social and hormonal relationships. In A. M. Schrier (Ed.), *Behavioral primatology: Advances in research and theory: Vol. 1.* Hillsdale, NJ: Lawrence Erlbaum Associates.

Goldin-Meadow, S., & Feldman, H. (1977). The development of language-like communication without a language model. *Science, 197,* 401–403.

Goldman, M. S., Brown, S. A., Christiansen, B. A., & Smith, G. T. (1991). Alcoholism and memory: Broadening the scope of alcohol-expectancy research. *Psychological Bulletin, 110,* 137–146.

Goldman, R. D., & Widawski, M. H. (1976). A within subjects technique for comparing college grading standards. *Educational Psychology Measurement, 36,* 381–390.

Goldman-Rakic, P. S. (1987). Development of cortical circuitry and cognitive function. *Child Development, 58,* 601–622.

Goldsmith, H. H. (1983). Genetic influences on personality from infancy to adulthood. *Child Development, 54,* 331–355.

Goldstein, B. (1989). *Sensation and perception* (3rd ed.), Belmont, CA: Wadsworth.

Goldstein, M. J., & Strachan, A. M. (1987). The family and schizophrenia. In T. Jacob (Ed.), *Family interaction and psychopathology: Theories, methods and findings.* New York: Plenum.

Goldstein, M. J., Kant, H. S., Judd, L., Rice, C., & Green, R. (1971). Experience with pornography: Rapists, pedophiles, homosexuals, transsexuals, and controls. *Archives of Sexual Behavior, 1,* 1–15.

Goleman, D. (1986, April 8). Studies point to the power of nonverbal signals. *New York Times.*

Gollwitzer, P. M., & Kinney, R. F. (1989). Effects of deliberative and implemental mind-sets on illusion of control. *Journal of Personality and Social Psychology, 56,* 531–542.

Goodale, M. A., & Milner, A. D. (1992). Separate visual pathways for perception and action. *Trends in Neuroscience, 15,* 20–25.

Goodale, M. A., Milner, A. D., Jakobson, L. S., & Carey, D. P. (1991). A neurobiological dissociation between perceiving objects and grasping them. *Nature, 349,* 154–156.

Goodenough, F. L. (1932). Expression of the emotions in a blind-deaf child. *Journal of Abnormal and Social Psychology, 27,* 328–333.

Goodkin, K., Blaney, N., Feaster, D., Fletcher, M. A., Baum, M., Mantero-Atienza, E., Klimas, N., Millon, C., Szapocznik, J., & Eisdorfer, C. (1992). Active coping style is associated with natural killer cell cytotoxicity in asymptomatic HIV-1 seropositive homosexual men. *Journal of Psychosomatic Research, 36,* 635–650.

Goodman-Gilman, A. G., Rall, T. W., Nies, A. S., & Taylor, P. (1990a). *Goodman and Gilman's the Pharmacological basis of therapeutics* (8th ed.). New York: Pergamon.

Goodman-Gilman, A., Rall, T. W., Nies, A. S., & Taylor, P. (1990b). *The pharmacological basis of therapeutics* (8th ed.). New York: Pergamon Press.

Goodwin, C. (1992). A conceptualization of motives to seek privacy for nondeviant consumption. *Journal of Consumer Psychology, 1,* 261–284.

Goodwin, D. W. (1979). Alcoholism and heredity: A review and hypothesis. *Archives of General Psychiatry, 36,* 57–61.

Goodwin, D. W., Crane, J. B., & Guze, S. B. (1973). Alcoholic "blackouts": A review and clinical study of 100 alcoholics. *American Journal of Psychiatry, 26,* 191–198.

Gopher, D., Weil, M., & Siegal, D. (1989). Practice under changing priorities: an approach to the training of complex skills. *Acta Psychologica, 1571,* 147–177.

Goplerud, E. N. (1980). Social support and stress during the first year of graduate school. *Professional Psychology, 11,* 283–290.

Gorassini, D., Sowerby, D., Creighton, A., & Fry, G. (1991). Hypnotic suggestibility enhancement through brief cognitive skill training. *Journal of Personality and Social Psychology, 61,* 289–297.

Gordon, N. P., Cleary, P. D., Parker, C. E., & Czeisler, C. A. (1986). The prevalence and health impact of shiftwork. *American Journal of Public Health, 76,* 1225–1228.

Gordon, T. (1970). *Parent effectiveness training: The no-lose program for raising responsible children.* New York: Wyden.

Gore, S. (1978). The effect of social support in moderating the health consequences of unemployment. *Journal of Health and Social Behavior, 19,* 157–165.

Gorenflo, D. W., & Crano, W. D. (1989). Judgmental subjectivity/objectivity and locus of choice in social comparison. *Journal of Personality and Social Psychology, 57,* 605–614.

Gorman, J. M., Liebowitz, M. R., Fyer, A. J., & Stein, J. (1989). A neuroanatomical hypothesis for panic disorder. *American Journal of Psychiatry, 146,* 148–161.

Gorman, J., Leibowitz, M., Fryer, A., & Stein, J. (1989). A neuroanatomical hypothesis of panic disorder. *American Journal of Psychiatry, 146,* 148–163.

Gorman, M. E. (1986). How the possibility of error affects falsification on a task that models scientific problem solving. *British Journal of Psychology, 77,* 85–96.

Gorn, G. J. (1982). The effects of music in advertising on choice behavior: A classical conditioning approach. *Journal of Marketing, 46,* 94–101.

Gottesman, A. (1992). Asking witness to point out suspect can court embarrassment. *Chicago Tribune,* July 19.

Gottesman, I. I. (1991). *Schizophrenia genesis.* New York: W. H. Freeman.

Gottesman, I., McGuffin, P., & Farmer, A. (1987). Clinical genetics as clues to the "real" genetics of schizophrenia. *Schizophrenia Bulletin, 13,* 23–47.

Gottfredson, L. S., & Crouse, J. (1986). Validity versus utility of mental tests: Example of the SAT. *Journal of Vocational Behavior, 29,* 363–378.

Gottfried, A. W. (1984). *Home environment and early cognitive development.* Orlando, FL: Academic Press.

Gottlieb, A. (1988). *Blood magic.* Berkeley: University of California Press.

Gottlieb, B. H. (Ed.) (1981). *Social networks and social support.* Beverly Hills, CA: Sage.

Gottlieb, B. H., & Peters, L. (1991). A national demographic portrait of mutual aid group participants in Canada. *American Journal of Community Psychology, 19,* 651–666.

Gottman, J. M. (1979). *Marital interaction: Experimental investigation.* New York: Academic Press.

Gottman, J. M., & Krokoff, L. J. (1989). Marital interaction and satisfaction: A longitudinal view. *Journal of Consulting and Clinical Psychology, 57,* 47–52.

Gottman, J. M., & Levenson, R. L. (1986). Assessing the role of emotion in marriage. *Behavioral Assessment, 8,* 31–48.

Gottman, J. M., & Levenson, R. W. (1992). Marital processes predictive of later dissolution: Behavior, physiology, and health. *Journal of Personality and Social Psychology, 63,* 221–233.

Gough, H. (1987). *California Psychological Inventory: Administrator's guide.* Palo Alto, CA: Consulting Psychologists Press.

Gould, S. J. (1983). *The mismeasure of man.* New York: W. W. Norton.

Graesser, A. C., & Nakamura, G. V. (1982). The impact of a schema on comprehension and memory. In G. H. Bower (Ed.), *The psychology of learning and motivation: Vol. 16.* New York: Academic Press.

Graesser, A. C., Woll, S. B., Kowalski, D. J., & Smith, D. A. (1980). Memory for typical and atypical actions in scripted activities. *Journal of Experimental Psychology: Human Learning and Memory, 6,* 503–515.

Graf, R. C., & Riddell, L. C. (1972). Helping behavior as a function of interpersonal perception. *Journal of Social Psychology, 86,* 227–231.

Graham, C., & Evans, F. J. (1977). Hypnotizability and the deployment of waking attention. *Journal of Abnormal Psychology, 86,* 631–638.

Graham, J. R. (1987). *The MMPI: A practical guide* (2nd ed.). New York: Oxford University Press.

Graham, S. (1992). "Most of the subjects were white and middle class." *American Psychologist, 47,* 629–639.

Granneman, J., & Friedman, M. J. (1980). Hepatic modulation of insulin-induced gastric acid secretion and EMG activity in rats. *American Journal of Physiology, 238,* 346–352.

Grant, S. G. N., O'Dell, T. J., Karl, K. A., Stein, P. L., Soriano, P., & Kandel, E. R. (1992). Impaired long-term potentiation, spatial learning, and hippocampal development in FYN mutant mice. *Science, 258,* 1903–1910.

Graubard, S. R. (Ed.) (1988). *The artificial intelligence debate.* Cambridge, MA: MIT Press.

Gray, A., Jackson, D. N., & McKinley, J. B. (1991). The relation between dominance, anger, and hormones in normally aging men: Results from the Massachusetts male aging study. *Psychosomatic Medicine, 53,* 375–385.

Gray, J. A., Feldon, J., Rawlins, J. N., Hemsley, D. R., & Smith, A. D. (1991). Neurophysiology of schizophrenia. *Behavior and Brain Science, 14,* 1–84.

Green, D. M., & Swets, J. A. (1965). *Signal detection theory and psychophysics.* New York: Wiley.

Green, E. J., Greenough, W. T., & Schlumpf, B. E. (1983). Effects of complex or isolated environments on cortical dendrites of middle-aged rats. *Brain Research, 264*(2), 233–240.

Green, M. (1991). Visual search, visual strains, and visual architecture. *Perception and Psychophysics, 50,* 388–404.

Green, R. (1987). *The "sissy boy syndrome" and the development of homosexuality.* New Haven: Yale University Press.

Green, R. G., & Stonner, D. (1971). Effects of aggressiveness habit strength on behavior in the presence of aggression-related stimuli. *Journal of Personality and Social Psychology, 17,* 149–153.

Greenberg, E., O'Neil, R., & Goldberg, W. (1991, September). Cited by T. Adler, Support and challenge: Both key for small kids. *APA Monitor,* p. 10.

Greenberg, J., & Cohen, R. L. (Eds.) (1982). *Equity and justice in social behavior.* New York: Academic Press.

Greenberg, J., & Mitchell, S. (1983). *Object relations in psychoanalytic theory.* Cambridge, MA: Harvard University Press.

Greenberg, L. (1986). Change process research. *Journal of Consulting and Clinical Psychology, 54,* 4–9.

Greenberg, M., & Stone, A. (1992). Emotional disclosure about trauma and its relation to health: Effects of previous disclosure and trauma severity. *Journal of Personality and Social Psychology, 63,* 75–84.

Greene, B. (1985, January 15). Less violence would be a big hit on TV. *Chicago Tribune.*

Greene, R. (1991). *The MMPI-2/MMPI: An interpretive manual.* Needham Heights, MA: Allyn & Bacon.

Greenfield, P. M., & Savage-Rumbaugh, E. S. (1990). Grammatical combination in *pan paniscus*: Processes of learning and invention in the evolution of language development. In S. Parker & K. Gibson (Eds.), *Comparative developmental psychology of language and intelligence in primates.* New York: Cambridge University Press.

Greenfield, P. M., & Childs, C. P. (1991). Developmental continuity in biocultural context. In R. Cohen & A. W. Siegel (Eds.), *Context and development* (pp. 135–159). Hillsdale, NJ: Lawrence Erlbaum Associates.

Greenfield, P., & Savage-Rumbaugh, E. S. (in press). Imitation, grammatical development, and the invention of protogrammar by an ape. In N. Krasnegor, D. M. Rumbaugh, M. Studdert-Kennedy, & D. Scheifelbusch (Eds.), *Biobehavioral foundations of language development.* Hillsdale: Lawrence Erlbaum Associates.

Greeno, J. G. (1989, February). A perspective on thinking. *American Psychologist, 44*(2), 134–141.

Greeno, J. G., Riley, M. S., & Gelman, R. (1984). Conceptual competence and children's counting. *Cognitive Psychology, 16,* 94–143.

Greenough, W. T. (1985). The possible role of experience-dependent synaptogenesis, or synapses on demand, in the memory process. In N. M. Weinberger, J. L. McGaugh, & G. Lynch (Eds.), *Memory systems of the brain.* New York: The Guilford Press.

Greenough, W. T., Black, J. E., & Wallace, C. S. (1987). Experience and brain development. *Child Development, 58,* 539–559.

Greenwald, A. (1980). The totalitarian ego: Fabrication and revision of personal history. *American Psychologist, 35,* 603–618.

Greenwald, A. G. (1992). Unconscious cognition reclaimed. *American Psychologist, 47*(6), 766–779.

Greenwald, A. G., & Pratkanis, A. R. (1984). The self. In R. S. Wyer & T. K. Srull (Eds.), *Handbook of social cognition* (Vol. 3). Hillsdale, NJ: Lawrence Erlbaum Associates.

Greenwald, A. G., & Spangenberg, E. R. (1991). Double-blind tests of subliminal self-help audiotapes. *Psychological Science, 2,* 119–122.

Greenwald, J. (1991). Smart as you wanna be. *Los Angeles Times Magazine,* December 22.

Greer, L. D. (1980). *Children's comprehension of formal features with masculine and feminine connotations.* Unpublished master's thesis, Department of Human Development, University of Kansas, Lawrence, KS.

Gregory, R. L. (1968). Visual illusions. *Scientific American, 219,* 66–67.

Gregory, R. L. (1973). *Eye and brain* (2nd ed.). New York: McGraw Hill.

Grencavage, L., & Norcross, J. C. (1991). Where are the commonalities among the therapeutic common factors. *Professional Psychology: Research and Practice, 21,* 372–378.

Griffiths, R. R., & Woodson, P. P. (1988). Caffeine physical dependence: A review of human and laboratory animal studies. *Psychopharmacology, 94,* 437–451.

Griffitt, W. B., & Guay, P. (1969). "Object" evaluation and conditioned affect. *Journal of Experimental Research in Personality, 4,* 1–8.

Griffitt, W. B., & Veitch, R. (1971). Hot and crowded: Influence of population density and temperature on interpersonal affective behavior. *Journal of Personality and Social Psychology, 17,* 92–98.

Grilo, C. M., Pogue-Geile, M. F. (1991). The nature of environmental influences on weight and obesity: A behavior genetic analysis. *Psychological Bulletin, 110,* 520–537.

Gritz, E., & St. Jeor, S. (1992). Task Force 3: Implications with respect to intervention and prevention. *Health Psychology, 11* (suppl.), 17–25.

Gross, W. B., & Colmano, G. (1969). The effect of social isolation on resistance to some infectious diseases. *Poultry Science, 48,* 514–520.

Grossberg, S. (1988). *Neural networks and natural intelligence.* Cambridge, MA: MIT Press.

Grossmann, K., Grossmann, K. E., Spangler, G., Suess, G., & Unzner, L. (1985). Maternal sensitivity and newborns' orientation responses as related to quality of attachment in Northern Germany. In I. Bretherton & E. Waters (Eds.), Growing points of attachment theory and research. *Monographs of the Society for Research in Child Development, 50*(1–2, Serial No. 209).

Grosz, H. I., & Zimmerman, J. (1970). A second detailed case study of functional blindness: Further demonstration of the contribution of objective psychological data. *Behavior Therapy, 1,* 115–123.

Grove, H. (1987). The reliability of psychiatric diagnosis. In C. G. Last & M. Hersen (Eds.), *Issues in diagnostic research* (pp. 99–119). New York: Plenum.

Grover, S. L., & Brockner, J. (1989). Empathy and the relationship between attitudinal similarity and attraction. *Journal of Research in Personality, 23,* 469–479.

Gruder, C. L., & Duslak, R. J. (1973). Elicitation of cooperation by retaliatory and nonretaliatory strategies in a mixed motive game. *Journal of Conflict Resolution, 17,* 162–174.

Grunberg, N. (1992). Cigarette smoking and body weight: A personal journey through a complex field. Health Psychology. 11, (suppl.) 26–31.

Guerin, B. (1986). Mere presence effects in humans: A review. *Journal of Experimental Social Psychology, 22,* 38–77.

Guerin, D., & Gottfried, A. W. (1986). Infant temperament as a predictor of preschool behavior problems. *Infant Behavior and Development, 9,* 152. (Special issue: abstracts of papers presented at the Fifth International Conference on Infant Studies.)

Guilford, J. P. (1959). Traits of creativity. In H. H. Anderson (Ed.), *Creativity and its cultivation.* New York: Harper & Row.

Guilford, J. P., & Hoepfner, R. (1971). *The analysis of intelligence.* New York: McGraw-Hill.

Guilleminault, C., Stroohs, R., & Quera-Salva, M. A. (1992). Sleep-related obstructive and nonobstructive apneas and neurologic disorders. *Neurology, 42,* 53–60.

Gunderson, J. G., & Mosher, L. R. (1975). The cost of schizophrenia. *American Journal of Psychiatry, 132,* 901–905.

Guntheroth, W. G., & Spiers, P. S. (1992). Sleeping prone and the risk of sudden infant death syndrome. *Journal of the American Medical Association, 267,* 2359–2362.

Gurin, G., Veroff, J., & Feld, S. (1960). *Americans view their mental health: A nationwide survey.* New York: Basic Books.

Gurman, A. S., Kniskern, D. P., & Pinsof, W. M. (1986). Research on marital and family therapies. In S. L. Garfield & A. E. Bergin (Eds.), *Handbook of psychotherapy and behavior change* (3rd ed.), pp. 565–624. New York: Wiley.

Guroff, G. (1980). *Molecular neurobiology.* New York: Marcel Dekker.

Gurtman, M. B. (1992). Construct validity of interpersonal personality measures: The interpersonal circumplex as a nomological net. *Journal of Personality and Social Psychology, 63,* 105–118.

Gustafson, B., & Wigstrom, H. (1988). Physiological mechanisms underlying long-term potentiation. *Trends in Neurosciences, 11,* 156–162.

Gustavson, C. R., Garcia, J., Hawkins, W. G., & Rusiniak, K. W. (1974). Coyote predation control by aversive conditioning. *Science, 184,* 581–583.

Gutierrez, L., Ortega, R., & Suarez, Z. (1990). Self-help and the Latino community. In T. J. Powell (Ed.), *Working with self-help.* Silver Spring, MD: NASW Press.

Guttfreund, D. G. (1990). Effects of language usage on the emotional experience of Spanish-English and English-Spanish bilinguals. *Journal of Consulting and Clinical Psychology, 58,* 604–607.

Guyton, A. C. (1991). *Textbook of medical physiology* (8th ed.). Philadelphia: Saunders.

Gwirtsman, H. E., & Germer, R. H. (1981). Abnormalities of dexamethasone suppression test and urinary MHPG in anorexia nervosa. *American Journal of Psychiatry, 138,* 650–653.

Ha, H., Tan, E. C., Fukunaga, H., & Aochi, O. (1981). Naloxone reversal of acupuncture analgesia in the monkey. *Experimental Neurology, 73,* 298–303.

Haaga, D., Dyck, M., & Ernst, D. (1991). Empirical status of the cognitive theory of depression. *Psychologial Bulletin, 110,* 215–236.

Haan, N., Aerts, E., & Cooper, B. A. B. (1985). *On moral grounds: The search for practical morality.* New York: New York University Press.

Haber, R. N. (1979). Twenty years of haunting eidetic imagery: Where's the ghost? *The Behavioral and Brain Sciences, 2,* 583–629.

Hackel, L. S., & Ruble, D. N. (1992). Changes in the marital relationship after the first baby is born: Predicting the impact of expectancy disconfirmation. *Journal of Personality and Social Psychology, 62,* 944–957.

Hagen, J. W., & Hale, G. H. (1973). The development of attention in children. In A. D. Pick (Ed.), *Minnesota symposia on child psychology* (Vol. 7). Minneapolis: University of Minnesota Press.

Hakuta, K., & Garcia, E. E. (1989). Bilingualism and education. *American Psychologist, 44,* 374–379.

Halbreich, U., Endicott, J., Goldstein, S., & Nee J. (1986). Premenstrual changes and changes in gonadal hormones. *Acta Psychiatrica Scandinavia, 74,* 576–586.

Haley, J. (1970). Family therapy. *International Journal of Psychiatry, 9,* 233–242.

Haley, J. (1971). Family therapy: A radical change. In J. Haley (Ed.), *Changing families: A family therapy reader.* New York: Grune & Stratton.

Hall, G. C. N., & Hirschman, R. (1991). Toward a theory of sexual aggression: A quadripartite model. *Journal of Consulting and Clinical Psychology, 59,* 662–669.

Hall, R. C., Hoffman, R. S., Beresford, T. P., Wooley, B., et al. (1989). Physical illness encountered in patients with eating disorders. *Psychosomatics, 30,* 174–191.

Hall, R. M., & Sandler, B. R. (1982). *The classroom climate: A chilly one for women?* Washington, DC: Association of American Colleges.

Haller, E. (1992). Eating disorders: A review and update. *Western Journal of Medicine, 157,* 658–662.

Hamburg, D. A., Elliot, G. R., & Parron, D. L. (1982). *Health and behavior: Frontiers of research in the biobehavioral sciences.* Washington, DC: National Academy Press.

Hamilton, D. L. (1988). Understanding impression formation: What has memory research contributed? In P. R. Solomon, G. R. Goethals, C. M. Kelley, & B. Stephens (Eds.), *Memory: An interdisciplinary approach.* New York: Springer-Verlag.

Hamilton, D. L., & Sherman, J. (1994). Social stereotypes. In R. S. Wyer & T. K. Srull (Eds.), *Handbook of social cognition* (2nd ed.). Hillsdale, NJ: Lawrence Erlbaum Associates.

Hamilton, P. (1989). *The interaction of depressed mothers and their 3-month-old infants.* Unpublished doctoral dissertation, Boston University.

Hamm, A. O., Vaitl, D., & Lang, P. J. (1989). Fear conditioning, meaning, and belongingness: A selective association analysis. *Journal of Abnormal Psychology, 98*, 395–406.

Hammarback, S., Damber, J. E., & Backstrom, T. (1989). Relationship between symptom severity and hormone changes in women with premenstrual syndrome. *Journal of Clinical Endocrinology and Metabolism, 68*, 125–130.

Hammel, E. (1968). Projective drawings. In A. I. Rabin (Ed.), *Projective techniques in personality assessment.* New York: Springer.

Hammock, T., & Brehm, J. W. (1966). The attractiveness of choice alternatives when freedom to choose is eliminated by a social agent. *Journal of Personality, 34*, 546–554.

Hammond, W. R., & Yung, B. (1993). Minority student recruitment and retention practices among schools of professional psychology: A national survey and analysis. *Professional Psychology: Research and Practice, 24*, 3–12.

Hammond, W. R., & Yung, B. R. (1991). Preventing violence in at-risk African-American youth. *Journal of Health Care for the Poor and Underserved, 2*, 359–373.

Hamner, W. C., & Yukl, G. A. (1977). The effectiveness of different offer strategies in bargaining. In D. Druckman, (Ed.), *Negotiations: Social-psychological perspectives.* London: Sage.

Hans, V. P. (1992). Judgments of justice. *Psychological Science, 3*, 218–221.

Hansel, C. E. M. (1966). *ESP: A scientific evaluation.* New York: Scribner.

Hansel, C. E. M. (1980). *ESP: A scientific evaluation.* New York: Scribner.

Hanson, S. J., & Burr, D. J. (1990). What connectionist models learn: Learning and representations in connectionist networks. *Behavioral and Brain Sciences, 13*, 471–518.

Harda, S., Misawa, S., Agarwal, D. P., & Goedde, H. W. (1980). Liver alcohol dehydrogenase and aldehyde dehydrogenase in the Japanese: Isozyme variation and its possible role in alcohol intoxication. *American Journal of Human Genetics, 32*, 8–15.

Hardaway, R. (1990). Subliminally activated symbiotic fantasies: Facts or artifacts. *Psychological Bulletin, 107*, 177–195.

Hardaway, R. A. (1990). Subliminally activated symbiotic fantasies: Facts and artifacts. *Psychological Bulletin, 107*, 177–195.

Hardimann, P. T., Dufresne, R., & Mestre, J. (1989). The relation between problem categorization and problem solving among experts and novices. *Memory & Cognition, 17*, 627–638.

Hare, R. (1991). The Hare Psychopathy Checklist—Revised. Toronto: Multi-Health Systems.

Hare, R. D. (1970). *Psychopathy: Theory and research.* New York: Wiley.

Hare, R. D. (1980). A research scale for the assessment of psychopathy in criminal populations. *Personality and Individual Differences, 1*, 111–119.

Hare, R. D., McPherson, L. M., & Forth, A. E. (1988). Male psychopaths and their criminal careers. *Journal of Consulting and Clinical Psychology, 56*, 710–714.

Hare, R., Hart, S., & Harpur, T. (1991). Psychopathy and the DSM-IV criteria for antisocial personality disorder. *Journal of Abnormal Psychology, 100*, 391–398.

Hari, R., & Lounasmaa, O. V. (1989). Recording and interpretation of cerebral magnetic fields. *Science, 244*, 432–436.

Harkins, S. G. (1987). Social loafing and social facilitation. *Journal of Experimental Social Psychology, 23*, 1–18.

Harkins, S. G., & Szymanski, K. (1987). Social loafing and social facilitation: New wine in old bottles. In C. Hendrick (Ed.), *Group processes and intergroup relations.* Newbury Park, CA: Sage.

Harlow, H. F. (1958). The nature of love. *American Psychologist, 13*, 673–685.

Harlow, H. F. (1959, June). Love in infant monkeys. *Scientific American*, 68–74.

Harlow, H. F., Harlow, M. K., & Suomi, S. J. (1971). From thought to therapy: Lessons from a private library. *American Scientist, 59*, 538–549.

Harper, R. C., Frysinger, J. D., Marks, J. X., & Zhang, R. B. (1988). Cardiorespiratory control during sleep. In P. J. Schwartz (Ed.), *The sudden infant death syndrome: Cardiac and respiratory mechanisms and interventions.* Annals of the New York Academy of Sciences, 533. New York: New York Academy of Sciences.

Harpur, T., Hare, R., & Hakstian, R. (1989). Two-factor conceptualization of psychopathy: Construct validity and assessment implications. *Psychological Assessment, 1*, 6–17.

Harris, J. E., & Morris, P. E. (Eds.) (1984). *Everyday memories, actions, and absent-mindedness.* New York: Academic Press.

Harris, M. J., Milich, R., Corbitt, E. M., Hoover, D. W., & Brady, M. (1992). Self-fulfilling effects of stigmatizing information on children's social interactions. *Journal of Personality and Social Psychology, 63*, 41–50.

Harris, P. L. (1974). Perseverative search at a visibly empty place by young infants. *Journal of Experimental Child Psychology, 18*, 535–542.

Harris, R. J., Sardarpoor-Bascom, F., & Meyer, T. (1989). The role of cultural knowledge in distorting recall for stories. *Bulletin of the Psychonomic Society, 27*, 9–10.

Harrison, A. A. (1976). *Individuals and groups.* Monterey, CA: Brooks/Cole.

Hart, J. T. (1965). Memory and the feeling-of-knowing experience. *Journal of Educational Psychology, 56*, 208–216.

Hart, J. T. (1967). Second-try recall, recognition, and the memory-monitoring process. *Journal of Educational Psychology, 58*, 193–197.

Hart, J., Jr., Berndt, R. S., & Caramazza, A. (1985). Category-specific naming deficit following cerebral infarction. *Nature, 316*, 439–440.

Hart, S. N., & Brassard, M. A. (1987). A major threat to children's health: psychological maltreatment. *American Psychologist, 42*, 160–165.

Harter, S., & Zigler, E. (1974). The assessment of effectance motivation in normal and retarded children. *Developmental Psychology, 10*, 169–180.

Hartman, B. K., Cozzari, C., Berod, A., Kalmbach, S. J., & Faris, P. L. (1986). Central cholinergic innervation of the locus coeruleus. *Society for Neuroscience Abstracts, 12*, 770.

Hartman, E., Baekeland, F., & Zwilling, G. (1972). Psychological differences between long and short sleepers. *Archives of General Psychiatry, 26*, 463–468.

Hartmann, H. (1939). Psychoanalysis and the concept of health. *International Journal of Psychoanalysis, 20*, 308–321.

Hartmann, H. (1958). *Ego psychology and the problem of adaptation.* New York: International Universities Press.

Hartup, W. W. (1983). Peer relations. In P. H. Mussen (Ed.), *Handbook of child psychology: Vol. 4.* New York: Wiley.

Haskell, I., & Wickens, C. D. (in press). Two- and three-dimensional displays for aviation. *International Journal of Aviation Psychology, 4.*

Hastie, R. (1986). Review essay: Experimental evidence on group accuracy. In B. Grofman & G. Owen (Eds.), *Information pooling and group decision making* (pp. 129–264). Greenwich, CT: JAI Press.

Hastie, R., Penrod, S. D., & Pennington, N. (1983). *Inside the jury.* Cambridge: Harvard University Press.

Hastie, R., Penrod, S. D., & Pennington, N. (1984). *Inside the jury.* Cambridge, MA: Harvard University Press.

Hatfield, E. (1986). *Mirror, mirror: The importance of looks in everyday life.* Albany: State University of New York Press.

Hatfield, E. (1988). Passionate and companionate love. In R. J.

Sternberg & M. L. Barnes (Eds.), *The psychology of love.* New Haven: Yale University Press.

Hatfield, E., Traupman, J., Sprecher, S., Utne, M., & Hay, T. (1984). Equity and intimate relations. In W. Ickes (Ed.), *Compatible and incompatible relationships.* New York: Springer-Verlag.

Hatfield, G., & Epstein, W. (1985). The status of the minimum principle in the theoretical analysis of visual perception. *Psychological Bulletin, 97,* 155–186.

Hauser, P., Zametkin, A. J., Martinez, P., Vitiello, B., Matochik, J. A., Mixson, J., & Weinstraub, B. D. (1993). Attention deficit hyperactivity disorder in people with generalized resistance to thyroid hormone. *The New England Journal of Medicine, 328,* 997–1001.

Haviland, S. E., & Clark, H. H. (1974). What's new? Acquiring new information as a process in comprehension. *Journal of Verbal Learning and Verbal Behavior, 13,* 512–521.

Hawkins, F. (1987). *Human factors in flight.* Brookfield, VT: Gower.

Hawkins, H. L., Kramer, A. R., & Capaldi, D. (1993). Aging, exercise, and attention. *Psychology and Aging, 7,* 643–653.

Hawkins, R. C. (1990). Dynamics of substance abuse: Nonlinearities in individual trajectories. *Network, 8,* 9–10.

Hawkins, R. P., Kashden, J., Hansen, D. J., & Sadd, D. L. (1992). The increasing reference to "cognitive" variables in behavior therapy: A 20-year empirical analysis. *The Behavior Therapist, 15,* 115–118.

Hawkins, S. A., & Hastie, R. (1990). Hindsight: Biased judgments of past events after the outcomes are known. *Psychological Bulletin, 107,* 311–327.

Hayes, A. S. (1992). Jurors' grasp of instructions may stir appeal. *Wall Street Journal,* July 16.

Hayes, J. R. M. (1952). *Memory span for several vocabularies as a function of vocabulary size.* Massachusetts Institute of Technology Acoustic Laboratory Progress Report. Cambridge: MIT.

Hays, R., Turner, H., & Coates, T. (1992). Social support, AIDS-related symptoms, and depression among gay men. *Journal of Consulting and Clinical Psychology, 60,* 463–469.

Hayslip, B., & Sterns, H. L. (1979). Age differences in relationships between crystallized and fluid intelligences and problem solving. *Journal of Gerontology, 14,* 404–414.

He, L. F. (1987). Involvement of endogenous opioid peptides in acupuncture analgesia. *Pain, 31,* 99–121.

Hearn, M., Murray, D., & Luepker, R. (1989). Hostility, coronary heart disease, and total mortality: A 33-year follow-up study of university students. *Journal of Behavioral Medicine, 12,* 105–121.

Hearold, S. (1986). A synthesis of 1043 effects of television on social behavior. In G. Comstock (Ed.), *Public communication and behavior.* New York: Academic Press.

Heath, A., Neale, M., Kessler, R., Eaves, L., & Kendler, K. (1992). Evidence for genetic influences on personality from self-reports and informant ratings. *Journal of Personality and Social Psychology, 63,* 85–96.

Heath, L., Kruttschnitt, C., & Ward, D. (1986). Television and violent criminal behavior: Beyond the Bobo doll. *Violence and Victims, 1,* 177–190.

Hebb, D. O. (1949). *The organization of behavior.* New York: Wiley.

Hebb, D. O. (1955). Drives and the C.N.S. (conceptual nervous system). *Psychological Review, 62,* 243–254.

Hebb, D. O. (1978, November). On watching myself get old. *Psychology Today,* pp. 15–23.

Hechtman, L., Weiss, G., & Perlman, T. (1984). Hyperactives as young adults: Past and current substance abuse and antisocial behavior. *American Journal of Orthopsychiatry, 54,* 415–425.

Heider, E. (1972). Universals of color naming and memory. *Journal of Experimental Psychology, 93,* 10–20.

Heilbrun, A. B., & Witt, N. (1990). Distorted body image as a risk factor in anorexia nervosa: Replication and clarification. *Psychological Reports, 66,* 407–416.

Heimberg, R., Dodge, C. L., Hope, D., Kennedy, C., & Zollo, L. (1990). Cognitive behavioral group treatment for social phobia: Comparison with a credible placebo control. *Cognitive Therapy and Research, 14,* 1–23.

Heinrichs, R. W. (1993). Schizophrenia and the brain. *American Psychologist, 48,* 221–233.

Heitler, J. B. (1976). Preparatory techniques in initiating expressive psychotherapy with lower-class, unsophisticated patients. *Psychological Bulletin, 83,* 339–352.

Helgeson, V. S., Shaver, P., & Dyer, M. (1987). Prototypes of intimacy and distance in same-sex and opposite-sex relationships. *Journal of Social and Personal Relationships, 4,* 195–233.

Heller, W. (1989, October). The neuropsychology of emotion: Self-awareness and personality development. Paper presented to the International Congress of Neurology, Symposium on States of Consciousness, New Delhi, India.

Helmes, E., & Reddon, J. R. (1993). A perspective on developments in assessing psychopathology: A critical review of the MMPI-2. *Psychological Bulletin, 113,* 453–471.

Helms, J. E. (1992). Why is there no study of cultural equivalence in standardized cognitive ability testing? *American Psychologist, 47,* 1083–1101.

Helson, R., & Moane, G. (1987). Personality change in women from college to midlife. *Journal of Personality and Social Psychology, 53,* 176–186.

Hendlin, H. (1975). Student suicide: Death as a life-style. *Journal of Nervous and Mental Disease, 160,* 204–219.

Hendrick, C., & Hendrick, S. (1986). A theory and method of love. *Journal of Personality and Social Psychology, 50,* 392–402.

Hendrick, C., & Hendrick, S. (1989). Research on love: Does it measure up? *Journal of Personality and Social Psychology, 56,* 784–794.

Hendrick, S., Hendrick, C., & Adler, N. L. (1988). Romantic relationships: Love, satisfaction, and staying together. *Journal of Personality and Social Psychology, 54,* 980–988.

Henig, R. M. (1988, August). How a body ages. *The Washingtonian,* pp. 59–65.

Henker, B., & Whalen, C. K. (1989). Hyperactivity and attention deficits. *American Psychologist, 44,* 216–223.

Hepworth, J. T., & West, S. G. (1988). Lynchings and the economy: A time-series reanalysis of Hovland and Sears (1940). *Journal of Personality and Social Psychology, 55,* 239–247.

Herink, R. (Ed.) (1980). *The psychotherapy handbook: The A to Z guide to more than 250 different therapies in use today.* New York: New American Library.

Herman, B. H., Hammock, M. K., Arthur-Smith, A., Egan, J., Chatoor, I., Zelnik, N., Carradine, M., Appelgate, K., Boecks, R., & Sharp, S. D. (1986, November). Role of opioid peptides in autism: Effects of acute administration of naltrexone. *Society for Neuroscience Abstracts, 12.*

Herman, C. P., & Polivy, J. (1975). Anxiety, restraint, and eating behavior. *Journal of Abnormal Psychology, 84,* 666–672.

Herman, J. H., & Roffwarg, H. P. (1983). Modifying oculomotor activity in awake subjects increases the amplitude of eye movement during REM sleep. *Science, 220,* 1074–1076.

Heron, W. (1957). The pathology of boredom. *Scientific American, 196,* 52–56.

Herrmann, D. J., & Searleman, A. (1992). Memory improvement and memory theory in historical perspective. In D. Herrmann, H. Weingartner, A. Searlman, & C. McEvoy (Eds.), *Memory improvement: Implications for memory theory.* New York: Springer-Verlag.

Herrnstein, R. J. (1989, May). IQ and falling birth rates. *Atlantic Monthly,* pp. 72–76.

Hersen, M., Bellack, A. S., Himmelhoch, J. M., & Thase, M. E. (1984). *Behavior Therapy, 15*, 21–40.

Hershenon, M. (1989). *The moon illusion.* Hillsdale, NJ: Lawrence Erlbaum Associates.

Hertel, P. T., & Hardin, T. S. (1990). Remembering with and without awareness in a depressed mood: Evidence of deficits in initiative. *Journal of Experimental Psychology: General, 119*, 45–59.

Hertzog, C. (1989). Influences of cognitive slowing on age differences in intelligence. *Developmental Psychology, 25*, 636–651.

Herzberg, F. (1966). *Work and the nature of man.* New York: Crowell.

Herzberg, F. (1968). One more time: How do you motivate employees? *Harvard Business Review, 46*, 53–62.

Herzog, D. B. (1982). Bulimia: The secretive syndrome. *Psychosomatics, 22*, 481–487.

Herzog, D. B., Keller, M. B, Lavori, P. W, Bradburn, I. S., & Ott, I. L. (1990). Course and outcome of bulimia nervosa. In M. M. Fichter (Ed.), *Bulimia nervosa: Basic research, diagnosis, and therapy.* Chichester, U.K.: Wiley.

Heston, L. L. (1966). Psychiatric disorders in foster home reared children of schizophrenic mothers. *British Journal of Psychiatry, 112*, 819–825.

Hetherington, E. (1989). Coping with family transitions: Winners, losers, and survivors. *Child Development, 60*, 1–14.

Hetherington, E. M., & Clingempeel, W. G. (1992). Coping with marital transitions. *Monographs of the Society for Research in Child Development, 57*(2–3, Serial No. 227).

Hever, F., & Reisberg, D. (1990). Vivid memories of emotional events: The accuracy of remembered minutiae. *Memory & Cognition, 18*, 496–506.

Higgins, E. T. (1987). Self-discrepancy: A theory relating self and affect. *Psychological Review, 94*, 319–340.

Higgins, E. T. (1989). Knowledge accessibility and activation: Subjectivity and suffering from unconscious sources. In J. S. Uleman & J. A. Bargh (Eds.), *Unintended thought.* New York: Guilford Press.

Hilgard, E. R. (1965). *Hypnotic susceptibility.* New York: Harcourt, Brace and World.

Hilgard, E. R. (1977). *Divided consciousness: Multiple controls in human thought and action.* New York: Wiley.

Hilgard, E. R. (1979). *Personality and hypnosis: A study of imaginative involvement.* Chicago: University of Chicago Press.

Hilgard, E. R. (1980). Consciousness in contemporary psychology. *Annual Review of Psychology, 31*, 1–26.

Hilgard, E. R. (1982). Hypnotic susceptibility and implications for measurement. *International Journal of Clinical and Experimental Hypnosis, 30*, 394–403.

Hilgard, E. R. (1992). Divided consciousness and dissociation. *Consciousness and Cognition, 1*, 16–31.

Hilgard, E. R., Morgan, A. H., & MacDonald, H. (1975). Pain and dissociation in the cold pressor test: A study of "hidden reports" through automatic key-pressing and automatic talking. *Journal of Abnormal Psychology, 84*, 280–289.

Hill, B. (1968). *Gates of horn and ivory.* New York: Taplinger.

Hill, C. E. (1990). Exploratory in-session process research in individual psychotherapy: A review. *Journal of Consulting and Clinical Psychology, 58*, 288–294.

Hill, D. L., & Mistretta, C. M. (1990). Developmental neurobiology of salt taste sensation. *Trends in Neuroscience, 13*, 188–195.

Hill, D. L., & Przekop, P. R., Jr. (1988). Influences of dietary sodium on functional taste receptor development: A sensitive period. *Science, 241*, 1826–1828.

Hill, D. L., Mistretta, C. M., & Bradley, R. M. (1986). Effects of dietary NaCl deprivation during early development on behavioral and neurophysiological taste responses. *Behavioral Neuroscience, 100*, 390–398.

Hill, T., Lewicki, P., Czyzewska, M., & Schuller, G. (1990). The role of learned inferential encoding rules in the perception of faces: Effects of nonconscious self-perpetuation of a bias. *Journal of Experimental Social Psychology, 26*, 350–371.

Hill, W. F. (1982). *Principles of learning.* Palo Alto, CA: Mayfield.

Hilton, H. (1986). *The executive memory guide.* New York: Simon & Schuster.

Hines, M., & Green, R. (1991). Human hormonal and neural correlates of sex-typed behavior. *Review of Psychiatry, 10*, 536–555.

Hinton, G. E. (1992, September). How neural networks learn for expense. *Scientific American, 267*, 145–151.

Hinton, J. (1967). *Dying.* Harmondsworth, UK: Penguin.

Hintzman, D. (1991). Human learning and memory. *Annual Review of Psychology, 110*–130.

Hintzman, D. L. (1978). *The psychology of learning and memory.* New York: W. H. Freeman.

Hintzman, D. L. (1986). Schema abstraction in a multiple trace memory model. *Psychological Review, 93*, 411–428.

Hintzman, D. L. (1988). Judgments of frequency and recognition memory in a multiple-trace memory model. *Psychological Review, 95*, 528–551.

Hiroto, D. S., & Seligman, M. E. P. (1975). Generality of learned helplessness in man. *Journal of Personality and Social Psychology, 31*, 311–327.

Hirsch, J., & Knittle, J. L. (1970). Cellularity of obese and nonobese human adipose tissue. *Federation of American Societies for Experimental Biology: Federation Proceedings, 29*, 1516–1521.

Hirsch-Pasek, K., Treiman, R., & Schneiderman, M. (1984). Brown and Hanlon revisited: Mothers' sensitivity to ungrammatical forms. *Journal of Child Language, 11*, 81–88.

Hirt, E. R., Deppe, R. K., & Gordon, L. J. (1991). Self-reported versus behavioral self-handicapping: Empirical evidence for a theoretical distinction. *Journal of Personality and Social Psychology, 61*, 981–991.

Hirtle, S. C., & Jonides, J. (1985). Evidence of hierarchies in cognitive maps. *Memory & Cognition, 13*, 208–217.

Hobfall, S. E. (1989). Conservation of resources: A new attempt at conceptualizing stress. *American Psychologist, 44*, 513–524.

Hochberg, J. E., & McAlister, E. (1955). Relative size versus familiar size in the perception of represented depth. *American Journal of Psychology, 68*, 294–296.

Hockey, G. R. (1984). Varieties of attentional state: The effects of environment. In R. Paraduraman & R. Davies (Eds.), *Varieties of attention.* New York: Academic Press.

Hockey, R. (1986). Changes in operator efficiency as a function of environmental stress. In K. Boff, L. Kaufman, & J. Thomas (Eds.), *Handbook of perception and human performance.* New York: Wiley.

Hodgkinson, S., Mullan, M. J., & Gurling, H. M. (1990). The role of genetic factors in the etiology of the affective disorders. *Behavior Genetics, 20*, 235–250.

Hoffert, M. J. (1992). The neurophysiology of pain. In G. M. Aronoff (Ed.), *Evaluation and treatment of chronic pain.* Baltimore: Williams & Wilkins.

Hoffman, C., & Hurst, N. (1990). Gender stereotypes: Perception or rationalization? *Journal of Personality and Social Psychology, 58*, 197–208.

Hoffman, L. (1991). The influence of the family environment on personality: Accounting for sibling differences. *Psychological Bulletin, 110*, 187–203.

Hoffman, L. R. (Ed.) (1979). *The group problem solving process: Studies of a valence model.* New York: Praeger.

Hoffman, L. R., & Maier, N. R. F. (1979). Valence in the adoption of solutions by problem-solving groups: Concept, method, and results. In L. R. Hoffman (Ed.), *The group problem solving process: Studies of a valence model.* New York: Praeger.

Hoffman, M. L. (1970). Moral development. In P. H. Mussen (Ed.), *Carmichael's manual of child psychology: Vol. 2.* New York: Wiley.

Hoffman, M. L. (1977). Sex differences in empathy and related behaviors. *Psychological Bulletin, 84,* 712–722.

Hofman, M. A., & Swaab, D. F. (1989). The sexually dimorphic nucleus of the preoptic area in the human brain: A comparative morphometric study. *Journal of Anatomy, 164,* 55–72.

Hogan, R., & Nicholson, R. A. (1988). The meaning of personality test scores. *American Psychologist, 43,* 621–626.

Hogarth, R. M., & Einhorn, H. J. (1992). Order effects in belief updating: The belief adjustment model. *Cognitive Psychology, 24,* 1–55.

Hogg, M. A., & Hardie, E. A. (1991). Social attraction, personal attraction, and self-categorization: A field study. *Personality and Social Psychology Bulletin, 17,* 175–180.

Hohmann, G. W. (1966). Some effects of spinal cord lesions on experienced emotional feelings. *Psychophysiology, 3,* 143–156.

Hoijer, U., Ejnell, H., Hedner, J., Petruson, B., & Eng, L. B. (1992). The effects of nasal dilation on snoring and obstructive sleep apnea. *Archives of Otolaryngology and Head and Neck Surgery, 118,* 281–284.

Holahan, C. J. (1986). Environmental psychology. *Annual Review of Psychology, 37,* 381–407.

Holahan, C. J., & Moos, R. H. (1987). Personality, coping, and family resources in stress resistance: A longitudinal analysis. *Journal of Personality and Social Psychology, 51,* 389–395.

Holahan, C. J., & Moos, R. H. (1990). Life stressors, resistance factors, and improved psychological functioning: An extension of the stress resistance paradigm. *Journal of Personality and Social Psychology, 58,* 909–917.

Holahan, C. K., Holahan, C. J., & Belk, S. S. (1984). Adjustment in aging: The role of life stress, hassles, and self-efficacy. *Health Psychology, 3,* 315–328.

Holahan, C., & Moos, R. (1991). Life stressors, personal and social resources and depressions: A 4-year structural model. *Journal of Abnormal Psychology, 100,* 31–38.

Holden, C. (1991). Probing the complex genetics of alcoholism. *Science, 251,* 163–164.

Holding, D. H. (1976). An approximate transfer surface. *Journal of Motor Behavior, 8,* 1–9.

Holding, D. H. (Ed.) (1989). *Human skills* (2nd ed.). New York: John Wiley & Sons.

Holender, D. (1986). Semantic activation without conscious identification. *Behavioral and Brain Sciences, 9,* 1–66.

Hollander, E. P. (1985). Leadership and power. In G. Lindzey & E. Aronson (Eds.), *The handbook of social psychology: Vol. 2* (3rd ed.). New York: Random House.

Hollander, E. P., & Offermann, L. R. (1990). Power and leadership in organizations: Relationships in transition. *American Psychologist, 45,* 179–189.

Hollon, S., Shelton, R., & Loosen, P. (1991). Cognitive therapy and pharmacotherapy for depression. *Journal of Consulting and Clinical Psychology, 59,* 88–99.

Holmes, D. S. (1984). Meditation and somatic arousal reduction: A review of the experimental evidence. *American Psychologist, 39,* 1–10.

Holmes, D. S. (1991). *Abnormal psychology.* New York: HarperCollins.

Holmes, T. H., & Masuda, M. (1974). Life change and illness susceptibility. In B. S. Dohrenwend & B. P. Dohrenwend (Eds.), *Stressful life events: Their nature and effects.* New York: John Wiley & Sons.

Holtzman, W. H. (1982). Cross-cultural comparison of personality development in Mexico and the United States. In D. A. Wagner & H. W. Stevenson (Eds.). *Cultural perspectives on child development* (pp. 225–247). San Francisco: W. H. Freeman.

Holway, A. H., & Boring, E. G. (1941). Determinants of apparent visual size with distance variant. *American Journal of Psychology, 54,* 21–37.

Honorton, C., & Harper, S. (1974). Psi-mediated imagery and ideation in an experimental procedure for regulating perceptual input. *Journal of the American Society for Psychical Research, 68,* 156–168.

Honorton, C., Berger, R. E., Varvoglis, M. P., Quant, M., Derr, P., Schechter, E. I., & Ferrari, D. C. (1990). Psi communication in the ganzfeld. *Journal of Parapsychology, 54,* 99–139.

Hooker, E. (1993). Reflections of a 40-year exploration: A scientific view on homosexuality. *American Psychologist, 48,* 450–453.

Horn, J. L. (1979). The rise and fall of human abilities. *Journal of Research and Development in Education, 12,* 59–78.

Horner, M. S. (1970). Femininity and successful achievement: A basic inconsistency. In J. M. Bardwicks (Ed.), *Feminine personality and conflict.* Monterey, CA: Brooks/Cole.

Horney, K. (1937). *Neurotic personality of our times.* New York: W. W. Norton.

Horowitz, A. V., & Horowitz, V. A. (1975). *The effects of task-specific instructions on the picture memory of children in recall and recognition tasks.* Paper presented at the Society for Research in Child Development, Denver, CO.

Horowitz, L. M., Rosenberg, S. E., Baer, B. A., Ureno, G., & Villasenor, V. S. (1988). The inventory of interpersonal problems: Psychometric properties and clinical applications. *Journal of Consulting and Clinical Psychology, 56,* 885–892.

Hosch, H. M., & Cooper, D. S. (1982). Victimization as a determinant of eyewitness accuracy. *Journal of Applied Psychology, 67,* 649–652.

House, J. S., Landis, K. R., & Umberson, D. (1988). Social relationships and health. *Science, 241,* 540–545.

House, J. S., Robbins, C., & Metzner, H. L. (1982). The association of social relationships and activities with mortality: Prospective evidence from the Tecumseh community health study. *American Journal of Epidemiology, 116,* 123–140.

House, J. S., Umberson, D., & Landis, K. R. (1988). Structures and processes of social support. *Annual Review of Sociology, 14,* 293–318.

Houston, B. K., & Snyder, C. R. (Eds.) (1987). *Type A behavior pattern: Current trends and future directions.* New York: Wiley.

Houston, B., & Vavac, C. (1991). Cynical hostility: Developmental factors, psychosocial correlates and health behaviors. *Health Psychology, 10,* 9–17.

Howard, D. V. (1983). *Cognitive psychology.* New York: Macmillan.

Howard, J. A., Blumstein, P., & Schwartz, P. (1987). Social or evolutionary theories? Some observations on preferences in human mate selection. *Journal of Personality and Social Psychology, 53,* 194–200.

Howard-Pitney, B., LaFramboise, T., Basil, M., September, B., & Johnson, M. (1992). Psychological and social indicators of suicide ideation and suicide attempts in Zuni adolescents. *Journal of Consulting and Clinical Psychology, 60,* 473–476.

Howe, M. J. A. (1970). Using students' notes to examine the role of the individual learner in acquiring meaningful subject matter. *Journal of Educational Research, 64,* 61–63.

Hoyer, W. J., & Plude, D. J. (1980). Attentional and perceptual processes in the study of cognitive aging. In L. W. Poon (Ed.), *Aging in the 1980s: Psychological issues.* Washington, DC: American Psychological Association.

Hsu, L. K. G. (1980). Outcome of anorexia nervosa: A review of the literature (1954 to 1978). *Archives of General Psychiatry, 37,* 1041–1046.

Hubel, D. H., & Wiesel, T. N. (1962). Receptive fields, binocular interaction and functional architecture in the cat's visual cortex. *Journal of Physiology, 160,* 106–154.

Hubel, D. H., & Wiesel, T. N. (1979). Brain mechanisms of vision. *Scientific American, 241,* 150–162.

Hudson, W. (1967). The study of the problem of pictorial representation among unacculturated groups. *International Journal of Psychology, 2,* 85–107.

Hudspeth, A. J. (1983). The hair cells of the inner ear. *Scientific American, 248,* 54–64.

Huesmann, L. R., Laperspetz, K., & Eron, L. D. (1984). Intervening variables in the TV violence-aggression relation: Evidence from two countries. *Developmental Psychology, 20,* 746–775.

Hugdahl, K., & Johnsen, B. H. (1989). Preparedness and electro-dermal fear-conditioning: Ontogenetic vs. phylogenetic explanations. *Behaviour Research and Therapy, 27,* 269–278.

Hughes, C. W., et al. (1984). Cerebral blood flow and cerebrovascular permeability in an inescapable shock (learned helplessness) animal model of depression. *Pharmacology, Biochemistry, and Behavior, 21,* 891–894.

Hughes, J. R., Gust, S. W., Skoog, K., Keenan, R. M., & Fenwick, J. W. (1991). Symptoms of tobacco withdrawal. *Archives of General Psychiatry, 48,* 52–59.

Hull, C. L. (1943). *Principles of behavior.* New York: Appleton-Century-Crofts.

Hull, C. L. (1951). *Essentials of behavior.* New Haven: Yale University Press.

Humphreys, K. (1993). Psychotherapy and the twelve-step approach for substance abusers: The limits of integration. *Psychotherapy, 30.*

Humphreys, L. G. (1984). General intelligence. In C. R. Reynolds & R. T. Brown (Eds.), *Perspectives on bias in mental testing.* New York: Plenum Press.

Humphreys, L. G. (1988). Trends in levels of academic achievement of blacks and other minorities. *Intelligence, 12,* 231–260.

Humphreys, L. G., & Davey, T. C. (1988). Continuity in intellectual growth from 12 months to 9 years. *Intelligence, 12,* 183–197.

Humphreys, M. S., Bain, J. D., & Pike, R. (1989). Different ways to cue a coherent memory system: A theory for episodic, semantic, and procedural tasks. *Psychological Review, 96,* 208–233.

Hunt, C. B. (1980). Intelligence as an information processing concept. *British Journal of Psychology, 71,* 449–474.

Hunt, E. (1983). On the nature of intelligence. *Science, 219,* 141–146.

Hunt, E. (1987). The next word on verbal ability. In P. A. Vernon (Ed.), *Speed of information-processing and intelligence* (pp. 347–392). Norwood, NJ: Ablex.

Hunt, E., & Lansman, M. (1983). Individual differences in intelligence. In R. Sternberg (Ed.), *Advances in the psychology of human intelligence.* Hillsdale, NJ: Lawrence Erlbaum Associates.

Hunt, M. (1982). *The universe within.* New York: Simon & Schuster.

Hunt, R., & Rouse, W. B. (1981). Problem solving skills of maintenance trainees in diagnosing faults in simulated power plants. *Human Factors, 23,* 317–328.

Hunter, E. J. (1979). *Combat casualties who remain at home.* Paper presented at Western Regional Conference of the Inter University Seminar, "Technology in Combat." Naval Postgraduate School, Monterey, CA.

Hunter, F. T., & Youniss, J. (1982). Changes in functions of three relations during adolescence. *Developmental Psychology, 18,* 806–811.

Hunter, J. E. (1986). Cognitive ability, cognitive aptitudes, job knowledge, and job performance. *Journal of Vocational Behavior, 29,* 340–362.

Hunter, J. E., & Hunter, R. F. (1984). Validity and utility of alternative predictors of job performance. *Psychological Bulletin, 96,* 72–98.

Hunter, M. A., & Ames, E. W. (1988). A multifactor model of infants' preferences for novel and familiar stimuli. In C. Rovee-Collier & L. P. Lipsitt (Eds.), *Advances in infancy research: Vol. 5* (pp. 69–91). Norwood, NJ: Ablex.

Hurd, M. W., & Ralph, M. R. (1992). Suprachiasmatic nucleus transplants normalize entrainment in aged *tau* mutant hamsters. *Society for Neuroscience Abstracts, 22,* 1223.

Hurst, R., & Hurst, L. (1982). *Pilot error.* London: Granada.

Huston, A. C. (1983). Sex-typing. In P. H. Mussen (Ed.), *Handbook of child psychology: Vol. 4* (4th ed.). New York: Wiley.

Huston, A. C., & Wright, J. C. (1989). The forms of television and the child viewer. In G. Comstock (Ed.), *Public communication and behavior* (Vol. 2). San Diego: Academic Press.

Huston, A. C., Carpenter, C. J., & Atwater, J. B. (1986). Gender, adult structuring of activities, and social behavior in middle childhood. *Child Development, 57,* 1200–1209.

Huston, J. P., Mueller, C. C., & Mondadore, C. (1977). Memory facilitation by post-trial hypothalamus stimulation and other reinforcements. *Biobehavioral Review, 13,* 171–180.

Huttenlocher, J. (1974). The origins of language comprehension. In R. L. Solso (Ed.), *Theories in cognitive psychology.* Hillsdale, NJ: Lawrence Erlbaum Associates.

Huttenlocher, P. R. (1979). Synaptic density in human frontal cortex: Developmental changes and effects of aging. *Brain Research, 163,* 195–205.

Hyde, J. S. (1986). Gender differences in aggression. In J. S. Hyde & M. C. Linn (Eds.), *The psychology of gender: Advances through meta-analysis.* Baltimore: Johns Hopkins University Press.

Hyde, J. S., & Phillis, D. E. (1979). Androgyny across the life span. *Developmental Psychology, 15,* 334–336.

Hyde, J. S., Fennema, E., & Lamon, S. J. (1990). Gender differences in mathematics performance: A meta-analysis. *Psychological Bulletin, 107,* 139–155.

Hyman, H., & Barmack, J. E. (1954). Special review: Sexual behavior in the human female. *Psychological Bulletin, 51,* 418–427.

Hyman, M. D. (1971). Disability and patients' perceptions of preferential treatment: Some preliminary findings. *Journal of Chronic Diseases, 24,* 329–342.

Ibrahim, F. (1991). Contributions of cultural worldview to generic counseling and development. *Journal of Counseling and Development, 70,* 13–19.

Ickovics, J., & Rodin, J. (1992). Women and AIDS in the United States: Epidemiology, natural history, and mediating mechanisms. *Health Psychology, 11,* 1–16.

Ilgen, D. R., & Klein, H. J. (1989). Organizational behavior. *Annual Review of Psychology, 40,* 327–351.

Infant Health and Development Program. (1990). Enhancing the outcomes of low-birth-weight, premature infants. *Journal of the American Medical Association, 263,* 3035–3042.

Ingham, A. G., Levinger, G., Graves, J., & Peckham, V. (1974). The Ringelmann effect: Studies of group size and group performance. *Journal of Experimental Social Psychology, 10,* 371–384.

Innes, C. A. (1988). *Profile of state prison inmates.* Washington, DC: Bureau of Justice Statistics.

Insko, C. A., Drenan, S., Solomon, M. R., Smith, R., & Wade, T. J. (1983). Conformity as a function of the consistency of positive self-evaluation with being liked and being right. *Journal of Experimental Social Psychology, 19,* 341–358.

Insko, C. A., Schopler, J., Hoyle, R. H., Dardis, G. J., & Graetz, K. A. (1990). Individual-group discontinuity as a function of fear and greed. *Journal of Personality and Social Psychology, 58,* 68–79.

Insko, C. A., Smith, R. H., Alicke, M. D., Wade, J., & Taylor, S. (1985). Conformity and group size: The concern with being right and the concern with being liked. *Personality and Social Psychology Bulletin, 11,* 41–50.

Irons, W. (1989). Mating preferences surveys: Ethnographic follow-up would be a good next step. *Behavioral and Brain Sciences, 12,* 24–26.

Irwin, M., Daniels, M., Smith, T., Bloom, E., & Weiner, H. (1987). *Brain, Behavior, and Immunity, 1,* 98–104.

Isabella, R. A., Belsky, J., & von Eye, A. (1989). Origins of infant-mother attachment: An examination of interactional synchrony during the infant's first year. *Developmental Psychology, 25,* 12–21.

Isenberg, D. J. (1986). Group polarization: A critical review and meta-analysis. *Journal of Personality and Social Psychology, 50,* 1141–1151.

Istomina, Z. M. (1975). The development of voluntary memory in pre-school age children. *Soviet Psychology, 13,* 5–64.

Ivancevich, J. M., Matteson, M. T., Freedman, S. M., & Phillips, J. S. (1990). Worksite stress management interventions. *American Psychologist, 45,* 252–261.

Izard, C. E. (1971). *The face of emotion.* New York: Appleton-Century-Crofts, New York.

Izard, C. E. (1977). *Human emotions.* New York: Plenum Press.

Izard, C. E. (1990). Facial expressions and the regulation of emotions. *Journal of Personality and Social Psychology, 58,* 487–498.

Jacklin, C. N. (1989). Female and male: Issues of gender. *American Psychologist, 44,* 127–133.

Jackson, D. (1980). Reunion of identical twins, raised apart, reveals some astonishing similarities. *Smithsonian,* 48–56.

Jackson, D. N. (1967). *Personality Research Form Manual.* Goshen, NY: Research Psychologists Press.

Jackson, D. N. (1984). *Personality Research Form Manual* (3rd ed.). Port Huron, MI: Research Psychologists Press.

Jackson, J. M., Buglione, S. A., & Glenwick, D. S. (1988). Major league baseball performance as a function of being traded: A drive theory analysis. *Personality and Social Psychology Bulletin, 14,* 46–56.

Jackson, S. E. (1991). Team composition in organizational settings: Issues in managing an increasingly diverse work force. In S. Worchel, W. Woods, & J. Simpson (Eds.), *Group process and productivity.* Newbury Park, CA: Sage.

Jacobs, B. L. (1987). How hallucinogenic drugs work. *American Scientist, 75,* 386–392.

Jacobs, M. K., & Goodman, G. (1989). Psychology and self-help groups: Predictions on a partnership. *American Psychologist, 44,* 536–545.

Jacobson, A., Kales, J., & Kales, A. (1969). Clinical and electrophysiological correlates of sleep disorders in children. In A. Kales (Ed.), *Sleep: Physiology and pathology.* Philadelphia: J. B. Lippincott.

Jacobson, E. (1938). *Progressive relaxation.* Chicago: University of Chicago Press.

Jacobson, N., & Truax, P. (1991). Clinical significance: A statistical approach to defining meaningful change in psychotherapy research. *Journal of Consulting and Clinical Psychology, 59,* 12–19.

Jacoby, L. L., Lindsay, D. S., & Toth, J. P. (1992). Unconscious influences revealed: Attention, awareness, and control. *American Psychologist, 47,* 802–809.

Jacoby, L. L., Marriott, M. J., & Collins, J. G. (1990). The specifics of memory and cognition. In T. K. Srull & R. S. Wyer (Eds.), *Advances in social cognition: Vol. III. Content and process specificity in the effects of prior experiences.* Hillsdale, NJ: Lawrence Erlbaum Associates.

Jacoby, T., & Padgett, T. (1989, August 7). Waking up the jury box. *Newsweek,* p. 51.

Jaffe, J. H. (1975). Drug addiction and drug abuse. In L. S. Goodman & A. Gilman (Eds.), *The parmacological basis of therapeutics* (5th ed.). New York: Macmillan.

Jahn, R. (1982). The persistent paradox of ESP: An engineering perspective. *Proceedings of the IEEE, 70,* 136–170.

James, W. (1890). *Principles of psychology.* New York: Holt.

James, W. (1892). *Psychology: Briefer course.* New York: Holt.

Jamison, K. R. (1984). Manic-depressive illness and accomplishment: Creativity, leadership, and social class. In F. K. Goodwin & K. R. Jamison (Eds.), *Manic-depressive illness.* New York: Oxford University Press.

Janicak, P. C., Davis, J. M., Gibbons, R. D., Ericksen, S., Chang, S., & Gallagher, P. (1985). Efficacy of ECT: A meta-analysis. *American Journal of Psychiatry, 142,* 297–302.

Janicak, P., Sharma, R., Israni, T., Dowd, S., Altman, E., & Davis, J. (1991). Effects of unilateral-nondominant vs. bilateral ECT on memory and depression: A preliminary report. *Psychopharmacology Bulletin, 27,* 353–357.

Janis, I. L. (1985). Sources of error in strategic decision making. In J. M. Pennings (Ed.), *Organizational strategy and change.* San Francisco: Jossey-Bass.

Jann, M. W. (1988). Buspirone: An update on a unique anxiolytic agent. *Pharmacotherapy, 8,* 100–116.

Janowitz, H. D. (1967). Role of gastrointestinal tract in the regulation of food intake. In C. F. Code (Ed.), *Handbook of physiology: Alimentary canal 1.* Washington, DC: American Physiological Society.

Janowitz, H. D., & Grossman, M. I. (1949). Some factors affecting the food intake of normal dogs and dogs with esophagostomy and gastric fistula. *American Journal of Physiology, 159,* 143–148.

Janowitz, H. D., & Grossman, M. I. (1951). Effect of prefeeding, alcohol and bitters on food intake of dogs. *American Journal of Physiology, 164,* 182–186.

Janz, N., & Becker, M. (1984). The health beliefs model: A decade later. *Health Education Monographs, 11,* 1–47.

Jellinek, E. M. (1960). *The disease concept of alcoholism.* New Haven: Hillhouse Press.

Jellison, J. M., & Oliver, D. F. (1983). Attitude similarity and attraction: An impression management approach. *Personality and Social Psychology Bulletin, 9,* 111–115.

Jemmott, J. B., & Locke, S. E. (1984). Psychosocial factors, immunologic mediation, and human susceptibility to infectious diseases: How much do we know? *Psychological Bulletin, 95,* 78–108.

Jemmott, J. B., III, & Magloire, K. (1988). Academic stress, social support, and secretory immunoglobulin A. *Journal of Personality and Social Psychology, 55,* 803–810.

Jenike, M., Baer, L., Ballantine, T., Martuza, R., Tynes, S., Giriunas, I., Buttolph, L., & Cassem, N. (1991). Cingulotomy for refractory obsessive-compulsive disorder: A long-term follow-up of 33 patients. *Archives of General Psychiatry, 48,* 548–555.

Jenkins, J. G., & Dallenbach, K. M. (1924). Oblivescence during sleep and waking. *American Journal of Psychology, 35,* 605–612.

Jenkins, J., & Karno, M. (1992). The meaning of expressed emotion: Theoretical issues raised by cross-cultural research. *American Journal of Psychiatry, 149,* 9–21.

Jensen, A. R. (1969). How much can we boost IQ and scholastic achievement? *Harvard Educational Review, 39,* 1–123.

Jensen, A. R. (1993). Why is reaction time correlated with psychometric g? *Current Directions in Psychological Science, 2,* 53–55.

Jensen, J. P., Bergin, A. E., & Greaves, D. W. (1990). The meaning of eclecticism: New survey and analysis of components. *Professional Psychology: Research and Practice, 21,* 124–130.

Jensen, M. R. (1987). Psychological factors predicting the course of breast cancer. *Journal of Personality, 55,* 317–342.

Jensen, M., & Karoly, P. (1991). Control beliefs, coping efforts, and adjustment to chronic pain. *Journal of Consulting and Clinical Psychology, 59,* 431–438.

Jeremy, R. J., & Hans, S. L. (1985) . Behavior of neonates exposed in utero to methadone as assessed on the Brazelton Scale. *Infant Behavior and Development, 8,* 323–336.

Jessop, J. J., West, G. L., & Sobotka, T. J. (1989). Immunomodulatory effects of footshock in the rat. *Journal of Immunology, 25,* 241–249.

Johansson, G., Hofsten, C. V., & Jansson, G. (1980). Event perception. *Annual Review of Psychology, 31,* 27–63.

John, R. (1982). The persistent paradox of psychic phenomena: An engineering perspective. *Proceedings of the IEEE, 70,* 136–170.

Johnson, B. T., & Eagly, A. H. (1989). Effects of involvement on persuasion: A meta-analysis. *Psychological Bulletin, 106,* 290–314.

Johnson, C., & Maddi, K. L. (1986). The etiology of bulimia: Bio-psycho-social perspectives. *Annals of Adolescent Psychiatry, 13,* 253–273.

Johnson, D. L. (1989). Schizophrenia as a brain disease. *American Psychologist, 44,* 553–555.

Johnson, H. H., & Torcivia, J. M. (1967). Group and individual performance on a single-stage task as a function of distribution of individual performance. *Journal of Experimental Social Psychology, 3,* 266–273.

Johnson, J. S., & Newport, E. L. (1989). Critical period effects in second language learning. *Cognitive Psychology, 21,* 60–99.

Johnson, J., Weissman, M., & Klerman, G. (1990). Panic disorder, comorbidity, and suicide attempts. *Archives of General Psychiatry, 47,* 805–808.

Johnson, M. A., Dziurawiec, S., Ellis, H., & Morton, J. (1991). Newborns' preferential tracking of face-like stimuli and its subsequent decline. *Cognition, 4,* 1–19.

Johnson, M. K., & Hasher, L. (1987). Human learning and memory. *Annual Review of Psychology, 38,* 631–668.

Johnson, R. E., Jaffe, J. H., & Fudala, P. J. (1992). A controlled trial of buprenorphine treatment for opioid dependence. *Journal of the American Medical Association, 267,* 2750–2755.

Johnson, S. L., McPhee, L., & Birch, L. L. (1991). Conditioned preferences: Young children prefer flavors associated with high dietary fat. *Physiology and Behavior, 50,* 1245–1251.

Johnson-Laird, P. N. (1983). *Mental models.* Cambridge: Harvard University Press.

Johnson-Laird, P. N., & Steedman, M. (1978). The psychology of syllogisms. *Cognitive Psychology, 10,* 64–99.

Johnston, L. D., O'Malley, P. M., & Bachman, J. G. (1987). *National trends in drug use and related factors among American high school students and young adults, 1975–1986.* Rockville, MD: National Institute on Drug Abuse.

Johnston, L. D., O'Malley, P. M., & Bachman, J. G. (1989). *Drug use, drinking, and smoking: National survey results from high school, college, and young adult populations, 1975–1988.* Rockville, MD: National Institute on Drug Abuse.

Jones, D. M. (1989). Culture and testing. *American Psychologist, 44,* 360–366.

Jones, G. V. (1989). Back to Woodworth: Role of interlopers in the tip-of-the-tongue phenomenon. *Memory & Cognition, 17,* 69–76.

Jones, G. V. (1990). Misremembering a common object: When left is not right. *Memory & Cognition, 18,* 174–182.

Jones, J. W. (1978). Adverse emotional reactions of nonsmokers to secondary cigarette smoke. *Environmental Psychology and Nonverbal Behavior, 3,* 125–127.

Jones, L. V., & Appelbaum, M. I. (1989). Psychometric methods. *Annual Review of Psychology, 40,* 23–44.

Jones, M. C. (1957). The later careers of boys who were early or late maturing. *Child Development, 28,* 113–128.

Jones, R. T. (1984). The pharmacology of cocaine. In J. Grabowski (Ed.), *Cocaine: Pharmacology, effects, and treatment of abuse.* Rockville, MD: National Institute on Drug Abuse.

Jordan, H. A. (1969). Voluntary intragastric feeding: Oral and gastric contributions to food intake and hunger in man. *Journal of Comparative and Physiological Psychology, 68,* 498–506.

Jordan, N. C., Huttenlocher, J., & Levine, S. C. (1992). Differential calculation abilities in young children from middle- and low-income families. *Developmental Psychology, 28,* 644–653.

Jordan, T. G., Grallo, R., Deutch, M., & Deutch, C. P. (1985). Long-term effects of enrichment: A 20-year perspective on persistence and change. *American Journal of Community Psychology, 13,* 393–414.

Josephs, R., Markus, R., & Tafarodi, R. (1992). Gender and self-esteem. *Journal of Personality and Social Psychology, 63,* 391–402.

Josephson, W. L. (1987). Television violence and children's aggression: Testing the priming, social script, and disinhibition predictions. *Journal of Personality and Social Psychology, 53,* 882–890.

Judd, C. M., Drake, R. A., Downing, J. W., & Krosnick, J. A. (1991). Some dynamic properties of attitude structures: Context-induced response facilitation and polarization. *Journal of Personality and Social Psychology, 60,* 193–202.

Julien, R. M. (1992). *A primer of drug action* (6th ed.). New York: W. H. Freeman.

Jung, C. G. (1916). *Analytical psychology.* New York: Moffat.

Jung, C. G. (1933). *Psychological types.* New York: Harcourt, Brace and World.

Jussim, L. (1989). Teacher expectations: Self-fulfilling prophecies, perceptual biases, and accuracy. *Journal of Personality and Social Psychology, 57,* 469–480.

Just, M., & Carpenter, P. (1992). A capacity theory of comprehension: Individual differences in working memory. *Psychological Review, 99,* 122–149.

Justice, A. (1985). Review of the effects of stress on cancer in laboratory animals: Importance of time of stress application and type of tumor. *Psychological Bulletin, 98,* 108–138.

Kadden, R. M., Cooney, N. L., Getter, H., & Litt, M. D. (1990). Matching alcoholics to coping skills or interactional therapies: Posttreatment results. *Journal of Consulting and Clinical Psychology, 57,* 698–704.

Kagan, J. (1984). *The nature of the child.* New York: Basic Books.

Kagan, J. (1988). The meanings of personality predicates. *American Psychologist, 43,* 614–620.

Kagan, J. (1989). Temperamental contributions to social behavior. *American Psychologist, 44,* 668–674.

Kagan, J., & Snidman, N. (1991). Temperamental factors in human development. *American Psychologist, 46,* 856–862.

Kagan, J., Kearsley, R. B., & Zelazo, P. R. (1978). *Infancy: Its place in human development.* Cambridge: Harvard University Press.

Kagan, J., Reznick, J. S., & Snidman, N. (1988). Biological bases of childhood shyness. *Science, 240,* 167–171.

Kagan, J., Reznick, J. S., Snidman, N., Gibbons, J., & Johnson, M. O. (1988). Childhood derivatives of inhibition and lack of inhibition to the unfamiliar. *Child Development, 59,* 1580–1589.

Kagitcibasi, C., & Berry, J. W. (1989). Cross-cultural psychology: Current research and trends. *Annual Review of Psychology, 40,* 493–531.

Kahn, A. S. (1984). *Social psychology.* Dubuque, IA: William C. Brown.

Kahneman, D., & Tversky, A. (1984). Choices values and frames. *American Psychologist, 39,* 341–356.

Kahneman, D., Beatty, J., & Pollack, I. (1967). Perceptual deficits during a mental task. *Science, 157,* 218–219.

Kahneman, D., Slovic, P., & Tversky, A. (Eds.) (1982). *Judgment under uncertainty: Heuristics and biases.* New York: Cambridge University Press.

Kalaska, J. F., & Crammond, D. J. (1992). Cerebral cortical mechanisms of reaching movements. *Science, 255*, 1517–1523.

Kales, A., & Kales, J. (1973). Recent advances in the diagnosis and treatment of sleep disorders. In G. Usdin (Ed.), *Sleep research and clinical practice.* New York: Brunner/Mazel.

Kalichman, S. C., Kelly, J. A., Hunter, T. L., Murphy, D. A., & Tyler, R. (1993). Culturally tailored HIV-AIDS risk-reduction messages targeted to African-American urban women: Impact on risk sensitization and risk reduction. *Journal of Consulting and Clinical Psychology, 61*, 291–295.

Kalick, S. M. (1988). Physical attractiveness as a status cue. *Journal of Experimental Social Psychology, 24*, 469–489.

Kalish, H. I. (1981). *From behavioral science to behavior modification.* New York: McGraw-Hill.

Kalivas, P. W., & Nemerroff, C. B. (Eds.) (1988). *The mesolimbic dopamine system: Annals of the New York Academy of Sciences: Vol. 537.* New York: New York Academy of Sciences.

Kamin, L. J. (1969). Predictability, surprise, attention and conditioning. In B. A. Campbell & R. M. Church (Eds.), *Punishment and aversive behavior.* New York: Appleton-Century-Crofts.

Kamin, L. J. (1986). Is there crime in the genes? The answer may depend on who chooses what evidence. *Scientific American, 254*, 22–27.

Kandel, D. B., Davies, M., Karus, D., & Yamaguchi, K. (1986). The consequences in young adulthood of adolescent drug involvement: An overview. *Archives of General Psychiatry, 43*, 746–754.

Kandel, E. (1976). *Cellular basis of behavior.* San Francisco: Freeman.

Kanfer, F. (1992). Motivation and emotion in behavior therapy. Paper presented at the Banff Conference on Behavior Therapy, Banff, Alberta, Canada, May.

Kaniasty, K., & Norris, F. H. (1993). A test of the social support deterioration model in the context of natural disaster. *Journal of Personality and Social Psychology, 64*, 395–408.

Kanner, A. D., Coyne, J. C., Schaefer, C., & Lazarus, R. S. (1981). Comparison of two modes of stress measurement: Daily hassles and uplifts versus major life events. *Journal of Behavioral Medicine, 4*, 1–39.

Kaplan, H. S. (1974). *The new sex therapy.* New York: Brunner/Mazel.

Kaplan, H. S. (1979). *Disorders of sexual desire.* New York: Brunner/Mazel.

Kaplan, M. F. (1987). The influencing process in group decision making. In C. Hendrick (Ed.), *Group processes.* Newbury Park, CA: Sage.

Kaplan, M. F., & Miller, C. E. (1987). Group decision making and normative vs. informational influence: Effects of type of issue and assigned decision rule. *Journal of Personality and Social Psychology, 53*, 306–313.

Kaplan, R. M., & Hartwell, S. L. (1987). Differential effects of social support and social network on physiological and social outcomes in men and women with Type II diabetes mellitus. *Health Psychology, 6*, 387–398.

Karasek, R., & Theorell, T. (1990). *Healthy work: Job stress, productivity, and the reconstruction of working life.* New York: Basic Books.

Karlins, M., Coffman, T. L., & Walter, G. (1969). On the fading of social stereotypes: Studies in three generations of college students. *Journal of Personality and Social Psychology, 13*, 1–16.

Karni, A., Tanne, D., Rubinstein, B. S., Askenasi, J. J. M., & Sagi, D. (1992). No dreams—no memory: The effect of REM sleep deprivation on learning a new perceptual skill. *Society for Neuroscience Abstracts, 22*, 387.

Karno, M., Hough, R. L., Burnam, M., Escobar, J. I., Timbers, D. M.,

Santana, F., & Boyd, J. (1987). Lifetime prevalence of specific psychiatric disorders among Mexican Americans and non-Hispanic whites in Los Angeles. *Archives of General Psychiatry, 44*, 695–701.

Kasper, S., Wehr, T., Bartko, J., Gaist, P., & Rosenthal, N. (1989). Epidemiological findings of seasonal changes in mood and behavior. *Archives of General Psychiatry, 46*, 823–833.

Kassin, S. M., Rigby, S., & Castillo, S. R. (1991). The accuracy-confidence correlation in eyewitness testimony: Limits and extensions of the retrospective self-awareness effect. *Journal of Personality and Social Psychology, 61*, 698–707.

Kastenbaum, R. (1965). Wine and fellowship in aging: An exploratory action program. *Journal of Human Relations, 13*, 266–275.

Kastenbaum, R., Kastenbaum, B. K., & Morris, J. (1989). Strengths and preferences of the terminally ill: Data from the National Hospice Demonstration Study.

Kathol, R., Jaekle, R., Lopez, J., & Meller, W. (1989). Pathophysiology of HPA axis abnormalities in patients with major depression: An update. *American Journal of Psychiatry, 146*, 311–317.

Kato, S., Wakasa, Y., & Yanagita, T. (1987). Relationship between minimum reinforcing doses and injection speed in cocaine and pentobarbital self-administration in crab-eating monkeys. *Pharmacology, Biochemistry, and Behavior, 28*, 407–410.

Katsanis, J., & Iacono, W. G. (1991). Clinical neuropsychological and brain correlates of smooth-pursuit eye tracking performance in chronic schizophrenia. *Journal of Abnormal Psychology, 100*, 526–534.

Katzell, R. A., & Thompson, D. E. (1990). Work motivation: Theory and practice. *American Psychologist, 45*, 144–153.

Katzenstein, L. (1992). Why do I feel so tired? *American Health,* May, 51–56.

Kauffman, J. M., Gerber, M. M., & Semmel, M. I. (1988). Arguable assumptions underlying the regular education initiative. *Journal of Learning Disabilities, 21*, 6–11.

Kaufman, A. S. & Harrison, P. L. (1991). Individual intellectual assessment. In E. E. Walker (Ed.), *Clinical psychology: Historical and research foundations.* New York: Plenum.

Kaufman, A. S., & Kaufman, N. L. (1983). *Kaufman assessment battery for children.* Circle Pines, MN: American Guidance Services.

Kaufman, L., & Rock, I. (1962). The moon illusion. *Science, 136*, 953–961.

Kaufman, M. T. (1980). Love upsetting Bombay's view of path to altar. *New York Times,* November 16.

Kaufman, R., Maland, J., & Yonas, A. (1981). Sensitivity of 5- and 7-month-old infants to pictorial depth information. *Journal of Experimental Child Psychology, 32*, 162–168.

Kavanaugh, R. D., & Jirkovsky, A. M. (1982). Parental speech to young children: A longitudinal analysis. *Merrill-Palmer Quarterly, 28*, 297–311.

Kawakami, K. (1987, July). Comparison of mother-infant relationships in Japanese and American families. Paper presented at the meetings of the International Society for the Study of Behavioral Development, Tokyo, Japan.

Kazdin, A. E. (1978). Evaluating the generality of findings in analogue therapy research. *Journal of Consulting and Clinical Psychology, 46*, 673–686.

Kazdin, A. E. (1982). The token economy: A decade later. *Journal of Applied Behavior Analysis, 15*, 431–445.

Kazdin, A. E. (1984). *Behavior modification in applied settings* (3rd ed.). Homewood, IL: Dorsey Press.

Kazdin, A. E., & Bootzin, R. R. (1972). The token economy: An evaluative review. *Journal of Applied Behavior Analysis, 5*, 343–372.

Kazdin, A. E., & Wilson, G. T. (1978). *Evaluation of behavior therapy: Issues, evidence, and research strategies.* Cambridge: Ballinger.

Kazdin, A. E., Bass, D., Siegel, T., & Thomas, C. (1989). Cognitive behavioral therapy and relationship therapy in the treatment of children referred for antisocial behavior. *Journal of Consulting and Clinical Psychology, 57,* 522–535.

Kazdin, A. E., Siegel, T., & Bass, D. (1992). Cognitive problem-solving skills training and parent management training in the treatment of antisocial behavior in children. *Journal of Consulting and Clinical Psychology, 60,* 733–747.

Keane, T. M., Lisman, S. A., & Kreutzer, J. (1980). Alcoholic beverages and their placebos: An empirical evaluation of expectancies. *Addictive Behavior, 4,* 313–328.

Keating, D. P. (1980). Thinking processes in adolescence. In J. Adelson (Ed.), *Handbook of adolescent psychology.* New York: Wiley.

Keele, S. W. (1973). *Attention and human performance.* Pacific Palisades, CA: Goodyear.

Keenan, S. A. (1992). Polysomnography: Technical aspects in adolescents and adults. *Journal of Clinical Neurophysiology, 9,* 21–31.

Keeney, T. J., Cannizzo, S. R., & Flavell, J. H. (1967). Spontaneous and induced verbal rehearsal in a recall task. *Child Development, 38,* 953–966.

Keesey, R. E. (1980). A set-point analysis of the regulation of body weight. In A. J. Stunkard (Ed.), *Obesity.* Philadelphia: W. B. Saunders.

Keesey, R. E., & Powley, T. L. (1975). Hypothalamic regulation of body weight. *American Scientist, 63,* 558–565.

Keesey, R. E., & Powley, T. L. (1986). The regulation of body weight. *Annual Review of Psychology, 37,* 109–133.

Keinan, G., Friedland, N., & Ben-Porath, Y. (1987). Decision making under stress: Scanning of alternatives under physical threat. *Acta Psychologica, 64,* 219–228.

Keller, A., Ford, L. H., & Meacham, J. A. (1978). Dimensions of self-concept in preschool children. *Developmental Psychology, 14,* 483–489.

Kelley, H. H. (1973). The processes of causal attribution. *American Psychologist, 28,* 107–128.

Kelley, J. A., St. Lawrence, J. S., Hood, H. V., & Brasfield, T. L. (1989). Behavioral intervention to reduce AIDS risk activities. *Journal of Consulting and Clinical Psychology, 57,* 60–67.

Kelley, K. W. (1985). Immunological consequences of changing environmental stimuli. In G. P. Moberg (Ed.), *Animal stress.* Bethesda, MD: American Physiological Society.

Kelley, K., Dawson, L., & Musialowski, D. M. (1989). Three faces of sexual explicitness: The good, the bad, and the useful. In D. Zillmann & J. Bryant (Eds.), *Pornography: Research advances and policy considerations.* Hillsdale, NJ: Sage.

Kellogg, R. T. (1988). Attentional overload and writing performance: Effects of rough draft and outline strategies. *Journal of Experimental Psychology: Learning, Memory, and Cognition, 14,* 355–365.

Kelly, D. H., & Burbeck, C. A. (1984). Critical problems in spatial vision (review). *Critical Reviews in Biomedical Engineering, 10,* 2, 125–177.

Kelly, G. A. (1955). *The psychology of personal contructs.* New York: W. W. Norton.

Kelly, J. A., & St. Lawrence, J. S. (1988). AIDS prevention and treatment: Psychology's role in the health crisis. *Clinical Psychology Review, 8,* 255–284.

Kelly, J., & Murphy, D. (1992). Psychological intervention with AIDS and HIV: Prevention and treatment. *Journal of Consulting and Clinical Psychology, 60,* 576–585.

Kelly, J., Murphy, D., Bahr, G., Brasfield, T., Davis, D., Hauth, A., Morgan, M., Stevenson, L., & Eilers, K. (1992). AIDS/HIV risk behavior among the chronically mentally ill. *American Journal of Psychiatry, 149,* 886–889.

Kelman, H. C., & Hamilton, V. L. (1989). *Crimes of obedience.* New Haven, CT: Yale University Press.

Kemp, J. S., & Thatch, B. T. (1991). Sudden death in infants sleeping on polystyrene-filled cushions. *New England Journal of Medicine, 324,* 1858–1864.

Kempe, H. C., & Helfer, R. E. (Eds.) (1972). *Helping the battered child and his family.* Philadelphia: Lippincott.

Kendall, P., & Lipman, A. (1991). Psychological and pharmacological therapy: Methods and modes for comparative outcome research. *Journal of Consulting and Clinical Psychology, 59,* 78–87.

Kendler, K. S., Heath, A., Martin, M. G., & Eaves, L. J. (1986). Symptoms of anxiety and depression in a volunteer twin population: The etiologic role of genetic and environmental factors. *Archives of General Psychiatry 43,* 213–221.

Kennedy, J. L., Giuffra, L. A., Moises, H. W., Cavalli-Sforza, L. L., Pakstis, A. J., Kidd, J. R., Castiglione, C. M., Sjogren, B., Wettermberg, L., & Kidd, K. K. (1988). Evidence against linkage of schizophrenia to markers on chromosome 5 in northern Swedish pedigree. *Nature, 336,* 167–170.

Kenrick, D. T. (1989). Selflessness examined: Is avoiding tar and feathers nonegoistic? *Behavioral and Brain Sciences, 12,* 711–712.

Kenrick, D. T., & Funder, D. C. (1988). Profiting from controversy: Lessons from the person-situation debate. *American Psychologist, 43,* 23–34.

Kenrick, D. T., & Keefe, R. C. (1990). Age preferences in mates reflect sex differences in reproductive strategies. Unpublished manuscript, Arizona State University.

Kent, S., Bluthe, R. M., Kelley, K. W., & Dantzer, R. (1992). Sickness behavior as a new target for drug development. *Trends in Pharmacological Sciences, 13,* 24–28.

Kernberg, O. (1976). *Object relations theory and clinical psychoanalysis.* New York: Jason Aronsen.

Kernis, M. H., Brockner, J., & Frankel, B. J. (1989). Self-esteem and reactions to failure: The mediating role of overgeneralization. *Journal of Personality and Social Psychology, 57,* 707–714.

Kerns, K. (1991). Data-link communication between controllers and pilots: A review and synthesis of the simulation literature. *The International Journal of Aviation Psychology, 1,* 181–204.

Kessler, M., & Albee, G. W. (1975). Primary prevention. *Annual Review of Psychology, 26,* 557–591.

Kessler, R. C., Downey, G., Milavsky, J. R., & Stipp, H. (1988). Clustering of teenage suicides after television news stories about suicides: A reconsideration. *American Journal of Psychiatry, 145,* 1379–1383.

Kety, S. S., Rosenthal, D., Wender, P. H., Schulsinger, F., & Jacobson, B. (1975). Mental illness in the biological and adoptive families of adopted individuals who have become schizophrenic: A preliminary report based on psychiatric interviews. In R. R. Fieve, D. Rosenthal, & H. Brill (Eds.), *Genetic research in psychiatry.* Baltimore: Johns Hopkins University Press.

Keys, A., Brozek, J., Henschel, A., Mickelson, O., & Taylor, H. (1950). *The biology of human starvation.* Minneapolis: University of Minnesota Press.

Kiecolt-Glaser, J. K., & Glaser, R. (1987). Psychosocial moderators of immune function. *Annals of Behavioral Medicine, 9,* 16–20.

Kiecolt-Glaser, J. K., Garner, W., Speicher, C. E., Penn, G. M., Holliday, J., & Glaser, R. (1984). Psychosocial modifiers of immunocompetence in medical students. *Psychosomatic Medicine, 46,* 7–14.

Kiecolt-Glaser, J., & Glaser, R., (1992). Psychoneuroimmunology: Can psychological interventions modulate immunity? *Journal of Consulting and Clinical Psychology, 60,* 569–575.

Kiesler, C. A. (1982). Mental hospitals and alternative care: Non-institutionalization as potential public policy for mental patients. *American Psychologist, 37,* 349–360.

Kiesler, C. A., & Sibulkin, A. E. (1989). *Mental hospitalization: Myths and facts about a national crisis.* Newbury Park, CA: Sage.

Kiesler, D. J. (1986). The 1982 interpersonal circle: An analysis of DSM-III personality disorders. In T. Millon & G. L. Klerman (Eds.), *Contemporary directions in psychopathology: Towards the DSM-IV.* New York: Guilford.

Kiesler, S., & Sproull, L. (1992). Group decision making and communications technology. *Organizational Behavior and Human Decision Processes, 52,* 96–123.

Kihlstrom, J. F. (1987). The cognitive unconscious. *Science, 237,* 1445–1452.

Kihlstrom, J. F. (1993). What does the self look like? In T. K. Srull & R. S. Wyer (Eds.), *The mental representation of trait and autobiographical knowledge about the self: Advances in social cognition: Vol. V.* Hillsdale, NJ: Lawrence Erlbaum Associates.

Kihlstrom, J. F., & Klein, S. B. (1994). The self as a knowledge structure. In R. S. Wyer & T. K. Srull (Eds.), *Handbook of social cognition* (2nd ed.). Hillsdale, NJ: Lawrence Erlbaum Associates.

Kihlstrom, J. F., Barnhardt, T. M., & Tataryn, D. J. (1992). The psychological unconscious. *American Psychologist, 47*(6), 788–791.

Kihlstrom, J. F., Cantor, N., Albright, J. S., Chew, B. R., Klein, S. B., & Niedenthal, P. M. (1988). Information processing and the study of the self. In L. Berkowitz (Ed.), *Advances in experimental social psychology* (Vol. 19). New York: Academic Press.

Kihlstrom, J. F., Schacter, D. L., Cork, R. C., Hurt, C. A., & Behr, S. E. (1990). Implicit and explicit recall following surgical anesthesia. *Psychological Science, 1,* 303–306.

Kim, J. J., & Fanselow, M. S. (1992). Modality-specific retrograde amnesia of fear. *Science, 256,* 675–677.

Kimble, G. A. (1989). Psychology from the standpoint of a generalist. *American Psychologist, 44,* 491–499.

Kimmel, A. J. (1991). Predictable biases in the ethical decision-making of American psychologists. *American Psychologist, 46,* 786–788.

Kimura, D. (1992). Sex differences in the brain. *Scientific American 267,* 118–125.

Kinchla, R. A. (1992). Attention. *Annual Review of Psychology, 43,* 711–742.

Kinnamon, S. C., & Cummings, T. A. (1992). Chemosensory transduction mechanisms in taste. *Annual Review of Physiology, 54,* 715–731.

Kinney, H. C., & Filiano, J. J. (1988). Brainstem research in sudden infant death syndrome. *Pediatrician, 15,* 240–250.

Kinsey, A. C., Pomeroy, W. R., & Martin, C. E. (1948). *Sexual behavior in the human male.* Philadelphia: W. B. Saunders.

Kinsey, A. C., Pomeroy, W. R., Martin, C. E., & Gebhard, P. H. (1953). *Sexual behavior in the human female.* Philadelphia: W. B. Saunders.

Kintsch, W. (1988). The use of knowledge in discourse processing: A construction-integration model. *Psychological Review, 95,* 163–182.

Kintsch, W., & Bates, E. (1977). Recognition memory for statements from a classroom lecture. *Journal of Experimental Psychology: Human Learning and Memory, 3,* 150–159.

Kirigin, K. A., Braukmann, C. J., Atwater, J. D., & Wolf, M. M. (1982). An evaluation of teaching-family (Achievement Place) group homes for juvenile offenders. *Journal of Applied Behavior Analysis, 15,* 1–16.

Kirmeyer, S. L., & Biggers, K. (1988). Environmental demand and demand engendering behavior: An observational analysis of the type A pattern. *Journal of Personality and Social Psychology, 54,* 997–1005.

Kirsch, I., Mobayed, C. P., Councill, J. R., & Kenny, D. A. (1992). Expert judgments of hypnosis from subjective state reports. *Journal of Abnormal Psychology, 101,* 657–662.

Kitano, H., Chi, I., Rhee, S., Law, C., & Lubben, J. (1992). Norms and alcohol consumption: Japanese in Japan, Hawaii, and California. *Journal of Studies on Alcohol, 53,* 33–39.

Kitayama, S., & Markus, H. R. (1992). Construal of self as cultural frame: Implications for internationalizing psychology. Paper presented to Symposium on Internationalization and Higher Education, Ann Arbor, May.

Kitcher, P. (1985). *Vaulting ambition: Sociobiology and the quest for human nature.* Cambridge: MIT Press.

Klagsbrun, F. (1976). *Too young to die: Youth and suicide.* Boston: Houghton Mifflin.

Klatzky, R. L. (1980). *Human memory: Structures and processes* (2nd ed.). San Francisco: W. H. Freeman.

Klaus, M. H., & Kennell, J. H. (1976). *Maternal infant bonding: The impact of early separation or loss on family development.* St. Louis: Mosby.

Klein, D. C., & Seligman, M. E. P. (1976). Reversal of performance deficits and perceptual deficits in learned helplessness and depression. *Journal of Abnormal Psychology, 85,* 11–26.

Klein, G. (1989). Recognition primed decisions. In W. Rouse (Ed.), *Advances in man machine systems research: Vol. 5* (pp. 47–92). Greenwich, CT: JAI Press.

Klein, G. A. (1989). Do decision biases explain too much? *Human Factors Society Bulletin, 32,* 1–3.

Klein, G. A. (1990). Recognition-primed decisions. In W. R. Rouse (Ed.), *Advances in man machine systems research.* Greenwich, CT: JAI Press.

Klein, J. G. (1991). Negativity effects in impression formation: A test in the political arena. *Personality and Social Psychology Bulletin, 17,* 412–418.

Klein, M. (1960). *The psychoanalysis of children.* New York: Grove Press.

Klein, M. (1975). *The writings of Melanie Klein: Vol. 3.* London: Hogarth Press.

Klein, M., & Tribich, D. (1981). Kernberg's object relations theory: A critical evaluation. *International Journal of Psychoanalysis, 62,* 27–43.

Klein, S. B., & Loftus, J. (1993a). The mental representation of trait and autobiographical knowledge about the self. In T. K. Srull & R. S. Wyer (Eds.), *The mental representation of trait and autobiographical knowledge about the self: Advances in social cognition: Vol. V.* Hillsdale, NJ: Lawrence Erlbaum Associates.

Klein, S. B., & Loftus, J. (1993b). Some lingering self-doubts: Reply to commentaries. In T. K. Srull & R. S. Wyer (Eds.), *The mental representation of trait and autobiographical knowledge about the self: Advances in social cognition: Vol. V.* Hillsdale, NJ: Lawrence Erlbaum Associates.

Klein, S. B., Loftus, J., & Burton, H. A. (1989). Two self-reference effects: The importance of distinguishing between self-descriptiveness judgments and autobiographical retrieval in self-referent coding. *Journal of Personality and Social Psychology, 56,* 853–865.

Kleinknecht, R. A. (1986). *The anxious self: Diagnosis and treatment of fears and phobias.* New York: Human Sciences Press.

Kleinknecht, R. A. (1991). *Mastering anxiety: The nature and treatment of anxious conditions.* New York: Plenum.

Kleinknecht, R., & Morgan, M. (1992). Treatment of posttraumatic stress disorder with eye movement desensitization. *Journal of Behavior Therapy and Experimental Psychiatry, 23,* 43–49.

Klerman, G. L. (1982). Practical issues in the treatment of depression and mania. In E. S. Paykel (Ed.), *Handbook of affective disorders.* New York: Guilford Press.

Klerman, G. L. (1983). The efficacy of psychotherapy as a basis for public policy. *American Psychologist, 38,* 929–934.

Klesges, R. C., Shelton, M. L., & Klesges, L. M. (1993). Effects of television on metabolic rate: Potential implications for childhood obesity. *Pediatrics, 91,* 281–286.

Klesges, R., & Shumaker, S. (1992). Understanding the relations between smoking and body weight and their importance to smoking cessation and relapse. *Health Psychology, 11* (suppl.), 1–3.

Kline, D. W., & Szafran, J. (1975). Age differences in backward monoptic masking. *Journal of Gerontology, 30,* 307–311.

Kline, S., & Groninger, L. D. (1991). The imagery bizarreness effect as a function of sentence complexity and presentation time. *Bulletin of the Psychonomic Society, 29,* 25–27.

Klosko, J. S., Barlow, D. H., Tassinari, R., & Cerny, J. A. (1990). A comparison of alprazolam and behavior therapy in treatment of panic disorder. *Journal of Consulting and Clinical Psychology, 58,* 77–84.

Kluft, R. P. (1987). An update on multiple personality disorder. *Hospital and Community Psychiatry, 38,* 363–373.

Knauft, B. M. (1989). Sociality versus self-interest in human evolution. *Behavioral and Brain Sciences, 12,* 712–713.

Knittle, J.L., Tinners, K., Ginsberg-Fellner, F., Brown, R. E., & Katz, D. P. (1979). The growth of adipose tissue in children and adolescents. *Journal of Clinical Investigation, 63,* 239–241.

Knoll, J., Dallo, J., & Yen, T. T. (1989). Striatal dopamine, sexual activity and lifespan. Longevity of rats treated with (-)deprenyl. *Life Sciences, 45,* 525–531.

Knox, R. E., & Safford, R. K. (1976). Group caution at the racetrack. *Journal of Experimental Social Psychology, 12,* 317–324.

Kobasa, S. C. (1979). Stressful life events, personality, and health: An inquiry into hardiness. *Journal of Personality and Social Psychology, 37,* 1–11.

Kobasa, S. C. (1982). The hardy personality: Toward a social psychology of stress and health. In G. S. Sanders & J. Suls (Eds.), *Social psychology of health and illness.* Hillsdale, NJ: Lawrence Erlbaum Associates.

Kobasa, S. C., Maddi, S. R., & Kahn, S. (1982). Hardiness and health: a prospective study. *Journal of Personality and Social Psychology, 42,* 168–177.

Kobasa, S. C., Maddi, S. R., & Zola, M. A. (1983). Type A and hardiness. *Journal of Behavioral Medicine, 6,* 41–51.

Kochanek, T. (1986). Background factors in child abuse and neglect. *The Brown University Child Behavior and Development Letter, 2, 12,* 1–3.

Koeske, R. D. (1987). Premenstrual emotionality: Is biology destiny? In M. R. Walsh (Ed.), *The psychology of women.* New Haven: Yale University Press.

Koestner, R., Bernieri, F., & Zuckerman, M. (1992). Self-regulation and consistency between attitudes, traits, and behavior. *Personality and Social Psychology Bulletin, 18,* 52–59.

Koestner, R., Zuckerman, M., & Koestner, J. (1989). Attributional focus of praise and children's intrinsic motivation: The moderating role of gender. *Personality and Social Psychology Bulletin, 15,* 61–72.

Kofta, M., & Sedek, G. (1989). Repeated failure: A source of helplessness or a factor irrelevant to its emergence? *Journal of Experimental Psychology: General, 118,* 3–12.

Kohen, D. P., Mahowald, M. W., & Rosen, G. M. (1992). Sleep-terror disorder in children: The role of self-hypnosis in management. *American Journal of Clinical Hypnosis, 34,* 233–244.

Kohlberg, L. (1966). A cognitive-developmental analysis of children's sex role concepts and attitudes. In E. E. Maccoby (Ed.), *The development of sex differences.* Stanford, CA: Stanford University Press.

Kohlberg, L., & Gilligan, C. (1971). The adolescent as a philosopher: The discovery of the self in a postconventional world. *Daedalus, 100,* 1051–1086.

Kohler, W. (1976). *The mentality of apes.* London: Routledge and Kegan Paul.

Kohn, M. L. (1977). *Class and conformity: A study in values* (2nd ed.). Chicago: University of Chicago Press.

Kohut, H. (1971). *Analysis of the self.* New York: International Universities Press.

Kohut, H. (1983). Selected problems of self-psychological theory. In J. D. Lichtenberg & S. Kaplan (Eds.), *Reflections on self psychology* (pp. 387–416). Hillsdale, NJ: Lawrence Erlbaum Associates.

Kohut, H. (1984). Selected problems of self-psychological theory. In J. D. Lichtenberg & S. Kaplan (Eds.), *Reflections on self psychology* (pp. 387–416). Hillsdale, NJ: Lawrence Erlbaum Associates.

Kolata, G. (1985). Why do people get fat? *Science, 227,* 1327–1328.

Komatsu, S-I., & Naito, M. (1992). Repetition priming with Japanese Kana scripts in word-fragment completion. *Memory & Cognition, 20,* 160–170.

Komorita, S. S. (1984). Coalition bargaining. In L. Berkowitz (Ed.), *Advances in experimental social psychology: Vol. 18.* New York: Academic Press.

Komorita, S. S., Parks, C. D., & Hulbert, L. G. (1992). Reciprocity and the induction of cooperation in social dilemmas. *Journal of Personality and Social Psychology, 62,* 607–617.

Komorita, S. S., Sweeney, J., & Kravitz, D. A. (1980). Cooperative choice in the N-person dilemma situation. *Journal of Personality and Social Psychology, 38,* 504–516.

Koob, G. F., & Bloom, F. E. (1988). Cellular and molecular mechanisms of drug dependence. *Science, 242,* 715–723.

Koppenaal, L., & Glanzer, M. (1990). An examination of the continuous distractor task and the "long-term recency effect." *Memory & Cognition, 18,* 183–195.

Korchin, S. J. (1976). *Modern clinical psychology: Principles of intervention in the clinic and community.* New York: Basic Books.

Korner, A. F. (1971). Individual differences at birth: Implications for early experience and later development. *American Journal of Orthopsychiatry, 41*(4).

Kornhaber, M., Krechevsky, M., & Gardner, H. (1990). Engaging intelligence. *Educational Psychologist, 25,* 177–199.

Korteling, J. (1991). Effects of skill integration and perceptual competition on age-related differences in dual-task performance. *Human Factors, 33,* 35–44.

Koskenvuo, M., Kaprio, J., Rose, R., Kesanieme, A., Sarna, S., Heikkila, K., & Langinvainio, H. (1988). Hostility as a risk factor for mortality and ischemic heart disease in men. *Psychosomatic Medicine, 50,* 330–340.

Kosslyn, S. (1976). Can imagery be distinguished from other forms of internal representation? Evidence from studies of information retrieval times. *Memory & Cognition, 4,* 291–297.

Kosslyn, S. (1983). *Ghosts in the mind's machine.* New York: Norton.

Kosslyn, S. M. (1988). Aspects of a cognitive neuroscience of mental imagery. *Science, 240,* 1621–1626.

Kozel, N. J., Grider, R. A., & Adams, E. H. (1982). National surveillance of cocaine use and related health consequences. *Morbidity and Mortality Weekly Report, 20,* 265–273.

Kraft, C. (1978). A psychophysical approach to air safety: Simulator studies of visual illusions in night approaches. In H. L. Pick, H. W. Leibowitz, J. E. Singer, A. Steinschneider, & H. W. Stevenson (Eds.), *Psychology: From research to practice.* New York: Plenum Press.

Kral, J. G. (1992). Overview of surgical techniques for treating obesity. *American Journal of Clinical Nutrition, 55,* 552S-555S.

Kramer, R. M. (1989). Windows of vulnerability or cognitive illusions? Cognitive processes and the nuclear arms race. *Journal of Experimental Social Psychology, 25,* 79–100.

Kramer, R. M., Meyerson, D., & Davis, G. (1990). How much is enough? Psychological components of "guns versus butter" decisions in a security dilemma. *Journal of Personality and Social Psychology, 58,* 984–993.

Krantz, D., & Durel, L. (1983). Psychobiological substrates of the Type A behavior pattern. *Health Psychology, 2,* 393–411.

Krantz, D., Contrada, R., Hill, D., & Friedler, E. (1988). Environmental stress and biobehavioral antecedents of coronary heart disease. *Journal of Consulting and Clinical Psychology,. 56,* 333–341.

Krauzlis, R. J., & Lisberger, S. G. (1991). Visual motion commands for pursuit eye movements in the cerebellum. *Science, 253,* 568–571.

Kravitz, D. A., & Martin, B. (1986). Ringelmann rediscovered: The original article. *Journal of Personality and Social Psychology, 50,* 936–941.

Krebs, D. L., & Miller, D. T. (1985). Altruism and aggression. In G. Lindzey & E. Aronson (Eds.), *Handbook of social psychology, Vol. 2* (3rd ed.). New York: Random House.

Krebs, R. L. (1967). *Some relations between moral judgment, attention, and resistance to temptation.* Unpublished doctoral dissertation, University of Chicago, Chicago, IL.

Krebs, R. L., & Kohlberg, L. (1973). Moral judgment and ego controls as determinants of resistance to cheating. Unpublished manuscript, Center for Moral Education, Harvard University

Krech, D. (1978). Quoted in M. C. Diamond, The aging brain: Some enlightening and optimistic results. *American Scientist, 66,* 66–71.

Kriger, S. F., & Kroes, W. H. (1972). Child-rearing attitudes of Chinese, Jewish, and Protestant mothers. *Journal of Social Psychology, 86,* 205–210.

Kristeller, J. L., Schwartz, G. E., & Black, H. (1982). The use of restricted environmental stimulation therapy (REST) in the treatment of essential hypertension: Two case studies. *Behaviour Research and Therapy, 20,* 561–566.

Kroll, J. (1973). A reappraisal of psychiatry in the middle ages. *Archives of General Psychiatry, 26,* 276–283.

Krosnick, J. A., & Judd, C. M. (1982). Transitions in social influence at adolescence: Who induces cigarette smoking? *Developmental Psychology, 18,* 359–368.

Krosnick, J. A., Betz, A. L., Jussim, L. J., & Lynn, A. R. (1992). Subliminal conditioning of attitudes. *Personality and Social Psychology Bulletin, 18,* 152–162.

Krosnick, J. A., Jussim, L. J., & Lynn, A. R. (1992). Subliminal conditioning of attitudes. *Personality and Social Psychology Bulletin, 18,* 152–162.

Kruglanski, A. W., & Mayseless, O. (1990). Classic and current social comparison research: Expanding the perspective. *Psychological Bulletin, 108,* 195–208.

Kruschke, J. K. (1992). ALCOVE: An exemplar-based connectionist model of category learning. *Psychological Review, 99,* 22–44.

Kryter, K. (1990). Aircraft noise and social factors in psychiatric hospital admission rates: A re-examination. *Psychological Medicine, 20,* 396–411.

Kryter, K. D. (1970). *The effects of noise on man.* New York: Academic Press.

Kuffler, S. W., & Nicholls, J. G. (1976). *From neuron to brain: A cellular approach to the function of the nervous system.* Sunderland, MA: Sinauer Associates.

Kuhn, D., Nash, S. C., & Brucken, L. (1978). Sex role concepts of two- and three-year-olds. *Child Development, 49,* 445–451.

Kuhs, H., & Tolle, R. (1991). Sleep deprivation therapy. *Biological Psychiatry, 29,* 1129–1148.

Kulka, R. A., Schlenger, W. E., Fairbank, J. A., Hough, R. L., Jordan, B. K., Marmar, C. R., & Weiss, D. S. (1988). *Contractual report of findings from the national Vietnam veterans readjustment study: Vol. 1.* Research Triangle Park, NC: Research Triangle Institute.

Kunda, Z. (1990). The case for motivated reasoning. *Psychological Bulletin, 108,* 480–498.

Kunst-Wilson, W. R., & Zajonc, R. B. (1980). Affective discrimination of stimuli that cannot be recognized. *Science, 207,* 557–558.

Kunz, P. R., & Woolcott, M. (1976). Season's greetings: From my status to yours. *Social Science Research, 5,* 269–278.

Kurtz, L. (1990). Twelve-step programs. In T. Powell (Ed.), *Working with self-help.* Silver Spring, MD: NASW Press.

Kutas, M., & Van Petten, C. (1988). Event-related brain potential studies of language. In P. K. Ackles, J. R. Jennings, & M. G. H. Coles (Eds.), *Advances in psychophysiology* (Vol. 3). Greenwich, CT: JAI Press.

Kwan, M., Greenleaf, W. J., Mann, J., Crapo, L., Davidson, J. M. (1983). The nature of androgen action on male sexuality: A combined laboratory-self-report study on hypogonadal men. *Journal of Clinical Endocrinology and Metabolism, 57,* 557–562.

LaBerge, D. (1991). Thalamic and cortical mechanisms of attention suggested by recent positron emission tomographic experiments. *Journal of Cognitive Neuroscience, 2,* 358–372.

Laberge, S. P., Nagel, L. E., Dement, W. C., & Zarcone, V. P. (1981). Lucid dreaming verified by volitional communication during REM sleep. *Perceptual and Motor Skills, 52,* 727–732.

Labouvie-Vief, G. (1982). Discontinuities in development from childhood. In T. M. Field, A. Huston, H. C. Quay, L. Troll, & G. E. Finley (Eds.), *Review of human development.* New York: Wiley.

Lachman, R., Lachman, J. L., & Butterfield, E. C. (1979). *Cognitive psychology and information processing.* Hillsdale, NJ: Lawrence Erlbaum Associates.

Lacks, P., Bertelson, A. D., Sugerman, J., & Kunkel, J. (1983). The treatment of sleep-maintenance insomnia with stimulus-control techniques. *Behaviour Research and Therapy, 21,* 291–295.

LaFromboise, T. D. (1992). An interpersonal analysis of affinity, clarification, and helpful responses with American Indians. *Professional Psychology: Research and Practice, 23,* 281–286.

LaFromboise, T. D., & Foster, S. (1989). Ethics in cross-cultural counseling. In J. Pederson, J. Draguns, W. Lonner, & J. Trimble (Eds.), *Counseling across cultures.* Honolulu: University of Hawaii Press.

Lagerspetz, K. M. J., & Lagerspetz, K. Y. H. (1983). Genes and aggression. In E. C. Simmel, M. E. Hahn, & J. K. Walters (Eds.), *Aggressive behavior: Genetic and neural approaches.* Hillsdale, NJ: Lawrence Erlbaum Associates.

Laird, J. D. (1984). The real role of facial response in the experience of emotion: A reply to Tourangeau and Ellsworth, and others. *Journal of Personality and Social Psychology, 29,* 909–917.

Lakey, B., & Cassady, P. (1990). Cognitive processes in perceived social support. *Journal of Personality and Social Psychology, 59,* 337–343.

Lamal, P. A. (1989). Attending to parapsychology. *Teaching of Psychology, 16,* 28–30.

Lamb, M. E. (1976). Parent-infant interaction in 8-month-olds. *Child Psychiatry and Human Development, 7,* 56–63.

Lamb, M. E. (1977). Father-infant and mother-infant interaction in the first year of life. *Child Development, 48,* 167–181.

Lambert, M. J. (1989). The individual therapist's contribution to psychotherapy process and outcome. *Clinical Psychology Review, 9,* 469–486.

Lambert, M. J., DeJulio, S. S., & Stein, D. M. (1978). Therapist interpersonal skills: Process, outcome, methodological considerations and recommendations for future research. *Psychological Bulletin, 85,* 467–489.

Lambert, M. J., Shapiro, D. A., & Bergin, A. E. (1986). The effectiveness of psychotherapy. In S. L. Garfield & A. E. Bergin (Eds.),

Handbook of psychotherapy and behavior change (3rd ed.). New York: Wiley.

Lambert, W. W., Solomon, R. L. C., & Watson, P. D. (1949). Reinforcement and extinction as factors in size estimation. *Journal of Experimental Psychology, 39,* 637–641.

Lamiell, J. T. (1981). Toward an idiothetic psychology of personality. *American Psychologist, 36,* 276–289.

Lamiell, J. T., & Trierweiler, S. J. (1986). Personality measurement and intuitive personality judgments from an idiothetic point of view. *Clinical Psychology Review, 6,* 471–491.

Land, M. F., & Fernald, R. D. (1992). The evolution of eyes.

Landers, S. (1989a, March). Colleges urged not to disclose average scores. *APA Monitor,* p. 12.

Landers, S. (1989b, April). NY: Scholarship awards are ruled discriminatory. *APA Monitor,* p. 14.

Landfield, P. W., Baskin, R. K., & Pitler, T. A. (1981). Brain aging correlates: retardation by hormonal-pharmacological treatments. *Science, 214,* 581–584.

Landman, J. T., & Dawes, R. M. (1982). Psychotherapy outcome: Smith and Glass' conclusions stand up under scrutiny. *American Psychologist, 36,* 937–952.

Landrine, H. (1991). Revising the framework of abnormal psychology. In P. Bronstein & K. Quina (Eds.), *Teaching a psychology of people.* Washington, DC: American Psychological Association.

Landrine, H., & Klonoff, E. (1992). Culture and health-related schemas: A review and proposal for interdisciplinary integration. *Health Psychology, 11,* 267–276.

Lang P. J. (1993). The network model of emotion: Motivational connections. In R. S. Wyer & T. K. Srull (Eds.), *Toward a general theory of anger and emotional aggression: Advances in social cognition, Vol. VI.* Hillsdale, NJ: Lawrence Erlbaum Associates.

Lang, A. R., Goeckner, D. J., Adesso, V. J., & Marlatt, G. A. (1975). Effects of alcohol on aggression in male social drinkers. *Journal of Abnormal Psychology, 84,* 508–518.

Lang, P. J., & Melamed, B. G. (1969). Avoidance conditioning therapy of an infant with chronic ruminative vomiting. *Journal of Abnormal Psychology, 74,* 1–8.

Langella, M., Colarieti, L., Ambrosini, M. V., and Giuditta, A. (1992). The sequential hypothesis of sleep function. IV. A correlative analysis of sleep variables in learning and nonlearning rats. *Physiology and Behavior, 51,* 227–238.

Langer, E. (1978). Rethinking the role of thought in social interaction. In J. H. Harvey, W. J. Ickes, & R. F. Kidd (Eds.), *New directions in attribution research* (Vol. 2). Hillsdale, NJ: Lawrence Erlbaum Associates.

Langer, E. (1989). *Mindfulness.* Reading, MA: Addison-Wesley.

Langlois, J. H., & Downs, A. C. (1980). Mothers, fathers, and peers as socialization agents of sex-typed play behavior in young children. *Child Development, 51,* 1237–1247.

Lanyon, R. (1984). Personality assessment. *Annual Review of Psychology, 35,* 667–701.

Lanzetta, J. T., & Englis, B. G. (1989). Expectations of cooperation and competition and their effects on observers' vicarious emotional responses. *Journal of Personality and Social Psychology, 56,* 543–554.

Lappiere, O., & Montplaisir, J. (1992). Polysomnographic features of REM sleep behavior disorder: Development of a scoring method. *Neurology, 42,* 1371–1374.

Larkin, J., McDermott, J., Simon, D., & Simon, H. (1981). Expert and novice performance in solving physics problems. *Science, 208,* 1335–1342.

Larsen, K. S. (1976). *Aggression: Myths and models.* Chicago: Nelson-Hall.

Larson, G. E., & Saccuzzo, D. P. (1989). Cognitive correlates of general intelligence: Toward a process theory of g. *Intelligence, 13,* 5–32.

Lashley, K. S. (1929). *Brain mechanisms and intelligence.* Chicago: University of Chicago Press.

Latane, B., & Darley, J. (1970). *The unresponsive bystander: Why doesn't he help?* New York: Appleton-Century-Crofts.

Latane, B., & Darley, J. M. (1968). Group inhibition of bystander intervention in emergencies. *Journal of Personality and Social Psychology, 10,* 215–221.

Latane, B., & Rodin, J. (1969). A lady in distress: Inhibiting effects of friends and strangers on bystander intervention. *Journal of Experimental Social Psychology, 5,* 189–202.

Latimer, P. R. (1983). Antidepressants and behavior therapy in agoraphobia and obsessive-compulsive disorders: A commentary. *Journal of Behavior Therapy and Experimental Psychiatry, 14,* 25–27.

Laudenslager, M. L., Ryan, S. M., Drugan, R. C., Hyson, R. L., & Maier, S. F. (1983). Coping and immunosuppression: Inescapable but not escapable shock suppresses lymphocyte proliferation. *Science, 221,* 568–570.

Lauer, J., & Lauer, R. (1985, June). Marriages made to last. *Psychology Today,* 22–26.

Laughlin, P. R., & Ellis, A. L. (1986). Demonstrability and social combination processes on mathematical intellective tasks. *Journal of Experimental Social Psychology, 22,* 177–189.

Laughlin, P. R., VanderStoep, S. W., & Hollingshead, A. B. (1991). Collective versus individual induction: Recognition of truth, rejection of error, and collective information processing. *Journal of Personality and Social Psychology, 61*(1), 50–67.

Law, D. J., Pellegrino, J. W., & Hunt, E. B. (1993). Comparing the tortoise and the hare: gender differences and experience in dynamic spatial reasoning tasks. *Psychological Science, 4,* 35–40.

Lawless, H. T., & Engen, T. (1977). Associations to odors: Interference, memories and verbal learning. *Journal of Experimental Psychology, 3,* 52–59.

Lawrence, R. (1989). *Guide to clinical preventive services.* Report of the U.S. Preventive Services Task Force. Baltimore: Williams & Wilkins.

Lawshe, C. H. (1975). A quantitative approach to content validity. *Personnel Psychology, 28,* 563–575.

Lawson, A. (1988). *Adultery: An analysis of love and betrayal.* New York: Basic Books.

Lazar, I., Darlington, R. B., Murray, H. W., & Snipper, A. S. (1982). Lasting effects of early education: A report from the consortium for longitudinal studies. *Monograph of Society for Research in Child Development, 47*(195, Serial No. 2–3).

Lazarus, A. A. (1971). *Behavior therapy and beyond.* New York: McGraw-Hill.

Lazarus, R. S. (1966). *Psychological stress and the coping process.* New York: McGraw-Hill.

Lazarus, R. S. (1985). Puzzles in the study of daily hassles. *Journal of Behavioral Medicine, 7,* 375–389.

Lazarus, R. S., & Folkman, S. (1984). *Stress, appraisal, and coping.* New York: Springer.

Lazarus, R. S., Opton, E. M., Nomikos, M. S., & Rankin, M. O. (1965). The principle of short-circuiting of threat: Further evidence. *Journal of Personality, 33,* 622–635.

Leary, M. R., Robertson, R. B., Barnes, B. D., & Miller, R. S. (1986). Self-presentations of small group leaders: Effects of role requirements and leadership orientation. *Journal of Personality and Social Psychology, 51,* 742–748.

Leary, T. (1957). *Interpersonal diagnosis of personality: A functional theory and methodology for personality evaluation.* New York: Ronald Press.

Leask, J., Haber, R. N., & Haber, R. B. (1969). Eidetic imagery in children: II. Longitudinal and experimental results. *Psychonomic Monograph Supplements, 3*(3, Whole No. 35).

Lederhouse, R. (1982). Territorial defense and lek behavior of the black swallowtail butterfly, Papilio polyxenes. *Behavioral Ecology and Sociobiology, 10,* 109–118.

LeDoux, J. E., Romanski, L., & Xagoraris, A. (1989). Indelibility of subcortical emotional memories. *Journal of Cognitive Neuroscience, 1,* 238–243.

LeDoux, J. E., Romanski, L., & Xagoraris, A. (1991). Indelibility of subcortical emotional memories. *Journal of Cognitive Neuroscience, 3,* 238–243.

Lee, V. E., Brooks-Gunn, J., & Schnur, E. (1988). Does Head Start work? A 1-year follow-up comparison of disadvantaged children attending Head Start, no preschool, and other preschool programs. *Developmental Psychology, 24,* 210–222.

Leeper, R. (1935). A study of a neglected portion of the field of learning: The development of sensory organization. *Journal of Genetic Psychology, 46,* 41–75.

Lefevre, V. A. (1982). *Algebra of consciousness.* Boston: Reidel.

Leff, J. P. (1976). Schizophrenia and sensitivity to the family environment. *Schizophrenia Bulletin, 2,* 566–574.

Lehman, D. R., Ellard, J. H., & Wortman, C. B. (1986). Social support for the bereaved: Recipients' and providers' perspectives on what is helpful. *Journal of Consulting and Clinical Psychology, 54,* 438–446.

Lehman, H. C. (1968). The creative production rates of present versus past generations of scientists. In B. L. Neugarten (Ed.), *Middle age and aging.* Chicago: University of Chicago Press.

Lehman, H. E. (1967). Schizophrenia: IV. Clinical features. In A. M. Freedman, H. I. Kaplan, & H. S. Kaplan (Eds.), *Comprehensive textbook of psychiatry.* Baltimore: Williams & Wilkins.

Lehrer, P. M., Sargunaraj, D., & Hochron, S. (1992). Psychological approaches to the treatment of asthma. *Journal of Consulting and Clinical Psychology, 60,* 639–643.

Leibowitz, H. W., & Pick, H. (1972). Cross cultural and educational aspects of the Ponzo perspective illusion. *Perception & Psychophysics, 12,* 430–432.

Leibowitz, H. W., Brislin, R., Perlmutter, L., & Hennessy, R. (1969). Ponzo perspective illusion as a manifestation of space perception. *Science, 166,* 1174–1176.

Leinhardt, G., Seewald, A., & Engel, M. (1979). Learning what's taught: Sex differences in instruction. *Journal of Educational Psychology, 71,* 432–439.

Leippe, M. R., Manion, A. P., & Romanczyk, A. (1992). Eyewitness persuasion: How and how well do fact finders judge the accuracy of adults' and children's memory reports? *Journal of Personality and Social Psychology, 63,* 181–197.

Lelwica, M., & Haviland, J. (1983, April). *Ten-week-old infants' reactions to mothers' emotional expressions.* Paper presented at the biennial meeting of the Society for Research in Child Development, Detroit.

LeMagnen, J. (1971). Advances in studies on the physiological control and regulation of food intake. In E. Stellar & J. M. Sprague (Eds.), *Progress in physiological psychology: Vol. 4.* New York: Academic Press.

Lenneberg, E. H. (1967). *Biological foundations of language.* New York: Wiley.

Lepore, S., Evans, G., & Schneider, M. (1991). Dynamic role of social support in the link between chronic stress and psychological distress. *Journal of Personality and Social Psychology, 61,* 899–909.

Lerner, R. M. (1984). *On the nature of human plasticity.* New York: Cambridge University Press.

Lesgold, A. M. (1984). Acquiring expertise. In J. R. Anderson & S. M. Kosslyn (Eds.), *Tutorials in learning and memory.* San Francisco: W. H. Freeman.

Lessne, G., & Venkatesan, M. (1989). Reactance theory in consumer research: The past, present, and future. *Advances in Consumer Research, 16,* 76–78.

Lett, J. (1992). The persistent popularity of the paranormal. *Skeptical Inquirer, 16,* 381–388.

Lettvin, J. Y., Maturana, H. R., McCulloch, W. S., & Pitts, W. H. (1959). What the frog's eye tells the frog's brain. *Proceedings of the Institute of Radio Engineers 47,* 1940–1951.

LeVay, S. (1991). A difference in hypothalamic structure between heterosexual and homosexual men. *Science, 253,* 1034–1037.

Levenkron, J. C., Cohen, J. D., Mueller, H. S., & Fisher, E. B. (1983). Modifying the Type A coronary-prone behavior pattern. *Journal of Consulting and Clinical Psychology, 51*(2), 192–204.

Levenson, A. H. (1981). *Basic psychopharmacology.* New York: Springer.

Levenson, R. W., & Ruef, A. M. (1992). Empathy: A physiological substrate. *Journal of Personality and Social Psychology, 63,* 234–246.

Levenson, R. W., Ekman, P., & Friesen, W. V. (in press). Voluntary facial action generates emotion-specific autonomic nervous system activity. *Psychophysiology.*

Leventhal, H. (1970). Findings and theory in the study of fear communications. In L. Berkowitz (Ed.), *Advances in experimental social psychology: Vol. 5.* New York: Academic Press.

Leventhal, H., & Tomarken, A. J. (1986). Emotion: Today's problems. *Annual Review of Psychology, 37,* 565–610.

Leventhal, H., Watts, J. C., & Pagano, F. (1967). Effects of fear and instructions on how to cope with danger. *Journal of Personality and Social Psychology, 6,* 313–321.

Levi, A. S., & Pryor, J. B. (1987). Use of the availability heuristic in probability estimates of future events. *Organizational Behavior and Human Decision Processes, 40,* 219–234.

Levin, D. N., Xiaoping, H., Tan, K. K., Galhotra, S., Pelizzari, C. A., Chen, G. T. Y., Beck, R. N., Chen, C. T., Cooper, M. D., Mullen, J. F., Hekmatpanah, & Spire, J. P. (Sept. 1989). The brain: Integrated three-dimensional display of MR and PET images. *Radiology, 786.*

Levin, I. P., Kao, S. F., & Wasserman, E. A. (1991). Biased information usage in contingency judgments. Paper presented at the Meeting of the Midwestern Psychological Association, Chicago.

Levine, J. D., Gordon, N. C., & Fields, H. L. (1979). Naloxone dose dependently produces analgesia and hyperalgesia in postoperative pain. *Nature, 278,* 740–741.

Levine, J. M. (1989). Reaction to opinion deviance in small groups. In P. B. Paulus (Ed.), *Psychology of group influence* (2nd ed.). Hillsdale, NJ: Lawrence Erlbaum Associates.

Levine, J., Warrenburg, S., Kerns, R., Schwartz, G., Delaney, R., Fontana, A., Gradman, A., Smith, S., Scott, A., & Cascione, R. (1987). The role of denial in recovery from coronary heart disease. *Psychosomatic Medicine, 49,* 109–117.

Levine, M. (1966). Hypothesis behavior by humans during discrimination learning. *Journal of Experimental Psychology, 71,* 331–338.

Levine, M. (1988). *Effective problem solving.* Englewood Cliffs, NJ: Prentice-Hall.

Levinger, G. (1988). Can we picture love? In R. J. Sternberg & M. L. Ba rnes (Eds.), *The psychology of love.* New Haven: Yale University Press.

Levinger, G., & Moles, O. C. (1979). *Divorce and separation: Context, causes, and consequences.* New York: Basic Books.

Levinger, G., & Snoek, J. D. (1972). *Attraction in relationship: A new look at interpersonal attraction.* Morristown, NJ: General Learning Press.

Levinson, D. J., Darrow, C. N., Klein, E. B., Levinson, M. H., & McKee, B. (1978). *The seasons of a man's life.* New York: Knopf.

Levy, S., Herberman, R., Lippman, M., & d'Angelo, T. (1987). Correlation of stress factors with sustained depression of natural killer cell activity and predicted prognosis in patients with breast cancer. *Journal of Clinical Oncology, 5,* 348–353.

Lewicki, P. (1992). Nonconscious acquisition of information. *American Psychologist, 47,* 796–801.

Lewicki, P., Czyzewska, M., & Hoffman, H. (1987). Unconscious acquisition of complex procedural knowledge. *Journal of Experimental Psychology: Learning, Memory, and Cognition, 13,* 523–530.

Lewicki, P., Hill, T., & Czyzewska, M. (1992). Nonconscious acquisition of information. *American Psychologist, 47*(6), 796–801.

Lewin, I. (1983). The psychological theory of dreams in the Bible. *Journal of Psychology and Judaism, 7,* 73–88.

Lewin, K. (1936). *Principles of topological psychology.* New York: McGraw-Hill.

Lewinsohn, P. H. (1974). A behavioral approach to depression. In R. J. Friedman & M. M. Katz (Eds.), *The psychology of depression: Contemporary theory and research.* Washington, DC: Winston-Wiley.

Lewinsohn, P. M. (1988). A prospective study of risk factors for unipolar depression. *Journal of Abnormal Psychology, 97,* 251–284.

Lewinsohn, P. M., & Rosenbaum, M. (1987). Recall of parental behavior by acute depressives, remitted depressives, and nondepressives. *Journal of Personality and Social Psychology, 52,* 611–619.

Lewis, M., & Goldberg, S. (1969). Perceptual-cognitive development in infancy: A generalized expectancy model as a function of the mother-infant interaction. *Merrill-Palmer Quarterly, 15,* 81–100.

Lewontin, R. (1976). Race and intelligence. In N. J. Block & G. Dworkin (Eds.), *The IQ controversy: Critical readings.* New York: Pantheon.

Lex, B. (1991). Some gender differences in alcohol and polysubstance users. *Health Psychology, 10,* 121–132.

Leyens, J. P., Camino, L., Parke, R. D., & Berkowitz, L. (1975). The effects of movie violence on aggression in a field setting as a function of group dominance and cohesion. *Journal of Personality and Social Psychology, 32,* 346–360.

Libet, B. (1992). Scientific approaches to conscious experience. *Consciousness and Cognition, 1,* 7.

Lichstein, K. L., & Fischer, S. M. (1985). Insomnia. In M. Hersen & A. S. Bellak (Eds.), *Handbook of clinical behaviour therapy with adults.* New York: Plenum.

Licht, B. G., & Dweck, C. S. (1984). Determinants of academic achievement: The interaction of children's achievement orientations with skill area. *Developmental Psychology, 20,* 628–636.

Lichenstein, E., & Glasgow, R. (1992). Smoking cessation: What have we learned over the past decade? *Journal of Consulting and Clinical Psychology, 60,* 518–527.

Lichtenstein E., & Penner, M. P. (1977). Long-term effects of rapid smoking treatment for dependent cigarette smokers. *Addictive Behaviors, 2,* 109–112.

Lichtman, S. W., Pisarska, K., Berman, E. R., Pestone, M., Dowling, H., Offenbacher, E., Weisel, H., Heshka, S., Matthews, D. E., & Heymsfield, S. B. (1992). Discrepancy between self-reported and actual caloric intake and exercise in obese subjects. *New England Journal of Medicine, 327,* 1893–1898.

Lickey, M. E., & Gordon, B. (1991a). *Medicine and mental illness: The use of drugs in mental illness* (2nd ed.). New York: W. H. Freeman & Co.

Lickey, M., & Gordon, B. (1991b). *Medicine and mental illness: The use of drugs in psychiatry.* San Francisco: W. H. Freeman.

Liddell, H. (1950). Some specific factors that modify tolerance for environmental stress. In H. G. Wolff, S. G. Wolff, & C. C. Hare (Eds.), *Life stress and bodily disease.* Baltimore: Williams & Wilkins.

Lieberman, A., & Pawl, J. (1988). Clinical applications of attachment theory. In J. Bellsky & T. Nezworski (Eds.), *Clinical applications of attachment.* Hillsdale, NJ: Lawrence Erlbaum Associates.

Lieberman, M. A., & Tobin, S. (1983). *The experience of old age.* New York: Basic Books.

Liebert, R. M., & Spiegler, M. D. (1982). *Personality: Strategies and issues* (4th ed.). Homewood, IL: Dorsey.

Liebert, R. M., & Sprafkin, J. (1988). *The early window* (3rd ed.). New York: Pergamon.

Lima, S. D., Hale, S., & Myerson, J. (1991). How general is general slowing? Evidence from the lexical domain. *Psychology and Aging, 6,* 416–425.

Lin, K-M., Poland, R., Smith, M., Strickland, T., & Mendoza, R. (1991). Pharmacokinetic and other factors affecting psychotropic responses in Asians. *Psychopharmacology Bulletin, 27,* 427–439.

Linde, L., & Bergstrom, M. (1992). The effect of one night without sleep on problem-solving and immediate recall. *Psychological Research, 54,* 127–136.

Lindsay, D. S. (1990). Misleading suggestions can impair eyewitnesses' ability to remember event details. *Journal of Experimental Psychology: Learning, Memory, and Cognition, 16,* 1077–1083.

Lindsay, D. S., & Johnson, M. K. (1989). The eyewitness suggestibility effect and memory of source. *Memory & Cognition, 17,* 349–358.

Lindsay, P. H., & Norman, D. A. (1977). *Human information processing* (2nd ed.). New York: Academic Press.

Lindsey, K. P., & Paul, G. L. (1989). Involuntary commitments to public mental institutions: Issues involving the overrepresentation of blacks and assessment of relevant functioning. *Psychological Bulletin, 106,* 171–183.

Lindvall, O., Brundin, P., Widner, H., Rehncrona, S., Gustavii, B., Frackowiak, R., Leenders, K. L., Sawle, G., Rothwell, J. C., Marsden, C. D., & Bjorklund, A. (1990). Grafts of fetal dopamine neurons survive and improve motor function in Parkinson's disease. *Science, 247,* 574–577.

Lindvall, O., Widner, H., Rehncrona, S., Brundin, P., Odin, P., Gustavii, B., Frackowiak, R., Leenders, K. L., Sawle, G., Rothwell, J. C., Bjorklund, A., & Marsden, C. D. (1992). Transplantation of fetal dopamine neurons in Parkinson's disease—One-year clinical and neurophysiological observations in 2 patients with putaminal implants. *Annals of Neurology, 31,* 155–165.

Lintern, G. (1991). An informational perspective on skill transfer in human-machine systems. *Human Factors, 33,* 251–266.

Lintern, G., & Gopher, D. (1978). Adaptive training of perceptual-motor skills. Issues, results and future directions. *International Journal of Man-Machine Studies, 10,* 521–551.

Linville, P. W. (1982). Affective consequences of complexity regarding the self and others. In M. S. Clark & S. T. Fiske (Eds.), *Affect and cognition.* Hillsdale, NJ: Lawrence Erlbaum Associates.

Linville, P. W. (1985). Self-complexity and affective extremity: Don't put all of your eggs in one cognitive basket. *Social Cognition, 3,* 94–120.

Linville, P. W. (1987). Self-complexity as a cognitive buffer against stress-related illness and depression. *Journal of Personality and Social Psychology, 52,* 663–676.

Linz, D. G., Donnerstein, E., & Penrod, S. (1988). Effects of long-term exposure to violent and sexually degrading depictions of women. *Journal of Personality and Social Psychology, 55,* 758–768.

Linz, D., & Donnerstein, E. (1989). The effects of counter-information on the acceptance of rape myths. In D. Zillmann & J. Bryant (Eds.), *Pornography: Research advances and policy considerations.* Hillsdale, NJ: Lawrence Erlbaum Associates.

Lips, H. (1988). *Sex and gender.* Mountain View, CA: Mayfield.

Lipton, A. A., & Simon, F. S. (1985). Psychiatric diagnosis in a state hospital: Manhattan State revisited. *Hospital Community Psychiatry, 36,* 368–373.

Lisak, D. & Roth, S. (1988). Motivational factors in nonincarcerated sexually aggressive men. *Journal of Personality and Social Psychology, 55,* 795–802.

Littman, M. S. (1989). *Poverty in the United States, 1987.* Washington, DC: U.S. Department of Commerce, Bureau of the Census.

Livingstone, M. S. (1988). Art, illusion and the visual system. *Scientific American, 258,* 78–85.

Livingstone, M. S., & Hubel, D. H. (1987). Psychological evidence for separate channels for the perception of form, color, movement and depth. *Journal of Neuroscience, 7,* 3416–3468.

Livingstone, M., & Hubel, D. (1988). Segregation of form, color, movement, and depth: Anatomy, physiology, and perception. *Science, 240,* 740–749.

Locurto, C. (1991a). Beyond IQ in preschool programs? *Intelligence, 15,* 295–312.

Locurto, C. (1991b). Hands on the elephant: IQ, preschool programs, and the rhetoric of inoculation—a reply to commentaries. *Intelligence, 15,* 335–349.

Loeb, G. E. (1989). Neural prosthetic interfaces with the nervous system. *Trends in Neuroscience, 12,* 195–201.

Loehlin, J. C. (1989). Partitioning environmental and genetic contributions to behavioral development. *American Psychologist, 44,* 1285–1292.

Loehlin, J. C., Horn, J. M., & Willerman, L. (1981). Personality resemblance in adoptive families. *Behavior Genetics, 11,* 309–330.

Loehlin, J. C., Willerman, L., & Horn, J. M. (1985). Personality resemblances in adoptive families when the children are late-adolescent or adult. *Journal of Personality and Social Psychology, 48,* 376–392.

Loftus, E. F. (1979). *Eyewitness testimony.* Cambridge: Harvard University Press.

Loftus, E. F. (1984). Eyewitness on trial. In B. D. Sales & A. Alwork (Eds.), *With liberty and justice for all.* Englewood Cliffs, NJ: Prentice-Hall.

Loftus, E. F. (1992). When a lie becomes memory's truth: Memory distortion after exposure to misinformation. *Psychological Science, 3,* 121–123.

Loftus, E. F. (1993a). The reality of repressed memories. *American Psychologist, 48,* 518–537.

Loftus, E. F. (1993b). Psychologists in the eyewitness world. *American Psychologist, 48,* 550–552.

Loftus, E. F., & Hoffman, H. G. (1989). Misinformation and memory: The creation of new memories. *Journal of Experimental Psychology: General, 118,* 100–104.

Loftus, E. F., & Klinger, M. R. (1992). Is the unconscious smart or dumb? *American Psychologist, 47*(6), 761–765.

Loftus, E. F., & Loftus, G. R. (1980). On the permanence of stored information in the human brain. *American Psychologist, 35,* 409–420.

Loftus, E., & Ketcham, K. (1991). *Witness for the defense.* New York: St. Martin's Press.

Loftus, G. R. (1983). The continuing persistence of the icon. *The Behavioral and Brain Sciences, 6,* 28.

Loftus, G. R. (1985). On worthwhile icons: Reply to DiLollo and

Haber. *Journal of Experimental Psychology: Human Perception and Performance, 11,* 384–388.

Loftus, G. R., & Hanna, A. M. (1989). The phenomenology of spatial integration: Data and models. *Cognitive Psychology, 21,* 363–397.

Loftus, G. R., & Hogden, J. (1988). Picture perception: Information extraction and phenomenological appearance. In G. H. Bower (Ed.), *The psychology of learning and motivation, Vol. 22.* San Diego, CA: Academic Press.

Logan, G. (1992). Attention and preattention in theories of automaticity. *American Journal of Psychology, 105,* 317–340.

Logothetis, N. K., & Schall, J. D. (1989). Neuronal correlates of subjective visual perception. *Science, 245,* 761–763.

Logue, A. W. (1985). Conditioned food aversion in humans. *Annals of the New York Academy of Sciences, 104,* 331–340.

Logue, A. W. (1991). *The psychology of eating and drinking.* New York: W. H. Freeman.

Lohman, D. A. (1989). Human intelligence: An introduction to advances in theory and research. *Review of Educational Research, 59,* 333–373.

Long, B. C. (1985). Stress-management interventions: A 15-month follow-up of aerobic conditioning and stress inoculation training. *Cognitive Therapy and Research, 9,* 471–478.

Long, G. M., & Beaton, R. J. (1982). The case for peripheral persistence: Effects of target and background luminance on a partial-report task. *Journal of Experimental Psychology: Human Perception and Performance, 8,* 383–391.

Long, P. (1986, January). Medical mesmerism. *Psychology Today.*

Lonner, W. J., & Malpass, R. S. (Eds.) (1994). *Psychology and culture.* Boston: Allyn & Bacon.

Loomis, A. L., Harvey, E. N., & Hobart, G. A. (1937). Cerebral states during sleep as studied by human brain potentials. *Journal of Experimental Psychology, 21,* 127–144.

Lopes, L. L. (1982). *Procedural debiasing* (Tech. Rep. WHIPP 15). Madison: University of Wisconsin, Human Information Processing Program.

Lopez, M., & Takemoto-Chock, N. (1992, April). Assessment of adolescent stressors: The adolescent Life Events Scale. Paper presented at the meetings of the Western Psychological Association, Portland, OR.

Lopez, S. R. (1989). Patient variable biases in clinical judgment: Conceptual overview and methodological considerations. *Psychological Bulletin, 106,* 184–203.

LoPiccolo, J. (1991). Post-modern sex therapy for erectile failure. In R. C. Rosen & S. R. Leiblum (Eds.), *Erectile failure: Diagnosis and treatment.* New York: Guilford.

Lore, R. K., & Schultz, L. A. (1993). Control of human aggression: A comparative perspective. *American Psychologist, 48,* 16–25.

Lorenz, K. (1981). *Foundations of ethology.* New York: Springer-Verlag.

Losch, M. E., & Cacioppo, J. T. (1990). Cognitive dissonance may enhance sympathetic tonus, but attitudes are changed to reduce negative affect rather than arousal. *Journal of Experimental Social Psychology, 26,* 289–304.

Lott, A. J., & Lott, B. E. (1974). The role of reward in the formation of positive interpersonal attitudes. In T. L. Houston (Ed.), *Foundations of interpersonal attraction.* New York: Academic Press.

Lovaas, O. I. (1987). Behavioral treatment and normal educational and intellectual functioning in young autistic children. *Journal of Consulting and Clinical Psychology, 55,* 3–9.

Lublin, J. S. (1992). Companies use cross-cultural training to help their employees adjust abroad *Wall Street Journal,* August 4.

Luborsky, L. (1954). A note on Eysenck's article, "The effects of psychotherapy: An evaluation." *British Journal of Psychology, 45,* 129–131.

Luborsky, L. (1972). Another reply to Eysenck. *Psychological Bulletin, 78,* 406–408.

Luborsky, L., Singer, B., & Luborsky, L. (1975). Comparative studies of psychotherapies: Is it true that everyone has won and all must have prizes? *Archives of General Psychiatry, 32,* 995–1008.

Lucas, F., & Sclafani, A. (1989). Flavor preferences conditioned by intragastric fat infusions in rats. *Physiology and Behavior, 46,* 403–412.

Lucas, R. (1975). The affective and medical aspects of different preoperative interventions with heart surgery patients. *Dissertation Abstracts International, 36,* 5763B.

Luce, G. G. (1971). *Body time.* New York: Random House.

Luce, S., & Hoge, R. (1978). Relations among teacher ratings, pupil-teacher interactions, and academic achievement: A test of teacher expectancy hypothesis. *American Educational Research Journal, 15,* 489–500.

Luchins, A. S. (1942). Mechanization in problem solving: The effect of Einstellung. *Psychological Monographs, 54*(6, Whole No. 248).

Ludwick-Rosenthal, R., & Neufeld, R. W. (1988). Stress management during noxious medical procedures: An evaluative review of outcome studies. *Psychological Bulletin, 104,* 326–342.

Ludwick-Rosenthal, R., & Neufeld, R. W. J. (1993). Preparation for undergoing an invasive medical procedure: Interacting effects of information and coping style. *Journal of Consulting and Clinical Psychology, 61,* 156–164.

Ludwig, A. M. (1969). Altered states of consciousness. In C. T. Tart (Ed.), *Altered states of consciousness.* New York: Wiley.

Luginbuhl, J., & Palmer, R. (1991). Impression management aspects of self-handicapping: Positive and negative effects. *Personality and Social Psychology Bulletin, 17,* 655–662.

Lundberg, U., Hedman, M., Melin, B., & Frankenhaeuser, M. (1989). Type A behavior in healthy males and females as related to physiological reactivity and blood lipids. *Psychosomatic Medicine, 51,* 113–122.

Luria, Z. (1992, February). Gender differences in children's play patterns. Paper presented at University of Southern California, Los Angeles.

Luria, Z., & Rubin, J. Z. (1974). The eye of the beholder: Parents' views on sex of newborns. *American Journal of Orthopsychiatry, 44,* 512–519.

Lutz, C. (1987). Goals, events and understanding in Ifaluk emotion theory. In N. Quinn & D. Holland (Eds.), *Cultural models in language and thought.* Cambridge: Cambridge University Press.

Lykken, D. T. (1979). *The detection of deception.* Psychological Bulletin, 86, 47–53.

Lynch, J. J. (1979). *The broken heart.* New York: Basic Books.

Lynch, K. (1960). *The image of the city.* Cambridge MA: MIT Press.

Lynn, D. B., & Cross, A. D. (1974). Parent preference of preschool children. *Journal of Marriage and the Family, 36,* 555–559.

Lynn, R. (1991). Race differences in intelligence. *Mankind Quarterly, 31,* 255–297.

Lynn, S. J., & Rhue, J. W. (1986). The fantasy-prone person: Hypnosis, imagination, and creativity. *Journal of Personality and Social Psychology, 51,* 404–408.

Lynn, S. J., & Rhue, J. W. (1988). Fantasy proneness: Hypnosis, developmental antecedents, and psychopathology. *American Psychologist, 43,* 35–44.

Lynn, S. J., & Rhue, J. W. (Eds.) (1991). *Theories of hypnosis: Current models and perspectives.* New York: Guilford Press.

Lynn, S. J., Weekes, J. R., & Milano, M. J. (1989). Reality versus suggestion: Pseudomemory in hypnotizable and simulating subjects. *Journal of Abnormal Psychology, 98,* 137–144.

Lytton, H. (1987, April). *Direction of effects in child socialization with particular reference to conduct disorder.* Paper presented at the meeting of the Society for Research in Child Development, Baltimore.

MacAndrew, C., & Edgerton, R. B. (1969). *Drunken comportment.* Chicago: Aldine.

Maccoby, E. E., & Feldman, S. S. (1972). Mother-attachment and stranger-reactions in the third year of life. *Monographs of the Society for Research in Child Development, 37*(1, Serial No. 146).

Maccoby, E. E., & Jacklin, C. N. (1974). *The psychology of sex differences.* Stanford, CA: Stanford University Press.

Maccoby, E. E., & Jacklin, C. N. (1987). Gender segregation in childhood. In H. W. Reese (Ed.), *Advances in child development and behavior* (Vol. 20). New York: Academic Press.

MacDonald, M. R., & Kuiper, N. A. (1983). Cognitive-behavioral preparations for surgery: Some theoretical and methodological concerns. Clinical Psychology Review, 3, 27–39.

MacDonald, M., & Bernstein, D. A. (1974). Treatment of a spider phobia with in vivo and imaginal desensitization. *Journal of Behavior Therapy and Experimental Psychiatry, 5,* 47–52.

Mace, W. M., & Turvey, M. T. (1983). The implications of occlusion for perceiving persistence. *The Behavioral and Brain Sciences, 6,* 29–31.

MacEvoy, B., Lambert, W. W., Karlberg, P., Karlberg, J., Klackenberg-Larsson, & Klackenberg, G. (1988). Early affective antecedants of adult type A behavior. *Journal of Personality and Social Psychology, 54,* 108–116.

MacEwan, K. E., & Barling, J. (1988). Multiple stressors, violence in the family of origin, and marital aggression: A longitudinal investigation. *Journal of Family Violence, 3,* 73–87.

MacKenzie, B. (1984). Explaining race differences in IQ: The logic, the methodology, and the evidence. *American Psychologist, 39,* 1214–1233.

MacLeod, C. M. (1988). Forgotten but not gone: Savings for pictures and words in long-term memory. *Journal of Experimental Psychology: Learning, Memory, and Cognition, 14,* 195–212.

MacQueen, G., Marshall, J., Perdue, M., Siegel, S., & Bienenstock, J. (1989). Pavlovian conditioning of rat mucosal mast cells to secrete rat mast cell protease II. *Science, 243,* 83–85.

Madni, A. (1988). The role of human factors in expert system design and acceptance. *Human Factors, 30,* 395–414.

Madrazo, I., Drucker-Colin, R., Diaz, V., Martinez-Mata, J., Torres, C., & Becerril, J. J. (1987). Open microsurgical autograft of adrenal medulla to the right caudate nucleus in two patients with intractable Parkinson's disease. *New England Journal of Medicine, 316,* 831–834.

Maeder, T. (1985). *Crime and madness.* New York: Harper & Row.

Magos, A. L., Brincat, M., & Studd, J. W. W. (1986). Treatment of the premenstrual syndrome by subcutaneous oestradiol implants and cyclical oral norethisterone: placebo controlled study. *British Medical Journal, 292,* 1629–1633.

Maher, B. A. (1966). *Principles of psychopathology: An experimental approach.* New York: McGraw-Hill.

Mahler, M. S., Pine, F., & Bergman, A. (1975). *The psychological birth of the human infant.* New York: Basic Books.

Mahrer, A. R., & Nadler, W. P. (1986). Good moments in psychotherapy: A preliminary review, a list, and some promising research avenues. *Journal of Consulting and Clinical Psychology, 54,* 10–15.

Maier, N. R. F. (1930). Reasoning in humans: I. On directions. *Journal of Comparative Psychology, 10,* 115–143.

Main, M., & George, C. (1985). Responses of abused and disadvantaged toddlers to distress in agemates: A study in the day care setting. *Developmental Psychology, 21,* 407–412.

Main, M., & Goldwyn, R. (1984). Predicting rejection of her infant from mother's representation of her own experience: Implica-

References

tions for the abused-abusing intergenerational cycle. *Child Abuse & Neglect, The International Journal, 8,* 203–217.

Majewska, M. D., Harrison, N. L., Schwartz, R. D., Barker, J. L., & Paul, S. M. (1986). Steroid hormone metabolites are barbiturate-like modulators of the GABA receptor. *Science, 232,* 1004–1007.

Malamuth, N. M., Sockloskie, R. J., Koss, M. P., & Tanaka, J. S. (1991). Characteristics of aggressors against women: Testing a model using a national sample of college students. *Journal of Consulting and Clinical Psychology, 59,* 670–681.

Malamuth, N. M. (1988). Predicting laboratory aggression against female and male targets: Implications for sexual aggression. *Journal of Research in Personality, 22,* 474–495.

Malatesta, C. Z., & Izard, C. E. (1984). The ontogenesis of human social signals: From biological imperative to symbol utilization. In N. A. Fox & R. J. Davidson (Eds.), *The psychobiology of affective development* (pp. 161–206). Hilsdale NJ: Lawrence Erlbaum Associates.

Manderscheid, R., & Barrett, S. (Eds.) (1987). *Mental health, United States, 1987* (National Institute of Mental Health, DHHS Pub. No. ADM 87–1518). Washington, DC: U.S. Government Printing Office.

Mane, A., Adams, J. A., & Donchin, E. (1989). Adaptive and part-whole training in the acquisition of a complex perceptual-motor skill. *Acta Psychologica, 71,* 179–196.

Manis, F., Keating, D. P., & Morrison, F. J. (1980). Developmental differences in the allocation of processing capacity. *Journal of Experimental Child Psychology, 29,* 156–159.

Mann, E., Ikeda, Y., Mueller, C., Takahashi, A., Tao, T., Humris, E., Ling li, B, & Chin, D. (1992). Cross-cultural differences in rating hyperactive-disruptive behaviors in children. *American Journal of Psychiatry, 149,* 1539–1542.

Mann, K., Roschke, J., Nink, M., Aldenhoff, J., Beyer, J., Benkert, O., & Lehnert, H. (1992). Effects of corticotropin-releasing hormone administration in patients suffering from sleep apnea syndrome. *Society for Neuroscience Abstracts, 22,* 196.

Manne, S. L., & Zautra, A. J. (1989). Spouse criticism and support: Their association with coping and psychological adjustment among women with rheumatoid arthritis. *Journal of Personality and Social Psychology, 56,* 608–617.

Mannuzza, S., Martin, L. Y., & Gallops, M. S. (1989). Reliability of anxiety assessment. *Archives of General Psychiatry, 46,* 1093–1101.

Mano, H. (1992). Judgments under distress: Assessing the role of unpleasantness and arousal in judgment formation. *Organizational Behavior and Human Decision Processes, 52,* 216–245.

Manson, S. M. (1994). Culture and depression: Discovering variations in the experience of illness. In W. J. Lonner & R. S. Malpass (Eds.), *Psychology and culture.* Boston: Allyn & Bacon.

Marantz, S. A., & Mansfield, A. F. (1977). Maternal employment and the development of sex-role stereotyping in five- to eleven-year-old girls. *Child Development, 48,* 668–673.

Marcel, A. J. (1983). Conscious and unconscious perception: Experiments on visual masking and word recognition. *Cognitive Psychology, 15,* 197–237.

Marchant, G., Robinson, J., Anderson, U., & Schadewald, M. (1991). Analogical transfer and expertise in legal reasoning. *Organizational Behavior and Human Decision Processes, 48,* 272–290.

Marcus, B., Rakowski, W., & Rossi, J. (1992). Assessing motivational readiness and decision making for exercise. *Health Psychology, 11,* 257–261.

Marek, P., Yirmiya, R., Panocka, I., and Liebeskind, J. C. (1989). Genetic influences on brain stimulation-produced analgesia in mice: I. Correlation with stress-induced analgesia. *Brain Research, 489*(1), 182–184.

Margolin, D. I. (1991). Cognitive neuropsychology: Resolving enigmas about Wernicke's aphasia and other higher cortical disorders. *Archives of Neurology, 48,* 751–765.

Margraf, J., Barlow, D., Clark, D., & Telch, M. (1992). Psychological treatment of panic work in progress on outcome, active ingredients, and follow up. *Behaviour Research and Therapy, 31,* 1–9.

Marini, Z., & Case, R. (1989). Parallels in the development of preschoolers' knowledge about their physical and social worlds. *Merrill-Palmer Quarterly, 35,* 63–88.

Marino, J., Gwynn, M. I., & Spanos, N. P. (1989). Cognitive mediators in the reduction of pain: The role of expectancy, strategy use, and self-presentation. *Journal of Abnormal Psychology, 98,* 256–262.

Markman, H. J., Renick, M. J., Floyd, F. J., Stanley, S. M., & Clements, M. (1993). Preventing marital distress through communication and conflict management training: A 4- and 5-year follow-up. *Journal of Consulting and Clinical Psychology, 61,* 70–77.

Marks, L. E., & Miller, G. A. (1964). The role of semantic and syntactic constraints in the memorization of English sentences. *Journal of Verbal Learning and Verbal Behavior, 3,* 1–5.

Markus, H. R., & Kitayama, S. (1991). Culture and the self: Implications for cognition, emotion, and motivation. *Psychological Review, 98,* 224–253.

Marlatt, G. A., & Gordon, J. R. (1985). *Relapse prevention.* New York: Guilford Press.

Marlatt, G. A., & Rohsenow, D. J. (1980). Cognitive processes in alcohol use: Expectancy and the balanced placebo design. In N. K. Mello (Ed.), *Advances in substance abuse: Behavioral and biological research.* Greenwich, CT: JAI Press.

Marlatt, G. A., Baer, J. S., Donovan, D. M., & Kivlahan, D. R. (1988). Addictive behaviors: Etiology and treatment. *Annual Review of Psychology, 39,* 223–252.

Marmar, C. R. (1990). Psychotherapy process research: Progress, dilemmas, and future directions. *Journal of Consulting and Clinical Psychology, 58,* 265–272.

Marr, D. (1982). *Vision.* New York: W. H. Freeman & Co.

Marsh, H. W. (1989). Sex differences in the development of verbal and mathmematics constructs: The high school and beyond study. *American Educational Research Journal, 26,* 191–225.

Marshall, G. D., & Zimbardo, P. G. (1979). Affective consequences of inadequately explained arousal. *Journal of Personality and Social Psychology, 37,* 970–985.

Marshall, J. C., & Halligan, P. W. (1988). Blindsight and insight into visuo-spatial neglect. *Nature, 336,* 766–767.

Marshall, P. (1990). Attention deficit disorder and allergy: A neurochemical model of the relation between the illnesses. *Psychological Bulletin, 106,* 434–446.

Marshall, S. L. A. (1947). *Men against fire.* New York: Morrow.

Marshall, W. L. (1989). Pornography and sex offenders. In D. Zillmann & J. Bryant (Eds.), *Pornography: Research advances and policy considerations.* Hillsdale, NJ: Lawrence Erlbaum Associates.

Martin, F. E. (1985). The treatment and outcome of anorexia nervosa in adolsecents: A prospective study and five year follow-up. *Journal of Psychiatric Research, 19,* 509–514.

Martin, G. (1989). Voice control: Review and data. *International Journal of Man-Machine Systems, 30,* 355–375.

Martindale, C. (1981). *Cognition and consciousness.* Homewood, IL: Dorsey Press.

Martindale, C. (1989). Personality, situation, and creativity. In J. A. Glover, R. R. Ronning, & C. R. Reynolds (Eds.), *Handbook of Creativity* (pp. 211–232). New York: Plenum.

Martindale, C. (1991). *Cognitive psychology: A neural-network approach.* Pacific Grove, CA: Brooks/Cole.

Martinez, J. L., Schulteis, G., & Weinberger, S. B. (1991). How to increase and decrease the strength of memory traces: The effects of drugs and hormones. In J. L. Martinez & R. P. Kesner (Eds.), *Learning and memory: A biological view* (2nd ed.). San Diego: Academic Press.

Maruyama, G., & Miller, N. (1975). *Physical attractiveness and classroom acceptance* (Research Report 75–2). Los Angeles: University of Southern California, Social Science Research Institute.

Marx, J. A., Zsuzsanna, K. G., Royalty, G. M., & Stern, T. E. (1992). Use of self-help books in psychotherapy. *Professional Psychology: Research and Practice, 23,* 300–305.

Maslach, C. (1979). Negative emotional biasing of unexplained arousal. *Journal of Personality and Social Psychology, 37,* 953–969.

Maslach, C., & Johnson, S. (1982). Burnout in health professionals: A social psychological analysis. In G. Sanders & J. Suls (Eds.), *Social psychology of health and illness.* Hillsdale, NJ: Lawrence Erlbaum Associates.

Maslach, C., Stapp, J., & Santee, R. T. (1985). Individuation: Conceptual analysis and assessment. *Journal of Personality and Social Psychology, 49,* 729–738.

Masling, J. (Ed.) (1982). *Empirical studies of psychoanalytical theories* (Vol. 1). Hillsdale, NJ: Lawrence Erlbaum Associates.

Masling, J. M., & Bornstein, R. F. (1991). Perception without awareness and electrodermal responding: A strong test of subliminal psychodynamic activation effects. *Journal of Mind and Behavior, 12,* 33–47.

Maslow, A. H. (1943). A theory of human motivation. *Psychological Review, 50,* 370–396.

Maslow, A. H. (1954). *Motivation and personality.* New York: Harper.

Maslow, A. H. (1962). *Toward a psychology of being.* Princeton, NJ: Van Nostrand.

Maslow, A. H. (1970). *Motivation and personality* (2nd ed.). New York: Harper & Row.

Maslow, A. H. (1971). *The farther reaches of human nature.* New York: McGraw-Hill.

Mason, A., & Blankenship, V. (1987). Power and affiliation motivation, stress, and abuse in intimate relationships. *Journal of Personality and Social Psychology, 52,* 203–210.

Mason, J. W. (1975). A historical view of the stress field. *Journal of Human Stress, I,* 22–36.

Mason, R. T., Fales, H. M., Jones, T. H., Pannell, L. K., Chinn, J. W., & Crews, D. (1989). Sex pheromones in snakes. *Science, 245,* 290–293.

Massaro, D. W. (1989). Testing between the TRACE model and the fuzzy logical model of speech perception. *Cognitive Psychology, 21,* 398–421.

Massaro, D. W., & Cowan, N. (1993). Information processing models: Microscopes of the mind. *Annual Review of Psychology, 44,* 383–425.

Masson, J. M. (1983). *Assault on the truth: Freud's suppression of the seduction theory.* New York: Farrar, Straus, & Giroux.

Masson, M. E. J., & MacLeod, C. M. (1992). Reenacting the route to interpretation: Enhanced perceptual identification without prior perception. *Journal of Experimental Psychology: General, 121,* 145–176.

Masters, J. C., Burish, T. G., Hollon, S. D., & Rimm, D. C. (1987). *Behavior therapy: Techniques and empirical findings* (3rd ed.). San Diego: Harcourt Brace Jovanovich.

Masters, W. H., & Johnson, V. E. (1966). *Human sexual response.* Boston: Little, Brown.

Matarazzo, J. (1984). Behavioral health: A 1990 challenge for the health sciences professions. In J. D. Matarazzo, S. M. Weiss, J. A. Herd, N. E. Miller, & S. E Weiss (Eds.), *Behavioral health: A handbook of health enhancement and disease prevention.* New York: Wiley.

Matarazzo, J. (1992). Psychological assessment versus psychological assessment: Validation from Binet to the school, to the clinic, to the courtroom. *American Psychologist, 45,* 999–1017.

Matarazzo, J. D. (1980). Behavioral health and behavioral medicine: Frontiers for a new health psychology. *American Psychologist, 35,* 807–817.

Matarazzo, J. D. (1983). The reliability of psychiatric and psychological diagnosis. *Clinical Psychology Review, 3,* 103–145.

Matarazzo, J. D. (1992). Psychological testing and assessment in the 21st century. *American Psychologist, 47,* 1007–1018.

Mathew, R. J., Wilson, W. H., Humphreys, D. F., Lowe, J. V., & Wiethe, K. E. (1992). Changes in middle cerebral artery velocity after marijuana. *Biological Psychiatry, 32,* 164–169.

Mathies, H. (1989). Neurobiological aspects of learning and memory. *Annual Review of Psychology, 40,* 381–404.

Matlin, M. (1993). The psychology of women (2nd ed.). Fort Worth, TX: Harcourt Brace Jovanovich.

Matlin, M. W. (1987). *Sensation and perception* (2nd ed.). Boston: Allyn & Bacon.

Matson, J., Sevin, J., Fridley, D., & Love, S. (1990). Increasing spontaneous language in autistic children. *Journal of Applied Behavior Analysis, 23,* 227–223.

Matsumoto, D., and Ekman, P. (1989). American-Japanese cultural differences in intensity ratings of facial expressions of emotion. *Motivation and Emotion, 13,* 143–157.

Matthews, K. (1988). Coronary heart disease and Type A behaviors: Update on and alternative to the Booth-Kewley and Friedman (1987) quantitative review. *Psychological Bulletin, 104,* 373–380.

Matthews, K. A. (1982). Psychological perspectives on the Type-A behavior pattern. *Psychological Bulletin, 91,* 293–323.

Matthews, K. A. (1988). Coronary heart disease and type A behaviors: Update on and alternative to the Booth-Kewley and Friedman (1987) quantitative review. *Psychological Bulletin, 104,* 373–380.

Matthews, K. A., & Siegel, J. M. (1983). Type A behaviors for children, social comparison, and standards for self-evaluation. *Developmental Psychology, 19,* 135–140.

Matthews, K., Weiss, S., Detre, T., Dembrowski, T., Falkner, B., Manuck, S., & Williams, R. (Eds.) (1986). *Handbook of stress reactivity and cardiovascular disease.* New York: Wiley.

Mattick, R. P., Peters, L., & Clarke, J. (1989). Exposure and cognitive restructuring for social phobia: A controlled study. *Behavior Therapy, 20,* 3–23.

Mauren, D. (1985). Infants' perception of facedness. In T. N. Field & N. Fox (Eds.), *Social perception in infants.* New York: Ablex.

Maurer, D., & Vogel, V. H. (1973). *Narcotics and narcotic addiction.* Springfield, IL: Charles C. Thomas.

Mayer, D. J., & Price, D. D. (1982). A physiological and psychological analysis of pain: A potential model of motivation. In D. W. Pfaff (Ed.), *The physiological mechanisms of motivation.* New York: Springer-Verlag.

Mayer, J. (1975). Obesity during childhood. In M. Winick (Ed.), *Childhood obesity.* New York: Wiley.

Mayer, J. D., Gayle, M., Meehan, M. E., & Haarman, A. (1990). Toward better specification of the mood-congruency effect in recall. *Journal of Experimental Social Psychology, 26,* 465–480.

Mayer, R. E. (1983). *Thinking, problem solving, and cognition.* San Francisco: W. H. Freeman.

Mayer, R. E., Tajika, H., & Stanley, C. (1991). Mathematical problem solving in Japan and the United States: A controlled comparison. *Journal of Educational Psychology, 83,* 69–72.

Mayer, W. (1983). Alcohol abuse and alcoholism: The psychologist's role in prevention, research, and treatment. *American Psychologist, 38,* 1116–1121.

Mayford, M., Barzilai, A., Keller, F., Schacher, S., & Kandel, E. R. (1992). Modulation of an ncam-related adhesion molecule with long-term synaptic plasticity in aplysia. *Science, 256,* 638–644.

Mazur, R. H. (1991). The future of synthetic sweeteners. In D. E. Walters et al. (Eds.), *Sweeteners, discovery, molecular design, and chemoreception.* Washington, DC: American Chemical Society.

Mazziotta, J. C., Phelps, M. E., Carson, R. E., & Kuhl, D. E. (1982). Tomographic mapping of human cerebral metabolism: Auditory stimulation. *Neurology, 32,* 921–937.

McAdams, D. (1992). The five-factor model in personality: A critical appraisal. *Journal of Personality, 60,* 329–361.

McCann, T., & Sheehan, P. W. (1988). Hypnotically induced pseudomemories—Sampling their conditions among hypnotizable subjects. *Journal of Personality and Social Psychology, 54,* 339–346.

McCarley, R. W. (1987). REM sleep generation: Intracellular studies of pontine reticular neurons. *Neuroscience, 22,* 387.

McCarthy, G., & Donchin, E. (1979). Event-related potentials: Manifestations of cognitive activity. In F. Hoffmeister & C. Muller (Eds.), *Bayer symposium: VIII. Brain function in old age.* New York: Springer.

McCartney, K., Harris, M., & Bernieri, F. (1990). Growing up and growing apart: A developmental meta-analysis of twin studies. *Psychological Bulletin, 107,* 226–237.

McCauley, C. (1989). The nature of social influence in groupthink: Compliance and internalization. *Journal of Personality and Social Psychology, 57,* 250–260.

McClelland, D. C. (1958). Risk-taking in children with high and low need for achievement. In J. W. Atkinson (Ed.), *Motives in fantasy, action, and society.* Princeton, NJ: Van Nostrand.

McClelland, D. C. (1985). *Human motivation.* Glenview, IL: Scott, Foresman.

McClelland, D. C. (1989). Motivational factors in health and disease. *American Psychologist, 44,* 675–683.

McClintock, C. G., & Liebrand, W. B. G. (1988). Role of interdependence structure, individual value orientation, and another's strategy in social decision making: A transformational analysis. *Journal of Personality and Social Psychology, 55,* 396–409.

McCloskey, D. I. (1978). *Kinesthetic sensibility.* Physiological Reviews, 58, 763.

McCloskey, M. (1983). Naive theories of motion. In D. Gentner & K. Stevens (Eds.), *Mental models.* Hillsdale, NJ: Lawrence Erlbaum Associates.

McCloskey, M., Wible, C. G., & Cohen, N. J. (1988). Is there a special flashbulb-memory mechanism? *Journal of Experimental Psychology: General, 117,* 171–181.

McConkie, G. W., Kerr, P. W., Reddix, M. D., & Zola, D. (1988). Eye movement control during reading: I. The location of the initial eye fixations on words. *Vision Research, 28,* 1107–1118.

McCormick, D. A., & Thompson, R. F. (1984). Cerebellum essential involvement in the classically conditioned eyelid response. *Science, 223,* 296–299.

McCrae, R. R., & Costa, P. T., Jr. (1982). Aging, the life course, and models of personality. In T. M. Field, A. Huston, H. C. Quay, L. Troll, & G. E. Finley (Eds.), *Review of human development.* New York: Wiley-Interscience.

McCrae, R., & John, O. (1992). An introduction to the five-factor model and its applications. *Journal of Personality, 60,* 175–215.

McDougall, W. (1904). The sensations excited by a single momentary stimulation of the eye. *British Journal of Psychology, 1,* 78–113.

McDougall, W. (1908). *An introduction to social psychology.* London: Methuen.

McDowd, J., Vercruyssen, M., & Birren, J. (1991). Aging, divided attention, and dual-task performance. In D. Damos (Ed.), *Multiple Task Performance.* Bristol, PA: Taylor & Francis.

McEwen, B. S. (1991). Steroid-hormones are multifunctional messengers to the brain. *Trends in Endocrinology and Metabolism, 2,* 62–67.

McFarland, C., Ross, M., DeCourville, N. (1989). Women's theories of menstruation and biases in recall of menstrual symptoms. *Journal of Personality and Social Psychology, 57,* 522–531.

McGarvey, R. (1989, February). Recording success. *USAIR Magazine,* pp. 94–102.

McGlashan, T., & Fenton, W. (1991). Classical subtypes for schizophrenia: Literature reveiw for DSM-IV. *Schizophrenia Bulletin, 17,* 610–632.

McGlone, J. (1980). Sex differences in human brain asymmetry: A critical survey. *The Behavioral and Brain Sciences, 3,* 215–263.

McGrady, A., Turner, J. W., Fine, T. H., Higgins, J. T. (1987). Effects of biobehaviorally-assisted relaxation training on blood pressure, plasma renin, cortisol, and aldosterone levels in borderline essential hypertension. *Clinical Biofeedback and Health: An International Journal, 10,* 16–25.

McGreevy, M. W. (1991). Virtual reality and planetary exploration. *29th AAS Goddard Memorial Symposium.* Washington, DC.

McGue, M., Pickens, R., & Svikis, D. (1992). Sex and age effects on the inheritance of alcohol problems: A twin study. *Journal of Abnormal Psychology, 101,* 3–17.

McGuire, W. J. (1968). Personality and susceptibility to social influence. In E. F. Borgatta & W. W. Lambert (Eds.), *Handbook of personality theory and research.* Chicago: Rand McNally.

McGuire, W. J. (1969). The nature of attitudes and attitude change. In G. Lindzey & E. Aronson (Eds.), *The handbook of social psychology: Vol. 3* (2nd ed.). Reading, MA: Addison-Wesley.

McGuire, W. J. (1985). Attitudes and attitude change. In G. Linzey & E. Aronson (Eds.), *The handbook of social psychology: Vol. 2* (3rd ed.). New York: Random House.

McGuire, W. J. (1989). The structure of individual attitudes and attitude systems. In A. R. Pratkanis, S. J. Breckler, & A. G. Greenwald (Eds.), *Attitude structure and function.* Hillsdale, NJ: Lawrence Erlbaum Associates.

McHugh, M., Koeske, R., & Frieze, I. (1986). Issues to consider in conducting nonsexist psychological research: A guide for researchers. *American Psychologist, 41,* 879–890.

McIntosh, J. L. (1991). Epidemiology of suicide in the U.S. In A. A. Leenaars (Ed.), *Life span perspectives on suicide.* New York: Plenum.

McKenna, D. J., & Peroutka, S. J. (1990). Neurochemistry and neurotoxicity of 3,4-methylendioxymethamphetamine (MDMA, "Ecstasy"). *Journal of Neurochemistry, 54,* 14–22.

McKenna, R. J. (1972). Some effects of anxiety level and food cues on the eating behavior of obese and normal subjects: A comparison of the Schachterian and psychosomatic conceptions. *Journal of Personality and Social Psychology, 22,* 311–319.

McMillen, D. (1991). The drunk driver: Personality and behavioral characteristics and intervention strategies. Paper presented at the 37th annual meeting of the Southeastern Psychological Association, March 20–23, New Orleans, LA.

McNally, R. J. (1987). Preparedness and phobias: A review. *Psychological Bulletin, 101,* 283–303.

McNally, R., Cassidy, K., & Calamari, J. (1990). *Taijin-Kyofu-Sho* in a Black American woman: Behavioral treatment of a "culture bound" anxiety disorder. *Journal of Anxiety Disorders, 4,* 83–87.

McNeal, E. T., & Cimbolic, P. (1986). Antidepressants and biochemical theories of depression. *Psychological Bulletin, 99,* 361–374.

McNeil, T. F., & Persson-Blennow, I. (1988). Stability of temperament characteristics in childhood. *American Journal of Orthopsychiatry, 58,* 622–626.

Mead, M. (1963). *Sex and temperament in three primitive societies.* New York: William Morrow.

Medin, D. L., & Ross, B. H. (1992). *Cognitive psychology.* Fort Worth, TX: Harcourt Brace Jovanovich.

Mednick, S. A. (1958). A learning theory approach to research in schizophrenia. *Psychological Bulletin, 55,* 316–327.

Mednick, S. A. (1970). Breakdown in individuals at high-risk for schizophrenia: Possible predispositional perinatal factors. *Mental Hygiene, 54,* 50–63.

Mednick, S. A., Gabrielli, W. F., & Hutchings, B. (1984). Genetic influences in criminal convictions: Evidence from adoption court. *Science, 224,* 891–894.

Mednick, S. A., Schulsinger, F., & Griffith, J. (1981). Children of schizophrenic mothers: The Danish high-risk study. In F. Schulsinger, S. A. Mednick, & J. Knop (Eds.), *Longitudinal research: Methods and uses in behavioral science.* Hingham, MA.: Martinus Nijhoff.

Meehan, P., Lamb, J., Saltzman, L., & O'Carroll, P. (1992). Attempted suicide among young adults: Progress toward a meaningful estimate of prevalence. *American Journal of Psychiatry, 149,* 41–44.

Mehle, T. (1982). Hypothesis generation in an automobile malfunction inference task. *Acta Psychologica, 52,* 87–116.

Meichenbaum, D. (1977). *Cognitive behavior modification: An integrative approach.* New York: Plenum Press.

Meichenbaum, D. (1985). *Stress-inoculation training.* New York: Pergamon Press.

Meijer, G. A., Westerterp, K. R., van Hulsel, A. M., & ten Hoor, F. (1992). Physical activity and energy expenditure in lean and obese adult human subjects. *European Journal of Applied Physiology and Occupational Physiology, 65,* 525–528.

Melamed, B. G., & Siegel, L. J. (1980). *Behavioral medicine.* New York: Springer.

Mello, N. K., Mendelson, J. H., Bree, M. P., & Lukas, S. E. (1989). Buprenorphine suppresses cocaine self-administration by rhesus monkeys. *Science, 245,* 859–862.

Mellsop, G., Varghese, F., Joshua, S., & Hicks, A. (1982). The reliability of Axis II of DSM-III. *American Journal of Psychiatry, 139,* 1360–1361.

Meltzer, H. Y. (1989). Duration of a clozapine trial in neuroleptic-resistant schizophrenic. *Archives of General Psychiatry, 46,* 668.

Meltzer, H. Y., & Stahl, S. M. (1976). The dopamine hypothesis of schizophrenia: A review. *Schizophrenia Bulletin, 2,* 19–76.

Meltzoff, A. N. (1988). Imitation of televised models by infants. *Child Development, 59,* 1221–1229.

Melzack, R., & Wall, P. D. (1965). Pain mechanisms: A new theory. *Science, 150,* 971–979.

Menditto, A. A., Baldwin, L. J., O'Neal, L. G., & Beck, N. C. (1991). *Journal of Behavior Therapy and Experimental Psychiatry, 22,* 265–269.

Mendoza, R., Smith, M., Poland, R., Lin, K-M., & Strickland, T. (1991). Ethnic psychopharmacology: The Hispanic and Native American perspective. *Psychopharmacology Bulletin, 27,* 449–461.

Mercer, J. R. (1988). Ethnic differences in IQ scores: What do they mean? (A response to Lloyd Dunn.) *Hispanic Journal of Behavioral Sciences, 10,* 199–218.

Merckelbach, H., de Ruiter, C., van den Hout, M. A., & Hoekstra, R. (1989). Conditioning experiences and phobias. *Behaviour Research & Therapy, 27,* 657–662.

Merikle, P. M. (1992). Perception without awareness. *American Psychologist, 47*(6), 792–795.

Merikle, P. M., & Reingold, E. M. (1990). Recognition and lexical decision without detection: Unconscious perception? *Journal of Experimental Psychology: Human Perception and Performance, 16,* 574–583.

Merritt, J. O. (1979). None in a million: Results of mass screening for eidetic ability using objective tests published in newspapers and magazines. *The Behavioral and Brain Sciences, 2,* 612.

Merton, R. (1948). *The self-fulfilling prophecy.* Antioch Review, 8, 193–210.

Merzenich, M. M., & Kass, J. H. (1980). Principles of organization of sensory-perceptual systems in mammals. In J. M. Sprague & A. N. Epstein (Eds.), *Progress in psychobiology and physiological psychology: Vol. 9.* New York: Academic Press.

Mesquita, B., & Frijda, N. H. (1992). Cultural variations in emotions: A review. *Psychological Bulletin, 112,* 179–204.

Messer, S. B., & Winokur, M. (1986). Eclecticism and the shifting visions of reality in three systems of psychotherapy. *International Journal of Eclectic Psychotherapy, 5,* 115–124.

Messick, D. M., & Mackie, D. M. (1989). Intergroup relations. *Annual Review of Psychology, 40,* 45–81.

Messick, S. (1980). *The effectiveness of coaching for the SAT: A review of and reanalysis of research from the fifties to the FTC.* Princeton, NJ: Educational Testing Services.

Messick, S., & Jungeblut, A. (1981). Time and method in coaching for the SAT. *Psychological Bulletin, 89,* 191–216.

Metalsky, G. I., Joiner, T. E., Jr., Hardin, T. S., & Abramson, L. Y. (1993). Depressive reactions to failure in a naturalistic setting: A test of the hopelessness and self-esteem theories of depression. *Journal of Abnormal Psychology, 102,* 101–109.

Metcalf, S. M., Livesey, J. H., Wells, J. E., Braiden, V., Hudson, S. M., & Bamber, L. (1991). Premenstrual syndrome in hysterectomized women: mood and physical symptom cyclicity. *Journal of Psychosomatic Research, 35,* 555–567.

Meuser, K. T., & Berenbaum, H. (1990). Psychodynamic treatment of schizophrenia: Is there a future? *Psychological Medicine, 20,* 253–262.

Meyer, R. G. (1975). A behavioral treatment of sleepwalking associated with test anxiety. *Journal of Behavior Therapy and Experimental Psychiatry, 6,* 167–168.

Meyer, R. G., & Hardaway-Osborne, Y. V. (1982). *Case studies in abnormal behavior.* Boston: Allyn & Bacon.

Meyer, R. W. (1992). New pharmacotherapies for cocaine dependence . . . revisited. *Archives of General Psychiatry, 49,* 900.

Meyers, J. K., Weissman, M. M., Tischler, G. L., Holzer, C. E., Leaf, P. J., Orvaschel, H., Anthony, J. C., Boyd, J. H., Burke, J. D., Jr., Kramer, M., & Stoltzman, R. (1984). Six-month prevalence of psychiatric disorders in three communities. *Archives of General Psychiatry, 41,* 959–967.

Michelson, L., Sugai, D. P., Wood, R. P., & Kazdin, A. E. (1983). *Social skills assessment and training with children.* New York: Plenum.

Middlestadt, S. E. (1990). The effect of background and ambient color on product attitudes and beliefs. *Advances in Consumer Research, 17,* pp. 244–249.

Mignard, M., & Malpeli, J. G. (1991). Paths of information flow through the visual cortex. *Science, 251,* 1249–1251.

Mikulincer, M. (1988). Reactance and helplessness following exposure to unsolvable problems: The effects of attributional style. *Journal of Personality and Social Psychology, 54,* 679–686.

Miles, T. R., & Miles, E. (1990). *Dyslexia: A hundred years of progress.* Philadelphia: Open University Press.

Milgram, S. (1963). Behavioral study of obedience. *Journal of Abnormal and Social Psychology, 67,* 371–378.

Milgram, S. (1965). Some conditions of obedience and disobedience to authority. *Human Relations, 18,* 57–76.

Milgram, S. (1972). Some conditions of obedience and disobedience to authority. *Human Relations, 18*(1), 63.

Milgram, S. (1974). *Obedience to authority.* New York: Harper & Row.

Milgram, S., & Jodelet, D. (1976). Psychological maps of Paris. In H. M. Proshansky, W. H. Itelson, & L. G. Revlin (Eds.), *Environmental psychology.* New York: Holt, Rinehart and Winston.

Milgram, S., Bickman, L., & Berkowitz, L. (1969). Note on the drawing power of crowds of different size. *Journal of Personality and Social Psychology, 13,* 79–82.

Milich, R., & Landau, S. (1982). Socialization and peer relations in hyperactive children. In K. D. Gadow & I. Bailer (Eds.), *Advances in learning and behavioral disabilities: A research annual* (Vol. 1, pp. 283–339). Greenwich, CT: JAI Press.

Millar, M. G., Millar, K. U., & Tesser, A. (1988). The effects of helping and focus of attention on mood states. *Personality and Social Psychology Bulletin, 14,* 536–543.

Miller, A. G. (1986). *The obedience experiments: A case study of controversy in social science.* New York: Praeger.

Miller, D. B., & Olson, D. (1978). *Typology of marital interaction and contextual characteristics: Cluster analysis of the I. M. C.* Unpublished paper available from D. Olson, Minnesota Family Study Center, University of Minnesota.

Miller, D. C. (1926). *The science of musical sounds.* New York: Macmillan.

Miller, D. T., & McFarland, C. (1987). Pluralistic ignorance: When similarity is interpreted as dissimilarity. *Journal of Personality and Social Psychology, 53,* 298–305.

Miller, D. T., Taylor, B., & Buck, M. (1991). Gender gaps: Who needs to be explained? *Journal of Personality and Social Psychology, 61,* 5–12.

Miller, G. A. (1956). The magical number seven, plus or minus two: Some limits on our capacity to process information. *Psychological Review, 63,* 81–97.

Miller, G. A. (1989). Scientists of the artificial. In D. Klahr & K. Kotovsky (Eds.), *Complex information processing.* Hillsdale, NJ: Lawrence Erlbaum Associates.

Miller, G. A., Heise, G. A., & Lichten, W. (1951). The intelligibility of speech as a function of the text and the test materials. *Journal of Experimental Psychology,* 329–335.

Miller, I. W., & Norman, W. H. (1979). Learned helplessness in humans: A review and attribution model. *Psychological Bulletin, 86,* 93–118.

Miller, J. G., & Bersoff, D. M. (1992). Culture and moral judgment: How are conflicts between justice and interpersonal responsibilities resolved? *Journal of Personality and Social Psychology, 62,* 541–554.

Miller, J. P. (1975). Suicide and adolescence. *Adolescence, 10*(37), 11–24.

Miller, L. T., & Vernon, P. A. (1992). The general factor in short-term memory, intelligence, and reaction time. *Intelligence, 16,* 5–29.

Miller, N. E. (1959). Liberalization of basic S-R concepts: Extensions to conflict behavior, motivation, and social learning. In S. Koch (Ed.), *Psychology: A study of science: Vol. 2.* New York: McGraw-Hill.

Miller, N. E., Bailey, C. U., & Stevenson, J. A. F. (1930). Decreased hunger but increased food intake resulting from hypothalmic lesions. *Science, 112,* 256–259.

Miller, N., & Brewer, M. (Eds.) (1984). *Groups in contact: The psychology of desegregation.* New York: Academic Press.

Miller, N., & Carlson, M. (1990). Valid theory-testing meta-analyses further question the negative state relief model of helping. *Psychological Bulletin, 107,* 215–225.

Miller, N., & Davidson-Podgorny, G. (1987). Theoretical models of intergroup relations and the use of cooperative teams as an intervention for desegregated settings. In C. Hendrick (Ed.), *Group processes and intergroup relations.* Newbury Park, CA: Sage.

Miller, N., Rogers, M., & Hennigan, K. (1983). Increasing interracial acceptance: Using cooperative games in desegregated elementary schools. In L. Bickman (Ed.), *Applied social psychology annual* (Vol. 4). Beverly Hills: Sage.

Miller, R. C., & Berman, J. S. (1983). The efficacy of cognitive-behavior therapies: A quantitative review of the research evidence. *Psychological Bulletin, 94,* 39–53.

Miller, S. M., Brody, D. S., & Summerton, J. (1988). *Journal of Personality and Social Psychology, 54,* 142–148.

Miller, S., & Nardini, R. M. (1977). Individual differences in the perception of crowding. *Environmental Psychology and Nonverbal Behavior, 2,* 3–13.

Miller, S., Rossbach, J., & Munson, R. (1981). Social density and affiliative tendency as determinants of dormitory residential outcomes. *Journal of Applied Social Psychology, 11,* 356–365.

Miller-Jones, D. (1989). Culture and testing. *American Psychologist, 44,* 360–366.

Millon, T. (1981). *Disorders of personality. DSMIII: Axis II.* New York: Wiley.

Millon, T. (1987). *Millon Clinical Multiaxial Inventory-II.* Minneapolis: National Computer Systems.

Milner, A. D., & Rugg, M. D. (Eds.) (1992). *The neuropsychology of consciousness.* San Diego, CA: Academic Press.

Milner, B. (1962). Les troubles de la memoire accompagnant des lesions hippocampiques bilaterales. In *Physiologie de l'hippocampe.* Paris: C.N.R.S., pp. 257–272. [English translation in P. M. Milner & S. Glickman (Eds.), *Cognitive processes and the brain.* Princeton, NJ: Van Nostrand, 1965, pp. 97–111.]

Milner, B. (1965). Visually-guided maze learning in man: Effects of bilateral hippocampal, bilateral frontal, and unilateral cerebral lesions. *Neuropsychologia, 3,* 317–338.

Milner, B. (1970). Memory and the medial temporal regions of the brain. In K. H. Pribram & D. E. Broadbent (Eds.), *Biology of memory.* New York: Academic Press.

Milner, B. R. (1966). Amnesia following operation on temporal lobes. In C. W. M. Whitty & O. L. Zangwill (Eds.), *Amnesia.* London: Butterworth.

Milner, D. (1983). *Children and race.* Beverly Hills, CA: Sage.

Mineka, S., & Hendersen, R. W. (1985). Controllability and predictability in acquired motivation. *Annual Review of Psychology, 36,* 495–529.

Minimi, H., & Dallenbach, K. M. (1946). The effect of activity upon learning and retention in the cockroach. *American Journal of Psychology, 59,* 1–58.

Minshew, N. J., Payton, J. B., & Sclabassi, R. J. (1986). Cortical neurophysiologic abnormalities in autism. *Neurology, 36* (Suppl. 1), 194.

Minuchin, S., & Fishman, H. (1981). *Family therapy techniques.* Cambridge, MA: Harvard University Press.

Minuchin, S., Rosman, B. L., & Baker, L. (1978). *Psychosomatic families: Anorexia nervosa in context.* Cambridge, MA: Harvard University Press.

Mischel, W. (1968). *Personality and assessment.* New York: Wiley.

Mischel, W. (1981). *Introduction to personality* (3rd ed.). New York: Holt, Rinehart, & Winston.

Mischel, W. (1984). Convergences and challenges in the search for consistency. *American Psychologist, 39,* 351–364.

Mischel, W. (1986). *Introduction to personality* (4th ed.). New York: Holt, Rinehart, & Winston.

Mischel, W., & Peake, P. K. (1983). Some facets of consistency: Replies to Epstein, Funder, and Bem. *Psychological Review, 90,* 394–402.

Mishkin, M., & Appenzeller, T. (1987). The anatomy of memory. *Scientific American, 256,* 80–89.

Mishkin, M., & Ungerleider, L. G. (1982). Contribution of striate inputs to the visuospatial functions of parieto-preoccipital cortex in monkeys. *Behavior and Brain Research, 6,* 57–77.

Mitchell, D. B. (1991). Implicit memory, explicit theories. *Contemporary Psychology, 36,* 1060–1061.

Mitchell, J. E., & Pyle, R. L. (1985). Characteristics of bulimia. In J. E. Mitchell (Ed.), *Anorexia nervosa and bulimia: Diagnosis and treatment.* Minneapolis: University of Minnesota Press.

Mitchell, J. E., Pyle, R. L., Eckert, E. D., Hatsukami, D., et al. (1990). Bulimia nervosa in overweight individuals. *Journal of Nervous and Mental Disease, 178,* 324–327.

Mitchell, J. V. (Ed.) (1985). *The ninth mental measurements yearbook.* Lincoln, NE: Buros Institute of Mental Measurements.

Miyake, K., Chen, S., & Campos, J. J. (1985). Infant temperament, mother's mode of interaction, and attachment in Japan: An interim report. In I. Bretherton & E. Waters (Eds.), Growing points of attachment theory and research. *Monographs of the Society for Research in Child Development, 50*(1–2, Serial No. 209).

Moergen, S., Merkel, W., and Brown, S. (1990) The use of covert sensitization and social skills training in the treatment of an obscene telephone caller. *Journal of Behavior Therapy and Experimental Psychiatry, 21,* 269–275.

Mogenson, G. J. (1976). Neural mechanisms of hunger: Current status and future prospects. In D. Novin, W. Wyrwicka, & G. Bray (Eds.), *Hunger: Basic mechanisms and clinical applications.* New York: Raven.

Mogg, K., Bradley, B. P., Williams, R., & Mathews, A. (1993). Subliminal processing of emotional information in anxiety and depression. *Journal of Abnormal Psychology, 102,* 304–311.

Molloy, D. W., Guyett, G. H., Wilson, D. B., Duke, R., Rees, L., & Singer, J. (1991). Effect of tetrahydroaminoacridine on cognition, function and behaviour in Alzheimer's disease. *Canadian Medical Association Journal, 144,* 29–34.

Monahan, J. (1981). *Predicting violent behavior: An assessment of clinical techniques.* Beverly Hills, CA: Sage.

Monahan, J. (1988). Risk assessment of violence among the mentally disordered: Generating useful knowledge. *International Journal of Law and Psychiatry, 11,* 249.

Monahan, J. (1993). Limiting therapist exposure to *Tarasoff* liability. *The American Psychologist, 48,* 242–250.

Money, J. (1987a). Human sexology and psychoneuroendocrinology. In D. Crews (Ed.), *Psychobiology of reproductive behavior: An evolutionary perspective.* Englewood Cliffs, NJ: Prentice-Hall.

Money, J. (1987b). Sin, sickness, or status? Homosexuality, gender identity, and psychoneuroendocrinology. *American Psychologist, 42,* 384–399.

Money, J., Schwartz, M., & Lewis, V. G. (1984). Adult erotosexual status and fetal hormonal masculinization and demasculinization: 46,XX congential virilizing adrenal hyperplasia and 46,XY androgen-insensitivity syndrome compared. *Psychoneuroendocrinology, 9,* 405–414.

Monk, T. H., Moline, M. L., & Graeber, R. C. (1988). Inducing jet lag in the laboratory patterns of adjustment to an acute shift in routine. *Aviation and Space Environmental Medicine, 59,* 703–710.

Monroe, S., & Simons, A. (1991). Diathesis-stress theories in the context of life stress research: Implications for the depressive disorders. *Psychological Bulletin, 110,* 406–425.

Monroe, S., Thase, M., & Simons, A. (1992). Social factors and psychobiology of depression: Relations between life stressand apid eye movement sleep latency. *Journal of Abnormal Psychology, 101,* 528–537.

Montemayor, R. (1983). Parents and adolescents in conflict: All families some of the time and some families most of the time. *Journal of Early Adolescence, 3,* 83–103.

Montgomery, K. C. (1953). Exploratory behavior as a function of "similarity" of stimulation situations. *Journal of Comparative and Physiological Psychology, 46,* 129–133.

Monti-Bloch, L., & Grosser, B. I. (1991). Effect of putative pheromones on the electrical activity of the human vomeronasal organ and olfactory epithelium. *Journal of Steroid Biochemistry and Molecular Biology, 39,* 573–582.

Moore, R. Y., & Bloom, F. E. (1979). Central catecholamine neuron systems: Anatomy and physiology of the norepinephrine and epinephrine systems. *Annual Review of Neuroscience, 2,* 113–168.

Moore-Ede, M. C., Sulzman, F. M., & Fuller, C. A. (1982). *The clocks that time us.* Cambridge: Harvard University Press.

Moos, R. H., & Billings, A. G. (1982). Conceptualizing and measuring coping resources and processes. In L. Goldberger & S. Breznitz (Eds.), *Handbook of stress.* New York: Macmillan.

Moos, R. H., & Schaefer, J. (1984). The crisis of physical illness: An overview and conceptual approach. In R. H. Moos (Ed.), *Coping with physical illness: New perspectives.* New York: Plenum

Morawitz, D. (1989). Behavioral self-help treatment for insomnia: A contolled evaluation. *Behavior Therapy, 20,* 365–379.

Moray, N. (1960). Attention in dichotic listening: Affective cues and influence of instructions. *Quarterly Journal of Experimental Psychology, 11,* 56–60.

Moreland, R. L., & Zajonc, R. B. (1977). Is stimulus recognition a necessary condition for the occurrence of exposure effects? *Journal of Personality and Social Psychology, 35,* 191–199.

Moreland, R. L., & Zajonc, R. B. (1982). Exposure effects in person perception. *Journal of Experimental Social Psychology, 18,* 395–415.

Morgan, C. D., & Murray, H. A. (1935). A method for investigating fantasy: The thematic apperception test. *Archives of Neurology and Psychiatry, 34,* 289–306.

Morgan, J. I., & Curran, T. (1991). Stimulus-transcription coupling in the nervous system: Involvement of the inducible proto-oncogenes *fos* and *jun. Annual Review of Neuroscience, 14,* 421–451.

Morgan, W. G. (1973). Situational specificity in altruistic behavior. *Representative Research in Social Psychology, 4,* 56–66.

Morris, C. D., Bransford, J. D., & Franks, J. J. (1977). Levels of processing versus transfer appropriate processing. *Journal of Verbal Learning and Verbal Behavior, 16,* 519–533.

Morrison, A. M., & Von Glinow, M. A. (1990). Women and minorities in management. *American Psychologist, 45,* 200–208.

Morrison, F., Holmes, D. L., & Haith, M. M. (1974). A developmental study of the effects of familiarity on short term visual memory. *Journal of Experimental Child Psychology, 18,* 412–425.

Morse, C. A., Dennerstein, L., Farrell, E., & Varnavides, K. (1991). A comparison of hormone therapy, coping skills training, and relaxation for the relief of premenstrual syndrome. *Journal of Behavioral Medicine, 14,* 469–489.

Mortimer, R. G., Goldsteen, K., Armstrong, R. W., & Macrina, D. (1988). *Effects of enforcement, incentives, and publicity on seat belt use in Illinois.* University of Illinois, Dept. of Health & Safety Studies, Final Report to Illinois Dept. of Transportation (Safety Research Report 88–11).

Moscovici, S. (1985). Social influence and conformity. In G. Lindzey & E. Aronson (Eds.), *The handbook of social psychology: Vol. 2* (3rd ed.). New York: Random House.

Moses, S. (1991, August). Researcher finds joy in helping kids learn. *APA Monitor,* 32.

Moses-Zirkes, S. (1993). Outcomes research: Everybody wants it. *APA Monitor,* March, pp. 22–23.

Moss, H. A., & Susman, E. J. (1980). Longitudinal study of personality development. In O. G. Brim & J. Kagan (Eds.), *Constancy and change in human development.* Cambridge, MA: Harvard University Press.

Mourant, R. R., & Rockwell, T. H. (1972). Strategies of visual search by novice and expert automobile drivers. *Human Factors, 14,* 325–336.

Mowbray, C. T., Herman, S. E., & Hazel, K. L. (1992). Gender and serious mental illness: A feminist perspective. *Psychology of Women Quarterly, 16,* 107–126.

Mowrer, O. H., & Ullman, A. D. (1945). Time as a determinant in integrative learning. *Psychological Review, 52,* 61–90.

Moyer, K. E. (1983). The physiology of motivation: Aggression as a model. In C. J. Scheier & A. M. Rogers (Eds.), *G. Stanley Hall Lecture Series: Vol. 3.* Washington, DC: American Psychological Association.

Moynihan, D. P. (1993). Defining deviancy down. *The American Scholar, 62,* 17–30.

Mueller, D., Edwards, D. W., & Yarvis, R. M. (1977). Stressful life events and psychiatric symptomatology: Change or undesirability? *Journal of Health and Social Behavior, 18,* 307–316.

Mueller, E. (1972). The maintenance of verbal exchanges between young children. *Child Development, 43,* 930–938.

Mueller, E. (1989). Toddlers' peer relations: Shared meaning and semantics. In W. Damon (Ed.), *Child development today and tomorrow* (pp. 312–331). San Francisco: Jossey-Bass.

Mueller, E., & Lucas, T. (1975). A developmental analysis of peer interaction among toddlers. In M. Lewis & L. A. Rosenblum (Eds.), *Friendship and peer relations.* New York: Wiley-Interscience.

Mueller, E., & Vandell, D. (1979). Infant-infant interaction. In J. D. Osofsky (Ed.), *Handbook of infant development.* New York: Wiley.

Mulder, H. E., Van Olphen, A. F., Bosman, A., & Smoorenburg, G. F. (1992). Phoneme recognition by deaf individuals using the multichannel nucleus cochlear implant. *Acta Otolaryngology, 112,* 946–955.

Munroe, R. H., & Munroe, R. L. (1994). Behavior across cultures: Results from observational studies. In W. J. Lonner & R. S. Malpass (Eds.), *Psychology and culture.* Boston: Allyn & Bacon.

Murray, E. A., & Mishkin, M. (1985). Amygdalectomy impairs crossmodal association in monkeys. *Science, 228,* 604–606.

Murray, H. A. (1938). *Explorations in personality.* New York: Oxford University Press.

Murray, H. A. (1962). *Explorations in personality.* New York: Science Editions.

Murray, H. A. (1971). *Thematic Apperception Test.* Cambridge: Harvard University Press.

Murrey, G. J., Cross, H. J., & Whipple. J. (1992). Hypnotically created pseudomemories: Further investigation into the "memory distortion or response bias" question. *Journal of Abnormal Psychology, 101,* 75–77.

Murstein, B. I. (1980). Mate selection in the 1970s. *Journal of Marriage and the Family, 42,* 777–792.

Murthy, C. V., & Panda, S. C. (1987). A study of intelligence, socioeconomic status and birth order among children belonging to SC-ST and non-SC-ST groups. *Indian Journal of Behaviour, 11,* 25–30.

Museo, E., Zocchi, A., & Pert, A. (1992). Cocaine and amphetamine: A comparison of their effects on dopamine overflow in the striatum and amygdala. *Society for Neuroscience Abstracts, 22,* 1079.

Musick, J. (1987, September 14). Press conference concerning the Ounce of Prevention Project, Chicago, IL.

Mussen, P. H., & Eisenberg-Berg, N. (1977). *The roots of caring.* New York: W. H. Freeman.

Myers, A. K., & Miller, N. E. (1954). Failure to find a learned drive based on hunger: Evidence for learning motivated by "exploration." *Journal of Comparative and Physiological Psychology, 47,* 428–436.

Myers, J. L., O'Brien, E. J., Balota, D. A., & Toyofuku, M. L. (1984). Memory search without interference: The role of integration. *Cognitive Psychology, 16,* 217–242.

Myles-Worsley, M., Johnston, W. A., & Simons, M. A. (1989). The influence of expertise on x-ray image processing. *Journal of Experimental Psychology: Learning, Memory, and Cognition, 14,* 553–557.

Mynatt, C., & Sherman, S. J. (1975). Responsibility attribution in groups and individuals: A direct test of the diffusion of responsibility hypothesis. *Journal of Personality and Social Psychology, 32,* 1111–1118.

Nagel, D. (1988) Human error in aircraft operations. In E. Wiener & D. Nagel (Eds.), *Human factors in aviation.* San Diego: Academic Press.

Naglieri, J. A., Das, J. P., Stevens, J. J., & Ledbetter, M. F. (1991). Confirmatory factor analysis of planning, attention, simultaneous, and successive cognitive processing tasks. *Journal of School Psychology, 29,* 1–17.

Nahemow, L., & Lawton, M. P. (1975). Similarity and propinquity in friendship formation. *Journal of Personality and Social Psychology, 32,* 205–213.

Nash, M., Drake, S., Wiley, S., Khalsa, S., & Lynn, S. (1986). Accuracy of recall by hypnotically age-regressed subjects. *Journal of Abnormal Psychology, 95,* 298–300.

Nathans, J. E., Thomas, D., & Hogness, D. (1986). Molecular genetics of human color vision: The genes encoding blue, green, and red pigments. *Science, 232,* 193–202.

National Academy of Sciences. (1982). *Marijuana and health.* Washington, DC: National Academy Press.

National Center for Health Statistics. (1988). *Advance report of final mortality statistics, 1986.* NCHS Monthly Vital Statistics Report, 37 (Suppl. 6).

National Commission on Marijuana and Drug Abuse, Raymond P. Shafer, Chair. (1972). *Marijuana: A signal of misunderstanding.* New York: New American Library.

National Computer Systems. (1992). *Catalog of assessment instruments, reports, and services.* Minneapolis: NCS.

National Institute of Mental Health. (1985). *Electroconvulsive therapy: Consensus development conference statement.* Bethesda, MD: U.S. Department of Health and Human Services.

National Institute of Mental Health. (1986). *Suicide.* Rockville, MD: U.S. Department of Health and Human Services.

National Institute on Drug Abuse. (1991). *National household survey on drug abuse.* Washington, DC: NIDA.

National Research Council. (1992). *Understanding and preventing violence.* Washington, DC: National Academy Press.

Navon, D., & Gopher, D. (1979). On the economy of the human processing system. *Psychological Review, 86,* 254–255.

Naylor, H., Halliday, R., & Callaway, R. (1992) Biochemical correlates of human information processing. In A. P. Vernon (Ed.), *Biological Approaches to the Study of Human Intelligence.* New Jersey: Ablex.

Neale, J. M., Oltmanns, T. F., & Winters, K. C. (1983). Recent developments in the assessment and conceptualization of schizophrenia. *Behavioral Assessment, 5,* 33–54.

Neher, A. (1991). Maslow's theory of motivation: A critique. *Journal of Humanistic Psychology, 31,* 89–112.

Neighbors, H., Elliot, K., & Gant, L. (1990). Self-help and Black Americans: A strategy for empowerment. In T. J. Powell (Ed.), *Working with self-help.* Silver Spring, MD: NASW Press.

Neimark, E. D. (1982). Adolescent thought: Transition to formal operations. In B. B. Wolman & G. Stircler (Eds.), *Hand-*

book of developmental psychology. Englewood Cliffs, NJ: Prentice-Hall.

Neisser, U. (1991). A case of misplaced nostalgia. *American Psychologist, 46,* 34–36.

Neisser, U., & Becklan, K. (1975). Selective looking: Attention to visually specified events. Cognitive Psychology, 7, 480–494.

Nelson, D. L., Schreiber, T. A., & McEvoy, C. L. (1992). Processing implicit and explicit representations. *Psychological Review, 99,* 322–348.

Nelson, K. (1986). Event knowledge and cognitive development. In K. Nelson (Ed.), *Event knowledge: Structure and function in development.* Hillsdale, NJ: Lawrence Erlbaum Associates.

Nelson, K. (1993). Developing self-knowledge from autobiographical memory. In T. K. Srull & R. S. Wyer (Eds.), *The mental representation of trait and autobiographical knowledge about the self: Advances in social cognition: Vol. V.* Hillsdale, NJ: Lawrence Erlbaum Associates.

Nelson, K. E., Denninger, M. M., Bonvillian, J. D., Kaplan, B. J., & Baker, N. (1983). Maternal input adjustments and nonadjustments as related to children's linguistic advances and to language acquisition theories. In A. D. Pellegrini & T. D. Yawkey (Eds.), *The development of oral and written languages: Readings in developmental and applied linguistics.* Norwood, NJ: Ablex.

Nelson, T. O., & Leonesio, R. J. (1988). Allocation of self-paced study time and the "labor-in-vain effect." *Journal of Experimental Psychology: Learning, Memory, and Cognition, 14,* 676–686.

Nelson, T. O., & Narens, L. (1980). A new technique for investigating the feeling of knowing. *Acta Psychologica, 46,* 69–80.

Nelson, T. O., Leoneslo, R. J., Shimamura, A. P., Landwehr, R. F., & Narens, L. (1982). Overlearning and the feeling of knowing. *Journal of Experimental Psychology: Learning, Memory, and Cognition, 8,* 279–288.

Nemeroff, C. B. (1989). Clinical significance of psychoneuroendocrinology in psychiatry: Focus on the thyroid and adrenal. *Journal of Clinical Psychiatry, 50,* 13–20.

Nemeth, C., & Chiles, C. (1988). Modelling courage: The role of dissent in fostering independence. *European Journal of Social Psychology, 18,* 275–280.

Neugarten, B. L. (1968). Adult personality: Toward a psychology of the life cycle. In B. L. Neugarten (Ed.), *Middle age and aging.* Chicago: University of Chicago Press.

Neugarten, B. L. (1977). Personality and aging. In J. E. Birren & K. W. Schaie (Eds.), *Handbook of the psychology of aging.* New York: Van Nostrand Reinhold.

Neugarten, B. L., & Neugarten, D. A. (1987). The changing meanings of age. *Psychology Today,* pp. 29–33.

Neugarten, B. L., Havighurst, D. J., & Tobin, S. S. (1968). Personality and patterns of aging. In B. L. Neugarten (Ed.), *Middle age and aging.* Chicago: University of Chicago Press.

Nevin, A., & Thousand, J. (1986). What the research says about limiting or avoiding referrals to special education. *Teacher Education and Special Education, 9,* 149–161.

Newcomb, M. D., & Bentler, P. M. (1989). Substance use and abuse among children and adolescents. *American Psychologist, 44,* 242–248.

Newell, A., & Simon, H. A. (1972). *Human problem solving.* Englewood Cliffs, NJ : Prentice-Hall.

Newlin, D. B., Carpenter, B., & Golden, C. J. (1981). Hemispheric asymmetries in schizophrenia. *Biological Psychiatry, 16,* 561–582.

Newman, J. P., & Kosson, D. S. (1986). Passive avoidance learning in psychopathic and nonpsychopathic offenders. *Journal of Abnormal Psychology, 95,* 252–256.

Newman, L. S., & Uleman, J. S. (1989). Spontaneous trait inference. In J. S. Uleman & J. A. Bargh (Eds.), *Unintended thought.* New York: Guilford Press.

Newman, L. S., & Uleman, J. S. (1990). Assimilation and contrast effects in spontaneous trait inference. *Personality and Social Psychology Bulletin, 16,* 224–240.

Niaura, R., Herbert, P., Petrie, C., McMahan, N., & Somerville, L. (1989). *Repressive coping and blood lipids: Gender and age effects.* Paper presented at the Tenth Annual Meeting of the Society of Behavioral Medicine, San Francisco.

Nicassio, P. (1985). The psychological adjustment of the Southeast Asian refugee: An overview of empirical findings and theoretical models. *Journal of Cross-Cultural Psychology, 16,* 153–173.

Nichols, D. E., & Oberlender, R. (1990). Structure-activity relationship of MDMA and related compounds: A new class of psychoactive drugs. *Annals of the New York Academy of Sciences, 600,* 613–625.

Nichols, R. (1978). Twin studies of ability, personality, and interests. *Homo, 29,* 158–173.

Nicholson, A. N., Pascoe, P. A., Spencer, M. B., Stone, B. M., Roehis, T., & Roth, T. (1986). Sleep after transmeridian fights. *Lancet, 2,* 1205–1208.

Nicholson, C. D. (1990). Pharmacology of nootropics and metabolically active compounds in relation to their use in dementia. *Psychopharmacology, 101,* 147–159.

Nicholson, I. R., & Neufeld, R. W. J. (1993). Classification of the schizophrenias according to symptomatology: A two factor model. *Journal of Abnormal Psychology, 102,* 259–270.

Nicholson, R. A., & Berman, J. S. (1983). Is follow-up necessary in evaluating psychotherapy? *Psychological Bulletin, 93,* 261–278.

Nickerson, R. A., & Adams, M. J. (1979). Long-term memory for a common object. *Cognitive Psychology, 11,* 287–307.

Niedenthal, P. M., Setterlund, M. B., & Wherry, M. B. (1992). Possible self-complexity and affective reactions to goal-relevant evaluation. *Journal of Personality and Social Psychology, 63,* 5–16.

Nielsen, S. (1990). Epidemiology of anorexia nervosa in Denmark from 1983 to 1987: A nationwide register study of psychiatric admission. *Acta Psychiatrica Scandinavica, 81,* 507–514.

Nielson Media. (1990). *1990 report on television.* New York: Nielson Media, Inc.

Nielson, E. B., Ginn, S. R., Cunningham, K. A., & Appeal, J. B. (1985). Antagonism of the LSD cue by putative serotonin antagonists: Relationship to inhibition of in vivo (-suo-3H) spiroperidol binding. *Behavioral Brain Research, 16*(2–3), 171–176.

Nietzel, M. T., & Bernstein, D. A. (1987). *Introduction to clinical psychology* (2nd ed.). New York: Prentice-Hall.

Nietzel, M. T., & Dillehay, R. C. (1987). *Psychological consultation in the courtroom.* New York: Pergamon.

Nietzel, M. T., & Harris, M. (1990). Relationship of dependency and achievement/autonomy to depression. *Clinical Psychology Review, 10,* 279–298.

Nietzel, M. T., Bernstein, D. A., & Milich, R. (1991). *Introduction to clinical psychology* (3rd ed.). Englewood Cliffs, NJ: Prentice Hall.

Nietzel, M. T., Bernstein, D. A., & Milich, R. (1994). *Introduction to clinical psychology* (4th ed.). Englewood Cliffs, NJ: Prentice-Hall.

Nietzel, M. T., Guthrie, P. R., & Susman, D. T. (1990). Utilization of community and social support resources. In F. H. Kanfer & A. P. Goldstein (Eds.), *Helping people change* (4th ed.). New York: Pergamon Press.

NIH (Technology Assessment Conference Panel) (1992). Methods for voluntary weight loss and control. *Annals of Internal Medicine, 116,* 942–949.

Nijhawan, R. (1991). Three dimensional Muller-Lyer illusion. *Perception and Psychophysics, 49,* 333–341.

Nilsson, L. (1989). Classification of human memory. In H. L. Roediger & F. I. M. Craik (Eds.), *Varieties of memory and consciousness*. Hillsdale, NJ: Lawrence Erlbaum Associates.

Nisbett, E. B. (1973). An escalator phobia overcome in one session of flooding in vivo. *Journal of Behavior Therapy and Experimental Psychiatry, 4,* 405–406.

Nisbett, R. E. (1972). Hunger, obesity, and the ventromedial hypothalamus. *Psychological Review, 79,* 433–453.

Nisbett, R. E., & Gordon, A. (1967). Self-esteem and susceptibility to social influence. *Journal of Personality and Social Psychology, 5,* 268–276.

Nisbett, R. E., & Wilson, T. D. (1977). Telling more than we can know: Verbal reports on mental processes. *Psychological Review, 84,* 231–259.

Nolen-Hoeksma, S. (1990). *Sex differences in depression.* Stanford, CA: Stanford University Press.

Nolen-Hoeksma, S., Morrow, J., & Fredrickson, N. (1993). Response styles and the duration of episodes of depressed mood. *Journal of Abnormal Psychology, 102,* 20–28.

Norman, D. (1987). Categorization of action slips. *Psychological Review, 88,* 1–15.

Norman, D. A. (1988). *The psychology of everyday things.* New York: Basic Books.

Norton, G. R., Cox, B., & Malan, J. (1992). Nonclinical panickers: A critical review. *Clinical Psychology Review, 12,* 121–139.

Nosofsky, R. M., Kruschke, J. K., & McKinley, S. C. (1992). Combining exemplar-based category representations and connectionist learning rules. *Journal of Experimental Psychology: Learning, Memory, and Cognition, 18,* 211–233.

Nottebohm, F. (1985). Neuronal replacement in adulthood. *Annals of the New York Academy of Science, 457,* 143–161.

Novak, M. A. (1991). Psychologists care deeply about animals. *APA Monitor,* July, p. 4.

Novick, L. R. (1988). Analogical transfer, problem similarity, and expertise. *Journal of Experimental Psychology: Learning, Memory, and Cognition, 14,* 510–520.

Nowicki, S., & Manheim, S. (1991). Interpersonal complementarity and time of interaction in female relationships. *Journal of Research in Personality, 25,* 322–333.

Nugent, F. (1994). *An introduction to the profession of counseling.* Columbus, OH: Merrill.

Nurnberger, J. I., & Gershon, E. S. (1984). Genetics of affective disorders. In R. M. Post & J. C. Ballenger (Eds.), *Neurobiology of mood disorders.* Baltimore: Williams & Wilkins.

O'Brien, T. L. (1991). Computers help thwart "groupthink" that plagues meetings. *Chicago Sun Times,* September 2.

O'Hare, D., & Roscoe, S. (1991). *Flight deck performance: The human factor.* Ames, IA: Iowa University Press.

O'Leary, D. K., & Wilson, T. G. (1987). Behavior therapy: Application and outcome (2nd ed.). Englewood Cliffs, NJ: Prentice-Hall.

O'Leary, K. D., Barling, J., Arias, I., Rosenbaum, A., Malone, J., & Tyree, A. (1989). Prevalence and stability of physical aggression between spouses: A longitudinal analysis. *Journal of Consulting and Clinical Psychology, 57,* 263–268.

O'Malley, S. S., Jaffe, A. J., Chang, G., Schottenfeld, R. S., Meyer, R. E., & Rounsaville, B. (1992). Naltrexone and coping skills therapy for alcohol dependence. *Archives of General Psychiatry, 49,* 881–887.

O'Reilly, K. R., & Higgins, D. L. (1991). AIDS community demonstration projects for HIV prevention among hard-to-reach groups. *Public Health Reports, 106,* 714–720.

O'Sullivan, C. S., & Durso, F. T. (1984). The effect of schema incongruent information on memory for stereotypical attributes. *Journal of Personality and Social Psychology, 47,* 55–70.

Oakes, J. (1989). Tracking in secondary schools. In R. E. Slavin (Ed.), *School and classroom organization.* Hillsdale, NJ: Lawrence Erlbaum Associates.

Oakland, T., & Glutting, J. J. (1990). Examiner observations of children's WISC-R test-related behaviors: Possible socioeconomic status, race, and gender effects. *Psychological Assessment, 2,* 86–90.

Oatley, K. (1993). Those to whom evil is done. In R. S. Wyer & T. K. Srull (Eds.), *Toward a general theory of anger and emotional aggression: Advances in social cognition, Vol. VI.* Hillsdale, NJ: Lawrence Erlbaum Associates.

Oatley, K., & Jenkins, J. M. (1992). Human emotions: Function and dysfunction. *Annual Review of Psychology, 43,* 55–85.

Offenbach, S. I. (1974). A developmental study of hypothesis testing and cue selection strategies. *Developmental Psychology, 10,* 484–490.

Offenbach, S., Chodzko-Zajko, W., & Ringel, R. (1990). Relationship between physiological status, cognition, and age in adult men. *Bulletin of the Psychonomics Society, 28,* 112–114.

Offerman, L. R., & Beil, C. (1992). Achievement styles of women leaders and their peers: Toward an understanding of women and leadership. *Psychology of Women Quarterly, 16,* 37–56.

Office of Technology Assessment. (1988). *Safe skies for tomorrow.* Washington, DC: U.S. Government Printing Office.

Ogloff, J., Wond, S., & Greenwood, A. (1990). Treating criminal psychopaths in a therapeutic community program. *Behavioral Sciences and the Law, 8,* 81–90.

Ohman, A., Dimberg, U., & Ost, L. G. (1985). Animal and social phobias: A laboratory model. In S. Reiss & R. R. Bootzin (Eds.), *Theoretical issues in behavior therapy.* Orlando, FL: Academic Press.

Ohman, A., Erixon, G., & Lofberg, I. (1975). Phobias and preparedness: Phobic versus neutral picture as conditioned stimuli for human autonomic responses. *Journal of Abnormal Psychology, 84,* 41–45.

Olds, J. (1973). Commentary on positive reinforcement produced by electrical stimulation of septal areas and other regions of rat brain. In E. S. Valenstein (Ed.), *Brain stimulation and motivation: Research and commentary.* Glenview, IL: Scott, Foresman.

Olds, J., & Milner, P. (1954). Positive reinforcement produced by electrical stimulation of septal areas and other regions of the rat brain. *Journal of Comparative and Physiological Psychology, 47,* 419–427.

Olds, M. E., & Fobes, J. L. (1981). The central basis of motivation: Intracranial self stimulus studies. *Annual Review of Psychology, 32,* 523–574.

Olney, J. W., Labruyere, J., & Price, M. T. (1989). Pathological changes induced in cerebrocortical neurons by phencyclidine and related drugs. *Science, 244,* 1360–1362.

Olpe, H. R., Steinmann, M. W., & Jones, R. S. G. (1985). Electrophysiological perspectives on locus coeruleus: Its role in cognitive versus vegetative functions. *Physiological Psychology, 13,* 179–187.

Olsen, K. M. (1969). *Social class and age-group differences in the timing of family status changes: A study of age-norms in American society.* Unpublished doctoral dissertation, University of Chicago, Chicago, IL.

Olson, G. M., & Sherman, T. (1983). Attention, learning, and memory in infants. In P. H. Mussen (Ed.), *Handbook of child psychology: Vol. 2. Infancy and developmental psychobiology.* New York: Wiley.

Olson, J. M. (1992). Self-perception of humor: Evidence for discounting and augmentation effects. *Journal of Personality and Social Psychology, 62,* 369–377.

Olson, L., Nordberg, A., Vonholst, H., Backman, L., Ebendal, T., Alafuzoff, I., Amberla, K., Hartvig, P., Herlitz, A., Lilja, A.,

Lundqvist, H., Langstrom, B., Meyerson, B., Persson, A., Viitanen, M., Winblad, B., & Seiger, A. (1992). Nerve growth factor affects C11-nicotine binding, blood flow, EEG, and verbal episodic memory in an Alzheimer patient. *Journal of Neural Transmission: Parkinson's Disease and Dementia Section, 4,* 79–95.

Olson, R. K., & Attneave, F. (1970). What variables produce stimulus grouping? *American Psychologist, 83,* 1–21.

Olson, R. P., Ganley, R., Devine, V. T., & Dorsey, G. C., Jr. (1981). Long-term effects of behavioral versus insight-oriented therapy with inpatient alcoholics. *Journal of Consulting and Clinical Psychology, 49,* 866–877.

Olweus, D. (1986). Aggression and hormones: Behavioral relationships with testosterone and adrenaline. In D. Olweus, J. Block, & M. Radke-Yarrow (Eds.), *Development of antisocial and prosocial behaviors.* Orlando, FL: Academic Press.

Orbell, J. M., van de Kragt, A. J. C., & Dawes, R. M. (1988). Explaining discussion-induced cooperation. *Journal of Personality and Social Psychology, 54,* 811–819.

Organ, D. W., & Bateman, J. S. (1991). *Organizational behavior* (4th ed.). Homewood, IL: Irwin.

Orme-Johnson, D. (1992). Personal communication, April 20.

Orne, M. T. (1970). Hypnosis, motivation and the ecological validity of the psychological experiment. In W. J. Arnold & M. M. Page (Eds.), *Nebraska symposium on motivation.* Lincoln: University of Nebraska Press.

Orne, M. T. (1977). The construct of hypnosis: Implications of definition for research and practice. In W. E. Edmonston, Jr. (Ed.), Conceptual and investigative approaches to hypnosis and hypnotic phenomena. *Annals of the New York Academy of Sciences, 296,* 14–33.

Orne, M. T. (1979). The use and misuse of hypnosis in court. *International Journal of Clinical and Experimental Hypnosis, 14,* 311–341.

Orne, M. T. (1980). On the construct of hypnosis: How its definition affects research and its clinical application. In G. D. Bowers & L. Dennerstein (Eds.), *Handbook of hypnosis and psychosomatic medicine.* Amsterdam: Elsevier.

Orne, M. T., & Evans, F. J. (1965). Social control in the psychological experiment: Antisocial behavior and hypnosis. *Journal of Personality and Social Psychology, 1,* 189–200.

Orne, M. T., & Holland, C. H. (1968). On the ecological validity of laboratory deceptions. *International Journal of Psychiatry, 6,* 282–293.

Orne, M. T., Sheehan, P. W., & Evans, F. J. (1968). Occurrence of posthypnotic behavior outside the experimental setting. *Journal of Personality and Social Psychology, 9,* 189–196.

Ornstein, R. (1985). *Psychology: The study of human experience.* San Diego: Harcourt Brace Jovanovich.

Ornstein, R. E. (1977). *The psychology of consciousness* (2nd ed.). New York: Harcourt Brace Jovanovich.

Ortega, K. A. (1989). Problem solving: Expert/novice differences. *Human Factors Society Bulletin, 32,* 1–5.

Ortony, A., Clore, G. L., & Collins, A. (1988). *The cognitive structure of emotions.* Cambridge, Eng.: Cambridge University Press.

Ory, J. (1986). *College, department, and course grade distribution for fall semester, 1985* (Research Memorandum No. 222). Champaign: University of Illinois, Office of Instructional Resources.

Öst, L-G. (1992). Blood and injection phobia: Background and cognitive, physiological and behavioral variables. *Journal of Abnormal Psychology, 101,* 68–74.

Öst, L-G., Hellström, K., & Kåver, A. (1992). One- versus five-session exposure in the treatment of needle phobia. *Behavior Therapy, 23,* 263–282.

Öst, L-G., Salkovskis, P. M., & Hellström, K. (1991). One-session therapist-directed exposure vs. self-exposure in the treatment of spider phobia. *Behavior Therapy, 22,* 407–422.

Öst, L-G. (1978). Behavioral treatment of thunder and lightning phobia. *Behaviour Research and Therapy, 16,* 197–207.

Öst, L-G. (1985). Ways of acquiring phobias and outcome of behavioral treatments. *Behaviour Research and Therapy, 23,* 683–689.

Oster, H. (1981). "Recognition" of emotional expression in infancy? In M. E. Lamb & L. R. Sherrod (Eds.), *Infant social cognition.* Hillsdale, NJ: Lawrence Erlbaum Associates.

Ostrom, T. M. (1989). Interdependence of attitude theory and measurement. In A. R. Pratkanis, S. J. Breckler, & A. G. Greenwald (Eds.), *Attitude structure and function.* Hillsdale, NJ: Lawrence Erlbaum Associates.

Ostrom, T. M. (1990). The maturing of social cognition. In T. K. Srull & R. S. Wyer (Eds.), *Advances in social cognition: Vol. 3. Content and process specificity in the effects of prior experiences.* Hillsdale, NJ: Lawrence Erlbaum Associates.

Otero, J., & Kintsch, W. (1992). Failures to detect contradictions in a text: What readers believe versus what they read. *Psychological Science, 3*(4), 229–235.

Otis, L. S. (1984). The adverse effects of meditation. In D. H. Shapiro & R. N. Walsh (Eds.), *Meditation: Classical and contemporary perspectives.* New York: Aldine.

Ottati, V. C., Riggle, E. J., Wyer, R. S., Schwarz, N., & Kuklinski, J. (1989). Cognitive and affective bases of opinion survey responses. *Journal of Personality and Social Psychology, 57,* 404–415.

Overton, D. A. (1984). State dependent learning and drug discriminations. In L. L. Iverson, S. D. Iverson, & S. H. Snyder (Eds.), *Handbook of psychopharmacology* (Vol. 18). New York: Plenum Press.

Pachella, R. (1974). The use of reaction time measures in information processing research. In B. H. Kantowitz (Ed.), *Human information processing.* Hillsdale, NJ: Lawrence Erlbaum Associates.

Padilla, A. M., Lindholm, K. J., Chen, A., Duran, R., Hakuta, K., Lambert, W., & Tucker, G. R. (1991). The English-only movement: Myth, reality and implications for psychology. *American Psychologist, 46,* 120–130.

Pagel, M. D., Erdley, W. W., & Becker, J. (1987). Social networks: We get by with (and in spite of) a little help from our friends. *Journal of Personality and Social Psychology, 53,* 793–804.

Paivio, A. (1986). *Mental representations: A dual coding approach.* New York: Oxford University Press.

Pallanti, S., & Mazzi, D. (1992). MDDMA (ecstasy) precipitation of panic disorder. *Biological Psychiatry, 32,* 91–95.

Palmer, D. L., & Kalin, R. (1991). Predictive validity of the dogmatic rejection scale. *Personality and Social Psychology Bulletin, 17,* 212–218.

Palmer, F. H., & Anderson, L. W. (1979). Long term gains from early intervention: Findings from longitudinal studies. In E. Zigler & J. Valentine (Eds.), *Project Head Start: A legacy of the war on poverty.* New York: Free Press.

Palmer, R. L. (Ed.) (1981). *Electroconvulsive therapy: An appraisal.* New York: Oxford University Press.

Palmer, S. E. (1975). The effects of contextual scenes on the identification of objects. *Memory & Cognition, 3,* 519–526.

Palmisano, M., & Herrmann, D. (1991). The facilitation of memory performance. *Bulletin of the Psychonomic Society, 29,* 557–559.

Pardo, J. V., Fox, P. T., & Raichle, M. E. (1991). Localization of a human system for sustained attention by positron emission tomography. *Nature, 349,* 61–64.

Park, B. (1989). Trait attributions as on-line organizers in person impressions. In J. N. Bassili (Ed.), *On-line cognition in person impression.* Hillsdale, NJ: Lawrence Erlbaum Associates.

Park, D. C., Smith, A. D., Dudley, W. N., & Lafronza, V. N. (1989). Effects of age and a divided attention task presented during encoding and retrieval on memory. *Journal of Experimental Psychology: Learning, Memory, and Cognition, 15,* 1185–1191.

Parke, R. D., Berkowitz, L., Leyens, J. P., West, S. G., & Sebastian, R. J. (1977). Some effects of violent and nonviolent movies on the behavior of juvenile delinquents. In L. Berkowitz (Ed.), *Advances in experimental social psychology: Vol. 10.* New York: Academic Press.

Parker, J. G., & Asher, S. R. (1987). Peer relations and later adjustment: Are low-accepted children "at risk"? *Psychological Bulletin, 102,* 358–389.

Parkes, C. M., & Brown, R. (1972). Health after bereavement: A controlled study of young Boston widows and widowers. *Psychosomatic Medicine, 34,* 449–461.

Parkes, J. D., & Locke, C. B. (1989). Genetic factors in sleep disorders. *Journal of Neurology, Neurosurgery, and Psychiatry,* June (Supplement), 101–108.

Parkes, K. R. (1984). Locus of control, cognitive appraisal, and coping in stressful episodes. *Journal of Personality and Social Psychology, 46*(3), 655–668.

Parkin, A. J., & Walter, B. M. (1991). Aging, short-term memory, and frontal dysfunction. *Psychobiology, 19,* 175–179.

Parloff, M. B. (1987). Psychotherapy: An import from Japan. *Psychology Today,* February, pp. 74–75.

Parten, M. B. (1932). Social participation among preschool children. *Journal of Abnormal and Social Psychology, 27,* 243–269.

Parten, M. B. (1971). Social play among preschool children. In R. E. Herron & B. Sutton-Smith (Eds.), *Child's play.* New York: Wiley. (Reprinted from *Journal of Abnormal and Social Psychology,* 1933, *28,* 136–147.)

Pascual-Leone, A., Dhuna, A., Altafullah, I., & Anderson, D. C. (1990). Cocaine-induced seizures. *Neurology, 40,* 404–407.

Patchev, V., Felszeghy, K., & Korranyi, L. (1991). Neuroendocrine and neurochemical consequences of long-term sleep deprivation in rats: Similarities to some features of depression. *Homeostasis in Health and Disease, 33,* 97–108.

Patel, V. L., Groen, G. J., & Arocha, J. F. (1990). Medical expertise as a function of task difficulty. *Memory & Cognition, 18,* 394–406.

Patrick, C. J., Bradley, M. M., & Lang, P. J. (1993). Emotion in the criminal psychopath: Startle reflex modulation. *Journal of Abnormal Psychology, 102,* 82–92.

Patrick, C. J., Craig, K. D., & Prkachin, K. M. (1986). Observer judgments of pain: Facial action determinants. *Journal of Personality and Social Psychology, 50,* 1291–1298.

Patterson, D. R., Everett, J. J., Burns, G. L., & Marvin, J. A. (1992). *Journal of Consulting and Clinical Psychology, 60,* 713–717.

Patterson, F. G. (1978). The gestures of a gorilla: Language acquisition in another pongid. *Brain and Language, 5,* 72–97.

Patterson, G. R. (1974). Intervention for boys with conduct problems: Multiple settings, treatments, and criteria. *Journal of Consulting and Clinical Psychology, 42,* 471–481.

Patterson, G. R. (1982). *Coercive family process.* Eugene, OR: Castalia Press.

Pattie, F. A. (1935). A report of attempts to produce uniocular blindness by hypnotic suggestion. *British Journal of Medical Psychiatry, 15,* 230–241.

Pauk, W., & Fiore, J. P. (1989). *Succeed in College!* Boston: Houghton Mifflin.

Paul, G. L. (1969a). Behavior modification research: Design and tactics. In C. M. Franks (Ed.), *Behavior therapy: Appraisal and status* (pp. 29–62). New York: McGraw-Hill.

Paul, G. L. (1969b). Physiological effects of relaxation training and hypnotic suggestion. *Journal of Abnormal Psychology, 74,* 425–437.

Paul, G. L. (1986). Can pregnancy be a placebo effect? Terminology, designs, and conclusions in the study of psychosocial and pharmacological treatments of behavior disorders. *Journal of Behavior Therapy and Experimental Psychiatry, 17,* 61–82.

Paul, G. L., & Lentz, R. J. (1977). *Psychosocial treatment of chronic mental patients: Milieu versus social learning programs.* Cambridge: Harvard University Press.

Paulus, P. B. (1988). *Prison crowding: A psychological perspective.* New York: Springer-Verlag.

Paulus, P. B., & Nagar, D. (1989). Environmental influences on groups. In P.B. Paulus (Ed.), *Psychology of group influence* (2nd ed.). Hillsdale, NJ: Lawrence Erlbaum Associates.

Paunonen, S., Jackson, D., Trzebinski, J., & Forsterling, F. (1992). Personality structure across cultures: A multimethod evaluation. *Journal of Personality and Social Psychology, 62,* 447–456.

Pavkov, T., Lewis, D., & Lyons, J. (1989). Psychiatric diagnosis and racial bias: An empirical investigation. *Professional Psychology: Research and Practice, 20,* 364–368.

Pavlov, I. P. (1927). *Conditioned reflexes* (G. V. Anrep, Trans.). London: Oxford University Press.

Pavlov, T. W., Lewis, D. A., & Lyons, J. S. (1989). Psychiatric diagnosis and racial bias: An empirical investigation. *Professional Psychology: Research and Practice, 20,* 364–368.

Paykel, E. S., Prusoff, B. A., & Myers, J. K. (1975). Suicide attempts and recent life events. *Archives of General Psychiatry, 32,* 327–333.

Payne, J. W., Bettman, J. R., & Johnson, E. J. (1992). Behavioral decision research: A constructive processing perspective. *Annual Review of Psychology, 43,* 87–131.

Peck, J. W. (1978). Rats defend different body weights depending on palatability and accessibility of their food. *Journal of Comparative and Physiological Psychology, 92,* 555–570.

Pedersen, D., & Wheeler, J. (1983). The Muller-Lyer illusion among Navajos. *Journal of Social Psychology, 121,* 3–6.

Pedersen, N. L., Plomin, R., McClearn, G. E., & Friberg, L. (1988). Neuroticism, extraversion, and related traits in adult twins reared apart and reared together. *Journal of Personality and Social Psychology, 55,* 950–957.

Pederson, P. (1994). A culture-centered approach to counseling. In W. J. Lonner & R. S. Malpass (Eds.), *Psychology and culture.* Boston: Allyn & Bacon.

Pederson, P., Draguns, J., Lonner, W., & Trimble, J. (Eds.) (1989). *Counseling across cultures* (3rd ed.). Honolulu: University of Hawaii Press.

Peele, S. (1988). Fools for love: The romantic ideal, psychological theory, and addictive love. In R. J. Sternberg & M. L. Barnes (Eds.), *The psychology of love.* New Haven: Yale University Press.

Peine, H., Liu, L., Blakelock, H., Jenson, W., & Osborne, J. (1991). The use of contingent water misting in the treatment of self-choking. *Journal of Behavior Therapy and Experimental Psychiatry, 22,* 225–231.

Penfield, W., & Rasmussen, T. (1968). *The cerebral cortex of man: A clinical study of localization of function.* New York: Hafner.

Pennebaker, J. W. (1985). Traumatic experience and psychosomatic disease: Exploring the roles of behavioural inhibition, obsession, and confiding. *Canadian Psychology, 26,* 82–95.

Pennebaker, J. W. (1990). *Opening up: The healing power of confiding in others.* New York: Morrow.

Pennebaker, J. W., & Beall, S. K. (1986). Confronting a traumatic event: Toward an understanding of inhibition and disease. *Journal of Abnormal Psychology, 95,* 274–281.

Pennebaker, J. W., & Chew, C. H. (1985). Deception, electrodermal activity, and inhibition of behavior. *Journal of Personality and Social Psychology, 49,* 1427–1433.

Pennebaker, J. W., & O'Heeron, R. C. (1984). Confiding in others and illness rate among spouses of suicide and accidental death victims. *Journal of Abnormal Psychology, 93,* 473–476.

Pennebaker, J. W., Colder, M., & Sharp, L. K. (1990). Accelerating the coping process. *Journal of Personality and Social Psychology, 58,* 528–537.

Pennebaker, J., Kiecolt-Glaser, J., & Glaser, R. (1988). Disclosure of trauma and immune function: Health implications for psychotherapy. *Journal of Consulting and Clinical Psychology, 56,* 239–245.

Pennington, B. F. (1991). *Diagnosing learning disorders.* New York: Guilford Press.

Pennington, N., & Hastie, R. (1990). Practical implications of psychological research on juror and jury decision making. *Personality and Social Psychology Bulletin, 16,* 90–105.

Peock, K. (1969). Pathophysiology of emotional disorders associated with brain damage. In P. J. Vinken and G. W. Bruyn (Eds.), *Handbook of clinical neurology* (Vol. 3). New York: American Elsevier.

Peper, R. J., & Mayer, R. E. (1978). Note taking as a generative activity. *Journal of Educational Psychology, 70,* 514–522.

Pepeu, G., Spignoli, G., Giovannini, M. G., & Magnani, M. (1989). The relationship between the behavioral effects of cognition-enhancing drugs and brain acetylcholine: Nootropic drugs and brain acetylcholine. *Pharmacopsychiatry, 22,* Supplement 2, 116–119.

Perfetti, C. A. (1991, March). The psychology, pedagogy, and politics of reading. *Psychological Science, 2*(2), 70.

Perloff, L. S., & Fetzer, B. K. (1986). Self-other judgments and perceived vulnerability to victimization. *Journal of Personality and Social Psychology, 50,* 502–511.

Perls, F. S. (1969). *Gestalt therapy verbatim.* Lafayette, CA: Real People Press.

Perls, F. S. (1970). Four lectures. In J. Fagan & I. L. Shepherd (Eds.), *Gestalt therapy now* (pp. 14–38). Palo Alto, CA: Science and Behavior Books.

Perls, F. S., Hefferline, R. F., & Goodman, P. (1951). *Gestalt therapy.* New York: Julian Press.

Peroutka, S. J. (1987). Incidence of recreational 3,4-methylene-dioxymethamphetamine (MDMA, "Ecstasy") on an undergraduate campus. *New England Journal of Medicine, 317,* 1542–1543.

Peroutka, S. J. (1989). "Ecstasy": A human neurotoxin? *Archives of General Psychiatry, 46,* 191.

Peroutka, S. J., Newman, H., & Harris, H. (1988). The subjective effects of 3, 4-methylenedioxymethamphetamine in recreational users. *Neuropharmacology, 1*(4), 273–277.

Perper, T. (1985). *Sex signals: The biology of love.* Philadelphia: ISI Press.

Pervin, L. (1989). *Personality: Theory and research* (5th ed.). New York: Wiley.

Pervin, L. A. (1989). Psychodynamic-systems reflections on a social-intelligence model of personality. In R. S. Wyer & T. K. Srull (Eds.), *Advances in social cognition: Vol. 2. Social intelligence and cognitive assessments of personality.* Hillsdale, NJ: Lawrence Erlbaum Associates.

Peters, J. J. (1977). The Philadelphia rape victim project. In D. Chappell, R. Geiss, & G. Geiss (Eds.), *Forcible rape: The crime, the victim, and the offenders.* New York: Columbia University Press.

Petersen, S. E., Fox, P. T., Snyder, A. Z., & Raichle, M. E. (1990). Activation of extrastriate and frontal cordical areas by visual words and word-like stimuli. *Science, 249,* 1041–1044.

Peterson, A. C. (1987, September). Those gangly years. *Psychology Today,* pp. 28–34.

Peterson, A., Compas, B., Brooks-Gunn, J., Stemmler, M., Ey, S., & Grant, K. (1993). Depression in adolescence. *American Psychologist, 48,* 155–168.

Peterson, C., & Seligman, M. E. P. (1984). Causal explanations as a risk factor for depression: Theory and evidence. *Psychological Review, 91,* 347–374.

Peterson, C., Seligman, M. E. P., & Vaillant, G. E. (1988). Pessimistic explanatory style is a risk factor for physical illness: A thirty-five-year longitudinal study. *Journal of Personality and Social Psychology, 55,* 23–27.

Peterson, L. (1989). Special series: Coping with medical illness and medical procedures. *Journal of Consulting and Clinical Psychology, 57,* 331–332.

Peterson, L. R., & Peterson, M. J. (1959). Short-term retention of individual verbal items. *Journal of Experimental Psychology, 58,* 193–198.

Peterson, S. E., Snyder, A., Fox, P. T., & Raichle, M. E. (1990). Activation of extrastriate and frontal cortical areas by visual words and word-like stimuli. *Science, 249,* 1041–1044.

Petitto, J., Folds, J., Ozer, H., Quade, D., & Evans, D. (1992). Abnormal diurnal variation in circulating natural killer cell phenotypes and cytotoxic activity in major depression. *American Journal of Psychiatry, 149,* 694–696.

Petri, H. L. (1986). *Motivation: Theory and research* (2nd ed.). Belmont, CA: Wadsworth.

Petty, R. E., & Cacioppo, J. T. (1981). *Attitudes and persuasion: Classic and contemporary approaches.* Dubuque, IA: William C. Brown.

Petty, R. E., Priester, J. R., & Wegener, D. T. (1994). Cognitive processes in attitude change. In R. S. Wyer & T. K. Srull (Eds.), *Handbook of social cognition* (2nd ed.). Hillsdale, NJ: Lawrence Erlbaum Associates.

Phares, E. J. (1973). *Locus of control: A personality determinant of behavior.* Morristown, NJ: General Learning Press.

Phares, E. J. (1991). *Introduction to personality* (3rd ed.). New York: Harper Collins.

Phelps, B. J., & Exum, M. E. (1992, Spring). Subliminal tapes: How to get the message across. *Skeptical Inquirer, 16,* 282–286.

Phelps, M. E., & Mazziotta, J. C. (1985). Positron emission tomography: Human brain function and biochemistry. *Science, 228,* 799–809.

Phinney, J. S. (1990). Ethnic identity in adolescents and adults: A review of research. *Psychological Bulletin, 108,* 499–514.

Phoenix, C. H., Goy, R. W., Gerall, A. A., & Young, W. C. (1959). Organizing action of prenatally administered testosterone propionate on the tissue mediating mating behavior in the female guinea pig. *Endocrinology, 65,* 369–382.

Piaget, J. (1952). *The origins of intelligence in children.* New York: International Universities Press.

Pickar, D., Owen, R., Litman, R., Konicki, P., Guiterrez, R., & Rapaport, M. (1992). Clinical and biologic response to clozapine in patients with schizophrenia. *Archives of General Psychiatry, 49,* 345–353.

Pickens, R. W., Svikis, D. S., McGue, M., Lykken, D. T., Heston, L. L., & Clayton, P. J. (1991). Heterogeneity in the inheritance of alcoholism. *Archives of General Psychiatry, 48,* 19–28.

Pierce, G., Sarason, B., & Sarason, I. (1992). General and relationship-based perceptions of social support: Are two constructs better than one? *Journal of Personality and Social Psychology, 61,* 1028–1039.

Pierce, G., Sarason, I., & Sarason, B. (1991). General and specific support expectations and stress as predictors of perceived supportivness: An experimental study. *Journal of Personality and Social Psychology, 63,* 297–307.

Pierce, J., Fiore, M., Novotny, T., Hatziandreu, E., & Davis, R. (1989). Trends in cigarette smoking in the United States: Projections to the year 2000. *Journal of the American Medical Association, 261,* 61–65.

Piliavin, I. M., Piliavin, J. A., & Rodin, J. (1975). Costs, diffusion, and the stigmatized victim. *Journal of Personality and Social Psychology, 32,* 429–438.

Pilisuk, M., Boylan, R., & Acredolo, C. (1987). Social support, life stress, and subsequent medical care utilization. *Health Psychology, 6,* 273–288.

Pillemer, D. B. (1990). Clarifying the flashbulb memory concept: Comment on McCloskey, Wible, and Cohen (1988). *Journal of Experimental Psychology: General, 119,* 92–96.

Pillemer, D. B., Goldsmith, L. R., Panter, A. T., & White, S. H. (1988). Very long-term memories of the first year in college. *Journal of Experimental Psychology: Learning, Memory, and Cognition, 14,* 709–715.

Pincus, H., Frances, A., Davis, W., First, M., & Widiger, T. (1992). DSM-IV and new diagnostic categories: Holding the line on proliferation. *American Journal of Psychiatry, 149,* 112–117.

Platt, S. A., & Sanislow, C. A. (1988). Norm-of-reaction: Definition and misinterpretation of animal research. *Journal of Comparative Psychology, 102,* 254–261.

Plomin, R. (1989). Environment and genes: Determinants of behavior. *American Psychologist, 44,* 105–111.

Plomin, R. (1990a). *Nature and nurture: An introduction to human behavioral genetics.* Belmont, CA: Brooks/Cole.

Plomin, R. (1990b). The role of inheritance in behavior. *Science, 248,* 183–188.

Plomin, R., & Daniels, D. (1987). Why are children in the same family so different from each other? *Behavioral and Brain Sciences, 10,* 1–16.

Plomin, R., & DeFries, J. C. (1985). *Origins of individual differences in infancy.* New York: Academic Press.

Plomin, R., & Foch, T. T. (1980). A twin study of objectively assessed personality in childhood. *Journal of Personality and Social Psychology, 39,* 680–688.

Plomin, R., & Neiderhiser, J. M. (1992). Genetics and experience. *Current Directions in Psychological Science, 1,* 160–163.

Plomin, R., DeFries, J. C., & Fulker, D. W. (1988). *Nature and nurture during infancy and early childhood.* New York: Cambridge University Press.

Plous, S. (1988). Modeling the nuclear arms race as a perceptual dilemma. *Philosophy and Public Affairs, 17,* 44–53.

Poeck, K. (1969). Pathophysiology of emotional disorders associated with brain damage. In P. J. Vinken & G. W. Bruyn (Eds.), *Handbook of clinical neurology: Vol. 3.* New York: American Elsevier.

Poggio, T, Gamble, E. B., & Little, J. J. (1988). Parallel integration of vision modules. *Science, 242,* 436–440.

Poincare, H. (1913). Mathematical creation. In G. H. Halstead (Trans.), *The foundations of science.* New York: Science Press.

Poland, R. E., Rubin, R. T., Lesser, I. M., Lane, L. A., & Hart, P. J. (1987). Neuroendocrine aspects of primary endogenous depression. *Archives of General Psychiatry, 44,* 790–796.

Pollack, I. (1953). The assimilation of sequentially coded information. *American Journal of Psychology, 66,* 421–435.

Pollard-Gott, L. (1983). Emergence of thematic concepts in repeated listening to music. *Cognitive Psychology, 15,* 66–94.

Polya, G. (1957). How to solve it. Garden City, NY: Anchor.

Pomerleau, O. (1992). Cigarette smoking as drug self-administration. *Health Psychology, 11* (suppl.), 49.

Ponzetti, J. J., Cate, R. M., & Koval, J. E. (1982). Violence between couples: Profiling the male abuser. *The Personnel and Guidance Journal, 61,* 222–224.

Poon, L. W., & Fozard, J. L. (1978). Speed of retrieval from long-term memory in relation to age, familiarity, and datedness of information. *Journal of Gerontology, 33,* 711–717.

Pope, H. G., & Katz, D. L. (1988). Affective and psychotic symptoms associated with anabolic steroid use. *American Journal of Psychiatry, 145,* 487–490.

Pope, K. S., & Vetter, V. A. (1992). Ethical dilemmas encountered by members of the American Psychological Association. *American Psychologist, 47,* 397–411.

Poppel, E. (1988). *Mindworks: Time and conscious experience.* Orlando: Harcourt Brace Jovanovich.

Porter, R. H. (1991). Human reproduction and the mother-infant relationship. In T. V. Getchell et al. (Eds.), *Taste and smell in health and disease.* New York: Raven Press.

Porter, R. H., Cernich, J. M., & McLaughlin, F. J. (1983). Maternal recognition of neonates through olfactory cues. *Physiology and Behavior, 30,* 151–154.

Posner, M. I. (1978). *Chronometric explorations of the mind.* Hillsdale, NJ: Lawrence Erlbaum Associates.

Posner, M. I., & Peterson, S. E. (1990). The attention system of the human brain. *Annual Review of Neurosciences, 13,* 25–42.

Posner, M. I., Nissen, M. J., & Klein, R. (1976). Visual dominance: An information processing account of its origins and significance. *Psychological Review, 83,* 157–171.

Posner, M., Petersen, S., Fox, P., & Raichle, M. E. (1988). Localization of cognitive operation in the human brain. *Science, 240,* 1627–1631.

Powell, G. J., Nabers, K., & Knight, M. (1992). Journal editors' attitudes toward statistical criteria for publication of manuscripts. Paper presented at the 4th annual convention of the American Psychological Society, San Diego, June.

Powell, T. J. (Ed.) (1990). *Working with self-help.* Silver Spring, MD: NASW Press.

Power, T. G., & Parke, R. D. (1983). Patterns of mother and father play with their 8-month-old infant: A multiple analysis approach. *Infant Behavior and Development, 6,* 453–459.

Powers, D. E. (1986). Relations of test item characteristics to test preparation/test practice effects: A quantitative summary. *Psychological Bulletin, 100,* 67–77.

Powley, T. L., & Keesey, R. E. (1970). Relationship of body weight to the lateral hypothalamic syndrome. *Journal of Comparative and Physiological Psychology, 70,* 25–36.

Pratkanis, A. R. (1992). The cargo-cult science of subliminal persuasion. *Skeptical Inquirer, 16,* 260–273.

Predmore, S. C. (1991). Micro-coding of cockpit communications in accident analyses: Crew coordination in the United Airlines flight 232 accident. In R. S. Jensen (Ed.), *Proceedings of the 6th International Symposium on Aviation Psychology.* Columbus: Ohio State University, Department of Aviation.

Premack, D. (1965). Reinforcement theory. In D. Levine (Ed.), *Nebraska symposium on motivation.* Lincoln: University of Nebraska Press.

Premack, D. (1971). Language in chimpanzees? *Science, 172,* 808–822.

Prentice-Dunn, S., & Rogers, R. W. (1989). Deindividuation and the self-regulation of behavior. In P. B. Paulus (Ed.), *Psychology of group influence* (2nd ed.). Hillsdale, NJ: Lawrence Erlbaum Associates.

President's Commission on Mental Health. (1978). *Report to the President.* Washington, DC: Superintendent of Documents, U.S. Government Printing Office.

Price, B. K., & McNeill, B. W. (1992). Cultural commitment and attitudes toward seeking counseling services in American Indian college students. *Professional Psychology, 23,* 376–381.

Price, R. (1992). Psychosocial impact of job loss on individuals and families. *Current Directions in Psychological Sciences,* 1–11.

Price, R. A., & Vanderberg, S. G. (1979). Matching for physical attractiveness in married couples. *Personality and Social Psychology Bulletin, 5,* 398–400.

Prinzmetal, W. (1992). The word superiority effect does not require a T-scope. *Perception and Psychophysics, 51,* 473–484.

Pritchard, W. S. (1981). The psychophysiology of P300. *Psychological Bulletin, 89,* 506–540.

Prochaska, J. O., & DiClemente, C. C. (1992). Stages of change in the modification of problem behaviors. In M. Hersen, R. M. Eisler, & P. M. Miller (Eds.), *Progress in behavior modification.* Sycamore, IL: Sycamore Press.

Prochaska, J. O., & DiClemente, C. C. (1992). Stages of change in the modification of problem behaviors. In M. Hersen, R. M. Eisler, & P. M. Miller (Eds.), *Progress in behavior modification.* Sycamore, IL: Sycamore Press.

Prochaska, J. O., DiClemente, C., & Norcross, J. (1992). In search of how people change: Application to addictive behaviors. *American Psychologist, 47,* 1102–1114.

Prochaska, J. O., DiClemente, C. C., Velicer, W. F., Rossi, J. S., & Guadagnoli, E. (1992). Patterns of change in smoking cessation: Between-variable comparisons. Unpublished manuscript, University of Rhode Island.

Prochaska, J. O., & Norcross, J. C. (1982). The future of psychotherapy: A Delphi poll. *Professional Psychology, 13,* 620–627.

Provence, S., & Lipton, R. C. (1962). *Infants in institutions.* New York: International Universities Press.

Psychology Teacher Network. (1992, January/February). APA task force emphasizes psychology's contributions to education (Vol. 2), pp. 1–10.

Purcell, D. G., & Stewart, A. L. (1991). The object-detection effect: Configuration enhances perception. *Perception and Psychophysics, 50,* 215–224.

Putallaz, M., & Gottman, J. (1981). An interactional model of children's entry into peer groups. *Child Development, 52,* 986–994.

Putnam, F. W., Zahn, T. P., & Post, R. M. (1990). Differential autonomic nervous system activity in multiple personality disorder. *Psychiatric Research, 31,* 251–260.

Pyle, R. L., Mitchell, J. E., & Eckert, E. D. (1981). Bulimia: A report of 34 cases. *Journal of Clinical Psychiatry, 42,* 60–64.

Qian, Z., Gilbert, M. E., Colicos, M. A., Kandel, E. R., & Kuhl, D. (1993). Tissue-plasminogen activator is induced as an immediate early gene during seizure, kindling and long-term potentiation. *Nature, 361,* 453–457.

Quartermain, D., Kissileff, H., Shapiro, R., & Miller, N. E. (1971). Suppression of food intake with intragastric loading: Relation to natural feeding cycle. *Science, 173,* 941–943.

Quattrochi, J. J., Mamelak, A. N., Madison, R. D., Macklis, J. D., & Hobson, J. A. (1989). Map inputs to REM sleep induction sites with carbachol-fluorescent microspheres. *Science, 245,* 984–986.

Quay, H. C. (1979). Classification. In H. C. Quay & J. S. Werry (Eds.), *Psychopathological disorders of childhood* (2nd ed.). New York: Wiley.

Rabbitt, P. (1977). Changes in problem solving ability in old age. In J. E. Birren & K. W. Schaie (Eds.), *Handbook of the psychology of aging.* New York: Van Nostrand Reinhold.

Rabkin, J. G., & Struening, E. L. (1976). Life events, stress, and illness. *Science, 194,* 1013–1020.

Rachman, S. (1989). *Fear and courage* (2nd ed.). New York: Freeman.

Rachman, S. J. (1990). *Fear and courage* (2nd ed.). San Francisco: W. H. Freeman.

Rachman, S. J., & Hodgson, R. J. (1980). *Obsessions and compulsions.* Englewood Cliffs, NJ: Prentice-Hall.

Rachman, S. J., & Wilson, G. T. (1980). *The effects of psychological therapy* (2nd ed.). New York: Pergamon Press.

Rada, J. B., & Rogers, R. W. (1973). *Obedience to authority: Presence of authority and command strength.* Paper presented at the annual convention of the Southeastern Psychological Association.

Radecki, T. E. (1990). Cartoon monitoring. *National Coalition on Television Violence News,* April-June, p. 9.

Rader, N., Spiro, D. J., & Firestone, P. B. (1979). Performance on a stage IV object permanence task with standard and nonstandard covers. *Child Development, 50,* 908–910.

Radloff, L. (1975). Sex differences in depression: The effects of occupation and marital status. *Sex Roles, 1,* 249–265.

Radner, D., & Radner, M. (1989). *Animal consciousness.* Buffalo, NY: Prometheus.

Ragland, D. R., & Brand, R. J. (1988). Type A behavior and mortality from coronary heart disease. *New England Journal of Medicine, 318,* 65–69.

Rahe, R., Romo, M., Bennett, L., & Siltanen, P. (1974). Recent life changes, myocardial infarction, and abrupt coronary death: Studies in Helsinki. *Archives of Internal Medicine, 133,* 221–228.

Raine, A., Venables, P., & Williams, M. (1990). Relationships between central and autonomic measures of arousal at age 15 years and criminality at age 24 years. *Archives of General Psychiatry, 47,* 1003–1007.

Rajecki, D. W. (1990). *Attitudes: Themes and advances* (2nd ed.). Sunderland, MA: Sinauer Associates.

Rakic, P., & Yaklovlev P. I. (1968). Development of the corpus callosum and the cavum septi in man. *Journal of Comparative Neurology, 132,* 45–72.

Rakowski, W., Dube, C., Marcus, B., Prochaska, J. O., Velicer, W., & Abrams, D. (1992). Assessing elements of women's decisions about mammography. *Health Psychology, 11,* 111–118.

Raloff, J. (1985). A sweet taste of success to drink in. *Science News, 127,* 262.

Ralph, M. R., Foster, R. G., Davis, F. C., & Menaker, M. (1990). Transplanted suprachiasmatic nucleus determines circadian period. *Science, 247,* 975–978.

Ramachandran, V. S. (1988, August). Perceiving shape from shading. *Scientific American,* pp. 76–83.

Ramey, C. T., Bryant, D. M., Wasik, B. H., Sparling, J. J., Fendt, K. H., & LaVange, L. M. (1992). Infant health and development program for low birth weight, premature infants: Program elements, family participation, and child intelligence. *Pediatrics, 89,* 454–465.

Randi, J. (1987). *Flim Flam!* Buffalo, NY: Prometheus Books.

Rao, K. R., & Palmer, J. (1987). The anomaly called Psi: Recent research and criterion. *Brain and Behavior Sciences, 10,* 539–643.

Rapoport, J. (1989). The biology of obsessions and compulsions. *Scientific American, 260,* 83–89.

Rappaport, J. (1977). *Community psychology: Values, research and action.* New York: Holt, Rinehart and Winston.

Rappaport, J. (1987). Terms of empowerment/exemplars of prevention: Toward a theory for community psychology. *American Journal of Community Psychology, 15,* 117–148.

Raschke, H. J. (1977). The role of social participation in postseparation and postdivorce adjustment. *Journal of Divorce, 1,* 129–140.

Raskin, D. C. (1986). The polygraph in 1986: Scientific, professional and legal issues surrounding applications and acceptance of polygraph evidence. *Utah Law Review 1986,* 29–74.

Raskin, D. C., & Podlesny, J. A. (1979). Truth and deception: A reply to Lykken. *Psychological Bulletin, 86,* 54–59.

Rasmussen, J. (1981). Models of mental strategies in process control. In J. Rasmussen & W. Rouse (Eds.), *Human detection and diagnosis of system failures.* New York: Plenum Press.

Rasmussen, J., Pejtersen, A. M., & Goodstein, L. P. (in press). *Cognitive engineering: Concepts and applications.* New York: John Wiley and Sons.

Ratcliff, R., & McKoon, G. (1989). Memory models, text processing, and cue-dependent retrieval. In H. L. Roediger & F. I. M. Craik (Eds.), *Varieties of memory and consciousness.* Hillsdale, NJ: Lawrence Erlbaum Associates.

Ray, D. W., Wandersman, A., Ellisor, J., & Huntington, D. E. (1982). The effects of high density in a juvenile correctional institution. *Basic and Applied Social Psychology, 3,* 95–108.

Raynor, J. O. (1970). Relationships between achievement-related motives, future orientation, and academic performance. *Journal of Personality and Social Psychology, 15,* 28–33.

Raz, S., & Raz, N. (1990). Structural brain abnormalities in the major psychoses: A quantitative review of the evidence from computerized imagining. *Psychological Bulletin, 108,* 93–108.

Reason, J. (1990). *Human error.* Cambridge, Eng.: Cambridge University Press.

Reber, A. S. (1992). The cognitive unconscious: An evolutionary perspective. *Consciousness and Cognition, 1,* 93–133.

Rechtschaffen, A., Gilliland, M. A., Bergmann, B. M., & Winter, J. B. (1983). Physiological correlates of prolonged sleep deprivation in rats. *Science, 221,* 180–184.

Redd, M., & de Castro, J. M. (1992). Social facilitation of eating: Effects of social instruction on food intake. *Physiology and Behavior, 52,* 749–754.

Redd, W. H. (1984). Psychological intervention to control cancer chemotherapy side effects. *Postgraduate Medicine, 75,* 105–113.

Redd, W. H., Jacobsen, P. B., Die-Trill, M., Dermatis, H., McEvoy, M., & Holland, J. C. (1987). Cognitive/attentional distraction in the control of conditioned nausea in pediatric cancer patients receiving chemotherapy. *Journal of Consulting and Clinical Psychology, 55,* 391–395.

Reder, L. M., & Anderson, J. R. (1980). A partial resolution of the paradox of interference: The role of integrating knowledge. *Cognitive Psychology, 12,* 447–472.

Reder, L. M., & Ritter, F. E. (1992). What determines initial feeling of knowing? Familiarity with question terms, not the answer. *Journal of Experimental Psychology: Learning, Memory, and Cognition, 18,* 435–451.

Ree, M. J., & Earles, J. A. (1992). Intelligence is the best predictor of job performance. *Current Directions in Psychological Science, 1,* 86–89.

Reed, S. K. (1992). *Cognition: Theory and applications* (3rd ed.). Pacific Grove, CA: Brooks/Cole.

Reed, T. (1980). Challenging some "common wisdom" on drug abuse. *International Journal of the Addictions, 15,* 359–373.

Reedy, M. N. (1983). Personality and aging. In D. S. Woodruff & J. E. Birren (Eds.), *Aging: Scientific perspectives and social issues* (2nd ed.). Monterey, CA: Brooks/Cole.

Reedy, M. N., Birren, J. E., & Schaie, K. W. (1981). Age and sex differences in satisfying love relationships across the adult life span. *Human Development, 24,* 52–56.

Regan, D., Kaufman, L., & Lincoln, J. (1986). Motion in depth and visual acceleration. In K. Boff, L. Kaufman, & J. Thomas (Eds.), *Handbook of perception and human performance.* New York: Wiley.

Regier, D. A., Narrow, W., Rae, D., Manderschied, R., Locke, B., & Goodwin, F. (1993). The de facto U.S. mental and addictive disorders service system: Epidemiologic catchment area prospective 1-year prevalence rates of disorders and services. *Archives of General Psychiatry, 50,* 85–94.

Reichel, F. D., & Todd, J. D. (1990). Perceived depth inversion of smoothly curved surface due to image orientation. *Journal of Experimental Psychology: Human Perception and Performance, 16,* 653–671.

Reicher, G. M. (1969). Perceptual recognition as a function of meaningfulness of stimulus material. *Journal of Experimental Psychology, 87,* 275–280.

Reiman, E. M., Fusselman, M. J., Fox, P. T., & Raichle, M. E. (1989). Neuroanatomical correlates of anticipatory anxiety. *Science, 243,* 1071–1074.

Reiman, E. M., Raichle, M. E., Butler, F. K., Herscovitch, P., & Robins, E. (1984). A focal brain abnormality in panic disorder, a severe form of anxiety. *Nature, 310,* 683–685.

Reinisch, J. M. (1981). Prenatal exposure to synthetic progestins increases potential for aggression in humans. *Science, 211,* 1171–1173.

Reinisch, J. M., Ziemba-Davis, M., & Sanders, S. A. (1991). Hormonal contributions to sexually dimorphic behavioral development in humans. *Psychoneuroendocrinology, 16,* 213–278.

Reis, H. T., & Shaver, P. (1988). Intimacy as an interpersonal process. In S. Duck (Ed.), *Handbook of personal relationships.* Chichester, UK: Wiley.

Reisberg, D., Heuer, F., McLean, J., & O'Shaughnessy, M. (1988). The quantity, not the quality of affect predicts memory vividness. *Bulletin of the Psychonomic Society, 26,* 100–103.

Reisenzein, R. (1983). The Schachter theory of emotion: Two decades later. *Psychological Bulletin, 94,* 239–264.

Reisman, J. M. (1976). *A history of clinical psychology.* New York: Irvington.

Reiss, S., & McNally, R. J. (1985). The expectancy model of fear. In S. Reiss & R. R. Bootzin (Eds.), *Theoretical issues in behavior therapy.* New York: Academic Press.

Reitman, J. S. (1971). Mechanisms of forgetting in short-term memory. *Cognitive Psychology, 2,* 185–195.

Reitman, J. S. (1974). Without surreptitious rehearsal, information in short-term memory decays. *Journal of Verbal Learning and Verbal Behavior, 13,* 365–377.

Renault, E. M., Signoret, J. L., Debruille, B., Breton, F., & Bolgert, F. (1989). Brain potentials reveal covert facial recognition in prosopagnosia. *Neuropsychologia, 27,* 905–912.

Rende, R. D., Slomkowski, C. L., Stocker, C., Fulker, D. W., & Plomin, R. (1992). Genetic and environmental influences on maternal and sibling interaction in middle childhood: A sibling adoption study. *Developmental Psychology, 28,* 484–490.

Repetti, R. L. (1989). Effects of daily workload on subsequent behavior during marital interaction: The roles of social withdrawal and spouse support. *Journal of Personality and Social Psychology, 57,* 651–659.

Report of the British Advisory Committee on Drug Dependence. (1968).

Rescorla, L. A. (1981). Category development in early language. *Journal of Child Language, 8,* 225–238.

Rescorla, R. (1988). Pavlovian conditioning: It's not what you think it is. *American Psychologist, 43,* 151–159.

Rescorla, R. A. (1968). Probability of shock in the presence and absence of CS in fear conditioning. *Journal of Comparative and Physiological Psychology, 66,* 1–5.

Rescorla, R. A., & Gillian, D. J. (1980). An analysis of the facilitative effect of similarity on second-order conditioning. *Journal of Experimental Psychology: Animal Behavior Processes, 6,* 339–352.

Rescorla, R. A., & Wagner, A. R. (1972). A theory of Pavlovian conditioning: Variations in the effectiveness of reinforcement and nonreinforcement. In A. H. Black & W. F. Prokasy (Eds.), *Classical conditioning II.* New York: Appleton Century Crofts.

Resnick, S. M., Berenbaum, S. A., Gottesman, I. I., & Bouchard, T. J. (1986). Early hormonal influences on cognitive functioning in congenital adrenal hyperplasia. *Developmental Psychology, 22,* 191–198.

Reveaux, T. (1993). Virtual reality gets real. *New Media.* January, 34–41.

Review Panel on Coronary-Prone Behavior and Coronary Heart Disease. (1981). Coronary-prone behavior and coronary heart disease: A critical review. *Circulation, 3,* 119–1215.

Revkin, A. C. (1989, September). Crack in the cradle. *Discover,* pp. 63–69.

Revusky, S. H. (1971). The role of interference in association over a delay. In W. K. Honig & P. H. R. James (Eds.), *Animal memory.* New York: Academic Press.

Revusky, S. H. (1977). The concurrent interference approach to delay learning. In L. M. Barker, M. R. Best, & M. Domjan (Eds.), *Learning mechanisms in food selection.* Waco, TX: Baylor University Press.

Reynolds, B. A., & Weiss, S. (1992). Generation of neurons and astrocytes from isolated cells of the adult mammalian central nervous system. *Science, 255,* 1707–1710.

Reynolds, D. V. (1969). Surgery in the rat during electrical analgesia induced by focal brain stimulation. *Science, 164,* 444–445.

Rheingold, H. (1991). *Virtual reality.* New York: Summit Books.

Rheingold, H. L., & Eckerman, C. O. (1971). Departures from the mother. In H. R. Schaffer (Ed.), *The origins of human social relations.* London: Academic Press.

Rheingold, H., & Cook, K. (1975). The contents of boys' and girls' rooms as an index of parents' behavior. *Child Development, 46,* 459–463.

Rhodes, N., & Wood, W. (1992). Self-esteem and intelligence affect influenceability: The mediating role of message reception. *Psychological Bulletin, 111,* 156–171.

Rhodewalt, F., & Zone, J. B. (1989). Appraisal of life change, depression, and illness in hardy and nonhardy women. *Journal of Personality and Social Psychology, 56,* 81–88.

Rholes, W. S., & Ruble, D. N. (1984). Children's understanding of dispositional characteristics of others. *Child Development, 55,* 550–560.

Rice, P. L. (1987). *Stress and health: Principles and practice for coping and wellness.* Pacific Grove, CA: Brooks/Cole.

Rice, P. L. (1992). *Stress and health* (2nd ed.). Pacific Grove, CA: Brooks/Cole.

Richardson, P. H., & Vincent, C. A. (1986). Acupuncture for the treatment of pain: A review of evaluative research. *Pain, 24,* 15–40.

Rickards, J. P. (1976). Interaction of position and conceptual level of adjunct questions in immediate and delayed retention of text. *Journal of Educational Psychology, 68,* 210–217.

Rickels, K., Schweizer, E., Weiss, S., & Zavodnick, S. (1993). Maintenance drug treatment of panic disorder. II: Short- and long-term outcome after drug taper. *Archives of General Psychiatry, 50,* 61–68.

Ridley, M., & Dawkins, R. (1981). The natural selection of altruism. In J. P. Rushton & R. M. Sorrentino (Eds.), *Altruism and helping behavior.* Hillsdale, NJ: Lawrence Erlbaum Associates.

Riegel, K. F. (1975). Toward a dialectical theory of development. *Human Development, 18,* 50–64.

Riese, M. L. (1986). Temperament stability between the neonatal period and 24 months in full-term and preterm infants. *Infant Behavior and Development, 9,* 305. (Special issue: abstracts of papers presented at the Fifth International Conference on Infant Studies.)

Riger, S. (1992). Epistemological debates, feminist voices: Science, social values, and the study of women. *American Psychologist, 47,* 730–740.

Riggar, T. F. (1985). *Stress burnout: An annotated bibliography.* Carbondale: Southern Illnois University Press.

Riggio, R. E. (1989). *Introduction to industrial/organizational psychology.* Glenview, IL: Scott Foresman.

Riggle. (1989). (See Ottati, et al., 1989.)

Ringold, D. J. (1988). Consumer response to product withdrawal: The reformulation of Coca-Cola. *Psychology & Marketing, 5,* 189–210.

Rinn, W. E. (1984). The neuropsychology of facial expression: A review of the neurological and psychological mechanisms for producing facial expressions. *Psychological Bulletin, 95,* 52–77.

Risby, E., Hsiao, J., Manji, H., Biran, J., Moses, F., Zhou, D., & Potter, W. (1991). The mechanisms of action of lithium: II. Effects of adenylate cyclase activity and b-adrenergic receptor binding in normal subjects. *Archives of General Psychiatry, 48,* 513–554.

Risley, T. R. (1968). The effects and side effects of punishing the autistic behaviors of a deviant child. *Journal of Applied Behavior Analysis, 1,* 21–34.

Robertson, J., & Robertson, J. (1971). Young children in brief sep-

aration: A fresh look. *Psychoanalytic Study of the Child, 26,* 264–315.

Robins, L. N., & Helzer, J. E. (1986). Diagnosis and clinical assessment: The current state of psychiatric diagnosis. *Annual Review of Psychology, 37,* 409–432.

Robins, L. N., Helzer, J. E., Weissman, M. M., Orvaschel, H., Gruenberg, E., Burke, J. D., Jr., & Regier, D. A. (1984). Lifetime prevalence of specific psychiatric disorders in three sites. *Archives of General Psychiatry, 41,* 949–958.

Robinson, J. H., & Pritchard, W. S. (1992). The role of nicotine in tobacco use. *Psychopharmacology, 108,* 397–407.

Rochat, P., Clifton, R. K., Litovsky, R., & Perris, E. (1989, April). Preparatory reaching for various sized objects in the light and the dark by 6-month-olds. Paper presented at the biennial meeting of the Society for Research in Child Development, Kansas City, MO.

Rock group not liable for deaths (1990, September 10). *National Law Journal,* p. 33.

Rock, I. (1975). *An introduction to perception.* New York: Macmillan.

Rock, I. (1978). *An introduction to perception.* New York: Macmillan.

Rock, I. (1983). *The logic of perception.* Cambridge, MA: MIT Press.

Rodgers, J. L., & Rowe, D. C. (1988). Influence of siblings on adolescent sexual behavior. *Developmental Psychology, 24,* 722–728.

Rodin, J. (1973). Effects of distraction on the performance of obese and normal subjects. *Journal of Comparative and Physiological Psychology, 83,* 68–78.

Rodin, J. (1980). Current status of the internal-external hypothesis of obesity: What went wrong? *American Psychologist, 36,* 361–372.

Rodin, J. (1986a). Aging and health: Effects of the sense of control. *Science, 233,* 1271–1276.

Rodin, J. (1986b). Health, control, and aging. In M. Baltes & P. Baltes (Eds.), *Aging and control.* Hillsdale, NJ: Lawrence Erlbaum Associates.

Rodin, J., & Langer, E. J. (1977). Long-term effects of a control-relevant intervention with the institutionalized aged. *Journal of Personality and Social Psychology, 35,* 879–902.

Rodin, J., & Salovey, P. (1989). Health psychology. *Annual Review of Psychology, 40,* 533–580.

Rodin, J., Bartoshuk, L., Peterson, C., & Shank, D. (1990). Bulimia and taste: Possible interactions. *Journal of Abnormal Psychology, 99,* 32–39.

Rodriguez, M. A. (1991). What makes a warning label salient? *Proceedings of the 35th Annual Meeting of the Human Factors Society* (pp. 1029–1033). Santa Monica, CA: Human Factors Society.

Roediger, H. L., III. (1990). Implicit memory: Retention without remembering. *American Psychologist, 45,* 1043–1056.

Roediger, H. L., III, & McDermott, K. B. (1992). Depression and implicit memory: A commentary. *Journal of Abnormal Psychology, 101,* 587–591.

Roff, J. D., & Knight, R. (1981). Family characteristics, childhood symptoms, and adult outcome in schizophrenia. *Journal of Abnormal Psychology, 90,* 510–520.

Roffman, R. A., Gilchrist, L. D., Stephens, R. S., & Kirham, M. A. (1988, November). *Relapse prevention with gay or bisexual males at risk of AIDS due to engaging in unsafe sexual behavior.* Paper presented at the annual meetings of the Association for the Advancement of Behavior Therapy, New York.

Roffwarg, H. P., Hermann, J. H., & Bowe-Anders, C. (1978). The effects of sustained alterations of waking visual input on dream content. In A. M. Arkin, J. S. Antrobus, & S. J. Ellman (Eds.), *The mind in sleep.* Hillsdale, NJ: Lawrence Erlbaum Associates.

Roffwarg, H. P., Muzio, J. N., & Dement, W. C. (1966). Ontogenetic development of the human sleep-dream cycle. *Science, 152,* 604–619.

Rogers, A. G. (1987). Gender differences in moral reasoning: A validity study of two moral orientations. Unpublished doctoral dissertation, Washington University, St. Louis, MO.

Rogers, C. R. (1942). *Counseling and psychotherapy.* Boston: Houghton Mifflin.

Rogers, C. R. (1951). *Client-centered therapy.* Boston: Houghton Mifflin.

Rogers, C. R. (1961). *On becoming a person.* Boston: Houghton Mifflin.

Rogers, C. R. (1970). *Carl Rogers on encounter groups.* New York: Harper & Row.

Rogers, C. R. (1980). *A way of being.* Boston: Houghton Mifflin.

Rogers, J., Madamba, S. G., Staunton, D. A., & Siggins, G. R. (1986). Ethanol increases single unit activity in the inferior olivary nucleus. *Brain Research, 385,* 253–262.

Rogers, M., & Miller, N. (1981). *The effect of school setting on cross-racial interaction.* Paper presented at the Annual Meeting of the American Psychological Association, Montreal.

Rogers, R., & Ewing, P. (1989). Ultimate opinion proscriptions: A cosmetic fix and a plea for empiricism. *Law and Human Behavior, 13,* 357–374.

Rogler, L. (1992). The role of culture in mental health diagnosis: The need for programmatic research. *Journal of Nervous and Mental Disease, 180,* 745–747.

Rogoff, B., & Waddell, K. J. (1982). Memory for information organized in a scene by children from two cultures. *Child Development, 53,* 1224–1228.

Rohde, P., Lawinsohn, P. M., Tilson, M., & Seeley, J. R. (1990). Dimensionality of coping and its relation to depression. *Journal of Personality and Social Psychology, 58,* 499–511.

Roitblat, H. L., & Van Fersen, L. (1992). Comparative cognition: Representations and processes in learning and memory. *Annual Review of Psychology, 43,* 671–710.

Ronis, D. L., Yates, J. F., & Kirscht, J. P. (1989). Attitudes, decisions, and habits as determinants of repeated behavior. In A. R. Pratkanis, S. J. Breckler, & A. G. Greenwald (Eds.), *Attitude structure and function.* Hillsdale, NJ: Lawrence Erlbaum Associates.

Rook, K. S. (1987). Social support versus companionship: Effects on life stress, loneliness, and evaluations by others. *Journal of Personality and Social Psychology, 52,* 1132–1137.

Rosch, E. (1975). Cognitive representations of semantic categories. *Journal of Experimental Psychology: General, 104,* 192–223.

Rosch, E., Mervis, C. B., Gray, W. D., Johnson, D. M., & Boyes-Braem, P. (1976). Basic objects in natural categories. *Cognitive Psychology, 8,* 382–439.

Roscoe, S. (1989). The zoom lens hypothesis. In M. Hershenon (Ed.), *The moon illusion.* Hillsdale, NJ: Lawrence Erlbaum Associates.

Rose, S. A., Feldman, J. F., & Wallace, I. F. (1988). Individual differences in infants' information processing: Reliability, stability, and prediction. *Child Development, 59,* 1177–1197.

Rosen, B. C., & D'Andrade, R. (1959). The psychosocial origins of achievement motivation. *Sociometry, 22,* 188–218.

Rosenbaum, M. E. (1980). Cooperation and competition. In P. B. Paulus (Ed.), *The psychology of group influence.* Hillsdale, NJ: Lawrence Erlbaum Associates.

Rosenbaum, M. E. (1986). The repulsion hypothesis: On the non-development of relationships. *Journal of Personality and Social Psychology, 51,* 1156–1166.

Rosenbaun, D. L., & Seligman, M. E. (1989). *Abnormal psychology* (2nd ed.). New York: Norton.

Rosenberg, M. B., Friedmann, T., Robertson, R. C., Tuszynski, M., Wolff, J. A., Breakefield, X. O., & Gage, F. H. (1988). Grafting genetically modified cells to the damaged brain: Restorative effects of NGF expression. *Science, 242,* 1575–1578.

Rosenhan, D. L. (1973). On being sane in insane places. *Science, 179,* 250–258.

Rosenhan, D. L., & Seligman, M. E. P. (1989). *Abnormal psychology* (2nd ed.). New York: Norton.

Rosenman, R. H., Brand, R. J., Jenkins, D., Friedman, M., Straus, R., & Wurm, M. (1975). Coronary heart disease in the Western Collaborative Group study: Final follow-up experience of 8 1/2 years. *Journal of the American Medical Association, 233,* 872–877.

Rosenstock, I. (1974). Historical origins of the health beliefs model. *Health Education Monographs, 2,* 328–335.

Rosenthal, D. (1977). Searches for the mode of genetic transmission in schizophrenia: Reflections and loose ends. *Schizophrenia Bulletin, 3,* 268–276.

Rosenthal, R. R. (1966). *Experimenter effects in behavioral research.* New York: Appleton-Century-Crofts.

Rosenthal, R. R., & Jacobson, L. (1968). *Pygmalion in the classroom.* New York: Holt, Rinehart and Winston.

Rosenzweig, M. R., Bennett, E. L., & Diamond, M. C. (1972). Brain changes in response to experiences. *Scientific American, 226,* 22–39.

Roskies, E., Seraganian, P., Oseasohn, R., Hanley, J. A., Collu, R., Martin, N., & Smilga, C. (1986). The Montreal type A intervention project: Major findings. *Health Psychology, 5,* 45–69.

Ross, B. H. (1984). Remindings and their effects in learning a cognitive skill. *Cognitive Psychology, 16,* 371–416.

Ross, C., & Currie, R. (1990). Dissociative experiences in the general population. *American Journal of Psychiatry, 147,* 1547–1552.

Ross, C., Joshi, S., & Currie, R. (1990). Dissociative experiences in the general population. *American Journal of Psychiatry, 147,* 1547–1552.

Ross, C., Miller, S., Reagor, P., Bjornson, L., Fraser, G., & Anderson, G. (1990). Structured interview data on 102 cases of multiple personality disorder from four centers. *American Journal of Psychiatry, 147,* 596–610.

Ross, D. M., & Ross, S. A. (1982). *Hyperactivity: Current issues, research, and theory.* New York: Wiley & Sons.

Ross, L. D. (1988). Situationist perspectives on the obedience experiments. *Contemporary Psychology, 33,* 101–104.

Ross, L., & Nisbett, R. E. (1991). *The person and the situation: Perspectives of social psychology.* New York: McGraw-Hill.

Ross, M. (1989). Relation of implicit theories to the construction of personal histories. *Psychological Review, 96,* 341–357.

Ross, S. I., & Jackson, J. M. (1991). Teachers' expectations for black males' and black females' academic achievement. *Personality and Social Psychology Bulletin, 17,* 78–82.

Ross, S. M., & Ross, L. E. (1971). Comparison of trace and delay classical eyelid conditioning as a function of interstimulus interval. *Journal of Experimental Psychology, 91,* 165–167.

Rossetti, Y. (1992). A multidisciplinary approach to consciousness: The mind-body problem and conscious-unconscious processing. *Trends in Neurosciences, 15,* 467–468.

Rossiter, J. R., & Percy, L. (1987). *Advertising and promotion management.* New York: McGraw-Hill.

Rotfeld, H. J. (1989). Fear appeals and persuasion: Assumptions and errors in advertising research. In J. H. Leigh & C. R. Martin (Eds.), *Current issues and research in advertising.* Ann Arbor: University of Michigan Press.

Rotter, J. B. (1954). *Social learning and clinical psychology.* Englewood Cliffs, NJ: Prentice-Hall.

Rotter, J. B. (1990). Internal versus external control of reinforcement: A case history of a variable. *American Psychologist, 45,* 489–493.

Rotton, J., & Frey, J. (1985). Air pollution, weather, and violent crimes: Concomitant time-series analysis of archival data. *Journal of Personality and Social Psychology, 49,* 1207–1220.

Rotton, J., Frey, J., Barry, T., Mulligan, M., & Fitzpatrick, M. (1979). The air pollution experience and physical aggression. *Journal of Applied Social Psychology, 9,* 397–412.

Roueche, B. (1986, December 8). Cinnabar. *The New Yorker.*

Rouse, W. B., & Morris, N. M. (1986). On looking into the black box: Prospects and limits in the search for mental models. *Psychological Bulletin, 100,* 349–363.

Rovee-Collier, C. (1987). Learning and memory in infancy. In J. D. Osofsky (Ed.), *Handbook of infant development* (pp. 98–148). New York: Wiley.

Rowlison, R. T., & Felner, R. D. (1988). Major life events, hassles, and adaptation in adolescence: Confounding in the conceptualization and measurement of life stress and adjustment revisited. *Journal of Personality and Social Psychology, 55,* 432–444.

Rozanski, A., Bairey, C. N., Krantz, D. S., Friedman, J., Resser, K. J., Morell, M., Hilton-Chalfen, S., Hestrin, L., Bietendorf, J., & Berman, D. S. (1988). Mental stress and the induction of silent myocardial ischemia in patients with coronary artery disease. *The New England Journal of Medicine, 318,* 1005–1012.

Rozin, P. (1976). The psychobiological approach to human memory. In M. R. Rosenzweig & E. L. Berrnet (Eds.), *Neural Mechanisms of Learning and Memory.* Cambridge, MA: MIT Press.

Rozin, P. (1982). "Taste-smell confusions" and the duality of the olfactory sense. *Perception and Psychophysics, 31,* 397–401.

Rubin, E. (1915). *Synsoplevede figure.* Copenhagen: Gyldendalske.

Rubin, J. Z., Provenzano, F. J., & Luria, Z. (1974). The eye of the beholder: Parents' views on the sex of newborns. *American Journal of Orthopsychiatry, 44,* 512–519.

Rubinow, D. R., & Roy-Byrne P. (1984). Premenstrual syndromes: Overview from a methodological perspective. *American Journal of Psychiatry, 141,* 163–172.

Rubinow, D. R., Roy-Byrne, P., Hoban, M. C., Grover, G. N., Stambler, N., & Post, R. M. (1988). Premenstrual mood changes: Characteristic patterns in women with and without premenstrual syndrome. *Journal of Affective Disorders, 10,* 85–90.

Rubinstein, T., & Mason, A. F. (1979, November). The accident that shouldn't have happened: An analysis of Three Mile Island. *IEEE Spectrum,* 37–57.

Ruble, D. N. (1977). Premenstrual symptoms: a reinterpretation. *Science, 197,* 291–292.

Ruble, D. N., Fleming, A. S., Hackel, L. S., & Stangor, C. (1988). Changes in the marital relationship during the transition to first time motherhood: Effects of violated expectations concerning division of household labor. *Journal of Personality and Social Psychology, 55,* 78–87.

Rudorfer, M. V., Ross, R., Linniola, M., Sherer, M., & Potter, W. (1985). Exaggerated orthostatic responsiveness of plasma norepinephrine in depression. *Archives of General Psychiatry, 42,* 1186–1192.

Ruehlman, L. S., & Wolchik, S. A. (1988). Personal goals and interpersonal support and hindrance as factors in psychological distress and well-being. *Journal of Personality and Social Psychology, 55,* 293–301.

Rumbaugh, D. M. (Ed.) (1977). *Language learning by a chimpanzee: The Lana project.* New York: Academic Press.

Rumelhart, D. E. (1984). Schemata and the cognitive system. In R. S. Wyer & T. K. Srull (Eds.), *Handbook of social cognition: Vol. 1.* Hillsdale, NJ: Lawrence Erlbaum Associates.

Rumelhart, D. E., & Todd, P. M. (1992). Learning and connectionist representations. In D. E. Meyer & S. Kornblum (Eds.), *Attention and performance XIV: Synergies in experimental psychology, artificial intelligence, and cognitive neuroscience.* Cambridge, MA: MIT Press (pp. 3–30).

Rumelhart, D. E., McClelland, J. L., & the PDP Research Group. (1986). *Parallel distributed processing: Vol. 1. Foundations.* Cambridge, MA: MIT Press.

Rundus, D. (1971). Analysis of rehearsal processes in free recall. *Journal of Experimental Psychology, 89,* 63–77.

Rusbult, C. E., Verette, J., Whitney, G. A., Slovik, L. F., & Lipkus, I. (1991). Accommodation processes in close relationships: Theory and preliminary empirical evidence. *Journal of Personality and Social Psychology, 60,* 53–78.

Rushton, J. P. (1988). Epigenic rules in moral development: Distal-proximal approaches to altruism and aggression. *Aggressive Behavior, 14,* 35–50.

Rushton, J. P. (1990). Creativity, intelligence, and psychoticism. *Personality and Individual Differences, 11,* 1291–1298.

Rushton, J. P., Fulker, D. W., Neale, M. C., Nias, D. K. B., & Eysenck, H. J. (1986). Altruism and aggression: The heritability of individual differences. *Journal of Personality and Social Psychology, 50,* 1192–1198.

Russek, M. (1971). Hepatic receptors and the neurophysiological mechanisms controlling feeding behavior. In S. Ehrenpreis (Ed.), *Neurosciences research: Vol. 4.* New York: Academic Press.

Russell, J. A. (1991). Culture and the categorization of emotions. *Psychological Bulletin, 110,* 426–450.

Russell, M. J. (1976). Human olfactory communication. *Nature, 260,* 520–522.

Russell, M. J., Dark, K. A., Cummins, R. W., Ellman, G., Callaway, E., & Peeke, H. V. S. (1984). Learned histamine release. *Science, 225,* 733–734.

Rutkowski, G. K., Gruder, C. L., & Romer, D. (1983). Group cohesiveness, social norms, and bystander intervention. *Journal of Personality and Social Psychology, 44,* 545–552.

Rutter, M., & Giller, H. (1984). *Juvenile delinquency: Trends and perspectives.* New York: Guilford.

Ryan, R. H., & Geiselman, R. E. (1991). Effects of biased information on the relationship between eyewitness confidence and accuracy. *Bulletin of the Psychonomic Society, 29,* 7–9.

Ryan, W. (1977). *Blaming the victim.* New York: Vintage Books.

Rymer, R. (1992, April 23). A silent childhood. *The New Yorker,* pp. 41–81.

Rynders, J., & Horrobin, J. (1980). Educational provisions for young children with Down's syndrome. In J. Gottlieb (Ed.), *Educating mentally retarded persons in the mainstream* (pp. 109–147). Baltimore: University Park Press.

Sachdev, P., Hay, P., & Cumming, S. (1992). Surgical treatment of obsessive-compulsive disorder. *Archives of General Psychiatry, 49,* 582–583.

Sachs, J. (1967). Recognition memory for syntactic and semantic aspects of connected discourse. *Perception and Psychophysics, 2,* 437–442.

Sackeim, H. A. (1985, June). The case for ECT. *Psychology Today,* pp. 36–40.

Sackeim, H. A. (1988). Mechanisms of action of electroconvulsive therapy. In A. J. Frances & R. E. Hales (Eds.), *Annual Review of Psychiatry* (Vol. 7). Washington, DC: American Psychiatric Press.

Sackeim, H. A., Gur, R. C. J., & Saucy, M. C. (1978). Emotions are expressed more intensely on the left side of the face. *Science, 202,* 434–436.

Sackoff, J., & Weinstein, L. (1988). The effects of potential self-inflicted harm on obedience to an authority figure. *Bulletin of the Psychonomic Society, 26,* 347–348.

Sacks, O. (1985). *The man who mistook his wife for a hat.* New York: Summit Books.

Sacks, O. (1992). The landscape of his dreams. *The New Yorker,* July 27.

Safer, D. J. (1991). Diet, behavior modification, and exercise: A review of obesity treatments from a long-term perspective. *Southern Medical Journal, 84,* 1470–1474.

Saghir, M. T., & Robins, E. (1973). *Male and female homosexuality: A comprehensive investigation.* Baltimore: Williams & Wilkins.

Sajwaj, T., Libet, J., & Agras, S. (1974). Lemon-juice therapy: The control of life-threatening rumination in a six-month infant. *Journal of Applied Behavioral Analysis, 7,* 557–563.

Sakitt, B., & Long, G. M. (1979). Spare the rod and spoil the icon. *Journal of Experimental Psychology: Human Perception and Performance, 5,* 19–30.

Sakmann, B. (1992) Elementary steps in synaptic transmission revealed by currents through single ion channels. *Science, 256,* 503–512.

Saks, M. J. (1992). Obedience versus disobedience to legitimate versus illegitimate authorities issuing good versus evil directives. *Psychological Science, 3,* 221–223.

Salas, E. (Ed.). (1991). Training theory, methods and technology. *Human Factors Special Issue, 3,* 249–362.

Salin-Pascual, R. J., Roehrs, T. A., Merlotti, L. A., Zorick, F., & Roth, T. (1992). Long-term study of the sleep of insomnia patients with sleep state misperception and other insomnia patients. *American Journal of Psychiatry, 149,* 904–908.

Salthouse, T. A. (1985). *A theory of cognitive aging.* Amsterdam: North Holland.

Salthouse, T. A. (1990). Working memory as a processing resource in cognitive aging. *Developmental Review, 10,* 101–124.

Salthouse, T. A., & Prill, K. A. (1987). Inferences about age impairments in inferential reasoning. *Psychology and Aging, 2,* 43–51.

Salthouse, T. A., Babcock, R. L., & Shaw, R. J. (1991). Effects of adult age on structural and operational capacities in working memory. *Psychology and Aging, 6,* 118–127.

Salzer, M. S., McFadden, L., & Rappaport, J. (in press). Professional views of self-help groups: A comparative and contextual analysis. *Administration and Policy in Mental Health.*

Samovar, L., & Porter, R. (Eds.) (1988). *Intercultural communication: A reader.* Belmont, CA: Wadsworth.

Sampson, H. A., & Jolie, P. L. (1984). Increased plasma histamine concentrations after food challenges in children with atopic dermatitis. *The New England Journal of Medicine, 311,* 372–376.

Sande, G. N., Goethals, G. R., & Radloff, C. E. (1988). Perceiving one's own traits and others': The multifaceted self. *Journal of Personality and Social Psychology, 54,* 13–20.

Sanderson, W. C., Rapee, R. M., & Barlow, D. H. (1989). The influence of an illusion of control on panic attacks induced via inhalation of 5.5 carbon dioxide-enriched air. *Archives of General Psychiatry 46,* 157–162.

Sanna, L. J. (1992). Self-efficacy theory: Implications for social facilitation and social loafing. *Journal of Personality and Social Psychology, 62,* 774–786.

Sanna, L. J., & Shotlund, L. (1990). Valence of anticipated evaluation and social facilitation. *Journal of Experimental Social Psychology, 26,* 82–92.

Sapolsky, B. S. (1984). Arousal, affect, and the aggression-moderating effect of erotica. In N. M. Malamuth & E. I. Donnerstein (Eds.), *Pornography and sexual aggression.* New York: Academic Press.

Sapolsky, R. M., Krey, L. C., & McEwen, B. S. (1985). Prolonged glucocorticoid exposure reduces hippocampal neurin number: Implications for aging. *Journal of Neuroscience, 5,* 1222–1227.

Sarafino, E. (1990) *Health psychology: Biopsychosocial interactions.* New York: John Wiley.

Sarason, I. G. (1978). The test anxiety scale concept and research. In C. D. Spielberger & I. G. Sarason (Eds.), *Stress and anxiety: Vol. 5* (pp. 193–216). Washington, DC: Hemisphere.

Sarason, I. G. (1984). Stress, anxiety, and cognitive interference: Reactions to tests. *Journal of Personality and Social Psychology, 46*(4), 929–938.

Sarason, I. G., & Sarason, B. R. (Eds.) (1985). *Social support: Theory, research and applications.* The Hague: Martinus Nijhof.

Sarason, I. G., Sarason, B. R., Keefe, D. E., Hayes, B. E., & Shearin, E. N. (1986). Cognitive interference: Situational determinants and traitlike characteristics. *Journal of Personality and Social Psychology, 51,* 215–226.

Sarason, I., Johnson, J., & Siegal, J. (1978). Assessing impact of life changes: Development of the life experiences survey. *Journal of Clinical and Consulting Psychology, 46,* 932–946.

Sarason, I., Sarason, B., Potter, E., & Antoni, M. (1985). Life events, social support, and illness. *Psychosomatic Medicine, 47,* 156–163.

Sarbin, T. R. (1950). Contributions to role-taking theory: I. Hypnotic behavior. *Psychological Review, 57,* 255–270.

Sarnoff, C. (1976). *Latency.* New York: Aronson.

Sartorius, N., Shapiro, R., & Jablensky, A. (1974). The international pilot study of schizophrenia. *Schizophrenia Bulletin, 1,* 21–35.

Satir, V. (1967). *Conjoint family therapy* (rev. ed.). Palo Alto, CA: Science and Behavior Books.

Satir, V. (1982). The therapist and family therapy: Process model. In A. M. Horne & M. M. Ohlsen (Eds.), *Family counseling and therapy.* Itasca, IL: Peacock.

Saufley, W. H., Otaka, S. R., & Bavaresco, J. L. (1985). Context effects: Classroom tests and context independence. *Memory & Cognition, 13,* 522–528.

Sauter, S., Murphy, L., & Hurrell, J. (1990). Prevention of work-related psychological disorders: A national strategy proposed by the National Institute for Occupational Safety and Health (NIOSH). *American Psychologist, 45,* 1146–1158.

Savage-Rumbaugh, E. S. (1990). Language acquisition in a non-human species: Implications for the innateness debate. *Developmental Psychobiology, 23*(7), 599–620.

Savage-Rumbaugh, E. S., McDonald, K., Sevcik, R. A., Hopkins, W. D., & Rubert, E. (1986). Spontaneous symbol acquisition and communicative use by pygmy chimpanzees. *Pan Journal of Experimental Psychology: General, 112,* 211–235.

Savage-Rumbaugh, E. S., Pate, J. L., Lawson, J., Smith, S. T., & Rosenbaum, S. (1983). Can a chimpanzee make a statement? *Journal of Experimental Psychology: General, 112,* 469–487.

Savin-Williams, R. C., & Demo, D. H. (1984). Developmental change and stability in adolescent self-concept. *Developmental Psychology, 20,* 1100–1110.

Sayers, S. L., & Baucom, D. H. (1991). Role of femininity and masculinity in distressed couples' communication. *Journal of Personality and Social Psychology, 61,* 641–647.

Scarr, S. (1989). Sociobiology: The psychology of sex, violence, and oppression. *Contemporary Psychology, 34,* 440–443.

Scarr, S., & Carter-Saltzman, L. (1982). Genetics and intelligence. In R. Sternberg (Ed.), *Handbook of human intelligence.* Cambridge: Cambridge University Press.

Scarr, S., & Weinberg, R. A. (1976). IQ test performance of black children adopted by white families. *American Psychologist, 31,* 726–739.

Scarr, S., Webber, P. L., Weinberg, R. A., & Wittig, M. A. (1981). Personality resemblance among adolescents and their parents in biologically related and adoptive families. *Journal of Personality and Social Psychology, 40,* 885–898.

Scattarella, C. (1992). Life beneath the roar. *Sunday Seattle Times/ Seattle Post Intelligencer,* March 15, B4.

Schachar, R., & Logan, G. (1990). Impulsivity and inhibitory control in normal development and childhood psychopathology. *Developmental Psychology, 26,* 710–720.

Schachter, S. (1959). *The psychology of affiliation.* Stanford, CA: Stanford University Press.

Schachter, S. (1971). Some extraordinary facts about obese humans and rats. *American Psychologist, 26,* 129–144.

Schachter, S., & Friedman, L. N. (1974). The effects of work and cue prominence on eating behavior. In S. Schachter & J. Rodin (Eds.), *Obese humans and rats.* Potomac, MD: Lawrence Erlbaum Associates.

Schachter, S., & Rodin, J. (Eds.) (1974). *Obese humans and rats.* Potomac, MD: Lawrence Erlbaum Associates.

Schachter, S., & Singer, J. (1962). Cognitive, social and physiological determinants of emotional state. *Psychological Review, 69,* 379–399.

Schacter, D. L., & Tulving, E. (1982). Amnesia and memory research. In L. S. Cermak (Ed.), *Human memory and amnesia.* Hillsdale, NJ: Lawrence Erlbaum Associates.

Schacter, D. L., Chiu, C.-Y. P., & Ochsner, K. N. (1993). Implicit memory: A selective review. *Annual Review of Neurosciences, 16,* 159–182.

Schacter, D. L., Cooper, L. A., Delaney, S. M., Peterson, M. A., & Tharan, M. (1991). Implicit memory for possible and impossible objects: Constraints on the construction of structural descriptions. *Journal of Experimental Psychology: Learning, Memory, and Cognition, 17,* 3–19.

Schaefer, C., Coyne, J. C., & Lazarus, R. S. (1982). The health-related functions of social support. *Journal of Behavioral Medicine, 4,* 381–406.

Schaefer, J., Sykes, R., Rowley, R., & Baek, S. (1988, November). *Slow country music and drinking.* Paper presented at the 87th annual meetings of the American Anthropological Association, Phoenix, AZ.

Schaeffer, M. A., Baum, A., Paulus, P. B., & Gaes, G. G. (1988). Architecturally mediated effects of social density in prison. *Environment and Behavior, 20,* 3–19.

Schafer, J., & Brown, S A. (1991). Marijuana and cocaine effect expectancies and drug use patterns. *Journal of Counsulting and Clinical Psychology, 59,* 558–565.

Schafer, R., & Murphy, G. (1943). The role of autism in a figure-ground relationship. *Journal of Experimental Psychology, 32,* 335–343.

Schaffer, C. E., Davidson, R. J., & Saron, C. (1983). Frontal and parietal EEG asymmetry in depressed and non-depressed subjects. *Biological Psychiatry, 18,* 753–762.

Schaie, K. W. (1979). The primary mental abilities in adulthood: An exploration in the development of psychometric intelligence. In P. B. Baltes & O. G. Brim, Jr. (Eds.), *Life-span development and behavior: Vol. 2.* New York: Academic Press.

Schaie, K. W., & Labouvie-Vief, G. (1974). Generational versus ontogenetic components of change in adult cognitive behavior. *Developmental Psychology, 10,* 305–320.

Schaie, K. W. (1989). Perceptual speed in adulthood: Cross-sectional and longitudinal studies. *Psychology and Aging, 4,* 443–453.

Schank, R. C., & Abelson, R. P. (1977). *Scripts, plans, goals and understanding.* Hillsdale, NJ: Lawrence Erlbaum Associates.

Schank, R. C., & Hunter, L. (1985, April). The quest to understand thinking. *Byte,* 143–155.

Schechtman, V. L., Harper, R. M., Wilson, A. J., & Southall, D. P. (1992). Sleep state organization in normal infants and victims of the sudden infant death syndrome. *Pediatrics, 89,* 865–870.

Scheerer, M., Rothmann, R., & Goldstein, K. (1945). A case of "idiot savant": An experimental study of personality organization. *Psychol. Monognomics, 58*(4).

Scheier, M. F., & Carver, C. S. (1985). Optimism, coping, and health: Assessment and implications of generalized outcome expectancies. *Journal of Personality, 4,* 219–247.

Scheier, M. F., & Carver, C. S. (1987). Dispositional optimism and physical well-being: The influence of generalized outcome expectancies on health. *Journal of Personality, 55,* 169–210.

Scheier, M. F., Matthews, K. A., Owens, J. F., Magovern, G. J., Lefebvre, R. C., Abbott, R. A., & Carver, C. S. (1989). Dispositional optimism and recovery from coronary artery bypass surgery: The beneficial effects on physical and psychological well-being. *Journal of Personality and Social Psychology, 57,* 1024–1040.

Scheier, M., Weintraub, J., & Carver, C. (1986) Coping with distress: Divergent strategies of optimists and pessimists. *Journal of Personality and Social Psychology, 51,* 1257–1264.

Schenck, C. H., Bundlie, S. R., Patterson, A. L., & Mahowald, M. W. (1987). Rapid eye movement sleep behavior disorder: A treatable parasomnia affecting older adults. *Journal of the American Medical Association, 257,* 1786–1789.

Schenck, C. S., & Mahowald, M. W. (1990). Polysomnographic, neurologic, psychiatric, and clinical outcome on 70 consecutive cases with the REM sleep behavior disorder (RBD): Sustained clonazepam efficacy in 89.5% of 57 treated patients. *Cleveland Clinical Journal of Medicine, 57* (Supplement), S10-S24.

Schick, R. R., Yaksh, T. L., & Go, V. L. W. (1986). An intragastric meal releases the putative satiety factor cholecystokinin from hypothalamic neurons in cats. *Brain Research, 370,* 349–353.

Schiff, M., Duyme, M., Dumaret, A., Stewart, J., Tomkiewicz, S., & Feingold, J. (1978). Intellectual status of working class children adopted early into upper-middle class families. *Science, 200,* 1503–1504.

Schindler, U. (1989). Pre-clinical evaluation of cognition-enhancing drugs. *Progress in Neuro-Psychopharmacology and Biological Psychiatry, 13* (Supplement), S99-S115.

Schleifer, S. J., Keller, S. E., Camerino, M., Thornton, J. C., & Stein, M. (1983). Suppression of lymphocyte stimulation following bereavement. *Journal of the American Medical Association, 250,* 374–377.

Schlesier-Stroop, B. (1984). Bulimia: A review of the literature. *Psychological Bulletin, 95,* 247–257.

Schlossberg, N. K. (1987, May). Taking the mystery out of change. *Psychology Today,* pp. 74–75.

Schmale, A. H., & Iker, H. P. (1966). The effect of hopelessness and the development of cancer. *Psychosomatic Medicine, 28,* 714–721.

Schmidt, H. (1969). Precognition of a quantum process. *Journal of Parapsychology, 33,* 99–108.

Schmidt, R. A., & Bjork, R. A. (1992, July). New conceptualizations of practice: Common principles in three paradigms suggest new concepts for training. *Psychological Science, 3*(4), 207–217.

Schmidt, S. R., & Bohannon, J. N. (1988). In defense of the flash-bulb-memory hypothesis: A comment on McCloskey, Wible, and Cohen (1988). *Journal of Experimental Psychology: General, 117,* 332–335.

Schnapf, J. L., & Baylor, D. A. (1987). How photoreceptor cells respond to light. *Scientific American, 256,* 40–47.

Schnapf, J. L., Kraft, T. W., & Baylor, D. A. (1987). Spectral sensitivity of human cone photoreceptors. *Nature, 325,* 439–441.

Schneider, B. (1985). Organizational behavior. *Annual Review of Psychology, 36,* 573–611.

Schneider, D. J., Roediger, H. L., III, & Khan, M. (1993). Diverse ways of accessing self knowledge. In T. K. Srull & R. S. Wyer (Eds.), *The mental representation of trait and autobiographical knowledge about the self: Advances in social cognition: Vol. V.* Hillsdale, NJ: Lawrence Erlbaum Associates.

Schneider, W. (1984). Developmental trends in the metamemory-behavior relationship. In D. L. Forrest-Pressley, G. E. MacKinnon, & P. G. Waller (Eds.), *Metacognition, cognition, and human performance.* New York: Academic Press.

Schneider, W., & Detweiler, M. (1988). The role of practice in dual-task performance: Toward workload modeling in a connectionist/control architecture. *Human Factors, 30,* 539–566.

Schneider-Rosen, K., Braunwald, K. G., Carlson, V., & Cicchetti, D. (1985). Current perspectives in attachment theory: Illustration from the study of maltreated infants. In I. Bretherton & E. Waters (Eds.), Growing points of attachment theory and research. *Monographs of the Society for Research in Child Development, 50*(1–2, Serial No. 209).

Schoenfeld, H. H. (1979). Explicit heuristic training as a variable in problem solving performance. *Journal for Research in Mathematical Education, 10,* 173–187.

Schopler, J., Lasko, C. A., Graetz, K. A., Drigotas, S. M., & Smith, V. A. (1991). The generality of the individual-group discontinuity effect: Variations in positivity-negativity of outcomes, players' relative power, and magnitude of outcomes. *Personality and Social Psychology Bulletin, 17,* 612–624.

Schroeder, D. A., Dovidio, J. F., Sibicky, M. E., Matthews, L. L., & Allen, J. L. (1988). Empathic concern and helping behavior: Egoism or altruism? *Journal of Experimental Social Psychology, 24,* 333–353.

Schroeder, D. H., & Costa, P. T. (1984). Influence of life event stress on physical illness: Substantive effects or methodological flaws? *Journal of Personality and Social Psychology, 46,* 853–863.

Schuckit, M. A. (1983). The genetics of alcoholism. In B. Tabakoff, P. B. Sutker, & C. L. Randall (Eds.), *Medical and social aspects of alcohol use.* New York: Plenum Press.

Schuckit, M. A., & Gold, E. (1988). Serum prolactin levels in sons of alcoholics and control subjects. *American Journal of Psychiatry, 144,* 854–859.

Schulz, R. (1978). *The psychology of death, dying, and bereavement.* Reading, MA: Addison-Wesley.

Schum, D. (1975). The weighing of testimony of judicial proceedings from sources having reduced credibility. *Human Factors, 17,* 172–203.

Schwartz, B., & Reisberg, D. (1991). *Learning and memory.* New York: W. W. Norton.

Schwartz, G. E. (1982). Testing the biopsychosocial model: The ultimate challenge facing behavioral medicine. *Journal of Consulting and Clinical Psychology, 50,* 6.

Schwartz, G. E., & Weiss, S. M. (1978). Behavioral medicine revisited: An amended definition. *Journal of Behavioral Medicine, 1,* 249–252.

Schwartz, J. T. (1988). The new connectionism: Developing relationships between neuroscience and artificial intelligence. In S. R. Graubard (Ed.), *The artificial intelligence debate.* Cambridge, MA: MIT Press.

Schwartz, R. M. (1982). Cognitive-behavior modification: A conceptual review. *Clinical Psychology Review, 2,* 267–293.

Schwartz, S., & Griffin, T. (1986). *Medical thinking: The psychology of medical judgment and decision-making.* New York: Springer-Verlag.

Schwarzwald, J., Bizman, A., & Raz, M. (1983). The foot-in-the-door paradigm: Effects of second request size on donation probability and donor generosity. *Personality and Social Psychology Bulletin, 9,* 443–450.

Schweinhart, L. J., & Weikart, D. P. (1991). Response to "Beyond IQ in preschool programs?" *Intelligence, 15,* 313–315.

Schweizer, E., Rickels, K., Weiss, S., & Zavodnick, S. (1993). Maintenance drug treatment of panic disorder 1: Results of a prospective, placebo-controlled comparison of alprazolam and impiramine. *Archives of General Psychiatry, 50,* 51–60.

Schwitzgebel, R. L., & Schwitzgebel, R. K. (1980). *Law and psychological practice.* New York: Wiley.

Scott, J. P. (1983). A systems approach to research on aggressive behavior. In E. C. Simmel, M. E. Hahn, & J. K. Walters (Eds.), *Aggressive behavior: Genetic and neural approaches.* Hillsdale, NJ: Lawrence Erlbaum Associates.

Scott, L. & O'Hara, M.W. (1993). Self-discrepancies in clinically anxious and depressed university students. *Journal of Abnormal Psychology, 102,* 282–287.

Scovern, A. W., & Kilmann, P. R. (1980). Status of electroconvulsive therapy: Review of the outcome literature. *Psychological Bulletin, 87,* 260–303.

Scribner, S. (1977). Modes of thinking and ways of speaking: Culture and logic reconsidered. In P. N. Johnson-Laird & P. C. Watson (Eds.), *Thinking: Readings in cognitive science.* New York: Cambridge University Press.

Seab, J. P., Jagust, W. J., Wong, S. T. S., Roos, M. S., Reed, B. R., & Budinger, T. F. (1988). Quantitative NMR measurements of hippocampal atrophy in Alzheimer's disease. *Magnetic Resonance in Medicine, 8,* 200–208.

Searle, J. (1990). Is the brain's mind a computer program? *Scientific American,* January, 26–31.

Searle, L. V. (1949). The organization of hereditary maze-brightness and maze dullness. *Genetic Psychology Monographs, 39,* 279–325.

Searles, J. S. (1985). A methodological and empirical critique of psychotherapy outcome meta-analysis. *Behaviour Research and Therapy, 23,* 453–463.

Sears, R. R. (1972). Attachment, dependency, and frustration. In J. L. Gewirtz (Ed.), *Attachment and dependency.* Washington, DC: Winston.

Secord, D., & Peevers, B. (1974). The development and attribution of person concepts. In T. Mischel (Ed.), *Understanding other persons.* Oxford: Blackwell.

Secretary of Health and Human Services. (1987). *Sixth special report to the U.S. Congress on alcohol and health* (DHHS Publication No. 87–1519). Rockville, MD: U.S. Department of Health and Human Services.

Secretary of Health, Education, and Welfare. (1980). *Marijuana and health.* Washington, DC: U.S. Government Printing Office.

Seeman, J. (1989). Toward a model of positive health. *American Psychologist, 44,* 1099–1109.

Seeman, P., & Lee, T. (1975). Antipsychotic drugs: Direct correlation between clinical potency and presynaptic action on dopamine neurons. *Science, 188,* 1217–1219.

Segal, M. W. (1974). Alphabet and attraction: An unobtrusive measure of the effect of propinquity in a field setting. *Journal of Personality and Social Psychology, 30,* 654–657.

Segal, M., & Bloom, F. E. (1976). The action of norepinephrine in the rat hippocampus: III. Hippocampal cellular responses to locus coeruleus stimulation in the awake rat. *Brain Research, 107,* 499–511.

Segall, M. H., Dasen, P. R., Berry, J. W., & Poortinga, Y. H. (1990). *Human behavior in global perspective: An introduction to cross-cultural psychology.* Elmwood, NY: Pergamon.

Seidenberg, M. S., & McClelland, J. L. (1989). A distributed, developmental model of word recognition and naming. *Psychological Review, 96,* 523–568.

Seidler, K., & Wickens, C. D. (1992). Distance and organizaiton in multifunction displays. *Human Factors, 34,* 555–569.

Seidman, L. J. (1990). The neuropsychology of schizophrenia: A neurodevelopmental and case study approach. *Journal of Neuropsychiatry and Clinical Neuroscience, 2,* 301–312.

Seifer, R., & Sameroff, A. (1989, January). Paper on the Rochester Longitudinal Study presented at the annual convention of the American Association for the Advancement of Science, San Francisco.

Seitz, V., Apfel, N. H., & Rosenbaum, L. (1981). Projects Head Start and Follow Through: A longitudinal evaluation of adolescents. In M. J. Begam, H. Garber, & H. C. Haywood (Eds.), *Prevention of retarded development in psychosocially disadvantaged children.* Baltimore: University Park Press.

Sejnowski, T. J. (1991). Back together again. *Nature, 352,* 669.

Sejnowski, T. J., & Rosenberg, C. R. (1987). Parallel networks that learn to pronounce English text. *Journal of Complex Systems, 1,* 145–168.

Sejnowski, T. J., Koch, C., & Churchland, P. S. (1988). Computational neuroscience. *Science, 241,* 1299–1306.

Seligman, M. E. P. (1970). On the generality of the laws of learning. *Psychological Review, 77,* 406–418.

Seligman, M. E. P. (1971). Phobias and preparedness. *Behavior Therapy, 2,* 307–320.

Seligman, M. E. P. (1975). *Helplessness: On depression, development, and death.* San Francisco: W. H. Freeman.

Seligman, M. E. P. (1991). *Learned optimism.* New York: Knopf.

Seligman, M. E. P., & Maier, S. F. (1967). Failure to escape traumatic shock. *Journal of Experimental Psychology, 74,* 1–9.

Seligman, M. E. P., Castellon, C., Cacciola, J., Shulman, P., Luborsky, L., Ollove, M., & Downing, R. (1988). Explanatory style change during cognitive therapy for unipolar depression. *Journal of Abnormal Psychology, 97,* 13–18.

Seligman, M. E. P., Klein, D. C., & Miller, W. R. (1976). Depression. In H. Leitenberg (Ed.), *Handbook of behavior modification and behavior therapy.* Englewood Cliffs, NJ: Prentice-Hall.

Seligman, M. E. P., Maier, S., & Geer, J. (1968). The alleviation of learned helplessness in a dog. *Journal of Abnormal and Social Psychology, 73,* 256–262.

Seligmann, J. (1992) The new age of aquarius. *Newsweek,* February 3, 65–67.

Selkoe, D. J. (1991). Amyloid protein and Alzheimer's disease. *Scientific American,* November, 68–78.

Selman, R. L. (1980). *The growth of interpersonal understanding: Developmental and clinical analyses.* New York: Academic Press.

Selman, R. L. (1981). The child as a friendship philosopher. In S. R. Asher & J. M. Gottman (Eds.), *The development of children's friendships.* New York: Cambridge University Press.

Selman, R. L., Schorin, M. Z., Stone, C. R., & Phelps, E. (1983). A naturalistic study of children's social understanding. *Developmental Psychology, 19,* 82–102.

Seltzer, J. A., & Kalmuss, D. (1988). Socialization and stress explanations for spouse abuse. *Social Forces, 67,* 473–491.

Selye, H. (1956). *The stress of life.* New York: McGraw-Hill.

Selye, H. (1974). *Stress without distress.* New York: Harper & Row.

Selye, H. (1976). *The stress of life* (2nd ed.). New York: McGraw-Hill.

Serbin, L. A., Conner, J. M., Burchardt, C. J., & Citron, C. C. (1979). Effects of peer presence on sex-typing of children's behavior. *Journal of Experimental and Child Psychology, 27,* 303–309.

Serpell, R. (1994). The cultural construction of intelligence. In W. J. Lonner & R. S. Malpass (Eds.), *Psychology and culture* Boston: Allyn & Bacon.

Servan-Schreiber, E., & Anderson, J. R. (1990). Learning artificial grammars with competitive chunking. *Journal of Experimental Psychology: Learning, Memory, and Cognition, 16,* 592–608.

Seta, J. J., Seta, C. E., & Donaldson, S. (1991). The impact of comparison processes on coactors' frustration and willingness to expend effort. *Personality and Social Psychology Bulletin, 17,* 560–568.

Shaffer, L. H. (1975). Multiple attention in continuous verbal tasks. In S. Dornic (Ed.), *Attention and performance: Vol. V.* New York: Academic Press.

Shank, R., & Abelson, R. (1977). *Scripts, plans, goals, and understanding.* Hillsdale, NJ: Lawrence Erlbaum Associates.

Shanks, D. R. (1991). Categorization by a connectionist network. *Journal of Experimental Psychology: Learning, Memory, and Cognition, 17,* 433–443.

Shapiro, D. H. (1980). *Meditation: Self-regulation strategy and altered states of consciousness.* New York: Aldine.

Shapiro, D. H., & Giber, D. (1978). Meditation and psychotherapeutic effects: Self regulation strategy and altered states of consciousness. *Archives of General Psychiatry, 35,* 294–302.

Shapiro, D. H., & Walsh, R. N. (Eds.) (1984). *Meditation: Classical and contemporary perspectives.* New York: Aldine.

Shapiro, F. (1989a). Eye movement desensitization: A new treatment for post-traumatic stress disorder. *Journal of Behavior Therapy and Experimental Psychiatry, 20,* 211–217.

Shapiro, F. (1989b). Efficacy of the eye movement desensitization procedure in the treatment of traumatic memories. *Journal of Traumatic Stress, 2,* 199–223.

Shapiro, F. (1991). Eye movement desensitization and reprocessing procedure: From EMD to EMD/R—A new treatment model for anxiety and related traumata. *The Behavior Therapist, 15,* 133–135.

Shapiro, K. L. (1991). Use morality as basis for animal treatment. *APA Monitor,* July, p. 5.

Shapiro, S., Skinner, E. A., Kessler, L. G., Von Korff, M., German, P. S., Tischler, G. L., Leaf, P. J., Beham, L., Cottler, L., & Legler, D. A. (1984). Utilization of health and mental health services. *Archives of General Psychiatry, 41,* 971–978.

Shaver, P., Hazan, C., & Bradshaw, D. (1988). Love as attachment: The integration of three behavioral systems. In R. J. Sternberg & M. L. Barnes (Eds.), *The psychology of love.* New Haven: Yale University Press.

Shaw, M. E. (1981). *Group dynamics: The psychology of small group behavior* (3rd ed.). New York: McGraw-Hill.

Shaw, M. E., Rothschild, G. H., & Strickland, J. F. (1957). Decision processes in communication nets. *Journal of Abnormal and Social Psychology, 54,* 323–330.

Shea, D. D., Ohnmeiss, D. D., Stith, W. J., Guyer, R. D., Rashbaum, R. F., Hochschuler, S. H., & Regan, J. J. (1991). The effect of sensory deprivation in the reduction of pain in patients with chronic low-back pain. *Spine, 16,* 560–561.

Shedler, J., & Block, J. (1990). Adolescent drug use and psychological health: A longitudinal inquiry. *American Psychologist, 45,* 612–630.

Sheehy, G. (1977). *Passages: Predictable crises of adult life.* New York: Bantam.

Sheehy, G. (1992). *The silent passage: Menopause.* New York: Random House.

Shepard, C., Kohut, J. J., & Sweet, R. (1989). *News of the weird*. New York: New American Library.

Shepard, R. & Metzler, J. (1971). Mental rotation of three dimensional objects. *Science, 171*, 701–703.

Shepard, R. N. (1984). Ecological constraints on internal representation: Resonant kinematics of perceiving, imagining, thinking, and dreaming. *Psychological Review, 91*, 417–447.

Shepherd-Look, D. L. (1982). Sex differentiation and the development of sex roles. In B. B. Wolman & G. Stricker (Eds.), *Handbook of developmental psychology*. Englewood Cliffs, NJ: Prentice-Hall.

Shepperd, J. A. (1993). Productivity loss in performance groups: A motivation analysis. *Psychological Bulletin, 113*, 67–81.

Sher, K. J., & Levenson, R. W. (1982). Risk for alcoholism and individual differences in the stress-response-dampening effects of alcohol. *Journal of Abnormal Psychology, 91*, 350–367.

Sher, K., Walitzer, K., Wood, P., & Brent, E. (1991). Characteristics of children of alcoholics: Putative risk factors, substance use and abuse, and psychopathology. *Journal of Abnormal Psychology, 100*, 427–448.

Sherer, M., Kumor, K., Cone, E., & Jaffe, J. (1988). Suspiciousness induced by four-hour intravenous infusions of cocaine. *Archives of General Psychiatry, 45*, 673–677.

Sherif, M. (1937). An experimental approach to the study of attitudes. *Sociometry, 1*, 90–98.

Sherman, S. S. (1980). On the self-erasing nature of errors of prediction. *Journal of Personality and Social Psychology, 16*, 388–403.

Sherrington, R., Brynjolfsson, J., Petursson H., Potter, M., Dudleston, K., Barraclough, B., Wasmuth, J., Dobbs, M., & Gurling, H. (1988). Localization of a susceptibility locus for schizophrenia on chromosome 5. *Nature, 336*, 164–167.

Sherwin, B. B. (1988). Affective changes with estrogen and androgen replacement therapy in surgically menopausal women. *Journal of Affective Disorders, 14*, 177–187.

Sherwin, B. B. (1991). The impact of different doses of estrogen and progestin on mood and sexual behavior in postmenopausal women. *Journal of Clinical Endocrinology and Metabolism, 72*, 336–343.

Sherwin, B. B., & Gelfand, M. M. (1987). The role of androgen in the maintenance of sexual functioing in oophorectomized women. *Psychosomatic Medicine, 49*, 397–409.

Sherwin, B. B., Gelfand, M. M., & Brender, W. (1985). Androgen enhances sexual motivation in females: A prospective crossover study of sex steroid administration in the surgical menopause. *Psychosomatic Medicine, 47*, 339–351.

Sherwin, R., & Sherry, C. (1985). Campus sexual norms and dating relationships: A trend analysis. *Journal of Sex Research, 21*, 258–274.

Shiffrin, R. M. (1973). Information persistence in short-term memory. *Journal of Experimental Psychology, 100*, 39–49.

Shimamura, A. P., & Squire, L. R. (1988). Long-term memory in amnesia: Cued recall, recognition memory, and confidence ratings. *Journal of Experimental Psychology: Learning, Memory, and Cognition, 14*, 763–770.

Shneidman, E. S. (1973). Suicide. In *Encyclopedia Britannica*. Chicago: Encyclopedia Britannica.

Shneidman, E. S. (1985). *Definition of suicide*. New York: Harper & Row.

Shneidman, E. S. (1987, March). At the point of no return. *Psychology Today*.

Shor, R. E., & Orne, M. T. (1963). Norms on the Harvard group scale of hypnotic susceptibility, Form A. *International Journal of Clinical and Experimental Hypnosis, 11*, 39–47.

Shore, M. F. (1992). Community mental health: Corpse or phoenix? Personal reflections on an era. *Professional Psychology: Research and Practice, 23*, 257–262.

Shortcliffe, E. H. (1983). Medical consultation systems: Designing for doctors. In M. E. Sime & M. J. Coombs (Eds.), *Designing for human computer communication*. New York: Academic Press.

Showers, C. (1992). Compartmentalization of positive and negative self-knowledge: Keeping bad apples out of the bunch. *Journal of Personality and Social Psychology, 62*, 1036–1049.

Shugan, S. M. (1980). The cost of thinking. *Journal of Consumer Research, 7*, 99–111.

Siegel, J. M. (1984). Type A behavior: Epidemiologic foundations and public health implications. *Annual Review of Public Health, 5*, 343–367.

Siegel, J. M. (1986). The Multidimensional Anger Inventory. *Journal of Personality and Social Psychology, 51*, 191–200.

Siegel, J. M., & Rogawski, M. A. (1988). A function for REM sleep: Regulation of noradrenergic receptor sensitivity. *Brain Research Review, 13*, 213–233.

Siegel, L. S., McCabe, A. E., Brand, J., & Matthews, J. (1978). Evidence for the understanding of class inclusion in preschool children: Linguistic factors and training effects. *Child Development, 49*, 688–693.

Siegel, S. (1984). Pavlovian conditioning and heroin overdose: Reports by overdose victims. *Bulletin of the Psychonomic Society, 22*, 428–430.

Siegel, S. (1985). Drug anticipatory response in animals. In L. White, B. Turskey, & G. Schwartz (Eds.), *Placebo: Theory, research and mechanisms*. New York: Guilford Press.

Siegel, S., & Ellsworth, D. W. (1986). Pavlovian conditioning and death from apparent overdose of medically prescribed morphine: A case report. *Bulletin of the Psychonomic Society, 24*, 278–280.

Siegel, S., Hirson, R. E., Krank, M. D., & McCully, J. (1982). Heroin "overdose" death: The contribution of drug associated environmental cues. *Science, 216*, 430–437.

Siever, L. J., & Davis, K. L. (1985). Overview: Toward a dysregulation hypothesis of depression. *American Journal of Psychiatry, 142*, 1017–1031.

Sifneos, P. (1979). *Short-term dynamic psychotherapy: Evaluating and technique*. New York: Plenum Press.

Sigman, M., Cohen, S., Beckwith, L., & Parmelee, A. (1986). Infant attention in relation to intellectual abilities in childhood. *Developmental Psychology, 6*, 788–792.

Silber, M., Carlstrom, K., & Larsson, B. (1989). Premenstrual syndrome in a group of hysterectomized women of reproductive age with intact ovaries. *Advances in Contraception, 5*, 163–171.

Silbert, M. H., & Pines, A. M. (1984). Pornography and sexual abuse of women. *Sex Roles, 10*, 857–868.

Silva, A. J., Paylor, R., Wehner, J. M., & Tonegawa, S. (1992). Impaired spatial learning in alpha-calcium-calmodulin kinsase-II mutant mice. *Science, 257*, 206–211.

Silver, R. L., & Wortman, C. B. (1980). Coping with undesirable life events. In J. Garber & M. E. P. Seligman (Eds.), *Human helplessness: Theory and applications* (pp. 279–340). New York: Academic Press.

Silverman, K., Evans, A. M., Strain, E. C., & Griffiths, R. R. (1992). Withdrawal syndrome after the double-blind cessation of caffeine consumption. *New England Journal of Medicine, 327*, 1109–1114.

Silverman, L. H. (1983). Subliminal psychodynamic activation method: Overview and comprehensive listing of studies. In J. Masling (Ed.), *Empirical studies in psychoanalysis* (Vol. 1). Hillsdale, NJ: Lawrence Erlbaum Associates.

Silverman, L. H. (1985). Research on psychodynamic propositions. *Clinical Psychology Review, 5*, 247–257.

Silverman, L. H., & Weinberger, J. (1985). Mommy and I are one: Implications for psychotherapy. *American Psychologist, 40,* 1296–1308.

Silverton, L., Mednick, S. A., Schulsinger, F., Parnas, J., & Harrington, M. E. (1988). Genetic risk for schizophrenia, birthweight, and cerebral ventricular enlargement. *Journal of Abnormal Psychology, 97,* 496–498.

Silviera, J. M. (1971). *Incubation: The effect of interruption timing and length on problem solution and quality of problem processing.* Unpublished doctoral dissertation. University of Oregon, Eugene.

Sime, W. E. (1984). Psychological benefits of exercise training in the healthy individual. In J. D. Matarazzo, S. M. Weiss, J. A. Herd, & N. Miller, (Eds.), *Behavioral health: A handbook of health enhancement and disease prevention.* New York: Wiley.

Simmons, R. G., Rosenberg, F., & Rosenberg, M. (1973). Disturbance in the self-image at adolescence. *American Sociological Review, 38,* 553–568.

Simon, H. A. (1974). How big is a chunk? *Science, 183,* 482–488.

Simon, H. A. (1990). A mechanism for social selection and successful altruism. *Science, 250,* 1665–1668.

Simons, C. (1987, December). A long-distance ticket to life. *Smithsonian,* pp. 44–52.

Simonton, D. K. (1991). Personality correlates of exceptional personal influence: A note on Thorndike's (1950) creators and leaders. *Creativity Research Journal, 4,* 67–78.

Simpson, J. A., Rholes, W. S., & Nelligan, J. S. (1992). Support seeking and support giving within couples in an anxiety-provoking situation: The role of attachment styles. *Journal of Personality and Social Psychology, 62,* 434–446.

Singer, J. (1976). *The inner world of daydreaming.* New York: Harper & Row.

Singley, M. K., & Anderson, J. R. (1989). *The transfer of cognitive skill.* Cambridge, MA: Harvard University Press.

Sizemore, C. C., & Pittillo, E. S. (1970). *I'm Eve.* New York: Doubleday.

Skinner, B. F. (1953). *Science and human behavior.* New York: Macmillan.

Skinner, B. F. (1961a). *Cumulative record* (3rd ed.). Englewood Cliffs, NJ: Prentice-Hall.

Skinner, B. F. (1961b). Teaching machines. *Scientific American* (November), pp. 91–102.

Skynner, A. (1981). An open-system group analytic approach to family therapy. In A. S. Gurman & D. P. Kniskern (Eds.), *Handbook of family therapy.* New York: Brunner/Mazel.

Slaby, R. G., & Frey, K. S. (1975). Development of gender constancy and selective attention to same-sex models. *Child Development, 46,* 849–856.

Slamecka, N. J., & McElree, B. (1983). Normal forgetting of verbal lists as a function of their degree of learning. *Journal of Experimental Psychology: Learning, Memory, and Cognition, 9,* 384–397.

Slater, A., Mattock, A., Brown, E., & Bremner, J. G. (1991). Form perception at birth. *Journal of Experimental Child Psychology, 51,* 395–406.

Slater, J., & DePue, R. A. (1981). The contribution of environmental events and social support to serious suicide attempts in primary depressive disorder. *Journal of Abnormal Psychology, 90,* 17–35.

Slavin, R. E. (1985). Cooperative learning: Applying contact theory in desegregated schools. *Journal of Social Issues, 41,* 45–62.

Slikker, W., Jr., Holson, R. R., Ali, S. F., Kolta, M. G., Paule, M. G., Scallet, A. C., McMillan, D. E., Bailey, J. R., Hong, J. S., & Scalzo, F. M. (1989). Behavioral and neurochemical effects of orally administered MDMA in the rodent and nonhuman primate. *Neurotoxicology, 10,* 529–542.

Sloane, R. B., Staples, F. R., Cristol, A. H., Yorkston, N. J., & Whipple, K. (1975). *Psychotherapy versus behavior therapy.* Cambridge: Harvard University Press.

Slobodyansky, E., Guidotti, A., Wambebe, C., Berkovich, A., & Costa, E. (1989). Isolation and characterization of a rat brain triakontatetraneuropeptide, a posttranslational product of diazepam binding inhibitor: Specific action at the Ro 5–4864 recognition site. *Journal of Neurochemistry, 53,* 1276–1284.

Slovic, P. (1984). *Facts versus fears: Understanding perceived risk.* In science and public policy seminar sponsored by the Federation of Behavioral and Psychological and Cognitive Sciences, Washington, DC.

Small, I. F., Small, J. G., & Milstein, V. (1986). Electroconvulsive therapy. In P. A. Berger & H. K. H. Brodie (Eds.), *American handbook of psychiatry: Biological psychiatry* (2nd ed., Vol. 8). New York: Basic Books.

Smeaton, G., Byrne, D., & Murnen, S. K. (1989). The repulsion hypothesis revisited: Similarity irrelevance or dissimilarity bias? *Journal of Personality and Social Psychology, 56,* 54–59.

Smith, A. C., III, & Kleinman, S. (1989). Managing emotions in medical school: Students' contacts with the living and the dead. *Social Psychology Quarterly, 52,* 56–69.

Smith, B., & Vetter, H. (1991). *Theories of personality* (2nd ed.). Englewood Cliffs, NJ: Prentice-Hall.

Smith, C. A. (1989). Dimensions of appraisal and physiological response in emotion. *Journal of Personality and Social Psychology, 56,* 339–353.

Smith, C. A., & Ellsworth, P. C. (1987). Patterns of appraisal and emotion related to taking an exam. *Journal of Personality and Social Psychology, 52,* 475–488.

Smith, D. (1982). Trends in counseling and psychotherapy. *American Psychologist, 37,* 802–809.

Smith, E. R. (1990). Content and process specificity in the effects of prior experiences. In T. K. Srull & R. S. Wyer (Eds.), *Advances in social cognition: Vol. III. Content and process specificity in the effects of prior experiences.* Hillsdale, NJ: Lawrence Erlbaum Associates.

Smith, E. R. (1994). Procedural knowledge and processing strategies in social cognition. In R. S. Wyer & T. K. Srull (Eds.), *Handbook of social cognition* (2nd ed.). Hillsdale, NJ: Lawrence Erlbaum Associates.

Smith, G. F., & Dorfman, D. D. (1975). The effect of stimulus uncertainty on the relationship between frequency of exposure and liking. *Journal of Personality and Social Psychology, 31,* 150–155.

Smith, G. P., & Gibbs, J. (1992). The development and proof of the cholecystokinin hypothesis of satiety. In C. T. Dourish, S. J. Cooper, S. D. Iversen, & L. L. Iversen (Eds.), *Multiple cholecystokinin receptors in the CNS.* Oxford: Oxford University Press.

Smith, J. (1993). *Understanding stress and coping.* New York: Macmillan.

Smith, J. C. (1975). Meditation as psychotherapy: A review of the literature. *Psychological Bulletin, 82,* 558–564.

Smith, M. (1988). Recall of spatial location by the amnesic patient HM. Special issue: Single case-studies in amnesia—Theoretical Advances. *Brain and Cognition, 7,* 178–183.

Smith, M. L., Glass, G. V., & Miller, T. I. (1980). *The benefits of psychotherapy.* Baltimore: Johns Hopkins University Press.

Smith, P. K., & Connolly, K. (1972). Patterns of play and social interaction in preschool children. In N. Blurton Jones (Ed.), *Ethological studies of child behaviour.* Cambridge: Cambridge University Press.

Smith, S. L. (1975). Mood in the menstrual cycle. In E. J. Sacher (Ed.), *Topics in psychoendocrinology.* New York: Grune & Stratton.

Smith, S. M., Brown, H. O., Toman, J. E. P., & Goodman, L. S. (1947). The lack of cerebral effects of d-tubocurarine. *Anesthesiology, 8,* 1–14.

Smith, S. M., Glenberg, A. M., & Bjork, R. A. (1978). Environmental context and human memory. *Memory & Cognition, 6,* 342–355.

Smith, S. M., Vela, E., & Williamson, J. E. (1988). Shallow input processing does not induce environmental context-dependent recognition. *Bulletin of the Psychonomic Society, 26,* 537–540.

Smith, S. R., & Meyer, R. G. (1987). *Law, behavior, and mental health: Policy and practice.* New York: New York University Press.

Smith, S. S., O'Hara, B. F., Persico, A. M., Gorelick, D. A., Newlin, D. B., Vlahov, D., Solomon, L., Pickens, R., & Uhl, G. R. (1992). Genetic vulnerability to drug abuse. The D_2 dopamine receptor *Taq* i B1 restriction fragment length polymorphism appears more frequently in polysubstance abusers. *Archives of General Psychiatry, 49,* 723–727.

Smith, S., & Freedman, D. G. (1983, April). *Mother-toddler interaction and maternal perception of child temperament in two ethnic groups: Chinese-American and European-American.* Paper presented at the meeting of the Society for Research in Child Development, Detroit, MI.

Smith, T. W. (1992). Hostility and health: Current status of a psychosomatic hypothesis. *Health Psychology, 11,* 139–150.

Smith, T. W., & Anderson, N. B. (1986). Models of personality and disease: An interactional approach to type A behavior and cardiovascular risk. *Journal of Personality and Social Psychology, 50,* 1166–1173.

Smith, T. W., Allred, K. D., Morrison, C. A., & Carlson, S. D. (1989). Cardiovascular reactivity and interpersonal influence: Active coping in a social context. *Journal of Personality and Social Psychology, 56,* 209–218.

Smith, T. W., & Brown, P. (1991). Cynical hostility, attempts to exert social control and cardiovascular reactivity in married couples. *Journal of Behavioral Medicine, 14,* 579–590.

Smith, T. W., McGonigle, M., Turner, C., Ford, M., & Slattery, M. (1991). Cynical hostility in adult male twins. *Psychosomatic Medicine, 53,* 684–692.

Snarey, J. (1987). A question of morality. *Psychological Bulletin, 97,* 202–232.

Sniezek, J. A. (1992). Groups under uncertainty: An examination of confidence in group decision making. *Organizational Behavior and Human Decision Processes, 52,* 124–155.

Snow, R. E., & Swanson, J. (1992). Instructional psychology: Aptitude, adoptation, and assessment. *Annual Review of Psychology, 43,* 583–626.

Snow, R. E., & Yallow, E. (1982). Education and intelligence. In R. Sternberg (Ed.), Handbook of human intelligence. Cambridge: Cambridge University Press.

Snowden, L. R., & Cheung, F. (1990). Use of inpatient mental health services by members of ethnic minority groups. *American Psychologist, 45,* 347–355.

Snowden, L. R., & Hines, A. M. (1994). Reaching the underserved: Mental health services systems and special populations. In W. J. Lonner & R. S. Malpass (Eds.), *Psychology and culture.* Boston: Allyn & Bacon.

Snowdon, C. T. (1969). Motivation, regulation, and the control of meal parameters with oral and intragastric feeding. *Journal of Comparative and Physiological Psychology, 69,* 91–100.

Snyder, C. R., & Forsythe, D. R. (Eds.) (1990). *Handbook of social clinical psychology: The health perspective.* New York: Pergamon Press.

Snyder, C. R., & Fromkin, H. L. (1980). *Uniqueness: The human pursuit of difference.* New York: Plenum.

Snyder, C. R., & Higgins, R. L. (1988). Excuses: Their effective role in the negotiation of reality. *American Psychologist, 104,* 23–35.

Snyder, D. K., & Wills, R. M. (1989). Behavioral versus insight-oriented marital therapy: Effects on individual and interspousal functioning. *Journal of Consulting and Clinical Psychology, 57,* 39–46.

Snyder, M. (1984). When belief creates reality. In L. Berkowitz (Ed.), *Advances in experimental social psychology* (Vol. 18). New York: Academic Press.

Snyder, M., Tanke, E. D., & Berscheid, E. (1977). Social perception and interpersonal behavior: On the self-fulfilling nature of social stereotypes. *Journal of Personality and Social Psychology, 35,* 656–666.

Snyder, S. H. (1978). Dopamine and schizophrenia. In L. C. Wynne, R. L. Cromwell, & S. Matthysse (Eds.), *The nature of schizophrenia: New approaches to research and treatment* (pp. 87–94). New York: Wiley.

Snyder, S. H. (1992). Nitric oxide: First in a new class of neurotransmitters? *Science, 257,* 494–496.

Snyderman, M., & Herrnstein, R. J. (1983). Intelligence tests and the Immigration Act of 1924. *American Psychologist, 38,* 986–995.

Sokoloff, L. (1981). Localization of functional activity in the central nervous system by measurement of glucose utilization with radioactive deoxyglucose. *Journal of Cerebral Blood Flow & Metabolism, 1,* 7–36.

Soloman, Z., Mikulincer, M., & Avitzur, E. (1988). Coping, loss of control, social support, and combat-related posttraumatic stress disorder: A prospective study. *Journal of Personality and Social Psychology, 55,* 279–285.

Solomon, R. L. (1980). The opponent-process theory of acquired motivation: The costs of pleasure and the benefits of pain. *American Psychologist, 35,* 691–712.

Solomon, R. L., & Corbit, J. D. (1974). An opponent-process theory of motivation: I. Temporal dynamics of affect. *Psychological Review, 81,* 119–145.

Solomon, R. L., Kamin, L. J., & Wynne, L. C. (1953). Traumatic avoidance learning: The outcomes of several extinction procedures with dogs. *Journal of Abnormal and Social Psychology, 48,* 291–302.

Solso, A. L. (1987). Inside the Russian mind. Unpublished manuscript.

Solso, A. L. (1991). *Cognitive psychology* (3rd ed.). Boston: Allyn & Bacon.

Sorce, J., Emde, R., & Frank, M. (1982). Maternal referencing in normal and Down's syndrome infants: A longitudinal study. In R. Emde & R. Harmon (Eds.), *The development of attachment and affiliative systems.* New York: Plenum Press.

Sorce, J., Emde, R., Campos, J., & Klinnert, M. (1981, April). *Maternal emotional signaling: Its effect on the visual cliff behavior of one-year-olds.* Paper presented at the meetings of the Society for Research in Child Development, Boston, MA.

Sorrentino, R. M., & Field, N. (1986). Emergent leadership over time: The functional value of positive motivation. *Journal of Personality and Social Psychology, 50,* 1091–1099.

Spangler, W. (1992). Validity of questionnaire and TAT measures of need for achievement: Two meta-analyses. *Psychological Bulletin, 112,* 140–154.

Spanier, G. B., & Lewis, R. A. (1980). Marital quality: A review of the seventies. *Journal of Marriage and the Family, 42,* 825–839.

Spanos, N. P., James, B., & de Groot, H. P. (1990). Detection of simulated hypnotic amnesia. *Journal of Abnormal Psychology, 99,* 179–182.

Spanos, N. P., Lush, N. I., & Gwynn, M. I. (1989). Cognitive skill-training enhancement of hypnotizability: Generalization effects and trance logic responding. *Journal of Personality and Social Psychology, 56,* 795–804.

Spearman, C. (1927). *The abilities of man.* London: Macmillan.

Speer, D. (1992). Clinically significant change: Jacobson & Truax revisited. *Journal of Consulting and Clinical Psychology, 60,* 402–408.

Spelke, E. S. (1982). Perceptual knowledge of objects in infancy. In J. Mehler, M. Garrett, & E. Walker (Eds.), *Perspectives on mental representation.* Hillsdale, NJ: Lawrence Erlbaum Associates.

Spelke, E. S., van Hofsten, C., & Kestenbaum, R. (1989). Object perception in infancy: Interaction of spatial and kinetic information for object boundaries. *Developmental Psychology, 25,* 185–196.

Speltz, M. L., & Bernstein, D. A. (1979). The use of participant modeling for claustrophobia: A case report. *Journal of Behavior Therapy and Experimental Psychiatry, 10,* 251–255.

Spence, M. J., & DeCasper, A. J. (1982, March). *Human fetuses perceive maternal speech.* Paper presented at the meeting of the International Conference on Infant Studies, Austin, TX.

Spencer, S. B., & Hemmer, R. C. (1993). Therapeutic bias with gay and lesbian clients: A functional analysis. *The Behavior Therapist, 16,* 93–97.

Sperling, G. (1960). The information available in brief visual presentations. *Psychological Monographs, 74,* 1–29.

Sperry, R. W. (1968). Hemisphere deconnection and unity in conscious awareness. *American Psychologist, 23,* 723–733.

Sperry, R. W. (1974). Lateral specialization in the surgically separated hemispheres. In F. O. Schmitt & F. G. Wordon (Eds.), *The neurosciences third study program.* Cambridge: MIT Press.

Spiegel, D., Bloom, J. R., Kraemer, H. C., & Gottheil, E. (1989, October 14). Effect of psychosocial treatment on survival of patients with metastatic breast cancer. *The Lancet 2* (8668), 888–891.

Spiegler, M. D., & Guevremont, D. C. (in press). *Contemporary behavior therapy (2nd ed.).* Pacific Grove, CA: Brooks/Cole.

Spielberger, C. (1979). *Understanding stress and anxiety.* New York: Harper & Row.

Spielberger, C. D. (1983). *State-Trait Anxiety Inventory (Form Y) manual.* Palo Alto, CA: Consulting Psychologists Press.

Spielberger, C. D. (1988). *State-Trait Anger Expression Inventory: Professional Manual.* Odessa, FL: Psychological Assessment Resources, Inc.

Spitz, H. H. (1991). Commentary on Locurto's "Beyond IQ in preschool programs?" *Intelligence, 15,* 327–333.

Spitzer, R. L., Gibbon, M., Skodol, A. E., Williams, J. B. W., & First, M. B. (1989). *DSM-III-R casebook.* Washington, DC: American Psychiatric Association.

Spitzer, R. L., Severino, S. K., Williams, J. B., & Parry, B. L. (1989). Late luteal phase dysphoric disorder and DSM-III-R. *American Journal of Psychiatry, 146,* 892–897.

Spitzer, R. L., Skodol, A. E., Gibbon, M., & Williams, J. B. W. (1983). *Psychopathology: A casebook.* New York: McGraw-Hill.

Spitzer, R., First, M., Williams, J., Kendler, K., Pincus, A., & Tucker, G. (1992). Now is the time to retire the term "Organic Mental Disorders." *American Journal of Psychiatry, 149,* 240–244.

Spoont, M. (1992). The role of serotonin in neural information processing: Implications for human psychopathology. *Psychological Bulletin, 112,* 330–350.

Sprafka, J., Folsom, A., Burke, G., Hahn, G., & Pirie, P. (1990). Type A behavior and its association with cardiovascular disease prevalence in blacks and whites: The Minnesota Heart Survey. *Journal of Behavioral Medicine, 13,* 1–13.

Springer, S. P., & Deutsch, G. (1989). *Left brain, right brain.* San Francisco: W. H. Freeman.

Squire, L. R. (1986). Mechanisms of memory. *Science, 232,* 1612–1619.

Squire, L. R. (1992). Memory and the hippocampus: A synthesis from findings with rats, monkeys, and humans. *Psychological Review, 99,* 195–231.

Squire, L. R., & McKee, R. (1992). The influence of prior events on cognitive judgments in amnesia. *Journal of Experimental Psychology: Learning, Memory, and Cognition, 18,* 106–115.

Squire, L. R., & Zola-Morgan, S. (1991). The medial temporal lobe memory system. *Science, 253,* 1380–1386.

Squire, S. (1987, November 22). Shock therapy's return to respectability. *New York Times Magazine,* pp. 78–89.

Squires, K. C., Donchin, E., Herning, R. I., & McCarthy, G. (1977). On the influence of task relevance and stimulus probability on event-related-potential components. *Electroencephalography and Clinical Neurophysiology, 42,* 1–14.

Squires, R. F., & Braestrup, C. (1977). Benzodiazepine receptors in rat brain. *Nature, 266,* 732–734.

Srull, T. K., & Gaelick, L. (1983). General principles and individual differences in the self as a habitual reference point: An examination of self-other judgements of similarity. *Social Cognition, 2,* 108–121.

Srull, T. K., & Wyer, R. S. (1983). The role of control processes and structural constraints in models of memory and social judgement. *Journal of Experimental Social Psychology, 19,* 497–521.

St. Lawrence, J. S. (1993). African-American adolescents' knowledge, health-related attitudes, sexual behavior, and contraceptive decisions: Implications for the prevention of adolescent HIV infection. *Journal of Counsulting Clinical Psychology, 61,* 104–112.

Staats, A. W. (1991). Unified positivism and unification psychology: Fad or new field? *American Psychologist, 46,* 899–912.

Stacy, A. W., Widaman, K. F., & Marlatt, G. A. (1990). Expectancy models of alcohol use. *Journal of Personality and Social Psychology, 58,* 918–928.

Staddon, J. E. R., & Ettinger, R. H. (1989). *Learning: An introduction to the principles of adaptive behavior.* San Diego: Harcourt Brace Jovanovich.

Standing, L., Conezio, J., & Haber, R. N. (1970). Perception and memory for pictures: Single-trial learning of 2500 visual stimuli. *Psychonomic Science, 19,* 73–74.

Stang, D. J. (1972). Conformity, ability and self-esteem. *Representative Research in Social Psychology, 3,* 97–103.

Stangor, C., & McMillan, D. (1992). Memory for expectancy-congruent and expectancy-incongruent information: A review of the social and social developmental literatures. *Psychological Bulletin, 111,* 42–61.

Stanislaw, H., & Rice, F. J. (1988). Correlation between sexual desire and menstrual cycle characteristics. *Archives of Sexual Behavior, 17,* 499–508.

Stankov, L. (1983). Attention and intelligence. *Journal of Educational Psychology, 75,* 471–490.

Stankov, L. (1988). Aging, attention and intelligence. *Psychology and Aging, 3,* 59–74.

Stankov, L. (1989). Attentional resources and intelligence: A disappearing link. *Personality and Individual Differences, 10,* 957–968.

Stanley, G., & Hall, R. (1973). Short term visual information processing in dyslexics. *Child Development, 44,* 841–844.

Stasser, G., Kerr, N. L., & Davis, J. H. (1989). Influence processes and consensus models in decision-making in groups. In P. B. Paulus (Ed.), *Psychology of group influence* (2nd ed.). Hillsdale, NJ: Lawrence Erlbaum Associates.

Staw, B. M., & Ross, J. (1989). Understanding behavior in escalation situations. *Science, 246,* 216–220.

Stearns, C. Z., & Stearns, P. N. (1986). *Anger: The struggle for emotional control in America's history.* Chicago: University of Chicago Press.

Steele, C. M. (1986, January). What happens when you drink too much? *Psychology Today.*

Steele, C. M., & Josephs, R. A. (1988). Drinking your troubles away II: An attention-allocation model of alcohol's effects on psychological stress. *Journal of Abnormal Psychology, 97,* 196–205.

Steinberg, L., Dornbusch, S. M., & Brown, B. B. (1992). Ethnic differences in adolescent achievement: An ecological perspective. *American Psychologist, 47,* 723–729.

Steinberger, L. (1986). Stability (and instability) of type A behavior from childhood to young adulthood. *Developmental Psychology, 22,* 393–402.

Steinmark, S. W., & Borkovec, T. D. (1974). Active and placebo treatment effects on moderate insomnia under counterdemand and positive demand conditions. *Journal of Abnormal Psychology, 83,* 157–163.

Stephan, W. G. (1985). Intergroup relations. In G. Lindzey & E. Aronson (Eds.), *Handbook of social psychology, Vol. 2* (3rd ed.). New York: Random House.

Stephens, J. H., & Kamp, M. (1962). On some aspects of hysteria: A clinical study. *Journal of Nervous and Mental Disease, 134,* 305–315.

Steriade, M., & McCarley, R. W. (1990). *Brainstem control of wakefulness and sleep.* New York: Plenum.

Stern, J., & Stern, M. (1992). Chiles (New Mexico). *The New Yorker,* p. 68.

Stern, R. (1983). Antidepressant drugs in the treatment of obsessive-compulsive disorders. *Journal of Behavior Therapy and Experimental Psychiatry, 14,* 19–23.

Sternberg, L., Dornbush, S. M., & Brown, B. B. (1992). Ethnic differences in adolescents' achievement. *American Psychologist, 47,* 723–729.

Sternberg, R. J. (1982). Reasoning, problem solving and intelligence. In R. J. Sternberg (Ed.), *Handbook of human intelligence.* Cambridge: Cambridge University Press.

Sternberg, R. J. (1985). *Beyond IQ: A triarchic theory of human intelligence.* Cambridge, MA: Cambridge University Press.

Sternberg, R. J. (1986a). A triangular theory of love. *Psychological Review, 93,* 119–135.

Sternberg, R. J. (1986b). Inside intelligence. *American Scientist, 74,* 137–143.

Sternberg, R. J. (1987). Liking versus loving: A comparative evaluation of theories. *Psychological Bulletin, 102,* 331–345.

Sternberg, R. J. (1988). *The triarchic mind.* New York: Cambridge Press.

Sternberg, R. J. (1988). *Triangulating love.* In R. J. Sternberg & M. L. Barnes (Eds.), *The psychology of love.* New Haven: Yale University Press.

Sternberg, R. J. (1989). Domain generality versus domain specificity: The life and impending death of a false dichotomy. *Merrill-Palmer Quarterly, 35,* 115–130.

Sternberg, R. J. (1990). Prototypes of competence and incompetence. In R. J. Sternberg & J. Kolligian, Jr. (Eds.), *Competence considered,* pp. 117–145. New Haven: Yale University Press.

Sternberg, R. J. (1991). Death, taxes, and bad intelligence tests. *Intelligence, 15,* 257–269.

Sternberg, R. J. (1992). Ability tests, measurements, and markets. *Journal of Educational Psychology, 84,* 134–140.

Sternberg, R. J. (1993). The g-ocentric view of intelligence and job performance is wrong. *Current Directions in Psychological Science, 2,* 1–4.

Sternberg, R. J., & Barnes, M. L. (Eds.) (1988). *The psychology of love.* New Haven: Yale University Press.

Sternberg, R. J., & Detterman, D. (1986). *What is intelligence?* Norwood, NJ: Ablex.

Sternberg, R. J., & Gastel, J. (1989). Coping with novelty in human intelligence: An empirical investigation. *Intelligence, 13,* 187–197.

Sternberg, R. J., & Grajeck, S. (1984). The nature of love. *Journal of Personality and Social Psychology, 47,* 312–329.

Sternberg, S. (1966). High-speed scanning in human memory. *Science, 153,* 652–654.

Sternberg, S. (1969). Mental processes revealed by reaction time experiments. *American Scientist, 57,* 421–457.

Sternglanz, S. H., & Serbin, L. A. (1974). Sex-role stereotyping in children's television programs. *Developmental Psychology, 10,* 710–715.

Stevens, A., & Coupe, P. (1978). Distortions in judged spatial relations. *Cognitive Psychology, 10,* 422–437.

Stevens, J. C., & Hooper, J. E. (1982). How skin and object temperature influence touch sensation. *Perception and Psychophysics, 32,* 282–285.

Stevens, S. S. (1957). On the psychophysical law. *Psychological Review, 64,* 153–181.

Stevenson, H. (1992). *A long way from being number one: What we have to learn from East Asia.* Washington, DC: Federation of Behavioral, Psychological and Cognitive Sciences.

Stevenson, H. W., Azuma, H., & Hakuta, K. (1986). *Child development and education in Japan.* New York: W. H. Freeman.

Stewart, A. J. (1989). Social intelligence and adaptation to life changes. In R. S. Wyer & T. K. Srull (Eds.), *Advances in social cognition: Vol. 2: Social intelligence and cognitive assessments of personality.* Hillsdale, NJ: Lawrence Erlbaum Associates.

Stewart, A. L., & Brook, R. H. (1983). Effects of being overweight. *American Journal of Public Health, 73,* 171–178.

Stewart, D. E. (1989). Positive changes in the premenstrual period. *Acta Psychiatrica Scandinavica, 79,* 400–405.

Stigler, J. (1992, March). Cultural differences in cognitive development and education. Paper presented at the Claremont Conference on Cognitive Development, Claremont CA.

Stigler, J. W. (1984). "Mental abacus": The effect of abacus training on Chinese children's mental calculation. *Cognitive Psychology, 16,* 145–176.

Stiles, W. B., Shapiro, D. A., & Elliott, R. (1986). "Are all psychotherapies equivalent?" *American Psychologist, 41,* 165–180.

Stoerig, P., & Cowey, A. (1992). Wavelength discrimination in blindsight. *Brain, 115,* 425–444.

Stokes, A. F., Wickens, C. D., & Kite, K. (1990). *Display technology: Human factors concepts.* Warrendale, PA: Society of Automotive Engineers, Inc.

Stone, A. A., Cox, D. S., Valdimarsdottir, H., Jandorf, N., & Neale, J. M. (1987). Evidence that secretory IgA antibody is associated with daily mood. *Journal of Personality & Social Psychology, 52,* 988–993.

Stone, A. A., Helder, L., & Schneider, M. S. (1988). Coping with stressful events: Coping dimensions and issues. In L. H. Cohen (Ed.), *Research on stressful life events: Theoretical and methodological issues.* New York: Sage.

Stone, M. H. (1986). Exploratory psychotherapy in schizophrenia-spectrum patients: A reevaluation in the light of long-term follow-up of schizophrenic and borderline patients. *Bulletin of the Menninger Clinic, 50,* 287–306.

Storms, M. D. (1980). Theories of sexual orientation. *Journal of Personality and Social Psychology, 38,* 783–792.

Storms, M. D. (1981). A theory of erotic orientation development. *Psychological Review, 88,* 340–353.

Strauman, T. J. (1989). Self-discrepancies in clinical depression and social phobia: Cognitive structures that underlie emotional disorders? *Journal of Abnormal Psychology, 98,* 14–22.

Straus, M. A., Gelles, R. J., & Steinmetz, S. K. (1980). *Behind closed doors.* Garden City, NY: Anchor Books.

Strayer, D. L., Wickens, C. D., & Braune, R. (1987). Adult age differences in the speed and capacity of information processing: 2. An electrophysiological approach. *Psychology and Aging, 2,* 99–110.

Streissguth, A. P., Barr, H. M., Sampson, P. D., Darby, B. L., & Martin, D. C. (1989). IQ at age 4 in relation to maternal alcohol use and smoking during pregnancy. *Developmental Psychology, 25,* 3–11.

Stretch, J. D. (1985). Posttraumatic stress disorder among U.S. Army Reserve Vietnam and Vietnam-era veterans. *Journal of Consulting and Clinical Psychology, 53,* 935.

Streufert, S. (1986). *Complexity, managers and organizations.* Orlando, FL: Academic Press.

Strickland, B. (1992). Women and depression. *Current Directions in Psychological Science, 1,* 132–135.

Strickland, B. R. (1989). Internal-external control expectancies: From contingency to creativity. *American Psychologist, 44,* 1–12.

Strickland, T., Ranganath, V., Lin, K-M., Poland, R., Mendoza, R., & Smith, M. (1991). Psychopharmacologic considerations in the treatment of Black American populations. *Psychopharmacology Bulletin, 27,* 441–448.

Strongman, K. T., & Kemp, S. (1991). Autobiographical memory for emotion. *Bulletin of the Psychonomic Society, 29,* 195–198.

Stroop, J. R. (1935). Studies of interference in serial verbal reactions. *Journal of Experimental Psychology, 18,* 643–662.

Strube, M. J., Boland, S. M., Manfredo, P. A., & Abdulrahman, A. (1987). Type A behavior pattern and the self-evaluation of abilities: Empirical tests of the self-appraisal model. *Journal of Personality and Social Psychology, 52,* 956–974.

Strube, M. J., Gardner, W., & Hartmann, D. P. (1985). Limitations, liabilities, and obstacles in reviews of the literature: The current status of meta-analysis. *Clinical Psychology Review, 5,* 63–78.

Strupp, H. H. (1989). Psychotherapy: Can the practitioner learn from the researcher? *American Psychologist, 44,* 717–724.

Strupp, H. H., & Hadley, S. W. (1977). A tripartite model of mental health and therapeutic outcomes. *American Psychologist, 32,* 187–196.

Stunkard, A. J., & Wadden, T. A. (1992). Psychological aspects of severe obesity. *American Journal of Clinical Nutrition, 55,* 524S-532S.

Suarez, E., Williams, R., Kuhn, C., Zimmerman, E., & Schanberg, S. (1991). Biobehavioral basis of coronary-prone behavior in middle-aged men. Part ii: Serum cholesterol, the Type A behavior pattern, and hostility as interactive modulators of physiological reactivity. *Psychosomatic Medicine, 53,* 528–537.

Suberi, M., & McKeever, W. F. (1977). Differential right hemispheric memory storage of emotional and non-emotional faces. *Neuropsychologia, 15,* 757–768.

Subhan, Z., & Hindmarch, I. (1985). Psychopharmacological effects of vinpocetine in normal healthy volunteers. *European Journal of Pharmacology, 28,* 567–571.

Suddath, R. L., Christison, G. W., Torrey, E. F., Casanova, M. F., & Weinberger, D. R. (1990). Anatomical abnormalities in the brains of monopsychotic twins discordant for schizophrenia. *New England Journal of Medicine, 322,* 789–794.

Sue, D. (1992). Asian and Caucasian subjects' preference for different counseling styles. Unpublished manuscript, Western Washington University.

Sue, D. W. (1990). Culture-specific strategies in counseling: A conceptual framework. *Professional Psychology: Research and Practice, 21,* 424–433.

Sue, S., & Okazaki, S. (1990). Asian-American educational achieve-

ments: A phenomenon in search of an explanation. *American Psychologist, 45,* 913–920.

Suedfeld, P. (1980). *Restricted environmental stimulation: Research and clinical applications.* New York: Wiley.

Suedfeld, P., & Baker-Brown, G. (1986). Restricted environmental stimulation therapy and aversion conditioning in smoking cessation: Active and placebo effects. *Behaviour Research & Therapy, 24,* 421–428.

Suedfeld, P., Roy, C., & Landon, P. B. (1982). Restricted environmental stimulation therapy in the treatment of essential hypertension. *Behaviour Research and Therapy, 20,* 553–560.

Suematsu, H., Ishikawa, H. Kuboki, T., & Ito, T. (1985). Statistical studies on anorexia nervosa in Japan: Detailed clinical data on 1,011 patients. *Psychotherapy and Psychosomatics, 43,* 96–103.

Sulin, R. A., & Dooling, D. J. (1974). Intrusion of a thematic idea in retention of prose. *Journal of Experimental Psychology, 103,* 255–262.

Sullivan, H. S. (1953). *The interpersonal theory of psychiatry.* New York: W. W. Norton.

Sullivan, H. S. (1954). *The psychiatric interview.* New York: W. W. Norton.

Sullivan, J. W., & Horowitz, F. D. (1983). The effects of intonation on infant attention: The role of the rising intonation contour. *Journal of Child Language, 10,* 521–534.

Sullivan, K., & Sullivan, A. (1980). Adolescent-parent separation. *Developmental Psychology, 10,* 93–99.

Sullivan, L. (1991). Study reported in *Daily Illini,* October 1. Washington, DC: National Center for Health Statistics and National Institute for Alcohol Abuse and Alcoholism.

Sullivan, L., & Stankov, L. (1990). Shadowing and target detection as a function of age: Implications for the role of processing resources in competing tasks and in general intelligence. *Australian Journal of Psychology, 42,* 173–185.

Suls, J., & Fletcher, B. (1985). The relative efficacy of avoidant and nonavoidant coping strategies: A meta-analysis. *Health Psychology, 4,* 249–288.

Suls, J., & Sanders, G. (1988). Type A behavior as a general risk factor for physical disorder. *Journal of Behavioral Medicine, 11,* 201–225.

Suls, J., & Wan, C. K. (1989). The relation between type A behavior and chronic emotional distress: A meta-analysis. *Journal of Personality and Social Psychology, 57,* 505–512.

Sundberg, N., & Sue, D. (1989). Research and research hypotheses about effectiveness in intercultural counseling. In P. Pederson, J. Draguns, W. Lonner, & J. Trimble (Eds.), *Counseling across cultures* (3rd ed.). Honolulu: University of Hawaii Press.

Susser, E., & Lin, S. (1992). Schizophrenia after prenatal exposure to the Dutch hunger winter of 1944–1945. *Archives of General Psychiatry, 49,* 983–988.

Suzdak, P. D., Glowa, J. R., Crawley, J. N., Schwartz, R. D., Skolnick, P., & Paul, S. M. (1986). A selective imidazobenzodiazepine antagonist of ethanol in the rat. *Science, 234,* 1243–1247.

Suzuki, K. (1991). Moon illusion simulated in complete darkness: Planetarium experiment reexamined. *Perception and Psychophysics, 49,* 349–354.

Swaab, D. F., & Fliers, E. (1985). A sexually dimorphic nucleus in the human brain. *Science, 228,* 1112–1115.

Swaab, D. F., & Hofman, M. A. (1990). An enlarged suprachiasmatic nucleus in homosexual men. *Brain Research, 537,* 141–148.

Swann, W. B., Stein-Seroussi, A., & Giesler, R. B. (1992). Why people self-verify. *Journal of Personality and Social Psychology, 62,* 392–401.

Swanson, L. W. (1976). The locus coeruleus: A cytoarchitectonic, Golgi, and immunohistochemical study in the albino rat. *Brain Research, 110,* 39–56.

Sweeney, P. D., Anderson, K., & Bailey, S. (1986). Attributional style in depression: A meta analytic review. *Journal of Personality and Social Psychology, 50,* 974–991.

Sweetland, R. C., & Keyser, D. J. (Eds.) (1986). *Tests: A complete reference for assessments in psychology, education, and assessment.* Kansas City, MO: Test Corporation of America.

Sweller, J., & Gee, W. (1978). Einstellung: The sequence effect and hypothesis theory. *Journal of Experimental Psychology: Human Learning and Memory, 4,* 513–526.

Swets, J., & Bjork, R.,A. (1990). Enhancing human performance: An evaluation of "New Age" techniques considered by the U.S. Army. *Psychological Science, 1,* 85–96.

Swets, J., & Druckman, D. (1988). *Enhancing human performance.* Washington, DC: National Academy of Sciences Press.

Swift, D. W., & Freeman, M. H. (1986, July). Application of head up displays to ears. *Displays,* pp. 107–110.

Synodinos, N. A. (1988). Subliminal stimulation: What does the public think about it? *Current Issues and Research in Advertising, 11,* 157–187.

Szasz, T. S. (1960). The myth of mental illness. *American Psychologist, 15,* 113–118.

Szasz, T. S. (1987). *Insanity: The idea and its consequences.* New York: Wiley.

Szasz, T. S. (Ed.) (1974). *The age of madness: The history of involuntary hospitalization.* New York: Jason Aronson.

Szmukler, G. I., & Russell, G. F. M. (1986). Outcome and prognosis of anorexia nervosa. In K. D. Brownell & J. P. Foreyt (Eds.), *Handbook of eating disorders.* New York: Basic Books.

Tabachnick, B. G., Keith-Spiegel, P., & Pope, K. S. (1991). Ethics of teaching: Beliefs and behaviors of psychologists as educators. *American Psychologist, 46,* 506–515.

Takahashi, T. (1989). Social phobia syndrome in Japan. *Comprehensive Psychiatry, 30,* 45–52.

Takeuchi, A. H., & Hulse, S. H. (1993). Absolute pitch. *Psychological Bulletin, 113,* 345–361.

Talbot, J. D., Marrett, S., Evans, A. C., Meyer, E., Bushnell, M. C., & Duncan, G. H. (1991). Multiple representations of pain in human cerebral cortex. *Science, 251,* 1355–1358.

Talley, P. F., Strupp, H. H., & Morey, L. C. (1990). Matchmaking in psychotherapy: Patient-therapist dimensions and their impact on outcome. *Journal of Consulting and Clinical Psychology, 58,* 182–188.

Tanford, S., & Penrod, S. (1984). Social influence model: A formal integration of research on majority and minority influence processes. *Psychological Bulletin, 95,* 189–225.

Tannen, D. (1990). *You just don't understand: Women and men in conversation.* New York: Ballantine Books.

Tanner, C. M. (1989). The role of environmental toxins in the etiology of Parkinson's disease. *Trends in Neurosciences, 12,* 49–54.

Tanouye, S. (1992). Social phobia and *Tai-jin kyofu sho* in Japanese Hawaiians. Unpublished master's thesis, Western Washington University, Bellingham, WA.

Tarler-Benlolo, L. (1978). The role of relaxation in biofeedback training: A critical review of the literature. *Psychological Bulletin, 85,* 727–755.

Tarpy, R. M., & Sawabini, F. L. (1974). Reinforcement delay: A selective review of the last decade. *Psychological Bulletin, 81,* 984–987.

Tavris, C. (1992). *The mismeasure of woman.* New York: Simon & Schuster.

Taylor J. W. (1979). Plasma progesterone, oestradiol 17 beta and premenstrual symptoms. *Acta Psychiatrica Scandinavica, 60,* 76–86.

Taylor, D. A., & Altman, I. (1987). Communication in interpersonal relationships: Social penetration processes. In M. Roloff & G. Miller (Eds.), *Exploration in interpersonal communication* (2nd ed.). Beverly Hills: Sage.

Taylor, D. M., & Jaggi, V. (1974). Ethnocentrism and causal attribution in a South Indian context. *Journal of Cross-Cultural Psychology, 5,* 162–171.

Taylor, R. L., & Richards, S. B. (1991). Patterns of intellectual differences of black, hispanic, and white children. *Psychology in the Schools, 28,* 5–8.

Taylor, S. (1991). *Health psychology* (2nd ed.). New York: McGraw-Hill.

Taylor, S. E. (1989). *Positive illusions: Creative self-deception and the healthy mind.* New York: Basic Books.

Taylor, S. E., & Brown, J. D. (1988). Illusion and well-being: A social psychological perspective on mental health. *Psychological Bulletin, 103,* 193–210.

Taylor, S. E., & Lobel, M. (1989). Social comparison activity under threat: Downward evaluation and upward contacts. *Psychological Review, 96,* 569–575.

Taylor, S. E., Buunk, B. P., & Aspinwall, L. G. (1990). Social comparison, stress, and coping. *Personality and Social Psychology Bulletin, 16,* 74–89.

Taylor, S. E., Kemeny, M. E., Aspinwall, L. G., Schneider, S. G., Rodriguez, R., & Herbert, M. (1992). Optimism, coping, psychological distress, and high-risk sexual behavior among men at risk for acquired immunodeficiency syndrome (AIDS). *Journal of Personality and Social Psychology, 63,* 460–473.

Tecoma, E. S., & Huey, L. Y. (1985). Psychic distress and the immune response. *Life Sciences, 36,* 1799–1812.

Teghtsoonian, R. (1992). In defense of the pineal gland. *Behavioral and Brain Sciences, 15,* 224–225.

Teitelbaum, P. (1957). Random and food-directed activity in hyperphagic and normal rats. *Journal of Comparative and Physiological Psychology, 50,* 486–490.

Teitelbaum, P. (1961). Disturbances in feeding and drinking behavior after hypothalamic lesions. In M. R. Jones (Ed.), *Nebraska symposium on motivation.* Lincoln: University of Nebraska Press.

Telch, M. J., Brouillard, M., Telch, C. F., Agras, W. S., & Taylor, C. B. (1989). Role of cognitive appraisal in panic-related avoidance. *Behaviour Research & Therapy, 27,* 373–383.

Tellegen, A., Lykken, D. T., Bouchard, T. J., Wilcox, K. J., Segal, N. L., & Rich, S. (1988). Personality similarity in twins reared apart and together. *Journal of Personality and Social Psychology, 54,* 1031–1039.

Tempel, D. L., Leibowitz, K. J., & Leibowitz, S. F. (1988). Effects of PVN galanin on macronutrient selection. *Peptides, 9,* 309–314.

Ter Riet, G., Kleijnen, J., & Knipschild, P. (1990). Acupuncture and chronic pain: A criteria-based meta-analysis. *Journal of Clinical Epidemiology, 43,* 1191–1199.

Terenius, L. (1988). Significance of opioid peptides and other potential markers of neuropeptide systems in cerebrospinal fluid. *Progress in Brain Research, 77,* 419–429.

Terkel, J., & Rosenblatt, J. S. (1972). Humoral factors underlying maternal behavior of parturition: Cross transfusion between freely moving rats. *Journal of Comparative and Physiological Psychology, 80,* 365–371.

Terman, L. M. (1916). *The measurement of intelligence.* Boston: Houghton Mifflin.

Terman, L. M. (1948). Kinsey's "Sexual behavior in the human male": Some comments and criticisms. *Psychological Bulletin, 45,* 443–459.

Terman, L. M., & Oden, M. (1959). *The gifted group at midlife.* Stanford, CA: Stanford University Press.

Terman, L. M., & Oden, M. H. (1947). *The gifted child grows up: Volume 4. Genetic studies of genius.* Stanford, CA: Stanford University Press.

Terrace, H. S. (1991). Chunking during social learning in progress. *Journal of Experimental Psychology: Aviation Behavior Processes, 17,* 94–106.

Terrace, H. S., Petitto, L. A., Sanders, D. L. & Berer, J. G. (1979). Can an ape create a sentence? *Science, 206,* 891–902.

Tetlock, P. E. (1986). Psychological advice in foreign policy: What do we have to contribute? *American Psychologist, 41,* 557–567.

Tetlock, P. E., Peterson, R. S., McGuire, C., Chang, S., & Feld, P. (1992). Assessing political group dynamics: A test of the groupthink model. *Journal of Personality and Social Psychology, 63,* 403–425.

Tetrud, J. W., & Langston, J. W. (1989). The effect of deprenyl (selegiline) on the natural history of Parkinson's disease. *Science, 245,* 519–522.

The World Alamanac. (1988). New York: Pharos Books.

Thibodeau, R., & Aronson, E. (1992). Taking a closer look: Reasserting the role of the self-concept in dissonance theory. *Personality and Social Psychology Bulletin, 18,* 591–602.

Thoits, P. A. (1986). Social support as coping assistance. *Journal of Personality and Social Psychology, 54,* 416–423.

Thomae, H. (1980). Personality and adjustment to aging. In J. E. Birren & R. B. Sloane (Eds.), *Handbook of mental health and aging.* Englewood Cliffs, NJ: Prentice-Hall.

Thomas, A., & Chess, S. (1977). *Temperament and development.* New York: Brunner/Mazel.

Thomas, E. L., & Robinson, H. A. (1972). *Improving reading in every class: A sourcebook for teachers.* Boston: Allyn & Bacon.

Thomas, K. W., & Schmidt, W. H. (1976). A survey of managerial interests with respect to conflict. *Academy of Management Journal, 19,* 315–318.

Thompson, C. P., & Cowan, T. (1986). Flashbulb memories: A nicer interpretation of a Neisser recollection. *Cognition, 22,* 199–200.

Thompson, L. L. (1990). Negotiation behavior and outcomes: Empirical evidence and theoretical issues. *Psychological Bulletin, 108,* 515–532.

Thompson, S. K. (1975). Gender labels and early sex role development. *Child Development, 46,* 339–347.

Thompson, T., & Grabowski, J. (Eds.) (1972). *Behavior modification of the mentally retarded.* New York: Oxford University Press.

Thoresen, C., & Powell, L. (1992). Type A behavior pattern: New perspectives on theory, assessment, and intervention. *Journal of Clinical and Consulting Psychology, 60,* 595–604.

Thorndike, E. L. (1898). Animal intelligence: An experimental study of the associative processes in animals. *Psychological Monographs, 2*(Whole No. 8).

Thorndike, R. L., Hagan, E., & Sattler, J. (1986). *Stanford-Binet* (4th ed.). Chicago: Riverside.

Thorne, B. (1986). Girls and boys together . . . but most apart: Gender arrangements in elementary school. In W. H. Hartup & Z. Rubin (Eds.), *Relationships and development.* Hillsdale, NJ: Lawrence Erlbaum Associates.

Thyer, B. A. (1992). The term "cognitive behavior therapy" is redundant. *The Behavior Therapist, 15,* 112, 128.

Tice, D. M. (1991). Esteem protection or enhancement? Self-handicapping motives and attributions differ by trait self-esteem. *Journal of Personality and Social Psychology, 60,* 711–725.

Tice, D. M., & Baumeister, R. F. (1990). Self-esteem, self-handicapping, and self-presentation: The strategy of inadequate practice. *Journal of Personality, 58,* 443–464.

Tiedemann, G. L., & Johnston, C. (1992). Evaluation of a parent training program to promote sharing between young siblings. *Behavior Therapy, 23,* 299–318.

Timberlake, W., & Farmer-Dougan, V. A. (1991). Reinforcement in applied settings: Figuring out ahead of time what will work. *Psychological Bulletin, 110*(3), 379–391.

Tinbergen, N. (1989). The study of instinct. Oxford: Clarendon.

Tinti, J. M., & Nofr, C. (1991). Design of sweeteners: A rational approach. In D. E. Walters et al. (Eds.), *Sweeteners, discovery, molecular design, and chemoreception.* Washington, DC: American Chemical Society.

Tolman, E. C., & Honzik, C. H. (1930). Introduction and removal of reward and maze performance in rats. *University of California Publication in Psychology, 4,* 257–275.

Tomarken, A. J., Mineka, S., & Cook, M. (1989). Fear-relevant selective associations and covariation bias. *Journal of Abnormal Psychology, 98,* 381–394.

Tooby, J., & Cosmides, L. (1989). Evolutionary psychologists need to distinguish between the evolutionary process, ancestral selection pressures, and psychological mechanisms. *Behavioral and Brain Sciences, 12,* 724–725.

Torgersen, S. (1983). Genetic factors in anxiety disorders. *Archives of General Psychiatry, 40,* 1085–1089.

Torgersen, S. (1990). Comorbidity of major depression and anxiety disorders. *American Journal of Psychiatry, 147,* 1199–1202.

Tourangeau, R., & Rasinski, K. A. (1988). Cognitive processes underlying context effects in attitude measurement. *Psychological Bulletin, 103,* 299–314.

Tourangeau, R., Rasinski, K. A., & D'Andrade, R. (1991). Attitude structure and belief accessibility. *Journal of Experimental Social Psychology, 27,* 48–75.

Tourangeau, R., Rasinski, K. A., Bradburn, N., & D'Andrade, R. (1989). Belief accessibility and context effects in attitude measurement. *Journal of Experimental Social Psychology, 25,* 401–421.

Trabasso, T., & Bower, G. H. (1968). *Attention in learning.* New York: Wiley.

Tracor, Inc. (1971). *Community reaction to aircraft noise: Vol. 1* (NASA Report CR-1761). Washington, DC: National Aeronautics and Space Administration.

Trafimow, D., Triandis, H. C., & Goto, S. G. (1991). Some tests of the distinction between the private self and the collective self. *Journal of Personality and Social Psychology, 60,* 649–655.

Tranel, D., & Damasio, A. R. (1985). Knowledge without awareness: An autonomic index of facial recognition by prosopagnosics. *Science, 228,* 1453–1454.

Treffert, D. A. (1988). The idiot savant: A review of the syndrome. *American Journal of Psychiatry, 145,* 563–572.

Treisman, A. (1988). Features and objects: The 14th Bartlett memorial lecture. *Quarterly Journal of Experimental Psychology, 40,* 201–237.

Treisman, A., & Gormican, S. (1988). Feature analysis in early vision: Evidence from search asymmetries. *Psychological Review, 95,* 15–48.

Treisman, A., Viera, A., & Hayes, A. (1992). Automaticity and preattentive processes. *American Journal of Psychology, 105,* 341–362.

Treisman, P. U. (1985). *A study of the mathematics performance of black students at the University of California, Berkeley.* Unpublished manuscript.

Tresnan, A., & Gelade, G. (1980). A feature integration theory of attention. *Cognitive Psychology, 12,* 97–136.

Triandis, H. C. (1964). Cultural influences upon cognitive processes. In L. Berkowitz (Ed.), *Advances in experimental social psychology.* New York: Academic Press.

Triandis, H. C. (1990). Theoretical concepts that are applicable to the analysis of ethnocentrism. In R. Brislin (Ed.), *Applied cross-cultural psychology.* Newbury Park, CA: Sage Publications.

Triandis, H. C., Kurowski, L. L., & Gelfand, M. J. (1993). Workplace diversity. In H. C. Triandis, M. D. Dunnette, L. Hough (Eds.), *Handbook of industrial and organizational psychology.* Palo Alto, CA: Consulting Psychologists Press.

Tronick, E. Z. (1989). Emotions and emotional communication in infants. *American Psychologist, 44,* 112–119.

Tronick, E. Z., Morelli, G. A., & Ivey, P. K. (1992). The Efe forager infant and toddler's pattern of social relationships: Multiple and simultaneous. *Developmental Psychology, 28,* 568–577.

Trope, Y. (1989). The multiple roles of context in dispositional judgment. In J. N. Bassili (Ed.), *On-line cognition in person perception.* Hillsdale, NJ: Lawrence Erlbaum Associates.

Trope, Y., Cohen, O., & Alfieri, T. (1991). Behavior identification as a mediator of dispositional inference. *Journal of Personality and Social Psychology, 61,* 873–883.

Trujillo, C. M. (1986). A comparative evaluation of classroom interactions between professors and minority and non-minority college students. *American Educational Research Journal, 23,* 629–642.

Trujillo, K. A., & Akil, H. (1991). Inhibition of morphine tolerance and dependence by the NMDA receptor antagonist MK-801. *Science, 251,* 85–87.

Tryon, R. C. (1940). Genetic differences in maze-learning ability in rats. *Yearbook of the National Society for the Study of Education, 39,* 111–119.

Tsang, P. S., & Wickens, C. D. (1988). The structural constraints and strategic control of resource allocation. *Human Performance, 1,* 45–72.

Tseng, W., Kan-Ming, M., Li-Shuen, L., Guo-Qian, C., Li-Wah, O., & Hong-Bo, Z. (1992). Koro epidemics in Guangdong China. *Journal of Nervous and Mental Disease, 180,* 117–123.

Tulving, E. (1972). Episodic and semantic memory. In E. Tulving & W. Donaldson (Eds.), *Organization of memory.* New York: Academic Press.

Tulving, E. (1974). Cue-dependent forgetting. *American Scientist, 62,* 74–82.

Tulving, E. (1979). Relation between encoding specificity and levels of processing. In L. S. Cermak & F. I. M. Craik (Eds.), *Levels of processing in human memory.* Hillsdale, NJ: Lawrence Erlbaum Associates.

Tulving, E. (1982). *Elements of episodic memory.* New York: Oxford University Press.

Tulving, E. (1985). How many memory systems are there? *American Psychologist, 40,* 385–398.

Tulving, E. (1993). Self-knowledge of an amnesic individual is represented abstractly. In T. K. Srull & R. S. Wyer (Eds.), *The mental representation of trait and autobiographical knowledge about the self: Advances in social cognition: Vol. V.* Hillsdale, NJ: Lawrence Erlbaum Associates.

Tulving, E., & Psotka, J. (1971). Retroactive inhibition in free recall: Inaccessibility of information available in the memory store. *Journal of Experimental Psychology, 87,* 1–8.

Tulving, E., & Schacter, D. L. (1990). Priming and human memory systems. *Science, 247,* 301–306.

Tulving, E., & Thomson, D. M. (1973). Encoding specificity and retrieval processes in episodic memory. *Psychological Review, 80,* 352–373.

Tulving, E., Hayman, C. A. G., & Macdonald, C. A. (1991). Long-lasting perceptual priming and semantic learning in amnesia: A case experiment. *Journal of Experimental Psychology: Learning, Memory, and Cognition, 17,* 595–617.

Tupes, E., & Christal, R. (1961). Recurrent personality factors based on trait ratings (USAF WADC Tech. Note No. 61–97). Lackland Air Force Base, TX: U.S. Air Force.

Turiel, E. (1966). An experimental test of the sequentiality of developmental stages in the child's moral judgments. *Journal of Personality and Social Psychology, 3,* 611–618.

Turk, D. C. (1978). Cognitive behavioral techniques in the management of pain. In P. J. Foreyt & D. P. Pathjen (Eds.), *Cognitive behavior therapy: Research and applications.* New York: Plenum Press.

Turkington, C. (1987). Special talents. *Psychology Today,* pp. 42–46.

Turkkan, J. S. (1989). Classical conditioning: The new hegemony. *Behavioral & Brain Sciences, 12,* 121–179.

Turner, A. M., & Greenough, W. T. (1985). Differential rearing effects on rat visual cortex synapses: I. Synaptic and neuronal density and synapses per neuron. *Brain Research, 329,* 195–203.

Turner, J. C. (1987). *Rediscovering the social group: A self-categorization theory.* New York: Basil Blackwell.

Turner, J. C., & Oakes, P. J. (1989). Self-categorization theory and social influence. In P. B. Paulus (Ed.), *Psychology of group influence* (2nd ed.). Hillsdale, NJ: Lawrence Erlbaum Associates.

Turnstall, O., Gudjonsson, G., Eysenck, H., & Haward, L. (1982). Professional issues arising from psychological evidence presented in court. *Bulletin of the British Psychological Society, 35,* 329–331.

Tversky, A. (1972). Elimination by aspects: A theory of choice. *Psychological Review, 79,* 281–299.

Tversky, A., & Kahneman, D. (1974). Judgment under uncertainty: Heuristics and biases. *Science, 185,* 1124–1131.

Tversky, A., & Kahneman, D. (1981). The framing of decisions and the psychology of choice. *Science, 211,* 453–458.

Tversky, A., & Kahneman, D. (1991). Loss aversion in riskless choice: A reference dependent model. *Quarterly Journal of Economics, 106,* 1039–1061.

Tversky, B. (1991). Spatial mental models. *The psychology of learning and motivation* (Vol. 27, pp. 109–145). Orlando, FL: Academic Press.

Tversky, B., & Tuchin, M. (1989). A reconciliation of the evidence on eyewitness testimony: Comments on McCloskey and Zaragoza. *Journal of Experimental Psychology: General, 118,* 86–91.

Tyler, S., & Elliott, C. D. (1988). Cognitive profiles of groups of poor readers and dyslexic children on British ability scales. *British Journal of Psychology, 79,* 493–508.

U.S. Bureau of the Census. (1991). Statistical abstract of the U.S.: 1991 (111th ed.). Washington, DC.

U.S. Congress. (1983). *Scientific validity of polygraph testing: A research review and evaluation* (Technical Memorandum OTA-TM-H-15). Washington, DC: U.S. Congress, Office of Technology Assessment.

U.S. Department of Commerce. (1986). *Statistical Abstract* (106th ed.). Washington, DC: U.S. Government Printing Office.

U.S. Department of Commerce, U.S. Bureau of the Census. (1992). *Statistical Abstract of the United States* (112th ed.). Washington, DC: U.S. Government Printing Office.

U.S. Department of Health and Human Services. (1988). *Nicotine addiction: A report of the Surgeon General.* US Department of Health and Human Services, Office of the Assistant Seecretary for Health. Office on Smoking and Health, Rockville, MD.

U.S. Department of Health and Human Services. (1990). *Healthy people 2000: National health promotion and disease prevention objectives.* Washington, DC: U.S. Government Printing Office.

U.S. Department of Health and Human Services. (1992). *NCPS AIDS community demonstration projects: What we have learned, 1985–1990.* Washington, DC: USDHHS.

U.S. Department of Health and Welfare. (1979). *Healthy people: The Surgeon General's report on health promotion and disease prevention.* Washington, DC: U.S. Government Printing Office.

Udry, J. R., Billy, J. O. G., Morris, N. M., Groff, T. R., & Raj, M. H. (1985). Serum androgenic hormones motivate sexual behavior in adolescent boys. *Fertility and Sterility, 43,* 90–94.

Ullmann, L., & Krasner, L. (1975). *A psychological approach to abnormal behavior* (2nd ed.). Englewood Cliffs, NJ: Prentice-Hall.

Ulrich, R. E., Stachnik, T. J., & Stainton, N. R. (1963). Student acceptance of generalized personality interpretations. *Psychological Reports, 13,* 831–834.

Vachon, M. L. S. Lyall, W. A. L., Rogers, J., Freeman-Letofsky, K., & Freeman, S. J. J. (1980). A controlled study of self-help intervention for widows. *American Journal of Psychiatry, 137,* 1380–1384.

Vaillant, G. E. (1977). *Adaptation to life: How the best and brightest came of age.* Boston: Little, Brown.

Valenstein, E. S. (Ed.) (1980). *The psychosurgery debate.* San Francisco: W. H. Freeman.

Van Bezooijen, R., Otto, S. A., & Heenan, T. A. (1983). Recognition of vocal expression of emotion: A three-nation study to identify universal characteristics. *Journal of Cross-Cultural Psychology, 14,* 387–406.

Van Buskirk, R. L., & Erickson, R. P. (1977). Odorant responses in taste neurons of the rat NTS. *Brain Research, 135,* 287–303.

van de Kragt, A. J. C., Orbell, J. M., Dawes, R. M., Braver, S., & Wilson, L. (1986). Doing well and doing good as ways of resolving social dilemmas. In H. Wilkie, D. Messick, & C. Rutte (Eds.), *Experimental social dilemmas.* Frankfurt: Verlag Peter Lang.

Van Der Heijden, A. C. (1992). *Selective attention in vision.* London: Routledge.

Van Dyke, C., & Byck, R. (1982). Cocaine. *Scientific American, 246,* 128–141.

Van Essen, D. C., Anderson, C. H., & Felleman, D. J. (1992). Information processing in the primate visual system: An integrated systems perspective. *Science, 255,* 419–423.

Van Sickel, A. D. (1992). Clinical hypnosis in the practice of anesthesia. *Nurse Anesthesiologist, 3,* 67–74.

Van Tol, H., Caren, M., Guan, H-C., Ohara, K., Bunzow, J., Civelli, O., Kennedy, J., Seeman, P., Niznik, H., & Jovanovic, V. (1992). Multiple dopamine D_4 receptor variants in the human population. *Nature, 358,* 149–152.

Vandell, D. L., Ramanan, J., & Lederberg, A. R. (1991, April). Mother-child pretend play and children's later competence with peers. Paper presented at the meetings of the Society for Research in Child Development, Seattle.

Vane, J. (1972). Intelligence and achievement test results of kindergarten children in England, Ireland and the United States. *Journal of Clinical Psychology, 29,* 191–193.

Vellmans, M. (1991). Is human information processing conscious? *Behavior and Brain Science, 14,* 651–726.

Vellutino, F. R. (1987). Dyslexia. *Scientific American, 256,* 20–27.

Vellutino, F. R. (1991). Has basic research in reading increased our understanding of developmental reading and how to teach reading? *Psychological Sciences, 2,* 70–83.

Verfaellie, M., & Cermak, L. S. (1991). Neuropsychological issues in amnesia. In J. L. Martinez & R. P. Kesner (Eds.), *Learning and memory: A biological view* (2nd ed.). San Diego: Academic Press.

Verma, A., Hirsch, D. J., Glatt, C. E., Ronnett, G. V., & Snyder, S. H. (1993). Carbon monoxide: A putative neural messenger. *Science, 259,* 381–384.

Vernon, P. A. (1983). Speed of information processing and general intelligence. *Intelligence, 7,* 53–70.

Vernon, P. A. (1987a). New developments in reaction time research. In P. A. Vernon (Ed.), *Speed of information-processing and intelligence* (pp. 1–20). Norwood, NJ: Ablex.

Vernon, P. A. (Ed.) (1987b). *Speed of information-processing and intelligence.* Norwood, NJ: Ablex.

Verny, T. R. (1984). *Inside groups: A practical guide to encounter groups and group therapy.* New York: McGraw-Hill.

Vicente, K., & Rasmussen, J. (1990). The ecology of human-machine systems. II: Mediating "direct perception" in complex work domains. *Ecological Psychology, 2,* 207–250.

Vicente, K., & Rasmussen, J. (1992). Ecological interface design:

Theoretical foundations. *IEEE Transactions on Systems, Man, & Cybernetics, 22,* 589–606.

Vincent, C. A., & Richardson, P. H. (1986). The evaluation of therapeutic acupuncture: Concepts and methods. *Pain, 24,* 1–13.

Vincent, J. P., Kartalovski, B., Geneste, P., Kamenka, J. M., & Lazdunski, M. (1979). Interaction of phencyclidine ("angel dust") with a specific receptor in rat brain membranes. *Proceedings of the National Academy of Sciences, 76,* 4678–4682.

Vincent, K. R. (1991). Black/white IQ differences: Does age make a difference? *Journal of Clinical Psychology, 47,* 266–270.

Vitiello, M. V., Carlin, A. S., Becker, J., Bradley, B., & Dutton, J. (1989). The effect of subliminal oedipal and competitive stimulation on dart throwing: Another miss. *Journal of Abnormal Psychology, 98,* 54–56.

Vokey, J. R., & Read, J. D. (1985). Subliminal messages: Between the devil and the media. *American Psychologist, 40,* 1231–1239.

Volkmar, F. R., & Greenough, W. T. (1972). Rearing complexity affects branching of dendrites in the visual cortex of the rat. *Science, 176,* 1445–1447.

Volpicelli, J. R., Alterman, A. I., Hayashida, M., & O'Brien, C. P. (1992). Naltrexone in the treatment of alcohol dependence. *Archives of General Psychiatry, 49,* 876–880.

von Bekesy, G. (1960). *Experiments in hearing.* New York: McGraw-Hill.

Voraver, J., & Ross, M. (1993). Exploring the nature and implications of functional independence: Do mental representations of the self become independent of their bases? In T. K. Srull & R. S. Wyer (Eds.), *The mental representation of trait and autobiographical knowledge about the self: Advances in social cognition: Vol. V.* Hillsdale, NJ: Lawrence Erlbaum Associates.

Vuchinich, R. E., & Sobell, M. B. (1978). Empirical separation of physiological and expected effects of alcohol on complex perceptual motor performance. *Psychopharmacology, 60,* 81–85.

Vygotsky, L. S. (1934/reprinted 1962). *Thought and language.* (E. Haufmann & G. Vaker, Eds. & Trans.) Cambridge MA: MIT Press.

Waaegenaar, W. (1986). My memory: A study of autobiographical memory over six years. *Cognitive Psychology, 18,* 225–252.

Waagenaar, W. A. (1989). *Paradoxes of gambling behavior.* Hillsdale, NJ: Lawrence Erlbaum Associates.

Wachs, T. D., & Gruen, C. E. (1982). *Early experience and human development.* New York: Plenum Press.

Wachtel, P. L. (1967). Conceptions of broad and narrow attention. *Psychological Bulletin, 68,* 417–419.

Wachtel, P. L. (1982). *Psychoanalysis and behavior therapy.* New York: Basic Books.

Wade, C. (1988, April). *Thinking critically about critical thinking in psychology.* Paper presented at the annual meeting of the Western Psychological Association, San Francisco, CA.

Wagner, D. A. (1978). Memories of Morocco: The influence of age, schooling, and environment on memory. *Cognitive Psychology, 10,* 1–28.

Wagner, H. L., MacDonald, C. J., & Manstead, A. S. R. (1986). Communication of individual emotions by spontaneous facial expressions. *Journal of Personality and Social Psychology, 50,* 737–743.

Waid, W. M., & Orne, M. T. (1981). Cognitive, social, and personality processes in the physiological detection of deception. In L. Berkowitz (Ed.), *Advances in experimental social psychology: Vol. 14.* New York: Academic Press.

Wainer, H. (1988). How accurately can we assess changes in minority performance on the SAT? *American Psychologist, 43,* 774–778.

Wakefield, J. C. (1992). The concept of mental disorder: On the boundary between biological facts and social values. *American Psychologist, 47,* 373–388.

Walberg, H. J. (1987). Studies show curricula efficiency can be attained. *NASSP Bulletin, 71,* 15–21.

Waldrop, M. M. (1984). Computer vision. *Science, 224,* 1225–1227.

Walker, L. (1991). The feminization of psychology. *Psychology of Women Newsletter of Division, 35,* 1, 4.

Walker, L. J. (1982). The sequentiality of Kohlberg's stages of moral development. *Child Development, 53,* 1330–1336.

Walker, L. J. (1989). A longitudinal study of moral reasoning. *Child Development, 60,* 157–166.

Walker-Andrews, A. (1988). Infants' perception of the affordances of expressive behaviors. In C. Rovee-Collier & L. P. Lipsitt (Eds.), *Advances in infancy research: Vol. 5* (pp. 173–221). Ablex.

Wall Street Journal (1992). GM says a worker sabotaged new autos at a plant in Canada. December 21, p. B10.

Wall, P. D., & Cronly-Dillon, J. R. (1960). Pain, itch and vibration. *AMA Archives of Neurology, 2,* 365–375.

Wallace, A. F. C. (1959). Cultural determinants of response to hallucinatory experience. *Archives of General Psychiatry, 1,* 58–69.

Wallace, C., Liberman, R., MacKain, S., Blackwell, G., & Eckman, T. (1992). Effectiveness and replicability of modules for teaching social and instrumental skills to the severely mentally ill. *American Journal of Psychiatry, 149,* 654–658.

Wallace, R. K., & Benson, H. (1972). The physiology of meditation. *Scientific American, 226,* 84–90.

Wallen, K. (1989). Mate selection: Economics and affection. *Behavioral and Brain Sciences, 12,* 37–38.

Wallen, K. (1990). Desire and ability: Hormones and the regulation of female sexual behavior. *Neuroscience and Biobehavioral Review, 14,* 233–241.

Wallen, K., & Lovejoy, J. (1993). Sexual behavior: Endocrine function and therapy. In J. Schulkin (Ed.), *Hormonal pathways to mind and brain.* New York: Academic Press.

Wallerstein, J. S., & Blakeslee, S. (1989). *Second chances: Men, women and children a decade after divorce.* New York: Ticknor and Fields.

Wallerstein, R. S. (1989). The psychotherapy research project of the Menninger Foundation: An overview. *Journal of Consulting and Clinical Psychology, 57,* 195–205.

Wallman, J., Gottlieb, M. D., Rajaram, V., & Fugate-Wentzek, L. A. (1987). Local retinal regions control local eye growth and myopia. *Science, 237,* 73–76.

Walster, E., & Festinger, L. (1962). The effectiveness of "overheard" persuasive communications. *Journal of Abnormal and Social Psychology, 65,* 395–402.

Walters, G. (1992). Drug-seeking behavior: Disease or lifestyle? *Professional Psychology, 23,* 139–145.

Waltz, D. L. (1988). The prospects for building truly intelligent machines. In S. R. Graubard (Ed.), *The artificial intelligence debate.* Cambridge, MA: MIT Press.

Warchol, M. E, Lambert, P. R., Goldstein, B. J., Forge, A., & Corwin, J. T. (1993). Regenerative proliferation in inner ear sensory epithelia from adult guinea pigs and humans. *Science, 259,* 1619–1622.

Ward, C. (1994). Culture and altered states of consciousness. In W. J. Lonner & R. S. Malpass (Eds.), *Psychology and culture.* Boston: Allyn & Bacon.

Ward, C. A. (Ed.) (1989). *Altered states of consciousness and mental health: A cross-cultural perspective.* Newbury Park, CA: Sage.

Ward, W. D. (1974). *Proceedings of the international congress on noise as a public health problem.* Washington, DC: U.S. Government Printing Office.

Warden, C. J. (1931). *Animal motivation: Experimental studies on the albino rat.* New York: Columbia University Press.

Warm, J. S. (Ed.) (1984). *Sustained attention in human performance.* London: Wiley.

Warm, J. S., & Parasuraman, R. (1987). Vigilance: Basic and applied. *Human Factors, 29,* 623–740.

Warner, R. A., & Sugarman, D. B. (1986). Attributions of personality based on physical appearance, speech, and handwriting. *Journal of Personality and Social Psychology, 50,* 792–799.

Warren, R., & Wertheimer, A. H. (1990). *Perception and control of self-motion.* Hillsdale, NJ: Lawrence Erlbaum Associates.

Wasik, B. H., Ramey, C. T., Bryant, D. M., & Sparling, J. J. (1990). A longitudinal study of two early intervention strategies: Project CARE. *Child Development, 61,* 1682–1696.

Waterman, A. S. (1982). Identity development from adolescence to adulthood: An extension of theory and a review of research. *Developmental Psychology, 18,* 341–358.

Watkins, B. (1989, June 14). Many campuses now challenging minority students to excel in math and science. *Chronicle of Higher Education,* pp. A13-A16.

Watkins, L. R., & Mayer, D. J. (1982). Organization of endogenous opiate and nonopiate pain control systems. *Science, 216,* 1185–1192.

Watkins, M. J. (1989). Willful and nonwillful determinants of memory. In H. L. Roediger & F. I. M. Craik (Eds.), *Varieties of memory and consciousness.* Hillsdale, NJ: Lawrence Erlbaum Associates.

Watkins, P. C., Mathews, A., Williamson, D. A., & Fuller, R. D. (1992). Mood congruent memory in depression: Emotional priming or elaboration? *Journal of Abnormal Psychology, 101,* 581–586.

Watson, D. (1976). *Molecular biology of the gene* (3rd ed.). Menlo Park, CA: Benjamin Cummings.

Watson, D., & Pennebaker, J. W. (1989). Health complaints, stress, and distress: Exploring the role of negative affectivity. *Psychological Review, 96,* 234–254.

Watson, J. B. (1913). Psychology as a behaviorist views it. *Psychological Review, 20,* 158–177.

Watson, J. B. (1924). *Behaviorism.* New York: W. W. Norton.

Watson, J. B. (1930). *Behaviorism* (rev. ed.). New York: Norton.

Watson, J. S. (1972). Smiling, cooing and "the game." *Merrill-Palmer Quarterly, 18,* 323–340.

Watson, M. W. (1981). The development of social roles: A sequence of social-cognitive development. *New Directions for Child Development, 12,* 33–41.

Weary, G., & Edwards, J. A. (1994). Social cognition and clinical psychology: Anxiety and the processing of social information. In R. S. Wyer & T. S. Srull (Eds.), *Handbook of social cognition* (2nd ed.). Hillsdale, NJ: Lawrence Erlbaum Associates.

Webb, W. B. (1968). *Sleep: An experimental approach.* New York: Macmillan.

Webb, W. B. (1975). *Sleep: The gentle tyrant.* Englewood Cliffs, NJ: Prentice-Hall.

Wechsler, D. (1949). *The Wechsler Intelligence Scale for children.* New York: Psychological Corporation.

Wedon, E., & Gargano, G. M. (1988). Cognitive loafing: The effects of accountability and shared responsibility on cognitive effort. *Personality and Social Psychology Bulletin, 14,* 159–171.

Weekes, J. R., Lynn, S. J., Green, J. P., & Brentar, J. T. (1992). Pseudomemory in hypnotized and task-motivated subjects. *Journal of Abnormal Psychology, 101,* 356–360.

Wehr, T. A., Sack, D., Rosenthal, N., Duncan, W., & Gillian, J. C. (1983). Circadian rhythm disturbances in manic-depressive illness. *Federation Practitioner, 42,* 2809–2814.

Weidner, G., Sexton, G., McLellarn, R., Connor, S., & Matarazzo, J. (1987). The role of Type A behavior and hostility in an elevation of plasma lipids in adult women and men. *Psychosomatic Medicine, 49,* 136–145.

Weinberg, J., & Levine, S. (1980). Psychobiology of coping in animals: The effects of predictability. In S. Levine & H. Ursin (Eds.), *Coping and health.* New York: Plenum.

Weinberg, R. A. (1989). Intelligence and IQ: Landmark issues and great debates. *American Psychologist, 44,* 98–104.

Weinberg, R. A., Scarr, S., & Waldman, I. D. (1992). The Minnesota transracial adoption study: A follow-up of IQ test performance at adolescence. *Intelligence, 16,* 117–135.

Weinberger, D. A., Schwartz, G. E., & Davidson, R. J. (1979). Low anxious, high anxious and repressive coping styles: Psychometric patterns and behavioral and physiological responses to stress. *Journal of Abnormal Psychology, 88,* 369–380.

Weinberger, D. R. (1988). Schizophrenia and the frontal lobe. *Trends in Neurosciences, 11,* 367–370.

Weinberger, D. R., Berman, K. F., & Zec, R. F. (1986). Physiologic dysfunction of dorsolateral prefrontal cortex in schizophrenia, I. Regional cerebral blood flow evidence. *Archives of General Psychiatry, 43*(2), 114–124.

Weinberger, D. R., Wagner, R. L., & Wyatt, R. J. (1983). Neuropathological studies of schizophrenia: A selective review. *Schizophrenia Bulletin, 9,* 193–212.

Weinberger, M., Hiner, S. L., & Tierney, W. (1987). In support of hassles as a measure of stress in predicting health outcomes. *Journal of Behavioral Medicine, 10,* 19–32.

Weiner, B. (1972). *Theories of motivation.* Chicago: Rand McNally.

Weiner, B. (1980). *Human motivation.* New York: Holt, Rinehart and Winston.

Weiner, R. D. (1984). Does electroconvulsive therapy cause brain damage? *The Behavioral and Brain Sciences, 7,* 1–53.

Weinstein, C. S. (1991). The classroom as a social context for learning. *Annual Review of Psychology, 42,* 527–562.

Weinstein, N. D. (1980). Unrealistic optimism about future life events. *Journal of Personality and Social Psychology, 39,* 806–820.

Weinstein, N. D. (1989). Effects of personal experience on self-protective behavior. *Psychological Bulletin, 105,* 31–50.

Weiskrantz, L. (1986). *Blindsight: A case study and implications.* Oxford: Oxford University Press.

Weiss, G., Hechtman, L., Milroy, T., & Perlman, T. (1985). Psychiatric status of hyperactives as adults: A controlled prospective 15-year follow-up of 63 hyperactive children. *Journal of American Academy of Child Psychiatry, 24,* 211–220.

Weiss, J. M. (1970). Somatic effects of predictable and unpredictable shock. *Psychosomatic Medicine, 32,* 397–409.

Weiss, S., & Moore, M. (1990) Cultural differences in the perception of magazine alcohol advertisements by Israeli Jewish, Moslem, Druze, and Christian high school students. *Drug and Alcohol Dependence, 26,* 209–215.

Weiss, V. (1986). From memory span and mental speed toward the quantum mechanics of intelligence. *Journal of Personality and Individual Differences, 7,* 737–749.

Weissman, M. M., Fox, K., & Klerman, G. L. (1973). Hostility and depression associated with suicide attempts. *American Journal of Psychiatry, 103,* 450–455.

Weisstein, N., & Harris, C. S. (1974). Visual detection of line segments: An object superiority effect. *Science, 186,* 752–755.

Weitzenhoffer, A. M., & Hilgard, E. R. (1962). *Stanford hypnotic suceptibility scale, Form C.* Palo Alto, CA: Consulting Psychologists Press.

Wekstein, L. (1979). *Handbook of suicidology: Principles, problems, and practice.* New York: Brunner/Mazel.

Wells, G. L. (1993). What do we know about eyewitness identification? *American Psychologist, 48,* 553–571.

Wells, G. L., & Leippe, M. R. (1981). How do triers of fact infer the accuracy of eyewitness identification? *Journal of Applied Psychology, 67,* 682–687.

Wells, R. S., & Higgins, E. T. (1989). Inferring emotions from multiple cues: Revealing age-related differences in "how" without differences in "can." *Journal of Personality, 57,* 747–771.

Wener, R., Frazier, W., & Farbstein, J. (1987, June). Building better jails. *Psychology Today.*

Wenk, G. L. (1989). An hypothesis on the role of glucose in the mechanism of action of cognitive enhancers. *Psychopharmacology, 99,* 431–438.

Wesnes, K., Simpson, P. M., & Kidd, A. (1987). The use of a scopolamine model to study the nootropic effects of tenilsetam (CAS 997) in man. *Medical Science Research: Psychology and Psychiatry, 15,* 1063–1064.

West, R. L., Crook, T. H., & Barron, K. L. (1992). Everyday memory performance across the life span: Effects of age and noncognitive individual differences. *Psychology and Aging, 7,* 72–82.

West, S. G., & Brown, T. J. (1975). Physical attractiveness, the severity of the emergency and helping: A field experiment and interpersonal simulation. *Journal of Experimental Social Psychology, 11,* 531–538.

West, S. G., & Graziano, W. G. (1989). Long-term stability and change in personality: An introduction. *Journal of Personality, 57,* 175–193.

West, S. G., Whitney, G., & Schnedler, R. (1975). Helping a motorist in distress: The effects of sex, race, and neighborhood. *Journal of Personality and Social Psychology, 31,* 691–698.

Wexley, K. N., & Yukl, G. A. (1984). *Organizational behavior and personnel psychology.* Homewood, IL: Richard D. Irwin.

Whalen, R., & Simon, N. G. (1984). Biological motivation. *Annual Review of Psychology, 35,* 257–276.

Wheeler, L., & Miyake, K. (1992). Social comparison in everyday life. *Journal of Personality and Social Psychology, 62,* 760–773.

Whimbey, A. (1976). *Intelligence can be taught.* New York: Bantam.

Whitbourne, S. K., Zuschlag, M. K., Elliot, L. B., & Waterman, A. D. (1992). Psychosocial development in adulthood: A 22-year sequential study. *Journal of Personality and Social Psychology, 63,* 260–271.

White, F. J., & Wang, R. Y. (1986). Electrophysiological evidence for the existence of both D-1 and D-2 dopamine receptors in the rat nucleus accumbens. *Journal of Neuroscience, 6,* 274–280.

White, G. L., & Mullen, P. E. (1990). *Jealousy: Theory, research, and clinical strategies.* New York: Guilford Press.

White, G. L., Fishbein, S., & Rutstein, J. (1981). Passionate love and the misattribution of arousal. *Journal of Personality and Social Psychology, 41,* 56–62.

White, K. R., Taylor, M. J., & Moss, V. D. (1992). Does research support claims about the benefits of involving parents in early intervention programs? *Review of Educational Research, 62,* 91–125.

White, M. (1987). *The Japanese educational challenge: A commitment to children.* New York: The Free Press.

White, N. M., & Milner, P. M. (1992). The psychobiology of reinforcers. *Annual Review of Psychology, 43,* 443–471.

White, S. R., & Paros, K. C. (1992). 3,4-methylenedioxymethamphetamine (MDMA) inhibits glutamate-evoked firing of nucleus accumbens cells. *Society for Neuroscience Abstracts, 22,* 1575.

Whitehouse, P. J., Struble, R. G., Hedreen, J. C., Clark, A. W., White, C. L., Parhad, I. M., & Price, D. L. (1983). Neuroanatomical evidence for a cholinergic deficit in Alzheimer's disease. *Psychopharmacology Bulletin, 19,* 437–440.

Whitla, D. (1991, May). Cited by T. Adler, Not all cognitive skills affected by age. *APA Monitor,* p. 16.

Whitley, B. E., & Hern, A. L. Perceptions of vulnerability to pregnancy and the use of effective contraception. Unpublished manuscript.

Whorf, B. L. (1956). *Language, thought and reality.* Cambridge and New York: MIT Press and Wiley.

Wichman, H. (1970). Effects of isolation and communication on cooperation in a two-person game. *Journal of Personality and Social Psychology, 16,* 114–120.

Wickelgren, W. (1977). Speed accuracy tradeoff and information processing dynamics. *Acta Psychologica, 41,* 67–85.

Wickens, C. D. (1989). Attention. In D. Holding (Ed.), *Human skills.* New York: Wiley.

Wickens, C. D. (1992). *Engineering psychology and human performance* (2nd ed.). New York: Harper Collins.

Wickens, C. D., Aretz, A., & Harwood, K. (1989). Frame of reference for electronic maps. In R. Jenson (Ed.), *Proceedings, 5th international symposium on aviation psychology.* Columbus, OH: Ohio State University.

Wickens, C. D., Heffley, E., Kramer, A., & Donchin, E. (1980). The event related brain potential as an index of attention allocation in visual displays. In *Proceedings, 24th Annual Meeting of the Human Factors Society.* Santa Monica: Human Factors.

Wickens, C. D., Stokes, A., Barnett, B., & Hyman, F. (1992). The effects of stress on pilot judgment in a MIDIS simulator. In O. Svenson & J. Maule (Eds.), *Time pressure and stress in human judgment and decision making.* New York: Plenum.

Wickens, D. D. (1938). Transference of conditioned excitation and conditioned inhibition from one muscle group to the antagonistic muscle group. *Journal of Experimental Psychology, 22,* 101–123.

Wickens, D. D. (1972). Characteristics of word encoding. In A. W. Melton & E. Martin (Eds.), *Coding processes in human memory.* Washington, DC: Winston.

Wickens, D. D. (1973). Some characteristics of word encoding. *Memory and Cognition, 1,* 485–490.

Wickless, C., & Kirsch, I. (1990). Effects of verbal and experiential expectancy manipulations on hypnotic susceptibility. *Journal of Personality and Social Psychology, 57,* 762–768.

Wickramasekera, I. (1985). A conditioned response model of the placebo effect: Predictions from the model. In L. White, B. Tursky, & G. E. Schwartz (Eds.), *Placebo: Theory, research, and mechanisms.* New York: Guilford Press.

Widiger, T. A., & Frances, A. (1985). The DSM-III personality disorders: Perspectives from psychology. *Archives of General Psychiatry, 42,* 615–623.

Widiger, T. A., & Kelso, K. (1983). Psychodiagnosis of Axis II. *Clinical Psychology Review, 3,* 491–510.

Widiger, T., & Shea, T. (1991). Differentiation of axis I and axis II disorders. *Journal of Abnormal Psychology, 100,* 399–406.

Widom, C. S. (1989). Does violence beget violence? A critical examination of the literature. *Psychological Bulletin, 106,* 3–28.

Wiebe, D. J., & McCallum, D. M. (1986). Health practices and hardiness as mediators in the stress-illness relationship. *Health Psychology, 5,* 425–438.

Wiedenfeld, S., O'Leary, A., Bandura, A., Brown, S., Levine, S., & Raska, K. (1990). Inpact of perceived self-efficacy in coping with stressors on components of the immune system. *Journal of Personality and Social Psychology, 59,* 1082–1094.

Wiegersma, S., & Meertse, K. (1990). Subjective ordering, working memory, and aging. *Experimental Aging Research, 16,* 73–77.

Wiener, E. L. (1977). Controlled flight into terrain accidents. *Human Factors, 19,* 171–180.

Wiener, E., & Nagel, D. (1988). *Human factors in aviation.* Orlando, FL: Academic Press.

Wiertelak, E. P., Maier, S. F., & Watkins, L. R. (1992). Cholecystokinin antianalgesia: Safety cues abolish morpine analgesia. *Science, 256,* 830–833.

Wiesenfeld, A. R., & Klorman, R. (1978). The mother's psychophysiological reactions to contrasting affective expressions by her own and an unfamiliar infant. *Developmental Psychology, 14,* 294–304.

Wiggins, J. S., & Broughton, R. (1985). The interpersonal circle: A structural model for the integration of personality research. In R. Hogan & W. C. Jones (Eds.), *Perspective in personality: Theory, measurement, and interpersonal dynamics* (Vol. 1). Greenwich, CT: JAI Press.

Wiggins, J. S., & Pincus, A. L. (1989). Conceptions of personality disorders and dimensions of personality. *Psychological Assessment: A Journal of Consulting and Clinical Psychology, 1,* 305–316.

Wiggins, J. S., Phillips, N., & Trapnell, P. (1989). Circular reasoning about interpersonal behavior: Evidence concerning some untested assumptions underlying diagnostic classification. *Journal of Personality and Social Psychology, 56,* 296–305.

Wiggins, J., & Pincus, A. (1992). Personality: Structure and assessment. *Annual Review of Psychology, 43,* 473–504.

Wightman, D. C., & Lintern, G. (1985). Part task training of tracking in manual control. *Human Factors, 27,* 267–283.

Wilder, D. A. (1977). Perception in groups, size of opposition, and social influence. *Journal of Experimental Social Psychology, 13,* 253–268.

Wilder, D. A., & Shapiro P. (1991). Facilitation of outgroup stereotypes by enhanced ingroup identity. *Journal of Experimental Social Psychology, 27,* 431–452.

Wilder, D. A., & Shapiro, P. N. (1989). Role of competition-induced anxiety in limiting the beneficial impact of positive behavior by an outgroup member. *Journal of Personality and Social Psychology, 56,* 60–69.

Wiley, J. A., & Camacho, T. C. (1980). Life-style and future health: Evidence from the Alameda County study. *Preventive Medicine, 9,* 1–21.

Wilkins, W. (1979). Expectations in therapy research: Discriminating among heterogeneous nonspecifics. *Journal of Consulting and Clinical Psychology, 47,* 837–845.

Wilkinson, A. C. (1984). Children's partial knowledge of the cognitive skill of counting. *Cognitive Psychology, 16,* 28–64.

Williams, C. D. (1959). Elimination of tantrum behavior by extinction procedures. *Journal of Personality and Social Psychology, 59,* 269.

Williams, D. E., & Page, M. M. (1989). A multi-dimensional measure of Maslow's hierarchy of needs. *Journal of Research in Personality, 23,* 192–213.

Williams, J. E., & Best, D. L. (1990). *Measuring stereotypes: A multination study* (Rev. ed.). Newbury Park, CA: Sage.

Williams, K. D., & Karau, S. J. (1991). Social loafing and social compensation: The effects of expectations on co-worker performance. *Journal of Personality and Social Psychology, 61,* 570–581.

Williams, M. H. (1992). Exploitation and inference: Mapping the damage from therapist-patient sexual involvement. *American Psychologist, 47,* 412–421.

Williams, R. C. (1985). *College, department, and course grade distribution for fall semester, 1984 (Research Memorandum No. 222).* Champaign: University of Illinois, Office of Instructional Resources.

Williams, R. J. (1967). The biological approach to the study of personality. In T. Million (Ed.), *Theories of psychopathology.* Philadelphia: W. B. Saunders.

Williams, R. L. (1972). The Black intelligence test of cultural homogeneity (BITCH)—A culture specific test. Paper presented at the annual meeting of the American Psychological Association, Honolulu.

Williams, R., Barefoot, J., Haney, T., Harrell, F., Blumenthal, J., Pryor, D., & Peterson, B. (1988). Type A behavior and angiographically documented coronary atherosclerosis in a sample of 2,289 patients. *Psychosomatic Medicine, 50,* 139–152.

Williams, R., Suarez, E., Kuhn, C., Zimmerman, E., & Schanberg, S. (1991). Biobehavioral basis of coronary-prone behavior in middle-aged men. Part I: Evidence for chronic SNS activation in Type As. *Psychosomatic Medicine, 53,* 517–527.

Willis, W. D., Jr. (1988). Dorsal horn neurophysiology of pain. *Annals of the New York Academy of Science, 531,* 76–89.

Wilson, B. A. (1987). *Rehabilitation of memory.* New York: Guilford Press.

Wilson, E. O. (1975). *Sociobiology: The new synthesis.* Cambridge, MA: Harvard University Press.

Wilson, G. T. (1984). Weight control treatments. In J. D. Matarazzo, S. M. Weiss, J. H. Herd, & N. E. Miller (Eds.) *Behavioral health: A handbook of health enhancement and disease prevention.* New York: Wiley.

Wilson, G. T. (1985). Limitations of meta-analysis in the evaluation of the effects of psychological therapy. *Clinical Psychology Review, 5,* 35–47.

Wilson, J. F. (1981). Behavioral preparation for surgery: Benefit or harm? *Journal of Behavioral Medicine, 4,* 79–102.

Wilson, L., & Rogers, R. W. (1975). The fire this time: Effects of race of target, insult and potential retaliation in black aggression. *Journal of Personality and Social Psychology, 32,* 857–864.

Wilson, M. A., Dwyer, K. D., & Roy, E. J. (1989). Direct effects of ovarian hormones on antidepressant binding sites. *Brain Research Bulletin, 22,* 181–185.

Wilson, S. C., & Barber, T. X. (1978). The creative imagination scale as a measure of hypnotic responsiveness: Applications to experimental and clinical hypnosis. *The American Journal of Clinical Hypnosis, 20,* 235–249.

Wimer, R. E., & Wimer, C. C. (1985). Animal behavior genetics: A search for the biological foundations of behavior. *Annual Review of Psychology, 36,* 171–218.

Winder, P. H., Kety, S. S., Rosenthal, D., Schulsinger, F., Ortmann, J., & Lunde, I. (1986). Psychiatric disorders in biological and adoptive families of adopted individuals with affective disorders. *Archives of General Psychiatry, 43,* 923–929.

Winefield, H. R. (1987). Psychotherapy and social support: Parallels and differences in the helping process. *Clinical Psychology Review, 7,* 631–644.

Winson, J. (1990). The meaning of dreams. *Scientific American,* November, 86–96.

Winterbottom, M. R. (1953). *The relation of childhood training in independence to achievement motivation.* Unpublished doctoral dissertation, University of Michigan, Ann Arbor.

Winton, W. M. (1987). Do introductory textbooks present the Yerkes-Dodson law correctly? *American Psychologist, 42,* 202–203.

Wise, R. A. (1978). Catecholamine theories of reward: A critical review. *Brain Research, 152,* 215–247.

Wise, R. A. (1988). The neurobiology of craving: Implications for the understanding and treatment of addiction. *Journal of Abnormal Psychology, 97,* 118–132.

Wise, R. A., & Rompre, P. P. (1989). Brain dopamine and reward. *Annual Review of Psychology, 40,* 191–225.

Wish, M., Deutsch, M., & Kaplan, S. J. (1976). Perceived dimensions of interpersonal relations. *Journal of Personality and Social Psychology, 33,* 409–420.

Wissler, C. (1901). The correlation of mental and physical traits. *Psychological Monographs, 3,* 1–62.

Witelson, S. F. (1992). Cognitive neuroanatomy: A new era. *Neurology, 42,* 709–713.

Wogalter, M. S., Rashid, R., Clarke, S. W., & Kalsher, M. J. (1991). Evaluating the behavioral effectiveness of a multimodal voice warning sign in a visually cluttered environment. *Proceedings of the 35th Annual Meeting of the Human Factors Society* (pp. 718–722). Santa Monica, CA: Human Factors Society.

Wolkin, A., Sanfilipo, M., Worlf, A., Angrist, B., Brodie, J., & Rotrosen, J. (1992). Negative symptoms and hypofrontality in chronic schizophrenia. *Archives of General Psychiatry, 49,* 959–965.

Wolpe, J. (1958). *Psychotherapy by reciprocal inhibition.* Stanford, CA: Stanford University Press.

Wolpe, J. (1982). *The practice of behavior therapy* (3rd ed.). New York: Pergamon Press.

Wolthuis, O. L. (1971). Experiments with UCB 6215, a drug which enhances acquisition in rats: Its effects compared with those of metamphetamine. *European Journal of Pharmacology, 16,* 283–297.

Wong, B. Y. L. (1986). Metacognition and special education: A review of a view. *The Journal of Special Education, 20,* 9–29.

Wong, D. F., Wagner, H. N., Tune, L. E., Dannals, R. F., Pearlson, G. D., Links, J. M., Tamminga, C. A., Broussolle, E. P., Ravert, H. T., Wilson, A. A., Toung, J. K. T., Malat, J., Williams, J. A., O'Tuama, L. A., Snyder, S. H., Kuhar, M. J., & Gjedde, A. (1986). Positron emission tomography reveals elevated D_2 dopamine receptors in drug-naive schizophrenics. *Science, 234,* 1558–1563.

Wong, M. M., & Csikszentmihalyi, M. (1992). *Journal of Personality and Social Psychology, 60,* 154–164.

Wong, S. E., Martinez-Diaz, J. A., Massel, H. K., Edelstein, B. A., Wiegand, W., Bowen, L., & Liberman, R. P. (1993). Conversational skills training with schizophrenic inpatients: A study of generalization across settings and conversants. *Behavior Therapy, 24,* 285–304.

Wood, J. V. (1989). Theory and research concerning social comparisons of personal attributes. *Psychological Bulletin, 106,* 231–248.

Wood, P. (1992, May 14). Old drivers, new concerns. *Champaign-Urbana News Gazette,* p. C1.

Wood, W., Wong, F. Y., & Chachere, G. (1991). Effects of media violence on viewers' aggression in unconstrained social interaction. *Psychological Bulletin, 109,* 371–383.

Woodall, K. L., & Matthews, K. A. (1993). Changes in and stability of hostile characteristics: Results from a 4-year longitudinal study of children. *Journal of Personality and Social Psychology, 64,* 491–499.

Woodhead, M. (1988). When psychology informs public policy: The case of early childhood intervention. *American Psychologist, 43,* 443–454.

Woods, D. D., O'Brien, J. F., & Hanes, L. F. (1987). Human factors challenges in process control: The case of nuclear power plants. In G. Salvendy (Ed.), *Handbook of human factors* (pp. 1724–1770). New York: Wiley.

Woodworth, R. S., & Schlosberg, H. (1954). *Experimental psychology.* New York: Holt.

Woody, E. Z., Costanzo, P. R., Liefer, H., & Conger, J. (1981). The effects of taste and caloric perceptions on the eating behavior of restrained and unrestrained subjects. *Cognitive Therapy and Research, 5,* 381–390.

Woolfolk, R. L., & McNulty, T. F. (1983). Relaxation treatment for insomnia: A component analysis. *Journal of Consulting and Clinical Psychology, 4,* 495–503.

Worchel, S., & Brehm, J. W. (1970). Effects of threats to attitudinal freedom as a function of agreement with the communicator. *Journal of Personality and Social Psychology, 14,* 18–22.

Worchel, S., & Shackelford, S. L. (1991). Groups under stress: The influence of group structure and environment on process and performance. *Personality and Social Psychology Bulletin, 17,* 640–647.

Worchel, S., & Simpson, J. A. (Eds.) (1993). *Conflict between people and groups*. Chicago: Nelson-Hall.

World Health Organizaton. (1979). *Schizophrenia: An international follow-up study*. Geneva, Switzerland: World Health Organization.

Wortman, C. B. (1984). Social support and the cancer patient: Conceptual and methodological issues. *Cancer, 53*, 2339–2360.

Wright, G. N., & Phillips, L. D. (1980). Cultural variation in probabilistic thinking: Alternative ways of dealing with uncertainty. *International Journal of Psychology, 15*, 239–257.

Wright, L. (1988). The type A behavior pattern and coronary artery disease: Quest for the active ingredients and the elusive mechanism. *American Psychologist, 43*, 2–14.

Wright, W. F., & Bower, G. H. (1992). Mood effects on subjective probability. *Organizational Behavior and Human Decision Processes, 52*, 276–291.

Wurtman, R. J., & Wurtman, J. J. (1989). Carbohydrates and depression. *Scientific American, 260*, 68–75.

Wyer, R. S., & Carlston, D. E. (1994). The cognitive representation of persons and events. In R. S. Wyer & T. K. Srull (Eds.), *Handbook of social cognition* (2nd ed.). Hillsdale, NJ: Lawrence Erlbaum Associates.

Wyer, R. S., & Srull, T. K. (1986). Human cognition in its social context. *Psychological Review, 93*, 322–359.

Wyer, R. S., & Srull, T. K. (Eds.) (1994). *Handbook of social cognition* (2nd ed.). Hillsdale, NJ: Lawrence Erlbaum Associates.

Wyer, R. S., Bodenhausen, G. V., & Gorman, T. F. (1985). Cognitive mediators to rape. *Journal of Personality and Social Psychology, 48*, 324–338.

Wyer, R. S., Strack, F., & Fuhrman, R. W. (1988). Erwerb von Informationen uber Personen: Einflusse von Aufgabenstellung und personlichen Erwartungen. *Zeitschrift fur experimentelle und angewandte Psychologie, 35*, 657–688.

Yakimovich, D., & Saltz, E. (1971). Helping behavior: The cry for help. *Psychonomic Science, 23*, 427–428.

Yalom, I. D. (1985). *The theory and practice of group psychotherapy* (3rd ed.). New York: Basic Books.

Yang, K., & Bond, M. (1990). Exploring implicit personality theories with indigenous or imported constructs: The Chinese case. *Journal of Personality and Social Psychology, 58*, 1087–1095.

Yassa, R., Nastase, C., Dupont, D., & Thibeau, M. (1992). Tardive dyskinesia in elderly psychiatric patients: A 5-year study. *American Journal of Psychiatry, 149*, 1209–1211.

Yates, F., Lee, J. W., & Shinotsuka, H. (1992). Cross-national variation in probability judgment. Paper presented at 33rd annual meeting of the psychonomic society, St. Louis.

Yates, J. F., Zhu, Y., Ronis, D. L., Wang, D. F., Shinotsuka, H., & Masanao, T. (1989). Probability judgement accuracy: China, Japan, and the United States. *Organizational Behavior and Human Decision Processes, 43*, 145–171.

Yau, T. Y., Sue, D., & Hayden, D. (1992). Counseling style preferences of international students. *Journal of Counseling Psychology, 39*, 100–104.

Yeh, C., Shiell, M., Lamke, J., & Volpe, M. (1992). Physical therapy: Evaluation and treatment of chronic pain. In G. M. Aronoff (Ed.), *Evaluation and treatment of chronic pain*. Baltimore: Williams & Wilkins.

Yerkes, R. M. (Ed.) (1921). Psychological examining in the U.S. Army. *Memoirs of the National Academy of Sciences*, No. 15.

Yesavage, J. A., Leirer, V. O., Denari, M., & Hollister, L. E. (1985). Carry-over effects of marijuana intoxication on aircraft pilot performance: A preliminary report. *American Journal of Psychiatry, 142*, 1325–1329.

Yonkers, K., Kando, J., Cole, J., & Blumenthal, S. (1992). Gender differences in pharmacokinetics and pharmacodynamics of psychotropic medication. *American Journal of Psychiatry, 149*, 587–595.

Young, A. W., & De Haan, E. H. F. (1992). Face recognition and awareness after brain injury. In A. D. Milner & M. D. Rugg (Eds.), *The neuropsychology of consciousness*. San Diego, CA: Academic Press.

Young, F. A., Leary, G. A., Baldwin, W. R., West, D. C., Box, R. A., Harris, E., & Johnson, C. (1969). The transmission of refractive errors within Eskimo families. *American Journal of Optometry, 46*, 676–685.

Young, M. (1966). Problem solving performance in two age groups. *Journal of Gerontology, 21*, 505–509.

Young, M. (1971). Age and sex differences in problem solving. *Journal of Gerontology, 26*, 331–336.

Youngstrom, N. (1991). Legal terms may elude jurors in capital cases. *American Psychological Association Monitor*, October.

Youngstrom, N. (1992). Field of psychoanalysis undergoes resurgence. *APA Monitor, 23*, 24–25.

Youtz, R. P. (1968). Can fingers "see" color? *Psychology Today*.

Zafiropoulou, M., & McPherson, F. M. (1986). "Preparedness" and the severity and outcome of clinical phobias. *Behavior Research and Therapy, 24*, 221–222.

Zahn-Waxler, C., Iannotti, R., & Chapman, M. (1982). Peers and prosocial development. In K. H. Rubin & H. S. Ross (Eds.), *Peer relationships and social skills in childhood*. New York: Springer-Verlag.

Zahn-Waxler, C., Radke-Yarrow, M., Wagner, E., & Chapman, M. (1992). Development of concern for others. *Developmental Psychology, 28*, 126–136.

Zajonc, R. B. (1965). Social facilitation. *Science, 149*, 269–274.

Zajonc, R. B. (1980). Feeling and thinking: Preferences need no inferences. *American Psychologist, 35*, 151–175.

Zajonc, R. B., & Markus, H. (1982). Affective and cognitive factors in preferences. *Journal of Consumer Research, 9*, 123–131.

Zanot, E. J., Pincus, J. D., & Lamp, E. J. (1983). Public perceptions of subliminal advertising. *Journal of Advertising, 12*, 37–45.

Zaragoza, M. S., & Koshmider, J. W. (1989). Misled subjects may know more than their performance implies. *Journal of Experimental Psychology: Learning, Memory, and Cognition, 15*, 246–255.

Zarski, J. J. (1984). Hassles and health: A replication. *Health Psychology, 3*, 243–251.

Zatorre, R. J., Evans, A. C., Meyer, E., Gjedde, A. (1992). Lateralization of phonetic and pitch discrimination in speech processing. *Science, 256*, 846–849.

Zautra, A. J., & Reich, J. W. (1983). Life events and the perceptions of life quality: Developments in a two-factor approach. *Journal of Community Psychology, 11*, 121–132.

Zax, M., & Stricker, G. (1963). *Patterns of psychopathology*. New York: Macmillan.

Zeig, J. K. (Ed.) (1987). *The evolution of psychotherapy*. New York: Bruner Mazel.

Zeki, S. (1992). The visual image in mind and brain. *Scientific American, 267*, 68–76.

Zellner, M. (1970). Self-esteem, reception, and influenceability. *Journal of Personality and Social Psychology, 15*, 87–93.

Zentall, S. S., & Zentall, T. R. (1983). Optimal stimulation: A model of disordered activity and performance in normal and deviant children. *Psychological Bulletin, 94*, 446–471.

Zhang, G., & Simon, H. A. (1985). STM capacity for Chinese words and idioms: Chunking and acoustical loop hypothesis. *Memory & Cognition, 13*, 193–201.

Zigler, E., & Seitz, V. (1982). Social policy and intelligence. In R.

J. Sternberg (Ed.), *Handbook of human intelligence.* Cambridge: Cambridge University Press.

Zigler, E., Taussig, C., & Black, K. (1992). Early childhood intervention: A promising preventive for juvenile delinquency. *American Psychologist, 47,* 997–1006.

Zillmann, D. (1978a). Attribution and misattribution of excitatory reactions. In J. H. Harvey, W. J. Ickes, & R. F. Kidd (Eds.), *New directions in attribution research: Vol. 2.* Hillsdale, NJ: Lawrence Erlbaum Associates.

Zillmann, D. (1978b). *Hostility and aggression.* Hillsdale, NJ: Lawrence Erlbaum Associates.

Zillmann, D. (1983). Arousal and aggression. In R. Geen & E. Donnerstein (Eds.), *Aggression: Theoretical and empirical reviews.* New York: Academic Press.

Zillmann, D. (1984). *Connections between sex and aggression.* Hillsdale, NJ: Lawrence Erlbaum Associates.

Zillmann, D. (1988). Cognition-excitation interdependencies in aggressive behavior. *Aggressive Behavior, 14,* 51–64.

Zillmann, D., & Weaver, J. B. (1989). Pornography and men's sexual callousness toward women. In D. Zillmann & J. Bryant (Eds.), *Pornography: Research advances and policy considerations.* Hillsdale, NJ: Lawrence Erlbaum Associates.

Zillmann, D., Baron, R. A., & Tamborini, R. (1981). Social costs of smoking: Effects of tobacco smoke on hostile behavior. *Journal of Applied Social Psychology, 11,* 548–561.

Zillmann, D., Katcher, A. H., & Milavsky, B. (1972). Excitation transfer from physical exercise to subsequent aggressive behavior. *Journal of Experimental Social Psychology, 8,* 247–259.

Zimbardo, P. G., Weisenberg, M., Firestone, I., & Levy, B. (1965). Communicator effectiveness in producing public conformity and private attitude change. *Journal of Personality, 33,* 233–255.

Zimmerman, B. J., & Schunk, D. H. (1989). *Self-regulated learning and academic achievement.* New York: Springer-Verlag.

Zimmerman, M., & Rappaport, J. (1988). Citizen participation, perceived control and psychological empowerment. *American Journal of Community Psychology, 16,* 725–750.

Zimmerman, M., Reischl, T., Seidman, E., Rappaport, J., Toro, P., & Salem, D. (1991). Expansion strategies of a mutual help organization. *American Journal of Community Psychology, 19,* 251–279.

Zinbarg, R. E., & Mineka, S. (1991). Animal models of psychopathology: II. Simple phobia. *The Behavior Therapist, 14,* 61–65.

Zinbarg, R., Barlow, D., Brown, T., & Hertz, R. (1992). Cognitive-behavioral approaches to the nature and treatment of anxiety disorders. *Annual Review of Psychology, 43,* 235–267.

Zinberg, N. E. (1974). *High states: A beginning study.* Washington, DC: Drug Abuse Council.

Zirkel, S., & Cantor, N. (1990). Personal construal of life tasks: Those who struggle for independence. *Journal of Personality and Social Psychology, 58,* 172–185.

Zitrin, C. M. (1983). Differential treatment of phobias: Use of imipramine for panic attacks. *Journal of Behavior Therapy and Experimental Psychiatry, 14,* 11–18.

Zola-Morgan, S., & Squire, L. R. (1990). Neuropsychological investigations of memory and amnesia: Findings from humans and nonhuman primates. In A. Diamond (Ed.), *The development and neural bases of higher cognitive functions.* New York: New York Academy of Sciences.

Zoller, C. L., Workman, J. S., & Kroll, N. E. A. (1989). The bizarre mnemonic: The effect of retention interval and mode of presentation. *Bulletin of the Psychonomic Society, 27,* 215–218.

Zook, A., II, & Walton, J. M. (1989). Theoretical orientations and work settings of clinical and counseling psychologists: A current perspective. *Professional Psychology: Research and Practice, 20,* 23–31.

Zorumski, C., & Isenberg, K. (1991). Insights into the structure and function of GABA-benzodiazepine receptors: Ion channels and psychiatry. *American Journal of Psychiatry, 148,* 162–173.

Zubek, J. P. (Ed.) (1969). *Sensory deprivation: Fifteen years of research.* New York: Appleton-Century-Crofts.

Zubin, J., & Spring, B. (1977). Vulnerability—A new view of schizophrenia. *Journal of Abnormal Psychology, 86,* 103–126.

Zuckerman, M. (1979). *Sensation seeking: Beyond the optimal level of arousal.* Hillsdale, NJ: Lawrence Erlbaum Associates.

Zuckerman, M. (1984). Sensation seeking: A comparative approach to a human approach. *The Behavioral and Brain Sciences, 7,* 413–471.

Zuckerman, M. (1990). Some dubious premises in research and theory on racial differences. *American Psychologist, 45,* 1297–1303.

Credits

Chapter 1: **p. 4:** Historical Pictures Collection/Stock Montage, Inc. **p. 6:** (*top*) Bettmann Archive; (*bottom*) J. H. Robinson/Animals, Animals. **p. 7:** (*top*) National Library of Medicine; (*bottom*) B. F. Skinner Foundation, Cambridge. **p. 8:** (*top*) Jay Freis/The Image Bank; (*bottom*) Courtesy Carl Rogers Memorial Library. **p. 9:** Michael Philip Manheim/First Light, Toronto. **p. 12:** James King-Holmes/Science Photo Library/Photo Researchers. **p. 13:** Santiago Lyon/Reuters/Bettmann.

Chapter 2: **p. 21:** (*top*) © 1992 Watterson. Distributed by Universal Press Syndicate, reprinted with permission. All rights reserved; (*bottom*) Myrleen Ferguson/Photo Edit. **p. 22:** Charles Gupton/Stock Boston. **p. 23:** Thomas McAvoy, *Life* Magazine c. Time Warner, Inc. **p. 24:** Spencer Grant/The Picture Cube. **p. 27:** John Elk/Stock, Boston. **p. 33:** David Young-Wolff/Photo Edit. **p. 34:** Meryl Joseph/The Stock Market. **p. 35:** Bob Daemmrich/Stock, Boston. **p. 38:** Christopher Brown/Stock, Boston.

Chapter 3: **p. 44:** Gabe Palmer/The Stock Market. **p. 46:** (*top*) Lennart Nilsson; (*bottom*) John Chiasson/Gamma Liaison. **p. 48:** Elizabeth Crews. **p. 51:** (*all*) George Zimbel/Monkmeyer Press Photos. **p. 56:** Bill Binzen/The Stock Market. **p. 59:** Anne Martens/The Image Bank. **p. 62:** (*both*) Harlow Primate Laboratory, University of Wisconsin. **p. 64:** Kevin Forest/The Image Bank. **p. 68:** Michael Hayman/Photo Researchers. **p. 69:** Lucy Rosenthal/Superstock. **p. 71:** Thomas Wanstall/The Image Works. **p. 73:** *Figure 3.8* Adapted from "Standards from Birth to Maturity for Height, Weight, Height Velocity: British Children" by Tanner, J. M., Whitehouse, R. H., and Takaishi, M., *Archives of Diseases in Childhood,* 1966, 41, 454–471. Reprinted with permission. **p. 74:** Katherine McGlynn/The Image Works. **p. 78:** The Farside © 1990 Farworks, Inc. Reprinted with permission of Universal Press Syndicate. All Rights Reserved. **p. 79:** *Figure 3.9* Colby, A., Kohlberg, L., Gibbs, J., & Lieberman, M. (1983). "A Longitudinal Study of Moral Judgment." *Monographs of the Society for Research in Child Development,* 48 (Whole nos. 1 & 2), (pp. 476, 477). **p. 84:** Steve Leonard/Black Star. **p. 87:** LLR Research. Photo by Joyce Kitchell.

Chapter 4: **p. 98:** *Figure 4.4* Micrograph produced by John E. Heuser of Washington University School of Medicine, St. Louis, MO. Reprinted by permission. **p. 100:** Max Planck Institute. **p. 104:** *Figure 4.10* Hinton, G. E. (1989) "Connectronist Learning Procedures." *Artificial Intelligence,* 40, 185–234. Reprinted by permission. **p. 105:** Peter Fox M.D. **p. 106:** D. N. Levin, H. Xiaoping, K. K. Tan, S. Galhotra, C. A. Pelizzare, G. T. Y. Chen, R. N. Beck, C-T Chen, M. D. Cooper, J. F. Mullan, J. Hekmatpanah and J-P. Spire (1989). *The Brain:* integrated three-dimensional display of MR and PET images. *Radiology,* 172: 783–789. By permission of the author. **p. 107:** Howard Sochurek/Medical Images. **p. 108:** Mimi Forsyth/Monkmeyer Press Photos. **p. 110:** J. P. Seab et al. (1988) "Magnetic Resonance in Medicine" 8, 200–208, Copyright 1988, Academic Press. **p. 113:** *Figure 4.18* Reprinted with permission of Macmillan Publishing Company, a Division of Macmillan, Inc. from *The Cerebral Cortex of Man* by Wilder Penfield and Theodore Rasmussen. Copyright 1950 Macmillan Publishing Company; copyright renewed © 1978 Theodore Rasmussen. **p. 114:** (*top*) The Farside. Copyright 1986 Universal Press Syndicate. Reprinted with permission; All rights reserved. (*bottom*) Fred McConnaughey/Photo Researchers. **p. 118:** Dan McCoy/Rainbow. **p. 121:** *Fig. 4.22* J. L. Conel, *The Postnatal Development of the Human Cerebral Cortex,* Vols. I, VIII, Harvard University Press, 1939, 1967. Reprinted by permission.

Chapter 5: **p. 136:** Dana Fineman/Sygma. **p. 139:** *Figure 5.6* Adapted from *Experiments In Hearing* by G. von Bekesy. Copyright © 1960. Reprinted with permission of McGraw-Hill Book Company. **p. 139:** Prof. J. E. Hawkins/Kresge Hearing Research Institute, University of Michigan. **p. 144:** H. Mark Weidman. **p. 150:** Peter Chapman. **p. 156:** *Figure 5.24* From Hubel, D. H., and Wiesel, T. N., 1962, 1965; redrawn by Kuffler, S. W. and Nicholls, A., 1976, *From Neuron to Brain,* Sinauer Associates, Inc. Reprinted by permission. **p. 157:** *Figure 5.25* From *Fundamentals of Sensation and Perception* by M. W. Levine and J. M. Shefner, Addison Wesley, 1981; and also from Leon B. Harmon and Bela Julesz (1973). *Science,* 180: 1194–97. Copyright 1973 by the AAAS. **p. 160:** The Farside. Copyright 1988 Universal Press Syndicate. Reprinted with permission. **p. 161:** Charles Kennard/Stock, Boston. **p. 163:** Bavaria Bildagentur. **p. 165:** UPI/Bettmann. **p. 166:** Courtesy of *The Daily Illini,* cartoon by Eric Smelroth © 1987. **p. 168:** Bruce Curtis/Peter Arnold.

Chapter 6: **p. 178:** *Table 6.1* Galanter, E. (1962), "Contemporary Psychophysics," in R. Brown (Ed.) *New Directions in Psychology.* New York: Holt, Rinehart & Winston. Reprinted by permission of the author. **p. 183:** Alan Carey/The Image Works. **p. 185:** © Will Barnet, Collection of Mr. & Mrs. Lee M. Oser, Jr. **p. 187:** (*top*) The Farside c. 1990 Farworks, Inc. Reprinted with permission of Universal Press Syndicate. All rights reserved; (*bottom*) Jim Anderson/Woodfin Camp. **p. 189:** AP/Wide World Photos. **p. 190:** (*bottom*) Larry Brownstein/Rainbow. **p. 194:** *Figure 6.17* Hudson, W. (1960). "Pictorial Depth Perception in Subcultural Groups in Africa." *Journal of Social Psychology,* 52, 183–208. Reprinted with permission of the Helen Dwight Reid Educational Foundation. Published by Heldref Publications, 1319 18th Street, N.W., Washington, DC 20030-1802. Copyright © 1960. **p. 195:** Leibowitz, H., Brislin, R., Perlmutter, L., & Hennessy, R. (1969). "Ponzo Perspective Illusion as a manifestation of Space Perception." *Science,* 166, 1174–1176. Copyright 1969 by the AAAS. **p. 196:** *Figure 6.19* Ronald C. James. **p. 198:** *Figure 6.21* Ronald C. James. **p. 199:** *Figure*

6.24 Romelhart, D. E. and McClelland, J. L. (1986). *Parallel Distributing Processing Volume 1: Foundations.* Cambridge, MA: MIT Press. Copyright 1986 by the Massachusetts Institute of Technology. Reprinted by permission. **p. 200:** Adamsmith Productions/First Light, Toronto. **p. 201:** *Fig. 6.26* Weisstein & Harris, *Science,* 1974, 186, 752–755. Copyright 1974 by The American Association for the Advancement of Science. **p. 203:** *Figure 6.28* Johnson, M. A., Dziurawiec, S., Ellis, H., & Morton, J. (1991). "Newborns' Preferential Tracking of Face-Like Stimuli and Its Subsequent Decline." *Cognition,* 4, 1–19. Reprinted by permission of Elsevier Science Publishing. **p. 203:** Enrico Ferorelli. **p. 205:** (*top*) Martin Handford, *Find Waldo Now,* Little, Brown Publishers, 1988; (*bottom*): Jim Pickerell. **p. 207:** Mike Surowiak/TSW, Click Chicago. **p. 210:** James King-Holmes/Science Photo Library/Photo Researchers.

Chapter 7: **p. 216:** (*top*) © 1986, Washington Post Writers Group. Reprinted with permission; (*bottom*) Figure 7.1 Schacter, D. L., Cooper, L. A., Delaney, S. M., Peterson, M. A., & Tharan, M. (1991). "Implicit Memory for Possible and Impossible Objects: Constraints on the Construction of Structural Descriptions." *Journal of Experimental Psychology: Learning, Memory, and Cognition,* 17, 3–19. Reprinted by permission. **p. 222:** Grant Leduc/Monkmeyer Press Photos. **p. 223:** *Figure 7.4* Reprinted with the permission of Macmillan Publishing Company from *Sleep: An Experimental Approach* by W. B. Webb. Copyright © 1968 by Wilse B. Webb. **p. 224:** *Figure 7.5* Adapted from Cartwright, *A Primer of Sleep and Dreaming,* Reading, Mass: Addison-Wesley, 1978. Reprinted by permission. **p. 225:** *Figure 7.6 Science,* Vol. 152, Page 606, 29 April 1966, (revised 1969), "Ontogenetic Development of the Human Sleep Dream Cycle." Copyright 1966 by the AAAS. Roffwarg et al., 1966. With author permission. **p. 226:** *Fig. 7.7* Adapted from Nicholson, A. N., Pascoe, P. A., Spencer, M. B., Stone, B. M., Roehis, T., & Roth, T. (1986). "Sleep After Tranmeridian Flights." *Lancet,* 2, 1205–1208. © 1986 by The Lancet Ltd. Reprinted by permission. **p. 229:** *The Engineer's Dream* by Thomas Hart Benton, 1931, Memphis Brooks Museum of Art, Memphis. **p. 230:** David Parker/Photo Researchers. **p. 231:** *Figure 7.10* Drucker-Colin, R. R. & McGaugh, J. L. (Eds.), 1977, *Neurobiology of Sleep and Memory.* San Diego: Academic Press. Reprinted by permission. **p. 231:** *Figure 7.11* From *Hypnotic Susceptibility* by Ernest R. Hilgard, copyright © 1965 by Harcourt Brace Jovanovich, Inc. Reprinted by permission of the author. **p. 232:** *Figure 7.12* Pattie, F. A. (1935). "A Report at Attempts to Produce Uniocular Blindness by Hypnotic Suggestion." *British Journal of Medical Psychiatry,* 15, 230–241. Reprinted by permission. **p. 236:** *Figure 7.13* From *Divided Consciousness: Multiple Controls in Human Thought and Action* by E. R. Hilgard. Copyright © 1977 John Wiley and Sons, Inc. Reprinted by permission of John Wiley and Sons, Inc. **p. 238:** *Figure 7.15* From "Effects of Alcohol on Aggression in Males." A. R. Lang, D. J. Goeckner, V. J. Adesso & G. A. Marlett, *Journal of Abnormal Psychology,* #84, pp. 508–516. Copyright 1975 by the American Psychological Association. Adapted by permission; and also from Kolata, G. (1986). "New drug counters alcohol intoxication" *Science,* 234, 1198–1199. Photo by Jules Asher at NIMH. **p. 239:** Kenneth Murray/Photo Researchers. **p. 240:** (*top*) *Figure 7.16* Kales, A.

& Kales, J. (1973). "Recent Advances in the Diagnosis and Treatment of Sleep Disorders." In G. Usdin (Ed.), *Sleep Research and Clinical Practice.* New York: Brunner/Mazel. Reprinted by permission; (*bottom*) Lawrence Migdale/Science/Photo Researchers.

Chapter 8: **p. 256:** Thomas Kitchin/Tom Stack and Associates. **p. 261:** Courtesy Pfizer, Inc. **p. 263:** *Figure 8.10* From *The Psychology of Learning and Memory* by Douglas L. Hintzman. Copyright © 1978 by W. H. Freeman and Company. Reprinted with permission. **p. 264:** (*top*) Frank Lotz Miller/Black Star; (*bottom*) Jim Davis/Photo Researchers. **p. 265:** Rick Smolan/Stock, Boston. **p. 266:** Lincoln Electric Company. **p. 267:** *Figure 8.12* Adapted from "Teaching Machines" by B. F. Skinner. Copyright © 1961 by Scientific American, Inc. All rights reserved. **p. 268:** Al Tielemans/Duomo. **p. 270:** J. Hillis Miller. **p. 272:** Robert Semenick/First Light, Toronto. **p. 275:** Kohler, W. 1976. *The Mentality of Apes.* London: Routledge and Kegan Paul Pic. **p. 276:** Albert Bandura/Stanford University.

Chapter 9: **p. 288:** Bob Daemmrich/Stock, Boston. **p. 290:** Elizabeth Crews/Stock, Boston. **p. 293:** *Figure 9.4* From "Contextual Prequisites for Understanding: Some Investigations of Comprehension and Recall" by Bransford and Johnson. *Journal of Verbal Learning and Verbal Behavior,* 61, pp. 717–726, 1972. With permission of Academic Press. **p. 295:** *Figure 9.5* Reprinted with permission of Macmillan Publishing Company from *Cognitive Psychology:* Memory, Language, and Thought by Darlene V. Howard. Copyright © 1983 by Darlene V. Howard. **p. 296:** (*top*) Chip Hires/Gamma Liasion; (*bottom*) Laima Druskis/Stock, Boston. **p. 298:** (*top*) *Figure 9.7* From "Long-Term Memory for a Common Object," by R. S. Nickerson and M. J. Adams. *Cognitive Psychology,* 1979, 11, 287–307. Reprinted by permission; (*bottom*) **p. 298:** (*top*) Franco Magnani; (*bottom*) Susan Schwartzenberg/The Exploratorium. **p. 299:** *Figure 9.9* From "Two Storage Mechanisms in Free Recall," by M. Glanzer and A. R. Cunitz. In *Journal of Verbal Learning and Verbal Behavior,* 1966, 5, 351–360. Copyright 1966 by Academic Press, Inc. Reprinted by permission. **p. 300:** (*top*) Bob Clay/Jeroboam; (*bottom*) Drawing by Lorenz; c. 1988 The New Yorker Magazine, Inc. **p. 304:** *Figure 9.12* From Minimi, H., and Dallenbach, K. M. (1946). "The Effect of Activity Upon Learning and Retention in the Cockroach," *American Journal of Psychology,* 59, 1–58. Copyright 1946 by the Board of Trustees of the University of Illinois. Reprinted by permission. **p. 306:** *Figure 9.13* From "Retroactive Inhibition in Free Recall: Inaccessibility of Information Available in the Memory Store" by Tulving and Psotka. *Journal of Experimental Psychology,* 87, pp. 1–8, 1971. Copyright © 1971 by the American Psychological Association. Adapted by permission. **p. 308:** *Figure 9.14* From *Cognitive Psychology: A Neural Network Approach* by Colin Martindale. Copyright © 1991 by Wadsworth, Inc. Reprinted by permission of Brooks/Cole Publishing Company, Pacific Grove, CA 93950. **p. 313:** Luc Delahaye/Sipa. **p. 317:** *Figure 9.17* Reprinted with permission from *Psychology Today* Magazine. Copyright © 1973 (Sussex Publishers, Inc.).

Chapter 10: **p. 325:** Seth Resnick/Stock, Boston. **p. 329:** (*left*) Joe Sohm/Chromosohm/Stock, Boston; (*right*) Scott An-

Silvester/Black Star. **p. 491:** Mary Cassatt, Baby's First Caress, 1891/New Britain Museum of American Art, Harriet Stanley Russell Fund. **p. 495:** *Figure 14.4* Eysenck, H. J., Rachman, S.: "The Causes and Cures of Neurosis: An Introduction to Modern Behavior Therapy Based on Learning Theory and the Principle of Conditioning." 1965. *Edits.* Reprinted by permission. **p. 499:** Jim Pickerell TSW - Click/Chicago. **p. 501:** Elena Rooraid/Photo Edit. **p. 502:** The Far Side, Copyright 1990 Farworks, Inc., Reprinted with permission of Universal Press Syndicate. All rights reserved. **p. 503:** *Figure 14.6* Reprinted from *Journal of Behavior Therapy and Experimental Psychiatry,* 13, "The Assessment and Predictive Generality of Self-Percepts of Efficacy," Bandura, A., 195–199. Copyright 1982, with kind permission from Pergamon Press Ltd., Headington Hill Hall, Oxford OX3 OBW, UK **p. 504:** David Madison **p. 505:** Bob Daemmrich/The Image Works. **p. 506:** Lee Snider/The Image Works. **p. 509:** *Figure 14.7* From Markus, H., & Kitayama, S. (1991). "Culture and the Self: Implications for Cognition, Emotion and Motivation." *Psychological Review,* 98, 224–253. Copyright 1991 by the American Psychological Association. Reprinted by permission. **p. 512:** *Figure 14.8* Minnesota Multiphasic Personality Inventory-2. Copyright © by the Regents of the University of Minnesota 1942, 1943 (renewed 1970), 1989. This profile form 1989. All rights reserved. "MMPI-2" and "Minnesota Multiphasic Personality Inventory-2" are trademarks owned by the University of Minnesota." **p. 513:** *Table 14.4* Reproduced by special permission of the publisher, Psychological Assessment Resources, Inc., Odessa, FL 33556, from the NEO Personality Inventory by Paul Costa and Robert McCrae. Copyright 1978, 1985, 1989, 1991 by PAR, Inc. **p. 514:** *Table 14.5* Material taken from the *Personality Research Form Manual, Second Edition* Copyright 1989, Douglas N. Jackson. Reproduced with permission of the Sigma Assessment Systems, Inc., Research Psychologists Press Division, Port Huron, MI. **p. 514:** *Figure 14.9* Emanuel F. Hammer, Ph.D, "Projective Drawings," in Rabin, ed., *Projective Techniques in Personality Assessment,* p. 375–376. Copyright © 1968 by Springer Publishing Company, Inc., New York. Used by permission.

Chapter 15: p. 522: Dan Hummel/The Image Bank. **p. 524:** Peter Turnley/Black Star. **p. 525:** Grox-J.M. News/Sipa Press. **p. 526:** Yves Coatsaliou/Sygma. **p. 527:** Culver Pictures. **p. 528:** Eric Roth/The Picture Cube. **p. 538:** The Far Side, Copyright 1985 Universal Press Syndicate, Reprinted by permission. **p. 539:** *(top)* Peter Chapman/Stock, Boston; *(bottom)* Ron Bradley/Photo Researchers. **p. 540:** Brian Potts. **p. 541:** Dr. Susan Mineka. **p. 544:** Debra Lex/People weekly Copyright 1989, Time, Inc. **p. 545:** Justin Kerr. **p. 546:** Miro Vintoniv/Stock, Boston. **p. 552:** Grunnitus/Monkmeyer Press. **p. 553:** Office of Scientific Information, National Institute of Mental Health. **p. 555:** *Figure 15.4* From J. Zubin and B. Spring, 1977, "A New View of Schizophrenia, *Journal of Abnormal Psychology,* 86, p. 103–126. Copyright © 1977 by the American Psychological Association. Adapted by permission. **p. 556:** UPI/Bettman. **p. 557:** Michael Weisbrot/Stock, Boston.

Chapter 16: p. 569: *(top)* Historical Pictures Collection/Stock Montage, *(bottom)* Bob Daemmrich/Stock, Boston **p. 571:**

David Young-Wolff/Photo Edit. **p. 573:** Michael Heron/Monkmeyer Press. **p. 575:** Stacy Pick/Stock, Boston. **p. 577:** Michael Weisbrot and family. **p. 579:** *Figure 16.1* From Bandura, Blanchard, Ritter. *Journal of Personality and Social Psychology,* 1969, 13, 173–199. Copyright © 1969 by the American Psychological Association. Adapted by permission of publisher and authors. **p. 580:** *Figure 16.2* After Matson, J., Sevin, J., Fridley, and Love, S. (1990). "Increasing Spontaneous Language in Autistic Children," *Journal of Applied Behavior Analysis,* 23, pp. 227–233. **p. 581:** *(top)* Michael Hayman/Stock, Boston; *(bottom)* Rich Friedman/Black Star. **p. 583:** Courtesy, Albert Ellis, Institute for Rational Emotive Therapy. **p. 584:** Courtesy, Dr. Aaron T. Beck, Center for Cognitive Therapy. **p. 585:** *(top)* Mary Kay Denny/Photo Edit; *(bottom)* Bob Daemmrich/Stock, Boston. **p. 587:** *Figure 16.3* From G. R. Patterson, "Intervention for Boys with Conduct Problems: Multiple Settings, Treatments, and Criteria," *Journal of Consulting and Clinical Psychology,* 1974, 42, 471–81. Copyright © 1974 by the American Psychological Association. Reprinted by permission. **p. 593:** Andrew Savulich/AP/Wide World. **p. 594:** Historical Pictures Service/Stock Montage. **p. 595:** Will McIntyre/Photo Researchers, Inc. **p. 602:** Snider/The Image Works.

Chapter 17: p. 610: Willie Hill/Stock, Boston. **p. 612:** Bill Gallery/Stock, Boston. **p. 613:** Drawing by Mankoff, ©1985 The New Yorker Magazine, Inc. **p. 614:** Rhoda Sidney/Photo Edit. **p. 619:** George Goodwin/Monkmeyer Press. **p. 620:** *Figure 17.3* D. Byrne and D. Nelson, "Attraction as a Linear Function of Proportion of Positive Reinforcements," *Journal of Personality and Social Psychology,* 1, 659–663. Copyright © 1965 by the American Psychological Association. Adapted by permission. **p. 622:** *(top)* David Young-Wolff/Photo Edit; *(bottom)* **p. 622:** *Figure 17.6* Sternberg, R. J. and Michael L. Barnes, Editors, (1986). "A Triangular Theory of Love," from *The Psychology of Love.* Copyright © 1988 by Yale University Press. Reprinted by permission of Yale University Press. **p. 625:** *Figure 17.8* Adapted with permission from Kahn, Arnold S., *Social Psychology,* © 1984 Wm. C. Brown Publishers, Dubuque, Iowa. All rights reserved. **p. 627:** Dennis Brack/Black Star. **p. 630:** *Figure 17.10* E. Aronson, J. A. Turner, and J. M. Carlsmith, "Communicator Credibility and Communicator Discrepancy as a Determinant of Opinion Change," *Journal of Abnormal and Social Psychology,* 67, 31–36. Copyright © 1963 by the American Psychological Association. Adapted by permission. **p. 631:** *Figure 17.11* From W. J. McGuire, 1968, "Personality and Susceptibility to Social Influence" in E. F. Borgatta and W. W. Lambert: *Handbook of Personality Theory and Research.* Reprinted by permission of the author. **p. 632:** Richard Brenner/Photo Edit. **p. 634:** Richard Hutchings/Photo Researchers.

Chapter 18: p. 640: *(left)* Paul Slaughter/The Image Bank; *(right)* Homer Sykes/Woodfin Camp. **p. 643:** *Figure 18.2* From "Opinions and Social Pressure" by Solomon E. Asch, November 1955. Illustration on p. 32 by Sara Love. Copyright © 1955 by Scientific American, Inc. All rights reserved. **p. 644:** Nabeel Turner/TSW/Click, Chicago. **p. 647:** *(top)* Shone/Gamma Liaison; *(bottom)* Peter Turnley/Black Star. **p. 648:** © Stanley Milgrim, 1972; By permission of Alexandra Milgrim. **p. 649:** *Figure 18.4* Courtesy of Alexandra Milgram.

Name Index

Goodenough, F. L., 443
Goodkin, K., 464
Goodman, G., 585
Goodman, P., 577
Goodman-Gilman, A. G., 112, 241
Goodwin, C., 639
Goodwin, D. W., 559
Goodwin, F. K., 548
Gopher, D., 206
Goplerud, E. N., 463
Gorassini, D., 230
Gordon, B., 548, 549, 567, 594, 597, 598, 600
Gordon, J. R., 582
Gordon, L. J., 617
Gordon, T., 507
Gorman, J., 539
Gorman, T. F., 616
Gorn, G. J., 627
Gottesman, A., 309
Gottesman, I. I., 552
Gottfried, A. W., 58, 59, 60
Gottlieb, B. H., 462, 585
Gottman, J. M., 23, 85, 623
Gould, S. J., 370, 385
Graesser, A. C., 612
Graf, R. C., 663
Graham, C., 230
Graham, D. P., 375, 380
Graham, S., 13, 568
Grajek, S., 623
Grant, S. G. N., 127, 314
Graubard, S. R., 361
Gray, A., 655
Graziano, W. G., 88
Greaves, D. W., 567, 572, 574
Green, B. G., 161
Green, B. L., 89, 317
Green, D. M., 179
Green, E. J., 121
Green, M., 177, 201
Green, R., 71, 421
Greenberg, E., 69
Greenberg, J., 572
Greenberg, M., 469, 622
Greene, B., 277
Greene, R., 513
Greene, R. L., 289, 312
Greenfield, P., 358
Greenfield, P. M., 61, 68
Greenough, W. T., 121, 314
Greenwald, A. G., 221
Greenwald, J., 111
Gregory, R. L., 193
Grencavage, L., 567, 588
Grider, R. A., 240
Griffith, J., 287
Griffiths, R. R., 241
Griffitt, W., 619
Griggs v. Duke Power Company, 374
Grilo, C. M., 414
Gritz, E., 473
Grobe, R., 58
Groninger, L. D., 316
Grossberg, S., 178, 201
Grosser, B. I., 160
Grossman, B. S., 390

Grossman, M. I., 410
Grossmann, K., 64
Grosz, H. I., 542
Grove, H., 534
Grover, S. L., 619
Gruder, C. L., 664, 667
Gruen, C. E., 381
Grunberg, N., 472
Guay, P., 619
Guerin, D., 60
Guilford, J. P., 390
Guilleminault, C., 225
Guloien, T. H., 659
Guntheroth, W. G., 225
Gur, R. C. J., 446
Gurling, H. M., 549
Gurman, A. S., 585
Guroff, G., 95
Gurtman, M. B., 620
Gustavson, C. R., 256
Guthrie, P. R., 585
Gutierrez, L., 585
Guyton, A. C., 125
Guze, S. B., 559
Gwirtsman, H. E., 415
Gwynn, M. I., 165, 230

Ha, H., 167
Haaga, D., 547
Haan, N., 80
Haber, R. N., 298
Hackel, L. S., 623
Hadley, S. W., 587
Hagan, E., 372
Hagen, J. W., 55
Haith, M. M., 55
Hakstian, R., 556
Hakuta, K., 58, 356
Hale, G. H., 55, 396
Hale, S., 396
Halford, W. K., 586
Hall, A., 28
Hall, G. C. N., 659
Hall, L. K., 298
Hall, R. C., 416
Hall, R. M., 424
Haller, E., 416
Halliday, R., 240
Halligan, P. W., 213
Halpern, J. N., 305
Hameroff, S. R., 215
Hamilton, D. L., 611, 630, 632, 633
Hamilton, V. L., 647
Hamm, A. O., 540
Hammersmith, S. K., 421
Hammond, W. R., 7, 591
Hamner, W. C., 667
Hans, S. L., 46
Hans, V. P., 647
Hansel, C. E. M., 183
Hanson, D. J., 237
Hanson, S. J., 281, 282
Harda, S., 238
Hardaway, R., 492
Hardie, E. A., 608
Hardimann, P. T., 393
Hardin, T. S., 312

Hare, R. D., 556
Hare Krishna Society, 639
Harkins, S. G., 642
Harlow, H. F., 61–63, 419
Harlow Primate Laboratory, 62
Harmon, L. B., 157
Harper, R. C., 225
Harper, S., 183
Harpur, T., 556
Harrington, D. M., 391
Harris, C. S., 200, 201
Harris, J. E., 316
Harris, M. J., 499, 563, 612
Harris, R. J., 307
Harrison, A. A., 653
Harrison, P. L., 397
Harrison, T., 436
Hart, D., 75
Hart, J., 75
Hart, S., 556
Hartley, A., 82
Hartman, B. K., 440
Hartman, E., 227
Hartmann, H., 490, 572
Hartup, W. W., 75
Harvey, E. N., 222
Harvey, R., 589
Haskell, I., 208
Hastie, R., 311, 341, 348, 349
Hatfield, E., 621, 622
Hatfield, G., 185
Hathaway, S., 511
Hauser, P., 560
Hawkins, F., 12, 208
Hawkins, H. L., 82
Hawkins, J. A., 70
Hawkins, R. P., 7
Hawkins, S. A., 341
Havighurst, D. J., 85
Hay, P., 595
Hayes, A. S., 205, 210, 295
Hayman, C. A. G., 315
Hays, R., 463
Hayslip, B., 396
Haythornwaite, J., 408
Hazel, K. L., 535
He, L. F., 167, 168
Hearn, M., 470
Hearold, S., 277
Heath, A., 497
Heath, L., 278
Hebb, D. O., 82, 408
Heenan, T. A., 443
Hefferline, R. F., 577
Heider, E., 360
Heilbrun, A. B., 416
Heinrichs, R. W., 555
Heise, G. A., 200
Hekmatpanah, J., 106
Helgeson, V. S., 622
Heller, W., 217
Hellstrm, K., 579, 581
Helmes, E., 513
Helmreich, R. L., 349
Helms, J. E., 375
Helson, R., 84
Helzer, J. E., 534

Subject Index

Abnormal behavior, 521–526, 563
  practical approach to, 524–526, 563
  statistical approach to, 522–523, 563
  valuative approach to, 523–524, 563
Abortion, 74
Absenteeism, 426
Absolute threshold, 178–179, 210
Abstract thought, 76, 90
Abuse, child. *See* Child abuse
Accessory structures, 131, 171
  auditory, 137, 140
  visual, 141, 158
Accidental reinforcement, 268
Accommodation
  in cognitive development, 50–51
  in eye structure, 142, 172, 190, 211
Acetylcholine, 102, 103, 109, 234, 235
  emotions and, 430
  memory and, 315
Achievement motivation, 422–424
Acoustic coding, 289, 294, 320
Acquired immune deficiency syndrome
  (AIDS), 463, 468
  drug abuse and, 559
  optimism and, 464
  preventing or coping with, 478–479
  unsafe sex and, 473
Acquisition, in classical conditioning,
  252, 257
ACTH (adrenocorticotropic hormone),
  124, 125, 458
Action potential, of axon, 97, 128, 133
Activational effects, of hormones, 418
Active listening, 575
Active sleep, 223, 246
Actor-observer bias, 616, 636
Actual self, 609–610
Acuity, visual, 144, 172
Acupuncture, 167–168
Adaptation
  to changing environments, 249
  in sensory system, 132, 162, 171
Adaptive reading, 208, 211
Additive color mixing, 148
A-delta fibers, 164, 173
Addiction, 240, 242, 565
  dependence and, 236, 557
  opponent-process theory and, 259
  See also Physical dependence
ADHD (attention deficit hyperactivity
  disorder), 204, 560
ADIS-R (Anxiety Disorders Interview
  Schedule—Revised), 511
Adjustment disorders, 534
Adolescence
  AIDS in, 479
  child abuse in, 74
  cognitive development in, 54, 76

identity in, 74–76, 90
  parents and peers in, 73–74
  puberty and, 73, 90
  sexual activity in, 74
Adoption studies, 37, 498
Adrenal cortex, 431
Adrenal glands, 124, 125, 431, 449, 457,
  470
Adrenaline, 103, 258, 259, 431
  stress and, 457–458, 470
Adrenal medulla, 431
Adrenergic neurons, 107
Adrenocorticotropic hormone (ACTH),
  124, 125, 458
Adulthood, 80–83, 91
  aging body in, 80–81, 91
  cognitive changes in, 81–83, 91
Affect, 544
Affection, in intimate relationships, 622
Affective disorders, 533, 544. *See also*
  Mood disorders
Afferent neurons, 105
African-Americans, 69, 471, 473, 530,
  535–536, 591, 598–599, 633, 634
Afterimages, 150, 152
Age-graded tasks, 368
Age regression, 230, 232, 246
Aggression, 3, 9, 653–661, 673
  androgens and, 124
  biological mechanisms in, 654–656,
  673
  circumstances for, 656–657, 673
  emotional factors in, 656–657
  environmental influences on, 660–661
  frustration and, 656–657
  gender differences in, 124, 655
  instinct theory of, 654
  learning and cultural mechanisms in,
  656, 673
  pornography and, 658–660
  stress and, 459
  television and, 277–278, 656
Aggressive pornography, 659
Agonists, receptor, 235, 246
Agoraphobia, 538, 564, 577, 596, 598
Agranulocytosis, 597
Agreeableness, 496
AI (artificial intelligence), 341–344, 363
AIDS. *See* Acquired immune deficiency
  syndrome
Air pollution, 660
Alarm reaction, 457
Alcohol
  abuse of, 473, 557–559
  aggressiveness and, 237
  antidepressants and, 596
  anxiolytics and, 239, 598
  as depressant, 238, 244

memory and, 304
  prenatal risks and, 46
  sleep disorders and, 224
  stress and, 459
Alcoholism, 557–559, 565, 581, 602
Algorithms, 334, 336, 362
Alpha waves, 222, 233
Alprazolam, 596, 598, 600
Altered state(s) of consciousness, 221,
  245–246
  dreaming as, 228–229, 246
  hypnosis as, 230–231, 234, 246
  meditation as, 232–233, 234, 246
  psychoactive drugs for, 233–243, 246
  sleep as, 222–229, 234, 246
Altruism, 661–665, 673
Alzheimer's disease, 82, 109–110, 112
  dementia and, 527
  memory and, 315
  treatment of, 110, 111–112
Ambiguity, conformity and, 644–645
American Sign Language (ASL), 357
Amino acids, 410
Amitriptyline, 596
Amnesia, 533
  anterograde, 217–218, 299, 315, 320
  dissociative, 543, 564
  posthypnotic, 230, 246
  retrograde, 300, 320
Amnesia fugue, 545
Amphetamines, 239–240, 244, 553, 557
Amplitude, 135, 171
Amygdala, 109, 128, 159
  aggression and, 655
  emotion and, 439
Analgesia, natural, 166, 173
Analogies, 337, 338
Anal stage, in personality development,
  487–488, 518
Analysis of variance, A-9
Analytic psychology, 489–490
Anandamide, 243
Anchoring heuristic, 334, 339, 343, 362,
  534
Androgens, 124, 417, 418, 419, 448, 420
Androgyny, 85
Anger, 434, 443, 444, 445, 458
  aggression and, 656, 659–660
  autonomic activity in, 434, 435
  emotional expression of, 443, 444, 445
  marital conflict and, 623
Animals
  brain research and, 118, 119
  language and, 357–360
Animal Welfare Act, 34
Anorexia nervosa, 415–416, 448, 533
ANS. *See* Autonomic nervous system
Antagonists, receptor, 235, 246, 601

Variable-ratio (VR) schedules, 266, 285
Variables, 21
    confounding, 26–28, 39
    dependent vs. independent, 25, 38
    intervening, 401
    random, 26–27, 39
Vasopressin, 111, 112
Venn diagrams, 337, 340
Ventricles, of brain, 553, 554
Ventromedial nucleus, 410–411
Verbal scale, 371, 398
Vesicles, of axons, 98
Vestibular sacs, 169, 173
Vestibular sense, 169, 173
Vestibular system, 161, 169
Vibrations, 162
Vicarious conditioning, 276, 285
Vinpocetine, 111
Violence, 3
    domestic, 459, 654
    environment and, 660–661
    pornography and, 659, 660
    television and, 25, 277–279, 656
    therapeutic relationship and, 592
Virtual reality, 210
Visible light, 141, 172
Vision, 141–157, 158, 172
    absolute threshold and, 178–179
    color and, 147–152
    depth perception and, 188–191

eye structure and, 141–147
light and, 141–147
pathways and representations in, 152–157
Visual cliff experiments, 203, 445
Visual coding, 289, 295, 298, 320
Visual cortex, 114, 154, 185, 217
Visual form agnosia, 217
Visual transduction, 142
Volley theory, 140, 172
Vomeronasal organ, 160, 172
Vulnerability model, of schizophrenia, 554–555

WAIS-R (Wechsler Adult Intelligence Scale—Revised), 371
"War of the Ghosts, The" (Bartlett), 309
Waveforms, 135, 156
Wavelengths, 135, 171, 172
    color and, 141, 147–149
Weber's law, 181–182, 210
Wechsler Adult Intelligence Scale—Revised (WAIS-R), 371
Wechsler Intelligence Scale for Children (WISC-III), 372
Wechsler Preschool and Primary Scale of Intelligence—Revised (WPPSI-R), 372
Wechsler scales, 371
Weight loss, 271, 415
Wernicke's area, 114, 356

Willingness, in hypnosis, 229
WISC-III (Wechsler Intelligence Scale for Children), 372
Withdrawal, 657, 662
Withdrawal syndrome, 236, 246
    barbituate, 239
    caffeine, 241
Wonderlic Personnel test, 372
Words, 331, 336, 350, 351–352
Word salad, 550
Word strings, 350
Word superiority effect, 200–201
Working backward, strategy of, 336–337, 340, 342
Working memory, 294, 320, 333, 338, 396. *See also* Short-term memory
Work motivation, 421–422, 425
WPPSI-R (Wechsler Preschool and Primary Scale of Intelligence—Revised), 372
Wundt illusion, 192

Yale University, 650
Yohimbine, 539
Yolk sac, 45
Young-Helmholtz theory, 149, 172

Zero-sum games, 667
Zollner illusion, 192
Zygote, 35